MW00783872

Puntos de partida

Thalia Dorwick

Ana M. Pérez-Gironés
WESLEYAN UNIVERSITY

Anne Becher
UNIVERSITY OF COLORADO, BOULDER

PUNTOS DE PARTIDA, ELEVENTH EDITION
Published by McGraw-Hill, 2 Penn Plaza, New York, NY 10121.

Some ancillaries, including electronic and print components, may not be available to customers outside the United States.

This book is printed on acid-free paper.

1 2 3 4 5 6 7 8 9 LKV 24 23 22 21 20

ISBN 978-1-259-99168-4 (bound edition)
MHID 1-259-99168-7 (bound edition)

ISBN 978-1-260-70758-8 (loose-leaf edition)
MHID 1-260-70758-X (loose-leaf edition)

ISBN 978-1-260-70761-8 (instructor's edition)
MHID 1-260-70761-X (instructor's edition)

Senior Portfolio Manager: Sadie Ray
Senior Product Developer: Shaun Bauer
Executive Marketing Manager: Ann Helgerson
Marketing Manager: Raúl J. Vázquez López
Lead Content Project Managers: Sandy Wille and Jodi Banowetz
Content Project Manager: Ryan Warczynski
Senior Buyer: Susan K. Culbertson
Design: Beth Blech
Content Licensing Specialist: Carrie Burger
Compositor: Lumina Datamatics, Inc.

All credits appearing on page or at the end of the book are considered to be an extension of the copyright page.

Library of Congress Cataloging-in-Publication Data
Names: Dorwick, Thalia, 1944– author.
Title: Puntos de partida / Thalia Dorwick, Ana M. Pérez-Gironés, Wesleyan University, Anne Becher, University of Colorado, Boulder.
Description: Eleventh edition. | New York, NY : McGraw Hill, [2021] | Includes index.
Identifiers: LCCN 2019024766 | ISBN 9781259991684 (student edition) | ISBN 9781260707618 (instructor's edition)
Subjects: LCSH: Spanish language—Textbooks for foreign speakers—English.
Classification: LCC PC4129.E5 P86 2021 | DDC 460.71—dc23
LC record available at https://lccn.loc.gov/2019024766

mheducation.com/highered

Puntos de partida has what you need.

In any language-learning setting, students require numerous and various opportunities to read, write, hear, and speak. *Puntos de partida* sets the standard for Spanish-language teaching with its concise grammar explanations, practical vocabulary, integration of cultures, and abundant resources. An innovative program that has been continuously refined for today's classroom, *Puntos* delivers proven pedagogy with clear and effective presentations, comprehensive teaching materials, and powerfully adaptive digital tools.

Puntos builds on the holistic, four-skills approach it pioneered, and offers a wealth of resources for every instructor and every learner. Your students are unique. *Puntos* has what they need.

©Kdonmuang/Shutterstock

Proven Approach

Puntos de partida has been the starting point for over a million students beginning to learn Spanish. Its winning combination is digital innovation plus proven approach.

Here is how *Puntos* sets the standard for Introductory Spanish programs:

Comprehensive scope and sequence

In *Puntos*, the hallmark approach to vocabulary and grammar focuses on the acquisition of vocabulary during the early stages of language learning (**Capítulo 1: Ante todo**) and then at the start of each chapter throughout the text. Grammar is introduced in thorough explanations, with careful attention given to skill development rather than grammatical knowledge alone.

To this end, the overall organization carefully progresses from formulaic expressions to vocabulary and grammar relevant to daily life and personal interests (studies, family, home, leisure activities), then goes on to prepare students for survival situations (ordering a meal, traveling), and finally branches out to broader themes (current events, social and environmental issues). This forward progress is reinforced by a cyclical structure where vocabulary, grammar, and language functions are continuously reviewed and recycled.

Students come to class ready

Our students tell us that, thanks to the clear, concise grammar explanations and recaps in *Puntos*, they are able to grasp new concepts more readily and feel better prepared. They love the conversational language, practical examples, and the organization of complex, dense explanations into manageable chunks. By making grammar concepts more approachable, *Puntos* helps raise students' confidence, and increased student confidence yields more active communication in the target language in your classroom.

Integrated four-skills approach with scaffolded activities and projects

One of the defining features of *Puntos* is its careful sequencing of activities, moving students from controlled to free-form tasks. Building off of the improved scaffolding in the tenth edition, the eleventh edition includes **Proyectos**, engaging communication tasks positioned at key moments in each chapter that guide students to create in the target language and accomplish a culturally significant goal.

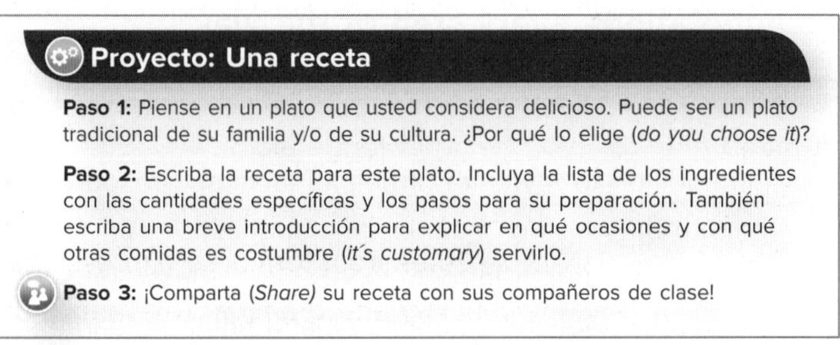

Proyecto: Una receta

Paso 1: Piense en un plato que usted considera delicioso. Puede ser un plato tradicional de su familia y/o de su cultura. ¿Por qué lo elige (*do you choose it*)?

Paso 2: Escriba la receta para este plato. Incluya la lista de los ingredientes con las cantidades específicas y los pasos para su preparación. También escriba una breve introducción para explicar en qué ocasiones y con qué otras comidas es costumbre (*it's customary*) servirlo.

Paso 3: ¡Comparta (*Share*) su receta con sus compañeros de clase!

Inclusion of all Spanish-speaking countries

The eleventh edition of *Puntos* highlights the proven concept that introducing students to the Spanish-speaking world goes beyond asking them to simply absorb information about each country. Instead, a few key cultural insights, appearing at various moments throughout each chapter, serve to spark students' interest and, by closing with a question that asks students to reflect on cultural comparisons, encourage them to create personal connections with the cultures of the Spanish-speaking world.

EL MUNDO HISPANOHABLANTE[a]
• Más de[b] 500 (quinientos) millones de personas hablan español.
• El español es la lengua oficial de 20 (veinte) naciones y de Puerto Rico.
[a]El... *The Spanish-speaking world*
[b]Más... *More than*

Comprehensive *Teaching Resources*

Puntos de partida was designed to provide novice and experienced instructors alike with the tools needed to enter the classroom—be it face-to-face or online—well-prepared to engage students in learning. As a comprehensive program, *Puntos* offers a wide array of resources and supporting materials to function as a flexible framework that can be tailored to individual teaching situations and goals. Whether you're using the program for your face-to-face, hybrid, or online class, the wealth of resources sets up both instructors and students for success.

Instructor's annotations every step of the way

Instructors can find teaching suggestions for each and every grammar presentation and practice activity in the text, with point-by-point guidance on presenting the material in class, in addition to a wealth of helpful facts and resources, variations on and supplements to the existing material, and suggestions for follow-up and extension. Taking into account that Introductory Spanish classrooms typically contain a mix of true beginners, false beginners, and heritage learners, *Puntos* offers a designated space for expanded suggestions for heritage speakers that makes it even easier to meet the needs of students with varying levels of language proficiency.

The Heritage Learner Support Modules referenced in the instructor's annotations are designed to help heritage learners avoid some common pitfalls. The modules are assignable on Connect and available in PowerPoint format, and may be accessed by going to the Library tab on Connect and navigating to "Instructor resources."

HERITAGE SPEAKERS

Heritage Learner Modules. En español las letras *b* y *v* se pronuncian de la misma manera. Pero, aunque suenen igual, hay que saber distinguir entre las palabras que se escriben con *b* y las que se escriben con *v*. Anime a los hispanohablantes a repasar la información sobre las letras *b* y *v* en español que se presenta en el *Módulo de aprendizaje para hispanohablantes* titulado «*The letters B and V*».

Flexible testing program

A key part of the instructor resources available with *Puntos* is the comprehensive testing program, available in both print and digital formats. Whether you use the testing program as a model to customize your own tests, or you want to quickly and easily assign existing exams or poolable questions, the testing program offers multiple versions for each chapter from which instructors can draw.

Updated supplemental activities manual

The eleventh edition can be accompanied by the updated *Supplementary Materials to Accompany* Puntos de partida, by Sharon Foerster. The supplementary materials are an updated teacher's guide to *Puntos* and consist of worksheets, short pronunciation practice activities, listening exercises, grammar worksheets, integrative communication-building activities, comprehensive chapter reviews, and language games.

New grammar tutorial videos

Short and engaging, the new grammar tutorial videos, which are conveniently available in the eBook, are hosted by a friendly cast of characters, who provide clear explanations in English with examples of Spanish grammatical concepts.

Engaging and Immersive **Digital Tools**

Connect is the most powerful and flexible course management system available. Rooted in research on effective student learning practices, the platform integrates adaptive learning tools with dynamic, engaging language practice activities. The result is better student learning of the Spanish language.

A personalized and adaptive learning and teaching experience

No two students learn a language the same way or at the same rate. Students enter the Introductory Spanish course with a wide range of knowledge and experience, from true beginners to heritage learners.

McGraw-Hill's adaptive learning tools provide each student with a personalized and adaptive learning experience based on individual needs. As the student works through a series of probes around the vocabulary and grammar presented in each chapter, our adaptive technology identifies what the student knows and doesn't know, and continuously tailors the subsequent probes to focus on those areas where the student needs the most help. Each student learns and masters core vocabulary and grammar at his or her own pace and comes to class better prepared to communicate in the target language.

And just as no two students learn a language the same way, no two Spanish courses are taught the same way. Connect provides the instructor with both the ability and flexibility to pull from the robust set of content available in the platform and craft a unique learning path based on the goals of the course. Be it in a face-to-face, hybrid, or fully online course, Connect can adapt to you and to your students to create the ideal learning environment.

Student-centered

Students learn best when they are involved and interested in the material being taught. *Practice Spanish: Study Abroad*, the market's first 3-D immersive language game designed exclusively by McGraw-Hill, brings the language to the students in a fun, engaging, and immersive gaming experience. Students "study abroad" virtually in Colombia where they will create their very own avatar, live with a host family, make new friends, and navigate a variety of real-world scenarios using their quickly developing Spanish language skills. Students earn points and rewards for successfully accomplishing these tasks, and instructors have the ability to assign specific tasks, monitor student achievement, and incorporate the game into the classroom experience. Your Learning Technology Representative can provide more information.

ReadAnywhere app

Our new ReadAnywhere app lets students access important course materials on their mobile device, both online and offline. ReadAnywhere includes the same functionality as the eBook offered in Connect with auto-sync across both platforms. Visit mheducation.com/ReadAnywhere to learn more.

New communication tools

The 11th edition of ***Puntos*** offers two new communication tools so students can easily interact in the target language with their classmates and instructors online.

Recordable Video Chat powered by GoReact, is a chat tool, now available on Connect, that allows students to practice live, synchronous communication. Up to six students can participate in a recorded conversation and instructors can provide personalized and on-the-spot feedback. Instructors can choose from a wide variety of pre-built activities or create their own.

Voice Board, also powered by GoReact, is our new asynchronous voice tool that gives students the chance to post video, audio, or text comments related to the topic and respond to their classmates' posts.

Robust data

Instructors and students alike want to know how students are performing in the course and where they can improve. The powerful reporting tools in Connect surface actionable data to both instructors and students so steps can be taken by both groups to ensure student success.

The first and only analytics tool of its kind, Connect Insight is a series of visual data displays—each framed by an intuitive question—to provide instructors at-a-glance information regarding how your class is doing. Connect Insight provides analysis on five key insights, available at a moment's notice from your Connect course.

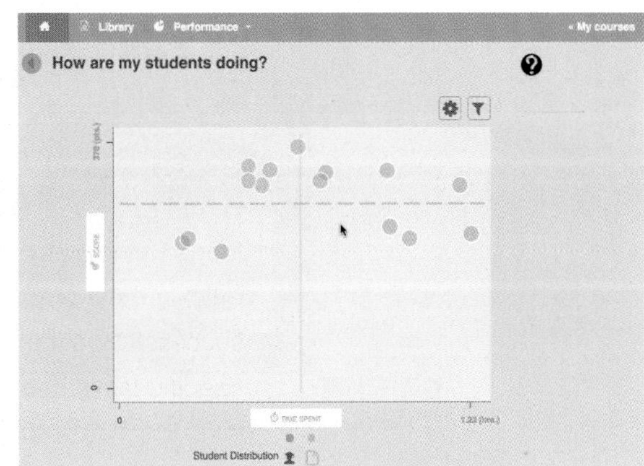

LearnSmart provides powerful reports to view student progress by module and detail with completion breakdown, along with class performance data, frequency of missed questions, and a view into the most challenging learning objectives. Metacognitive reports allow instructors to view statistics on how knowledgeable their students are about their own comprehension and learning. What's more, LearnSmart provides students their own progress reports so they can take full responsibility for their own learning.

Practice Spanish: Study Abroad is a 3-D language game designed for college and university students looking to make the Spanish language come to life in an engaging, motivating, and immersive environment.

Practice Spanish: Study Abroad

Attend a fictional study abroad program in Colombia and live with a host family, make friends, and experience life in a Spanish-speaking environment.

Choose and customize an avatar and interact with non-player game characters in a variety of real-life quests to earn points and rewards.

Fun, adaptive mini-games are also available to practice the target vocabulary and grammar.

WHAT'S NEW

Functional design and increased accessibility

- Visually fresh: Many new photos, realia, and updated drawings.
- Colorblind-friendly text: Now all red text used as a call-out is also underlined.
- Language-tagged eBook: Our eBook is now coded to allow screen readers to flip seamlessly from Spanish to English pronunciations, as appropriate.

New opportunities for communication in the target language

- **Mundo hispano (*The Hispanic World*):** This five-part capstone section delves deeper into each chapter's country of focus and presents authentic materials, including literature, from the Spanish-speaking world. **Textos orales** presents authentic listening tasks, **Escritura** contains writing assignments and other real-world writing tasks in Spanish, and **Más ideas para su portafolio** offers ideas for creating a portfolio to showcase what students can do in Spanish.
- **En acción:** Brief communication tasks tied to the chapter themes and topics of the readings encourage student production in the target language.
- **Proyectos:** Engaging communication tasks guide students to accomplish culturally significant goals in Spanish.
- Open-ended tests on Connect: The eleventh edition welcomes our open-ended tests, formerly available only in print, to Connect.

En acción

En parejas, entérense del (*find out about the*) pronóstico del tiempo para los próximos dos días en el estado donde viven y preparen un breve pronóstico en español. Intenten (*Try*) usar el vocabulario que se usa en el pronóstico del tiempo argentino.

Integrated culture

- Culturally based activities: More grammar and vocabulary exercises center on cultural context.
- **Lectura** (formerly **A leer**): Readings are simplified and include more interactive activities.
- **Todo junto** (formerly **Un poco de todo**): Each section starts with a **Lengua y cultura** activity to practice newly acquired and recycled grammar and vocabulary.

Digital tools

- Vocabulary toggle: EBook vocabulary presentations now can toggle to reveal an unlabeled version for convenient review.
- New grammar tutorial videos: Engaging, brief videos offer students concise grammar explanations in English.
- *Practice Spanish: Study Abroad*: This interactive 3-D game immerses students in a virtual study abroad experience in Colombia. *Practice Spanish* facilitates real-world application that integrates culture, grammar, and vocabulary, and now launches directly from Connect.
- New communication tools: Our new Recordable Video Chat and Voice Board powered by GoReact allow for easy synchronous and asynchronous communication in the target language.

ABOUT THE AUTHORS

Thalia Dorwick retired as McGraw-Hill's Editor-in-Chief for Humanities, Social Sciences, and Languages. For many years she was also in charge of McGraw-Hill's World Languages college list in Spanish, French, Italian, German, Japanese, and Russian. She has taught at Allegheny College, California State University (Sacramento), and Case Western Reserve University, where she received her Ph.D. in Spanish in 1973. She was recognized as an Outstanding Foreign Language Teacher by the California Foreign Language Teachers Association in 1978. Dr. Dorwick is the coauthor of several textbooks and the author of several articles on language teaching issues. She was a frequent guest speaker on topics related to language learning, and she was also an invited speaker at the *II Congreso Internacional de la Lengua Española*, in Valladolid, Spain, in October 2001. In retirement, she consulted for McGraw-Hill, especially in the area of world languages, which is of personal interest to her. She was a Vice President of the Board of Trustees of Case Western Reserve University and a past President of the Board of Directors of Berkeley Repertory Theatre.

Ana María Pérez-Gironés a native of Seville, Spain, is an Adjunct Full Professor of Spanish at Wesleyan University, Middletown, Connecticut. She received a Licenciatura en Filología Anglogermánica from the Universidad de Sevilla, and an M.A. in General Linguistics from Cornell University. At Wesleyan, she teaches and coordinates Spanish language courses at all levels, including Spanish for heritage speakers. She has also served as resident director of the Vassar-Wesleyan Program in Madrid. She has published a variety of pedagogical material, including the series En una palabra (Georgetown University Press), and Más, Español Intermedio (McGraw-Hill).

Anne Becher received her M.A. in Hispanic Linguistics in 1992 from the University of Colorado—Boulder, and now coordinates first-year Spanish courses and teaches pedagogy and methods courses for the Department of Spanish and Portuguese there. She has taught beginning through advanced levels of Spanish since 1996, including several years teaching Modified Spanish classes for students with difficulty learning languages. She presents frequently at the Colorado Congress of Foreign Language Teachers (CCFLT) and other conferences on language teaching, and serves on the board of the Colorado chapter of American Association of Teachers of Spanish and Portuguese. Recently she won teaching excellence awards from CCFLT and the Southwest Conference on Language Teaching (SWCOLT). She co-edited the bilingual literary journal *La selva subterranea* from 1987–1996.

ACKNOWLEDGMENTS

We would like to thank the many friends and colleagues who served on boards of advisors or as consultants, completed reviews or surveys, and attended symposia or focus groups. Their feedback was indispensible in creating the *Puntos* program. The appearance of their names in the following lists does not necessarily constitute their endorsement of the program or its methodology.

Symposia

Austin, TX

Julia Bussade
University of Mississippi
Sara Casler
Sierra College
Elsa Castillo
CSU, Fresno
Manuel Cortés-Castañeda
Eastern Kentucky University
Marina Crouse
Diablo Valley College
Jabier Elorrieta
New York University
Mandy Faretta-Stutenberg
Northern Illinois University
Leah Fonder-Solano
University of Southern Mississippi
Donna Gillespie
College of DuPage
José Juan Gómez-Becerra
Eastern Kentucky University
Marga Kelly
Sierra College
Alejandro Muñoz-Garcés
Coastal Carolina University
Lynn Pearson
Bowling Green State University
Marianela Rivera
Florida Gulf Coast University
Mary Sobhani
University of Arkansas–Fort Smith
Helga Winkler
Moorpark College
Evangeline Velez-Cobb
Palo Alto College
Marcy Ziska
University of Arizona

Chicago, IL

Suzanne Buck
Central New Mexico Community College
Araceli Canalini
Chicago State University
Sara Casler
Sierra College
Esther Castro
San Diego State
An Chung Cheng
University of Toledo
Scott Gibby
Austin Community College
Steven Sheppard
University of North Texas Denton
Jen Vojtko Rubi
University of Cincinnati
Germán Zárate
Western Michigan University

Reviewers

Ana Afzali
Citrus College
Pilar Alcalde
The University of Memphis
Tim Altanero
Austin Community College
Dorothy Álvarez
Wright State University
Javier Alvarez-Jaimes
Eastern Kentucky University
Deisy Anderson
Kankakee Community College
Collin Ashmore
Washington College
Bárbara Ávila-Shah
University at Buffalo, SUNY
Margarita Balentine
Phoenix College
Maria Barker
Sam Houston State University
Wanda Baumgartel
Snead State Community College
Clare Bennett
University of Alaska Southeast Ketchikan
Lisa Bischoff
La Roche College
Nicolas Bordage
Long Beach State
Donna Boston Ross
Catawba Valley Community College
Ana Bouloy
Broward College
Chris Bourg
Regis University
Steven Byrd
University of New England
Maria C. Campos Fuentes
DeSales University
Gabriela Carrión
Regis University

Carmen Del Castillo-Zerbe
York College of PA

Isabel Castro
Towson University

Rosa María Chism
Penn State Abington College

Robert L. Colvin
Brigham Young University–Idaho

Marcos Contreras
Modesto Junior College

Rachel Cortest
University of Oklahoma

Mayra Cummings
Paris Junior College

Tonka Curtis
Eastern Arizona College

Kit Decker
Piedmont Virginia Community College

David Detwiler
MiraCosta College

Elizabeth Díaz
Belmont Abbey College

T. Dickerson
Indiana Wesleyan University

Margaret Eomurian
Houston Community College

Edward Erazo
Broward College

Dina A. Fabery
University of Central Florida

Timothy J. Foxsmith
University of Texas at Arlington

Daniel Fulmer
Snead State Community College

Scott Gibby
Austin Community College

Rafael Gómez
California State University Monterey Bay

José Juan Gómez-Becerra
Eastern Kentucky University

Yolanda Gonzalez
Valencia College

Elena Grajeda
Pima Community College

Charlene M. Grant
Skidmore College

Sergio Guzmán
College of Southern Nevada

Alan G. Hartman
Mercy College

Mary Hartson
Oakland University

Maria Hasler-Barker
Sam Houston State University

Valerie Hecht
College of Southern Nevada

D. Eric Holt
University of South Carolina

Elena Iglesias-Villamel
Hiram College

Becky Jaimes
Austin Community College

Ana Juarez
Brigham Young University–Idaho

Gioia Marie Kerlin
Rogers State University

Jeremy Larochelle
University of Mary Washington

Tim Lee
Catawba Valley Community College

Joseph López-Marrón
Bronx Community College–CUNY

Karen Malcolm
University of Colorado Boulder

Pablo Antonio Martinez
The University of the District of Columbia

Carlos David Martínez
University of Houston

Pablo A. Martínez
The University of the District of Columbia

Michael Martínez-Raguso
Colby College

Rob Martinsen
Brigham Young University

Francesco Masala-Martínez
Florida Gulf Coast University

Thomas J. Mathews
Weber State University

Marco Mena
Massbay Community College

Wendy Mendez-Hasselman
Palm Beach State College

José Mendoza
Campbell University

Joseph Menig
Valencia College

Ryan Minier
Danville Area Community College

Charles H. Molano
Lehigh Carbon Community College

Joshua Mora
Wayland Baptist University

Javier M. Morin
Del Mar College Corpus Christi

Donald Mueller
Pellissippi State Community College

Raquel Olivera
Moorpark College

Michelle Orecchio
University of Michigan

M. Patricia Orozco Watrel
University of Mary Washington

Elizabeth Osborne
Worcester State University

Tika H. Owens
Winston-Salem State University

Beatriz Perez Reyes
University of Louisville

Rosa M. Pillcurima
Clemson University

Dora Y. Romero
Broward College

Susan Salazar-Kleiner

Roman Santos
Mohawk Valley Community College

Julie A. Sellers
Benedictine College

Georgia Seminet
St. Edward's University

Natalie Sobalvarro
Merced College

Adriana Sommerville
Johnson County Community College

Samuel Sommerville
Johnson County Community College

Alexander Steffanell
Lee University

Kerri Stephenson
Johnson County Community College

Rosa Maria Tamayo Chism

Patricia Tello
University of Oklahoma

Encarna Turner
Wake Forest University

Elinor A Torda
University of California Merced

Bernardo Vallejo
Houston Community College Central

Daniel Vargas
Arizona State University–SILC

Titania Vargas
Illinois Central College

Edgar Mauricio Vargas Blanco
Community College of Aurora

Kimberly Vinall
De Anza College

Tina Ware-Walters
Oklahoma Christian University

Sandra Watts
The University of North Carolina at Charlotte

Justin P. White
Florida Atlantic University

The authors wish to thank the following friends and professional colleagues. Their feedback, support, and contributions are greatly appreciated.

- The colleagues of Ana Pérez-Gironés at Wesleyan University, for answering many dialectal questions and much more
- Anne Becher's colleagues—graduate students, lecturers, faculty, and administrators—at the University of Colorado, Boulder
- Laura Chastain, for her meticulous work on the language and linguistic accuracy of the manuscript, over many editions but especially this one
- Shaun Bauer, of McGraw-Hill, who has been a wonderful collaborator in all ways on this edition

Finally, the authors would like to thank their families and close personal friends for all of their love, support, and patience throughout the creation of this edition. **¡Los queremos mucho!**

Contributors

Soraya Alem, Nicole Casnettie, Laura Chastain, Kevin Donnelly, A. Raymond Elliott, Allison Hawco, Ana Vanesa Hidalgo Del Rosario, Margaret Hines, Juliana Jiménez, Jae Johnson, Constance Kihyet, Avi Kotzer, Christopher LaFond, Gabriella Licata, Misha Maclaird, Celia Meana, Ron Nelms, Pennie Nichols, Juan Sebastián Ospina León, María Sabló-Yates, Julie A. Sellers, Nina Tunac Basey

Product Team

Editorial and Marketing: Janet Banhidi, Shaun Bauer, Margaryta Bondarenko, Katie Crouch, Dawn Groundwater, Ann Helgerson, Miranda Hency, Amanda Hirt, Jamie Laferrera, Sadie Ray, Amy Reed, Kim Schroeder-Freund, Katie Stevens, Raúl J. Vázquez-López

Art, Design, and Production: Jodi Banowetz, Beth Blech, Carrie Burger, Kelly Heinrichs, Ryan Warczynski, Sandy Wille

Media Partners: Aptara, BBC Motion Gallery, Cenveo, Eastern Sky Studios, Hurix, Klic Video Productions, Inc., Laserwords, Latinallure Voiceover, LearningMate, Lumina Datamatics

CONTENTS

	VOCABULARY & PRONUNCIATION	GRAMMAR
3 La familia *64*  ©UpperCut Images/Alamy  México	La familia y los parientes 66 Los números del 31 al 100 68 **Nota comunicativa** Cómo expresar la edad: **tener... años** 69 Los adjetivos 70 **Pronunciación** Stress and Written Accent Marks (Part 1) 72	**5** Describing • Adjectives: Gender, Number, and Position 73 **Nota comunicativa** Otras nacionalidades 77 **6** Expressing *to be* • Present Tense of **ser**; Summary of Uses (Part 2) 79 **Nota comunicativa** Cómo dar explicaciones : Porque y para + infinitive 83 **7** Expressing Possession • Unstressed Possessive Adjectives (Part 1) 84 **8** Expressing Actions • Present Tense of **-er** and **-ir** Verbs; Subject Pronouns (Part 2) 88 **Nota comunicativa** Cómo expresar la frecuencia de las acciones 92
4 De compras *102*  ©Danny Lehman/Getty Images  Guatemala  Honduras	De compras: La ropa 104 **Nota comunicativa** Preguntas coletilla (*tag*) 106 Los colores: ¿De qué color es? 107 Los números a partir del 100 109 **Pronunciación** Stress and Written Accent Marks (Part 2) 112	**9** Pointing Out People and Things • Demonstrative Adjectives (Part 2) and Pronouns 114 **10** Expressing Actions and States • **Tener, venir, poder, preferir, querer;** Some Idioms with **tener** 118 **Nota comunicativa** **Mucho** y **poco** 121 **11** Expressing Destination and Future Actions • **Ir;** The Contraction **al; Ir** + **a** + infinitive 123
5 En casa *134*  ©Jon Arnold Images Ltd/ Alamy  El Salvador  Nicaragua	Los muebles, los cuartos y otras partes de la casa 136 ¿Qué día es hoy? 138 **Nota comunicativa** Cómo expresar *on* con los días de la semana 139 ¿Cuándo? • Las preposiciones (Part 1) 140	**12** Expressing Actions • **Hacer, oír, poner, salir, traer, ver** 143 **13** Expressing Actions • Present Tense of Stem-changing Verbs (Part 2) 149 **14** Expressing *-self/-selves* • Reflexive Pronouns (Part 1) 153 **Nota comunicativa** Cómo expresar una secuencia de acciones 156

VIDEO, LISTENING, AND WRITING

READING AND CULTURE

©McGraw-Hill Education/Klic Video Productions

©McGraw-Hill Education/Klic Video Productions

©McGraw-Hill Education/Klic Video Productions

©McGraw-Hill Education/Klic Video Productions

©McGraw-Hill Education/Klic Video Productions

©McGraw-Hill Education/Klic Video Productions

	VOCABULARY & PRONUNCIATION	GRAMMAR
6 Las estaciones y el tiempo *168*  ©Paul Souders/The Image Bank/Getty Images  Costa Rica	¿Qué tiempo hace hoy? 170 **Nota comunicativa** Otras expresiones con **tener** 171 Los meses y las estaciones del año 172 ¿Dónde está?: Las preposiciones (Part 2) 174	**15** ¿Qué están haciendo? • Present Progressive: **Estar** + **-ndo** 177 **Nota comunicativa** El gerundio con otros verbos 181 **16** **¿Ser** o **estar**? • Summary of the Uses of **ser** and **estar** 182 **Nota comunicativa** El uso de adjetivos + **por** 185 **17** Describing • Comparisons 189
7 ¡A comer! *204*  ©The Visual Explorer/ Shutterstock  Panamá	La comida y las comidas 206 **Nota comunicativa** Más vocabulario para hablar de la comida 207 ¿Qué sabe usted y a quién conoce? 209	**18** Expressing *what* or *who(m)* • Direct Objects: The Personal **a;** Direct Object Pronouns 213 **Nota comunicativa** Cómo expresar una acción muy reciente: **acabar** + **de** + *infinitivo* 218 **19** Expressing Negation • Indefinite and Negative Words 219 **20** Influencing Others • Commands (Part 1): Formal Commands 223
8 De viaje *236*  ©Giuseppe Crimeni/ Shutterstock  La República Dominicana	De viaje 238 De vacaciones 240 **Nota comunicativa** Otro uso de la palabra **se:** para expresar acciones impersonales 242	**21** Expressing *to whom* or *for whom* • Indirect Object Pronouns; **Dar** and **decir** 245 **22** Expressing Likes and Dislikes • **Gustar** (Part 2) 250 **Nota comunicativa** Otras maneras de expresar los gustos y preferencias 254 **23** Talking About the Past (Part 1) • Preterite of Regular Verbs and of **dar, hacer, ir,** and **ser** 255

VIDEO, LISTENING, AND WRITING

©McGraw-Hill Education/Klic Video Productions

©McGraw-Hill Education/Klic Video Productions

©McGraw-Hill Education/Klic Video Productions

©McGraw-Hill Education/Klic Video Productions

©McGraw-Hill Education/Klic Video Productions

©McGraw-Hill Education/Klic Video Productions

READING AND CULTURE

VOCABULARY & PRONUNCIATION	GRAMMAR

9 Los días festivos *270*

©Evelyn Paley/Alamy

Cuba

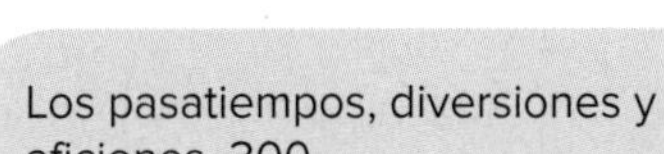

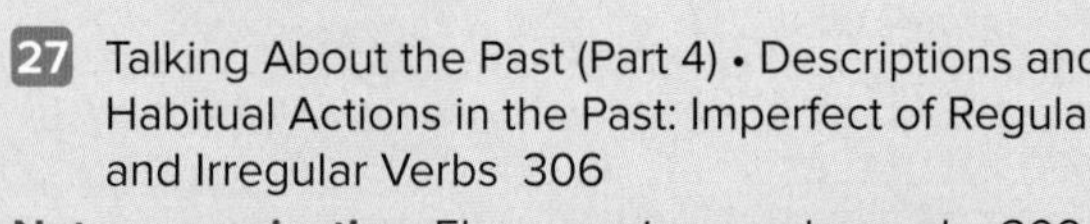

10 El tiempo libre *298*

©Alfred Wekelo/Shutterstock

Puerto Rico

11 La salud *326*

©ZUMA Press, Inc/Alamy

Venezuela

	VOCABULARY & PRONUNCIATION	GRAMMAR
12 ¡Conectad@s! *356*  ©Radius/SuperStock  Colombia	En el centro de una ciudad 358 La tecnología 360	33 Influencing Others (Part 2) • **Tú** (Informal) Commands 364 **Nota comunicativa** Verbos derivados de **poner, tener** y **venir** 367 34 Expressing Subjective Actions or States • Present Subjunctive (Part 1): An Introduction 369 35 Expressing Desires and Requests • Use of the Subjunctive (Part 2): Influence 375
13 El arte y la cultura *388*  ©Bernai Velarde  El Ecuador  Bolivia	Las artes 390 **Nota comunicativa** Más sobre los gustos y preferencias 391 Los ordinales 394	36 Expressing Feelings • Use of the Subjunctive (Part 3): Emotion 396 **Nota comunicativa** Cómo expresar los deseos con **ojalá** 399 37 Expressing Uncertainty • Use of the Subjunctive (Part 4): Doubt and Denial 401 **Nota comunicativa** Verbos que requieren preposiciones 404 38 Expressing Influence, Emotion, Doubt, and Denial • The Subjunctive (Part 5): A Summary 405

VIDEO, LISTENING, AND WRITING

©McGraw-Hill Education/Klic Video Productions

©McGraw-Hill Education/Klic Video Productions

READING AND CULTURE

©McGraw-Hill Education/Klic Video Productions

©McGraw-Hill Education/Klic Video Productions

VIDEO, LISTENING, AND WRITING

©McGraw-Hill Education/Klic Video Productions

©McGraw-Hill Education/Klic Video Productions

©McGraw-Hill Education/Klic Video Productions

©McGraw-Hill Education/Klic Video Productions

©McGraw-Hill Education/Klic Video Productions

©McGraw-Hill Education/Klic Video Productions

READING AND CULTURE

VOCABULARY & PRONUNCIATION | GRAMMAR

VIDEO, LISTENING, AND WRITING

©McGraw-Hill Education/Klic Video Productions

©McGraw-Hill Education/Klic Video Productions

READING AND CULTURE

©McGraw-Hill Education/Klic Video Productions

©McGraw-Hill Education/Klic Video Productions

Appendices

Vocabulary

An Invitation to Puntos de partida

Puntos de partida means *points of departure* in Spanish. This program will be your point of departure for learning Spanish and for learning about Hispanic cultures. With *Puntos de partida*, you will get ready to communicate with Spanish speakers in this country and in other parts of the Spanish-speaking world. To speak a language means much more than just learning its grammar and vocabulary. To know a language is to know the people who speak it. For this reason, *Puntos de partida* will provide you with cultural information to help you understand and appreciate the traditions and values of Spanish-speaking people all over the world. Get ready for the adventure of learning Spanish!

1

Ante todo°

Ante... *First of all*

En este capítulo°

En... *In this chapter*

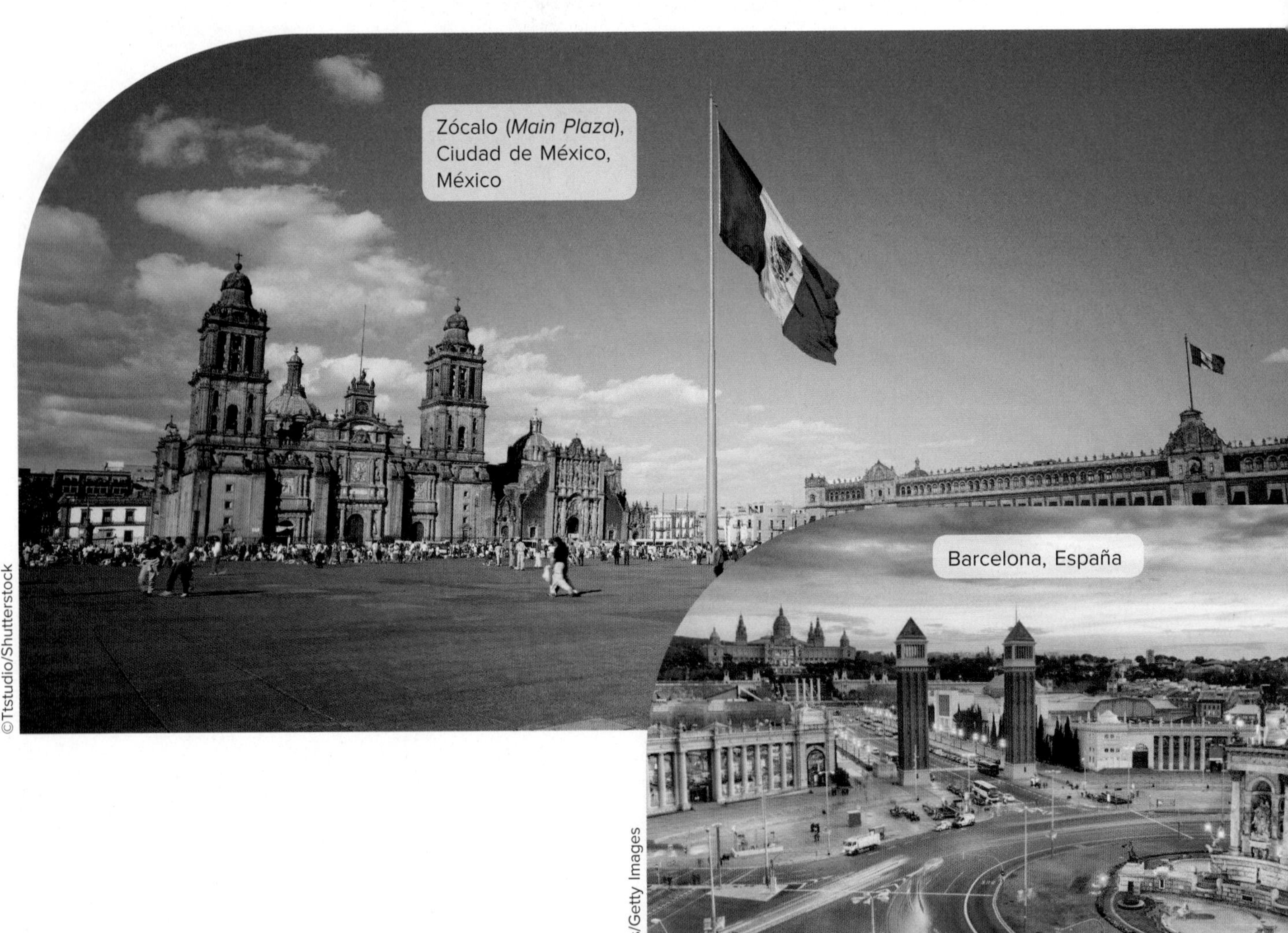

Zócalo (*Main Plaza*), Ciudad de México, México

Barcelona, España

©Ttstudio/Shutterstock

©Mark Lewis/Getty Images

EL MUNDO HISPANOHABLANTE[a]

- Más de[b] 500 (quinientos) millones de personas hablan español.
- El español es la lengua oficial de 20 (veinte) naciones y de Puerto Rico.

[a]El... *The Spanish-speaking world*
[b]Más... *More than*

ENTREVISTA° *Interview*

Here are some questions that a native speaker of Spanish has answered. When you have completed this chapter, you will be able to give your own answers to the same questions.

- ¡Hola! ¿Cómo está usted?[a]
- ¿Cómo se llama?[b]
- ¿De dónde es?[c]
- ¿Cómo es usted?[d]

[a]¡Hola!... *Hello! How are you?* [b]¿Cómo... *What's your name?* [c]¿De... *Where are you from?* [d]¿Cómo... *What are you like?*

Alejandra Hernández Soto contesta las preguntas.[a]

- ¡Hola! Estoy[b] muy bien. ¿Y usted?[c]
- Me llamo Alejandra Hernández Soto.
- Soy de[d] Guanajuato, México.
- ¿Cómo soy?[e] Optimista, responsable, sentimental y muy independiente. ¿Y cómo es usted?

[a]contesta... *answers the questions* [b]*I am* [c]¿Y... *And (how are) you?* [d]Soy... *I'm from* [e]¿Cómo... *What am I like?*

PRIMERA° PARTE

First

You can hear the pronunciation of theme vocabulary words and phrases in the Connect eBook.

Saludos° y expresiones de cortesía

Greetings

Here are some words, phrases, and expressions for meeting and greeting others in Spanish. Can you tell the difference between those that are formal and those that are more informal or familiar (as on a first-name basis)?

Situaciones formales

©iakovenko/123RF

1. ELISA VELASCO: Buenas tardes, señor Gómez.
MARTÍN GÓMEZ: Muy buenas, señora Velasco. ¿Cómo está?
ELISA VELASCO: Bien, gracias. ¿Y usted?
MARTÍN GÓMEZ: Muy bien, gracias. Hasta luego.
ELISA VELASCO: Adiós.

©Tom Fowlks/Getty Images

2. LUPE: Buenos días, profesor.
JUAN PÉREZ: Buenos días. ¿Cómo se llama usted, señorita?
LUPE: Me llamo Lupe Carrasco.
JUAN PÉREZ: Mucho gusto, Lupe.
LUPE: Igualmente.

©GoGo Images Corporation/Alamy

Situaciones informales

3. JOSÉ: ¡Hola, Carmen!
CARMEN: ¿Qué tal, José? ¿Cómo estás?
JOSÉ: Muy bien. ¿Y tú?
CARMEN: Regular. Nos vemos mañana, ¿eh?
JOSÉ: Bien. Hasta mañana.

©Radius/SuperStock

4. MIGUEL RENÉ: Hola. Me llamo Miguel René. ¿Y tú? ¿Cómo te llamas?
KARINA: Me llamo Karina. Mucho gusto.
MIGUEL RENÉ: Encantado, Karina. Y, ¿de dónde eres?
KARINA: Soy de Venezuela. ¿Y tú?
MIGUEL RENÉ: Yo soy de México.

Translations of short dialogues like the ones on this page will always be at the foot of the page, but you should try to read them without the translations first!

---

1. *EV: Good afternoon, Mr. Gómez. MG: Afternoon, Mrs. Velasco. How are you? EV: Fine, thank you. And you? MG: Very well, thanks. See you later. EV: Bye.*
2. *L: Good morning, professor. JP: Good morning. What's your name, miss? L: My name is Lupe Carrasco. JP: Nice to meet you, Lupe. L: Likewise.*
3. *J: Hi, Carmen! C: How's it going, José? How are you? J: Very well. And you? C: OK. See you tomorrow, OK? J: Fine. Until tomorrow.*
4. *MR: Hello. My name is Miguel René. And you? What's your name? K: My name is Karina. Nice to meet you. MR: Nice to meet you, Karina. And where are you from? K: I'm from Venezuela. And you? MR: I'm from Mexico.*

Note the use of **red and underlined** text to highlight aspects of Spanish that you should pay special attention to.

	Formal		Informal	
Títulos	**señor (Sr.)** **señora (Sra.)** **señorita (Srta.)** **profesor** (*for a man*) **profesora** (*for a woman*)	Mr. Mrs., ma'am Miss		
Saludos	**buenos días** **buenas tardes** **buenas noches** **(muy) buenas**	good morning good afternoon/evening good evening/night good day (*any time*)	**hola**	hi
Preguntas (*Questions*)	**¿Cómo está?** **¿Y usted?**	How are you? And you?	**¿Cómo estás?** **¿Qué tal?** **¿Y tú?**	How are you? And you?
	—¿Cómo se llama (usted)? **—Me llamo...** "What's your name?" "My name is . . . "		**—¿Cómo te llamas (tú)?** **—Me llamo...** "What's your name?" "My name is . . . "	
	—¿De dónde es (usted)? **—(Yo) Soy de...** "Where are you from?" "I'm from . . . "		**—¿De dónde eres (tú)?** **—(Yo) Soy de...** "Where are you from?" "I'm from . . . "	

¡OJO! means *Watch out!* or *Pay attention!* in Spanish.

¡OJO!

There is no Spanish equivalent for *Ms.;* use **Sra.** or **Srta.,** as appropriate.

¡OJO!

Note the accent marks on Spanish words that ask questions.

¡OJO!

Pay attention to the endings and other words associated with **tú** and **usted**.

Nota cultural

©Hola Images/age fotostock

¿Qué pasa, hombre? (*What's up, man?*)

Los saludos en el mundo° hispano

°*world*

Hispanics all over the world hug and kiss when they are greeting each other a lot more frequently than do non-Hispanics in this country. Younger people especially greet in this way, even when they have just met. Two men will typically hug or pat each other on the back, and if they are family, they will sometimes give a kiss on the cheek and embrace, just like women do.

 **How do you greet your friends? Your relatives?**

Así se dice (*That's how it's said*) introduces optional vocabulary from the Spanish-speaking world.

Así se dice

The following greetings express *What's up?*, *What's happening?*, or *How's it going?*

¿Qué hay? ¿Qué pasa?
¿Qué hubo? ¿Qué onda? (*Mexico*)

The phrase **por nada** is an alternative to **de nada.**

Nota comunicativa

Más° expresiones de cortesía

° More

—Encantado. (*for a man*) —Encantada. (*for a woman*) —Mucho gusto.	"Nice to meet you."	**por favor**	please (*also used to get someone's attention*)
—Igualmente.	"Likewise."	**perdón**	pardon me, excuse me (*to ask forgiveness or to get someone's attention*)
Gracias.	Thanks. Thank you.	**(con) permiso**	pardon me, excuse me (*to request permission to pass by or through a group of people*)
Muchas gracias.	Thank you very much.		
De nada. / No hay de qué.	You're welcome.		

You will use these expressions in **Comunicación.**

Comunicación

A. Expresiones de cortesía. How many different ways can you respond to the following greetings and phrases?

1. Buenas tardes.
2. Adiós.
3. ¿Qué tal?
4. Hola.
5. ¿Cómo está?
6. Buenas noches.
7. Muchas gracias.
8. Hasta mañana.
9. ¿Cómo se llama usted?
10. Mucho gusto.
11. ¿De dónde eres?
12. Buenos días.

B. Situaciones. If the following people met or passed each other at the times given, what might they say to each other? Role-play the situations with a classmate.

1. Mr. Santana and Miss Pérez, at 5:00 P.M.
2. Mrs. Ortega and Pablo, at 10:00 A.M.
3. Professor María Hernández and Olivia, at 11:00 P.M.
4. you and a classmate, just before your Spanish class

C. Situaciones. What would you say in Spanish in the following situations?

1. Your classmate passes you a handout from the professor.
2. You need to be excused from class to go to the restroom.
3. You just dropped your drink on a friend's book.
4. Your professor thanks you for opening the door for her.
5. You need your professor's attention.

D. Más (*More*) situaciones. Are the people in this drawing saying **por favor, con permiso,** or **perdón? ¡OJO!** More than one response is possible for some items.

E. Entrevista (*Interview*)

Paso (*Step*) 1. Turn to a person sitting next to you and do the following.

- Greet him or her appropriately, that is, with informal forms.
- Ask how he or she is.
- Find out his or her name.
- Ask where he or she is from.
- Conclude the exchange.

Paso 2. Now have a similar conversation with your instructor, using the appropriate formal or familiar forms, according to your instructor's request.

Pronunciación: Las vocales:° *a, e, i, o, u*

°vowels

There is a very close relationship between the way Spanish is written and the way it is pronounced. This makes it relatively easy to learn the basics of Spanish spelling and pronunciation.

Many Spanish sounds, however, do not have an exact equivalent in English, so you can't always trust English to be your guide to Spanish pronunciation. Even words that are spelled the same in both languages are usually pronounced quite differently.

English vowels can have many different pronunciations or may be silent. Spanish vowels are almost always pronounced, and they are almost always pronounced in the same way. They are always short and tense. They are never drawn out with a *u* or *i* glide as in English: **lo** ≠ *low;* **de** ≠ *day.*

a: pronounced like the *a* in *father,* but short and tense
e: pronounced like the *e* in *they,* but without the *i* glide
i: pronounced like the *i* in *machine,* but short and tense
o: pronounced like the *o* in *home,* but without the *u* glide
u: pronounced like the *u* in *rule,* but short and tense

¡OJO!

In English, most unstressed vowels are pronounced like an *uh* sound or schwa: c**a**nal, wait**e**d, at**o**m. This sound does not exist in Spanish.

¡OJO!

The word **y** (*and*) is pronounced like the letter **i**, as is the letter **y** at the end of a word: **¡ay!**

Práctica

A. Palabras. (*Words.*) Repeat the following words after your instructor.

1. hasta	tal	nada	mañana	natural	normal	fascinante
2. me	qué	Pérez	Elena	rebelde	excelente	elegante
3. sí	señorita	permiso	terrible	imposible	tímido	Ibiza
4. yo	con	como	noches	profesor	señor	generoso
5. uno	usted	tú	mucho	Perú	Lupe	Úrsula

B. Nombres. Here is a table of the 10 Spanish names most frequently given to Hispanic babies (male and female) in the U.S. in 2016 (**dos mil dieciséis**).

Los 10 nombres de bebé preferidos por los hispanos en 2016	
Niña	**Niño**
Sofía	Mateo
Isabela	Santiago
Valentina	Matías
Emma	Sebastián
Martina	Benjamín
Lucía	Martín
Victoria	Nicolás
Luciana	Alejandro
Valeria	Lucas
Camila	Diego

Source: Hispana Global

(Continúa.)

Paso 1. Can you find the Spanish word for *boy*? for *girl*? for the phrase *preferred by Hispanics*?

Paso 2. Working in pairs, try to give the English version of some of these names. Say the Spanish names aloud and, as you do, focus on the different pronunciation and spelling as compared to English. **¡OJO!** One name in the list is not really Spanish. After studying **El alfabeto español**, you will know which one it is.

Paso 3. In pairs, make a list of other Hispanic first names you know and say them out loud, trying to pronounce them in Spanish.

¡OJO!

The **ll** and **rr** combinations occur frequently in Spanish, but they are not separate letters. The only other consonants that are ever doubled are **c** and **n**, but they don't have a special sound.

El alfabeto español

The Spanish *alphabet* (**el alfabeto** or **el abecedario**) is slightly different from the English alphabet.

- It has 27 letters (not 26).
- The extra letter is **ñ**.
- The letters **k** and **w** appear only in words borrowed from other languages.

Letters	Names of Letters	Examples			Pronunciation
a	a	Antonio	Ana	la Argentina	
b	be	Benito	Blanca	Bolivia	
c	ce	Carlos	Cecilia	Cáceres	**c + a/o/u** = like English *k*; **c + e/i** = like English *s* (in Spain, a *th* sound)
d	de	Domingo	Dolores	Durango	
e	e	Eduardo	Elena	el Ecuador	
f	efe	Felipe	Francisca	Florida	
g	ge	Gerardo	Gloria	Guatemala	**g + e/i** = like hard English *h*; **g + a/o/u** and **gue/gui** = like English *g* in *got*
h	hache	Héctor	Hortensia	Honduras	always silent; in **ch** combination = like English *cheese*
i	i	Ignacio	Inés	Ibiza	
j	jota	José	Juana	Jalisco	like hard English *h*; similar to **g + e/i**
k	ca (ka)	(Karl)	(Karina)	(Kansas)	like English *k*
l	ele	Luis	Lola	Lima	like English *l*; when doubled (**ll**), like *y* in English *yes*
m	eme	Manuel	María	México	
n	ene	Nicolás	Nati	Nicaragua	
ñ	eñe	Íñigo	Begoña	España	close to *ny* in English *canyon*
o	o	Octavio	Olivia	Oviedo	
p	pe	Pablo	Pilar	Panamá	
q	cu	Enrique	Raquel	Quito	like English; appears only in the combinations **que** and **qui**, like English *ke* and *ki*
r	ere	Álvaro	Rosa	Monterrey	like *tt* in English *butter*; trilled at beginning of a word or as **rr**
s	ese	Salvador	Sara	San Juan	
t	te	Tomás	Teresa	Toledo	
u	u	Agustín	Úrsula	el Uruguay	
v	uve	Víctor	Victoria	Venezuela	like Spanish **b**
w	doble uve	(Oswaldo)	(Wilma)	(Washington)	like English *w*
x	equis	Xavier	Ximena	Extremadura	like English *x*; at beginning of a word and in **México, mexicano**, **x** = Spanish **j**
y	ye	Pelayo	Yolanda	el Paraguay	like *y* in English *yes*
z	zeta	Gonzalo	Zoila	Zaragoza	like English *s* (in Spain, a *th* sound); never like English *z*

©dynamicgraphics/Jupiterimages

Práctica

A. Pronunciación. Match the Spanish letters with their equivalent pronunciation and pronounce the example words.

EXAMPLES/SPELLING	PRONUNCIATION
1. _____ mucho: **ch**	**a.** like the *g* in English *garden*
2. _____ Geraldo: **ge** (also: **gi**); Jiménez: **j**	**b.** similar to *tt* of *butter* when pronounced very quickly
3. _____ hola: **h**	**c.** like *ch* in English *cheese*
4. _____ gusto: **gu** (also: **ga, go**)	**d.** like Spanish **b**
5. _____ me llamo: **ll**	**e.** similar to a "strong" English *h*
6. _____ señor: **ñ**	**f.** like *y* in English *yes*
7. _____ profesora: **r**	**g.** a trilled sound, several Spanish **r**'s in a row
8. _____ Ramón: **r** (to start a word); burro: **rr**	**h.** like the *ny* sound in *canyon*
9. _____ nos vemos: **v**	**i.** never pronounced

B. ¿Cómo se escribe... ? *(How do you write. . . ?)*

Paso 1. Pronounce these U.S. place names in Spanish. Then spell the names aloud in Spanish. All of them are of Hispanic origin: **Toledo, Los Ángeles, Montana, Colorado, El Paso, Florida, Las Vegas, Amarillo, San Francisco.**

Paso 2. Spell your own name aloud in Spanish, and listen as your classmates spell their names. Try to remember as many of their names as you can.

MODELO: Me llamo María: M (eme) **a** (a) **r** (ere) **í** (i con acento) **a** (a).

Nota comunicativa

Los cognados

As you study Spanish, note that many Spanish and English words are similar or identical in form and meaning. These related words are called *cognates* (**los cognados**). It's useful to begin recognizing and using cognates immediately; they will help you enrich your Spanish vocabulary and develop language proficiency more quickly. Here are some examples.

TO DESCRIBE PEOPLE			TO NAME PLACES AND THINGS		
cruel	inteligente	responsable	alcohol	estudiante	parque
elegante	interesante	sentimental	bar	examen	teatro
idealista	optimista	terrible	café	hotel	teléfono
importante	paciente	tolerante	clase	museo	televisión
independiente	pesimista		diccionario	oficina	

You will practice this vocabulary throughout this chapter.

©robertharding/Alamy

El Teatro Juárez, Guanajuato, México

¿Cómo es usted?° (Part 1) ¿Cómo... *What are you like?*

©Kevin Peterson/Getty Images

Ángela Suárez del Pino

©Andersen Ross/Getty Images

Ismael Figueroa García

—¿Quién **es usted** y cómo **es**?
—**Soy** Ángela Suárez del Pino. **Soy** optimista y tolerante.

Remember to watch for the words in **red and underlined.** Check the translation at the bottom of the page only if you need to.

—¿Quién **eres tú**?
—Me llamo Ismael Figueroa García y **soy** estudiante de universidad.
—Ismael, ¿cómo **eres**?
—**Soy** inteligente, romántico y responsable.

a verb / **un verbo** = a word that describes an action or a state of being

¡OJO!

In Spanish, subject pronouns are not always used because the verb form indicates the person. See how this works in the dialogues on this page.

Use the following verb forms to describe yourself or another person.

Subject Pronouns / Pronombres personales*	*ser* (to be):[†] Formas singulares	
yo	**soy**	I am
tú	**eres**	you (*familiar*) are
usted	**es**	you (*formal*) are
él	**es**	he is
ella	**es**	she is

Comunicación

A. ¿Cómo es usted?

Paso 1. Indique todas (*all*) las palabras apropiadas (*appropriate words*).

(Yo) Soy...

________ diligente	________ pesimista	________ independiente
________ idealista	________ materialista	________ estudiante
________ impaciente	________ normal	________ diferente
________ extravagante	________ profesor	________ profesora
________ elegante	________ importante	________ ¿ ?

"Who are you and what are you like?" "I'm Ángela Suárez del Pino. I'm optimistic and tolerant." "Who are you?" "My name is Ismael Figueroa García, and I'm a university (college) student." "Ismael, what are you like?" "I'm intelligent, romantic, and responsible."

You will learn more about subject pronouns in* **Gramática 3 (Capítulo 2) *and* **Gramática 8 (Capítulo 3).**
†You will learn more about **ser** *in* **Gramática 6 (Capítulo 3).**

Paso 2. With a classmate, use the adjectives and nouns in **Paso 1** to ask each other what you are like and who you are.

MODELO: diligente →
ESTUDIANTE 1: ¿Eres / Es usted diligente?
ESTUDIANTE 2: Sí, soy diligente. / No, no soy diligente.

B. ¿Quién es... ?

Paso 1. With a classmate, take turns asking and answering questions.

MODELO: arrogante →
ESTUDIANTE 1: ¿Quién es arrogante?
ESTUDIANTE 2: **Enrique Iglesias** es arrogante.

Personas

Enrique Iglesias Selena Gómez Penélope Cruz ¿ ?

1. arrogante
2. independiente
3. paciente
4. materialista
5. impresionante
6. interesante
7. elegante
8. terrible
9. fascinante

Paso 2. Now describe the people in negative terms, using **no** in front of the verb.

MODELO: Enrique Iglesias **no** es arrogante.

C. Una encuesta (*A poll*)

Paso 1. Use cognates from **Nota comunicativa** (page 9) and others you have heard or seen to describe the following people and things.

MODELO: Jennifer López → Jennifer López es **independiente.**

1. Jennifer López
2. este país (*this country*)
3. ________ (programa de televisión)
4. ________ (una persona famosa)

Paso 2. Now poll two classmates about the same four items. Write their answers in the chart.

MODELO: To ask: ESTUDIANTE 1: En tu opinión, ¿cómo es Jennifer López?
To answer: ESTUDIANTE 2: Es independiente.

Estudiantes (nombre)	Jennifer López	este país	________ (programa de televisión)	________ (persona famosa)

©America/Alamy

La Misión Basílica San Diego de Alcalá, cerca de (*near*) San Diego, California

MUNDO HISPANO°

Mundo... *The Hispanic world*

¡Aquí se habla español! If you sometimes have the feeling that Spanish is everywhere, that's because it's true, and it may become even more so during your lifetime. Here are some interesting facts.

- Spanish is spoken as a first or second language by more than 500 million people. This makes Spanish the second most widely spoken language in the world. (Chinese is the most widely spoken.) Some Spanish speakers also speak another language, like **náhuatl** in Mexico, **mapuche** in Chile, or **catalán** in Spain.
- Spanish is an official language of 20 countries.
- Over 43 million people in the United States speak Spanish, making it the fourth largest Spanish-speaking country in the world. About 15 million are bilingual.
- Spanish is the official language (along with English) of Puerto Rico, a commonwealth (**un estado libre asociado**) of the United States.

Comparing Origins of U.S. Hispanic Population
Total Hispanic Population
2017 Estimate*
57.5 Million

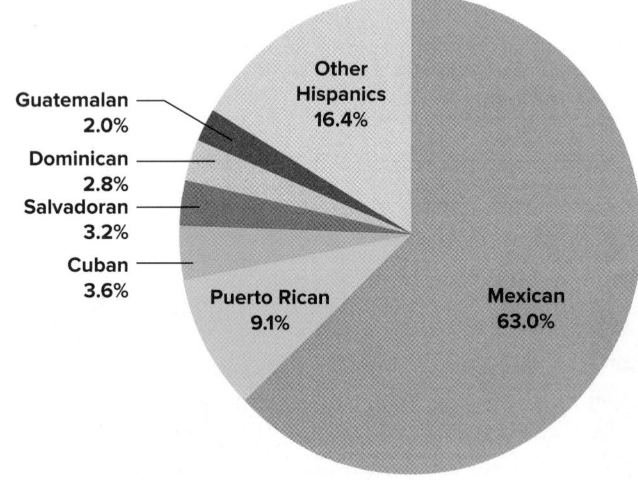

* Source: 2017 U.S. Census

- Spanish is present in Equatorial Guinea (where it is an official language), in the Philippines as a heritage from the not so distant past when the islands were colonies of Spain, and in Canada.
- Spanish is second only to English in terms of the number of people studying it worldwide.

Knowing a second language has many personal and professional advantages. If you live in a country like the United States, there is no need to explain to you why it's a good thing to study Spanish. The language and its cultures are part of the country's historical and cultural past. And, from an economic standpoint, Spanish speakers provide a huge market of consumers of all kinds of goods and services, including the entertainment industry and the world of art.

Spanish is also a great asset for traveling for business or pleasure, within this country or abroad. Like all languages spoken by a large number of people, modern Spanish varies from region to region. The Spanish of Madrid is different from that spoken in Mexico City, Buenos Aires, or Los Angeles. Although these differences are most noticeable in pronunciation ("accent"), they are also found in vocabulary and special expressions used in different areas of the world. But the majority of structures and vocabulary is common to the many varieties of Spanish.

Knowing Spanish also opens the door to a fascinating culture. Actually, *cultures*, plural, would be more accurate. Spanish was the language of one of the most impressive intersections of culture and civilization the world has ever known, when a small group of Spaniards landed on an island in the Caribbean over 500 years ago. No two of the Spanish-speaking American countries that arose from that fusion of European and indigenous cultures (including those of Africans, brought to work as slaves) are alike. They offer a rich and diverse cultural panorama, one that you will learn about in every chapter of *Puntos de partida*.

So . . . welcome to the Spanish-speaking world! Actually, you know, you're already in it.

(Alaska) ESTADOS UNIDOS
CANADÁ
ESTADOS UNIDOS
ESPAÑA
(Hawái) ESTADOS UNIDOS
MÉXICO
CUBA
REPÚBLICA DOMINICANA
PUERTO RICO
GUATEMALA
HONDURAS
EL SALVADOR
VENEZUELA
NICARAGUA
COSTA RICA
PANAMÁ
COLOMBIA
ISLAS FILIPINAS
GUINEA ECUATORIAL
ECUADOR
PERÚ
BOLIVIA
PARAGUAY
CHILE
URUGUAY
ARGENTINA

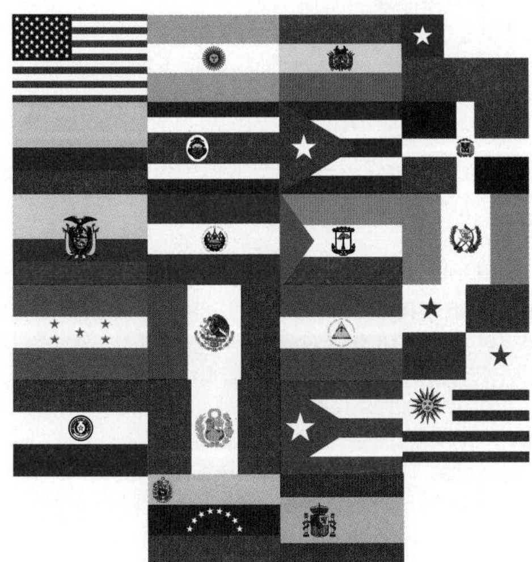

Comprensión

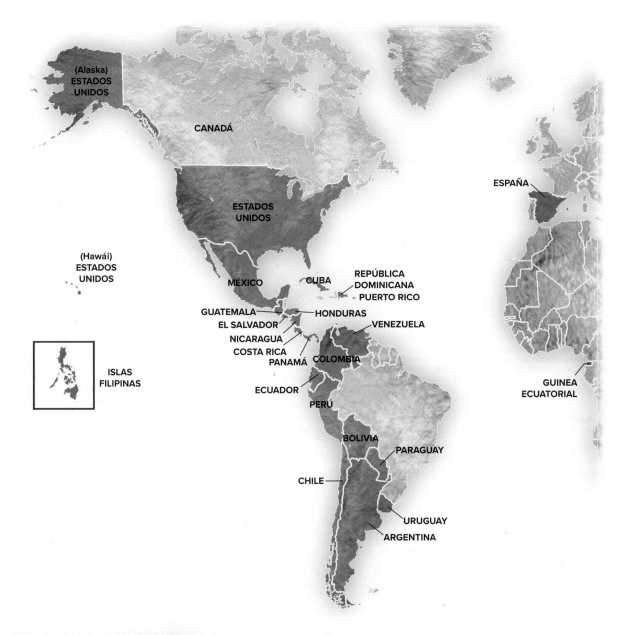

¿Cierto o falso? (*True or false?*)

1. There are more than 500 million Spanish speakers in the world.
2. There are more than 43 million Spanish speakers in the U.S.
3. Only indigenous and European cultures contributed to the culture of Spanish-speaking countries in the Americas.
4. Speakers of one variety of Spanish usually cannot understand what speakers of another variety of Spanish say.
5. The Spaniards brought Spanish to the Americas about 300 years ago.

En acción

Identify the flags or the colors of the flags of at least three Spanish-speaking countries. You can find them on the chapter-opening pages of Chapters 2–18 of *Puntos de partida.*

SEGUNDA° PARTE

Second

Los números del 0 al 30; *Hay*

Algo sobre... (*Something about . . .*) offers cultural information, often about the chapter's country of focus.

En un salón de clase

Hay una profesora.
Hay cinco estudiantes.

Algo sobre ...

los números

In Spanish-speaking countries, hand-written numbers may look a little different from the way they do in the U.S.

 **Do you notice any differences in the way the numbers are written in these photos and the way you write them?**

Los números del 0 al 30

0 cero		
1 uno	11 once	21 veintiuno
2 dos	12 doce	22 veintidós
3 tres	13 trece	23 veintitrés
4 cuatro	14 catorce	24 veinticuatro
5 cinco	15 quince	25 veinticinco
6 seis	16 dieciséis	26 veintiséis
7 siete	17 diecisiete	27 veintisiete
8 ocho	18 dieciocho	28 veintiocho
9 nueve	19 diecinueve	29 veintinueve
10 diez	20 veint<u>e</u>	30 treint<u>a</u>

a noun / **un sustantivo** = a word that denotes a person, place, thing, or idea

¡OJO!

uno, dos,... veinti**<u>uno</u>,** veintidós,...
but
un señor, veinti**<u>ún</u>** señores
una señora, veinti**<u>una</u>** señoras

Nota comunicativa

El género (*gender*) y los números

The number *one* has several forms in Spanish. **Uno** is the form used in counting. The forms **un** and **una** are used before *nouns* (**los sustantivos**). How will you know which one to use? It depends on the *gender* (**el género**) of the noun.

All Spanish nouns are either masculine or feminine. For example, the noun **señor** is masculine (*m.*) in gender, and the noun **señora** is feminine (*f.*). (As you will learn, even nouns that are not sex-linked have gender.) Here is how *one* is expressed with these nouns: **un señor**, **una señora**. The number **veintiuno** has similar forms before nouns: **veintiún señores, veintiuna señoras.** Just get used to using **un** and **una** with nouns now. You'll learn more about gender and number in **Capítulo 2.**

Hay

The word **hay** expresses both *there is* and *there are* in Spanish. It can be made negative (**no hay**) and can also be used to ask a question: **¿Hay... ?** (*Is there . . . ? Are there . . . ?*)

hay = there is / there are

Hay un teatro en esta universidad, pero **no hay** un museo.	There's a theater at this university, but there isn't a museum.
—¿Cuántos estudiantes hay en la clase?	"How many students are there in the class?"
—(Hay) Treinta.	"(*There are*) Thirty."

Práctica y comunicación

A. Una canción infantil. (*A children's song.*) This is a popular song for children from all over the Spanish-speaking world. Complete it with the missing numbers. It's basic math!

Dos y dos son ____________, cuatro y dos son __________,
seis y dos son ____________, y ocho __________,
y ocho ____________, y __________treinta y dos...

B. Los números. Practique los números, según (*according to*) el modelo. **¡OJO!** *f.* = femenino; *m.* = masculino.

MODELO: 1 señor → Hay **un** señor.

1. 4 señoras
2. 12 pianos
3. 1 café (*m.*)
4. 21 cafés (*m.*)
5. 14 días
6. 1 idea (*f.*)
7. 21 ideas (*f.*)
8. 11 personas
9. 15 estudiantes
10. 13 teléfonos
11. 28 naciones
12. 5 guitarras
13. 1 león (*m.*)
14. 30 señores
15. 20 oficinas

C. Problemas de matemáticas. Express the following simple mathematical equations in Spanish. Note: + (**y**), − (**menos**), = (**son**).

MODELOS: 2 + 2 = 4 → Dos y dos son cuatro.
4 − 2 = 2 → Cuatro menos dos son dos.

1. 2 + 4 = 6
2. 8 + 17 = 25
3. 11 + 1 = 12
4. 3 + 18 = 21
5. 9 + 6 = 15
6. 5 + 4 = 9
7. 1 + 13 = 14
8. 15 − 2 = 13
9. 9 − 9 = 0
10. 13 − 8 = 5
11. 14 + 12 = 26
12. 23 − 13 = 10
13. 1 + 4 = 5
14. 1 + 3 − 1 = 3
15. 8 − 7 = 1
16. 13 − 9 = 4
17. 2 + 3 + 10 = 15
18. 28 − 6 = 22
19. 30 − 17 = 13
20. 28 − 5 = 23
21. 19 − 7 = 12

D. Intercambios. (*Exchanges.*) With a classmate, ask and answer the following questions.

1. ¿Cuántos (*How many*) estudiantes hay en la clase de español? ¿Cuántos estudiantes hay en clase hoy (*today*)? ¿Hay tres profesores o un profesor / una profesora?
2. ¿Cuántos días hay en una semana (*week*)? ¿Hay seis? **(No, no hay...)** ¿Cuántos días hay en un fin de semana (*weekend*)? ¿Cuántos días hay en febrero? ¿en junio? ¿Cuántos meses hay en un año (*year*)?
3. En esta (*this*) universidad, ¿hay una cafetería? **(Sí, hay... / No, no hay...)** ¿un teatro? ¿un laboratorio de lenguas (*languages*)? ¿un bar? ¿una clínica? ¿un hospital? ¿un museo? ¿muchos (*many*) estudiantes? ¿muchos profesores?

Los gustos° y preferencias (Part 1)*

Los... *Likes*

¡OJO!

En español, **fútbol** = *soccer* en inglés y **fútbol americano** = *football.*

©Monkey Business Images/Shutterstock

—¿**Te gusta** el fútbol?
—Sí, ¡**me gusta** mucho!

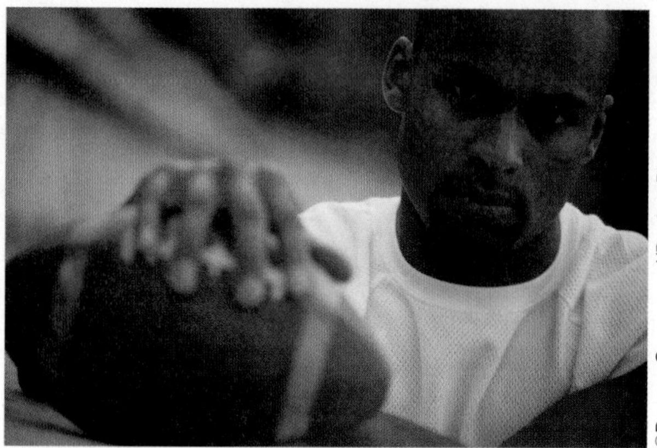

©Darren Greenwood/Design Pics

—Y **a usted,** señor, ¿**le gusta** el fútbol también?
—No, **no me gusta** mucho el fútbol, pero sí **me gusta** el fútbol americano.

Use these patterns with the verb **gustar** to express likes and dislikes.

Me gusta ________.	*I like ________.*
No **me** gusta ________.	*I don't like ________.*
(No) **Te** gusta ________. (*familiar*) (No) **Le** gusta ________. (*formal*)	*You (don't) like ________.*
¿**Te** gusta ________? (*familiar*) ¿(**A usted**) **Le** gusta ________? (*formal*)	*Do you like ________?*

an infinitive / **un infinitivo** = a verb form that indicates action or state of being without referring to a specific person or time

In the following activities you will use **el** to mean *the* with masculine nouns and **la** with feminine nouns. Don't try to memorize which words are masculine or feminine at this time. You will also use Spanish verbs in the infinitive form, which always ends in **-r.** Here are some examples: **estudiar** = *to study*, **comer** = *to eat*. You will be able to guess the meaning of other infinitives from context (the surrounding words).

Práctica y comunicación

A. ¿Yo, tú o usted? Indicate which pronoun you associate with each question or statement.

1. ¿Te gusta la pizza?
2. ¿Le gusta la Coca-Cola?
3. Me gusta mucho el chocolate.

B. Versión bilingüe. Match the ideas.

1. _____ —¿Te gusta esquiar?
   —No, no me gusta.
2. _____ —¿Le gusta esquiar?
   —Sí, me gusta.
3. _____ —Me gusta esquiar.
   —¿Sí? A mí no me gusta.

a. "Do you (*formal*) like to ski?" "Yes, I like to."
b. "I like to ski." "Yeah? I don't like to."
c. "Do you (*familiar*) like to ski?" "No, I don't like to."

"Do you like soccer?" "Yes, I like it a lot!" "And (what about) you, sir, do you also like soccer?" "No, I don't like soccer that much, but I do like football."

You will learn more about* **gustar *in* **Gramática 22 (Capítulo 8).**

C. Los gustos y preferencias

Paso 1. Make a list of six things you like and six things you don't like, following the model. You may choose items from the **Vocabulario útil** box.

MODELO: Me gusta **la clase de español.** No me gusta **la clase de matemáticas.**

Vocabulario útil

Vocabulario útil is not active; that is, you don't need to focus on learning it. But it will help you do this activity.

el actor _____, **la actriz** _____
el café, el té, la limonada, la Coca-Cola®
el/la cantante (*singer*) _____
el cine (*movies*), **el teatro, la ópera, el arte abstracto, el fútbol**
la música moderna, la música clásica, *el hip hop,* la música *country*
la pizza, la pasta, la comida (*food*) **mexicana, la comida de la cafetería**
__________ **(programa de televisión)**
__________ **(ciudad** [*city*]**)**

¡OJO!

The word **cantante** is used for both men *and* women.

1. Me gusta _____. No me gusta _____.
2. ____________________
3. ____________________
4. ____________________
5. ____________________
6. ____________________

Paso 2. Now ask a classmate if he or she shares your likes and dislikes.

MODELO: **ESTUDIANTE 1:** ¿Te gusta la clase de español?
ESTUDIANTE 2: Sí, me gusta (la clase de español). (No me gusta la clase de español.)
ESTUDIANTE 1: ¿Y la clase de matemáticas?
ESTUDIANTE 2: Sí, también me gusta (la clase de matemáticas). (No me gusta la clase de matemáticas.)

D. Más (*More*) gustos y preferencias

Paso 1. Here are some useful verbs and nouns to talk about what you like. For each item, combine an infinitive (shaded) with a noun to form a sentence that is true for you. The verb **estudiar** is an easily recognizable cognate. Use context to guess the meaning of verbs that are not cognates.

MODELO: Me gusta _________. → Me gusta **estudiar inglés.**

1. beber — café chocolate limonada té
2. comer — enchiladas ensalada hamburguesas pasta pizza
3. estudiar — computación (*computer science*) español historia inglés matemáticas
4. hablar — con mis amigos (*with my friends*) por teléfono (*on the phone*) español
5. jugar — al basquetbol al béisbol al fútbol al fútbol americano al tenis
6. tocar — la guitarra el piano el violín

Paso 2. Ask a classmate about his or her likes, using your own preferences as a guide.

MODELO: ¿Te gusta **comer enchiladas**?

Paso 3. Now ask your professor if he or she likes certain things. **¡OJO!** Remember to address your professor in a formal manner if that is his or her preference.

MODELO: ¿Le gusta **jugar al tenis**?

¿Qué hora es?

Es la una.

Son las dos.

Son las cinco.

¿Qué hora es? is used to ask *What time is it?* In telling time, one says ***Es* la una** but ***Son* las dos (las tres, las cuatro,** and so on).

Es la una **y** { **cuarto**. / **quince**. }

Son las dos **y** { **media**. / **treinta**. }

Son las cinco **y diez**.

Son las ocho **y veinticinco**.

Note that from the hour to the half-hour, Spanish, like English, expresses time by adding minutes or a portion of an hour to the hour.

Son las dos **menos** { **cuarto**. / **quince**. }

Son las ocho **menos diez**.

Son las once **menos veinte**.

From the half-hour to the hour, Spanish usually expresses time by subtracting minutes or a part of an hour from the *next* hour.

¡OJO!

Es la... / Son las... = to tell time

A la... / A las... = to tell *at* what time something happens

Nota comunicativa

Cómo expresar la hora

de la mañana	A.M., in the morning
de la tarde	P.M., in the afternoon (and early evening)
de la noche	P.M., in the evening
en punto	exactly, on the dot, sharp
¿a qué hora... ?	(at) what time . . . ?
a la una (las dos,...)	at 1:00 (2:00, . . .)
Son las cuatro **de la tarde en punto.**	It's exactly 4:00 P.M.
—¿**A qué hora** es la clase de español?	"What time is Spanish class (at)?"
—Es **a las** once **de la mañana.**	"It's at 11:00 A.M."

You will practice these phrases in **Práctica y comunicación**.

Práctica y comunicación

A. ¡Atención! Listen as your instructor says a time of day. Find the clock face that corresponds to the time you heard and say its number in Spanish.

1. 2. 3. 4.

5. 6. 7.

B. ¿Qué hora es? Express the time in full sentences in Spanish.

1. 1:00
2. 6:00
3. 11:00
4. 1:30 P.M.
5. 3:15 A.M.
6. 7:45 P.M.
7. 4:15 A.M.
8. 11:45 exactly
9. 9:10 on the dot
10. 9:50 sharp

C. ¡Atención! With a classmate, ask and answer questions about the drawings (**los dibujos**) in **Actividad A.**

MODELO: **ESTUDIANTE 1:** Son las nueve y media de la mañana.
ESTUDIANTE 2: Es el dibujo 6.
ESTUDIANTE 1: ¡Correcto! (No es correcto.)

D. Situaciones en la calle (*street*). Complete los diálogos con un compañero / una compañera.

Diálogo 1: Por la mañana, en la calle

SR. ROLDÁN: Buenos días, Sra. Valdés. ¿Cómo __________ ?
SRA. VALDÉS: Muy bien. ¿ __________, Sr. Roldán?
SR. ROLDÁN: __________. Perdón, ¿qué hora __________?
SRA. VALDÉS: __________ las __________ (*10:30*), señor.
SR. ROLDÁN: __________ gracias, señora.

Diálogo 2: Por la tarde

SILVIA: ¡Hola!, muy __________, Julio. ¿Cómo __________?
JULIO: Bien, ¿y __________? ¡Huy!, perdón, ¿qué hora __________?
SILVIA: __________ las __________.
JULIO: ¡Ay! La clase de historia es a las __________ y diez. Me voy corriendo.[a] ¡Hasta luego!
SILVIA: Oye,[b] ¿nos vemos el sábado[c] en la fiesta?
JULIO: ¡Sí, sí!

[a]Me... *I have to run.* [b]*Hey* [c]*Saturday*

E. Intercambios (*Exchanges*)

Paso 1. Read and practice pronouncing the words in **Vocabulario útil.**

Vocabulario útil

¿cuándo?	when?
los días de la semana*	the days of the week
el lunes	on Monday
el martes	on Tuesday
el miércoles	on Wednesday
el jueves	on Thursday
el viernes	on Friday
el sábado	on Saturday
el domingo	on Sunday

Paso 2. With a partner, take turns asking and answering questions about when the following events or activities take place, according to the schedule. Can you guess the meaning of the new words in the schedule?

Esta *(This)* semana

L	M	X	J	V	S	D
español: 9 a.m.		*español: 9 a.m.*		*español: 9 a.m.*	*excursión: 8:45 a.m.*	
física: 11:50 a.m.	*historia: 11:50 a.m.*	*física: 11:50 a.m.*	*historia: 11:50 a.m.*	*física: 11:50 a.m.*		*tenis: 10 a.m.*
	laboratorio: 3:10 p.m.		*laboratorio: 3:10 p.m.*			*concierto: 7:30 p.m.*
					fiesta: 10 p.m.	

MODELO: la clase de español →

ESTUDIANTE 1: ¿Cuándo es la clase de español?

ESTUDIANTE 2: El lunes, el miércoles y el viernes a las nueve de la mañana.

1. la clase de español
2. la clase de física
3. la clase de historia
4. la sesión de laboratorio
5. la excursión
6. la fiesta
7. el partido (*game*) de tenis
8. el concierto

Paso 3. Now ask when your partner likes to perform the following activities on a given day.

MODELO: cenar (*to have dinner*) →

ESTUDIANTE 1: ¿Cuándo te gusta cenar **el sábado**?

ESTUDIANTE 2: El sábado me gusta cenar **a las seis y media**.

1. cenar
2. estudiar español
3. mirar (*to watch*) la televisión
4. ir al (*to go to the*) gimnasio
5. ir al cine
6. ir a una fiesta

*You will learn more about the days of the week in Spanish in **Capítulo 5.***

desde° Los Ángeles *from*

Antes de mirar° Antes... *Before watching*

What is a morning news and talk television show usually like? Check all of the phrases that apply

- ☐ un poco (*a little*) cómico
- ☐ un poco serio
- ☐ informativo
- ☐ muy dramático
- ☐ para (*for*) una audiencia diversa
- ☐ solo para las personas mayores (*only for older people*)

El presentador (*anchor*) Víctor Gutiérrez y la presentadora Ana García Blanco. *Salu2* es un programa sobre (*about*) la comunidad global de hispanohablantes (*Spanish speakers*).

Este° programa *This*

This is the introductory program of a new morning show, based in Los Angeles, California.

Reading part of the script before watching each segment of *Salu2* will help you understand more of the show.

Fragmento del guion° del... *of the script*

VÍCTOR: Muchas gracias, Laura. La presencia del español en la ciudad de Los Ángeles es impresionante, ¿no crees,[a] Ana?

ANA: Absolutamente. Y personas de todo tipo hablan español, no solo[b] los hispanos. Bueno, es hora de decir[c] adiós por hoy. Espero que les haya gustado nuestro primer programa.[d] Nos vemos muy pronto.[e]

VÍCTOR: Desde el estudio de *Salu2* en la ciudad de Los Ángeles, California, les mandamos[f] saludos a todos los telespectadores y esperamos verlos en nuestro próximo programa.[g] ¡Hasta entonces![h]

[a]¿no... *don't you think* [b]no... *not only* [c]es... *it's time to say* [d]Espero... *I hope you liked our first program.* [e]muy... *very soon* [f]les... *we send* [g]esperamos... *we hope to see you at our next program* [h]¡Hasta... *Until then!*

These words and phrases in **Vocabulario del programa** (given in the order in which they appear in the show) will help you understand more when you watch this episode.

Vocabulario del° programa *of the*

hoy les presentamos	today we're introducing . . . to all of you
un nombre	a name
antiguo	former
la ciudad	the city
el país	the country, nation
el tema	the topic, subject
dentro y fuera de	within and outside of
vamos a hablar/escuchar	we're going to talk/listen to
cuarenta y ocho	forty-eight
les saludo	I'm greeting all of you
la playa	the beach
disculpa	pardon me
¿de dónde vienes?	**¿de dónde eres?**
(yo) vengo de	**(yo) soy de**
¿cuántos años tienes?	how old are you?

Estrategia

You will not understand every word in *Salu2*. In fact we never catch everything in any program even in our native language. But you will be able to get the gist of the show by catching some key words and phrases that you *do* know and by using context, both in the program as well as in the text and images in this section.

If you scan **Después de mirar** *before* watching the show, you will understand more of what is in the program.

Después de mirar°

°Después... *After watching*

Laura Sánchez Tejada es reportera. Es de México pero hoy está en California.

A. ¿Está claro? ¿Cierto o falso? Corrija (*Correct*) las oraciones (*sentences*) falsas, según (*according to*) el video.

	CIERTO	FALSO
1. *Salu2* es un programa matinal (*morning*) de televisión.	☐	☐
2. Es un programa informativo para un público hispanohablante diverso.	☐	☐
3. El estudio está en San Francisco.	☐	☐
4. Hay tres presentadores (*anchors*) y una reportera.	☐	☐
5. Pocas (*Few*) personas hablan español en Los Ángeles.	☐	☐

B. ¿Quién lo dice? (*Who says it?*) Indique el presentador: **A** = Ana o **V** = Víctor.

1. «...el Pueblo de Nuestra Señora la Reina de los Ángeles de Porciúncula.» ________
2. «...el nombre de Los Ángeles es un nombre español...» ________
3. «Y vamos a escuchar a personas hispanohablantes de varios países...» ________
4. «...vamos a escuchar a miembros de la comunidad hispana de Los Ángeles.» ________
5. «...es evidente que muchas personas no hispanas sí hablan español.» ________
6. «Y hoy vamos a escuchar los saludos de algunos angelinos...» ________

C. Un poco más. (*A little more.*) Match each person with her/his place of origin.

ORIGEN

a. Chicago **b.** Los Ángeles **c.** México **d.** Puerto Rico **e.** no se sabe (*not known*)

PERSONAS

1. _____ Ricardo
4. _____ Michelle y Amy

2. _____ Wally

5. _____ Miriam y Verónica

3. _____ Jennifer

6. _____ Rubí

En acción

Filme los saludos de dos o tres personas en español.

D. Y ahora, ustedes. (*And now it's your turn.*) Practique su (*your*) pronunciación y su talento como presentador(a). Haga el papel (*Play the role*) de Laura y complete el fragmento con su propia (*your own*) información.

Buenos días a todos. ¿Cómo están ustedes? Yo estoy muy bien. Me llamo ________ y soy **el reportero / la reportera** del programa *Salu2*. Les saludo desde[a] ________, en el estado de ________.

[a]Les... *I'm speaking to you (lit. I'm greeting you from)*

MUNDO HISPANO°

Mundo… *The Hispanic world*

Antes de leer°

Antes… *Before reading*

This reading consists of a series of photos and captions. In it, you will learn the names of important geographical features in the Spanish-speaking world. Before you read each photo caption, study the image and identify what is in it. This will help you understand the key words in the caption, which are underlined. These words are often cognates; if not, they are guessable in the context provided by the photo.

As you read, you will probably "get" a lot of information from the captions without actually knowing or understanding all of the words. This happens even when you read in your native language.

Finally, it's a good idea to read the captions more than once. Start by reading them all through quickly, without looking up any words, then start back at the beginning again. You will be surprised by how much more you will understand the second time around.

La geografía del mundo hispanohablante°

mundo… *Spanish-speaking world*

La diversidad del mundo hispano es fabulosa. Lea[a] el texto, mire[b] las fotos ¡y consulte los mapas en la página 13 y al final del libro[c]!

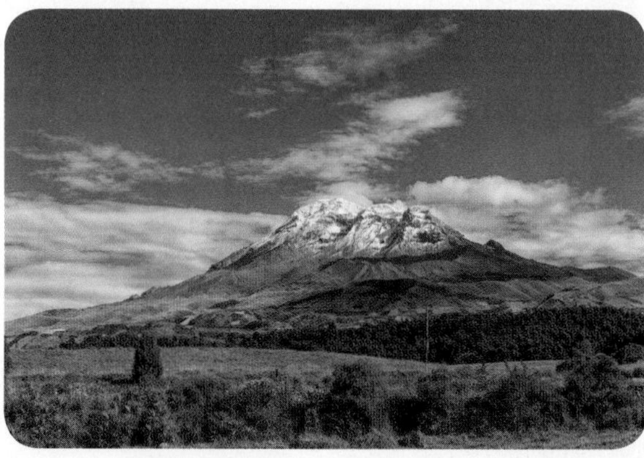

1.
El volcán Chimborazo (en el Ecuador), en la cordillera de Los Andes. Los Andes forman la cordillera más larga[d] del mundo (ocho mil quinientos[e] kilómetros), y se extienden por[f] siete naciones de Sudamérica.

2.
Una playa en la península de Samaná, República Dominicana. En el mar Caribe hay tres islas de habla española. El mundo hispano también tiene[g] costas en el océano Atlántico y en el Pacífico.

[a]*Read* [b]*look at* [c]al… *at the back of the book* [d]más… *longest* [e]ocho… *8,500* [f]se… *they pass through* [g]*has*

(Continúa.)

3.
Una selva[h] en México. Hay selvas también en otros países[i] en Centroamérica y Sudamérica.

4.
El desierto de Atacama, Chile. Es el más árido[j] del mundo. También hay zonas desérticas en otros países hispanos de Norteamérica a Sudamérica: México, el Perú, Bolivia, la Argentina, Colombia. Y también en España.

5.
El glaciar Perito Moreno, en la Patagonia argentina. Chile y la Argentina tienen[k] territorio en la Patagonia y en el continente de la Antártida.

6.
Madrid, la capital de España, en Europa. Es una ciudad de gran[l] importancia histórica y cultural. En Latinoamérica también hay muchas ciudades grandes,[m] como la Ciudad de México, Buenos Aires, Santiago,...

[h]*jungle* [i]naciones [j]más... *driest* [k]*have* [l]*great* [m]*large*

Comprensión

A. ¿Qué significa? (*What does it mean?*)

Paso 1. In pairs, decide on the meaning of the Spanish words for geographical features that are underlined in the reading.

Paso 2. With your partner, give examples of these geographical features in the U.S (or other part of the world) and in the Spanish-speaking world.

1. un volcán
2. una cordillera
3. una playa
4. una península
5. un mar
6. un océano
7. un desierto

B. Los nombres de las regiones del mundo. ¿Cómo se dice *(How do you say it)* en español?

1. Latin America
2. Central America
3. North America
4. South America
5. Europe
6. Antarctica

EN RESUMEN En este capítulo°

En... *In this chapter*

AFTER STUDYING THIS CHAPTER I CAN . . .

- ☐ meet and greet others appropriately in Spanish (4–6)
- ☐ pronounce words in Spanish and say the alphabet (7–8)
- ☐ recognize the meaning of many Spanish cognates (9)
- ☐ describe myself and others (10)
- ☐ say numbers 0–30 and use **hay** (14–15)
- ☐ talk about some of my likes and dislikes (16)
- ☐ tell time (18)
- ☐ recognize/describe at least 2–3 facts about the Spanish-speaking world

Vocabulario

This is the active vocabulary for **Capítulo 1**. Be sure that you know all the words, including the meaning of the group titles, before beginning **Capítulo 2.**

Saludos y expresiones de cortesía

Buenos días. Buenas tardes. Buenas noches.
Buenas. Muy buenas.

Hola. ¿Qué tal?
¿Cómo estás? ¿Cómo está?

Bien. Muy bien. Regular.
¿Y tú? ¿Y usted?

Adiós. Hasta luego. Hasta mañana. Nos vemos.

(Continúa.)

¿Cómo te llamas? ¿Cómo se llama usted?
Me llamo ______.

¿De dónde eres (tú)? ¿De dónde es (usted)?
(Yo) Soy de ______.

señor (Sr.), señora (Sra.), señorita (Srta.)
profesor, profesora

Gracias. Muchas gracias.
De nada. No hay de qué.
Por favor. Perdón. (Con) Permiso.
Mucho gusto. Igualmente. Encantado/a.

el saludo	greeting

¿Cómo es usted?

All forms of infinitives in red and underlined can be found in Appendix 5.

ser: soy, eres, es

¿Cómo es usted?	What are you like?

Los gustos y preferencias

¿Te gusta ______? ¿(A usted) Le gusta ______?
(Sí,) Me gusta ______. (No,) No me gusta ______.

los gustos	likes

Los números del 0 al 30

cero	**diez**	**veinte**	**treinta**
uno	**once**	**veintiuno**	
dos	**doce**	**veintidós**	
tres	**trece**	**veintitrés**	
cuatro	**catorce**	**veinticuatro**	
cinco	**quince**	**veinticinco**	
seis	**dieciséis**	**veintiséis**	
siete	**diecisiete**	**veintisiete**	
ocho	**dieciocho**	**veintiocho**	
nueve	**diecinueve**	**veintinueve**	

¿Qué hora es?

es la... , son las...
y/menos cuarto (quince)
y media (treinta)

en punto
de la mañana (tarde, noche)
¿a qué hora... ?, a la(s)...

¿qué hora es?	what time is it?

Las palabras interrogativas

¿cómo?	how?; what?
¿dónde?	where?
¿qué?	what?
¿quién?	who?
la palabra	word

Palabras adicionales

sí/no	yes/no
hay	there is/are
no hay	there is not / are not
¿hay?	is there / are there?
hoy/mañana	today/tomorrow
y/o	and/or
a	to; at (*with time*)
de	of; from
en	in; on; at
muy	very
pero	but
también	also

Vocabulario personal

Use this space for other words and phrases you learn in this chapter.

ESPAÑOL	INGLÉS

An Introduction to the Rest of Puntos de partida

Each chapter of the rest of this textbook has a chapter theme and follows a consistent organization. In addition, every chapter focuses on one or more countries of the Spanish-speaking world.

- **The opening pages of the chapter:** Here you will begin to learn about each chapter's theme and geographical focus. A Spanish speaker will provide a model of things you will be able to say after studying the vocabulary and grammar in the chapter, which are previewed in **En este capítulo.**
- **Vocabulario: Preparación:** This section presents vocabulary related to each chapter's theme.
- **Pronunciación:** Found in **Capítulos 2–4,** this section presents important aspects of Spanish pronunciation and orthography (spelling).
- **Salu2 Segmento 1:** This section will help you to understand a segment of the ***Salu2*** morning show.
- **Gramática:** This section presents grammar points in context and offers many opportunities for you to practice Spanish, alone and with a partner or group. In a subsection of **Gramática** called **Todo junto** (***All together***), you will practice all of the grammar points from the chapter plus review important grammar topics from previous chapters.
- ***Salu2* Segmento 2:** Here is another segment of the show.
- **Mundo hispano (*The Hispanic World*):** This section of each chapter has five parts. You will learn more about the chapter's country of focus (**Enfoque cultural**) and also read authentic materials from the Spanish-speaking world (**Lectura**), including literature. In **Textos orales**, you will practice authentic listening tasks. In **Escritura**, you will write essays and do other real-world writing tasks in Spanish. In **Más ideas para su portafolio**, you will find some final ideas for creating a portfolio to showcase what you can do in Spanish.
- **En resumen: En este capítulo:** This section shows you vocabulary and grammar you need to know from each chapter.

2

En la universidad

En este capítulo°

En... *In this chapter*

En un salón de clase universitario

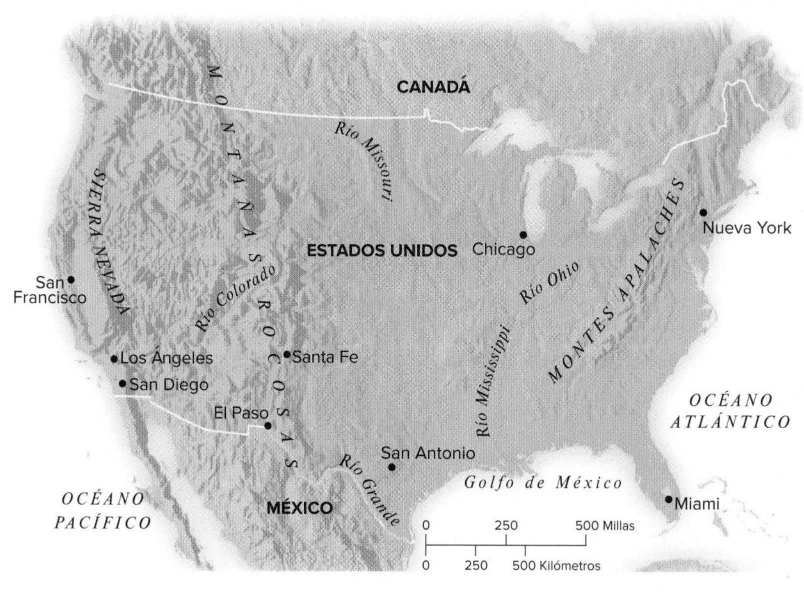

LOS ESTADOS UNIDOS DE AMÉRICA

326,8 (trescientos veintiséis coma ocho) millones de habitantes

- En los Estados Unidos hay más de 57,5 (cincuenta y siete coma cinco) millones de personas de origen hispano.
- Es el quinto[a] país del mundo por[b] número de hispanohablantes.
- Hay muchos estados y ciudades con nombres[c] en español.

[a]*fifth* [b]país... *country in the world in* [c]muchos... *many states and cities with names*

ENTREVISTA° *Interview*

Here are some questions that a native speaker of Spanish has answered. When you have completed this chapter, you will be able to give your own answers to the same questions.

- ¿En qué universidad estudia usted[a]?
- ¿Qué materias[b] estudia este[c] semestre/trimestre?
- ¿Cuál[d] es su[e] clase favorita? **(Mi clase...)**

[a]estudia... *are you studying* [b]*subjects* [c]*this* [d]*Which* [e]*your*

Alejandra Hernández Soto contesta las preguntas.

- Estudio Relaciones Internacionales en la UNAM, la Universidad Nacional Autónoma de México.
- Este semestre tomo[a] seis clases: estadística, historia, geografía, economía, sistemas políticos, teorías de las relaciones internacionales. ¡Ah! Y también estudio inglés.
- ¿Mi materia favorita este semestre? No sé[b]. ¡Me gusta todo[c]!

[a]*I'm taking* [b]No... *I don't know.* [c]*everything*

VOCABULARIO: PREPARACIÓN

You can hear the pronunciation of theme vocabulary words and phrases in the Connect eBook.

En el salón de clase

¿Dónde? Lugares en la universidad

la biblioteca	the library
la cafetería	the cafeteria
el edificio	the building
la librería	the bookstore
la oficina	the office
la residencia	the dormitory
el salón de clase	the classroom

¿Quién? Personas

el bibliotecario	the (male) librarian
la bibliotecaria	the (female) librarian
el compañero (de clase)	the (male) classmate
la compañera (de clase)	the (female) classmate
el compañero de cuarto	the (male) roommate
la compañera de cuarto	the (female) roommate
el consejero	the (male) advisor
la consejera	the (female) advisor
el hombre	the man
la mujer	the woman
el secretario	the (male) secretary
la secretaria	the (female) secretary

¿Qué? Objetos

la computadora (portátil)	(laptop) computer
el dinero	money
el pizarrón (blanco)	(white)board
el teléfono (celular)	(cellular) telephone

Comunicación

A. Identificaciones. ¿Es hombre o mujer?

MODELO: ¿El profesor? → Es hombre.

1. ¿La consejera?
2. ¿La estudiante?
3. ¿El secretario?
4. ¿El estudiante?
5. ¿La bibliotecaria?
6. ¿El compañero de cuarto?

B. ¿Dónde están (*are they*)? Tell where these people are and identify the numbered people and things.

MODELO: El dibujo (*drawing*) 1: **Están** en el salón de clase.
1 → la profesora, 2 → la estudiante,...

Así se dice

el bolígrafo = la pluma, el birome, el esfero
la calculadora = la máquina de calcular
la computadora = el computador (*Latin America*), el ordenador (*Spain*)
la computadora portátil = el/la portátil (*Latin America, Spain*)
el escritorio = el mesabanco, el pupitre
el pizarrón = el encerado, la pizarra, el tablero
el salón de clase = el aula, la sala (de clase)

In general, use **el profesor / la profesora** to refer to a college teacher, or **el doctor / la doctora**, as appropriate. However, there are many institutional and national differences in usage. Ask what title to use to address your instructor.

Young people often shorten some words. Can you guess what **el boli** and **la profe** mean?

1.

2.

3.

Algo sobre...°

Algo... *Something about*

la universidad

En el mundo[a] hispanohablante no llaman[b] **colegio** a una institución universitaria. La palabra **colegio** se usa para referirse a[c] la educación preuniversitaria, aunque[d] con nombres diferentes en diferentes países.[e] También se usa en el nombre de asociaciones de profesionales, como el «Colegio de Arquitectos».

¿Cómo se llama su[f] colegio?

[a]*world* [b]*no... they don't call* [c]*se... is used for talking about* [d]*although* [e]*countries* [f]*your*

Nota cultural

Las universidades más antiguas° del mundo hispano°

más... *oldest* / del... *of the Spanish-speaking world*

En España

- la Universidad de Salamanca, Salamanca (1218 = mil doscientos dieciocho)

En Latinoamérica

- la Universidad Nacional Mayor de San Marcos, Lima, Perú (1551 = mil quinientos cincuenta y uno)
- la Universidad Nacional Autónoma de México (UNAM), en la Ciudad de México, México (1551 = mil quinientos cincuenta y uno)
- la Universidad Nacional de Córdoba, Argentina (1621 = mil seiscientos veintiuno)
- la Universidad San Francisco Xavier de Chuquisaca, Sucre, Bolivia (1624 = mil seiscientos veinticuatro)
- la Universidad de San Carlos de Guatemala, Antigua, Guatemala (1676 = mil seiscientos setenta y seis)
- la Universidad Nacional de San Antonio Abad del Cusco, Perú (1692 = mil seiscientos noventa y dos)
- la Universidad Central de Venezuela (1721 = mil setecientos veintiuno)
- la Universidad de San Gerónimo, ahora la Universidad de La Habana, Cuba (1728 = mil setecientos veintiocho)

¿Cuál[a] es la universidad más antigua de su país[b]?

[a]*What* [b]su... *your country*

El campus de la Universidad de San Marcos, en Lima, Perú

Las materias°

Las... *Subject areas*

The names for most of these subject areas are cognates. See if you can recognize their meaning without looking at the English equivalent. You should learn in particular the names of subject areas that are of interest to you.

la administración de empresas	business administration
las comunicaciones	communications
la economía	economics
el español	Spanish
la filosofía	philosophy
la literatura	literature
las matemáticas	mathematics
la sociología	sociology
las ciencias	sciences
naturales	natural
políticas	political
sociales	social
las humanidades	humanities
las lenguas (extranjeras)	(foreign) languages

Así se dice

la administración de empresas = el comercio, los negocios (*U.S.*)
la computación = la informática (*Spain*)
el español = el castellano (*Spain, Latin America*)

Comunicación

A. Asociaciones. ¿Qué materia(s) asocia usted con (*with*) las siguientes (*following*) personas y cosas (*things*)?

1. la zoología, la botánica, la química
2. Sigmund Freud, Carl Jung, B.F. Skinner
3. CNN, NBC, ESPN
4. la ética, la moral, la esencia de la realidad
5. Shakespeare, J.K. Rowling, Isabel Allende
6. Frida Kahlo, Pablo Picasso, Salvador Dalí
7. Apple, Microsoft, Google
8. la Guerra (*War*) de la Independencia, la presidencia de Barak Obama, el Imperio Romano

B. ¿Qué estudia usted? Create sentences about your academic interests by using one word or phrase from each column. Can you guess the meaning of the phrases in the left-hand box? If you need help, they are translated at the bottom of the page*.

MODELOS: Deseo estudiar **español y antropología.**
Necesito estudiar **matemáticas.**

1. (No) Estudio ______. **2.** (No) Deseo estudiar ______. **3.** (No) Necesito estudiar ______. **4.** (No) Me gusta estudiar ______.	+	español, francés (*French*), inglés arte, filosofía, literatura, música ciencias políticas, historia antropología, sicología, sociología biología, física, química computación, matemáticas ¿ ?

¡OJO!

The word **no** before the verb or verb phrase makes the sentence negative.

Vocabulario útil

la contabilidad	accounting
la ingeniería	engineering
el mercadeo	marketing
el periodismo	journalism

These **¿Recuerda usted?** boxes will help you review content you already know on which new material is based.

 ¿Recuerda usted?°

°¿Recuerda... *Do you remember?*

In **Capítulo 1,** you used a number of interrogative words to get information: **¿cómo?, ¿dónde?, ¿qué?,** and **¿quién?** Tell what those words mean in these questions. Then answer the questions.

1. ¿Cómo estás?
2. ¿Cómo es usted?
3. ¿De dónde eres?
4. ¿Qué hora es?
5. ¿Quién es la profesora/el profesor?

As you listen to your instructor say questions with those words, you will notice that, in Spanish, the voice falls at the end of questions that begin with interrogative words.

¿Qué hora es? ¿Cómo es usted?

You will learn more about asking questions in the **Nota comunicativa** on the next page and in **Gramática 4** in this chapter.

an interrogative word / **una palabra interrogativa** = a word used to ask a question about specific information (*who?, where?,* and so on)

---

*__1.__ *I'm studying (I'm not studying)* **2.** *I want to study (I don't want to study)* **3.** *I need to study (I don't need to study)* **4.** *I like to study (I don't like to study)*

Nota comunicativa

Más° palabras interrogativas

° More

What? can be expressed with two different words in Spanish.

- **¿Qué?** = asks for a definition or explanation

  ¿Qué es un hospital? **¿Qué** es esto (*this*)?

- **¿Cuál?** = used for other contexts

  ¿Cuál es la capital de Colombia? **¿Cuál** es tu materia favorita?

You will learn more about using these words in **Gramática 28 (Capítulo 10)**.

Here are more interrogative words. Guess their meaning from the context in which they appear.

1. —**¿Cuándo** es la clase? —Es mañana, a las nueve.
2. —**¿Cuánto** cuesta (*costs*) el cuaderno? —Dos dólares.
3. —**¿Cuántos** estudiantes hay en la clase? —Hay quince.
4. —**¿Cuántas** naciones hay en Centroamérica? —Hay siete.

Remember to drop your voice at the end of a question that begins with a Spanish interrogative word, the opposite of what happens in English, where the voice usually rises. This feature of Spanish may cause you to "hear" a Spanish question as a statement. Compare these questions.

¿Qué es un tren? *What's a train?*

¿Cuándo es el programa? *When is the program?*

You will use many of the preceding interrogative words in **Comunicación C** and **D**.

C. Preguntas. (*Questions.*) Choose the appropriate interrogative words to create meaningful questions, then answer the questions.

Cómo Cuál Cuándo Cuántos Dónde Qué Quién

1. ¿__________ hay clase de español, por (*in*) la mañana, por la tarde o por la noche (*night*)?
2. ¿__________ es una mochila, un objeto o una persona?
3. ¿__________ libros hay en su (*your*) mochila o bolsa (*bag*)? **(En mi mochila/bolsa...**)
4. ¿__________ es su (*your*) número de teléfono? (**Es el...**)
5. ¿__________ se llama su universidad? (**Mi...**)
6. ¿__________ está la universidad?
7. ¿__________ es el presidente / la presidenta?

¿Dónde le gusta estudiar a usted?

D. Intercambios (*Exchanges*)

Paso 1. Answer the following questions. Pay attention to the words and endings in bold; you have seen most of them before and should be able to guess what they mean.

1. —¿Qué **estudias** este (*this*) semestre/trimestre?
   —**Estudio** ____________________.
2. —¿Cuál es **tu** (*your*) materia favorita?
   —**Mi** materia favorita es el/la ____________________.
3. —¿Quién es **tu** profesor(a) en la clase de español?
   —Es el profesor / la profesora ____________________.
4. —¿Cuántas horas **estudias** al día (*per day*)?
   —**Estudio** ____________ horas al día.
5. —¿Dónde **estudias**?
   —**Estudio** en ____________________ (la residencia, la biblioteca, mi cuarto, mi apartamento, la cafetería...).
6. —¿**Te gusta** estudiar por (*in*) la mañana, por la tarde o por la noche (*at night*)?
   —**Me gusta** estudiar por ____________________.

Estrategia

Use **el** or **la** with a title when talking about a person, as in item 3.
el profesor Arana
la señora Castellano
el doctor Brook

Paso 2. Now practice the conversation in **Paso 1** with a classmate. Use **¿Y tú?** to ask about your partner.

MODELO: **ESTUDIANTE 1:** ¿Qué **estudias** este semestre/trimestre?
ESTUDIANTE 2: **Estudio** matemáticas, historia, literatura y español. ¿Y tú?
ESTUDIANTE 1: **Yo estudio** español, biología, física y arte.

«¡Qué bacán!°» Segmento 1

¡Qué... *How great!*

Antes de mirar°

Antes... *Before watching*

What do you think Víctor and Ana will talk about as they introduce the show? Check all of the phrases that apply.

_____________ su (*their*) familia
_____________ su concentración/carrera (*major*) en la universidad
_____________ el nombre de su universidad
_____________ el tráfico en Los Ángeles
_____________ el costo de una educación universitaria

Víctor y Ana, los presentadores de *Salu2*, que (*who*) hablan de sus (*talk about their*) estudios universitarios

Este° segmento

This

Los presentadores introducen el tema (*topic*) del programa: la universidad en el mundo (*world*) hispanohablante.

Vocabulario del segmento

bienvenidos	welcome	**el país**	the country
los telespectadores	the TV viewers	**el/la periodista**	the journalist
los universitarios	the university students	**estudiaste**	did you study
los padres	the parents	**pasé**	I spent
con frecuencia pagan	frequently pay for	**en el extranjero**	abroad
		marca tu vida	changes your life
bien cara	quite expensive	**vamos a ver**	we're going to see
la maestría	the master's degree		

Estrategia

Before you watch the segment, be sure to read the photo caption and go over the vocabulary list. Don't expect to remember most of the words while watching; they're new and may be difficult for you. But just reading the list will enhance your comprehension, giving you ideas about what to watch for.

Después de mirar°

Después... *After watching*

A. ¿Está claro? Empareje a (*Match*) los presentadores, Ana (**A**) y Víctor (**V**) o a **los dos** (*both*), con las carreras o concentraciones y universidades apropiadas.

LAS CARRERAS O CONCENTRACIONES	LAS UNIVERSIDADES
_________ sociología	_________ UCLA
_________ comunicación	_________ la Universidad de Panamá
_________ inglés	

B. Un poco más. (*A little more.*) ¿Cierto o falso? Corrija (*Correct*) las oraciones (*sentences*) falsas, según (*according to*) el video.

	CIERTO	FALSO
1. El programa no es interesante para los padres.	☐	☐
2. La universidad es cara.	☐	☐
3. Victor pasó (*spent*) un semestre en España.	☐	☐
4. Ana es de Panamá.	☐	☐

C. Y ahora, ustedes. (*And now it's your turn.*) Practique su (*your*) pronunciación y su talento como presentador(a). Complete el fragmento con su propia (*your own*) información y con vocabulario del programa.

Buenos días desde[a] _________. Soy _________. Es es un placer[b] presentar un nuevo programa de *Salu2*. El tema del programa de hoy es la universidad, un tema muy ___________ (adjetivo) para[c] los ___________ (personas) y los ___________ (personas). Estamos en la Universidad de _________, donde yo estudio _________ (materias). ¡Bienvenidos!

[a]*from* [b]*pleasure* [c]*for*

PRONUNCIACIÓN

Diphthongs and Linking

¿Recuerda usted?

Review what you already know about the pronunciation of Spanish vowels by saying the following names and nicknames aloud.

1. Ana **2.** Pepe **3.** Pili **4.** Momo **5.** Lulú

a diphthong / **un diptongo** = a combination of two vowel sounds in one syllable

Two successive weak vowels **(i, u)** or a combination of a strong vowel **(a, e, o)** and a weak vowel **(i, u)** are pronounced as a single syllable in Spanish, forming a *diphthong* **(un diptongo): L*ui*s, s*ie*te, c*ua*derno.**

When words are combined to form phrases, clauses, and sentences, they are linked together in pronunciation. In spoken Spanish, it is often difficult to hear the word boundaries—that is, where one word ends and another begins.

Práctica

A. Vocales. Más práctica con las vocales.

1. hablar	regular	reservar	compañera
2. trece	clase	papel	general
3. pizarrón	oficina	bolígrafo	libro
4. hombre	profesor	dólares	los
5. universidad	gusto	lugar	mujer

B. Diptongos. Practique las siguientes (*following*) palabras.

1. historia	secretaria	gracias	estudiante	materia
2. bien	Oviedo	siete	ciencias	diez
3. secretario	biblioteca	adiós	diccionario	Antonio
4. cuaderno	Eduardo	el Ecuador	Guatemala	Managua
5. bueno	nueve	luego	pueblo	Venezuela

C. Frases y oraciones (*sentences*). Practice saying each phrase or sentence as if it were one long word, pronounced without a pause.

1. el papel y el lápiz
2. la profesora y la estudiante
3. las ciencias y las matemáticas
4. la historia y la sicología
5. la secretaria y el profesor
6. el inglés y el español
7. la clase en la biblioteca
8. el libro en la librería
9. Es la una y media.
10. Hay siete estudiantes en la oficina.
11. No estoy muy bien.
12. No hay consejero aquí (*here*).

GRAMÁTICA

¿Recuerda usted?

As you know, in English and in Spanish, a noun is the name of a person, place, thing, or idea. You have been using nouns since the beginning of *Puntos de partida*. Remember that **el** and **la** mean *the* before nouns. If you can change the Spanish words for *the* to *one* in the following phrases, you already know some of the material in **Gramática 1.**

1. el libro **2. la mesa** **3. el profesor** **4. la estudiante**

1 Naming People, Places, Things, and Ideas (Part 1)

Singular Nouns: Gender and Articles*

Gramática en acción: La lista de la profesora Lifante para el primer día de clase

Note the use of text in **red and underlined** in **Gramática en acción** to indicate examples of the grammar point of focus.

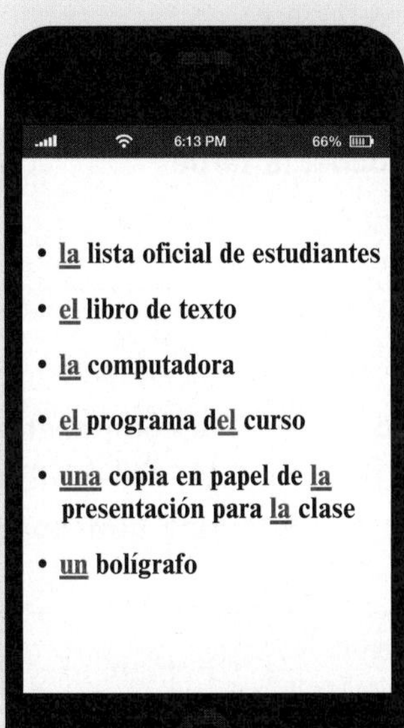

6:13 PM
66%
• la lista oficial de estudiantes
• el libro de texto
• la computadora
• el programa del curso
• una copia en papel de la presentación para la clase
• un bolígrafo

Comprensión

Según (*According to*) la lista, ¿es posible o no?

	SÍ	NO
1. La materia de la profesora Lifante es el Español Elemental.	☐	☐
2. La materia es la Historia de América.	☐	☐
3. Hay una presentación de PowerPoint en clase hoy.	☐	☐
4. Hay un libro de texto obligatorio.	☐	☐

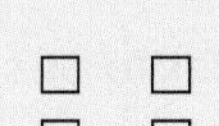

©McGraw-Hill Education

La profesora Lifante

You use nouns to name people, places, things, and ideas. In Spanish, all *nouns* (**los sustantivos**) have either masculine or feminine *gender* (**el género**). This is a purely grammatical feature; it does not mean that Spanish speakers perceive things or ideas as having male or female attributes.

Since the gender of all nouns must be memorized, it is best to learn the definite article along with the noun; that is, learn **el lápiz** rather than just **lápiz.** The definite article is given with nouns in vocabulary lists in this book.

Professor Lifante's list for the first day of class ■ *the official list of students* ■ *the textbook* ■ *the computer* ■ *the course syllabus* ■ *a paper copy of the class presentation* ■ *a pen*

*The grammar sections of **Puntos de partida** are numbered consecutively throughout the book. If you need to review a particular grammar point, the index will refer you to its page number.

an article / **un artículo** = a determiner that sets off a noun

a definite article / **un artículo definido** = an article that indicates a specific noun (*the*)

an indefinite article / **un artículo indefinido** = an article that indicates an unspecified noun (*a, an*)

Nouns / **Los sustantivos**				
	Masculine / **Masculino**		Feminine / **Femenino**	
Definite Articles / **Los artículos definidos**	**el hombre** **el libro**	the man the book	**la mujer** **la mesa**	the woman the table
Indefinite Articles / **Los artículos indefinidos**	**un hombre** **un libro**	a man a book	**una mujer** **una mesa**	a woman a table

Note the two-column format of grammar explanations. Explanations are on the left, examples are on the right, and text in **red and underlined** will help you see what's important.

Gender / **El género**

1. **Masculine Nouns**
   Nouns that refer to male beings and most other nouns that end in **-o** are *masculine* (**masculino**) in gender.

   Sustantivos masculinos
   hombre, libro

2. **Feminine Nouns**
   Nouns that refer to female beings and most other nouns that end in **-a, -ción, -sión, -xión, -tad,** and **-dad** are *feminine* (**femenino**) in gender.

   Sustantivos femeninos
   mujer, mesa, silla
   nación, misión, conexión
   libertad, universidad

3. **Other Endings**
   Nouns that have other endings and that do not refer to either male or female beings may be masculine or feminine. The gender of these words must be memorized.

   el lápiz, el papel, el salón de clase
   la clase, la noche, la tarde

4. **Spelling Changes**
   Many nouns that refer to people indicate gender . . .
   - by changing the last vowel

     el compañero → **la compañera**
     el bibliotecario → **la bibliotecaria**

   OR
   - by adding **-a** to the last consonant of the masculine form to make it feminine

     un profesor → **una profesora**

5. **Some Nouns that Refer to People**
   Many other nouns that refer to people have a single form for both masculine and feminine genders. Gender is made clear by context or by an article.

   However, a few such nouns that end in **-e** also have a feminine form that ends in **-a.**

Masculino	Femenino
el estudiante	**la estudiante**
el dentista	**la dentista**
el presidente	**la presidenta**
el cliente	**la clienta**
el dependiente (*clerk*)	**la dependienta**

¡OJO!

A common exception to the normal rules of gender is the word **el día,** which is masculine in gender. Many words ending in **-ma** are also masculine: **el problema, el programa, el sistema,** and so on.

Articles / **Los artículos**

1. **Definite Articles**
   In English, there is only one *definite article* (**el artículo definido**): *the.*

   In Spanish, there are two definite articles for singular nouns, one masculine (**el**) and one feminine (**la**).

Artículo definido: *the*		
m. sing.	→	**el**
f. sing.	→	**la**

---

2. **Indefinite Articles**
   In English, the singular *indefinite article* (**el artículo indefinido**) is *a* or *an.*

   In Spanish, the indefinite article, like the definite article, must agree with the gender of the noun: **un** for masculine nouns, **una** for feminine nouns.

   Un and **una** can mean *one* or *a/an*, depending on context.

Artículo indefinido: *a, an*		
m. sing.	→	**un**
f. sing.	→	**una**

¡OJO!

The word **hay** is only followed by the indefinite articles, singular or plural: **Hay una computadora / unas computadoras en la mesa.** You will learn about plural articles in *Gramática 2.*

One of the first two activities in **Práctica y comunicación** will always include a brief **Autoprueba** (*Self-test*). Take it to see if you understand the basics of the grammar point. The answers are at the bottom of the page.

Gender Summary

MASCULINO	FEMENINO
el, un	**la, una**
-o	-a
	-ción, -sión, -xión
	-dad, -tad

Práctica y comunicación

A. Autoprueba. Escoja (*Choose*) el artículo definido apropiado.

1. __ (el / la) libro
2. __ (el / la) mujer
3. __ (el / la) oficina
4. __ (el / la) escritorio
5. __ (el / la) libertad
6. __ (el / la) acción

B. Los artículos

Paso 1. Dé (*Give*) el artículo definido apropiado **(el, la).**

1. edificio
2. biblioteca
3. bolígrafo
4. mochila
5. hombre
6. diccionario
7. universidad
8. estudiante
9. señora
10. nación
11. bibliotecario
12. calculadora

Paso 2. Ahora (*Now*) dé el artículo indefinido apropiado (**un, una**).

1. día
2. mañana
3. problema
4. lápiz
5. clase
6. dentista
7. condición
8. programa

C. Escenas de la universidad

Paso 1. Haga una oración (*Form a sentence*) con las palabras indicadas.

MODELO: estudiante / librería → **Hay un** estudiante **en la** librería.

1. consejero / oficina
2. profesora / salón de clase
3. lápiz / mesa
4. cuaderno / escritorio
5. libro / mochila
6. bolígrafo / silla
7. palabra / papel
8. oficina / residencia
9. compañero / biblioteca
10. diccionario / librería

Paso 2. Now create new sentences by changing one of the words in each item in **Paso 1.** Try to come up with as many variations as possible.

MODELOS: Hay un estudiante en **la residencia**. Hay **una profesora** en la librería.

***Prác. A:* Answers: *1.* el *2.* la *3.* la *4.* el *5.* la *6.* la**

D. Definiciones. En parejas (*pairs*), definan las siguientes (*following*) palabras en español como (*as*) **edificio**, **materia**, **objeto** o **persona**, según (*according to*) el modelo.

MODELO: biblioteca → ESTUDIANTE 1: ¿Qué es una biblioteca?
ESTUDIANTE 2: Es **un edificio**.

1. cliente
2. bolígrafo
3. residencia
4. dependienta
5. hotel (*m.*)
6. computadora
7. computación
8. inglés
9. ¿ ?

E. Nuestra (Our) universidad. En parejas, hagan oraciones (*form sentences*) sobre su (*about your*) universidad.

Estrategia

Remember to use the article **el** or **la** to refer to someone who has a title: **el profesor Márquez.**

MODELOS: mi consejero/a → El profesor Márquez es mi consejero.
cafetería → Hay una cafetería. Se llama (*It's called*) Foster Hall. (No hay una cafetería.)

1. mi consejero/a
2. mi profesor(a) de ______ (materia)
3. residencia
4. biblioteca principal
5. cafetería
6. edificio de clases

2 Naming People, Places, Things, and Ideas (Part 2)

Nouns and Articles: Plural Forms

Gramática en acción: Un anuncio

You don't have to understand all of the words in this ad (**anuncio**) to get its general meaning. What is it an ad for?

[a]en... *abroad*

Comprensión

1. How many nouns (including proper nouns) can you find in the ad? Can you guess the meaning of most of them?
2. Some of the nouns in the ad are plural. Can you tell how to make nouns plural in Spanish?
3. Look for the Spanish equivalent of these words: *adults, preparation, program, courses.*
4. The word **idioma** is a false cognate; it never means *idiom*. What do you think it means?

	Singular	Plural	
Nouns Ending in a Vowel / **Los sustantivos que terminan en una vocal**	**el libro** **la mesa** **un libro** **una mesa**	**los libros** **las mesas** **unos libros** **unas mesas**	the books the tables some books some tables
Nouns Ending in a Consonant / **Los sustantivos que terminan en una consonante**	**la universidad** **un papel** **un lápiz**	**las universidades** **unos papeles** **unos lápices**	the universities some papers some pencils

1. **Plural Endings**
Spanish nouns that end in a vowel form plurals by adding **-s.** Nouns that end in a consonant add **-es.** Nouns that end in the consonant **-z** change the **-z** to **-c** before adding **-es: lápiz → lápices.**

Sustantivos plurales

vowel + **-s**

consonant + **-es**

-z → -ces

---

2. **Plural of Articles**
The definite and indefinite articles also have plural forms: **el → los, la → las, un → unos, una → unas.**
Unos and **unas** mean *some, several,* or *a few.*

Artículos plurales

el → los **un → unos**

la → las **una → unas**

---

3. **Groups of People**
In Spanish, the masculine plural form of a noun is used to refer to a group that includes both males and females.

los amigos = *the friends* (all male or both male and female)
las amigas = *the friends* (only female)
unos extranjeros = *some foreigners* (all male or both male and female)
unas extranjeras = *some foreign women*

Práctica y comunicación

Plural Forms Summary

el → los **un → unos**
la → las **una → unas**
vowel + **-s**
consonant + **-es**
-z → -ces

A. Autoprueba. Empareje (*Match*) los sustantivos con los artículos apropiados.

1. libros
2. hombre
3. librería
4. profesoras

a. el
b. las
c. unos
d. una

B. Cambios (*Changes*)

Paso 1. Singular → plural.

1. la mesa
2. el papel
3. el amigo
4. la oficina
5. un cuaderno
6. un lápiz
7. una universidad
8. un bolígrafo
9. un teléfono

Paso 2. Plural → singular.

1. los profesores
2. las computadoras
3. las bibliotecarias
4. los estudiantes
5. unos hombres
6. unas tardes
7. unas residencias
8. unas sillas
9. unos escritorios

***Prác. A: Answers 1.** c **2.** a **3.** d **4.** b*

¡OJO!

Remember:
hay = there **is**
= there **are**

Vocabulario útil

el experimento
el laboratorio

C. Identificaciones. Nombre (*Name*) las personas, los objetos y los lugares.

MODELOS: Hay _______ en _______. → Hay **unos estudiantes** en **el salón de clase.**
Hay **un profesor** en **el laboratorio.**

1.

2.

D. ¡Ojo alerta!*

Paso 1. ¿Cuáles son las semejanzas (*similarities*) y las diferencias entre (*between*) los dos salones de clase? Hay por lo menos (*at least*) seis diferencias.

En el dibujo A, hay _______.
En el dibujo B, hay solo (*only*) _______.
En el escritorio del dibujo A, hay _______.
En el escritorio del dibujo B, (no) hay _______.

A.

B.

Paso 2. Ahora indique qué hay en su propio (*your own*) salón de clase.

MODELO: En mi salón de clase hay _______. En mi escritorio hay _______.

In Spanish, activities like this one are often called **¡Ojo alerta!** = *Eagle Eye!*

¿Recuerda usted?

These sentences contain Spanish verbs that you have already used. Pick them out.

1. Soy estudiante en la Universidad de _______.
2. Este (*This*) semestre/trimestre, estudio español.
3. En el futuro, deseo estudiar francés.

If you selected **estudiar** in addition to three other words, you did very well! You will learn more about Spanish verbs and how they are used in **Gramática 3.**

3 Expressing Actions

Subject Pronouns (Part 1): Present Tense of **-ar** Verbs; Negation

Gramática en acción: ¿Una escena típica?

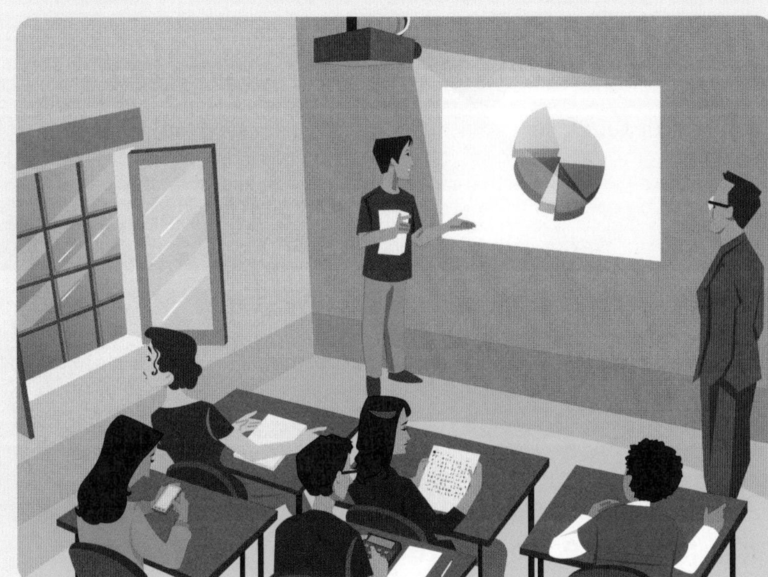

Manu **habla** enfrente de la clase porque hoy es su presentación. Pero... ¡varias personas **no escuchan**!

- Laila **manda** un mensaje de texto.
- Kevin y Lisa **trabajan** en otras materias.
- Teresa **mira** por la ventana.
- ¿Y **usted**? ¿También **desea estar** en otro lugar?

Comprensión

En la escena...

1. ¿Cuántos estudiantes **hablan?**
2. ¿Cuántas personas **escuchan** la presentación?
3. ¿Quién **manda** un mensaje de texto?
4. ¿Quién **estudia** chino?

Subject Pronouns / **Los pronombres personales**

Singular		Plural	
yo	I	**nosotros / nosotras**	we
tú	you (*familiar*)	**vosotros / vosotras**	you (*familiar, Spain*)
usted (Ud.)*	you (*formal*)	**ustedes (Uds.)***	you (*formal*)
él	he	**ellos**	they (*m., m. + f.*)
ella	she	**ellas**	they (*f.*)

a subject / **un sujeto** = the person or thing that performs the action in a sentence

a pronoun / **un pronombre** = a word that takes the place of a noun or represents a person

A typical scene? *Manu is talking in front of the class because today is his presentation. But . . . several people are not listening! • Laila is sending a text message. • Kevin and Lisa are working on other subjects. • Teresa is looking out the window. • And you? Do you want to be somewhere else too?*

***Usted** *and* **ustedes** *are frequently abbreviated in writing as* **Ud.** *or* **Vd.,** *and* **Uds.** *or* **Vds.,** *respectively.*

1. **Subject Pronouns and Gender**
The person that performs the action in a sentence is expressed by *subject pronouns* (**los pronombres personales**).
In Spanish, the equivalents of *he* and *she* and all plural subject pronouns have masculine and feminine forms. The masculine plural form is used to refer to a group of males as well as to a group of males and females.

Manuel	→	**él**	*he*
Sara	→	**ella**	*she*
Manuel + Juan	→	**ellos**	*they*
Manuel + Sara	→	**ellos**	*they*
María + Sara	→	**ellas**	*they*

¡OJO!

As in English-speaking countries, Spanish speakers are creating multiple ways of expressing non-binary gender identities.

---

2. **Pronouns for *you***
Spanish has different words for *you*. In general,
- **tú** is used with a friend or a family member.
- **usted** is used with people with whom the speaker has a more formal or distant relationship.

The situations in which **tú** and **usted** are used also vary among different countries and regions.

tú	→	friend, family member
usted	→	formal or distant relationship

---

3. **Plural of *you***
In Latin American Spanish, the plural for both **usted** and **tú** is **ustedes.**
In Spain, however, **vosotros/vosotras** is the plural of **tú,** while **ustedes** is used as the plural of **usted** exclusively.

Latinoamérica		
tú / **usted**	→	**ustedes**

España		
tú	→	**vosotros/vosotras**
usted	→	**ustedes**

---

4. **Omitting Subject Pronouns**
Subject pronouns are not used as frequently in Spanish as they are in English, and they may usually be omitted. You will learn more about the uses of Spanish subject pronouns in **Gramática 8 (Cap. 3).**

Present Tense of **-ar** Verbs / **El tiempo presente de los verbos *-ar***

1. **Infinitives**
As you know, the *infinitive* (**el infinitivo**) of a verb indicates the action or state of being, with no reference to who or what performs the action or when it is done (present, past, or future).
Infinitives in English are indicated by *to: to* speak, *to* eat, *to* live.
In Spanish, all infinitives end in **-ar, -er,** or **-ir.**

-ar:	**hablar**	to speak
-er:	**comer**	to eat
-ir:	**vivir**	to live

an infinitive / **un infinitivo** = a verb form that indicates action or state of being without reference to person, tense, or number

a tense / **un tiempo** = the quality of a verb form that indicates time: present, past, or future

---

2. **Conjugating Verbs**
To *conjugate* (**conjugar**) a verb means to give the various forms of the verb with their corresponding subjects: *I speak, you speak, she speaks,* and so on.
All regular Spanish verbs are conjugated by adding *personal endings* (**las terminaciones personales**) that reflect the subject doing the action. These are added to the *stem* (**la raíz**), which is the infinitive minus the infinitive ending.

Infinitive / **Infinitivo**		Stem / **Raíz**
hablar	→	**habl-**
comer	→	**com-**
vivir	→	**viv-**

3. Present Tense Endings

The personal endings that are added to the stem of all regular **-ar** verbs to form the *present tense* (**el presente**) are listed at the right. The chart below shows those same endings attached to the stem of the infinitive **hablar** (**habl-**).

Las terminaciones *-ar* del tiempo presente
-o, -as, -a, -amos, -áis, -an

hablar (*to speak; to talk*): **habl-**					
Singular			**Plural**		
(yo)	**hablo**	I speak	**(nosotros)** **(nosotras)**	**hablamos**	we speak
(tú)	**hablas**	you speak	**(vosotros)** **(vosotros)**	**habláis**	you speak
(usted) **(él)** **(ella)**	**habla**	you speak he speaks she speaks	**(ustedes)** **(ellos)** **(ellas)**	**hablan**	you speak they (*m., m.* + *f.*) speak they (*f.*) speak

4. Important *-ar* Verbs

Here are some **-ar** verbs used in this chapter.

Los verbos *-ar*	
bailar	to dance
buscar	to look for
cantar	to sing
comprar	to buy
desear	to want
enseñar	to teach
escuchar	to listen (to)
estudiar	to study
hablar	to speak; to talk
hablar por teléfono	to talk on the phone
mandar un mensaje (de texto)	to (send a) text
necesitar	to need
pagar	to pay (for)
practicar	to practice
regresar	to return (*to a place*)
tocar	to play (*a musical instrument*)
tomar	to take; to drink
trabajar	to work

¡OJO!

Note that in Spanish the meaning of the English word *for* is included in the verbs **buscar** (*to look* ***for***) and **pagar** (*to pay* ***for***); *to* is included in **escuchar** (*to listen* ***to***).

5. Conjugated Verb + *Infinitive*

As in English, when two Spanish verbs are used in a row and there is no change of subject, the second verb is usually in the infinitive form.

Necesito mandar un mensaje de texto.
I need to send a text (message).

Me gusta bailar.
I like to dance.

6. **Tense**

In both English and Spanish, conjugated verb forms also indicate the *time* or *tense* (**el tiempo**) of the action: *I speak* (present), *I spoke* (past).

Some English equivalents of the present tense forms of Spanish verbs are shown at the right.

hablo	I speak	Simple present tense
	I am speaking	Present progressive (indicates an action in progress)
	I will speak	Near future action

¡OJO!

The exact English equivalent of a Spanish verb form depends on the context in which the verb appears. In the following sentence, the word **mañana** indicates a future action, so **hablo** means *I will speak:* **Hablo con Juan mañana.**

Negation / **La negación**

In Spanish the word **no** is placed before the conjugated verb to make a negative sentence.

subject + **no** + *verb*

El estudiante **no habla** español.	*The student doesn't speak Spanish.*
No, **no necesito** dinero.	*No, I don't need money.*

Summary of *-ar* Verb Endings

(yo)	**-o**	**(nosotros/as)**	**-amos**
(tú)	**-as**	**(vosotros/as)**	**-áis**
(usted, él/ella)	**-a**	**(ustedes, ellos/as)**	**-an**

Práctica y comunicación

A. Asociaciones. ¿Qué verbos asocia usted con las siguientes (*following*) ideas? Dé (*Give*) infinitivos.

MODELO: la música → escuchar, tocar, bailar, ...

1. español
2. mucho (*a lot of*) dinero
3. en la librería
4. en el salón de clase
5. un coche (*car*)
6. a la residencia
7. Coca-Cola® o café (*coffee*)
8. la música

B. Mi compañero/a y yo

Paso 1. Autoprueba. Complete los verbos con las terminaciones apropiadas.

1. (yo) pag_______
2. (tú) toc_______
3. (ella) habl_______
4. (nosotras) compr_______
5. (usted) escuch_______
6. (ellos) trabaj_______

Paso 2. ¿Sí o no? Complete las oraciones de forma personal con la forma **yo** de los verbos. Use **no** delante del (*in front of the*) verbo si es necesario.

MODELO: **1.** Necesit___ un coche. → Necesit**o** un coche. (**No** necesit**o** un coche.)

1. Necesit___ un coche.
2. Trabaj___ en la biblioteca de la universidad
3. Cant___ en un coro (*choir*).
4. Tom___ una clase de ciencias sociales este (*this*) semestre/trimestre.
5. Bail___ salsa en las fiestas.
6. Habl___ inglés como (*as a*) lengua nativa.
7. Mand___ muchos mensajes todos los días (*every day*).
8. Toc___ un instrumento musical.

Paso 3. En parejas (*pairs*), hagan y contesten preguntas (*ask and answer questions*) basadas en el **Paso 2.**

MODELO: Necesito un coche. → ESTUDIANTE 1: ¿**Necesitas** un coche?
ESTUDIANTE 2: Sí, **necesito** un coche. (No, **no necesito** un coche.)

***Prác. A:* Answers, Paso 1.** *1. pago 2. tocas 3. habla 4. compramos 5. escucha 6. trabajan*

C. Una o más personas

Paso 1. Cambie por (*Change to*) un sujeto plural.

MODELOS: Él no desea tomar café. →
Ellos no **desean** tomar café.
Yo no deseo tomar café. →
Nosotros no **deseamos** tomar café.

1. Ella no desea estudiar francés.
2. Usted baila muy bien el tango.
3. ¿Mandas mensajes con frecuencia?
4. Escucho la radio con frecuencia.

Paso 2. Ahora cambie por un sujeto singular. En los números 2 y 4 hay más de una opción.

1. Ellas no buscan el dinero.
2. Los estudiantes no necesitan seis clases.
3. Pagamos mucho dinero de matrícula (*tuition*).
4. ¿Compran ustedes muchos libros?

D. La fiesta de Marcos

Paso 1. Complete el párrafo con las formas apropiadas de los verbos entre paréntesis.

¿A usted le gustan las fiestas?

Esta noche[a] hay una fiesta en casa de Marcos.[b] Marcos es de Guatemala y su compañero de apartamento, Julio, es de Honduras. Hay quince amigos en la fiesta. Una persona __________ (tocar[1]) la guitarra y las otras personas __________ (cantar[2]) o __________ (escuchar[3]). ¡Yo solo __________ (desear[4]) bailar!

Marta __________ (hablar[5]) con Nati mucho tiempo.[c] Pero Nati __________ (desear[6]) bailar con Miguel, el estudiante mexicano, porque[d] él __________ (bailar[7]) muy bien. Eduardo, Marcos y yo __________ (bailar[8]) en grupo.

A las once de la noche Julio __________ (buscar[9]) pizza para todos.[e] Pero todos __________ (pagar[10]).

¡La fiesta es fantástica! __________ (*Yo*: Practicar[11]) español toda la noche[f] porque todos los amigos de Marcos __________ (hablar[12]) español. ¡Eduardo y yo __________ (regresar[12]) a casa[g] a las dos de la mañana!

[a]Esta... *Tonight* [b]en... *at Marco's place (lit., house)* [c]mucho... *for a long time* [d]*because* [e]para... *for everyone* [f]toda... *all night* [g]a... *home*

Paso 2. Comprensión. Indique si las siguientes (*following*) oraciones son **ciertas, falsas** o **no se sabe** (*not known*). Luego (*Then*) indique dónde está la información correcta en el texto.

	CIERTO	FALSO	NO SE SABE
1. La persona que (*who*) habla es hispanohablante.	☐	☐	☐
2. Nati baila muy bien.	☐	☐	☐
3. Marcos y Julio compran la pizza.	☐	☐	☐
4. Todos tocan la guitarra y bailan.	☐	☐	☐
5. Marta habla mucho (*a lot*) en la fiesta.	☐	☐	☐

E. Oraciones lógicas. Form eight complete logical sentences by using one word or phrase from each column. Many combinations are possible. Use the correct form of the verbs and make any sentences negative.

MODELO: Yo no estudio francés.

yo
tú (un[a] estudiante)
nosotros (los miembros de esta clase)
los estudiantes de aquí
el extranjero
un secretario
una profesora de español
una dependienta

\+ (no) { buscar, comprar, enseñar, estudiar, hablar, mandar, pagar, regresar, tocar, tomar, trabajar } +

la guitarra, el piano, el violín
el edificio de ciencias
en la cafetería, en la universidad, en casa (*at home*)
en una oficina, en una librería
a casa muy tarde (*very late*)/temprano (*early*)
a la biblioteca a las dos
muchos/pocos mensajes
francés, alemán (*German*), italiano, inglés
bien el español
los libros de texto, la matrícula
libros y cuadernos en la librería

\+ (no) { desear, necesitar } +

tomar una clase de computación
hablar bien el español
estudiar más
comprar una calculadora, una mochila
pagar la matrícula en septiembre

¡OJO!

Remember that the verb form that follows **desear** or **necesitar** is the infinitive, just as in English.

¡OJO!

Remember that **de la mañana (tarde, noche)** are used when a specific hour of the day is mentioned. Also, remember to use **a la una / a las dos (tres...)** to express a specific time of day.

Generalmente estudio en casa **por** la mañana.

Hoy estudio con Javier en la biblioteca **a las** diez **de** la mañana.

Nota comunicativa

Cómo expresar las partes del día

You can use the preposition **por** to mean *in* or *during* when expressing the part of the day in which something happens.

Estudio **por** la mañana y trabajo **por** la tarde. **Por** la noche, estoy en casa.
I study in the morning and I work in the afternoon. At night I'm at home.

You will practice these phrases in **Práctica F.**

F. Intercambios (*Exchanges*)

Paso 1. Use los siguientes verbos y frases para crear (*create*) cinco preguntas (*questions*) interesantes.

MODELO: **¿Cantas** bien?

1. cantar o bailar
2. estudiar o trabajar
3. necesitar
4. tomar
5. tomar

\+

bien/mal (*poorly*), mucho/poco (*a little*)
muchas/pocas (*few*) horas, todos los días
dinero, libros, una computadora, pagar la matrícula
_______ (número de clases) / café o té por la mañana
clases por la mañana / por la tarde / por la noche

Paso 2. En parejas, túrnense (*take turns*) para hacer y contestar (*answer*) sus (*your*) preguntas del **Paso 1.**

MODELO: ESTUDIANTE 1: ¿Cantas bien?
ESTUDIANTE 2: Sí, **canto** bien. (No, **canto** mal.)

Nota comunicativa

El verbo *estar*

Estar is a Spanish **-ar** verb that means *to be*. You have already used forms of it to ask how others are feeling or to tell where things are located. Here is the complete present tense conjugation of **estar.** Note that the **yo** form is irregular. The other forms take regular **-ar** endings, and some have an accent to maintain the stress pattern.

(yo)	**estoy**	I am	**(nosotros/as)**	**estamos**	we are
(tú)	**estás**	you are	**(vosotros/as)**	**estáis**	you are
(usted)	**está**	you are	**(ustedes)**	**están**	you are
(él/ella)	**está**	he/she is	**(ellos/ellas)**	**están**	they are

You will learn the uses of the verb **estar,** along with those of **ser** (a second Spanish verb that means *to be*) gradually, over the next several chapters. Review what you already know by answering these questions.

1. ¿Cómo está usted en este momento (*right now*)?
2. ¿Cómo están sus (*your*) compañeros? (**Mis** compañeros…)
3. ¿Dónde está usted en este momento?

You will use **estar** in **Práctica G**.

G. ¿Dónde están? Tell where these people are and what they are doing.

MODELO: **FOTO 1:** La Srta. Martínez _______. →
La Srta. Martínez **está en una oficina. Trabaja por la tarde. Necesita…**

Vocabulario útil

buscar información
hablar por teléfono
mandar un mensaje
preparar la lección
pronunciar las palabras
tomar apuntes to take notes
usar una computadora

¡OJO!

Remember to use the definite article with titles when you are talking *about* a person: **el señor Santana, la profesora Aguilar,** and so on.

1. La Srta. Martínez _______.
   Trabaja por _______.
   Necesita _______.

2. Estas (*These*) personas _______.
   El profesor _______.
   Una estudiante _______.
   Muchos (*Many*) estudiantes _______.

Algo sobre...

¿América?

En los países hispanohablantes América es un continente que incluye[a] Norteamérica, Centroamérica y Sudamérica. Por eso,[b] el término **americano/a** define a las personas y cosas de todo el continente, no solo de los Estados Unidos. La palabra **estadounidense** es específica para los Estados Unidos.

Para abreviar el nombre de los Estados Unidos hay varias formas comunes (según[c] los países): E.U., EU, E.U.A, EE.UU., EEUU. *USA* no es una abreviatura del español.

 **¿Cuántos continentes hay en este[d] hemisferio, según se enseña[e] en los Estados Unidos?**

[a]que... *that includes* [b]Por... *That's why* [c]*according to* [d]*this* [e]según... *as is taught*

4 Getting Information (Part 1)

Asking Yes/No Questions

Gramática en acción: La matriculación

©Digital Vision/Getty Images

PENÉLOPE: ... y ahora necesito una clase más por la mañana. ¿Hay espacio en la clase de Sociología 2?

JAVIER: A ver... No, no hay.

PENÉLOPE: ¿Hay una clase de historia o de matemáticas?

JAVIER: Solo por la noche. ¿Deseas tomar una clase por la noche?

PENÉLOPE: ¡Ay, chico, es imposible! Trabajo por la noche.

JAVIER: Pues... ¿qué tal la clase de Literatura Hispana en los Estados Unidos?

PENÉLOPE: ¡Perfecto! ¡Me gusta mucho la literatura! ¿Cuándo es la clase?

Comprensión

1. ¿Necesita Penélope dos clases más?
2. ¿Hay espacio en Sociología 2?
3. ¿Cuál es el problema con los cursos de historia y matemáticas?
4. ¿Qué curso recomienda Javier por fin?

You have been asking questions since the beginning of *Puntos de partida*, and you learned more about asking questions in **Nota comunicativa** (page 34). This section will help you review all that you know about this topic as well as learn another way to ask questions in Spanish.

Registration *PENÉLOPE: . . . and now I need one more class in the morning. Is there room in Sociology 2? JAVIER: Let's see . . . No, there isn't (room). PENÉLOPE: Is there a history or a math class? JAVIER: Only at night. Do you want to take a night class? PENÉLOPE: Come on, that's impossible! I work at night. JAVIER: Well . . . what about the class about Hispanic Literature in the United States? PENÉLOPE: Perfect! I love literature! When is the class?*

Types of Questions / **Tipos de preguntas**

There are two kinds of *questions* (**las preguntas**) in English and in Spanish.

1. *Information questions* ask for information, for facts. They typically begin with *interrogative words* **(las palabras interrogativas)**. You have already learned a number of them.

Preguntas informativas

—¿**Qué** lengua habla usted?
—Hablo español.

2. *Yes/No questions* can be answered by a simple **sí** or **no.**

Preguntas sí/no

—¿Habla usted francés?
—No.

¡OJO!

Remember that intonation drops at the end of an information question in Spanish, whereas it rises in English.

Forming Yes/No Questions / **La formación de preguntas sí/no**

There are two ways to form this kind of question.

1. *Rising intonation:* The simplest way is to make your voice rise at the end of a statement. Doing so makes the statement into a question.

STATEMENT: Usted trabaja aquí todos los días.
You work here every day.

QUESTION: ¿Usted trabaja aquí todos los días?
Do you work here every day?

2. *Inversion:* Another way to form yes/no questions is to invert (transpose) the order of the subject and verb, in addition to making your voice rise at the end of the question. You can also put the subject all the way at the end of the question.

STATEMENT: **Usted** trabaja aquí todos los días.

QUESTION: ¿Trabaja **usted** aquí todos los días?

STATEMENT: **María** toca el piano.

QUESTION: ¿Toca el piano **María**?

Subjects in Questions and Answers / **Los sujetos en las preguntas y respuestas**

1. When a question is asked about a third person or persons (**Tomás, ella, ellos, los amigos,** ...), the subject and the verb of the question and answer *are the same*. However, the subject is usually not repeated in the answer. In fact, the subject may not even appear in the question if it is clear to whom the question refers to.

SUBJECT: **Tomás**
VERB: **toca**

¿**Toca** el piano Tomás?
¿**Toca** Tomás el piano? →
¿Tomás **toca** el piano?

Sí, **toca** el piano muy bien.

Does Tom play the piano? →
Yes, he plays the piano very well.

¿**Toca** más instrumentos? →
Sí, **toca** la trompeta también. / No, no **toca** más instrumentos.

Does he play more instruments? →
Yes, he also plays the trumpet. / No, he doesn't play any more instruments.

(Continúa.)

SUBJECTS: **Ángela y Carlos** VERB: **toman**	¿**Toman** cálculo Ángela y Carlos? ¿**Toman** Ángela y Carlos cálculo? ¿Ángela y Carlos **toman** cálculo? → Sí, **toman** cálculo y álgebra. *Are Angela and Carlos taking calculus?* → *Yes, they're taking calculus and algebra.*

¡OJO!

Notice that the subjects (**Tomás, Ángela y Carlos**) are not expressed in the answers, and no subject pronouns (**él, ellos**) are needed in the Spanish answers because **toca** = *he plays* and **toman** = *they are taking* in this context.

---

2. When asking a question directly *to* a person with whom you are speaking, the subject and verb *are different* in the question and answer.

QUESTION SUBJECT: **tú** VERB: **cantas**	¿**Cantas** bien? → *Do you sing well?* →
ANSWER SUBJECT: **yo** VERB: **canto**	Sí, **canto** bien. *Yes, I do (sing well).*
QUESTION SUBJECT: **ustedes** VERB: **desean**	¿**Desean** ustedes trabajar más? → *Do you want to continue working?* →
ANSWER SUBJECT: **nosotros** VERB: **deseamos**	No, **deseamos** regresar a casa. *No, we want to go home.*

¡OJO!

Notice how the subjects change: **¿tú? → yo, ¿ustedes? → nosotros.**
The Spanish verbs also change **¿cantas? → canto, ¿desean? → deseamos**.

Summary of Question Formation

- with interrogative words
- with intonation
- by inverting the subject and verb

Práctica y comunicación

A. Preguntas

Paso 1. Autoprueba. ¿Cómo se dice (*How do you say it*) en inglés?

1. ¿Habla usted inglés?
2. ¿Necesitan ustedes otra clase?
3. ¿Tomas biología?
4. ¿Trabajo mañana?

Paso 2. Ahora exprese las siguientes oraciones como preguntas. **¡OJO!** Hay dos o tres formas.

MODELO: Alicia toca el violín. → ¿**Toca Alicia** el violín? ¿**Toca** el violín **Alicia**? ¿**Alicia toca** el violín?

1. Susana toca la guitarra.
2. Los estudiantes compran muchos libros.
3. Ustedes miran el teléfono en clase.
4. Diego manda mensajes en clase.
5. Ustedes toman cinco clases este semestre/trimestre.

Paso 3. Ahora, en parejas, usen las oraciones del **Paso 2** para hacer y contestar preguntas. **¡OJO!** No es necesario usar los pronombres **tú** y **yo** en la pregunta o en la respuesta (*answer*).

MODELO: tocar la guitarra →
ESTUDIANTE 1: ¿**Tocas** la guitarra?
ESTUDIANTE 2: Sí, **toco** la guitarra. (No, no **toco** la guitarra.)

Prác. A: Answers, Paso 1. 1. *Do you speak English?* ***2.*** *Do you (pl.) need another class?* ***3.*** *Are you taking (a) biology (class)?* ***4.*** *Do (Will) I work tomorrow?*

B. Una conversación inventada. Imagine that you have just met Diego and Irene, new students on campus. You asked them some questions and they gave you the following answers. What were the questions that you asked?

MODELO: Sí, estudiamos antropología. → ¿**Estudian** antropología?

1. Sí, tomamos una clase de español.
2. Sí, estudiamos en la biblioteca con frecuencia.
3. No, no tocamos el piano.
4. No, no deseamos trabajar más horas.
5. No, no hablamos francés, pero hablamos italiano un poco.
6. ¡Sí, estamos muy bien en esta (*this*) universidad!

C. Intercambios: Sus (*Your*) actividades

Paso 1. Use the following cues as a guide to form questions that you will ask a classmate. You may ask other questions as well. Write the questions on a sheet of paper. **¡OJO!** Use the **tú** form of the verbs.

MODELO: escuchar música por la mañana →
¿**Escuchas** música por la mañana?

1. estudiar en la biblioteca todos los días
2. practicar español con un amigo o amiga
3. tomar mucho / un poco de (*a little bit of*) café por la mañana
4. bailar mucho en las fiestas
5. cantar en la ducha (*shower*)
6. regresar a casa muy tarde los fines de semana (*on the weekends*)
7. comprar los libros en la librería de la universidad
8. mandar muchos mensajes
9. trabajar los fines de semana
10. usar (*to use*) un diccionario bilingüe online

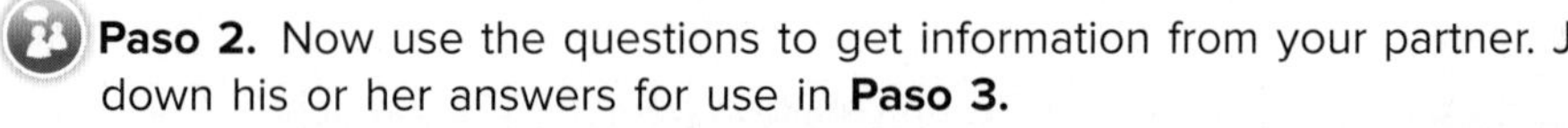

Paso 2. Now use the questions to get information from your partner. Jot down his or her answers for use in **Paso 3.**

MODELO: ESTUDIANTE 1: ¿Escuchas música por la mañana?
ESTUDIANTE 2: Sí, (No, no) **escucho** música por la mañana.

Paso 3. With the information you gathered in **Paso 2,** report your partner's answers to the class. (You will use the **él/ella** form of the verbs when reporting.)

MODELO: Jenny no **escucha** música por la mañana.

D. Una encuesta (*poll*): ¿Qué clases tomas?

Paso 1. Make a list in Spanish of the classes you are taking. Ask your instructor or use a dictionary to find the names of classes you don't know how to say in Spanish. If you ask your instructor, remember to ask in Spanish: **¿Cómo se dice _______ en español?**

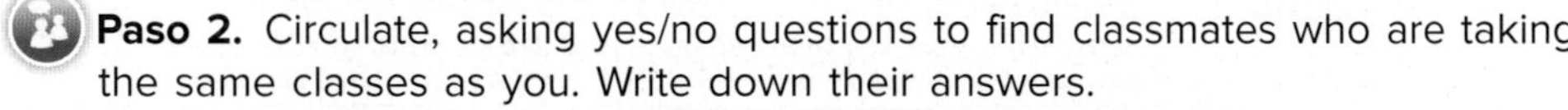

Paso 2. Circulate, asking yes/no questions to find classmates who are taking the same classes as you. Write down their answers.

MODELO: ESTUDIANTE 1: Carlos, ¿tomas una clase de matemáticas?
ESTUDIANTE 2: Sí, tomo matemáticas. Tomo Cálculo 2.

Paso 3. Report back the information you have learned to the whole class.

MODELO: Carlos y yo tomamos matemáticas. Jennie y yo... Solo yo tomo geología.

Algo sobre°...

Algo... *Something about*

los Departamentos de Estudios Latinos en las universidades de los Estados Unidos

La importancia de la población hispana en los Estados Unidos se refleja[a] en el mundo[b] académico. Muchas universidades tienen[c] departamentos o concentraciones[d] que investigan[e] y enseñan temas[f] relacionados con los latinos en los Estados Unidos. En los estados del Suroeste,[g] se ofrecen[h] regularmente Estudios Chicanos, especializados en la población norteamericana de origen mexicano.

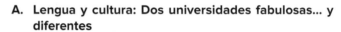

¿? **En su universidad, ¿hay un programa o un área de concentración de estudios especializados en los latinos? (En mi universidad...)**

[a]se... *is reflected* [b]*world* [c]*have* [d]*majors* [e]que... *that research* [f]*topics* [g]*Southwest* [h]se... *are offered* [i]*your*

Todo junto

La Colección Latinoamericana Benson, una colección comprensiva de libros, documentos, revistas (*magazines*) y periódicos (*newspapers*) relacionados con (*related to*) Latinoamérica

A. Lengua y cultura: Dos universidades fabulosas... y diferentes

Paso 1. Completar. Complete the following description of two well-known universities. Give the correct form of the verbs in parentheses, as suggested by context. When the subject pronoun is in *italics,* don't use it in the sentence. When two possibilities are given in parentheses, select the correct word.

¿Cómo es la universidad perfecta? Hay muchas[a] opciones. Aquí ____________ (hay / es[1]) dos ejemplos de ____________ (universidad / universidades[2]) muy famosas en los Estados Unidos. La primera[b] es ____________ (el / la[3]) Universidad de Texas, en Austin. ¡Es ____________ (un / una[4]) universidad muy grande[c]! Hay veinticuatro grupos sociales para estudiantes hispanos y una ____________ (librería / biblioteca[5]) con una colección latinoamericana fantástica, la Colección Latinoamericana Benson. ____________ (Los / Las[6]) materias más populares en la UT son: administración de empresas, ingeniería, humanidades y comunicaciones. Muchos estudiantes ____________ (tomar[7]) cursos en ____________ (el / la[8]) Instituto de Estudios Latinoamericanos y en ____________ (el / la[9]) Centro para Estudios Mexicoamericanos.

Stanford, en ____________ (el / la[10]) estado de California, es una universidad más pequeña.[d] Tiene[e] una residencia para estudiantes de español, la Casa Zapata. Allí,[f] ____________ (los / las[11]) estudiantes ____________ (practicar[12]) español y ____________ (participar[13]) en celebraciones hispanas. Las materias más populares en Stanford son:[g] biología, economía, inglés y ciencias políticas. ____________ (El / La[14]) problema en Stanford es que los estudiantes ____________ (pagar[15]) mucho por[h] la matrícula.

¿Prefiere usted la UT o Stanford? ____________ ¿(*Usted:* Desear[16]) ____________ (estudia / estudiar[17]) en California o en Texas?

[a]*many* [b]La... *The first one* [c]*big* [d]más... *smaller* [e]*It has* [f]*There* [g]*are* [h]*for*

Paso 2. Comprensión. Las siguientes oraciones son falsas. Corríjalas. (*Correct them.*)

1. En la Universidad de Texas hay dos grupos sociales para estudiantes hispanos.
2. En el Instituto de Estudios Latinoamericanos hay pocos (*few*) estudiantes.
3. La Universidad de Stanford está en Texas.
4. La Casa Zapata es una biblioteca importante.

Paso 3. En acción

Ahora complete la siguiente información sobre su (*about your*) universidad.

Mi universidad est__ en el estado de _______.

En mi universidad...

1. muchos / pocos (*many/few*) estudiantes tom__ clases de español.
2. hay / no hay un centro o un / una programa de estudios latinoamericanos.
3. hay / no hay organizaciones de estudiantes latinos
4. las materias más populares son: _______.
5. los estudiantes pag__ mucho / poco dinero.

B. Proyecto: Perfil° académico de la clase

°*Profile*

Working in groups, create a profile of the academic preferences of your class by polling your classmates about how many and which classes they are taking and when. When you analyze the results, you will determine which are the most popular subjects among the classmates you interviewed and at what times.

Paso 1. Preparación. In your group, prepare one question for each member of the group. You will use these questions in **Paso 2** to interview some classmates. Some questions can elicit yes/no answers, while other questions will use interrogative words such as **¿cuándo... ?, ¿a qué hora... ?,** and so on.

(Continúa.)

Estrategia

Use the question **¿Cuántas clases tomas?** to find out how many classes someone is taking.

Use the question **¿Cómo se dice ______ en español?** when you need help with a new word.

Paso 2. Encuesta. ***(Poll.)*** Each member of your group should poll as many classmates as possible using his/her particular question. Before you start polling, create a table on which to record the answers. And don't forget to ask for and record the names of the classmates you poll.

MODELO: ¿Cuántas clases tomas por la mañana (tarde, noche)?

nombre / número de clases	por la mañana	por la tarde	por la noche

Paso 3: Análisis de datos (*data*). Gather the information from your group's polling, and prepare 4 to 5 statements to share with the rest of the class. Here are some examples of statements. You can use them or create your own.

1. En nuestra (*Our*) encuesta hay información de ___________ (número) estudiantes.
2. ___________ (número) estudiantes de la clase toman ___________ (número) clases. ___________ (número) estudiantes toman ___________ clases....
3. Las tres materias más (*most*) / menos (*least*) populares son ___________.
4. Muchos/Pocos (*Many/Few*) estudiantes toman clases por ___________.

¡Ahora, yo!

A. Entrevista. Use de (*as a*) modelo las preguntas y respuestas (*answers*) de la página 29 de este capítulo para hablar de sus propios estudios universitarios (*own university studies*).

B. Proyecto audiovisual. Con las preguntas de la página 29 como modelo, filme una o dos entrevistas con compañeros de clase sobre (*about*) las materias que estudian y su especialización universitaria.

SALU'

«¡Qué bacán!°» Segmento 2

¡Qué... *How great!*

Antes de mirar°

Antes... *Before watching*

Conteste (*Answer*) las siguientes preguntas.

1. ¿Desea usted estudiar en un país (*country*) hispanohablante? ¿En qué país(es)?
2. En ese (*that*) país, ¿desea vivir (*to live*) con una familia o en una residencia de estudiantes?

Este° segmento

This

Desde (*From*) Lima, Perú, Laura presenta un reportaje sobre la Universidad del Pacífico, un lugar muy interesante para estudiar español.

Muchos (*Many*) estudiantes extranjeros viven (*live*) con familias peruanas hospitalarias (*welcoming*). Así (*So*), practican el español todo el tiempo (*all the time*) y aprenden (*they learn*) por experiencia la cultura de manera directa y personal.

Vocabulario del segmento

la ciudad	city	**los negocios**	business
el sitio	place, site	**la mercadotecnia**	marketing
el barrio	neighborhood	**la contabilidad**	accounting
lindo/a	pretty, cute	**pequeño/a**	small
se especializa	it specializes	**se sienten como miembros**	feel like members
la carrera	concentration, major		

Fragmento del guion°

script

Esta universidad limeña[a] atrae[b] a numerosos estudiantes internacionales por varias razones.[c] Primero,[d] la universidad cuenta con[e] modernas instalaciones,[f] como la biblioteca. Segundo,[g] está muy cerca del[h] centro histórico de Lima. Pero lo más importante es que la universidad tiene[i] un estupendo Centro de Idiomas.

[a]*in Lima* [b]*attracts* [c]por... *for various reasons* [d]*First* [e]cuenta... *has* [f]*facilities* [g]*Second* [h]muy... *very close to the* [i]*has*

Después de° mirar

Después... *After*

A. ¿Está claro? ¿Cierto o falso? Corrija (*Correct*) las oraciones falsas según (*according to*) el video.

	CIERTO	FALSO
1. La ciudad de Lima...		
a. es pequeña.	☐	☐
b. tiene (*has*) barrios modernos.	☐	☐
c. tiene sitios arqueológicos de los incas.	☐	☐
2. La Universidad del Pacífico...		
a. es rural.	☐	☐
b. es pública.	☐	☐
c. tiene un centro para estudiar lenguas.	☐	☐
d. se especializa en humanidades.	☐	☐

B. Un poco más. Conteste las siguientes preguntas.

1. ¿En qué materias se especializa la Universidad del Pacífico?
2. ¿Cuándo hay clases para los estudiantes extranjeros, por la mañana o por la tarde? ¿Qué hay por la tarde?

C. Y ahora, ustedes. En parejas, usen algunas (*some*) ideas del programa y del capítulo para hablar de su universidad.

MODELO: Esta (*This*) universidad es pública/privada. Se especializa en...

MUNDO° HISPANO *World*

Enfoque cultural: Los Estados Unidos

Antes de leer° Antes... *Before reading*

¿Hay muchos estudiantes de origen hispano en su (*your*) universidad? ¿Hay organizaciones para ellos? ¿Es usted miembro de una organización estudiantil?

El mural *Resurrection of the Green Planet,* del artista chicano Ernesto de la Loza, en *East Los Angeles*

Presencia latina en las universidades

En la actualidad[a] hay muchos estudiantes latinos en las universidades de los Estados Unidos.

La experiencia universitaria típica en los Estados Unidos incluye[b] la participación en organizaciones de estudiantes con diversos intereses. Por eso,[c] las universidades estadounidenses tienen[d] una variada representación de organizaciones latinas.

- Algunas[e] son para todos los hispanos de la universidad, como **Latinos Unidos.**
- Otras son para un grupo específico, como **Fuerza Quisqueyana** (estudiantes dominicanos) o **(La) Raza** (estudiantes mexicanoamericanos o chicanos).

Las organizaciones latinas coordinan eventos sociales y académicos: bailes de gala[f] con música hispana, conferencias de escritores[g] hispanohablantes, servicios sociales, etcétera. Con frecuencia, también hay una Casa Latina, donde miembros de la organización viven juntos.[h]

[a]En... *Currently* [b]*includes* [c]Por... *For this reason* [d]*have* [e]*Some (organizations)* [f]bailes... *formal dances* [g]*writers* [h]viven... *live together*

Un símbolo latino en los Estados Unidos: Los murales y el arte urbano

La tradición muralista mexicana está muy presente en las comunidades latinas de los Estados Unidos, especialmente en California y los estados del Suroeste.[a] Presenta motivos indigenistas,[b] históricos y sociales. Ahora hay ejemplos del arte urbano en los grandes[c] museos, desde[d] grafitis hasta[e] murales.

[a]*Southwest* [b]motivos... *indigenous* (*native*) *themes or elements* [c]*great* [d]*from* [e]*to*

Comprensión

Empareje (*Match*) la información de las dos columnas.

A	B
1. la Raza	**a.** ejemplos del arte latino
2. los murales	**b.** estudiantes dominicanos
3. bailes de gala	**c.** estudiantes mexicoamericanos
4. Fuerza Quisqueyana	**d.** un evento social

En otros países° hispanos *countries*

En todo el mundo[a] hispanohablante Hay universidades nacionales que son gratuitas[b] o muy económicas en comparación con las universidades privadas. Las universidades nacionales son con frecuencia las más prestigiosas y antiguas[c] del país.

[a]*world* [b]que... *that are free* [c]las... *the most prestigious and oldest*

En acción

Haga (*Make*) una lista de organizaciones para los estudiantes latinos de su (*your*) universidad. ¿Son (*Are they*) para una comunidad hispana específica, como la comunidad dominicana o la chicana?

Lectura°

Reading

Antes de leer°

Antes... *Before reading*

What is a good way for an adult to learn another language? On the job (**el trabajo**), with friends who speak the language, in school (**una escuela**)? Can you think of other ways? Explain your answer. In a school, how many other learners would there ideally be in each class? How many days per week would the class meet? How many hours per day?

Un anuncio° de Inglés USA

Un... *An ad*

Comprensión

A. Traducciones. (***Translations.***) Empareje (*Match*) las frases en español del anuncio con sus equivalentes en inglés.

1. ________	una hora de descanso	**a.**	*more*
2. ________	el almuerzo	**b.**	*an hour-long break*
3. ________	semanas	**c.**	*weeks*
4. ________	mayor	**d.**	*lunch*

B. En el anuncio. Busque (*Look for*) la siguiente información en el anuncio.

1. ¿Cómo se llama la escuela?
2. ¿Dónde está la escuela?
3. ¿Cuántos estudiantes hay en una clase?
4. ¿Qué tipo de estudiantes hay en la escuela?
5. ¿Cuántas horas de clase hay al (*per*) día?

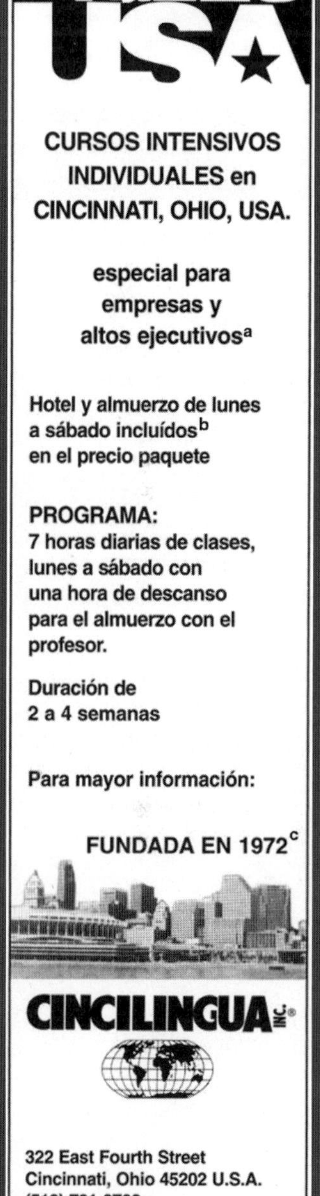

[a]para... *for business and corporate executives* [b]*included* [c]mil novecientos setenta y dos

 Proyecto: ¿Y en su° universidad?

your

Create a similar advertisement for the Spanish program at your college or university.

Paso 1. Información. Answer the following questions to gather information about your Spanish program. You may need to ask your instructor some questions.

1. ¿Cuántos niveles (*levels*) de cursos de español hay?
2. Cómo máximo, ¿cuántos estudiantes hay por sección en los cursos para principiantes (*for beginners*)?
3. ¿Son las clases para principiantes presenciales (*face-to-face*)? ¿virtuales? ¿semipresenciales?
4. ¿Son las clases por la mañana, por la tarde o por la noche?
5. ¿Cuántos días por semana (*days a week*) hay clase? ¿Cuántos créditos vale (*is worth*) cada (*each*) curso?
6. ¿Hay actividades extracurriculares relacionadas con el (*related to*) español en el *campus*? (Por ejemplo: cine [*movies*), teatro, horas de conversación...]
7. ¿Hay otras oportunidades para los estudiantes de español? (Por ejemplo: estudiar en países (*countries*) hispanohablantes, participar en actividades para voluntarios, ...)

Paso 2. El anuncio. Now that you have some information about your institution's Spanish program, create an advertisement for it, similar to the ad for **Cincilingua**.

Textos orales

Un anuncio° para los cursos de verano° de una universidad

ad / summer

Antes de escuchar°

Antes... *Before listening*

What kind of information do you expect to hear in an ad for a summer course?

Vocabulario para escuchar

el anuncio	ad
el verano	summer
mayo	May
la semana	week
julio	July
agosto	August

Comprensión

A. Información básica. Indique las respuestas (*answers*) apropiadas.

1. El período de matrícula es en...

   ____ mayo ____ junio ____ julio ____ agosto

2. Hay cursos de...

   ____ 2 semanas ____ 4 semanas ____ 8 semanas ____ 10 semanas

3. Con seguridad (*For sure*) hay cursos de... según (*according to*) el anuncio.

   ____ sociología ____ arte ____ matemáticas ____ literatura

4. Por internet se ofrecen (*are offered*) cursos de...

   ____ alemán ____ filosofía ____ italiano ____ portugués

B. Más información. Según (*According to*) el anuncio, ¿cuál es el nombre de la residencia? ¿la dirección (*address*) de la página web? ¿el teléfono de contacto?

En acción

Create a short Facebook® ad about your university. Here is a basic model to which you can add ideas based on **Comprensión A.**

MODELO: ¿Desea estudiar con estudiantes fantásticos?
La Universidad de ______________ es perfecta.
Hay un extenso catálogo que incluye (*that includes*) ...
Visitar la página web ...

Proyecto en su° comunidad

your

As you know, all Spanish-speaking countries use the word **universidad** to refer to colleges or universities, big or small, public or private. But there is a lot of variation in the words that Spanish speakers use for *elementary school*, *middle school*, and *high school*. There is also variation in how the following words and phrases are expressed: (*academic*) *grade* (and the symbols used to give grades), *to pass, to fail.*

Preguntas posibles

- Ask someone who was raised in a Hispanic country what language is used in his or her country to express different levels of schooling and the grading system.
- Ask the person to describe his or her educational experience in the country of origin.
- If relevant, ask for a comparison with the educational system in this country.

Escritura°

Writing

Proyecto: Un ensayo sobre este° semestre/trimestre

ensayo... *essay about this*

¿Qué estudia usted? ¿Trabaja? ¿Es su horario (*schedule*) este semestre/trimestre muy diferente del (*from the*) horario de sus (*your*) compañeros de clase? ¿O es similar?

©Andersen Ross/Getty Images

Estudiantes universitarios que escriben (*who are writing*) un ensayo juntos (*together*)

Antes de escribir°

Antes... *Before writing*

Primero (*First*), complete la columna de la izquierda (*left-hand column*) con información personal. Luego entreviste a (*Then interview*) un compañero / una compañera y complete la columna de la derecha.

Yo	Mi compañero/a
Mi especialización[a] es / puede ser[b]:	Su[c] especialización es / puede ser:
Clases que[d] tomo este semestre/ trimestre:	Clases que toma este semestre/ trimestre:
Mi clase favorita es:	Su clase favorita es:
No trabajo. / Trabajo en...	No trabaja. / Trabaja en...
(No) Me gusta este (*this*) semestre/ trimestre.	(No) Le gusta[e] este semestre/trimestre.

[a]*major* [b]puede... *might be* [c]*His/ Her* [d]*that* [e]Le... *He/She likes*

A escribir°

A... *Let's write*

Ahora combine la información para escribir (*to write*) un ensayo. Hay más ayuda (*help*) en Connect.

Más ideas para su portafolio

- Make a list of reasons why you are studying Spanish. No reason is too silly or too small!
- Make a list of things you'd like to be able to do eventually with your Spanish. Let your imagination run wild!
- If you have been playing Practice Spanish: Study Abroad, in Quest 1 you saw the importance of the **plaza.** Where can **plazas** generally be found? How do people use them within their communities?

©McGraw-Hill Education

Sugerencia: You are now ready to play Quest 1 in Practice Spanish: Study Abroad.

EN RESUMEN En este capítulo

AFTER STUDYING THIS CHAPTER I CAN . . .

- ☐ name people, places, and things in the classroom and the university (30–31)
- ☐ name academic subject areas (32)
- ☐ recognize nouns and articles as masculine or feminine, singular or plural (37–39, 40–41)
- ☐ talk about actions with **-ar** verbs and subject pronouns (43–46)
- ☐ ask questions with interrogatives and yes/no questions with proper intonation (34, 50–52)
- ☐ recognize/describe at least 2–3 aspects of the Hispanic population of the U.S.

Gramática en breve

1. Singular nouns: Gender and Articles

Noun Endings

Masculine:	**-o**
Feminine:	**-a, -ción, -sión, -xión, -dad, -tad**
Masculine or feminine:	**-e**, other consonants

2. Nouns and Articles: Plural Forms

Plural Endings

-o →	**-os**
-a →	**-as**
-e →	**-es**
z →	**-ces**
consonant	**+-es**

	Definite Articles			Indefinite Articles		
Masculine	**el**	→	**los**	**un**	→	**unos**
Feminine	**la**	→	**las**	**una**	→	**unas**

3. Subject Pronouns; Present Tense of *-ar* Verbs; Negation

Subject Pronouns

yo, tú, usted, él, ella, nosotros/as, vosotros/as, ustedes, ellos/as

Regular -ar Verb Endings

-o, -as, -a, -amos, -áis, -an

4. Asking Yes/No Questions

- Rising intonation
- Inversion of word order: *subject* + *verb* → *verb* + *subject*

Vocabulario

¡OJO!

- Infinitives listed in **red and underlined** in **Vocabulario** lists are conjugated in all tenses and moods in Appendix 5.
- Be sure that you know the meaning of the group headings in addition to the meaning of the words in each group.
- If you are not sure of the meaning of a word, you can look it up in the end-of-book Spanish-English Vocabulary.)

Los verbos

bailar	to dance
buscar	to look for
cantar	to sing
comprar	to buy
desear	to want
enseñar	to teach
escuchar	to listen (to)
estar (estoy, estás,...)	to be
estudiar	to study
hablar	to speak; to talk
hablar por teléfono	to talk on the phone
mandar un mensaje (de texto)	to (send a) text
necesitar	to need
pagar	to pay (for)
practicar	to practice
regresar	to return (*to a place*)
regresar a casa	to go home
tocar	to play (*a musical instrument*)
tomar	to take; to drink
trabajar	to work

Las personas

el/la amigo/a	friend
el/la bibliotecario/a	librarian
el/la cliente/a	client
el/la compañero/a (de clase)	classmate
el/la compañero/a de cuarto	roommate
el/la consejero/a	advisor
el/la dependiente/a	clerk
el/la estudiante	student
el/la extranjero/a	foreigner
el hombre	man
la mujer	woman
el/la secretario/a	secretary

Repaso: el/la profesor(a)

Repaso (*Review*) indicates vocabulary listed as active in this chapter that you learned in previous chapters.

Los lugares

la biblioteca	library
el cuarto	room
el edificio	building
la fiesta	party
la librería	bookstore
la residencia	dormitory
el salón de clase	classroom
la universidad	university
el lugar	place

Cognados: el apartamento, la cafetería, la oficina

Cognado(s) lists vocabulary you should be able to recognize because the words are close cognates of English.

Los objetos

el bolígrafo	pen
la calculadora	calculator
la computadora (portátil)	(laptop) computer
el cuaderno	notebook
el diccionario	dictionary
el dinero	money
el escritorio	desk
el lápiz (*pl.* lápices)	pencil
el libro (de texto)	(text)book
la mesa	table
la mochila	backpack
el papel	paper
el pizarrón (blanco)	(white)board
la puerta	door
la silla	chair
el teléfono (celular)	(cell) phone
la ventana	window

Las materias

la administración de empresas	business administration
la ciencia	science
la computación	computer science
la física	physics
la materia	subject area
la química	chemistry
la sicología	psychology

Cognados: el arte, las ciencias (naturales/políticas/sociales), las comunicaciones, la economía, la filosofía, la historia, las humanidades, la literatura, las matemáticas, la sociología

Las lenguas (extranjeras)

el alemán	German
el español	Spanish
el francés	French
el inglés	English
el italiano	Italian
la lengua (extranjera)	(foreign) language

Otros sustantivos

el café	coffee
la clase	class (*of students*); class, course (*academic*)
el día	day
la matrícula	tuition
la oración	sentence *(gram.)*

Las palabras interrogativas

¿cuál?	what?; which?
¿cuándo?	when?
¿cuánto?	how much?
¿cuántos/as?	how many?

Repaso: ¿cómo?, ¿(de) dónde?, ¿qué?, ¿quién?

¿Cuándo?

ahora	now
con frecuencia	frequently
el fin de semana	weekend
por la mañana/tarde	in the morning/afternoon
por la noche	at night, in the evening
tarde/temprano	late/early
todos los días	every day

Los pronombres personales

yo	I
tú	you (*fam. sing.*)
usted	you (*form, sing.*)
él	he
ella	she
nosotros/as	we
vosotros/as	you (*fam., plural*)
ustedes	you (*form., plural*)
ellos/as	they

Palabras adicionales

aquí	here
con	with
en casa	at home
mal	poorly
más	more
mucho (*adverb*)	much; a lot
poco (*adverb*)	(a) little
un poco (de)	a little bit (of)
solo	only

Repaso: no

Vocabulario personal

Use this space for other words and phrases you learn in this chapter.

ESPAÑOL **INGLÉS**

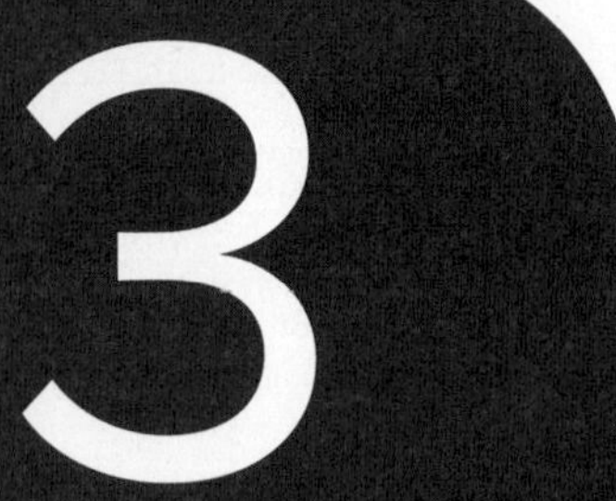

3 La familia

En este° capítulo

this

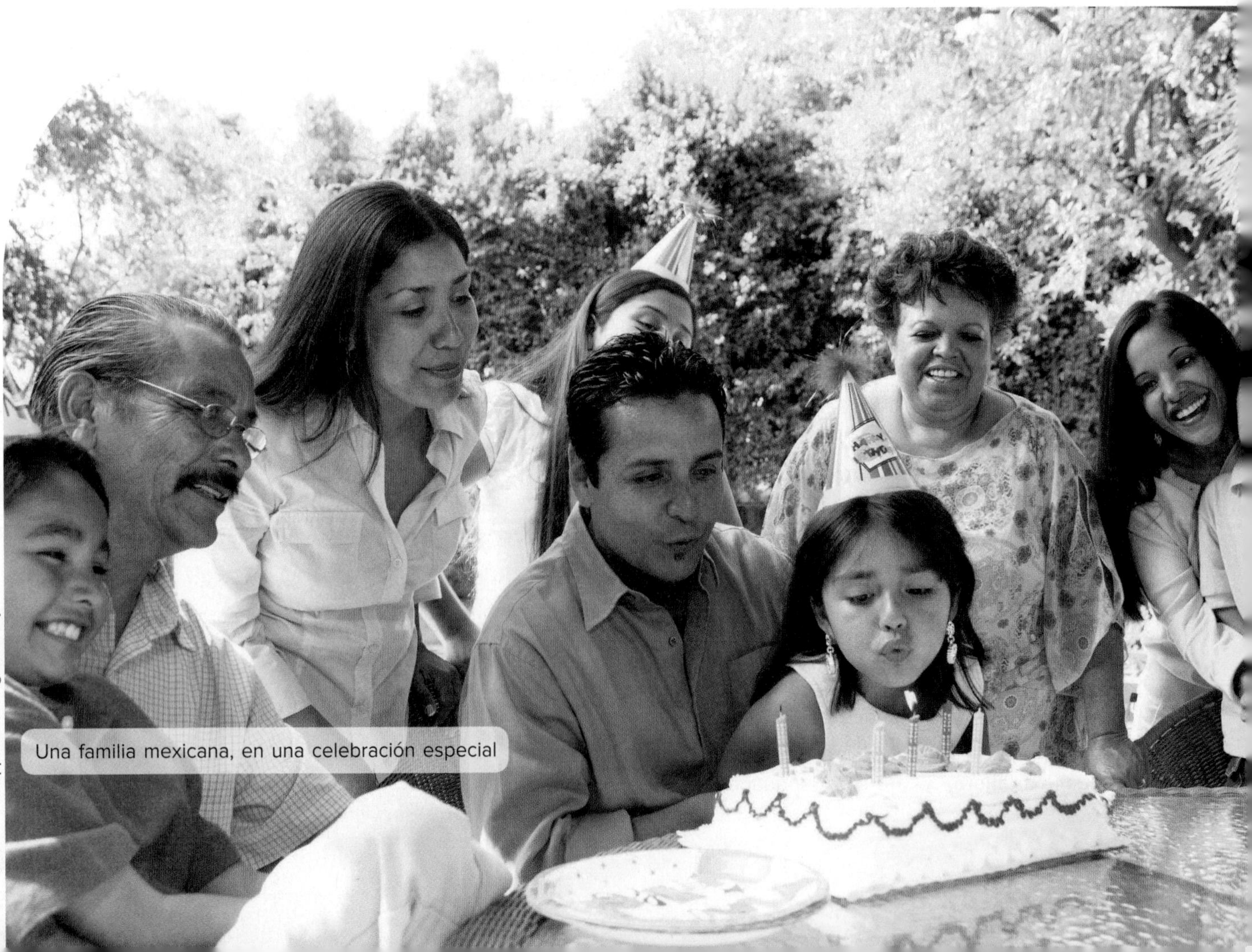

Una familia mexicana, en una celebración especial

MÉXICO

127 (ciento veintisiete) millones de habitantes

- El nombre oficial de México es Estados Unidos Mexicanos. Hay 31 estados mexicanos.
- Es el primer país del mundo por[a] número de hispanohablantes.
- Un 64% (sesenta y cuatro por ciento) de los hispanos de los Estados Unidos de América son de origen mexicano.

[a]*el... the number one country in the world by*

ENTREVISTA

- ¿Cómo es su[a] familia, grande[b] o pequeña[c]? (**Mi** familia...)
- ¿Cuántas personas hay en su familia más cercana[d]?
- ¿Cómo se llama su padre[e]/madre? (**Mi** padre/madre...)
- ¿Le gusta celebrar su cumpleaños[f] con sus amigos? (...con **mis** amigos) ¿con su familia? (...con **mi** familia)

[a]*your* [b]*big* [c]*small* [d]más... *closest* [e]*father* [f]*birthday*

 Alejandra Hernández Soto contesta las preguntas.

- Mi familia más cercana es pequeña porque[a] soy hija única.[b]
- Pero mi familia extendida es muy grande: tengo seis tías[c] y tíos y doce primos.[d]
- Mi padre se llama Juan y mi madre se llama Susana. Yo me llamo como mi abuela[e] materna.
- Me gusta celebrar mi cumpleaños con mis padres y también con mis amigos pero ¡por separado!

[a]*because* [b]hija... *an only child* [c]*aunts* [d]*cousins* [e]*grandmother*

VOCABULARIO: PREPARACIÓN

You can hear the pronunciation of theme vocabulary words and phrases in the Connect eBook.

La familia y los parientes°

° *relatives*

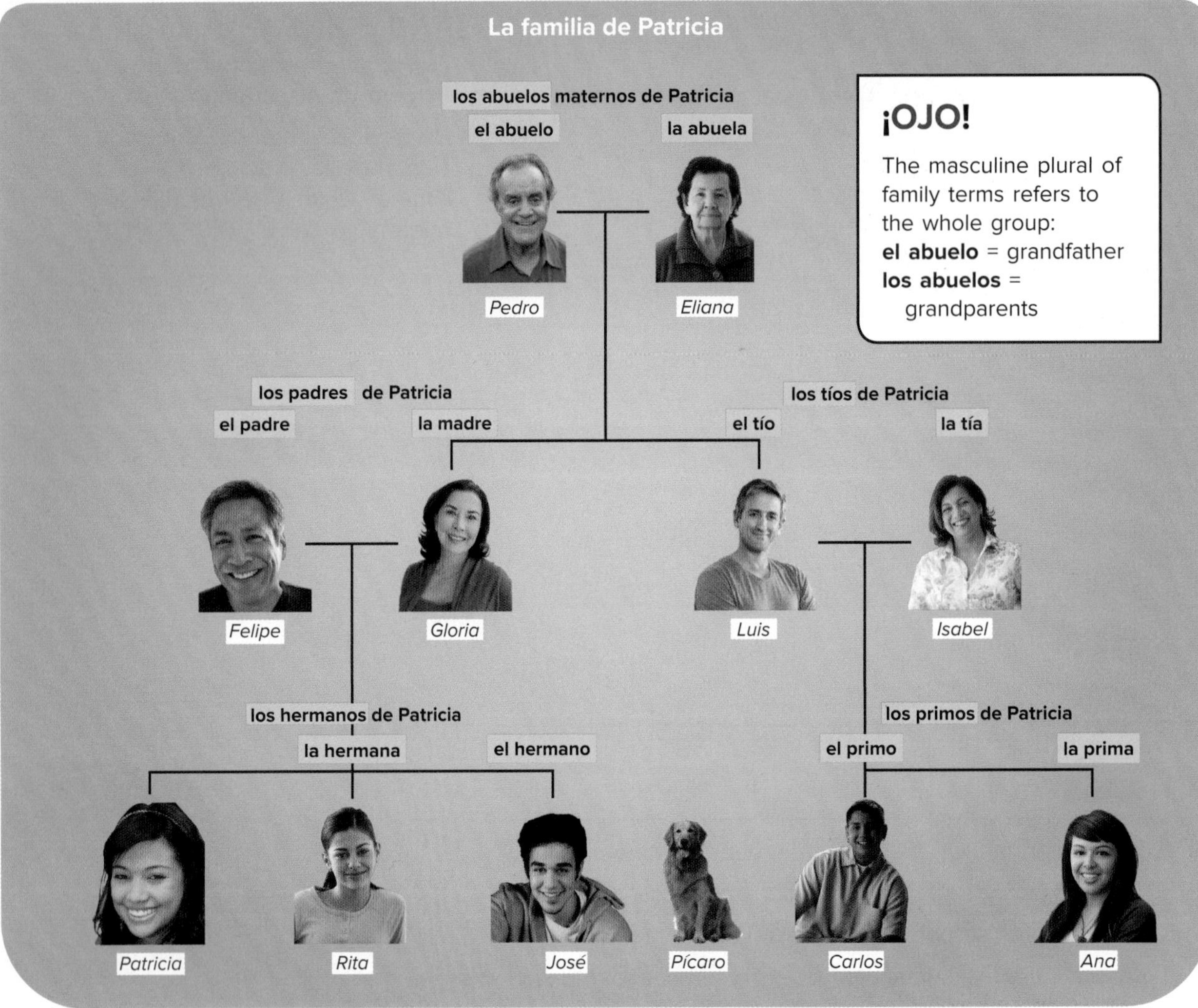

¡OJO!

The masculine plural of family terms refers to the whole group:
el abuelo = grandfather
los abuelos = grandparents

la madre (mamá)	mother (mom)
el padre (papá)	father (dad)
los padres	parents
la hija	daughter
el hijo	son
los hijos	children
la esposa / la mujer	wife
el esposo / el marido	husband
la pareja	partner; significant other; couple
la nieta	granddaughter
el nieto	grandson
la sobrina	niece
el sobrino	nephew

Las mascotas°

° Las... *Pets*

el gato	cat
el pájaro	bird
el perro	dog

Remember that the complete conjugation of infinitives in **red and underlined** is given in Appendix 5.

Formas del verbo tener°

° *to have*

tengo	I have
tienes	you (*fam.*) have
tiene	you (*form.*) have, he/she/it has

Más parientes

Learn as many of the following terms for additional family relationships as you need to describe your own family as completely as possible. Write the terms you learn in **Vocabulario personal** on the **En resumen** page at the end of the chapter.

el padrastro / la madrastra	stepfather / stepmother
el hijastro / la hijastra	stepson / stepdaughter
el hermanastro / la hermanastra	stepbrother / stepsister
el medio hermano / la media hermana	half-brother / half-sister
el suegro / la suegra	father-in-law / mother-in-law
el yerno / la nuera	son-in-law / daughter-in-law
el cuñado / la cuñada	brother-in-law / sister-in-law
ser adoptado/a	to be adopted
...(ya) murió	...has (already) died

Así se dice

The terms **mamá/mami** and **papá/papi** are used to speak *to* one's parents.

Many Spanish speakers use the terms **abuelito/tata** and **abuelita/nana** to speak *to* their grandparents.

Here is vocabulary for referring to non-traditional families:

- **una familia reconstituida** (family whose parents were previously married and have other children with previous spouses)
- **una unión civil**
- **una pareja de hecho** (non-married couple with formalized status)
- **un matrimonio entre personas del mismo** (*same*) **sexo**

Comunicación

A. La familia de Patricia. Mire (*Look at*) el árbol (*tree*) genealógico de Patricia en la página de **Vocabulario: Preparación**. Indique si las siguientes oraciones son ciertas o falsas. Corrija (*Correct*) las oraciones falsas.

	CIERTO	FALSO
1. José es el hermano de Ana.	☐	☐
2. Eliana es la abuela de Patricia.	☐	☐
3. Ana es la sobrina de Felipe y Gloria.	☐	☐
4. Patricia y José son (*are*) primos.	☐	☐
5. Gloria es la tía de José.	☐	☐
6. Carlos es el sobrino de Isabel.	☐	☐
7. Pedro es el padre de Luis y Gloria.	☐	☐
8. Isabel y Gloria son las esposas de Luis y Felipe, respectivamente.	☐	☐

B. ¿Quién es?

Paso 1. Complete las siguientes oraciones lógicamente.

1. La madre de mi (*my*) padre es mi ________.
2. El hijo de mi tío es mi ________.
3. La hermana de mi padre es mi ________.
4. El esposo (marido) de mi abuela es mi ________.

Paso 2. Ahora defina la relación de estas (*these*) personas, según (*according to*) el modelo de las oraciones del **Paso 1.**

MODELOS: El _____ de mi _____ es mi _____.
La _____ de mi _____ es mi _____.

1. prima **2.** sobrino **3.** tío **4.** abuelo

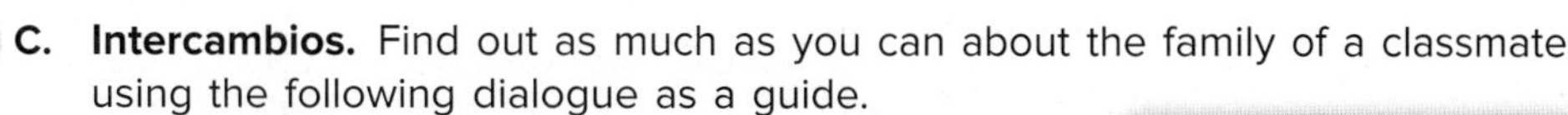

C. Intercambios. Find out as much as you can about the family of a classmate, using the following dialogue as a guide.

MODELO: **E1:** ¿Cuántos hermanos tienes?
E2: Bueno,[a] tengo dos hermanos.
E1: ¿Cómo se llaman tus hermanos?
E2: Se llaman Dixon y Lisa.
E1: ¿Y cuántos primos tienes?
E2: ¡Uf! Tengo un montón.[b] Más de[c] veinte.
E1: ¿Tienes una mascota?
E2: Sí, tengo un perro. Se llama Bear.

[a]*Well* [b]*bunch* [c]*Más... More than*

From this point on in the text, **ESTUDIANTE 1** *and* **ESTUDIANTE 2** *will be abbreviated as* **E1** *and* **E2**, *respectively.*

¡OJO!

¿cuántos? (*with male relatives*)

¿cuántas? (*with female relatives*)

En esta credencial para votar, de México, están el nombre y los dos apellidos de la persona: primero, los apellidos y después (*next*), el nombre.

Source: National Electoral Institute, Mexico

Nota cultural

El sistema hispano de apellidos° *last names*

En los países hispanos las personas llevan sistemáticamente dos apellidos oficiales. Típicamente, el primer[a] apellido es el del[b] padre y el segundo,[c] el de la madre.

PADRE
Antonio **Lázaro** Ochoa

MADRE
Marina **Aguirre** Salmero

HIJOS
Marta **Lázaro Aguirre**
Jacobo **Lázaro Aguirre**

 **Según el sistema hispano, ¿cómo se llamaría usted?**[d]

[a]*first* [b]*el... that of the* [c]*second* [d]*¿cómo... what would your name be?*

Los números del 31 al 100

Continúe las secuencias:

- treinta y uno, treinta y dos...
- ochenta y cuatro, ochenta y cinco...

31	treinta y uno	**40**	cuarenta
32	treinta y dos	**50**	cincuenta
33	treinta y tres	**60**	sesenta
34	treinta y cuatro	**70**	setenta
35	treinta y cinco	**80**	ochenta
36	treinta y seis	**90**	noventa
37	treinta y siete	**100**	cien
38	treinta y ocho		
39	treinta y nueve		

setenta y ocho años
cincuenta y cinco años
treinta y nueve años
cuarenta y cinco años
cuarenta y siete años
ochenta y cinco años
«El abuelito Pedro tiene 85 años.»
«La abuelita Eliana tiene 78 años.»

(top left) ©pxhidalgo/123RF; (bottom left) ©Caia Image/Glow Images; (top middle) ©Seth Joel/Getty Images; (middle) ©Monkey Business Images/Shutterstock; (bottom middle) ©Glow Images/SuperStock; (top right) ©John Henley/Getty Images; (bottom right) ©Jack Hollingsworth/Getty Images

Beginning with 31, Spanish numbers are *not* written in a combined form. **Treinta y uno, cuarenta y dos, sesenta y tres,** and so on, must be three separate words.

Cien is used before nouns and in counting.

cien casas	a (one) hundred houses
noventa y ocho, noventa y nueve, cien	ninety-eight, ninety-nine, one hundred

Remember that when **uno** is part of a compound number (**treinta y uno**, **cuarenta y uno**, and so on), it becomes **un** before a masculine noun and **una** before a feminine noun.

setenta y un hombres **cincuenta y una mesas**

Comunicación

A. Más problemas de matemáticas. Recuerde (*Remember*): + **y,** − **menos,** = **son.**

1. 30 + 50 = 80
2. 45 + 45 = 90
3. 68 − 28 = 40
4. 77 + 23 = 100
5. 100 − 40 = 60
6. 55 + 15 = 70

B. Bingo

Paso 1. Mire el cartón (*card*) de bingo mexicano. Observe el patrón (*pattern*) de organización de los números y cree su propio (*create your own*) cartón con números de su elección (*of your choice*).

	12		32		56		74	88
7		27			59	61		90
	18		34	44		68	77	

 **Paso 2.** Ahora, en parejas, lean sus números. ¿Hay repetición de números?

Nota comunicativa

Cómo expresar la edad:° *tener... años* °age

In Spanish, age is expressed with the phrase **tener... años** (literally, *to have . . . years*).

NORA: ¿Cuántos **años tienes**, abuela?
ABUELA: Setenta y ocho. ¿Y cuántos **años tienes** tú?
NORA: Yo **tengo** ocho.

You will practice telling how old people are in **Comunicación C**.

©Sam Edwards/Glow Images

C. Hablemos (*Let's talk*) de la edad (*age*)

Paso 1. Complete las siguientes oraciones.

1. Yo tengo _______ años.
2. La persona mayor (*oldest*) de mi familia es **mi** _______. Tiene _______ años.
3. La persona más joven (*youngest*) de mi familia es **mi** _______. Tiene _______ años.
4. En mi opinión, una persona es vieja (*old*) cuando tiene _______ años.
5. La edad ideal para casarse (*for getting married*) es a los _______ años.
6. La edad ideal para tener hijos es a los _______ años.

Paso 2. Ahora haga preguntas basadas en las oraciones del **Paso 1** y haga (*conduct*) una encuesta (*poll*) entre (*with*) un mínimo de seis compañeros de clase.

Estrategia

En el **Paso 2**, cambie (*change*) la palabra **mi** para formar las preguntas, según el modelo:

mi → tu

MODELO: **2. E1:** ¿Quién es la persona mayor de **tu** familia? ¿Cuántos años tiene?
E2: Es **mi** abuela. Tiene noventa y siete años.

Paso 3. Finalmente, presente sus (*your*) resultados a la clase.

Algo sobre...

los estados[a] mexicanos

El escudo (símbolo) de los Estados Unidos Mexicanos es un águila sobre un nopal.

Source: Federal Government of Mexico

México tiene 32 entidades federativas: 31 estados y 1 distrito federal, que[b] es la capital, la Ciudad de México. Los mexicanos la llamaban[c] el D.F.

¿? ¿Cuántos estados hay en los Estados Unidos? La capital, Washington D.C., ¿es un estado?

[a]*states* [b]*which* [c]la... *used to call it (i.e., the capital)*

Los adjetivos

guapo	handsome, good-looking (*people*)
bonito	pretty (*people and things*)
feo	ugly
grande	large, big
pequeño	small
simpático	nice, likeable (*people*)
antipático	unpleasant, unlikeable (*people*)
corto	short (*in length*)
largo	long
bueno	good
malo	bad
listo	smart; clever
tonto	silly, foolish
trabajador	hardworking
perezoso	lazy
rico	rich
pobre	poor
delgado	thin, slender
gordo	fat

¡OJO!

You will learn how to describe feminine and plural nouns in **Gramática 5.**

Comunicación

A. Descripciones

Paso 1. En parejas, describan estas (*these*) imágenes opuestas (*opposite*).

MODELO: Un _____ es _____ y el otro es _____.

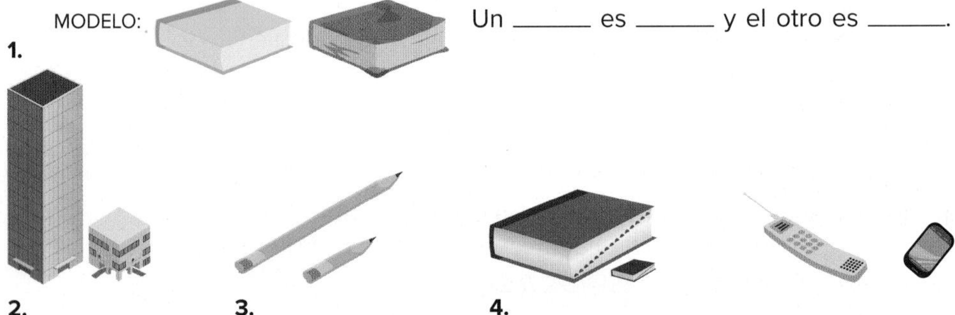

Paso 2. Ahora describan las siguientes (*following*) palabras.

MODELO: fumar (*to smoke*) → Fumar es malo. No es bueno.

1. bailar
2. Stephen Hawking
3. Bill Gates
4. estudiar toda la noche (*all night*)
5. el edificio Empire State
6. el monstruo de Frankenstein
7. un átomo

B. ¿Cómo es? Describe a famous male personality, using as many adjectives as possible so that your classmates can guess who the person is. You can also use cognate adjectives that you have seen in **Capítulos 1** and **2.**

MODELO: Es un hombre importante; controla una compañía de *software* muy importante. Es muy trabajador y muy rico. → Bill Gates

SALU2 «Padres modernos» Segmento 1

Antes de mirar°

Antes... *Before watching*

¿Tiene usted.... ?

_______ abuelos que viven cerca (*who live nearby*)
_______ muchos parientes
_______ hijos
_______ padrinos (*godparents*) (un padrino / una madrina)
_______ ahijados (*godchildren*) (un ahijado / una ahijada)

Hoy Víctor toma una taza grande (*big cup*) de café. ¿Por qué? (*Why?*

Este° segmento

This

Ana García Blanco y Víctor Gutiérrez presentan un programa sobre (*about*) la familia. También hablan de personas importantes en su vida familiar (*their family life*).

Vocabulario del segmento

disfrutar	to enjoy	**cuidar a**	to take care of
enfermo/a	sick	**¡Vivan las abuelas!**	Hooray for grandmothers!
cansado/a	tired	**los amigos íntimos**	very close friends

Estrategia

Before you watch, scan **Actividades A** and **B** in **Después de mirar.** Knowing what tasks you need to do after watching will help you focus on information to pay attention to as you watch the segment.

Después de mirar°

Después... *After watching*

A. ¿Está claro? Empareje (*Match*) las personas con las relaciones familiares del segmento.

LAS PERSONAS	LAS RELACIONES FAMILIARES
____ **1.** Víctor	**a.** la esposa de Víctor
____ **2.** la abuela	**b.** la mamá de Víctor
____ **3.** Sarita	**c.** la hija de Víctor
____ **4.** Marina	**d.** la tía y madrina de Leticia
____ **5.** Ana	**e.** la sobrina de Ana
____ **6.** Leticia	**f.** el papá de Sarita

B. Un poco más. ¿Cierto o falso? Corrija las oraciones falsas, según el video.

	CIERTO	FALSO
1. Víctor toma aspirinas porque (*because*) está cansado.	☐	☐
2. Víctor está enfermo.	☐	☐
3. La esposa de Víctor cuida a Sarita hoy.	☐	☐
4. Los padrinos y los amigos íntimos son (*are*) personas importantes y fundamentales en muchas familias.	☐	☐

C. Y ahora, ustedes. Practique su (*your*) pronunciación y su talento como presentador(a). Complete el fragmento con su propia (*your own*) información y con vocabulario del programa.

Muy buenos días desde nuestro estudio en _______. ¿Cómo están ustedes? Yo estoy _______ hoy. El tema del programa de hoy es la familia. ¿Qué personas son[a] muy importantes en su[b] familia, además de[c] los padres? ¿Son importantes también los _______ (personas)? En mi caso, mi _______ y mi _______ son personas fundamentales. ¡Viva mi _______ ! ¡Vivan mis _______ !

[a]*are* [b]*your* [c]además... *besides*

PRONUNCIACIÓN

Stress and Written Accent Marks (Part 1)

Some Spanish words have *written accent marks* over one of the vowels. That mark is called **el acento (ortográfico).** It means that the syllable containing the accented vowel is stressed when the word is pronounced, as in the word **bolígrafo (bo-LÍ-gra-fo),** for example.

Although all Spanish words of more than one syllable have a stressed vowel, most words do not have a written accent mark. Most words have the spoken stress exactly where native speakers of Spanish would predict it. These two simple rules tell you which syllable is stressed when there is no written accent on the word.

1. **Las palabras llanas**- words ending in a vowel, **-n**, or **-s**

Las palabras llanas have the word stress on the *next-to-last syllable* (**la penúltima sílaba**). When they end in a vowel, **-n,** or **-s,** they don't need a written accent mark. This is the largest group of Spanish words; it includes most nouns and adjectives as well as their plurals, most verb forms, and so on. Here are some examples.

me-sa   me-xi-ca-no   e-xa-men   gra-cias   e-res

¡OJO!

You will learn about words that have a written accent mark in **Capítulo 4.**

2. **Las palabras agudas**- words ending in a consonant other than **-n** or **-s**

Las palabras agudas have the word stress on the *last syllable* (**la última sílaba**). When they end in consonants other than **-n** or **-s** (typically **-d, -l,** and **-r**), they don't need a written accent mark. This group includes all infinitives and many common words that end in **-dad, -or,** and **-al.** Here are some examples.

us-ted   es-pa-ñol   pro-fe-sor   es-tar   doc-tor

Práctica

Estrategia

llana (ends in a vowel, **-n**, or **-s**) = stress on the second-to-last syllable

aguda (ends in a consonant other than **-n** or **-s**) = stress on the last syllable

A. Tipos de palabras: ¿Llanas o agudas? None of these words needs a written accent mark. Categorize each one as **llana** or **aguda,** then pronounce the word.

1. can-tan
2. ar-te
3. cla-se
4. mu-jer
5. me-sa
6. es-pa-ñol
7. a-mi-gos
8. us-ted
9. se-ñor
10. na-tu-ral
11. com-pu-ta-do-ra
12. bai-las

B. Vocales. Indicate the stressed vowel in the following words.

1. mo-chi-la
2. me-nos
3. re-gu-lar
4. i-gual-men-te
5. E-cua-dor
6. e-le-gan-te
7. li-be-ral
8. hu-ma-ni-dad

GRAMÁTICA

5 Describing

Adjectives: Gender, Number, and Position

Gramática en acción: Un poema sencill<u>o</u>

©oliveromg/Shutterstock

Amig<u>o</u>
Fiel
Amable
Simpátic<u>o</u>
¡Lo admiro!

Amig<u>a</u>
Fiel
Amable
Simpátic<u>a</u>
¡La admiro!

Comprensión

Which of the following adjectives can be used to describe Mario? And Marta?

fiel **amable** **simpátic<u>a</u>** **simpátic<u>o</u>**

Adjectives (**Los adjetivos**) are words used to talk about nouns or pronouns. Adjectives may describe or tell how many of something there are.

an adjective / **un adjetivo** = a word used to describe a noun or a pronoun

large *desk*	***few*** *desks*
tall *woman*	***several*** *women*

You have been using adjectives to describe people since **Capítulo 1.** In this section, you will learn more about describing the people and things around you.

Adjectives with **ser** / **Los adjetivos con *ser***

In Spanish, forms of **ser** are used with adjectives that describe basic, inherent qualities or characteristics of the nouns or pronouns they modify. **Ser** establishes the "norm," that is, what is considered basic reality: *snow is cold, water is wet.*

El diccionario **<u>es</u> grande.**
The dictionary is big.

Mi hermana **<u>es</u> trabajadora.**
My sister is hardworking.

¡<u>Eres</u> muy amable!
You are very kind!

A simple poem *Friend Loyal Kind Nice I admire him/her!*

Forms of Adjectives / **Las formas de los adjetivos**

Spanish adjectives "agree" with the noun or pronoun they modify. This agreement is shown in two ways:

- gender agreement (masculine or feminine): **una amiga alta**
- number agreement (singular or plural): **los amigos ricos**

agreement / **la concordancia** = when one word "agrees," or must be coordinated, with an aspect of another (for example, *he + speaks* but *you + speak*)

For this reason, Spanish adjectives have more than one form.

1. **Adjectives Ending in *-o***
   Adjectives that end in **-o** (**alto**) have four forms, showing gender and number.

Adjetivos con 4 formas		
	Masculino	**Femenino**
Singular	**amigo alto**	**amiga alta**
Plural	**amigos altos**	**amigas altas**

2. **Adjectives Ending in *-e* or a Consonant**
   Adjectives that end in **-e** (**amable**) or in most consonants (**fiel**) have only two forms, a singular and a plural form. The plural of adjectives is formed in the same way as that of nouns, by adding **-s** or **-es.**

Adjetivos con 2 formas		
	Masculino	**Femenino**
Singular	**amigo amable** **amigo fiel**	**amiga amable** **amiga fiel**
Plural	**amigos amables** **amigos fieles**	**amigas amables** **amigas fieles**

¡OJO!

When the adjective **joven** is made plural, an accent mark is added to retain the original word stress: **joven → jóvenes**.

3. **Adjectives Ending in *-dor***
   Like adjectives that end in **-o,** these adjectives also have four forms.

Adjetivos con 4 formas		
	Masculino	**Femenino**
Singular	**amigo trabajador**	**amiga trabajadora**
Plural	**amigos trabajadores**	**amigas trabajadoras**

4. **Nationality Adjectives**
   Many adjectives of nationality have four forms.

	Masculino	**Femenino**
Singular	**el doctor** **mexicano** **español**	**la doctora** **mexicana** **española**
Plural	**los doctores** **mexicanos** **españoles**	**las doctoras** **mexicanas** **españolas**

¡OJO!

Nationality adjectives ending in **-e** generally have only two forms: **estadounidense(s)** (from the United States), **canadiense(s).**

5. **Names of Languages**
   The names of many languages—which are masculine in gender—are the same as the masculine singular form of the corresponding adjective of nationality.

Lengua	Adjetivo
el inglés	**inglés, inglesa, ingleses, inglesas**
el francés	**francés, francesa, franceses, francesas**
el italiano	**italiano, italiana, italianos, italianas**
el alemán	**alemán, alemana, alemanes, alemanas**

¡OJO!

Note that in Spanish the names of languages and adjectives of nationality are not capitalized, but the names of countries are: **el español, española,** but **España.**

¡OJO!

When the last syllable of an adjective has a written accent mark (**inglés**, **alemán**), the accent is dropped in the feminine and plural forms, as shown in the box above.

Position of Adjectives / **La posición de los adjetivos**

As you have probably noticed, adjectives do not always precede the noun in Spanish as they do in English. Note the following rules for adjective placement.

1. Adjectives of Quantity

Like numbers, adjectives of quantity *precede* the noun, as do the interrogatives **¿cuánto/a?** and **¿cuántos/as?**

> **¡OJO!**
>
> **Otro/a** is an adjective of quantity. By itself it means *another* or *other*. The indefinite article is never used with **otro/a.**

¿Cuántas sillas hay?
How many chairs are there?

Hay **muchas sillas** y también **dos escritorios**.
There are many chairs and also two desks.

¿Cuánto dinero necesitas?
How much money do you need?

Busco **otro coche.**
I'm looking for another car.

---

2. Adjectives of Quality

Adjectives that describe the qualities of a noun and distinguish it from others generally *follow* the noun. Adjectives of nationality are included in this category.

un **perro listo**
un **dependiente trabajador**
una **mujer delgada** y **morena**
un **profesor español**

---

3. *Bueno* and *malo*

The adjectives **bueno** and **malo** may *precede or follow* the noun they modify. When they precede a masculine singular noun, they shorten to **buen** and **mal,** respectively.

un **buen perro** / un **perro bueno**
una **buena perra** / una **perra buena**

un **mal día** / un **día malo**
una **mala noche** / una **noche mala**

---

4. *Grande*

The adjective **grande** may also *precede or follow* the noun.

- When it precedes a singular noun—masculine or feminine—it shortens to **gran** and means *great* or *impressive*.
- When it follows the noun, it means *large* or *big*.

Nueva York es una **gran** ciudad.
New York is a great (impressive) city.

Nueva York es una **ciudad grande**.
New York is a large city.

Forms of *this/these* / **Formas de *este/estos* (Part 1)**

1. *This/These*

The adjective *this/these* has four forms in Spanish. Learn to recognize them when you see them.

You will learn all forms of this type of adjective (*this, that, these, those*) in **Gramática 9** (**Cap. 4**).

este hijo	this son
esta hija	this daughter
estos hijos	these sons
estas hijas	these daughters

---

2. Esto

You have already seen the neuter demonstrative **esto.** It refers to something that is as yet unidentified.

¿Qué es **esto**?
What is this?

Algo sobre...

una gran ciudad mexicana

Más de[a] 21 millones de personas viven en el área metropolitana de la Ciudad de México. Su abreviatura es CDMX.

 **¿Cuántos habitantes hay en su ciudad?**

[a]Más... *More than*

©Pixtal/age fotostock

Ciudad de México

Adjective Agreement Summary

SINGULAR ENDINGS	PLURAL ENDINGS
-o, -a	**-os, -as**
-e	**-es**
-[consonant]	-[consonant] + **-es**
-dor, -dora	**-dores, -doras**

Práctica y comunicación

A. La familia

Paso 1. Autoprueba. Complete los adjetivos con la forma apropiada.

1. El padre es alt_______ y trabajador_______.
2. La madre es baj_______ y amabl_______.
3. Los abuelos son viej_______ y simpátic_______.
4. Las hijas son pequeñ_______ y adorabl_______.
5. Hay much_______ parientes en la familia.
6. La familia tiene buen_______ amigos.

Paso 2. Ahora complete las siguientes oraciones según la familia de usted.

1. Mi padre/hermano/tío es _______ y _______.
2. Mi madre/hermana/tía es _______ y _______.
3. Mis abuelos son (*are*) _______ y _______. (Mi abuelo/a es _______ y _______.)
4. _______ (nombre) y _______ (nombre) son buen_______ amigos/amigas de mi familia

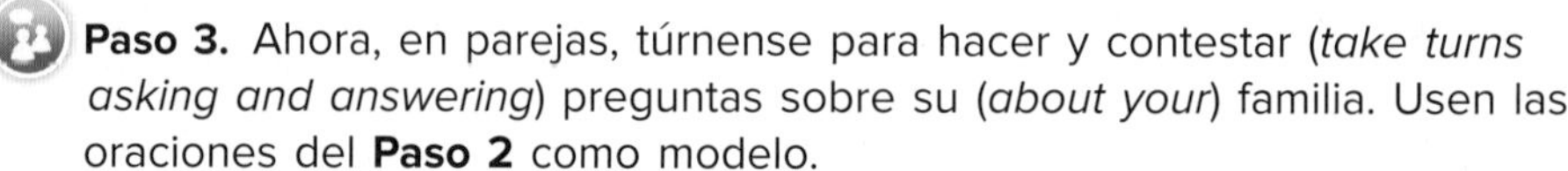

Paso 3. Ahora, en parejas, túrnense para hacer y contestar (*take turns asking and answering*) preguntas sobre su (*about your*) familia. Usen las oraciones del **Paso 2** como modelo.

MODELO: **E1:** Mis abuelos son mexicanos y simpáticos. ¿Y tus abuelos?
E2: Mis abuelos son estadounidenses y viejos.

B. Descripciones

Paso 1. Haga oraciones con los siguientes adjetivos para describirse (*to describe yourself*). **¡OJO!** Use la forma apropiada del adjetivo.

Soy...
No soy...

1. alto
2. trabajadora
3. estadounidense
4. rico
5. rubia
6. fiel
7. simpático
8. europeo
9. delgado
10. hispana (latina)
11. dedicado
12. social
13. estudiosa
14. listo

Paso 2. Ahora haga oraciones para describir a su (*your*) padre/madre, a su esposo/a o a su mejor amigo/a (*best friend*).

MODELOS: **Mi** mejor amiga es moren**a,** simpátic**a** y pobre.
Mi esposo es alt**o,** trabaja**dor** y muy dedicad**o.**

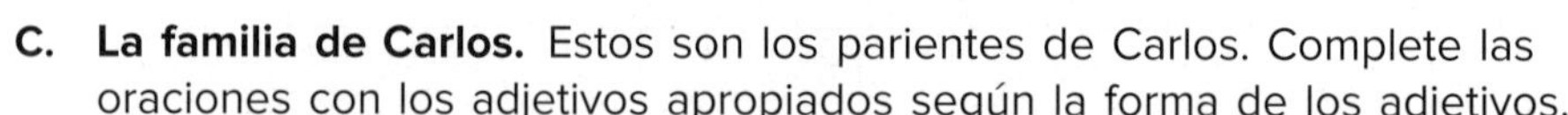

C. La familia de Carlos.

Estos son los parientes de Carlos. Complete las oraciones con los adjetivos apropiados según la forma de los adjetivos.

1. **El tío Felipe** es _______. (trabajador / alto / joven / gran / amable)
2. **Los abuelos** son _______. (rubio / antipático / inteligentes / viejos / religiosos / sinceras)
3. **Mi tía Gloria,** la madre de Patricia, es _______. (rubio / elegante / sentimental / buenas / hispanas / simpática)
4. **Mis primos** son _______. (trabajadores / morenos / lógica / bajas / mala)

©Ryan McVay/Getty Images

Carlos, un estudiante mexicano

Prác. A, Paso 1: Answers: *1. alto, trabajador* (no change) *2. baja, amable 3. viejos, simpáticos 4. pequeñas, adorables 5. muchos 6. buenos*

D. ¡Dolores es igual! Cambie (*Exchange*) **Diego** por **Dolores.**

Diego es un buen estudiante. Es listo y trabajador y estudia mucho. Es estadounidense de origen mexicano, y por eso[a] habla español. Desea ser profesor de antropología. Diego es moreno, guapo y atlético. Le gustan las fiestas grandes y tiene buenos amigos en la universidad. Tiene parientes estadounidenses y mexicanos. Diego tiene 20 años.

[a]por... *for that reason*

Nota comunicativa

Otras nacionalidades

You learned some nationality adjectives on page 74. Here are some more. If you don't find the adjective(s) you need to describe yourself and your family, ask your instructor. Write the adjectives you need in **Vocabulario personal** on the **En resumen** page.

Norteamérica	Centroamérica y el Caribe	Sudamérica		Europa y Asia	
canadiense	costarricense	argentino/a	ecuatoriano/a	chino/a	japonés, japonesa
mexicano/a	cubano/a	boliviano/a	paraguayo/a	coreano/a	pakistaní (*pl.* pakistaníes)
	dominicano/a	brasileño/a	peruano/a	indio/a	palestino/a
	guatemalteco/a	chileno/a	uruguayo/a	israelí (*pl.* israelíes)	ruso/a
	hondureño/a	colombiano/a	venezolano/a	iraní (*pl.* iraníes)	tailandés, tailandesa
	nicaragüense			iraquí (*pl.* iraquíes)	vietnamita
	panameño/a				
	salvadoreño/a				

You will use many of these adjectives in **Práctica E.**

E. Países (*Countries*) y nacionalidades del mundo (*world*)

Paso 1. Diga (*Tell*) la nacionalidad de las siguientes personas.

1. Monique es de Francia; es __________.
2. Piero y Andri son (*are*) del Uruguay; son (*they are*) ___________.
3. Indira y su (*her*) hermana son de la India; son ________.
4. Ronaldo y Ronaldinho son del Brasil; son ___________.
5. Saji es un hombre del Japón; es _________.
6. La familia Musharraf es de Pakistán; son ___________.
7. Paul es de Inglaterra; es ________.
8. Samuel y su (*his*) hermana son de Guatemala; son _____________.
9. Sonia es de la Argentina; es __________.
10. Ramón y José son de Colombia; son ____________.
11. Jimena es de Costa Rica; es _____________.
12. Bill y Susan son de California; son _______________.

¡OJO!

Remember that adjectives of nationality and the names of languages don't start with a capital letter in Spanish.

Paso 2. En parejas, hagan oraciones con las nacionalidades hispanas, según el modelo. Busquen (*Look for*) los nombres de las naciones hispanas en el mapa de la página 13.

MODELO: **E1:** ¿Una mujer de Costa Rica?
E2: Es **costarricense.** ¿Y un hombre?
E1: Es **costarricense.** ¿Una mujer de El Salvador?
E2: Es...

Sor Juana Inés de la Cruz, 1651 – 1695 (mil seiscientos cincuenta y uno hasta mil seiscientos noventa y cinco)

F. Una mujer sorprendente (*surprising*)

Paso 1. Complete con las terminaciones apropiadas la siguiente descripción de una mujer muy especial.

Sor[a] Juana Inés de la Cruz es una mujer religios___[1] mexican___[2] del siglo[b] XVII. Es una gran__[3] poeta y una mujer muy inteligent___[4] y muy ilustrad___[c5] para su[d] época. Es muy famos___[6] internacionalmente. Escribió[e] much___[7] poemas important___[8] de la literatura hispan___[9].

[a]*Sister* [b]*century* [c]ilustrado/a = *educated* [d]para... *for her* [e]*She wrote*

Paso 2. Comprensión. ¿Cierto o falso? Corrija las oraciones falsas.

	CIERTO	FALSO
1. Sor Juana es de Nicaragua.	☐	☐
2. Escribió poemas en español.	☐	☐
3. Es famosa solamente en México.	☐	☐

G. Asociaciones. En grupos, hablen (*talk*) de las personas o cosas (*things*) que (*that*) asocian con las siguientes frases. Expresen acuerdo (*agreement*) o desacuerdo (*disagreement*) con **(No) Estoy de acuerdo.**

MODELO: un gran hombre →
E1: Creo que (*I believe that*) **mi padre** es un gran hombre.
E2: Estoy de acuerdo.

1. un mal restaurante
2. un buen programa de televisión
3. una gran mujer, un gran hombre
4. un buen libro (¿una novela?), un libro horrible
5. un buen coche
6. una buena computadora

H. Descripciones. En parejas, describan a su (*your*) familia, haciendo (*forming*) oraciones completas con estas palabras, con cualquier (*any*) otro adjetivo que conozcan (*that you may know*) y con los adjetivos de nacionalidad. **¡OJO!** Cuidado (*Be careful*) con la forma de los adjetivos.

MODELO: Mi familia no es grande. Es pequeña. Mi padre tiene 50 años. Es pakistaní de nacimiento (*by birth*).

mi familia mi padre/madre mi esposo/esposa mi ¿ ? (otro pariente) mi perro/gato	+ (no) es + + tiene... años	agresivo amable animado (*lively*) antipático bueno cariñoso (*affectionate*) comprensivo (*understanding*) difícil (*difficult*)	famoso grande (im)paciente importante inteligente interesante malo nuevo	pequeño sensible (*sensitive*) sentimental serio simpático tolerante travieso (*mischievous*) viejo

¿Recuerda usted?

Before beginning **Gramática 6,** review the forms and uses of **ser** that you know already by answering these questions.

1. ¿Es usted estudiante o profesor(a)?
2. ¿Cómo es usted? ¿Es una persona sentimental? ¿inteligente? ¿paciente? ¿elegante?
3. ¿Qué hora es? ¿A qué hora es la clase de español?
4. ¿Qué es un hospital? ¿Es una persona? ¿un objeto? ¿un edificio?

6 Expressing *to be*

Present Tense of **ser**; Summary of Uses (Part 2)

Gramática en acción: Presentaciones

©Corbis/SuperStock

Lea lo que dice Francisco y luego complete su descripción de su esposa.

— Hola. Me llamo Francisco Durán Ferrer, pero todos me llaman Pancho.

- **Soy** profesor de la universidad.
- **Soy** alto y moreno.
- **Soy** de Guanajuato, México.

—¿Y Lola Benítez Velasco, mi esposa?

- **Es** _______ (profesión).
- **Es** _______ y _______ (descripción).
- **Es** de _______ (origen).

Vocabulario útil

guapa, pesimista, muy inteligente
Jalisco (un estado de México)
médica en el Hospital Central, profesora también

©Lifesize/Getty Images

ser (*to be*)			
(yo)	**soy**	**(nosotros/as)**	**somos**
(tú)	**eres**	**(vosotros/as)**	**sois**
(usted)		**(ustedes)**	
(él)	**es**	**(ellos)**	**son**
(ella)		**(ellas)**	

As you know, two Spanish verbs mean *to be:* **ser** and **estar.** They are not interchangeable; the meaning the speaker wants to convey determines their use. Here, you will review the uses of **ser** that you already know and learn some new ones. Remember to use **estar** to express location and to ask how someone is feeling. You will learn more about **estar** in **Gramática 15–16 (Cap. 6).**

Some basic uses of **ser** are presented on the following pages. You have used or seen all of them already in this and previous chapters.

Introductions *Read what Francisco says and then complete his description of his wife. Hello! My name is Francisco Durán Ferrer, but everyone calls me Pancho. ■ I'm a university professor. ■ I'm tall and brunet. ■ I'm from Guanajuato, Mexico. And Lola Benítez Velasco, my wife? ■ She's _______. ■ She's _______ and _______. ■ She's from _______.*

Identification / **La identificación**

To *identify* people (including their profession) and things

> **¡OJO!**
>
> Note that the indefinite article is not used after **ser** before unmodified (undescribed) nouns of profession: **Carmen es profesora.** *but* **Carmen es una buena profesora.**

> **¡OJO!**
>
> Note the use of **e** instead of **y** when the next word starts with the sound **i-**. Also note the use of **u** instead of **o** when the next word starts with the sound **o-**.

Soy estudiante.
I'm a student.

Esto **es un libro**.
This is a book.

—¿Quiénes **son**?
—**Son Camila e Ismael**.
"Who are they?"
"They're Camila and Ismael."

—**¿Es Mateo u Omar**?
—Es Omar.
"Is he Mateo or Omar?"
"He's Omar?

Description / **La descripción**

To *describe* people and things

You practiced this use of **ser** in **Gramática 5** in this chapter.

Soy sentimental.
I'm sentimental (*a sentimental person*).

El coche **es muy viejo.**
The car is very old.

Origin / **El origen**

With **de,** to express *origin*

Somos de Chile, pero nuestros padres **son de la Argentina. ¿De dónde es** usted?
We're from Chile, but our parents are from Argentina. Where are you from?

Generalizations / **Las generalizaciones**

To express *generalizations* (with **es** + *adjective*)

> **¡OJO!**
>
> Note that **es** + *adjective* is followed by an infinitive in this context, just like in English.

Es necesario estudiar. Por eso no **es posible** mirar la televisión todos los días.
It's necessary to study. For that reason (That's why) it's not possible to watch television every day.

Here are two basic functions of **ser** that you have not yet practiced.

Possession / **Las posesiones**

With **de,** to express *possession*, to whom something belongs.

> **¡OJO!**
>
> Note that there is no **'s** in Spanish.

—Este **es** el perro **de Carla. ¿De** quién **son** las gatas?
—**Son** las gatas **de Jorge.**
"This is Carla's dog. Whose are those cats?"
"They're Jorge's cats."

The masculine singular article **el** contracts with **de** to form **del**. (No other article contracts with **de**.)

Esta **es** la casa **del** abuelo.
Esta **es** la casa **de la** abuela.

Use **¿de quién es… ?** to ask to whom something belongs.

> **¡OJO!**
>
> The subject pronoun **él** never contracts with **de**: **Es la casa de él.**

—**¿De quién es** esta casa?
—**Es del** abuelo.
"Whose house is this?"
"It's grandfather's."

Destination / **El destino**

With **para,** to tell for whom or what something *is intended*

¿Romeo y Julieta? **Es para** la clase de inglés.
Romeo and Juliet? *It's for English class.*

—¿**Para** quién **son** los regalos? ¿**Para** mi nieto?
"Who are the presents for? For my grandson?"

Práctica y comunicación

A. Así es mi familia (*That's what my family is like*)

Paso 1. Autoprueba. Complete las frases con las formas apropiadas del verbo **ser.**

1. yo _______
2. tú _______
3. usted _______
4. Pedro _______
5. tú y yo _______
6. Pedro y Alicia _______
7. usted y sus (*your*) amigos _______
8. tú y tus amigos _______

Paso 2. Complete las siguientes oraciones con formas del verbo **ser** y el adjetivo o frase apropiados.

1. Yo ______ miembro de una familia _______ (grande/pequeña).
2. Mi familia _____ de origen (*f.*) _______ (adjetivo de nacionalidad).
3. Mi familia más cercana (*closest*) y yo _________ ______ (estado o país).
4. Otros parientes de mi familia ______ de ______ (estado o país).
5. Mi _______ (abuelo paterno/materno / abuela paterna/materna) _____ de _______ (estado o país).
6. En mi familia, (no) _____ normal _______ celebrar fiestas familiares / bailar en las fiestas familiares / estar en contacto con frecuencia...

Paso 3. Ahora use formas del verbo **ser** y las ideas del **Paso 2** para entrevistar (*interview*) a un compañero o una compañera.

1. ¿_______ miembro de una familia grande o pequeña?
2. ¿De qué nacionalidad _____ tu familia?
3. ¿De qué estado o país ______ tu familia y tú?
4. ¿De dónde ______ otros de tus parientes?
5. ¿De dónde _____ tu abuelo paterno/materno / tu abuela paterna/materna?
6. En tu familia, ¿_____ normal _______ (celebrar los cumpleaños [*birthdays*] / comer pizza /...)?

Summary of Uses of *ser*

- to identify
- to describe
- to express origin
- to express generalizations
- to express possession
- to express whom or what something is intended for

B. Nacionalidades

Paso 1. ¿De dónde son, según los nombres, apellidos y ciudades?

MODELO: João Gonçalves, Lisboa → João Gonçalves **es de** Portugal.

1. John Doe, Nueva York
2. Karl Lotze, Berlín
3. Graziana Lazzarino, Roma
4. Mongkut, Bangkok
5. María Gómez, San Salvador
6. Claudette Moreau, París
7. Timothy Windsor, Londres
8. Hai Chow, Beijing

Paso 2. Ahora, dé su (*your*) información personal: ¿De dónde es usted? ¿De este estado / una metrópoli / un área rural? ¿Es de otro país?

Naciones

Alemania
China
El Salvador
los Estados Unidos
Francia
Inglaterra
Italia
Portugal
Tailandia

Prác. A, Paso 1: Answers: *1. soy 2. eres 3. es 4. es 5. somos 6. son 7. son 8. sois/son*

Estrategia

Form complete sentences by supplying the missing verbs (indicated by /), as in the model.

C. Personas extranjeras

Paso 1. ¿Quiénes son, de dónde son y dónde trabajan ahora?

MODELO: **Teresa**: actriz / de Madrid / en Cleveland →
Teresa **es** actriz. **Es** de Madrid. **Ahora trabaja** en Cleveland.

1. **Carlos Miguel:** médico / de Cuba / en Milwaukee
2. **Pilar:** profesora / de Barcelona / en Miami
3. **Mariela:** dependienta / de Buenos Aires / en Nueva York
4. **Juan:** dentista* / de Lima / en Los Ángeles

Paso 2. Ahora hable sobre (*talk about*) un amigo o pariente, según el modelo del **Paso 1.** También puede (*you can*) usar el verbo **estudiar**.

D. ¿De quién es? Las siguientes cosas (*things*), ¿son de la rica actriz Jennifer Sánchez o de Martín Osborne, el estudiante (pobre, naturalmente)? En parejas, hagan y contesten preguntas. Las respuestas pueden (*can*) variar.

MODELO: la mochila →
E1: ¿De quién es la mochila?
E2: Es la mochila **del** estudiante. (La mochila es **del** estudiante.)

Estrategia

Use **son** with plural items: **¿De quién son los… ? Son…**

1. la casa grande
2. la computadora
3. la limusina
4. los libros de texto
5. el Óscar
6. los exámenes
7. los ex esposos
8. el teléfono celular
9. los mensajes

E. ¡Somos como una familia!

Paso 1. Complete el párrafo con las formas correctas de **ser** o con **hay**.

Me llamo Antonia y ______[1] de Chicago. (Yo) ______[2] estudiante de ingeniería en la Universidad de Illinois. En mis clases ______[3] estudiantes de todas partes[a] y muchos de ellos ______[4] hispanos. Mi familia ______[5] de origen mexicano y aunque nunca he vivido[b] en México, hablo bastante bien[c] el español. Me gusta hablar español con mi amigo Javier. Javier ______[6] de Costa Rica y estudia ingeniería también. Javier y yo ______[7] los asistentes del profesor Thomas; por eso pasamos mucho tiempo juntos.[d] Javier ______[8] muy guapo y simpático, pero nosotros solo ______[9] buenos amigos. Javier ______[10] el novio[e] de mi mejor[f] amiga.

[a]*places* [b]aunque… *although I have never lived* [c]bastante… *rather well* [d]pasamos… *we spend a lot of time together* [e]*boyfriend* [f]*best*

Paso 2. Comprensión. ¿Cierto o falso? Corrija las oraciones falsas.

	CIERTO	FALSO
1. Javier es costarricense.	☐	☐
2. Antonia es de México.	☐	☐
3. Antonia y Javier son novios.	☐	☐

*A number of professions end in **-ista** in both masculine and feminine forms. The article indicates gender: **el/la dentista, el/la artista,** and so on.*

F. Frida Kahlo

Paso 1. Complete las oraciones para hablar de Kahlo.

Frida Kahlo fue (*was*)...

1. ______________________ (profesión).
2. ______________________ (país).
3. ______________________ (adjetivo).
4. ______________________ (relación familiar).

Paso 2. Ahora use el modelo del **Paso 1** para hablar de una persona de su (*your*) familia.

Algo sobre...

una pintora mexicana

Frida Kahlo es una pintora mexicana muy famosa. Fue[a] la esposa del famoso muralista mexicano Diego Rivera. Los dos vivieron[b] por un tiempo en los Estados Unidos, en Nueva York y San Francisco.

En sus obras,[c] Frida se enfoca en sí misma.[d] Sus obras son autorretratos[e] que incluyen elementos de la cultura mexicana.

¿Hay pintoras famosas en los Estados Unidos?

[a]*She was* [b]*lived* [c]sus... *her works* [d]se... *looks inward at herself* [e]*self-portraits*

Frida Kahlo con su esposo, Diego Rivera

Nota comunicativa

Cómo dar° explicaciones: Porque y para + *infinitive* *to give*

porque = because

—¿Por qué trabajas tanto?
—¡**Porque** necesito el dinero!

"Why do you work so much?"
"Because I need the money!"

para + *inf.* = in order to (*do something*)

—¿Por qué necesitamos otro paquete de canales de televisión?
—Pues... **para** mirar los partidos de fútbol...

"Why do we need another package of TV channels?"
"Well ... (in order) to watch the soccer games...

You will practice using these words in **Práctica G.**

¡OJO!

Note: **porque** (one word, no accent) versus the interrogative **¿por qué?** (two words, accent on **qué**), meaning *why?*

G. El regalo (*gift*) ideal

Paso 1. Look at Diego's list of gifts and what his family members like. With a partner, decide who receives each gift and why. A sample item is done for you.

MODELO: la camiseta (*t-shirt*) de la selección (*team*) nacional de México →
E1: **¿Para quién** es la camiseta de la selección nacional de México?
E2: **Es para** la prima.
E1: **¿Por qué?**
E2: **Porque** le gusta (*she likes*) el fútbol.

LOS REGALOS DE DIEGO	LOS MIEMBROS DE LA FAMILIA DE DIEGO
1. _____ una calculadora grande	**a.** el primo: Desea estudiar en el extranjero (*abroad*).
2. _____ unas entradas (*tickets*) para un concierto	**b.** el padre: Le gusta mucho el fútbol.
3. _____ un teléfono celular	**c.** los abuelos: Les gusta mucho la música clásica.
4. _____ la última (*latest*) novela de Isabel Allende	**d.** el hermano: Estudia ingeniería y toma clases de matemáticas
5. _____ un balón (*ball*) oficial de la Copa del Mundo	**e.** la hermana pequeña: Tiene 11 años y no tiene teléfono propio (*of her own*).
6. _____ dinero	**f.** la madre: Le gusta mucho leer (*to read*).

Paso 2. With a partner, exchange ideas about good gifts for members of your family and also about good gifts for you.

MODELO: Para mi mamá, deseo comprar ropa, porque ella necesita ropa nueva. Yo necesito ropa nueva también.

Vocabulario útil

el coche	car
los audífonos	earphones
la ropa	clothing

H. ¿Qué opina usted? Exprese opiniones originales, afirmativas o negativas, con estas palabras como base.

MODELO: En mi opinión, **es importante hablar español en la clase de español.**

(no) es importante (no) es muy práctico (no) es necesario (no) es absurdo (no) es fascinante (no) es una molestia (*bother, pain*) (no) es posible	+	mirar la televisión todos los días hablar español en la clase tener muchas mascotas llegar (*to arrive*) a clase puntualmente tomar café en el salón de clase hablar con los animales / las plantas tomar mucho café y fumar cigarrillos trabajar dieciocho horas al día tener muchos hermanos ser amable con todos los miembros de la familia estar mucho tiempo (*a lot of time*) con la familia

¿Recuerda usted?

You have already learned one way to express possession in Spanish: **de** + *noun*. Express these ideas in Spanish.

1. Juan's house
2. Jorge and Estela's grandfather
3. the man's niece
4. the student's book

You will learn another way to express possession in **Gramática 7.**

7 Expressing Possession

Unstressed Possessive Adjectives (Part 1)*

Gramática en acción: Invitación y posesión

A. «¡Pasen, por favor! <u>Nuestra</u> casa es <u>su</u> casa.»

B. «¡No son <u>tus</u> juguetes! ¡Son <u>mis</u> juguetes!»

Comprensión

En el dibujo A:

1. ¿De quién es la casa?
2. ¿Quiénes visitan la casa?

En el dibujo B:

3. ¿De quién son los juguetes?
4. ¿Quién desea jugar (*to play*) con los juguetes?

Possessive adjectives (**Los adjetivos posesivos**) are words that tell *to whom* or *to what* something belongs: *my*, *her*, *their* . . . You have already seen and used several possessive adjectives in Spanish. Here is the complete set.

Invitation and Ownership A. "Come in, please! Our house is your house." ***B.*** "They're not your toys! They're my toys!"

Another kind of possessive is called the stressed possessive adjective. *It can be used as a noun. You will learn more about using stressed possessive adjectives in* **Capítulo 17.**

Los adjetivos posesivos				
my	**mi hijo/hija** **mis hijos/hijas**	our	**nuestro hijo** **nuestros hijos**	**nuestra hija** **nuestras hijas**
your (*fam.*)	**tu hijo/hija** **tus hijos/hijas**	your (*fam.*)	**vuestro hijo** **vuestros hijos**	**vuestra hija** **vuestras hijas**
your (*form.*), his, her, its	**su hijo/hija** **sus hijos/hijas**	your (**ustedes.**), their	**su hijo / hija** **sus hijos / hijas**	

a possessive adjective / **un adjetivo posesivo** = an adjective that expresses who owns or has something

¡OJO!

The possessive adjective **tu** has no accent, but the subject pronoun **tú** does.

1. Agreement with Person or Thing Possessed
In Spanish, the ending of a possessive adjective agrees in form with the person or thing owned, not with the owner or possessor. Note that these possessive adjectives are placed before the noun.

The possessive adjectives **mi(s), tu(s),** and **su(s)** show agreement in number only (as seen in the chart above and to the right). **Nuestro/a/os/as** and **vuestro/a/os/as,** like all adjectives that end in **-o,** show agreement in both number and gender.

Es {**mi** / **tu** / **su**} hermano.

Son {**mis** / **tus** / **sus**} hermanos.

Es {**nuestra** / **vuestra** / **su**} familia.

Son {**nuestras** / **vuestras** / **sus**} familias.

---

2. *Su*(*s*)
As you have seen, the word **su(s)** has several equivalents in English: *your* (sing.), *his, her, its, your* (pl.), and *their.* Usually its meaning is clear in context. When the meaning is not clear, the construction **de** + *pronoun* is used to indicate possession.

su hijo = **el** hijo **de** {usted, ustedes / él/ella / ellos/ellas}

sus hijos = **los** hijos **de** {usted, ustedes / él/ella / ellos/ellas}

---

3. *Su*(*s*) versus *vuestro/a/os/as*
The forms **vuestro/a/os/as** are the possessives that correspond to the subject pronoun **vosotros.** They are used only in Spain.

Latin America
ustedes → su, sus

Spain	
vosotros/as	**→ vuestro/a/os/as**
ustedes	**→ su, sus**

Summary of Possessive Adjectives

mi(s)	**nuestro/a(s)**
tu(s)	**vuestro/a(s)**
su(s)	

Práctica y comunicación

A. Las posesiones

Paso 1. Autoprueba. Complete la tabla con los posesivos apropiados. **¡OJO!** Preste atención a (*Pay attention to*) las personas y los sustantivos. ¿Son masculinos o femeninos? ¿singulares o plurales? Siga (*Follow*) el modelo del número 1.

Personas	Adjetivos posesivos	Sustantivos
1. yo	**mi**	compañero de clase
2. nosotros/as = mi compañero/a y yo		computadoras
3. usted		mesa
4. los otros compañeros de clase		escritorios
5. tú		teléfono celular
6. Luisa		profesoras

Paso 2. Ahora indique los sustantivos posibles para cada (*each*) adjetivo posesivo según su forma.

1. **su:** problema primos dinero tías escritorios familia
2. **tus:** perro idea hijos profesoras abuelo examen
3. **mi:** ventana médicos cuarto coche abuela gatos
4. **sus:** animales oficina nietas padre hermana abuelo
5. **nuestras:** guitarra libros materias lápiz sobrinas tía
6. **nuestros:** gustos consejero parientes puertas clases residencia

Paso 3. Ahora, en parejas, indiquen tres sustantivos para cada uno de los siguientes adjetivos posesivos.

MODELO: tu → **computadora, tía, perro**

Adjetivos posesivos (personas)	Tres sustantivos
1. mis	
2. su (de los compañeros de clase)	
3. sus (del profesor / de la profesora)	
4. nuestras (de nosotros dos)	

B. ¿Cuáles son sus hijos? Empareje (*Match*) las fotos de padres e hijos.

LOS PADRES

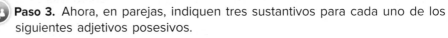

1. Su hija es ________.

2.  Sus hijos son ________.

3.  Sus hijas son ________.

4.   Su hijo es ________.

LOS HIJOS

a. David

b. Sara

c.  Maribel y Julia

d.  Joaquín y Rosa

Prác. A, Paso 1: Answers: 2. nuestras 3. su 4. sus 5. tu 6. sus

C. David y su familia

Paso 1. Describa a la familia de David.

MODELO: familia / pequeño →
Su familia **es** pequeñ**a**.

1. hijo / guapo
2. perro / feo
3. hija / rubio
4. padre / simpático
5. esposa / bonito

Paso 2. Ahora imagine que usted es David y modifique (*change*) las respuestas (*answers*).

MODELO: familia / pequeño →
Mi familia es pequeñ**a**.

Paso 3. Ahora imagine que usted es la esposa de David. Hable por (*Speak for*) usted y por su esposo. Modifique solo las respuestas del 1 al 3.

MODELO: familia / pequeño →
Nuestra familia es pequeñ**a**.

Estrategia

You must provide a possessive adjective for the noun, then a verb, as in the model. Then be sure that the adjective agrees with the noun!

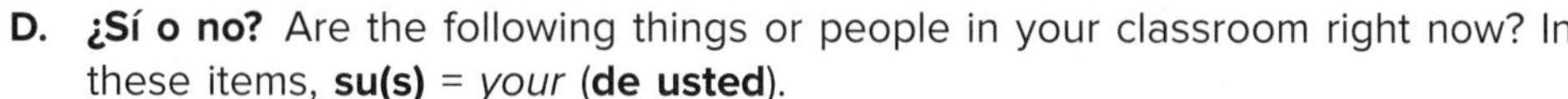

D. ¿Sí o no? Are the following things or people in your classroom right now? In these items, **su(s)** = *your* (**de usted**).

MODELOS: ¿su libro? → Sí, **mi** libro está en mi mochila. (No, **mi** libro está en casa.)
¿los amigos de ustedes? → No, **nuestros** amigos no están en el salón de clase. Están en la cafetería.

1. ¿su computadora portátil?
2. ¿los libros de ustedes?
3. ¿el profesor / la profesora de ustedes?
4. ¿la computadora del profesor / de la profesora de ustedes?
5. ¿los teléfonos celulares de ustedes?
6. ¿su silla?
7. ¿sus padres? / ¿su esposo/a?
8. ¿la mochila de otro estudiante?
9. ¿su dinero? (la cartera = *wallet*)

Estrategia

Remember to use forms of **estar** to express location.

¿Recuerda usted?

The personal endings used with **-ar** verbs share some characteristics with **-er** and **-ir** verbs, which you will learn in **Gramática 8.** Review the present tense endings of **-ar** verbs by telling which subject pronoun(s) you associate with each of these endings.

1. -amos 2. -as 3. -áis 4. -an 5. -o 6. -a

E. Intercambios

Paso 1. With a partner, take turns asking and answering questions about your families. Talk about what family members are like, their ages, some things they do, and so on. Use the model as a guide. Take notes on what your partner says.

MODELO: tu abuela →
E1: Mi abuela es alta. ¿Y tu abuela? ¿Es alta?
E2: Bueno, no. Mi abuela es baja.
E1: ¿Cuántos años tiene?...

1. tu familia en general
2. tus padres
3. tus abuelos
4. tus hermanos/hijos
5. tu esposo/a / compañero/a de cuarto/casa

Paso 2. Tell the class one thing that you and your partner have in common.

MODELO: Nuestras abuelas tienen 75 años.

8 Expressing Actions

Present Tense of **-er** and **-ir** Verbs; Subject Pronouns (Part 2)

Gramática en acción: Un estudiante típico

- Se llama Samuel Flores Toledo.
- Estudia en la UNAM (Universidad Nacional Autónoma de México).
- Vive con su familia en la Ciudad de México.
- Come pizza y tacos con frecuencia.
- Bebe café por la mañana.
- Recibe muchos e-mails de sus primos del Canadá.
- Lee y escribe mucho para su especialización.
- Aprende inglés porque desea visitar a su familia en Ontario.

Samuel Flores Toledo

¿Y usted?

Complete las oraciones con formas verbales que terminan en **-o** (= **yo**) y con información personal.

1. Yo (no) vivo con mi familia.
2. (No) Com_____ muchos tacos.
3. Recib_____ muchos e-mails de _____
4. Le_____ y escrib_____ mucho para mi clase de _____.
5. Aprend_____ español en esta clase.

In **Capítulo 2** you learned a number of verbs whose infinitive ends in **-ar**. Remember that in Spanish verbs have three types of infinitive endings: **-ar**, **-er**, and **-ir**. These endings are very important in Spanish, because they determine the verb conjugation, that is, the endings for the different persons of the conjugation. In this section you will learn about verbs whose infinitive ends in **-er** or **-ir**.

Present Tense of **-er/-ir** Verbs / **El tiempo presente de los verbos *-er/-ir***

1. **Present Tense Endings**
   The present tense of **-er** and **-ir** verbs is formed by adding personal endings to the stem of the verb (the infinitive minus its **-er/-ir** ending). The personal endings for **-er** and **-ir** verbs are the same except for the first and second person plural.

Las terminaciones *-er/-ir* del tiempo presente

-er		-ir	
-o	-emos	-o	-imos
-es	-éis	-es	-ís
-e	-en	-e	-en

¡OJO!

Only the endings for **nosotros** and **vosotros** are different for **-er** and **-ir** verbs.

comer (*to eat*)				**vivir** (*to live*)			
(yo)	**como**	(nosotros/as)	**comemos**	(yo)	**vivo**	(nosotros/as)	**vivimos**
(tú)	**comes**	(vosotros/as)	**coméis**	(tú)	**vives**	(vosotros/as)	**vivís**
(usted) (él) (ella)	**come**	(ustedes) (ellos) (ellas)	**comen**	(usted) (él) (ella)	**vive**	(ustedes) (ellos) (ellas)	**viven**

A typical student ■ *His name is Samuel Flores Toledo.* ■ *He studies at UNAM (the National Autonomous University of Mexico).* ■ *He lives with his family in Mexico City.* ■ *He frequently eats pizza and tacos.* ■ *He drinks coffee in the morning.* ■ *He gets a lot of e-mails from his cousins in Canada.* ■ *He reads and writes a lot for his major.* ■ *He's learning English because he wants to visit his family in Ontario.*

2. Important *-er/-ir* Verbs

These are the frequently used **-er** and **-ir** verbs you will find in this chapter.

-er verbs		**-ir** verbs	
aprender	to learn	**abrir**	to open
aprender +a + *inf.*	to learn how to (*do something*)	**asistir (a)**	to attend, go to (*a class, a function*)
beber	to drink	**escribir**	to write
comer	to eat	**recibir**	to receive
comprender	to understand	**vivir**	to live
creer (en)	to think; to believe (in)		
deber + *inf.*	should, must, ought to (*do something*)		
leer	to read		
vender	to sell		

- **Deber,** like **desear** and **necesitar,** is followed by an infinitive.

Debes leer tus e-mails todos los días.
You should read your e-mails on a daily basis.

- **Aprender** + **a** +*infinitive* means *to learn how to* (*do something*).

Muchos niños **aprenden a hablar** español con sus abuelos.
Many children learn to speak Spanish with their grandparents.

3. English Equivalents of the Present Tense

Remember that the Spanish present tense has a number of present tense equivalents in English. It can also be used to express future meaning.

como = *I eat, I am eating, I will eat*

Uses of Subject Pronouns / **Los usos de los pronombres personales**

In English, a verb must have an expressed subject (a noun or pronoun): ***the train** arrives*, ***she** says*. In Spanish, however, as you have probably noticed, an expressed subject is not required. Verbs are accompanied by a subject pronoun only for clarification, emphasis, or contrast.

- *Clarification:* When the context does not make the subject clear, the subject pronoun is expressed. This happens most frequently with third person singular and plural verb forms.

Unclear: Escribe cartas. Nunca **escribe** cartas. → **Ella** escribe cartas. **Él** nunca escribe cartas.
She writes letters. He never writes letters.

- *Emphasis:* Subject pronouns are used in Spanish to emphasize the subject when in English you would stress it with your voice.

—¿Quién debe pagar? "*Who should pay?*"
—¡**Tú** debes pagar! "***You*** should pay!"

- *Contrast:* Contrast is a special case of emphasis. Subject pronouns are used to contrast the actions of two individuals or groups.

Ellos leen mucho; **nosotros** leemos poco.
***They** read a lot; **we** read little.*

¡OJO!

Avoid using subject pronouns in Spanish when they are not necessary. The overuse of subject pronouns sounds overbearing to native speakers of Spanish.

Unnecessary: Yo soy de Tampa. Yo soy estudiante universitario. Yo vivo con mi familia.
Natural: (Yo) Soy de Tampa. Soy estudiante universitario. Vivo con mi familia.

Práctica y comunicación

Summary of *-er/-ir* Verb Endings

(yo)	**-o**	**(nosotros/as)**	**–emos / -imos**
(tú)	**-es**	**(vosotros/as)**	**-éis / -ís**
(ustedes, el/ella)	**-e**	**(ustedes, ellos/as)**	**-en**

A. Asociaciones. Empareje (*Match*) las ideas y cosas (*things*) con el verbo más lógico. Luego (*Then*) dé otras ideas para cada (*each*) verbo.

MODELO: 1. abrir → e: abrir **una puerta** También: abrir **una ventana**...

VERBOS

1. abrir
2. aprender
3. asistir a
4. beber
5. comer
6. deber
7. escribir
8. leer
9. vivir

IDEAS Y COSAS

a. una revista (*magazine*)
b. una composición
c. un té
d. las materias
e. una puerta
f. un concierto
g. tacos
h. estudiar más
i. en un apartamento

Algo sobre...

la comida[a] de México

El maíz[b] es el producto esencial en la comida de los mexicanos y otros pueblos[c] americanos desde[d] 1500 a. e. c. (mil quinientos antes de la era común). Es la base para las tortillas y los tamales. El tamal consiste en masa[e] de maíz con otros ingredientes, envuelta[f] y cocida[g] en hojas[h] de maíz (u hojas de otras plantas, como el plátano[i]).

 **En su opinión, ¿qué ingrediente(s) son esenciales en la comida de su país de origen?**

[a]*food* [b]*corn* [c]*peoples* [d]*since* [e]*dough* [f]*wrapped* [g]*steamed* [h]*leaves* [i]*plantain*

©Sergio Salvador/Getty Images

Un delicioso tamal mexicano

B. En la clase de español

Paso 1. Autoprueba. Complete los verbos con las terminaciones apropiadas.

1. yo: com_______, viv_______
2. tú: aprend_______, escrib_______
3. él: cre_______, abr_______
4. nosotros: le_______, asist_______
5. ustedes: comprend_______, recib_______

Paso 2. Ahora use las siguientes ideas para expresar acciones que usted hace (*do*) o no hace en la clase de español.

MODELO: comer en clase → **Como** en clase. (No **como** en clase.)

1. escribir respuestas en el libro de texto
2. aprender palabras nuevas
3. asistir a clase todos los días
4. beber café en clase
5. comprender las instrucciones para las actividades
6. abrir regalos

Paso 3. Ahora, en parejas, túrnense para hacer y contestar preguntas basadas en el **Paso 2.** Luego (*Then*), digan (*tell*) a la clase algo (*something*) que ustedes tienen en común.

MODELO: escribir respuestas en el libro texto →

E1: ¿Escribes respuestas en el libro de texto?

E2: No, no escribo respuestas en el libro de texto.

E2: Yo tampoco. (*Me neither.*) (Yo sí.)

EN COMÚN: Nosotros/as dos (no) escribimos respuestas en el libro de texto.

***Prác. B, Paso 1:* Answers:** *1.* como, vivo *2.* aprendes, escribes *3.* cree, abre *4.* leemos, asistimos *5.* comprenden, reciben

C. Diego habla de su padre. Complete el siguiente párrafo con la forma correcta de los verbos entre paréntesis.

Mi padre ___________ (vender[1]) coches y trabaja mucho. Mis hermanos y yo ___________ (aprender[2]) mucho de papá. Según mi padre, los jóvenes ___________ (deber[3]) ___________ (asistir[4]) a clase todos los días, porque es su obligación. Papá también ___________ (creer[5]) que no es necesario mirar la televisión por la noche. Es más interesante ___________ (leer[6]) el periódico,[a] una revista o un buen libro. Por eso ___________ (*nosotros*: leer[7]) o ___________ (escribir[8]) por la noche y no miramos la televisión. Yo admiro a mi papá y ___________ (creer[9]) que él ___________ (comprender[10]) la importancia de la educación.

[a]*newspaper*

Comprensión. ¿Cierto o falso? Corrija las oraciones falsas.

	CIERTO	FALSO
1. Diego y sus hermanos venden coches.	☐	☐
2. Diego mira mucho la televisión.	☐	☐
3. El padre de Diego lee mucho.	☐	☐

D. Este domingo, tamalada

Paso 1. Una tamalada consiste en hacer (*making*) y comer tamales. Hay familias que hacen una tamalada en ocasiones especiales.

Complete las siguientes oraciones con la forma apropiada de un verbo de **Vocabulario útil.** El número 2 entre paréntesis indica que usted debe usar el verbo dos veces (*twice*) en las oraciones.

©Charlie Neuman/U-T San Diego/ZUMA Wire/Alamy

Una escena típica de una tamalada

¡OJO!

Hay verbos de todos tipos en la lista: **-ar, -er, -ir,** irregular.

Vocabulario útil

aprender, asistir, beber, celebrar, comprender, creer, deber, leer (2), **mirar, preparar, ser** (2), **vivir**

1. Hoy todos nosotros __________[1] el cumpleaños (*birthday*) de mi abuela y hay una tamalada.
2. Toda la familia __________[2] a la tamalada en nuestra casa.
3. Mis padres y mis tíos __________[3] los tamales, con la ayuda (*help*) de las mujeres de la familia.
4. Después de comer (*After eating*), los adultos __________[4] café.
5. Muchos __________[5] la tele y mi padre __________[6] el periódico.
6. Yo __________[7] un libro a los niños pequeños. Mi prima Lucy __________[8] descansar (*rest*) porque solo tiene 2 años.
7. Mi primo Rudy, que (*who*) __________[9] en Oklahoma, no __________[10] todo porque su español no __________[11] perfecto. Pero __________[12] rápido.
8. Yo __________[13] que todos mis tíos __________[14] cocineros (*cooks*) excelentes.

Paso 2. Comprensión. Complete las oraciones con información del **Paso 1.**

1. ________________ es un ejemplo de una fiesta familiar.
2. Esta familia celebra ________________ de la abuela.
3. ________________ preparan los tamales; ________________ ayudan (*help*).
4. Después de comer, unos ________________ y ________________.
5. La persona que narra la historia (*story*) ________________
6. Rudy no ________________ bien el español.

Nota comunicativa

Cómo expresar la frecuencia de las acciones

AT THE BEGINNING OR END OF A SENTENCE

a veces	sometimes, at times
con frecuencia	frequently
siempre	always
todos los días	every day
una vez a la semana	once a week

AT THE BEGINNING OF A SENTENCE

casi nunca	almost never
nunca	never

Hablo con mis amigos **todos los días.** Hablo con mis padres **una vez a la semana. Casi nunca** hablo con mis abuelos. Y **nunca** hablo con mis tíos que viven en Italia.

You will use these expressions in **Práctica E.**

Estrategias

- Use **nunca** and **casi nunca** at the beginning of the sentence instead of **no.**
- Don't use **yo** in front of the verbs.
- Adjust the possessive adjectives, as needed.

E. ¿Con qué frecuencia?

Paso 1. Indique con oraciones completas la frecuencia con que usted hace (*do*) las siguientes actividades.

EXPRESIONES DE FRECUENCIA:

todos los días **con frecuencia** **a veces** **casi nunca** **nunca**

MODELO: 1. recibir un e-mail de **sus** padres/abuelos →
Todos los días recibo e-mails de **mis** abuelos. / **Nunca recibo** un e-mail de **mis** abuelos.

1. recibir un e-mail de sus padres/abuelos
2. escribir en su Facebook
3. usar la computadora en una clase
4. comer pizza
5. leer revistas
6. beber café
7. comprar cosas por (cosas… *things on the*) internet
8. vender sus libros al final del semestre/trimestre

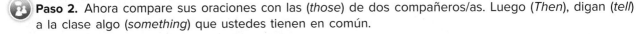

 **Paso 2.** Ahora compare sus oraciones con las (*those*) de dos compañeros/as. Luego (*Then*), digan (*tell*) a la clase algo (*something*) que ustedes tienen en común.

MODELO: 1. recibir un e-mail de **sus** padres/abuelos →
EN COMÚN: Todos los días los/las tres recibimos un e-mail de **nuestros** abuelos. (Nunca recibimos un e-mail de **nuestros** abuelos.)

 **F. Intercambios.** Use las siguientes frases para entrevistar (*interview*) a un compañero o una compañera. Use expresiones de frecuencia cuando sea (*it is*) apropiado. Luego (*Then*) digan (*tell*) a la clase algo (*something*) que ustedes tienen en común.

MODELO: leer + novelas de terror
→ Carmen, ¿lees novelas de terror a veces?
EN COMÚN: Los/Las dos leemos novelas de terror a veces. (Nunca leemos novelas de terror.)

(nombre de estudiante), (tú) tus padres/hijos tus abuelos tu mejor (*best*) amigo/a	+	abrir beber comprender escribir leer recibir vender vivir ¿ ?	+	mucho / poco la situación / los problemas de los estudiantes Coca-Cola/café antes de (*before*) la clase tu ropa (*clothing*), un auto viejo la puerta a (*for*) las mujeres / los hombres novelas de ciencia ficción / de terror el periódico / una revista todos los días muchas/pocas cartas, novelas, revistas muchos/pocos ejercicios, libros, regalos en una casa / un apartamento / una residencia en otra ciudad / en otro estado/país en un cuaderno / con un bolígrafo/lápiz
	+	deber	+	mirar mucho/poco la televisión llegar a casa tarde/temprano

 **G. Una fiesta.** There is a Spanish saying, **«Una fiesta se hace** (*is made*) **con tres personas: una canta, otra baila y la otra toca.»** In pairs, use this saying as a model to tell what the following things are "made of."

MODELO: una clase → Una clase **se hace con** un profesor o una profesora. Esta persona enseña la clase. También hay unos estudiantes. Desean aprender la materia y estudian mucho. Leen su libro de texto y escriben informes (*papers*). También hay un salón de clase, un pizarrón...

¿Cómo se hace... ?

1. una clase de español
2. una fiesta en esta universidad
3. una universidad
4. una familia

Estrategia

Use...
- all of the **-ar/-er/-ir** verbs that you know
- the irregular verbs **ser** and **estar**
- forms of **tener: tengo, tienes, tiene**
- the verb form **hay**

Todo junto

A. Lengua y cultura: Las familias

Paso 1. Completar. Complete the following paragraphs about families. Give the correct form of the words in parentheses, as suggested by context.

¿Existe la familia hispana típica? La idea de que las familias hispanas son muy _______[1] (grande) es un estereotipo del pasado,[a] especialmente en las _______[2] (grande) ciudades. Ahora, la norma _______[3] (ser) una familia con uno o dos hijos. Es difícil tener _______[4] (mucho) hijos cuando las madres y los padres _______[5] (trabajar) fuera de la casa,[b] y cuando los abuelos o tías no _______[6] (vivir) en casa para cuidar[c] a los niños.

A pesar de[d] la reducción en el número de hijos, los hispanos _______[7] (creer) que la familia es su institución _______[8] (principal). Muchos hispanos mantienen[e] relaciones con parientes que _______[9] (estar) en otro país y muchos les mandan[f] dinero y regalos para ayudarlos.[g] En las reuniones _______[10] (familiar) también es frecuente incluir a parientes de _______[11] (vario) generaciones.

En su opinión, ¿hay _______[12] (mucho) diferencias entre su familia y las familias hispanas que conoce[h]?

[a]*past* [b]fuera... *outside the home* [c]cuidar... *care for* [d]A... *In spite of* [e]*keep up, maintain* [f]les... *send them* [g]*help them* [h]*you know*

Una familia mexicana que celebra un día especial

Paso 2. Comprensión. ¿Cierto o falso? Corrija las oraciones falsas.

	CIERTO	FALSO
1. Todas las familias hispanas son grandes.	☐	☐
2. Por lo general (*Generally*), las familias urbanas son pequeñas.	☐	☐
3. Para los hispanos, la familia es una institución social fundamental.	☐	☐

Paso 3. En acción

 Ahora, en parejas, contesten la pregunta del final del **Paso 1**. Deben escribir 3 o 4 oraciones para expresar su opinión. Usen las oraciones de **Lengua y cultura** como modelo y hagan los cambios (*changes*) necesarios. **¡OJO!** No es necesario usar todo el texto original.

MODELOS: En **nuestra** opinión (no) hay muchas diferencias entre **nuestras** familias y las familias hispanas.
No estamos de acuerdo. Yo creo que... pero mi compañera cree...
En la familia típica estadounidense/mexicana, hay...

B. Proyecto: Las familias de las personas de la clase

Working in groups, create a profile of the types of families your classmates have and/or their ideas about family.

Vocabulario útil

juntos/as	together
mismo/a	same
para ti/usted	for you, in your case
la tradición	

Paso 1. Preparación. In groups, think of characteristics or actions that are relevant to family life. Make a list of one or two ideas for each member of your group. Ideas to consider: if parents live together, proximity to or interaction with grandparents, actions family members do together, the presence of another language or traditions, and so on.

MODELOS: Los abuelos (no) viven en la misma ciudad.
(No) Es importante comer juntos todos los días.

Now use those ideas to create questions to poll your classmates. Use different polling options. For example: **cierto o falso**, open-ended questions (like **¿Cuántos/as... ?**), or a series of options (asking about frequency with **todos los días**, **con frecuencia**, ...) You can also ask for opinions using **creer** + **que**... **¡OJO!** Don't forget to use the appropriate possessive adjectives.

MODELOS: Los abuelos (no) viven en la misma ciudad. →
¿Viven **tus** abuelos en la misma ciudad?
¿Cierto o falso para ti? **Mis** abuelos viven en la misma ciudad.
Es importante comer juntos todos los días. →
¿Crees que es importante comer juntos todos los días?

Paso 2. Encuesta. ***(Poll.)*** Each member of your group should poll as many classmates as possible using his/her particular question(s). Before you start polling, create a table on which to record the answers. And don't forget to ask for and record the names of the classmates you poll.

Nombre	Los abuelos viven en la misma ciudad. Sí No	Cree que es importante comer juntos todos los días. Sí No

Paso 3: Análisis de datos (***data***). Gather the information from your group's polling, and prepare 4 or 5 statements to share with the rest of the class. Here are some examples of statements. You can use them or create your own.

1. En nuestra encuesta / Para esta pregunta hay información de __________ (número) estudiantes.
2. Los abuelos de __________ (número) estudiantes viven en la misma ciudad.
3. __________ (número) estudiantes creen que es importante comer juntos todos los días. __________ creen que no es importante.

¡Ahora, yo!

A. Entrevista. Use de (*as a*) modelo las preguntas y respuestas de la página 65 de este capítulo para hablar de su propia (*own*) familia.

B. Proyecto audiovisual. Con las preguntas de la página 65 como modelo, filme una o dos entrevistas con personas que hablan de sus familias.

«Padres modernos» Segmento 2

Antes de mirar°

Antes... *Before watching*

Conteste las siguientes preguntas.

1. ¿De dónde es su familia?
2. ¿Tiene parientes en otro país?
3. ¿Cree que su familia es muy unida (*close*)?

Este segmento

Laura entrevista (*interviews*) a los miembros de una familia mexicana que vive en Los Ángeles.

Las hermanas Minerva (de blanco [*in white*]) y Araceli Rubio, con sus hijos. Todos extrañan (*miss*) a los parientes que están en México.

Vocabulario del segmento

único/a	unique
una vida mejor	a better life
mil novecientos noventa y nueve	1999
mayor	oldest
estar solo/a	to be alone
han crecido juntos	they've grown up together
dejar atrás	to leave behind

Fragmento del guion°

script

El año pasado hubo[a] una celebración especial en México. Una sobrina de Minerva y Araceli cumplió 15 años.[b] Mine fue[c] a México para estar en la celebración de la quinceañera[d] de su prima. Fue[e] una buena oportunidad de estar cerca del[f] resto de su familia y ver[g] a todos los parientes: abuelos, tíos, primos. ¡Fue una fiesta fantástica!

[a]El... *Last year there was* [b]cumplió... *turned 15* [c]*went* [d]*fifteenth birthday* [e]*It was* [f]cerca... *close to the* [g]*to see*

Después de mirar°

Después... *After watching*

A. ¿Está claro? ¿Cierto o falso? Corrija las oraciones falsas según el video.

	CIERTO	FALSO
1. Minerva tiene dos hijas.	☐	☐
2. Las hijas de Minerva viven en California.	☐	☐
3. Araceli tiene 3 hijos.	☐	☐
4. Los hijos de Araceli y de Minerva no son unidos.	☐	☐

B. Un poco más. Conteste las siguientes preguntas.

1. ¿Qué miembros de esta familia viven en los Estados Unidos?
2. ¿Qué celebración importante para la familia de Minerva y Araceli hubo en México?

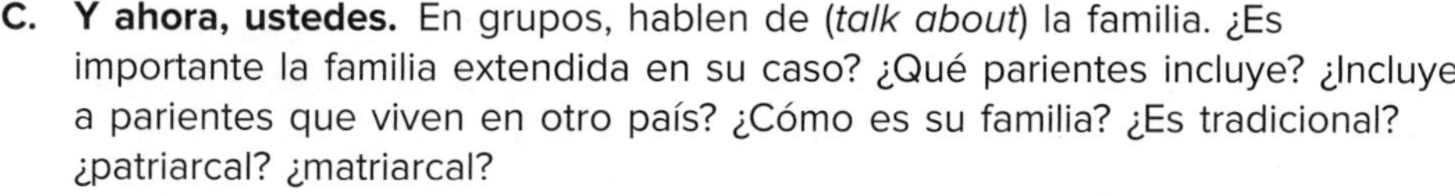

C. Y ahora, ustedes. En grupos, hablen de (*talk about*) la familia. ¿Es importante la familia extendida en su caso? ¿Qué parientes incluye? ¿Incluye a parientes que viven en otro país? ¿Cómo es su familia? ¿Es tradicional? ¿patriarcal? ¿matriarcal?

MUNDO° HISPANO

World

Enfoque cultural: México

Antes de leer

¿Es normal para los jóvenes estadounidenses vivir con su familia cuando tienen 20 años o más? Si usted vive con su familia, ¿le gusta? ¿Le gusta vivir cerca de (*close to*) su familia?

La institución de la familia

Por tradición,[a] las familias en México son muy unidas.[b] Esto tiene ventajas[c] para los niños y adolescentes: tienen el apoyo[d] de sus padres, hermanos y parientes cercanos.[e] Pero hay personas que creen que esta unión familiar presenta problemas. Cuando los jóvenes viven con sus padres hasta que[f] son adultos, pueden perder[g] parte de su identidad individual. Muchos jóvenes viven con su familia hasta que contraen matrimonio.[h] Y si no contraen matrimonio, siempre viven en casa de sus padres.

Aquí hay unas cifras para pensar.[i]

- El 89% (por ciento) de los hogares[j] mexicanos son de tipo familiar, es decir,[k] entre[l] las personas que los forman[m] existe una relación familiar.
- El 17% de los hogares familiares son monoparentales. Las mujeres son responsables de su familia[n] en la inmensa mayoría[ñ] de los hogares monoparentales.
- El número promedio[o] por hogar familiar es de casi cuatro personas.

[a]Por... *Traditionally* [b]*close* [c]*advantages* [d]*support* [e]*close* [f]hasta... *until* [g]pueden... *they can lose* [h]hasta... *until they marry* [i]cifras... *numbers to think about* [j]*homes* [k]es... *that is* [l]*among* [m]los... *make them up* [n]responsables... *the heads of the household* [ñ]la... *the great majority* [o]*average*

En otros países hispanos

En todo el mundo hispanohablante Es impresionante cómo los hispanos de todos los países coinciden en cuanto a[a] la importancia de la familia. También es típico en todo el mundo hispano que los hijos se independicen[b] tarde.

[a]en... *with regard to* [b]se... *become independent*

©Anuska Sampedro/Getty Images

La Pirámide del Sol (*Sun*) en la antigua ciudad de Teotihuacán, cerca de (*close to*) la Ciudad de México. Tiene 63,5 metros de altura (*height*).

Un símbolo mexicano: Los centros arqueológicos

Hay muchos por todo el país, pero los más importantes son las ruinas mayas de Chichén Itzá (cerca de[a] Cancún), el complejo[b] de Teotihuacán (cerca de la Ciudad de México) y las ruinas zapotecas (cerca de Oaxaca).

[a]cerca... *close to* [b]*building complex*

Comprensión

¿Cierto o falso? Identifique la parte de los textos donde aparece la información.

	CIERTO	FALSO
1. La unidad de la familia mexicana tiene aspectos positivos para los hijos.	☐	☐
2. Para los jóvenes, vivir con la familia es siempre ideal.	☐	☐
3. La estructura familiar mexicana es única en el mundo hispanohablante.	☐	☐
4. En México hay ruinas de solo una cultura indígena.	☐	☐

En acción

Haga una lista de los centros arqueológicos importantes de su estado o en este país. ¿Qué lugares deben visitar los turistas interesados en la historia y la arqueología? Recomiende dos o tres lugares importantes.

Lectura

Antes de leer

1. ¿Cómo es su familia? Identifique el modelo apropiado en la Infografía. Explique.
2. ¿Tiene usted idea de cuántas personas viven en los hogares *(households)* de los Estados Unidos y el Canadá? Seleccione el número correcto para cada (*each*) espacio: **16, 23, 27, 34.**

- ______% (por ciento) de la población vive sola *(alone)*.
- ______% de los hogares consiste en *(consists of)* dos personas.
- ______% de los hogares consiste en tres personas.
- ______% de los hogares consiste en cuatro personas o más (*more*).

Vocabulario útil

cuidar	to care for
solo/a	single

Infografía: La familia en México

En México las familias están evolucionando.[a] Este tipo de evolución es representativa de la institución de la familia por todo el mundo.[b]

Roles diversificados

Madres y padres trabajan fuera de la casa[c] y también cuidan a sus hijos.

Microfamilias

Hogares que consisten en una sola persona, una tendencia creciente[d] en todo el mundo.

Amigos y mascotas

La estructura familiar incluye más que[e] parientes.

Datos clave[f]

- El 97% de los mexicanos viven en familia.
- Menos del[g] 50% de las familias mexicanas son tradicionales (padre + madre + hijos).
- El 1% de las familias mexicanas son homoparentales, y casi el 70% de estas familias tienen hijos.

Más allá de[h] la familia nuclear tradicional: Otros tipos de hogares comunes

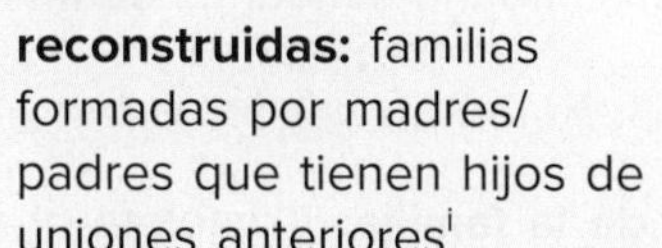

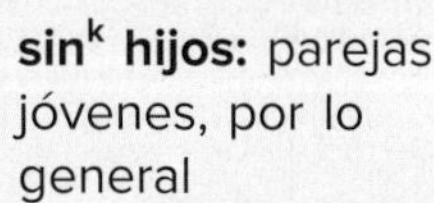

monoparentales: solo la madre o el padre con sus hijos

reconstruidas: familias formadas por madres/padres que tienen hijos de uniones anteriores[i]

homoparentales: los padres son personas del mismo[j] sexo

sin[k] hijos: parejas jóvenes, por lo general

mayores de[l] 60 años: si tienen hijos, no están en el hogar familiar

multigeneracionales: varias generaciones cohabitan en una casa

unipersonales: personas que viven solas

[a]están... *are evolving* [b]por... *worldwide* [c]fuera... *outside of the home* [d]*growing* [e]más... *more than* [f]Datos... *Key facts* [g]Menos... *Less than* [h]Más... *Beyond* [i]*previous* [j]*same* [k]*without* [l]mayores... *older than*

Comprensión

A. ¿Cierto o falso? Según la infografía, ¿son ciertas o falsas las siguientes oraciones?

	CIERTO	FALSO
1. Casi todos los mexicanos viven con su familia nuclear: padre, madre e hijo(s).	☐	☐
2. No son muy comunes las familias en las que *(which)* las madres y los padres trabajan y cuidan a sus hijos.	☐	☐
3. Las mascotas no son importantes para los mexicanos.	☐	☐
4. Las parejas sin hijos son viejas por lo general.	☐	☐

B. Clasificación. Mire los siete tipos de familias de la infografía. ¿De qué tipo es cada (*each*) una de las siguientes familias?

1. Matías tiene dos hijos y está divorciado. Sofía tiene una hija y está divorciada. Ahora Matías y Sofía viven juntos (*together*) con sus tres hijos.
2. Juan Carlos y Alonso son esposos. No tienen hijos.
3. Diego y Camila son ancianos (*elderly*). Sus hijos viven en otro estado.
4. Ana y Martín tienen tres hijos pequeños de 3, 5 y 7 años. Viven con los padres de Martín.
5. Lucía vive sola con su perro Atila.
6. Samuel está divorciado; vive con sus dos hijas, Elena y Emilia.

Proyecto: La demografía de las familias de la clase

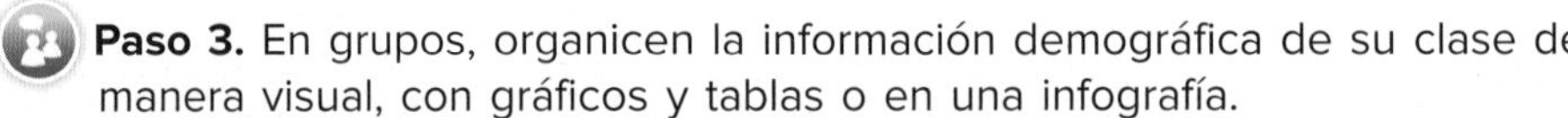

Paso 1. ¿Cómo son las familias de sus compañeros de clase? Mire la infografía y determine la información que desea recoger *(to gather)* de sus compañeros de clase. Después prepare unas preguntas específicas.

Paso 2. Use las preguntas del **Paso 1** para entrevistar a varias personas de su clase.

Paso 3. En grupos, organicen la información demográfica de su clase de manera visual, con gráficos y tablas o en una infografía.

Vocabulario para escuchar

la escuela	school
la cuñada	sister-in-law
travieso/a	troublemaker
las mellizas	twins
juntos/as	together

En acción

Complete las siguientes ideas sobre usted y su familia.

1. La mayor parte de mi familia vive en (el área de) ___________.
2. Muchas personas de mi familia son __________ y __________ (adjetivos).
3. Creo que mi familia es / no es muy unida.
4. En mi familia existe / no existe la tradición de madrinas y padrinos (*godparents*).

Textos orales

La familia de Lucía Jiménez Flores

Antes de escuchar

¿Cómo es su familia? ¿Tiene usted hermanos casados (*married*)? ¿Tiene buenas relaciones con sus cuñados (*in-laws*)? ¿Tiene padrinos (*godparents*) o es padrino o madrina de un niño?

Comprensión

A. El árbol genealógico de la familia. Complete el árbol genealógico con los nombres de los miembros de la familia.

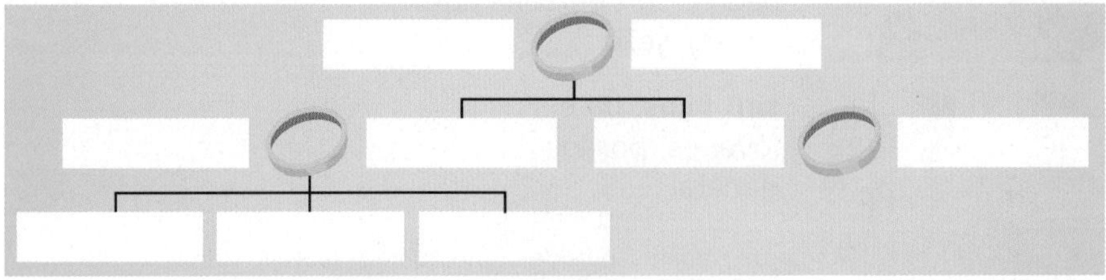

B. ¿Quién es quién? Complete las oraciones.

1. La cuñada de Lucía se llama ________.
2. El cuñado de José se llama ________.
3. Lucía tiene tres ________.
4. La abuela de Camila tiene ________ años.
5. El nombre del padre de Lucía es ________.
6. La familia de Lucía es de ________ (ciudad).
7. En México, Lucía tiene muchos ________.

Proyecto en su comunidad

Entreviste a (*Interview*) una persona hispana sobre (*about*) su familia.

Preguntas posibles

- ¿Tiene esta persona una familia grande o pequeña? ¿Cuáles son los miembros de la familia?
- ¿Cuál es el país de origen de los abuelos de la persona? ¿Viven solos (*alone*) o con un pariente?
- ¿Los parientes se reúnen (*get together*) con frecuencia? ¿En qué ocasiones?

©Erik Isakson/Getty Images

¿Una familia típica?

Escritura

Proyecto: Un ensayo sobre° la familia

ensayo... *essay about*

¿Cómo son las familias estadounidenses? ¿Hay una familia estereotípica? ¿Qué une (*unites*) a los miembros de una familia?

Antes de escribir

Decida un enfoque (*focus*) para su ensayo. Luego (*Then*) use las siguientes preguntas y otras más para entrevistar (*interview*) a varios miembros de la clase. Las respuestas pueden (*can*) ser útiles para documentar las diferentes estructuras familiares y usar como ejemplos en su ensayo. Repase (*Review*) el vocabulario de **Más parientes** (pág. 67).

- ¿Viven tus padres en el mismo domicilio (*same residence*)?
- ¿Cuántos hermanos tienes?
- ¿Tienes padrastro / madrastra / hermanastro/a(s) / hijastro/a(s) / medio/a(s) hermano/a(s) / ?
- ¿Viven tus abuelos cerca (*nearby*)?
- ¿Cuál es el país de origen de tu familia?
- _______ (una pregunta propia [*of your own*])

A escribir

Ahora use sus opiniones y las respuestas de sus compañeros para escribir un ensayo sobre (*about*) la familia moderna. Hay más ayuda (*help*) en Connect.

Estrategias

As you learn Spanish, you will often need to look up words in the dictionary. Here are a few suggestions for using the dictionary efficiently.

- Pay attention to the gender of nouns (nouns are typically marked with *m.* for masculine or *f.* for feminine).
- Don't settle for the first translation given; words in all languages can have more than one meaning. The extra seconds spent looking at all of the translations can be very informative!
- Notice if the word has an accent mark.
- Take full advantage of online dictionaries and listen to the pronunciation of the words you look up.

Más ideas para su portafolio

- Busque (*Look for*) una fotografía de su familia y seleccione un adjetivo especial para cada (*each*) persona de la foto.
- Escriba un breve poema sobre (*about*) una persona de su familia que es muy especial para usted. Use el modelo de la página 73.
- Dé tres palabras favoritas de este capítulo para usted. ¿Por qué son interesantes para usted? ¿Con qué las asocia usted (*do you associate them*)?
- Si ha estado jugando (*you have been playing*) Practice Spanish: Study Abroad, en Quest 2, usted conoció (*met*) a un fantasma (*ghost*) que se llama la Mancarita. Dibuje (*Draw*) a la Mancarita y luego escriba cuatro oraciones que la describen (*that describe her*).

©McGraw-Hill Education

Sugerencia: You are now ready to play Quest 2 in **Practice Spanish: Study Abroad.**

EN RESUMEN En este capítulo

AFTER STUDYING THIS CHAPTER I CAN . . .

- ☐ name family members (66–67)
- ☐ count from 31 to 100 (68)
- ☐ describe people, places, things, and ideas using adjectives and the verb **ser** (70, 73–75)
- ☐ also use **ser** to identify and to express origin, generalizations, possession, and destination (79–81)
- ☐ use possessive adjectives to distinguish what's mine and what belongs to others (84–85)
- ☐ talk about more actions with **-er** and **-ir** verbs (88–89)
- ☐ avoid subject pronouns but use them to clarify or emphasize the subject (89)
- ☐ recognize/describe at least 2–3 aspects of Mexican cultures

Gramática en breve

5. Adjectives: Gender, Number, and Position

Adjective Endings

Singular	Plural
-o	**-os**
-a	**-as**
-e	**-es**
-[consonant]	-[consonant] + **-es**

6. Present Tense of *ser*; Summary of Uses

ser: soy, eres, es, somos, sois, son

Uses of **ser:** identification, description, origin, generalizations, possession, destination

de + el → del

7. Unstressed Possessive Adjectives

yo	**→ mi(s)**	**nosotros**	**→ nuestro/a(s)**
tú	**→ tu(s)**	**vosotros**	**→ vuestro/a(s)**
usted, él, ella	**→ su(s)**	**ustedes, ellos, ellas**	**→ su(s)**

8. Present Tense of *-er* and *-ir* Verbs; Subject Pronouns

Regular* -er *Verb Endings

-o, -es, -e, -emos, -éis, -en

Regular* -ir *Verb Endings

-o, -es, -e, -imos, -ís, -en

When to use subject pronouns: for clarification, emphasis, and contrast

Vocabulario

Los verbos

abrir	to open
aprender	to learn
aprender a + *inf.*	to learn how to (*do something*)
asistir (a)	to attend, go to (a *class, a function*)
beber	to drink
comer	to eat
comprender	to understand
creer (en)	to think; to believe (in)
deber + *inf.*	should, must, ought to (*do something*)
escribir	to write
leer	to read
llegar	to arrive
mirar	to look at; to watch
mirar la tele(visión)	to watch television
recibir	to receive
ser (soy, eres,...)	to be (I am, you are . . .)
vender	to sell
vivir	to live

La familia y los parientes

el/la abuelo/a	grandfather/grandmother
los abuelos	grandparents
el/la esposo/a	husband/wife
el/la hermano/a	brother/sister
los hermanos	siblings
el/la hijo/a	son/daughter
los hijos	children
la madre (mamá)	mother (mom)
el marido	husband
la mujer	wife
el/la nieto/a	grandson/granddaughter
el/la niño/a	small child; boy/girl
el padre (papá)	father (dad)
los padres	parents
la pareja	partner; significant other; couple
el/la primo/a	cousin
los primos	cousins
el/la sobrino/a	nephew/niece
el/la tío/a	uncle/aunt
los tíos	aunts and uncles
el pariente	relative

Las mascotas

el gato	cat
el pájaro	bird
el perro	dog
la mascota	pet

Otros sustantivos

la carta	letter
la casa	house, home
la ciudad	city
el coche	car
el estado	state
el/la médico/a	(medical) doctor
el mundo	world
el país	country
el periódico	newspaper
el regalo	present, gift
la revista	magazine

Los adjetivos

alto/a	tall
amable	kind; nice
antipático/a	unpleasant, unlikeable (*people*)
bajo/a	short (*in height*)
bonito/a	pretty (*people and things*)
buen, bueno/a	good
corto/a	short (*in length*)
delgado/a	thin, slender
este/a	this
estos/as	these
feo/a	ugly
fiel	faithful
gordo/a	fat
gran, grande	large, big; great
guapo	handsome, good-looking (*people*)
joven	young
largo/a	long
listo/a	smart; clever
mal, malo/a	bad
moreno/a	brunet(te)
mucho/a	a lot (of)
muchos/as	many
nuevo/a	new
otro/a	other, another
pequeño/a	small
perezoso/a	lazy
pobre	poor
rico/a	rich
rubio/a	blond(e)
simpático/a	nice, likeable (*people*)
todo/a	all; every
tonto/a	silly, foolish
trabajador(a)	hardworking
viejo/a	old

Cognados: hispano/a, inteligente, necesario/a, posible

Los adjetivos de nacionalidad

alemán/alemana	German
español(a)	Spanish
estadounidense	U.S.
inglés/inglesa	English
mexicano/a	Mexican

Los adjetivos posesivos

mi(s)	my
tu(s)	your (*fam. sing.*)
nuestro/a(s)	our
vuestro/a(s)	your (*fam. pl., Sp.*)
su(s)	his, hers, its; your (*form. sing.*); their; your (*form. pl.*)

Los números del 31 al 100

treinta, cuarenta, cincuenta, sesenta, setenta, ochenta, noventa, cien

¿Con qué frecuencia... ?

a veces	sometimes, at times
casi	almost
casi nunca	almost never
nunca	never
siempre	always
una vez a la semana	once a week
¿con qué frecuencia... ?	how often . . . ?

Repaso: con frecuencia, todos los días

Palabras adicionales

¿de quién?	whose?
del (de + el)	of the, from the
e	and (*before words beginning with the sound* ***i-***)
estar de acuerdo / no estar de acuerdo	to agree / to disagree
esto	this (*neuter*)
para	(intended) *for*
para + *inf.*	in order to (*do something*)
por eso	for that reason
¿por qué?	why?
porque	because
que	that, which; who
según	according to
tener... años (tengo, tienes, tiene)	to be . . . years old
u	or (*before words beginning with the sound* ***o-***)

Repaso: ¿de dónde es usted?

Vocabulario personal

Remember to use this space for other words and phrases you learn in this chapter.

ESPAÑOL	**INGLÉS**

4

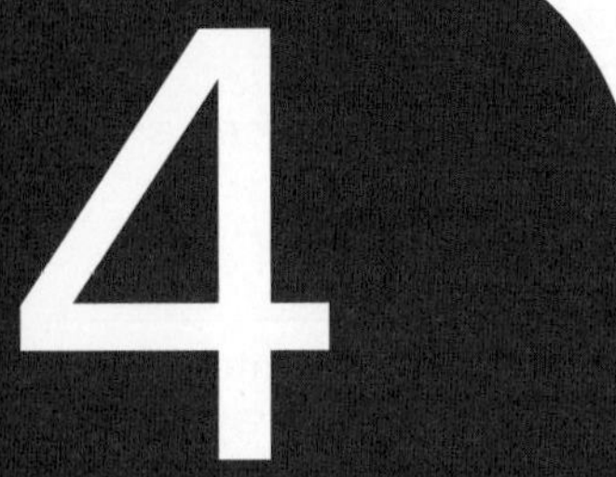

De compras°

De... *Shopping*

En este capítulo

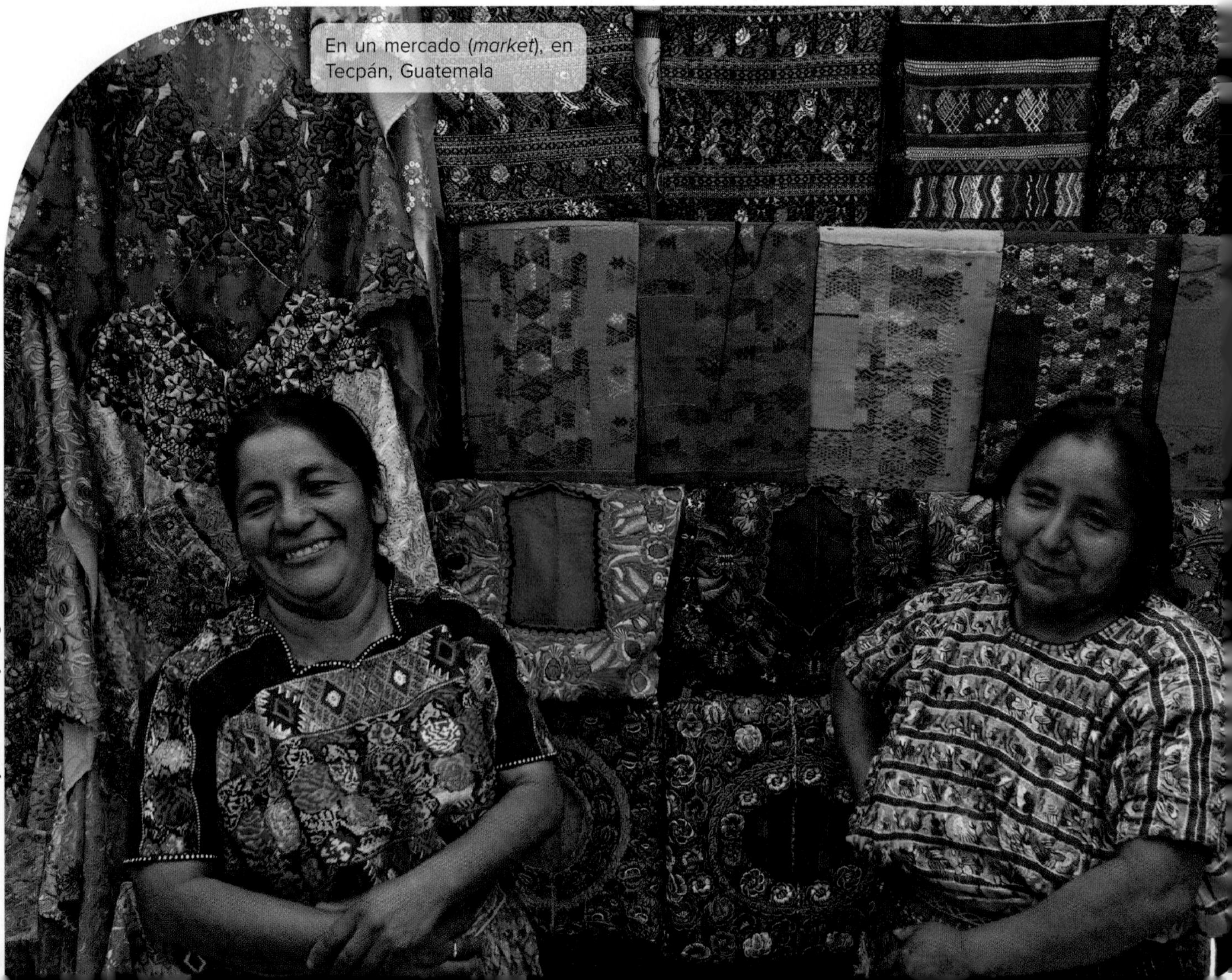

En un mercado (*market*), en Tecpán, Guatemala

GUATEMALA

17,3 (coma tres) millones de habitantes

- Guatemala es el centro de la civilización maya. También hay población maya en Honduras, México, El Salvador y Belice.

HONDURAS

9 millones de habitantes

- Honduras tiene una población afroindígena[a] muy grande: los garífunas, que viven a lo largo del[b] Golfo de Honduras, de Belice a Nicaragua.

[a]*native African* [b]a... *along the*

ENTREVISTA

- ¿Qué tipo de ropa[a] le gusta llevar[b] con más frecuencia, ropa formal o informal?
- ¿Prefiere usar ropa de muchos colores o prefiere la ropa de colores muy básicos, como el blanco y el negro[c]? (**Prefiero...**)
- ¿Le gusta ir de compras[d] o prefiere comprar por[e] internet? Cuando va[f] de compras, ¿va a centros comerciales o a pequeñas tiendas[g] locales? (**Voy...**)

[a]*clothing* [b]*to wear* [c]el... *white and black* [d]ir... *to go shopping* [e]*on the* [f]*you go* [g]*shops*

Alejandra Hernández Soto contesta las preguntas.

- Me gusta todo tipo de ropa. Para ir[a] a la universidad todos los días, llevo ropa cómoda:[b] *jeans*, camisetas[c] y suéteres grandes, zapatos bajos o deportivos.[d] Pero me gusta la ropa elegante para ocasiones especiales.
- Me gusta mucho combinar el negro con el blanco y colores vivos,[e] como el rojo[f] y el turquesa.
- Prefiero ir de compras. Con frecuencia voy a un centro comercial. Pero a veces, voy[g] a tiendas pequeñas en el centro que tienen cosas un poco diferentes. ¡Nunca compro por internet!

[a]Para... *To go* [b]*comfortable* [c]*T-shirts* [d]zapatos... *low or sporty shoes* [e]*strong, vibrant* [f]*red* [g]*I go*

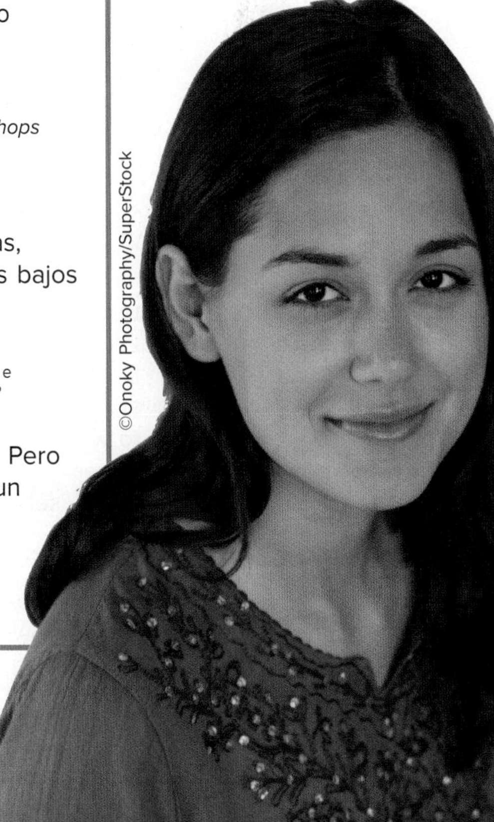

VOCABULARIO: PREPARACIÓN

You can hear the pronunciation of theme vocabulary words and phrases in the Connect eBook.

De compras: La ropa°

De... *Shopping: Clothing*

©drbimages/Getty Images
©Glow Images RM/Alamy
©Peopleimages/Getty Images

Los verbos

comprar	to buy
comprar por internet	to buy online
llevar	to wear; to carry; to take
regatear	to haggle; to bargain
usar	to wear; to use
vender	to sell
venden de todo	they sell (have) everything

Los lugares

el almacén	department store
el centro	downtown
el centro comercial	shopping mall
el mercado	market(place)
la plaza	plaza
la tienda	shop, store

¿Cuánto cuesta(n)?°

¿Cuánto... *How much does it (do they) cost?*

la ganga	bargain
el precio	price
el precio fijo	fixed (set) price
las rebajas	sales, reductions
barato/a	inexpensive
caro/a	expensive
cómodo/a	comfortable

Otras palabras y expresiones útiles

el abrigo	coat
los aretes	earrings
las botas	boots
los calcetines	socks
la cartera	wallet; handbag
la chaqueta	jacket (*for a woman or a man*)
la corbata	tie
las gafas de sol	sunglasses
la gorra	baseball cap
el impermeable	raincoat
los *jeans*	blue jeans, jeans
las medias	stockings
el reloj	watch
la ropa interior	underwear
las sandalias	sandals
el sombrero	hat
la sudadera	sweatshirt
el suéter	sweater
el traje	suit
el traje de baño	bathing suit
el vestido	dress
de cuadros, de lunares, de rayas	plaid, polka-dot, striped
Es de (algodón, cuero, lana, oro, plata, seda).*	it is made of (cotton, leather, wool, gold, silver, silk).
Es de última moda. / Está de moda.	It's trendy (hot).

Así se dice

el almacén = los grandes almacenes (*Spain*)
el bolso = la bolsa (*Mexico*)
la camiseta = la polera (*Argentina*), la playera (*Mexico*), el polo (*Peru*)
la cartera = la billetera (*Argentina, El Salvador*); *coin purse* = el monedero
la falda = la pollera (*Argentina, Uruguay*)
los *jeans* = los mahones (*Puerto Rico, Dominican Republic*), los vaqueros (*Spain*)
el suéter = el jersey (*Spain*), el pulóver (*Argentina*)

To talk about sales, you can say **hay rebajas** or say that something **está de/en rebaja** or **está en liquidación/venta.**

Comunicación

A. La ropa

Paso 1. ¿Qué ropa llevan estas personas?

©Andresr/Getty Images
1.

©drbimages/Getty Images
2.

©4x6/Getty Images
3.

Paso 2. De estas personas, ¿quién trabaja hoy? ¿Quién probablemente no trabaja en este momento? ¿Quién va a (*is going to*) una fiesta?

Vocabulario útil

la chica	girl
el chico	guy
el hombre	
la mujer	

*Note another use of **ser** + **de:** to tell what material something is made of.

B. Asociaciones. Complete las siguientes oraciones lógicamente con palabras de **De compras: La ropa.**

1. Un ______ es una tienda grande, con muchos departamentos.
2. No es posible __________ cuando hay precios fijos.
3. En la librería, _________ de todo: textos y otros libros, cuadernos, lápices,...
4. Hay grandes _________ en las tiendas al final de la temporada (*season*), en las cuales (*in which*) todo es muy barato.
5. Siempre hay *boutiques* en los _________________.
6. El ________ de una ciudad es con frecuencia la parte histórica.
7. Esta ropa es para fiestas formales: __________.
8. La ropa de _________ (materia) es muy elegante.

Estrategia

Remember that the preposition **para** followed by an infinitive can be used to express *in order to.*

Para ir al centro, me gusta llevar pantalones, una camiseta y sandalias.
(*In order*) *To go downtown, I like to wear pants, a T-shirt, and sandals.*

C. El estilo personal. Complete las siguientes oraciones lógicamente para hablar de sus preferencias con relación a la ropa.

1. Para ir a la universidad, llevo _________.
2. Para ir a las fiestas con los amigos, llevo _________.
3. Para pasar un día en la playa (*beach*), me gusta llevar _________.
4. Para estar en casa todo el día, me gusta llevar _________.
5. Nunca uso _________.
6. No puedo vivir sin (*I can't live without*) _____ y _____.

¡OJO!

The inverted question mark comes immediately before the tag question, not at the beginning of the statement.

Nota comunicativa

Preguntas coletilla° — °*tag*

Tag phrases can change statements into questions.

Aquí venden de todo, { **¿no?** / **¿verdad?** }	*They sell everything here, right? (don't they?)*
No necesito impermeable hoy, **¿verdad?**	*I don't need a raincoat today, do I?*

¿Verdad? is found after affirmative or negative statements; **¿no?** is usually found after affirmative statements only.

You will practice using tag phrases in **Comunicación D.**

D. Intercambios. En parejas, usen las coletillas **¿no?** y **¿verdad?** para intercambiar (*exchange*) información de sus hábitos y preferencias sobre (*about*) las compras.

MODELO: Hay un buen centro comercial cerca de (*close to*) tu casa. →
E1: Hay un buen centro comercial cerca de tu casa, ¿no? (¿verdad?)
E2: Sí, hay un centro comercial muy grande a cinco millas (*five miles away*) de mi casa. (No, no hay un buen centro comercial cerca de mi casa.)

1. Hay un buen centro comercial cerca de tu casa.
2. Te gusta la ropa deportiva (*sports*) más que (*more than*) la ropa elegante.
3. Tienes muchos zapatos.
4. Te gusta llevar ropa de moda.
5. No compras en las tiendas de ropa usada (*used*).
6. Compras muchas cosas (*things*) por internet.
7. No hay muchos mercados en esta ciudad.

Los colores: ¿De qué color es?

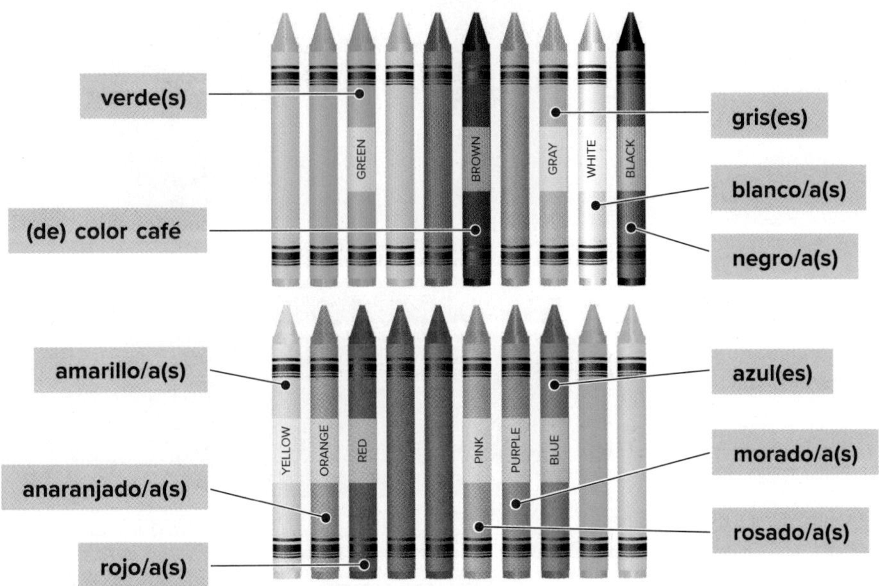

- Because of their ending, some adjectives of color (**verde, azul**, and **gris**) have only two forms, singular and plural.

  la camisa gris   el traje gris   las cosas gris<u>es</u>

- The expression **(de) color café** is invariable; that is, it does not show gender or number agreement. Sometimes **de** is not used.

  el sombrero (de) color café   las gorras (de) color café

- Another way to express colors is to just say **de color (rojo, verde…)**.
- When the colors are used as nouns, they are always masculine, and are preceded by an article:

  Me gusta **el** rojo. — *I like (the color) red.*
  El azul y **el** verde son mis colores favoritos. — *(The color) Blue and (the color) green are my favorite colors.*

Así se dice

anaranjado = naranja
(de) color café = marrón, pardo
morado = (de) color violeta, púrpura, purpúreo
rosado = (de) color rosa, rosa
Note that **naranja, violeta,** and **púrpura** do not take different gender endings.

Note that some Spanish speakers use **marrón** for objects and **pardo** for animals. Brown hair and eye color are often expressed with **castaño.**

Comunicación

A. Un cuadro colorido (*colorful painting*). Hay muchos colores en este cuadro de Edwin Guillermo. ¿Cuáles son?

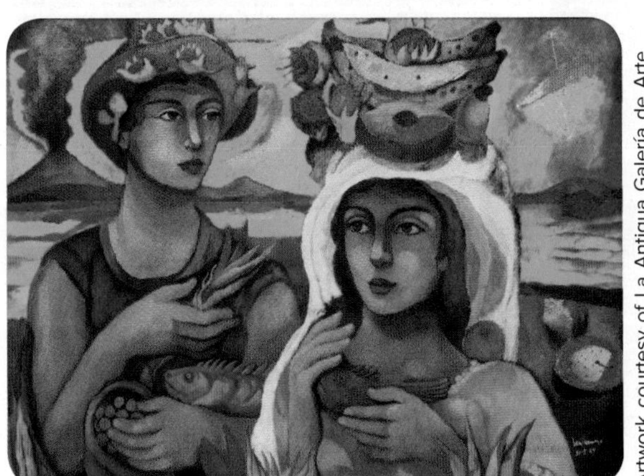

Artwork courtesy of La Antigua Galería de Arte Antigua Guatemala, www.artintheamericas.com

El cortejo (*Courting*), de Erwin Guillermo

Algo sobre...

un artista guatemalteco

Erwin Guillermo (1951– [mil novecientos cincuenta y uno]) vive y trabaja en la Ciudad de Guatemala. Su estilo es representativo del arte contemporáneo guatemalteco: es muy expresivo y simbólico. Con frecuencia, como se ve[a] en este cuadro,[b] las figuras de Guillermo tienen una forma estilizada y sensual, con muchos colores.

¿Le gusta el estilo del cuadro de Guillermo? ¿Qué pintor(a) le gusta mucho a usted?

[a]se... *is seen* [b]*painting*

Nota cultural

La ropa tradicional en el mundo hispano

La ropa tradicional en el mundo hispano es muy diversa, porque hay muchos países y regiones diferentes. Algunas prendas[a] son ahora conocidas[b] en todo el mundo:

- la guayabera[c] (Caribe)
- el poncho (los Andes)
- los huaraches (México)

En los países de cultura maya (México, Guatemala y Honduras, principalmente) hay tejidos muy bellos y coloridos.[d] Varían según la región y forman parte de la ropa habitual de las mujeres indígenas. Una prenda distintiva es el huipil, una especie de blusa.

¿Hay ropa tradicional en este país?

[a]*articles of clothing* [b]*known* [c]*elegant short-sleeved shirt worn outside the pants* [d]tejidos... *beautiful and colorful textiles*

©John Mitchell/Alamy

Un huipil

©bponline/Getty Images

Unos huaraches

©trappy76/Shutterstock

Un poncho

©Roberto Machado Noa/Getty Images

Una guayabera

Vocabulario útil

una flor	*flower*
una fruta	
un limón	
un pingüino	

Vocabulario útil

multicolor	
un par de	a pair of

B. Asociaciones. ¿Qué asocia usted con los siguientes colores?

1. gris
2. verde
3. blanco y negro
4. amarillo
5. rojo
6. azul

C. ¡Ojo alerta! ¿Escaparates *(Window displays)* idénticos? These window displays are almost alike . . . but not quite! Can you find at least nine differences between them?

MODELO: En el dibujo A hay _______, pero en el dibujo B hay _______.

A.

B.

D. ¿De qué color es?

Paso 1. Describa el color de la ropa y de las cosas (*things*) de sus compañeros.

MODELO: El bolígrafo de Anita es amarillo. Un libro de Anita es azul...

Paso 2. Ahora describa la ropa que lleva una persona de la clase sin decir (*without saying*) su nombre. Sus compañeros tienen que (*have to*) identificar a la persona de la descripción.

MODELO: **E1:** Lleva botas negras, una camiseta blanca y *jeans*.
E2: Es Anne.

Los números a partir del 100°

Continúe las secuencias:

- noventa y nueve, cien, ciento uno...
- mil, dos mil...
- un millón, dos millones...

100	cien, ciento	**700**	setecientos/as
101	ciento uno/una	**800**	ochocientos/as
200	doscientos/as	**900**	novecientos/as
300	trescientos/as	**1.000**	mil
400	cuatrocientos/as	**2.000**	dos mil
500	quinientos/as	**1.000.000**	un millón
600	seiscientos/as	**2.000.000**	dos millones

©brianlatino/Alamy

Este huipil guatemalteco hecho a mano (*handmade*) cuesta 750 (setecientos cincuenta) quetzales.

- **Cien** is used in counting: ...**noventa y nueve, cien.** It is also used to refer to exactly one hundred of something: **cien** dólares.
- **Ciento** is used in combination with numbers from 1 to 99 to express the numbers 101 to 199: cien, **ciento** uno, **ciento** dos...
- **Cien** is used before numbers greater than 100: **cien mil, cien millones.**
- When counting, the masculine form of words containing **cientos** is used: **...doscientos uno, doscientos dos...**
- When the numbers 200 to 900 modify a noun, they must agree in gender: **doscientos veintiún dólares, quinientas ocho sillas.**
- **Mil** means *one thousand* or *a thousand*. It does not have a plural form in counting, but **millón** does. When followed directly by a noun, **millón** (**dos millones,** and so on) must be followed by **de.**

mil gracias	
3.000 habitantes	**tres mil habitantes**
14.000.000 de habitantes	**catorce millones de habitantes**

- Years are expressed like regular numbers in Spanish, and they are written without any separation, just as in English.

1899	**mil ochocientos noventa y nueve**
2008	**dos mil ocho**

¡OJO!

In many parts of the Spanish-speaking world, a period **(punto)** is used where a comma **(coma)** is used in English and viceversa.

$1.500 **$1.000.000**
$10,45 **65,9%**

Comunicación

A. La población de varios países. ¿Cuánto sabe usted (*do you know*) del mundo hispano? Practique los números grandes emparejando (*matching*) los países con su población (estimaciones de 2017). ¡No debe buscar la información!

1. 122.900.000	**a.** la Argentina
2. 49.000.000	**b.** Colombia
3. 43.800.000	**c.** Guatemala
4. 17.000.000	**d.** Honduras
5. 8.800.000	**e.** México
6. 3.500.000	**f.** el Uruguay

°a... *from 100 on*

Answers, Com. A 1. e **2.** b **3.** a **4.** c **5.** d **6.** f

B. ¿Cuánto cuestan?

Paso 1. Empareje de manera lógica las cantidades con las cosas (*things*) de la lista y exprese los precios. **¡OJO! el dólar → los dólares.**

CANTIDADES	COSAS
1. \$100	**a.** un coche de lujo (*luxury*)
2. \$150	**b.** un anillo (*ring*) de diamantes
3. \$225	**c.** un edificio de apartamentos
4. \$330	**d.** un bolso de una diseñadora (*designer*) famosa
5. \$2.500	**e.** unos aretes de oro
6. \$75.000	**f.** un apartamento en San Francisco
7. \$2.600.000	**g.** unos tenis de moda
8. \$15.800.000	**h.** unos boletos (*tickets*) para un concierto

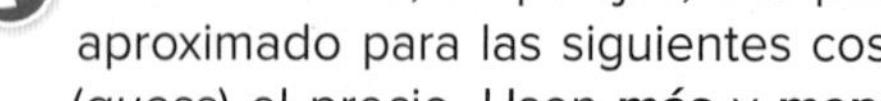

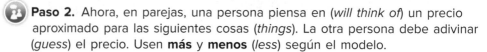

Paso 2. Ahora, en parejas, una persona piensa en (*will think of*) un precio aproximado para las siguientes cosas (*things*). La otra persona debe adivinar (*guess*) el precio. Usen **más** y **menos** (*less*) según el modelo.

MODELO: unos *jeans* de moda muy caros →

E2: \$75.
E1: No, más.
E2: \$200.
E1: No, menos.
E2: \$175.
E1: ¡Correcto!

1. un Tesla™
2. la matrícula de esta universidad
3. un libro de texto de biología
4. un iPhone de última generación
5. un viejo coche usado (*used*)
6. una cena (*dinner*) en un restaurante elegante

C. Precios en otras divisas (*currency*)

Paso 1. ¿Cuánto cuestan estas cosas (*things*) de OLX Guatemala (un sitio web como eBay)? **¡OJO! Q = el quetzal / los quetzales**, la divisa de Guatemala.

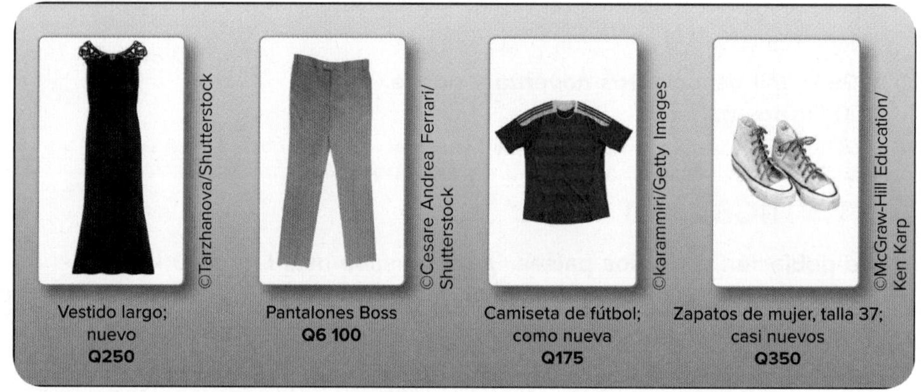

Paso 2. Ahora, en parejas, calculen los precios del **Paso 1** en las divisas de otros países. Las siguientes correspondencias son aproximadas.

1 quetzal = 3 lempiras hondureños
7 quetzales = 1 dólar estadounidense
9 quetzales = 1 euro

D. Fechas *(Dates)* importantes. Exprese las siguientes fechas en español.

1. este año, el año pasado y el próximo (*next*) año
2. el año de su nacimiento (*birth*)
3. 1821, el año de la independencia de Guatemala y Honduras (de España)
4. 1776, el año de la independencia de los Estados Unidos (de Inglaterra)

«¡Moda,° moda, moda!» Segmento 1

°Fashion

Antes de mirar

¿Qué estilo de ropa prefiere usted? Indique sus preferencias después de leer (*after reading*) la descripción del estudio de Vilma (foto).

_______ siempre ropa cómoda e informal
_______ ropa elegante de alta costura y de tiendas exclusivas
_______ ropa variada, a veces informal, a veces elegante
_______ ropa muy juvenil y deportiva (*youthful and sporty*)

«En el estudio de Vilma, vemos (*we see*) vestidos (*costumes*) de épocas históricas para obras de teatro (*plays*), vestidos de alta costura (*designer*) y su nueva línea de prendas (*garments*) reversibles de cuero.»

Este segmento

El tema de este programa es la moda. El segmento incluye una entrevista (*interview*) con una diseñadora (*designer*) puertorriqueña.

Vocabulario del segmento

te ves	you look	**acá/allá**	here/there
no creas	don't get the idea	**mismo/a**	same
el significado	meaning	**la marca**	brand, label
Cuéntanos.	Tell us (about it).	**hablé**	I spoke
primero vamos	first let's go	**Ropajes**	Apparel
el clima	climate	**desarrollamos**	we develop
la playa	beach	**la enseñanza**	teaching
Colón llegó	Columbus arrived	**todo el mundo**	everybody
el segundo viaje	second voyage		

Estrategia

You can pick up vocabulary that will be in the segment by reading the photo caption, **Este segmento,** and **Vocabulario del segmento,** doing **Antes de mirar,** and scanning **Después de mirar** before you watch the segment!

Después de mirar

A. ¿Está claro? Las siguientes oraciones son falsas. Corríjalas (*Correct them*), según el video.

1. Ana y Víctor están hoy en Puerto Rico.
2. Víctor lleva una camiseta hoy porque va (*he's going*) a la playa.
3. Solo hay influencia de España en Puerto Rico.
4. El estilo de Ropajes Inc. es juvenil e informal.

B. Un poco más. Empareje (*Match*) las ideas de la **Columna A** con la forma correcta de una palabra de la **Columna B.**

COLUMNA A	COLUMNA B
1. ____ el clima de Puerto Rico	**a.** bonito
2. ____ las playas de Puerto Rico	**b.** relajado (*relaxed*)
3. ____ la apariencia de Víctor hoy, en camiseta	**c.** reversible
4. ____ la diseñadora Vilma Martínez	**d.** fundador (*founder*)
5. ____ las prendas de cuero de la nueva línea	**e.** suave (*mild*)

C. Y ahora, ustedes. En parejas, imaginen que son los presentadores del programa de hoy sobre la ropa y la moda. Sigan el modelo de este segmento y hagan una breve introducción al programa, incluyendo (*including*):

- un saludo + una presentación personal + el lugar donde ustedes están
- un comentario informal sobre la ropa de uno de ustedes o su estilo (o sobre la ropa que ustedes llevan hoy o su propio [*own*] estilo). (Usen vocabulario de **Antes de mirar** y de **Vocabulario: Preparación.**)
- una breve introducción al próximo (*upcoming*) reportaje sobre la moda o sobre una tienda en particular

PRONUNCIACIÓN

Stress and Written Accent Marks (Part 2)

 ¿Recuerda usted?

In the **Pronunciación** section of **Capítulo 3**, you learned that most Spanish words do not need a written accent mark because their pronunciation is completely predictable. Review the two basic rules of Spanish word stress in words that do not have a written accent mark by looking at the examples and completing the rules. The stressed syllable is underlined.

- Examples: **libro, mesa, examen, imagen, eres, gracias**

  A word that ends in a ____, ____, or ____ is stressed on the next-to-last syllable.

- Examples: **bailar, usted, papel, estoy**

  A word that ends in ____________________ is stressed on the last syllable.

In Spanish, the written accent mark is used in the following situations.

1. A written accent mark is needed when a word does not follow the two basic rules reviewed in **¿Recuerda usted?**

   Look at the words in this group.

ta-bú	a-le-mán	in-glés
ca-fé	na-ción	es-tás

   The preceding words end in a vowel, **-n,** or **-s,** so one would predict that they would be stressed on the *next-to-last syllable* (**la penúltima sílaba**). But the written accent mark shows that they are in fact accented on the *last syllable* (**la última sílaba**).

   Now look at the words in this group.

   lá-piz   dó-lar   ál-bum   á-gil   dó-cil

   The preceding words end in a consonant (other than **-n** or **-s**), so one would predict that they would be stressed on the last syllable. But the written accent mark shows that they are in fact accented on the next-to-last syllable.

2. All words that are stressed on the *third-to-last syllable* (**la antepenúltima sílaba**) must have a written accent mark, regardless of which letter they end in. These are called **palabras esdrújulas.**

   bo-lí-gra-fo   ma-trí-cu-la   ma-te-má-ti-cas

3. When two consecutive vowels do not form a diphthong (see **Pronunciación, Cap. 2**), the weak vowel (**i, u**) that receives the spoken stress will have a written accent mark. This pattern is very frequent in words that end in **-ía.**

Ma-rí-a	po-li-cí-a	as-tro-no-mí-a
dí-a	bio-lo-gí-a	

¡OJO!

Contrast the pronunciation of the words in **Point 3.** with the following words in which the vowels **i** and **a** *do* form a diphthong: **Patricia, Francia, infancia, distancia.**

4. Accent marks are also added to preserve the original stress of a word when the word is changed in some way, for example, when it becomes plural. Here are some examples:

   joven → jóvenes   examen → exámenes

   You will learn about other situations in which accents are added for this reason in upcoming chapters.

¡OJO!

As you know, the accent mark is sometimes dropped when a word is made plural.

pantalón → pantalones
francés → franceses
nación → naciones

5. Some one-syllable words have accents to distinguish them from other words that are pronounced the same but have different meanings. This type of accent does not follow the general rules of accentuation; it is called the *diacritic accent* (**el acento diacrítico**). Here are some of the most common examples.

   él (*he*) / el (*the*)
   sí (*yes*) / si (*if*)
   tú (*you*) / tu (*your*)
   mí (*me*) / mi (*my*)

6. Interrogative and exclamatory words have a written accent on the stressed vowel. For example:

   ¿quién?
   ¿dónde?
   ¡Qué ganga! (*What a bargain!*)

Práctica

A. Sílabas. The following words have been separated into syllables for you. Read them aloud, paying careful attention to where the spoken stress should fall. Don't worry about the meaning of words you haven't heard before. The rules you have learned will help you pronounce them correctly.

1.	a-quí	pa-pá	a-diós	bus-qué
2.	prác-ti-co	mur-cié-la-go	te-lé-fo-no	ar-chi-pié-la-go
3.	Ji-mé-nez	Ro-drí-guez	Pé-rez	Gó-mez
4.	si-co-lo-gí-a	so-cio-lo-gí-a	sa-bi-du-rí-a	e-ner-gí-a
5.	his-to-ria	te-ra-pia	Pre-to-ria	me-mo-ria

B. Reglas. ***(Rules.)*** Indicate the stressed vowel of each word in the following list. Explain your answer by referring to the rules given on page 112.

1. exámenes
2. lápiz
3. necesitar
4. perezoso
5. actitud
6. acciones
7. dólares
8. francés
9. están
10. hombre
11. peso
12. mujer
13. plástico
14. María
15. Rodríguez
16. Patricia

GRAMÁTICA

¿Recuerda usted?

You learned the four forms of the demonstrative adjective **este** in **Gramática 5 (Cap. 3).** Review them now by completing these phrases.

1. est_____ pantalones **2.** est_____ falda **3.** est_____ blusas **4.** est_____ abrigo

9 Pointing Out People and Things

Demonstrative Adjectives (Part 2) and Pronouns

Gramática en acción: Suéteres a buenos precios

Susana busca un suéter con su amigo Jorge.

SUSANA: ¿Cuánto cuesta este suéter?

VENDEDOR: Bueno, ese que usted tiene en la mano cuesta 800 quetzales. Este aquí cuesta 700 quetzales.

SUSANA: ¡Qué caros!

VENDEDOR: Es que todos son de pura lana. Mire aquellos suéteres de rayas sobre aquella mesa. Solo cuestan 300 quetzales. Son acrílicos.

SUSANA: Muchas gracias.

Comprensión

¿Quién habla, Susana, su amigo Jorge o el vendedor?

1. «Estos suéteres de rayas son bonitos. Y solo cuestan 300 quetzales.»
2. «Los suéteres en aquella mesa no son de pura lana.»
3. «Compro este suéter. Me gusta la ropa de lana.»
4. «Estos suéteres acrílicos son más baratos que aquellos de lana.»

Demonstrative Adjectives / **Los adjetivos demostrativos**

Singular			**Plural**			Adverbs / **Los adverbios**
this	**este abrigo**	**esta gorra**	these	**estos abrigos**	**estas gorras**	**aquí** = here
that	**ese abrigo**	**esa gorra**	those	**esos abrigos**	**esas gorras**	**allí** = there
	aquel abrigo	**aquella gorra**		**aquellos abrigos**	**aquellas gorras**	**allá** = way over there

¡OJO!

Note that the final **-e** in the singular forms **este** and **ese** changes to an **-o-** in the plural: **estos, esos.**

a demonstrative adjective / **un adjetivo demostrativo** = an adjective used to indicate a particular person, place, thing, or idea

Sweaters at good prices *Susana is looking for a sweater with her friend Jorge. SUSANA: How much is this sweater? SALESMAN: Well, that one that you have in your hand costs 800 quetzales. This one here costs 700 quetzales. SUSANA: (They're) So expensive! SALESMAN: It's because they're all made of pure wool. Take a look at those striped sweaters on that table (over there). They only cost 300 quetzales. They're acrylic. SUSANA: Thanks a lot.*

1. **Agreement**
Demonstrative adjectives are used to indicate a specific noun or nouns. In Spanish, **los adjetivos demostrativos** precede the nouns they modify. They also agree in number and gender with the nouns.

2. **Using *este* and *ese***
Forms of **este** (*this, these*) and **ese** (*that, those*) are used just like *this/these* and *that/those* in English.

- When two people are speaking, forms of **este** are used to refer to nouns that are close to the speaker in space or time.
- Forms of **ese** refer to nouns that are close to the person spoken *to*.
- When the noun is distant from both speakers, forms of **ese** are used.

3. **Using *ese* and *aquel***
There are two ways to say *that/those* in Spanish.

- Forms of **ese** refer to nouns that are not close to the speaker(s) (point 2).
- Forms of **aquel** refer to nouns that are even farther away from the speaker(s).

an adverb / **un adverbio** = a word (such as *very* and *quickly*) that modifies a verb, adjective, or another adverb

In the chart on page 114, the *adverbs* (**los adverbios**) **aquí, allí,** and **allá** are associated with the forms of **este, ese,** and **aquel,** respectively. However, it is not obligatory to use these words with the demonstrative adjectives.

<u>Este</u> niño es mi hijo. <u>Ese</u> joven allí es mi otro hijo. Y <u>aquel</u> señor allá es mi esposo.
This boy is my son. That young man there is my other son. And that man way over there is my husband.

Demonstrative Pronouns / **Los pronombres demostrativos**

1. **Demonstrative Pronouns**
In English, the *demonstrative pronouns* are the demonstrative adjective + the word *one*(*s*), as in the examples to the right. In Spanish, **los pronombres demostrativos** are the same as demonstrative adjectives, except that the noun is not used and there is no direct equivalent for English *one*(*s*).

—¿Te gusta <u>aquella</u> casa allá?
—¿Cuál?
—<u>**Aquella**</u>, la de las ventanas grandes.
—Sí, me gusta mucho. Mucho más que <u>esta</u>...

*"Do you like **that** house way over there?"*
"Which one?"
*"**That one,** the one with the big windows."*
*"Yes, I like it a lot. A lot more than **this one** . . ."*

2. **Agreement**
In Spanish, demonstrative pronouns agree in gender and number with the noun they are replacing.

<u>ese</u> libro, en la mesa → <u>ese</u> en la mesa
<u>aquellos</u> señores, en el café → <u>aquellos</u> en el café

3. **Neuter Demonstrative Pronouns**
Use the neuter demonstrative pronouns **esto, eso,** and **aquello** to refer to as yet unidentified objects or to a whole idea, concept, or situation.

¿Qué es <u>esto</u>?
What is this?

<u>Eso</u> es todo.
That's it. / That's all.

¡<u>Aquello</u> es terrible!
That's terrible!

¡OJO!

<u>Esto</u> es una mochila. (to identify in general)
This is a backpack.

<u>Esta</u> es mi mochila. (to identify one out of a group)
This (*one*) *is my backpack.*

Summary of Demonstratives

near	**este/a, estos/as, esto**
far	**ese/a, esos/as, eso**
farther	**aquel(la), aquellos/as, aquello**

Práctica y comunicación

A. Una cuestión de perspectiva

Paso 1. Autoprueba. Empareje (*Match*) las palabras con su significado apropiado en inglés.

1. estas	**a.** *that*
2. aquellos	**b.** *those* (*over there*)
3. ese	**c.** *these*
4. esas	**d.** *this*
5. este	**e.** *those*

Paso 2. Autoprueba. Ahora empareje los siguientes demostrativos con los objetos apropiados, según la perspectiva de la mujer.

1. esta _______
2. estas _______
3. este _______
4. aquel _______
5. aquellos _______
6. esos _______

Paso 3. Ahora, en parejas, desde (*from*) el lugar donde ustedes están, usen los siguientes demostrativos para identificar los objetos de la clase.

1. estos _______ y esta _______
2. ese _______ y esas _______
3. aquel _______ y aquellos _______

B. Cambios (*Changes*)

Paso 1. Cambie (*Change*) las formas de **este** por **ese** y añada (*add*) **también,** según el modelo.

MODELO: Este abrigo es muy grande. →
Ese abrigo **también** es muy grande.

1. Esta falda es muy corta.
2. Este reloj es muy caro.
3. Este bolso es muy bonito.
4. Esta corbata es muy fea.

Paso 2. Ahora cambie **este** por **aquel** y añada **allá** también.

MODELO: Este abrigo es muy grande. →
Aquel abrigo **allá también** es muy grande.

Paso 3. Finalmente, cambie las oraciones del singular al plural.

MODELO: Este abrigo es muy grande. →
Est**os** abrigo**s** **son** muy grande**s**.

***Prác. A: Answers, Paso 1. 1.** c **2.** b **3.** a **4.** e **5.** d*
***Answers, Paso 2. 1.** gorra **2.** chanclas **3.** traje de baño **4.** suéter **5.** zapatos/tenis **6.** pantalones*

C. Situaciones. Empareje (*Match*) cada (*each*) situación de la columna A con un comentario de la columna B.

	A		B
1.	_____ Aquí hay un regalo para usted.	**a.**	¡Eso es un desastre!
2.	_____ Ocurre un accidente de coche.	**b.**	¡Eso es magnífico!
3.	_____ No hay clases mañana.	**c.**	¿Qué es esto?
4.	_____ La matrícula cuesta más este semestre/ trimestre.	**d.**	¡Eso es terrible!
5.	_____ Usted tiene A en su examen de español.		

D. En una tienda

Paso 1. Complete el siguiente diálogo con los demostrativos apropiados. Asuma (*Take*) el punto de vista (*point of view*) del vendedor y el cliente.

VENDEDOR: ¿Qué suéter le gusta? ¿_____[1] rojo que está aquí?

CLIENTE: No, el rojo no.

VENDEDOR: ¿_____[2] suéter amarillo?

CLIENTE: No, tampoco[a] el amarillo. ¡Me gusta _____[3] anaranjado de allá!

[a]No... *No, not* [*the yellow one*] *either*

Paso 2. Ahora indique el demostrativo apropiado para los pantalones de cada maniquí, según la perspectiva de los dos hombres.

1. _____ pantalones negros
2. _____ pantalones azules
3. _____ pantalones color kaki

E. En la alcoba (*bedroom*) de Ernesto. Working with a partner, imagine that you are the person depicted in the drawing, who is looking into Ernesto's bedroom. Some objects and items of clothing are close to you, some are a bit farther away, and some are at the other end of the room. Describe them as accurately as you can, using the appropriate demonstrative adjectives and all of the vocabulary you have learned so far.

MODELOS: _____ gato es blanco y
_____ gato es negro.
_____ libro es verde.

Vocabulario útil

la cama	bed
el estante	book shelf
la mesita	nightstand

F. En el salón de clase

Paso 1. En parejas, usen demostrativos para identificar cinco pares (*pairs*) de personas o cosas en el salón de clase.

MODELO: Esta joven es rubia. Aquella joven cerca de la puerta es morena.

Paso 2. Ahora compartan (*share*) sus oraciones con el resto de la clase. Sus compañeros deben adivinar (*guess*) a qué personas u objetos se refieren ustedes.

Vocabulario útil

cerca de	near
lejos de	far from

¿Recuerda usted?

You began using the singular forms of the verb **tener** in **Capítulo 3.** Review them by completing the following verb forms.

1. tú t__nes **2.** yo te__o **3.** Julio t__ne

You will learn about similar patterns in **Gramática 10.**

10 Expressing Actions and States

Tener, venir, poder, preferir, querer; Some Idioms with tener

Gramática en acción: Un mensaje telefónico

Hola, Jorge. Soy Jaqui. Esta tarde tengo que comprar un regalo para Miguel y no quiero ir sola. ¿Vienes conmigo? Podemos encontrarnos en ese centro comercial que está cerca de tu casa. O si prefieres, puedo pasar por ti antes. ¡Llámame!

Comprensión

Ahora vuelva a contar (*retell*) el mensaje de Jaqui. Estas formas verbales son como **tiene**.

1. Jaqui tien____ que comprar un regalo.
2. Quier____ ir de compras con Jorge.
3. Pued____ encontrarse con Jorge en el centro comercial.
4. O si Jorge prefier____, Jaqui pued____ pasar por la casa de él.

Tener, venir, poder, preferir, querer

Remember that infinitives in **red and underlined** are conjugated in their entirety in Appendix 5.

tener (*to have*)		**venir** (*to come*)		**poder** (*to be able, can*)		**preferir** (*to prefer*)		**querer** (*to want*)	
tengo	tenemos	vengo	venimos	puedo	podemos	prefiero	preferimos	quiero	queremos
tienes	tenéis	vienes	venís	puedes	podéis	prefieres	preferís	quieres	queréis
tiene	tienen	viene	vienen	puede	pueden	prefiere	prefieren	quiere	quieren

The five verbs shown on the preceding page share a number of characteristics.

- The **yo** forms of **tener** and **venir** are irregular.
- In other forms of **tener** and **venir,** and in **preferir** and **querer,** when the stem vowel **e** is stressed, it becomes **ie.**
- Similarly, the stem vowel **o** in **poder** becomes **ue** when stressed.

tener: yo **tengo,** tú **tienes (e → ie)…**
venir: yo **vengo,** tú **vienes (e → ie)…**

preferir, querer: (e → ie)

poder: (o → ue)

In vocabulary lists, these changes are shown like this in parentheses after the infinitive: **poder (puedo).**

¡OJO!

The **nosotros** and **vosotros** forms of these verbs do not have changes in the stem vowel because it is not stressed.

A phone message *Hello, Jorge. It's Jaqui. This afternoon I have to buy a gift for Miguel, and I don't want to go alone. Will you come with me? We can meet at that shopping center that's near your house. Or if you prefer, I can come by for you ahead of time. Call me!*

- Like **deber**, **desear**, and **necesitar**, the verbs **poder**, **preferir**, and **querer** can be followed by an infinitive.

Verbs like these are called *stem-changing verbs.* You will learn more verbs of this type in **Gramática 13 (Cap. 5).**

> **¡OJO!**
>
> You will learn to use the verb **hacer** (*to do or to make*) in **Gramática 12 (Cap. 5).** Learn to recognize it in questions and direction lines.

¿**Puedes correr** muy rápido?
Can you run very fast?

¿Qué **quieres/prefieres hacer** hoy?
What do you want/prefer to do today?

Prefiero no ir a la biblioteca el sábado por la noche.
I prefer not to go to the library Saturday night.

Some Idioms with **tener** / **Algunos modismos con *tener***

1. Conditions or States

Many ideas expressed in English with the verb *to be* are expressed in Spanish with *idioms* (**los modismos**) that use **tener.**

Idioms are often different from one language to another. For example, in English, *to pull Mary's leg* usually means *to tease her*, not *to grab her leg and pull it.* In Spanish, *to pull Mary's leg* is **tomarle el pelo a Mary** (lit., *to take hold of Mary's hair*).

You already know one **tener** idiom: **tener... años.** Here are some more **tener** idioms. They all describe a condition or state. Based on the drawings, can you guess what these idioms mean?

> *an idiom* / **un modismo** = an expression whose meaning cannot be inferred from the literal meaning of the words that form it

tener sueño

tener prisa

tener razón

no tener razón

tener miedo (de)

Note that **de** (in **tener miedo de**) can be followed by an infinitive or a noun.

Tengo miedo **de estar** solo aquí. ¡Tengo miedo **de la oscuridad**!
I'm afraid of being alone here. I'm afraid of the dark!

---

2. *Tener* Idioms + *infinitive*

Other **tener** idioms include the following:

> **¡OJO!**
>
> Note that the English equivalent of the infinitive in expressions with **tener ganas** is expressed with *-ing*, not with the infinitive as in Spanish.

tener ganas de + *infinitive* = to feel like (*doing something*)

tener que + *infinitive* = to have to (*do something*)

Tengo ganas de comer.
I feel like eating.

¿No **tiene** usted **que leer** este capítulo?
Don't you have to read this chapter?

Summary of Verbs

tener: tengo, tienes...
venir: vengo, vienes...
poder: puedo...
preferir: prefiero...
querer: quiero...

Práctica y comunicación

A. Esta semana

Paso 1. Autoprueba. Complete los siguientes verbos.

1. p_______do, p_______des, p_______demos
2. pref_______ro, pref_______mos, pref_______ren
3. qu_______ro, qu_______re, qu_______remos
4. t_______o, t_______nes, t_______nemos
5. v _______o, v_______ne, v_______nimos

Paso 2. Ahora complete las siguientes oraciones con uno de los verbos o frases. Debe añadir (*add*) información de sus actividades esta semana y el nombre de un día de la semana. Solo debe repetir el verbo **tener.**

Verbos: poder preferir querer tener tener ganas venir

Esta semana (yo)...

1. ______ clase de _______ (materia) el _______.
2. (no) ______ que estudiar mucho el _______.
3. (no) ___________ estudiar en la biblioteca el _______.
4. _______ (no) estudiar en la biblioteca el _______ por la noche.
5. (no) ___________ de mirar ______ (programa de televisión) el _______.
6. (no) _______ a la universidad el _______ / todos los días.

Paso 3. Finalmente, en parejas, usen sus oraciones del **Paso 2** como base para hacer y contestar preguntas. Luego (*Then*) digan (*tell*) a la clase algo (*something*) que ustedes tienen en común.

MODELO: 1. Tengo clase de chino el martes. →
E1: ¿**Tienes** clase de chino el martes?
E2: No, no estudio chino. Pero **tengo** clase de química el martes.

B. Situaciones

Paso 1. Empareje las situaciones con los comentarios apropiados.

SITUACIONES	COMENTARIOS
1. _____ El niño es muy pequeño.	a. Tengo mucho sueño.
2. _____ En esa casa, hay un perro muy grande.	b. Tengo miedo de ese perro.
3. _____ Son las tres de la mañana.	c. Solo tiene dos años.
4. _____ «Dos y dos son... seis».	d. Tienes razón.
5. _____ «Buenos Aires es la capital de la Argentina».	e. Por eso tienen que estudiar esta noche.
6. _____ Tenemos que estar en el centro a las tres y ya son (*it's already*) las tres menos cuarto.	f. No tienes razón.
7. _____ Mañana estos estudiantes tienen un examen.	g. Por eso tenemos mucha prisa.

Paso 2. ¿Qué quieren decir (*mean*) estos emoticonos en un mensaje de texto? **¡OJO!** Pueden significar más de una idea.

1.  
2. 
3. 
4. 

MODELO: El número 1 quiere decir...

Prác. A, Paso 1: Answers: 1. puedo, puedes, podemos 2. prefiero, preferimos, prefieren 3. quiero, quiere, queremos 4. tengo, tienes, tenemos 5. vengo, viene, venimos

Nota comunicativa

Mucho* y *poco

In this chapter, you learned that words like **aquí, allí,** and **allá** are *adverbs* (**los adverbios**), words that modify a verb (*run **quickly***), an adjective (***very** smart*), or another adverb (***very** quickly*). One very common Spanish adverb that you have used frequently is **muy** (*very*).

In the first chapters of *Puntos de partida*, you have used the words **mucho** and **poco** as both adjectives and adverbs. In English and in Spanish, adverbs are invariable in form. Spanish adjectives, however, agree in gender and number with the words they modify, as you know.

ADVERBIOS:	**mucho**	Rosa estudia **mucho.**	*Rosa studies a lot.*
	poco	Julio come **poco.**	*Julio doesn't eat much.*
ADJETIVOS:	**mucho/a(s)**	Rosa tiene **mucha** ropa. Tiene **muchos** zapatos.	*Rosa has a lot of clothes.* *She has a lot of shoes.*
	poco/a(s)	Julio come **poca** pasta. Come **pocos** postres.	*Julio doesn't eat much pasta.* *He eats few desserts.*

You will use these words in **Práctica C**, **D**, and **E.**

Algo sobre...

Tikal

Las ruinas mayas en Tikal (Guatemala) son una de las maravillas[a] de la época prehispánica. Muchos turistas visitan las ruinas. Algunos[b] descendientes de los mayas todavía[c] celebran sus ceremonias religiosas en este sitio.

©Lissa Harrison

El Templo del Gran Jaguar

¿Le gusta visitar sitios históricos en sus vacaciones? ¿O prefiere las ciudades modernas?

[a]*marvels, wonders* [b]*Some* [c]*still*

C. En mi armario (*closet*)

Paso 1. Haga rápidamente una lista aproximada de su ropa y complementos (*accessories*). Escriba (*Write*) **muchos, muchas, pocos, pocas** o **no tengo,** según sea (*is*) apropiado.

	MUCHOS/AS	POCOS/AS	NO TENGO
camisas/blusas			
camisetas			
pantalones largos			
pantalones cortos			
faldas			
vestidos			
chaquetas			
zapatos (de todo tipo)			
botas			
complementos			
¿ ?			

Paso 2. Ahora, en parejas, túrnense para hacer y contestar preguntas sobre cuánta ropa tienen y de qué tipo.

MODELO: E1: ¿Tienes muchas camisas?
E2: No, no tengo muchas camisas. Solo tengo dos o tres. ¿Y tú?
E1: Yo tengo más de 6.

Paso 3. Para terminar, hagan una evaluación mutua de su vestuario (*wardrobe*). ¿Qué es obvio que prefieren llevar o no llevar? ¿Tienen su propio (*own*) estilo? ¿Qué tienen en exceso? ¿Qué tienen que comprar?

Vocabulario útil

demasiados/as	too many
deportivo/a	sporty
más/menos de + *number*	more/less than

D. Circunstancias personales

Paso 1. Choose a partner. Before doing *Paso 1*, try to predict the choices your partner will make in the following circumstances.

MODELO: tener muchos / pocos libros en su cuarto →
Mi compañero tiene muchos libros en su cuarto.

1. estudiar ________ (mucho / poco) este semestre/trimestre
2. querer tomar ________ (muchas / pocas) clases de ciencias en la universidad
3. venir ________ (en coche / en autobús / a pie [*on foot*]) a la universidad todos los días
4. preferir estudiar en ________ (la biblioteca / casa / la residencia)
5. tener ________ (muchas / pocas) cosas con el logotipo (*logo*) de la universidad
6. poder correr (*run*) una milla en ________ (menos / más) de (*than*) cinco minutos
7. tener muchas ganas de ________ (estudiar / bailar) esta noche
8. tener ________ (mucha / poca) ropa
9. preferir el ________ (verde / rojo / amarillo)
10. preferir usar ________ (botas / zapatos / sandalias / tenis / chanclas)

Paso 2. Now, using tag questions (**preguntas coletilla**), ask your partner questions to find out if you guessed correctly in **Paso 1.**

MODELO: E1: Tienes muchos libros en tu cuarto, ¿verdad?
E2: Sí, tengo muchos libros en mi cuarto. (No, tengo pocos libros.)

E. Intercambios. En parejas, túrnense para entrevistarse (*take turns interviewing each other*) sobre los siguientes temas (*topics*). Deben añadir (*add*) una pregunta original para cada (*each*) verbo.

VERBO INICIAL	OPCIONES
preferir	¿los gatos o los perros? ¿mirar una película (*movie*) en casa o en el cine (*movie theater*)? ¿la ropa elegante o la ropa cómoda? ¿ ?
tener	¿mucho dinero o muchas deudas (*debts*)? ¿una familia grande o pequeña? ¿sueño en clase con frecuencia? ¿ ?
venir	¿a clase muy tarde o temprano? ¿de una familia anglosajona, hispana o de otro origen? ¿a clase todos los días? ¿ ?
(¿qué?) querer	¿comprar esta semana? ¿comprar en el futuro? ¿mirar en la tele esta noche? ¿ ?
poder	¿hablar una lengua extranjera? ¿vivir sin (*without*) dinero? ¿escribir poemas? ¿ ?

F. ¿Deseos u obligaciones? En parejas, usen **tener ganas de** + ***infinitivo*** y **tener que** + ***infinitivo*** para entrevistarse sobre su semana.

MODELOS: ¿Qué tienes ganas de comer hoy?
¿Qué tienes que hacer esta noche?

ACCIONES POSIBLES

aprender el vocabulario sobre la ropa
bailar salsa/reguetón
dormir to sleep
hablar con ______ **(una persona)**
mirar ______ **(una serie o una película** [*movie*]**)**
trabajar

Vocabulario útil

esta noche
este fin de semana
este ________ **(día de la semana)**

11 Expressing Destination and Future Actions

Ir; The Contraction **al**; **Ir** + **a** + infinitive

Gramática en acción: ¿Adónde vas?

©Diego Lezama/Lonely Planet Images/Getty Images

El Mercado Central, Ciudad de Guatemala

Rosa y Casandra son compañeras de casa.

CASANDRA: ¿Adónde vas?
ROSA: Voy al Mercado Central.
CASANDRA: ¿Qué vas a comprar allá?
ROSA: Voy a comprar unos regalos para mi familia en Nueva Jersey.
CASANDRA: ¿Vas a viajar a los Estados Unidos pronto?
ROSA: Sí, en quince días. ¿Por qué no vienes conmigo al Mercado?
CASANDRA: ¡Sí! Vamos.

Comprensión

¿Cierto o falso? Corrija las oraciones falsas.

	CIERTO	FALSO
1. Rosa va a estudiar.	☐	☐
2. Rosa va a comprar regalos.	☐	☐
3. Casandra va a los Estados Unidos.	☐	☐

The Verb **ir** / **El verbo *ir***

ir (*to go*)			
(yo)	voy	(nosotros/as)	vamos
(tú)	vas	(vosotros/as)	vais
(usted, él, ella)	va	(ustedes, ellos/as)	van

The irregular Spanish verb **ir** expresses *to go*.

Rosa **va** al centro.
Rosa is going downtown.
¿Adónde **vas** tú?
Where are you going?

The first person plural of **ir, vamos** (*we go, are going, do go*), is also used to express *let's go*.

Vamos a clase ahora mismo.
Let's go to class right now.

The Contraction **al** / **La contracción *al***

As you can see in the preceding examples, the verb **ir** is often used with the preposition **a** to indicate where someone is going (to).

When **a** is followed by **el,** it contracts to **al,** just as **de + el → del (Capítulo 3). Al** and **del** are the only *contractions* (**las contracciones**) in Spanish.

a + el → al

Voy **al** centro comercial.
I'm going to the mall.

Vamos a la tienda.
We're going to the store.

Where are you going? *Rosa and Casandra are housemates.* ***CASSANDRA:*** *Where are you going?* ***ROSA:*** *I'm going to the Central Market.* ***CASSANDRA:*** *What are you going to buy there?* ***ROSA:*** *I'm going to buy some presents for my family in New Jersey.* ***CASSANDRA:*** *Are you going to travel to the United States soon?* ***ROSA:*** *Yes, in two weeks. Why don't you come to the Market with me?* ***CASSANDRA:*** *Yes! Let's go.*

Using **ir** to Talk About the Future / **El uso de *ir* para hablar del futuro**

You can use the verb **ir** + **a** + *infinitive* to talk about the future in Spanish.

<u>**Van a**</u> **venir** a la fiesta esta noche.
They're coming to the party tonight.
<u>**Voy a**</u> **comer** en un restaurante en el centro.
I'm going to eat at a downtown restaurant.

¡OJO!

This structure is like **aprender** + **a** + *infinitive,* which you learned in **Gramática 8 (Cap. 3).**

This use of the preposition **a** is different from the use of **a** to indicate where someone is going. Compare these two sentences.

<u>**Voy al**</u> **centro** para comer.
I'm going downtown *to eat.*

<u>**Voy a**</u> **ir** <u>**al**</u> **centro** para comer.
I'm going to go downtown to eat.

Práctica y comunicación

Summary of *ir*

voy, vas...
<u>ir</u> + a + infinitivo

A. Mañana

Paso 1. Autoprueba. Complete las siguientes frases con formas del verbo **ir.**

1. tú _______
2. nosotros _______
3. yo _______
4. ustedes _______
5. usted _______

Paso 2. Ahora use las siguientes frases para expresar lo que (*what*) usted va a hacer o no hacer mañana.

MODELO: estudiar → Mañana **no voy a** estudiar.

1. ir de compras (*to go shopping*)
2. comer en la cafetería de la universidad
3. estudiar en la biblioteca
4. escribir e-mails
5. venir a la clase de español
6. poder hacer toda mi tarea (*homework*)
7. bailar en una discoteca

Paso 3. Ahora use las frases del **Paso 2** para entrevistar (*interview*) a un compañero o una compañera.

MODELO: estudiar → ¿**Vas a** estudiar mañana?

B. ¿Adónde van de compras? Haga oraciones completas, usando (*using*) **ir. ¡OJO! a** + **el** → **al.**

MODELO: Marta / el centro → Marta **va al** centro.

1. tú y yo / la *boutique* Regalitos
2. Francisco / el almacén Goya
3. Juan y Raúl / el centro comercial
4. (tú) / el Mercado Central
5. usted / la tienda Gómez
6. yo / ¿ ?

C. ¿Adónde va usted si... ? ¿Cuántas oraciones puede hacer?

Vocabulario útil

el cine	movie theater
el mercadillo	flea market

Me gusta	+	leer. ir de compras. buscar gangas y regatear. hablar con mis amigos. comer en restaurantes. mirar programas de detectives. ver películas (*movies*).	+	Por eso voy a _______.

***Prác. A, Paso 1: Answers: 1.** vas **2.** vamos **3.** voy **4.** van **5.** va*

D. Intercambios

Paso 1. En parejas, túrnense para hacer y contestar preguntas sobre sus planes para el fin de semana. Aquí hay unas actividades posibles. Traten de obtener (*Try to get*) mucha información. **¡OJO! ¿adónde?** = *where to?*

MODELO: ir de compras → **¿Vas a ir** de compras **este fin de semana**? **¿Adónde** vas a ir? **¿Por qué** vas a ese centro comercial? **¿Qué** vas a comprar?

1. ir de compras
2. leer una novela
3. asistir a un concierto
4. estudiar para un examen
5. ir a una fiesta
6. escribir una carta
7. ir a bailar
8. escribir un ensayo (*essay*)
9. practicar un deporte (*sport*)
10. mirar mucho la televisión

Paso 2. Ahora digan (*tell*) al resto de la clase un plan que ustedes tienen en común y otra actividad para la que (*which*) tienen distintos planes.

Algo sobre...

las compras en Guatemala y Honduras

Igual que[a] en los Estados Unidos, en el mundo hispano abundan[b] los centros comerciales. De hecho,[c] en algunos[d] países, como en Guatemala y Honduras, se llaman «malls». Algunos centros comerciales están en el centro de la ciudad y otros en las afueras.[e] En las tiendas de los centros comerciales los precios son siempre fijos.

¿Hay grandes centros comerciales en el centro de su ciudad? ¿O están en las afueras?

[a]Igual... *Similar to* [b]*there are many* [c]De... *In fact* [d]*some* [e]en... *in the outskirts*

City Mall, San Pedro Sula, Honduras. Es probablemente el centro comercial más grande y moderno de todo el país.

Todo junto

A. Lengua y cultura: Pero, ¿no se puede (*can't one*) regatear?

Paso 1. Completar. Complete the following paragraphs about shopping. Give the correct form of the words in parentheses, as suggested by context. When two possibilities are given in parentheses, select the correct word.

¿A usted le gusta ir de compras? En ________ (los / las[1]) ciudades hispanas, hay una ________ (grande[2]) variedad de tiendas para ________ (ir[3]) de compras. Hay almacenes, centros comerciales y *boutiques* ________ (elegante[4]), como en ________ (este[5]) país, en donde los precios son siempre ________ (fijo[6]).

También hay tiendas que ________ (vender[7]) un solo[a] producto. Por ejemplo,[b] en una zapatería solo hay zapatos. En español el sufijo **-ería** se usa[c] para ________ (formar[8]) el nombre de la tienda. ¿Dónde ________ (creer[9]) usted que venden papel y ________ (otro[10]) artículos de escritorio[d]? ¿A qué tienda ________ (ir[11]) a ir usted a comprar fruta?

Finalmente, vamos ________ (a / de[12]) mencionar los mercados porque hay muchos en el mundo hispano. En ________ (este[13]) mercados hay ________ (pequeño[14]) tiendas permanentes o temporales[e] donde usted ________ (poder[15]) encontrar[f] desde comida[g] típica hasta artesanías[h] locales o ropa interior. Allí los compradores[i] ________ (regatear[16]) los precios, porque el primer[j] precio casi siempre ________ (ir[17]) a ser muy alto.

[a]*single* [b]Por... *For example* [c]se... *is used* [d]artículos... *writing implements* [e]*temporary* [f]*find* [g]*food* [h]*arts and crafts* [i]*shoppers, buyers* [j]*first*

(Continúa.)

©Diego Lezama/Lonely Planet Images/Getty Images

Una zapatería, en Quetzaltenango, Guatemala

Paso 2. Comprensión. Complete las oraciones.

1. En las ciudades hispanas hay *boutiques*, tiendas, __________, __________ y __________.
2. El nombre de muchas tiendas especializadas en un tipo de producto termina en ______.
3. Una tienda de zapatos se llama una __________.
4. Si a usted le gusta practicar español y regatear, debe ir a __________.

Paso 3. En acción

 En parejas, hagan una lista de los lugares para ir de compras en la ciudad donde ustedes estudian. No olviden (*Don't forget*) su propio *campus*. ¿Hay muchas opciones o pocas? ¿Son fijos los precios en todos los lugares? ¿Tienen una tienda favorita entre todas? Luego (*Then*) comparen sus respuestas con las (*those*) de otras parejas. ¿Hay una tienda favorita de toda la clase?

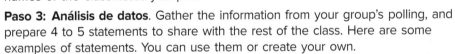

B. Proyecto: Encuesta sobre las preferencias de la clase con relación a la moda y los estilos

Vocabulario útil

el brazo	arm
el labio	lip
la lengua	tongue
nadie	no one
la nariz	nose
la oreja	ear
el piercing	piercing
los pantalones muy bajos (*low*) / **muy estrechos** (*tight*)	
el tatuaje	tattoo

Create a profile of the fashion preferences of your class.

Paso 1. Preparación In groups, think of style and fashion trends; they may be current or not. Express them as phrases, as in the model. Create one to two phrases for each member of your group.

MODELO: llevar un arete en la nariz

Now turn those phrases into questions to poll your classmates. Consider your polling options: **cierto o falso**, open-ended questions, or a series of options.

MODELOS: llevar un arete en la nariz →
¿Llevas un arete en la nariz? / ¿Quieres llevar un arete en la nariz?
¿Cierto o falso para ti? Te gustan los aretes en la nariz.
¿Cuál es tu opinión sobre la idea de llevar aretes en la nariz?
Es bonito / absurdo / irrelevante.

©charlie bonallack/Alamy

¿Le gustan los tatuajes?

Paso 2. Encuesta. Working individually, poll as many of your classmates as possible using the questions you created. Before you start polling, create a table on which to record the answers. Remember to ask for and record the names of the classmates you poll.

Paso 3: Análisis de datos. Gather the information from your group's polling, and prepare 4 to 5 statements to share with the rest of the class. Here are some examples of statements. You can use them or create your own.

1. __________ (número) personas tienen un arete en la nariz, __________ (número) quieren tener un arete en la nariz y __________ (número) no quieren.
2. __________ (número) estudiantes piensan que tener un arete en la nariz es bonito, __________ (número) piensan que es absurdo y __________ (número) piensan que es irrelevante.

¡Ahora, yo!

 **A. Entrevista.** Use de (*as a*) modelo las preguntas y respuestas de la página 103 de este capítulo para hablar de su ropa favorita y su propio estilo de vestir.

 **B. Proyecto audiovisual.** Con las preguntas de la página 103 como modelo, filme una o dos entrevistas con personas que hablan de su estilo de vestir y de sus tiendas de ropa favoritas.

©Onoky Photography/SuperStock

SALU2

«¡Moda, moda, moda!» Segmento 2

Antes de mirar

Conteste las siguientes preguntas.

1. ¿Prefiere usted las camisetas con diseños o mensajes o sin nada (*with nothing* [*on them*])? ¿Tiene una camiseta muy especial?
2. En general, ¿hay marcas (*brands*) que usted prefiere? ¿Qué le gusta especialmente de esas marcas? ¿los diseños? ¿los colores? ¿el precio?

Javier Claudio es dueño (*owner*) de la tienda Icónica, que se especializa en diseños (*designs*) de camisetas.

Este segmento

En este segmento del programa, Laura entrevista a otro diseñador puertorriqueño y los presentadores hablan del tipo de ropa de su preferencia.

Fragmento del guion

Yo creo que en Puerto Rico por la condición del Caribe, que es un clima tropical y es caluroso,[a] pues los jóvenes universitarios mayormente andan[b] siempre en *T-shirts* y mahones,[c] quizás[d] andan también en pantalones cortos, ¿no? y tenis. De hecho, eso fue lo que me llevó a mí a hacer[e] la marca Icónica.

[a]*hot* [b]mayormente... *mostly wear* [c]*jeans (only in Puerto Rico)* [d]*maybe* [e]De... *In fact, that's what motivated me to create*

Vocabulario del segmento

se hace	becomes	**nos recuerda**	it reminds us
como dice el nombre	as the name suggests	**importantísimos**	very important
nos representan	represent us	**¡Ay, mi'jo!**	Oh, boy!
la venta	sale	**en todas partes**	everywhere
¡Bien padres!	Very cool!	**vestida impecablemente**	impeccably dressed

Después de mirar

A. ¿Está claro? ¿Quién dice (*says*) las siguientes oraciones? Conteste con la inicial del nombre de la persona: Ana (**A**), Javier (**J**), Laura (**L**) o Víctor (**V**).

1. «...donde el viejo San Juan se hace global con los diseños de camisetas.»
2. «...como dice el nombre, son íconos de la cultura popular, ... »
3. «Icónica es otro ejemplo (*example*) de globalización, en este caso de productos hispanos.»
4. «Nos recuerda que en el mundo de la alta costura (*high fashion*) hay nombres hispanos importantísimos, ... »
5. «El próximo segmento nos lleva a una tienda aquí en Los Ángeles.»

B. Un poco más. Conteste las siguientes preguntas.

1. ¿Cómo se llama la tienda de Javier? ¿Por qué se llama así (*like that*)?
2. ¿Qué diseñadores importantes nombra Ana?
3. ¿Dónde compra ropa Ana?

C. Y ahora, ustedes. En parejas, hablen de los estilos o marcas de ropa que se mencionan en el programa y de los estilos o marcas que ustedes prefieren. Expliquen por qué. Luego digan (*tell*) a la clase una cosa que ustedes tienen en común o una en que son muy diferentes.

MUNDO HISPANO

Enfoque cultural: Guatemala y Honduras

Antes de leer

¿Hay mercados en su ciudad o en la zona donde usted vive? ¿Qué se vende (*is sold*) allí: productos locales, artesanías (*arts and crafts*), ropa y zapatos ... ?

Los mercados

En Guatemala y Honduras hay mercados donde se puede comprar artículos de artesanía a buen precio. Son famosos los mercados guatemaltecos de las ciudades de Guatemala, Antigua, Chichicastenango y Quetzaltenango. En estos mercados existe la costumbre[a] del «regateo»: el comprador[b] de un artículo debe negociar el precio con el vendedor.[c] Los vendedores invitan a los compradores a regatear y con frecuencia se escucha decir:[d] « ...pero tiene rebaja, ofrezca un precio[e]».

En Guatemala, los tejidos[f] de tradición maya son especialmente populares entre los turistas por su colorido y belleza.[g] En Honduras, además de[h] artesanías, los turistas también compran café, ron,[i] vainilla, cerámica y puros.[j]

[a]*custom* [b]*buyer, customer* [c]*seller* [d]se... *one hears people say* [e]pero... *but a discount is possible, make an offer* [f]*weavings* [g]por... *for their colors and beauty* [h]además... *besides* [i]*rum* [j]*cigars*

En otros países hispanos

- **En todo el mundo hispanohablante** En los países hispanohablantes es común encontrar[a] ropa con tallas[b] similares a las[c] de los Estados Unidos (XS, S, M, L y XL). Pero si la ropa es hecha[d] en un país hispano, se usan las iniciales de los adjetivos en español:

  CH = chico (México y Latinoamérica)
  P = pequeño (España)
  M = mediano
  G = grande
  EG = extra grande

- En varios países los números de las tallas de zapatos van del 35 al 46: 36–39 son comunes para las mujeres y 40–43 para los hombres.
- **En los países andinos** En estos países hay una lana excelente que viene de los camélidos[e] de la región: la llama, la vicuña, la alpaca y el guanaco. La lana de estos animales es de excelente calidad y se utiliza para hacer[f] suéteres, gorras,[g] guantes,[h] ponchos, mantas,[i] etcétera.

[a]*to find* [b]*sizes* [c]*those* [d]*made* [e]*camel-like animals* [f]*making* [g]*knitted caps* [h]*gloves* [i]*blankets*

Ilustración de Diego de Rivera, basada en la creación de la humanidad según el *Popol Vuh*

Un símbolo guatemalteco y hondureño: El *Popol Vuh*

La cultura maya es el sustrato[a] fundamental de Guatemala y Honduras. El *Popol Vuh* es el libro sagrado[b] de los mayas, escrito en el siglo XVI.[c] Es la historia de la creación del mundo, según las creencias[d] mayas.

[a]*essence* [b]*sacred* [c]escrito... *written in the 16th century* [d]*beliefs*

Comprensión

Conteste las siguientes preguntas.

1. ¿En qué ciudades de Guatemala hay mercados de artesanías?
2. ¿Qué es el regateo?
3. ¿Cómo se indica la talla de la ropa y de los zapatos en el mundo hispanohablante?
4. ¿Dónde hay muchos productos de lana?
5. ¿Qué texto describe la creación del mundo, según los mayas?

En acción

Haga una lista de los productos más típicos de la zona donde usted vive. ¿Son productos agrícolas (*agricultural*), artesanales o industriales? ¿Qué productos u objetos compran los turistas cuando visitan la zona? Use el diccionario si no sabe (*you don't know*) las palabras.

Lectura

Antes de leer

Conteste las siguientes preguntas.

1. ¿Qué significa para usted la frase «ropa activa»? ¿Cuándo y dónde es buena idea usar «ropa activa»? ¿Tiene usted ropa de este tipo?
2. Para usted, ¿son importantes estas características en la ropa? ¿Por qué?
   - Repeler los mosquitos.
   - Proveer (*Provide*) protección solar.
   - Ser impermeable.
   - Neutralizar malos olores (*odors*).

Algo[a] más que ropa

por Gregori Dolz

Desde[b] las calles[c] de Manhattan a las colinas nevadas[d] de Aspen, Exofficio proporciona[e] a sus clientes algo más que ropa activa. Parte de sus beneficios ayudan a[f] causas medioambientales[g] como la Conservation Alliance o World Concern, que auxilian[h] a comunidades necesitadas[i] de todo el mundo. Además,[j] sus prendas[k] proporcionan protección contra los insectos, contra el sol[l] y el agua, contra los olores corporales[m] y muchas otras inconveniencias.

» www.exofficio.com

[a]*Something* [b]*From* [c]*streets* [d]colinas... *snowy hills* [e]*offers* [f]ayudan... *help* [g]*environmental* [h]*help* [i]*needy* [j]*In addition* [k]ropa [l]*sun* [m]*bodily*

Comprensión

A. Un resumen del artículo. Las tres oraciones del artículo «Algo más que ropa» describen tres de las características de la compañía Exofficio y de la ropa que vende. Empareje (*Match*) las tres oraciones del artículo con los siguientes resúmenes.

_____ **a.** La compañía dona (*donates*) parte de sus ganancias (*earnings*) a organizaciones conservacionistas y humanitarias.

_____ **b.** La ropa de Exofficio protege (*protects*) contra diversos inconvenientes.

_____ **c.** La ropa de Exofficio es apropiada en muchos lugares diferentes.

B. Usted y Exofficio. Indique la importancia que tienen para usted las siguientes características de Exofficio y la ropa que produce. Luego explique sus respuestas.

	MUY IMPORTANTE	IMPORTANTE	POCO IMPORTANTE	NADA (*NOT*) IMPORTANTE
1. La compañía dona parte de sus ganancias a varias causas.	☐	☐	☐	☐
2. Es ropa protectora.	☐	☐	☐	☐
3. Es «ropa activa» que uno puede usar en muchas situaciones.	☐	☐	☐	☐

 Proyecto: Preferencias de la clase con respecto a la ropa

Paso 1. Haga una lista de tres de las características que usted prefiere en la ropa. Incluya al menos (*Include at least*) un aspecto diferente de los que aparecen (*from those that appear)* en el anuncio de Exofficio. Use el modelo y un diccionario si es necesario.

MODELO: Para mí, la ropa debe ser elegante.

 **Paso 2.** Ahora, en grupos, hagan una lista completa de las características que prefieren los compañeros de su grupo en su ropa.

 **Paso 3.** Comenten las características preferidas por (*by*) los miembros del grupo o de toda la clase. Usen la escala *(scale)* de opinión de **Comprensión B** para evaluar cada (*each*) preferencia. ¿Cuáles son las características más *(most)* importantes? ¿Y las menos (*least*) importantes? ¿Hay tendencias generales?

Textos orales

Dos amigas hacen planes para ir de compras

Vocabulario para escuchar

la llamada	(telephone) call
¿Qué onda?	What's up? (*Mexico*)
conmigo	with me
empiezan	they start
¡Qué padre!	Great! (*Mexico*)

Antes de escuchar

¿Espera usted (*Do you wait for*) las rebajas para ir de compras? ¿Para comprar qué tipo de cosas (*things*) busca usted rebajas? ¿ropa? ¿objetos electrónicos?

Comprensión

A. ¿Cierto o falso? Las siguientes oraciones son falsas. Corríjalas. (*Correct them.*)

1. Las rebajas empiezan hoy.
2. Cristina tiene clases mañana por la mañana.
3. Lidia no tiene clases mañana.
4. Cristina y Lidia van a encontrarse (*meet up*) en la universidad.
5. Lidia no tiene hermanos.

B. Intercambios. Invente la parte que falta (*is missing*), usando expresiones del diálogo.

1. — ______
—Hola, soy yo.

2. — __________
—Muy bien. ¿Y tú?

3. — ______________________
—Perfecto. En Zara, a las 7.

En acción

En parejas, creen (*create*) un pequeño diálogo similar a la conversación de Lidia y Cristina para hacer planes para ir de compras a un centro comercial o a las tiendas locales.

Proyecto en su comunidad

Entreviste a una persona hispana de su universidad o ciudad para informarse de (*find out about*) sus preferencias con respecto a las compras y la moda.

Preguntas posibles

- ¿Cuáles son las tiendas favoritas de esta persona para comprar ropa?
- ¿Hay mercados en su país de origen? ¿Qué venden en los mercados? ¿Se puede regatear allí?
- En su opinión, ¿dónde hay más preocupación por la ropa, en este país o en su país de origen?

Escritura

©Ed Suter/Africa Media Online/The Image Works

Proyecto: Un ensayo sobre los estilos en el campus

¿Cree usted que hay un estilo de ropa que llevan los estudiantes universitarios en general o hay más de un estilo? En su opinión, ¿se ven (*are seen*) en este campus las tendencias de la moda (*fashion*) que predominan en el resto del país?

Antes de escribir

En parejas, hagan una lista del estilo o los estilos de moda típicos en su universidad. Para cada (*each*) estilo, hagan una lista de la ropa más característica del estilo, con una descripción básica (por ejemplo: pantalones elásticos muy estrechos [*tight*]...). La siguiente tabla va a ayudarles (*help you*) a organizar sus ideas. ¡Deben incluir el estilo de los profesores también! Pónganle (*Give*) un nombre a cada estilo si no lo tiene todavía (*yet*). ¡Sean (*Be*) originales!

©Blue Jean Images/Alamy

	El más (*most*) popular	Segundo (*2nd*) más popular	Tercero (*3rd*) más popular
¿Nombre del estilo?			
Personas (estudiantes, profesores, personal administrativo...)			
Descripción de la ropa			

A escribir

Ahora use sus ideas para escribir un ensayo sobre la moda en su universidad. Incluya unas oraciones sobre su propio estilo. Hay más ayuda (*help*) en Connect.

Más ideas para su portafolio

- Busque (*Find*) una fotografía reciente de usted llevando (*wearing*) ropa bonita o interesante en una ocasión especial y descríbala (*describe it*).
- Busque la página web de su tienda o marca favorita y determine si tiene una página en español. Si la tiene (*If it has one*), incluya (*include*) unos detalles de la página.
- Si ha estado jugando (*you have been playing*) Practice Spanish: Study Abroad, en Quest 2 usted pasó su primer día (*spent your first day*) en el Instituto de Lenguas y tuvo que aprender (*had to learn*) información sobre sus clases y el campus. Ahora cree (*create*) un folleto (*brochure*) para estudiantes nuevos sobre la universidad a la que (*that*) asiste usted. Incluya (*Include*) detalles (*details*) sobre las clases y las actividades que ofrece (*that it offers*).

©McGraw-Hill Education

Sugerencia: You are now ready to play Quest 2 in **Practice Spanish: Study Abroad.**

EN RESUMEN En este capítulo

AFTER STUDYING THIS CHAPTER I CAN . . .

- ☐ name items of clothing and use color adjectives (104–105, 107)
- ☐ talk about shopping (104–105)
- ☐ count beyond 100 and express years (109)
- ☐ use demonstratives to describe people and things at different distances (114–115)
- ☐ talk about more actions with a different kind of **-er** and **-ir** verbs (118–119)
- ☐ use very frequent expressions with **tener** (119)
- ☐ talk about where I'm going and what I'm going to do in the near future, using the verb **ir** (123–124)
- ☐ recognize/describe at least 2–3 aspects of Guatemalan and Honduran cultures

Gramática en breve

9. Demonstrative Adjectives and Pronouns

this → *these*	*that/those*	*that/those* (*over there*)
este → estos	**ese → esos**	**aquel → aquellos**
esta → estas	**esa → esas**	**aquella → aquellas**
neuter: **esto**	neuter: **eso**	neuter: **aquello**

10. *Tener, venir, poder, preferir, querer;* Some Idioms with *tener*

tener: tengo, tienes, tiene, tenemos, tenéis, tienen

venir: vengo, vienes, viene, venimos, venís, vienen

poder: puedo, puedes, puede, podemos, podéis, pueden

preferir: prefiero, prefieres, prefiere, preferimos, preferís, prefieren

querer: quiero, quieres, quiere, queremos, queréis, quieren

Idioms with **tener:**

tener miedo de / prisa / razón / sueño / no tener razón

tener ganas de + *inf.* **/ que** + *inf.*

11. *Ir;* The Contraction *al; Ir* + *a* + *inf.*

ir: voy, vas, va, vamos, vais, van

a + **el** → **al**

Vocabulario

Remember that changes like **e → ie** and **o → ue** will be shown like this in vocabulary lists.

Los verbos

ir (voy, vas,...)	to go
ir a + *inf.*	to be going to (*do something*)
poder (puedo)	to be able, can
preferir (prefiero)	to prefer
querer (quiero)	to want
tener (tengo, tienes,...)	to have
venir (vengo, vienes,...)	to come

La ropa

llevar	to wear; to carry; to take
usar	to wear; to use
el abrigo	coat
los aretes	earrings
la blusa	blouse
el bolso	purse
las botas	boots
los calcetines	socks
la camisa	shirt
la camiseta	T-shirt
la cartera	wallet; handbag
las chanclas	flip-flops
la chaqueta	jacket (*for a woman or a man*)
el cinturón	belt
la corbata	tie
la falda	skirt
las gafas de sol	sunglasses
la gorra	baseball cap
el impermeable	raincoat
las medias	stockings
los pantalones	pants
los pantalones cortos	shorts
el reloj	watch
la ropa interior	underwear
las sandalias	sandals
el sombrero	hat
la sudadera	sweatshirt
el traje	suit
el traje de baño	swimsuit
el vestido	dress
los zapatos	shoes
la ropa	clothing

Cognados: los *jeans*, el suéter, los tenis

De compras

comprar por internet	to buy online
ir (voy, vas...) de compras	to go shopping
regatear	to haggle; to bargain

Repaso: comprar, vender

la ganga	bargain
el precio (fijo)	(fixed, set) price
las rebajas	sales, reductions
¿cuánto cuesta(n)?	how much does it (do they) cost?
de todo	everything
Es de última moda. / **Está de moda.**	It's trendy (hot).

Las materias

de...	
cuadros	plaid
lunares	polka-dot
rayas	striped
es de...	it is made of . . .
algodón (*m.*)	cotton
cuero	leather
lana	wool
oro	gold
plata	silver
seda	silk
la materia	material

Los lugares

el almacén	department store
el centro	downtown
el centro comercial	shopping mall
el mercado	market(place)
la tienda	shop, store

Cognado: la plaza

Los colores

amarillo/a	yellow
anaranjado/a	orange
azul	blue
blanco/a	white
(de) color café	brown
gris	gray
morado/a	purple
negro/a	black
rojo/a	red
rosado/a	pink
verde	green

Otros sustantivos

el/la chico/a	guy/girl
el examen	exam, test

Cognado: el dólar

Los adjetivos

barato/a	inexpensive
caro/a	expensive
cómodo/a	comfortable
poco/a	little, few
propio/a	own, one's own
último/a	last; latest

Repaso: mucho/a

Los números a partir del 100

ciento, ciento uno/una, ciento dos... ciento noventa y nueve, doscientos/as, trescientos/as, cuatrocientos/as, quinientos/as, seiscientos/as, setecientos/as, ochocientos/as, novecientos/as, mil, un millón (de)

Repaso: cien

Las formas demostrativas

aquel, aquella, aquellos/as	that, those ([way] over there)
aquello (neuter)	that ([way] over there)
ese/a, esos/as	that, those
eso (neuter)	that

Repaso: este/a, esto (neuter)**, estos/as**

Palabras adicionales

¿adónde?	where (to)?
al (a + el)	to the
allá	(way) over there
allí	there
si	if
sobre	about
tener...	
ganas de + *inf.*	to feel like (*doing something*)
miedo (de)	to be afraid (of)
prisa	to be in a hurry
que + *inf.*	to have to (*do something*)
razón	to be right
sueño	to be sleepy
no tener razón	to be wrong
vamos	let's go
¿verdad?, ¿no?	right, don't they (you, and so on)?

Repaso: aquí, mucho (*adv.*), **poco** (*adv.*), **tener... años**

Vocabulario personal

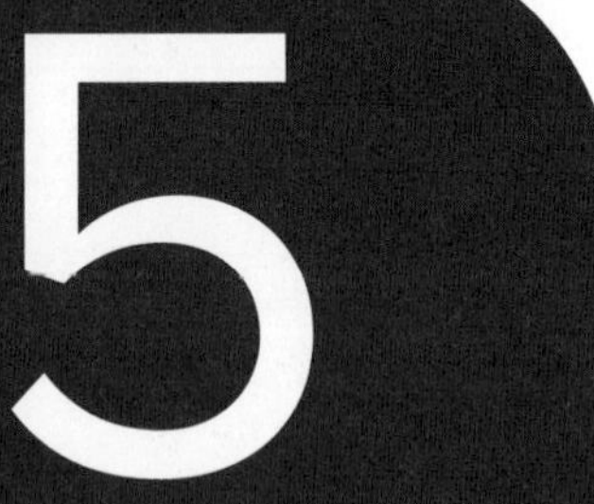

5 En casa

En este capítulo

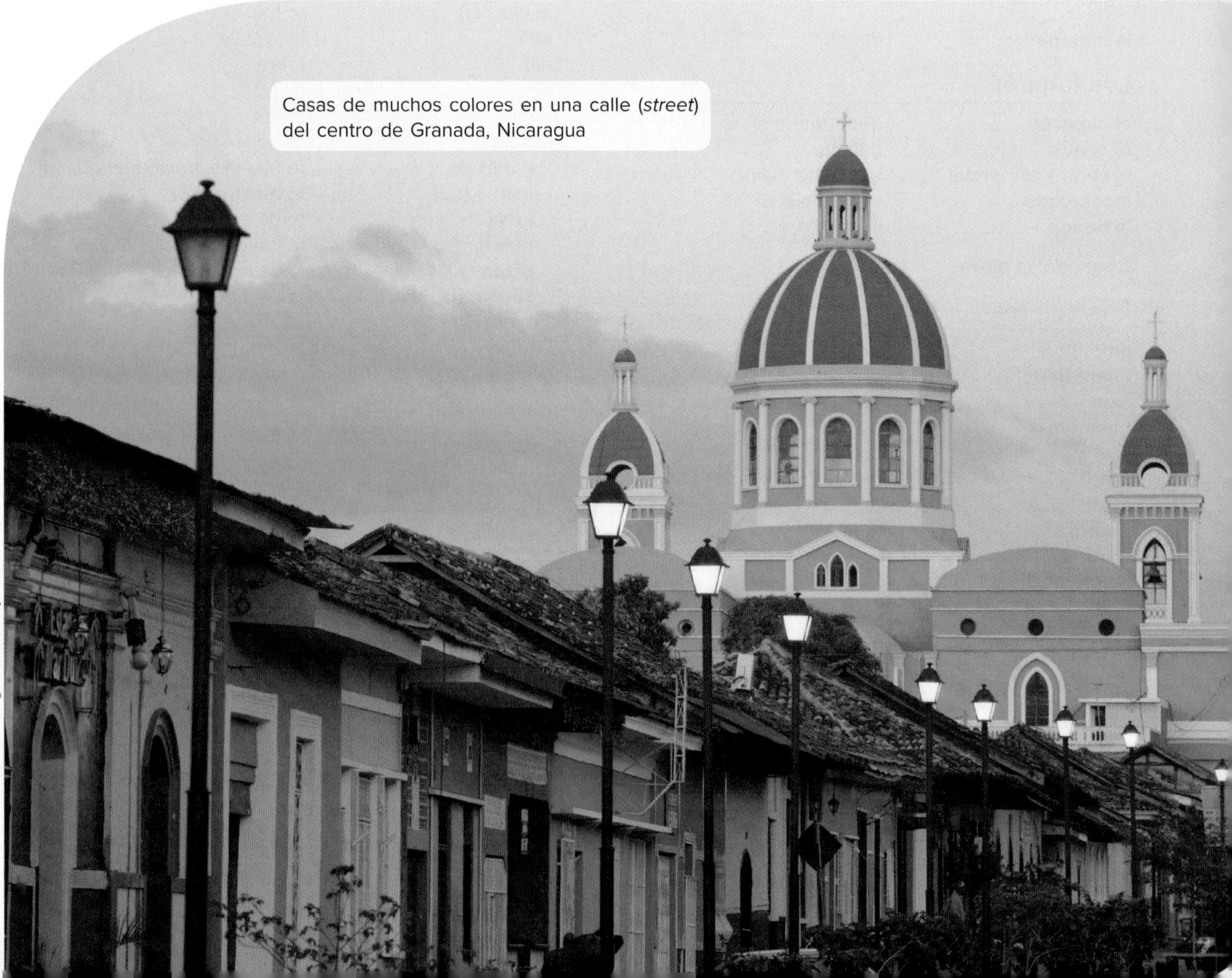

Casas de muchos colores en una calle (*street*) del centro de Granada, Nicaragua

EL SALVADOR

6,3 (coma tres) millones de habitantes

- El Salvador es el país más pequeño de Centroamérica, pero tiene la densidad de población más alta.

NICARAGUA

6,3 (coma tres) millones de habitantes

- Nicaragua tiene diecisiete volcanes y dos lagos inmensos.

ENTREVISTA

- ¿Dónde vive usted? ¿En qué parte de la ciudad? ¿en el centro, en la zona universitaria o en una zona residencial? ¿Vive en una residencia, en una casa o en un apartamento?
- ¿Cómo es su alcoba,[a] grande o pequeña? ¿Tiene un cuarto de baño[b] propio?
- ¿Cómo se siente usted[c] cuando está en casa? (**Me siento...**)

[a]*bedroom* [b]cuarto... *a bathroom* [c]se... *do you feel*

Manuel Gil del Valle contesta las preguntas.

- Vivo en Managua, en un apartamento en una zona residencial que está a 5 kilómetros del centro de la ciudad.
- Es un apartamento muy cómodo, con tres alcobas y dos baños. Mi mujer y yo tenemos la alcoba de matrimonio,[a] que es muy amplia y luminosa y tiene su propio baño. La alcoba de mis hijas también está muy bien, pero no tiene cuarto de baño propio. La otra alcoba es más pequeña y funciona como un estudio.
- Me gusta mucho estar en casa. Allí me siento bien porque puedo descansar y relajarme.[b] Pero sobre todo[c] porque en mi casa estoy con mi mujer y mis hijas, que son lo más importante en mi vida.[d]

[a]alcoba... *master bedroom (lit., of the marriage)* [b]descansar... *rest and relax* [c]sobre... *especially* [d]lo... *the most important thing in my life*

©Purestock/Getty Images

VOCABULARIO: PREPARACIÓN

You can hear the pronunciation of theme vocabulary words and phrases in the Connect eBook.

Los muebles,° los cuartos y otras partes de la casa

Los... *Furniture*

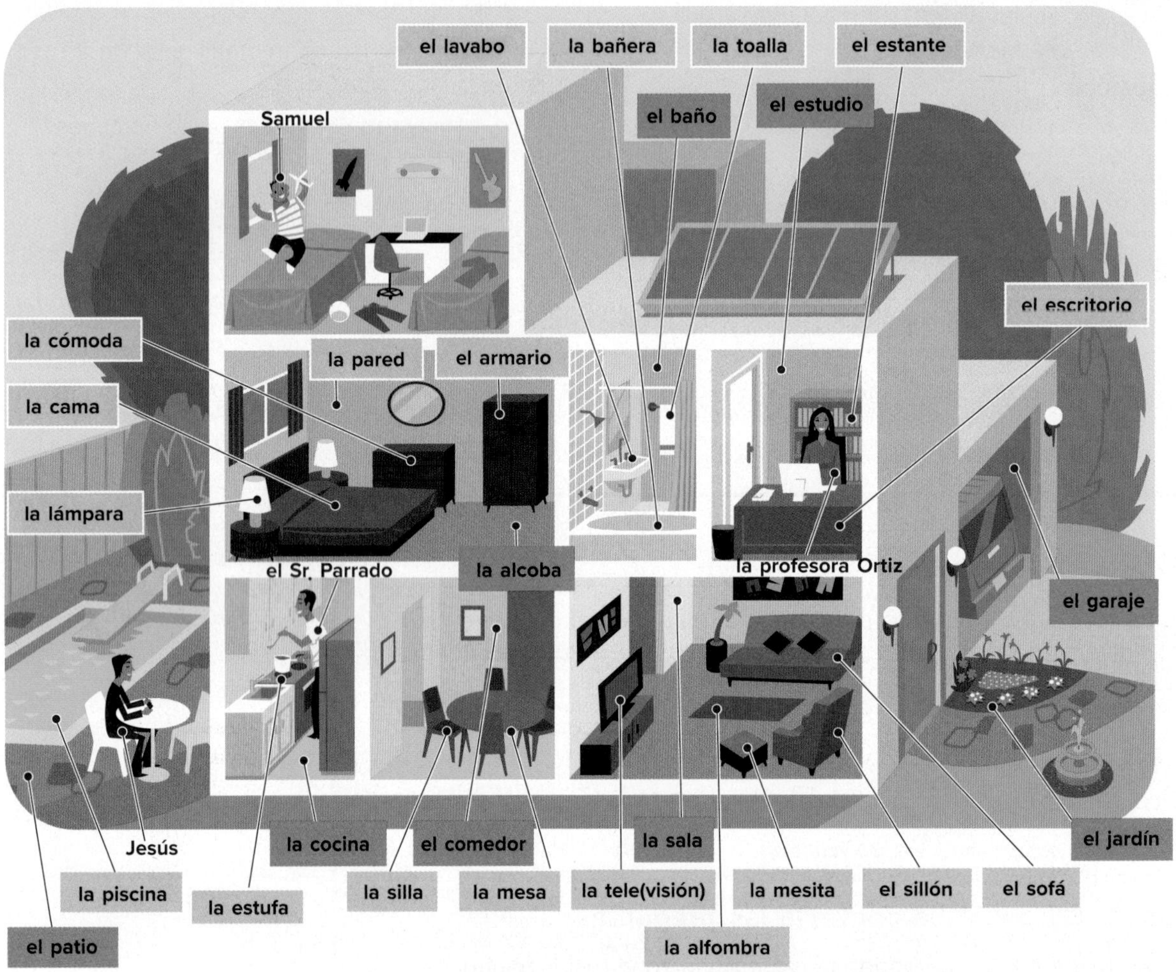

Así se dice

el armario = el ropero
la bañera = la tina
el estudio = el despacho (*Sp.*)
el lavabo = la pileta (*L.A.*)
la piscina = la alberca (*Mex.*), la pileta (*Arg.*)
la sala = el living
la televisión = el televisor

There is great variation in the ways in which Spanish speakers refer to the bedroom. It is called **la habitación** (also a synonym for any room of a house) by many native speakers, **el dormitorio** by Argentines, and **la recámara** by Mexicans.

This is the first group of words you will learn for talking about where you live and the things found in your room, house, or apartment. You will learn additional vocabulary for those topics in* **Capítulos 10 *and* **12**.

Comunicación

A. ¿Dónde? ¿En qué cuarto o parte de la casa hace usted estas actividades? **¡OJO! se** + *verb* = *one (does something).*

1. Es donde se trabaja en la computadora.
2. Es donde se come con toda la familia.
3. Allí se guarda (*one keeps*) el coche.
4. Allí se nada (*one swims*).
5. Allí se duerme (*one sleeps*).
6. Es donde se prepara la comida (*food*).

B. Asociaciones

Paso 1. En parejas, hagan una lista de los muebles o partes de la casa que ustedes asocian con las siguientes actividades.

1. estudiar para un examen
2. dormir la siesta (*to take a nap*) por la tarde
3. pasar (*to spend*) una noche en casa con la familia
4. celebrar con una comida (*meal*) especial
5. lavar (*to wash*) el perro
6. hablar de temas (*topics*) serios con los amigos (padres, esposo/a, hijos)

Paso 2. Ahora comparen sus respuestas con las (*those*) del resto de la clase. ¿Tienen todos las mismas costumbres (*same customs*)?

C. ¿Qué necesita? ¿Qué muebles u objetos se necesitan lógicamente en estas situaciones?

1. No puedo leer bien porque hay poca luz (*light*). Necesito ____________.
2. Para hacer la tarea (*homework*) en casa necesito ____________.
3. Para mi ropa interior necesito ____________.
4. Para todos mis libros necesito ____________.
5. Después de bañarme (*After bathing*) necesito ____________.

Vocabulario útil

la bicicleta
las cortinas
la planta

D. Esta casa

Paso 1. En parejas, identifiquen las partes de esta casa y lo que (*what*) hay en cada (*each*) una. Usen colores también.

MODELO: **E1:** El número 1 corresponde al **garaje.**
E2: ¿Qué hay en el garaje?
E1: Hay **un coche verde** y…

Paso 2. Ahora expandan el plano de esta casa para incorporar dos partes más. Deben pensar (*think*) en la utilidad (*purpose*) que tienen esas partes y poner (*put in*) los muebles apropiados. Luego (*Then*) prepárense para describir sus cambios.

Paso 3. Describan al resto de la clase las nuevas partes de la casa sin (*without*) leer.

MODELO: Las nuevas partes de nuestra casa son… En el/la ________ hay…

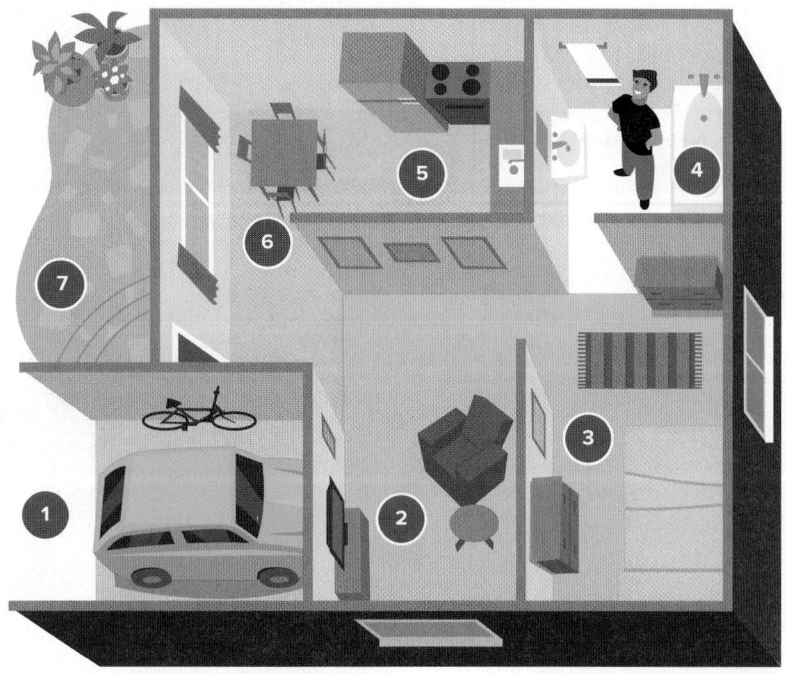

Nota cultural

Las casas en el mundo hispano

La palabra **casa** se usa de manera genérica en español para significar hogar,[a] como en estos ejemplos.

ir/regresar a casa	to go/return home
estar en casa	to be at home
Estás en tu casa.	Welcome. (*Lit.*, You're in your home.)

Hay una gran variedad de tipos de casas en el mundo hispano y no se puede decir que haya[b] «una casa típica». Las construcciones dependen del[c] uso, de la zona (rural o urbana), del clima y de las tradiciones históricas y culturales. Y, por supuesto,[d] del factor económico.

En las ciudades, la mayoría de las personas no vive en casas sino[e] en apartamentos. Otras palabras para apartamento son **piso** (España) y **departamento** (México, Argentina).

El Museo Casa Natal (*Birthplace*) de Rubén Darío, en Ciudad Darío, Nicaragua

¿? En su ciudad, ¿es más común vivir en un apartamento o en una casa? En su estado o país, ¿hay un estilo de casas predominante o tradicional?

[a]*home* [b]decir... *say that there is* [c]*on the* [d]por... *of course* [e]*but rather*

¿Qué día es hoy?

¡OJO!

To express *on* with days of the week, use **el** (for singular) or **los** (to generalize), as appropriate. The word **en** is not used with days of the week in Spanish. See **Nota comunicativa**, page 139.

1. Javier asiste a clase el lunes a las ocho.

2. Javier mira la televisión el martes.

3. Javier va al gimnasio el miércoles.

4. Javier trabaja cuatro horas el jueves.

5. El viernes va al mercado con unos amigos.

6. El fin de semana juega al basquetbol con sus amigos.

Hoy es viernes (domingo,...).	Today is Friday (Sunday, . . .).
Mañana es sábado (lunes,...).	Tomorrow is Saturday (Monday, . . .).
Ayer fue martes (miércoles,...).	Yesterday was Tuesday (Wednesday, . . .).
el fin de semana	the weekend
pasado mañana	the day after tomorrow
anteayer	the day before yesterday
el próximo jueves (viernes,...) **el jueves (viernes,...) que viene**	next Thursday (Friday, . . .)
la próxima semana **la semana que viene**	next week

- In Spanish-speaking countries, the week usually starts with **lunes.**
- The days of the week are not capitalized in Spanish.
- The words **sábado** and **domingo** have plural forms: **sábados**, **domingos.** All other days of the week end in **-s**; they use the same form for the plural as they do for the singular. See examples in **Nota comunicativa.**

Nota comunicativa

Cómo expresar *on* con los días de la semana

The definite article (singular or plural) is used to express **on** with the days of the week in Spanish.

el + *day* = on (Monday, Tuesday . . .)
Esta semana, tengo que ir al mercado **el** lunes.
This week, I have to go to the market on Monday.

los + *day* (plural form, if any) = on (Mondays, Tuesdays . . .)
Por lo general voy al mercado **los** viernes o **los** sábados.
I generally go to the market on Fridays or on Saturdays.

You will use **el** and **los** with days of the week in **Comunicación A** and **B**.

Comunicación

A. La semana

Paso 1. Complete las oraciones.

1. Hoy es ________. Mañana es ________.
2. Ayer fue ________ y anteayer fue ________.
3. Si hoy es sábado, mañana es ________. Ayer fue ________.
4. Si ayer fue domingo, hoy es ________ y mañana es ________.
5. Hay clase de español los ________, ________ y ________.
6. No tengo clases los ________ ni (*nor*) los ________.
7. Mi próximo examen de ________ es este ________.
8. Trabajo los ________ por la mañana/tarde/noche.
9. Los ________ por la tarde nunca estudio en la biblioteca.
10. Casi todos los ________ salgo (*I go out*) con mis amigos.

Paso 2. En parejas, intercambien (*exchange*) la información de los números 6–10. Luego digan (*tell*) a la clase las actividades que tienen en común.

B. Mi semana. Primero (*First*), indique lo que usted va a hacer **el** (lunes...) que viene. Luego indique una actividad típica de todos **los** (lunes...). Siga los modelos.

MODELOS: **El lunes** tengo que ir al gimnasio. (Voy a ir al gimnasio **el lunes.**)
Por lo general (Generalmente) voy al gimnasio **los lunes.**

Estrategia

Remember to use an infinitive after **ir a** if you want to use a verb. To express a place after **ir a,** remember to form the contraction **al** if necessary. The infinitive is used after all of the other verbs in the middle column.

lunes martes miércoles jueves viernes sábado domingo	+	ir a + *place* ir a + *inf.* deber desear necesitar poder preferir tener ganas de tener que	+	el bar la biblioteca el centro el cine (*movies*) el gimnasio el museo el parque ¿ ? descansar (*to rest*) en cama hasta muy tarde jugar (*to play*) al (tenis, golf, voleibol, basquetbol) ¿ ?

¿Cuándo? • Las preposiciones (Part 1)*

1. Antes de la fiesta, Rosa prepara la ensalada.

2. Durante la fiesta, Rosa baila y baila hasta el final.

3. Después de la fiesta, Rosa limpia la sala.

a preposition / **una preposición** = a word or phrase that specifies the relationship of one word to another

Prepositions link words or phrases to other words or phrases. The prepositions are indicated in the following sentences. Can you tell what words or phrases are linked by them?

1. The book is **on** the table.
2. The homework is **for** tomorrow.
3. Los sábados siempre descanso **hasta** muy tarde.
4. Voy a mirar la tele **después de** comer.

---

*You will learn prepositions that express spatial relationships in the **Vocabulario: Preparación** section of **Capítulo 6.***

You have already used many common Spanish prepositions, including: **a, con, de, en, hasta** (as in **hasta mañana**), **para, por** (*in*, *during*, as in **por la mañana**), and **sobre**.

In English, prepositions are often followed by the *-ing* form of a verb. However, in Spanish, the infinitive is the only verb form that can follow a preposition. You learned this with the expressions **para** + *inf.* and **ir a** + *inf.*

¿Adónde vas **después de** estudiar?	*Where are you going after studying (after you study)?*
Tengo ganas de comer **antes de** ir a la biblioteca esta noche.	*I feel like eating before going / (before I go) to the library tonight.*

Comunicación

A. ¿Cuándo?

Paso 1. Complete las siguientes oraciones lógicamente. Puede usar sustantivos, infinitivos, días de la semana, etcétera.

1. Por lo general, prefiero estudiar ______ (antes de / después de) las nueve de la noche.
2. Siempre tengo mucho sueño durante la clase de ______.
3. Voy a la clase de español ______ (antes de / después de) la clase de ______.
4. El/Los ______ (día o días), estoy en la universidad hasta ______ (hora).
5. No puedo ir a fiestas durante la semana. Voy el/los ______ (día o días).
6. Tengo que estudiar en esta universidad hasta el año ______.
7. Antes de / Después de mi primera (*first*) clase los ______ (día), voy a ______.

Paso 2. Ahora entreviste (*interview*) a un compañero o una compañera, usando (*using*) las oraciones del **Paso 1.**

MODELOS: ¿Prefieres estudiar antes de las nueve de la noche?
¿Prefieres estudiar antes o después de las nueve de la noche?
¿Cuándo prefieres estudiar, antes o después de las nueve de la noche?

B. Intercambios. En parejas, túrnense para entrevistarse. Hagan sus preguntas, usando una palabra o frases de cada columna.

estudiar hablar por teléfono leer trabajar ¿ ?	+	antes de después de durante hasta	+	tu serie favorita (de televisión) las clases las conferencias (*lectures*) de ______ los viernes por la noche, los domingos por la mañana... estudiar, mirar la tele,... las tres de la mañana, medianoche (*midnight*), muy tarde,... ¿ ?

Algo sobre...

la costa centroamericana

Los países centroamericanos tienen costa en los océanos Pacífico y Atlántico (el mar Caribe), excepto El Salvador, que solo tiene costa en el Pacífico. El Salvador es un poco más pequeño que el estado de Massachusetts. Así que aunque[a] solo tiene costa en el Pacífico, ¡el mar nunca está muy lejos[b] para ir a bañarse[c]!

©Nicholas Gill/Alamy

Playa la Paz, El Salvador, un lugar ideal para bañarse y surfear

¿Tiene su estado (o país) costa marítima? ¿En qué océano o mar?

[a]Así... *So although* [b]*far* [c]*swimming*

SALU'

«Vivir con la familia» Segmento 1

©McGraw-Hill Education/Klic Video Productions

«Bueno, mientras (*while*) asisto a la universidad vivo con mis padres. Lo mejor (*The best part*) de vivir con mis padres es la convivencia (*living together*) con ellos y lo peor (*the worst thing*) es que tengo que acatar sus reglas (*follow their rules*).»

Antes de mirar

Conteste las siguientes preguntas.

1. ¿Dónde vive usted ahora mientras asiste a la universidad? ¿En una residencia universitaria? ¿en un apartamento compartido (*shared*) con otros estudiantes? ¿con su familia?
2. ¿Dónde vive la mayoría (*majority*) de los estudiantes de su universidad?

Este segmento

El tema del reportaje (*report*) de este segmento es dónde viven los estudiantes universitarios estadounidenses y mexicanos.

Estrategia

Remember to go over everything on this page before watching the segment for the first time. As you watch, make a mental note of words or expressions that are repeated in the segment. What are they?

Vocabulario del segmento

les vuelven a dar la bienvenida	welcome you again
¡En efecto!	You're so right!
lejos de	far from
en cambio	in contrast
no deja su hogar	don't leave home
la colonia	neighborhood (*Mex.*)
lo más céntrico	very centrally located
el apoyo que me dan	the support they give me
la novia	girlfriend
los familiares	relatives
las facilidades	conveniences

Después de mirar

A. ¿Está claro? Complete las siguientes oraciones según el video.

1. Según Víctor, _________ (muchos/pocos) estudiantes estadounidenses asisten a una universidad que está lejos de su casa.
2. La mayoría de los estudiantes entrevistados (*interviewed*) _________ (vive/no vive) con su familia.
3. Según unos estudiantes, uno _________ (tiene que/no tiene que) acatar las reglas de la familia.
4. Para estos estudiantes, la compañía o convivencia _________ (es/no es) importante.
5. Según un estudiante, cuando uno vive con la familia, hay muchas _________ (facilidades/familiares) porque no es necesario pagar muchas cosas (*things*).

B. Un poco más. Conteste las siguientes preguntas.

1. Según los estudiantes mexicanos entrevistados, ¿qué es lo mejor de vivir con la familia? ¿Y lo peor?
2. Según Víctor, ¿por qué es caro asistir a la universidad en los Estados Unidos?

C. Y ahora, ustedes. En grupos, expresen sus opiniones sobre la idea de vivir con la familia mientras uno asiste a la universidad. ¿Qué es lo mejor y lo peor?

GRAMÁTICA

¿Recuerda usted?

Most of the verbs presented in **Gramática 12** share a first person singular irregularity with two verbs that you learned in **Capítulo 4.** Review what you know about those two verbs by completing their first person forms.

(yo) ven_______o (yo) ten_______o

12 Expressing Actions

Hacer, oír, poner, salir, traer, ver

Gramática en acción: Aspectos de la vida de Rigoberto

1. Traigo mi portátil al salón de clase.

2. No oigo bien. Por eso hago muchas preguntas en clase.

3. Pongo la tele y veo mi programa favorito.

4. Salgo con Elena los fines de semana.

Comprensión

1. ¿Qué trae Rigoberto al salón de clase?
2. ¿Por qué hace muchas preguntas en clase? ¿Ve bien? ¿Oye bien?
3. ¿A qué hora pone la tele? ¿Por qué prefiere mirar la tele a esa hora?
4. ¿Con quién sale?

hacer (*to do; to make*)		**oír** (*to hear*)		**poner** (*to put; to place*)		**salir** (*to leave [a place]; to go out*)		**traer** (*to bring*)		**ver** (*to see*)	
hago	**hacemos**	**oigo**	**oímos**	**pongo**	**ponemos**	**salgo**	**salimos**	**traigo**	**traemos**	**veo**	**vemos**
haces	**hacéis**	**oyes**	**oís**	**pones**	**ponéis**	**sales**	**salís**	**traes**	**traéis**	**ves**	**veis**
hace	**hacen**	**oye**	**oyen**	**pone**	**ponen**	**sale**	**salen**	**trae**	**traen**	**ve**	**ven**

Aspects of Rigoberto's life 1. *I bring my laptop to class.* ***2.*** *I don't hear well. That's why I ask a lot of questions in class.* ***3.*** *I turn on the TV and watch my favorite program.* ***4.*** *I go out with Elena on weekends.*

1. **hacer** = *to do; to make*

Pero, Julio, ¿qué **haces**?
But, Julio, what are you doing?

Siempre **hago** la tarea en la cafetería.
I always do my homework in the cafeteria.

Alicia **hace** unos tamales deliciosos.
Alicia makes delicious tamales.

Hacer is also used in a number of common idioms.

hacer un viaje
hacer una pregunta

Quieren **hacer un viaje** al Perú.
They want to take a trip to Peru.

Los niños siempre **hacen muchas preguntas.**
Children always ask a lot of questions.

Hacer is also used to express *to do* with physical and academic exercises.

Irene **hace ejercicio** todos los días.
Irene exercises every day.

En la clase de matemáticas **hacemos** muchos **ejercicios** y problemas.
In math class, we do a lot of exercises and problems.

---

2. **oír** = *to hear*
The command forms of **oír** are used to attract someone's attention in the same way that English uses *Listen up!* or *Hey!*

oye (tú) **oiga** (usted) **oigan** (ustedes)

> **¡OJO!**
>
> **oír** = to hear **escuchar** = to listen (to)
> Some native speakers of Spanish use **oír** to mean *to listen to* things like music or the news. But **escuchar** can never mean *to hear*.

No **oigo** bien a la profesora.
I can't hear the professor well.

Oye, Juan, ¿vas a la fiesta?
Hey, Juan, are you going to the party?

¡**Oigan**! ¡Silencio, por favor!
Listen up! Silence, please!

Oímos/Escuchamos música en clase.
We listen to music in class.

No **oigo** bien por el ruido.
I can't hear well because of the noise.

---

3. **poner** = *to put; to place*
Many Spanish speakers use **poner** with appliances to express *to turn on*.

Voy a **poner** la televisión.
I'm going to turn on the TV.

Siempre **pongo** leche y mucho azúcar en el café.
I always put milk and a lot of sugar in my coffee.

---

4. **salir** = *to leave* (a place); *to go out*
Note in the examples at the right how different prepositions are used with it to express different meanings.

salir de + *place*
salir con + *person*
salir para + *destination*

Salgo con el hermano de Cecilia.
I'm going out with / dating Cecilia's brother.

Salimos para la sierra pasado mañana.
We're leaving for the mountains the day after tomorrow.

Salen de clase ahora.
They're leaving class now.

Here's another useful expression: **salir bien/mal,** which means *to turn/come out well/poorly, to do well/poorly.*

Todo va a **salir bien.**
Everything is going to turn out OK (well).

No quiero **salir mal** en esta clase.
I don't want to do poorly in this class.

5. **traer** = *to bring*

> **¡OJO!**
>
> **Traer** and **llevar** are somewhat related in meaning, but they are actually antonyms, like *bring* and *take* in English. **Traer** expresses *to bring* as in *to have* something *with* or *on* one. It also expresses *to bring* something *to* the person who is speaking. **Llevar** means *to take* someone or something *to* a place.

¡Por favor! ¿Me **traes** una toalla?
Please! Can you bring me a towel?

Lo siento, pero no **traigo** dinero.
Sorry, but I have no money on me/didn't bring any money.

¿Por qué no me **traes** una de las sillas del comedor?
Why don't you bring me one of the chairs from the dining room?

Este año voy a **llevar** a mi familia a Nicaragua.
This year I'm going to take my family to Nicaragua.

---

6. **ver** = *to see*
Ver can also mean *to watch* as in watching television or a movie, which is also expressed with the verb **mirar.**

> **¡OJO!**
>
> **Mirar** never expresses *to see* (except with movies). It only means *to watch, look at.*

No **veo** bien sin mis lentes.
I don't see well without my glasses.

Los niños **ven/miran** una película.
The kids are watching a movie.

Práctica y comunicación

A. Mi rutina

Paso 1. Autoprueba. Dé la forma indicada para cada verbo.

1. hacer: yo
2. oír: ellos
3. poner: yo
4. salir: yo
5. traer: yo
6. ver: yo

Verb Summary

hacer	
oír	
poner	**-go**
salir	
traer	
oír	**oyes, oyen**
ver	**veo, ves...**

Paso 2. Ahora complete las siguientes oraciones lógicamente usando los verbos del **Paso 1** solo una vez. Añada (*Add*) una expresión de tiempo a cada oración y la palabra **no,** si es necesario.

Expresiones de tiempo

Before or after the verb: **los lunes/martes..., los fines de semana, (casi) todos los días, a veces...**

Before the verb: **(casi) siempre, (casi) nunca**

1. ________ ejercicio en el gimnasio ________.
2. ________ a mis amigos los ________ por la ________.
3. ________ de casa antes de las ________ de la mañana.
4. ________ mi libro de texto a la clase de español ________.
5. ________ las noticias (*news*) por la tele ________.
6. ________ la ropa en la cómoda y el armario ________.

Paso 3. Ahora, en parejas, túrnense para hacer y contestar preguntas basadas en las oraciones del **Paso 2.** Luego digan (*tell*) a la clase algo (*something*) que ustedes tienen en común o que hacen de manera muy diferente o peculiar.

MODELO: Hago ejercicio en el gimnasio casi todos días. →
¿Con qué frecuencia haces ejercicio en el gimnasio? (¿Haces ejercicio en el gimnasio todos los días?) →
Hannah y yo casi nunca hacemos ejercicio en el gimnasio.

***Prác. A, Paso 1: Answers: 1.** hago **2.** oyen **3.** pongo **4.** salgo **5.** traigo **6.** veo*

B. Lógicamente

Paso 1. Complete las siguientes oraciones con la forma apropiada de **hacer, oír, poner, salir, traer** o **ver.** Use **no** cuando es necesario para que (*so that*) las oraciones sean (*will be*) apropiadas para usted.

MODELO: Los estudiantes de esta clase ________ mucha tarea. →
Los estudiantes de esta clase **hacemos/hacen** mucha tarea.

1. (Yo) __________ la tele por la noche.
2. Los sábados por la noche siempre (tú) __________ solo/a (*alone*) / con tus amigos.
3. (Nosotros) __________ el libro de texto de español a clase.
4. Muchas personas no __________ ejercicio.
5. Los hispanos __________ mucho la radio.
6. Yo __________ azúcar (*sugar*) en mi café.
7. Mi amigo va a __________ un viaje a Nicaragua en diciembre.
8. En general, (yo) __________ bien en los exámenes.
9. Me gusta __________ películas extranjeras.

Paso 2. Use las respuestas del **Paso 1** para hacerle preguntas a un compañero o una compañera. ¿Está siempre de acuerdo con usted su compañero/a?

MODELO: Los estudiantes de esta clase **hacemos** mucha tarea. →
¿**Crees que** los estudiantes de esta clase hacemos mucha tarea?

C. Los nuevos verbos

Paso 1. Lea (*Read*) el siguiente afiche, que ilustra una expresión idiomática.

Vocabulario útil

el afiche	poster
sabio/a	wise

LOS TRES MONOS SABIOS
NO OÍR, NO VER, NO HABLAR

©Jan Stromme/Alamy

1. ¿Qué dicen los monos sabios en inglés?
2. ¿Qué diría (*would say*) cada mono en español hablando (*speaking*) en primera persona?
3. ¿Dónde sería (*would it be*) apropiado colgar (*to hang*) un afiche como este?

Paso 2. Los nuevos verbos se usan en más expresiones idiomáticas. Pero el significado (*meaning*) de los modismos no es siempre transparente. ¿Puede usted emparejar cada expresión con su significado?

EXPRESIONES

1. _____ poner en duda
2. _____ poner un límite
3. _____ salir en las noticias
4. _____ hacer un papel (*role*)
5. _____ ver para creer

SIGNIFICADOS

a. ¡tener sus 15 minutos de fama!
b. pensar que una información no es cierta
c. necesitar la observación personal para aceptar que una cosa es verdad
d. decidir hasta dónde puede llegar una situación
e. actuar en una película o una obra de teatro (*play*)

Algo sobre...

los lagos de Nicaragua

En Nicaragua hay dos lagos inmensos: el lago de Nicaragua (o Cocibolca) y el lago de Managua (o Xolotlán). Los dos están unidos por el río[a] Tipitapa. El Cocibolca es el lago más grande[b] de Centroamérica y, después del lago Titicaca en Bolivia, es el lago más grande de Latinoamérica. En el Cocibolca hay volcanes e islas.

 **¿Cómo se llama el lago más grande de este país? ¿y el río más grande?**

[a]*river* [b]*más... biggest*

©Paul Taylor/Getty Images

El lago de Nicaragua, con el volcán Maderas al fondo (*in the background*)

 **D. Consecuencias lógicas.** En parejas, indiquen acciones lógicas o consecuencias relacionadas con cada situación. No se limiten a usar los verbos de esta sección del libro. ¡Sean (*Be*) creativos y audaces (*daring*)!

1. Me gusta nadar (*to swim*) en los lagos. Por eso...
2. Todos los días usamos este libro en la clase de español. Por eso...
3. Mis hijos / compañeros de cuarto hacen mucho ruido en la sala. Por eso...
4. La televisión no funciona. Por eso...
5. Hay mucho ruido en el salón de clase. Por eso...
6. Estoy en la biblioteca y ¡no puedo estudiar más! Por eso...
7. Queremos bailar y necesitamos música. Por eso...
8. No comprendo la lección. Por eso...
9. Me gusta hacer ecoturismo y hablar español. Por eso...

Vocabulario útil

gritar «¡silencio!»	to shout "silence!"
hacer una cita	to make an appointment
los vecinos	neighbors

 **E. Intercambios**

Paso 1. En parejas, hagan y contesten las siguientes preguntas.

EN CASA

1. ¿Qué pones en el armario? ¿y en la cómoda? ¿en el cajón (*drawer*) del escritorio?
2. ¿Pones la televisión con frecuencia cuando estás en casa? ¿Qué programa(s) ves todos los días? ¿Qué programa o serie muy popular no ves nunca? (**Nunca veo...**) ¿Cuál es el canal de televisión que más miras? ¿Por qué te gusta tanto (*so much*)?
3. ¿Pones el radio con frecuencia? ¿Prefieres oír las noticias por radio o verlas (*to see them*) en la televisión? ¿Cuál es la estación de radio que más escuchas? ¿Por qué te gusta tanto?

MIS ACTIVIDADES

4. ¿Qué haces los ________ (día) por la noche? ¿Cuándo sales con los amigos? ¿Adónde van cuando salen juntos (*together*)? ¿Cuándo sales solo/a?
5. ¿Te gusta hacer ejercicio? ¿Haces ejercicios aeróbicos? ¿Dónde haces ejercicio?

(Continúa.)

PARA LAS CLASES

6. Generalmente, ¿qué traes a clase todos los días? ¿Crees que traes más cosas (*things*) que (*than*) tus compañeros o menos? ¿Sales a veces para la clase sin tu libro de texto? ¿sin dinero? ¿Qué trae tu profesor(a) de español a clase?
7. ¿A qué hora sales para las clases los lunes? ¿A qué hora sales de clase los viernes?
8. ¿Cuándo haces la tarea? ¿Por la mañana? ¿Dónde haces la tarea? ¿En casa? ¿Haces la tarea mientras (*while*) ves la televisión? ¿mientras oyes música?
9. ¿Siempre sales bien en los exámenes? ¿En qué clase no sales bien? ¿Qué haces si sales mal en un examen?

Paso 2. Ahora digan (*tell*) a la clase dos o tres cosas que ustedes tienen en común.

MODELO: Jim y yo nunca ponemos la ropa en el armario. Hacemos ejercicio todos los días: Jim hace ejercicios aeróbicos y yo voy al gimnasio. Los dos vemos el programa ________ los lunes por la noche; es nuestro programa favorito.

Algo sobre...

las casas tradicionales centroamericanas

En Centroamérica y en otros países latinoamericanos hay casas de bajareque, un tipo de construcción tradicional de origen prehispánico.[a] Se usan materiales locales y económicos: paredes sostenidas por palos[b] y rellenas de barro y cañas.[c] Las casas de bajareque son generalmente humildes,[d] pero también son construcciones ecológicas y sismorresistentes,[e] una característica importante para una región de alta actividad sísmica como es Centroamérica.

En los Estados Unidos, ¿es la construcción de las casas típicas del norte diferente de la (*that*) de las casas del sur?

[a]*pre-Hispanic (before the arrival of Columbus)* [b]sostenidas... *held up by sticks or logs* [c]rellenas... *filled with mud and reeds* [d]*humble* [e]*resistant to earthquakes*

©BrazilPhotos.com/Alamy

Una casa de bajareque, en Nicaragua

¿Recuerda usted?

The change in the stem vowels of **preferir, querer,** and **poder** was presented in **Gramática 10.** Review the forms of **preferir, querer,** and **poder** now.

poder: o → __ **preferir: e → __** **querer: e → __**

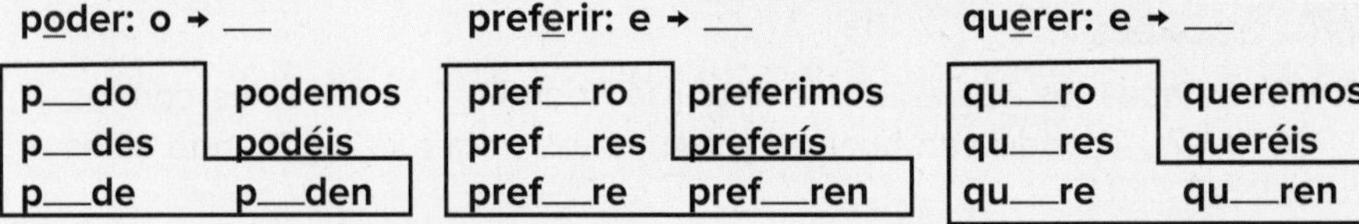

poder		preferir		querer	
p__do	podemos	pref__ro	preferimos	qu__ro	queremos
p__des	podéis	pref__res	preferís	qu__res	queréis
p__de	p__den	pref__re	pref__ren	qu__re	qu__ren

If you could complete those verb forms correctly, you already know most of the important information in **Gramática 13.**

13 Expressing Actions

Present Tense of Stem-changing Verbs (Part 2)

Gramática en acción: ¿Una fiesta exitosa?

Es la noche del sábado y todos están en una fiesta en casa de Ernesto.

- Aurora duerme en el sofá.
- Samuel juega a las cartas... a solas.
- Ernesto sirve las bebidas. Kevin pide una Coca-Cola.
- Noemí sale y vuelve con más amigas.
- ¿Es una fiesta exitosa? ¿Qué piensa usted? ¿Por qué?

¿Y usted? ¿Qué hace en las fiestas?

1. ¿Duerme usted en el sofá?
2. ¿Juega a las cartas?
3. ¿Sirve las bebidas?
4. ¿Pide Coca-Cola?
5. ¿Sale y vuelve con más amigos?

e → ie: pensar (*to think*)		**o → ue: volver** (*to return*)		**e → i: pedir** (*to ask for; to order*)	
pienso	**pensamos**	**vuelvo**	**volvemos**	**pido**	**pedimos**
piensas	**pensáis**	**vuelves**	**volvéis**	**pides**	**pedís**
piensa	**piensan**	**vuelve**	**vuelven**	**pide**	**piden**

1. **Stem-changing Verbs**
You have already used three *stem-changing verbs* **(los verbos que cambian el radical): poder**, **preferir**, and **querer.** And you also know two other verbs that are similar (**tener** and **venir**), but whose first person singular forms are irregular.

2. **Stem Vowel Changes**
There are three groups of stem-changing verbs. You already know about the first two.
   - verbs like **preferir** and **querer,** in which the stem vowel **e** becomes **ie** in stressed syllables
   - verbs like **poder,** in which the stem vowel **o** becomes **ue** in stressed syllables

   Here is the third group.
   - verbs in which the stem vowel **e** becomes **i**

   The stem-changing pattern of all three groups is shown at the right. The stem vowels are stressed (and so they change) in all present tense forms except **nosotros** and **vosotros.** All three groups follow this regular pattern, which looks like a boot.

Las vocales que cambian el radical

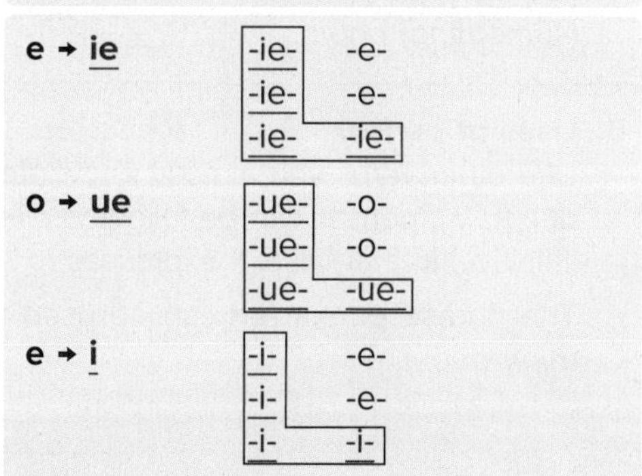

e → ie	-ie-	-e-
	-ie-	-e-
	-ie-	-ie-
o → ue	-ue-	-o-
	-ue-	-o-
	-ue-	-ue-
e → i	-i-	-e-
	-i-	-e-
	-i-	-i-

¡OJO!

Nosotros and **vosotros** forms *do not* have a stem vowel change.

A successful party? *It's Saturday night and everybody is at a party at Ernesto's house. • Aurora is sleeping on the couch. • Samuel is playing cards ... alone. • Ernesto is serving beverages. Kevin asks for a Coke. • Noemí leaves and comes back with more friends. • Is it a successful party? What do you think? Why?*

3. Important Stem-changing Verbs

Some stem-changing verbs practiced in this chapter include the following.

e → ie

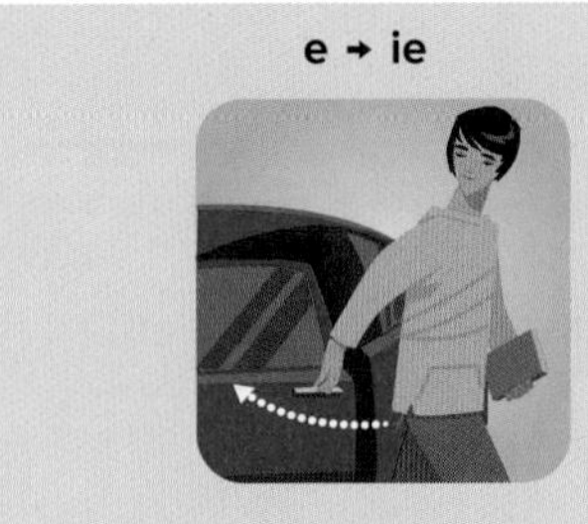

cerrar (cierro)

cerrar (cierro)	to close
empezar (empiezo)	to begin, start
entender (entiendo)	to understand
pensar (pienso)	to think
perder (pierdo)	to lose; to miss (*an event*)

o (u) → ue

dormir (duermo)

almorzar (almuerzo)	to have lunch
dormir (duermo)	to sleep
jugar (juego)	to play (*a game, sport*)
volver (vuelvo)	to return (*to a place*)

e → i

servir (sirvo) (para)

pedir (pido)	to ask for; to order
servir (sirvo) (para)	to serve; to be used (for)

As you learned with **poder, preferir,** and **querer,** stem-changing verbs will be indicated in vocabulary lists with the **yo** form in parentheses, as shown here.

¡OJO!

Jugar is the only **u → ue** stem-changing verb in Spanish. **Jugar** is usually followed by **al** when used with the name of a sport: **Juego al tenis.** Some Spanish speakers, however, omit the **al.** Games expressed in the plural use **a los** or **a las** after **jugar**: **Juego a las cartas.**

4. Verb + *a* + Infinitive

Like **aprender** and **ir,** the stem-changing verbs **empezar** and **volver** are followed by **a** before an infinitive.

Ustedes **empiezan a hablar** muy bien el español.
You're starting to speak Spanish very well.

The meaning of **empezar** does not change in this structure, but **volver a** + *infinitive* expresses *to do (something) again.*

¿Cuándo **vuelves a jugar** al tenis?
When are you going to play tennis again?

5. Uses of *pensar*

Like other verbs you already know (**desear, necesitar, deber,...**), **pensar** can be followed directly by an infinitive. In that case, it expresses *to intend, plan.*

¿Cuándo **piensas almorzar**?
When do you plan to eat lunch?

The phrase **pensar en** can be used to express *to think about.*

—¿**En** qué **piensas**?
—**Pienso en** las cosas que tengo que hacer el domingo.
"What are you thinking about?"
"I'm thinking about the things I have to do on Sunday."

Pensar de indicates one's opinion about someone or something. The answer to a question with **pensar de** usually starts with **Pienso que...**

—¿Qué **piensas de** esa situación?
—¡**Pienso que** es un desastre!
"What do you think about that situation?"
"I think (that) it's a real mess!"

—¿Qué **piensas del** nuevo apartamento de Cristina?
—**Pienso que** es elegante. . . pero ¡muy caro!
"What do you think of/about Cristina's new apartment?"
"I think (that) it's fancy. . . but very expensive!"

6. **Present Tense Equivalents**
Remember that the Spanish present tense has a number of present tense equivalents in English. It can also be used to express future meaning.

cierro = *I close, I am closing, I will close*

Práctica y comunicación

Stem-Change Summary

empezar (empiezo) **jugar (juego)**
volver (vuelvo) **pedir (pido)**

A. Asociaciones

Paso 1. Dé por lo menos un infinitivo que asocia con las siguientes ideas y cosas.

1. una bebida
2. una lección (*lesson*)
3. a casa
4. una cama
5. una hamburguesa
6. el tenis
7. una opinión
8. una puerta
9. las llaves (*keys*)
10. la cocina
11. una siesta
12. un favor
13. las cartas
14. una palabra o frase
15. la música

Paso 2. Explique para qué sirven las siguientes cosas.

MODELO: las cartas → **Sirven para** jugar.

1. las llaves
2. una almohada (*pillow*)
3. una bandeja (*tray*)
4. un menú
5. un diccionario
6. el cerebro (*brain*)

B. La vida (*Life*) en la universidad

Paso 1. Autoprueba. Dé la forma de cada verbo para **yo** y para **nosotros.**

1. almorzar
2. entender
3. pedir
4. perder
5. dormir
6. jugar
7. pensar
8. volver

Paso 2. Ahora complete las siguientes oraciones lógicamente usando los verbos del **Paso 1** solo una vez. Añada (*Add*) una expresión de tiempo y/o la palabra **no,** si es necesario.

Expresiones de tiempo

Before or after the verb: **los lunes/martes... , los fines de semana, (casi) todos los días, a veces, constantemente** (*constantly*)...

Before the verb: **(casi) siempre, (casi) nunca**

MODELO: **1.** _______ la siesta _______. → **Duermo** la siesta **casi todos los días.**

1. _________ la siesta _______.
2. __________ en la cafetería _______.
3. _______ pizza para almorzar _______.
4. ________ a las cartas con mi familia _______.
5. _________ en mis notas (*grades*) _______.
6. _________ mi carnet de identificación de la universidad _______.
7. _________ a casa de mis padres / de mi familia _______.
8. __________ muchas cosas en mi clase de _______ (materia).

Paso 3. Ahora, en parejas, túrnense para hacer y contestar preguntas basadas en las oraciones del **Paso 2.** Luego digan (*tell*) a la clase algo (*something*) que ustedes tienen en común o que hacen de manera muy diferente o peculiar.

MODELOS: Duermo la siesta casi todos días. →
¿Con qué frecuencia duermes la siesta? (¿Duermes la siesta todos los días?) →
Jacob y yo dormimos la siesta casi todos los días.

Prác. B, Paso 1: Answers: 1. almuerzo, almorzamos 2. entiendo, entendemos 3. pido, pedimos 4. pierdo, perdemos 5. duermo, dormimos 6. juego, jugamos 7. pienso, pensamos 8. vuelvo, volvemos

C. Una tarde típica en casa. ¿Cuáles son las actividades de todos? Haga oraciones completas, usando una palabra o frase de cada columna.

(yo)	+	(no) almorzar	+	descansar, dormir
mi padre/madre		dormir		solo/a
mi esposo/a		empezar a		en un sillón / en la cocina
los niños		entender		toda la tarde / la siesta
mi amigo/a ______ y yo		jugar a / al		su pelota (*ball*), sus llaves, su mochila
el perro/gato		pedir		tarde/temprano a casa
mi compañero/a (de cuarto)		pensar		en el patio / en la piscina / afuera (*outside*)
		pensar en		golf (tenis, voleibol...), las cartas
		perder		las películas viejas/recientes
		preferir		mis notas, mis clases, los exámenes
		volver		la lección, la oración
		volver a		hablar bien el español
		¿ ?		ver una película con frecuencia
				¿ ?

D. Una semana ideal... ¡y posible!

Paso 1. ¿Qué va a hacer usted la semana que viene? Organice la próxima semana en la siguiente agenda. Escriba frases con el infinitivo, por ejemplo: **ver la televisión.** Incluya actividades que tiene que hacer, pero también algunas (*some*) que tiene ganas de hacer.

	por la mañana	por la tarde	por la noche
lunes			
martes			
miércoles			
jueves			
viernes			
sábado			
domingo			

Paso 2. En parejas, hablen de su horario (*schedule*) para esta semana, basándose (*based on*) en la agenda del **Paso 1.** Luego digan (*tell*) algunas (*some*) respuestas interesantes a la clase.

Estrategia

e → ie
o → ue
e → i

MODELO: ver la televisión →
E1: ¿Qué **piensas** hacer el domingo por la tarde?
E2: **Pienso** ver la televisión. Y tú, ¿qué haces el domingo?
E1: El domingo **juego** al tenis con mi amigo Alex.

E. Intercambios. En parejas, túrnense para hacer y contestar preguntas sobre los temas siguientes con las frases sugeridas (*suggested*).

Estrategia

generalizations: present tense
future: **ir** + **a** + *inf.*
definite plans: **pensar** + *inf.*

MODELOS: almorzar (¿dónde? ¿con quién? ¿a qué hora?) →
Por lo general, ¿dónde **almuerzas** de lunes a viernes?
¿Con quién **vas a almorzar** hoy?
¿A qué hora **piensas almorzar** el domingo?

1. almorzar (¿dónde? ¿con quién? ¿a qué hora?)
2. perder (¿qué? ¿dónde? ¿con frecuencia? ¿siempre?)
3. dormir (¿cuántas horas? ¿mucho o poco? ¿siestas frecuentes o infrecuentes? ¿largas o cortas?)
4. jugar (¿juegos de mesa [*board games*]? ¿cuáles? ¿con quién? ¿dónde?)

¿Recuerda usted?

In **Capítulo 1,** you learned how to ask what someone's name is and express your own name by using phrases with the verb **llamar.** Show what you remember by completing the following phrases.

1. (yo) ____ llamo **2.** (tú) ____ llamas **3.** usted ____ llama

The words with which you completed those phrases are part of a pronoun system that you will learn about in **Gramática 14.**

14 Expressing *-self/-selves*

Reflexive Pronouns (Part 1)*

Gramática en acción: La rutina diaria de Andrés

La rutina de Andrés empieza a las siete y media.

1.

2.

3.

4.

(1) Me despierto a las siete y media y me levanto en seguida. Primero, (2) me ducho y luego (3) me cepillo los dientes. (4) Me peino, (5) me pongo la bata y (6) voy al cuarto a vestirme. Por fin, (7) salgo para la universidad. No tomo nada antes de salir porque, por lo general, ¡tengo prisa!

5.

6.

7.

¿Y usted? ¿Cómo es su rutina diaria?

1. Yo me levanto a las ________.
2. Me ducho por la mañana / noche.
3. Me visto en el baño / mi cuarto.
4. Me peino antes de / después de vestirme.
5. Antes de salir para las clases, tomo / no tomo el desayuno (*breakfast*).

Andrés's daily routine *Andrés's routine begins at seven-thirty. (1) I wake up at seven-thirty and I get up right away. First, (2) I take a shower and then (3) I brush my teeth. (4) I comb my hair, (5) I put on my robe, and (6) I go to my room to get dressed. Finally, (7) I leave for the university. I don't eat or drink anything before leaving because I'm generally in a hurry!*

You will learn how to use reflexive pronouns to express* each other *in* **Gramática 32 (Cap. 11).

Verbs Used Reflexively / **Los verbos que se usan con pronombres reflexivos**

bañarse (*to take a bath, bathe*)					
(yo)	**me baño**	I take a bath	(nosotros)	**nos bañamos**	we take a bath
(tú)	**te bañas**	you take a bath	(vosotros)	**os bañáis**	you take a bath
(usted)	**se baña**	you take a bath	(ustedes)	**se bañan**	you take a bath
(él)		he takes a bath	(ellos)		they take a bath
(ella)		she takes a bath	(ellas)		they take a bath

1. Reflexive Pronouns
In Spanish, some verbs are used reflexively. This means that they are used with reflexive pronouns that indicate that the subject is doing something *to* or *for oneself.* The reflexive pronouns that correspond to the subject accompany the verb and must come before it.

The pronoun **-se** at the end of an infinitive indicates that the verb is used reflexively: **bañarse** (to take a bath; to bathe oneself).

> **¡OJO!**
>
> Verbs used reflexively often do not have an exact parallel in English, and there is not always a reflexive pronoun in the translation.

Los pronombres reflexivos		
yo	**me**	myself
tú	**te**	yourself (*fam., sing.*)
usted/ él/ella	**se**	himself, herself, itself; yourself (*form. sing.*)
nosotros/as	**nos**	ourselves
vosotros/as	**os**	yourselves (*fam. pl. Sp.*)
ustedes/ ellos/as	**se**	themselves; yourselves (*form. pl.*)

me baño = I take a bath (bathe myself)
me ducho = I shower (take a shower)

2. Important Verbs Used Reflexively
Many English verbs that describe parts of one's daily routine—to get up, to take a bath, and so on—are expressed in Spanish with a reflexive construction. Here are some that are frequently used.

> **¡OJO!**
>
> Notice that some of these reflexive verbs also have stem changes: **e → ie, o → ue, e → i.**

despertarse (me despierto)

ducharse

afeitarse

vestirse (me visto)

sentarse (me siento)

Note the **-se** on the end of these infinitives. This is how reflexive verbs will be shown in vocabulary lists.

acostarse (me acuesto)	to go to bed	**levantarse**	to get up (out of bed); to stand up
afeitarse	to shave	**llamarse**	to be called
bañarse	to take a bath, bathe	**peinarse**	to do (brush/comb) one's hair
cepillarse los dientes	to brush one's teeth	**ponerse (me pongo)**	to put on (*an article of clothing*)
despertarse (me despierto)	to wake up	**quitarse**	to take off (*an article of clothing*)
divertirse (me divierto)	to have a good time, enjoy oneself		
dormirse (me duermo)	to fall asleep	**sentarse (me siento)**	to sit down
ducharse	to take a shower	**vestirse (me visto)**	to get dressed

> **¡OJO!**
>
> After **ponerse** and **quitarse**, the definite article, not the possessive as in English, is used with articles of clothing.

Me siento y **me quito** los zapatos. Luego **me quito** los pantalones y la camisa y **me pongo** la pijama.
I sit down and take off my shoes. Then I take off my pants and shirt and put on my pajamas.

3. Placement of Reflexive Pronouns

- Reflexive pronouns are placed before a conjugated verb.

Me levanto temprano todos los días.
I get up early every day.

- In a negative sentence, the reflexive pronoun is placed between **no** and the conjugated verb.

Matías **no se levanta** temprano los domingos.
Matías doesn't get up early on Sundays.

- When a conjugated verb is followed by an infinitive that is used reflexively, the reflexive pronoun may either precede the conjugated verb or be attached to the infinitive.

Pienso **acostarme** temprano esta noche.
Me pienso **acostar** temprano esta noche.
I plan to go to bed early tonight.

- Remember that the infinitive form follows prepositions in Spanish—the reflexive pronouns are attached at the end of the infinitive: **antes de acostarse**, **después de ducharme**.

Me cepillo los dientes y **me peino** antes de **vestirme**.
I brush my teeth and do my hair before dressing (before I get dressed).

> **¡OJO!**
>
> The reflexive pronoun must be repeated with each verb in a series of verbs.

Mi esposo **se baña,** yo **me ducho** y los dos **nos peinamos** antes de las seis.
My husband takes a bath, I shower, and the two of us do our hair before six o'clock.

4. Nonreflexive Use of Verbs

All of these verbs can also be used nonreflexively, often with a different meaning. Here are some examples.

dormir = to sleep	**dormirse** = to fall asleep
poner = to put, place	**ponerse** = to put on

Antonio **se pone** un suéter.

Su mamá **pone** la ropa en la lavadora.

Práctica y comunicación

A. Asociaciones. ¿Cuántas palabras puede usted asociar con los siguientes infinitivos? Piense (*Think*) en grupos de palabras que usted ya conoce (*you already know*): los cuartos de una casa, los muebles, la ropa, otros verbos, los adverbios, etcétera.

1. llamarse
2. levantarse
3. bañarse
4. sentarse
5. ponerse
6. despertarse
7. divertirse
8. acostarse

Reflexive Pronoun Summary

yo	→	me
tú	→	te
usted, él, ella	→	se
nosotros/as	→	nos
vosotros/as	→	os
ustedes, ellos, ellas	→	se

B. Su rutina diaria

Paso 1. Autoprueba. Empareje los pronombres reflexivos con los verbos apropiados.

PRONOMBRES

1. me ________
2. te ________
3. se ________
4. nos ________

VERBOS

a. acuesta
b. baño
c. ponemos
d. duermen
e. despierta
f. vistes

Paso 2. Escoja (*Choose*) el verbo apropiado para completar las siguientes oraciones. Luego use verbos en la primera persona singular (**yo**) para describir su propia rutina. No repita los verbos.

VERBOS: acostarse, despertarse, divertirse, ducharse, levantarse, ponerse

1. ____________ a la(s) ____________ (hora) con la ayuda (*help*) del reloj despertador (*alarm clock*).
2. ¡Siempre/Nunca ____________ inmediatamente cuando escucho el despertador!
3. ____________ después de levantarme por la mañana / antes de acostarme por la noche.
4. ____________ después de la(s) ____________ (hora) los días de entresemana (*weekdays*).
5. ____________ con mis amigos / mi familia los fines de semana.
6. Generalmente, para ir a clase (no) ____________ ropa deportiva (*sports*) y tenis.

Paso 3. Ahora, en parejas, túrnense para hacer y contestar preguntas basadas en las oraciones del **Paso 2**. Luego digan (*tell*) a la clase algo (*something*) que ustedes tienen en común o que hacen de manera muy diferente o peculiar.

MODELO: 1. Me despierto a las siete con la ayuda del reloj despertador. →
¿Te despiertas a las siete con la ayuda del reloj despertador? →
Sam y yo nos despertamos con la ayuda del reloj despertador. Pero yo me despierto a las siete y Sam no se despierta hasta las diez.

C. La oración correcta. Elija (*Choose*) la mejor oración para cada dibujo.

1.

a. La mamá baña a los niños.
b. Los niños se bañan.

2.

a. Un joven despierta a otro.
b. Los dos jóvenes se despiertan.

3.

a. El papá sienta a su hijo a la mesa.
b. El papá se sienta a la mesa.

4.

a. Elena se viste para el frío.
b. Elena viste a su perro para el frío.

Nota comunicativa

Cómo expresar una secuencia de acciones

The following adverbs and expressions will help you indicate the sequence of actions or events.

primero	first	**en seguida**	immediately	**por fin**	finally
luego, después	then, later, next	**finalmente**	finally		

Primero, me ducho y me visto. **Luego,** tomo un café y leo el periódico. **Después,** me cepillo los dientes. **Finalmente,** salgo para el trabajo.

First, I shower and get dressed. Then I drink a cup of coffee and read the paper. Afterwards, I brush my teeth. Finally, I leave for work.

You will use these words and phrases in **Práctica D** and **E.**

***Prác. B, Paso 1:* Answers: *1.* b *2.* f *3.* a, d, e *4.* c**

D. El día de Ángela. Ángela es dependienta en una tienda de ropa para jóvenes en El Paso. ¿Cómo es un día normal de trabajo para ella? Complete la narración con los verbos apropiados, según los dibujos. **¡OJO!** Algunos (*Some*) verbos se usan más de una vez (*more than once*).

1. Verbos: **comer, levantarse, vestirse (me visto)**

Me despierto a las nueve de la mañana y ________ en seguida. (Yo) ________ rápidamente y salgo de casa sin ________. Llego a la tienda a las diez menos diez de la mañana con mis compañeras de trabajo.

2. 

Verbos: **empezar (empiezo), ser**

Primero (yo) ________ mi trabajo, ordenando (*putting in order*) la ropa. La ropa de la tienda ________ muy bonita.

3. 

Verbos: **almorzar (almuerzo), dormir (duermo), pedir (pido), sentarse (me siento), volver (vuelvo)**

(Yo) ________ a las doce y media con mi amiga Susie, que trabaja en una zapatería. Generalmente podemos ________ en la pizzería San Marcos y casi siempre ________ pizza. Luego, (yo) ________ a la tienda y ________ a trabajar. Nunca ________ la siesta.

4. 

Verbos: **cerrar (cierro), dormirse (me duermo), pensar (pienso), ponerse, quitarse, volver (vuelvo)**

Por fin, la supervisora ________ la tienda a las seis en punto. Luego yo ________ a casa. ________ la ropa de trabajo (*work clothes*) y ________ un vestido y zapatos elegantes. ________ salir a bailar con unos amigos... ¡y no pienso ir a ________ hasta muy, muy tarde!

E. Un día típico

Paso 1. Complete las siguientes oraciones lógicamente para describir su rutina diaria. Use el pronombre reflexivo cuando sea necesario. **¡OJO!** Use el infinitivo después de las preposiciones.

1. Me levanto después de ________ la(s) ________ (hora).
2. Inmediatamente después de levantarme, (yo) ________ y luego ________. (verbos)
3. Generalmente, me visto antes de / después de ________ (verbo).
4. Me gusta estudiar antes de ________ o después de ________. (verbos)
5. Por la noche me divierto y luego ________ (verbo).
6. Me acuesto antes de / después de ________ y finalmente ________. (verbos)

Paso 2. Con las oraciones del **Paso 1,** describa los hábitos de su esposo/a, su compañero/a de cuarto/casa, sus hijos…

F. Intercambios: Su rutina

Paso 1. En parejas, túrnense para entrevistarse. Hagan preguntas, usando las ideas de las tres columnas y otras de su imaginación. Usen una palabra o frase de cada columna y traten de (*try to*) explicar sus acciones.

MODELO: **E1:** ¿A qué hora te acuestas?
E2: Siempre me acuesto muy tarde porque trabajo hasta las once de la noche en un restaurante. Luego tengo que estudiar un poco.

¿a qué hora? ¿cuándo? ¿dónde? ¿durante ______ ? ¿hasta qué hora?	+	acostarse afeitarse cepillarse los dientes despertarse dormirse ducharse/bañarse levantarse peinarse sentarse vestirse/ponerse ______ volver	+	los días de la semana los fines de semana los lunes (martes…) todos los días tarde/temprano solo/a

Paso 2. Ahora digan (*tell*) a la clase un detalle (*detail*) interesante, raro o indiscreto de la vida (*life*) de su compañero/a.

MODELO: Sebastián se duerme a la una todas las noches con su perro y con sus dos gatos. ¡Debe tener una cama muy grande!

La ciudad de San Salvador, capital de El Salvador

Todo junto

A. Lengua y cultura: ¿Dónde viven los hispanohablantes?

Paso 1. Completar. Complete the following paragraphs about different types of living arrangements in the Spanish-speaking world. Give the correct form of the words in parentheses, as suggested by context. When two possibilities are given in parentheses, select the correct one.

Como es de imaginar, en los países hispanohablantes hay una gran variedad de viviendas.[a] __________ (Este[1]) variaciones corresponden a diferencias socioeconómicas y también tienen relación con el urbanismo[b] y el clima.

Las ______ (grande[2]) ciudades ______ (tener[3]) muchos edificios de apartamentos que ______ (poder[4]) acomodar la ______ (alto[5]) densidad de población (el 80 por ciento de los latinoamericanos vive en zonas urbanas). Sin embargo,[c] los gobiernos[d] ______ (entender[6]) la necesidad de tener ciudades más ______ (verde[7]) y habitables para todas las personas. Cada día hay más preocupación ______ (e / y[8]) interés por tener más parques, ______ (jardín[9]), carriles[e] para bicicletas, excelentes sistemas de transporte, etcétera.

En contraste, las casas predominan en las áreas ______ (rural[10]) y en las zonas residenciales fuera de[f] una ciudad. Por cierto,[g] la palabra *suburbio* es un falso cognado en español: significa una zona fuera de la ciudad, pero no un ______ (bueno[11]) lugar para vivir.

También se pueden encontrar[h] muchas casas en los centros históricos de las ciudades, donde ______ (a / en[12]) veces hay viviendas en muy ______ (malo[13]) estado habitadas por[i] personas de bajos recursos[j] cerca de[k] ______ (precioso[14]) casas antiguas que ______ (costar[15]) mucho dinero.

No solo hay mucha variedad de viviendas, sino que[l] también cada país hispanohablante ______ (preferir[16]) nombres diferentes para las viviendas y las zonas donde están. Por ejemplo, los distritos de una ciudad en México ______ (llamarse[17]) colonias. Pero no se preocupe.[m] ¡ ______ (*Usted:* Poder[18]) aprender ese vocabulario fácilmente[n] si ______ (*usted:* pensar[19]) comprar una vivienda en un país hispanohablante!

[a]*housing* [b]*urban development* [c]Sin... *However* [d]*governments* [e]*lanes* [f]fuera... *outside of* [g]Por... *By the way* [h]se... *one can find* [i]habitadas... *inhabited by* [j]bajos... *low income* [k]cerca... *close to* [l]sino... *but* [m]no... *don't worry* [n]*easily*

Paso 2. Comprensión. ¿Cierto o falso? Corrija las oraciones falsas.

	CIERTO	FALSO
1. El clima afecta los tipos de vivienda.	☐	☐
2. En Latinoamérica hay una gran población rural.	☐	☐
3. En los centros históricos todas las casas están en un estado excelente.	☐	☐
4. Las ciudades latinoamericanas tienen interés en tener viviendas habitables para todas las personas.	☐	☐

Paso 3. En acción

Conteste las siguientes preguntas con información y ejemplos específicos. Prepare la información para presentarla *(present it)* a la clase de manera concisa y eficiente.

1. ¿Hay una gran densidad de población en su estado? ¿Tiene muchas grandes ciudades o muchas personas que viven en zonas rurales? ¿Cuáles son las ciudades más grandes (*biggest)*?
2. ¿Qué tipos de viviendas hay en su ciudad? ¿Qué es más común: vivir en un gran edificio de apartamentos o en casas unifamiliares (*single family)*? ¿vivir en el centro (histórico) o en una zona residencial fuera de la ciudad?

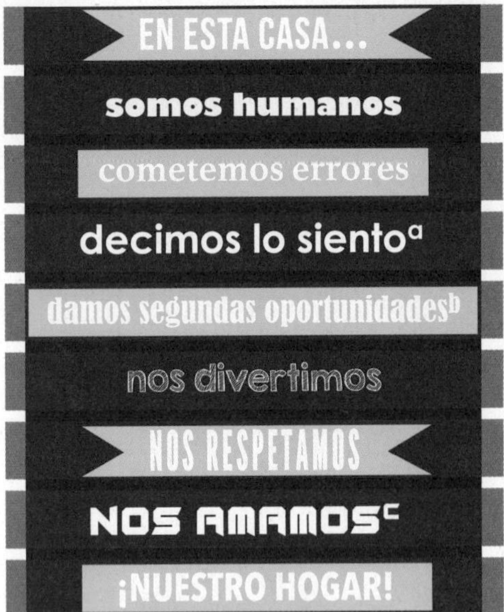
EN ESTA CASA...
somos humanos
cometemos errores
decimos lo siento[a]
damos segundas oportunidades[b]
nos divertimos
NOS RESPETAMOS
NOS AMAMOS[c]
¡NUESTRO HOGAR!

[a]decimos... *we say I'm sorry* [b]damos... *we give second chances* [c]nos... *we love each other*

B. Proyecto: Hogar dulce hogar°

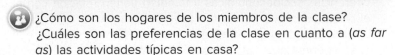

°Hogar... *Home Sweet Home*

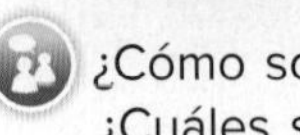

¿Cómo son los hogares de los miembros de la clase? ¿Cuáles son las preferencias de la clase en cuanto a (*as far as*) las actividades típicas en casa?

Paso 1. Preparación. En grupos, piensen en ideas (1 to 2 por miembro del grupo) relacionadas con el hogar para encuestar (*poll*) al resto de la clase. Pueden hacer preguntas sobre cómo es su casa, si hacen ciertas actividades o dónde las hacen (*you do them*), si hay muebles u otras cosas que desean para mejorar (*improve*) su hogar, etcétera.

MODELOS: tener sótano (*basement*)
quitarse los zapatos para entrar en la casa

Ahora preparen las preguntas para hacer la encuesta. Consideren varias opciones: cierto o falso, preguntas directas o una serie de opciones.

MODELOS: tener sótano → ¿Hay sótano en tu casa?
¿Cierto o falso para ti? Hay sótano en mi casa o edificio.
¿Cuál es tu opinión de los sótanos? Son necesarios / poco útiles (*not very useful*) / irrelevantes.

Paso 2. Encuesta. Cada miembro de su grupo debe hacerles su pregunta / sus preguntas a varios compañeros de clase. Antes de empezar a preguntar, deben tener un plan para apuntar (*write down*) las respuestas.

Paso 3: Análisis de datos. Analicen la información y preparen varias oraciones para presentar los datos al resto de la clase.

MODELOS:
__________ (número) personas de la clase viven en una casa o en un edificio con sótano.
__________ (número) estudiantes desean tener una casa con sótano.
__________ (número) estudiantes creen que los sótanos son poco útiles.

¡Ahora, yo!

A. Entrevista. Use de (*as a*) modelo las preguntas y respuestas de la página 135 de este capítulo para hablar de su casa y su alcoba.

B. Proyecto audiovisual. Con las preguntas de la página 135 como modelo, filme una o dos entrevistas con estudiantes de su universidad que hablan del lugar donde viven mientras (*while*) asisten a la universidad.

«Vivir con la familia» Segmento 2

Lorena Campos Verduzco quiere alquilar *(to rent)* un cuarto en su casa a un estudiante extranjero, porque su hija se va a casar (*get married*) y no quiere quedarse sola (*to be left alone*).

Antes de mirar

Conteste las siguientes preguntas.

1. ¿Piensa usted pasar un tiempo en otro país mientras (*while*) completa sus estudios universitarios? ¿A qué país piensa ir? ¿Por qué quiere ir a ese país?
2. ¿Cuáles son las ventajas (*advantages*) y desventajas de vivir con una familia en otro país?

Este segmento

Desde la Ciudad de México Laura ofrece un reportaje sobre una mujer que espera recibir (*hopes to house*) a estudiantes extranjeros en su casa.

Vocabulario del segmento

bienvenidos	welcome	**por lo regular**	generally
mostrarnos	showing us	**la carrera**	university studies
el próximo curso	next academic year	**hasta que no se casan**	until they get married
disfrutar	to enjoy	**la costumbre**	custom
la actual habitante	the current inhabitant	**los grandes**	adults
debido a que	due to (the fact) that	**la gente**	people
la luz	light	**el hogar**	home
cuentas con	you have	**hasta cierto punto**	up to a point
se la va a pasar	he/she is going to be	**nos despedimos**	we'll say good-bye

Fragmento del guion

Bueno,[a] aquí en casa va a tener todas las comodidades[b] como si estuviera[c] en su propia casa. Porque a mí me gusta tener ordenado el cuarto,[d] entonces no va a haber necesidad de que él vaya a pagar lavandería,[e] aquí mismo lo podemos hacer. Va a comer comida casera[f] muy rica.[g] Y aparte[h] va a tener compañía...

[a]*Well* [b]*comforts* [c]como... *as if he were* [d]tener... *to have the room tidy* [e]entonces... *so there is no need for him to pay for laundry* [f]*homemade* [g]muy... *very tasty* [h]*besides*

Después de mirar

A. ¿Está claro? ¿Cierto o falso? Corrija las oraciones falsas.

	CIERTO	FALSO
1. Lorena y su familia viven en Guadalajara, México.	☐	☐
2. Lorena tiene tres hijos.	☐	☐
3. La hija de Lorena que se va a casar se llama Luisa.	☐	☐
4. Por lo general, los jóvenes mexicanos viven con sus padres durante y después de sus estudios universitarios.	☐	☐

B. Un poco más. Describa el cuarto para un estudiante extranjero. ¿De quién es ahora el cuarto? ¿Cómo es? ¿Qué tiene?

C. Y ahora, ustedes. En parejas, imaginen que son los presentadores de *Salu2*. Preparen un cierre (*closing*) diferente para este segmento, incluyendo:

- una idea general como resumen del segmento
- una despedida (*sign-off*) con el nombre del programa y la ciudad de origen
- un anticipo (*preview*) del próximo programa (¡tienen libertad de imaginar!)

MUNDO HISPANO

Enfoque cultural: El Salvador y Nicaragua

Antes de leer

En la zona o ciudad donde usted vive, ¿qué tipo de vivienda (*housing*) es más común, casas o apartamentos?

La vivienda[a]

Como en todo el mundo, la vivienda en El Salvador y Nicaragua puede variar mucho. Hay lujosas[b] mansiones para las personas ricas y casas muy pobres y humildes[c] con un solo cuarto para toda una familia. En las ciudades principales hay edificios de apartamentos, como en cualquier[d] otro país.

En las ciudades de León y Granada, en Nicaragua, hay hermosas[e] casas de la época colonial. Estas casas cuentan con[f] muchos cuartos y tienen techos de tejas,[g] un jardín en medio de la casa y un patio trasero.[h]

[a]La... *Housing* [b]*luxurious* [c]*humble, simple* [d]*any* [e]*beautiful* [f]cuentan... tienen [g]techos... *tiled roofs* [h]*out back*

En otros países hispanos

En todo el mundo hispanohablante Los hispanos en general tienen un concepto muy generoso de la hospitalidad en su hogar[a] y les gusta ofrecer algo[b] de comer y beber a sus invitados.[c] Otra característica es que la hospitalidad en los hogares hispanos es más formal que en los Estados Unidos, una formalidad que los hispanos comprenden bien. Por ejemplo, es una falta[d] de respeto abrir el refrigerador en la casa de un amigo sin su permiso, aun si[e] se trate de[f] la casa de un amigo íntimo.

[a]*home* [b]ofrecer... *to offer something* [c]*guests (in their home)* [d]*lack* [e]aun... *even if* [f]se... *it involves*

El volcán Izalco, también llamado (*called*) «el Faro (*Lighthouse*) del Pacífico», todo un símbolo salvadoreño

Un símbolo de El Salvador y Nicaragua: Los volcanes

Los volcanes son una imagen representativa en estos dos países, que están dentro del llamado[a] Arco[b] Volcánico Centroamericano. En Nicaragua solamente,[c] hay diecinueve volcanes. Por eso, los escudos de las banderas[d] nicaragüense y salvadoreña muestran[e] una cordillera[f] con cinco volcanes.

[a]dentro... *inside the so-called* [b]*Rim, Arch* [c]En... *In Nicaragua alone* [d]escudos... *shields on the flags* [e]*show* [f]*mountain range*

Comprensión

Conteste las siguientes preguntas.

1. ¿En qué manera es similar la situación de la vivienda en El Salvador y Nicaragua a la (*to that*) del resto del mundo?
2. En general, ¿cómo es la hospitalidad de los hispanos?
3. ¿Por qué se consideran los volcanes un símbolo del país en Nicaragua y El Salvador?

En acción

En su región o estado, ¿qué se destaca (*stands out*) en la geografía? ¿Volcanes, montañas, ríos (*rivers*), colinas (*hills*) ... ? ¿Están en la bandera (*flag*) de su estado? Si no, diseñe (*design*) una bandera con ese ícono geográfico. ¿Puede crear (*create*) un lema (*motto*) en español?

Lectura

Antes de leer

¿Le gustan los colores de su casa? ¿Cuáles son los colores de las paredes exteriores de su propia casa o edificio? ¿De qué color o colores son las paredes interiores? ¿Son todas las paredes del mismo (*same*) color o hay toques de color (*color accents*) en diferentes cuartos?

La sicología de los colores en la decoración interior

Los colores que tenemos en nuestro hogar[a] nos afectan.[b] Cada color estimula diferentes asociaciones y estados de ánimo.[c] Por eso debemos estar conscientes a la hora de elegir[d] los colores para los diferentes espacios de nuestra casa.

Colores: Sus efectos sicológicos

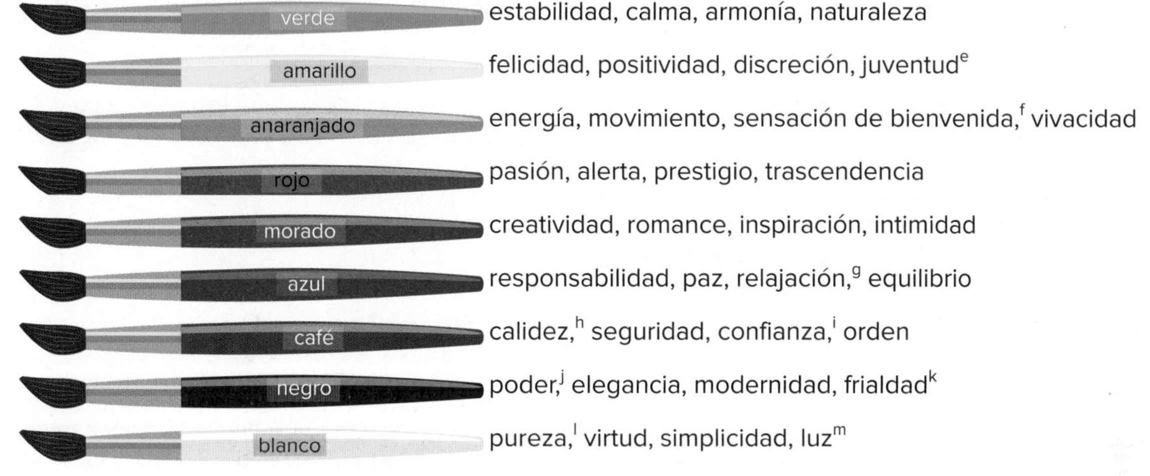

estabilidad, calma, armonía, naturaleza

felicidad, positividad, discreción, juventud[e]

energía, movimiento, sensación de bienvenida,[f] vivacidad

pasión, alerta, prestigio, trascendencia

creatividad, romance, inspiración, intimidad

responsabilidad, paz, relajación,[g] equilibrio

calidez,[h] seguridad, confianza,[i] orden

poder,[j] elegancia, modernidad, frialdad[k]

pureza,[l] virtud, simplicidad, luz[m]

---

[a]*home* [b]nos... *affect us* [c]estados... *moods* [d]seleccionar [e]*youth* [f]*welcoming* [g]*relaxation*
[h]*warmth* [i]*confidence* [j]*power* [k]*coldness* [l]*purity* [m]*light*

Comprensión

A. ¿Qué color deben usar? Use la información en la tabla de colores y su propia intuición para ayudar a las siguientes personas a elegir los colores ideales para pintar (*paint*) sus hogares. Explique las razones de cada decisión.

MODELO: Amalia trabaja duro (*hard*) todo el día y cuando regresa a casa necesita descansar. → Debe pintar su sala de color **azul** porque **tiene el efecto de paz y relajación.**

1. Ricardo trabaja en el estudio de su apartamento. Su trabajo es repetitivo; por eso se distrae fácilmente (*he gets distracted easily*).
2. Marta está sola en casa todo el día con sus tres hijos pequeños, que (*who*) son muy activos.
3. Arturo es inversionista (*investor*) y hace cenas (*dinners*) elegantes en su apartamento para clientes importantes.
4. Gloria es sicóloga y recibe clientes en casa. Muchos de ellos sufren de depresión y ansiedad.
5. Marcos tiene un pequeño gimnasio en su garaje, donde enseña clases de pilates a personas mayores (*older*).

B. Colores complementarios. Es común pintar un cuarto de dos o tres colores: un color de base y otro(s) de acento. Piense en uno de sus propios espacios y describa una buena combinación de colores para ese lugar. Explique sus razones para seleccionar esos colores.

Proyecto: Decoración de un espacio interior

Imagine que usted es experto/a en decoración de interiores.

Paso 1: Invente a un cliente/una clienta que es dueño/a (*owner*) de una casa, una tienda o una oficina donde recibe a clientes. ¿Cómo es su cliente/clienta? ¿Qué tipo de atmósfera necesita en su espacio?

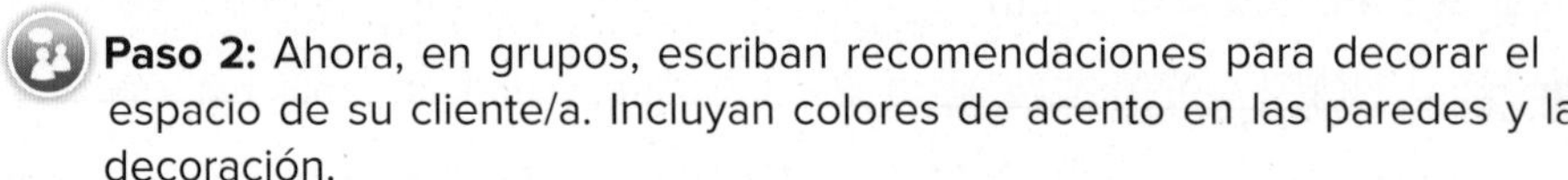

Paso 2: Ahora, en grupos, escriban recomendaciones para decorar el espacio de su cliente/a. Incluyan colores de acento en las paredes y la decoración.

Paso 3: Finalmente, hagan una breve presentación a la clase sobre su diseño (*design*). ¿Qué grupo tiene los diseños más creativos (*most creative*)? ¿más atractivos? ¿más prácticos?

Textos orales

Vocabulario para escuchar

amueblar	to furnish
ya	already
la plasma	flat-screen TV

Enrique y Víctor necesitan muebles

Antes de escuchar

¿Qué es más usual entre los estudiantes universitarios: alquilar (*to rent*) un apartamento amueblado o uno sin amueblar (*furnished or unfurnished*)? ¿Tiene usted muchos muebles propios donde usted vive? En su cuarto, casa o apartamento, ¿qué cosas son de usted?

Comprensión

A. ¿Qué necesitan? Enrique y Víctor acaban de alquilar (*have just rented*) un apartamento que tiene muy pocos muebles, pero no importa porque ellos tienen varias cosas. Dibuje (*Draw*) o escriba en el plano del apartamento el nombre de los muebles y cosas que ellos ya tienen para cada cuarto.

B. Más detalles. Conteste las siguientes preguntas.

1. ¿Qué cosas tienen que comprar Víctor y Enrique para sus alcobas?
2. ¿Qué parte de la casa no mencionan en la conversación?
3. ¿Qué muebles no necesitan comprar para la sala comedor?
4. ¿Cuántos televisores tienen entre los dos?

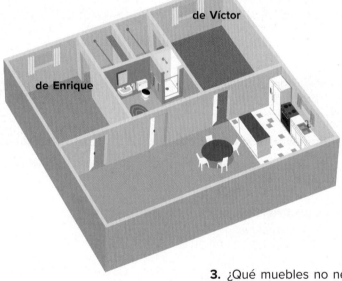

En acción

En parejas, imaginen que tienen que compartir (*share*) un pequeño apartamento el próximo semestre/trimestre. ¿Qué cosas tienen? ¿Qué muebles pueden compartir? ¿Qué necesitan?

Proyecto en su comunidad

Entreviste a (*Interview*) una persona hispana de su universidad o ciudad sobre las viviendas (*housing*) de su país de origen.

Preguntas posibles

- ¿En qué tipo de vivienda vive la mayoría de las personas en su país de origen?
- ¿Hay un tipo o estilo de casa «típico»? ¿Cómo es?
- ¿Dónde vive su familia?

Escritura

Proyecto: Un ensayo sobre una semana típica de los estudiantes universitarios

¿Cree usted que los estudiantes universitarios en general tienen una manera típica de vivir? Y, en particular, ¿los estudiantes de su universidad? ¿Por qué?

Un joven que estudia mucho

Antes de escribir

En una hoja de papel aparte, complete una tabla como la siguiente con información sobre 5 o 6 actividades que usted hace de lunes a viernes y durante el fin de semana en una semana típica. Luego entreviste (*interview*) a dos compañeros de clase sobre sus actividades y complete la tabla con su respectiva información.

	de lunes a viernes	fines de semana
usted		
estudiante A		
estudiante B		

A escribir

Ahora use la información para escribir un ensayo sobre la semana típica de los estudiantes de su universidad, si cree que es posible hablar de una semana típica. Hay más ayuda (*help*) en Connect.

Más ideas para su portafolio

- Incluya (*Include*) una foto de su cuarto o alcoba y descríbalo (*describe it*).
- Describa con muchos detalles la casa de sus sueños (*dreams*).
- Describa un día ideal para usted. ¿Qué día de la semana es, dónde está usted y qué hace durante todo el día?
- Si ha estado jugando (*you have been playing*) Practice Spanish: Study Abroad, en Quest 3 usted almorzó (*you had lunch*) en la casa de su familia colombiana. ¿Cómo es la casa? Dibuje el plano (*Draw the floorplan*) de la casa de su familia colombiana, incluyendo (*including*) todos los cuartos que usted recuerde (*remember*). Luego, nombre (*name*) dos actividades que se hacen (*are done*) en cada cuarto.

Sugerencia: You are now ready to play Quest 3 in **Practice Spanish: Study Abroad.**

EN RESUMEN En este capítulo

AFTER STUDYING THIS CHAPTER I CAN. . .

- ☐ name the parts of a house or apartment and furniture (136)
- ☐ use the names of the days of the week as well as other time expressions (138–139)
- ☐ use some words and expressions that put actions in sequence (140–141, 156)
- ☐ use important irregular and stem-changing verbs (143–145, 149–151)
- ☐ talk about my daily routine and other actions that require reflexive pronouns (153–155)
- ☐ recognize/describe at least 2–3 aspects of Salvadoran and Nicaraguan cultures

Gramática en breve

12. Present Tense of *hacer, oír, poner, salir, traer, ver*

hacer: hago, haces, hace, hacemos, hacéis, hacen

oír: oigo, oyes, oye, oímos, oís, oyen

poner: pongo, pones, pone, ponemos, ponéis, ponen

salir: salgo, sales, sale, salimos, salís, salen

traer: traigo, traes, trae, traemos, traéis, traen

ver: veo, ves, ve, vemos, veis, ven

13. Present Tense of Stem-changing Verbs

Stem-changing Patterns

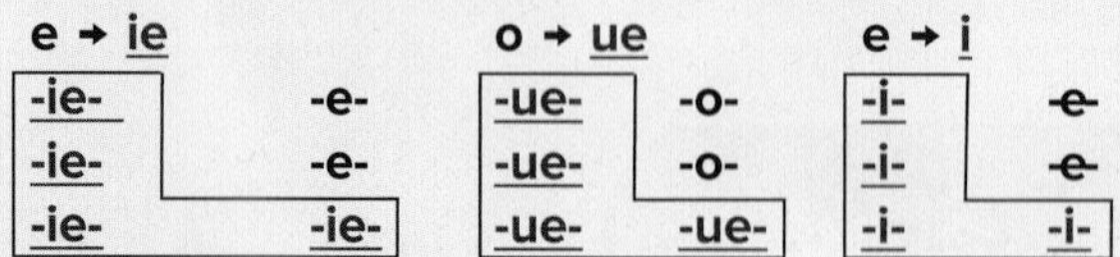

e → ie
-ie- -e-
-ie- -e-
-ie- -ie-
o → ue
-ue- -o-
-ue- -o-
-ue- -ue-
e → i
-i- -e-
-i- -e-
-i- -i-

14. Reflexive Pronouns

yo → me	**nosotros/as → nos**
tú → te	**vosotros/as → os**
usted/él/ella → se	**ustedes/ellos/ellas → se**

Vocabulario

Los verbos

almorzar (almuerzo)	to have lunch
cerrar (cierro)	to close
descansar	to rest
dormir (duermo)	to sleep
dormir la siesta	to take a nap
empezar (empiezo)	to begin, start
empezar a + *inf.*	to begin to (*do something*)
entender (entiendo)	to understand
hacer	to do; to make
hacer ejercicio	to exercise
hacer un viaje	to take a trip
hacer una pregunta	to ask a question
jugar (juego) (a; al)	to play (*a game; a sport*)
oír (oigo, oyes,...)	to hear; to listen to (*music, the radio*)
pedir (pido)	to ask for; to order
pensar (pienso) (en)	to think (about)
pensar de/que	to think of, have an opinion about/that
pensar + *inf.*	to intend, plan to (*do something*)
perder (pierdo)	to lose; to miss (*an event*)
poner (pongo)	to put; to place; to turn on (*an appliance*)
salir (salgo) (de)	to leave (*a place*); to go out
salir bien/mal	to turn/come out well/poorly; to do well/poorly
salir con	to go out with, date
salir para	to leave for (*a place*)
servir (sirvo)	to serve
servir para	to be used for
traer (traigo)	to bring
ver (veo)	to see; to watch (*a program, movie*)
volver (vuelvo)	to return (*to a place*)
volver a + *inf.*	to (*do something*) again

Los verbos que se usan con pronombres reflexivos

acostarse (me acuesto)	to go to bed
afeitarse	to shave
bañarse	to take a bath, bathe
cepillarse los dientes	to brush one's teeth
despertarse (me despierto)	to wake up
divertirse (me divierto)	to have a good time, enjoy oneself
dormirse (me duermo)	to fall asleep
ducharse	to take a shower
levantarse	to get up (out of bed); to stand up
llamarse	to be called
peinarse	to brush/comb one's hair
ponerse (me pongo)	to put on (*an article of clothing*)
quitarse	to take off (*an article of clothing*)
sentarse (me siento)	to sit down
vestirse (me visto)	to get dressed

Los cuartos y otras partes de una casa

la alcoba	bedroom
el baño	bathroom
la cocina	kitchen
el comedor	dining room
el estudio	office (*in a home*)
el jardín	garden
la pared	wall
el patio	patio; yard
la piscina	swimming pool
la sala	living room

Cognado: el garaje

Repaso: la casa, el cuarto

Los muebles y otras cosas de una casa

la alfombra	rug
el armario	armoire, free-standing closet
la bañera	bathtub
la cama	bed
la cómoda	bureau; dresser
el estante	bookshelf
la estufa	stove
la lámpara	lamp
el lavabo	(bathroom) sink
la mesita	end table
el sillón	armchair
la toalla	towel
el mueble	piece of furniture

Cognado: el sofá

Repaso: el escritorio, la mesa, la silla, la tele(visión)

Otros sustantivos

la bebida	drink
el cine	movies; movie theater
la cosa	thing
el diente	tooth
el ejercicio	exercise
la llave	key
la nota	grade
las noticias	news
la película	movie
la pregunta	question
el ruido	noise
la rutina	routine
la tarea	homework
el viaje	trip

Los adjetivos

cada *inv.**	each, every
diario/a	daily
primero/a[†]	first
siguiente	following
solo/a	alone

Las preposiciones

antes de	before
después de	after
durante	during
sin	without

Repaso: a, con, de, en, hasta, para, por (*in, during*), **sobre**

¿Qué día es hoy?

los días de la semana:
lunes, martes, miércoles, jueves, viernes, sábado, domingo

anteayer	the day before yesterday
ayer fue (miércoles...)	yesterday was (Wednesday. . .)
el lunes (martes...)	on Monday (Tuesday. . .)
los lunes (los martes...)	on Mondays (Tuesdays. . .)
pasado mañana	the day after tomorrow
el próximo (martes...)	next (Tuesday. . .)
la próxima semana	next week
la semana (el lunes...) que viene	next week (Monday. . .)

Repaso: el día, el fin de semana, hoy, mañana

Palabras adicionales

después *adv.*	then, later, next
en seguida	immediately
finalmente	finally
lo que	what, that which
luego	then, later, next
por fin	finally
por lo general	generally
primero *adv.*	first

Vocabulario personal

*The abbreviation inv. means invariable, unchanging (in form). The adjective **cada** is used with masculine and feminine nouns **(cada libro, cada mesa)**, and since its meaning (each) is singular, it is never used with plural nouns.*

[†]*The adjective **primero** shortens to **primer** before masculine singular nouns: **el primer libro**, but **la primera clase**.*

Las estaciones y el tiempo°

Las... *Seasons and the weather*

En este capítulo

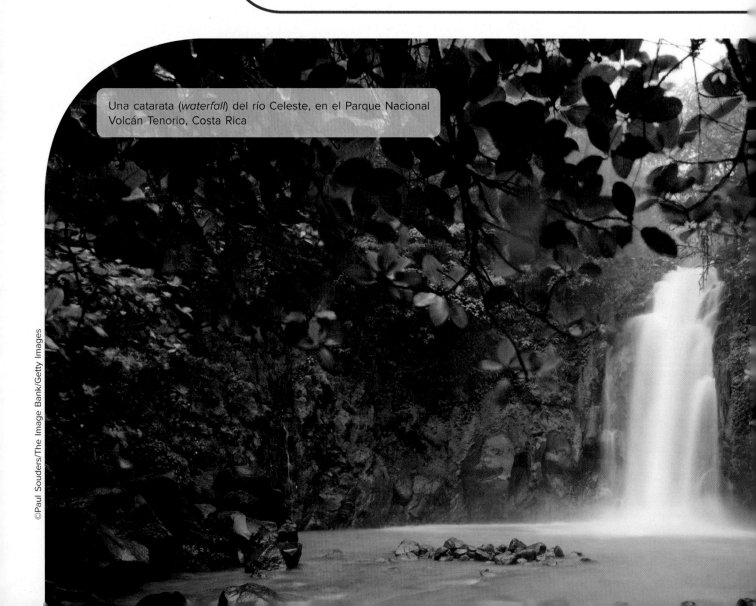

Una catarata (*waterfall*) del río Celeste, en el Parque Nacional Volcán Tenorio, Costa Rica

COSTA RICA

4,9 (coma nueve) millones de habitantes

- La Constitución de Costa Rica prohíbe la organización de fuerzas armadas.[a]
- El ecoturismo es fundamental para la economía de Costa Rica y para preservar sus bosques[b] y selvas,[c] que cubren[d] un 30% (por ciento) de su territorio.

[a]fuerzas... *armed forces* [b]*forests* [c]*jungles* [d]*cover*

ENTREVISTA

- ¿Cómo es el clima de su país?
- ¿Qué le gusta hacer cuando el tiempo[a] es bueno?
- ¿Cuál es su estación[b] favorita?

[a]*weather* [b]*season*

Manuel Gil del Valle contesta las preguntas.

- El clima de Managua es poco variado. Solo hay dos estaciones, una lluviosa[a] y otra seca.[b] La temperatura diaria varía poco: alrededor de[c] 30 grados de máxima y 21 de mínima. Es decir,[d] hace calor[e] todo el año.
- Bueno,[f] no hago nada[g] en especial, porque no hay una estación de calor y otra de frío.[h]
- Prefiero la estación seca. Es que[i] puede llover[j] mucho durante la estación lluviosa y no me gusta estar mojado.[k]

[a]una... *a rainy one* [b]otra... *a dry one* [c]alrededor... *around* [d]Es... *That is* [e]hace... *it's hot* [f]*Well* [g]no... *I don't do anything* [h]*cold* [i]Es... *That's because* [j]*rain* [k]*wet*

VOCABULARIO: PREPARACIÓN

You can hear the pronunciation of theme vocabulary words and phrases in the Connect eBook.

¿Qué tiempo hace hoy?°

¿Qué... *What's the weather like today?*

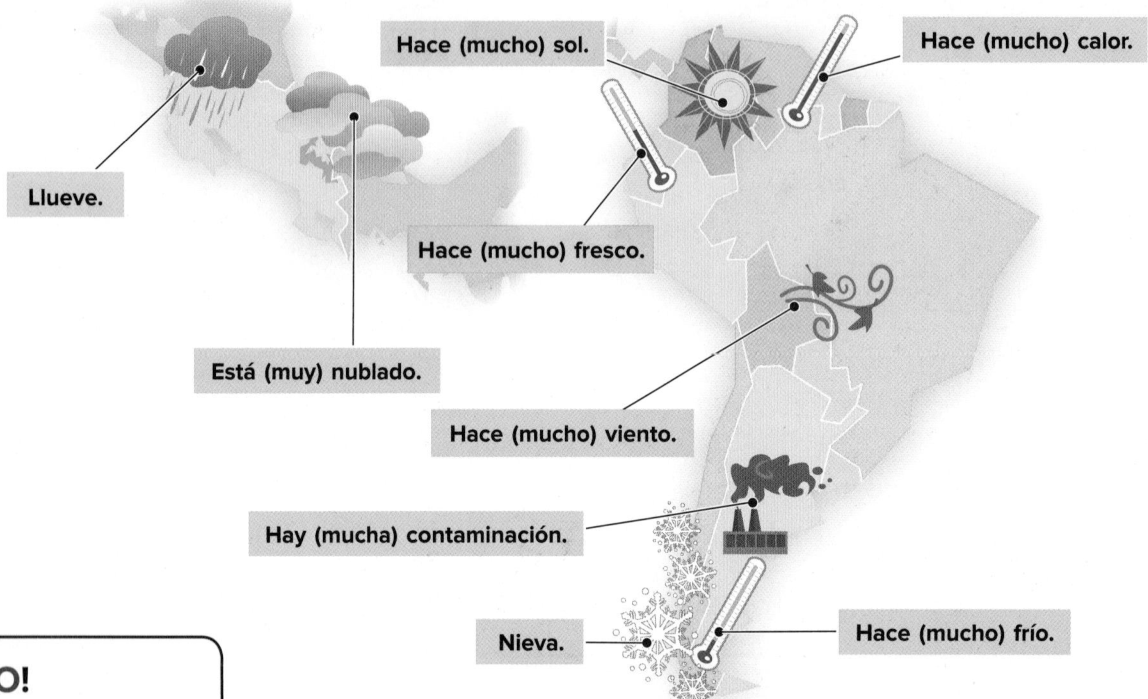

Hace (mucho) sol.
Hace (mucho) calor.
Llueve.
Hace (mucho) fresco.
Está (muy) nublado.
Hace (mucho) viento.
Hay (mucha) contaminación.
Nieva.
Hace (mucho) frío.

¡OJO!

el tiempo = *weather* and *time* in general, but: *What time is it?* = **¿Qué hora es?**

¡OJO!

There is no Spanish equivalent for the English subject *it* in these weather expressions. The verb alone (**hace**, **está**, **hay**) is sufficient.

- Many weather conditions are expressed with **hace** (**hacer**).

Hace (muy) buen/mal tiempo	It's (very) good/bad weather. It's (very) nice/bad out.
Hace (mucho) calor/fresco/frío/sol/viento.	It's (very) hot/cool/cold/sunny/windy.

- The words **calor** (*heat*), **fresco** (*coolness*), **frío** (*cold*), **sol** (*sun*), and **viento** (*wind*) are all nouns, which is why the adjective **mucho** is used with them, and not an adverb (as in English, which uses *very*).
- *To rain* and *to snow* are expressed with stem-changing verbs. Only the third person singular is used.

llover: llueve it rains, it's raining **nevar: nieva** it snows, it's snowing

- There are also weather expressions with the verbs **está** and **hay.**

Está (muy) nublado.	It's (very) cloudy.
Hay (mucha) contaminación.	There's (a lot of) pollution.

Así se dice

Here are some other weather expressions that you might hear.

Está nublado. = Está nubloso.
Nieva. = Está nevoso.
Llueve. = Está lluvioso.
Hace sol. = Está soleado.

Comunicación

A. El tiempo y la ropa. Diga qué tiempo hace, según la ropa de cada persona.

MODELO: Todos llevan traje de baño y chanclas. → Hace calor. (Hace buen tiempo.)

1. María lleva pantalones cortos y camiseta.
2. Juan lleva suéter, pero no lleva chaqueta.
3. Roberto lleva sudadera y chaqueta.
4. Ramón lleva impermeable y botas y también tiene paraguas (*umbrella*).
5. Todos llevan abrigo, botas y sombrero.

B. El clima en el mundo

Paso 1. ¿Qué clima o condición metereológica asocia usted con las siguientes ciudades?

1. Seattle, Washington
2. Los Ángeles, California
3. San José, Costa Rica
4. Buffalo, Nueva York
5. Waikiki, Hawái
6. Chicago, Illinois

Paso 2. ¿Qué clima o condición asocia usted con los siguientes lugares?

1. un desierto
2. una playa (*beach*)
3. una montaña muy, muy alta
4. una ciudad grande
5. la Antártida
6. una zona tropical
7. una zona templada (*temperate*)
8. Londres

C. El tiempo y las actividades. Haga oraciones completas, indicando una actividad apropiada para cada situación. Es necesario conjugar los verbos a la derecha (*right*).

MODELO: Cuando hace buen tiempo, almuerzo afuera / muchos estudiantes almuerzan afuera.

cuando hace buen/mal tiempo
cuando hace calor
cuando hace frío
cuando hay mucha contaminación
cuando llueve
cuando nieva

\+ 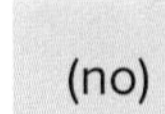 (no) +

jugar al basquetbol/voleibol con mis amigos
almorzar afuera (*outside*) / en el parque
divertirse en el parque / en la playa con mis amigos
salir de casa
volver a casa
trabajar o estudiar
quedarse (*to stay*) en casa

Nota comunicativa

Otras expresiones con *tener*

In addition to those you have already learned, some other conditions are expressed in Spanish with **tener** idioms—not with *to be,* as in English.

tener (mucho) calor	to be/feel (very) warm, hot
tener (mucho) frío	to be/feel (very) cold

These expressions are used to describe people or animals only. *To be comfortable*—neither hot nor cold—is expressed with **estar bien.**

You will use these expressions in **Comunicación D.**

D. ¿Tienen frío o calor? ¿Están bien? En parejas, describan el tiempo que hace en cada dibujo. También deben indicar cómo están las personas. Si ustedes creen que no tienen ni (*neither*) frío ni (*or*) calor, pueden decir (*say*): **«Está(n) bien».**

1.

2.

3.

4.

5.

6.

Los meses y las estaciones° del año *seasons*

Las cuatro estaciones en el hemisferio norte

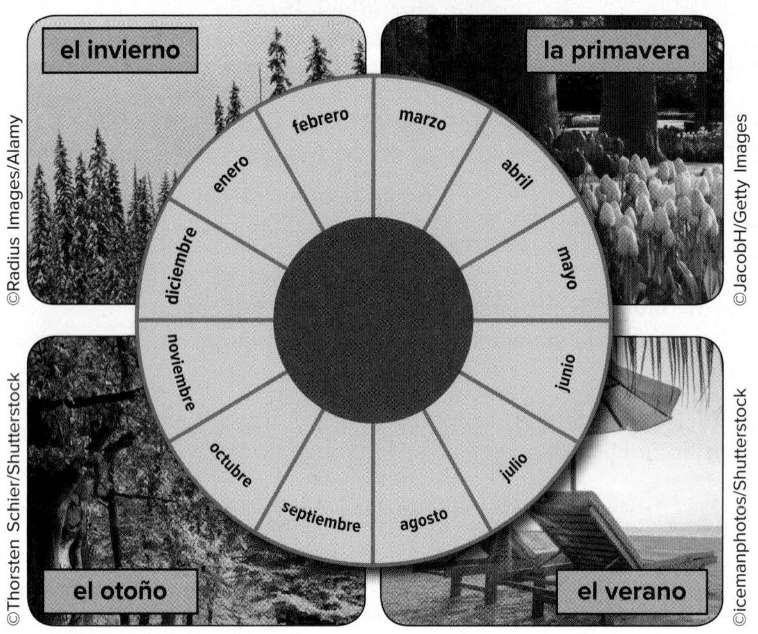

¿Cuál es la fecha de hoy? **¿Qué fecha es hoy?**	What's today's date?
(Hoy) Es el primero de abril.	(Today is) It's the first of April.
(Hoy) Es el cinco de febrero.	(Today is) It's the fifth of February.

- The ordinal number **primero (1°)** is used to express the first day of the month. Cardinal numbers (**dos, tres,** and so on) are used for other days.
- The definite article **el** is used before the date. However, when the day of the week is expressed, **el** is omitted: **Hoy es jueves, 3 de octubre.**
- As you know, **mil** is used to express the year (**el año**) after 999.

1950 mil novecientos cincuenta   2020 dos mil veinte

Así se dice

Other ways to ask what day it is include:

¿Qué día es hoy?
¿A cuántos estamos?

In the last sentence, **cuántos** is masculine because it refers to **días** (*m.*).

Comunicación

A. ¿Cuántos días hay en cada mes? Piense en el poema que se usa en inglés para recordar (*remember*) el número de días en cada mes: *Thirty days . . .* Aquí está el poema en español. Para completarlo (*complete it*), usted tiene que hacer rimar los dos primeros versos (*lines*).

Treinta días tiene __________,
Con abril, __________ y __________.
De veintiocho solo hay uno,
Y los demás,[a] treinta y uno.

[a]los... *the rest*

B. Las fechas

Paso 1. Exprese estas fechas en español. ¿En qué estación caen (*do they fall*)?

MODELO: February 15 → Es **el** quince **de** febrero. Cae (*It falls*) en invierno.

1. March 7
2. August 24
3. December 1
4. June 5
5. September 19, 1997
6. May 30, 1842
7. January 31, 1660
8. July 4, 1776

Paso 2. ¿Cuándo se celebran (día y mes)?*

Se celebra...

1. el Día del Año Nuevo
2. el Día de los Enamorados (de San Valentín)
3. la Navidad (*Christmas*)
4. el Día de los Inocentes (*Fools*), en los Estados Unidos
5. su cumpleaños (*birthday*)
6. el cumpleaños de su pareja, novio/a (*boyfriend/girlfriend*), esposo/a, mejor (*best*) amigo/a,...

¡OJO!

Remember: **el... de** = *on the . . . of*

Nota cultural

El clima en el mundo hispano

El mundo hispanohablante es inmenso. Se extiende en las Américas desde los Estados Unidos hasta la Argentina. Por eso, el clima de los países hispanohablantes es muy variado.

- No todos los países tienen cuatro estaciones. Costa Rica y otros países centroamericanos y sudamericanos solo tienen dos: una estación seca[a] y otra húmeda, con mucha lluvia. Esto es normal en los países de la zona tropical.
- El Niño, un fenómeno meteorológico, afecta directamente a varios países hispanos. Está caracterizado por temperaturas más calientes de lo normal[b] en la zona ecuatorial del océano Pacífico. El fenómeno se llama El Niño porque se presenta típicamente alrededor de[c] Navidad, época en que nace el Niño Jesús[d] (para los cristianos).

La costa del Perú, donde se descubrió (*was discovered*) el fenómeno de El Niño en el siglo (*century*) XIX

©DEA/S. Buonamici/Getty Images

[a]*dry* [b]más... *warmer than normal* [c]alrededor... *around* [d]nace... *the Baby Jesus is born*

¿Cómo es el clima de su estado o país? ¿Están las estaciones bien diferenciadas?

C. Intercambios

Paso 1. En parejas, túrnense para entrevistarse sobre los siguientes temas. Deben obtener detalles interesantes y personales de su compañero/a.

MODELO: la fecha de su cumpleaños →
¿Cuál es la fecha de tu cumpleaños? ¿Qué tiempo hace, generalmente, ese día? ¿Cómo celebras tu cumpleaños?

1. la fecha de su cumpleaños
2. su signo del horóscopo
3. su estación favorita
4. una estación que no le gusta

Paso 2. Digan a la clase lo que ustedes tienen en común.

MODELO: Nosotras tenemos el cumpleaños en abril. La fecha de María es el 16 y mi fecha es el 18. Nuestro signo es Aries. Las dos (*Both of us*) preferimos la primavera. ¿Por qué? Porque nuestro cumpleaños es en primavera y es una estación muy bonita.

Los signos del horóscopo

Aries	Libra
Tauro	Escorpión
Géminis	Sagitario
Cáncer	Capricornio
Leo	Acuario
Virgo	Piscis

Remember that the word **se** *before a verb changes the verb's meaning slightly.* **¿Cuándo se celebran?** = *When are they celebrated? You will see this construction throughout* **Puntos de partida**. *You will learn about this usage in* **Capítulo 8.**

¿Dónde está? Las preposiciones (Part 2)

cerca de	close to
lejos de	far from
debajo de	below
encima de	on top of
al lado de	alongside of
entre	between; among
delante de	in front of
detrás de	behind
a la derecha/ izquierda de	to the right/ left of
al norte/ sur/este/ oeste de	to the north/ south/east/ west of

Nueva York está al norte de Miami. México está al sur de los Estados Unidos.
Canadá
Estados Unidos
Nueva York
Miami
México
la maestra
Pablito
Luis
Carmen
Teresa
Los estudiantes están delante de la maestra.
Teresa está entre Carmen y Pablito.
El libro está encima de la mesa.
La mochila está debajo de la mesa.
Pablito está a la derecha de Teresa.

¡OJO!

Note that **mí** has a written accent, but **ti** does not. This diacritical accent (**Capítulo 4**) distinguishes the object of a preposition (**mí**) from the possessive adjective (**mi**).

- In Spanish, the *pronoun objects of prepositions* (**los pronombres preposicionales**) are identical in form to the subject pronouns, except for **mí** and **ti.**

Julio está delante de mí.	Julio is in front of me.
María está detrás de ti.	María is behind you.
Me siento a la izquierda de ella.	I sit on her left.

- The pronouns **mí** and **ti** combine with the preposition **con** to form **conmigo** (*with me*) and **contigo** (*with you*), respectively.

—¿Vienes conmigo?	"Are you coming with me?"
—Sí, voy contigo.	"Yes, I'll go with you."

¡OJO!

As in English, possessives are often used instead of the article to express location.

María está a **mi** izquierda.
Luis se sienta a **tu** derecha.

Comunicación

A. En el salón de clase

Paso 1. Describa a las personas o cosas de su clase en relación con usted. Siga el modelo. Use **nadie** (*no one*) cuando sea (*it's*) necesario.

MODELO: está cerca de la puerta. → **Jaime** está cerca de la puerta.

Una persona o una cosa que...

1. está cerca/lejos de la puerta.
2. está detrás de la mesa del profesor / de la profesora.
3. está delante del pizarrón.
4. se sienta a su izquierda/ derecha.
5. habla con usted en la clase.
6. hoy trabaja con usted.

Paso 2. Con un compañero / una compañera, escoja (*choose*) a una persona o un objeto en el salón de clase. Luego, sin nombrarlo/la (*without naming him/her/it*), use las preposiciones de lugar para explicar dónde está. Su compañero/a va a adivinar (*guess*) qué persona, objeto o mueble es.

MODELO: Está a la derecha de Paul ahora, pero generalmente se sienta detrás de mí. Siempre llega a clase conmigo. ¿Quién es?

B. ¿De qué país se habla?

Paso 1. Escuche la descripción de un país de Latinoamérica que da (*gives*) su profesor(a). ¿Cuál es ese país?

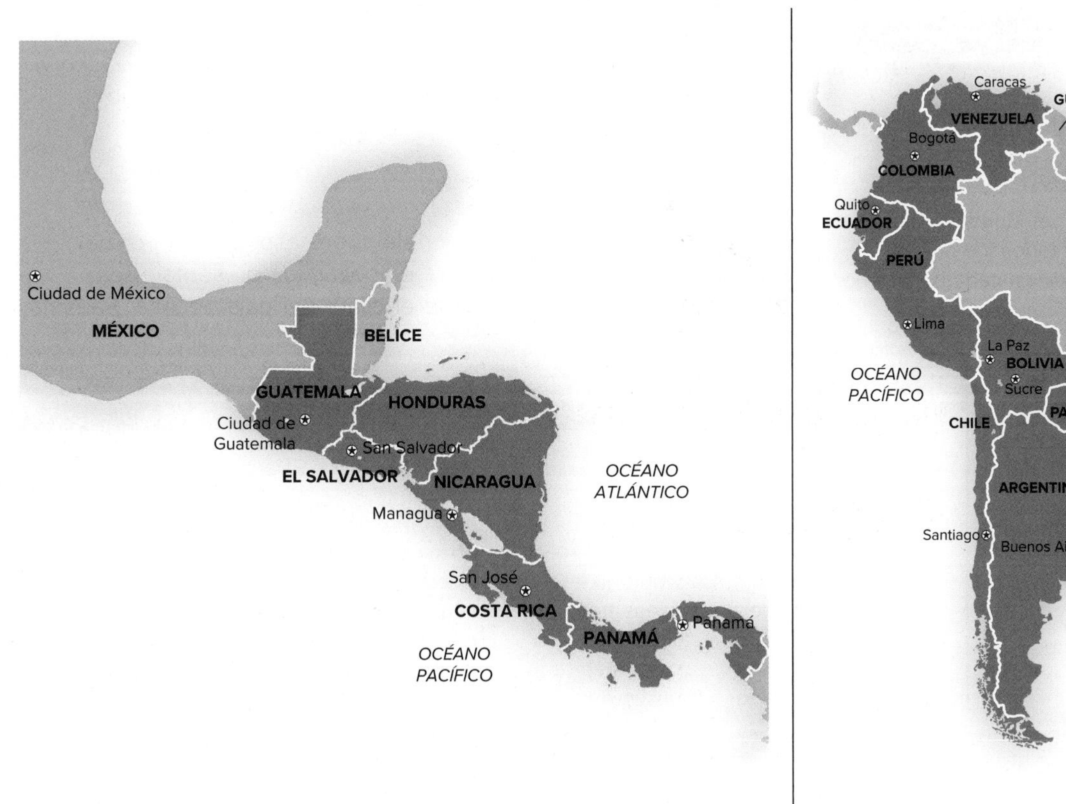

Paso 2. Ahora describa un país de Latinoamérica. Sus compañeros de clase van a decir cuál es. Siga (*Follow*) el modelo, usando todas las frases que sean (*are*) apropiadas.

MODELO: Este país está al norte/sur/este/oeste de _______. También está cerca de _______. Pero está lejos de _______ . Está entre _______ y _______. Su capital es _______. ¿Cómo se llama?

C. Intercambios. En parejas, túrnense para entrevistarse. Deben averiguar (*find out*) información sobre la ubicación (*location*) de las ciudades y los estados o países de donde son ustedes, y sobre su clima.

MODELO: E1: ¿De dónde eres?
E2: Soy de Tylertown.
E1: ¿Dónde está Tylertown?
E2: Está en el estado de _______, al oeste de _______.
E1: ¿Cómo es el clima?

«En la Mitad del Mundo°» Segmento 1 Mitad... *Middle of the World*

El monumento a la Mitad del Mundo: «Aquí turistas ecuatorianos y de todos los países vienen a poner un pie (*foot*) en cada hemisferio.»

Antes de mirar

Indique todas las opciones que son ciertas para usted.

- ☐ Donde yo vivo hay cuatro estaciones.
- ☐ Me gusta el clima cálido (*warm*) y seco (*dry*). ¡Me gusta el sol!
- ☐ Prefiero el invierno porque me gusta el frío y la nieve (*snow*).
- ☐ Llueve mucho aquí. Afortunadamente me gusta mucho la lluvia (*rain*).

Este segmento

Este segmento incluye un reportaje sobre aspectos del clima y la geografía del Ecuador. Para empezar, los presentadores intercambian comentarios sobre el clima del país de Ana, Panamá.

Estrategia

This segment includes a lot of vocabulary that you learned in **Vocabulario: Preparación.** You will understand the segment more easily if you review that vocabulary before watching. Consider adding some additional weather-related vocabulary to **Vocabulario personal** (at the end of the chapter).

Vocabulario del segmento

rico/a	beautiful	**reflejar**	to reflect
disfrutando	enjoying	**olvidar**	to forget
la temporada	season	**montañoso/a**	mountainous
mejor te quedas	you better stay	**atravesar (atraviesо)**	to cross
me gustaría	I would like	**el corazón**	heart
la infatigable viajera	tireless traveler	**segundo/a**	second
lluvioso/a	rainy	**rodear**	to surround
a nivel del mar	at sea level	**contrarrestar**	to react (with), counteract
el grado centígrado	Celsius degree		
la humedad	humidity		

Después de mirar

A. ¿Está claro? Las siguientes oraciones son falsas. Corríjalas. (*Correct them.*)

1. A Ana no le gusta la nieve.
2. El clima de Panamá es muy diferente del clima del Ecuador.
3. La Mitad del Mundo es una ciudad del Ecuador.
4. En los países tropicales hay dos temporadas, una cálida y otra fría.
5. En Quito no llueve mucho.

B. Un poco más. Conteste las siguientes preguntas.

1. ¿Es muy cálido el clima en todas las zonas tropicales del mundo? Dé un ejemplo.
2. ¿Qué factor geográfico afecta el clima del Ecuador?

C. Y ahora, ustedes En parejas, hablen sobre si les gustaría (*you would like*) vivir en un lugar con un clima como el (*like that*) de Quito o como el de la costa ecuatoriana, que es mucho más cálido. Expliquen por qué.

MODELO: Me gustaría vivir en un lugar con un clima similar al (*to that*) de Quito porque me gusta la lluvia...

GRAMÁTICA

15 *¿Qué están haciendo?*

Present Progressive: **Estar + -ndo**

Gramática en acción: ¿Qué está haciendo Elisa esta tarde?

©Janis Christie/Getty Images

Elisa es periodista. Por eso escribe y habla mucho por teléfono en su trabajo. Pero ahora mismo no está trabajando. Está descansando en casa. Está escuchando música, leyendo una novela y tomando un café.

¿Y usted?

En el salón de clase, ¿quién está haciendo las siguientes cosas en este momento? **¡OJO! nadie** = *nobody*.

1. _______ está hablando por teléfono.
2. _______ está leyendo un periódico.
3. _______ está tomando un café.
4. _______ está mandando mensajes.
5. _______ está escuchando música.

The Progressive / **El progresivo**			
estoy **estás** **está** **estamos** **estáis** **están**	**tomando** **comiendo** **abriendo**	I am you (*fam.*) are he, she, it, you (*form.*) are we are you (*pl. fam.*) are they, you (*pl. form.*) are	drinking eating opening

Uses of the Progressive / **Los usos del progresivo**

the progressive / **el progresivo** = a verb form that expresses continuing or developing action

1. **The Progressive**
   Spanish and English form the *progressive* (**el progresivo**) in similar ways, as you can see in the preceding chart, but the use of the progressive is not the same in both languages.

What's Elisa doing this afternoon? *Elisa is a journalist. That's why she writes and talks a lot on the phone in her job. But she's not working right now. She's resting at home. She's listening to music, reading a novel, and having a cup of coffee.*

2. Uses of the Progressive

As shown in the example sentences, English uses the present progressive to tell:

- what is happening *right now* (1)
- what is happening *over a period of time* (2)
- what is *going to* happen (3)

In Spanish, the present progressive is always used primarily to express an action that *is happening right now* (1).

To express actions that are happening over a period of time, Spanish uses the present progressive or the simple present tense (2).

To express actions that are going to happen, Spanish uses the simple present tense or **ir** + **a** + *infinitive* (3), but never the progressive.

1. *Ramón is eating right* now.
   Ramón **está comiendo** ahora mismo.
2. *Adelaida is studying chemistry this semester.*
   Adelaida **está estudiando** química este semestre.
   Adelaida **estudia** química este semestre.
3. *We're buying the house tomorrow.*
   Compramos (Vamos a comprar) la casa mañana.

Forming the Present Progressive / **La formación del presente progresivo**

1. Spanish Present Progressive

The Spanish *present progressive* (**el presente progresivo**) is formed with **estar** plus the *present participle* (**el gerundio**).

The present participle is formed by adding **-ando** to the stem of **-ar** verbs and **-iendo** to the stem of **-er** and **-ir** verbs.

The present participle never varies; it always ends in **-o.**

a present participle / **un gerundio** = the verb form that ends in *-ing* in English

estar + *present participle*

tomar → **tomando**		taking; drinking
comprender → **comprendiendo**		understanding
abrir → **abriendo**		opening

¡OJO!

Unaccented **i** between two vowels becomes the letter **y.**

leer: le + **iendo** → **leyendo**
oír: o + **iendo** → **oyendo**

---

2. Present Participle of *-ir* Stem-changing Verbs

-Ir stem-changing verbs also have a stem change in the present participle.

- The stem vowel **e** changes to **i.**
- The stem vowel **o** changes to **u.**

As you can see, sometimes that change is the same as in the present tense (as in **pedir**) and sometimes it is different (as in **preferir** and **dormir**).

The verbs you have learned so far that show this second change are: **divertirse, dormir(se), pedir, preferir, servir,** and **vestirse.**

preferir (prefiero) (i) → **prefiriendo**
pedir (pido) (i) → **pidiendo**
dormir (duermo) (u) → **durmiendo**

Note that (**duermo**) shows you the present tense stem change for **dormir: o** → **ue.** The **(u)** shows you the change in the present participle of **dormir: o** → **u (durmiendo).**

In vocabulary lists from this point on in *Puntos de partida*, this second stem change will be shown in parentheses after the first person singular form of the verb.

---

3. Position of Reflexive Pronouns

Reflexive pronouns can be attached to a present participle or precede the conjugated form of **estar.** Note the accent that is added to the present participle when pronouns are attached.

Pablo **se está** bañando. Pablo **está bañándose.**	*Pablo is taking a bath.*
Estoy empezando a vestir**me.** **Me estoy empezando** a vestir.	*I'm starting to get dressed.*

Práctica y comunicación

A. Un sábado típico

Paso 1. Autoprueba. Complete el gerundio de los siguientes verbos con una de las siguientes terminaciones.

a. -ando **b. -iendo** **c. -yendo**

1. acost_______
2. bañ_______
3. durm_______
4. hac_______
5. le_______
6. pid_______
7. prefir_______
8. divirt_______
9. cre_______
10. empez_______

Paso 2. Ahora piense en su rutina de un sábado típico. Indique dos acciones que es posible que usted esté (*might be*) haciendo a las siguientes horas. Hay una lista de **Frases útiles,** pero usted puede modificarlas (*modify them*) o añadir otras.

MODELO: a las ocho de la mañana →
A las ocho de la mañana estoy durmiendo o duchándome.

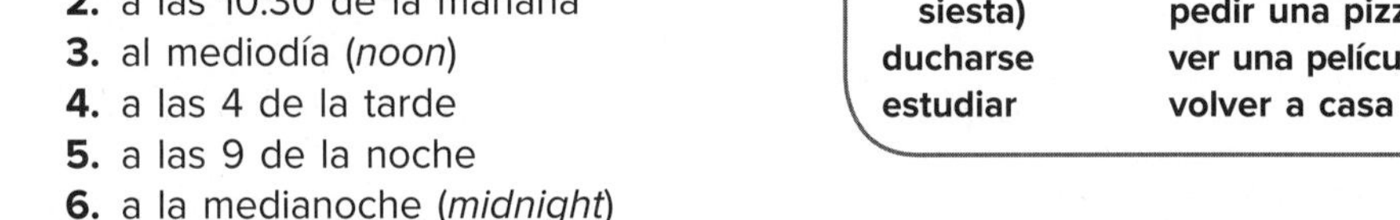

1. a las 8 de la mañana
2. a las 10:30 de la mañana
3. al mediodía (*noon*)
4. a las 4 de la tarde
5. a las 9 de la noche
6. a la medianoche (*midnight*)

Frases útiles

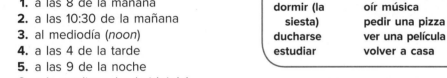

almorzar	**hacer ejercicio**
despertarse	**levantarse**
dormir (la siesta)	**oír música**
ducharse	**pedir una pizza**
estudiar	**ver una película**
	volver a casa

Paso 3. Ahora, en parejas, túrnense para determinar si hacen las mismas (*same*) cosas a la misma hora.

MODELO: E1: A las ocho de la mañana los sábados, ¿estás durmiendo?
E2: No, a esa hora estoy trabajando.

B. Hoy, en casa de Lola.

Hoy, en casa de Lola. Hoy no es un día como todos los días para la familia de Lola, porque su tío de Costa Rica está de visita. Complete las siguientes oraciones para expresar lo que está pasando (*happening*).

MODELO: Casi siempre, Lola almuerza con su hija. Hoy Lola... (**almorzar** con su tío en un restaurante) →
Hoy Lola **está almorzando** con su tío en un restaurante.

1. Generalmente, Lola pasa la mañana en la universidad. Hoy Lola... (**pasar** el día con su tío Ricardo)
2. Casi siempre, Lola toma un café en la cafetería después de sus clases. Hoy Lola y su tío... (**tomar** un café en casa)
3. De lunes a viernes, Marta, la hija de Lola, va a la escuela (*school*) por la tarde. Pero esta tarde ella... (**jugar** con Ricardo)
4. Generalmente, la familia cena (*has dinner*) a las nueve. Esta noche todos... (**cenar** a las diez)

Summary of Present Progressive

estar + -ando
-iendo
-yendo

Algo sobre...

los valores[a] de los costarricenses

©imagebroker/Alamy

El Parque Nacional Rincón de la Vieja, parte de la importante industria ecoturística de Costa Rica

Dos cualidades caracterizan el país de Costa Rica. Una es la paz.[b] Esta nación no tiene fuerzas armadas[c] desde 1948. Hay una expresión que ilustra este sentimiento nacional: «Donde haya[d] un costarricense, habrá[e] paz.» La segunda[f] característica es la importancia que la ecología tiene para el país. Costa Rica no solo preserva su biodiversidad; también la explota.[g]

¿Qué cualidades caracterizan este país? ¿Es la paz un valor estadounidense?

[a]*values* [b]*peace* [c]fuerzas... *armed forces* [d]Donde... *Wherever there is* [e]*there will be* [f]*second* [g]la... *she develops it*

Prác. A, Paso 1: **Answers:** *1.* a *2.* a *3.* b *4.* b *5.* c *6.* b *7.* b *8.* b *9.* c *10.* a

C. **En casa con la familia Duarte**

Paso 1. Describa lo que pasa en cada dibujo, explicando quién está haciendo la acción —el padre, la madre, la hija, los gemelos (*twins*), el perro— y a qué hora. Use los verbos de la lista u otros verbos, si desea. Puede hacer más de (*than*) una oración para cada dibujo, si quiere. **¡OJO!** Hay verbos reflexivos en las listas.

MODELO: salir de la ducha (*shower*) → El padre **está saliendo** de la ducha a las seis de la mañana.

Por la mañana: A las seis de la mañana

Acciones

dormir todavía still
leer el periódico
levantarse
salir de la ducha
tomar un café

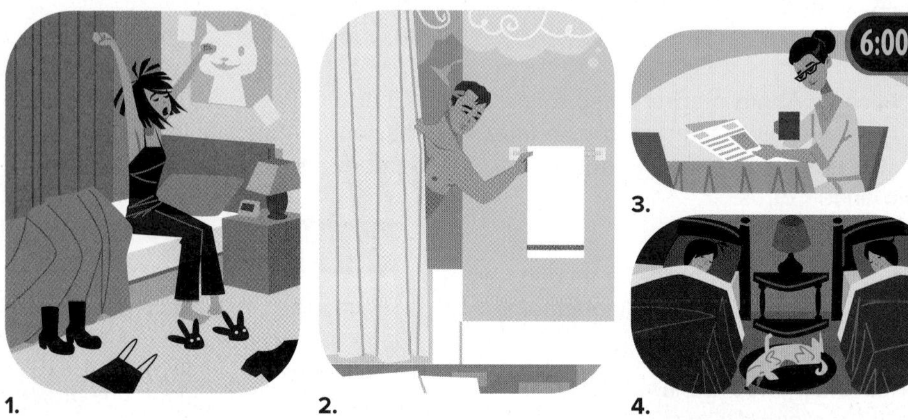

Más tarde: A las ocho de la mañana

Acciones

desayunar
leer sus e-mails
pensar en el examen que tiene hoy
salir para la universidad
trabajar en la oficina
vestirse

Por la tarde: A las seis y media de la tarde

Acciones

hacer la tarea
jugar
leer un libro de texto
preparar la cena dinner
quitarse la ropa

Paso 2. Ahora explique qué hacen usted y otros miembros de su familia o sus compañeros de cuarto/casa a la misma hora que ve en los dibujos.

Nota comunicativa

El gerundio con otros verbos

As in English, the Spanish *present participle* **(el gerundio)** can be used with verbs other than **estar.** The following verbs are commonly followed by the present participle.

- **pasar tiempo** + *present participle* — *to spend time* (doing something)
  - ¿**Pasas** mucho tiempo **haciendo** la tarea? — *Do you spend a lot of time doing homework?*
- **seguir (sigo) (i) / continuar (continúo)** + *present participle* — *to continue* (doing something)
  - **Sigue lloviendo** mucho. — *It continues to rain / raining a lot.*
- **divertirse (me divierto) (i)** + *present participle* — *to enjoy* (doing something)
  - ¿Te **diviertes** mucho **bailando** salsa? — *Do you have a good time dancing salsa?*

Remember that the letter in parentheses indicates the change in the present participle of the verb, which in this case would be **siguiendo** and **divirtiendo.**

You will use these verbs in **Práctica D** and **E.**

¡OJO!

Note the present tense forms of **continuar,** which have an accent on the **u** when it is stressed (like the boot pattern of stem-changing verbs):

continúo	**continuamos**
continúas	**continuáis**
continúa	**continúan**

¡OJO!

If the second verb in these constructions is reflexive, its reflexive pronoun must agree with the subject.

Me divierto **bañándome** en el mar.
I enjoy swimming in the sea.

D. Intercambios

Paso 1. Use las siguientes ideas para hacer cinco oraciones sobre sus hábitos.

		infinitivo → gerundio
continuar/seguir divertirse estar pasar más tiempo pasar mucho/poco tiempo	+	**bailar** hasta la medianoche **estudiar / leer** / ¿ ? **hablar** español después de la clase **mandar** mensajes **mirar** series en Netflix™ / **escuchar** música (con los audífonos) **ser** amigo/a de mi mejor (*best*) amigo/a de la escuela primaria **trabajar** (en ¿ ?) ¿ ?

Paso 2. Ahora, en parejas, túrnense para entrevistarse sobre los mismos temas. Luego compartan (*share*) con la clase algo (*something*) que tienen en común.

MODELOS: ¿Pasas mucho tiempo mirando series en Netflix ¿Cuántas horas al (*per*) día? ¿Cuál es tu serie favorita?

E. ¿Qué están haciendo? Imagine lo que están haciendo las siguientes personas ahora mismo. También puede decir (*say*) si pasan tiempo o se divierten haciendo esas acciones. Use una palabra o frase de cada columna y la forma progresiva.

(yo) mi mejor (*best*) amigo/a mis padres mi equipo (*team*) deportivo favorito el presidente / la presidenta de este país el profesor / la profesora de español _______ (un compañero / una compañera que está ausente hoy)	+	descansar, dormir(se), escribir, hacer, jugar (al), leer, pasar (mucho) tiempo, practicar, trabajar, ¿ ? divertirse + *pres. part.*, seguir + *pres. part.*	+	fútbol/basquetbol un libro / una novela a los estudiantes / a sus consejeros la tarea / un informe (*report*) ejercicio físico ¿ ?

¿Recuerda usted?

You have been using forms of **ser** and **estar** since **Capítulo 1.** The following section will help you consolidate everything you know so far about these two verbs, both of which express *to be* in Spanish. You will learn a bit more about using them as well.

Before you begin **Gramática 16,** think in particular about the following questions: **¿Cómo está usted? ¿Cómo es usted?** What do these questions tell you about the difference between **ser** and **estar**?

16 *¿Ser o estar?*

Summary of the Uses of **ser** and **estar**

Gramática en acción: Una conversación a larga distancia

©Stockbyte/Getty Images

©XiXinXing/Getty Images

Aquí hay un lado de la conversación entre una esposa que **está** en un viaje de negocios y su esposo, que **está** en casa. Habla el esposo.

«Aló. [...] ¿Cómo **estás**, querida? [...] ¿Dónde **estás** ahora? [...] ¿Qué hora **es** allí? [...] ¡Huy!, **es** muy tarde. Y el hotel, ¿cómo **es**? [...] Oye, ¿qué **estás** haciendo ahora? [...] Ay, lo siento. **Estás** muy ocupada. ¿Con quién tienes cita mañana? [...] ¿Quién **es** el dueño de la compañía? [...] Ah, él **es** de Costa Rica, ¿verdad? [...] Bueno, ¿qué tiempo hace allí? [...] Muy bien. Hasta luego, ¿eh? [...] Adiós.»

Comprensión

Complete las oraciones con **es** o **está**.

1. El esposo _____ en casa.
2. La esposa _____ una mujer de negocios.
3. La esposa _____ en un viaje de negocios.
4. No sabemos (*We don't know*) cómo _____ el hotel.
5. _____ muy tarde donde _____ la esposa.
6. La esposa _____ trabajando ahora.
7. El dueño de la compañía _____ de Costa Rica.

A long-distance conversation *Here is one side of a conversation between a wife who is on a business trip and her husband, who is at home. The husband is speaking. "Hello . . . How are you, dear? . . . Where are you now? . . . What time is it there? . . . Wow, it's very late. And how's the hotel? . . . Hey, what are you doing now? . . . Gosh, I'm sorry. You're very busy. Whom do you have an appointment with tomorrow? . . . Who's the owner of the company? . . . Ah, he's from Costa Rica, isn't he? . . . Well, what's the weather like there? . . . Great. See you later, OK? . . . Good-bye."*

Summary of the Uses of ser / **Resumen de los usos de ser**	
• To *identify* people (including their profession) and things	Ella **es doctora.** Tikal **es una ciudad maya.**
• To express *nationality;* with **de** to express *origin*	**Son cubanos.** **Son de** La Habana.
• With **de** to tell of what *material* something is made	Este bolígrafo **es de plástico.**
• With **de** to express *possession*	**Es de** Carlota.
• With **para** to tell *for whom something is intended*	El regalo **es para** Sara.
• To tell *time* and give the *date*	**Son las once.** **Es la una y media.** Hoy **es martes,** tres de octubre.
• With *adjectives* that describe *basic, inherent characteristics*	Ramona **es inteligente.**
• To form many *generalizations* or *impersonal expressions* (only **es**)	**Es necesario** llegar temprano. **Es importante** estudiar.

Summary of the Uses of estar / **Resumen de los usos de estar**	
• To tell *location*	El libro **está en la mesa.**
• To describe *health* and *condition* with adverbs	**Estoy** muy **bien,** gracias. Las respuestas **están mal.**
• With *adjectives* that describe *conditions*	**Estoy** muy **ocupada.**
• In a number of *fixed expressions*	**(No) Estoy de acuerdo.** **Está bien.** (*It's fine, OK.*)
• With *present participles* to form the *progressive tense*	**Estoy estudiando** ahora mismo.

Ser and **estar** with Adjectives / ***Ser* y *estar* con adjetivos**

1. ***Ser* = Fundamental Characteristics**
   Ser is used with adjectives that describe the *fundamental qualities* (**las características fundamentales**) of a person, place, or thing.

   Esa mesa **es** muy **baja.**
   That table is very short.

   Sus calcetines **son morados.**
   His socks are purple.

   Este sillón **es cómodo.**
   This armchair is comfortable.

   Sus padres **son cariñosos.**
   Their parents are affectionate people.

---

2. ***Estar* = Conditions**
   Estar is used with adjectives to express *conditions* (**las condiciones**) or observations that are true at a given moment but that do not describe inherent qualities of the noun. The adverbs **bien** and **mal** are often used in this context. The adjectives on the next page are generally used with **estar.**

(Continúa.)

Temporary Conditions / **Las condiciones temporales**					
abierto/a	open	**desordenado/a**	messy	**ocupado/a**	busy
aburrido/a	bored	**enfermo/a**	sick	**ordenado/a**	neat
alegre	happy	**furioso/a**	furious, angry	**preocupado/a**	worried
cansado/a	tired	**limpio/a**	clean	**seguro/a**	sure, certain
cerrado/a	closed	**loco/a**	crazy	**sucio/a**	dirty
congelado/a	frozen; very cold	**molesto/a**	annoyed	**triste**	sad
contento/a	content, happy	**nervioso/a**	nervous		

3. ***Ser* or *estar*?**
Many adjectives can be used with either **ser** or **estar,** depending on what the speaker intends to communicate. In general, when *to be* implies *looks, feels,* or *appears,* **estar** is used. Compare the use of **ser** and **estar** in the sample sentences.

Daniel **es guapo.**
Daniel is handsome. (*He is a handsome person.*)
Daniel **está muy guapo** esta noche.
Daniel looks very nice (*handsome*) *tonight.*

Amalia **es muy simpática**, pero hoy **está muy seria**.
Amalia is very nice, but she's very serious today.

Summary of *ser* and *estar*

ser = inherent qualities
identification
nationality, origin
material
possession
for whom
time, date
generalizations

estar = conditions
location
present progressive
fixed expressions

Práctica y comunicación

A. *¿Soy o estoy?*

Paso 1. Autoprueba. ¿Ser o **estar**? ¿Cuál es el verbo apropiado para cada caso?

____ **1.** to describe a health condition
____ **2.** to tell time
____ **3.** to describe inherent characteristics
____ **4.** to tell where a thing or person is located
____ **5.** to tell someone's profession
____ **6.** to say to whom something belongs
____ **7.** to tell where someone is from
____ **8.** to describe a temporary condition
____ **9.** to make a generalization
____ **10.** to tell what something is intended for

Paso 2. Ahora complete las siguientes oraciones con **estoy** o **soy.** También identifique la razón para usar cada verbo, usando los números de las explicaciones del **Paso 1.**

		RAZÓN DEL **Paso 1**
a.	_____ bien.	_____
b.	_____ simpático/a.	_____
c.	_____ contento/a de tomar español este semestre/trimestre.	_____
d.	_____ estudiante universitario/a.	_____
e.	_____ de_____ (ciudad, estado o país).	_____

Paso 3. Ahora, en parejas, túrnense para hacer y contestar preguntas basadas en el **Paso 2.** Luego digan a la clase algo (*something*) que ustedes tienen en común.

MODELO: a. Estoy bien. →
E1: ¿Cómo estás?
E2: Estoy muy bien. ¿Y tú?
EN COMÚN: Los dos estamos bien hoy.

Prác. A Paso 1: Answers: 1. *estar* ***2.*** *ser* ***3.*** *ser* ***4.*** *estar* ***5.*** *ser* ***6.*** *ser* ***7.*** *ser* ***8.*** *estar* ***9.*** *ser (es)* ***10.*** *ser*

B. Un regalo estupendo. Use **es** o **está** para describir la computadora que los padres de su compañero/a de cuarto acaban de comprarle (*just bought for him/her*).

La computadora…

1. _____ en la mesa del comedor.
2. _____ un regalo de cumpleaños.
3. _____ para mi compañero de cuarto.
4. _____ de la tienda Computec.
5. _____ en una caja (*box*) verde.
6. _____ de los padres de mi compañero.
7. _____ un regalo muy caro, pero estupendo.
8. _____ de metal y plástico gris.
9. _____ una IBM último modelo.
10. _____ muy fácil (*easy*) de usar.

Nota comunicativa

El uso de adjetivos + *por*

Por often expresses *because of* or *about* (as in *due to*), especially with adjectives such as **contento/a, furioso/a, nervioso/a,** and **preocupado/a.**

Amalia está preocupada **por** los exámenes finales.
Amalia is worried about her final exams.

You will use **por** in this way in **Práctica C** and **D.**

C. ¿Quiénes son? En parejas, inventen detalles para describir a las personas de la foto, haciendo oraciones con **ser** o **estar.**

1. ¿quiénes?
2. ¿de qué país?
3. simpáticos/antipáticos / ¿ ?
4. en este momento, contentos/ tristes / ¿ ?
5. molestos/cansados por el viaje / ¿ ?
6. aquí por un mes / una semana / ¿ ?
7. ¿ ?

©Paul Burns/Getty Images

Algo sobre…

¡Pura vida[a]!

Cada país hispanohablante tiene expresiones típicas y ¡Pura vida! es la más típica de Costa Rica. Los costarricenses usan esta frase para expresar que algo[b] es bueno, y también para decir[c] «hola» y «adiós». Como muchas expresiones, la traducción[d] literal no tiene mucho sentido[e] y no es aplicable en otra lengua.

Otra cosa típica del país: los costarricenses usan el pronombre **vos** en lugar de[f] **tú**. El uso de **vos** no es exclusivo de Costa Rica, sino que[g] es prevalente en la Argentina, el Uruguay, el Paraguay y en Centroamérica, excepto en Panamá.

—¿Cómo estás vos?
—¡Pura vida!

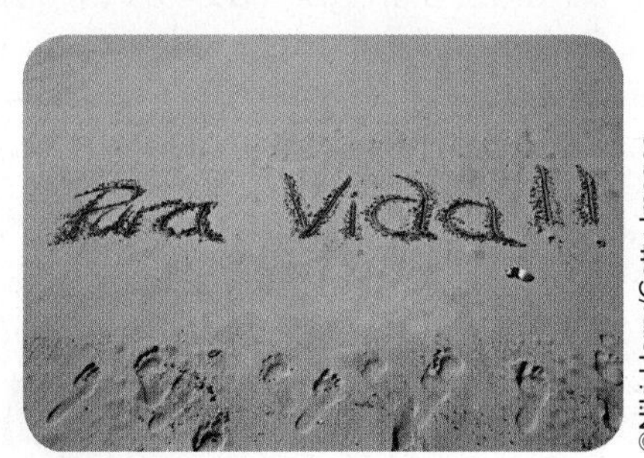

©Niki Harry/Getty Images

[a]*life* [b]*something* [c]*say* [d]*translation* [e]no… *doesn't make much sense*
[f]en… *instead of* [g]sino… *but*

¿Qué expresión es típica de la región donde usted vive?

D. Publicidad

Paso 1. Complete el siguiente anuncio (*ad*) con la forma apropiada de **ser**, **estar** o **hay**, según el contexto.

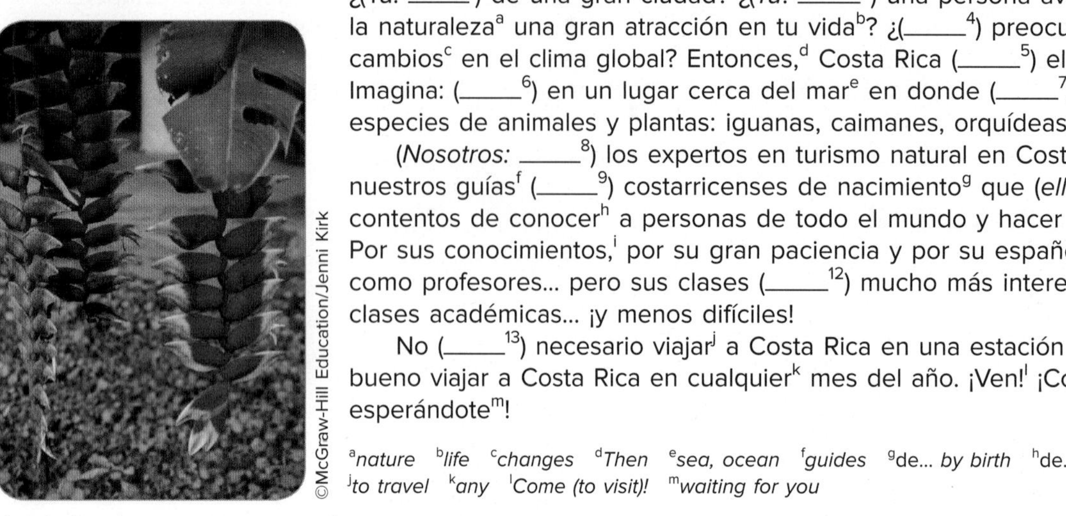

Una heliconia

Costa Rica, ¡pura vida!

¿(Tú: ______[1]) de una gran ciudad? ¿(*Tú*: ______[2]) una persona aventurera? ¿(______[3]) la naturaleza[a] una gran atracción en tu vida[b]? ¿(______[4]) preocupado/a por los cambios[c] en el clima global? Entonces,[d] Costa Rica (______[5]) el país para ti. Imagina: (______[6]) en un lugar cerca del mar[e] en donde (______[7]) increíbles especies de animales y plantas: iguanas, caimanes, orquídeas, heliconias...

(*Nosotros:* ______[8]) los expertos en turismo natural en Costa Rica. Todos nuestros guías[f] (______[9]) costarricenses de nacimiento[g] que (*ellos:* ______[10]) contentos de conocer[h] a personas de todo el mundo y hacer nuevos amigos. Por sus conocimientos,[i] por su gran paciencia y por su español, (*ellos:* ______[11]) como profesores... pero sus clases (______[12]) mucho más interesantes que las clases académicas... ¡y menos difíciles!

No (______[13]) necesario viajar[j] a Costa Rica en una estación específica. (______[14]) bueno viajar a Costa Rica en cualquier[k] mes del año. ¡Ven![l] ¡Costa Rica (______[15]) esperándote[m]!

[a]*nature* [b]*life* [c]*changes* [d]*Then* [e]*sea, ocean* [f]*guides* [g]de... *by birth* [h]de... *to meet* [i]*knowledge* [j]*to travel* [k]*any* [l]*Come (to visit)!* [m]*waiting for you*

Paso 2. Comprensión. ¿Cierto o falso? Corrija las oraciones falsas.

	CIERTO	FALSO
1. En Costa Rica, la naturaleza tiene mucha importancia para el turismo	☐	☐
2. El turista no va a ver animales exóticos allí.	☐	☐
3. El turista puede aprender español allí.	☐	☐
4. No todas las estaciones son apropiadas para el turismo.	☐	☐

E. Una conversación entre esposos

Paso 1. En parejas, organicen el diálogo entre el marido de la página 182 (**Columna A**) y su esposa (**Columna B**), que está en un viaje de negocios. Primero, emparejen los elementos de las dos columnas. El esposo empieza el diálogo, contestando el teléfono.

A

1. ______ Aló.
2. ______ Bien. ¿Cómo estás tú, querida?
3. ______ ¿Dónde estás ahora?
4. ______ ¿Qué hora es allí?
5. ______ ¡Huy!, es muy tarde. Y el hotel, ¿cómo es?
6. ______ Oye, ¿qué estás haciendo ahora?
7. ______ Ay, lo siento. Estás muy ocupada. ¿Con quién tienes cita mañana?
8. ______ ¿Quién es el dueño de la compañía?
9. ______ Ah, él es de Costa Rica, ¿verdad?
10. ______ Bueno, ¿qué tiempo hace allí?
11. ______ Bueno. Mañana hablamos más. Buenas noches.

B

a. ______ muy moderno y ______ muy limpio.
b. Sí, pero ahora ______ trabajando en Nueva York.
c. ______ las once de la noche.
d. Hola, querido. ¿Qué tal?
e. El señor Cortina.
f. ______ leyendo unos informes (*reports*) para la reunión de mañana. ______ que leer uno más todavía.
g. Sí. Hasta mañana.
h. ______ en el hotel, en Nueva York.
i. ______ un poco cansada por el viaje y ______ sueño.
j. ______ fresco y ______ nublado.
k. Con un señor de Computec.

Paso 2. Ahora completen las oraciones de la señora con la forma correcta de **estar, hacer, ser** o **tener**. Luego practiquen la conversación completa.

F. Una tarde terrible

Paso 1. Hoy es un día desastroso para la familia Castañeda. Usted va a describir lo que está pasando en su casa en el **Paso 2.** Para prepararse, repase (*review*) primero unos adjetivos, cambiando (*exchanging*) las palabras subrayadas (*underlined*) por antónimos en las siguientes oraciones.

1. No hace buen tiempo; hace ________________ tiempo.
2. El bebé no está bien; está ________________.
3. El gato no está limpio; está ________________.
4. El esposo no está tranquilo; está ________________ por el bebé.
5. El garaje no está cerrado; está ________________.
6. Los niños no están tranquilos; están ________________, porque tienen miedo.
7. La esposa no está contenta; está ________________ por el tiempo.
8. El grifo (*faucet*) del baño no está cerrado; está ________________.

Paso 2. Ahora use los adjetivos del **Paso 1** y otros que usted conozca (*you know*) para expresar lo que **están haciendo** todos los miembros de la familia en este momento. Póngales (*Give*) nombres a todos y exprese su **estado de ánimo** (*their feelings*) o sus deseos. ¡Use su imaginación! Si puede, diga también **lo que usualmente hacen** estas personas a esta hora.

Estrategia

lo que están haciendo = el presente progresivo

el estado de ánimo = **el presente simple**

lo que usualmente hacen = **el presente simple**

Vocabulario útil

la cena	dinner	**ladrar**	to bark
cenar	to have dinner	**llorar**	to cry
cocinar	to cook	**los truenos y relámpagos**	thunder and lightning
conducir (conduzco)*	to drive		

*Only the first person singular of the verb **conducir** is irregular, as noted. The other forms of the present tense are regular: **conduces, conduce...***

G. **Compañeras ideales**

Paso 1. Conteste las preguntas para describir el siguiente dibujo de un cuarto de dos estudiantes. **¡OJO!** Invente otros detalles necesarios.

Vocabulario útil

el cajón drawer
el cartel poster
la foto

1. ¿Quiénes son las dos compañeras de cuarto?
2. ¿Dónde estudian? ¿Qué estudian?
3. ¿De dónde son?
4. ¿Cómo son?
5. ¿Dónde están en este momento?
6. ¿Qué hay en el cuarto?
7. ¿Cómo está el cuarto?
8. ¿Son ordenadas las dos o desordenadas?

 **Paso 2.** Ahora, en parejas, hablen de las características que prefieren en un compañero / una compañera de cuarto o de casa. Idealmente, ¿cómo debe ser esa persona?

 H. **Intercambios.** ¿Cómo están ustedes en estas situaciones? En parejas, túrnense para hacer y contestar preguntas, según el modelo.

MODELO: cuando / tener mucha tarea →
E1: ¿Cómo estás cuando **tienes** mucha tarea?
E2: Estoy cansado y estresado, como ahora. ¿Y tú?
E3: Yo también.

Vocabulario útil

agobiado/a	overwhelmed
deprimido/a	depressed
desahogado/a	relieved
estresado/a	

1. cuando / tener mucha tarea / una tarea fácil/difícil
2. cuando / no tener trabajo (*work*) académico
3. cuando / sacar (*to get*) A/D en un examen
4. en verano/invierno
5. cuando llueve/nieva
6. los lunes por la mañana / los domingos por la tarde / los...
7. después de una fiesta / un examen
8. durante la clase de _______
9. ¿ ?

17 Describing

Comparisons

Gramática en acción: Buenos Aires y San José

©Image Source

El centro de Buenos Aires, Argentina

- Buenos Aires es más grande que San José.
- Tiene más edificios altos que San José.
- Generalmente, en Buenos Aires no hace tanto calor como en San José.

Pero…
- San José es menos antigua que Buenos Aires.
- No tiene tantos habitantes como Buenos Aires.
- Sin embargo, los costarricenses son tan simpáticos como los argentinos.

¿Y usted?

1. Mi ciudad/pueblo…
- (no) es tan grande como Chicago.
- es más/menos cosmopolita que San Francisco.

2. Me gusta _____ (nombre de mi ciudad/pueblo)…
- más que _____ (nombre de otra ciudad).
- menos que _____ (nombre de otra ciudad).
- tanto como _____ (nombre de otra ciudad).

©mtcurado/Getty Images

El centro de San José, Costa Rica

Algo sobre…

San José y Buenos Aires

San José
- Fundada en 1738 y capital de Costa Rica desde 1823
- Población: 333.980 habitantes
- Clima: 2 estaciones; 23° C (grados Celsius) promedio[a] todo el año

Buenos Aires
- Fundada en 1580 y capital de la Argentina desde 1853
- Población: 2.891.000 habitantes
- Clima: 4 estaciones; 26° C de máximas temperaturas (diciembre–febrero) y 14° C de mínimas (junio–agosto).

La ciudad donde usted vive, ¿es una ciudad capital? ¿Cuántos habitantes tiene, aproximadamente? ¿Cuántas estaciones hay?

[a]*average*

In English *comparisons* (**las comparaciones**) are formed in a variety of ways. Equal comparisons are expressed with the word *as*. Unequal comparisons are expressed with the adverbs *more* or *less,* or by adding *-er* to the end of the adjective.

as** cold **as
as** many **as

***more** intelligent,*
***less** important*
*tall**er**, smart**er***

a comparative / **un comparativo** = a form of or structure with nouns, adjectives, and adverbs used to compare nouns, qualities, or actions

Buenos Aires and San José *Buenos Aires is bigger than San José. • It has more tall buildings than San José. • It is not as hot in Buenos Aires as it is in San José, generally. But . . . • San José is newer (lit., less ancient) than Buenos Aires. • It doesn't have as many inhabitants as Buenos Aires. • Nevertheless, Costa Ricans are as nice as Argentines.*

Comparatives / **Los comparativos**					
Inequality / **La desigualdad**				Equality / **La igualdad**	
más... que	more . . . than	**menos... que**	less . . . than	**tan... como**	as . . . as
más que	more than	**menos que**	less than	**tanto/a/os/as... como**	as much/many . . . as
				tanto como	as much as

Inequality / **La desigualdad: más/menos... que, más/menos que**

1. Comparing Adjectives, Adverbs, and Verbs

Elena habla: «Juan es **más alto que yo**. Y corre **más rápido que yo**.»

Para describir

más/menos + *adjective* + **que**

more/less + *adjective* } + *than*
adjective + **-er** }

Juan es **más alto que** Elena.
Juan is taller than Elena.

Elena es **menos alta que** Juan.
Elena is shorter than Juan.

Para describir cómo se hace una acción

más/menos + *adverb* + **que**

more/less + *adverb* } + *than*
adverb + **-er** }

Juan corre **más rápido que** Elena.
Juan runs faster (more quickly) than Elena.

Elena corre **menos rápido que** Juan.
Elena runs slower (less quickly) than Juan.

> **¡OJO!**
>
> Look at the examples under the drawings and notice the use of **yo**, (never **mí**) as the second term of the comparison.

Para expresar la frecuencia o intensidad de una acción

verb + **más/menos que**

verb + *more/less than*

Juan **corre más que** Elena.
Juan runs more than Elena.

Elena **corre menos que** Juan.
Elena runs less than Juan.

2. Comparing Nouns

Carmen habla: «Rigoberto tiene **más coches que yo**.»

Para comparar la cantidad

más/menos + *noun* + **que**

more/less (fewer) + *noun* + *than*

Rigoberto tiene **más coches que** Carmen.
Rigoberto has more cars than Carmen.

Carmen tiene **menos coches que** Rigoberto.
Carmen has fewer cars than Rigoberto.

3. *More/Fewer than* + number

Juan habla: «Elena tiene **menos lápices que yo**.»

> **¡OJO!**
>
> The preposition **de** is used instead of **que** when the comparison is followed by a number.

Para expresar una cantidad

más/menos de + ***number*** + ***noun***

more/fewer than + *number* + *noun*

Juan tiene **más de dos** lápices.
Juan has more than two pencils.

Elena tiene **menos de dos** lápices.
Elena has fewer than two pencils.

Equality / **La igualdad: tan... como, tanto como, tanto/a/os/as... como**

1. Comparing Adjectives, Adverbs, and Verbs

Patricia habla: «Ernesto es **tan alto** y **tan delgado como yo**»

Para describir

tan + *adjective* + **como**
as + *adjective* + *as*

Patricia es **tan alta como** Ernesto. También es **tan delgada como** él.
Patricia is as tall as Ernesto (is). She's also as thin as him.

Ernesto habla: «Patrica juega **tan agresivamente como yo**. También juega **tanto como yo**.»

Para describir cómo se hace una acción

tan + *adverb* + **como**
as + *adverb* + *as*

Ernesto juega al tenis **tan bien como** Patricia. También juega **tan agresivamente como** *ella.*
Ernesto plays tennis as well as Patricia (does). He also plays as aggressively as her.

Para expresar la frecuencia o intensidad de una acción

verb + **tanto como**
verb + *as much as*

Patricia **juega** al tenis **tanto como** Ernesto. También **gana tanto como** él.
Patricia plays tennis as much as Ernesto. She also wins as much (often) as him.

2. Comparing Nouns

> **¡OJO!**
>
> Like all adjectives, **tanto** must agree in gender and number with the noun it modifies: **tanto dinero, tanta prisa, tantos abrigos, tantas hermanas.**

Para comparar la cantidad

tanto/a/os/as + *noun* + **como**
as much/many + *noun* + *as*

Ernesto tiene **tantos trofeos como** Patricia. También tiene **tantas raquetas de tenis como** ella.
Ernesto has as many trophies as Patricia. He also has as many tennis rackets as her.

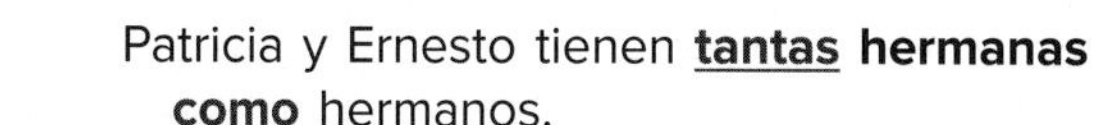

Patricia y Ernesto tienen **tantas hermanas como** hermanos.
Patricia and Ernesto each have as many sisters as (they have) brothers.

Patricia habla: «Ernesto tiene **tantos hermanos como yo**.»

Irregular Forms / **Las formas irregulares**

- **bueno/a/os/as** *adj.* → **mejor, mejores (que)** Estos coches son **buenos,** pero esos son **mejores** (que estos). *These cars are good, but those are better (than these).*
- **bien** *adv.* → **mejor (que)** Yo hablo español **bien,** pero mi amigo Dennis lo habla **mejor** (que yo). *I speak Spanish well, but my friend Dennis speaks it better (than I [do]).*
- **malo/a/os/as** *adj.* → **peor, peores (que)** La nueva película de este director es **mala,** pero la primera es **peor**. *This director's new movie is bad, but his first one is worse.*
- **mal** *adv.* → **peor (que)** La profesora canta **mal,** pero yo canto **peor** (que ella). *The professor sings badly, but I sing worse (than her).*
- **viejo/a/os/as** → **mayor, mayores (que)** La abuela es **viejita,** pero el abuelo es **mayor** (que ella). *Grandmother is old, but grandfather is older than she (is).*
- **joven, jóvenes** → **menor, menores (que)** Delia es **joven,** pero su esposo es **menor** (que ella). *Delia is young, but her husband is younger than her.*

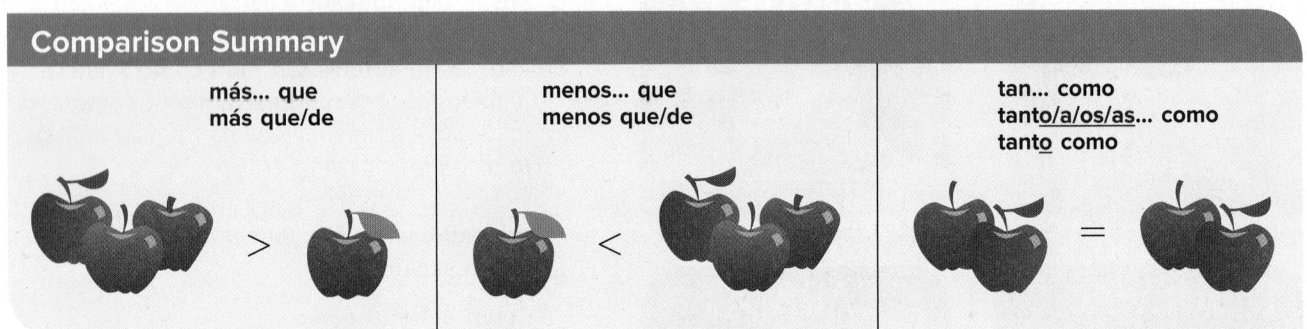

Comparison Summary
más... que
más que/de
menos... que
menos que/de
tan... como
tanto/a/os/as... como
tanto como
>
<
=

Práctica y comunicación

A. Comparaciones

Paso 1. Autoprueba. Complete las frases con la palabra comparativa apropiada.

a. como **b.** que

1. más _______ **3.** peor _______ **5.** menos _______
2. tantos _______ **4.** tan _______ **6.** tanta _______

Paso 2. Ahora compárese *(compare yourself)* con su mejor amigo/a, haciendo oraciones con los siguientes verbos y las formas comparativas del **Paso 1** u otras.

MODELO: tener años → Tengo **tantos años como** mi mejor amiga. (Soy [un año] **mayor/menor que** mi mejor amiga.)

1. tener años
2. tomar cursos
3. bailar
4. tener dinero
5. ser inteligente
6. tener pasión por el/la _______

Paso 3. Ahora, en parejas, usen las oraciones del **Paso 2** para entrevistarse. Luego digan a la clase algo (*something*) que tienen en común.

MODELO: **E1:** Tengo tantos años como mi mejor amiga. ¿Y tú?
E2: Sí, tengo tantos años como mi mejor amiga. (No, soy [un año] mayor que mi mejor amiga.)
EN COMÚN: Las dos tenemos tantos años como nuestras mejores amigas. (Las dos no tenemos tantos años como nuestras mejores amigas.)

Prác. A, Paso 1: Answers:* 1. *b* 2. *a* 3. *b* 4. *a* 5. *b* 6. *a

B. Alfredo y Gloria

©John Lund/Sam Diephuis/Blend Images

Alfredo
San José, Costa Rica
Profesor universitario
Casado. (*Married.*) Vive en una casa cerca del campus.
Dos hijos

©Pixtal/age fotostock

Gloria
Punta Arenas, Chile
Estudiante universitaria
Vive en una casa en el centro con ocho compañeros.
No tiene hijos.

Paso 1. ¿Quién probablemente tiene más de las siguientes cosas y cualidades y quién tiene menos? **¡OJO!** Los dos son similares en los números 4, 5 y 6.

1. botas de invierno
2. camisas de manga (*sleeves*) corta
3. chanclas
4. inteligencia
5. parientes
6. camisetas

Paso 2. ¿Quién probablemente hace más o hace menos? **¡OJO!** Los dos son similares en los números 4, 5 y 6.

1. ganar (*to earn*) dinero
2. salir con sus amigos
3. dormir
4. levantarse temprano
5. hacer ejercicio
6. trabajar

Paso 3. Use los comparativos irregulares para hablar de Alfredo y Gloria.

1. Es obvio que Alfredo tiene más años: es ______ ______ Gloria.
2. Los padres de Alfredo tienen más de 65 años. Probablemente, los padres de Gloria son ______ ______ los padres de Alfredo.
3. Gloria toma clases de danza. Así que (*So*), Gloria baila ______ ______ Alfredo.

C. Opiniones

Paso 1. Complete las siguientes declaraciones para expresar su opinión.

MODELO: el cine / la televisión : ser / interesante →
El cine **es más** interesante **que** la televisión. (**tan... como**)

1. el fútbol / el fútbol americano: ser / divertido (*amusing*)
2. la clase de historia / la clase de español: ser / interesante
3. en esta universidad, las artes / los deportes (*sports*): ser / importante
4. el español / el inglés: ser / difícil
5. mis amigos / mis padres: divertirse con
6. los niños / los adultos: dormir
7. los profesores / los estudiantes: trabajar
8. en primavera / en otoño: llover

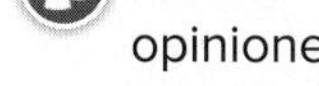

Paso 2. Ahora, en parejas, comparen sus respuestas y expliquen sus opiniones. Luego digan a la clase una idea que los dos comparten (*share*).

D. Más opiniones

Paso 1. Compare las siguientes personas y cosas para expresar su opinión sobre ellas. Puede añadir (*add*) más palabras si quiere.

MODELO: el basquetbol y el golf: interesante, rápido, fácil de aprender →
El basquetbol es **menos** interesante **que** el golf.

1. Meryl Streep y Millie Bobby Brown: joven, bonito, tener premios Óscar
2. Usted y sus padres (hijos): joven, conservador, tener experiencia, desordenado
3. un Prius™ y un Cadillac™: grande, barato, gastar (*to use*) gasolina, elegante
4. los perros y los gatos: independiente, inteligente, cariñoso, activo
5. Texas y Delaware: grande, tener habitantes, petróleo, estar lejos de California

(Continúa.)

Paso 2. En parejas, comparen sus opiniones. Traten de (*Try to*) explicar sus razones. Luego digan a la clase algo (*something*) que tienen en común.

MODELO: el basquetbol y el golf: interesante, rápido →
E1: El basquetbol es **menos** interesante **que** el golf.
E2: No estoy de acuerdo. El basquetbol es **más** interesante **que** el golf porque es **más** rápido.

E. Comparaciones. Complete las siguientes oraciones según su experiencia personal.

1. En mi familia, yo soy mayor que _____ y menor que _____.
2. En esta clase, _____ estudia(n) tanto como yo.
3. En esta universidad, los estudiantes _____ más que _____.
4. _____ es más guapo que Luis Fonsi.
5. _____ es más guapa que Shakira.
6. _____ tiene tanto talento como Bruno Mars.

F. La familia de Lucía y Miguel

Paso 1. En parejas, miren la foto e identifiquen a los miembros de la familia de Lucía. Piensen en la edad (*age*) de cada persona.

Lucía, con su esposo, sus padres y sus hijos

MODELO: Sancho es mayor que sus hermanos.

Paso 2. Comparen a cada miembro de la familia con otra persona.

MODELO: Amalia es menor que Sancho pero es más alta que él.

Paso 3. Ahora comparen a los miembros de su propia familia. Haga por lo menos cinco declaraciones.

MODELOS: **E1:** Mi hermana Mary es mayor que yo, pero yo soy más alto que ella.
E2: Mi abuela es mayor que mi abuelo, pero ella es más activa que él.

G. La rutina diaria... en invierno y en verano

Paso 1. ¿Es diferente nuestra rutina diaria en cada estación? Complete las siguientes oraciones sobre su rutina.

	EN INVIERNO	EN VERANO
1. Me levanto a _____ (hora).	_____	_____
2. Almuerzo en _____.	_____	_____
3. Me divierto con mis amigos / mi familia en _____.	_____	_____
4. Estudio _____ horas todos los días.	_____	_____
5. Estoy / me quedo en _____ (lugar) por la noche.	_____	_____
6. Me acuesto a _____ (hora).	_____	_____

Vocabulario útil

afuera outside
el gimnasio
el parque

Paso 2. En parejas, comparen sus actividades de invierno con las de verano.

MODELO: **E1:** En invierno, ¿te levantas más temprano que en verano?
E2: No, en invierno, me levanto tan temprano como en verano. (No, en invierno, me levanto a la misma hora que en verano.)

Paso 3. Ahora digan a la clase una o dos cosas que ustedes tienen en común.

MODELO: Nosotros nos levantamos más tarde en verano que en invierno. En verano no hay clases y, por lo general, nos acostamos más tarde.

Todo junto

A. Lengua y cultura: Dos hemisferios

Paso 1. Completar. Complete the following paragraphs with the correct forms of the words in parentheses, as suggested by context. When two possibilities are given in parentheses, select the correct word.

¿Sabe usted[a] algo de las diferencias entre el clima del hemisferio norte y sur? Hay ______ (mucho[1]) diferencias.

Cuando ______ (ser / estar[2]) invierno en este país, por ejemplo, ______ (ser / estar[3]) verano en la Argentina, en Bolivia, en Chile... Cuando yo ______ (salir[4]) para la universidad en enero, con frecuencia tengo que ______ (llevar[5]) abrigo y botas. En ______ (los / las[6]) países del hemisferio sur, un estudiante ______ (poder[7]) asistir ______ (a / de[8]) un concierto en febrero llevando solo pantalones ______ (corto[9]), camiseta y sandalias.

Es diciembre en Buenos Aires. ¿Qué tiempo hace?

En muchas partes de este país, ______ (antes de / durante[10]) las vacaciones de diciembre, casi siempre ______ (hacer[11]) frío y a veces ______ (nevar[12]). En ______ (grande[13]) parte de Sudamérica, al otro lado del ecuador, hace calor y ______ (muy / mucho[14]) sol durante ______ (ese[15]) mes. A veces en los periódicos, hay fotos de personas que ______ (tomar[16]) el sol y nadan[b] en las playas sudamericanas en enero.

Tengo un amigo que ______ (ir[17]) a ______ (hacer / tomar[18]) un viaje a Buenos Aires. Él me dice[c] que allí la Navidad[d] ______ (ser / estar[19]) una fiesta de verano y que todos ______ (llevar[20]) ropa como la que[e] llevamos nosotros en julio. Parece[f] increíble, ¿verdad?

[a]¿Sabe... *Do you know* [b]*are swimming* [c]Él... *He tells me* [d]*Christmas* [e]la... *that which* [f]*It seems*

Paso 2. Comprensión. ¿Probable o improbable?

	PROBABLE	IMPROBABLE
1. Los estudiantes argentinos van a la playa en julio.	☐	☐
2. Muchas personas sudamericanas hacen viajes de vacaciones en enero.	☐	☐
3. En Santiago (Chile) hace frío en diciembre.	☐	☐

Paso 3. En acción

En parejas, lean el anuncio (*ad*) del inicio del año escolar (*school*) en el Perú. Luego contesten las siguientes preguntas y escriban un párrafo comparando el año escolar en los dos países.

1. ¿En qué mes cae (*occurs*) el inicio del año escolar en los Estados Unidos? ¿En qué estación cae?
2. ¿En qué mes empieza en el Perú? ¿En qué estación cae?
3. ¿Por qué la escuela empieza en meses diferentes en los dos países?
4. ¿Cuándo son las vacaciones de verano en los Estados Unidos?
5. ¿Cuándo creen ustedes que empiezan las vacaciones de verano en el Perú?

Buen inicio del año escolar
10 de marzo

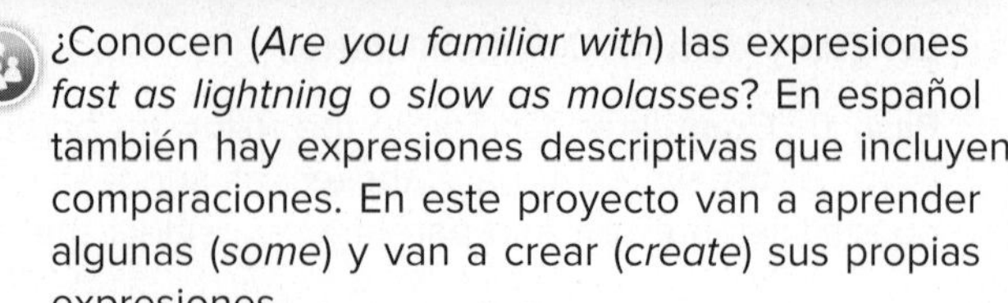

B. Proyecto: Expresiones comparativas

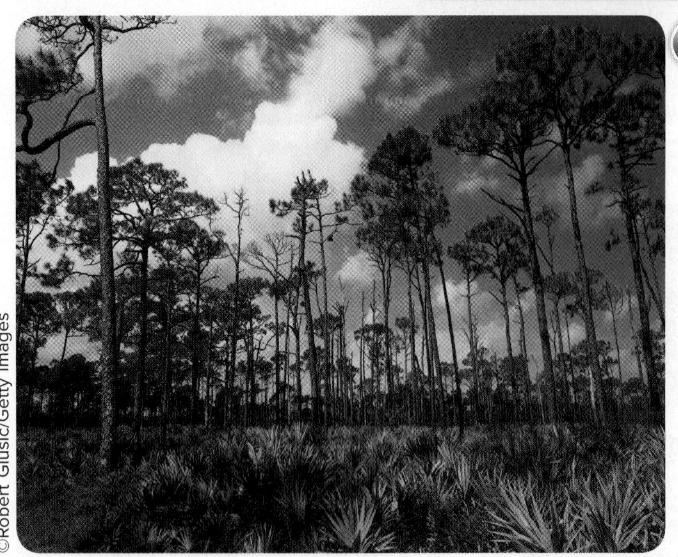

©Robert Glusic/Getty Images

Unos pinos altos

¿Conocen (*Are you familiar with*) las expresiones *fast as lightning* o *slow as molasses*? En español también hay expresiones descriptivas que incluyen comparaciones. En este proyecto van a aprender algunas (*some*) y van a crear (*create*) sus propias expresiones.

Paso 1. Preparación. En grupos, lean las siguientes comparaciones que son aplicables a personas y cosas. Intenten (*Try to*) explicar lo que significan. ¿Creen que son positivas, negativas o neutras? ¿Tienen equivalentes en inglés? ¿Hay algún (*any*) símbolo en particular muy positivo?

1. ser más alto/a que un pino (*pine tree*)
2. ser delgado/a como un espagueti
3. ser más bueno/a que el pan (*bread*)
4. ser más largo/a que una semana sin carne (*meat*)
5. estar más claro que el agua (*water*)
6. ser más viejo/a que Matusalén (una persona de la Biblia)

©McGraw-Hill Education

Un vaso de agua

Paso 2. Creación. Ahora, en grupos, creen (*create*) varias comparaciones similares a las (*those*) del **Paso 1** para describir personas, cosas o situaciones. Pueden usar como base expresiones e ideas comunes en su cultura o pueden inventarlas (*invent them*). Luego, den un ejemplo concreto del uso de cada expresión en su entorno (*environment*) universitario. Consideren bien los siguientes factores.

- la estructura de las comparaciones en español
- el uso de los verbos (**ser** / **estar** + adjetivos, expresiones con **tener** + sustantivo…)

MODELO: Comparación: más lento (*slow*) que la melaza (*molasses*)
Ejemplo concreto: Podemos decir que una persona trabaja más lento que la melaza.

Paso 3: Competición. Escuchen las comparaciones de los otros grupos. ¿Cuáles son las expresiones más interesantes y divertidas de todas? ¿Cuál es el grupo más creativo?

Vocabulario útil

ser **divertido/a**	to be fun
ser **pesado/a**	to be overbearing or boring

¡Ahora, yo!

A. Entrevista. Use de modelo las preguntas y respuestas de la página 169 de este capítulo para hablar del clima donde usted vive y de su estación del año favorita y lo que le gusta hacer en esa estación.

B. Proyecto audiovisual. Mire el pronóstico del tiempo de su ciudad para los próximos tres días y filme su propio informe metereológico. Puede tener un tono serio o cómico.

©Purestock/Getty Images

«En la Mitad del Mundo» Segmento 2

Antes de mirar

Indique todas las palabras que usted asocia con las artesanías (*crafts*). ¿Tiene otras asociaciones?

_______ la tradición
_______ mercados al aire libre (*open air*)
_______ la gente (*people*) mayor
_______ su país
_______ la modernidad
_______ centros comerciales
_______ la gente joven
_______ otros países

©McGraw-Hill Education/Klic Video Productions

El Sr. José Cotocachi, maestro tejedor (*master weaver*) de tercera (*third*) generación que mantiene (*maintains*) la tradición textil de su familia

Este segmento

Laura presenta un reportaje sobre la tradición artesanal textil en la ciudad ecuatoriana de Otavalo y habla con un maestro tejedor.

Fragmento del guion

LAURA: La lengua materna de José es el quechua, la lengua que hablaban[a] los incas y que hoy siguen hablando muchas personas desde Ecuador hasta Chile. José nos enseñó[b] cómo él mismo[c] hace los tintes[d] para la lana que usa en los tejidos de su taller.[e] Estos tintes son completamente naturales y los colores son increíbles. Vemos cómo un insecto tan pequeño, la cochinilla, produce un intenso color rojo.

JOSÉ: Si es que le guardo[f] un año o dos años mejor todavía más fuerte[g]... y bueno un poco de ácido natural... llegó [a ser] un poquito claro.[h]

[a]*used to speak* [b]nos... *showed us* [c]él... *he himself* [d]*dyes* [e]tejidos... *fabrics of his shop* [f]Si... *If I keep it* [g]todavía... *even stronger* [h]llegó... *it got lighter*

Vocabulario del segmento

rodeado/a de	surrounded by
sobre todo	especially
la bufanda	scarf
tuve	I had
la transmite	he teaches it
era	it was
duro/a	hard, difficult
no ha cambiado	has not changed
la venta masiva	mass distribution
nos explicó	explained to us
los negocios	businesses
la feria	fair
trabajábamos	used to work
ya salíamos	we were already leaving
ya no es así	it's not that way anymore

Después de mirar

A. ¿Está claro? Las siguientes oraciones son falsas. Corríjalas (*Correct them*) según el video.

1. Otavalo está en la costa del Ecuador.
2. Allí hace mucho calor.
3. Otavalo es famosa por su gran centro comercial.
4. La ciudad no tiene población indígena.
5. José es el único (*only*) tejedor en su familia.

B. Un poco más. Conteste las siguientes preguntas.

1. Además del (*Besides*) español, ¿qué otra lengua se habla en el Ecuador?
2. ¿Qué prendas (*articles of clothing*) textiles producen los artesanos otavaleños?
3. ¿Qué pasa en una feria?

C. Y ahora, ustedes. En parejas, preparen un resumen informativo de este segmento de *Salu2*. Deben crear (*create*) un texto que pudiera (*could*) ser útil a turistas.

MUNDO HISPANO

Enfoque cultural: Costa Rica

Antes de leer

¿Es muy variado el clima en el país donde usted vive? ¿Cómo es el clima de su estado o región? ¿Varía mucho durante el año?

Diversidad climática

Se puede decir[a] que el clima de Costa Rica es tropical. Esto significa que propiamente[b] no tiene una estación de invierno. Lo que sí tiene son dos temporadas:[c] una seca[d] y otra lluviosa.[e] En la mayor parte del país, esta última[f] ocurre entre mayo y noviembre. En las zonas más lluviosas del país, las lluvias son muy copiosas[g] y llegan a ocasionar muchas inundaciones.[h]

Sin embargo, el clima de Costa Rica es muy diverso. Esto llama mucho la atención de los turistas, ya que[i] en pocas horas se puede pasar de un clima lluvioso en las montañas a uno caluroso[j] en la playa.

[a]*say* [b]*really* [c]*seasons* [d]*dry* [e]*rainy* [f]esta... *the latter* [g]*heavy* [h]llegan... *they cause a lot of floods* [i]ya... *since* [j]uno... *a warm one (i.e., warm climate)*

En otros países hispanos

- **En Chile** En este país se encuentra[a] el desierto de Atacama, el más seco[b] del mundo.
- **En España** La diversidad climática y geográfica de este país europeo es espectacular para su tamaño.[c] La zona más caliente de Europa (el área de Córdoba y Sevilla) coexiste con una de las cordilleras[d] más altas del continente (la Sierra Nevada). Hasta hay[e] una zona desértica (en Almería).

[a]se... *is found* [b]mas... *driest* [c]*size* [d]*mountain ranges* [e]Hasta... *There's even*

Un símbolo costarricense: La carreta

Como método de transporte tradicional, las carretas no son exclusivas de Costa Rica. Allí su uso se asocia con las plantaciones de café. Sin embargo, sí es puramente costarricense decorar las carretas con bellos diseños[a] y colores. Por eso, las carretas son un símbolo nacional del trabajo y la cultura costarricense. La ciudad de Sarchí, al norte de la capital, es el centro artesanal de estas carretas.

Una carreta de Sarchí, Costa Rica

[a]bellos... *beautiful designs*

Comprensión

Conteste las siguientes preguntas.

1. ¿Por qué no tiene el clima costarricense cuatro estaciones?
2. ¿Cuáles son los meses secos en Costa Rica?
3. ¿Dónde está el desierto de Atacama?
4. ¿Qué aspecto del clima y la geografía de España es interesante?
5. ¿Para qué sirve una carreta?

En acción

Usted ya tiene mucha información sobre la geografía y el clima del mundo hispanohablante. Seleccione un país que usted considera ideal para vivir y hablar español. Describa su clima y geografía en unas oraciones y luego escriba una lista de razones para vivir allí.

Lectura

Antes de leer

El siguiente artículo presenta información que probablemente va a ser familiar para usted. Contiene muchas palabras sobre el clima y el tiempo. Intente *(Try)* leer el texto sin mirar *(without looking at)* el **Vocabulario útil.**

Vocabulario útil

el giro	movimiento	**la tormenta**	storm	**templado/a**	warm, temperate
la lluvia	rain				
la nube	cloud	**cálido/a**	warm	**calentar(se) ([me] caliento)**	to warm
el ojo	eye	**caliente**	hot	**subir**	to rise

Ciclones, huracanes y tifones: Qué son y cómo se forman

1 Los ciclones, huracanes y tifones son diferentes nombres para el mismo tipo de fenómeno. Estas violentas tormentas surgen[a] en aguas tropicales y la única diferencia entre ellas es su origen: los huracanes se originan en el océano Atlántico, los tifones en el Pacífico y los ciclones en el Índico. El nombre genérico para todos ellos es «ciclón tropical».

2 Los ciclones tropicales son perturbaciones atmosféricas caracterizadas por fuertes[b] giros de aire que generan abundantes lluvias, siempre alrededor de[c] un «ojo» de baja presión[d] (menos aire).

3 Los ciclones tropicales se forman cuando el aire que está cerca de la superficie de los océanos se hace caliente y húmedo. Este aire sube, dejando[e] entrar aire más frío. Es un proceso circular que crea una columna giratoria[f] de aire.

4 Cuando el aire cálido y húmedo se eleva, apartándose[g] del agua templada del océano, se enfría y así se forman nubes. Todo este proceso forma un gran sistema que va girando alrededor de su centro, el ojo, que es, irónicamente, un espacio muy tranquilo y calmado de baja presión.

[a]*emerge, appear* [b]*strong* [c]alrededor... *around* [d]baja... *low pressure* [e]allowing [f]*spinning* [g]*moving away* [h]*god* [i]*fire*

Source: NASA-NOAA GOES project

Una curiosidad

La palabra «huracán» viene de la lengua de los taínos, habitantes indígenas de las islas del Caribe. Y también de los mayas, quienes tienen un dios[h] llamado Hun-r-akan, el dios del fuego[i], del viento y de las tormentas.

Source: Adapted from "¿Cómo se forman los huracanes y por qué son tan peligrosos?," *CNNEspañol*, 6 octubre, 2016.

Comprensión

A. ¿Dónde está la información? Las siguientes oraciones resumen (*summarize*) la información del artículo. Indique el número del párrafo (*paragraph*) donde aparece (*it appears*).

_____ Los ciclones tropicales incluyen estos fenómenos: aire que gira y lluvia.
_____ El centro de este sistema se llama «el ojo».
_____ Para la formación de un ciclón tropical se necesita aire cálido y húmedo.
_____ Aire nuevo entra en el espacio que deja el aire que sube, y se forma una columna de aire que gira verticalmente.
_____ Los huracanes y los tifones también son ciclones tropicales; el nombre depende de su lugar de origen.

B. Ideas incorrectas. Corrija las oraciones según la información del artículo.

1. En un ciclón tropical, el aire frío cerca de la superficie del océano sube.
2. Cuando el aire caliente sube, deja (*it leaves*) espacio para más agua.
3. El aire húmedo que sube hacia arriba se transforma en nieve (*snow*).
4. El ojo del huracán se forma en el exterior de la tormenta.
5. El ojo del huracán es la parte más violenta de este sistema.

Proyecto: Cómo prevenir el impacto de eventos climáticos extremos

Algunos (*Some*) fenómenos climáticos pueden causar graves desastres. ¿Cómo podemos prepararnos para esos desastres?

Paso 1. Haga una lista de los eventos climáticos extremos que más afectan la región donde usted vive. Luego indique una posible consecuencia negativa de cada fenómeno para la zona.

MODELO: Fenómeno: No llueve por muchos días.
Consecuencia negativa: Hay restricciones en el uso del agua.

Paso 2. Elija un fenómeno natural de su lista del **Paso 1** y haga una lista de las medidas (*measures*) que pueden tomar los habitantes para prepararse. ¿Dónde deben ir o estar antes o durante el desastre? Si es apropiado tener un equipo (*kit*) de emergencia, ¿qué cosas debe contener?

Paso 3. Comparen sus ideas con las (*those*) de sus compañeros de clase. Luego preparen una lista completa de recomendaciones.

Textos orales

El pronóstico° del tiempo en la Argentina

°forecast

Antes de escuchar

¿Mira usted el pronóstico del tiempo todos los días? ¿Le gustan los pronósticos con muchos detalles o solo quiere saber (*know*) la información básica, como la temperatura máxima y mínima y si va a hacer sol o va a llover?

Vocabulario para escuchar

despejado	clear, no clouds	**el granizo**	hail
se espera(n)	is/are expected	**la borrasca**	storm
los grados	degrees	**la bajada**	dip, lowering
soleado	sunny	**bajo**	below
la franja	coastal area		

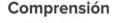

Comprensión

A. Temperaturas y condiciones atmosféricas. Complete los espacios en blanco (*blanks*) en el mapa con las temperaturas máximas y mínimas y las condiciones atmósfericas que se mencionan: granizo, lluvia, nieve, sol.

B. El pronóstico en general. Conteste las siguientes preguntas.

1. ¿Qué tiempo va a hacer el domingo en la mayoría de las regiones argentinas?
2. ¿Qué estación es hoy en la Argentina?

En acción

En parejas, entérense del (*find out about the*) pronóstico del tiempo para los próximos dos días en el estado donde viven y preparen un breve pronóstico en español. Intenten (*Try*) usar el vocabulario que se usa en el pronóstico del tiempo argentino.

Proyecto en su comunidad

Entreviste (*Interview*) a una persona hispana de su universidad o ciudad sobre el clima de su país de origen y los horarios (*schedules*) de clases durante el año.

Preguntas posibles

- ¿Hay en su país cuatro estaciones o solo dos?
- ¿Coinciden con las estaciones del lugar donde usted vive ahora?
- ¿Cómo es el clima en cada estación?
- ¿En qué mes empiezan las clases en las escuelas? ¿Y en qué mes terminan?

Escritura

Proyecto: Un ensayo sobre preferencias climáticas

En este ensayo, va a escribir sobre sus preferencias con respecto al tiempo y las preferencias de sus compañeros. ¿Cuál es su estación favorita? ¿Con qué la asocia (*do you associate it*)? ¿Cuál es la estación del año que menos le gusta? ¿Por qué? ¿Cree que hay una estación más o menos popular, en general? ¿Puede justificar su opinión?

Antes de escribir

Entreviste a dos compañeros de clase sobre la estación del año que más les gusta y la que (*that which*) menos les gusta. También debe preguntarles por qué. Complete el cuadro con la información respectiva.

nombre	estación preferida	estación que menos le gusta	¿por qué?
yo			
compañero/a 1			
compañero/a 2			

©Elena Zajchikova/Shutterstock

Las cuatro estaciones del año

A escribir

Ahora use sus opiniones y las respuestas de sus compañeros para escribir su ensayo. Hay más ayuda (*help*) en Connect.

Más ideas para su portafolio

- Incluya una imagen del mapa del tiempo de una ciudad donde usted desea vivir. Explique por qué le gusta (o no le gusta) el tiempo de esta ciudad.
- Dé tres palabras que usted asocia con el clima del estado donde vive y tres palabras que asocia con el clima del estado o país donde le gustaría (*you would like*) vivir en el futuro. Incluya una foto que represente el clima de su estado o el clima del país de su futuro.
- Si ha estado jugando (*you have been playing*) Practice Spanish: Study Abroad, en Quest 4 usted participó (*participated*) en una telenovela (*soap opera*) sobre una compañía que se especializa en la moda. Busque información en internet sobre dos hispanos famosos en la industria de la moda y escriba por lo menos seis oraciones que los comparen (*compare them*). Incluya (*Include*) una foto de cada uno y escriba dos o tres oraciones sobre la ropa que llevan en la foto.

©McGraw-Hill Education

Sugerencia: You are now ready to play Quest 4 in **Practice Spanish: Study Abroad.**

EN RESUMEN En este capítulo

AFTER STUDYING THIS CHAPTER I CAN . . .

- ☐ talk about the weather (170)
- ☐ talk about months and seasons of the year and express dates (172)
- ☐ use prepositions and cardinal points to locate people, places, and things (174)
- ☐ use the present progressive to express what I'm doing right now (177–178)
- ☐ use the verbs **ser** and **estar** correctly, especially with adjectives (182–184)
- ☐ compare people, places, things, and actions (189–192)
- ☐ recognize/describe at least 2–3 aspects of Costa Rican cultures

Gramática en breve

15. Present Progressive **estar + -ndo**
-ar → -ando
-er/-ir → -iendo

unaccented **-i- → -y- (leyendo)**

-ir Stem-changing Verbs: **e → i (pidiendo)**
o → u (durmiendo)

16. Summary of the Uses of *ser* and *estar*

ser	**estar**
inherent qualities, characteristics	mental, physical, health conditions
identification (including profession)	location
nationality, origin	present progressive
material	fixed expressions
possession	
for whom intended	
time and date	
generalizations	

Idioms with tener (expressing *to be*)
tener (mucho) calor, (mucho) frío

17. Comparisons

Comparisons of Inequality	Comparisons of Equality
más/menos... que	**tan... como**
más/menos que	**tanto/a/os/as... como**
más/menos de + ***número***	
mayor/menor que	
mejor/peor que	

Vocabulario

Los verbos

celebrar	to celebrate
continuar (continúo)	to continue
pasar	to happen
pasar tiempo	to spend time
quedarse	to stay, remain (*in a place*)
seguir (sigo) (i)	to continue

Repaso: divertirse (me divierto) (i)

Remember that the parenthetical letter gives you the stem change for the present participle.

¿Qué tiempo hace?

el clima	climate
está (muy) nublado	it's (very) cloudy, overcast
hace...	it's ...
(muy) buen/mal tiempo	(very) good/bad weather (very) nice out
(mucho) calor	(very) hot
(mucho) fresco	(very) cool
(mucho) frío	(very) cold
(mucho) sol	(very) sunny
(mucho) viento	(very) windy
hay (mucha) contaminación	there's (lots of) pollution
llover: llueve	to rain: it rains, it's raining
nevar: nieva	to snow: it snows, it's snowing
el tiempo	weather; time
¿qué tiempo hace?	what's the weather like?

Los meses del año

la fecha	date (*calendar*)
el mes	month
¿Cuál es la fecha de hoy? / **¿Qué fecha es hoy?**	What's today's date?
el primero de	the first of (*month*)

enero	**abril**	**julio**	**octubre**
febrero	**mayo**	**agosto**	**noviembre**
marzo	**junio**	**septiembre**	**diciembre**

el año	year

Las estaciones del año

la primavera	spring
el verano	summer
el otoño	fall, autumn
el invierno	winter
la estación	season

Los lugares

la capital capital city
la playa beach

Otros sustantivos

el cumpleaños birthday
la medianoche midnight
el mediodía noon
el/la novio/a boyfriend/girlfriend
la respuesta answer

Los adjetivos

abierto/a open
aburrido/a bored
alegre happy
cansado/a tired
cariñoso/a affectionate
cerrado/a closed
congelado/a frozen; very cold
contento/a content, happy
desordenado/a messy
difícil hard, difficult
enfermo/a sick
fácil easy
furioso/a furious, angry
limpio/a clean
loco/a crazy
mismo/a same
molesto/a annoyed
nervioso/a nervous
ocupado/a busy
ordenado/a neat
preocupado/a worried
querido/a dear
seguro/a sure, certain
sucio/a dirty
triste sad

Las comparaciones

más/menos de + *number* more/fewer than + *number*
más/menos que more/less than
más/menos... que more/less (-er) . . . than
tan... como as . . . as
tanto como as much as
tanto/a(os/as) ... como as much/many . . . as
mayor(es) (que) older (than)
mejor(es) (que) better (than); best
menor(es) (que) younger (than)
peor(es) (que) worse (than)

Las preposiciones

a la derecha de to the right of
a la izquierda de to the left of
al lado de alongside of
cerca de close to
debajo de below
delante de in front of
detrás de behind
encima de on top of
entre between; among
lejos de far from

Los puntos cardinales

el norte, el sur, el este, el oeste

Palabras adicionales

afuera *adv.* outdoors
ahora mismo right now
conmigo with me
contigo with you (*fam.*)
esta noche tonight
está bien it's fine, OK
estar bien to be comfortable (*temperature*)
mí (*obj. of prep.*) me
por because of; about
sin embargo nevertheless
tener (mucho) calor to be (very) warm, hot
tener (mucho) frío to be (very) cold
ti (*obj. of prep.*) you (*fam.*)
todavía still

Repaso: estar de acuerdo

Vocabulario personal

7

¡A comer!°

°¡A... *Let's eat!*

En este capítulo

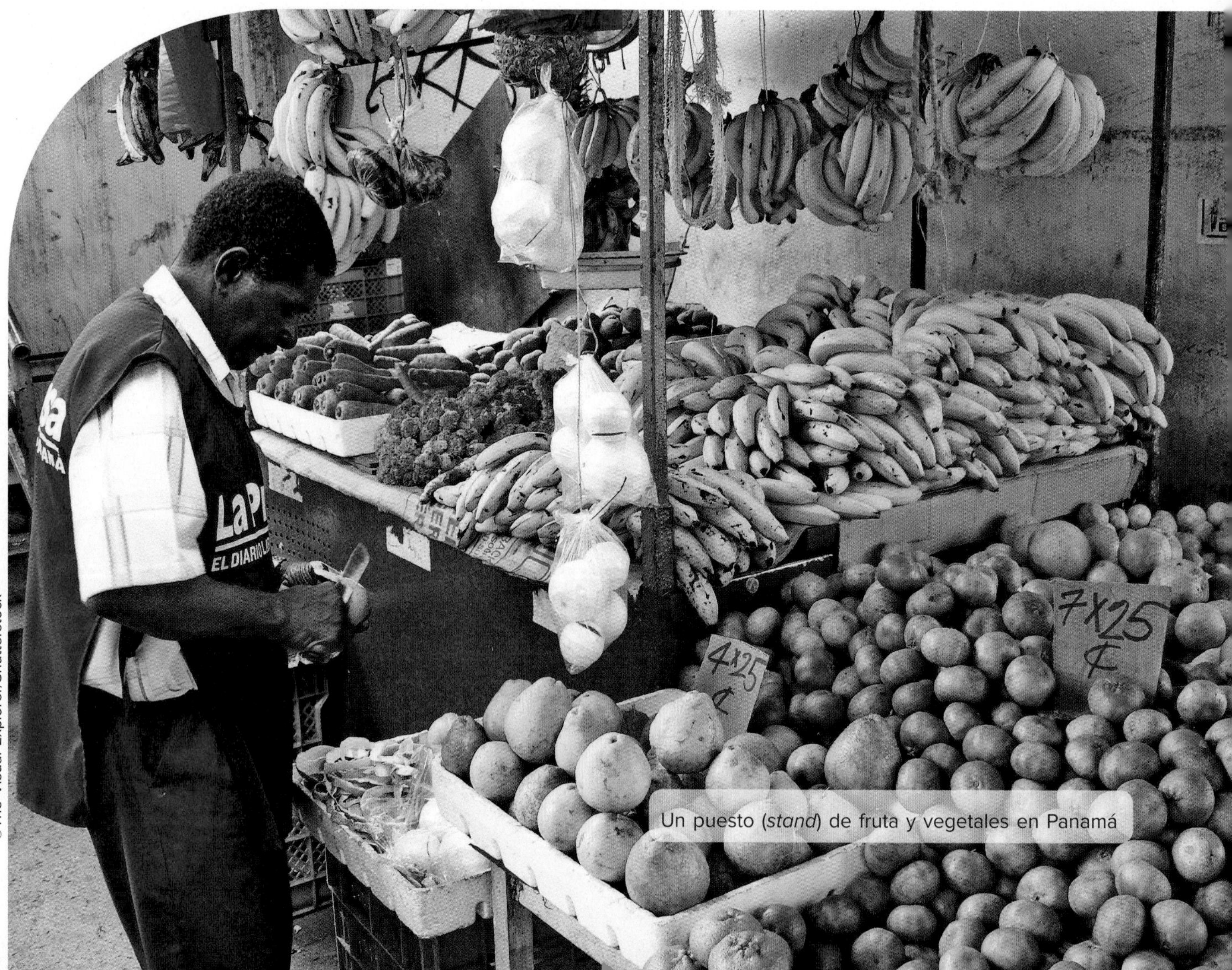

Un puesto (*stand*) de fruta y vegetales en Panamá

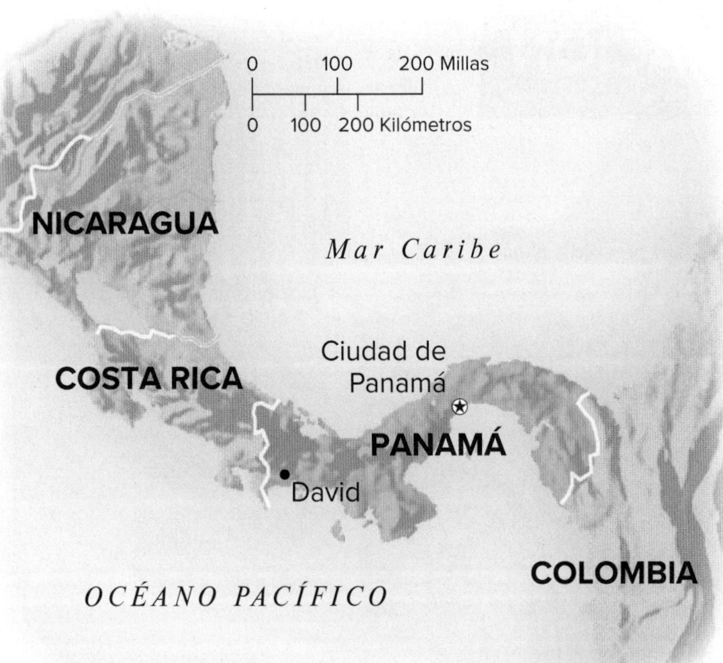

PANAMÁ

4,1 (coma un) millones habitantes

- Vasco Núñez de Balboa fue[a] el primer europeo que vio[b] el océano Pacífico en 1514, desde una colina[c] de Panamá. Este descubrimiento[d] cambió[e] la comprensión[f] de la geografía de nuestro planeta.
- El arroz con pollo[g] es uno de los platos[h] panameños más típicos. Es también típico el sancocho, un tipo de sopa que muestra[i] la influencia de varias culturas: la indígena, la hispana, la africana y la afroantillana.[j]

[a]*was* [b]*saw* [c]*hill* [d]*discovery* [e]*changed* [f]*understanding* [g]arroz... *chicken with rice* [h]*dishes* [i]*shows* [j]*Afro-Caribbean*

ENTREVISTA

- ¿Cuál es su comida[a] favorita?
- ¿Cuáles son algunos[b] de los platos[c] típicos de su país?
- ¿Dónde y a qué hora almuerza y cena[d] usted, por lo general?

[a]*food* [b]*some* [c]*dishes* [d]*have dinner*

Manuel Gil del Valle contesta las preguntas.

- Eso es difícil de contestar porque me gusta comer bien y me gusta casi todo. Pero si tengo que elegir un plato, elijo la paella de mariscos.[a]
- Los «nacatamales» son muy populares. Son tamales muy grandes, rellenos de carne, verduras, arroz, ciruelas[b] y otros ingredientes más. Una bebida típicamente nicaragüense es el pinolillo, una especie de horchata hecha de harina de maíz.[c] Pero en Nicaragua también son populares las comidas originarias de otros países, como la española, italiana, mexicana, china, etcétera.
- Trabajo en el centro de Managua. Así que,[d] por lo general, almuerzo en uno de los muchos restaurantes pequeños que hay en el centro. La hora siempre depende del trabajo, pero con frecuencia almuerzo al mediodía. ¿Y la cena? Casi siempre cenamos en casa con toda la familia, a eso de[e] las ocho. Mi esposa es una cocinera[f] estupenda.

[a]paella... *seafood paella* [b]rellenos... *stuffed with meat, vegetables, rice, plums* [c]hecha... *made with corn flour* [d]Así... *So* [e]a... *around* [f]*cook*

VOCABULARIO: PREPARACIÓN

You can hear the pronunciation of theme vocabulary words and phrases in the Connect eBook.

La comida y las comidas°

La... *Food and meals*

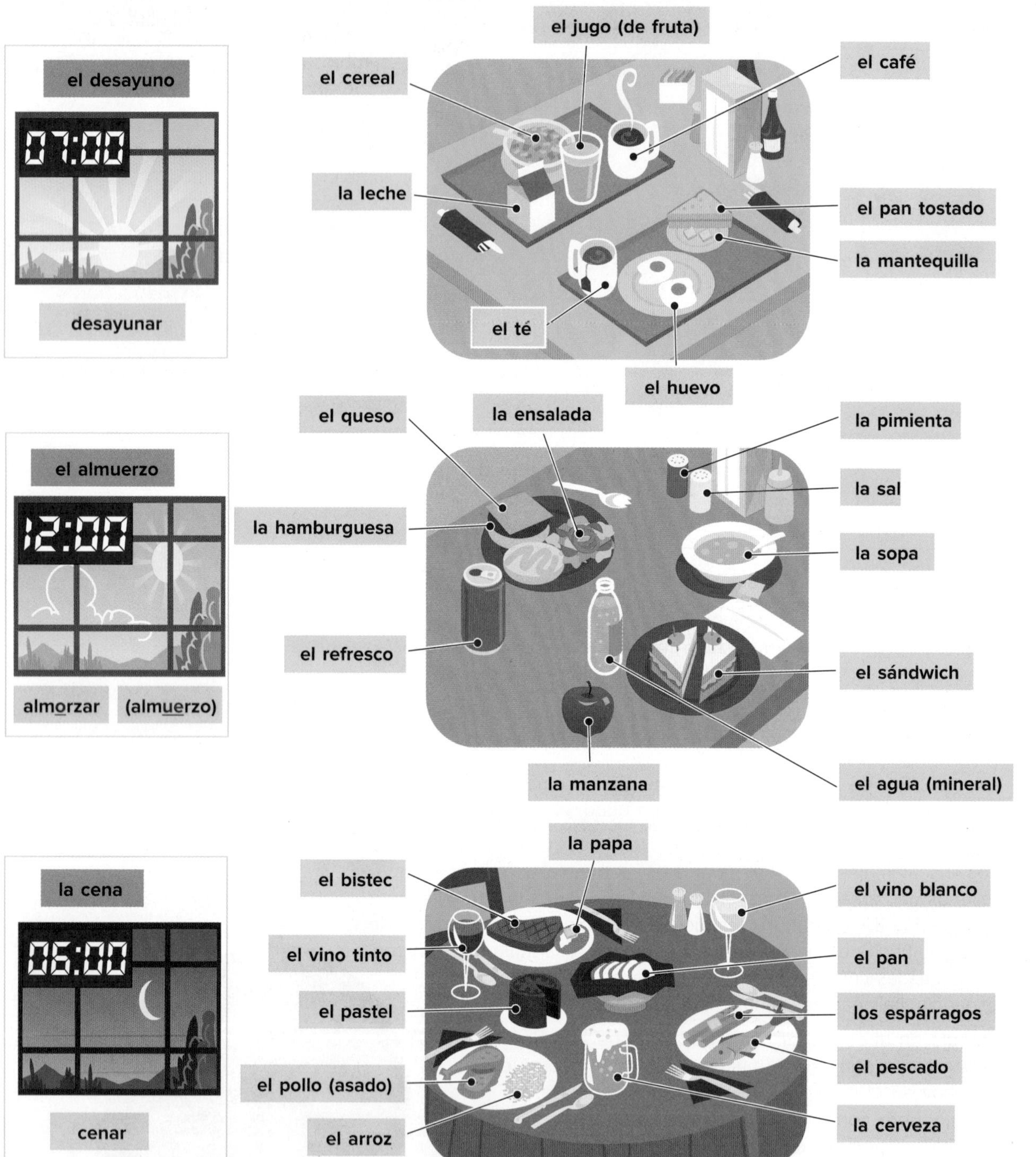

¡OJO!

The noun **agua** is feminine, but it is used with masculine articles in the singular and feminine adjectives: **el agua fría**. This occurs with all feminine nouns that begin with a stressed **a-**. Other examples**: el águila** (*eagle*), **el alma** (*soul*).

Otras frutas

la banana banana
la naranja orange

Otras verduras

el aguacate avocado
las arvejas green peas
la cebolla onion
los champiñones mushrooms
los frijoles beans
los garbanzos chickpeas
la lechuga lettuce
el pepino cucumber
el tomate tomato
la zanahoria carrot

Otras carnes

la barbacoa barbeque
la chuleta (de cerdo) (pork) chop
el jamón ham
el pavo turkey
la salchicha sausage; hot dog

Otros pescados y mariscos

el atún tuna
los camarones shrimp
la langosta lobster
el salmón salmon

Otros postres

los dulces sweets; candy
el flan (baked) custard
la galleta cookie
el helado ice cream

Otras comidas

el aceite (de oliva) (olive) oil
el azúcar sugar
la salsa salsa
el yogur yogurt

Los verbos

almorzar (almuerzo) to have (eat) lunch
cenar to have (eat) dinner, supper
cocinar to cook
desayunar to have (eat) breakfast

Así se dice

There is great variety in the words used to refer to foods in the Spanish-speaking world. The following are only a few of the most common ones.

las arvejas = los guisantes (*Sp.*)
los camarones = las gambas (*Sp.*)
el jugo = el zumo (*Sp.*)
la papa = la patata (*Sp.*)
el refresco = la gaseosa, la soda
(**¡OJO!** = *soda water* in some areas)

There are many ways to express **la tienda de comestibles** (*grocery store*): **la abacería, el almacén** (which you have learned means *department store* in most areas), **la bodega** (popular in the Caribbean), **la pulpería** (*C.A., S.A.*), **la trucha** (*C.A.*).

Nota comunicativa

Más vocabulario para hablar de la comida

¡Buen provecho! Bon appetit!
tener (mucha) hambre to be (very) hungry
tener (mucha) sed to be (very) thirsty

merendar (meriendo) to snack
la merienda snack

la cocina cuisine
los comestibles groceries, foodstuff
el plato dish (*food prepared in a particular way*); course;
el plato principal main course

caliente hot (*in temperature, not taste*)
frito/a fried
picante hot, spicy
rico/a tasty, savory; rich (*in calories*)

La merienda (typically a late afternoon snack) is a traditional custom in those countries where the dinner hour is quite late, such as Spain, for example, where people may have dinner at 10:00 or 11:00 P.M. or even later. **La merienda** tides people over until the late evening meal.

You will use these words and phrases in **Comunicación A** and **B.**

Comunicación

A. ¿Qué quiere tomar? Empareje las descripciones con las comidas.

DESCRIPCIONES

1. ____ una sopa fría, langosta, espárragos, ensalada de lechuga y tomate, vino blanco y, para terminar, un pastel
2. ____ jugo de fruta, huevos con jamón, pan tostado y café
3. ____ un vaso (*glass*) de leche y unas galletas
4. ____ pollo asado, arroz, arvejas, agua mineral y, para terminar, una manzana
5. ____ una hamburguesa con papas fritas, un refresco y un helado

COMIDAS

a. un menú ligero (*light*) para una dieta
b. una comida rápida
c. una cena elegante
d. un desayuno estilo estadounidense
e. una merienda

B. Definiciones

Paso 1. Dé las palabras definidas.

1. un plato de lechuga y tomate
2. una bebida alcohólica blanca o roja
3. una verdura anaranjada
4. una carne típica para una barbacoa en este país
5. la comida favorita de los ratones (*mice*)
6. una verdura que se come frita con las hamburguesas
7. una fruta roja o verde

Paso 2. Ahora, en parejas, túrnense para crear (*create*) definiciones de comidas y bebidas, según el modelo del **Paso 1.** Una persona da (*gives*) la definición y la otra da la palabra correspondiente.

Nota cultural

La comida del mundo hispano

No se puede hablar de una sola comida hispana, porque en el mundo hispanohablante hay una gran variedad culinaria.

- La comida cambia de país a país, dependiendo de los productos locales y de influencias nativas y externas. Sin embargo, sí hay productos de origen americano que se utilizan[a] en prácticamente todas las cocinas latinoamericanas: el maíz, las papas, los frijoles, los tomates, los aguacates.
- El arroz es también fundamental, pero es de origen asiático. Fue introducido en América por[b] los españoles.

Una de las influencias básicas en la cocina de todos los países latinoamericanos es la cocina española. Se combina con la tradición culinaria indígena de cada región y, en algunos[c] países, también con la tradición culinaria africana, gracias a la influencia de los esclavos[d] que fueron traídos[e] a América.

©Nicholas Gill/Alamy

El maíz, uno de los ingredientes básicos de casi todos los países latinoamericanos

¿? ¿Cuáles son los ingredientes básicos de la cocina de su familia o su país?

[a]se... *are used* [b]*by* [c]*some* [d]*slaves* [e]fueron... *were brought*

C. Consejos (*Advice*) a la hora de comer. ¿Qué puede comer o beber su compañero/a en las siguientes situaciones? Dé consejos, según el modelo.

MODELO: Tengo mucha/poca hambre (sed). →
E1: Tengo mucha hambre.
E2: Puedes comer un bistec con papas fritas.

1. Tengo mucha/poca hambre (sed).
2. Tengo hambre a las cuatro de la mañana, después de una fiesta.
3. Estoy a dieta.
4. Estoy de vacaciones en Maine (Texas, California, la Florida,...).
5. Es hora de merendar. Estoy en casa (la universidad).
6. Soy vegano/a.

D. Las preferencias gastronómicas

Paso 1. Complete las siguientes oraciones para describir lo que usted come y no come.

1. Por la mañana siempre como ____________.
2. En el desayuno me gusta comer ____________.
3. Para cenar, prefiero comer ____________.
4. Nunca como ____________ y nunca bebo ____________.
5. No me gusta comer ____________, pero lo/la como (*I eat it*) en casa de mis padres/hijos/abuelos.

Paso 2. Haga una lista de los tres tipos de cocinas que usted prefiere.

Paso 3. Entre todos, comparen las listas. ¿Cuáles son los platos, lugares para comer y cocinas favoritos de la clase? ¿Cuáles son los ingredientes más necesarios para cocinar sus platos favoritos?

¿Qué sabe usted y a quién conoce?°

°¿Qué... *What do you know and who do you know?*

As you know, two Spanish verbs express *to be:* **ser** and **estar.** They are not interchangeable, and their use depends on the meaning the speaker wishes to express. Similarly, two Spanish verbs express *to know:* **saber** and **conocer.** Note their uses in the drawings and text below.

saber = to know (*facts, information*)
+ *inf.* = to know how to (*do something*)

conocer = to know (*a person*)
to meet (*a person*)
to be acquainted, familiar with (*a place or thing*)

sé	**sabemos**
sabes	**sabéis**
sabe	**saben**

conozco	**conocemos**
conoces	**conocéis**
conoce	**conocen**

¡OJO!

Note the **a** before the phrase **una persona**, and before **quién** in the title of this section (**¿a quién conoce?**). You will learn about this **a** in **Gramática 18** in this chapter. For now, always use it when you see it in the text.

Algo sobre...

Rubén Blades

©John Parra/Getty Images

Rubén Blades, en un concierto en Miami

El panameño Rubén Blades (1948–) es uno de los cantautores[a] de salsa más conocidos[b] en todo el mundo. Su álbum *Siembra*[c] se considera uno de los más importantes de la historia salsera. Además de[d] músico, Blades es actor, abogado[e] y político.

¿Tiene usted un cantautor favorito? ¿Quién es?

[a]*singer-songwriters* [b]más... *best known, most famous* [c]*Planting time* [d]Además... *Besides being a* [e]*lawyer*

Comunicación

A. ¿Cuánto sabe usted de Panamá?

Paso 1. ¿Cierto o falso? Complete las oraciones con la forma **yo** del verbo **saber** o **conocer.** Luego diga si las oraciones son ciertas o falsas para usted.

		CIERTO	FALSO
1.	_______ Panamá.	☐	☐
2.	_______ dónde está Panamá.	☐	☐
3.	_______ el nombre de la capital de Panamá.	☐	☐
4.	_______ a una persona panameña famosa.	☐	☐
5.	_______ quién es Rubén Blades.	☐	☐
6.	_______ la música de Blades.	☐	☐
7.	_______ la letra de una canción de Blades.	☐	☐
8.	_______ bailar salsa.	☐	☐
9.	_______ un restaurante panameño.	☐	☐

Paso 2. Ahora, en parejas, túrnense para hacer y contestar preguntas basadas en las oraciones del **Paso 1.**

MODELO: **E1:** ¿Conoces Panamá?
E2: No, no conozco Panamá. ¿Y tú?
E1: Yo sí. / Yo tampoco. (*Me neither.*)

B. Los usos de *saber* y *conocer*

Paso 1. Llene (*Fill in*) los espacios en blanco con la forma apropiada de **saber.** Luego dé su equivalente en inglés.

—¿(Tú) _______[1] si hay un restaurante panameño cerca de aquí?

—¡Cómo no![a] Hay uno en la calle[b] Park. El chef, Felipe, _______[2] hacer unos platos muy originales.

—¿(Tú) _______[3] a qué hora abren los sábados?

—(Yo) No _______[4] exactamente. ¡Pero _______[5] que tiene una página web!

[a]¡Cómo... *Of course!* [b]*street*

Paso 2. Ahora llene los espacios en blanco con la forma apropiada de **conocer.** Luego dé su equivalente en inglés.

—¿(Tú) _______[1] ese restaurante panameño que está en la calle Park?

—Sí, y también (yo) _______[2] al chef, Felipe.

—¿Ah sí? Yo lo[a] quiero _______[3]. Es muy famoso.

[a]*him*

C. ¿Dónde cenamos?

Paso 1. Lola y Manolo quieren salir a cenar. Complete su diálogo con las formas apropiadas de **saber** o **conocer.**

LOLA: ¿(Tú) _______[1] adónde quieres ir a cenar?
MANOLO: No _______.[2] ¿Y tú?
LOLA: No, pero hay un restaurante nuevo en la calle Betis. Creo que se llama Guadalquivir. ¿ _______[3] el restaurante?
MANOLO: No, pero (yo) _______[4] que tiene mucha fama. Es el restaurante favorito de Pepa. Ella _______[5] al dueño.[a]
LOLA: ¿(Tú) _______[6] qué tipo de comida tienen?
MANOLO: Creo que española. Tenemos que llamar[b] a Pepa porque quiere venir con nosotros. ¿(Tú) _______[7] su teléfono?
LOLA: Sí, está en mi celular.

[a]*owner* [b]*call*

Paso 2. Comprensión. Conteste las siguientes preguntas.

1. ¿Saben Lola y Manolo dónde quieren cenar?
2. ¿Conocen el nuevo restaurante?
3. ¿Saben qué tipo de comida se sirve allí?
4. ¿Saben el número de teléfono de Pepa?
5. ¿Conocen al dueño del restaurante?

D. ¿Sabe usted mentir (*to lie*) bien?

Paso 1. Escriba dos oraciones con **saber** sobre algunas (*some*) cosas que sabe hacer y dos oraciones con **conocer** sobre personas interesantes que conoce. Algunas oraciones deben ser falsas. **¡OJO!** No olvide (*Don't forget*) usar la **a** con **conocer.**

Paso 2. En grupos de tres, túrnense para presentar sus oraciones. Los compañeros que escuchan deben adivinar (*guess*) cuáles son las oraciones falsas.

Vocabulario útil

la mentira lie, falsehood

¡OJO!

conocer a (una persona)

Conozco **a** Rubén Blades.

E. Encuesta (*Poll*) sobre los talentos especiales de la clase

Paso 1. Haga una lista de tres cosas interesantes que usted sabe hacer bien. Use infinitivos, según el modelo.

MODELO: tocar el acordeón, hacer paella, esquiar

Paso 2. Ahora haga una encuesta entre las personas de clase para ver si los talentos de usted son únicos o comunes en su clase. Si sus compañeros tienen un talento que usted también tiene, deben firmar (*sign*) en el espacio indicado.

MODELO: tocar el acordeón → ¿**Sabes** tocar el acordeón? Si **sabes, firma** aquí.

Talento 1: ________	**Talento 2:** ________	**Talento 3:** ________

Este joven sabe tocar el acordeón.

Paso 3. Finalmente, entre todos los miembros de la clase, decidan qué tipos de talentos son más comunes y cuáles son únicos o extraordinarios. ¡Quizá alguien (*Perhaps someone*) puede hacer una demostración!

F. Intercambios

1. ¿Qué restaurantes conoces en esta ciudad? ¿Cuál es tu restaurante favorito? ¿Por qué es tu favorito? ¿Es buena la comida allí? ¿Qué tipo de comida sirven? ¿Te gusta el ambiente (*atmosphere*)? ¿Comes allí con frecuencia? ¿Llamas para hacer reservaciones?
2. ¿Qué platos sabes hacer? ¿Tacos? ¿enchiladas? ¿pollo frito? ¿hamburguesas? ¿Te gusta cocinar? ¿Cocinas con frecuencia? ¿Qué ingredientes usas con más frecuencia? ¿Tienes una receta (*recipe*) favorita?

SALU

«¡Qué rico!°» Segmento 1

°¡Qué... *How delicious!*

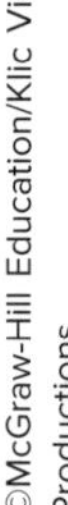

Ana saluda tomando café: «Me entusiasmé con (*I became a fan of*) el café cubano durante los meses que viví (*I lived*) en Miami. Y va muy bien con el primer segmento de hoy... »

Antes de mirar

Indique con qué comida del día se relacionan las siguientes comidas y bebidas. Y si le gusta mucho una comida o bebida, Márquela con una estrella (*star*)! Si no conoce una comida o bebida, escriba **no sé.**

D = el desayuno **A** = el almuerzo **C** = la cena **M** = la merienda

1. _____ el café
2. _____ la leche
3. _____ el chocolate
4. _____ el arroz
5. _____ el jamón
6. _____ el queso
7. _____ las tapas
8. _____ los mariscos

Este segmento

En este segmento Laura va a Miami y después a Barcelona para hablar de comidas... ¡y de bebidas!

Estrategia

To maximize your comprehension of *Salu2*, go beyond actively looking at the texts and photo on this page. Try to imagine what you will see in the segment. What do you expect to see and hear in a show devoted to food?

Vocabulario del segmento

fuerte	strong	**la sartén**	frying pan
¡a mí me encanta!	I love it!	**se cocina**	it is cooked
la calle	street	**vine**	I came
cortado/a con	diluted, cut with	**para que la vean**	for you to see
un poquito de	a little bit of	**no es nada barato**	not at all cheap
yo no sabía nada	I didn't know anything	**una auténtica delicia**	a true delicacy
Se ve bien rico.	It looks great (very delicious).	**algo dulce**	something sweet
estuvo	was	**espeso/a**	thick, dense
dicen	(they) say	**¡Riquísimo!**	Very delicious!

Después de mirar

Vocabulario útil

¿Has probado... ?	Have you tried . . . ?
Ya he probado...	I have already tried . . .
Me/Te gustaría probar...	I'd/You'd like to try . . .

A. ¿Está claro? Empareje las palabras de las dos columnas para describir las comidas que se mencionan en el segmento.

1. _____ la «medianoche»
2. _____ los churros
3. _____ la paella
4. _____ el jamón serrano

a. una tapa
b. el chocolate
c. los mariscos
d. un sándwich cubano

B. Un poco más. Conteste las siguientes preguntas.

1. ¿Qué adjetivos usan los presentadores para hablar del café cubano?
2. ¿Qué ingredientes varían en la paella? ¿Cuál es la paella favorita de Laura?
3. ¿Cómo es el chocolate español? Según Laura, ¿cuándo se toma un chocolate con churros?

C. Y ahora, ustedes. En parejas, hablen de las comidas y bebidas que se presentan en el segmento. ¿Son ustedes *gourmets* o se resisten a probar (*trying*) cosas nuevas?

MODELO: **E1:** Ya he probado el café cortado.
E2: ¿Te gusta?
E1: ¡Me encanta! Es intenso.

GRAMÁTICA

18 Expressing *what* or *who(m)*

Direct Objects; The Personal **a;** Direct Object Pronouns

Gramática en acción: La pirámide alimenticia

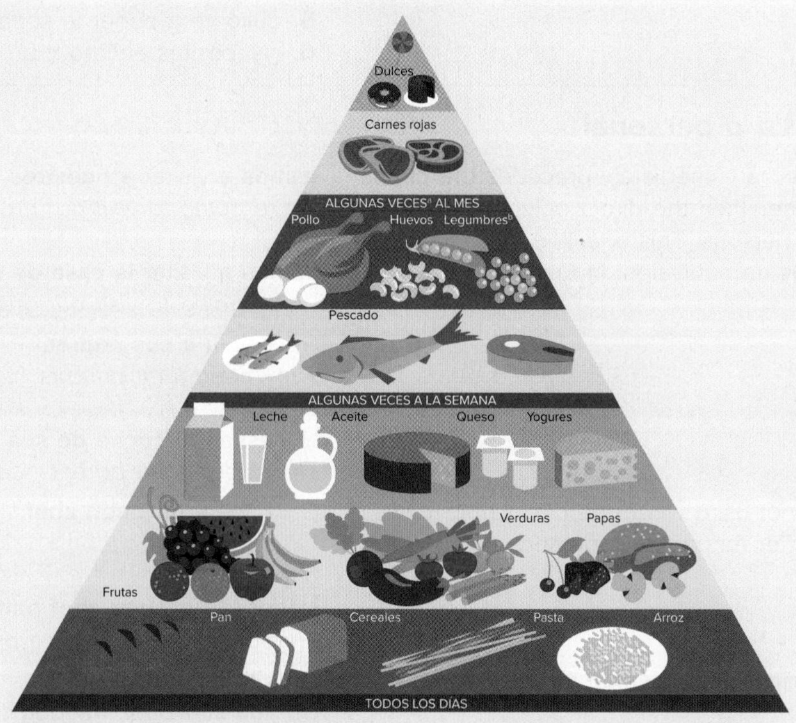

[a]Algunas... *Sometimes* [b]*Legumes*

¿Y usted?

Indique cuáles de estas declaraciones expresan lo que usted hace.

1. **el pollo**
   - **Lo** como todos los días. Por eso tengo que comprar**lo** con frecuencia.
   - **Lo** como de vez en cuando (*once in a while*). Por eso no **lo** compro a menudo (*often*).
   - Nunca **lo** como. No necesito comprar**lo**.
2. **la fruta**
   - **La** como todos los días. Por eso tengo que comprar**la** con frecuencia.
   - **La** como de vez en cuando. Por eso no **la** compro a menudo.
   - Nunca **la** como. No necesito comprar**la**.
3. **los refrescos**
   - **Los** bebo todos los días. Por eso tengo que comprar**los** con frecuencia.
   - **Los** bebo de vez en cuando. Por eso no **los** compro a menudo.
   - Nunca **los** bebo. No necesito comprar**los**.
4. **las bananas**
   - **Las** como todos los días. Por eso tengo que comprar**las** con frecuencia.
   - **Las** como de vez en cuando. Por eso no **las** compro a menudo.
   - Nunca **las** como. No necesito comprar**las**.

Direct Objects / **Los complementos directos**

In English and in Spanish, the *direct object* (**el complemento directo**) of a sentence answers the question *what?* or *who(m)?* in relation to the subject and verb.

the direct object / **el complemento directo** = the noun or pronoun that receives the action of the verb

SUBJECT (S)	VERB (V)	DIRECT OBJECT (DO)
Ana	is preparing	**dinner.**
They	can't hear	**the waiter.**

What is Ana preparing? → **dinner**
Who(m) can't they hear? → **the waiter**

Indicate the subjects, verbs, and direct objects in the following sentences.

1. *I don't see Betty and Mary here.*
2. *We don't have any money.*
3. No veo a Betty y María aquí.
4. No tenemos dinero.
5. Julio va a poner la sopa en la mesa.
6. ¿Necesitas el libro y un bolígrafo?

The Personal **a** / **La *a* personal**

In Spanish, the word **a** immediately precedes the direct object of a sentence when the direct object refers to a specific person or persons. This **a,** called the *personal **a*** **(la *a* personal),** has no equivalent in English.

Vamos a visitar a **nuestros abuelos.**
We're going to visit our grandparents.
but
Vamos a visitar **la casa de nuestros abuelos.**
We're going to visit our grandparents' house.

Necesitan a **sus padres.**
They need their parents.
but
Necesitan **el coche de sus padres.**
They need their parents' car.

The personal **a** is not used when the direct object is a nonspecific person or an unknown person.

Conozco a **un buen chef.**
I know a great chef.
but
Necesito **un buen chef para una fiesta.**
I need a great chef for a party.

Pets (but not all animals) are treated like people and take the personal **a.**

¿Ves a **Bear**, mi perro?
Do you see Bear, my dog?
but
¿Ves **el perro** allí?
Do you see the dog over there?

¡OJO!

The personal **a** is used before the interrogative words **¿quién?** and **¿quiénes?** when they function as direct objects.

¿A quién llamas? **¿al** camarero?
Who(m) are you calling? The waiter?

¡OJO!

The English verbs *to listen **to*** / *look **at*** / *look **for*** / *wait **for*** require prepositional phrases (a *preposition* + *noun* or *pronoun*). However, the Spanish equivalents of those verbs (**escuchar, mirar, buscar,** and **esperar**) are not followed by prepositions. They *are* followed by the personal **a** before a specific person or pet. Compare these pairs of sentences.

Miro el menú. *I'm looking at the menu.*
Miro **al** niño. *I'm looking at the boy.*

Espero el autobús. *I'm waiting for the bus.*
Espero **al** niño. *I'm waiting for the boy.*

¡OJO!

Don't confuse the personal **a** with other uses of the word **a** that you have learned so far.

- **a** = the preposition *to*
- **a** = used after some verbs before an infinitive

Voy a la universidad.
En esta clase **aprendemos** a hablar español.
Vamos a salir mañana.

Direct Object Pronouns / **Los pronombres del complemento directo**

me	me	**nos**	us
te	you (*fam. sing.*)	**os**	you (*fam. pl.*)
lo	you (*form. sing.*), him, it (*m.*)	**los**	you (*form. pl.*), them (*m., m. + f.*)
la	you (*form. sing.*), her, it (*f.*)	**las**	you (*form. pl.*), them (*f.*)

1. Direct Object Pronouns

Like direct object nouns, *direct object pronouns* (**los pronombres del complemento directo**) are the first recipient of the action of the verb.

If the direct object noun were repeated in the English answer to the right, it would sound very repetitive: *"Where are the carrots?" "Do you need the carrots right now?"* Direct object pronouns avoid that kind of unnecessary repetition: *"Do you need **them** right now?"*

—¿Dónde están **las zanahorias**?
—¿**Las** necesitas ahora mismo?
*"Where are **the carrots**?"*
*"Do you need **them** right now?"*

---

2. Placement of Direct Object Pronouns with Conjugated Verbs and *no*

In Spanish, direct object pronouns are placed:

- before a conjugated verb
- after the word **no** when it appears

—¿Quién **te** llama más por teléfono?
—Mi madre **me** llama más.
"Who calls you the most?"
"My mother calls me the most."

—¿Conoces a **Diego**?
—No, no **lo** conozco.
"Do you know Diego?"
"No, I don't know him."

---

3. With Infinitives or Present Participles

When the conjugated verb is followed by an infinitive or a present participle, the pronouns either precede the conjugated verb *or* follow (and are attached to):

- the infinitive
- the present participle

Las tengo que leer. / Tengo que **leerlas.** } *I have to read them.*

Lo estoy comiendo. / Estoy **comiéndolo.** } *I am eating it.*

¡OJO!

When the pronoun is added to the end of a present participle, an accent mark is added to retain the original stress: **mirando → mirándolo**.

---

4. Multiple Meanings of *lo/la/los/las*

Note that the direct object pronouns **lo/la/los/las** have different meanings depending on the context. In the sentences to the right, it is impossible to know what **lo** and **las** mean.

No **lo** veo.

lo = { el pan (*it*) / a usted (*you form., sing., masc.*) / al niño (*him*) }

Las oigo bien.

Las = { las guitarras (*them*) / a las niñas (*them*) / a ustedes (*you form., pl., fem.*) }

---

5. The Pronoun *lo*

The direct object pronoun **lo** can also refer to actions, situations, or ideas in general. When used in this way, **lo** expresses English *it* or *that*.

Lo comprende muy bien.
He understands it (that) very well.

No **lo** creo.
I don't believe it (that).

Lo sé.
I know (it).

Summary of Direct Object Pronouns

yo →	<u>me</u>
tú →	<u>te</u>
usted, él →	<u>lo</u>
usted, ella →	<u>la</u>
nosotros/as →	<u>nos</u>
vosotros/as →	<u>vos</u>
ustedes, ellos →	<u>los</u>
ustedes, ellas →	<u>las</u>

Práctica y comunicación

A. Correspondencias

Paso 1. Autoprueba. Complete las siguientes oraciones. **¡OJO!** Use la **a** personal cuando sea (*whenever it is*) necesaria.

Conozco...

1. una persona famosa.
2. la ciudad de Nueva York.
3. el estado de Montana.
4. el profesor / la profesora de ______.
5. los padres de mi compañero/a de cuarto.

Necesito...

6. el libro de texto en esta clase.
7. más clases para graduarme.
8. mi familia.
9. mis buenos amigos.
10. mi perro/gato.

Paso 2. Ahora complete las oraciones del **Paso 1** con el pronombre del complemento directo apropiado.

MODELO: Conozco... al profesor de historia latinoamericana. → **Lo** conozco.

 **Paso 3.** Ahora, en parejas, túrnense para hacer preguntas usando las oraciones del **Paso 1** y contestarlas usando pronombres como en el **Paso 2**.

MODELO: Conozco... al profesor de historia latinoamericana. →
E1: ¿Conoces al profesor de historia latinoamericana?
E2: Sí, **lo** conozco. (No, no **lo** conozco.) ¿Y tú?
E1: Yo sí/también. / Yo tampoco. (*Me neither.*)

B. Más correspondencias. Empareje los pronombres del complemento directo con las personas. A veces hay más de una correspondencia posible.

PRONOMBRES

1. ______ los
2. ______ la
3. ______ te
4. ______ lo
5. ______ las
6. ______ nos

PERSONAS

a. Ana
b. tú
c. Pedro y Carolina
d. María y yo
e. Jorge
f. Elena y Rosa
g. ustedes
h. usted

C. ¿Qué comen los vegetarianos? Aquí hay una lista de diferentes comidas. ¿Cree usted que las come un vegetariano? Conteste según los modelos.

MODELOS: el bistec → No **lo** come.
la banana → **La** come.

1. las papas
2. el arroz
3. las chuletas de cerdo
4. las zanahorias
5. las manzanas
6. los camarones
7. los champiñones
8. los frijoles
9. la ensalada

D. La cena de Lola y Manolo

Paso 1. La siguiente descripción de la cena de Lola y Manolo es muy repetitiva. Combine las oraciones, según el modelo.

MODELO: El camarero (*waiter*) trae un menú. Lola lee **el menú**. →
El camarero trae un menú y Lola **lo** lee.

1. El camarero trae una botella de vino tinto. Pone **la botella** en la mesa.
2. Lola quiere la especialidad de la casa. Va a pedir **la especialidad de la casa**.
3. Manolo prefiere el pescado fresco (*fresh*). Pide **el pescado fresco**.
4. Lola quiere una ensalada también. Por eso pide **una ensalada**.
5. El camarero trae la comida. Sirve **la comida**.
6. «¿La cuenta (*bill*)? El dueño está preparando **la cuenta** para ustedes».
7. Manolo quiere pagar con tarjeta (*card*) de crédito. Pero no tiene **su tarjeta**.
8. Por fin, Lola toma la cuenta. Paga **la cuenta**.

Prác. A, Paso 1: Answers: 1. *a una* **2.** *ø* **3.** *ø* **4.** *al / a la* **5.** *a los* **6.** *ø* **7.** *ø* **8.** *a* **9.** *a* **10.** *a*

Paso 2. Las siguientes oraciones describen la cena de Lola y Manolo. Diga en español a qué se refieren los pronombres indicados. Luego diga quién hace cada acción.

1. **Lo** pide.
2. **La** sirve.
3. No **la** tiene.
4. **La** paga.

E. Minidiálogos

Paso 1. Complete los siguientes minidiálogos con los pronombres del complemento directo que faltan (*are missing*).

1. —¿Me quieres (*do you love*)?
   —¡ ______ quiero muchísimo!
2. —Voy a Panamá y tengo un boleto (*ticket*) de avión gratis. ¿Me acompañas?
   —¡Claro que ______ acompaño! ¿Cuándo nos vamos?
3. —Buenas noches, señor. ¿ ______ atienden ya? (*Is someone already helping you?*)
   —No, todavía no, gracias.
   —Perdón. Entonces (*Then*) voy a atender ______ yo.
4. —¡Mi hija nunca me llama por teléfono!
   —¡Tu hija solo tiene 19 años! Seguro que ______ llama si necesita dinero.
5. —¿Cuándo van a visitarlos a ustedes sus primos panameños?
   —______ van a visitar este verano.
6. —Buenos días, señora. ¿En qué puedo ayudar______ (*to help*)?
   —Buenos días. Busco una blusa negra de mi talla (*size*).
7. —¡Qué perro tan bonito (*What a beautiful dog*) tienes!
   —Si quieres, puedes tocar______ (*to touch*).

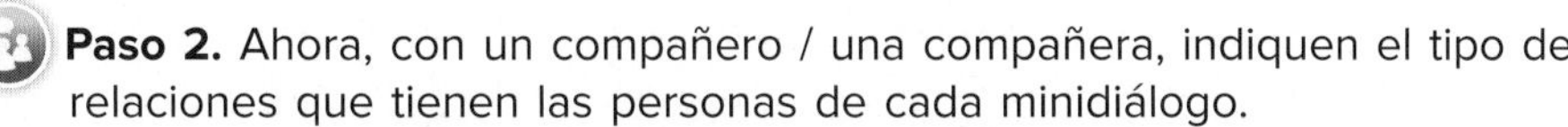

Paso 2. Ahora, con un compañero / una compañera, indiquen el tipo de relaciones que tienen las personas de cada minidiálogo.

MODELO: 1. Puede ser una pareja con una relación romántica o...

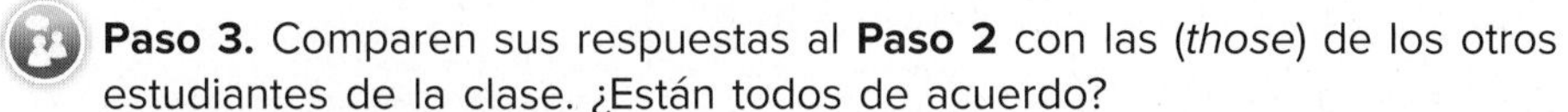

Paso 3. Comparen sus respuestas al **Paso 2** con las (*those*) de los otros estudiantes de la clase. ¿Están todos de acuerdo?

F. ¿Quién lo hace?

Paso 1. Mire cada dibujo y complete cada oración con la mejor opción.

1. El papá ______
   a. la baña.
   b. se baña.

2. La niña ______
   a. la peina.
   b. se peina.

3. A su nuevo perro, el niño ______
   a. lo llama Max.
   b. se llama Max.

Paso 2. Ahora conteste las siguientes preguntas personales. Ponga (*Pay*) atención a los pronombres.

1. ¿Cómo se llama su mejor amigo/a? ¿Cómo lo/la llama usted algunas veces (*sometimes*)?
2. ¿A qué hora se despierta usted los días de clase? ¿Lo/La despierta el reloj despertador o puede despertarse sin la alarma?
3. ¿Tiene usted perro? ¿Con qué frecuencia lo baña y lo cepilla?

Algo sobre...

la Ciudad de Panamá

©Image Source

La Ciudad de Panamá: una imagen de la moderna y urbana zona metropolitana (1,8 [coma ocho] habitantes)

La capital panameña es el primer lugar de asentamiento[a] europeo en la costa del Pacífico. La fundó[b] el español Pedro Arias Dávila en 1519 para usarla como punto de partida para la conquista del Perú. La parte antigua de la ciudad, llamada Panamá la Vieja, mezcla[c] la arquitectura colonial española con el estilo de las casas antillanas[d] de la época de la construcción del canal de Panamá. Hoy día la ciudad de Panamá se destaca por[e] sus altos rascacielos.[f]

¿Sabe usted cuándo fue fundada[g] su ciudad? ¿Qué se destaca[h] en su ciudad?

[a]lugar... *settlement* [b]*founded* [c]*mixes* [d]*of the Antilles, the Caribbean islands* [e]se... *is noted for* [f]*skyscrapers* [g]fue... *was founded* [h]se... *stands out*

Nota comunicativa

Cómo expresar una acción muy reciente: *acabar* + *de* + *infinitivo*

To talk about what you have *just* done, use the phrase **acabar** + **de** + *infinitive*. The verb **acabar** literally means *to finish*.

Acabo de almorzar con Beto.	*I just had lunch with Beto.*
Acabas de celebrar tu cumpleaños, ¿verdad?	*You just celebrated your birthday, didn't you?*

Note that the infinitive follows the preposition **de.**

You will practice talking about what you have *just* done in **Práctica F.**

G. ¡Acabo de hacerlo! En parejas, túrnense para practicar cómo se expresan las acciones que uno acaba de hacer. Sigan el modelo.

MODELO: E1: ¿Por qué no haces la ensalada? →
E2: Acabo de hacer**la.** (**La** acabo de hacer.)

1. ¿Por qué no preparas las chuletas para la fiesta?
2. ¿Vas a comprar la fruta hoy?
3. ¿Por qué no pagas los cafés?
4. ¿Vas a cocinar la comida para la cena?
5. ¿Quieres ayudarme?
6. ¿Por qué no me invitas a cenar?

Vocabulario útil

ayudar + **a** + *inf.* to help to (*do something*)

Estrategia

Use the word **nadie** before the object pronoun and verb to express that *no one* does something. For example, in item 1: **Nadie me ayuda con las cuentas.**

Vocabulario útil

la cafeína
las calorías
el colesterol
la grasa fat

<u>estar</u> **a dieta**
<u>ser</u> **alérgico/a a**
<u>ser</u> **bueno/a para la salud** (health)
<u>ser</u> **celíaco/a**

me pone(n) nervioso/a it/they make me nervous
me sienta(n) mal it/they don't agree with me
lo/la/los/las detesto

H. ¡Ayuda! (*Help!*)

Paso 1. Todos necesitamos ayuda alguna vez (*at some point*), ¿no? ¿Quién lo/la ayuda a usted en los siguientes casos?

MODELO: con el coche → **Mi padre me** ayuda con el coche.

1. con las cuentas (*bills*)
2. con la tarea
3. con la matrícula
4. con el horario de clases
5. con el español
6. pagar las deudas (*debts*)
7. estudiar para los exámenes
8. resolver los problemas personales

Paso 2. Ahora, en parejas, túrnense para hacer y contestar preguntas basadas en el **Paso 1.**

MODELO: con el coche →
E1: ¿Quién **te** ayuda con el coche?
E2: Generalmente, **mis padres me** ayudan un poco. A veces también **me** ayudan **mis abuelos.**

I. Intercambios. En parejas, túrnense para hacer y contestar preguntas sobre los alimentos (*foods*) que consumen y con qué frecuencia. Expliquen por qué tienen esos hábitos. Luego digan a la clase algo (*something*) que tienen en común.

MODELO: E1: ¿Comes pan sin gluten?
E2: No, no **lo** como porque no soy celíaco.

1. pan sin gluten
2. refrescos sin azúcar
3. productos bajos en sodio
4. frutas y verduras orgánicas
5. pescados y mariscos
6. hamburguesas
7. bebidas alcohólicas
8. café
9. productos lácteos (*milk*)
10. comidas congeladas (*frozen*)

¿Recuerda usted?

You have been using a few words that express indefinite and negative qualities since the first chapter of this text. Review what you already know about the content of **Gramática 19** by giving the English equivalent of the following words.

1. siempre ________ **2.** nunca ________ **3.** también ________

19 Expressing Negation

Indefinite and Negative Words

Gramática en acción: ¿Un refrigerador típico?

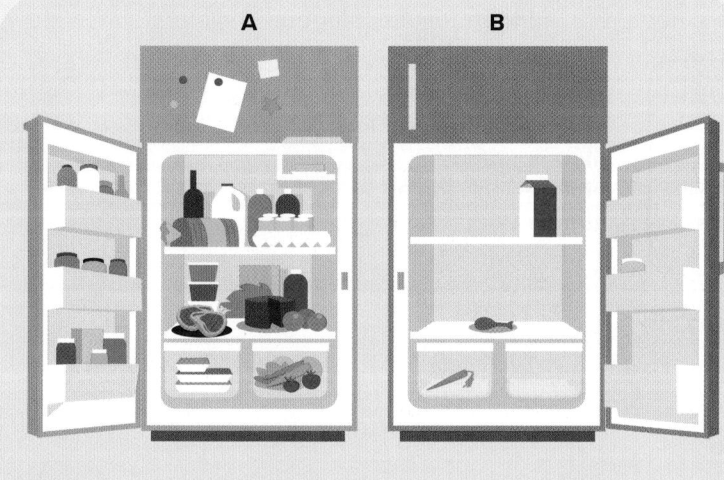

Comprensión

Empareje las siguientes respuestas con el refrigerador A o el B.

1. ¿Hay algo bueno de comer en este refrigerador?
_____ Sí, hay algo.
_____ No, no hay nada.

2. ¿Hay fruta y pan?
_____ Sí, hay fruta y pan.
_____ No, no hay fruta. Tampoco hay pan.

3. ¿Hay chuletas de cerdo?
_____ No, no hay ninguna chuleta.
_____ Sí, hay algunas chuletas.

4. En esta casa, ¿alguien compra comida con frecuencia?
_____ No, nadie la compra.
_____ Sí, alguien la compra.

¿Y usted?

¿Cuál de los dos refrigeradores se parece (*resembles*) más al refrigerador de su casa o apartamento? ¿Cuál se parece más al típico refrigerador de los estudiantes? ¿de una familia con hijos? ¿de jóvenes profesionales?

Indefinite and Negative Words / **Las palabras indefinidas y negativas**

Los adverbios indefinidos y negativos		
siempre	always	**Siempre** estudio en casa. Estudio en casa **siempre**.
nunca, jamás	never	**Nunca** estudio en la biblioteca. **No** estudio **nunca** en la biblioteca.
también	also	Yo **también** sé preparar una paella. Yo sé preparar una paella **también**.
tampoco	neither, not either	**Tampoco** sé preparar una paella. Yo **no** sé preparar una paella **tampoco**.

A typical refrigerator? **1.** *Is there something good to eat in this refrigerator? Yes, there is something. No, there is nothing.* **2.** *Is there (some) fruit and bread? Yes, there is (some) fruit and bread. No, there is no fruit. There isn't any bread either.* **3.** *Are there pork chops? No, there aren't any chops. (Lit., No, there is no chop.) Yes, there are some chops.* **4.** *In this house, does anyone buy food frequently? No, no one buys it. Yes, someone buys it.*

Los sustantivos indefinidos y negativos		
alguien **nadie**	someone, anyone no one, nobody, not anybody	En esta clase **alguien** habla chino. En esta clase **nadie** habla chino. En esta clase **no** habla chino **nadie**. Conozco **a alguien** en esa fiesta. **No** conozco **a nadie** en esa fiesta.
algo **nada**	something, anything nothing, not anything	Sé **algo** de la cocina panameña. **No** sé **nada** de la cocina panameña.

¡OJO!

The personal **a** is used with **alguien** and **nadie** when they function as direct objects, as in the examples.

Pronunciation Hint: Pronounce the **d** in **nada** and **nadie** as a fricative, that is, like the *th* sound in *the*: [**na-đa**], [**na-đie**].

Los adjetivos indefinidos y negativos		
algún, alguna, algunos/as	some, any	**algún** tomate, **algunas** chuletas
ningún, ninguna	no, not any	**ningún** tomate, **ninguna** chuleta

¡OJO!

Note how **alguno** and **ninguno** shorten (**algún, ningún**) before masculine singular nouns. You've seen something similar with **uno (→ un), bueno (→ buen), grande (→ gran)**, and **primero (→ primer).**

algún / ningún problema
alguna / ninguna cosa
algunos problemas
algunas cosas

The Double Negative / **La negativa doble**

A double negative is avoided in English but is often necessary in Spanish.

- When the negative word comes *before* the conjugated verb, that is all that is needed.
- When the negative word comes *after* the conjugated verb, another negative word—usually **no**—must be placed before the verb.

negative word + verb
no + *verb + negative word*

¿**Nadie estudia**?
¿**No estudia nadie**? — *Isn't anyone studying?*

Nunca estás en clase.
No estás en clase **nunca.** — *You're never in class.*

Tampoco quieren cenar aquí.
No quieren cenar aquí **tampoco.** — *They don't want to have dinner here either.*

The Adjectives **algún** and **ningún** / **Los adjetivos *algún* y *ningún***

The indefinite words **algún/alguna/algunos/algunas** and the negative **ningún/ninguna** are adjectives. That's why they must agree with the noun they modify.

The singular negative forms **ningún/ninguna** are used to indicate that there is none of something. The plural forms are used only with words that are always plural, like **las gafas** or **los pantalones**: **ningunas gafas, ningunos pantalones.**

—¿Hay **algún** mensaje para mí hoy?
—No, no hay **ningún** mensaje para usted.
"Are there any messages for me today?"
"No, there are no messages for you today."
(*"There is not a single message for you today."*)

—¿Ves a **algunas** de tus amigas aquí?
—No, no veo a **ninguna**.
"Do you see any of your friends here?"
"No, I don't see any (of them)."

—¿Hay **algún** problema?
—No, **ninguno**.
"Is there a problem?"
"No, none."

¡OJO!

Algún and **ningún** change to **alguno** and **ninguno**, respectively, when referring to a masculine noun that is not expressed.

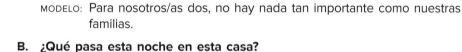

Summary of Indefinite and Negative Words

algo	**nada**	**siempre**	**nunca, jamás**
alguien	**nadie**	**también**	**tampoco**
algún/alguna/os/as	**ningún, ninguna**		

Práctica y comunicación

A. Cosas esenciales

Paso 1. Autoprueba. Dé la palabra negativa correspondiente.

1. siempre **2.** también **3.** algo **4.** alguien **5.** alguna

Paso 2. Complete las siguientes oraciones para que sean (*so that they are*) verdaderas para usted. Siga (*Follow*) las indicaciones en paréntesis.

1. Siempre tengo ______ (algo) en mi cuarto y también tengo ______ (algo más).
2. (Yo) Nunca ______ (una acción) temprano por la mañana. Tampoco me gusta ______ (otra acción en infinitivo).
3. Algo que siempre hay en mi refrigerador es ______. Algo que nunca hay es ______.
4. Para mí, no hay nada tan importante como mi(s) ______ (algo).
5. En este momento, nadie es tan importante en mi vida (*life*) como mi(s) ______ (alguien).

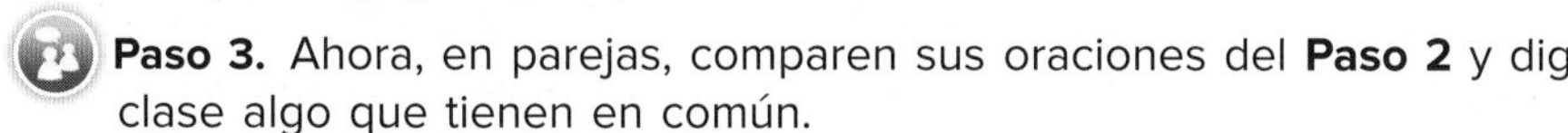

Paso 3. Ahora, en parejas, comparen sus oraciones del **Paso 2** y digan a la clase algo que tienen en común.

MODELO: Para nosotros/as dos, no hay nada tan importante como nuestras familias.

B. ¿Qué pasa esta noche en esta casa?

Paso 1. Complete las siguientes oraciones con la palabra indefinida o negativa apropiada según el dibujo.

1. Hay ______ cantando en el baño.
2. Hay ______ niños jugando en su alcoba.
3. Hay ______ en la mesa del comedor.
4. Hay ______ comida en la barbacoa.
5. Hay ______ personas en la sala.
6. No hay ______ en la cocina.
7. No hay ______ plato en la mesa del comedor.

Paso 2. Ahora haga otras oraciones ciertas, pero contrarias a las (*those*) del **Paso 1**.

MODELO: **1. No** hay **nadie** cantando en **el jardín**.

Estrategia

Remember that **ninguno** is always used in the singular and that it shortens to **ningún** before a masculine, singular noun.

C. ¡Nadie come allí! Exprese negativamente, usando la negativa doble.

MODELO: Hay alguien en el restaurante. → **No** hay **nadie** en el restaurante.

1. Hay algo interesante en el menú.
2. Tienen algunos platos típicos.
3. El profesor cena allí también.
4. Mis amigos siempre almuerzan allí.
5. Preparan algo especial para grupos.
6. Siempre hacen platos nuevos.
7. Y también sirven paella, mi plato favorito.

Prác. A, Paso 1: Answers: 1. nunca 2. tampoco 3. nada 4. nadie 5. ninguna

D. Extremos

Paso 1. Modifique las siguientes declaraciones para hacerlas negativas.

MODELO: Hay muchas personas antipáticas en mi familia. →
No hay **ninguna persona** antipática (**No** hay **nadie** antipático) en mi familia.

1. Tengo muchos planes interesantes para este fin de semana.
2. Todas mis clases este semestre/trimestre son maravillosas (*wonderful*).
3. Me gusta toda la comida de la cafetería.
4. Hay muchas noticias (*news*) buenas últimamente (*lately*).
5. Siempre estudio en la biblioteca.
6. Todos los estudiantes de esta universidad son internacionales.

Paso 2. Ahora modifique las oraciones del **Paso 1** para que expresen (*so that they express*) su opinión.

MODELOS: Hay muchas personas antipáticas en mi familia. →
No hay ninguna persona antipática en mi familia.
En mi familia hay algunas personas antipáticas, pero muy pocas.

Paso 3. Ahora, en parejas, túrnense para hacer y contestar preguntas basadas en las oraciones del **Paso 2.**

MODELO: En mi familia hay algunas personas antipáticas, pero muy pocas. →
E1: En tu familia ¿hay alguna persona antipática (alguien antipático)?
E2: Sí, mi tío Gerry es muy antipático. (No, no hay nadie antipático.)

E. Intercambios

Paso 1. En parejas, túrnense para entrevistarse sobre los siguientes temas. Deben obtener detalles interesantes y personales de su compañero/a.

MODELO: **E1:** ¿Tienes alguna buena excusa para no ir al gimnasio esta semana?
E2: No, no tengo ninguna buena excusa esta semana. (Sí, tengo una buena excusa. ¡No tengo tiempo!)

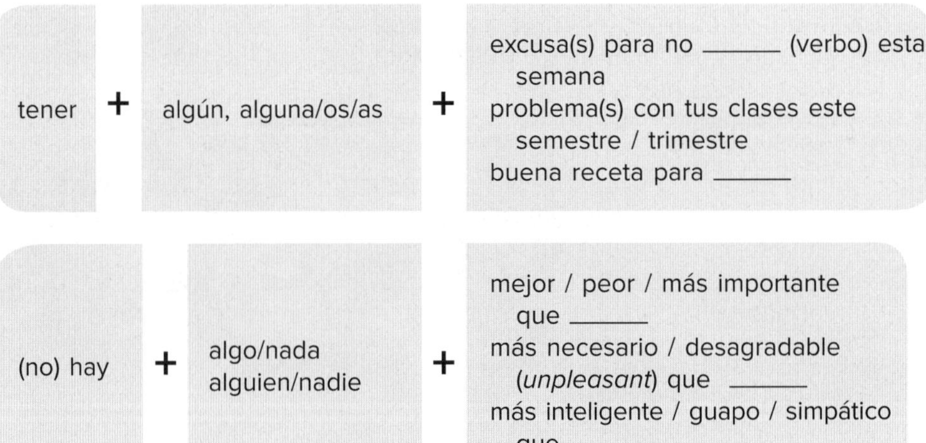

tener	+	algún, alguna/os/as	+	excusa(s) para no ______ (verbo) esta semana problema(s) con tus clases este semestre / trimestre buena receta para ______
(no) hay	+	algo/nada alguien/nadie	+	mejor / peor / más importante que ______ más necesario / desagradable (*unpleasant*) que ______ más inteligente / guapo / simpático que ______

Paso 2. Ahora digan a la clase una respuesta interesante o peculiar.

MODELOS: Algo interesante de Jim es que tiene una excusa muy buena para no hacer la tarea esta noche. Va a...
Algo interesante de Aurora es que, en su opinión, no hay nada más desagradable que la arrogancia.

Algo sobre...

los emberás

©Lissa Harrison

Unas casas típicas de los emberás

Los emberás son un pueblo amerindio del este de Panamá y también de la región noroeste de Colombia y del Ecuador. Tradicionalmente viven en la selva,[a] junto a ríos,[b] en zonas donde llueve todo el año. Por eso sus casas están en alto.[c] Están cubiertas[d] de hojas[e] de palma.

¿Hay algún pueblo indígena en su estado? ¿Qué sabe de ellos?

[a]*jungle* [b]*junto... next to rivers* [c]*en... raised up* [d]*covered* [e]*leaves*

¿Recuerda usted?

Review what you already know about irregular first person present tense forms by giving the **yo** form of the following infinitives. You will need to know this information in **Gramática 20.**

1. salir ________ **3.** conocer ________ **5.** hacer ________ **7.** perder ________
2. tener ________ **4.** pedir ________ **6.** dormir ________ **8.** traer ________

20 Influencing Others

Commands (Part 1): Formal Commands

Gramática en acción: Receta para guacamole

El guacamole

1 aguacate
1 diente de ajo,[a] prensado[b]
1 tomate
jugo de un limón[c]
sal
un poco de cilantro fresco

Cómo se prepara

Corte el aguacate y el tomate en trozos[d] pequeños. Añada el jugo del limón, el ajo, el cilantro y la sal a su gusto. Mezcle bien todos los ingredientes y sírvalo con tortillas de maíz[e] fritas.

©Purestock/Getty Images

[a]diente... *clove of garlic* [b]*crushed* [c]*lemon* [d]*pieces* [e]*corn*

En español, los mandatos se usan con frecuencia en las recetas. Los siguientes verbos se usan en forma de mandato en esta receta. ¿Puede encontrarlos?

añadir	to add
cortar	to cut
mezclar	to mix
servir (sirvo) (i)	

¿Y usted?

¿Le gusta el guacamole? ¿Lo pide o lo hace con frecuencia? ¿Con qué lo come?

Formal Command Forms / **Los mandatos formales (usted, ustedes)**

a command or *imperative* / **un mandato** = a verb form used to tell someone to do something

In *Puntos de partida* you have seen formal commands in the direction lines of activities since the beginning of the text: **haga, complete, conteste,** and so on.

Commands (imperatives) are verb forms used to tell someone to do something. In Spanish, *formal commands* (**los mandatos formales**) are used with people whom you address as **usted** or **ustedes.*** Here are some of the basic forms.

	hablar	**comer**	**escribir**	**volver**	**poner**
usted	**hable**	**coma**	**escriba**	**vuelva**	**ponga**
ustedes	**hablen**	**coman**	**escriban**	**vuelvan**	**pongan**
	speak	*eat*	*write*	*come back*	*put, place*

1. Regular Verbs
Most formal command forms can be derived from the **yo** form of the present tense.

Note that the "opposite" vowel is used:
-ar → **e**
-er/-ir → **a**

-ar: -o	→	-e, -en	*-er/-ir:* -o	→	-a, -an
hablo	→	**hable**, **hablen**	**como**	→	**coma**, **coman**
			escribo	→	**escriba**, **escriban**

2. Stem-changing Verbs
Formal commands for stem-changing verbs show the stem change, since the stem vowel is stressed. Base the command on the **yo** form to get the stem change right.

pensar (pienso) → **piense, piensen**
volver (vuelvo) → **vuelva, vuelvan**
pedir (pido) → **pida, pidan**

*You will learn how to form informal (**tú**) commands in* **Gramática 36 (Cap. 13).**

3. **Verbs Ending in *-car, -gar, -zar***
   These verbs have a spelling change to preserve the **-c-**, **-g-**, and **-z-** sounds of the infinitives.

c → qu	**buscar: busque, busquen**
g → gu	**pagar: pague, paguen**
z → c	**empezar: empiece, empiecen**

¡OJO!

From this chapter on, these three spelling changes for verbs in formal commands will be indicated in parentheses in vocabulary lists. If these three verbs were active in this chapter, they would be listed in the end-of-chapter vocabulary list as follows: **buscar (qu), pagar (gu), empezar (empiezo) (c).**

---

4. **Verbs with Irregular Present Tense *yo* Forms**
   Verbs that have an irregular **yo** form in the present tense will keep the irregularity in the **usted/ustedes** commands.

conocer: **conozco**	→ **conozca, conozcan**
decir* (*to say, tell*): **digo**	→ **diga, digan**
hacer: **hago**	→ **haga, hagan**
oír: **oigo**	→ **oiga, oigan**
salir: **salgo**	→ **salga, salgan**
tener: **tengo**	→ **tenga, tengan**
traer: **traigo**	→ **traiga, traigan**
venir: **vengo**	→ **venga, vengan**
ver: **veo**	→ **vea, vean**

---

5. **Irregular Formal Commands**
   A few verbs have irregular **usted/ustedes** command forms.

dar* (*to give*)	→ **dé**, *but* **den**
estar	→ **esté, estén**
ir	→ **vaya, vayan**
saber	→ **sepa, sepan**
ser	→ **sea, sean**

Position of Pronouns / **El lugar de los pronombres**

1. **Pronouns with Affirmative Commands**
   Direct object pronouns and reflexive pronouns must *follow* affirmative commands and are attached to them. In order to maintain the original stress of the verb form, an accent mark is added to the stressed vowel if the original command has two or more syllables.

1 palabra: *mandato* + *pronombre*

Pídalo usted.	*Order it.*
Siéntense, por favor.	*Sit down, please.*

---

2. **Pronouns with Negative Commands**
   Direct object and reflexive pronouns must *precede* the verb form in negative commands.

3 palabras: **no** + *pronombre* + *mandato*

No lo pida usted.	*Don't order it.*
No se levanten, por favor.	*Don't get up.*

¡OJO!

Now that you know how to form formal commands, be sure to use them carefully when speaking to native speakers of Spanish. Commands are strong forms in any language. It is wise to soften formal commands with **por favor** and by using a polite tone, just as you would in English. Example: **Abra la puerta, por favor.**

***Decir** *and* **dar** *are used primarily with indirect objects. Both of these verbs and indirect object pronouns will be formally introduced in* **Gramática 21 (Cap. 8)**.

Práctica y comunicación

A. Mandatos de esta clase

Paso 1. Autoprueba. Complete los siguientes mandatos formales de **usted** con las terminaciones apropiadas. **¡OJO!** Es necesario escribir más de una letra en algunos casos.

1. habl_______
2. escrib_______
3. lleg_______
4. aprend_______
5. cierr_______
6. duerm_______
7. le_______
8. ha_______
9. empie_______
10. bus_______

Summary of Formal Commands

-ar → -e(n)
-er/-ir → -a(n)

Affirmative: *command* + *pronoun* (1 word)
Negative: no + *pronoun* + *command* (3 words)

Paso 2. Cambie las siguientes frases en mandatos lógicos y típicos de una clase de español. **¡OJO!** Pueden ser afirmativos o negativos.

MODELO: abrir los libros en la página x →
Abr**an** los libros en la página x.

1. cerrar los libros
2. traer la tarea mañana
3. sentarse en círculo
4. dormirse
5. leer el texto
6. hacer preguntas
7. hablar en inglés
8. repetir (*like* pedir) más alto (*louder*)

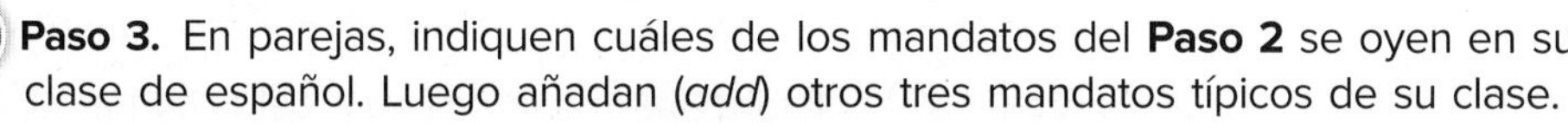

Paso 3. En parejas, indiquen cuáles de los mandatos del **Paso 2** se oyen en su clase de español. Luego añadan (*add*) otros tres mandatos típicos de su clase.

B. El mundo al revés (*The world upside down*)

Paso 1. Hoy, los estudiantes son los «jefes» (*bosses*)... pero ¡solo por un día! Cambie las siguientes acciones en mandatos «lógicos» para todos sus profesores, no solo para su profesor(a) de español. Haga mandatos afirmativos y negativos.

1. llegar a tiempo
2. venir a la universidad
3. pedir la tarea
4. volver a casa
5. poner música de _______
6. pensar en _______
7. traer _______ (¿comida?) a clase
8. sentarse en _______
9. hacer _______
10. dar _______ a los estudiantes

Vocabulario útil

el examen
la nota grade (*academic*)
la prueba quiz

Paso 2. ¿Qué otros mandatos pueden dar a sus profesores hoy? En parejas, inventen tres mandatos para ellos.

C. ¡Pobre Sr. Casiano!

Paso 1. El Sr. Casiano no se siente (*feel*) bien. Lea la descripción que él da de las cosas que hace.

Trabajo[1] muchísimo[a] —¡me gusta trabajar! En la oficina, **soy**[2] impaciente y **critico**[3 b] bastante[c] a los otros. En mi vida personal, a veces **soy**[4] un poco impulsivo. **Fumo**[5 d] bastante y también **bebo**[6] cerveza y otras bebidas alcohólicas, a veces sin moderación... **Almuerzo**[7] y **ceno**[8] fuerte,[e] y **desayuno**[9] poco. Por la noche, con frecuencia **salgo**[10] con los amigos —me gusta ir a las discotecas— y **vuelvo**[11] tarde a casa.

[a]*a great deal* [b]critico → criticar [c]*a good deal* [d]Fumo → fumar (*to smoke*) [e]*a lot*

(Continúa.)

Prác. A, Paso 1: **Answers:** *1. hable 2. escriba 3. llegue 4. aprenda 5. cierre 6. duerma 7. lea 8. haga 9. empiece 10. busque*

Paso 2. Comprensión. ¿Cierto o falso?

	CIERTO	FALSO
1. El Sr. Casiano es una persona muy simpática.	☐	☐
2. Tiene algunos hábitos malos.	☐	☐
3. Por la noche, siempre está en casa.	☐	☐

Paso 3. ¿Qué *no* debe hacer el Sr. Casiano? Aconséjelo (*Advise him*) y dígale (*tell him*) lo que no debe hacer. Use los verbos en **negrilla** o cualquier (*any*) otro.

MODELOS: **1. Trabajo** → Sr. Casiano, **no trabaje** tanto.
2. soy → **No sea** tan impaciente.

D. Estrategias para adelgazar (*lose weight*). ¿Qué debe o no debe comer y beber una persona que quiere adelgazar? En parejas, imaginen una conversación entre esa persona y su médico.

MODELOS: ensalada → E1: ¿Ensalada?
E2: Cómа**la**.

postres → E1: ¿Postres?
E2: No **los** coma.

1. bebidas alcohólicas
2. verduras
3. pan
4. dulces
5. leche entera (*whole*)
6. hamburguesas con queso
7. frutas frescas
8. refrescos dietéticos

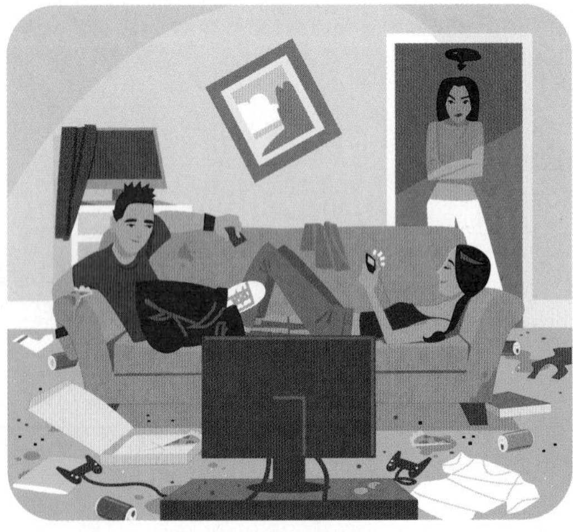

E. ¡Qué desastre! Imagine los mandatos que esta madre va a darles a sus hijos adolescentes. ¿Le resultan (*Do they sound*) familiares a usted estos mandatos?

MODELO: **no acostarse** muy tarde →
¡**No se acuesten** muy tarde!

1. **levantarse** más temprano
2. **bañarse** todos los días
3. **quitarse** esa ropa sucia
4. **ponerse** ropa limpia
5. **no divertirse** todas las noches con los amigos
6. **ir** más a la biblioteca y **estudiar** más
7. ¿ ?

Vocabulario útil

con la boca llena	with one's mouth full
la cuchara	spoon
el cuchillo	knife
la mano	hand
la servilleta	napkin
el tenedor	fork
masticar (qu)	to chew
servirse (me sirvo) (i) a uno mismo	to help one's self
despacio	slowly

F. Consejos sobre los buenos modales (*good manners*) en la mesa

Paso 1. Use las siguientes ideas para dar consejos en forma de mandatos formales sobre cómo se debe comer en una ocasión formal. **¡OJO!** Algunos consejos son normas en los países hispanos y *no* coinciden con las normas que se practican en este país. ¿Puede decir cuáles son las normas específicamente hispanas?

1. **poner** las dos manos en la mesa
2. no **poner** los codos (*elbows*) en la mesa
3. para cortar, **agarrar** (*to hold*) el tenedor con la mano izquierda y el cuchillo con la derecha
4. **cortar** solo el pedazo (*piece*) de comida que puede poner en la boca
5. no **cambiar** (*to change*) de mano el tenedor para llevar la comida a la boca
6. no **eructar** (*to burp*) en público

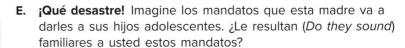

Paso 2. Ahora, en grupos, inventen por lo menos (*at least*) cuatro consejos más.

Todo junto

A. Lengua y cultura: La cocina panameña

Paso 1. Completar. Complete the following paragraphs with the correct form of the words in parentheses, as suggested by context. When two possibilities are given in parentheses, select the correct word. **¡OJO!** As you conjugate the verbs in this activity, note that you will make formal commands with some infinitives.

©Ildi.Food/Alamy

El ceviche, un típico plato panameño

¿Creen ustedes que la comida panameña es similar a la[a] de México y que los tacos y las tortillas ______ (ser / estar[1]) parte de la comida típica de los panameños? Si creen eso, entonces[b] no ______ (*ustedes:* saber / conocer[2]) ______ (algo / nada[3]) de la comida de ______ (este[4]) nación. ______ (*Ustedes:* Seguir[5]) ______ (leer[6]), porque van a aprender mucho.

La influencia ______ (extranjero[7]) en la comida de la cosmopolita Ciudad de Panamá es muy visible. Hay ______ (mucho[8]) restaurantes que ______ (servir[9]) comida italiana, china, ______ (francés[10]), etcétera.

Sin embargo, los panameños no ______ (perder[11]) su identidad nacional, y frecuentemente ______ (preferir[12]) la comida tradicional. En la cocina panameña hay muchos platos de mariscos y pescados, entre ellos el ceviche. Las personas vegetarianas no ______ (tener[13]) problema ______ (también / tampoco[14]) porque hay una variedad de platos ______ (preparado[15]) con arroz y verduras. El arroz es un ingrediente importante en la comida de Panamá. Si usted desea ______ (saber / conocer[16]) cuál es el plato nacional de Panamá, los panameños ______ (contestar[17]): «el arroz con pollo.» ______ (*Usted:* Pedirlo[18]). Le va a gustar.

[a]*a... to that* [b]*then*

Paso 2. Comprensión. Conteste las siguientes preguntas.

1. ¿Cómo se sabe que la Ciudad de Panamá es cosmopolita?
2. ¿Cuál es el plato que representa mejor la cocina panameña?
3. ¿Qué ingredientes son comunes en la comida de Panamá?

(Continúa.)

Paso 3. En acción

En parejas, den consejos a turistas extranjeros sobre dónde pueden encontrar las siguientes comidas, que son típicas de algunas partes de los Estados Unidos. Den sus recomendaciones en forma de mandatos. Luego comparen sus recomendaciones con las (*those*) del resto de la clase para ver si todos están de acuerdo.

MODELO: la mejor sopa de almejas (*clams*) → Vayan a los estados del noreste, a la región de Nueva Inglaterra. Pidan la sopa que se llama *clam chowder*. Tiene almejas y con frecuencia tiene leche.

1. la mejor barbacoa
2. los mejores mariscos
3. la mejor comida china
4. la mejor comida hispana
5. el mejor queso
6. la mejor langosta

B. Proyecto: ¿Cómo come esta clase?

MANIFIESTO DE LA COMIDA
AGRADECE LOS ALIMENTOS QUE VAS A RECIBIR NO TODOS LOS TIENEN
COME SÓLO CUANDO TENGAS HAMBRE
COMIENZA CON UNA ENSALADA
COME DESPACIO Y CONSCIENTEMENTE
LLENA SOLO EL 80% Y DEJA EL 20% DEL ESTÓMAGO VACIO
COME CON UNA BUENA COMPAÑIA
NO HABLES TEMAS QUE TE ALTEREN
APAGA EL CELULAR TODOS MERECEMOS UNA COMIDA TRANQUILA
COME SENTADO
SI COMES SOLO NO TRATES DE DISTRAERTE MIENTRAS COMES
DEJA DE COMER CUANDO YA NO SIENTAS HAMBRE
COME COMIDA... NO PRODUCTOS

Para este proyecto van a documentar los hábitos relacionados con la comida de las personas de la clase.

Paso 1. Preparación. En grupos, piensen en ideas (1-2 por miembro del grupo) relacionadas con los hábitos de comer para encuestar al resto de la clase: qué comen, dónde, con quién, con qué frecuencia, qué hacen mientras (*while*) comen, etcétera. Hay algunas ideas en el **Manifiesto de la comida**. Para hacer las preguntas, consideren varias opciones, como se muestran (*are shown*) en los modelos.

MODELOS: comer verduras → ¿Con qué frecuencia comes verduras? En todas las comidas. En algunas comidas. Casi nunca.

tener una dieta sana → Evalúa tu dieta del 1 al 5: 1 significa mala y 5 significa excelente.

actividades durante la comida → Indica dos de las acciones que haces con más frecuencia mientras comes: hablar con otra persona, ver algún programa en una pantalla (*screen*), leer, concentrarte en la comida.

Paso 2. Encuesta. Ahora háganles sus preguntas a varias personas de la clase (¡o a todas!). Recuerden (*Remember*) preparar un método para apuntar (*note down*) las respuestas.

Paso 3. Análisis de datos. Analicen las respuestas y preparen una serie de oraciones para presentar los datos al resto de la clase.

MODELOS: Un total de ______ (número) de ______ (número) personas encuestadas prefiere...Más del 50% (por ciento) de los encuestados...

¡OJO!

You have just learned formal commands, which use the opposite vowel. But you may want to use informal commands in this activity. Two of them are shown in the models (**Evalúa, Indica),** and several others appear in **Manifiesto de la comida.**

¡Ahora, yo!

A. Entrevista. Use de modelo las preguntas y respuestas de la página 205 de este capítulo para hablar de la comida de su país y de sus preferencias culinarias.

B. Proyecto audiovisual. Filme un programa culinario en el que (*which*) presente al menos (*at least*) dos platos o ingredientes tradicionales de una cocina nacional o regional.

«¡Qué rico!» Segmento 2

Antes de mirar

Conteste las siguientes preguntas.

1. ¿Hay restaurantes de comida hispana donde usted vive? ¿En qué tipo de cocina se especializan?
2. ¿Se puede comprar comida en la calle (*street*) donde usted vive? ¿Hay muchos *food trucks*?

Este segmento

Los presentadores introducen un reportaje sobre la comida que se puede comprar en la calle (*street*). Luego cierran el programa haciendo planes para almorzar.

«Sin duda (*Undoubtedly*), los tacos son la comida callejera (*street*) por excelencia. Los hay de muchos tipos: al pastor, de carne, de pescado, etcétera. En efecto, cualquier alimento sabroso envuelto (*any tasty food wrapped*) en tortillas de esta manera puede llamarse taco.»

Fragmento del guion

¡Esa paella! Este reportaje de Laura me ha abierto el apetito.[a] El castellano[b] y la comida son la herencia[c] más positiva que nos dejó[d] la colonización española. Y lo mejor es que la comida española se adaptó fácilmente[e] a los ingredientes locales de cada país. Y se mezcló[f] con las tradiciones indígenas y también con las africanas que llegaron con los esclavos.[g] Y para qué hablar[h] del efecto de los productos americanos en la cocina de España y de toda Europa.

[a]me... *has whet my appetite* [b]*Spanish language* [c]*heritage, inheritance* [d]nos... *gave (lit., left) to us* [e]se... *easily adapted itself* [f]se... *it mixed* [g]llegaron... *arrived with the slaves* [h]para... *what can we say*

Vocabulario del segmento

neoyorquino/a	**de Nueva York**
el chorizo	type of sausage
la empanada	turnover
relleno/a	stuffed
el horneado de puerco	pork roast
me dijo	told me
el vendedor ambulante	street vendor
ya se imaginarán	you can imagine
cuidado con	(be) careful with
me muero de hambre	I'm starving
te apetece	do you feel like
la pupusa	filled corn tortilla
nos despedimos	that's all
¡No se lo pierdan!	Don't miss it!
¿Nos acompañan?	Won't you come with us?

Después de mirar

A. ¿Está claro? Empareje las siguientes comidas con su lugar de origen.

COMIDAS	LUGARES DE ORIGEN
1. ____ el horneado de puerco	a. la Argentina
2. ____ el choripán	b. América
3. ____ el chocolate y el tomate	c. el Ecuador
4. ____ el taco	d. El Salvador
5. ____ la pupusa	e. México

B. Un poco más. Conteste las siguientes preguntas.

1. ¿Qué es el choripán? ¿Cuál es el origen de su nombre?
2. ¿Cuál es la comida callejera por excelencia en México?
3. ¿Cómo se siente (*feels*) Víctor al final del programa? ¿Por qué?

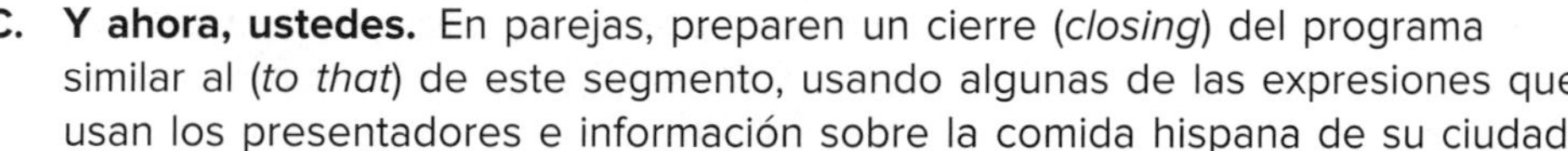

C. Y ahora, ustedes. En parejas, preparen un cierre (*closing*) del programa similar al (*to that*) de este segmento, usando algunas de las expresiones que usan los presentadores e información sobre la comida hispana de su ciudad.

MUNDO HISPANO

Enfoque cultural: Panamá

Antes de leer

¿Cuáles son algunos de los platos típicos de su país? ¿Hay alguna comida típica de su ciudad o estado?

La comida panameña

El arroz con pollo al estilo panameño es uno de los platos más típicos de Panamá. Otro plato típico es el sancocho, una sopa que también es parte de la cocina de otros países caribeños y que lleva algún tipo de carne, verduras y legumbres.[a] Y es necesario mencionar también las frituras, es decir,[b] la comida frita. Hay gran variedad de frituras: la yuca frita, las carimañolas (unas bolas de masa[c] de yuca con carne dentro[d]), los patacones (rebanadas[e] de plátano frito), las empanadas[f] al estilo panameño, etcétera.

De beber, se debe probar[g] las chichas, que son refrescos naturales de frutas panameñas, como el coco, la guanábana y el maracuyá.[h]

[a]*legumes* [b]es... *that is* [c]bolas... *balls of dough* [d]*inside* [e]*slices* [f]*see* **En otros países hispanos** [g]*try* [h]coco... *coconut, soursop, and passion fruit*

En otros países hispanos

- **En todo el mundo hispanohablante** Las empanadas son probablemente la constante culinaria más notable de todos los países hispanohablantes. Consisten en una masa de pan[a] rellena[b] de algo dulce o salado.[c] Pueden ser pequeñas e individuales o grandes para ser compartidas.[d] Las empanadas son de procedencia española... y los españoles las heredaron[e] de los árabes. ¡Una larga y deliciosa tradición!
- **En los Estados Unidos** La comida latina es omnipresente en los Estados Unidos hoy día. La cocina mexicana es muy popular, como también lo es su variante *Tex-Mex,* genuinamente estadounidense. Pero también se puede encontrar la comida de casi todas las otras cocinas hispanas: las pupusas[f] salvadoreñas, la tortilla[g] española (con papas y cebollas), el arroz con gandules[h] puertorriqueño, el dulce de leche[i] (una comida panhispánica), etcétera.

[a]masa... *bread dough* [b]*filled* [c]*salty* [d]*shared* [e]*inherited* [f]*corn masa stuffed with cheese, refried beans, or meat, then fried like a tortilla* [g]*omelet* [h]*pigeon peas* [i]dulce... *caramel*

©Gonzalo Azumendi/The Image Bank/Getty Images

El canal de Panamá: 48 millas de canales y esclusas (*locks*)

Un símbolo panameño: El canal

Es una de las obras[a] de ingeniería más importantes del mundo por su impacto en el transporte mundial. Une el mar Caribe con el océano Pacífico. Fue inaugurado[b] en 1914. Antes de su existencia, los barcos tenían que dar la vuelta por el estrecho de Magallanes.[c] La ruta del canal fue descubierta[d] en 1514 por el explorador español Vasco Núñez de Balboa. Desde entonces[e] los españoles tuvieron[f] la idea de construir un canal. Pero su construcción no se hizo[g] realidad hasta principios del siglo XX.[h] En la actualidad,[i] el canal se está ampliando.[j]

[a]*works* [b]*opened* [c]tenían... *had to go around the Strait of Magellan* [d]*discovered* [e]Desde... *Since then* [f]*had* [g]no... *didn't become* [h]principios... *the beginning of the 20th century* [i]En... *Currently* [j]se... *is being enlarged*

Comprensión

1. ¿Qué son las frituras panameñas?
2. ¿Qué es la chicha?
3. ¿Qué comida es muy típica de todo el mundo hispano?
4. ¿Qué cocina genuinamente estadounidense es de origen hispano?
5. ¿Cuándo empezó (*began*) a funcionar el canal de Panamá? ¿Cuándo empezaron los españoles a pensar en hacer un canal?

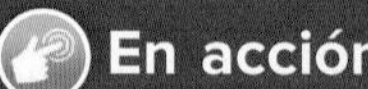

En acción

Haga dos listas: una de los cinco platos más tradicionales de los Estados Unidos, y la otra de los cinco productos más representativos de este país. Si no sabe el nombre de alguno, use un diccionario. Prepárese para justificar su selección.

Lectura

Antes de leer

Piense en la lasaña, un plato italiano tradicional. ¿Cuáles de estos ingredientes contiene una lasaña típica? ¿pollo, aceite de oliva, papas, pimienta, pasta, tomates, sal, champiñones, tortillas, frijoles, agua, salchicha, lechuga, queso?

Una receta

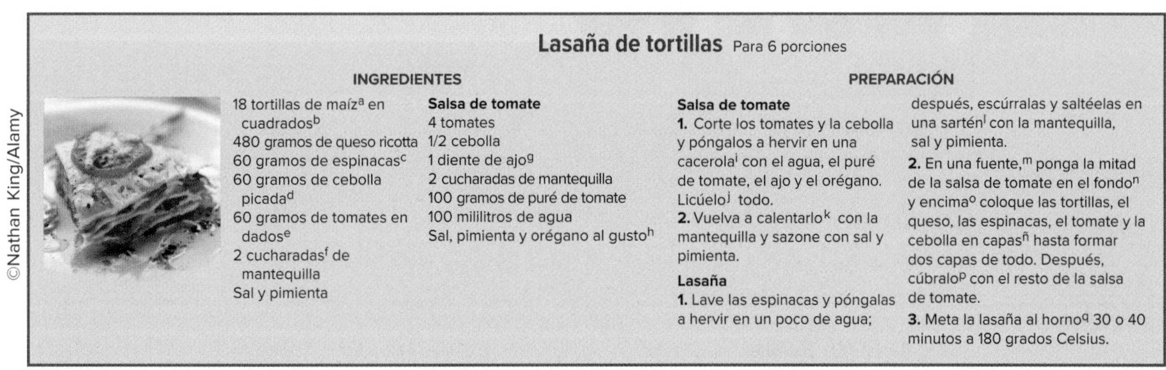

Lasaña de tortillas Para 6 porciones

INGREDIENTES

18 tortillas de maíz[a] en cuadrados[b]
480 gramos de queso ricotta
60 gramos de espinacas[c]
60 gramos de cebolla picada[d]
60 gramos de tomates en dados[e]
2 cucharadas[f] de mantequilla
Sal y pimienta

Salsa de tomate
4 tomates
1/2 cebolla
1 diente de ajo[g]
2 cucharadas de mantequilla
100 gramos de puré de tomate
100 mililitros de agua
Sal, pimienta y orégano al gusto[h]

PREPARACIÓN

Salsa de tomate

1. Corte los tomates y la cebolla y póngalos a hervir en una cacerola[i] con el agua, el puré de tomate, el ajo y el orégano. Licúelo[j] todo.

2. Vuelva a calentarlo[k] con la mantequilla y sazone con sal y pimienta.

Lasaña

1. Lave las espinacas y póngalas a hervir en un poco de agua; después, escúrralas y saltéelas en una sartén[l] con la mantequilla, sal y pimienta.

2. En una fuente,[m] ponga la mitad de la salsa de tomate en el fondo[n] y encima[o] coloque las tortillas, el queso, las espinacas, el tomate y la cebolla en capas[ñ] hasta formar dos capas de todo. Después, cúbralo[p] con el resto de la salsa de tomate.

3. Meta la lasaña al horno[q] 30 o 40 minutos a 180 grados Celsius.

[a]*corn* [b]*squares* [c]*spinach* [d]*chopped* [e]*cubes* [f]*tablespoons* [g]diente... *clove of garlic* [h]al... *to taste* [i]póngalos... *boil them in a pot* [j]*Blend it* [k]Vuelva... *Reheat it* [l]escúrralas... *drain them* (*the spinach leaves*) *and sauté them in a frying pan* [m]*serving dish* [n]*bottom* [ñ]*on top* [o]*layers* [p]*cover it* [q]*oven*

Comprensión

A. Los mandatos de la receta. Todos los verbos para preparar esta receta son mandatos formales. Empareje los siguientes mandatos con su traducción en inglés, según el contexto de la receta.

MANDATOS	TRADUCCIONES
1. _____ corte	**a.** *put* (*into*)
2. _____ sazone	**b.** *wash*
3. _____ lave	**c.** *place, arrange*
4. _____ coloque	**d.** *cut*
5. _____ meta	**e.** *season*

B. Paso por *(by)* paso. Ponga en orden cronológico (de 1 a 4) los siguientes pasos para la lasaña, según la receta.

_____ Cocinar la lasaña en el horno.
_____ Hervir las espinacas y luego cocinarlas en una sartén.
_____ Preparar la salsa de tomate.
_____ Poner en una fuente, en capas, todos los ingredientes preparados para formar la lasaña.

Proyecto: Una receta

Paso 1: Piense en un plato que usted considera delicioso. Puede ser un plato tradicional de su familia y/o de su cultura. ¿Por qué lo elige (*do you choose it*)?

Paso 2: Escriba la receta para este plato. Incluya la lista de los ingredientes con las cantidades específicas y los pasos para su preparación. También escriba una breve introducción para explicar en qué ocasiones y con qué otras comidas es costumbre (*it´s customary*) servirlo.

Paso 3: ¡Comparta (*Share*) su receta con sus compañeros de clase!

Textos orales

En un restaurante

Antes de escuchar

¿Sale con frecuencia a comer en restaurantes? ¿Tiene algún restaurante favorito? ¿En qué se especializa?

Vocabulario para escuchar

la carta	menu	**mixto/a**	mixed (with **paella** = having both meat and seafood)
los entrantes	starters, first courses		
el segundo plato	main course	**cómo no**	of course

Comprensión

A. **¿Qué desean?** Los señores Robles cenan esta noche en un restaurante elegante. ¿Qué piden?

1. El Sr. Robles:
   Entrante ______________________ Segundo plato __________
2. La Sra. Robles:
   Entrante ________________ Segundo plato ________________
3. De beber:
   ____

B. **Más detalles.** Conteste las siguientes preguntas.

1. ¿Qué platos tienen fama en este restaurante?
2. ¿Cuándo van a pedir el postre los Sres. Robles?

En acción

Escriba un párrafo para una página web sobre restaurantes, dando su opinión sobre un restaurante en particular. Además de dar (*Besides giving*) el nombre del restaurante, explique en qué tipo de comida se especializa, cuáles son sus platos favoritos (con algunos detalles) y por qué usted lo recomienda... ¡o no lo recomienda!

Proyecto en su comunidad

Entreviste a una persona hispana de su universidad o ciudad sobre la cocina y la comida de su país.

Preguntas posibles

- ¿Cuáles son los ingredientes más importantes?
- ¿Puede encontrar estos ingredientes en los supermercados de aquí?
- ¿Cuál es la comida principal del día? ¿Comen un desayuno fuerte (*heavy*)?
- ¿Cuáles son algunos de los platos típicos?
- ¿Hay muchos restaurantes especializados en la comida de su país en este estado? ¿Cuál es su favorito?

Escritura

Proyecto: Las opciones de comida en esta universidad

Usted va a escribir un ensayo sobre cómo y dónde comen los estudiantes en su universidad y si, en general, hay satisfacción con las opciones para comer en el campus.

Antes de escribir

En parejas, compartan (*share*) sus ideas sobre las opciones que se ofrecen en su campus para comer. La conversación los/las ayudará (*will help you*) a clarificar sus propias ideas y determinar un enfoque para su ensayo.

- ¿Ofrecen las cafeterías y otros restaurantes una buena variedad de comidas? Ejemplos: platos vegetarianos, comida baja en calorías.
- ¿Hay buenos planes de comida?
- ¿Cuáles son los platos que más piden los estudiantes?
- En general, ¿está rica la comida? ¿Es cara o barata?
- ¿Hay alguna cafetería mejor que otra?
- ¿Creen que hay bastante satisfacción entre los estudiantes con respecto a las opciones que se ofrecen? Justifiquen sus respuestas.

¿Come usted con frecuencia en la cafetería universitaria?

A escribir

Ahora use sus opiniones y las (*those*) de su compañero/a (recuerde citarlo/la [*remember to quote him or her*]) para escribir su ensayo. Escoja (*Choose*) un enfoque desde el principio (*from the beginning*) para organizar bien su texto. Hay más ayuda en Connect.

Más ideas para su portafolio

- Incluya una lista de sus comidas y bebidas favoritas. Incluya los lugares (restaurantes, la casa de alguien) donde las come o las bebe porque son mejores.
- Incluya una receta familiar favorita.
- Entreviste a un(a) hispanohablante sobre los platos más tradicionales de su cultura y pídale (*ask him/her for*) una receta fácil.
- Si ha estado jugando (*you have been playing*) Practice Spanish: Study Abroad, en Quest 4 usted participó (*participated*) en una telenovela (*soap opera*) sobre una compañía que se especializa en (*specializes in*) la moda. En grupos, escriban una escena (*scene*) de una telenovela que tenga lugar (*takes place*) en un restaurante. Usen vocabulario de este capítulo ¡y sean creativos (*creative*)! Después, ustedes pueden interpretar (*act out*) su escena para la clase.

Sugerencia: You are now ready to play Quest 4 in **Practice Spanish: Study Abroad.**

EN RESUMEN En este capítulo

AFTER STUDYING THIS CHAPTER I CAN. . .

- ☐ talk about food and the meals of the day (206–207)
- ☐ use the verbs **saber** and **conocer** to express *to know* (209)
- ☐ use direct object pronouns to avoid repetition in conversation (213–215)
- ☐ use negative and indefinite words (219–220)
- ☐ give and understand formal commands (223–224)
- ☐ recognize/describe at least 2–3 aspects of Panamanian cultures

Gramática en breve

18. Direct Object Pronouns

me, te, lo/la, nos, os, los/las

19. Indefinite and Negative Words

algo	**nada**
alguien	**nadie**
algún (alguna/os/as)	**ningún (ninguna)**
siempre	**nunca, jamás**
también	**tampoco**

no + *verb* + *negative word*
negative word + *verb*

20. Formal Commands

-ar → -e(n)
-er/-ir → -a(n)

Affirmative: *command* + *pronoun* (1 word)
Negative: no + *pronoun* + *command* (3 words)

Vocabulario

Los verbos

acabar de + *inf.*	to have just (*done something*)
ayudar	to help
ayudar a + *inf.*	to help to (*do something*)
conocer (conozco)	to know (*a person*); to be acquainted, familiar with (*a place or thing*); to meet (*a person*)
contestar	to answer
esperar	to wait (for); to expect
invitar	to invite
llamar	to call
saber (sé)	to know (*facts, information*)
saber + *inf.*	to know how to (*do something*)

La comida

cenar	to have/eat dinner, supper
cocinar	to cook
desayunar	to have/eat breakfast
merendar (meriendo)	to snack
preparar	to prepare

Repaso: almorzar (almuerzo) (c)

Remember that this letter (c) indicates the spelling change that happens in the formal commands of verbs that end in **-car, -gar,** or **-zar.**

el aceite (de oliva)	(olive) oil
el aguacate	avocado
el arroz	rice
las arvejas	green peas
el atún	tuna
el azúcar	sugar
el bistec	steak
los camarones	shrimp
la carne	meat
la cebolla	onion
los champiñones	mushrooms
la chuleta (de cerdo)	(pork) chop
los dulces	sweets; candy
los espárragos	asparagus
el flan	(baked) custard
los frijoles	beans
la galleta	cookie
los garbanzos	chickpeas
el helado	ice cream
el huevo	egg
el jamón	ham
la langosta	lobster
la lechuga	lettuce
la mantequilla	butter
la manzana	apple
los mariscos	shellfish
la naranja	orange
el pan	bread
el pan tostado	toast
la papa (frita)	(French fried) potato
el pastel	cake; pie
el pavo	turkey
el pepino	cucumber
el pescado	fish
la pimienta	pepper
el pollo (asado)	(roast) chicken
el postre	dessert
el queso	cheese
la sal	salt
la salsa	salsa; sauce
la salchicha	sausage; hot dog
la sopa	soup
las verduras	vegetables
la zanahoria	carrot

la comida	food

Cognados: la banana, la barbacoa, el cereal, la ensalada, la fruta, la hamburguesa, el salmón, el sándwich, el tomate, el yogur

Las bebidas

el agua (*but f.*) (mineral)	(mineral) water
la cerveza	beer
el jugo (de fruta)	(fruit) juice
la leche	milk
el refresco	soft drink
el vino (blanco, tinto)	(white, red) wine

Cognado: el té

Repaso: la bebida, el café

Las comidas

el almuerzo	lunch
la cena	dinner, supper
el desayuno	breakfast
la merienda	snack
la comida	meal

En un restaurante

el/la camarero/a	waiter/waitress
la cuenta	check, bill
el plato	dish (*food prepared in a particular way*); course; plate
el plato principal	main course

Cognado: el menú

Otros sustantivos

la ayuda	help
la canción	song
la cocina	cuisine
los comestibles	groceries, foodstuff
el consejo	(piece of) advice
la dirección	address
el/la dueño/a	owner
la letra	lyrics (*of a song*)
el mandato	command
el nombre	name
la receta	recipe
la tarjeta de crédito	credit card

Los adjetivos

asado/a	roast(ed), grilled
caliente	hot (*in temperature, not taste*)
fresco/a	fresh
frito/a	fried
ligero/a	light, not heavy
picante	hot, spicy
rico/a	tasty, savory; rich (*in calories*)
tostado/a	toasted

Las palabras indefinidas y negativas

algo	something, anything
alguien	someone, anyone
algún (alguna/os/as)	some, any
jamás	never
nada	nothing, not anything
nadie	no one, nobody, not anybody
ningún (ninguna)	no, not any
tampoco	neither, not either

Repaso: nunca, siempre, también

Palabras adicionales

¡Buen provecho!	Bon appetit!
estar a dieta	to be on a diet
tener (mucha) hambre	to be (very) hungry
tener (mucha) sed	to be (very) thirsty

Vocabulario personal

8

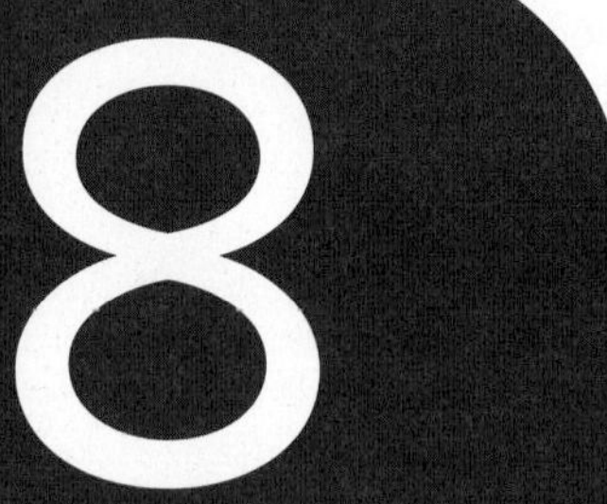

De viaje°

De... *On a trip, Traveling*

En este capítulo

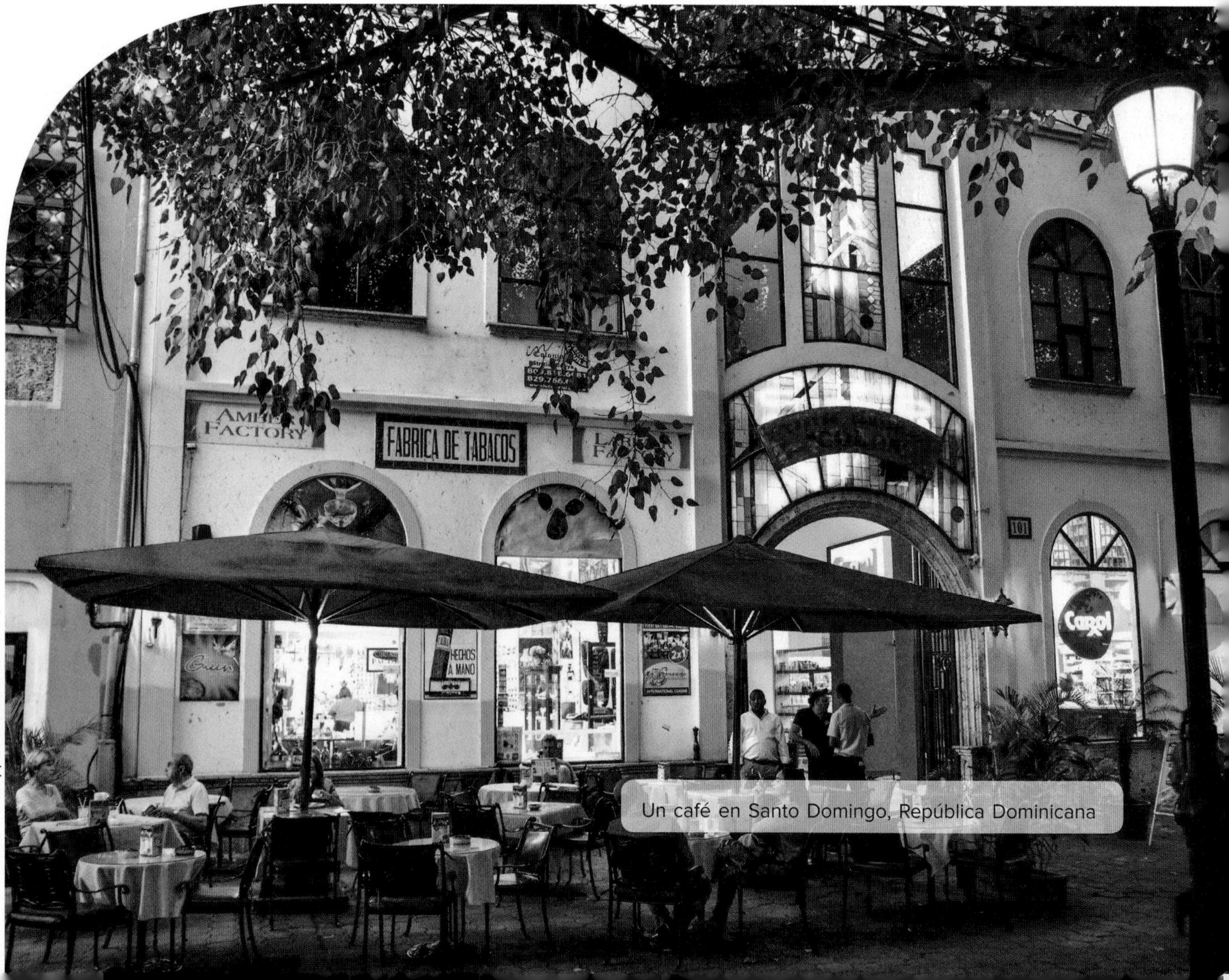

Un café en Santo Domingo, República Dominicana

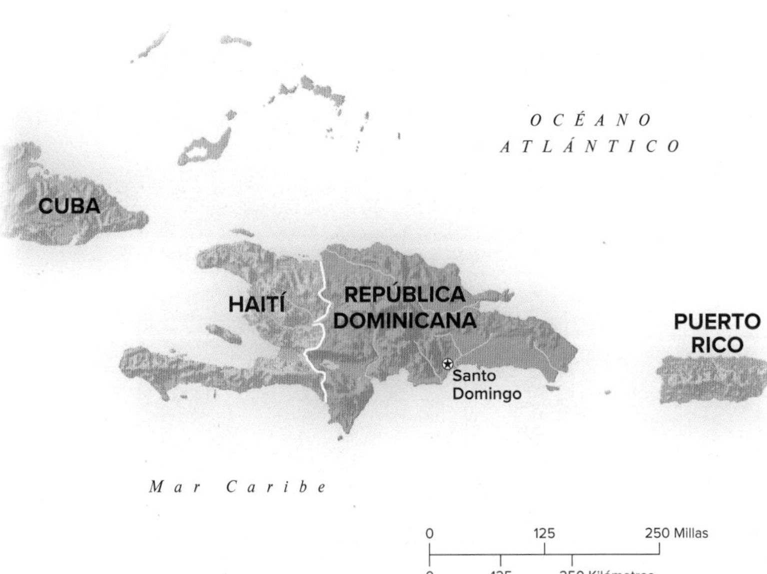

LA REPÚBLICA DOMINICANA

10,8 (coma ocho) millones de habitantes

- La República Dominicana comparte[a] la isla de La Española (*Hispaniola,* en inglés) con el país de Haití.
- La ciudad de Santo Domingo, capital del país, fue fundada[b] por el hermano de Cristóbal Colón en 1496. Es la más antigua de todas las ciudades fundadas por los europeos en América.

[a]*shares* [b]*founded*

ENTREVISTA

- ¿Dónde le gusta pasar las vacaciones? ¿En la playa? ¿en las montañas? ¿visitando una ciudad o un país que usted no conoce? (¿una nueva ciudad o un nuevo país?)
- ¿Qué le gusta hacer cuando está en la playa? ¿nadar[a]? ¿tomar el sol[b]? ¿surfear u otros deportes[c]?
- ¿Qué es lo peor[d] de hacer un viaje, hacer la maleta,[e] el viaje mismo[f] o volver a casa?

[a]*swim* [b]tomar... *sunbathe* [c]*sports* [d]lo... *the worst part* [e]hacer... *packing* [f]el... *the trip itself*

Cecilia Figueroa Martín contesta las preguntas.

- Prefiero ir de viaje a otros países y también visitar a mis parientes en los Estados Unidos. Como[a] soy de Puerto Rico y tengo el mar[b] y el calor todo el tiempo, me gusta ir de vacaciones a lugares con un clima diferente. ¡Me encanta[c] ver la nieve!
- Cuando voy a la playa, me gusta nadar y estar en la arena[d] leyendo.
- Para mí, lo peor de un viaje es tener que trasladarse.[e] Odio[f] especialmente los viajes en avión.[g] Pero si el viaje es muy divertido,[h] ¡odio volver!

[a]*Since* [b]*ocean* [c]¡Me... *I love* [d]*sand* [e]*change locations* [f]*I hate* [g]en... *by plane* [h]muy... *a lot of fun*

VOCABULARIO: PREPARACIÓN

You can hear the pronunciation of theme vocabulary words and phrases in the Connect eBook.

De viaje°

De... *On a trip, Traveling*

Los medios de transporte

la cabina	cabin (*on a ship; of a plane*)
el crucero	cruise (ship)
la estación	station
de autobuses	bus station
de trenes	train station
el puerto	port
la sala de espera	waiting room
la sala de fumar / de fumadores	smoking area
el vuelo	flight
ir en...	to go/travel by . . .
autobús	bus
avión	plane
barco	boat, ship
tren	train

El viaje

el asiento	seat
el billete (*Sp.*) / **el boleto** (*L.A.*)	ticket
de ida	one-way ticket
de ida y vuelta	round-trip ticket
el billete/boleto electrónico	e-ticket
la demora	delay
el destino	destination
la llegada	arrival
el pasaje	fare, price (*of a transportation ticket*)
el pasaporte	passport
el pasillo	aisle
la puerta de embarque	boarding gate
la salida	departure
la tarjeta de embarque	boarding pass
la ventanilla	small window (*on a plane*)

anunciar	to announce	**ir al extranjero**	to go abroad
bajarse (de)	to get down (from); to get off (of) (*a vehicle*)	**pasar por**	to go/pass through
		la aduana	customs
		el control de seguridad	security (check)
estar atrasado/a	to be late	**quejarse (de)**	to complain (about)
facturar el equipaje	to check baggage	**salir/llegar (gu) a tiempo**	to depart/arrive on time
guardar (un puesto)	to save (a place [*in line*])	**subir (a)**	to go up; to get on (*a vehicle*)
hacer cola	to stand in line	**viajar**	to travel
hacer escala/parada	to make a stop	**volar (vuelo) en avión**	to fly; to go by plane
hacer la(s) maleta(s)	to pack one's suitcase(s)		
hacer un viaje	to take a trip		

Comunicación

A. Hablando de medios de transporte. ¿Con qué medio de transporte relaciona usted las siguientes personas y cosas? Hay más de una respuesta posible en algunos casos.

1. un crucero
2. un(a) asistente de vuelo
3. un puerto
4. una estación
5. una cabina
6. una agencia de viajes
7. un asiento
8. un(a) piloto
9. un capitán / una capitana
10. la llegada

B. Un viaje al extranjero

Paso 1. Use los números del 1 al 9 para organizar un viaje de manera lógica.

a. _____ subir al avión cuando se anuncia el vuelo
b. _____ pasar por el control de seguridad
c. _____ hacer cola para obtener la tarjeta de embarque y facturar el equipaje
d. _____ pedir un taxi y llegar al aeropuerto
e. _____ oír el anuncio de la salida del vuelo
f. _____ hacer la maleta y poner el pasaporte en el bolso
g. _____ esperar en la puerta de embarque mandando mensajes
h. _____ sentarse en el asiento junto a la ventanilla
i. _____ llegar al aeropuerto de destino y pasar por el control de inmigración y la aduana

Paso 2. Ahora narre la secuencia en primera persona (**yo**).

C. En el aeropuerto. En parejas, nombren o describan las cosas y acciones representadas en este dibujo.

Así se dice

El autobús is expressed in a variety of ways in different parts of the Spanish-speaking world. Here are a few of the most common ones.

el camión (*Mex.*)
el bus (*C.A.*)
la guagua (*Cuba, P.R.*)
el colectivo (*Arg.*)

Here are some other common travel-related variations.

la maleta = la valija (*Arg.*), la petaca (*Mex.*)

El boleto is generally understood to express ticket throughout the Spanish-speaking world. The word **el tiquete** is heard in Mexico and Central America, as well as in this country, and **el billete** is used in Spain.

Estrategia

Pay attention to the phrases used in **Paso 1** to define and describe. Here are some more.

Es el sinónimo de...
Es el lugar donde...
Es cuando...
Es lo que...

D. Definiciones

Paso 1. Dé las palabras definidas.

1. Es necesario pasar por este control al llegar a otro país.
2. Es la cosa que se compra antes de hacer un viaje.
3. Es el antónimo de **subir a.**
4. Se va allí cuando se hace un viaje en avión.
5. Se va allí cuando se hace un viaje en tren.
6. Es la persona que nos ayuda durante un vuelo.

Paso 2. Ahora prepare dos definiciones para leer a toda la clase. Sus compañeros van a dar (*give*) la palabra que usted define.

De vacaciones°

De... *On vacation*

el *camping*	campground
el mar	sea
el océano	ocean
estar de vacaciones	to be on vacation
hacer *camping*	to go camping
ir de vacaciones a...	to (go on) vacation to/in . . .
pasar las vacaciones en...	to spend one's vacation in . . .
salir de vacaciones	to leave on vacation
tomar unas vacaciones	to take a vacation

Así se dice

la camioneta = la ranchera, la rubia, el coche rural, el coche familiar, el monovolumen (*Sp.*)
el *camping* = el campamento
hacer *camping* = acampar
sacar fotos = tomar fotos
la tienda de campaña = la tienda de acampar, la carpa, la casa de campaña

Comunicación

A. ¿Qué hace usted?

Paso 1. Diga si las siguientes declaraciones son ciertas o falsas para usted. Corrija las declaraciones falsas.

	CIERTO	FALSO
1. Cuando estoy de vacaciones, tomo el sol.	☐	☐
2. Prefiero ir de vacaciones a las montañas.	☐	☐
3. Duermo muy bien en una tienda de campaña.	☐	☐
4. Saco muchas fotos cuando estoy de vacaciones.	☐	☐
5. Es fácil ir a playas bonitas desde (*from*) aquí.	☐	☐
6. Escribo muchas tarjetas postales.	☐	☐

Paso 2. En parejas, túrnense para hacer y contestar preguntas basadas en las oraciones del **Paso 1.**

Nota cultural

Tipos de turismo en el mundo hispano

En el mundo hispano hay ciudades y lugares impresionantes que visitar y playas maravillosas donde pasar las vacaciones. Pero hay también una gran variedad de lugares de destino para las personas que desean disfrutar de[a] unas vacaciones excepcionales.

- **El ecoturismo**
  Consiste en visitar lugares poco explotados por los seres[b] humanos. La selva costarricense y la selva amazónica (en el Ecuador y el Perú) son destinos populares, así como[c] la Patagonia (en la Argentina y Chile) y las Islas Galápagos. En el norte de España, muchos caminantes[d] de todas partes del mundo hacen el Camino de Santiago.[e] Su origen fue como un camino de peregrinación,[f] pero ahora muchas personas lo hacen sin motivo religioso. Es una actividad física no extrema que le permite a uno[g] hacer compañeros de viaje interesantes y variados.
- **El agroturismo**
  Este tipo de vacaciones implica pasar las vacaciones en un lugar rural. Los turistas pueden quedarse[h] en casas renovadas que ofrecen la experiencia de hacer trabajo agrícola y excursiones educativas. En la isla chilena de Chiloé, por ejemplo, hay ofertas agroturísticas interesantes.
- **El aventurismo**
  Es para aquellos[i] que buscan aventuras emocionantes y físicas. Se puede esquiar en los Andes o en las montañas españolas, hacer ciclismo de montaña, navegar en rápidos, etcétera.

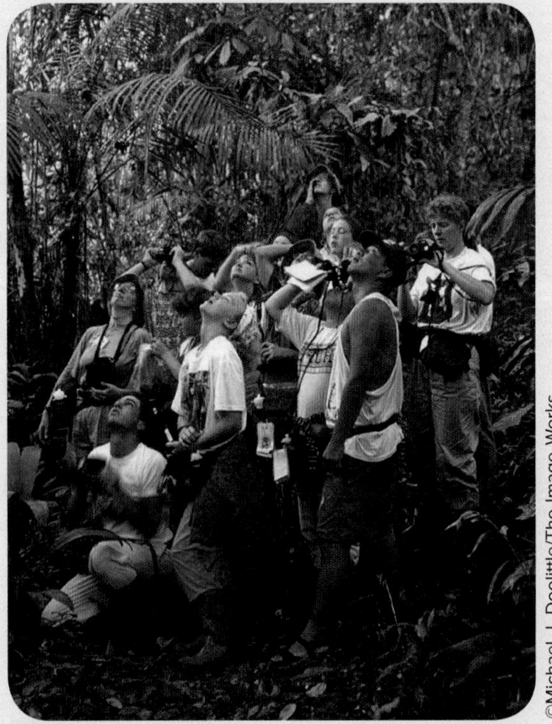

Un grupo de estudiantes en una excursión ecoturística en la selva (*jungle*) amazónica, Perú

¿? ¿Practica usted alguno de estos tipos de turismo? ¿Dónde lo hace?

[a]disfrutar... *to enjoy* [b]*beings* [c]así... *as are* [d]*hikers* [e]Camino... *St James's Trail, Way* [f]un... *a (religious) pilgrimage* [g]le... *allows one* [h]*be lodged* [i]*those (people)*

B. Intercambios

Paso 1. Complete los siguientes párrafos sobre sus vacaciones típicas y sus vacaciones más memorables.

En mis vacaciones típicas, voy a _______[1] en _______[2] (medio de transporte) en el mes de _______.[3] Voy con _______[4] (personas) y esto es lo que hago: _______.[5]

En mis vacaciones más memorables, fui[a] a _______[6] en _______[7] en el mes de _______.[8] Fui con _______.[9] Hice[b] las siguientes actividades: _______[10] (infinitivos).

[a]*I went* [b]*I did*

Vocabulario útil

(tú) fuiste you went

Paso 2. Ahora, en parejas, túrnense para hacer y contestar preguntas basadas en las ideas del **Paso 1.** Obtengan (*Get*) mucha información de su compañero/a.

MODELOS: ¿Adónde vas para tus vacaciones, generalmente? ¿Prefieres algún lugar en especial? ¿Vas allí todos los años? ¿Por qué vas allí? Y para tus vacaciones más memorables, ¿a qué lugar fuiste (*did you go*)?

Nota comunicativa

Otro uso de la palabra *se*: para expresar acciones impersonales

If there are native Spanish speakers living in your area, you probably have seen signs like the one in the photo: **Se habla español.** The word **se** in front of the verb (rather than a specific subject, like **Juan** or **ellos**) changes the English equivalent of the verb. In English, **se habla español** can mean: *Spanish is spoken here. We/They speak Spanish here. People speak Spanish here.* You have already seen this use of **se** in direction lines and readings in *Puntos de partida*.

©Elena Rooraid/PhotoEdit

Here are some additional examples of this use of **se** to talk about things that "people," rather than specific individuals, do.

Se va al aeropuerto para tomar un vuelo. *One goes / People go / You go to the airport to catch a flight.*

Se aprende mucho viajando. *One learns / People learn / You learn a lot by traveling.*

Be alert to this use of **se** in *Puntos de partida* as well as in real-life Spanish; it is very frequent and you need to understand it. You will practice it in **Comunicación C.** You will also see (and hear) plural verbs, but you will not practice using them in this text.

Algo sobre...

el colmado dominicano

En todo el mundo hispanohablante hay tiendas en los barrios[a] donde se venden comestibles, bebidas y las cosas que en este país se compran en los supermercados. En la República Dominicana, estas tiendas se llaman «colmados». Un colmado es un punto de encuentro[b] para la gente[c] del barrio. A veces es como un bar-discoteca, donde se baila merengue y bachata[d] y otros tipos de música.

Un colmado dominicano

©Jane Sweeney/AWL Images/ Getty Images

¿Existe en el lugar donde usted vive alguna tienda similar a los colmados? ¿Qué se hace allí?

[a]*neighborhoods* [b]punto... *meeting place* [c]*people* [d]*dance music (typically Dominican but danced in all Spanish-speaking countries)*

C. ¿Dónde se hace esto? Indique el lugar (o los lugares) donde se hacen las siguientes actividades.

MODELO: Se come. → Se come en un restaurante, en casa, en la cafetería…

1. Se factura el equipaje y se anuncia el vuelo.
2. Se hace la maleta.
3. Se compra un boleto.
4. Se espera el avión.
5. Se pide una bebida.
6. Se mira una película.
7. Se nada y se toma el sol.
8. Se habla francés.
9. Se habla portugués.
10. Se viaja en barco.

D. Los viajes y la vida (*life*)

Paso 1. Elija (*Choose*) una experiencia o etapa (*phase*) importante o interesante en la vida de una persona y descríbala con dos o tres oraciones impersonales. Siga el modelo de esta descripción de los viajes.

Vocabulario útil

Experiencias y etapas de la vida

la adolescencia	
la comida de la cafetería	
la compra de…	
la maternidad	
la paternidad	
la primera cita	first date
el trabajo	work

Acciones

evitar	to avoid
experimentar	to experience
planear	to plan
recordar (recuerdo)	to remember
soñar (sueño)	to dream
sufrir	to suffer, endure

Un viaje se vive tres veces:
cuando se sueña[a]
cuando se vive
y cuando se recuerda[b]

[a]se… *it is dreamed* [b]se… *it is remembered*

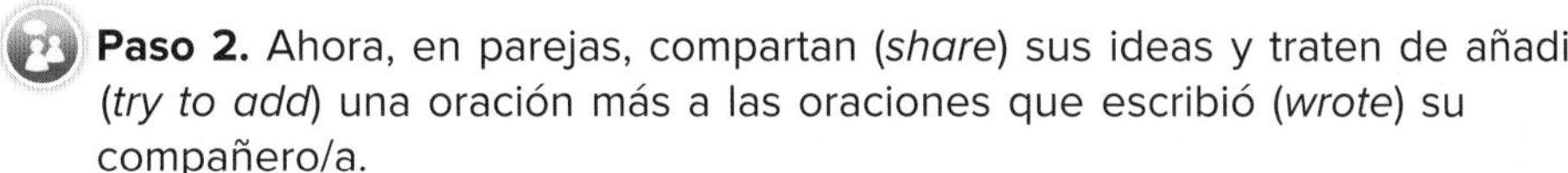

Paso 2. Ahora, en parejas, compartan (*share*) sus ideas y traten de añadir (*try to add*) una oración más a las oraciones que escribió (*wrote*) su compañero/a.

SALU'

«¡De viaje!» Segmento 1

Un arcoíris (*rainbow*) en las cataratas (*Falls*) del Iguazú: «La caída (*plunging*) de agua desde una altura de ochenta metros es simplemente indescriptible... Hay que estar allí para oír el rugido (*roar*) de las cataratas, sentir (*to feel*) el vapor del agua... »

Antes de mirar

¿Qué espera usted ver en un programa de viajes?

- ☐ la gente (*people*) del lugar que se visita
- ☐ el ambiente en las calles (*the atmosphere in the streets*)
- ☐ la naturaleza (selvas [*jungles*], animales autóctonos [*native*])
- ☐ la comida
- ☐ otras cosas: ___________

Estrategia

So far you have talked almost exclusively about the present time. What verb tense do you think a traveler would use to talk about a trip?

Este segmento

Este segmento introduce un programa que muestra (*shows*) videos filmados por telespectadores sobre sus viajes favoritos a lugares de Latinoamérica. El primer video es sobre la Argentina.

Vocabulario del segmento

la elección	choice	**visité**	I visited	**me pareció**	it seemed
estar listo/a	to be ready	**enterrado/a**	buried	**impresionante**	impressive
la voz	voice	**me encantó**	I loved	**me gustó**	I liked
hice	I took, made	**fui/encontré**	I went / I found	**estuve**	I was
el año pasado	last year	**el puesto**	stall, stand		
llegué	I arrived	**vi**	I saw		

Después de mirar

A. **¿Está claro?** Empareje los lugares con las descripciones de Jaime.

LUGARES

1. 

2.

3. 

4.

DESCRIPCIONES DE JAIME

a. _____ la tumba de Eva Perón en el Cementerio de la Recoleta
b. _____ un espectáculo (*show*) de gauchos en la Feria de Mataderos
c. _____ las increíbles cataratas del Iguazú
d. _____ la famosa Plaza de Mayo

B. **Un poco más.** Las siguientes oraciones son falsas. Corríjalas, según el video.

1. Ana y Víctor recibieron (*received*) más de mil videos para este programa.
2. El video que se ve en este segmento es sobre Chile.
3. El turista solo fue (*went*) a las cataratas del Iguazú.
4. Los gauchos son similares a los tucanes.

C. **Y ahora, ustedes.** En parejas, escojan un lugar que a los dos les gustaría (*you would both like*) visitar. Luego completen la siguiente descripción del viaje.

En el futuro, nos gustaría[a] ir a ________ en el/la (estación del año) porque nos gusta ________ (infinitivos). Nos gustaría ir con ________ y pasar ________ (período de tiempo) allí.

[a]nos... *we would like*

GRAMÁTICA

¿Recuerda usted?

In **Gramática 18 (Cap. 7),** you learned how to use direct object pronouns to avoid repetition. Can you identify the direct object pronouns in the following exchange? To what or to whom do these pronouns refer?

ROBERTO: ¿Tienes los boletos?
ANA: No, no los tengo, pero mi agente de viajes ya los tiene listos (*ready*).
ROBERTO: Si quieres, te acompaño a la agencia.
ANA: Encantada. Casi nunca te veo.

21 Expressing *to whom* or *for whom*

Indirect Object Pronouns; **Dar** and **decir**

Gramática en acción: En el aeropuerto

En el mostrador

—¿**Me** puede dar un asiento de ventanilla, por favor?
—Lo siento, pero ya no hay. Pero sí puedo asignar**le** un asiento de pasillo.

En el control de seguridad

—¿**Le** enseño la tarjeta de embarque?
—No es necesario, señorita.
—¿**Le** enseño el pasaporte?
—Tampoco es necesario.

Comprensión

¿Dónde se oye, en el mostrador o en el control de seguridad?

1. «¿Puede enseñar**me** (*show me*) lo que hay en su bolso?»
2. «No **me** gusta sentarme en el asiento de en medio (*middle*).»
3. «En un momento **le** doy la nueva tarjeta de embarque.»
4. «¿**Me** enseña el pasaporte, por favor?»

Indirect Object Pronouns / **Los pronombres del complemento indirecto**

me	to/for me	**nos**	to/for us
te	to/for you (*fam. sing.*)	**os**	to/for you (*fam. pl.*)
le	to/for you (*form. sing.*), him, her, it	**les**	to/for you (*form. pl.*), them

the indirect object / **el complemento indirecto** = the noun or pronoun that indicates *to whom* or *for whom* an action is performed

¡OJO!

Note that indirect object pronouns have the same form as direct object pronouns, except in the third person: **le, les.**

At the airport At the counter: *"Could you please give me a window seat?" "I'm sorry, but there aren't any more (available). But I* ***can*** *give you an aisle seat."* ***At the security check:*** *"Do I show you my boarding pass?" "That's not necessary, miss." "Do I show you my passport?" "That isn't necessary either."*

1. Indirect Objects

Indirect object nouns and pronouns are the person affected by the action of the verb. They usually answer the question *to whom?* or *for whom?* in relation to the verb. The word *to* is frequently omitted in English.

	INDIRECT	DIRECT	
Ana is preparing	**them**	dinner.	
I'll give	**her**	the gift	tomorrow.

For whom is Ana preparing dinner? → **(for) them**
To whom am I giving the gift? → **(to) her**

Indicate the direct and indirect objects in the following sentences.

1. *He'll give me the car tomorrow.*
2. *Please tell me the answer now.*
3. Me va a dar el coche mañana.
4. Dígame la respuesta ahora, por favor.
5. El profesor nos va a hacer algunas preguntas.
6. ¿No me compras una revista ahora?

---

2. Placement of Indirect Object Pronouns

Like direct object pronouns, *indirect object pronouns* (**los pronombres del complemento indirecto**) precede the conjugated verb.

No, no **te presto** el coche.
No, I won't lend you the car.

When the conjugated verb is followed by an infinitive or a present participle, the pronouns either precede the conjugated verb *or* follow (and are attached to):

- the infinitive
- the present participle

Voy a **guardarte** el asiento.
Te voy a guardar el asiento.
I'll save your seat for you.

Remember to add an accent mark to the present participle when you attach a pronoun to it.

Le estoy escribiendo un e-mail a Marisol.
Estoy **escribiéndole** un e-mail a Marisol.
I'm writing Marisol an email.

---

3. With Commands

As with direct object pronouns, indirect object pronouns:

- are attached to the affirmative command form.
- precede the negative command form.

Remember to add an accent to most affirmative commands when you attach a pronoun.

Sírvanos un café, por favor.
Serve us some coffee, please.

No me dé su número de teléfono ahora.
Don't give me your phone number now.

---

4. Redundancy of the Indirect Object

Even when a sentence has a third person indirect object *noun*, it must also have a third person indirect object *pronoun*. The noun object is preceded by **a,** which expresses *to* or *for*. This redundancy may sound repetitive to you, but it is what happens in Spanish most of the time.

Vamos a **mandarle** un mensaje **a Juan.**
Let's send Juan a message.
(Lit., *Let's send* ***to him*** *a message* ***to Juan***.)

¿Les guardo los asientos **a los niños?**
Shall I save the seats for the kids?
(Lit., *Shall I* ***for them*** *save the seats* ***for the kids?***

---

5. Multiple Meanings of *le(s)*

Le and **les** can have several different meanings. When context does not make the meaning clear, the meaning is clarified with a prepositional phrase: **a** + *pronoun object of a preposition.* This redundancy is appropriate in Spanish.

> **¡OJO!**
>
> Object of prepositions = subject pronouns, except for **mí** and **ti**.

Voy a **mandarle** un telegrama. = meaning of **le** unclear unless specified
Voy a **mandarle** un telegrama **a usted** / ...**a él.** / ...**a ella.**
I'm going to send you/him/her a telegram.

---

6. Clarification or Emphasis of Indirect Object Pronouns

To clarify or emphasize the indirect object pronouns **me, te, nos,** and **os,** a phrase with **a** + *object pronoun* is also used. English accomplishes this by tone of voice, but Spanish does it with redundancy.

¿Usted **me** habla **a mí**?
Are you talking to ***me****?*

Pedro **te** dio el pasaporte **a ti,** no **a mí.**
Pedro gave ***you*** *the passport, not (to)* ***me.***

7. **Verbs Often Used with Indirect Objects**
Here are some verbs frequently used with indirect objects. You already know the meaning of the ones marked with *.

contar (cuento)	to tell; to narrate	***pedir (pido) (i)**	to ask for
entregar (gu)	to hand in	**preguntar**	to ask (*a question*)
***escribir**	to write	**prestar**	to lend
explicar (qu)	to explain	**prometer**	to promise
***hablar**	to speak	**recomendar (recomiendo)**	to recommend
***mandar**	to send	**regalar**	to give (*as a gift*)
mostrar (muestro)	to show	***servir (sirvo) (i)**	to serve
ofrecer (ofrezco)	to offer		

Dar and *decir*

Juan **dice** que tiene muchos gastos (*expenses*) en la universidad. Por eso Juan les **dice** a sus padres que necesita dinero.

dar (*to give*)		**decir** (*to say; to tell*)	
doy	**damos**	**digo**	**decimos**
das	**dais**	**dices**	**decís**
da	**dan**	**dice**	**dicen**

Sus padres le **dan** un cheque.

1. ***dar***
Dar means *to give*. It is almost always used with indirect object pronouns.

> **¡OJO!**
> Another Spanish verb expresses *to give* as a gift: **regalar.**

Los profesores **nos dan** mucha tarea en todas las clases.
Professors give us a lot of homework in all my classes.

Mis abuelos **me regalan** dinero para mi cumpleaños.
My grandparents give me money for my birthday.

2. ***decir***
Decir means *to say* or *to tell*. When **decir** means *to tell*, it is almost always used with indirect object pronouns, like **dar.**

> **¡OJO!**
> Other verbs related to speaking are used to express different meanings.
> **hablar** — to speak
> **contar** (**cuento**) — to tell; to narrate

Mi profesor **dice** que la historia es fascinante.
My professor says that history is fascinating.

Y **nos dice** que tenemos mucho que aprender de la historia.
And he tells us that we have a lot to learn from history.

El profesor **habla** varias lenguas.
The professor speaks several languages.

A veces **nos cuenta** algunas de sus experiencias en Latinoamérica.
At times he tells us (about) some of his experiences in Latin America.

3. **Formal Commands of *dar* and *decir***
As you know, **dar** and **decir** also have irregular formal command forms. There is a written accent on **dé** to distinguish it from the preposition **de.**

Mandatos formales
dar → dé, den
decir → diga, digan

Summary of Indirect Object Pronouns

a mí → **me**
a nosotros/as → **nos**

a ti → **te**
a vosotros/as → **os**

a usted, él, ella → **le**
a ustedes, ellos, ellas → **les**

Práctica y comunicación

A. Asociaciones. ¿Qué verbos asocia usted con los siguientes objetos y situaciones?

1. un coche, el dinero
2. la comida en un restaurante
3. las fotos
4. hacer algo por (*for*) alguien
5. la gramática, un profesor
6. la tarea, un informe (*report, paper*)
7. algo para un cumpleaños
8. un restaurante, una película, un libro
9. flores (*flowers*), un e-mail
10. un secreto, un chiste (*joke*)

B. Dar y recibir

Paso 1. Autoprueba. Complete las siguientes oraciones con el pronombre del objeto indirecto apropiado de la lista: **me, te, le, nos, les.**

1. _______ presto el coche a ti, Carolina, no a tu hermano.
2. Los señores Gómez _______ mandan saludos a su amigo dominicano.
3. No _______ dé más galletas a los niños, por favor.
4. ¿ _______ pasas el pan, por favor? Está muy lejos de mí.
5. Profesora, no podemos terminar el examen si no _______ da más tiempo.
6. El tío Juan siempre _______ dice a mis hermanos y a mí que la ciudad de Santa Domingo es muy bonita.

Paso 2. Complete las siguientes declaraciones sobre su vida (*life*) con el pronombre del objeto indirecto apropiado. Si la oración no es cierta para usted, hágala negativa usando **no** u otras palabras negativas.

1. Todos los años _____ doy una tarjeta de cumpleaños a mi mejor amigo/a.
2. Todos los años mi mejor amigo/a _____ da una tarjeta de cumpleaños.
3. Todos los días _____ escribo un mensaje a mis padres o a mis abuelos.
4. Todos los días mis padres o mis abuelos (mis hijos) _____ mandan un mensaje.
5. Todos mis profesores _____ cuentan chistes en clase con frecuencia.
6. Con frecuencia, _____ cuento historias a mis profesores y compañeros de clase.
7. Mis abuelos/hijos _____ regalan dinero con frecuencia.
8. _____ regalo dinero a mis abuelos/hijos con frecuencia.

Paso 3. Ahora, en parejas, túrnense para hacer y contestar preguntas, usando las oraciones del **Paso 2.** Luego díganle al resto de la clase algo que ustedes tienen en común. **¡OJO!** Hagan los cambios necesarios, según el modelo.

MODELO: Todos los años _______ doy una tarjeta de cumpleaños a mi mejor amigo/a. →

E1: ¿Todos los años **le das** una tarjeta de cumpleaños a **tu** mejor amiga?
E2: No, nunca **le doy** una tarjeta de cumpleaños a **mi** mejor amiga. ¿Y tú?
E1: Yo tampoco. →

Nosotros nunca **les damos** una tarjeta de cumpleaños a **nuestras** mejores amigas.

C. De vuelta (*Returning*) a la República Dominicana

Paso 1. Unos amigos dominicanos necesitan ayuda para arreglar (*arrange*) su vuelta (*return*) a casa. Explíqueles cómo usted los puede ayudar.

MODELO: imprimir (*to print*) el boleto electrónico → **Les** imprimo el boleto electrónico.

1. llamar un taxi
2. bajar (*to carry down*) las maletas de su habitación
3. guardar (*to keep an eye on*) el equipaje
4. guardar un puesto en la cola
5. comprar una revista
6. por fin dar un abrazo (*hug*)

Prác. B, Paso 1: Answers: *1. Te 2. le 3. les 4. Me 5. nos 6. nos*

Paso 2. Ahora describa las acciones, pero desde el punto de vista (*point of view*) de sus amigos.

MODELO: imprimir el boleto electrónico → **Nos** imprimes el boleto electrónico.

D. ¿Qué hacen estas personas? Complete las siguientes oraciones lógicamente con un verbo y un pronombre del complemento indirecto.

MODELO: El vicepresidente ________ consejos al presidente.

→ El vicepresidente **le ofrece** consejos al presidente.

1. Romeo ______ flores a Julieta.
2. Snoopy ______ besos (*kisses*) a Lucy... ¡Y a ella no le gusta!
3. Eva ______ una manzana a Adán.
4. Los psicólogos ______ consejos a la gente (*people*) que los necesita.
5. Los bancos ______ dinero a las personas que quieren comprar una casa.
6. Los asistentes de vuelo ______ bebidas a los pasajeros.
7. Yo siempre ______ la verdad a todos.

Vocabulario útil

dar
decir
ofrecer (ofrezco)
prestar
regalar
servir (sirvo) (i)

E. En un restaurante. Explíquele al pequeño Benjamín, que solo tiene 4 años, lo que se hace en un restaurante. Llene los espacios en blanco con pronombres del complemento indirecto.

Primero el camarero ____[1] ofrece una mesa desocupada.[a] Luego tú ____[2] pides el menú al camarero. También ____[3] haces preguntas sobre los platos y las especialidades de la casa y ____[4] dices lo que quieres comer. El camarero ____[5] trae la comida. Por fin tu papá ____[6] pide la cuenta al camarero. Si tú quieres pagar, ____[7] pides dinero a tu papá y ____[8] das el dinero al camarero.

[a]*vacant*

F. Intercambios. En parejas, túrnense para entrevistarse sobre los siguientes temas. Traten de (*Try to*) continuar la conversación.

MODELO: hacer buenos regalos →

E1: **¿Quién te** hace buenos regalos?
E2: Mis padres siempre me hacen buenos regalos.
E1: **¿Qué te** regalan, por ejemplo?
E2: Bueno, me regalan dinero, ropa, cosas para mi apartamento...

1. hacer buenos / interesantes regalos / regalar cosas feas
2. decir la verdad / mentiras (*lies*)
3. contar secretos / los secretos de otras personas
4. hacer favores / recomendaciones / la cena
5. escribir e-mails / poemas de amor / tarjetas postales cuando están de vacaciones
6. mostrar las fotos de sus vacaciones / las notas de sus exámenes
7. servir la comida / bebidas
8. pedir / dar ayuda / consejos
9. prestar dinero / ropa / su coche
10. prometer cosas que luego no hace
11. recomendar películas / restaurantes / clases en la universidad
12. ¿ ?

Algo sobre...

el casabe

El casabe, un producto que representa la cultura de la República Dominicana

El casabe es una especie de tortilla que se hace con la yuca.[a] Es un producto básico de alimentación[b] de los dominicanos. Como comida, el casabe es una tradición que viene de los taínos, los indígenas de la isla de La Española (hoy día, Haití y la República Dominicana).

En su cultura, ¿qué alimento se puede comparar con el casabe?

[a]*manioc, cassava root* [b]*diet, what people eat*

¿Recuerda usted?

In **Capítulo 1** you started to use forms of **gustar** to express your likes and dislikes. Review what you know by answering the following questions. Then, changing their form as needed, interview your instructor.

1. ¿Te gusta el café (el vino, el té...)?
2. ¿Te gusta jugar al béisbol (al golf, al voleibol, al...)?
3. ¿Te gusta viajar en avión (fumar, viajar en tren...)?
4. ¿Qué te gusta más, estudiar o ir a fiestas (trabajar o descansar, cocinar o comer)?

22 Expressing Likes and Dislikes

Gustar (Part 2)

Gramática en acción: Vacaciones en la República Dominicana

En la República Dominicana se puede hacer de todo en las vacaciones.

- A algunas personas les gusta relajarse en la playa.
- A otras personas les gustan las vacaciones que les permiten hacer actividades deportivas (*sporting*).
- A algunos turistas les gustan los museos y los monumentos históricos.
- A mucha gente le gusta hacer de todo un poco.

¿Y a usted?

¿Qué le gusta hacer en sus vacaciones? ¿Le gusta ir a un sitio donde hace buen tiempo? ¿Le gustan las actividades deportivas o las culturales (*cultural ones*)?

Using **gustar** / **Los usos de *gustar***

Spanish	English Phrasing	Literal Equivalent
Me gusta la playa.	*I like the beach.*	The beach is pleasing to me.
No le gustan esos cursos.	*You* (form.)*/He/She doesn't like those courses.*	Those courses are not pleasing to you (form.)/him/her.
Nos gusta esquiar.	*We like to ski.*	Skiing is pleasing to us.

You have been using the verb **gustar** since the beginning of *Puntos de partida* to express likes and dislikes. However, **gustar** does not literally mean *to like*, but rather *to be pleasing*.

Me gusta viajar.
Traveling is pleasing to me. (*I like to travel.*)

Me gustan los viajes de aventura.
Adventure trips are pleasing to me. (*I like adventure trips.*)

1. ***Gustar* + Indirect Object Pronouns**

Gustar is always used with an indirect object pronoun: something is pleasing *to* someone. The verb agrees with the subject of the sentence = the thing that is pleasing. In the first two examples, **gusta** is used with the singular noun **asiento, gustan** with the plural **asientos**.

¡OJO!

An infinitive is a singular subject in Spanish. **Gusta** is used even if there are two or more infinitive subjects.

(**no**) *indirect object pronoun* + **gusta(n)** + *subject*

Me gusta **este asiento** de pasillo.
This aisle seat is pleasing to me. (I like this aisle seat.)

No **me** gustan **los asientos** de ventanilla.
Window seats are not pleasing to me. (I don't like window seats.)

Me gusta mucho **volar** en avión.
Flying is really pleasing to me. (I really like to fly.)

Me gusta nadar y **tomar** el sol.
I like to swim and sunbathe.

2. **Redundancy of Indirect Object**

When the person pleased is a noun or a proper name, the indirect object pronoun is still used. This redundancy (repetition) is the same concept you learned with **le** and **les** in **Gramática 21**.

¡OJO!

Remember: The indirect object pronoun *must* be used with **gustar** even when the prepositional phrase **a** + *noun* or *pronoun* is used.

a + *noun* + **(no) le / les gusta(n)** + *subject*
(no) le / les gusta(n) + *subject* + **a** + *noun*

Al niño no **le** gustan los aviones.
No **le** gustan los aviones **al niño**.
The child doesn't like airplanes.

A Raquel y a Arturo les gusta viajar juntos.
Les gusta viajar juntos **a Raquel y Arturo**.
Raquel and Arturo like to travel together.

3. **Clarification or Emphasis**

A phrase with **a** + *pronoun* is often used for clarification or emphasis. The prepositional phrase can appear before the indirect object pronoun or after the verb.

¡OJO!

Remember that subject pronouns (**usted, él, ella**...) are used as the object of prepositions, except for **mí** (accent) and **ti** (no accent). (Exceptions: **conmigo**, **contigo**.)

CLARIFICATION

¿**Le** gusta **a usted** viajar? ¿**A usted le** gusta viajar?
Do you like to travel?

¿**Le** gusta **a él** viajar? ¿**A él le** gusta viajar?
Does he like to travel?

EMPHASIS

A mí me gusta viajar en avión, pero **a mi esposo le** gusta viajar en coche. Y **a ti,** ¿en qué **te** gusta viajar?
I like to travel by plane, but my husband likes to travel by car. How do you like to travel?

4. ***Gustar* + determiner + noun**

When the thing liked is a noun, it is always preceded by a determiner of some kind: an article, an adjective of quantity (like **muchos**), a possessive, or a demonstrative.

¡OJO!

In English, the definite article is omitted with the verb *like*. The definite article is *never* omitted with **gustar** unless another determiner is used.

Me gusta **el** chocolate. Me gustan **los** dulces.
I like chocolate. I like sweets.

Me gustan **muchas** canciones de Shakira.
I like many of Shakira's songs.

Me gustan **tus** sugerencias, pero no me gusta **ese** tipo de vacaciones.
I like your suggestions, but I don't like that type of vacation.

*Would Like / Wouldn't Like = **Gustaría***

To express what you *would* or *would not* like to do, use **gustaría** + *infinitive* with the appropriate indirect objects.

A mí me gustaría viajar a Colombia.
I would like to travel to Colombia.

No nos gustaría hacer *camping* este verano.
We would not like to go camping this summer.

Summary of the Uses of *gustar*

me (te...) **gusta** + singular noun or infinitive(s)
me (te...) **gustan** + plural noun

Práctica y comunicación

A. Los gustos y preferencias para las vacaciones

Paso 1. Autoprueba. Complete las siguientes oraciones con **-a** or **-an.**

1. Me gust______ nadar.
2. Por eso me gust______ las playas caribeñas.
3. A mi familia y a mí nos gust______ esquiar.
4. Por eso nos gust______ las vacaciones de invierno.
5. A mi mejor amigo le gust______ el sol.
6. Por eso siempre le gust______ la República Dominicana para las vacaciones.
7. ¿A ti te gust______ las vacaciones activas o relajantes (*relaxing*)?

Paso 2. Use las siguientes frases en oraciones completas para expresar sus gustos.

MODELOS: ¿viajar? → (No) Me **gusta** viajar.
¿los aviones? → (No) Me **gustan** los aviones.

1. ¿viajar?
2. ¿los viajes con mi familia?
3. ¿los vuelos?
4. ¿el calor?
5. ¿el invierno?
6. ¿las playas caribeñas?
7. ¿los aeropuertos?
8. ¿viajar en coche?

Paso 3. Ahora, en parejas, túrnense para entrevistarse sobre las ideas del **Paso 2.** Luego díganle al resto de la clase algo que ustedes tienen en común.

MODELO: E1: A mí me gusta viajar. ¿Y a ti?
E2: A mí también. →
A nosotros nos gusta viajar.

Vocabulario útil

A mí también.	So do I.
A mí tampoco.	I don't either. / Neither do I.
Pues a mí, sí.	Well, I do.
Pues a mí, no.	Well, I don't.

B. Vacaciones y viajes. Complete las oraciones con el pronombre de objeto indirecto apropiado y la forma apropiada del verbo **gustar.**

1. A la profesora / Al profesor ______ ______ viajar en primera clase... ¡pero nunca puede!
2. A mí ______ ______ los viajes a otros países y a todos mis amigos ______ ______ también.
3. A ti no ______ ______ el mar y a tu amiga no ______ ______ tampoco.
4. ¡A todos los estudiantes de esta clase ______ ______ las vacaciones! ¡Y también ______ ______ viajar!

C. ¿Cómo van a organizar las vacaciones los Soto?

Paso 1. Los Soto tienen gustos muy diversos. Explique el gusto de cada persona con oraciones completas. Luego nombre una actividad que probablemente le gusta hacer en las vacaciones.

MODELO: 1. la madre: las novelas de Julia Álvarez →
A la madre **le gustan** las novelas de Julia Álvarez. **Seguro que** (*For sure*) **le gusta** leer en la playa.

1. la madre: las novelas de Julia Álvarez
2. el padre: los deportes (*sports*) acuáticos
3. los abuelos: el arte
4. Lucas: la naturaleza (*nature*)
5. Elena, la hija adolescente: la música pop
6. los mellizos (*twins*) de 11 años: jugar en la piscina

Vocabulario útil

surfear
la discoteca
el hotel
el museo
el parque nacional

Prác. A, Paso 1: Answers: 1. gusta 2. gustan 3. gusta 4. gustan 5. gusta 6. gusta 7. gustan

 **Paso 2.** Ahora, en parejas, nombren un lugar al que (*to which*) a cada una de esas personas les gustaría ir para las vacaciones.

MODELO: A la madre le **gustaría** ir a una playa tranquila.

 **Paso 3.** Finalmente, escojan un destino en el que (*which*) todos los miembros de la familia puedan (*can*) hacer algo que les gusta.

D. ¿Conoce bien a... ?

Paso 1. ¿Cree usted que conoce bien a su profesor(a) de español? Haga oraciones completas para decir si a él/ella le gustan o no las siguientes cosas.

MODELO: **1.** la música clásica →
(No) Le gusta la música clásica.

1. la música clásica
2. bailar salsa
3. los niños pequeños
4. las canciones de los años 80
5. viajar
6. los destinos exóticos
7. el arte surrealista
8. ¿ ?

 **Paso 2.** Ahora entreviste a su profesor(a) para saber si le gustan las cosas del **Paso 1** o no.

MODELOS: ¿A usted le gusta la música clásica?
A usted le gusta la música clásica, ¿verdad?

 **Paso 3.** Ahora entreviste a un compañero o una compañera sobre las mismas cosas.

MODELO: E1: ¿Te gusta la música clásica?
E2: Sí. ¿Y a ti?

 **E. Perfiles (*Profiles*) personales**

Paso 1. En parejas, inventen un perfil más o menos realista para cada una de las personas de los dibujos: quiénes son, dónde están, por qué están allí y, finalmente, tres de las cosas y actividades que les gustan.

Vocabulario útil

el arte
el *rap* / el *hip hop*
hacer senderismo to hike

Paso 2. Ahora, digan con cuál de los personajes (*characters*) que inventaron (*you invented*) en el **Paso 1** se identifican más y expliquen por qué.

MODELO: Me identifico más con el hombre/la mujer del dibujo _____ porque...

Nota comunicativa

Otras maneras de expresar los gustos y preferencias

Here are some ways to express intense likes and dislikes. Note that most of these verbs are used like **gustar**.

> Verbs that are used like **gustar** will be noted in vocabulary lists with the parenthetical note (like **gustar**).

INTENSE LIKES

- **mucho/muchísimo** (with **gustar**)

Me gusta **mucho/muchísimo.**	*I like it a lot / a whole lot.*

- **encantar** (*like* **gustar**), **interesar** (*like* **gustar**)

Me encantan las películas extranjeras.	*I love foreign films.*
Me interesa aprender otras lenguas.	*I'm interested in learning other languages.*

INTENSE DISLIKES

- **no... (para) nada** (with **gustar**)

No me gusta **(para) nada** la comida japonesa.	*I don't like Japanese food at all.*

- **odiar**

Unlike **encantar** and **interesar,** which are used like **gustar, odiar** is conjugated like regular **-ar** verbs. It is a transitive verb, that is, a verb that can take a direct object.

Odio los champiñones.	*I hate mushrooms.*
Mi madre **odia** viajar sola.	*My mother hates traveling alone.*

Use as many of these verbs and expressions as you can in **Práctica F.**

F. Intercambios. En parejas, túrnense para describir lo que les gusta y lo que odian cuando están en las siguientes situaciones. Inventen los detalles necesarios.

MODELO: en la playa → Cuando estoy en la playa, me encanta nadar en el mar, pero no me gusta el sol ni me gusta la arena (*sand*). Por eso odio pasar todo el día en la playa. Prefiero nadar en una piscina.

Situaciones

en un autobús	**en el salón de clase**
en un avión	**en el coche**
en la biblioteca	**en una discoteca**
en una cafetería	**en una fiesta**
en casa con mis amigos	**en un parque**
en casa con mis padres/hijos	**en la playa**
en un centro comercial	**en un tren**

¿Recuerda usted?

You have already learned one of the irregular past tense verb forms that is presented in **Gramática 23.** Review it now by telling what day yesterday was: **Ayer...**

23 Talking About the Past (Part 1)

Preterite of Regular Verbs and of **dar, hacer, ir,** and **ser**

Gramática en acción: Un viaje a la República Dominicana

Elisa Velasco es reportera. Hace poco, fue a la República Dominicana para escribir un artículo sobre la isla de La Española. Elisa nos cuenta su experiencia.

- «Hice el viaje en avión.
- El vuelo fue largo porque el avión hizo escala en Miami.
- Pasé una semana entera en la Isla.
- Visité muchos sitios de interés turístico e histórico.
- Comí mucha comida típica del Caribe.
- Tomé el sol, nadé en el mar y escribí muchas tarjetas postales.
- ¡Lo pasé muy bien!»

Comprensión

¿Cierto o falso? Corrija las oraciones falsas.

	CIERTO	FALSO
1. Elisa fue a la República Dominicana para pasar sus vacaciones.	☐	☐
2. El avión hizo escala en los Estados Unidos.	☐	☐
3. Elisa no visitó ningún lugar importante de la Isla.	☐	☐
4. No lo pasó bien en la playa.	☐	☐

So far, you have almost always spoken in the present tense. In this section, you will use forms of the preterite, one of the past tenses in Spanish.

To talk about the past in Spanish, there are two simple tenses: the preterite and the imperfect. In this chapter, you will learn the regular forms of the preterite and those of four irregular verbs: **dar, hacer, ir,** and **ser.** Then in **Capítulos 9, 10,** and **11,** you will learn more about both tenses.

> a simple tense / **un tiempo simple** = a tense formed without an auxiliary or "helping" verb (*I ate* versus *I have eaten*)

Preterite: Regular Verbs / **El pretérito: Los verbos regulares**

***-ar* Verbs**		***-er/-ir* Verbs**			
hablar		**comer**		**vivir**	
hablé	I spoke (did speak)	**comí**	I ate (did eat)	**viví**	I lived (did live)
hablaste	you spoke	**comiste**	you ate	**viviste**	you lived
habló	you/he/she spoke	**comió**	you/he/she ate	**vivió**	you/he/she lived
hablamos	we spoke	**comimos**	we ate	**vivimos**	we lived
hablasteis	you spoke	**comisteis**	you ate	**vivisteis**	you lived
hablaron	you/they spoke	**comieron**	you/they ate	**vivieron**	you/they lived

A trip to the Dominican Republic *Elisa Velasco is a reporter. A little while ago, she went to the Dominican Republic to write an article about the island of Hispaniola. Elisa tells us about her experience. ■ "I made the trip by plane. ■ The flight was long because the plane made a stop in Miami. ■ I spent a whole week on the Island. ■ I visited a lot of interesting tourist and historical sites. ■ I ate a lot of typical Caribbean food. ■ I sunbathed, swam in the ocean, and wrote a lot of postcards. ■ I had a really good time!"*

1. **Uses of the Preterite**

As you saw in the chart on p. 255, the *preterite* (**el pretérito**) has several English equivalents.

hablé = I spoke, I did speak

The preterite is used to report finished, completed actions or states of being in the past. If the action or state of being is viewed as completed—no matter how long it lasted or took to complete—it will be expressed with the preterite. A two-month period is specified in the first example sentence; that period is over. No time span is specified in the second sentence, but the action is clearly over since it took place *last summer*.

Pasé dos meses en el Caribe.
I spent two months in the Caribbean.

El verano pasado **hicimos** *camping* en Puerto Rico.
Last summer we went camping in Puerto Rico.

---

2. ***Nosotros* forms**

Note that the **nosotros** forms of regular preterites for **-ar** and **-ir** verbs are the same as the present tense forms. Context usually helps determine meaning. If the translation were not available, what words would tell you that the first **hablamos** means *we spoke* and the second one *we'll speak*?

Ayer **hablamos** del viaje con nuestros amigos. Hoy, más tarde, **hablamos** con el agente de viajes a las dos de la tarde.
Yesterday we spoke about the trip with our friends. Today, later on, we'll speak with the travel agent at 2:00 P.M.

---

3. **Accent Marks**

Note the accent marks on the first and third person singular of the preterite tense. These accent marks are not used in the conjugation of **ver: vi, vio.**

bailé, bailó
bebí, bebió
asistí, asistió

but

vi, vio

---

4. **Verbs ending in *-car*, *-gar*, and *-zar***

These verbs show a spelling change in the first person singular (**yo**) of the preterite. This is the same change you have already learned to make in formal commands, **Gramática 20 (Cap. 7)**.

-car → qu	**busqué**	**buscamos**
buscar	**buscaste**	**buscasteis**
	buscó	**buscaron**
-gar → gu	**pagué**	**pagamos**
pagar	**pagaste**	**pagasteis**
	pagó	**pagaron**
-zar → c	**empecé**	**empezamos**
empezar	**empezaste**	**empezasteis**
	empezó	**empezaron**

---

5. **Unstressed *-i-***

An unstressed **-i-** between two vowels becomes **-y-.** Also, note the accent on the **í** in the **tú, nosotros,** and **vosotros** forms.

creer		**leer**	
creí	**creímos**	**leí**	**leímos**
creíste	**creísteis**	**leíste**	**leísteis**
creyó	**creyeron**	**leyó**	**leyeron**

---

6. ***-ar* and *-er* Stem-changing Verbs**

Stem-changing verbs that end in **-ar** and **-er** do not show the stem change in the preterite. However, the preterite of **-ir** stem-changing verbs is not regular. You will learn the preterite of those verbs in **Gramática 25 (Cap. 9).**

despertar (despierto): desperté, despertaste,...
volver (vuelvo): volví, volviste,...

Irregular Forms / **Las formas irregulares**

1. *Dar*

The preterite endings for **dar** are the same as those used for regular **-er/-ir** verbs, except that the accent marks are dropped.

dar	
di	dimos
diste	disteis
dio	dieron

2. *Hacer*

All forms of **hacer** are irregular in the preterite, especially the third person singular, **hizo,** which is spelled with a **z** rather than a **c** to keep the [s] sound of the infinitive.

hacer	
hice	hicimos
hiciste	hicisteis
hizo	hicieron

3. *Ir* and *ser*

These verbs have identical forms in the preterite. Context will make the meaning clear. For example, in the first sentence to the right, the word **a** is a clue that **Fui** means *I went*, since forms of the verb **ir** are often followed by **a**. In the second sentence, **Fui** is followed directly by a noun; forms of **ir**/*to go* are never *directly* followed by a noun, so **fui** must mean *I was*.

ir/ser	
fui	fuimos
fuiste	fuisteis
fue	fueron

Fui a la playa el verano pasado.
I went to the beach last summer.

Fui agente de viajes.
I was a travel agent.

Práctica y comunicación

A. El verano pasado

Paso 1. Autoprueba. Dé la forma apropiada del pretérito para cada sujeto.

1. **tú:** comprar, ir, acostarse, beber, hacer, llegar
2. **usted:** comprender, empezar, creer, afeitarse, dar, volar
3. **nosotros:** hacer, ser, ir, pagar, leer, subir
4. **ellas:** asistir, volver, terminar, despertarse, salir, viajar

Summary of Preterite Endings

-ar: **-é, -aste, -ó, -amos, -asteis –aron**

-er/-ir: **-í, -iste, -ió, -imos, -isteis, -ieron**

dar: **di...** hacer: **hice...** ir/ser: **fui...**

Paso 2. Complete las siguientes oraciones sobre el verano pasado con las terminaciones apropiadas de la primera persona singular (**yo**). Si es necesario, use **no** para hacer oraciones que son ciertas para usted.

El verano pasado...

1. tom_______ clases en la universidad.
2. asist_______ a un concierto en otra ciudad.
3. trabaj_______ mucho y gan_______ mucho dinero. (**ganar** = to earn)
4. hi_______ *camping* con unos amigos.
5. viv_______ todo el tiempo con mi familia.
6. me qued_______ trabajando y estudiando en la universidad.
7. fu_______ a la playa.
8. me levant_______ tarde casi todos los días.

Paso 3. Ahora, en parejas, túrnense para entrevistarse sobre las ideas del **Paso 2.** Luego díganle a la clase dos cosas que ustedes tienen en común.

MODELO: tomé clases en la universidad. →
E1: El verano pasado, ¿**tomaste** alguna clase en la universidad?
E2: No, ¿y tú?
E1: Yo tampoco. →
Nosotros no **tomamos** ninguna clase el verano pasado.

Práct. A, Paso 1:* Answers: *1. *compraste, fuiste, te acostaste, bebiste, hiciste, llegaste* ***2.*** *comprendió, empezó, creyó, se afeitó, dio, voló* ***3.*** *hicimos, fuimos, fuimos, pagamos, leímos, subimos* ***4.*** *asistieron, volvieron, terminaron, se despertaron, salieron, viajaron*

B. El viernes pasado por la tarde

Paso 1. Narre la secuencia de las acciones que hizo Julio el viernes pasado por la tarde. **¡OJO! Julio** es el sujeto de muchas oraciones, pero no de todas. A veces el sujeto es **ellos** (Julio y su amigo Roberto).

El viernes por la tarde, Julio...

1. **volver** a casa después de trabajar todo el día

2. **llamar** a su amigo Roberto y los dos: **decidir** ir al cine juntos

3. **ducharse** y **afeitarse**

4. **salir** de casa rápidamente e **ir** al cine en autobús

5. los dos: **hacer** cola para comprar las entradas (*tickets*) y **comprar** palomitas (*popcorn*)

6. **entrar** en la sala y **sentarse**

7. **ver** la película pero no **gustarles** para nada

8. **ir** a un restaurante a cenar y **quedarse** conversando hasta muy tarde

Paso 2. Comprensión. ¿Cierto, falso o no lo dice?

	CIERTO	FALSO	NO LO DICE
1. El amigo de Julio se llama Roberto.	☐	☐	☐
2. Son compañeros de clase.	☐	☐	☐
3. A los dos amigos les interesa el cine.	☐	☐	☐
4. Vieron una película extranjera.	☐	☐	☐
5. Odiaron la película.	☐	☐	☐
6. Comieron después de la película.	☐	☐	☐
7. Julio regresó a casa en autobús.	☐	☐	☐

Paso 3. Ahora, en parejas, vuelvan a contar la historia. Use palabras de **Estrategia**.

Estrategia

Use these words to put the part of a story into a logical progression.

primero	
segundo	second
después / luego	
entonces	then
finalmente	
por último	finally

C. Un semestre en la República Dominicana

Paso 1. Cuente la siguiente historia en primera persona, usando el pretérito de los verbos.

MODELO: *yo*: viajar a la República Dominicana el año pasado → **Viajé** a la República Dominicana el año pasado.

1. *yo:* pasar todo el semestre en Santo Domingo
2. mis padres: pagarme el vuelo
3. *yo:* trabajar para ganar el dinero para los otros gastos (*expenses*)
4. vivir con una familia dominicana
5. aprender mucho sobre la la cultura dominicana
6. mis amigos: escribirme con frecuencia
7. comprarles recuerdos (*souvenirs*) a todos
8. volver a casa a fines de junio

Paso 2. Ahora, piense en las cosas que posiblemente hacen los turistas en la República Dominicana y añada dos acciones más a la lista de lo que hizo la persona que narra su experiencia en el **Paso 1.**

D. El día de ayer de dos compañeras

Paso 1. Teresa y Liliana son compañeras de apartamento en la universidad. Haga oraciones completas según el modelo para describir su día.

MODELO: 7:30 **levantarse** → **Se levantó a** las siete y media.

TERESA

1. 8:00 **ducharse** y **desayunar**
2. 9:00 **salir** de casa / **ir** a la universidad
3. 10:00 **estudiar** toda la mañana
4. 12:00 **almorzar** con unos compañeros de la universidad
5. 1:00 **hacer** experimentos en el laboratorio de química
6. 3:15 **volver** a casa

LILIANA

7. 9:45 **despertarse**, pero no **levantarse** pronto
8. 10:30 **desayunar** y **empezar** a hacer la tarea de matemáticas
9. 12:30 **terminarla** y **ver** la tele
10. 2:00 **empezar** a hacer un pastel para el cumpleaños de Miriam
11. 2:30 **mandar** unos e-mails.
12. 4:30 **terminar** el pastel / **decorar**lo

TERESA Y LILIANA

13. 5:00 **ir** al gimnasio cerca de su apartamento / allí **hacer** ejercicio por una hora
14. 6:30 **volver** a casa / **ducharse** y **hablar** de la fiesta de Miriam
15. 9:30 **ir** a casa de Miriam / **cantar**le «Cumpleaños feliz» / **dar**le su regalo y **comer** el pastel

¿Quién es, Teresa o Liliana? ¿Cómo lo sabe?

Paso 2. En parejas, túrnense para hacer y contestar preguntas basadas en las oraciones del **Paso 1.**

MODELO: E1: ¿**Te duchaste** a las ocho, como Teresa?
E2: No, **me duché** por la noche. ¿Y tú?
E1: No **me duché.** Me bañé.

Algo sobre...

las hermanas Mirabal

©H.S. Photos/Alamy

Un billete[a] de 200 pesos dominicanos con fotos de las hermanas Mirabal

Patria (1924–1960), Minerva (1926–1960) y María Teresa (1935–1960) Mirabal son heroínas dominicanas que lucharon[b] contra la terrible dictadura[c] de Rafael Trujillo. (Se conocen también como las Mariposas.[d]) Las tres fueron brutalmente asesinadas por orden del dictador. La hermana sobreviviente,[e] Dedé, dedicó el resto de su vida a preservar la memoria de sus hermanas. Ahora hay una provincia dominicana con el nombre de Hermanas Mirabal. Las Mariposas también aparecen[f] en los billetes de 200 pesos dominicanos.

La Asamblea General de las Naciones Unidas designó el día de la muerte[g] de las Mirabal como el Día Internacional de la No Violencia Contra la Mujer.

¿Cuáles son algunos de los héroes y heroínas nacionales más importantes de su país? ¿Por qué son importantes?

[a]*bill* [b]*fought* [c]*dictatorship* [d]*Butterflies* [e]*surviving* [f]*appear* [g]*death*

E. La última vez

Paso 1. Conteste las siguientes preguntas. Añada más detalles si puede.

MODELO: La última vez que usted fue a una fiesta, ¿le llevó un regalo al anfitrión / a la anfitriona (*host/ hostess*)? →
Sí, **le** llevé flores / una botella de vino. (No, no **le** llevé nada.)

La última vez que usted...

1. hizo un viaje, ¿le mandó una tarjeta a alguien?
2. tomó el autobús/metro, ¿le ofreció su asiento a una persona mayor?
3. vio a su profesor(a) de español en público, ¿le habló en español?
4. comió en un restaurante, ¿le recomendó algún plato a su compañero/a?
5. entró en un edificio, ¿le abrió la puerta a otra persona?
6. voló en avión, ¿le pidió algo a uno de los asistentes de vuelo?
7. le regaló algo a alguien, ¿le gustó el regalo a la persona?
8. le prometió a alguien hacer algo, ¿lo hizo?
9. se quejó de algo, ¿a quién habló?

Paso 2. Ahora, en parejas, túrnense para hacer y contestar preguntas basadas en las oraciones del **Paso 1.** Después, díganle al resto de la clase una o dos cosas interesantes de su compañero/a.

F. Intercambios

Paso 1. Escriba una lista de diez de las acciones que usted hizo ayer. Use los siguientes verbos y cuatro más de su preferencia en oraciones completas.

MODELO: levantarse → Ayer **me levanté** a las seis de la mañana.

1. levantarse
2. empezar
3. leer
4. dar
5. hacer
6. ir

Paso 2. En parejas, túrnense para entrevistarse sobre las acciones de su lista del **Paso 1.** Después, compartan con la clase una acción en la que (*which*) coincidieron ayer.

MODELO: E1: Ayer **me levanté** a las seis de la mañana. ¿A qué hora **te levantaste tú**?
E2: **Me levanté** a las diez.

G. Más intercambios

Paso 1. En parejas, túrnense para entrevistarse sobre su último viaje. Deben obtener información relacionada con las siguientes preguntas.

1. ¿cuándo?
2. ¿adónde?
3. ¿en qué medio de transporte?
4. ¿cuántos días?
5. ¿con quién?

Paso 2. Ahora cuéntenles a todas las personas de la clase los detalles esenciales del viaje de su compañero/a.

MODELO: Susie fue a Puerto Rico el verano pasado. Hizo el viaje en avión. Se quedó en Puerto Rico una semana. Viajó con su novio y su familia.

Todo junto

A. Lengua y cultura: Mi abuela dominicana

Paso 1. En acción. Complete the following paragraphs with the correct form of the words in parentheses, as suggested by context. When two possibilities are given in parentheses, select the correct word. **¡OJO!** The verbs in the paragraphs will be present tense or preterite; the context will indicate which tense to use.

Ayer llegó de visita mi abuela Manuela. Ella vive en Santo Domingo, con mi tía Zaira, la ______ (hermana / sobrina[1]) de mi mamá. ______ (*Nosotros*: Ir[2]) a recibir______ (la / le[3]) al aeropuerto y nos ______ (*ella*: dar[4]) un abrazo[a] muy fuerte. ______ (Mi / Mí[5]) abuela va ______ (a / de[6]) pasar dos meses con nosotros en Connecticut, y luego ______ (ir[7]) a quedarse un mes con el tío Julián en Nueva York. Así es la vida[b] de muchas abuelas con hijos en otro país.

A mi abuela le ______ (gusta / gustaría[8]) tener a todos sus hijos y ______ (nietos / sobrinos[9]) en Santo Domingo y siempre ______ (ser / estar[10]) muy triste cuando ______ (volver[11]) a la República Dominicana ______ (antes de / después de[12]) visitarnos. Pero también ______ (le / la[13]) gusta mucho la vida en los Estados Unidos. ______ (*Ella*: Decir[14]) que aquí se vive muy bien y que las casas ______ ser / estar[15]) muy buenas. (______El / La[16]) problema es que no le ______ (gustan / gustarían[17]) los inviernos de ______ (este / esto[18]) país. ¡Es lógico! A ella le ______ (gusta / gustan[19]) las playas y las palmeras, porque es lo que ______ (conoce / sabe[20]) bien.

Una abuela con su hija y su nieta

©Medioimages/Photodisc/Getty Images

Cuando mi abuela regresa a Santo Domingo, ______ (les / los[21]) mandamos con ella muchos regalos a nuestros ______(padres / parientes[22]). Casi todos los años mi familia ______ (viaje / viaja[23]) a la República Dominicana, porque mis padres ______ (vivir[24]) allá hasta que ______ (ir[25]) a estudiar a la Universidad de Massachusetts. ______ ¡(A / –[26]) mí me encanta ir de vacaciones a la República Dominicana!

[a]*hug* [b]Así... *Such is the life*

Paso 2. Comprensión. Conteste las siguientes preguntas.

1. ¿Quién habla en la narración? ¿Se sabe si es hombre o mujer?
2. ¿Dónde vive la tía Zaira?
3. ¿Qué le gusta de la vida en los Estados Unidos a la abuela?
4. ¿Qué no le gusta?
5. ¿Cuándo emigraron a los Estados Unidos los padres del narrador / de la narradora?

Paso 3. En acción

Casi todos los estadounidenses son descendientes de inmigrantes; muchos son inmigrantes recientes. En parejas, túrnense para saber algo de un pariente o un amigo / una amiga de su compañero/a que llegó a este país como inmigrante. Usen las siguientes preguntas.

1. ¿Quién es el pariente o amigo/a? ¿Dónde nació (*was he/she born*)?
2. ¿Cuándo llegó a los Estados Unidos?
3. ¿Vino solo/a? ¿A quién(es) dejó (*did he/she leave behind*) en su país de origen?
4. Si ese pariente o amigo/a vive todavía, ¿visita a veces su país de origen? Si ya murió (*he/she is already deceased*), ¿volvió a visitar su país de origen antes de morir (*die*)? ¿Cuántas veces fue?

B. Proyecto: Turismo en la República Dominicana

Van a preparar un guion (*script*) para un video sobre el turismo en la República Dominicana que muestre (*shows*) la variedad de lo que les ofrece a los turistas este país. El video debe narrar lo que hicieron unos turistas en un viaje reciente, desde su punto de vista (*point of view*).

Paso 1. Preparación. En parejas o grupos, preparen los siguientes aspectos del proyecto.

Aspecto 1: Inventar el perfil (*profile*) de unos de los turistas de la siguiente lista.

- la familia Ortiz, de la Ciudad de Nueva York, con raíces (*roots*) dominicanas
- Jordan y Jay, una pareja en su luna de miel (*honeymoon*)
- cuatro amigas que estudian español en la universidad

Aspecto 2: Investigar lugares dominicanos interesantes por diferentes razones para los turistas. Usen la siguiente tabla, pero pueden añadir (*add*) más categorías si quieren. Piensen en unas vacaciones de una semana.

Lugar(es)	Cómo llegar	Qué ver / Qué hacer	Dónde comer

Paso 2. Desarrollo. ***(Development.)*** Ahora desarrollen el guion, narrándolo en el pretérito desde el punto de vista de los personajes que eligieron (*you chose*).

Paso 3. Competición. Enseñen (*Show*) su guion a la clase. Pueden hacer su presentación con fotos de los lugares que visitaron sus turistas ficticios. ¿Qué grupo tiene el mejor plan? ¿Por qué es tan bueno su plan?

Estrategia

You have not yet learned the irregular preterite forms of a few frequently used verbs. Here are their first person forms.

estar: estuve, estuvimos
poner: puse, pusimos
tener: tuve, tuvimos
venir: vine, vinimos

¡Ahora, yo!

A. Entrevista. Use de modelo las preguntas y respuestas de la página 237 de este capítulo para hablar de sus vacaciones favoritas.

B. Proyecto audiovisual. Haga un fotomontaje con voz en off (*voiceover*) sobre un destino turístico. Puede ser un destino que usted ya conoce o uno que le gustaría visitar.

«¡De viaje!» Segmento 2

Antes de mirar

¿Le gustaría visitar el Perú? ¿Por qué? ¿Qué sabe del país?

Este segmento

Este segmento muestra otro video filmado por un telespectador de *Salu2*. Este turista hizo un viaje inolvidable (*unforgettable*) al Perú.

«Primero estuvimos (*we were*) varios días en Cusco, la antigua capital del Imperio inca. Está a más de 3.000 metros de altitud, y esta altitud puede provocar malestar (*discomfort*) físico. ¡Pero el malestar no es nada comparado a la belleza (*beauty*) de la ciudad!»

Vocabulario del segmento

con razón	rightly so	**el fuerte**	fort
la piedra	stone	**al final**	at the end
rodeado/a de	surrounded by	**la fuente**	fountain
permanecer oculto/a	to remain hidden	**el espectáculo**	show
descubrir	to discover	**no dejen de visitar**	don't miss out on visiting

Fragmento del guion

De Cusco nos fuimos al Valle Sagrado[a] de los Incas para visitar un santuario de llamas. Estuvimos[b] con personas de esta comunidad mientras hacían tejidos tradicionales.[c] Es un arte que ha pasado[d] de generación en generación y un gran ejemplo de la hermosa[e] artesanía peruana. Pero lo mejor[f] del viaje fue Machu Picchu, considerada una de las siete maravillas del mundo actual.[g]

[a]Valle... *Sacred Valley* [b]*We were* [c]mientras... *while they made traditional weavings* [d]ha... *has been passed down* [e]*beautiful* [f]lo... *the best part* [g]*modern*

Después de mirar

A. ¿Está claro? Ponga los lugares que visitó el turista en el orden de su visita. Luego empareje cada lugar con las frases del video.

LUGARES

1. _______ Machu Picchu
2. _______ Cusco
3. _______ Lima
4. _______ el Valle Sagrado de los Incas

FRASES DEL VIDEO

a. «la ciudad más visitada de todo Perú»
b. «el nuevo Parque de las Fuentes»
c. «un santuario de llamas»
d. «una de las siete maravillas del mundo actual (*modern*)»

B. Un poco más. Conteste las siguientes preguntas.

1. ¿Por qué se puede sentir (*feel*) malestar físico en Cusco?
2. ¿Qué tipo de artesanía hacen en el Valle Sagrado de los Incas?
3. ¿Por qué es misterioso Machu Picchu?

C. Y ahora, ustedes. En parejas, preparen un resumen de este segmento de *Salu2*, contando lo que hizo este turista e incluyendo algo interesante que vio o aprendió en cada sitio. También deben decir lo que más le gusto a él.

MODELO: Primero fue a la ciudad de Cusco. Allí...

MUNDO HISPANO

Enfoque cultural: La República Dominicana

Antes de leer

¿Es el turismo un sector económico muy importante en su ciudad o estado?

El turismo en la República Dominicana

El turismo es el sector económico más importante de la República Dominicana. Es un país que ofrece lugares de interés para cualquier[a] visitante: bosques,[b] parques nacionales, ríos, lagos, playas, ciudades y zonas rurales. Uno de los destinos turísticos más populares es Punta Cana, al este del país. Allí se puede disfrutar de[c] un clima tropical y de bellas[d] playas de arena[e] blanca y fina. Santo Domingo, la capital del país, tiene una hermosa[f] zona colonial con museos, casas antiguas y otros monumentos históricos. En 1990, fue reconocida[g] como Patrimonio Cultural de la Humanidad[h] por la UNESCO.

[a]*any* [b]*forests* [c]disfrutar... *enjoy* [d]*beautiful* [e]*sand* [f]*beautiful* [g]*recognized* [h]Patrimonio... *World Cultural Heritage site*

En otros países hispanos

- **En todo el mundo hispanohablante** En muchos países hispanos, y no solo en los países tropicales, hay playas maravillosas.[a] El Uruguay, la Argentina y Chile tienen costas fabulosas sin estar en el trópico.
- **En España** La industria del turismo es un importante motor[b] de la economía española. España es el cuarto[c] país del mundo receptor de turistas extranjeros, después de China, Francia y los Estados Unidos.
- **En los Estados Unidos** Gran parte del actual[d] territorio estadounidense fue antes territorio español. Así que podría[e] visitar lugares históricos en Florida, Texas, California, etcétera, para saber de la historia del mundo hispano... ¡sin salir de este país!

[a]*wonderful* [b]*engine* [c]*fourth* [d]*present-day* [e]Así... *So you could*

©Jon McLean/Alamy

Un grupo de merengueros dominicanos

Un símbolo dominicano: El merengue

El merengue es un tipo de música de origen dominicano que se conoce y se baila en todo el mundo hispano. Empezó a tocarse[a] con instrumentos de cuerda,[b] pero se incorporó el acordeón (de influencia europea), el güiro[c] (de origen taíno) y la tambora[d] (de origen africano). Hoy se incluyen el piano y los instrumentos de viento.

[a]Empezó... *It was first played* [b]*string* [c]*percussion instrument made of the gourd of the calabash tree* [d]*bass drum*

Comprensión

1. ¿Cuáles son dos de los lugares turísticos importantes en la República Dominicana?
2. ¿Qué país hispanohablante está muy alto en la lista de países receptores de turistas?
3. ¿Por qué se puede decir que en los Estados Unidos es muy importante la presencia histórica de los países hispanos?
4. ¿En qué países hispanos no tropicales hay playas fabulosas?
5. ¿Qué es el merengue?

En acción

Hay lugares en los Estados Unidos que también pueden ser un destino turístico hispano porque gran parte del actual (*present-day*) territorio estadounidense fue antes territorio español y/o mexicano. Elija un estado o una ciudad estadounidense con raíces (*roots*) hispanas y entérese de (*find out about*) su historia. ¿Por cuánto tiempo fue un territorio dominado por hispanohablantes? ¿Qué lugares se debe visitar para saber su historia anterior a formar parte de los Estados Unidos?

Lectura

Antes de leer

¿Le interesa a usted el aventurismo? (Vea la Nota cultural en la página 241.) ¿Por qué? En su opinión, ¿cómo son las personas que practican este estilo de viajar?

Vocabulario para leer

la belleza	beauty
descubrir	to discover
disfrutar de	to enjoy
encontrar (encuentro)	to find
salvaje	wild, untamed

I love viajes

©Ingram Publishing/SuperStock

©Lissa Harrison

©Exactostock/SuperStock

Norte de África en 4x4[a]
Explora el Marruecos[b] más desconocido[c] y aventúrate[d] en 4x4 entre las dunas del Sahara. Descubre oasis perdidos[e] en lo más profundo[f] del desierto y disfruta de una flora que no esperarías[g] encontrar en estas latitudes. ¡Pon rumbo a[h] la aventura!

Tierra del Fuego
Lugar de belleza única con sus nevados picos[i], montañas, bosques[j] y maravillosos lagos. Ushuaia es la ciudad más al sur del mundo. Tierra del Fuego es una isla de belleza extrema que une[k] el Pacífico y el Atlántico. Parajes vírgenes[l] por explorar.

Safari por África
El espectacular parque natural del delta del Okavango (Botsuana) es una gran concentración de animales salvajes. Visita las cataratas[m] Victoria (en Zimbabue) donde observarás[n] la cortina[ñ] de agua más caudalosa[o] del mundo. ¡Refréscate![p]

[a]*four-wheel drive* [b]*Morocco* [c]*unknown* [d]*venture out* [e]*lost* [f]lo... *the deepest part* [g]no... *you wouldn't expect* [h]¡Pon... *Get ready for* [i]nevados... *snowy peaks* [j]*forests* [k]conecta [l]Parajes... *Virgin expanses, territories* [m]*Falls* [n]vas a observar [ñ]*curtain* [o]más... *fastest flowing* [p]*Cool off!*

Comprensión

A. ¡Sea agente de viajes! ¿Adónde deben ir de viaje las siguientes personas? Dé una recomendación lógica para cada caso, explicando por qué hace esa sugerencia. Use **Le recomiendo...** o **Les recomiendo...** , según el caso.

MODELO: **El profesor Legrán:** «Tengo todo el verano para viajar. Quiero escaparme del calor de Nuevo México en el verano y visitar lugares remotos.» → Le recomiendo Tierra del Fuego, porque allí no hace calor y está en el extremo sur de Sudamérica. Hay montañas, lagos y bosques allí. También hay una ciudad interesante.

1. **Los Sres. Ávila:** «Queremos viajar a un lugar cálido (*warm*) y seco (*dry*) durante el invierno.»
2. **El Sr. Sorkin:** «Me gusta observar los animales y verlos en su espacio natural.»
3. **Alejandra:** «Conozco Norteamérica, Europa y África. Para mis próximas vacaciones, quiero visitar un continente totalmente nuevo para mí.»
4. **Jorge y Jimena:** «Somos especialistas en la flora tropical. Pero para estas vacaciones queremos algo diferente.»

B. Preferencias personales. En parejas, hagan y contesten las siguientes preguntas sobre los destinos turísticos.

1. De los tres destinos que sugiere (*suggests*) la lectura, ¿cuál es el más atractivo para ti? ¿Por qué? ¿Cuál es la mejor estación del año para visitar ese lugar? ¿Por qué?
2. ¿Hay algún lugar de los tres destinos que no te gustaría visitar? ¿Por qué?
3. ¿Qué otros lugares conoces o puedes nombrar donde se pueda (*one can*) hacer el mismo tipo de turismo de los destinos mencionados en los anuncios?

(Continúa.)

 Proyecto: Una solicitud° para una beca de un viaje educativo

°proposal

Para este proyecto, van a planear un viaje educativo a una ciudad hispanohablante y solicitar una beca de la universidad para el viaje.

Paso 1. En grupos, elijan la ciudad hispana que quieren visitar. Después, hagan una investigación en internet para identificar: varios destinos de interés (museos, monumentos, parques y otros sitios naturales, etcétera), otras actividades culturales que hay oportunidad de hacer en la ciudad y un hotel donde quedarse (*in which to stay*).

Paso 2. Escriban la solicitud, especificando:

- una breve explicación de por qué quieren viajar a ciudad que seleccionaron
- un itinerario de 7 días con los destinos de interés y descripciones concisas de las actividades que piensan hacer en cada lugar
- un presupuesto *(budget)* aproximado, pero realista, por cada participante, incluyendo los costos del vuelo, del hotel y de la comida

Paso 3. Ahora, van a cambiar de papel (*change roles*). Imaginen que forman parte del comité que evalúa las solicitudes. ¿A qué solicitudes deben darse las becas? ¡Los fondos son limitados!

Textos orales

Las actividades de Arturo y David

Antes de escuchar

Por lo general, ¿qué hace usted en su tiempo libre (*free time*)? ¿Qué actividades le gusta hacer cuando va a la playa? ¿Y cuando va al centro de su ciudad?

Vocabulario para escuchar

¡No me digas que... !	Don't tell me that . . . !
apagado/a	turned off
¿De veras?	Really?
corriendo	running (in a hurry)

©Westend61/Getty Images

David habla por teléfono

Comprensión

A. **¿Qué pasó ayer?** Conteste las siguientes preguntas según la conversación telefónica para decir lo que hicieron ayer unos amigos dominicanos.

1. ¿Qué hicieron David y Paula?
2. ¿Qué hicieron Arturo y Cristina?
3. ¿Cuál de los cuatros amigos hizo la actividad más relajada (*relaxing*)?

B. **¿Qué va a pasar hoy?** ¿Cierto o falso? Corrija las oraciones falsas.

	CIERTO	FALSO
1. Arturo y Cristina no quieren salir con David y Paula.	☐	☐
2. Hace viento hoy.	☐	☐
3. Van a la playa en coche.	☐	☐
4. No van a llevar nada de comer.	☐	☐

 En acción

Haga una lista de las actividades que usted hizo el fin de semana pasado. ¿Hizo algo como lo que hicieron Arturo y David?

Proyecto en su comunidad

Entreviste a una persona hispana de su universidad o ciudad sobre sus últimas vacaciones y los lugares más populares de su país para ir de vacaciones.

Preguntas posibles

- ¿Cuándo fue de vacaciones a su país la última vez? ¿Con quién fue? ¿Cuánto tiempo pasó allá? ¿Se quedó en casa de su familia o en un hotel? ¿Con cuánta frecuencia va de vacaciones a su país?
- ¿Cuáles son los lugares de vacaciones más famosos de su país? ¿Los visitan solo los turistas extranjeros o los nacionales también? ¿Cuál es su lugar favorito? ¿Por qué?

Escritura

Proyecto: Un ensayo sobre el verano pasado

¿Qué hizo usted el verano pasado? ¿Fue un buen verano? Para este proyecto, va a escribir un ensayo descriptivo sobre el último verano.

©Aurora Open/SuperStock

©Image Source

©Purestock/Superstock

©Fancy/Veer/Corbis/Glow Images

©Brand X Pictures/age fotostock

Antes de escribir

En parejas, hagan una lista de las preguntas básicas que se pueden hacer para hablar de lo que hicieron el verano pasado. Después, usen esas preguntas para entrevistarse mutuamente, buscando detalles interesantes, como por ejemplo, lo que más les gustó del verano y lo que menos les gustó.

A escribir

Con esa información, escriba un ensayo individual sobre cómo pasaron el verano. Hay más ayuda en Connect.

Más ideas para su portafolio

- Haga una lista de seis palabras que usted asocia con la palabra **vacaciones.**
- Incluya una imagen de unas vacaciones memorables, explicando qué hizo durante ese tiempo.
- Ponga la foto de un lugar que le gustaría conocer y diga qué cosas se ven y se hacen allí típicamente.
- Si ha estado jugando (*you have been playing*) Practice Spanish: Study Abroad, en Quest 5 usted fue a un mercado al aire libre en Colombia y tuvo que regatear (*had to haggle*). En parejas, conversen sobre la costumbre de regatear. ¿Dónde se hace típicamente? ¿Es aceptable regatear en el país donde ustedes viven? ¿En qué situaciones es aceptable regatear (o incluso esperado [*even expected*])? Luego, hagan una lista de instrucciones para una persona que quiera aprender a regatear.

©McGraw-Hill Education

Sugerencia: You are now ready to play Quest 5 in **Practice Spanish: Study Abroad.**

EN RESUMEN En este capítulo

AFTER STUDYING THIS CHAPTER I CAN. . .

- ☐ talk about travel, transportation, and vacations (238–240)
- ☐ understand and use pronouns to explain *to* or *for whom* an action is done (245–247)
- ☐ use **gustar** and other verbs to talk about likes and dislikes in more detail (250–251)
- ☐ talk about actions in the past with many types of verbs (255–257)
- ☐ recognize/describe at least 2–3 aspects of Dominican culture

Gramática en breve

21. Indirect Object Pronouns; *Dar* and *decir*

me, te, le, nos, os, les

dar: doy, das, da, damos, dais, dan

decir: digo, dices, dice, decimos, decís, dicen

22. *Gustar*

(no) *indirect object pronoun* + **gusta** + *singular subject*

(no) *indirect object pronoun* + **gustan** + *plural subject*

Would like: **gustaría**

23. Preterite of Regular Verbs and of *dar, hacer, ir,* and *ser*

-ar Verbs: **-é, -aste, -ó, -amos, -asteis, -aron**

-er/-ir Verbs: **-í, -iste, -ió, -imos, -steis, -ieron**

dar: di diste, dio, dimos, disteis, dieron

hacer: hice, hiciste, hizo, hicimos, hicisteis, hicieron

ir/ser: fui, fuiste, fue, fuimos, fuisteis, fueron

Vocabulario

Los verbos

contar (cuento)	to tell; to narrate
dar (doy)	to give
decir (digo) (i)	to say; to tell
encantar (*like* gustar)	to like very much; to love
entregar (gu)	to hand in
explicar (qu)	to explain
gustar	to be pleasing
interesar (*like* gustar)	to interest (*someone*)
mostrar (muestro)	to show
odiar	to hate
ofrecer (ofrezco)	to offer
preguntar	to ask (*a question*)
prestar	to lend
prometer	to promise
recomendar (recomiendo)	to recommend
regalar	to give (*as a gift*)

Repaso: escribir, hablar, mandar, pedir (pido) (i), servir (sirvo) (i)

De viaje

la aduana	customs (*at a border*)
el aeropuerto	airport
el asiento	seat
el/la asistente de vuelo	flight attendant
el autobús	bus
el avión	airplane
el barco	boat, ship
el billete (*Sp.*) / **el boleto** (*L.A.*)	ticket
de ida	one-way ticket
de ida y vuelta	round-trip ticket
electrónico	e-ticket
la cola	line (*of people*)
el control de seguridad	security (check)
el crucero	cruise (ship)
la demora	delay
el destino	destination
el equipaje	baggage, luggage
la escala	stop
la estación	station
de autobuses	bus station
de trenes	train station
la llegada	arrival
la maleta	suitcase
el maletero	porter
el medio de transporte	means of transportation
el mostrador	counter
la parada	stop
el pasaje	fare, price (*of a transportation ticket*)
el/la pasajero/a	passenger
el pasillo	aisle
la puerta de embarque	boarding gate
el puerto	port
el puesto	place (*in line*)

la sala de espera	waiting room
la sala de fumar / de fumadores	smoking area
la salida	departure
la tarjeta (postal)	(post)card
la tarjeta de embarque	boarding pass
la ventanilla	small window (*on a plane*)
el vuelo	flight
de viaje	on a trip, traveling

Cognados: el/la agente, la cabina, el pasaporte, el/la piloto, el tren

Repaso: el viaje

anunciar	to announce
bajarse (de)	to get down (from); to get off (of) (*a vehicle*)
facturar el equipaje	to check baggage
fumar	to smoke
guardar (un puesto)	to save (a place [*in line*])
hacer cola	to stand in line
hacer escala/parada	to make a stop
hacer la(s) maleta(s)	to pack one's suitcase(s)
ir al extranjero	to go abroad
ir en...	to go/travel by . . .
autobús	bus
avión	plane
barco	boat, ship
tren	train
pasar por	to go/pass through
la aduana	customs
el control de seguridad	security (check)
quejarse (de)	to complain (about)
subir (a)	to go up; to get on (*a vehicle*)
viajar	to travel
volar (vuelo) en avión	to fly; to go by plane

Repaso: hacer un viaje, ir

De vacaciones

el bloqueador solar	sunscreen
la camioneta	(mini)van
el *camping*	campground
la foto(grafía)	photo(graph)
el mar	sea
la montaña	mountain
el océano	ocean
la tienda (de campaña)	tent
de vacaciones	on vacation

Repaso: la playa, el sol

estar de vacaciones	to be on vacation
hacer *camping*	to go camping
ir de vacaciones a...	to go on vacation to/in . . .
nadar	to swim
pasar las vacaciones en...	to spend one's vacation in . . .
sacar (qu) fotos / fotografías	to take photos
salir de vacaciones	to leave on vacation
tomar el sol	to sunbathe
tomar unas vacaciones	to take a vacation

Repaso: salir

Otros sustantivos

el chiste	joke
la flor	flower
la gente	people
la historia	story

Los adjetivos

atrasado/a (*with* estar)	late
juntos/as	together

Palabras adicionales

a tiempo	on time
entonces	then; in that case
me gustaría (mucho)...	I would (really) like . . .
muchísimo	an awful lot
(para) nada	at all
por	through; for

Vocabulario personal

Los días festivos°

Los... *Holidays*

En este capítulo

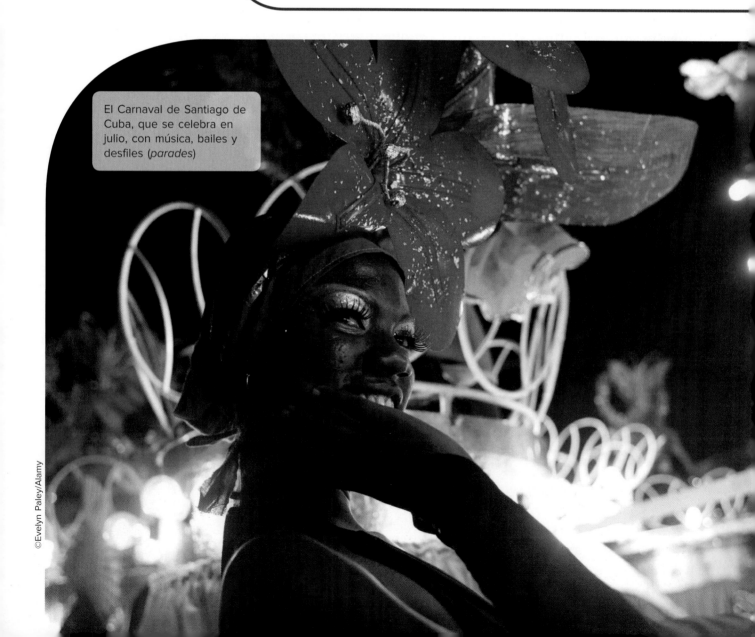

El Carnaval de Santiago de Cuba, que se celebra en julio, con música, bailes y desfiles (*parades*)

CUBA

11,5 (y medio) millones de habitantes

- La isla de Cuba está a solo 150 kilómetros (90 millas) de la costa sur de Florida.
- Cuba es un destino turístico importante para europeos y canadienses.
- Es un país con una tradición musical impresionante y que también se destaca[a] en el béisbol y en la danza.

[a]se... *excels*

ENTREVISTA

- ¿Cuáles son las celebraciones más importantes de su país?
- ¿Qué días celebran más usted y su familia? ¿Cómo los celebran ustedes?
- ¿Tuvo usted[a] una fiesta en su último cumpleaños? ¿Quién se la dio[b]?

[a]¿Tuvo... *Did you have* [b]se... *gave it for you*

Cecilia Figueroa Martín contesta las preguntas.

- En Puerto Rico celebramos las fiestas de los Estados Unidos: el Día de los Presidentes, el Cuatro de Julio, el Día de Gracias, la Navidad. Y luego hay las fiestas patronales[a] de cada ciudad.
- Para nosotros la Navidad es un día muy importante de reunión familiar. Aunque,[b] en realidad,[c] nosotros festejamos[d] en Nochebuena.[e] La familia se reúne,[f] vienen amigos, comemos, bebemos, cantamos, bailamos...
- ¡Sí! Mi marido me hizo una fiesta muy grande para mi cumpleaños. Invitó a toda la familia y a nuestros amigos. ¡Estuvimos[g] de fiesta hasta las 4 cuatro de la mañana!

[a]fiestas... *holidays of the patron saints* [b]*Although* [c]en... *actually*
[d]nosotros... *we celebrate* [e]*Christmas Eve* [f]se... *gets together* [g]*We were*

VOCABULARIO: PREPARACIÓN

Una fiesta de cumpleaños para Javier

You can hear the pronunciation of theme vocabulary words and phrases in the Connect eBook.

Para comer y beber

las botanas (*Mex.*) / **las tapas**	appetizers

Otros sustantivos

el anfitrión / la anfitriona	host (*of an event*)
el cumpleaños	birthday
el día festivo	holiday
el invitado / la invitada	guest

Los verbos

celebrar	to celebrate
comer/beber (demasiado)	to eat/drink (too much)
cumplir años	to have a birthday
darle una fiesta (a alguien)	to give (someone) a party; to have a party (for someone)
divertirse (me divierto) (i)	to have a good time, enjoy oneself
faltar (a)	to be absent (from); to not attend
gastar	to spend (*money*)
hacerle una fiesta (a alguien)	to give (someone) a party; to have a party (for someone)
invitar	to invite
pasarlo bien/mal	to have a good/bad time
regalar	to give (*as a gift*)
reunirse (me reúno) con	to get together (with)
ser + **en** + *place*	to take place in/at (*a place*)
¿Dónde es la fiesta?	Where is the party (at)?

¡OJO!

Note the accent that occurs on **-u-** in forms of **reunirse** when the weak vowel **-u-** is stressed: **me reúno**, **te reúnes**, **se reúne**, **nos reunimos**, **os reunís**, **se reúnen**. This pattern is like that of stem-changing verbs (that is, the stem vowel changes when it is stressed.)

Palabras adicionales

¡Felicitaciones!	Congratulations!
gracias por + *noun*	thanks for + *noun*
Gracias por el regalo.	Thanks for the present.
gracias por + *inf.*	thanks for + *verb* (*-ing*)
Gracias por invitarme.	Thanks for inviting me.

Algunos días festivos

¡OJO!

Only the highlighted items are active vocabulary. Learn the Spanish names of the holidays that you need to talk about your activities and those of your family and write them in **Vocabulario personal** at the end of the chapter.

Los días festivos hispanos

el Día de los Reyes Magos	Day of the Magi (Three Kings) (Jan. 6)
la Pascua	Easter
la Pascua judía	Passover
el Día de la Raza	Columbus Day (Oct. 12)
el Día de Muertos	Day of the Dead (Nov. 2)
el Janucá	Hanukkah
la Nochebuena	Christmas Eve
la Navidad	Christmas
la Nochevieja	New Year's Eve
la quinceañera	young woman's fifteenth birthday party

Los días festivos estadounidenses

el Día de San Patricio, el Cinco de Mayo, el Cuatro de Julio, el Día de (Acción de) Gracias

Note that **el Día de la Raza** corresponds to *Columbus Day* in the U.S. In some areas, it is called *Hispanic Awareness Day.* In some areas, **el Día de la Raza** is celebrated as **el Día de los Pueblos Indígenas** or **el Día de las Comunidades Indígenas.**

Algo sobre...

©Adalberto Roque/AFP/Getty Images

Una parranda en Remedios, Cuba

las parrandas cubanas

Las parrandas son grandes fiestas navideñas[a] típicas de los pueblos y ciudades de una región de la Cuba central. Las más famosas son las[b] de Remedios. La costumbre de las parrandas data del siglo XVIII.[c] Cada barrio[d] de una ciudad monta[e] una parranda y hay una competición entre los barrios para ver cuál es la mejor.[f] Estas fiestas incluyen fuegos artificiales y disfraces,[g] como las fiestas de carnaval.

 **¿En qué fiestas de su país hay fuegos artificiales? ¿y disfraces?**

[a]*Christmas* [b]*those* [c]data... *dates back to the 18th century* [d]*neighborhood* [e]*throws, organizes* [f]la... *the best one* (parranda) [g]fuegos... *fireworks and costumes*

Así se dice

hacer una fiesta = hacer una juerga (*Sp.*), armar (un) bochinche (*Cuba*)
la quinceañera = la fiesta de quince años
el pastel = la torta, la tarta, el queque (*L.A.*)
la Pascua = la Pascua Florida
el Día de Muertos = el Día de los Difuntos
la Navidad = las Pascuas

The figure of **Santa Claus** is a familiar one in Hispanic countries. That is what he is called in Mexico and Puerto Rico. In other parts of the Spanish-speaking world, he is more often called **Papá Noel.**

Comunicación

A. Una fiesta de cumpleaños para Javier. Conteste las siguientes preguntas sobre el dibujo de la página anterior (*previous*).

1. ¿Qué tipo de fiesta es? ¿Dónde es la fiesta?
2. ¿Quiénes son los anfitriones de la fiesta? ¿Quién es el invitado de honor?
3. ¿Qué hay de comer y de beber? ¿Qué hacen los invitados?
4. ¿Qué le dan los invitados a Javier, además de (*besides*) regalos?
5. ¿Quién falta a la fiesta? ¿Quién lo invita por teléfono?
6. ¿Qué le van a decir todos a Javier cuando corte (*he cuts*) el pastel?
7. ¿Qué cree usted que Javier les va a decir a Carmen y Pedro después de la fiesta?

B. Asociaciones. ¿Qué palabras asocia usted con las siguientes ideas? Dé por lo menos (*at least*) dos palabras asociadas con cada idea.

1. un cumpleaños
2. una fiesta
3. los fuegos artificiales (*fireworks*)
4. un árbol (*tree*)
5. los regalos
6. una comida grande

C. Definiciones

Paso 1. Dé las palabras definidas.

1. Algo de comer o beber que se sirve en las fiestas.
2. El día en que, por tradición, algunas personas visitan los cementerios.
3. La fiesta de una muchacha (*girl*) que cumple 15 años.
4. Lo que uno le dice a un amigo que celebra algo.
5. Una fiesta de los judíos (*Jewish people*) que dura 8 días.

Vocabulario útil

el fin	end
el nacimiento	birth

Paso 2. Ahora, en parejas, creen (*create*) por lo menos dos definiciones como las del **Paso 1.** La clase va a adivinar (*guess*) la palabra definida.

Nota cultural

Los días festivos importantes del mundo hispano

Algunas fiestas se celebran en casi todos los países hispanos.

- **La Nochebuena**
  Esta fiesta se celebra con una gran cena en casa. Luego los hispanos cristianos van a la Misa del Gallo,[a] un servicio religioso que se celebra a medianoche. En algunos países, esa misma noche se reciben regalos del Niño Jesús o el Niño Dios.
- **La Nochevieja**
  Es una ocasión para grandes celebraciones, tanto entre familia como en lugares públicos. En España y otros países algunos siguen la tradición de comer una uva[b] por cada una de las doce campanadas[c] de medianoche.
- **El Día de los Reyes Magos**
  Esta fiesta se celebra en muchos países el 6 de enero. Los Reyes Magos son los encargados[d] de traer regalos. Muchos niños ponen sus zapatos en la ventana o balcón antes de acostarse la noche del 5 de enero. Los Reyes llegan en camellos durante la noche y llenan los zapatos con regalos y dulces.
- **El Día de la Independencia**
  Todos los países latinoamericanos celebran el día de la declaración de su independencia de España. Por ejemplo, Cuba celebra su independencia el 10 de octubre; México, el 16 de septiembre; Bolivia, el 6 de agosto; el Paraguay, el 15 de mayo; El Salvador, el 15 de septiembre.

Unos bailarines (*dancers*) durante las celebraciones del Día de los Reyes Magos, en La Habana, Cuba

- **La quinceañera**
  Esta fiesta, celebrada en muchos países latinoamericanos y en este país, celebra la llegada de las niñas a los 15 años, es decir, su transición de niña a mujer. La familia y los amigos de la joven le dan una gran fiesta, en la que[e] ella se viste de largo.[f] A veces se celebra una misa especial, pero siempre hay una cena y una fiesta con música para bailar.

¿Cuáles de estas fiestas se celebran en su familia? Si no se celebra ninguna de ellas, ¿cuáles son las fiestas familiares de más importancia para usted?

[a]Misa... *Midnight Mass* [b]*grape* [c]*bell strokes*
[d]los... *in charge* [e]la... *which* [f]se... *dresses up (in a gown)*

Vocabulario útil

el árbol	tree
el barrio	neighborhood
la corona	wreath
el desfile	parade
el globo	balloon

D. Hablando de fiestas

Paso 1. ¿Cuáles de estas fiestas le gustan a usted? ¿Cuáles no le gustan? Explique por qué. Compare sus respuestas con las (*those*) de sus compañeros de clase.

MODELO: el Cuatro de Julio → Me gusta mucho el Cuatro de Julio porque vemos fuegos artificiales (*fireworks*) en el parque y...

1. el Cuatro de Julio
2. el Día de (Acción de) Gracias
3. la Nochevieja
4. la Navidad

Paso 2. Ahora piense en su fiesta favorita. Piense en cómo celebra usted esa fiesta, para explicárselo (*explain it*) luego a la clase. Debe pensar en lo siguiente.

- los preparativos que usted hace de antemano (*beforehand*)
- la ropa que lleva
- las comidas o bebidas que compra o hace
- el lugar donde se celebra
- la decoración especial que hay o que usted pone

Paso 3. Ahora, en parejas, compartan (*share*) sus respuestas. Luego díganle a la clase las preferencias o tradiciones que tienen en común.

Las emociones y los estados afectivos°

estados... *emotional states*

llorar

discutir con (alguien) por/sobre (algo)

enojarse con (alguien) por (algo)

ponerse rojo/a

Para expresar *to become/get* y *to feel*

estarse/sentirse (me siento) (i) + *adj./adv.*	to be / to feel + *adj./adv.*
ponerse + *adj./adv.*	to become/get + *adj./adv.*

Me pongo triste cuando escucho malas noticias y luego **estoy triste** todo el día.
I get sad when I hear bad news, and then I'm sad all day long.

Cuando **me pongo enfermo/a, me siento muy mal**.
When I get sick, I feel awful.

Otros verbos

olvidar	to forget
portarse bien/mal	to (mis)behave
quejarse de	to complain about
recordar (recuerdo)	to remember
reírse (me río) (i) (de)	to laugh (about)
sonreír (sonrío) (i)	to smile

Adjetivos

enojado/a	angry; upset
feliz (*pl.* **felices**)	happy
tranquilo/a	calm

Repaso: alegre, contento/a, furioso/a, nervioso/a, triste

¡OJO!

The verbs **reír** and **sonreír** are **e → i** stem-changing verbs. An accent is required on all present tense forms of these verbs (as well as on the infinitives) to show the breaking of dipthongs **io, ie, ei** by stressing the weak vowel **i: (son)río, (son)ríes, (son)ríe, (son)reímos, (son)reís, (son)ríen**. No accent mark is needed on the present participle, in which the **i** is not stressed: **(son)riendo.**

Comunicación

A. Asociaciones

Paso 1. ¿Con qué verbos asocia usted las siguientes cosas y situaciones? Use verbos de **Las emociones...** o cualquier (*any*) otro.

1. ver un bebé
2. una situación injusta
3. un número de teléfono nuevo
4. algo memorable que pasó
5. tener un examen importante
6. un chiste muy bueno
7. un perro muy joven
8. un desacuerdo (*disagreement*) con un amigo
9. conocer a una persona muy interesante
10. estar equivocado (*wrong*) en público / enfrente de una clase

(Continúa.)

Paso 2. Ahora, en parejas, digan las palabras o frases que ustedes asocian con los siguientes verbos o frases.

1. recordar
2. sonreír
3. ponerse nervioso/a
4. discutir con alguien

Nota comunicativa

Cómo enfatizar: *-ísimo*

To emphasize the quality described by an adjective or an adverb in English, you can put *very very* or *really really* before the word: *I tried very very hard. I really really like it.* This is expressed in Spanish by adding **-ísimo** to an adverb and **-ísimo/a(os/as)** to an adjective. You already know one adverb formed like this: **muchísimo.**

Mi madre se emocionó **muchísimo** porque las tarjetas y los regalos eran **lindísimos**.
My mother got very very emotional because the cards and gifts were super nice.

- If the word ends in a consonant, **-ísimo** is added to the singular form and any accents on the original word are dropped: **difícil → dificilísimo.**

Estas tapas son **dificilísimas** de preparar.
These appetizers are very, very hard to prepare.

- If the word ends in a vowel, that vowel is dropped before adding **-ísimo** and any accents on the original word are also dropped.

tarde → tardísimo   **rápida → rapidísima**

- There are spelling changes when the final consonant is a **c, g,** or **z.** This is the same spelling change you have learned to make in the formal command and preterite forms of verbs that end in **-car, -gar,** and **-zar.**

rico → riquísimo   **largas → larguísimas**
feliz → felicísimo

You can use adjectives and adverbs formed in this way in **Comunicación B** and **C.**

Vocabulario útil

avergonzado/a embarrassed
de buen/mal humor
contento/a
feliz/triste
furioso/a
impaciente
nervioso/a
preocupado/a

B. Reacciones. ¿Cómo se pone o se siente usted en estas situaciones? Use los adjetivos y verbos que usted sabe y también algunas formas enfáticas (**-ísimo**). ¿Cuántas emociones puede usted describir?

MODELO: Llueve todo el día. → Me pongo / Me siento **triste/tristísima.**

1. Llueve el día de su cumpleaños.
2. Es Navidad. Alguien le hace un regalo carísimo.
3. Usted quiere bañarse. No hay agua caliente.
4. Usted está solo/a en casa una noche y oye un ruido.
5. Usted da una fiesta en su apartamento. Los invitados están aburridísimos.
6. Usted tiene un examen importantísimo pero no estudió nada la noche anterior (*before*).
7. Usted cuenta un chiste pero nadie se ríe.
8. Usted acaba de terminar un examen difícil. Cree que lo hizo muy mal.

C. ¿Cuándo... ?

Paso 1. En parejas, completen las siguientes oraciones con un lugar y una acción o situación, según su experiencia. Sigan el modelo.

MODELO: Me quejo en... (lugar) cuando... (acción o situación) →
E1: Me quejo en **el aeropuerto** cuando **tengo que hacer cola... ¡y la cola es larguísima!**
E2: Yo también, y también me quejo en **una tienda cuando tengo que esperar demasiado tiempo.**

1. Me quejo en... cuando...
2. Me río muchísimo en... cuando...
3. Sonrío en... cuando...
4. Lloro en... cuando...
5. Mis padres se enojan en... cuando... (Mis hijos... Mi esposo/a... Mi novio/a...)
6. Los niños se portan bien/malísimo en... cuando...
7. Las mascotas se portan bien/mal en... cuando...
8. Me pongo rojo/a en... cuando...

Paso 2. Ahora comparen sus respuestas con las (*those*) del resto de la clase. ¿En qué son similares o diferentes las respuestas de todos?

«De fiesta en fiesta» Segmento 1

Antes de mirar

Indique las religiones más representadas en su comunidad.

- ☐ el budismo
- ☐ el cristianismo
  - **a.** ☐ católicos
  - **b.** ☐ evangélicos
  - **c.** ☐ protestantes
  - **d.** ☐ otros
- ☐ el islam
- ☐ el judaísmo

Mucha gente limeña (*from Lima*) participa en la procesión del Señor de los Milagros (*Our Lord of the Miracles*). Es una imagen de un Cristo crucificado (*Christ on the cross*) muy venerada (*worshipped*) por más de cinco siglos (*centuries*).

Este segmento

En este segmento Víctor y Ana presentan datos estadísticos sobre la afiliación religiosa de los hispanos estadounidenses y hablan de las fiestas que celebran. Luego Laura presenta un reportaje desde (*from*) el Perú.

Vocabulario del segmento

de nuevo nos encontramos	here we are again	**el/la muchacho/a**	boy/girl
aunque	although	**el/la esclavo/a**	slave
el/la seguidor(a)	follower	**el muro**	wall
atraer (like **traer**)	to attract	**el terremoto**	earthquake
la escuela	school	**asolar**	to devastate
conocido/a	known	**rendir (rindo) (i) culto**	to worship
la fe	faith	**caminar despacio**	to walk slowly
alrededor de	circa, about	**la mantilla**	lace veil

Estrategia

The following Christian holidays are mentioned in **Segmento 1.** You do not need to know any details about them, but this list will help you recognize their names when you hear them.

- **la Navidad** (the celebration of the birth of Christ)
- **la Semana Santa** (*Holy Week* = the week leading up to Easter Sunday)
- **el Viernes Santo** (*Good Friday* = the day Christ was crucified on the cross)
- **el Domingo de Pascua de Resurrección** (*Easter Sunday* = the celebration of Christ's resurrection)

Después de mirar

A. ¿Está claro? Empareje los siguientes porcentajes con la explicación apropiada.

PORCENTAJES Y FECHAS	FRASES
1. 60% (por ciento)	**a.** población hispana cristiana pero no católica
2. 22%	**b.** población hispana religiosa pero no cristiana
3. 12%	**c.** población hispana católica
4. 1%	**d.** población hispana sin afiliación religiosa

B. Un poco más. Conteste las siguientes preguntas.

1. ¿En qué mes se celebra el Mes Morado? ¿Cuál es el origen del nombre de la celebración?
2. ¿Quién pintó la imagen del Señor de los Milagros? ¿En qué año?
3. En Panamá, ¿qué representan las fechas 3/11 y 28/11?

C. Y ahora, ustedes. En grupos, hablen de las fiestas más importantes que se celebran en su ciudad o estado. Por ejemplo, ¿hay grandes celebraciones para el Día de la Independencia (el Cuatro de Julio)? ¿Cómo lo celebra su familia? ¿Qué otros días de fiesta se celebran en su ciudad o estado?

GRAMÁTICA

¿Recuerda usted?

You already know the irregular preterite stem and endings for **hacer.** All verbs presented in **Gramática 24** have irregular stems used with the same preterite endings as **hacer.** Review those endings by completing these forms.

1. yo: hic_____ 2. nosotros: hic_____ 3. usted: hiz_____ 4. ellos: hic_____

24 Talking About the Past (Part 2)

Irregular Preterites

Gramática en acción: ¿Qué pasó en la fiesta de fin de año en casa de Sofía y Paco?

Mire con atención los verbos en rojo. Son formas del pretérito. Dé el infinitivo y luego conteste las preguntas.

1. ¿Quién estuvo hablando por teléfono?
2. ¿Quién dio la fiesta?
3. ¿Quién no pudo ir a la fiesta?
4. ¿Quién puso su copa sobre la televisión?
5. ¿Quién hizo mucho ruido?
6. ¿Quién no quiso beber más?
7. ¿Quién probablemente tuvo que irse temprano?

¿Y usted?

1. ¿Estuvo usted alguna vez en una fiesta de fin de año como esta? (**Estuve**...)
2. ¿Tuvo que irse temprano de la fiesta? (**Tuve...**) ¿O se quedó hasta medianoche?
3. ¿Recuerda qué ropa se puso para la fiesta? (**Me puse**...)

Irregular Forms / **Las formas irregulares**

1. **Additional Irregular Forms**
   You have already learned the irregular preterite forms of **hacer.** The verbs to the right are also irregular in the preterite, like **hacer.**
   - Their stem (shown in red and underlined) is irregular.
   - They use the same preterite endings as **hacer.**

   Only the first and third person singular endings are irregular (they have no accent marks). The verb **estar** is conjugated for you. The other verbs listed are conjugated like **estar.**

estar	
estuve	**estuvimos**
estuviste	**estuvisteis**
estuvo	**estuvieron**

¡OJO!

There are no accents on **-e** and **-o.**

estar:	**estuv-**
poder:	**pud-**
poner:	**pus-**
querer:	**quis-**
saber:	**sup-**
tener:	**tuv-**
venir:	**vin-**

Las terminaciones irregulares	
-e	**-imos**
-iste	**-isteis**
-o	**-ieron**

2. **Preterite of *decir* and *traer***
The irregular preterite stems of these two verbs end in **-j-**. They use the same endings as the verbs on page 278, except that the **-i-** of the third person plural is omitted: **dijeron, trajeron.**

decir: dij-
traer: traj-
} **-e, -iste, -o, -imos, -isteis, -eron**

---

3. **Preterite of** hay: hubo
Hay (*There is/are*) comes from the infinitive **haber.** Its preterite form is **hubo** = *there was/were.*

Hubo un accidente ayer en el centro.
There was an accident yesterday downtown.

Hubo muchas fiestas de Navidad el año pasado.
There were a lot of Christmas parties last year.

Changes in Meaning / **Cambios de significado**

The following Spanish verbs have an English equivalent in the preterite tense that is different from that of the infinitive.

Infinitive	Present Tense	Preterite Meaning
saber =	to know (*facts, information*)	to find out, learn
	Ya lo **sé.** *I already know it.*	Lo **supe** ayer. *I found it out (learned it) yesterday.*
conocer =	to know, be familiar with (*people, places*)	to meet (*for the first time*)
	Ya la **conozco.** *I already know her.*	La **conocí** ayer. *I met her yesterday.*
querer =	to want	to try
	Quiero hacerlo hoy. *I want to do it today.*	**Quise** hacerlo ayer. *I tried to do it yesterday.*
no querer =	not to want	to refuse
	No quiero hacerlo hoy. *I don't want to do it today.*	**No quise** hacerlo anteayer. *I refused to do it the day before yesterday.*

Práctica y comunicación

A. La última Nochevieja

Paso 1. Autoprueba. Dé la forma indicada del pretérito.

1. yo: saber
2. ellos: tener
3. tú: venir
4. él: poner
5. nosotros: querer
6. usted: poder
7. ellos: decir
8. haber

Summary of Irregular Preterites

Endings: **-e, -iste, -o, -imos, -isteis, -ieron**
Irregular stems: **dij-, estuv-, hic-, pud-, pus-, quis-, sup-, traj-, tuv-, vin-**

Paso 2. Ahora diga lo que usted hizo o no hizo el último día del año pasado. Haga oraciones completas con la forma apropiada del pretérito.

MODELO: 1. (no) querer hacer algo / nada especial ese día →
Quise hacer **algo** especial ese día. **No quise** hacer **nada** especial ese día.

El último día del año pasado, (yo)...

1. (no) querer hacer algo / nada especial ese día
2. (no) dar una fiesta en mi casa / apartamento
3. (no) estar con unos buenos amigos
4. (no) tener que hacer algo / nada de comida

***Prác. A, Paso 1: Answers: 1.** supe **2.** tuvieron **3.** viniste **4.** puso **5.** quisimos **6.** pudo **7.** dijeron **8.** hubo*

(Continúa.)

5. (no) conocer a alguien / nadie interesante
6. (no) decirle ¡Feliz Año Nuevo! a alguien / nadie
7. (no) poder quedarme despierto/a (*awake*) hasta la medianoche
8. (no) ponerse ropa elegante esa noche

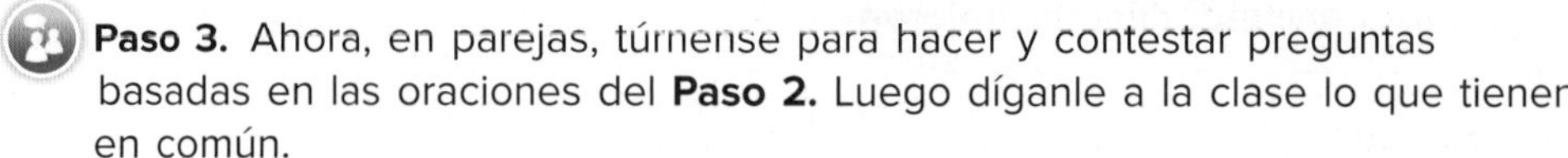

Paso 3. Ahora, en parejas, túrnense para hacer y contestar preguntas basadas en las oraciones del **Paso 2.** Luego díganle a la clase lo que tienen en común.

MODELO: **E1:** ¿**Quisiste** hacer algo especial ese día?
E2: No, no **quise** hacer nada especial. ¿Y tú?
E1: Yo tampoco. →
Ninguno de nosotros **quiso** hacer nada especial ese día.

B. En una fiesta. ¿Cómo se dice en inglés?

1. Conocí al primo cubano de una amiga.
2. Quise abrir una botella de champán.
3. Supe algo interesante sobre los anfitriones.
4. No quise bailar. ¡La música era (*was*) malísima!

Estrategia

Not all of the verbs in this story are irregular in the preterite. As you conjugate each infinitive, first ask yourself if its preterite is regular or irregular.

C. Una Nochebuena en Santiago de Cuba

Paso 1. Complete la siguiente narración sobre la celebración de la Nochebuena de una familia cubana de la ciudad de Santiago, al sur de la isla de Cuba. Habla Manuel, el padre de la familia. Use el pretérito de los verbos.

El lechón (*suckling pig*) con moros (= frijoles) y cristianos (= arroz)

El año pasado mi esposa y yo celebramos la Nochebuena en casa con toda la familia. ______ (Estar[1]) con nosotros mi primo Andrés, de la Florida, quien ______ (quedarse[2]) con nosotros toda la semana. ______ (Venir[3]) mis padres, mis suegros,[a] hermanos y cuñados[b] con sus hijos. También ______ (*nosotros*: invitar[4]) a nuestros vecinos[c] de toda la vida,[d] los Benjumea. Pero ellos no ______ (poder[5]) asistir porque ______ (irse[6]) a La Habana para estar con su hija, que ______ (tener[7]) un niño en noviembre.

Mi esposa ______ (preparar[8]) lechón asado, moros y cristianos, yuca y tostones.[e] ¡Todo ______ (estar[9]) riquísimo! Mi cuñado ______ (traer[10]) turrón[f] español y cava.[g] A las 10:30, mi hermana ______ (decir[11]) que era[h] hora de ir a la Misa del Gallo[i] y ______ (llevar[12]) a los abuelos a la iglesia.[j] Los demás[k] no ______ (querer[13]) ir y seguimos armando bochinche hasta que ______ (volver[14]) los otros. Todo ______ (ir[15]) bien chévere.[l] Como regalo de Navidad, mi primo Andrés me ______ (dar[16]) un álbum con fotos y cartas de mis parientes en la Florida y Nueva Jersey. Yo ______ (ponerse[17]) tan emocionado[m] que ______ (llorar[18]).

[a]*in-laws* [b]*brothers- and sisters-in-law* [c]*neighbors* [d]de... *long-time (lit., of one's whole life)* [e]*fried plantains* [f]*almond Christmas candy* [g]*Spanish sparkling wine* [h]*it was* [i]Misa... *Midnight Mass* [j]*church* [k]Los... *The others* [l]*great* [m]*touched, emotional*

Paso 2. Comprensión

1. ¿Qué tuvo de especial la Nochebuena del año pasado para Manuel?
2. ¿Por qué no pudieron asistir los Benjumea?
3. ¿Quiénes fueron a la Misa del Gallo?
4. ¿Qué comieron y bebieron todos?

Paso 3. Ahora complete las siguientes oraciones basadas en lo que pasó en la celebración de la pasada Navidad, Pascua judía u otra fiesta de importancia para su familia. Conjugue los verbos en el pretérito, añadiendo el sujeto y otra información apropiada.

MODELO: **celebrar** _______ (fiesta) en _______ (lugar) →
Mi familia **celebró** la Nochebuena en casa de mis abuelos.

1. **celebrar** _______ (fiesta) en _______ (lugar)
2. **querer** asistir / (no) **poder**
3. **ir** _______ (servicio religioso) **antes / después** de cenar
4. **comer** _______ (platos) y **beber** _______ (bebidas)
5. **ponerse** muy emocionado/a porque _______
6. **dar**le un regalo a _______ (persona)

D. Hechos (*Events*) históricos. Describan ustedes algunos hechos históricos, usando el pretérito de los verbos y una palabra o frase de cada columna. Su profesor(a) los puede ayudar con los datos (*information*) que no saben.

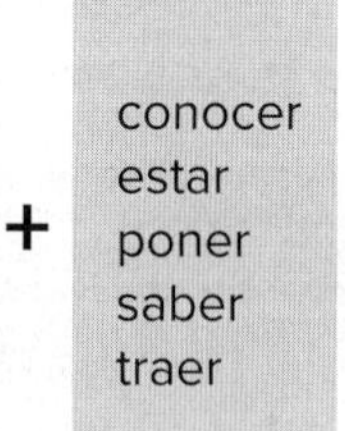

en 1957 los rusos				en Valley Forge con sus soldados
en 1969 los estadounidenses		conocer		a un hombre en la luna (*moon*)
Adán y Eva		estar		un satélite en el espacio por primera vez
George Washington	+	poner	+	el significado (*meaning*) de un árbol especial
los europeos		saber		a Livingston en África
los aztecas		traer		el caballo (*horse*) al Nuevo Mundo
Stanley				a Hernán Cortés en Tenochtitlán

E. Intercambios

Paso 1. Haga preguntas en el pretérito con los siguientes verbos. En el **Paso 2,** usted va a usar las preguntas para entrevistar a un compañero o una compañera de clase.

MODELO: conocer → ¿Cuándo **conociste** a tu mejor amigo/a?

1. conocer
2. saber
3. estar
4. tener
5. hacer
6. dar

Paso 2. En parejas, túrnense para hacer y contestar sus preguntas. Luego díganle a la clase algo que los/las dos tienen en común.

MODELO: conocer → Los dos **conocimos** a nuestros mejores amigos en la escuela secundaria.

F. La última fiesta

Paso 1. Haga una lista de todos los detalles (*details*) que usted recuerda de la última fiesta a la que (*which*) fue. Puede ser una fiesta que usted organizó o que otra persona dio. Use los siguientes verbos: **conocer, dar, estar, invitar, organizar, poder, saber, ser, venir.**

MODELO: Di una fiesta para el cumpleaños de mi mejor amigo.
Mi amigo Clark y yo organizamos la fiesta...

Paso 2. Ahora entreviste a un compañero o una compañera sobre la última fiesta a la que (*to which*) fue o que dio. Haga preguntas con las palabras interrogativas y el pretérito.

Palabras interrogativas: ¿cuándo?, ¿dónde?, ¿quién?, ¿con quién?, ¿qué?, ¿por qué?

MODELOS: ¿**Quién dio** la fiesta?
¿**Qué hubo** de comer y beber?

Paso 3. Luego díganle a la clase dos detalles interesantes sobre las últimas fiestas a las que (*to which*) ustedes fueron o que ustedes organizaron.

¿Recuerda usted?

You learned in **Gramática 15 (Cap. 6)** to make a change in the **-ndo** form of **-ir** stem-changing verbs. That same change occurs in some forms of the preterite of that type of verb. Review the change in the present participle by completing the following forms.

1. pedir: p_____diendo **2.** dormir: d_____rmiendo

You will learn about this change in the preterite in **Grámatica 25.**

25 Talking About the Past (Part 3)

Preterite of Stem-changing Verbs

Gramática en acción: Una fiesta de quinceañera

Escoja las respuestas más lógicas para describir la fiesta de quinceañera de Lupe Carrasco. Al leer (*As you read*), mire con atención los verbos en rojo. Son formas del pretérito. ¿Puede usted dar el infinitivo de esos verbos?

1. Para su fiesta, Lupe se vistió con...
   - ☐ un vestido blanco muy elegante.
   - ☐ una camiseta y *bluejeans.*
2. Mientras Lupe cortaba[a] el pastel de cumpleaños, la madre de ella...
   - ☐ empezó a llorar.
   - ☐ se rio mucho.
3. Lupe pidió un deseo[b] al cortar[c] el pastel. Ella...
   - ☐ les dijo a todos qué fue lo que pidió.
   - ☐ prefirió guardarlo en secreto.
4. En la fiesta sirvieron...
   - ☐ champán y refrescos.
   - ☐ solo té y café.
5. Todos los invitados...
   - ☐ se divirtieron mucho.
   - ☐ se quejaron.
6. A las tres de la mañana, el último invitado
   - ☐ se despidió.[d]
   - ☐ sonrió.

[a]Mientras... *While Lupe was cutting* [b]*wish* [c]al... *as she cut*
[d]se... *said good-bye*

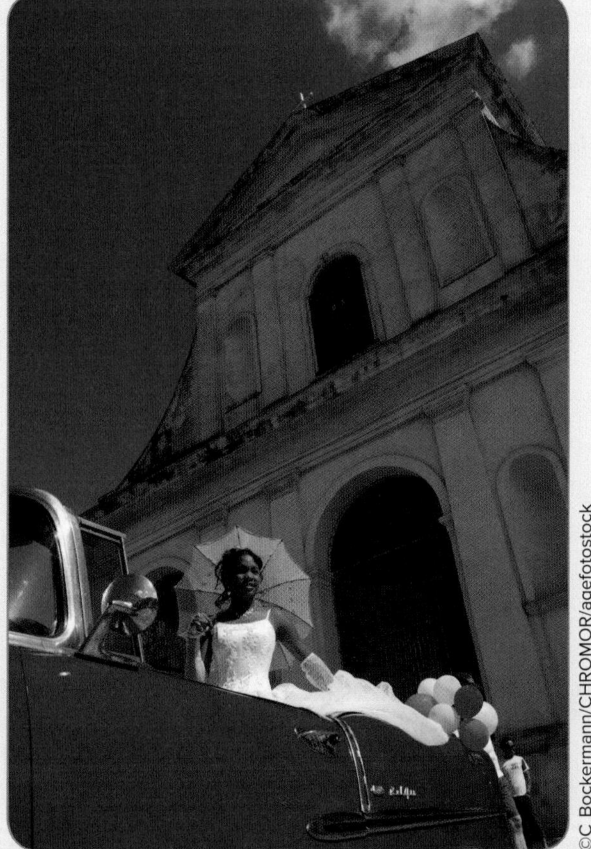

Otra costumbre (*custom*) de quinceañera común en Cuba: ir por la ciudad en coche, como los recién casados (*newlyweds*) en este país

¿Y usted?

1. ¿Recuerda usted qué hizo cuando cumplió 15 años?
2. ¿Qué regalos pidió? (**Pedí...**)
3. ¿Qué sirvieron en la fiesta? (**Sirvieron...**)
4. ¿Se divirtió? (**Me divertí...**)
5. ¿Cómo se sintió ese día? (**Me sentí...**)

1. Preterite of *-ar* and *-er* Stem-changing Verbs
In **Gramática 23** (**Cap. 8**) you learned that **-ar** and **-er** stem-changing verbs have no stem change in the preterite (or in the present participle).

El pretérito de los verbos en *-ar*/*-er*			
recordar (recuerdo)		**perder (pierdo)**	
recordé	**recordamos**	**perdí**	**perdimos**
recordaste	**recordasteis**	**perdiste**	**perdisteis**
recordó	**recordaron**	**perdió**	**perdieron**
recordando		**perdiendo**	

2. Preterite of *-ir* Stem-changing Verbs
-Ir stem-changing verbs *do* have a stem change in the preterite.

- The change occurs only in the third person singular and plural forms.
- The stem vowels **e** and **o** change to **i** and **u,** respectively. This is the same change that occurs in the present participle of **-ir** stem-changing verbs.

El pretérito de los verbos en *-ir*			
e → i **pedir (pido) (i)**		**o → u** **dormir (duermo) (u)**	
pedí	**pedimos**	**dormí**	**dormimos**
pediste	**pedisteis**	**dormiste**	**dormisteis**
pidió	**pidieron**	**durmió**	**durmieron**
pidiendo		**durmiendo**	

¡OJO!

Remember that this change is indicated in parentheses after the infinitive in vocabulary lists: **pedir (pido) (i), dormir (duermo) (u).** Now you know that it indicates two different changes: (1) in the present participle, and (2) in the third person singular and plural of the preterite.

3. Important *-ir* Stem-changing Verbs
You already know or have seen many of these verbs. New ones are indicated with*.

***conseguir (consigo) (i)**	to get; to obtain
conseguir + *inf.*	to succeed in (*doing something*)
***despedirse (me despido) (i) (de)**	to say good-bye (to)
divertirse (me divierto) (i)	to have a good time
dormir (duermo) (u)	to sleep
dormirse	to fall asleep
***morirse (me muero) (u)**	to die
pedir (pido) (i)	to ask for; to order
preferir (prefiero) (i)	to prefer
reírse (me río) (i) (de)	to laugh (at)
seguir (sigo) (i)	to continue; to follow
sentirse (me siento) (i)	to feel
servir (sirvo) (i)	to serve
sonreír (sonrío) (i)	to smile
***sugerir (sugiero) (i)**	to suggest
vestirse (me visto) (i)	to get dressed

¡OJO!

The verbs **reírse** and **sonreír** are **e → i** stem-changing verbs, but they drop the **e** completely in the third persons of the preterite and in the present participle.

(me reí, te reíste) **se rio**	**(nos reímos, os reísteis)** **se rieron → riendo**
(sonreí, sonreíste) **sonrió**	**(sonreímos, sonreísteis)** **sonrieron → sonriendo**

Práctica y comunicación

A. ¿Quién lo hizo?

Paso 1. Autoprueba. Complete las siguientes formas del pretérito.

1. nos divert___mos
2. se d___rmieron
3. tú s___rviste
4. se v___stió
5. yo sug___rí
6. ustedes p___dieron

Summary of the Preterite of Stem-changing Verbs

-ar / -er = no change
-ir = change in the third persons singular and plural
e → i
o → u

(Continúa.)

Prác. A, Paso 1: Answers: 1. *nos divertimos* ***2.*** *se durmieron* ***3.*** *tú serviste* ***4.*** *se vistió* ***5.*** *yo sugerí* ***6.*** *ustedes pidieron*

Paso 2. Ahora indique quiénes de sus compañeros de clase hicieron las siguientes acciones la semana pasada (*last week*). Use verbos en el pretérito. Si nadie lo hizo, simplemente diga **Nadie...** Si más de una persona lo hizo, use el verbo en plural.

MODELO: 1. ______ **vestirse** con ropa **elegante / extravagante** para venir a clase → Tom **se vistió** con ropa **elegante** para venir a clase.

1. ______ **vestirse** con ropa **elegante / extravagante** para venir a clase
2. ______ **dormirse** en clase
3. ______ **pedirle** al profesor / a la profesora más tarea
4. ______ **sentirse bien / mal** con el resultado de un examen
5. ______ **divertirse** muchísimo en un concierto
6. ______ **reírse** a carcajadas (*out loud*)
7. ______ **sugerir** tener la clase afuera (*outside*)
8. ______ no **recordar** traer la tarea a clase
9. ______ **despedirse** en español de sus amigos de la clase
10. ______ **morirse** de vergüenza (*embarrassment*) por algo

Paso 3. Ahora, en parejas, comparen sus respuestas del **Paso 2.** Luego díganle a la clase una o dos de las respuestas que tienen en común. Mencionen el día, si lo recuerdan.

MODELO: Pensamos que Tom **se vistió** con ropa **elegante** para venir a clase **el miércoles de la semana pasada.**

B. José Martí

Paso 1. Complete la siguiente narración con formas del pretérito para saber más sobre José Martí.

José Martí ______ (servir[1]) la causa de la independencia cubana toda su vida.[a] Siempre ______ (pedir[2]) la libertad de Cuba, de España, y se opuso a la esclavitud.[b] Nació[c] en 1853 en Cuba, hijo de españoles. ______ (Estudiar[3]) en España, donde ______ (recibir[4]) el título de abogado[d] en 1874. Pero no ______ (poder[5]) ejercer[e] esta profesión en Cuba. Luego ______ (vivir[6]) en México, Guatemala y los Estados Unidos.

En 1876 ______ (conocer[7]) a la mujer que luego ______ (ser[8]) su esposa, María, y se casaron.[f] ______ (*Ellos:* Tener[9]) un hijo, pero el matrimonio se separó y Martí ______ (perder[10]) contacto con su hijo.

En 1895 ______ (decidir[11]) empezar una guerra de independencia en Cuba. ______ (Morirse[12]) luchando[g] en su querida[h] isla.

Algunos de sus versos son especialmente famosos en todo el mundo gracias a la canción «Guantanamera».

[a]*life* [b]*se... he opposed slavery* [c]*He was born* [d]título... *law degree* [e]*practice* [f]se... *they got married* [g]*fighting* [h]*beloved*

Paso 2. Ahora, haga cinco preguntas usando verbos en el pretérito que se puedan contestar (*can be answered*) con información del texto.

MODELO: ¿Cuántos años vivió Martí?

C. Las historias que todos conocemos

Paso 1. Empareje los personajes (*characters*) de la columna de la izquierda con las acciones de la columna de la derecha para crear oraciones en el pretérito basadas en unos cuentos o historias muy famosos. ¿Puede adivinar (*guess*) quiénes son Caperucita Roja, la Cenicienta y Blancanieves?

Algo sobre...

José Martí

©Carl DeAbreu/Alamy

José Martí, llamado el Apóstol (*founding voice*) de la independencia cubana

José Martí fue un escritor[a] y periodista[b] cubano que se considera un héroe nacional por su lucha[c] por la independencia y por la libertad de su país. Fue uno de los grandes intelectuales hispanohablantes del siglo XIX.[d]

¿Hay algún héroe político o social que usted admire mucho? ¿Por qué lo/la admira?

[a]*writer* [b]*journalist* [c]*fight* [d]siglo... *19th century*

PERSONAJES	ACCIONES
1. Caperucita Roja	**a.** conocer a una mujer misteriosa en un baile
el lobo (*wolf*)	**b.** divertirse bailando con un joven muy guapo
2. la Cenicienta	**c.** dormirse después de comer una manzana
el Príncipe	**d.** morirse por el amor de su novia
las hermanastras de la Cenicienta	**e.** perderse en el bosque (*forest*)
	f. perder un zapato muy bonito
3. Blancanieves	**g.** encontrar (*to find*) un zapato de cristal (*glass*)
los siete enanos (*dwarfs*)	**h.** sentirse preocupados por su amiga
	i. vestirse de (*as a*) abuela
4. Romeo	**j.** no conseguir ponerse el zapato de cristal
Julieta	**k.** hablar con un joven guapo desde su balcón

Paso 2. Ahora, en parejas, inventen dos acciones más en el pretérito para cada historia, pero sin incluir el nombre del personaje. La clase va a adivinar a qué personaje, cuento o historia se refieren sus oraciones.

MODELO: Una mujer **quiso** ponerse el zapato de cristal, pero no **pudo** ponérselo. → la hermanastra de la Cenicienta

D. Una entrevista indiscreta

Paso 1. Lea las siguientes preguntas y escriba una respuesta para cada una. **¡OJO!** Tres de sus respuestas deben ser falsas.

1. ¿A qué hora te dormiste anoche?
2. ¿Perdiste mucho dinero alguna vez?
3. ¿Con qué programa o serie de televisión te divertiste mucho en los días o meses pasados... pero te avergüenzas de (*you're ashamed*) admitirlo?
4. ¿Seguiste haciendo algo después de que tu padre/madre (compañero/a, esposo/a) te dijo que no lo hicieras (*not to do it*)?
5. ¿Pediste una bebida alcohólica antes de tener 21 años?
6. ¿Qué cosa o tarea no conseguiste terminar el mes pasado?

Paso 2. En parejas, usen las preguntas del **Paso 1** para entrevistarse. Traten de (*Try to*) adivinar las respuestas falsas de su compañero/a.

Paso 3. Ahora presenten a la clase una de las respuestas interesantes de su compañero/a. La clase va a adivinar si la respuesta es cierta o falsa.

MODELO: **E1:** Julie, ¿a qué hora te dormiste anoche?
E2: Me dormí a las tres de la mañana.
E1: (*a la clase*): Julie se durmió a las tres de la mañana anoche.
CLASE: No es cierto.
E1: Tienen razón. No es cierto. Me dormí a las once.

E. Una fiesta de Halloween

Paso 1. En grupos, usen las siguientes ideas como guía para entrevistarse sobre la última fiesta de Halloween a la que (*which*) asistieron.

MODELO: **vestirse** de → **E1:** ¿De qué **te vestiste**?
E2: **Me vestí** de vampiro. ¿Y tú?
E3: **Yo me vestí** de bruja.

1. la fiesta: **ser** en ______ (lugar)
2. **llegar** ______ (modo de transporte)
3. **vestirse** de (*as*) ______ (disfraz)
4. **ir** con ______ (persona[s])
5. **pedir / conseguir / dar** ______ (comida)
6. **bailar / hablar / beber / ¿ ?**
7. **divertirse** mucho/poco
8. **despedirse** a la(s) ______ (hora)
9. ¿ ?

Paso 2. Escojan a la persona que asistió a la mejor fiesta y luego díganle a toda la clase dos cosas interesantes que esa persona hizo en la fiesta.

Vocabulario útil

la bruja witch
el disfraz costume
el esqueleto
el fantasma ghost
la máscara
la momia
el monstruo
el vampiro / la vampira

¿Recuerda usted?

In **Gramática 18 (Cap. 7)** you learned about direct object nouns and pronouns. In **Gramática 21 (Cap. 8),** you learned about indirect object nouns and pronouns. Review both types of object pronouns by identifying the indicated pronouns in the following sentences.

	DIRECT OBJECT	INDIRECT OBJECT
1. El profesor **les** dio la tarea.	☐	☐
2. El profesor **la** asignó para hacer en casa.	☐	☐
3. La profesora **me** vio.	☐	☐
4. La profesora **me** dio la tarea.	☐	☐

26 Avoiding Repetition

Expressing Direct and Indirect Object Pronouns Together

Gramática en acción: La fiesta de Anita

1 Berta le hizo un pastel a Anita y **se lo** dio en la fiesta.

2 Anita le prestó unos aretes a Berta.

3 Berta le sacó una foto a Anita y **se la** mostró.

Comprensión

¿Quién lo dijo? ¿De qué habla?

1. «Me lo hizo para mi cumpleaños.»
2. **«Me los prestó para la fiesta.»**
3. «Se la mostré en el celular.»

¿Y usted?

Describa los siguientes detalles de su último cumpleaños.

1. ¿Un pastel? ¿Alguien se lo hizo? **(Alguien / Nadie me...)**
2. ¿Unas fotos? ¿Alguien se las sacó?
3. ¿Algo de vestir? ¿Alguien se lo prestó?

complemento indirecto		complemento directo
me	+	lo / la / los / las
te	+	lo / la / los / las
(le →) se	+	lo / la / los / las

complemento indirecto		complemento directo
nos	+	lo / la / los / las
os	+	lo / la / los / las
(les) → se	+	lo / la / los / las

Order of Pronouns / **La secuencia de los pronombres**

1. Both Object Pronouns in the Same Sentence

When both an indirect and a direct object pronoun appear in the same sentence, the indirect object pronoun comes first, followed by the direct object pronoun. (This is the opposite of English.) You can remember the order of the Spanish pronouns by thinking of **ID** = **(1)** **I**ndirect **(2)** **D**irect).

¿El almuerzo? **Te lo** sirvo ahora mismo.
Lunch? I'll serve it to you you right now.

¿El trofeo? No **nos lo** dieron.
The trophy? They didn't give it to us.

---

2. Position of Double Object Pronouns

The placement of double object pronouns in relation to the verb is the same as for single object pronouns. The pronouns come:

- before a conjugated verb — ¿El libro? **Me lo dio.**
- after an infinitive or present participle — ¿La carta? Acaban de **mandármela**. Están **mandándomela** hoy.

or

- before the conjugated verb that precedes them — ¿Las cartas? **Me las acaban** de mandar. **Me las están** mandando hoy.
- before a negative command — ¿La comida? **No me la traiga** ahora.
- after an affirmative command — ¿Las bebidas? **Tráigamelas**, por favor.

Using **se** instead of **le** or **les** / **El uso de *se* en vez de *le* o *les***

1. Use of *se*

When both the indirect and the direct object pronouns begin with the letter **l,** the indirect object pronoun *always* changes to **se.**

This change from **le/les** to **se** happens when the indirect object refers to **usted / ustedes** or to a third person singular or plural (**él, ella, ellos, ellas**), the equivalents of English *(I'll give) it/them to you/him/her/them.*

Four pronoun combinations with **se** instead of **le/les** are possible: **se lo, se la, se los, se las.** In these combinations:

- **se** = indirect object pronoun (**le** or **les**)
- **lo/la/los/las** = direct object pronouns (no change)

(1) indirect (2) direct

Les dimos el coche (a ustedes).	*We gave you the car.*
(les lo)	
Se lo dimos.	*We gave it to you.*
Le escribí la carta ayer (a ella).	*I wrote her the letter yesterday.*
(le la)	
Se la escribí ayer.	*I wrote it to her yesterday.*
Le regaló esos zapatos (a él).	*He gave him those shoes.*
(le los)	
Se los regaló.	*He gave them to him.*
Les mandamos a todos las invitaciones. (les las)	*We sent all of them the invitations.*
Se las mandamos.	*We sent them to them.*

---

2. Clarifying *se*

Since **se** can stand for **le** (*to/for you* [sing.], *him, her*) or **les** (*to/for you* [pl.], *them*), it is often necessary to clarify its meaning by using **a** plus the prepositional pronoun.

You learned to clarify the indirect object pronouns **le** and **les** in this way in **Capítulo 8.** This is exactly the same thing, since **se** represents **le** and **les.**

¿La carta de recomendación? Voy a escribír**sela**.
(meaning of **se** unclear unless specified)

¿La carta de recomendación? Voy a escribír**sela** **a usted** / **a ustedes**.
a él / **a ellos.**
a ella / **a ellas.**

Práctica y comunicación

A. Oraciones «familiares»

Paso 1. Autoprueba. Complete las siguientes oraciones con los pronombres apropiados del complemento directo e indirecto: **se lo, se la, se los, se las.**

1. Le dieron el libro. → _______ _______ dieron.
2. Les sirvieron la paella. → _______ _______ sirvieron.
3. Le di las direcciones. → _______ _______ di.
4. Les trajo los boletos. → _______ _______ trajo.

(Continúa.)

Summary of Indirect and Direct Object Pronouns

INDIRECT	DIRECT
me/te/nos/os	+ **lo/la/los/las**
le(s) → **se**	+ **lo/la/los/las**

Prác. A, Paso 1: Answers: 1. *Se lo* ***2.*** *Se la* ***3.*** *Se las* ***4.*** *Se los*

Paso 2. Complete las oraciones con información personal. Las oraciones en **a** se refieren a las acciones que usted hace por otros = usted es el sujeto de la oración. Las oraciones en **b** se refieren a lo que otras personas hacen por usted = esas personas son el sujeto.

1. «¡Te quiero!»:	**a.** Se lo digo a _____.	**b.** Me lo dice _____.
2. «¡Te lo dije!»:	**a.** Se lo digo a _____.	**b.** Me lo dice _____.
3. Regalos:	**a.** Se los doy a _____.	**b.** Me los dan _____.
4. Favores:	**a.** Se los hago a _____.	**b.** Me los hacen _____.

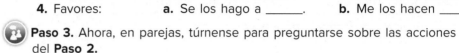

Paso 3. Ahora, en parejas, túrnense para preguntarse sobre las acciones del **Paso 2.**

MODELO: «¡Te quiero!» →
E1: ¿Le dices «¡Te quiero!» a alguien?
E2: Sí, se lo digo a mi madre. ¿Y tú?
E1: Yo también se lo digo a mi madre. / Yo no se lo digo a nadie.

B. En la mesa. Usted todavía tiene hambre. Pida más comida, según el modelo. Preste atención al uso del tiempo presente para pedir algo de manera informal.

MODELO: ensalada → ¿Hay más **ensalada**? ¿Me **la** pasas, por favor?

1. pan	**3.** tomates	**5.** vino
2. tortillas	**4.** fruta	**6.** jamón

C. En el aeropuerto. Cambie los sustantivos por pronombres para evitar (*avoid*) la repetición.

MODELO: ¿La maleta? Van a prestarme **la maleta** mañana. →
Van a prestá**mela** (**Me la** van a prestar) mañana.

1. ¿La hora de la salida? Acaban de decirnos **la hora de la salida**.
2. ¿El horario (*schedule*)? Sí, léame **el horario**, por favor.
3. ¿Los boletos? No, no tiene que darle **los boletos** aquí.
4. ¿El equipaje? ¡Claro que le guardo **el equipaje!**
5. ¿Los boletos? Ya te compré **los boletos**.
6. ¿El puesto? No te preocupes. Te puedo guardar **el puesto**.

Algo sobre...

el son cubano

El son es un género musical cubano que dio lugar[a] al mambo, a la rumba y a la salsa, entre otros bailes. También está presente en el *latin jazz*.

El son se originó en el este de Cuba a finales del siglo XIX[b] con elementos musicales africanos y españoles. A principios[c] del siglo XX llegó a La Habana y de allí salió al mundo. Los grupos soneros originales tocaban[d] con un tres cubano (una guitarra con tres pares de cuerdas[e]), bongós y maracas. Después empezaron a usar la guitarra, el contrabajo[f] y la trompeta.

¿? En su opinión ¿cuál es el género musical de su país que más influencia tiene en el mundo? ¿Qué sabe de esa música?

[a]dio... *gave rise, created* [b]siglo... *19th century* [c]A... *At the beginning* [d]*played* [e]*strings* [f]*string bass*

Celia Cruz (1925–2003), la gran cantante cubana que llevó el son por todo el mundo

D. Minidiálogos

Paso 1. Complete las respuestas usando los pronombres necesarios.

1. —¿Me vas a dar dinero? —¡No! No ______.
2. —¿Por qué no me dices la verdad? —¡Yo siempre ______!
3. —¿Podemos hacerle una fiesta a Paula por su cumpleaños?
   —¡Por supuesto (*Of course*) que ______!
4. —¿Les doy (*Shall I give*) una buena nota final a todos ustedes?
   —Por favor, ¡______!

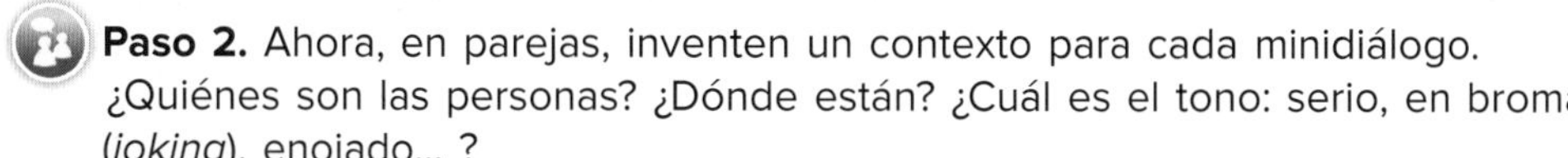

Paso 2. Ahora, en parejas, inventen un contexto para cada minidiálogo. ¿Quiénes son las personas? ¿Dónde están? ¿Cuál es el tono: serio, en broma (*joking*), enojado... ?

E. Regalos

[a]Cartero... *Royal Mail Deliverer*

Paso 1. Conteste las preguntas usando los pronombres del complemento directo e indirecto necesarios en vez de las palabras subrayadas.

1. Según sus tradiciones, ¿los Reyes Magos les traen los regalos a los niños en la madrugada (*night/early morning*) del día 6 de enero?
2. En su familia, ¿Papá Noel les trae regalos en la Nochebuena?
3. ¿Les da regalos usted a sus amigos en diciembre o enero? ¿En qué día?
4. ¿Le da su mejor amigo/a un regalo en diciembre o enero? ¿En qué día?

Paso 2. Ahora, haga una lista de los tres mejores regalos que le han hecho a usted (*you've received*) en su vida (*life*). Piense en los siguientes detalles en cada caso: ¿Quién se lo regaló? ¿Cuándo y por qué se lo dio?

Paso 3. Finalmente, en parejas, túrnense para hablar de los regalos más especiales de su vida. Recuerden usar pronombres para evitar la repetición.

Todo junto

A. Lengua y cultura: La Virgen de Guadalupe, quince siglos (*centuries*) de historia

Paso 1. Completar. Complete the following paragraphs with the correct form of the words in parentheses, as suggested by context. When two possibilities are given in parentheses, select the correct word. Use the present tense or the preterite of the infinitives, according to context.

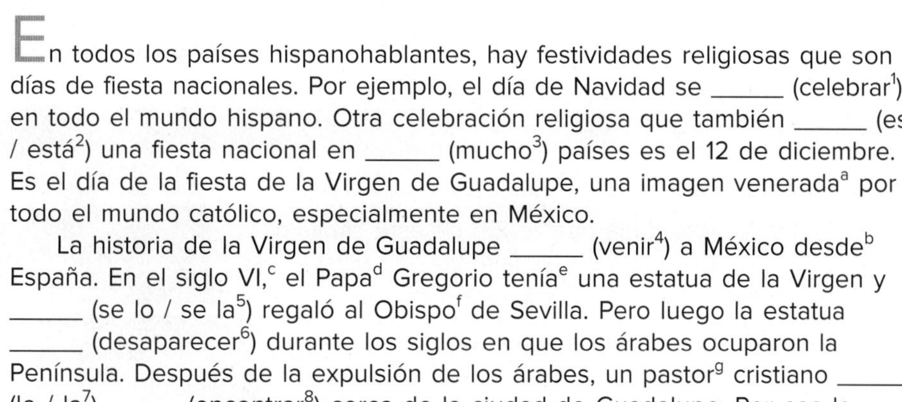

En todos los países hispanohablantes, hay festividades religiosas que son días de fiesta nacionales. Por ejemplo, el día de Navidad se ______ (celebrar[1]) en todo el mundo hispano. Otra celebración religiosa que también ______ (es / está[2]) una fiesta nacional en ______ (mucho[3]) países es el 12 de diciembre. Es el día de la fiesta de la Virgen de Guadalupe, una imagen venerada[a] por todo el mundo católico, especialmente en México.

La historia de la Virgen de Guadalupe ______ (venir[4]) a México desde[b] España. En el siglo VI,[c] el Papa[d] Gregorio tenía[e] una estatua de la Virgen y ______ (se lo / se la[5]) regaló al Obispo[f] de Sevilla. Pero luego la estatua ______ (desaparecer[6]) durante los siglos en que los árabes ocuparon la Península. Después de la expulsión de los árabes, un pastor[g] cristiano ______ (le / la[7]) ______ (encontrar[8]) cerca de la ciudad de Guadalupe. Por eso la estatua ______ (tomar[9]) el nombre de la Virgen de Guadalupe.

[a]imagen... *image venerated, adored* [b]*from* [c]el... *the sixth century* [d]*Pope* [e]*had* [f]*Bishop* [g]*shepherd*

©Beren Patterson/Alamy

La tilma (*shawl*) de Juan Diego en la Basílica de Nuestra Señora (*Lady*) de Guadalupe, en la Ciudad de México

(Continúa.)

En lo que hoy es México, en el siglo XVI, un campesino[h] indígena, Juan Diego, se convirtió[i] al cristianismo. Un día ______ (*él*: ver[10]) a la Virgen en un lugar llamado Tepeyac. Por un milagro,[j] la Virgen ______ (dejar[k11]) su imagen impresa[l] en la tilma de Juan Diego. Esta imagen ______ (recibir[12]) el nombre de Virgen de Guadalupe porque Tepeyac ______ (es / está[13]) cerca del pueblo mexicano de Guadalupe.

La tilma de Juan Diego, con la imagen de la Virgen, todavía se puede ______ (ver[14]) en la Basílica[m] de Nuestra Señora de Guadalupe, en la Ciudad de México.

[h]*peasant* [i]*se... converted* [j]*miracle* [k]*to leave* [l]*imprinted* [m]*large church*

Paso 2. Comprensión. ¿Cierto o falso? Corrija las oraciones falsas.

	CIERTO	FALSO
1. La Virgen de Guadalupe española es una estatua.	☐	☐
2. El Papa Gregorio vio a la Virgen en Tepeyac.	☐	☐
3. El campesino Juan Diego era (*was*) de origen español.	☐	☐
4. La tilma de Juan Diego ya no (*no longer*) existe.	☐	☐

Paso 3. En acción

En parejas, vuelvan a contar la historia de la Virgen de Guadalupe. Primero, hagan una lista de los hechos importantes en la historia, usando infinitivos. Ejemplo: **venir de España.** Luego, cuenten la historia.

B. Proyecto: El Día de...

Para este proyecto van a inventar un día de fiesta nuevo para celebrar algo que no se celebra todavía o no se celebra lo suficiente. Sean creativos: puede ser sobre algo serio o divertido, relacionado con (*related to*) su universidad, su localidad, este país o algo global.

Día de la Madre
¿Quiere decirle a su mamá «gracias, te quiero»?
¡Dígaselo con flores!

Paso 1. Idea. En grupos, elijan un motivo de celebración y un día para celebrarlo. Justifiquen sus elecciones.

Paso 2. Desarrollo. (*Development.*) Ahora desarrollen esa celebración e inventen un mensaje (*slogan*). Piensen en los siguientes detalles.

- La celebración: ¿Qué se puede hacer para celebrar ese día? ¿Con quién se celebra? ¿Dónde?
- Publicidad y mensaje: Creen (*Create*) un mensaje para animar (*urge*) a la gente a celebrar ese día con entusiasmo. Para esto, consideren modelos como el (*that*) de la imagen para el Día de la Madre y de otros días festivos que ustedes conocen (el Día del Padre, el Día de Acción de Gracias, etcétera).

Paso 3. Competición. Toda la clase va a hacer de comité para seleccionar los dos días festivos nuevos del calendario.

¡Ahora, yo!

A. Entrevista. Use de modelo las preguntas y respuestas de la página 271 de este capítulo para hablar de los días festivos que usted celebra.

B. Proyecto audiovisual. Filme una entrevista con una persona hispana no estadounidense en su universidad o su comunidad. Hágale preguntas sobre un día festivo muy especial que se celebra en su ciudad o país, pero que no se celebra en los Estados Unidos.

«De fiesta en fiesta» Segmento 2

Antes de mirar

¿Qué asocia usted con una gran fiesta nacional?

_______ música
_______ comida
_______ mucha gente
_______ banderas (*flags*)
_______ colores patrióticos
_______ celebraciones en la calle (*street*)
_______ ¿ ?

La Fiesta Broadway, una celebración que conmemora una victoria mexicana

Este segmento

Laura presenta un reportaje sobre el Cinco de Mayo, y los presentadores, Ana y Víctor, cierran el programa.

Vocabulario del segmento

sino	but rather	**la manzana**	(city) block
la fuerza invasora	invading force	**el escenario**	stage
ha llegado a ser	has become	**¡Órale!**	Right on!
en grande	in a big way		

Fragmento del guion

ANA: Bueno, con sabor a[a] fiesta mexicana, despedimos[b] el programa de hoy. No se olviden que nos volvemos a ver aquí muy, muy pronto.

VÍCTOR: Hasta entonces, cuídense mucho.[c] Nos vemos pronto.

[a]con… *with the taste of… in mind* [b]*we close* [c]cuídense… *take good care of yourselves*

Después de mirar

A. ¿Está claro? Complete las siguientes oraciones con las cifras (números) que se oyen en el segmento.

1. _____________ fue el año de una victoria mexicana.
2. En la Fiesta Broadway hay _____________ escenarios musicales diferentes.
3. Se calcula que _____________ de personas asisten a la Fiesta Broadway.
4. La Fiesta Broadway ocupa _____________manzanas.

B. Un poco más. Conteste las siguientes preguntas.

1. ¿Dónde tiene lugar (*takes place*) la Fiesta Broadway?
2. ¿Qué tiene de raro (*What's odd about*) la celebración del Cinco de Mayo?
3. ¿Qué otra fiesta muy conocida (*well known*) en los Estados Unidos está asociada con otro grupo nacional?

C. Y ahora, ustedes. En parejas, preparen un segmento informativo sobre una fiesta que se celebra en su ciudad o estado. El segmento debe comenzar con un saludo a los telespectadores y la introducción de ustedes, los presentadores del programa. El segmento debe cerrarse formalmente. Usen el **Fragmento del guion** como modelo para el cierre.

MUNDO HISPANO

Enfoque cultural: Cuba

Antes de leer

¿Hubo en este país alguna época de intolerancia política o religiosa?

Dos días festivos cubanos

En Cuba se conmemoran dos días muy importantes. El primero es el 10 de octubre, que se conoce como el Día de la Independencia Nacional. En este día de 1868, el patriota cubano Carlos Manuel de Céspedes declaró libres a todos los esclavos.[a] También llamó a todos los cubanos a liberarse del dominio[b] colonial de España. Esto marca el inicio[c] de la primera guerra[d] de independencia de Cuba.

El otro día festivo de mucha importancia para los cubanos es la Navidad. Como resultado del cambio[e] político de 1959 y durante muchos de los años bajo el régimen de Fidel Castro, no se les permitió a los cubanos celebrar la Navidad de manera oficial. Todo cambió[f] con la visita a Cuba del Papa[g] Juan Pablo II (segundo) en el año 1998. Desde[h] entonces los cubanos pueden asistir a la iglesia y celebrar este día tan importante con su familia y amigos.

[a]*slaves* [b]*control* [c]*beginning* [d]*war* [e]*change (that is, the regime of Fidel Castro)* [f]*changed* [g]*Pope (Head of the Catholic Church)* [h]*Since*

En otros países hispanos

En todo el mundo hispanohablante Estas festividades se celebran en todas partes.

- **La Semana Santa** Así[a] se llama a la semana que va desde el Domingo de Ramos[b] hasta el Domingo de Pascua. En muchas ciudades hay procesiones[c] para conmemorar la pasión, muerte[d] y resurrección de Jesús. Tiene lugar[e] entre marzo y abril.
- **El Carnaval** Esta fiesta precede al comienzo de la Cuaresma.[f] El Carnaval más famoso del mundo es el[g] de Río de Janeiro (Brasil), pero hay Carnavales hispanos que también son famosos por la exuberancia de su música, bailes y colorido, como los Carnavales de Cádiz (España), Barranquilla (Colombia) y Santiago de Cuba (Cuba).

[a]*That's how* [b]el... *Palm Sunday* [c]*street processions* [d]la... *passion (that is, suffering), death* [e]Tiene... *It takes place* [f]*Lent (period from Ash Wednesday to Good Friday)* [g]*that*

©Purestock/Superstock

Unas palmas reales en La Habana, Cuba

Un símbolo cubano: La palma

La palma real[a] (también llamada palmera en otros países) es un ícono nacional que se encuentra por toda la isla. Forma parte del escudo[b] nacional como símbolo del espíritu cubano: siempre alto y orgulloso.[c] José Martí la menciona en sus famosos versos[d]:

> Yo soy un hombre sincero
> De donde crece[e] la palma,
> Y antes de morirme quiero
> Echar[f] mis versos del alma.[g]

[a]*royal* [b]*coat of arms* [c]*proud* [d]*lines (of a poem)* [e]*grows* [f]*Release* [g]*soul*

Comprensión

1. ¿Cuáles son los días festivos más importantes de Cuba?
2. ¿Desde cuándo se permite celebrar la Navidad sin restricciones otra vez en Cuba?
3. ¿Cuáles son otros de los días festivos importantes del mundo hispano?
4. ¿Cuándo se celebra la Semana Santa?
5. ¿Por qué es la palma un símbolo apropiado del espíritu cubano?

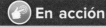

En acción

En parejas, hagan una lista de seis de las cosas que ustedes consideran más simbólicas de este país. Pueden ser un animal, una planta, una canción, un objeto... Busquen en el diccionario las palabras que no saben.

Lectura

Antes de leer

Es muy común hacerse algunos propósitos (*resolutions*) cuando un año empieza. ¿Se los hace usted generalmente? Haga una lista de cuatro propósitos que usted hizo en años pasados o quiso hacer. Use infinitivos en su lista. ¿Pudo cumplirlos todos?

Una declaración de propósitos

12 propósitos para el Año Nuevo

Complete la siguiente declaración:

Yo, ______________________ (nombre), me comprometo[a] a cumplir ________ (número) propósitos de esta lista en los próximos 365 días.

- Leer un libro cada dos meses.
- No excederte en tus horas de trabajo.
- Comer más sano.[b]
- Asistir a una muestra[c] de cine o de arte.
- Comprar la membresía[d] de un gimnasio.
- Tomar dos litros de agua diariamente.
- Ir a una ceremonia religiosa ajena a la tuya.[e]
- Regalar sin razón.
- Desayunar bien.
- Ir a votar.
- Ir de excursión a un lugar remoto.
- Separar la basura[f] en orgánica e inorgánica.

©Ingram Publishing/SuperStock ©Ingram Publishing ©Comstock/PunchStock, ©Royalty Free/Masterfile ©Ekaterina V. Ryabikina/Shutterstock

[a]me... *I promise* [b]más... *in a more healthy manner* [c]*exhibition* [d]*membership* [e]ajena... *different from yours* [f]*garbage*

Vocabulario para leer

cumplir
to meet an expectation/promise

diariamente
daily

Comprensión

A. Tipos de propósitos. Clasifique los propósitos de esta lectura según las tres categorías a continuación (*following*), dando su justificación. (Algunos se pueden poner en más de un grupo.)

1. Los que pueden mejorar la salud (*health*) física
2. Los que pueden mejorar la salud mental o espiritual
3. Los que pueden mejorar las relaciones con otras personas y con el medio ambiente (*environment*)

B. Actitudes hacia el cambio. ¿Se identifica usted con una (o más) de estas actitudes? Explique.

1. Es imposible cambiar (*to change*) los hábitos. Somos como somos y no podemos cambiar.
2. Siempre podemos tener una vida (*life*) mejor y debemos hacer lo posible para conseguirlo (*attain it*).
3. Es difícil cambiar nuestros hábitos, pero es posible hacerlo con un propósito firme y mucho apoyo (*support*) de la familia y los amigos.

Proyecto: Cumplir un propósito para el Año Nuevo

Paso 1. Elija (*Choose*) un propósito de la lista de la lectura u otro diferente que usted se compromete (*commit*) a cumplir para el Año Nuevo (o antes).

Paso 2. Escriba un plan que usted puede seguir para cumplir su propósito. Incluya por lo menos tres de las cosas que debe hacer y el tipo de ayuda que va a necesitar de sus amigos, parejas o parientes.

Paso 3. Comparta (*Share*) su plan con sus compañeros de clase para saber cómo reaccionan y oír sus sugerencias.

Textos orales

El mensaje telefónico de Pilar

Antes de escuchar

¿Qué actividades generalmente se hacen en una boda (*wedding*)? Haga una lista de todas las actividades que pueda imaginar. Consulte el **Vocabulario para escuchar** al hacer (*while making*) su lista.

Vocabulario para escuchar

¡qué lástima!	what a shame!	**tirar**	to throw, toss
los novios	bride and groom	**lo sintió mucho**	was very sorry
cortar	to cut	**el recuerdo**	souvenir, party favor
ensuciarse la cara	to dirty each other's faces		

Comprensión

A. ¿Quién hizo qué? Indique quién hizo qué, emparejando las acciones con las personas que las hicieron. Hay más de una opción en algunos casos.

	ACCIONES	PERSONAS
________	**1.** bailar	**a.** Estela
________	**2.** cortar el pastel y tirarlo	**b.** un conjunto (*group*) musical
________	**3.** llorar	**c.** Pilar
________	**4.** mandar un recuerdo	**d.** la mamá de Estela
________	**5.** tocar salsa	**e.** los novios
________	**6.** no ir a la boda	**f.** la amiga de Pilar y de Estela

B. Más información. ¿Qué más se sabe o deduce usted del mensaje?

1. La amiga de Pilar, ¿es amiga de Estela también?
2. ¿Cómo se llama el novio?
3. ¿Por qué no fue la amiga de Pilar a la boda?
4. ¿Por qué cree Pilar que su amiga no contesta su llamada (*call*)?
5. ¿Cuál es la profesión de la amiga de Pilar?

En acción

Describa algo curioso o diferente que ocurrió en una celebración reciente. ¿Qué y cómo ocurrió? ¿Dónde? ¿Cuándo? ¿Quién lo hizo? ¿A quién o a quiénes afectó?

Proyecto en su comunidad

Entreviste a una persona hispana de su universidad o ciudad sobre las celebraciones tradicionales de su país y de su familia.

Preguntas posibles

- ¿Cuáles son los días festivos más importantes de su país? ¿Son celebraciones de origen civil o religioso? ¿Se celebran en familia? ¿También hay eventos en la ciudad?
- ¿Cuáles son las celebraciones más importantes en su familia? ¿Y sus favoritas?
- ¿Cuál fue la última fiesta que usted celebró en su país? ¿Cómo y con quién la celebró?

Escritura

Proyecto: Un ensayo sobre una celebración memorable

¿Cuál es la celebración más memorable de su vida (*life*)? ¿un baile de fin de curso (*prom night*)? ¿una boda (*wedding*)? ¿un cumpleaños? ¿una fiesta de Nochevieja? ¿el bautizo (*baptism*) de una hija o un hijo? ¿Qué es memorable de esa celebración?

©moodboard/Alamy

©Purestock/Superstock

©Cultura Creative/Alamy

©Ariel Skelley/Blend Images LLC

Antes de escribir

En parejas, hagan una lista de los aspectos que su ensayo debe incluir, sin olvidar lo que más le gustó.

A escribir

Use las ideas de **Antes de escribir** para escribir su ensayo. Debe expresar sus sentimientos o los (*those*) de otras personas que estuvieron o no estuvieron en la celebración. Hay más ayuda en Connect.

Más ideas para su portafolio

- Escriba una o dos oraciones sobre unos momentos emocionantes de su vida (*life*): cuándo se puso más feliz (rojo/a, triste...), cuándo lloró más desconsoladamente (*nonstop*) o se rio con más ganas (*most uproariously*), etcétera.
- Escriba unas oraciones sobre una fiesta de un país hispanohablante a la que (*which*) usted quiere asistir algún día.
- Si ha estado jugando (*you have been playing*) Practice Spanish: Study Abroad, en Quest 6 usted pasó tiempo en el museo del pueblo. Si hay una galería de arte en su ciudad o en el campus de su universidad haga un afiche (*poster*) o un folleto (*brochure*) con información sobre la galería para la comunidad hispanohablante.

©McGraw-Hill Education

Sugerencia: You are now ready to play Quest 6 in **Practice Spanish: Study Abroad.**

EN RESUMEN En este capítulo

AFTER STUDYING THIS CHAPTER I CAN . . .

- ☐ talk about holidays (272–273)
- ☐ express more feelings and emotions (275)
- ☐ use more types of verbs in the preterite (278–279, 282–283)
- ☐ understand double object pronouns and use them to avoid repetition (286–287)
- ☐ recognize/describe at least 2–3 aspects of Cuban cultures

Gramática en breve

24. Irregular Preterites

Irregular Preterite Endings

Stems		Endings	
estuv-, pud-, pus-, quis-, sup-, tuv-, vin-	=	-e	-imos
		-iste	-isteis
		-o	-ieron
dij-, traj-	=	-e	-imos
		-iste	-isteis
		-o	-eron

hay: haber ⟶ hubo (*there was/were*)

25. Preterite of Stem-changing Verbs

Preterite Stem-changing Patterns

-ar/-er = no change

-ir = change in the third person singular and plural

e ⟶ i

o ⟶ u

26. Direct and Indirect Object Pronouns Together

Indirect	Direct
me/te/nos/os	**lo/la/los/las**
le(s) ⟶ se	

Vocabulario

Los verbos

adivinar	to guess
conseguir (*like* **seguir**)	to get; to obtain
conseguir +*inf.*	to succeed in (*doing something*)
despedirse (*like* **pedir**) **(de)**	to say good-bye (to)
encontrar (encuentro)	to find
morirse (me muero) (u)	to die
sugerir (sugiero) (i)	to suggest

Repaso: divertirse (me divierto) (i), dormir(se) ([me] duermo) (u), pedir (pido) (i), preferir (prefiero) (i), seguir (sigo) (i), servir (sirvo) (i), vestirse (me visto) (i)

Los días festivos y las fiestas

el anfitrión, la anfitriona	host (*of an event*)
las botanas (*Mex.*)	appetizers
el champán	champagne
el/la invitado/a	guest
el pastel de cumpleaños	birthday cake
las tapas	appetizers
la vela	candle
el día festivo	holiday

Repaso: el cumpleaños, la fiesta, el pastel, el refresco, el regalo, la tarjeta

cumplir años	to have a birthday
darle una fiesta (a alguien)	to give (someone) a party; to have a party (for someone)
faltar (a)	to be absent (from); to not attend
gastar	to spend (*money*)
hacerle una fiesta (a alguien)	to give (someone) a party; to have a party (for someone)
pasarlo bien/mal	to have a good/bad time
reunirse (me reúno) (con)	to get together (with)
ser en + *place*	to take place in/at (*a place*)

Repaso: bailar, beber, celebrar, comer, divertirse (me divierto) (i), invitar, regalar

Las emociones y los estados afectivos

el estado afectivo	emotional state
discutir con (alguien) por/sobre (algo)	to argue with (someone) about (something)
enojarse con (alguien) por (algo)	to get angry with (someone) about (something)
llorar	to cry
olvidar	to forget (about)
ponerse + *adj./adv.*	to become, get + *adj./adv.*
ponerse rojo/a	to blush
portarse bien/mal	to (mis)behave
recordar (recuerdo)	to remember
reírse (me río) (i) (de)	to laugh (about)
sentirse (me siento) (i) + *adj./adv.*	to feel + *adj./adv.*
sonreír (sonrío) (i)	to smile

Repaso: estar, quejarse (de)

Otros sustantivos

el árbol	tree
el detalle	detail
el fin de año	end of the year
el hecho	fact; event

Los adjetivos

avergonzado/a	embarrassed
enojado/a	angry; upset
feliz (*pl.* **felices**)	happy
festivo/a	festive, celebratory
tranquilo/a	calm
-ísimo/a	very very

Repaso: alegre, contento/a, furioso/a, nervioso/a, triste

Algunos días festivos

la Navidad	Christmas
la Nochebuena	Christmas Eve
la Nochevieja	New Year's Eve
la Pascua	Easter
la quinceañera	young woman's fifteenth birthday party

Palabras adicionales

demasiado (*adv.*)	too; too much
¡Felicitaciones!	Congratulations!
gracias por + *noun* or *inf.*	thanks for
por lo menos	at least
ya	already
-ísimo (*adv.*)	very very

Repaso: muchísimo

Vocabulario personal

El tiempo libre°

El... *Free time*

En este capítulo

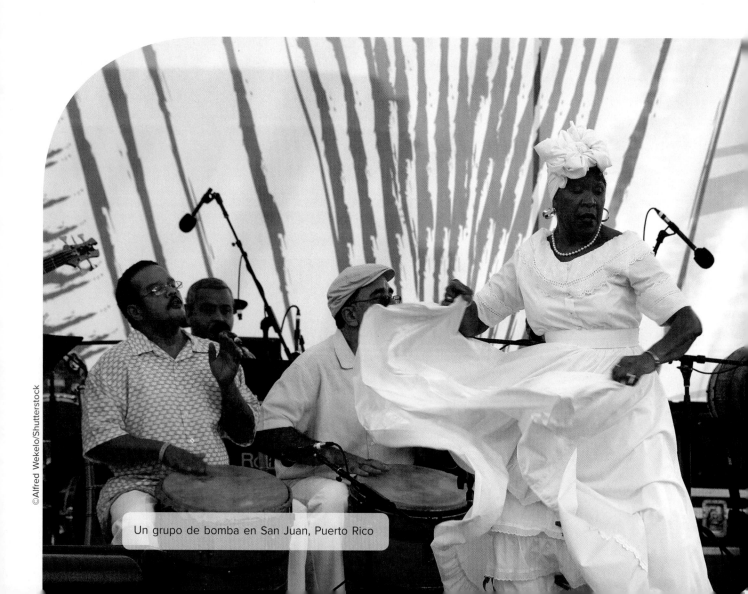

Un grupo de bomba en San Juan, Puerto Rico

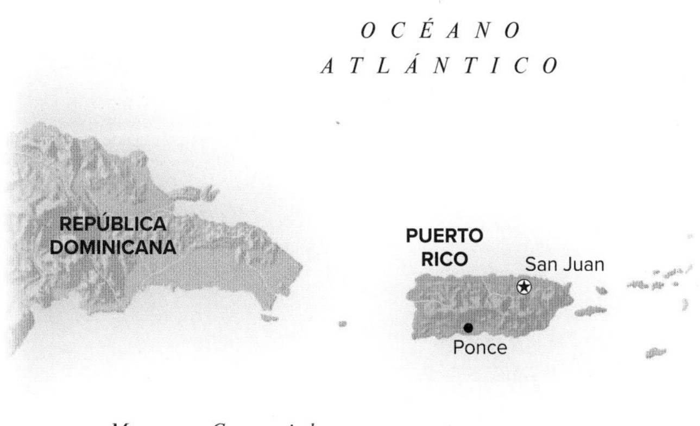

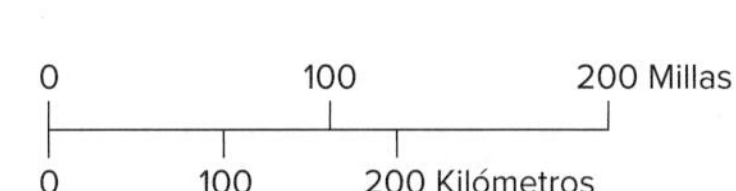

PUERTO RICO

3,6 (coma seis) millones de habitantes

- Puerto Rico es un Estado Libre Asociado a los Estados Unidos. Esto significa que Puerto Rico no es independiente, pero sí tiene autonomía interna. Los puertorriqueños son ciudadanos[a] estadounidenses.
- Los puertorriqueños tienen una gran conciencia[b] de su historia y de la importancia de su cultura. Se sienten muy orgullosos[c] de su herencia indígena, africana e hispana.

[a]*citizens* [b]*awareness* [c]*proud*

ENTREVISTA

- ¿Qué le gusta a usted hacer en su tiempo libre? ¿Prefiere las actividades al aire libre[a]? ¿O prefiere las actividades sedentarias?
- ¿Es el baile una de sus diversiones preferidas? ¿Qué tipo de música le gusta más para bailar?
- ¿Tiene que pasar a veces parte de su tiempo libre haciendo quehaceres domésticos[b]?

[a]al... *outdoor* [b]quehaceres... *household tasks*

Cecilia Figueroa Martín contesta las preguntas.

- En mi tiempo libre, además de[a] descansar, me gusta hacer cosas con mi familia y con mis amigos. Algunas de las actividades que me gustan son sedentarias, como leer, ver películas, jugar al dominó y a las cartas. Pero también juego al tenis y me encanta nadar en el mar.
- ¡Claro que sí![b] Ahora no bailo tanto como cuando era[c] joven, pero me encanta bailar siempre que[d] puedo. Cualquier[e] tipo de música: pop, rock, salsa, merengue... lo que sea.[f]
- ¡Quién no! Tengo dos niños chicos.[g] Pero, en mi opinión, hacer los quehaceres domésticos no es parte del tiempo libre. ¡Es otro trabajo[h]!

[a]además... *besides* [b]¡Claro... *Of course!* [c]*I was* [d]siempre... *whenever* [e]*Any* [f]lo... *whatever* [g]niños... *small, young kids* [h]*job*

VOCABULARIO: PREPARACIÓN

You can hear the pronunciation of theme vocabulary words and phrases in the Connect eBook.

Los pasatiempos, diversiones y aficiones°

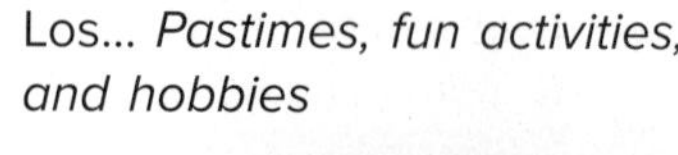
Los... *Pastimes, fun activities, and hobbies*

©Comstock Images/Alamy

montar a caballo

©David Planchet

caminar

©Ingram Publishing/SuperStock

hacer (el) yoga

©IM_photo/Shutterstock

esquiar (esquío), el esquí

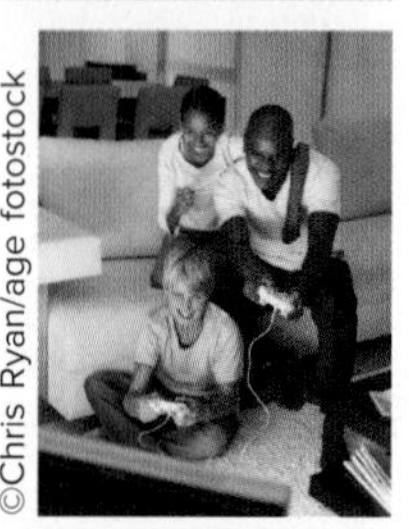
©Chris Ryan/age fotostock

jugar (juego) (gu) a los videojuegos

©Mark Andersen/Getty Images

correr

©Image Source/Alamy

dar una caminata

©Chris Ryan/age fotostock

ir a una fiesta

Los pasatiempos

los ratos libres	spare (free) time
dar/hacer una fiesta	to give a party
dar un paseo	to take a walk
hacer *camping*	to go camping
hacer planes (*m.*) **para** + *inf.*	to make plans to (*do something*)
hacer un pícnic	to have a picnic
ir...	to go . . .
a un bar / a una discoteca	to a bar / to a disco
a un museo	to a museum
a ver una película	to see a movie
al cine	to the movies
al teatro / a un concierto	to the theatre / to a concert
jugar (juego) (gu) a las cartas / al ajedrez	to play cards/chess
sacar (qu) fotos/fotografías	to take pictures
tomar el sol	to sunbathe
aburrirse	to get bored
ser...	to be . . .
aburrido/a	boring
divertido/a	fun

Los deportes

el ciclismo	bicycling
el fútbol	soccer
el fútbol americano	football
montar/pasear en bicicleta	to ride a bicycle
nadar	to swim
la natación	swimming
el patinaje	skating
patinar	to skate
surfear	to surf

Cognados: el basquetbol, el béisbol, el golf, el hockey, el tenis, el voleibol

el equipo	team
el jugador / la jugadora	player
el partido	game, match
la pelota	ball
entrenar	to practice; to train
ganar	to win
jugar (juego) (gu) al + *sport*	to play (*a sport*)
perder (pierdo)	to lose
practicar (qu)	to participate (*in a sport*)
ser aficionado/a (a)	to be a fan (of)

Comunicación

A. El tiempo libre

Paso 1. ¿Cierto o falso? Corrija las oraciones falsas, según su opinión.

	CIERTO	FALSO
1. Es más aburrido ver un partido en la tele que en el estadio.	☐	☐
2. Lo paso mejor con mi familia que con mis amigos.	☐	☐
3. Las actividades creativas y artísticas me gustan más que las deportivas (*sport-related ones*).	☐	☐
4. Odio el béisbol tanto como el fútbol.	☐	☐
5. Los estudiantes universitarios tienen tanto tiempo libre como los (*those*) de la escuela secundaria.	☐	☐
6. La mejor actividad para un viernes por la noche es estudiar.	☐	☐
7. Jugar al ajedrez es más aburrido que jugar a las cartas.	☐	☐
8. No me gustan las actividades al aire libre (*outdoor*).	☐	☐

Paso 2. Ahora haga una lista de sus pasatiempos favoritos y de los que usted odia o no le interesan.

Paso 3. Compare su lista con la (*that*) de un compañero o una compañera de clase con quien usted no habla con frecuencia. ¿Les gustan los mismos pasatiempos?

B. Definiciones

Paso 1. Dé las palabras definidas.

MODELO: entrar en un lugar para ver una película → ir al cine

1. un grupo de jugadores
2. salir bien en una competencia; salir mal
3. practicar un deporte intensamente
4. asistir a todos los partidos de un equipo en particular
5. un deporte que se practica en una piscina

Paso 2. Ahora defina las siguientes palabras, según el modelo del **Paso 1.**

1. un jugador
2. un partido
3. aburrirse
4. hacer un pícnic
5. dar un paseo

Así se dice

el basquetbol = el baloncesto (*Sp.*)
dar una caminata = hacer senderismo (*Sp.*)
hacer *camping* = hacer acampada, acampar
pasear en bicicleta = andar en bicicleta, montar en bicicleta
la película = el filme, el film
surfear = hacer *surf* (*P.R.*)
el voleibol = el vólibol, el volibol

Nota cultural

Los deportes más populares del mundo hispano

Dos deportes predominan en el panorama deportivo del mundo hispano: el fútbol y el béisbol.

- **El fútbol** Sin duda este es el rey[a] de los deportes en el mundo hispano, como en el resto del mundo. Ningún evento deportivo se compara en seguimiento[b] a la Copa Mundial de Fútbol, en la cual[c] compiten regularmente muchas naciones hispanohablantes. En todos los países hispanos, el fútbol se juega en cualquier calle,[d] plaza o espacio abierto y hay innumerables ligas[e] de todo tipo.
- **El béisbol** Un deporte inmensamente popular en los países de la costa caribeña es el béisbol. En las grandes ligas estadounidenses hay muchos jugadores de primer orden con apellidos hispanos. Muchos de estos «peloteros[f]», como se les llama[g] en muchos países, vienen de las ligas de sus respectivos países de origen, como la República Dominicana, Venezuela y México.
- **El basquetbol, el tenis y el ciclismo** Estos deportes también tienen gran seguimiento en el mundo hispano. El basquetbol está creciendo[h] en cuanto al[i] número de espectadores y tiene dos grandes potencias[j] hispanas: España y la Argentina. Estos países tienen varios jugadores en la NBA estadounidense.

©UPI/Terry Schmitt/Newscom

El equipo nacional de béisbol puertorriqueño, que celebra una victoria

¿Qué otros deportistas hispanos puede usted nombrar?

[a]*king* [b]*following* [c]la... *which* [d]cualquier... *any street* [e]*leagues* [f]*ball-players* [g]se... *they are called*

[h]*growing* [i]en... *as far as the* [j]*superpowers*

C. ¿Cómo pasa usted su tiempo?

Paso 1. Complete la tabla con el tiempo medio (*average*) que usted pasa diariamente haciendo las actividades indicadas.

Paso 2. Ahora, en parejas, hagan comparaciones sobre el tiempo que ustedes pasan haciendo las actividades de cada categoría. Díganle a la clase algo que tienen en común.

MODELO: **E1:** ¿Cuánto tiempo pasas en los estudios?
E2: Paso cinco horas aproximadamente. ¿Y tú?
E1: Yo paso seis horas. Yo paso más horas estudiando que tú.

Actividad	Media[a] de tiempo diario (aproximada)
Estudios	
Vida[b] social con los amigos (en persona o a distancia)	
Vida familiar	
Tareas domésticas	
Deportes	
Ver medios de comunicación[c]	
Leer por placer	
Otras actividades	

[a]*Average* [b]*Life* [c]medios... *media*

D. Actividades del año pasado

Paso 1. Indique todas las actividades en que usted participó o que hizo por lo menos una vez el año pasado.

1. Fui a una fiesta. ☐
2. Di una caminata por el bosque (*forest*). ☐
3. Hice *camping*. ☐
4. Jugué a un juego de mesa (las cartas, el ajedrez, *Life*™...) ☐
5. Saqué fotos. ☐
6. Monté en bicicleta. ☐
7. Hice yoga. ☐
8. Corrí. ☐
9. Nadé. ☐
11. Entrené con un equipo. ☐
12. Gané/Perdí un partido/una competición. ☐

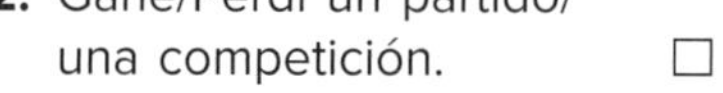

Paso 2. En parejas, comparen sus respuestas y compartan (*share*) con la clase dos de las actividades que hicieron y dos de las (*those*) que no hicieron. También deben dar unos detalles interesantes.

MODELO: Ernesto y yo hicimos caminatas y corrimos. No hicimos *camping*. Tampoco sacamos fotos. Yo entrené con el equipo de natación de la universidad. Perdí todas las competiciones. Ernesto fue a muchas fiestas y también jugó al ajedrez con frecuencia.

Los quehaceres domésticos°

Los... *Household chores*

limpiar (la casa)°

limpiar... *to clean (house)*

barrer el piso

pasar la aspiradora

planchar la ropa

hacer la cama

sacar (qu) la basura

lavar los platos

poner la mesa

quitar la mesa

Algunos aparatos domésticos

la aspiradora	vacuum cleaner	**la lavadora**	washing machine
la cafetera	coffee maker	**el lavaplatos**	dishwasher
el congelador	freezer	**el refrigerador**	refrigerator
la estufa	stove	**la secadora**	clothes dryer
el horno de microondas	microwave oven	**la tostadora**	toaster

Comunicación

A. Los quehaceres domésticos. ¿En qué cuarto o parte de la casa se hacen las siguientes actividades? Hay más de una respuesta en muchos casos.

1. Se hace la cama en _____.
2. Se saca la basura de _____ y se pone en _____.
3. Uno se baña en _____ pero baña al perro en _____.
4. Se barre el piso del / de la _____.
5. Se pasa la aspiradora en _____.
6. Se lava y se seca la ropa en _____.
7. La ropa se plancha en _____.
8. Se usa la cafetera en _____.

B. Las marcas. (*Brand names.*) ¿Para qué se usan o para qué sirven los siguientes productos?

MODELO: Mr. Coffee™ → Mr. Coffee sirve para hacer el café.

1. Windex™
2. Glad™ bags
3. Lysol™
4. Tide™
5. Cascade™
6. Palmolive™

C. Intercambios

Paso 1. En parejas, túrnense para hacer y contestar preguntas sobre cómo pasan ustedes el fin de semana. Basen sus preguntas en las siguientes ideas. Deben obtener detalles interesantes y personales de su compañero/a.

1. qué día y a qué hora (más o menos) empiezan el fin de semana
2. cómo se divierten
3. cuánta tarea hacen
4. cuánto duermen (¿por la noche? ¿la siesta?)
5. los quehaceres domésticos que tienen que hacer
6. cómo se sienten el domingo por la noche

Paso 2. Díganle a la clase dos detalles interesantes sobre lo que hace su compañero/a.

Así se dice

el congelador = la nevera
la estufa = la cocina
hacer la cama = tender la cama
lavar los platos = fregar los platos
el refrigerador = el frigorífico, la heladera, la nevera, la refrigeradora

Vocabulario útil

se usa para...
sirve para

el fregadero sink

Algo sobre...

el coquí

Los coquíes son ranas[a] de varias especies de un género[b] nativo de Puerto Rico. Son muy pequeños (alrededor de una pulgada[c]) y viven en los árboles.[d] Su nombre es una versión onomatopéyica del sonido[e] que algunas especies de coquíes machos[f] hacen cuando cantan desde la caída del sol[g] hasta el amanecer.[h] La canción del coquí se puede oír por toda la isla y por eso esta ranita es uno de los grandes símbolos puertorriqueños. Desgraciadamente, los coquíes están en peligro[i] de extinción.

¿Qué animales son considerados símbolos de su estado o país? ¿Por qué lo representan?

[a]*frogs* [b]*genus* [c]alrededor... *about an inch* [d]*trees* [e]*sound* [f]*male* [g]caída... *sunset* [h]*dawn* [i]*danger*

©Geordie Torr/Alamy

Un coquí puertorriqueño

Nota comunicativa

Cómo expresar la obligación

You already know several ways to express the obligation to do something.

Tengo que **Necesito** **Debo**	barrer el piso.	*I have to* *I need to* *I should, must*	*sweep the floor.*

Of the three, **deber** + *infinitive* expresses the strongest sense of obligation (like a moral obligation), and **tener que** expresses the greatest sense of urgency or immediacy. **Tener que** is the most frequently used for everyday commitments.

The concept *to be someone's turn or responsibility* (to do something) is expressed in Spanish with the verb **tocar (qu)** plus an indirect object.

—**¿A quién le toca** lavar los platos esta noche?	*"Whose turn is it to wash the dishes tonight?"*
—**A mí me toca** sacar la basura. Creo que **a papá le toca** lavar los platos.	*"It's my turn to take out the garbage. I think it's Dad's turn to wash the dishes."*

You will use these expressions in **Comunicación D** and **E.**

D. Las tareas domésticas de esta semana

Paso 1. ¿Tiene usted que hacer los quehaceres de la siguiente lista esta semana? Conteste usando los verbos de la **Nota comunicativa.** Si tiene que hacerlos, diga cuándo. Si no tiene que hacerlos, puede decir: **No me toca ________ (quehacer) esta semana.**

MODELO: 1. hacer la cama →
Necesito / Tengo que hacer la cama todos los días.

1. hacer la cama
2. poner la mesa
3. lavar los platos
4. lavar la ropa
5. planchar la ropa
6. sacar la basura
7. pasar la aspiradora
8. barrer el piso
9. limpiar el piso
10. ¿ ?

Paso 2. Ahora, en parejas, túrnense para entrevistarse sobre sus hábitos domésticos, basándose en el **Paso 1.** De los dos, ¿quién se preocupa más por su hogar (*home*)? ¿por la limpieza (*cleanliness*)? ¿Quién mantiene (*keeps*) más limpia la casa?

MODELO: hacer la cama →
E1: ¿Con qué frecuencia haces la cama? (¿A quién **le toca** hacer las camas en tu casa?)
E2: La hago todos los días. / La hago a veces. (En mi casa, **le toca** a mi madre hacer las camas.)

E. Las obligaciones. Piense en las cosas que todos tenemos que hacer, no solo las tareas domésticas. ¿Cuáles son las obligaciones que no le gustan a usted para nada? ¿Cuáles son las (*those*) que hace de buena gana (*willingly*)? Dígale a la clase una de las obligaciones en cada categoría.

«Deportes que mueven masas» Segmento 1

Antes de mirar

¿Qué deportes le gustan a usted? ¿Es usted aficionado/a o lo(s) practica?

- ☐ el basquetbol
- ☐ el béisbol
- ☐ el fútbol
- ☐ el fútbol americano
- ☐ la lucha libre (*wrestling*)
- ☐ otros: _______

El Museo del Deporte de Puerto Rico es un lugar maravilloso (*wonderful*) para las personas de todas las edades (*ages*) y especialmente para los aficionados al béisbol, el deporte rey (*number one*) de los puertorriqueños.

Este segmento

Ana y Víctor introducen un programa sobre los deportes, que incluye un reportaje sobre el Museo del Deporte en Puerto Rico.

Vocabulario del segmento

veamos	let's see	**de primer orden**	first rate	**el campeonato**	championship
de hecho	in fact	**el pelotero**	**el beisbolista**	**las destrezas**	skills
yo jugaba	I played	**el lanzador**	pitcher	**recaen en**	fall on, are the responsibility of
la magnitud	size	**el compromiso**	commitment		
los comienzos	beginnings	**el fuerte de enseñanza**	teaching strength	**han practicado**	have played
el lugar de nacimiento	birthplace				

Después de mirar

A. ¿Está claro? Empareje los años con los acontecimientos (*events*) importantes del béisbol.

LOS AÑOS

____ **1.** 1942
____ **2.** 1898
____ **3.** 1973
____ **4.** a fines del siglo XIX (*at the end of the 19th century*)
____ **5.** la década de 1940

LOS ACONTECIMIENTOS

a. Los norteamericanos empezaron a llegar a Puerto Rico.
b. Los Estados Unidos tomaron posesión de Puerto Rico después de ganar una guerra (*war*) contra España.
c. El primer pelotero puertorriqueño jugó para los Chicago Cubs en las Grandes Ligas (*Leagues*).
d. Terminó la segregación entre blancos y negros en los equipos estadounidenses de béisbol.
e. El primer beisbolista hispano entró en el Salón de la Fama.

B. Un poco más. Conteste las siguientes preguntas.

1. ¿Qué deportes le gustan a Víctor? ¿Y qué equipos?
2. ¿A qué pelotero se le otorga (*is awarded*) anualmente el Premio (*Prize*) Roberto Clemente?
3. Según el Director del Museo, ¿quiénes son las personas más importantes en la enseñanza de los jóvenes beisbolistas puertorriqueños?
4. ¿Qué tipo de visitantes recibe el museo?

C. Y ahora, ustedes. En parejas, hablen sobre los deportes más populares en su universidad. ¿Cuáles son? ¿De qué manera son populares, por el número de aficionados o por el número de jugadores? ¿Eran (*Were*) esos mismos deportes los más populares en su escuela secundaria?

GRAMÁTICA

¿Recuerda usted?

In **Capítulos 8** and **9,** you learned the forms and some uses of the preterite. Before you learn the other simple past tense (in **Gramática 27**), you might want to review the forms of the preterite in those chapters. The verbs in the following sentences are in the preterite. Can you identify any words in the sentences that emphasize the completed nature of the actions expressed by the verbs?

1. Esta mañana me levanté a las seis.
2. Ayer fui al cine con un amigo.
3. La semana pasada saqué la basura todos los días.

27 Talking About the Past (Part 4)

Descriptions and Habitual Actions in the Past: Imperfect of Regular and Irregular Verbs

Gramática en acción: Los indígenas taínos

Antillas Mayores

- Los taínos eran los habitantes originales de las Antillas Mayores, que son las islas de Jamaica, Puerto Rico, Cuba y La Española (que incluye los países de la República Dominicana y Haití).
- Estos indígenas vivían allí cuando llegaron los españoles en el siglo XV.
- El pueblo taíno era pacífico y generoso.
- Tenían una sociedad matrilineal.
- Llamaban «cacique» a su jefe y «Borinquen» a su isla.
- Las palabras *hamaca, huracán, canoa, tabaco* y *barbacoa* eran parte de la lengua que hablaban.

Comprensión

1. ¿De cuántas islas están formadas las Antillas Mayores?
2. ¿Cómo era el pueblo taíno?

¿Y usted?

1. ¿Qué significan en inglés las últimas palabras del párrafo?
2. ¿Conoce algunos de los pueblos que vivían en lo que hoy son los Estados Unidos cuando llegaron los europeos?

The Taíno Indians *The Taíno Indians were the original inhabitants of the Greater Antilles, which are the islands of Jamaica, Puerto Rico, Cuba, and Hispaniola (which includes the countries of the Dominican Republic and Haiti). • These natives were living there when the Spanish arrived in the 15th century. • The Taíno people were peaceful and generous. • They had a matrilineal society. • They called their leader* "cacique" *and their island* "Borinquen." *• The words* hamaca, huracán, canoa, tabaco, *and* barbacoa *were part of the language they spoke.*

You have already used the *preterite* (**el pretérito**) to express events in the past. The *imperfect* (**el imperfecto**) is the second simple past tense in Spanish. The preterite is used when you view actions or states of being as begun or completed in the past. The imperfect is used when you view past actions or states of being as habitual or as "in progress." It is also used for describing the past, especially for giving background details.

Forms of the Imperfect / **Las formas del imperfecto**

hablar		comer		vivir	
hablaba	**hablábamos**	**comía**	**comíamos**	**vivía**	**vivíamos**
hablabas	**hablabais**	**comías**	**comíais**	**vivías**	**vivíais**
hablaba	**hablaban**	**comía**	**comían**	**vivía**	**vivían**

¡OJO!

Note that the first and third person singular forms are identical for **-ar, -er,** and **-ir** verbs. When context does not make meaning clear, subject pronouns are used.

Los sábados **yo jugaba** al tenis y **él paseaba** en bicicleta.
On Saturdays I used to play tennis and he used to ride his bike.

Pronunciation Hints

- The **b** between vowels, such as in the imperfect ending **-aba,** is pronounced as a *soft* [b] sound.
- In **-er/-ir** imperfect forms, it is important not to pronounce the ending **-ía** as a diphthong, but to pronounce the **i** and the **a** in separate syllables. The accent mark over the **í** helps remind you of this.

Los verbos en *-ar*		Los verbos en *-er/-ir*	
-aba	**-ábamos**	**-ía**	**-íamos**
-abas	**-abais**	**-ías**	**-íais**
-aba	**-aban**	**-ía**	**-ían**

1. English Equivalents

As you can see at the right, the imperfect has several English equivalents. Most of them indicate that the action was still in progress (*was/were -ing*) or that it was habitual (*used to, would*).

yo hablaba = *I spoke, I was speaking, I used to speak, I would speak*
comíamos = *we ate, we were eating, we used to eat, we would eat*
él vivía = *he lived, he was living, he used to live, he would live*

¡OJO!

The simple English equivalents in the box (*I spoke, we ate, he lived*) can correspond to either the preterite or the imperfect, but it usually corresponds to the preterite. You'll learn more about this in **Capítulo 11.**

The word *would* is also an English equivalent of the imperfect. But keep in mind that *would* expresses two different things in English: a repeated action in the past and a hypothetical situation. The Spanish imperfect is used only in the first case. (Hypothetical situations are expressed with other tenses in Spanish. You have learned to use **gustaría** to express *I would like*. You will learn more about this in **Capítulo 18**.)

¡OJO!

would = repeated action → imperfect

Comíamos allí todos los domingos.
We would eat there every Sunday.

¡Cuando era joven, **jugaba** al fútbol todo el día en el verano!
When I was young, I would play soccer all day long in the summer!

BUT

Me **gustaría** dar un paseo hoy.
I would like to take a walk today.

2. Stem-changing Verbs and *hay*

Stem-changing verbs do not show a change in the imperfect.

almorzar (almuerzo) → almorzaba, almorzabas,...
perder (pierdo) → perdía, perdías,...
pedir (pido) (i) → pedía, pedías,...

The imperfect of **hay** is **había**. It means *there was, there were,* or *there used to be*, and its form never changes.

Había muchos estudiantes en el salón de clase.
There were a lot of students in the class.

3. Irregular Imperfect Forms
Only three verbs are irregular in the imperfect: **ir**, **ser**, and **ver**.

ir		ser		ver	
iba	íbamos	era	éramos	veía	veíamos
ibas	ibais	eras	erais	veías	veíais
iba	iban	era	eran	veía	veían

Uses of the Imperfect / **Los usos del imperfecto**

If you know when to use the imperfect, it will be easy to understand when the preterite is used. When talking about the past, the preterite *is* used when the imperfect *isn't.* That's an oversimplification, but at the same time it's a general rule of thumb that will help you out at first.

The imperfect has the following uses. Notice that the first three have clear English equivalents. Also, pay attention to the words that indicate time and frequency.

1. To describe *repeated habitual actions* in the past

used to / would } + *verb*

De niños, **siempre jugábamos** en el parque todas las tardes.
As children, we always played (used to play, would play) in the park in the afternoon.

Todos los agostos, mi familia **iba** a la playa.
Every August my family went (used to go, would go) to the beach.

2. To describe an *action that was in progress* (when something else happened)

was/were + *-ing*

Ramón **pedía** la cena (cuando Cristina **llamó**).
Ramón was ordering dinner (when Cristina called).

Los taínos **vivían** en Puerto Rico (cuando **llegó** Colón).
The Taíno Indians were living in Puerto Rico (when Columbus arrived).

3. To describe two *simultaneous past actions in progress,* with **mientras**

was/were + *-ing*

Tú **leías mientras** Juan **escribía** la carta.
You were reading while Juan was writing the letter.

Mientras yo **veía** la tele, los niños **jugaban** a las cartas.
While I was watching TV, the kids were playing cards.

4. To describe ongoing *physical, mental,* or *emotional states* in the past

Estaban muy **distraídos.**
They were very distracted.

Él la **quería** muchísimo.
He loved her a lot.

Hacía calor, pero Luis **tenía** frío.
It was hot (out) but Luis was cold.

5. To tell *time* in the past and to express *age* with **tener**

Era la una. / **Eran las dos.**
It was one o'clock. / It was two o'clock.

Tenía 18 años.
She / He was 18 years old.

¡OJO!

Just as in the present, the singular form of the verb **ser** is used with one o'clock, the plural form from two o'clock on.

Summary of the Uses of the Imperfect

used to, would
was/were + *-ing*
simultaneous actions (**mientras**)
physical, mental, and emotional states
time
age

Práctica y comunicación

A. Cuando yo tenía 16 años...

Paso 1. Autoprueba. Dé la terminación apropiada del imperfecto para cada verbo.

1. yo habl_______ **2.** ustedes er_______ **3.** nosotros com_______ **4.** Pedro ib_______ **5.** tú ten_______

Paso 2. Haga oraciones basadas en las siguientes frases, usando el imperfecto para hablar de su vida a los 16 años. Si alguna oración no es cierta para usted, use **No...** .

1. **ser** muy estudioso/a
2. **saber** conducir (*to drive*)
3. **tener** que ___________ (quehacer doméstico)
4. **ir** a la escuela secundaria en autobús
5. **levantarse** muchos domingos antes de las 10
6. **tocar** un instrumento en la orquesta de la escuela
7. **ver** mis programas favoritos en internet
8. **querer** un celular mejor que el que (*the one*) tenía

Paso 3. Ahora, en parejas, túrnense para entrevistarse usando como base las oraciones del **Paso 2.** Luego díganle a la clase algo que ustedes tenían en común.

MODELO: **E1:** Cuando tenías 16 años, ¿eras muy estudioso?
E2: No, no era nada estudioso. ¿Y tú?
E1: Yo sí.

B. La vida a los 7 años

Paso 1. Haga oraciones sobre la vida de Tina Acevedo, que vivía en Puerto Rico cuando tenía 7 años. Use el imperfecto de los verbos.

1. Tina: **vivir** en Bayamón, Puerto Rico
2. **asistir** a una escuela católica
3. **hablar** español todo el tiempo
4. **aprender** inglés en la escuela
5. **dibujar** (*to draw*) mucho en clase
6. **jugar** con sus compañeros en el parque
7. **ir** a casa de sus abuelos después de la escuela
8. **ver** sus programas favoritos en la tele
9. sus padres: **llegar** por ella a las 7:30
10. sus padres: **llevarla** a casa

Paso 2. Ahora haga oraciones similares a las oraciones del **Paso 1** pero con información de su propia vida a los 7 años.

MODELO: Tina: **vivir** en Bayamón, Puerto Rico. →
Yo **vivía** en St. Louis, Missouri.

Nota comunicativa

El progresivo en el pasado

Just like the present progressive, the *past progressive* (**el imperfecto progresivo**) emphasizes that an action was happening at that very moment. The past progressive is formed with the imperfect of **estar** plus the present participle (-**ndo**) of another verb.

Cuando mi tío llamó, **estábamos cenando.**
When my uncle called, we were having dinner.

El sábado a las 10 de la noche, ¿**estabas estudiando**?
Saturday night at 10, were you studying?

You will use the past progressive in **Práctica C.**

Prác. A, Paso 1: **Answers: 1.** *hablaba* **2.** *eran* **3.** *comíamos* **4.** *iba* **5.** *tenías*

Vocabulario útil

el bebé	
el timbre	doorbell
gritar	to shout
ladrar	to bark
pelear	to fight
sonar	to ring;
(suena)	to sound

C. Trabajos (*Jobs*) de adolescentes

Paso 1. Muchos adolescentes trabajan de niñeros (*babysitters*), un trabajo que puede ser pesado (*boring*) o difícil. ¿Qué estaba pasando cuando esta niñera perdió por fin la paciencia? Describa todas las acciones que pueda (*you can*), usando **estaba(n)** + *present participle* (**-ndo**).

MODELO: El bebé **estaba llorando.**

Vocabulario útil

caerse (cayendo)	to fall down
cuidar	to take care of
sacar (qu)	to take something out

Paso 2. De adolescentes, ¿tenían ustedes un trabajo? ¿Tenían que cuidar a sus hermanos menores o a otros niños? En parejas, túrnense para hablar de sus experiencias de trabajo cuando tenían 15, 16 o 17 años. Háganse preguntas para obtener mucha información.

MODELO: **E1:** Cuando yo tenía 15 años, cuidaba a mi hermano menor.
E2: ¿Lo cuidabas todos los días? ¿Cuánto te pagaban tus padres? ¿Se portaba bien tu hermano o era mucho trabajo?

1900

HOY

D. Los tiempos cambian (*change*). Las siguientes oraciones describen aspectos de la vida de hoy. En parejas, comparen estos aspectos con el estilo de vida alrededor del (*around the*) año 1900. Luego, describan dos cambios más.

MODELO: **E1:** Ahora la gente se comunica electrónicamente. →
E2: Alrededor del año 1900, la gente **se comunicaba por carta.**

1. Ahora muchísimas mujeres trabajan fuera de (*outside of the*) casa.
2. Hoy día la gente lee libros en formato electrónico.
3. Ahora la gente puede escuchar música en casa todo el tiempo.
4. Hoy día las mujeres se ponen pantalones.
5. Ahora hay hombres enfermeros (*nurses*) y maestros (*grade school teachers*).
6. Hoy, tenemos más máquinas y por eso hacemos menos trabajo físicamente.
7. Las familias son más pequeñas.
8. Muchas parejas viven juntas sin estar casadas (*married*).

E. Descripción de un momento en el pasado

Paso 1. Conteste las siguientes preguntas, pensando en el mediodía de ayer.

1. ¿Qué tiempo hacía?
2. ¿Dónde estaba usted?
3. ¿Qué estaba haciendo?
4. ¿Qué ropa llevaba?
5. ¿Con quién estaba?
6. ¿Cómo se sentía usted? ¿Por qué?

Vocabulario útil

agobiado/a de trabajo overwhelmed by work
con mucha/poca energía
listo/a para + *inf.* ready to + *inf.*

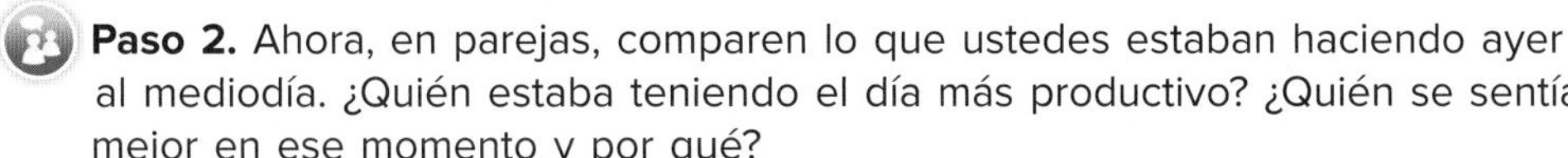

Paso 2. Ahora, en parejas, comparen lo que ustedes estaban haciendo ayer al mediodía. ¿Quién estaba teniendo el día más productivo? ¿Quién se sentía mejor en ese momento y por qué?

F. Este semestre/trimestre

Paso 1. En parejas, comparen el semestre/trimestre pasado con el presente (*the current one*), hablando de los siguientes temas.

1. hacer ejercicio o deportes
2. la primera clase del día
3. la última clase de la semana
4. las actividades extracurriculares
5. su cuarto / residencia / apartamento / casa
6. sus hábitos de estudio y/o de comer

Paso 2. Ahora díganle al resto de la clase algo que ustedes tenían en común el semestre/trimestre pasado y algo que tienen en común este semestre/trimestre.

Algo sobre...

Borinquen

Borinquen es el nombre que los taínos, los habitantes originales de Puerto Rico, le daban a su isla. El pueblo taíno se extinguió[a] en el siglo XVI, como consecuencia de la colonización. Pero los puertorriqueños están muy orgullosos[b] de su origen taíno. Los términos[c] **boricua** y **borinqueño/a** se usan con frecuencia para referirse a las personas, instituciones y tradiciones de la Isla. De hecho,[d] el himno oficial[e] puertorriqueño se llama «La borinqueña».

¿Sabe usted quiénes eran los habitantes originales de su estado? ¿Está presente su herencia en el folclore de su estado?

[a]se... *died out* [b]*proud* [c]*terms* [d]De... *In fact* [e]himno... *national anthem*

United States Coast Guard

El emblema de la Guardia Costera de Puerto Rico, que lleva dos símbolos puertorriqueños: el coquí y el nombre Borinquen

¿Recuerda usted?

You have been using interrogative words since the beginning of *Puntos de partida*, so not much will be new for you in **Gramática 28.** Review what you already know by telling which interrogative word or phrase you associate with the following phrases.

1. un lugar
2. la hora
3. una persona
4. la manera de hacer algo
5. una selección
6. la razón (*reason*) por algo
7. el lugar de origen de una persona
8. un destino
9. una cantidad
10. ser el dueño de algo

28 Getting Information (Part 2)

Summary of Interrogative Words

Gramática en acción: Un restaurante de Connecticut

1. ¿Cómo se llama el restaurante?
2. ¿En qué ciudad de Connecticut está?
3. ¿En qué tipo de cocina se especializa el restaurante?
4. ¿Qué grupo toca el viernes, 6 de octubre?
5. ¿Cuál es la dirección del restaurante?

¿Y usted?

¿Cuántas preguntas más puede usted hacer sobre este restaurante, por (*based on*) lo que dice el anuncio?

Here are all of the interrogatives that you have learned so far. Only more information about using **¿qué?** and **¿cuál(es)?,** both of which express *what?* or *which?* in Spanish, is new.

¡OJO!

Remember that interrogative words always have an accent mark in Spanish, and that questions have two question marks: **¿ ?**

¿Cómo?	How?	**¿Dónde?**	Where?
		¿De dónde?	From where?
¿Cuándo?	When?	**¿Adónde?**	Where (to)?
¿A qué hora?	At what time?		
¿Qué?	What? Which?	**¿Cuánto/a?**	How much?
¿Cuál(es)?	What? Which one(s)?	**¿Cuántos/as?**	How many?
¿Por qué?	Why?	**¿Quién(es)?**	Who?
		¿De quién(es)?	Whose?

Uses of **¿qué?** and **¿cuál?** / **Los usos de *¿qué?* y *¿cuál?***

1. **¿Qué? + es/son = Definition/Explanation**
   Use **¿Qué es/son... ?** to ask for a definition or for the explanation of what something is.

   ¿Qué es esto?
   What is this?

   ¿Qué son las Antillas?
   What are the West Indies?

2. **¿Qué? +** *verb* **= Information**
   Use ¿**Qué...** ? with any verbs to ask for information.

   ¿Qué quieres comer?
   What do you want to eat?

   ¿Qué hacen ustedes por la mañana?
   What do you do in the morning?

3. **¿Qué? +** *noun* **= Choice**
   Use a question with **¿qué?** + a *noun* to ask the listener to specify a preference or make a choice.

   ¿Qué deporte prefieres?
   What (Which) sport do you prefer?

   ¿Qué playa te gusta más?
   What (Which) beach do you like most?

   ¿Qué instrumento musical tocas?
   What (Which) musical instrument do you play?

4. **¿Cuál(es)?** + *verb* = **Choice**

Use **¿cuál(es)?** + a *verb* to express *what* when it means *which one*, that is, when it calls for a choice. Sometimes a phrase like **de los dos (tres...**) makes the choice more obvious.

> **¡OJO!**
>
> ¿**Qué**?, not ¿**cuál**?, is followed by a noun. Compare these sentences:
>
> ¿**Qué** **libro** quieres? = *which book?*
> ¿**Cuál** (es el libro que) **quieres?** = *which one?*
> ¿**Cuál de los dos** **quieres?** = *which one of the two?*

¿**Cuál** **prefieres**?
Which one do you prefer?

¿**Cuál** **es** la cafetería más grande?
What (Which [one]) is the biggest cafeteria?

¿**Cuáles** **son** tus jugadores favoritos?
What (Which [ones]) are your favorite players?

¿**Cuál** **es** tu (número de) teléfono?
What is your phone number?

¿**Cuál** **de los dos coches** vas a comprar?
Which of the two cars are you going to buy?

Práctica y comunicación

Summary of ¿qué? Versus ¿cuál?

¿qué? + **es/son** = definition/explanation
+ *verb* = information
+ *noun* = choice

¿cuál(es)? + *verb* = choice

A. Preguntas personales

Paso 1. Autoprueba. Empareje las palabras interrogativas con la información que piden.

1. ¿Cuándo?
2. ¿Dónde?
3. ¿Qué?
4. ¿Cuánto?
5. ¿Cuál?

a. un lugar
b. una selección
c. un número o una cantidad
d. una definición
e. la hora
f. información

Paso 2. Complete las siguientes preguntas con **qué** o **cuál(es)** y contéstelas.

1. ¿Tiene usted un segundo nombre (*middle name*)? ¿_______ es? ¿_______ son sus dos apellidos, según el sistema hispano de apellidos?
2. ¿_______ es su número de teléfono?
3. ¿_______ es su dirección postal? ¿_______ es su e-mail?
4. ¿_______ clase le gusta más?
5. ¿_______ son las materias que usted toma este semestre/trimestre? ¿_______ es su favorita?
6. ¿_______ de las redes (*networks*) sociales mira usted más?
7. ¿_______ tarea doméstica odia más?
8. ¿_______ es un equipo? ¿_______ es su equipo de fútbol americano favorito?

Paso 3. Ahora, en parejas, túrnense para hacer y contestar las preguntas del **Paso 2.** Luego díganle a la clase algo que ustedes tienen en común.

B. Intercambios

Paso 1. En parejas, túrnense para entrevistarse sobre los siguientes temas. Empiecen las preguntas con **¿Qué... ?** or **¿Cuál(es)... ?** Hablen de sus preferencias actuales (*current*) o de sus preferencias de niño/a (usando el imperfecto).

MODELOS: estaciones del año →
¿**Qué** estación del año **prefieres**? (¿**Qué** estación del año **preferías** de niño/a?)
¿**Cuál es / Cuál era** tu estación del año favorita?

1. estilo de música
2. pasatiempos o deportes
3. programas de televisión
4. materias este semestre/trimestre
5. colores
6. tipos de comida

Paso 2. Ahora, díganle a la clase una cosa que tienen en común y otra en la que (*which*) no están de acuerdo.

Prác. A, Paso 1: Answers: 1. e 2. a 3. d, f 4. c 5. b

¿Recuerda usted?

You learned how to make comparisons in **Gramática 17** (**Cap. 6**). Before you start **Gramática 29,** review what you remember about comparisons by completing the following comparative phrases with the appropriate word.

1. más dinero ________ tú
2. tan simpáticos ________ ellos
3. ________ hermanas como...
4. menos libros ________ Cecilia
5. correr ________ como usted
6. tener un hermano ________

29 Expressing Extremes

Superlatives

Gramática en acción: Los puertorriqueños más famosos

©Stephane Cardinale/Sygma/Getty Images

©Stefanie Keenan/WireImage/Getty Images

©Focus on Sport/Getty Images

¿Está usted de acuerdo? Corrija las declaraciones falsas, según su opinión.

	CIERTO	FALSO
1. Jennifer López es la cantante puertorriqueña más conocida del mundo.	☐	☐
2. Benicio del Toro es el actor puertorriqueño más famoso del mundo.	☐	☐
3. Roberto Clemente, de origen puertorriqueño, es el mejor beisbolista hispano de todos los tiempos.	☐	☐

¿Y usted?

Complete las siguientes declaraciones para expresar su opinión.

1. El cantante hispano / La cantante hispana más popular del momento es ________.
2. La mejor actriz (*actress*) del momento es ________.
3. En la actualidad (*Currently*), la música más popular es ________ (la música de ________, la música de estilo ________).

Comparatives / Los comparativos	Superlatives / Los superlativos
Julio es **más** alto **que** Juanito.	Julio es el niño más alto de la clase. (Julio es el más alto de la clase.*)
El fútbol es **más** popular **que** el golf.	El fútbol es el deporte más popular del mundo. (El fútbol es el más popular del mundo.*)
La comida italiana es **buena,** pero la comida mexicana es **mejor**.	La comida mexicana es la mejor comida de todas las comidas del mundo. (La comida mexicana es la mejor de todas las comidas del mundo.*)

the superlative / **el superlativo** = an adjective or adverb that expresses an extreme

The most famous Puerto Ricans *Do you agree?* **1.** *Jennifer Lopez is the best known Puerto Rican singer in the world.* **2.** *Benicio del Toro is the most famous Puerto Rican actor in the world.* **3.** *Roberto Clemente, of Puerto Rican descent, is the best Hispanic baseball player of all time.*

Notice how adjectives can be used as nouns:* **el niño más alto *(the tallest child)* → **el más alto** *(the tallest), and so on. You can learn more about using adjectives in this way in Appendix 2, Using Adjectives as Nouns.*

Superlatives / **Los superlativos**

1. **Forming the Superlative**
   To express the *most/best/least/worst,* and so on, the comparative forms are used with the definite article.

> **¡OJO!**
> *in/of* = **de**

el / la / los / las + *noun* + **más / menos** + *adjective* + **de**

El basquetbol es **el deporte más competitivo del** mundo.
Basketball is the most competitive sport in the world.

El golf es **el deporte menos peligroso de** todos.
Golf is the least dangerous sport of all.

2. **Irregular Superlatives**
   Mejor and **peor** generally precede the noun.

el / la / los / las + **mejor(es) / peor(es)** + *noun* (+ **de**)

La verdad es que es **el peor jugador del** equipo.
The truth is that he's the worst player on the team.

Son **las mejores lavadoras**.
They're the best washing machines.

Note that **mejor** and **peor** are often used with possessives instead of the articles.

Ana es **mi mejor** amiga.
Ana is my best friend.

Mayor and **menor** are often used without the noun.

Lorenzo es **el mayor de** los hermanos y Leticia es **la menor**.
Lorenzo is the oldest of the siblings and Leticia is the youngest.

Práctica y comunicación

Summary of Superlatives

el / la / los / las + *noun* + **más / menos** + *adjective* + **de**

el / la / los / las + { **mejor(es) / peor(es)** | **mayor(es) / menor(es)** } + *noun* + **de**

A. Opiniones personales

Paso 1. Autoprueba. Ordene las palabras para hacer oraciones con sentido (*meaningful*) que expresan ideas superlativas.

1. **Es...** ciudad / más / el / grande / la / parque / de
2. **Son...** clase / los / difíciles / de / niños / la / más
3. **Visité...** del / los / mundo / museos / mejores
4. **Vi...** peor / año / película / la / del

Paso 2. Use las siguientes ideas para dar su opinión sobre lo que es «más» en cada categoría.

MODELO: una estación del año (frío) → El invierno es **la** estación **más fría del** año.

1. un día festivo del año (divertido)
2. una materia de este semestre/trimestre (difícil)
3. una persona de la familia (vieja)
4. una persona de la familia (joven)
5. un mes del año (bueno)
6. un día de la semana (malo)
7. un amigo / una amiga (bueno/a)

Paso 3. Ahora, en parejas, usen las ideas del **Paso 2** para entrevistarse. Luego, díganle a la clase algo que tienen en común.

MODELO: E1: ¿Cómo se llama tu mejor amigo o amiga?
E2: Mi mejor amigo es Jacobo. ¿Y tu mejor amigo?
E1: (Es) Luis.

***Prác. A, Paso 1: Answers: 1.** Es el parque más grande de la ciudad. **2.** Son los niños más difíciles de la clase. **3.** Visité los mejores museos del mundo. **4.** Vi la peor película del año.*

B. Superlativos

Paso 1. Modifique las siguientes oraciones para hacer una forma superlativa.

MODELO: Es una estudiante muy **alta. (la clase)** →
Es **la** estudiante **más alta de la clase.**

1. Son unos días festivos muy **divertidos. (el año)**
2. Es una clase muy **interesante. (todas mis clases)**
3. Es una persona muy **inteligente. (todos mis amigos)**
4. Son ciudades muy **grandes. (los Estados Unidos)**
5. Es un estado muy **pequeño. (el país)**
6. Es un perro muy **pequeño. (el mundo)**
7. Es una residencia muy **ruidosa** (*noisy*). **(la universidad)**
8. Es una montaña muy **alta. (el mundo)**

Paso 2. Ahora repita cada oración con información verdadera.

MODELO: **Carla** es la estudiante más alta de la clase.

C. Intercambios. En parejas, túrnense para expresar sus opiniones sobre las siguientes ideas. Luego compartan (*share*) sus opiniones con la clase.

MODELO: el peor / mejor restaurante de la ciudad →
E1: Yo creo que ______ es **el peor** restaurante **de** la ciudad.
E2: En mi opinión, **el peor** restaurante **de** la ciudad es ______.
→ No estamos de acuerdo. Yo creo que ______ es **el peor** restaurante **de** la ciudad. Mi compañero/a cree que **el peor** es ______.

Estrategia

Emphatic forms formed with **-ísimo/a** cannot be used in a superlative construction. You can use **-ísimo/a** adjectives in this activity, but only as shown in the mode.

1. el **peor / mejor** restaurante de la ciudad
2. un libro **interesantísimo / aburridísimo**
3. un plato **riquísimo / malísimo**
4. un programa de televisión **interesantísimo / pesadísimo**
5. un lugar **tranquilísimo / animadísimo / peligrosísimo** (*very dangerous*)
6. la canción más **bonita / fea** del año
7. la **mejor / peor** película del año

Nota comunicativa

Los diminutivos

In Spanish, it is very common to add a suffix to nouns and adjectives to express littleness or affection. The most common diminutive ending is **-ito/a.**

- If the word ends in a consonant, **-ito/a** is added to the singular form (and any accent on the word is dropped): **papel → papelito, fácil → facilito.**
- If the word ends in a vowel, the final vowel is dropped before adding **-ito/a** (and any accent on the word is dropped): **guapo → guapito, libro → librito (libros →libritos), rápido → rapidito.**
- Spelling changes occur when the final consonant is **c, g,** or **z**: **poco → poquito, amiga → amiguita, pedazos** (*chunks*) **→ pedacitos.**

You will use diminutives in **Práctica D.**

D. ¿Diminutivos para usted? Los diminutivos se usan para hablar de algo con afecto y ternura (*tenderness*). ¿Usarían ustedes (*Would you use*) un diminutivo para hablar de las siguientes personas y cosas? Expliquen sus respuestas.

MODELO: 1. ¿su cuarto? →
E1: Sí, mi **cuartito,** porque es muy pequeño / es un lugar especial.
E2: No, no quiero llamarlo **cuartito,** porque no es pequeño / no me gusta.

1. ¿su cuarto?
2. ¿su libro de español?
3. ¿su hermano/a (sobrino/a) menor?
4. ¿su gorra favorita?
5. ¿su abuelo/a?
6. ¿su perro/a?

Algo sobre...

la bomba y la plena

©Helen H. Richardson Denver Post/Getty Images

Un grupo puertorriqueño con sus congas

La bomba y la plena son dos géneros musicales de Puerto Rico que son productos del sincretismo[a] musical típico del Caribe. La bomba está marcada por la herencia[b] africana, mientras que la plena muestra la influencia de la tradición española. La bomba es un diálogo entre los bailarines y los tambores.[c] La plena incluye instrumentos como el cuatro (una evolución de la guitarra española) y la pandereta.[d]

¿Cuál es el origen de un género musical típico de los Estados Unidos? ¿Qué instrumentos se usan en esa música?

[a]*blending* [b]*heritage* [c]*drums* [d]*tambourine*

Todo junto

A. Lengua y cultura: Un poco de la historia de Puerto Rico

Paso 1. Completar. Complete the following passage with the correct form of the words in parentheses, as suggested by context. When two possibilities are given in parentheses, select the correct word. **¡OJO!** Give the preterite form of the verbs marked *P* and the imperfect of those marked *I*.

En la isla de Puerto Rico, como en todas las Antillas Mayores, __________ (*I:* vivir[1]) los indígenas taínos. Cristóbal Colón __________ (*P:* llegar[2]) a la isla en 1493, en su segunda[a] expedición al Nuevo Mundo. __________ (Se / Le[3]) dice que el jefe[b] de los taínos, que __________ (*I:* tener[4]) el título de cacique, __________ (*P:* recibir[5]) a Colón con un collar[c] de oro. __________ (Por / Para[6]) eso Colón pensó que __________ (*I:* haber[7]) mucho oro en la isla, pero no tenía __________ (razón / prisa[8]). De todas formas,[d] los españoles explotaron la isla intensamente. En poco tiempo, la población taína prácticamente __________ (*P:* desaparecer[e9]) debido a[f] tres factores: __________ (el / la[10]) explotación física causada por labores intensas,[g] las rebeliones de los nativos y las enfermedades[h] que los españoles __________ (*P:* llevar[11]) consigo,[i] que __________ (*I:* ser[12]) nuevas para los taínos. La población africana, que los españoles llevaron al Caribe como esclavos,[j] __________ (*P:* empezar[13]) a llegar en el siglo XVI.

En el siglo XIX, por toda Latinoamérica, __________ (*P:* haber[14]) guerras[k] contra España para obtener la independencia. Pero las Antillas no __________ (*P:* independizarse[15]). En 1898 Puerto Rico se convirtió en[l] territorio de los Estados Unidos, después de que España __________ (*P:* perder[16]) la guerra que en los Estados Unidos __________ (*P:* recibir[17]) el nombre de «*the Spanish-American War*» (la Guerra hispanoamericana).

En 1917 los puertorriqueños __________ (*P:* ser[18]) declarados ciudadanos[m] __________ (estadounidense[19]) y, desde 1953, su país es un Estado Libre Asociado a los Estados Unidos de América. Esto significa que no es independiente.

©Glyn Genin/Alamy

Estatua y fuente (*fountain*) de La India Taína, en Caguas, Puerto Rico

[a]*second* [b]*chief* [c]*necklace* [d]De... *In any case* [e]*to disappear* [f]debido... *due to* [g]labores... *hard labor* [h]*illnesses* [i]*with them* [j]*slaves* [k]*wars* [l]se... *became a* [m]*citizens*

Paso 2. Comprensión. Conteste las siguientes preguntas.

1. ¿De qué grupo de islas forma parte Puerto Rico?
2. ¿Quiénes eran los habitantes originales de Puerto Rico?
3. ¿Cuándo llegaron los españoles a Puerto Rico por primera vez?
4. Después del siglo XVI, ¿qué otros grupos raciales había en la isla?
5. ¿Desde cuándo es Puerto Rico territorio de los Estados Unidos?
6. ¿Cuál es la situación política actual de Puerto Rico?

(Continúa)

Paso 3. En acción

Ahora, en parejas, den información histórica sobre su estado (o país) comparable a la información sobre Puerto Rico. Aquí hay unas sugerencias.

1. qué pueblo(s) vivía(n) en su estado (país) originalmente
2. qué otros pueblos llegaron más tarde y cuándo
3. si hubo guerra(s) con otro país y cuándo
4. si ganó su independencia de otro país y cuándo
5. cuándo se convirtió en estado de la Unión estadounidense

B. Proyecto: Reacciones y actitudes de la adolescencia

Hay muchos estereotipos que se asocian con la adolescencia. Van a hacer una encuesta (*poll*) para ver si esos estereotipos son de verdad (*really*) muy comunes.

cambios independencia imagen grupos celular niñez adolescencia actitud juventud familia rebeldía acné amigos *selfies*

Paso 1. Preparación. En parejas o grupos, hagan una lista de cinco de las reacciones o actitudes que generalmente se asocian con los jóvenes entre los 14 y 18 años.

Paso 2. Encuesta. Ahora, usen las ideas del **Paso 1** para hacerles preguntas a varias personas de la clase sobre sus hábitos o actitudes cuando eran adolescentes. Recuerden establecer un formato para preguntar (sí/no, escala de posibilidades, etcétera) y un método para apuntar (*note down*) las respuestas.

MODELO: discutir con los padres/hermanos → ¿Discutías mucho con tus padres? 1 = nunca o casi nunca 5 = todo el tiempo

Paso 3. Análisis de datos. Según los resultados de su encuesta, ¿son válidos los estereotipos que ustedes eligieron (*chose*)? Preparen un breve informe (*report*) para la clase que incluya (*includes*) la lista de preguntas, el número de personas encuestadas (*polled*) por cada pregunta y un resumen (*summary*) de las respuestas.

Vocabulario útil

discutir con los padres/hermanos
encerrarse (me encierro) *(to shut oneself up)* en su cuarto
preocuparse (*to worry*) mucho por la imagen que se proyecta
sacar(se) *selfies* con frecuencia
sentirse (me siento) (i) cohibido/a por *(self-conscious about)*
tener acné

¡Ahora, yo!

A. Entrevista. Use de modelo las preguntas y respuestas de la página 299 de este capítulo para hablar de su tiempo libre y de sus pasatiempos favoritos.

B. Proyecto audiovisual. Filme una entrevista con un(a) atleta hispanohablante de su universidad. Si no encuentra ninguno/a, entreviste a un(a) atleta anglohablante (*English-speaking*) y use su voz en off (*voiceover*) para traducir al español las ideas principales de lo que dice el/la atleta.

©Rafael Guerrero/Photolibrary/Getty Images

«Deportes que mueven masas» Segmento 2

Antes de mirar

Conteste las siguientes preguntas.

¿Vio usted recientemente la final de algún campeonato (*championship*) importante?
¿Qué equipos se disputaron (*fought for*) el campeonato? ¿Cuál ganó?

Este segmento

Laura presenta un reportaje sobre el deporte rey (*number one*) en México.

«Y muchos [mexicanos] se unen a una porra (*fan club*) para acompañar a su equipo hasta el campo de fútbol y defenderlo a gritos (*with shouts* [*of support*]).»

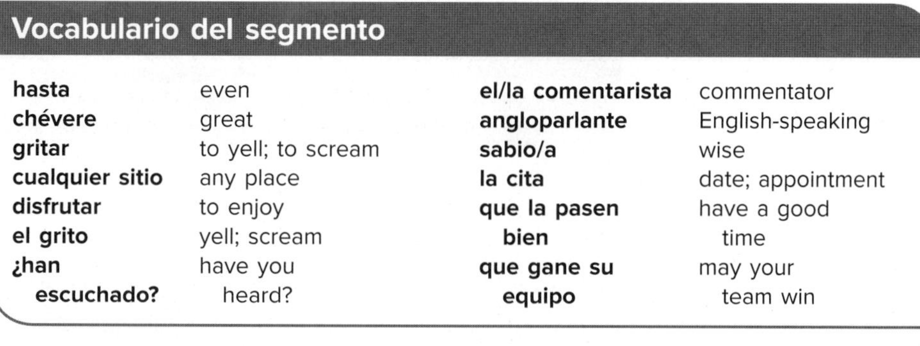

Vocabulario del segmento

hasta	even	**el/la comentarista**	commentator
chévere	great	**angloparlante**	English-speaking
gritar	to yell; to scream	**sabio/a**	wise
cualquier sitio	any place	**la cita**	date; appointment
disfrutar	to enjoy	**que la pasen bien**	have a good time
el grito	yell; scream	**que gane su equipo**	may your team win
¿han escuchado?	have you heard?		

Fragmento del guion

Pero el auténtico deporte rey del planeta es el fútbol. Les voy a dar un dato[a] fascinante: se calcula que más de mil millones de personas en todo el mundo vieron la final de la Copa Mundial[b] de Fútbol del año 2010, que se disputaron[c] España y Holanda. ¡Más de mil millones!

[a]*fact* [b]Copa... *World Cup* [c]se... *was fought out by*

Después de mirar

A. ¿Está claro? Complete las oraciones con información del video.

1. El ___________ por ciento de los beisbolistas de las grandes ligas es de origen hispano.
2. El deporte rey del planeta es el ___________.
3. El deporte rey en México es el ___________.
4. ___________ ganó la Copa Mundial en 2010.
5. Los comentaristas ___________ no saben gritar bien «¡gol!».

B. Un poco más. Conteste las siguientes preguntas.

1. ¿Dónde vio Ana la final de la Copa del Mundo?
2. ¿Qué hizo Ana durante el partido?
3. ¿Quién prefería ver los partidos de fútbol en español? ¿Por qué?

C. Y ahora, ustedes En parejas, escojan uno de los dos deportes de este programa (el béisbol, **Segmento 1**, o el fútbol, este **Segmento**) y hablen de la situación de este deporte en su país. ¿Es este deporte uno de los más populares? ¿Es popular por el número de espectadores o por el número de personas que lo practican? ¿Dónde se practica?

MUNDO HISPANO

Enfoque cultural: Puerto Rico

Antes de leer

¿Hay playas muy frecuentadas por la gente cerca de su ciudad o estado? En la zona donde usted vive, ¿cuáles son los lugares que más visita la gente en el tiempo libre?

El tiempo libre en Puerto Rico

A muchos puertorriqueños les gusta pasar el tiempo junto al[a] mar. Es lógico: Puerto Rico y sus islas más pequeñas, como Vieques y Culebra, están rodeadas de[b] deliciosas aguas cálidas[c] y hermosas[d] playas. Muchas son de arena[e] fina y mar tranquilo, ideales para relajarse y nadar. Otras, especialmente en el norte, son excelentes para surfear. Y otras (al este y al sur) ofrecen el espectáculo natural de la bioluminiscencia: unos microorganismos llamados dinoflagelados iluminan el agua del mar en la noche.

Aunque[f] en Puerto Rico hace buen tiempo todo el año, es en los meses de verano (de mayo a septiembre) cuando los puertorriqueños van más a la playa. Amigos y familia, música, comida, una hamaca entre palmas... ¿Qué más se puede pedir?

[a]*junto... next to the* [b]*rodeadas... surrounded by* [c]*warm* [d]*beautiful* [e]*sand* [f]*Although*

En otros países hispanos

- **En todo el mundo hispanohablante** Jugar al dominó y hacer la sobremesa son pasatiempos muy populares en muchos países hispanos. El dominó es un juego muy fácil de aprender, pero el juego se complica muchísimo —y también se hace más interesante— jugando en parejas. La sobremesa es el tiempo que se pasa charlando[a] en la mesa después de la comida. No es nada extraño[b] que un grupo de parientes o amigos hispanos pase dos o tres horas sentados[c] a la mesa, primero comiendo, luego tomando café y charlando, hasta unir el almuerzo con la merienda.
- **En la Argentina** En este país sudamericano hay gran afición por el deporte del polo. La Argentina domina ese deporte en el panorama mundial.

[a]*chatting* [b]*strange* [c]*seated*

El Fuerte de San Felipe del Morro, que guardaba el puerto de la bahía de San Juan, Puerto Rico

Un símbolo puertorriqueño: El Viejo San Juan

Los puertorriqueños se sienten muy orgullosos[a] de su herencia cultural y de sus tradiciones, heredadas de los taínos, africanos y españoles. El Viejo San Juan representa la cultura y tradición españolas. Sus edificios coloniales, sus calles adoquinadas,[b] el Fuerte[c] San Felipe del Morro, la Catedral y otros edificios históricos representan la historia de la Isla.

[a]*proud* [b]*cobblestone* [c]*Fort*

Comprensión

1. ¿Cuáles son los meses en que los puertorriqueños van más a la playa?
2. ¿Qué es la bioluminiscencia?
3. ¿Dónde están las mejores playas puertorriqueñas para surfear?
4. ¿Cuáles son dos de los pasatiempos populares en algunos países hispanohablantes?
5. ¿Qué deporte es muy popular en la Argentina?
6. ¿Con qué herencia cultural se identifica el Viejo San Juan?

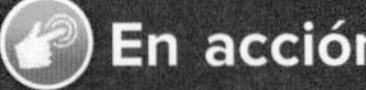 En acción

Haga una lista de los pasatiempos familiares que usted considera típicos de su país y otra lista de los pasatiempos más comunes de su familia. ¿Cree usted que su familia es una familia típica?

Lectura

Antes de leer

Piense en cómo usa usted su teléfono celular. ¿Cuáles son los aspectos positivos y negativos de su uso?

Vocabulario para leer

apagado/a	turned off
el dispositivo	device
la llamada	(phone) call
la pantalla	screen
quedar con	to meet, make a date with
saludable	healthy
sano/a	healthy

Volver a conectar

Aunque[a] tabletas, *smartphones* y otros dispositivos están pensados y diseñados[b] para servirnos, los estudios realizados[c] hasta ahora constatan[d] nuestra «dependencia electrónica». Sin embargo, desconectar es posible. El psicólogo Fernando Azor nos aporta[e] algunas sugerencias:

PRIORIZAR Hay que atender[f] primero a aquellos que se dirigen a[g] nosotros en persona; después las llamadas; después los mensajes instantáneos y, por último, los correos electrónicos.

RESPONDER MÁS TARDE No responder de inmediato es un buen entrenamiento[h] para combatir la ansiedad. Ni nosotros estamos obligados a contestar al instante,[i] ni ellos pueden sentirse cuestionados[j] porque no se les escriba en el acto.[k]

ABSTENERSE[l] Ser capaz[m] de pasar un fin de semana o un día entero con el teléfono apagado es una señal[n] de sana independencia. Si este período es demasiado largo, hay que tratar de desconectar todas las redes[ñ] (si no, al menos[o] el wifi) en determinados momentos del día, por ejemplo durante la noche.

CONFIGURAR Configure su dispositivo para que los nuevos correos o mensajes instantáneos solo lleguen cuando usted actualice[p] manualmente. Evitará así[q] las constantes miradas a la pantalla en busca de notificaciones.

HUMANIZAR La tecnología crea una ilusoria sensación de intimidad y contacto. Por ello[r] es aconsejable,[s] al menos una vez a la semana, «desvirtualizar» nuestras relaciones y quedar con ese interlocutor[t] para tomar un café o dar un paseo real.

SELECCIONAR A menudo[u] mantenemos relaciones virtuales que, en realidad, no aportan[v] nada a nuestra vida,[w] o que incluso nos restan[x] energía y tiempo. Por ello, es muy saludable ser un poco más darwinistas* con nuestra agenda de contactos, y no dudar a la hora de dejar de[y] ser «amigo» de aquellas personas a las que, en el fondo, no nos une nada.[z]

[a]*Although* [b]pensados… *imagined and designed* [c]*completed* [d]*show* [e]ofrece [f]*pay attention* [g]se… *address* [h]*training* [i]al… *immediately* [j]*let down* [k]en… *immediately* [l]*Abstain* [m]*capable* [n]*sign* [ñ]hay… *it's necessary to try to disconnect the networks* [o]al… *at least* [p]*refresh, update* [q]Evitará… *That way you will avoid* [r]Por… Por eso [s]*advisable* [t]*conversation partner* [u]A… Con frecuencia [v]contribuyen [w]*life* [x]incluso… *even take away from us* [y]no… *not hesitate when it comes to stop* [z]a… *who, in the final analysis, we have no ties with*

Comprensión

A. Ideas principales. ¿Cuál de las siguientes oraciones resume mejor la lectura? Señale (*Point out*) evidencia en el texto para la respuesta que seleccione.

1. Los teléfonos celulares son dispositivos esenciales para la vida moderna y no se puede vivir sin ellos.
2. La dependencia de los teléfonos celulares y otros dispositivos es un problema, pero es posible controlarla.
3. Es mejor vivir sin teléfonos celulares y otros dispositivos.

B. Aplicación personal. De las seis sugerencias que ofrece la lectura, ¿cuáles implementa usted ahora? ¿Cuáles quiere implementar? ¿Cuáles no son ni (*neither*) apropiadas ni (*nor*) aceptables para usted? Explique sus respuestas.

Proyecto: Una encuesta° sobre «la dependencia electrónica»

°*survey*

En este proyecto, va a realizar una encuesta para determinar si usted y el resto de la clase sufren de «la dependencia electrónica».

(Continúa.)

*Darwinistas *refers to Charles Darwin, the nineteenth-century theorist of biological evolution. In this context, the term refers to an action that will lead to self-preservation.*

Paso 1. Escriba varias preguntas para la encuesta, basadas (*based*) en las sugerencias de la lectura **Volver a conectar**.

MODELO: ¿Te sientes obligado/a a contestar mensajes de texto de inmediato?

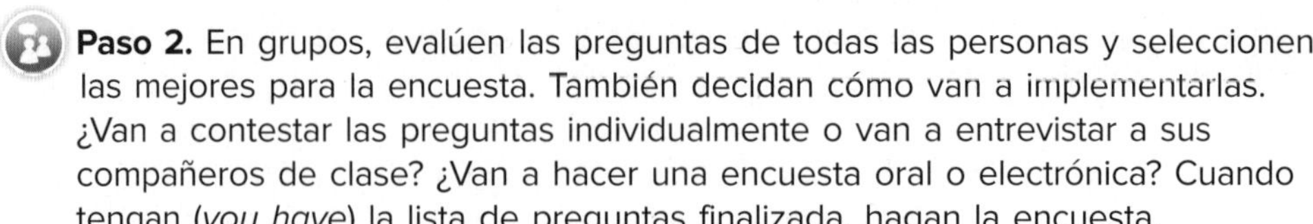

Paso 2. En grupos, evalúen las preguntas de todas las personas y seleccionen las mejores para la encuesta. También decidan cómo van a implementarlas. ¿Van a contestar las preguntas individualmente o van a entrevistar a sus compañeros de clase? ¿Van a hacer una encuesta oral o electrónica? Cuando tengan (*you have*) la lista de preguntas finalizada, hagan la encuesta.

Paso 3. Analicen las respuestas y compartan los resultados con toda la clase. ¿Hay tendencias y/o problemas frecuentes en su clase? ¿Creen ustedes que sufren de «la dependencia electrónica»?

Textos orales

Unos compañeros hablan de «un desastre»

Antes de escuchar

¿Qué quehaceres hace usted para mantener limpio su apartamento o alcoba? ¿Cuál de los quehaceres hace con más frecuencia? ¿Cuál le molesta más hacer?

Vocabulario para escuchar

verdadero/a	real
no te preocupes	don't worry
arreglar	to tidy up
no discutamos	let's not argue
yo me encargo de	I'll take care of
¡muévete!	move it!, get a move on!

Comprensión

A. ¿Quién lo va a hacer? Empareje cada tarea con la persona que la va a hacer.

TAREAS	PERSONAS
1. _____ limpiar la cocina	**a.** Jorge
2. _____ limpiar el baño	**b.** Hilda
3. _____ pasar la aspiradora	**c.** Ana
4. _____ sacar la basura	

B. Otros detalles. Conteste las siguientes preguntas según el diálogo.

1. ¿Por qué es urgente limpiar el apartamento?
2. ¿Quién está dispuesto (*willing*) a ayudar?
3. ¿Quién no tiene muchas ganas de ayudar?

En acción

Haga un horario (*schedule*) para este fin de semana empezando por el viernes por la tarde. Incluya (*Include*) pasatiempos, tarea y quehaceres domésticos. ¡Seguro que hay por lo menos (*Surely there must be at least*) una cosa que usted tiene que hacer en su cuarto o en su casa/apartamento!

Proyecto en su comunidad

Entreviste a una persona hispana de su universidad o ciudad sobre lo que hace en su tiempo libre.

Preguntas posibles

- ¿Practica algún deporte? ¿Es su deporte favorito uno de los deportes más populares de su cultura?
- ¿Cuáles son sus pasatiempos favoritos? ¿Cuáles eran sus pasatiempos favoritos cuando era niño/a?

- ¿Hace muchos quehaceres domésticos? ¿Cuáles son? ¿Cuáles son los quehaceres que más odia? ¿Qué tareas domésticas tenía que hacer cuando tenía 12 o 13 años?

©Hola Images/Getty Images

En el Bosque (*Forest*) Nacional el Yunque, en Puerto Rico

Escritura

Proyecto: Un ensayo sobre los pasatiempos y diversiones

¿Cuáles son las actividades típicas de los estudiantes de su universidad? ¿Y qué hacía usted cuando era más joven? ¿Era similar a lo que hace ahora? Usted va a escribir un ensayo sobre estas ideas.

Antes de escribir

En parejas, piensen en las actividades típicas de la gente de su edad (*age group*) y en concreto de los estudiantes de su universidad. La tabla sugiere (*suggests*) algunas categorías, pero ustedes las pueden ampliar o modificar.

	Actividades durante el tiempo libre	La gente de nuestra edad, en general	Los estudiantes de esta universidad
Físicas			
Intelectuales			
Sociales			
Otras			

A escribir

Ahora use la información de **Antes de escribir** para escribir un ensayo comparativo. ¿Es usted una persona representativa de su generación y de su universidad? Cuando usted era más joven, ¿hacía las mismas cosas? Hay más ayuda en Connect.

Más ideas para su portafolio

- Si usted juega en un equipo o hace un deporte a nivel competitivo, incluya una foto suya (*of yourself*) haciendo ese deporte. Describa su posición en el equipo y otros detalles importantes (*ranking*, nombre del entrenador / de la entrenadora, etcétera). Si no practica ningún deporte, describa el tipo de ejercicio físico que hace, incluyendo una foto si es posible. Y si no hace ningún tipo de ejercicio físico, explique cómo pasa su tiempo libre.
- Incluya dos imágenes de lugares favoritos o especiales que usted relaciona con el tiempo libre y los pasatiempos de su infancia o adolescencia. Explique por qué iba allí, y qué hacía, con quiénes, etcétera.
- Si ha estado jugando (*you have been playing*) Practice Spanish: Study Abroad, en Quest 7 usted supo que su amigo David está leyendo *El ingenioso hidalgo don Quijote de la Mancha*, de Miguel de Cervantes Saavedra, en su tiempo libre. Busque información sobre la trama (*plot*), el autor, el contexto histórico, los personajes (*characters*), etcétera, de esta novela. ¿Por qué cree usted que esta novela es tan famosa? ¿Ve paralelos entre los personajes de *Don Quijote* y los personajes del juego? Escriba un informe (*report*) y entrégueselo (*hand it in*) a su profesor(a) o presente sus ideas en clase.

©McGraw-Hill Education

Sugerencia: You are now ready to play Quest 7 in **Practice Spanish: Study Abroad**.

EN RESUMEN En este capítulo

AFTER STUDYING THIS CHAPTER I CAN . . .

- ☐ talk about sports and other pastimes (300–301)
- ☐ talk about household chores (302–303)
- ☐ use the imperfect to describe past actions (306–308)
- ☐ use interrogatives more effectively, especially **¿qué?** and **¿cuál(es)?** (312–313)
- ☐ use superlatives to describe "the most" in a category (314–315)
- ☐ recognize/describe at least 2–3 aspects of Puerto Rican cultures

Gramática en breve

26. The Imperfect

Regular -ar *Endings*
-aba, -abas, -aba, -ábamos, -abais, -aban

Regular -er/-ir *Endings*
-ía, -ías, -ía, -íamos, -íais, -ían

Verbs Irregular in the Imperfect
ir: iba, ibas, iba, íbamos, ibais, iban
ser: era, eras, era, éramos, erais, eran
ver: veía, veías, veía, veíamos, veíais, veían

27. Superlatives

el/la/los/las + *noun* + **más/menos** + *adjective* + **de**
el/la/los/las + **mejor(es)/peor(es)** + *noun* + **de**

28. Interrogative Words

¿qué? { = definition, explanation; = identification: + *noun* = *what/which* . . . ?
¿cuál(es)? = choice: + *verb* = *what/which (one)* . . . ?

Vocabulario

Los verbos

pelear	to fight
sonar (suena)	to ring; to sound
tocarle (qu) a uno (like **gustar**)	to be someone's turn

Repaso: deber, necesitar, tener que

Los pasatiempos, diversiones y aficiones

la afición	hobby
la diversión	fun activity
el pasatiempo	pastime
los ratos libres	spare (free) time
el tiempo libre	free time
aburrirse	to get bored
caminar	to walk
dar un paseo	to take a walk
dar una caminata	to hike; to go for a hike
hacer planes (*m.*) **para** + *inf.*	to make plans to (*do something*)
hacer un pícnic	to have a picnic
hacer (el) yoga	to do yoga
ir...	to go . . .
a un bar / a una discoteca	to a bar / to a disco
a un museo	to a museum
al teatro / a un concierto	to the theater / to a concert
jugar (juego) (gu) a las cartas / a los videojuegos / al ajedrez	to play cards / videogames / chess
ser...	to be . . .
aburrido/a	boring
divertido/a	fun

Repaso: dar/hacer una fiesta, hacer *camping*, ir a una fiesta / al cine / a ver una película, jugar (juego) (gu), sacar (qu) fotos / fotografías, tomar el sol

Los deportes

correr	to run
entrenar	to practice; to train
esquiar (esquío)	to ski
ganar	to win
montar a caballo	to ride a horse
montar/pasear en bicicleta	to ride a bicycle
patinar	to skate
ser aficionado/a (a)	to be a fan (of)
surfear	to surf

Repaso: jugar (juego) (gu) al + *sport,* **nadar, perder (pierdo), practicar (qu)**

el ciclismo	bicycling
el equipo	team
el fútbol	soccer
el fútbol americano	football
el/la jugador(a)	player
la natación	swimming
el partido	game, match
el patinaje	skating
la pelota	ball
el deporte	sport

Cognados: el basquetbol, el béisbol, el esquí, el golf, el hockey, el tenis, el voleibol

Algunos aparatos domésticos

la aspiradora	vacuum cleaner
la cafetera	coffee maker
el congelador	freezer
el horno de microondas	microwave oven
la lavadora	washing machine
el lavaplatos	dishwasher
el refrigerador	refrigerator
la secadora	clothes dryer
la tostadora	toaster
el aparato doméstico	home appliance

Repaso: la estufa

Los quehaceres domésticos

el quehacer doméstico	household chore
barrer el piso	to sweep the floor
hacer la cama	to make the bed
lavar	to wash
limpiar (la casa)	to clean (house)
pasar la aspiradora	to vacuum
planchar	to iron
poner la mesa	to set the table
quitar la mesa	to clear the table
sacar (qu) la basura	to take out the trash

Repaso: la cama, la casa, hacer, la mesa, los platos, poner, la ropa

Otros sustantivos

la escuela	school
el/la niñero/a	babysitter
el siglo	century
el trabajo	work; job

Los adjetivos

deportivo/a	sporting, sports (*adj.*); sports-loving
doméstico/a	domestic, related to the home
libre	free, unoccupied
pesado/a	boring
-ito/a	small, little

Palabras adicionales

al aire libre	outdoors
de adolescente	as an adolescent
de niño/a	as a child
en la actualidad	currently, right now
mientras	while

Repaso: ¿a qué hora?, ¿adónde?, ¿cómo?, ¿cuál(es)?, ¿cuándo?, ¿cuánto/a?, ¿cuántos/as?, ¿de dónde?, ¿de quién(es)?, ¿dónde?, ¿por qué?, ¿qué?, ¿quién(es)?

Vocabulario personal

La salud°

°La... *Health*

En este capítulo

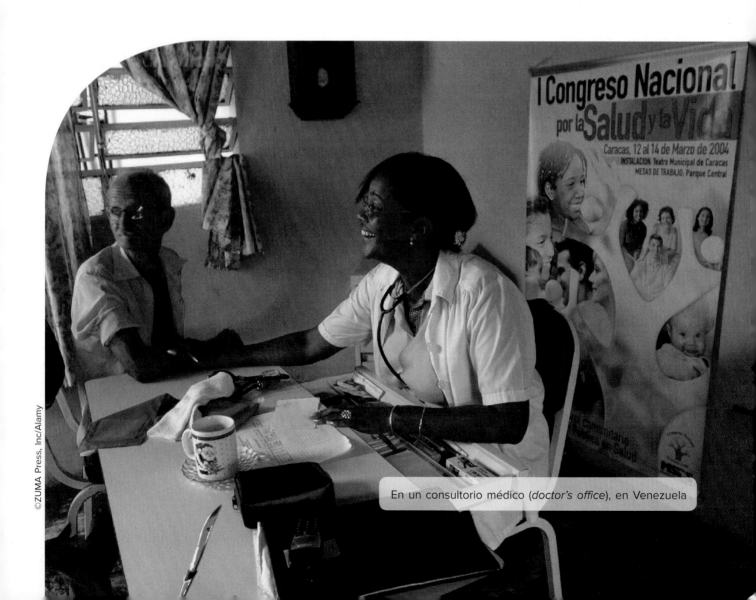

En un consultorio médico (*doctor's office*), en Venezuela

VENEZUELA

32,4 (coma cuatro) millones de habitantes

- Venezuela es un país muy rico en petróleo. Petróleos de Venezuela S.A.* (PDVSA) es una de las empresas (compañías) petroleras más grandes del mundo. Es una corporación del estado que controla la exploración, producción y venta[a] de todo el petróleo del país.
- La Fundación del Estado para el Sistema Nacional de las Orquestas Juveniles e Infantiles de Venezuela (FESNOJIV) es una iniciativa que fomenta la instrucción musical «como instrumento de organización social y desarrollo[b] comunitario».

[a]*sale* [b]*development*

ENTREVISTA

- ¿Cómo es su salud[a] en general? ¿Lleva usted una vida sana[b]?
- ¿Hace usted ejercicio con frecuencia? ¿Hizo usted ejercicio ayer?
- ¿Cuándo fue la última vez que usted fue al médico? ¿Fue por algo grave o fue una visita rutinaria?

[a]*health* [b]*healthy*

Cecilia Figueroa Martín contesta las preguntas.

- Creo que mi salud es excelente, afortunadamente. ¡Toco madera![a] La verdad es que llevo una vida sana por lo general. Como bien, no bebo mucho, no fumo nada...
- Sí, trato de[b] hacer ejercicio por lo menos tres o cuatro días a la semana: voy al gimnasio o corro tres o cuatro millas. Ayer corrí.
- La última vez que fui al médico fue el mes pasado, para mi chequeo anual.

[a]¡Toco... *Knock on wood!* [b]trato... *I try to*

*S.A. = Sociedad Anónima (*Inc.*)

VOCABULARIO: PREPARACIÓN

You can hear the pronunciation of theme vocabulary words and phrases in the Connect eBook.

La salud y el bienestar°

La... *Health and well-being*

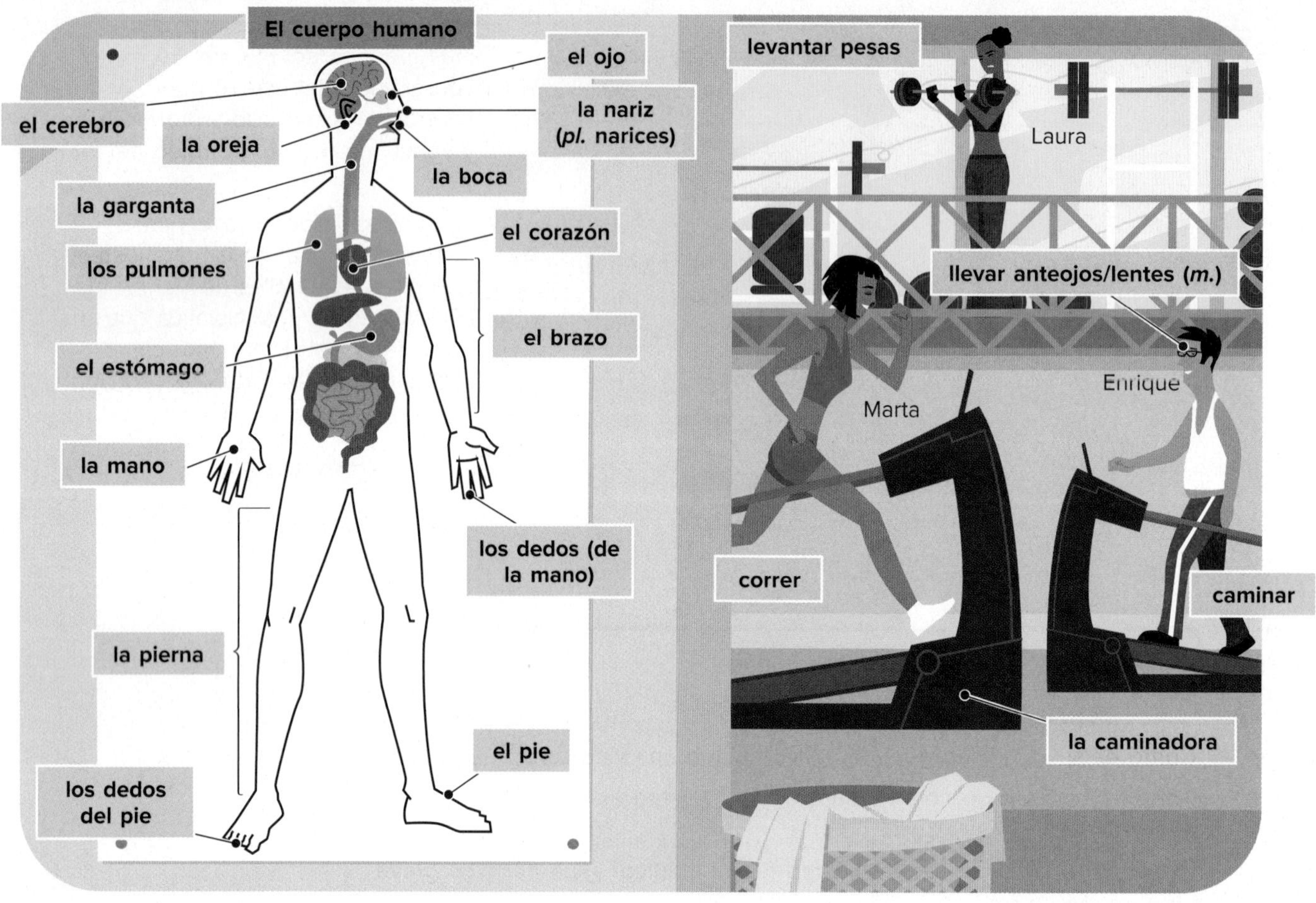

El cuerpo humano

la cabeza head
el oído inner ear

Para cuidar de la salud

comer comidas sanas to eat healthy food
cuidarse to take care of oneself
dejar de + *inf.* to stop (*doing something*)
dormir (duermo) (u) lo suficiente to get enough sleep
hacer ejercicio to exercise; to get exercise
hacer... to do . . .
  ejercicios aeróbicos aerobics
  (el método) Pilates Pilates
llevar lentes (*m.*) de contacto to wear contact lenses
llevar una vida sana/tranquila to lead a healthy/calm life
practicar (qu) deportes to practice, play sports
respirar to breathe

Así se dice

los anteojos, los lentes = las gafas (*Sp.*)
los lentes de contacto = las lentes de contacto (*Sp.*), las lentillas (*Sp.*)
la caminadora = la cinta de andar (*Sp.*), la cinta de correr, la cinta rodante, la trotadora (*P.R.*), la rueda de molino

Comunicación

A. Asociaciones

Paso 1. ¿Qué partes del cuerpo humano asocia usted con las siguientes palabras? **¡OJO!** A veces hay más de una respuesta posible.

1. un ataque
2. comer
3. cantar
4. los anteojos
5. pensar
6. la digestión
7. el amor (*love*)
8. fumar
9. la música
10. el perfume
11. caminar
12. una flor

Paso 2. ¿Qué verbos asocia usted con las siguientes partes del cuerpo?

1. los ojos
2. los dedos
3. la boca
4. el oído
5. el estómago
6. los pulmones

B. Hablando de la salud.

¿Qué significan para usted las siguientes oraciones?

MODELOS: Se debe comer comidas sanas. →
Eso quiere decir (*means*) que es necesario comer muchas verduras, que...
También significa que no debemos comer muchos dulces o...

1. Se debe dormir lo suficiente todas las noches.
2. Hay que hacer ejercicio.
3. Es necesario llevar una vida tranquila.
4. En general, uno debe cuidarse mucho.
5. Es importante llevar una vida sana.

Vocabulario útil

Eso quiere decir...
Esto significa que...
También...

C. ¿Cómo vive usted?

Paso 1. Indique las cosas que usted hace para mantener la salud y el bienestar.

	SÍ	NO
1. comer comidas sanas en general	☐	☐
2. no comer muchos dulces	☐	☐
3. comer muchas frutas y verduras	☐	☐
4. hacer ejercicio moderado diariamente	☐	☐
5. beber agua suficiente todos los días	☐	☐
6. dormir por lo menos ocho horas por noche	☐	☐
7. tomar bebidas alcohólicas en moderación	☐	☐
8. no beber mucho café o té	☐	☐
9. no fumar	☐	☐

Paso 2. Escriba un hábito malo que debe dejar y uno bueno que desea adquirir (*to acquire*).

Paso 3. Ahora, en parejas, entrevístense sobre los hábitos de los **Pasos 1** y **2**. Luego díganle a la clase algo que tienen en común.

MODELO: E1: Yo como comidas sanas, pero como muchos dulces. ¿Y tú?
E2: Yo también. Comer muchos dulces es un hábito que quiero dejar. →
Nosotros comemos muchos dulces y es un hábito que queremos dejar.

D. Consejos expertos

Paso 1. Usando los verbos que usted acaba de aprender sobre el cuidado (*care*) de la salud, haga una lista de cinco consejos que cree que son importantes para toda la comunidad universitaria. Delos usando la forma de **ustedes** de los mandatos.

Paso 2. En parejas, comparen sus consejos y combínenlos para crear una lista finalizada. Luego preséntenla a la clase. ¿Son similares todas las listas?

Vocabulario útil

fumar to smoke
tomar cerveza / bebidas alcohólicas
usar drogas

Una cita en el consultorio°

°Una... *An appointment at the doctor's office*

Javier está sano. El enfermero le toma la temperatura.

Rosa está enferma. Se siente mal. Le duele la cabeza y todo el cuerpo. Tiene fiebre. Tiene la gripe.

el antibiótico	antibiotic
la cita	appointment; date
el dolor (de)	pain, ache (in)
el diente / la muela	tooth / molar
la enfermedad	illness
el enfermero / la enfermera	nurse
el farmacéutico / la farmacéutica	pharmacist
la fiebre	fever
la gripe	flu
el jarabe	(cough) syrup
la medicina	medicine
el médico / la médica	doctor, physician
la pastilla	pill
la receta	prescription
el resfriado	cold (*illness*)
la tos	cough
el tratamiento	treatment
la vacuna	vaccination; shot

Cognados: el/la dentista, la visita

doler (duele)	to hurt, ache
enfermarse	to get sick
estar enfermo/a	to be sick
mareado/a	to be dizzy; nauseated
resfriado/a	to be congested, stuffed up
sano/a	to be healthy
guardar cama	to stay in bed
molestar	to bother
resfriarse (me resfrío)	to get/catch a cold
sacar (qu) la lengua	to stick out one's tongue
sentirse (me siento) (i)	to feel
tener dolor de cabeza	to have a headache
dolor de estómago	to have a stomachache
dolor de muela	to have a toothache
tener fiebre	to have a fever
toser	to cough

¡OJO!

Use the term **el médico / la médica** to talk *about* doctors in general and **el/la dentista** for the dentist. However, when you use the doctor or dentist's name, you should use the definite article plus the title: **el doctor Gómez, la dentista Velázquez.** To speak directly *to* him or her, just use the title **doctor(a).**

¡OJO!

Doler and **molestar** are used like **gustar**: **Me duele la cabeza. Me molestan los ojos.**

Así se dice

el resfriado = el catarro, el resfrío
estar resfriado/a = estar constipado/a (*Sp.*)

la gripe = la gripa
el consultorio = la consulta

Comunicación

A. Estudio de palabras. Complete las siguientes oraciones con una palabra derivada de la palabra en rojo y subrayada.

1. Si me resfrío, tengo ______.
2. La respiración ocurre cuando alguien ______.
3. Si me ______, estoy enfermo/a. Un(a) ______ me toma la temperatura.
4. Cuando alguien tose, es porque tiene ______.
5. Si me duele el estómago, tengo ______ de estómago.

B. Enfermedades comunes

Paso 1. ¿Con qué enfermedad se relacionan las siguientes situaciones, con la gripe, con el resfriado común o con un virus gastrointestinal?

1. tener tos
2. tener fiebre
3. tener dolor de garganta
4. ponerse una vacuna
5. tomar antibióticos
6. ir al médico
7. tener vómitos y diarrea
8. tener dolor de estómago
9. tomar pastillas
10. guardar cama

Paso 2. En parejas, hablen de la última vez que sufrieron (*you had*) una enfermedad común. ¿Cuándo fue? ¿Cómo se sentían? ¿Fueron al médico?

Nota cultural

El cuidado° médico en el mundo hispano

°*care*

En el mundo hispano el cuidado médico puede ser muy variado. Depende principalmente del[a] nivel económico del país y después (como ocurre en este país) del nivel económico del individuo. Pero en todos los países hispanos hay excelentes médicos en todo tipo de especialidades, bien preparados[b] en las universidades de su país o en el extranjero. Aquí hay unos aspectos interesantes del cuidado médico en el mundo hispanohablante.

- **Los farmacéuticos y practicantes** Los hispanos consultan con frecuencia a estos profesionales cuando no pueden o no sienten la necesidad de acudir[c] a un médico. Por ejemplo, cuando uno tiene una enfermedad leve,[d] puede ir a la farmacia para pedir consejo sobre una medicina o conseguir un remedio, sin tener receta. Cuando se necesita un tratamiento simple, como ponerse una inyección, se puede llamar a un practicante, que es más o menos como un enfermero.
- **Los remedios tradicionales o alternativos** Homeópatas, naturópatas, sanadores,[e] tiendas de botánica[f]... Hay una importante tradición, de gran diversidad en el mundo hispanohablante, de consultar a personas que tienen conocimiento[g] de los remedios naturales o de curaciones basadas en la fe,[h] especialmente para las molestias y menores enfermedades más frecuentes.

[a]*on the* [b]*trained* [c]*go* [d]*minor, mild* [e]*healers* [f]*herbs*

©David R. Frazier Photolibrary, Inc./Alamy

A diferencia de las farmacias en este país, en las farmacias de muchos países hispanos no se venden muchos productos para la higiene personal ni comestibles.

¿A quién consulta usted cuando está enfermo/a?

[g]*knowledge* [h]*faith*

C. **Hablando de la salud**

Paso 1. Complete las oraciones lógicamente para describir la situación de las personas de las fotos.

©Fuse/Getty Images

1. Irene está _____ ahora. _____ muy sana y siempre _____ bien. Todos los días _____. Nunca le duele _____ y nunca tiene _____.

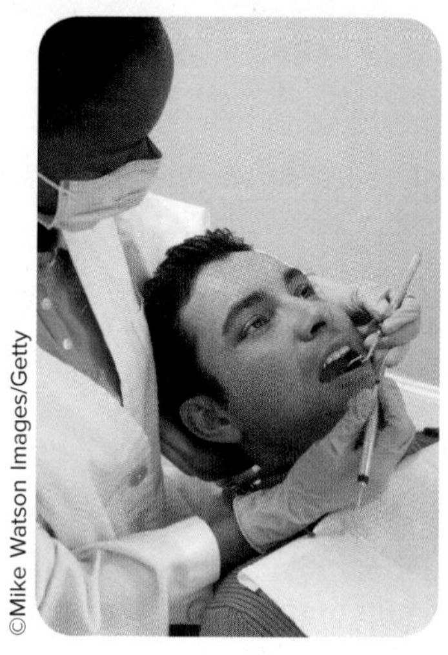

©Mike Watson Images/Getty

2. Martín está con su _____. Ayer tuvo que hacer una _____ urgente porque le dolía mucho una _____.

Paso 2. ¿Y ustedes? En parejas, hablen de cómo se sienten últimamente (*lately*). ¿Les duele alguna parte del cuerpo? ¿Toman pastillas para el dolor u otras medicinas? ¿Se ponen la vacuna de la gripe regularmente?

Algo sobre...

la harina[a] de maíz blanco

©bonchan/Getty Images

Una arepa

La harina de maíz blanco es el ingrediente básico para hacer dos platos típicos venezolanos: las arepas y las hallacas. Las arepas son similares al pan de pita y se pueden comer como sándwiches. Las hallacas son parecidas[a] a los tamales; son una comida tradicional de la Navidad y la Nochevieja.

¿Hay algo similar a las arepas o a las hallacas en la cocina de su familia?

[a]*flour* [b]*similar*

Nota comunicativa

Cómo expresar una cualidad general: *lo* + *adjetivo*

To describe the general qualities or characteristics of something, use **lo** with the masculine singular form of an adjective.

lo bueno/malo **lo más importante** **lo mejor/peor** **lo menos interesante**

This structure has a number of English equivalents, especially in colloquial speech.

lo bueno = the good thing/part/news, what's good

lo más importante = the most important thing/part/news, what's most important

You will use expressions of this type in **Comunicación C.**

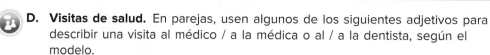

D. **Visitas de salud.** En parejas, usen algunos de los siguientes adjetivos para describir una visita al médico / a la médica o al / a la dentista, según el modelo.

MODELO: **peor** → **Lo** peor de ir a mi dentista es tener que esperar antes de mi cita.

1. malo / bueno 2. peor / mejor 3. más importante

E. **Refranes hispanos.** Empareje una frase de la columna A con otra de la columna B para formar algunos refranes muy comunes en el mundo hispano. En algunos casos lo/la puede ayudar la rima. Luego explique lo que significan los refranes. ¿Cuál es el equivalente en inglés?

COLUMNA A	COLUMNA B
1. _____ La salud no se compra:	a. engorda (*fattens*).
2. _____ Músculos de Sansón,	b. no tiene precio (*is priceless*).
3. _____ Si quieres vivir sano,	c. y cerebro de mosquito.
4. _____ Para enfermedad de años,	d. no hay medicina.
5. _____ Ojos que no ven,	e. acuéstate y levántate temprano.
6. _____ Lo que no mata (*doesn't kill*),	f. corazón que no siente.

«Remedios para todos» Segmento 1

Antes de mirar

Cuando usted tiene problemas de salud, ¿a quién consulta? Indique a todas las personas de la lista que usted haya consultado (*may have consulted*) por razones de salud por lo menos una vez.

- ☐ mi madre/padre
- ☐ mi abuelo/a
- ☐ un médico / una médica
- ☐ un(a) homeópata
- ☐ un(a) naturópata
- ☐ ¿ ?

En esta botánica (*herb store*) se venden velas (*candles*), imágenes, collares (*necklaces*), rosarios, incienso, agua florida (*aromatic essences*) y mucho más. ¡Hasta (*Even*) imágenes de Buda para la buena suerte (*luck*)!

Este segmento

Laura presenta un reportaje sobre una botánica, una tienda tradicional típica del Caribe.

Vocabulario del segmento

desde luego	certainly
ahorrar	to save
mezclarse	to mix up/in with
han visitado	have you visited
tuvo la amabilidad de concedernos	was kind enough to give us
sobar	to rub
la sávila	aloe vera
la quemada	burn
el catarro	**el resfriado**
broncear la piel	to tan (one's skin)
la tuna	cactus
el riñón	kidney
la limpieza	cleaning, cleansing
la hoja	leaf

Después de mirar

A. ¿Está claro? Complete las siguientes oraciones con información del video.

1. Las botánicas son tiendas típicas de los países ________.
2. En una botánica se compran ingredientes naturales para hacer tés y ________ tradicionales.
3. Los viejos y los ________ van a las botánicas.
4. La tuna se usa para problemas del estómago y de los ________.

B. Un poco más. Conteste las siguientes preguntas.

1. ¿Por qué se llaman «botánicas» las tiendas como la (*that*) de la Sra. Santiago?
2. ¿En qué tipo de tratamientos se especializan las botánicas?
3. ¿Qué objetos se puede comprar en una botánica? ¿Para qué sirven?

C. Y ahora, ustedes. En grupos, hablen de las comidas y bebidas que ustedes toman cuando no se sienten bien y de las cosas que hacen cuando quieren conseguir buena suerte o necesitan calmarse. Por ejemplo, ¿soban o tocan ustedes algo, como una imagen de Buda?

GRAMÁTICA

¿Recuerda usted?

Since **Capítulo 8** you have been using first the preterite and then the imperfect in appropriate contexts. Indicate which tense you use to do each of the following.

	PRETERITE	IMPERFECT
1. to tell what you did yesterday	☐	☐
2. to tell what you used to do when you were in grade school	☐	☐
3. to describe background details, like physical or mental states	☐	☐
4. to tell about a completed action	☐	☐
5. to talk about the way things used to be	☐	☐
6. to describe an action that was in progress	☐	☐

If you understand these uses of the preterite and the imperfect, the summary of their uses in **Gramática 30** will be very easy for you.

30 Talking About the Past (Part 5)

Using the Preterite and the Imperfect

Gramática en acción: En el consultorio de la Dra. Méndez

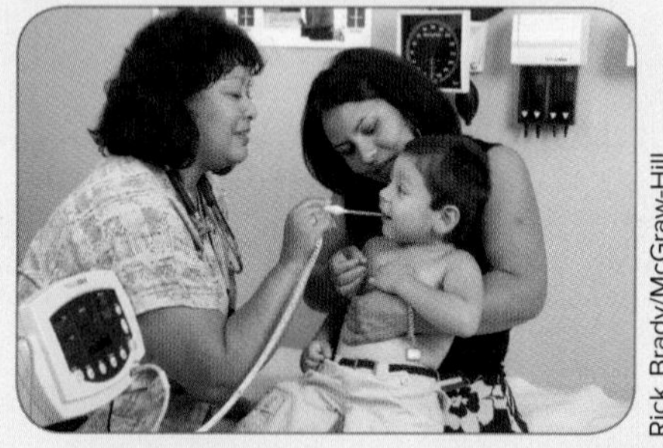

Rick Brady/McGraw-Hill

DRA. MÉNDEZ: ¿Cuándo empezó a sentirse mal su hijo?

MADRE: Ayer por la tarde. Estaba resfriado, tosía mucho y se quejaba de que le dolían el cuerpo y la cabeza.

DRA. MÉNDEZ: ¿Y le notó algo de fiebre?

MADRE: Sí. Por la noche le tomé la temperatura y tenía treinta y nueve grados.*

DRA. MÉNDEZ: A ver... Abre la boca, por favor.

grados Celsius	36	37	38	39	40	41
grados Fahrenheit	96.8	98.6	100.4	102.2	104	105.8

¿Y usted?

1. ¿Cómo se sentía usted ayer por la noche?
2. ¿A qué hora se acostó?

You have already learned and used the preterite (**Capítulos 8** and **9**) and imperfect tenses (**Capítulo 10**). In this chapter you will begin to use them together to talk about the past.

Keep the following points in mind.

1. The preterite and the imperfect are both past tenses.
2. They are both used to talk about the same point in the past.

In Dr. Méndez's office *DR. MÉNDEZ: When did your son begin to feel ill? MOTHER: Yesterday afternoon. He was stuffed up, he was coughing a lot, and he was complaining that his body and head were hurting. DR. MÉNDEZ: And did you notice any fever? MOTHER: Yes. At night I took his temperature, and it was thirty-nine degrees. DR. MÉNDEZ: Let's see . . . Open your mouth, please.*

**Normal body temperature is 37°C (98.6°F).*

They *differ* in the point of view (aspect) about the past that they each convey. This is the same as with English usage. When you decide to say *I ran, I used to run,* or *I was going to run,* you are making a decision about the aspect of the past action that you want to communicate.

Here is a summary of the main uses of the two tenses. You will learn about them on the next pages.

Pretérito	Imperfecto
• beginning/end of an action • completed action • series of completed actions • the action on the "stage"	• habitual/repeated action • ongoing action • background information • the setting for the action

Note: I, II, III = completed actions in the past, one, two, three or more
~~~~ = ongoing or repeated actions in the past, background detail

Differences between the Preterite and the Imperfect / **Las diferencias entre el pretérito y el imperfecto**

1. Beginning/End vs. Habitual

Use the **preterite** to tell about the beginning or the end of a past action. III

El sábado pasado, el partido de fútbol **empezó** a la una. **Terminó** a las cuatro. El entrenador **habló** a las cinco.
Last Saturday, the soccer game began at one. It ended at four. The coach spoke (began to speak) at five.

Use the imperfect to talk about the habitual nature of an action (something you always did). ~~~~

Había un partido **todos los sábados.** Muchas personas **jugaban todas las semanas.**
There was a game every Saturday. Many people played every week.

---

2. Completed vs. Ongoing

Use the **preterite** to express an action that is viewed as completed. II

El partido **duró** tres horas. **Ganaron** Los Lobos.
The game lasted three hours. The Lobos won.

Use the imperfect to tell about simultaneous events (with **mientras** = *while*).
~~~~ mientras ~~~~
Mientras ~~~~, ~~~~

Yo **estaba** en la cocina **mientras** todos **miraban** el partido.
I was in the kitchen while everyone was watching the game.

Mientras mi amigo **veía** el partido, **hablaba** con su novia.
While my friend was watching the game, he was talking with his girlfriend.

Use the imperfect and the preterite in the same sentence to tell what was happening when another action took place. I ~~~~ I

Yo no **vi** el final del partido. **Estaba** en la cocina cuando **terminó.** (El partido **terminó** cuando **estaba** en la cocina.)
I didn't see the end of the game. I was in the kitchen when it ended. (The game ended while I was in the kitchen.)

---

3. Series of Completed Actions vs. Background Details

Use the **preterite** to express a series of completed actions.

Durante el partido, los jugadores **corrieron, saltaron** y **gritaron.**
During the game, the players ran, jumped, and shouted.

Use the imperfect to give background details of many kinds: time, location, weather, mood, age, physical and mental characteristics.

Todos los jugadores **eran** jóvenes; **tenían** 17 o 18 años. ¡Y todos **esperaban** ganar!
All the players were young; they were 17 or 18 years old. And all of them hoped to win!

4. Action vs. the Setting

The **preterite** and imperfect are also used together in the presentation of an event.

- The imperfect sets the stage, describes the conditions that caused the action, or emphasizes the continuing nature of a particular action.
- The preterite narrates the actions.

Era un día hermoso. **Hacía** mucho sol, pero no **hacía** mucho calor. Como no **tenía** que trabajar en la oficina, **salí** a comprar unas flores. Luego **me puse** camiseta y pantalones cortos y **decidí** trabajar todo el día en el jardín.
It was a beautiful day. It was very sunny, but it wasn't very hot. Since I didn't have to work at the office, I went out to buy some flowers. Then I put on a T-shirt and shorts and decided to work in the garden all day.

Changes in Meaning / **Los cambios de significado**

Remember that, when used in the **preterite**, **saber, conocer,** and **querer** have English equivalents different from that of their infinitives. (See page 279.) In the **imperfect**, the English equivalents of these verbs do not differ from the infinitive meanings.

—¿Ya **sabías** que se murió el abuelo de Miguel?
—Sí, lo **supe** el mes pasado.
*"**Did** you already **know** that Miguel's grandfather passed away?"*
*"Yes, **I found out** (**learned**) about it last month."*

—Anoche **conocí** a Roberto.
—¿Anoche? Yo pensaba que ya lo **conocías.**
*"Last night **I met** Roberto."*
*"Last night? I thought you already **knew** him."*

—¿No **querías** hablar con el profesor ayer?
—Sí, **quise** llamarlo, pero no estaba en su oficina.
*"Didn't you **want** to talk to the professor yesterday?"*
*"Yes, I **tried** to call him but he wasn't in his office."*

Preterite vs. Imperfect Summary

Beginning/middle vs. habitual/repeated
Completed vs. ongoing
Actions vs. background
Action vs. setting

Práctica y comunicación

A. En la escuela secundaria

Paso 1. Autoprueba. ¿Se usa el pretérito (P) o el imperfecto (I) ?

1. para dar detalles de fondo (*background details*) y descripciones como el tiempo y la hora ______
2. para hablar de acciones habituales ______
3. para narrar acciones completadas ______
4. para hablar de hábitos personales ______
5. para hablar de una acción en progreso ______
6. para narrar una secuencia de acciones ______
7. para decir lo que pasaba cuando otra acción ocurrió ______
8. para describir condiciones y estados físicos o afectivos ______

***Prác. A, Paso 1: Answers:** 1. I 2. I 3. P 4. I 5. I 6. P 7. I 8. I*

Paso 2. ¿Cómo era su salud cuando usted estaba en la secundaria? Complete las siguientes oraciones con la forma apropiada del imperfecto o el pretérito. Use **no** cuando sea (*it's*) necesario.

Cuando estaba en la secundaria...

1. ________ (resfriarse) con frecuencia
2. ________ (tener) alergias
3. ________ (tener) una operación
4. ________ (ir) al dentista con regularidad
5. ________ (tener) la gripe / mononucleosis
6. ________ (hacer) mucho ejercicio
7. ________ (sufrir) (*to have*) un accidente de coche
8. ________ (gustar me) quedarme en casa y no ir a la escuela

Paso 3. Ahora, en parejas, túrnense para hacer y contestar preguntas basadas en las oraciones del **Paso 2.** Luego díganle a la clase algo que tienen en común.

MODELO: **E1:** Cuando estabas en la escuela secundaria, ¿te resfriabas con frecuencia?
E2: No, no me resfriaba con frecuencia. ¿Y tú?
E1: Yo tampoco.

B. En el consultorio. Estos son algunos de los pacientes que el Dr. Sánchez vio ayer en el consultorio. Describa cómo **se sentía** cada paciente. Luego empareje cada caso con lo que **hizo** el Dr. Sánchez y complete esas oraciones.

LOS SÍNTOMAS DE LOS PACIENTES (IMPERFECTO)

1. Un paciente: **tener** mucho frío
2. A otro le: **doler** la garganta
3. Un señor: **creer** que estaba anémico
4. Una señora: **sentirse** muy mal sin saber por qué
5. Un señor mayor: **querer** más medicinas
6. Un niño: **estar** muy alto para su edad (*age*)
7. A un hombre le: **doler** el pecho (*chest*)

POR ESO, EL DR. SÁNCHEZ... (PRETÉRITO)

a. _____ **hacerle** muchas preguntas.
b. _____ **darle** una nueva receta.
c. _____ **tomarle** la temperatura.
d. _____ **escucharle** los sonidos (*sounds*) de los pulmones y del corazón.
e. _____ **pedirle** un análisis de sangre (*blood*).
f. _____ **hacerle** sacar la lengua.
g. _____ **decirle** que su chequeo (*check-up*) mostraba que estaba muy bien.

Nota comunicativa

Algunas palabras y expresiones asociadas con el pretérito y el imperfecto

Certain words and expressions are frequently associated with the preterite, others with the imperfect. Only the words that are translated are new.

Some words often associated with the **preterite** are:

ayer, anteayer, anoche (*last night*)	**de repente** (*suddenly*)
una vez, dos veces (*twice*)...	**en seguida**
el año pasado (*last*), **el lunes pasado...**	

Some words often associated with the **imperfect** are:

todos los días, todos los lunes...	**mientras**
siempre, frecuentemente (*frequently*)	**de niño/a, de adolescente**

As you continue to practice using the preterite and imperfect, these expressions can help you determine which tense to use. These words do not *automatically* cue either tense, however. The most important consideration is the meaning that you want to express.

Ayer cenamos temprano.	*Yesterday we had dinner early.*
Ayer cenábamos cuando Juan llamó.	*Yesterday we were having dinner when Juan called.*
Jugaba al fútbol **de niño.**	*He played soccer as a child.*
Empezó a jugar al fútbol **de niño.**	*He began to play soccer as a child.*

You will see these words and expressions in activities in the rest of this section and throughout the rest of *Puntos de partida*.

Algo sobre...

Simón Bolívar

©DEA/M. Seemuller/De Agostini/Getty Images

Simón Bolívar (1783–1830), el Libertador

Simón Bolívar fue un general y político venezolano que es conocido[a] en Latinoamérica como el Libertador. Fue la figura principal en el movimiento por la independencia de España de varios países latinoamericanos (Venezuela, Colombia, Panamá, el Perú, Bolivia y el Ecuador). Desde 1819 hasta 1830 fue presidente de la Gran Colombia, una unión de naciones hispanohablantes que se estableció después de ganar su independencia de España. La Gran Colombia duró[b] solo hasta 1831.

¿Quién es el gran héroe de la independencia de los Estados Unidos? ¿Qué cargos[c] tuvo?

[a]*known* [b]*lasted* [c]*positions*

C. La última vez que...

Paso 1. Complete las siguientes oraciones con detalles personales verdaderos. Luego añada otros detalles.

La última vez que alguien me llamó por teléfono...

1. La última vez que alguien me llamó por teléfono fue ______ (ayer, anoche, esta mañana...).
2. Cuando sonó el teléfono yo estaba ______ (estudiando, durmiendo, ...) y estaba ______ (solo/a, con un amigo / una amiga, con...).
3. La persona que me llamó era ______ y hablamos por ______ (tiempo).
4. Cuando colgué (*I hung up*) el teléfono, me sentía ______ (contento/a, preocupado/a...) y quería ______.

La última vez que me reí a carcajadas (*I laughed out loud*)...

1. La última vez que me reí a carcajadas fue ______.
2. Estaba en... y estaba ______ (acción).
3. Me reí tanto (*so much*) porque ______.
4. Después de reírme tanto, ______ (me sentí bien, me dolía el estómago...).

Paso 2. Ahora, en parejas, compartan (*share*) sus oraciones. Escojan (*Choose*) las respuestas más interesantes y compártanlas con la clase.

D. Pequeñas historias

Paso 1. Complete el siguiente párrafo con una de las palabras o frases de la lista. Antes de empezar, mire la foto que acompaña el párrafo para tener una idea general del tema de la historia.

VOCABULARIO: íbamos, nos gustó, nos quedábamos, nos quedamos, nuestra familia decidió, vivíamos

©Imagesource/Getty Images

Cuando éramos niños, Jorge y yo ______[1] en la Argentina. Siempre ______[2] a la playa, a Mar del Plata, para pasar la Navidad. Allí casi siempre ______[3] en el Hotel Fénix. Un año, ______[4] quedarse en otro hotel, el Continental. No ______[5] tanto como el Fénix y por eso, al año siguiente, ______[6] en el Fénix otra vez.

Paso 2. Ahora, para completar la siguiente historia, debe escoger (*choose*) entre el pretérito y el imperfecto en cada caso. Antes de empezar, mire el dibujo que acompaña el párrafo.

Eran las once de la noche y yo (**estaba** / **estuve**[1]) leyendo un libro, cuando de repente se (**apagaban** / **apagaron**[a2]) todas las luces[b] de la casa. (**Ponía** / **Puse**[3]) el libro en el suelo[c] y luego (**usaba** / **usé**[4]) mi celular para tener algo de luz. La verdad es que (**tenía** / **tuve**[5]) mucho miedo. Por eso, (**salía** / **salí**[6]) a la calle.[d] Entonces (**podía** / **pude**[7]) ver que (**había** / **hubo**[8]) un apagón por todo el barrio.[e] La luz (**volvía** / **volvió**[9]) media hora después.

[a]apagar = *to go out* [b]*lights* [c]*floor* [d]*street* [e]un... *a power outage in the whole neighborhood*

E. La historia afectiva de Simón Bolívar

Paso 1. Complete los siguientes párrafos con la forma apropiada de los infinitivos, en el pretérito o el imperfecto.

Simón Bolívar (1783–1830) fue el gran héroe de la independencia sudamericana. Bolívar no _______ (tener[1]) una vida personal muy afortunada. _______ (Ser[2]) hijo de una familia aristocrática española. _______ (Tener[3]) tres hermanos mayores. Sus padres _______ (morirse[4]) cuando Bolívar _______ (ser[5]) muy pequeño y por eso _______ (vivir[6]) varios años con otros parientes.

En 1798, cuando _______ (tener[7]) 15 años, _______ (irse[8]) a estudiar a Madrid. Allí _______ (conocer[9]) a María Teresa, con quien _______ (casarse[a][10]) en 1802. Bolívar _______ (regresar[11]) a Venezuela con su joven esposa. Pero María Teresa _______ (morir[12]) ocho meses después, víctima de la fiebre amarilla. Bolívar _______ (empezar[13]) su carrera[b] como líder nacional viajando por Europa para poder soportar[c] la muerte[d] de María Teresa. Nunca _______ (volver[14]) a casarse.

[a]*to marry* [b]*career* [c]*to deal with* [d]*death*

Paso 2. Comprensión. Conteste las siguientes preguntas.

1. En la familia de Bolívar, ¿era él hermano mayor o el menor (*the younger one*)?
2. ¿Cuántos años tenía Bolívar cuando se casó con María Teresa?
3. ¿De qué murió María Teresa?
4. ¿Por qué empezó a viajar Bolívar?

Estrategia

Una pregunta *no* se contesta siempre con el mismo tiempo verbal de la pregunta. Por ejemplo, si es necesario explicar por qué ocurrió algo (pretérito), se usa el imperfecto.

F. Rubén y Soledad

Paso 1. Complete el párrafo con la forma apropiada de los infinitivos, en el pretérito o en el imperfecto.

Rubén estaba estudiando cuando Soledad entró en el cuarto. Ella le _______ (preguntar[1]) a Rubén si _______ (querer[2]) ir al cine. Rubén le _______ (decir[3]) que sí porque _______ (sentirse[4]) un poco aburrido de estudiar. Los dos _______ (salir[5]) en seguida para el cine. _______ (Ver[6]) una película cómica y _______ (reírse[7]) mucho. Luego, como _______ (hacer[8]) frío, _______ (entrar[9]) en su café favorito, El Gato Negro, y _______ (tomar[10]) churros y chocolate. _______ (Ser[11]) las dos de la mañana cuando por fin _______ (regresar[12]) a casa. Soledad _______ (acostarse[13]) en seguida porque _______ (estar[14]) cansada, pero Rubén _______ (empezar[15]) a estudiar otra vez.

©Boston Globe/Getty Images

Una merienda típicamente española: churros (*fried dough rolled in sugar*) y chocolate

Paso 2. Comprensión. Ahora conteste las siguientes preguntas, según el párrafo.

1. ¿Qué hacía Rubén cuando Soledad entró?
2. ¿Qué le preguntó Soledad a Rubén? (**Le preguntó si...**)
3. ¿Por qué le contestó Rubén que sí?
4. ¿Les gustó la película? ¿Cómo se sabe?
5. ¿Por qué tomaron churros y chocolate después de salir del cine?
6. ¿Qué hora era cuando regresaron a casa?
7. ¿Qué hicieron cuando llegaron a casa?

G. Una enfermedad durante la Navidad

Paso 1. Haga oraciones completas con la forma apropiada de los infinitivos, en el pretérito o el imperfecto.

1. Cuando yo _______ (ser) niño, _______ (pensar) que lo mejor de estar enfermo _______ (ser) pasar el día en casa.
2. Lo peor _______ (ser) que yo _______ (resfriarse) con frecuencia durante las vacaciones.
3. Una vez _______ (*yo:* ponerse) muy enfermo durante la Navidad.
4. Mi madre _______ (llamar) al médico porque yo _______ (tener) una fiebre muy alta.
5. El Dr. Matamoros _______ (venir) a casa en seguida y _______ (ponerme) una inyección de antibióticos porque yo _______ (tener) una infección de garganta.
6. Desgraciadamente (*Unfortunately*), mis padres _______ (tener) que darme un baño de agua fría para bajarme la fiebre, y eso no _______ (gustarme) para nada.
7. Tengo que decir que no _______ (ser) la mejor Navidad de mi vida.
8. Mis primos _______ (venir) a casa, pero yo _______ (estar) demasiado enfermo para jugar.
9. ¡Pero esa Navidad mis abuelos _______ (regalarme) mi primera PlayStation™!

Paso 2. Ahora, en parejas, hablen de la última vez que no se sintieron bien. No olviden usar los verbos en la forma de **tú** para entrevistarse y en la forma de **yo** para contestar.

MODELO: E1: ¿Cuándo te enfermaste la última vez?
E2: Me enfermé el mes pasado. ¿Y tú?

1. ¿Cuándo se enfermaron la última vez?
2. ¿Fue algo serio? ¿Qué síntomas tenían?
3. ¿Fueron al médico? ¿Pudieron ir a clase o al trabajo?
4. ¿Qué hicieron para cuidarse? ¿Alguien los cuidó?
5. ¿Tomaron alguna medicina?

H. Una historia famosa

Paso 1. En la siguiente historia, los verbos se dan en el presente. Póngalos en el pretérito para narrar la historia en el pasado.

La niña _______ (abre[1]) la puerta y _______ (entra[2]) en la casa. _______ (Ve[3]) tres sillas. _______ (Se sienta[4]) en la primera silla, luego en la segunda[a], pero no le _______ (gusta[5]) ninguna. Por eso _______ (se sienta[6]) en la tercera.[b] _______ (Ve[7]) tres platos de comida en la mesa y _______ (decide[8]) comer el más pequeño. Luego, _______ (va[9]) a la alcoba para descansar un poco. Después de probar[c] las camas grandes, _______ (se acuesta[10]) en la cama más pequeña y _______ (se queda[11]) dormida.[d]

[a]*second* [b]*third* [c]*trying* [d]*asleep*

Paso 2. ¿Reconoce usted la historia? Es el cuento de Ricitos de Oro (lit., *Little Golden Curls*) y los tres osos (*bears*). Pero el cuento es un poco aburrido tal como está escrito (*as it is written*) en el **Paso 1.** Mejórelo (*Improve it*) con palabras de **Vocabulario útil** y dando detalles y descripciones (usando el imperfecto). También debe terminar el cuento: ¿Qué pasó al final?

MODELO: Había una vez una niña que **se llamaba** Ricitos de Oro. Un día la niña **fue...**

Vocabulario útil

Había una vez... + *imp.* Once upon a time there was ...
Un día... + *pret.*

el bosque forest
la casita little house

huir to flee*

Present tense forms of* **huir *have a* **y** *(rather than an* **i***) in the stem-changing pattern:* **huyo, huyes**... **Y** *is also used in the preterite third person singular and plural forms (like* **leer***):* **huyó, huyeron**. *The present participle is* **huyendo.**

I. Intercambios

Paso 1. ¿Cuántos años tenían ustedes cuando sus padres los dejaron (*allowed*) hacer las siguientes cosas? Hagan y contesten preguntas sobre ese tema, según el modelo.

MODELO: te dejaron cruzar la calle (*street*) solo/a →
E1: ¿Cuántos años **tenías** cuando tus padres te dejaron cruzar la calle sola?
E2: **Tenía** 7 u 8 años cuando mis padres me dejaron cruzar la calle sola.

¿Cuánatos años tenías cuando tus padres... ?

1. te dejaron cruzar la calle solo/a
2. te permitieron ir de compras solo/a
3. te dejaron acostarte después de las nueve
4. te dejaron estar en casa sin niñero/a
5. te permitieron usar la estufa para cocinar
6. te dejaron ver una película para mayores de 17 años («*R*»)
7. te dejaron buscar tu primer trabajo

Paso 2. Ahora hagan preguntas basadas en las ideas de la siguiente lista para saber cuántos años tenía su compañero/a cuando hizo las cosas de la lista.

MODELO: (aprender) a pasear en bicicleta →
¿Cuántos años tenías cuando aprendiste a pasear en bicicleta?

¿Cuántos años tenías cuando...?

1. ______ (aprender) a pasear en bicicleta
2. ______ (hacer) su primer viaje en avión
3. ______ (tener) su primera cita romántica
4. ______ (empezar) a afeitarse / ______ (teñirse) el pelo (*dye his/her hair*)
5. ______ (conseguir) la licencia de manejar (*driver's license*)
6. ______ (abrir) una cuenta (*account*) en el banco

Paso 3. Ahora, en grupos de cuatro, comparen sus respuestas. Entre todos, ¿quién tenía los padres más estrictos? ¿los menos estrictos?

J. Un evento increíble: Cuando conocí a... Imagine que usted conoció recientemente a su persona famosa favorita. Conteste las siguientes preguntas de su amigo/a, que siente mucha curiosidad y envidia (*envy*). ¡Sea creativo/a y diviértase imaginando!

—¿Qué? ¿Es verdad que conociste a ______? ¿Cómo fue?
—¿Dónde estabas?
—¿Qué hora era?
—¿Con quién estabas? ¿Y con quién estaba él/ella?
—¿Qué estaban haciendo?
—¿Cómo se conocieron? ¿Alguien los presentó (*introduced*)?
—¡No me digas! ¿Qué te dijo? Y tú, ¿qué le dijiste?
—¿Y entonces qué pasó?

¿Recuerda usted?

Que is one of the most frequently used words in the Spanish language, and it has several meanings. Review what you already know about **que** by expressing the following sentences in English.

1. ¿Qué estudias?
2. Tengo que hacer la tarea.
3. No entiendo lo que usted me dice.
4. Creo que la fórmula es correcta.

In **Gramática 31,** you will learn more about **que** and other related terms that you have been using for a while: **quien** and **lo que.**

31 Recognizing *que, quien(es), lo que*

Relative Pronouns

Gramática en acción: Tus médicos, tus mejores amigos

La Organización de Médicos Hispanohablantes: Siempre contigo

Tus médicos pueden ser tus mejores amigos.

- Son personas con quienes puedes hablar de TODO.
- Son personas que pueden ayudarte y explicarte TODO lo que tú necesitas saber de tu salud.
- Tienen consultorios que están CERCA de ti.
- Y además, ¡hablan ESPAÑOL!

¿Y usted?

Complete las oraciones con el nombre de una persona que usted conoce. Incluya la relación que tiene con usted, por ejemplo: **mi madre.**

1. Una persona que tiene mi total confianza es ______.
2. Una persona con quien hablo si necesito ayuda, no importa en qué situación, es ______.
3. Una persona que sabe todo —o casi todo— lo que pasa en mi vida es ______.

a relative pronoun / **un pronombre relativo** = a pronoun that refers back to a noun or phrase already mentioned

Relative Pronouns / **Los pronombres relativos**

Relative pronouns (**Los pronombres relativos**) are words that connect ideas within one sentence. Most frequently they refer back to a noun or an idea that has already been mentioned. In both English and Spanish, these words make communication more efficient and fluid because they help to avoid unnecessary repetition by linking ideas. Notice how this happens in the sentences on the next page.

Your doctors, your best friends *The Organization of Spanish-speaking Doctors: Always with you. Your doctors can be your best friends. ■ They're people with whom you can talk about ANYTHING. ■ They're people that can help you and explain (to you) EVERYTHING that you need to know about your health. ■ They have offices that are CLOSE TO you. ■ And besides, they speak SPANISH!*

Conozco a una **médica**. Es de Venezuela. → Conozco a una médica que es de Venezuela.

I know a **doctor**. *She is from Venezuela.* → *I know a doctor* **who** *is from Venezuela.*

The Spanish language has many relative pronouns. You will learn only three of them in this section.

1. Relative Pronouns

There are four principal *relative pronouns* in English: *that, which, who,* and *whom.* They are usually expressed in Spanish by the relative pronouns at the right, all of which you already know.

Los pronombres relativos		
que =	refers to things and people	*that, which, who*
quien(es) =	refers only to people	*who(m)*
lo que =	refers to a situation	*what, that which*

2. *que* = *that, which, who*

Que is by far the most frequently used relative pronoun in Spanish. It refers to people and things.

> **¡OJO!**
>
> **Que** cannot be used after a preposition to refer to people. See Point 3.

Tuve **una cita** con el médico **que** duró una hora.
I had an appointment with the doctor ***that*** *lasted an hour.*

Es **un buen médico** **que** tiene mucha experiencia.
He's a good doctor ***who*** *has a lot of experience.*

3. *quien, quienes* = *who(m)*

Quien and **quienes** can refer only to people. They are almost always used after a preposition.

La mujer **con quien** hablaba es mi médica.
The woman ***with whom*** *I was speaking is my doctor. (The woman I was speaking with is my doctor.)*

Las enfermeras **a quienes** les dimos las flores cuidaron a mi padre.
The nurses ***to whom*** *we gave the flowers took care of my dad. (The nurses we gave the flowers to took care of my dad.)*

4. *lo que* = *what, that which, the thing that*

Lo que always refers to a whole situation or idea. It can refer to something that has been mentioned before or to something that will be referred to later in the sentence. It frequently starts sentences.

> **¡OJO!**
>
> If you can substitute *that which* for *what* in a sentence, use **lo que,** not **que.**

No entiendo **lo que** **dijo.**
I don't understand ***what (that which)*** *he said.*

Lo que necesito es **estudiar más.**
What (The thing that) *I need is to study more.*

5. Relative Pronouns versus Interrogatives

Que and **quien(es)** sound like **¿qué?** and **¿quién(es)?,** but they are not the same.

- **Que** and **quien(es)** link words within a sentence.
- **¿Qué?** and **¿quién(es)?** ask questions (and they have an accent mark to distinguish them from the relative pronouns).

—**¿Qué** es eso?
—Es una cosa **que** sirve para ver mejor.
"***What*** *is this?*
"It's something ***that*** *helps you see better."*

—**¿Quién** es ese señor?
—Es el profesor con **quien** tengo la clase de psicología.
"***Who*** *is that man?"*
"He's the professor ***with whom*** *I take Psychology."*

Summary of Relative Pronouns

que = that, which, who
quien(es) = *preposition* + whom
lo que = what, that which, the thing that

Práctica y comunicación

A. *¿Que, quien(es) o lo que?*

Paso 1. Autoprueba. Empareje los conceptos con el pronombre relativo apropiado.

1. ______ una cosa		**a.** que
2. ______ una idea		**b.** quien
3. ______ a una persona		**c.** quienes
4. ______ con dos amigos		**d.** lo que

Paso 2. Empareje los elementos de las dos columnas. **¡OJO!** Puede repetir las personas de la Columna B.

COLUMNA A	COLUMNA B
1. ______ Es lo que me dijo mi madre antes de salir para la universidad.	**a.** «Come bien y duerme lo suficiente.»
2. ______ Es la persona en quien yo más confío.	**b.** mi mejor amigo/a
3. ______ Es lo que más me importa en la vida.	**c.** mi familia
4. ______ Es la persona que más me apoya (*supports*).	**d.** mi consejero/a
5. ______ Es lo que necesito hacer para graduarme.	**e.** mi madre/padre
6. ______ Es la persona que me da los mejores consejos académicos.	**f.** sacar notas aceptables

Paso 3. Ahora, en parejas, túrnense para hacer y contestar preguntas usando las ideas de la Columna A en el **Paso 2.**

MODELO: **E1:** ¿Quién es la persona **que** te da los mejores consejos académicos?
E2: (Es) Mi consejero académico. ¿Quién te los da a ti?
E1: (Es) Mi consejero también.

B. El estrés, la condición humana. Lea la siguiente tira cómica y complete las oraciones.

[a]cansancio... *fatigue, restlessness, worry, nervousness,* (*emotional*) *imbalance, and anxiety* [b]*as yet*

1. Lo que quiere el padre de Libertad es ______.
2. Lo que su padre tiene es ______.
3. Según el médico, lo que tiene su padre es ______.

C. En la preadolescencia

Paso 1. Complete las siguientes oraciones con detalles de su vida personal.

Cuando yo tenía diez años más o menos...

1. lo que más me divertía/molestaba era ______.
2. el programa de televisión que más me gustaba era ______.
3. la persona / las personas que yo más quería (*loved*) era(n) ______.

Paso 2. Ahora, en parejas, comparen sus respuestas.

Prác. A, Paso 1: Answers: *1. a 2. d 3. b 4. c*

¿Recuerda usted?

Before learning how to express reciprocal actions in **Gramática 32,** review the reflexive pronouns in **Gramática 14 (Cap. 5),** then provide the correct reflexive pronouns for the following sentences.

1. ___ levanté a las ocho y media.
2. Laura ___ puso el vestido.
3. Mis amigos y yo ___ sentamos en un café.
4. ¿Prefieres duchar___ o bañar___?

32 Expressing *each other* (Part 2)

Reciprocal Actions with Reflexive Pronouns

Gramática en acción: La amistad

©Hola Images/Getty Images

Los buenos amigos...

- se conocen bien.
- se respetan.
- se quieren.
- se recuerdan siempre.

En las culturas hispanas, cuando las buenas amigas se encuentran, se besan en la mejilla.

¿Y usted?

Cuando usted y sus amigos se encuentran, ¿cómo se saludan (*do you greet each other*)? ¿Se dan la mano? ¿Se besan?

Reciprocal Actions / **Las acciones recíprocas**

1. Reciprocal Actions

Reciprocal actions (**Las acciones recíprocas**) are actions that involve two or more people doing something *to* or *for* each other. They are usually expressed in English with *each other* or *one another*. In Spanish, reciprocal actions are expressed with pronouns that are identical to the plural reflexive pronouns.

nos = each other (**nosotros/as**)
os = each other (**vosotros/as**)
se = each other (**ustedes, ellos/as**)

Nos queremos.	*We love each other.*
¿**Os** ayudáis?	*Do you help one another?*
Se miran con ternura.	*They're looking at each other tenderly.*

2. Verbs Frequently Used to Express Reciprocal Actions

Verbs frequently used in this way include those at right, but any verb to whose meaning the phrase *each other* can be added may express a reciprocal action: **hablarse, mirarse, pelearse,** and so on.

abrazarse (c)	to embrace
besarse	to kiss each other
darse la mano	to shake hands
encontrarse (se encuentran)	to meet (*someone somewhere*)
quererse	to love each other; to be fond of each other
saludarse	to greet each other

¡OJO!

Sometimes a preposition is added in English to express the meaning of these verbs: **hablarse** = *to talk to each other*, **mirarse** = *to look at each other*, **pelearse** = *to fight with each other*. But no preposition is needed in Spanish.

Most of these verbs are new. The verbs **darse, encontrarse,** and **quererse** are new to you with their reciprocal meaning.

Friendship *Good friends . . . • know each other well. • respect each other. • are fond of each other. • always remember each other. In Hispanic cultures, when close women friends meet, they kiss each other on the cheek.*

Reciprocal Action Summary

nos, os, se + verb = each other, one another

Práctica y comunicación

A. Los buenos amigos

Paso 1. Autoprueba. Dé el pronombre apropiado para expresar acciones recíprocas.

1. ______ miramos
2. ______ pelearon
3. ______ conocen
4. ______ llamaban
5. ______ saludamos

Paso 2. ¿Qué hace usted con sus buenos amigos? Conteste usando **nos** (el pronombre recíproco). Si una oración no es cierta para usted, use **no.**

MODELO: abrazar cuando ver → **Nos abrazamos** cuando **nos vemos.**

1. ______ (ver) con frecuencia
2. ______ (conocer) bien
3. ______ (respetar) mucho
4. ______ (ayudar) cuando necesitamos ayuda
5. ______ (mandar) muchos mensajes
6. ______ (hablar) por teléfono con frecuencia
7. ______ (decir) la verdad siempre, lo bueno y lo malo
8. ¿ ?

Paso 3. Ahora, en parejas, túrnense para hacer y contestar preguntas basadas en el **Paso 2.** Luego, díganle a la clase algo que tienen en común.

MODELO: E1: ¿Tus amigos y tú **se abrazan** cuando **se ven**?
E2: Sí, con frecuencia **nos abrazamos** cuando **nos vemos** después de un tiempo. ¿Y ustedes?
E1: Nosotros también **nos abrazamos.**

B. ¿Qué pasa entre ellos?

¿Qué pasa entre ellos? Describa las siguientes relaciones familiares o sociales, haciendo oraciones completas con una palabra o frase de cada columna.

MODELO: Los buenos amigos **se conocen** bien.

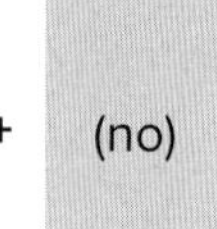

los buenos amigos los parientes los esposos los padres y los niños los amigos que no viven en la misma ciudad los profesores y los estudiantes los compañeros de cuarto/casa	+	(no)	+	visitarse con frecuencia quererse, respetarse, necesitarse, conocerse bien ayudarse mutuamente (en los quehaceres domésticos, cuando tienen problemas económicos o problemas personales) verse (todos los días, con frecuencia) llamarse por teléfono, escribirse mirarse (con cariño [*affection*]) saludarse, darse la mano quejarse sinceramente, escucharse

C. Intercambios

Paso 1. Haga una pregunta en el presente con cada una de las siguientes frases. En el **Paso 2,** va a usar esas preguntas para entrevistar a alguien de la clase sobre sus relaciones con su pareja, sus amigos, sus padres y sus parientes.

MODELOS: besarse → ¿Tu pareja y tú se besan en público?

1. verse
2. escribirse
3. mantenerse en contacto
4. llamarse por teléfono
5. abrazarse
6. besarse
7. saludarse dándose la mano
8. pelearse

Paso 2. Ahora, en parejas, túrnense para hacerse las preguntas del **Paso 1.** Luego, díganle a la clase lo que tienen en común.

Prác. A, Paso 1: **Answers:** *1.* nos *2.* se *3.* se *4.* se *5.* nos

Todo junto

Algo sobre...

el lago de Maracaibo

El lago de Maracaibo ocupa el puesto[a] 19 entre los lagos más grandes del mundo. En la actualidad, conecta con el golfo de Venezuela en el norte, que lo hace una bahía semicerrada salobre.[b] Pero está documentado que fue originalmente un lago cerrado, uno de los más antiguos de la Tierra. Numerosos ríos[c] vierten[d] sus aguas en el lago de Maracaibo.

¿Cuál es el lago más grande de su estado? ¿Y del país?

[a]*spot* [b]bahía... *semi-closed brackish bay* [c]*rivers* [d]*empty*

El lago de Maracaibo, el más grande de toda Latinoamérica

A. Lengua y cultura: La leyenda del lago de Maracaibo

Paso 1. Completar. Complete the following legend with the correct form of the word in parentheses, as suggested by context. The verbs will be in the preterite or imperfect. When two possibilities are given in parentheses, select the correct word.

Había una vez[a] un cacique[b] indígena que se llamaba Zapara. Este[c] tenía una hija, Maruma, que ______ (ser[1]) muy bonita. Al padre y a la hija ______ (se / les[2]) ______ (gustar[3]) pasar tiempo juntos y caminar por el bosque.[d]

Un día Zapara ______ (comprender[4]) que su hija ya ______ (ser[5]) una mujer y ______ (se / le[6]) ______ (decir[7]): «Debes escoger[e] esposo, pues ya tienes edad[f] para formar una familia. Pero ______ (su / tu[8]) esposo debe ser guerrero,[g] como todos los hombres de nuestra familia».

Un día, mientras su padre ______ (estar[9]) ausente, Maruma ______ (salir[10]) sola a cazar[h] en el bosque. Estaba a punto de dispararle a un ciervo[i] cuando ______ (un / —[11]) otro cazador[j] ______ (matar[k12]) al animal. Maruma ______ (ponerse[13]) muy enojada, pero el joven, ______ (que / quienes[14]) ______ (ser[15]) guapo y simpático, dijo: «El ciervo es para ______ (tú / ti[16]). Solo quiero conocerte. Me llamo Tamaré». A partir de ese día[l] los ______ (joven[17]) ______ (hacerse[m18]) amigos. Pronto se enamoraron.[n]

Desgraciadamente, el joven no era un buen guerrero y por eso el padre de Maruma ______ (enojarse[19]) mucho cuando ______ (saber[20]) que ella ______ (querer[21]) casarse con él. Se enfadó tanto[ñ] que la naturaleza reaccionó y ______ (haber[22]) grandes terremotos[o] e inundaciones:[p] las aguas cubrieron[q] las tierras del cacique Zapara y también a Maruma y Tamaré, formando así el lago de Maracaibo. Zapara se convirtió en una de sus pequeñas islas.

[a]Había... *Once upon a time there was* [b]*chief* [c]*He* [d]*forest* [e]*choose* [f]ya... *you're old enough* [g]*a warrior* [h]*hunt* [i]Estaba... *She was about to shoot a deer* [j]*hunter* [k]*to kill* [l]A... *From that day on* [m]*to become* [n]se... *they fell in love* [ñ]Se... *He was so angry* [o]*earthquakes* [p]*floods* [q]*covered*

(Continúa)

Paso 2. Comprensión. Conteste las siguientes preguntas.

1. ¿Quién era Zapara?
2. ¿De quién se enamoró (*fell in love*) Maruma?
3. ¿Por qué se enojó Zapara?
4. ¿Cómo se formó el lago de Maracaibo?

Paso 3. En acción

Ahora, en parejas, cuenten una versión sencilla (*simple*) de una leyenda de su país. Si no saben una leyenda, pueden contar un cuento (*story*) tradicional.

Estrategia

Aquí hay varias sugerencias (*suggestions*) para contar la leyenda.

- Para empezar la historia (*story*): Había una vez... + imperfecto (Use más de un verbo para describir a los protagonistas o el lugar donde estaban.)
- Para empezar con la acción: Un día/Una noche... + pretérito
- Para continuar con la secuencia de acciones: Entonces/Después/Luego... + pretérito
- Para terminar: Finalmente/Afortunadamente/Desgraciadamente... + pretérito

B. Proyecto: Un anuncio° de prevención contra una enfermedad común

°*announcement*

En grupos, van a trabajar juntos para crear y grabar (*create and record*) un anuncio informativo audiovisual sobre una enfermedad común y cómo prevenirla. Imaginen que están haciendo el anuncio para la población hispanohablante en general.

Paso 1. Preparación. Primero, elijan una enfermedad o condición física común. Busquen en internet un artículo o documento de algún país hispanohablante sobre una campaña de prevención de esa enfermedad o condición. Ese texto va a ser útil para aprender el vocabulario necesario.

Paso 2. Organización. Identifiquen la información más importante que deben darles a sus oyentes (*listeners*) y preparen el texto. Consideren:

- en qué forma van a dar la información (Recuerden que es un anuncio para la población en general, entonces no deben usar palabras muy difíciles y especializadas.)
- las formas de los mandatos para dar instrucciones
- qué tipo de imágenes van a usar
- la pronunciación de las palabras nuevas

Paso 3. Creación. Finalmente, graben su anuncio y preséntenlo a la clase.

¡Ahora, yo!

A. Use de modelo las preguntas y respuestas de la página 327 de este capítulo para hablar del tipo de vida que usted lleva y de su salud en general.

B. Filme a una persona que habla de un remedio casero (*homemade*) que se usa en su familia. Puede ser algo serio o cómico.

©Rafael Guerrero/Photolibrary/Getty Images

«Remedios para todos» Segmento 2

Antes de mirar

Cuando usted tiene resfriado, ¿va al médico generalmente? ¿Qué hace para curarse y sentirse mejor? ¿Tiene algún remedio casero? ¿Quién se lo enseñó?

Este segmento

En este segmento final del programa, una reportera española enseña un remedio casero contra el resfriado. Luego Ana y Víctor hablan de otros remedios caseros.

Un remedio casero (*homemade*) contra el catarro (resfriado): un empaste de mostaza (*mustard plaster*) con harina de trigo (*wheat flour*)

Fragmento del guion

Luego, lo que tenéis que poner es aceite de oliva, que lo frotáis[a] así[b] en el pecho,[c] para que la masa[d]... lo coja[e] mejor. Entonces, podéis poner la pasta así directamente con la cuchara. Y así lo dejáis[f] unas horas. Luego así ya te puedes ir a trabajar lo que queráis,[g] pero sobre todo no os lo quitéis.[h]

[a]*you rub* [b]*like this* [c]*chest* [d]*para... so that the paste* [e]*lo... sticks to it* [f]*you leave* [g]*lo... whatever you want* [h]*no... don't take it off*

Vocabulario del segmento

la miel	honey	**tapar**	to cover
pon atención	pay attention	**ensuciarse**	to get dirty
la risa	laughter	**espero que os funcione**	I hope it works for you
constipado/a (*Spain*)	**resfriado/a**	**el ajo crudo**	raw garlic
probar (pruebo)	to try	**fíjate**	look
el/la bisabuelo/a	great-grandparent	**tuyo/a**	of yours
el tercio	third part (*measure*)	**la planta**	sole (*of the foot*)
espeso/a	thick		

Después de mirar

A. ¿Está claro? ¿Cierto o falso? Corrija las oraciones falsas.

	CIERTO	FALSO
1. Es un remedio de su abuela.	☐	☐
2. El primer ingrediente del empaste es el aceite de oliva.	☐	☐
3. El empaste debe estar bastante (*rather*) espeso.	☐	☐
4. Se pone aceite de oliva en la mano.	☐	☐
5. La persona enferma debe llevar el empaste solo unos minutos.	☐	☐

B. Un poco más. Conteste las siguientes preguntas.

1. ¿Qué le pasa a Víctor hoy?
2. ¿Qué remedio casero le recomienda Ana a Víctor?
3. ¿Qué remedio prefiere Víctor? ¿Por qué?

C. Y ahora, ustedes. En grupos, hablen de los remedios y productos que no necesitan receta médica que ustedes usan por razones de salud. ¿Qué tipo de remedios son? ¿farmacéuticos, herbales, homeopáticos,... ? ¿Confían ustedes (*Do you trust*) en sus beneficios? ¿Les preocupan los posibles efectos secundarios?

MUNDO HISPANO

Enfoque cultural: Venezuela

Antes de leer

¿Tiene usted seguro (*insurance*) médico? ¿Lo tiene a través de (*through*) la universidad, de su trabajo o del trabajo de sus padres?

Un país en crisis

Desde el cambio[a] de milenio Venezuela sufre una grave crisis política y económica. La situación empeoró[b] en 2013, cuando hubo un cambio de presidente y un descenso[c] en la producción de petróleo, la fuente de ingresos[d] más importante del país. Para el 2020 (año de publicación de esta edición de *Puntos de partida*), existe la opinión generalizada de que Venezuela vive una crisis humanitaria que está causando la emigración de millones de venezolanos. Muchos venezolanos desean y promueven[e] un cambio de gobierno.[f]

Uno de los sectores más afectados por la crisis es el[g] de la salud, que es, en general, muy deficiente. Existía un sistema público de salud que cubría[h] a la gente que no podía pagar un seguro[i] médico privado.

Había consultorios médicos, clínicas y hospitales que proveían de[j] todo tipo de servicios relacionados con la salud a las personas que los necesitaban. Pero en la actualidad el país no tiene recursos[k] suficientes para mantener[l] los hospitales y clínicas. Y, desgraciadamente, pocos venezolanos tienen dinero suficiente para pagar los tratamientos que necesitan.

[a]Desde... *Since the change* [b]*became worse* [c]*decline* [d]fuente... *source of income* [e]*support* [f]*government* [g]*that* [h]*covered* [i]*insurance policy* [j]proveían... *provided* [k]*resources* [l]*maintain*

En otros países hispanos

- **En Latinoamérica** Es muy diversa la manera en que cada país provee de asistencia sanitaria[a] a sus habitantes: a través de[b] un sistema exclusivamente gubernamental[c] o por medio de[d] una combinación de sistemas públicos y privados. El acceso al cuidado médico también varía mucho de país a país. Hay países como la Argentina, Cuba y Costa Rica que proporcionan[e] acceso a todas las personas. Desgraciadamente, en otros países hay un considerable número de personas que no tienen acceso fácil a médicos y medicinas.

[a]*health* [b]a... *via* [c]*government-run* [d]por... *through* [e]*provide*

- **En España** España tiene un sistema nacional de seguridad social y médico para todos los ciudadanos.[f] Este sistema, con otros factores, contribuye a que los españoles tengan una de las esperanzas de vida[g] más largas del mundo.

[f]*citizens* [g]esperanzas... *life expectancies*

©Paula Bronstein/Getty Images

Un venezolano que baila el limbo durante una fiesta en Caracas

Un símbolo venezolano: «La rumba»

Al espíritu fiestero[a] de los venezolanos se le dice[b] «la rumba». Venezuela es el principal mercado de consumo de la música popular caribeña. A la gente venezolana le gusta organizar y celebrar fiestas en las cuales[c] siempre se baila salsa, merengue o cualquier otro ritmo caribeño hasta el amanecer.[d]

[a]*party-loving* [b]se... *(it) is called* [c]las... *which* [d]*dawn*

Comprensión

1. ¿Qué problema tiene Venezuela en la actualidad?
2. ¿Cómo era el sistema de salud en Venezuela en el pasado?
3. ¿Los habitantes de qué país hispanohablante tienen una de las esperanzas de vida más largas del planeta?
4. ¿Qué es «la rumba» en Venezuela?
5. ¿Qué bailan los venezolanos?

En acción

Haga una lista de seis tipos de profesionales especializados en medicina (no debe usar médico/a, enfermero/a o dentista). Puede buscar en internet o preguntarle a una persona hispanohablante. ¿Hay muchos cognados?

Lectura

Antes de leer

Las relaciones sentimentales pueden ser complicadas y a veces difíciles. ¿Puede usted pensar en algunos consejos o sugerencias para darle a una persona que está en una relación sentimental que le está causando mucho estrés *(stress)*?

«Prescripción», de Daisy Zamora

Ni acupuntura,
ni infusión de hierbas[a],
ni antidepresivos,
ni inyecciones —señora—
la jaqueca se cura[b] solamente
dejando[c] a su marido

[a]infusión... *herbal tea* [b]la... *you'll cure your migraine* [c]*leaving*

Comprensión

A. Un problema de salud. Identifique lo siguiente en el poema.

1. un problema de salud
2. cuatro tratamientos posibles
3. una cura

B. Un problema del corazón. Imagine la situación, entre la señora y su marido, implícita en este poema.

1. En su opinión, ¿son apropiados para curar una jaqueca los tratamientos mencionados en los primeros cuatro versos (*lines*) del poema? Explique.
2. ¿Está usted de acuerdo con la cura que se sugiere en este poema? ¿Hay situaciones donde la única solución apropiada es dejar a la pareja?
3. ¿Cuál es el tono del poema? ¿Es dramático, humorístico, irónico? ¿Por qué piensa usted así (*so*)?

Proyecto: Una cura infalible

Ahora usted va a escribir su propio poema describiendo tratamientos posibles e infalibles para curar algún problema de salud.

Paso 1. Identifique un problema de salud física o mental muy común.

Paso 2. Luego piense en dos o tres tratamientos inútiles (*useless*) y una solución más efectiva para el problema que ha identificado (*you have identified*).

Paso 3. Ahora escriba un poema para una persona que sufre este problema, siguiendo el mismo formato de «Prescripción».

Textos orales

Campaña de vacunación contra la gripe

Antes de escuchar

¿Qué precauciones toma usted para no enfermarse? ¿Tuvo usted algún resfriado el año pasado? ¿alguna gripe? ¿Fue al médico con frecuencia durante el último año?

Vocabulario para escuchar

vacunarse	to get a shot	**de alto riesgo**	high-risk
la muerte	death	**embarazadas**	pregnant
contraer (*like* **traer**)	to get; to contract (*an illness*)	**peligroso/a**	dangerous

Comprensión

A. La gripe. Conteste las siguientes preguntas sobre esta enfermedad, según la información en el anuncio.

1. ¿Aproximadamente cuántas personas van al hospital cada año en los Estados Unidos a causa de la gripe?
2. ¿Cuántas personas mueren anualmente en los Estados Unidos a causa de la gripe, aproximadamente?
3. ¿Hay solo un tipo de virus de gripe?

B. La vacuna. Conteste las siguientes preguntas sobre la campaña de vacunación.

1. ¿Quiénes deben vacunarse contra la gripe?
2. ¿Quiénes se consideran personas de alto riesgo?
3. ¿Quiénes no pueden recibir la vacuna?

En acción

Haga una encuesta entre las personas de la clase para ver quién ya se vacunó contra la gripe y si se vacuna todos los años. ¿Cree que el porcentaje de personas de la clase vacunadas es alto, normal o bajo en comparación con el (*that*) del resto del país?

Proyecto en su comunidad

Entreviste a una persona hispana de su universidad o ciudad sobre el cuidado médico en su país de origen.

Preguntas posibles

- En su país de origen, ¿qué hace una persona cuando tiene una enfermedad que no es muy seria? ¿Va al médico? ¿Habla con el farmacéutico? ¿Va a alguna persona que cura con remedios naturales?
- ¿Qué alimentos se consideran muy sanos en su país? ¿Se usan algunos productos naturales? ¿Cuáles son? ¿Para qué sirven de remedio?
- ¿Cómo se dice *flu* en su país? ¿Y *cold*?

Escritura

Proyecto: La historia de una enfermedad

Usted ya ha hablado (*You've already talked*) en este capítulo de sus enfermedades. Ahora va a escribir un ensayo sobre una enfermedad que sufrió un compañero / una compañera de clase.

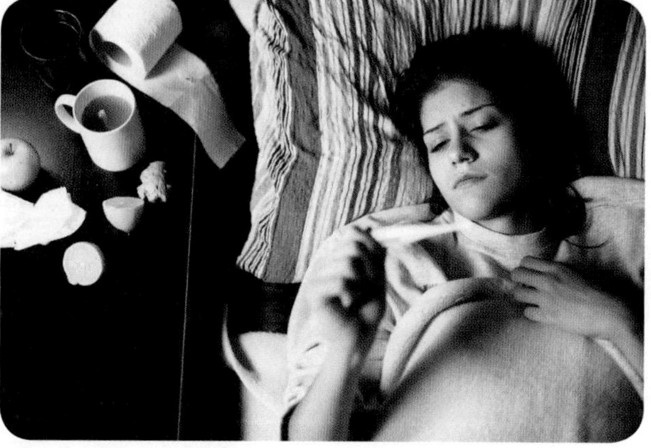

©eldarnurkovic/123RF

Tenía fiebre y y tuvo que guardar cama.

Antes de escribir

En parejas, entrevístense sobre una enfermedad que sufrieron. Piensen en la información que van a necesitar para escribir la narración de un episodio de una enfermedad. Aquí hay algunos ejemplos. Ustedes deben añadir por lo menos 3 o 4 preguntas. **¡OJO!** Usen el pretérito y el imperfecto con cuidado.

1. ¿Fue una enfermedad grave o leve (*minor*)? ¿O era crónica?
2. ¿Cuándo ocurrió? ¿Cuántos años tenías?
3. ¿Cuáles eran los síntomas?
4. ¿ ?

A escribir

Ahora escriba la narración, usando la información que consiguió en **Antes de escribir.** O, si usted prefiere, puede escribir sobre la enfermedad de un amigo o un pariente. Hay más ayuda en Connect.

Más ideas para su portafolio

- Incluya 5 consejos que usted considera fundamentales para estar bien físicamente.
- Dé un resumen de su historia favorita (de un libro o una película) cuando usted era pequeño/a.
- Si ha estado jugando (*you have been playing*) Practice Spanish: Study Abroad, en Quest 8 usted leyó la historia de los dos cadejos (animales fantásticos), una leyenda que trata del equilibrio (*deals with the balance*) entre lo bueno y lo malo. ¿Conoce usted otras historias sobre la armonía entre el bien y el mal? Escriba un informe (*report*) que resuma la leyenda de los dos cadejos y compárela con leyendas, cuentos o creencias (*beliefs*) de su propia cultura o de otras culturas que usted conoce sobre el bien y el mal.

©McGraw-Hill Education

Sugerencia: You are now ready to play Quest 8 in **Practice Spanish: Study Abroad.**

EN RESUMEN En este capítulo

AFTER STUDYING THIS CHAPTER I CAN . . .

- ☐ name many parts of the body and activities related to a healthy life (328)
- ☐ talk about illnesses and medical exams (330)
- ☐ use the preterite and imperfect together to talk about the past and tell stories (334–336)
- ☐ use **que, quien,** and **lo que** to avoid repetition (342–343)
- ☐ express the concept of "each other" with pronouns (345)
- ☐ recognize/describe at least 2–3 aspects of Venezuelan cultures

Gramática en breve

30. Using the Preterite and the Imperfect

Uses of the Preterite	Uses of the Imperfect
beginning/end of an action	habitual/repeated action
completed action	ongoing action
series of completed actions	background information
the action on the "stage"	the setting for the action

31. Relative Pronouns

que = refers to things and people
quien(es) = refers only to people
lo que = refers to a situation

32. Reciprocal Actions with Reflexive Pronouns

each other = **nos, os, se**

Vocabulario

Los verbos

abrazarse (c)	to embrace
besarse	to kiss each other
darse la mano	to shake hands
encontrarse (me encuentro) (con)	to meet (*someone somewhere*)
quererse	to love each other; to be fond of each other
saludarse	to greet each other

La salud y el bienestar

los anteojos	glasses
la caminadora	treadmill
los lentes	glasses
los lentes de contacto	contact lenses
el bienestar	well-being
la salud	health

Repaso: la comida, el deporte, llevar (to wear)

cuidar de	to take care of
cuidarse	to take care of oneself
dejar de + *inf.*	to stop (*doing something*)
doler (duele) (*like* **gustar)**	to hurt; to ache
enfermarse	to get sick
guardar cama	to stay in bed
hacer ...	to do . . .
ejercicios aeróbicos	aerobics
(el método) Pilates	Pilates
levantar pesas	to lift weights
llevar una vida sana/tranquila	to lead a healthy/calm life
molestar (*like* **gustar)**	to bother
ponerle una inyección / una vacuna	to give (*someone*) a shot / a vaccination
resfriarse (me resfrío)	to get/catch a cold
respirar	to breathe
sacar (qu) sacar la lengua	to stick out one's tongue
tener dolor de	to have a pain/ache in
tomarle la temperatura	to take someone's temperature
toser	to cough

Repaso: caminar, comer, correr, dormir (duermo) (u), hacer ejercicio, practicar (qu), sentirse (me siento) (i)

El cuerpo humano

la boca	mouth
el brazo	arm
la cabeza	head
el cerebro	brain
el corazón	heart
el dedo (de la mano)	finger
el dedo del pie	toe
el estómago	stomach
la garganta	throat
la lengua	tongue
la mano	hand
la muela	molar, back tooth
la nariz (*pl.* **narices)**	nose
el oído	inner ear
el ojo	eye
la oreja	(outer) ear

el pie foot
la pierna leg
los pulmones lungs
la sangre blood

el cuerpo humano human body

Repaso: el diente

Las enfermedades

el chequeo check-up
el consultorio (medical) office
el dolor (de) pain, ache (in)
la fiebre fever
la gripe flu
el jarabe (cough) syrup
la pastilla pill
la receta prescription
el resfriado cold (*illness*)
el síntoma symptom
la tos cough
el tratamiento treatment

la enfermedad illness, sickness

Cognados: el antibiótico, la medicina, la temperatura, la visita

El personal médico

el/la enfermero/a nurse
el/la farmacéutico/a pharmacist

Cognado: el/la dentista, el/la paciente

Repaso: el/la médico/a

Otros sustantivos

la cita appointment; date
la vida life

Los adjetivos

mareado/a dizzy; nauseated
pasado/a past, last
resfriado/a congested, stuffed up
rutinario/a routine
sano/a healthy
suficiente enough

Repaso: enfermo/a, todo/a, tranquilo/a

Palabras adicionales

anoche last night
de repente suddenly
desgraciadamente unfortunately
dos veces twice
eso quiere decir... that means . . .
frecuentemente frequently
lo bueno the good thing/news
lo malo the bad thing/news
lo suficiente enough

Repaso: anteayer, ayer, de adolescente, de niño/a, en seguida, lo que, mientras, que, quien(es), siempre, todos los días, una vez

Vocabulario personal

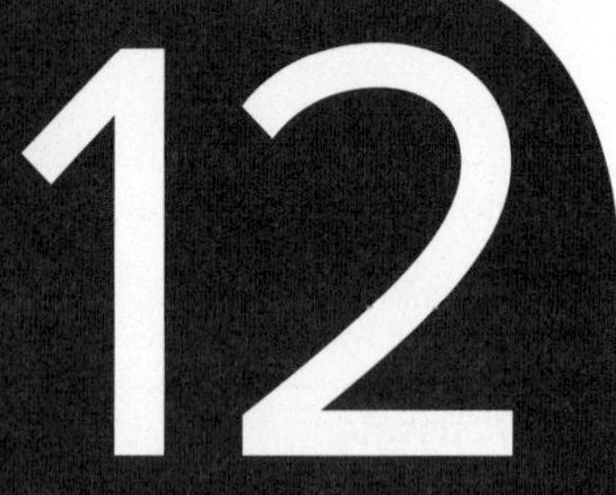

12 ¡Conectad@s!°

Connected!

En este capítulo

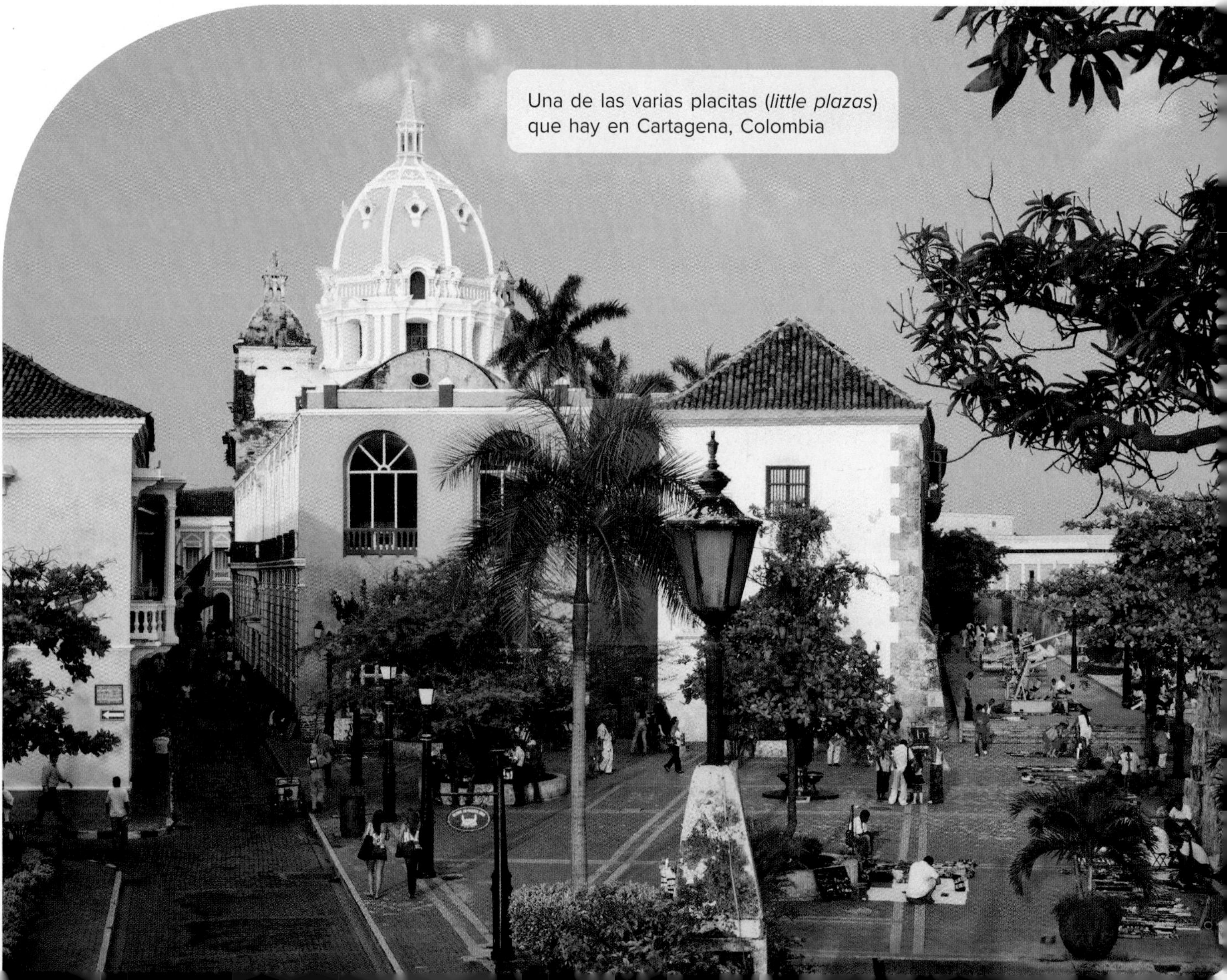

Una de las varias placitas (*little plazas*) que hay en Cartagena, Colombia

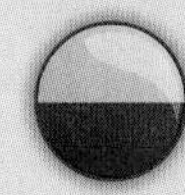

COLOMBIA

49,4 (coma cuatro) millones de habitantes

- La diversidad natural de Colombia es magnífica. Este país comprende[a] territorio caribeño, andino[b] y amazónico.
- Además,[c] Colombia tiene muchísimos recursos naturales: petróleo, oro, platino y esmeraldas. Es uno de los principales productores y exportadores de café del mundo. También exporta flores.

[a]*includes* [b]*Andean* [c]*In addition*

ENTREVISTA

- ¿Dónde vive usted? ¿Vive en una zona bien comunicada[a] con el resto de la ciudad?
- ¿Se mantiene usted[b] en contacto con sus parientes y amigos que no viven cerca? ¿Cómo lo hace?
- Después de su computadora y su celular, ¿qué aparato electrónico considera usted más necesario en su vida diaria? ¿Por qué?

[a]*connected* [b]*¿Se... Do you stay*

Ismael Pérez Mendizábal contesta las preguntas.

- Mi carrera es Estudios Urbanos, en la Universidad Nacional de Colombia, en Bogotá, y vivo bastante[a] cerca de la Universidad. Vivo con mi familia en un barrio[b] que está muy bien comunicado, así que[c] puedo llegar a la universidad en bus.
- Bueno, mis abuelos y la mayoría de mis tíos viven en Bogotá, así que nos vemos con frecuencia en las reuniones familiares. Pero ahora mi hermana está estudiando en España. Por eso nos comunicamos por *WhatsApp*™ y nos hablamos por *Skype*™.
- Pues me gusta mucho mi *Kindle*™, porque me encanta leer y es más cómodo leer con el *Kindle* que con un libro tradicional.

[a]*rather* [b]*neighborhood* [c]*así... so*

VOCABULARIO: PREPARACIÓN

You can hear the pronunciation of theme vocabulary words and phrases in the Connect eBook.

En el centro de una ciudad

La vivienda	Housing
la residencia de ancianos	nursing home
el dueño / la dueña	owner; landlord, landlady
el inquilino / la inquilina	tenant; renter
el portero / la portera	building manager; doorman
el ascensor	elevator
el piso	floor (*of a building*)
el primer piso	first floor (*second story*)
el segundo piso	second floor (*third story*)
la planta baja	ground floor
la vista (a, de)	view (of)

La zona	
las afueras	outskirts; suburbs
el barrio	neighborhood
la calle	street
la dirección	address
mudarse	to move (*residences*)

Los gastos	Expenses
alquilar	to rent
el alquiler	rent
la calefacción	heat
la electricidad	electricity
el gas	gas (*residential; not for cars*)

¡OJO!

The word **suburbio** is a false cognate; it means *slum*. To say you live in the suburbs, say **vivo en las afueras.**

Así se dice

el apartamento = el departamento (*Mex., Arg.*), el piso (*Sp.*)
el ascensor = el elevador

El barrio is the word most generally used to express *neighborhood* in Spanish, although it is often said by Hispanics with more affection than its English counterpart. To talk about **mi barrio** is to talk about a place to which one is emotionally linked, not just the area where one lives. Many other words are used regionally and can depend on the kind of neighborhood. **La colonia** and **el fraccionamiento** are used in Mexico. Other common terms are **el vecindario** and **la zona residencial.**

Comunicación

Estrategia

Es una persona que...
Es un lugar donde...
Es una cosa que...
Es lo que...

A. Definiciones. Defina las siguientes palabras en español, según el modelo.

MODELO: la residencia de estudiantes →
Es un lugar donde viven muchos estudiantes. Por lo general está situada en el campus universitario.

1. el inquilino
2. el centro
3. el alquiler
4. el portero
5. la vecina
6. la dueña
7. la dirección
8. las afueras
9. el barrio
10. el ascensor
11. la avenida
12. la residencia de ancianos
13. la planta baja
14. la vista
15. la electricidad

B. Buscamos un apartamento. Lea los siguientes avisos de venta (*sale ads*) de viviendas en Bogotá y conteste las preguntas. **¡OJO!** $ = el peso colombiano

ZONA NORTE

Casa bien ubicada,[a] cerca de la Calle 170. Buenas rutas y cerca de colegios,[b] centros comerciales y supermercados. Zona de alta valorización.[c] 130 mts2.[d] Parqueadero privado con acceso directo a casa. 3 niveles;[e] 4 alcobas, 3 baños, sala-comedor, estudio y ático. $450.000.000 Celular: 3005566177

A.

BARRIO TEUSAQUILLO

Apartamento de 2 alcobas, 1 baño, cocina y sala-comedor. 3er[f] piso en edificio de 5 pisos con ascensor. Excelente ubicación cerca de bancos, supermercados, centros médicos y parque. $325.000.000 Celular: 3104488776 E-mail: micasa@gmail.com

B.

BARRIO PRADERA NORTE–TORRE[g] DE MADRID

2 habitaciones, dos baños, estudio, sala-comedor, pisos laminados, ascensor, garaje cubierto,[h] balcón. 100 mts2, 4°[i] piso. Adicionales: piscina, gimnasio, sauna, cancha de *squash*. $350.000.000 Tel. fijo[j] 6688775 Celular: 3169545650 E-mail: micasa@gmail.com

C.

[a]*situated, located* [b]*schools* [c]alta... *high property values* [d]metros cuadrados (*square meters*) [e]*levels* [f]tercer (*third*) [g]*Tower* [h]*covered* [i]cuarto (*fourth*) [j]Tel.... *Landline*

1. ¿Qué tipo de vivienda se vende en cada anuncio?
2. ¿Cuántas alcobas tiene cada vivienda?
3. ¿Cuál de las viviendas sería (*would be*) mejor para una famila con dos hijas adolescentes? ¿para una pareja de profesionales sin hijos y sin planes para tenerlos? ¿para una mujer profesional que ya tiene su primer trabajo, bien pagado (*well paying*)?

C. Mi situación de vivienda

Paso 1. Haga seis preguntas que usted puede hacerle a un compañero / una compañera de clase sobre su vivienda familiar o sobre su vivienda actual (*current*) si vive fuera de la universidad (*off campus*). Temas que se relacionan con la vivienda: **la dirección, el alquiler, el tipo de edificio, los gastos, los vecinos,...**

Paso 2. Ahora, en parejas, túrnense para entrevistarse sobre su vivienda actual, usando las preguntas del **Paso 1.** Luego hablen de dónde les gustaría vivir si el dinero se lo permitiera (*if you could financially*). Traten de (*Try to*) usar palabras y frases de los anuncios (**Comunicación B**).

MODELOS: ¿Cuántos pisos hay en la casa de tus padres?
¿Dónde te gustaría vivir, en el centro o en las afueras?

Paso 3. Díganle a la clase lo que ustedes tienen en común.

La tecnología

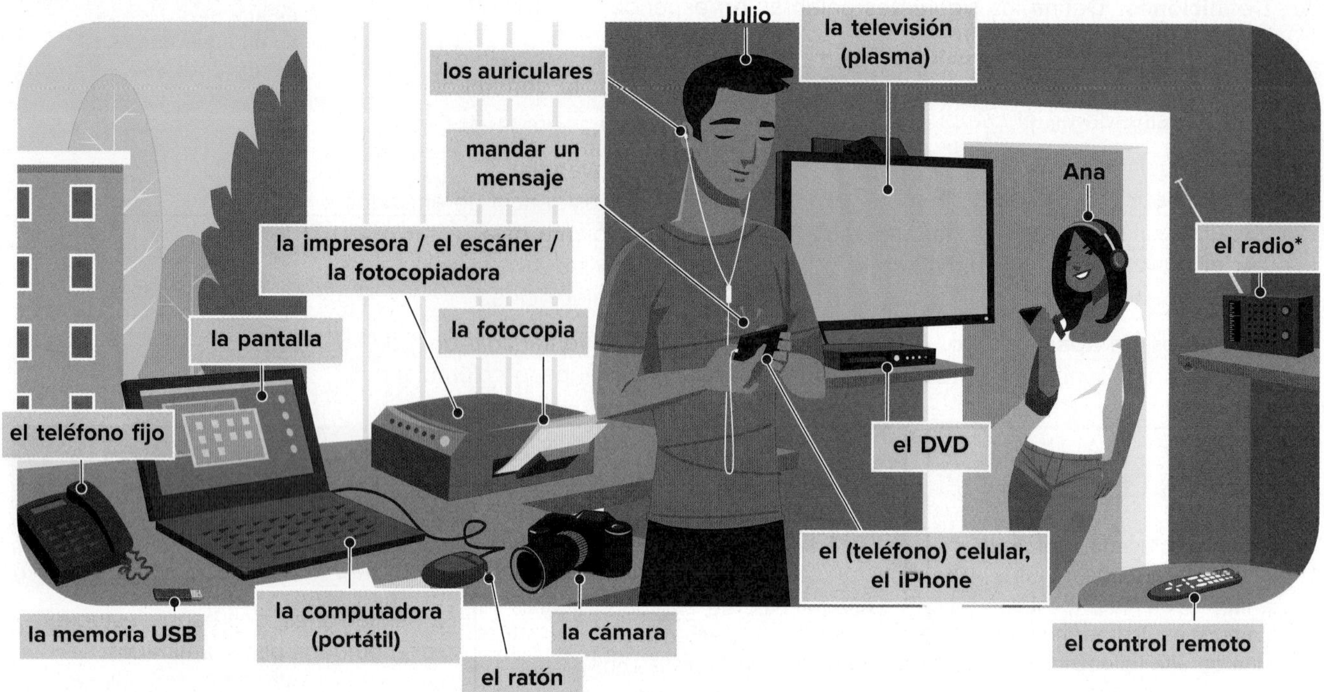

El equipo electrónico

el archivo (computer) file
el buzón de voz voice mailbox
la carpeta (computer) folder
la contraseña password
el disco duro hard drive
el equipo equipment
el espacio (de almacenamiento) (storage) space
la pantalla (grande/plana) (big/flat) screen (monitor)

Cognados: el android, la app, el CD, el CD-ROM, el documento, el fax, la memoria, el módem, el video, el wifi

En internet (*m.*)

la arroba @
el buscador search engine
el correo electrónico e-mail
la página web web page
la red social social network
el sitio web website
el usuario / la usuaria user

Cognados: el blog, el chateo, el e-mail, Facebook (*m.*), **el tuit, Twitter**™ (*m.*)

Los verbos

almacenar to store; to save
apagar (gu) to turn off (*a machine*)
bajar/descargar (gu) to download
buscar (qu) en internet to look up on the internet
cambiar (de canal [*m.*], **de ropa...)** to change (channels, clothing . . .)
conseguir (*like* **seguir)** to get, obtain
copiar/hacer (foto)copia to copy
encender (ie), poner to turn on (*a machine*)
entrar/estar en internet to go/be online
entrar/estar en Facebook to go/be on Facebook
fallar to "crash" (*computer*)
funcionar to work, function; to run (*machines*)
grabar to record; to tape
guardar to keep; to save (*documents*)
imprimir to print
mandar to send
manejar to operate (*a machine*)
navegar (gu) la red to surf the internet
obtener (*like* **tener)** to get, obtain
publicar (qu) to post (*as on Facebook*); to publish

Cognados: conectarse, hacer clic, instalar, tuitear

Usage regarding the word* **radio *is changing in the Spanish-speaking world. Many countries use* **el radio** *for the apparatus and* **la radio** *for the medium of radio.*

Comunicación

Así se dice

mandar = enviar (envío)
el internet = la internet
el (teléfono) celular = el (teléfono) móvil (*Sp.*)
el video (*L.A.*) = el vídeo (*Sp.*)

A. Lo que tenemos y lo que necesitamos

Paso 1. Haga una lista de todas las cosas electrónicas que usted tiene.

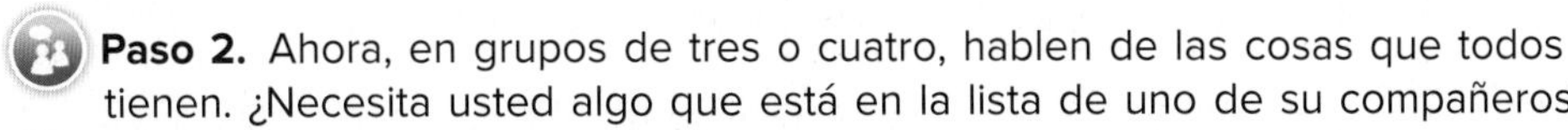

Paso 2. Ahora, en grupos de tres o cuatro, hablen de las cosas que todos tienen. ¿Necesita usted algo que está en la lista de uno de su compañeros?

Paso 3. Ahora usted y sus compañeros del **Paso 2** deben escoger los cinco aparatos electrónicos que ustedes consideran esenciales para los estudiantes de hoy. Luego compartan (*share*) su lista con la clase y expliquen sus decisiones.

B. Asociaciones. ¿Qué cosas asocia usted con los siguientes verbos?

1. mandar	**3.** conseguir	**5.** guardar	**7.** imprimir
2. fallar	**4.** grabar	**6.** cambiar	**8.** instalar

C. Definiciones

Paso 1. Dé la palabra definida. **¡OJO!** Puede haber (*There can be*) más de una respuesta en algunos casos.

1. Es un aparato que hace copias de un documento.
2. Es un aparato que sirve para hacer una copia electrónica de un documento.
3. Es lo que usamos para cambiar el programa de televisión sin levantarnos del sofá.
4. Este sistema recibe mensajes cuando no podemos (o no queremos) contestar el teléfono.
5. Es lo que usamos para escuchar música sin hacer ruido.
6. Esto se hace cuando hay en la tele una película que queremos ver pero que ahora mismo no podemos verla.
7. Es un sinónimo de guardar, como guardar un documento en el disco duro.

Paso 2. Ahora le toca a usted darles una o dos definiciones a sus compañeros de clase. Siga el modelo del **Paso 1.**

D. La tecnología y yo

Paso 1. Complete las siguientes oraciones para describir su relación con la tecnología.

1. No puedo imaginar la vida sin mi(s) ______ (aparato) porque...
2. Estoy conectado/a a internet ______ (¿con qué frecuencia?) porque...
3. Entro en internet sobre todo (*especially*) para...

Paso 2. Ahora, en parejas, comparen sus respuestas. ¿Son muy similares sus preferencias y hábitos con relación a la tecnología?

E. Actitudes sobre el uso de la tecnología

Paso 1. Lea la tabla **Porcentajes de adultos**... y conteste las siguientes preguntas.

1. ¿Está usted entre la mayoría de los adultos con respecto a lo que piensa sobre esos usos y actitudes?
2. ¿Actúa usted de acuerdo con su propia opinión?
3. ¿En qué otros lugares y situaciones sociales usa usted el celular?

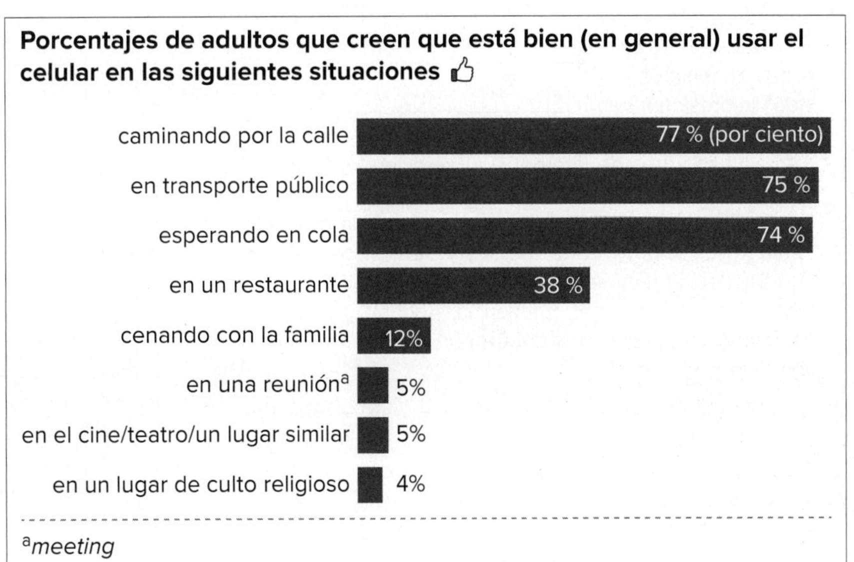

Source: Based on Perrin, Andrew, "10 Facts about smartphone as the iPhone turns 10," *Pew Research Center*, June 28, 2017.

(Continúa.)

Paso 2. En parejas, indiquen cuáles de los usos y actitudes de la tabla **Los estudiantes y el uso...** son ciertos para ustedes. ¿Con cuáles de ellos están más/menos de acuerdo? ¿Por qué? Finalmente, comenten entre ustedes si creen que una universidad debe prohibir o restringir (*restrict*) algunos usos de los aparatos personales. Si creen que sí, ¿cómo se pueden implementar estas restricciones?

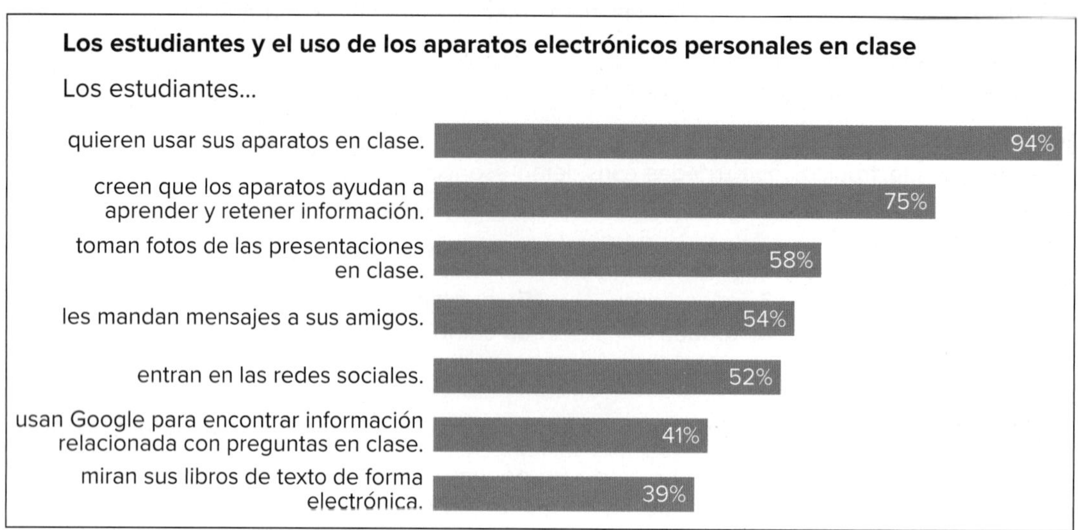

Los estudiantes y el uso de los aparatos electrónicos personales en clase
Los estudiantes...
quieren usar sus aparatos en clase. 94%
creen que los aparatos ayudan a aprender y retener información. 75%
toman fotos de las presentaciones en clase. 58%
les mandan mensajes a sus amigos. 54%
entran en las redes sociales. 52%
usan Google para encontrar información relacionada con preguntas en clase. 41%
miran sus libros de texto de forma electrónica. 39%

Source: Kelly, Rhea, "Survey: 94% of Students Want to Use Their Cell Phones in Class," *Campus Technology*, December 12, 2017.

Nota cultural

El español y la tecnología

El español ocupa el tercer[b] puesto entre las lenguas por número de internautas,[c] depués del inglés y el chino, con casi el 8% de los usuarios en total (según datos de 2017). El crecimiento[d] en número de usuarios hispanohablantes ha sido[e] impresionante en la última década. Y el acceso y uso de internet sigue creciendo,[f] gracias a los teléfonos celulares inteligentes.

E	Significado	Atajo de teclado[a]	E	Significado	Atajo de teclado
	Sonrisa	:-) :) :] =)		Guiño	;-) ;)
	Carcajada	:-D :D =D		Inseguro	:/ :-/ :\ :-\
	Tristeza	:-(:(:[=(		Ángel	O:) O:-)
	Llanto	:'(		Demonio	3:) 3:-)
	Confusión	o.O O.o		Corazón	<3
	Sacar la lengua	:-P :P :-p :p =P		Felicidad	^_^
	Susto	:-O :O :-o :o		Beso	:-‡ :‡

Como ocurre en inglés, la lengua española que aparece[g] en textos, redes sociales y otros sitios web es con frecuencia muy «oral» y poco pulida[h] y los emoticonos se usan con frecuencia. Aquí hay algunas características y ejemplos del español de textos y redes sociales:

- muchas abreviaturas: **que = k, q; para = p; por = x; porque = pq; besos = bss; te = t**
- onomatopeyas: **jeje, jaja, uf**
- falta de signos de puntuación y acentos: **q tal?**
- abuso[i] de las mayúsculas y signos de interrogación y admiración: **COMO??? Bien!!!!**

Por otro lado,[j] el inglés es una fuente[k] interminable de vocabulario relacionado con la tecnología, tanto para el español como para todas las otras lenguas del mundo. La lista de vocabulario de **La tecnología** (pág. 360) pone en evidencia[l] esta situación. Algunos de estos términos luego encuentran una traducción directa al español, como el disco duro por *hard drive*, o terminan escribiéndose y pronunciándose en una manera que es normal para el español, como **hacer clic, cliquear** o **clicar** por *to click*.

¿Usa usted algunas convenciones específicas cuando escribe mensajes de texto o chateo?? ¿Cuáles son?

[a]Atajo... *Key shortcut* [b]*third* [c]*internet users* [d]*growth* [e]ha... *has been* [f]*growing* [g]*appears* [h]*polished* [i]*overuse* [j]Por... *On the other hand* [k]*source* [l]pone... *illustrates, proves*

«¡No sin mi celular!» Segmento 1

Antes de mirar

Conteste las siguientes preguntas.

1. ¿Recuerda cuándo tuvo usted su primer celular?
2. ¿Cuándo compró el celular que tiene ahora?
3. ¿Hay un teléfono fijo en su casa o apartamento?
4. ¿Cuáles son las compañías de telefonía móvil más usadas hoy día?

Telmex, ahora parte de América Móvil, la compañía de telefonía móvil más grande de Latinoamérica

Este segmento

Este segmento trata de (*is about*) la tecnología y sobre todo de los teléfonos celulares. Laura trae un reportaje desde México sobre una compañía muy grande.

Vocabulario del segmento

¿Qué tal han estado?	How have you been?
inconcebible	inconceivable
cierto/a	certain
a ver	let's see
que no tenga	who doesn't have
por todas partes	everywhere
tercero/a	third
el nacimiento	birth
libanés/libanesa	Lebanese
cuarto/a	fourth
sino que	but rather
estrecho/a	narrow
lleno/a	full
a pesar de	in spite of
el consumo	consumption, use

Después de mirar

A. ¿Está claro? Complete las siguientes oraciones con información del video.

1. Carlos Slim Helú es ________, de origen ________.
2. Slim es el ________ de Telmex.
3. La Ciudad de México es la ________ ciudad más grande del mundo.
4. América Móvil es la ________ compañía de telefonía móvil más grande del mundo.

B. Un poco más. Conteste las siguientes preguntas.

1. Según Laura, ¿cómo son las ciudades de la Ciudad de México y Guanajuato? Compárelas según la descripción de ellas.
2. ¿Cómo es Carlos Slim Helú, según el segmento?

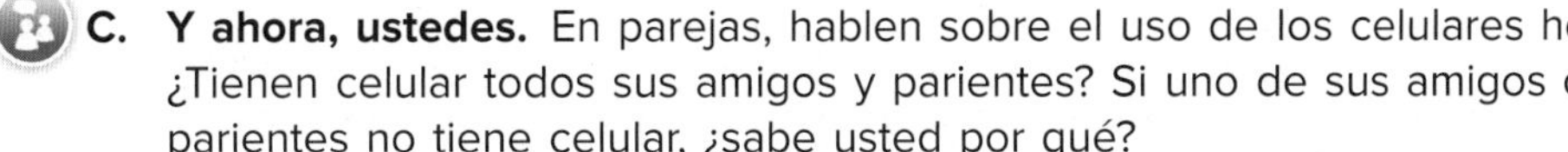

C. Y ahora, ustedes. En parejas, hablen sobre el uso de los celulares hoy día. ¿Tienen celular todos sus amigos y parientes? Si uno de sus amigos o parientes no tiene celular, ¿sabe usted por qué?

GRAMÁTICA

¿Recuerda usted?

In **Gramática 20 (Cap. 7)** you learned how to form **usted** and **ustedes** (formal) commands with the "opposite" vowel. Remember that the commands are based on the **yo** form of the present tense of irregular and stem-changing verbs, and that verbs that end in **-car, -gar,** and **-zar** have spelling changes in the command forms.

hablar → hable	comer → coman	vivir → viva
jugar → jueguen	poner → ponga	volver → vuelvan

Also remember that object pronouns (direct, indirect, reflexive) must follow and be attached to affirmative commands; they must precede negative commands: **Háblele usted. No le hable usted.**

Give the indicated command forms, affirmative and negative.

1. sentarse (usted)
2. dárselo (usted)
3. llamarnos (usted)
4. acostarse (ustedes)
5. escucharme (ustedes)
6. vestirse (ustedes)

You'll learn how to form informal commands in **Gramática 33.**

33 Influencing Others (Part 2)

Tú (Informal) Commands

Gramática en acción: Mandatos para situaciones sociales

¿Llegaste? ¡Saluda!
¿Alguien te habló? ¡Contesta!
¿Te vas? ¡Di adiós!
¿No vas a ayudarme? ¡No me molestes!

¿Alguien te hizo un favor? ¡Dale las gracias!

¿Ofendiste a alguien? ¡Pídele perdón!

¿Y usted?

Pensando en la clase de español, ¿qué preguntas puede usted hacer para los siguientes mandatos, según el modelo de las imágenes?

1. ¡Pregunta!
2. ¡Estúdialos!

a command or imperative / **un mandato** = a verb form used to tell someone to do something

In English, the command forms are the same regardless of whom you're giving them to: *Go. . . , Put. . . , Don't touch. . .* In Spanish, however, the forms for formal **(usted, ustedes)** commands are different from those you use with a person whom you address as **tú**. And unlike **usted** and **ustedes** commands, whose form is the same whether affirmative or negative, the negative **tú** commands have different forms than the affirmative commands.

Commands for social situations ■ *Did you arrive? Say hello!* ■ *Are you leaving? Say good-bye!* ■ *Someone spoke to you? Answer!* ■ *Aren't you going to help me? Don't bother me!* ■ *Someone did you a favor? Say thanks to them!* ■ *Did you offend someone? Ask them for forgiveness!*

Negative **tú** Commands / **Los mandatos informales negativos**

-ar → no + -es

-er/-ir → no + -as

-ar verbs		**-er/-ir verbs**	
no hables	don't speak	**no comas**	don't eat
no bailes	don't dance	**no escribas**	don't write
no empieces	don't start	**no pidas**	don't order
no toques	don't play	**no salgas**	don't leave
no juegues	don't play	**no vayas**	don't go

1. **Formation of Negative Informal Commands**

   Negative **tú** commands are basically the same as **usted/ustedes** commands.

   They use the "opposite" vowel but with the **-s** that is characteristic of **tú** forms.

   No lo **guardes** en esa carpeta. No **imprimas** ese documento.
   Don't save it in that folder. Don't print that document.

   All of the irregularities that you have already learned for **usted/ustedes** commands apply to the negative **tú** commands.

   - Stem-changing verbs show the stem change: **no cierres, no vuelvas, no sirvas.**
   - Verbs that end in **-car, -gar**, and **-zar** have a spelling change: **no busques, no descargues, no almuerces.**
   - Verbs with irregular **yo** forms show the irregularity in the command: **no pongas, no digas.**
   - The same verbs that have irregular **usted/ustedes** commands have irregular negative **tú** commands, identical to the **usted/ustedes** form but with characateristic **-s** of **tú** forms.

dar	→	**no des**
estar	→	**no estés**
ir	→	**no vayas**
saber	→	**no sepas**
ser	→	**no seas**

2. **Position of Pronouns**

   As with negative **usted/ustedes** commands, object pronouns—direct, indirect, and reflexive—precede negative **tú** commands.

   No lo mires.
   Don't look at him.

   No te levantes.
   Don't get up.

   No les escribas.
   Don't write to them.

   No se lo des.
   Don't give it to them.

Affirmative **tú** Commands / **Los mandatos informales afirmativos**

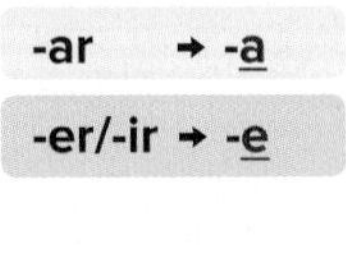

-ar → -a

-er/-ir → -e

-ar verbs		**-er/-ir verbs**	
habla	speak	**come**	eat
empieza	start	**escribe**	write
toca	play	**pide**	order
juega	play	**oye**	listen

1. **Formation of Regular Informal Affirmative Commands**

   Most affirmative **tú** commands are identical to the third person singular (**usted, él, ella**) form of the present tense. All stem-changes appear (because they occur in that person in the present), but there are no changes in verbs ending in **-car, -gar,** and **-zar**.

   Descarga otra app, por favor.
   Download another app, please.

   Enciende la computadora.
   Turn on the computer.

2. Irregular Informal Affirmative Commands

Some verbs have irregular affirmative **tú** command forms.

decir	→	**di**	**salir**	→	**sal**
hacer	→	**haz**	**ser**	→	**sé**
ir	→	**ve**	**tener**	→	**ten**
poner	→	**pon**	**venir**	→	**ven**

Sé puntual, pero **ten** cuidado.
Be there on time, but be careful.

> **¡OJO!**
>
> **Sé,** the informal affirmative command of **ser,** has an accent mark to distinguish it from the pronoun **se.**

> **¡OJO!**
>
> The affirmative **tú** commands for **ir** and **ver** are identical: **ve.** Context will clarify meaning. The command form of **ver** is rarely used.

¡**Ve** esa película!
See that movie!

Ve a casa ahora mismo.
Go home right now.

---

3. Position of Pronouns

As with affirmative **usted/ustedes** commands, object and reflexive pronouns follow affirmative **tú** commands and are attached to them. Accent marks are necessary except when a single pronoun is added to a one-syllable command.

One pronoun: **Lée**lo. **Levánta**te. **Di**me la verdad.
Two pronouns: **Dá**selo. **Regála**mela. **Dí**mela.

Summary of Informal Commands

Negative:	-ar → -es	-er/-ir → -as
Affirmative:	-ar → -a	-er/-ir → -e

Affirmative: *command* + *pronoun(s)* (1 word)
Negative: **no** + *pronoun(s)* + *command* (3 words)

Práctica y comunicación

A. Mandatos frecuentes

Paso 1. Autoprueba. Complete las siguientes oraciones con el mandato apropiado.

1. ______me qué quieres.		**a.** di
2. No ______ al parque sola.		**b.** digas
3. No le ______ nada de la fiesta.		**c.** pon
4. ______te un abrigo.		**d.** pongas
5. ______ a la fiesta.		**e.** vayas
6. No ______ eso en mi cama.		**f.** ve

Paso 2. Haga mandatos informales basados en las siguientes frases.

1. **buscar** la información en Google
2. **lavar** los platos
3. **ir** al gimnasio con más frecuencia
4. **imprimir** la tarea
5. **salir** con nosotros el viernes por la noche
6. no: **entrar** en esa página web
7. no: **hacer** eso
8. no: **encender** el celular
9. no: **decirle** esta información a nadie
10. no: **descargar** esa app de internet

Paso 3. Ahora, en parejas, díganse cuáles son los mandatos de la lista que se oyen con frecuencia. También deben decirse quiénes se los dicen y en qué situaciones.

PPrác. A, Paso 1: Answers: *1. a 2. e 3. b 4. c 5. f 6. d*

B. Recuerdos de la niñez

Paso 1. Haga mandatos informales basados en las siguientes frases. ¿Oía usted estos mandatos cuando era niño/a? ¿Quién se los daba?

1. **limpiar** tu cuarto
2. **hacer** la tarea
3. **lavarse** las manos
4. **decirme** la verdad
5. **ser** bueno
6. **irse** a la cama
7. ¡**acostarse** ahora mismo!
8. no: **cruzar** (*to cross*) la calle solo/a
9. no: **jugar** con mis cosas
10. no: **darles** tu comida a los otros niños
11. no: **decir** mentiras (*lies*)
12. no: **ponerse** esa camiseta sucia

Paso 2. Finalmente, en parejas, den otros mandatos afirmativos y negativos que ustedes oían con frecuencia en casa o en la escuela cuando eran niños y cuando eran adolescentes. Traten de (*Try to*) recordar tres mandatos en cada categoría.

Nota comunicativa

Verbos derivados de *poner, tener* y *venir*

Many Spanish verbs are formed with a prefix (a syllable or syllables added to the beginning of a word) plus **poner, tener,** and **venir.** You already know one verb of this kind: **obtener.** Can you infer the meaning of the following infinitives? **Componer** (*to compose; to form, make up*) is harder to guess, but the others should be obvious.

poner: <u>com</u>poner, <u>pro</u>poner, <u>su</u>poner

tener: <u>con</u>tener, <u>man</u>tener

venir: <u>inter</u>venir, <u>pre</u>venir

These verbs are conjugated just like the verbs on which they are based. The only difference is that they need an accent mark in the **tú** affirmative commands. Here are some of the forms of **componer.**

Present: **compongo, compones...**
Imperfect: **componía, componías...**
Preterite: **compuse, compusiste...**
Present participle: **componiendo**
Commands: **componga usted, compongan ustedes no compongas, compón**

You will practice some of these verbs in **Práctica C.** Recognizing and using them will increase your Spanish vocabulary. Only **obtener** is listed in the end-of-chapter **Vocabulario** list.

C. Modo avión

Paso 1. ¿Cree usted que estamos demasiado «conectad@s»? Compare lo que hacemos y sentimos hoy día con lo que hacía y sentía la gente a finales del siglo XX.

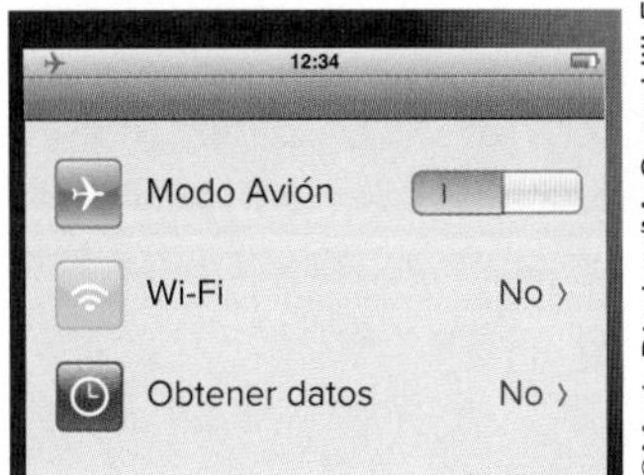

©Mark Dierker/McGraw-Hill Education

1. ¿Qué hacía la gente para obtener información sobre algo que no sabía?
2. ¿Qué hacía la gente para mantenerse en contacto con los amigos, la familia, etcétera? ¿Y ahora?
3. ¿Cree usted que las personas del siglo XX se sentían culpables (*guilty*) por estar desconectadas durante las vacaciones? ¿Y ahora?

Paso 2. Ahora use las siguientes ideas para dar consejos en forma de mandatos informales para vivir «en modo avión», por lo menos temporalmente (*temporarily*). Es decir (*That is*), den consejos sobre cómo usar la tecnología sin dejarse absorber por ella.

1. no **tener** el celular al lado de la almohada (*pillow*) toda la noche / **poner**lo lejos de la cama
2. no **mantener** el celular encendido (*on*) todo el tiempo / **desconectar** a veces
3. **proponer** actividades físicas para hacer con los amigos en lugar de mirar una pantalla / **hacer** ejercicio.
4. **contenerse** las ganas de contestar todos los mensajes inmediatamente / **ser** paciente

Paso 3. Finalmente, en parejas, inventen un mandato importantísimo para todo el mundo con respecto al uso de tecnología en la vida diaria.

Algo sobre...

la cumbia

©Kobby Dagan/Shutterstock

Un grupo folclórico de cumbia

La cumbia es un género[a] musical y un baile tradicional de la costa caribeña de Colombia y Panamá. Se cree que su origen fue una danza de cortejo[b] africana. La cumbia combina el ritmo y percusión de origen africano con instrumentos indígenas, como la gaita[c] colombiana, y europeos, como la guitarra. La cumbia es tan famosa como la salsa en algunos países de Sudamérica.

¿Qué géneros musicales de los Estados Unidos son populares fuera de[d] este país? ¿Son bailables? ¿Qué tipos de instrumentos se usan?

[a]*genre, type* [b]*courtship*
[c]*woodwind instrument*
[d]fuera... *outside of*

D. Entre compañeros de casa. En parejas, hagan una lista de los cinco mandatos que se oyen con más frecuencia en su casa (apartamento, residencia). Piensen en los mandatos que ustedes oyen y también en los que ustedes les dan a los demás (*others*).

Vocabulario útil

apagar (gu) la computadora	**no ser...**	**poner, encender (enciendo) la tele**
contestar el teléfono	**así** (like that), **bobo/a** (dumb),	**prestarme dinero**
lavar los platos	**impaciente, impulsivo/a,**	**sacar (qu) la basura**
no hacer ruido	**loco/a, pesado/a,**	
	precipitado/a (hasty), **tonto/a**	

E. Un anuncio turístico. Los mandatos se usan con frecuencia en los anuncios, como este que nos invita a visitar Colombia. En parejas, inventen por lo menos ocho mandatos que podrían (*might*) ser útiles para un anuncio turístico sobre los Estados Unidos. ¡No repitan verbos, por favor!

Colombia te invita.
¡Ven y conócenos!

©Digital Archive Japan/Alamy

F. Mandatos y preguntas

Paso 1. Imagine que estas personas son sus amigos. Deles consejos en forma de mandatos informales.

1. Su amiga Mariana trabaja demasiado. Duerme poco y bebe muchísimo café. Jamás hace ejercicio. Siempre está mirando su iPhone.
2. Su prima Sara vive sola en una casa grande en la mejor zona de la ciudad, con dos perros y dos gatos. Tiene demasiados gastos para su sueldo (*salary*). Antes, sus abuelos le mandaban dinero, pero ahora no pueden seguir mandándoselo.
3. Celia quiere salir a divertirse, especialmente los viernes por la noche. Pero su novio está muy cansado los viernes después de la semana de trabajo.

Paso 2. Ahora, en parejas, digan cómo se expresarían (*you would express yourselves*) en las siguientes situaciones. **¡OJO!** Consideren bien si es mejor usar la forma de **tú** o de **usted** en cada situación. Recuerden que no se debe usar mandatos en ciertas situaciones, incluso (*even*) con los buenos amigos y familiares.

1. A la profesora de español: usted no entendió lo que acaba de decir.
2. A un compañero de clase que quiere usar las respuestas de usted porque no hizo la tarea.
3. A una compañera de cuarto o de casa que nunca contribuye con nada para la comida... y hoy quiere tomarse la leche que usted tiene en el refrigerador.
4. A un señor en la calle: usted necesita saber dónde está la parada del autobús.
5. A un amigo en la mesa: usted quiere la sal.
6. A una persona joven en el campus: usted quiere saber dónde esta el edificio X.
7. A una compañera de clase: usted quiere saber la hora.
8. A un profesor que no puede encontrar una aplicación en la computadora: usted le dice cómo hacerlo.

34 Expressing Subjective Actions or States

Present Subjunctive (Part 1): An Introduction

Gramática en acción: Manuela busca apartamento

©Glowimages/Getty Images

—Por supuesto, **quiero que** el apartamento esté en un buen barrio.

—Claro, por eso **es muy importante que** haya una parada del autobús cerca.

—Sí, ¡**espero que** mi sueldo sea suficiente para el alquiler y todos los gastos mensuales!

—¿El depósito? **Es probable que** mis padres me den el dinero para pagarlo.

Comprensión

Según lo que dice Manuela por teléfono, **¿es probable que...**

1. Manuela esté hablando con su mejor amiga?
2. Manuela tenga un perro?
3. Manuela no tenga coche?
4. Manuela viva en una ciudad grande?
5. los padres de Manuela estén preocupados por la situación económica de su hija?

Present Subjunctive / **El presente de subjuntivo**

1. Indicative Mood

Except for **usted/ustedes** and negative **tú** commands, all the verb forms you have learned so far in *Puntos de partida* are part of the *indicative mood* (**el modo indicativo**). In both English and Spanish, the indicative is used to state facts and to ask questions; it objectively expresses what the speaker considers to be true.

El modo indicativo

Prefiero llegar temprano a casa.
I prefer getting home early.

¿**Vienes** a la fiesta, ¿verdad?
You're coming to the party, right?

2. Subjunctive Mood

Spanish has another verb system called the *subjunctive mood* (**el modo subjuntivo**). The subjunctive is used to express the attitude of the speaker with respect to what he/she says. These include things that the speaker

- wants to happen or wants others to do
- reacts to emotionally
- does not yet know to be true

To sum up:

- indicative = objective reality (speaker knows it)
- subjunctive = subjective or conceptual (that is, in the mind of the speaker)

El modo subjuntivo

Prefiero que **llegues** temprano a casa.
I prefer for you to be (that you be) home early.

Espero que **vengas** a la fiesta.
I hope (that) you're coming to the party.

Es probable que **vengas** a la fiesta, ¿no?
You're probably coming (It's probable that you will come) to the party, aren't you?

Manuela is looking for an apartment *—"Naturally, I want the apartment to be (lit., that the apartment be) in a good neighborhood." —"Of course, that's why it's really important for there to be (lit., that there be) a bus stop nearby." —"Yes, I hope (that) my salary will be enough for the rent and all the monthly expenses!" —"The deposit? It's probable that my parents will give me the money to pay it."*

3. Simple vs. Complex Sentences

In English and in Spanish, sentences may be simple or complex.

- A *simple sentence* (**una oración simple**) has one conjugated verb.

Oraciones simples

Vienes a la fiesta.
You are coming to the party.

Alicia **está** en casa.
Alicia is at home.

- A *complex sentence* (**una oración compleja**) has two or more *clauses* (**las cláusulas**), each with a conjugated verb.

Oraciones complejas

Yo **sé** que **vienes** a la fiesta.
I know that you're coming to the party.

Miguel **piensa** que Alicia **está** en casa.
Miguel thinks (that) Alicia is at home.

¡OJO!

As you can see in the example sentences, in English the word *that* introduces the second clause, but it can be and is often omitted. The word **que** is never omitted in Spanish.

---

4. Two Types of Clauses

In English and in Spanish, there are two types of clauses: main and subordinate.

- *Main clauses* (**Las cláusulas principales**) (under ① in the sentences to the right) express an idea that controls the subordinate clause. These are also called independent clauses.
- *Subordinate clauses* (**Las cláusulas subordinadas**) (under ② in the sentences to the right) contain an incomplete thought and cannot stand alone. They require a main clause to form a complete sentence. Because they depend on the main clause, they are also called dependent clauses.

a clause / **una cláusula** = a group of words that contains a subject and a verb

¡OJO!

In English, there are different ways to express Spanish sentences that contain the subjunctive, as you can see in the examples.

Oraciones complejas

El indicativo

①		②
Yo **sé** *I know*	**que** *(that)*	esta impresora no **funciona**. *this printer doesn't work.*
Miguel **piensa** *Miguel thinks*	**que** *(that)*	Alicia **está** en casa. *Alicia is at home.*

El subjuntivo

①		②
Quiero *I want*	**que** *(for)*	**leas** mi blog. *you to read my blog.*
Miguel **espera** *Miguel hopes*	**que** *(that)*	Alicia **esté** en casa. *Alicia is at home.*
Dudo *I doubt*	**que** *(that)*	esta impresora **funcione**. *this printer works.*

---

5. Use of the Subjunctive in Subordinate Clauses

As you can see in the sentences in Point 4, when the subjects of the clauses in a complex sentence are different, the subjunctive is often used in the subordinate clause in Spanish.

①		②
first subject = **indicative**	**que**	second subject = **subjunctive**

---

6. Same Subject → Infinitive

As you already know, when there is no change of subject in the sentence, the infinitive often follows the conjugated verb and no conjunction is necessary. In this type of sentence, the infinitive is the direct object of the conjugated verb.

Quiero ir a la fiesta.
I want to go to the party.

Necesitan estudiar para el examen.
They need to study for the test.

Es necesario **estudiar** para los exámenes.
It's necessary to study for tests.

7. Common Uses of the Subjunctive

In Spanish, the subjunctive is commonly used in the subordinate clause:

- when the main clause verb expresses *influence*, *emotion*, or *doubt* or *denial*

AND

- when there is a different subject in the main and subordinate clauses.

You will practice all these uses of the subjunctive in this section, and learn more about them in **Gramática 38, 39,** and **40.**

Influencia: **Necesito** que mis padres me **den** más dinero.
Emoción: **Espero** que mis padres me **den** más dinero.
Duda: **Dudo** que mis padres me **den** más dinero.
Negación: **No creo** que mis padres me **den** más dinero.

Forms of the Present Subjunctive / **Las formas del presente de subjuntivo**

The **usted/ustedes** and negative **tú** command forms that you have already learned are part of the subjunctive system.

Terminaciones del presente de subjuntivo
-ar: -e, -es, -e, -emos, -éis, -en
-er/-ir: -a, -as, -a, -amos, -áis, -an

	-ar verbs	**-er** verbs	**-ir** verbs	stem-changing verbs	irregular verbs
	hablar: habl-	**comer: com-**	**escribir: escrib-**	**volver: vuelv-**	**decir: dig-**
Singular	**hable** **hables** **hable**	**coma** **comas** **coma**	**escriba** **escribas** **escriba**	**vuelva** **vuelvas** **vuelva**	**diga** **digas** **diga**
Plural	**hablemos** **habléis** **hablen**	**comamos** **comáis** **coman**	**escribamos** **escribáis** **escriban**	**volvamos** **volváis** **vuelvan**	**digamos** **digáis** **digan**

1. Present Indicative *yo* Stem + Present Subjunctive Endings

The personal endings of the present subjunctive are formed with the "opposite" vowel. They are added to the first person singular (**yo**) of the present indicative, minus its **-o** ending: **habl-, com-, escrib-, vuelv-, dig-,** as shown in the preceding chart.

¡OJO!

present subjunctive stem = present indicative **yo** form minus **-o**

---

2. *-ar* and *-er* Stem-changing Verbs

These verbs follow the stem-changing pattern of the present indicative.

pensar (pienso):	**piense** **pienses** **piense**	**pensemos** **penséis** **piensen**
poder (puedo):	**pueda** **puedas** **pueda**	**podamos** **podáis** **puedan**

---

3. *-ir* Stem-changing Verbs

The present subjunctive of **-ir** stem-changing verbs has the same stem change as that of the present indicative when the stem vowel is stressed.

- **preferir: e → ie**
- **pedir: e → i**
- **dormir: o → ue**

- **preferir (prefiero) (i)**

prefiera	**prefiramos**
Prefieras	**prefiráis**
prefiera	**prefieran**

prefiriendo / prefirió, prefirieron

Remember that when infinitives appear in vocabulary lists, the stem changes are always indicated. All you have to do is remember where they occur.

(Continúa.)

In addition, these verbs show a second stem change in the **nosotros** and **vosotros** forms. This change is highlighted in the verbs on the previous page and to the right.

- e → i
- o → u

This is *the same change* that happens in the present participle (**-ndo**) and in the third person singular and plural of the preterite of **-ir** stem-changing verbs, so you have already learned to make it.

- **pedir (pido) (i)**

pida	**pidamos**
pidas	**pidáis**
pida	**pidan**

pidiendo / pidió, pidieron

- **dormir (duermo) (u)**

duerma	**durmamos**
duermas	**durmáis**
duerma	**duerman**

durmiendo / durmió, durmieron

---

4. Verbs Ending in *-car, -gar,* and *-zar*

These verbs have a spelling change in *all* persons of the present subjunctive to preserve the **c, g,** and **z** sounds. This is the same change that happens in the **usted/ustedes** commands, in the negative **tú** commands, and in the first person singular of the preterite of these verbs.

- **-car: c → qu**
- **-gar: g → gu**
- **-zar: z → c**

buscar (qu)		pagar (gu)		empezar (c)	
busque	**busquemos**	**pague**	**paguemos**	**empiece**	**empecemos**
busques	**busquéis**	**pagues**	**paguéis**	**empieces**	**empecéis**
busque	**busquen**	**pague**	**paguen**	**empiece**	**empiecen**
busque(n), no busques / busqué		**pague(n), no pagues / pagué**		**empiece(n), no empieces / empecé**	

---

5. Verbs with Irregular *yo* Forms

Since the present subjunctive stem is the **yo** form of the present indicative (minus **-o**), verbs with irregular **yo** forms in the present indicative show that irregularity in *all* persons of the present subjunctive.

conocer: conozca, conozcas, conozca, conozcamos, conozcáis, conozcan

decir:	**diga,...**	tener:	**tenga,...**
hacer:	**haga,...**	traer:	**traiga,...**
oír:	**oiga,...**	venir:	**venga,...**
poner:	**ponga,...**	ver:	**vea,...**
salir:	**salga,...**		

---

6. Irregular Verbs

A few verbs have irregular present subjunctive forms.

dar:	**dé, des, dé, demos, deis, den**
estar:	**esté, estés, estés, estemos, estéis, estén**
ir:	**vaya, vayas, vaya, vayamos, vayáis, vayan**
saber:	**sepa, sepas, sepa, sepamos, sepáis, sepan**
ser:	**sea, seas, sea, seamos, seáis, sean**

---

7. Present Subjunctive of *haber: haya*

Remember that the infinitive form of **hay** is **haber.** The present subjunctive of **hay** is **haya.**

No creo que **haya** clases hoy.
I don't think there are any classes today.

Práctica y comunicación

Endings of the Present Subjunctive

-ar → -e   -er/-ir → -a

A. El próximo semestre/trimestre

Paso 1. Autoprueba. Dé las formas indicadas del presente de subjuntivo de los siguientes verbos. **¡OJO!** Hay unos cambios ortográficos (*spelling changes*).

1. conocer: nosotros **3.** sacar: tú **5.** conseguir: yo
2. decir: ustedes **4.** entregar: ella **6.** morir: ellos

Paso 2. Complete las siguientes oraciones con la forma apropiada de los infinitivos. En algunos casos el infinitivo es la forma apropiada, pero en otros casos es necesario usar el presente de subjuntivo. Si alguna oración es falsa para usted, use **no** antes del verbo principal (es decir, el verbo en el indicativo).

El próximo semestre/trimestre...

1. quiero ________ (tomar) otra clase de español.
2. mi padre/madre (esposo/a, hijo/a, amigo/a...) quiere que yo ________ (tomar) una clase de economía.
3. mi consejero/a recomienda que yo ________ (tomar) una clase de matemáticas.
4. deseo ________ (vivir) fuera del campus.
5. espero ________ (encontrar) un apartamento o una casa cerca del campus.
6. espero que mis padres/amigos ________ (ayudarme) con el alquiler.
7. deseo que mi mejor amigo/a ________ (vivir) conmigo fuera del campus.
8. dudo que ________ (haber) problemas en encontrar una casa o un apartamento.

Paso 3. Ahora, en parejas, entrevístense sobre las oraciones del **Paso 2** para ver si las oraciones son ciertas o falsas para ustedes. Luego díganle al resto de la clase algo que ustedes tienen en común.

MODELO: **E1:** ¿Tu padre quiere que **tomes** una clase de economía el próximo trimestre?
E2: No, mi padre no quiere que **tome** una clase de economía. ¿Y tu padre?
E1: Mi padre tampoco. → Nuestros padres no quieren que **tomemos** una clase de economía el próximo trimestre.

B. En el trabajo. Complete las oraciones de la columna de la izquierda con la cláusula más lógica de la columna de la derecha.

1. La jefa (*boss*) quiere que ___.
2. Y duda que ___.
3. Prohíbe que ___.
4. Para ella, es importante ___.
5. Yo espero que ___.
6. Pero no creo que ___.

a. me dé un aumento de sueldo (*raise*) pronto.
b. tengamos que trabajar los sábados este mes.
c. seamos diligentes durante las horas de trabajo.
d. usemos el escáner para las cosas personales durante las horas de trabajo.
e. eso ocurra (*will happen*) este mes.
f. tener una reunión (*meeting*) semanal con todo el equipo.

C. Cosas importantes. Haga oraciones completas conectando las dos frases. En algunos casos no es necesario hacer cambios, pero en otros casos es necesario añadir la palabra **que** y conjugar el segundo verbo en el presente de subjuntivo.

MODELOS: Es necesario / **saber** cuáles son los gastos de electricidad y gas antes de alquilar un apartamento → Es necesario **saber** cuáles son los gastos de electricidad y gas antes de alquilar un apartamento.

Mi compañero espera / yo: **saber** cuáles son los gastos de un apartamento antes de alquilarlo → Mi compañero espera **que yo sepa** cuáles son los gastos de un apartamento antes de alquilarlo.

Sobre una vivienda

1. Es importante / **informarse** sobre las zonas de una ciudad antes de alquilar un apartamento
2. Se recomienda / **leer** en internet los anuncios clasificados de viviendas
3. Todo el mundo espera / sus vecinos: **ser** personas amables
4. A alguna gente no le importa / **haber** mucho tráfico en su calle

Sobre internet y celulares

5. Mucha gente quiere / **tener** cientos de amigos en Facebook
6. Otros no quieren / gente desconocida (*unknown*): **saber** de su vida por Facebook
7. A los profesores les molesta / sus estudiantes: **mandar** mensajes en clase
8. Es dudoso (*doubtful*) / alguien en este país: no **tener** acceso a internet hoy día

---

Prác. A, Paso 1: **Answers:** *1. conozcamos 2. digan 3. saques 4. entregue 5. consiga 6. mueran*

D. ¿Puede usted substituir a su profesor(a) en el salón de clase? Demuéstrele a su profesor(a) que usted lo/la conoce bien, haciendo oraciones como las (*those*) que dice él/ella en clase. (Solo tiene que cambiar el infinitivo.)

quiero que espero que prohíbo que dudo que es necesario que me alegro de (*I'm glad*) que no creo que recomiendo que	+	(nombre de un[a] estudiante) todos ustedes nadie alguien de la clase yo	+	(no)	+	copiar en un examen dormirse / entrar en internet / estar en Facebook en clase estudiar hacer la tarea llegar a tiempo saber el subjuntivo sacar notas mejores tener un blog ¿ ?

E. Cómo dar una buena fiesta

Paso 1. Haga una lista de las cosas que hay que hacer para dar una fiesta exitosa (*successful*), en su opinión. Use infinitivos en su lista.

MODELOS: llamar a los amigos con anticipación (*ahead of time*), comprar...

Paso 2. En parejas, comparen sus listas del **Paso 1** y hagan una sola lista de por lo menos diez acciones.

Paso 3. Luego conviertan la lista en una serie de recomendaciones para dar una buena fiesta.

MODELO: Recomendamos que llamen a los amigos con anticipación.

Vocabulario útil

Es necesario/ bueno/importante/ esencial que...
Recomendamos que...
Sugerimos que...
} + *subjuntivo*

Algo sobre...

la ciudad de Medellín

Con una población de 3.5 millones de habitantes en el área metropolitana, Medellín es la capital del departamento[a] de Antioquia y la segunda ciudad más grande de Colombia. Está considerada como una de las mejores ciudades para vivir en Latinoamérica. Para empezar, tiene vistas fabulosas de las montañas y un clima templado[b] que le da el título de Ciudad de la eterna primavera. Además,[c] es un importante centro de desarrollo[d] e innovación, así como[e] una ciudad modelo por sus soluciones para la sostenibilidad ambiental y su excelente sistema de transporte.

Medellín, Colombia

En su país, ¿hay alguna ciudad comparable con Medellín por su clima, su interés como centro de innovación o como modelo de ciudad sostenible?

[a]región [b]*mild* [c]*In addition* [d]*development* [e]así... *as well as*

¿Recuerda usted?

In **Gramática 35** and in the grammar sections of **Capítulo 13,** you will learn more about the three major uses of the subjunctive. Summarize what you have learned so far by completing the following sentences.

1. In Spanish, there are at least ________________ clauses in a sentence that contains the subjunctive.
2. The subjunctive appears in the ________________ clause.
3. The indicative appears in the ________________ clause.
4. The word ________________ must always appear.
5. The verb subjects in each clause are ________________.

35 Expressing Desires and Requests

Use of the Subjunctive (Part 2): Influence

Gramática en acción: ¿Quién debe hacerlo?

Comprensión

Escoja la oración que describa cada dibujo.

1. _____ **a.** No quiero usar el celular ahora.
   b. No quiero que usen el celular ahora.

2. _____ **a.** Es necesario tomar clases de arte.
   b. Es necesario que tome clases de arte.

3. _____ **a.** ¡Quiero bajar el volumen!
   b. ¡Te pido que bajes el volumen!

1. Features of the Subjunctive

So far, as you know, you have learned to identify the subjunctive by the features listed at the right.

In addition, the subjunctive is associated with three concepts or conditions that "trigger" the use of it in the subordinate clause: influence, emotion, and doubt or denial.

- It is conjugated with the "opposite" vowel.
- It appears in a complex sentence, one that has at least two clauses and thus two conjugated verbs.
- It is used in the dependent clause when the subject of that clause is different from the subject of the main clause.
- It is preceded by **que.**

2. The Subjunctive after Verbs of Influence

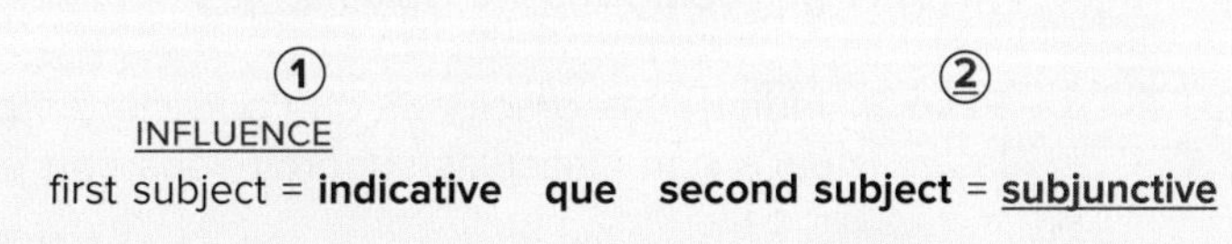

One trigger for the use of the subjunctive in the subordinate clause is the concept of *influence* (**la influencia**). The subject of the main clause *wants*, *prefers*, *insists*, and so on, that the subject of the subordinate clause do something, expressed by a verb in the subjunctive. The verb in the main clause is always in the indicative.

①		**La influencia** ②
Yo **quiero** *I want*	**que**	tú **pagues** la cuenta. *you to pay the bill.*
La profesora **prefiere** *The professor prefers*	**que** *that*	no **lleguemos** tarde. *we don't don't arrive late.*

3. Verbs of Influence

There are many verbs of influence, some very strong and direct, some very soft and polite. The verbs marked with * are new.

STRONG(ER)		SOFT(ER)
***insistir en**		**desear**
***mandar**	to order	**pedir (pido) (i)**
***permitir**	to permit, allow	**preferir (prefiero) (i)**
***prohibir (prohíbo)**		**recomendar (recomiendo)**
querer (quiero)		**sugerir (sugiero) (i)**

4. Impersonal Expressions of Influence

An impersonal generalization (**es** + *adjective*) can also be the main clause that triggers the subjunctive. The subject of the impersonal expression is *it* (expressed by the verb **es**), and the subjunctive is used when there is another subject in the sentence.

Es necesario que / **Es urgente** que / **Es mejor** que } Paco **estudie** español.

> **¡OJO!**
>
> As you know, when there is no second subject, the infinitive follows verbs of influence and impersonal expressions of influence.

Quiero/Deseo/Prefiero estudiar español.
Es necesario/urgente/mejor/importante estudiar español.

5. Indicative in two-clause sentences

Not all sentences that have two clauses contain the subjunctive. You have been using two-clause sentences with two different subjects like the ones to the right for some time. What is lacking in these sentences is one of the three subjunctive "triggers."

Sé que la clase **es** a las ocho de la mañana.
Creo/Pienso que esa computadora vieja **va** a fallar pronto.

Summary of Influence

influence + **que** + change of subject → **subjunctive**

Práctica y comunicación

A. Opiniones sobre la tecnología

Paso 1. Autoprueba. Indique cuál(es) de los siguientes conceptos *no* se asocia(n) con el subjuntivo.

1. un infinitivo ☐
2. la influencia en la cláusula independiente ☐
3. dos sujetos ☐
4. dos cláusulas ☐
5. **que** para unir dos cláusulas ☐

Paso 2. Indique las oraciones que son ciertas para usted. Indique también las oraciones con cláusulas subordinadas con el subjuntivo.

	CIERTO PARA MÍ	SUBJUNTIVO
1. Muchos de mis profesores quieren que los estudiantes usemos la computadora en clase.	☐	☐
2. Algunos de mis profesores prefieren que no usemos la computadora en clase.	☐	☐
3. Todos mis profesores insisten en que no usemos el celular en clase.	☐	☐
4. Es mejor que haya una multa (*fine*) muy grande para las personas que mandan mensajes mientras conducen (*they drive*).	☐	☐
5. Es necesario que los padres y los maestros (*teachers*) prohíban a los menores el uso frecuente de los celulares.	☐	☐
6. Quiero eliminar varias aplicaciones de mi celular.	☐	☐

Prác. A, Paso 1: Answers: 1

 **Paso 3.** Ahora, en parejas, entrevístense sobre las ideas del **Paso 1.**

MODELO: E1: ¿Quieren muchos de tus profesores que los estudiantes usen la computadora en clase?
E2: Sí, muchos de mis profesores quieren eso. ¿Y tus profesores?
E1: También.

B. Gabriel García Márquez. Complete las siguientes oraciones sobre el escritor colombiano con el verbo apropiado.

1. Es importante que todo el mundo ______ (sabe / sepa / saber) quién es Gabriel García Márquez.
2. Todos los profesores de literatura quieren que sus estudiantes ______ (conocen / conozcan / conocer) la obra de este escritor.
3. Los profesores de español sugieren que todo el mundo ______ (lee / lea / leer) algo escrito (*written*) por García Márquez.
4. Mi amiga colombiana insiste en que yo ______ (busco / busque / buscar) un cuento de García Márquez en español.
5. Pero yo prefiero ______ (leo / lea / leer) algo traducido (*translated*) al inglés.
6. ¿Con qué novela de García Márquez me recomiendas que ______ (*yo*: empiezo / empiece / empezar)?

 **C. ¿Qué quiere usted?**

Paso 1. En parejas, hablen de cómo desean afectar las acciones de otras personas.

MODELO: E1: ¿Qué quieres que haga tu padre?
E2: **Quiero que** mi padre me **compre** una computadora.

insistir en mandar permitir preferir prohibir querer recomendar	+	padre/madre amigos/as hermano/a profesor(a) novio/a esposo/a compañero/a de cuarto hijo/a, hijos ¿ ?	+	comprarme... (una televisión, rosas, ¿ ?) visitarme... (mañana, el jueves, ¿ ?) invitarme... (al cine, a cenar, ¿ ?) (no) dar tarea... (hoy, mañana, ¿ ?) ayudarme... (a hacer la tarea, ¿ ?) salir con... (otra persona, ¿ ?) llamarme... (el viernes, ¿ ?) explicarme... (la gramática, ¿ ?) ¿ ?

Paso 2. Ahora hablen de las cosas que otras personas quieren, prefieren, permiten, etcétera, que ustedes hagan.

MODELO: E1: ¿Qué quieren tus hijos que hagas?
E2: Quieren que yo compre una computadora nueva.

Algo sobre...

Gabriel García Márquez

©Ulf Andersen/Getty Images

Gabriel García Márquez (1927–2014), un escritor[a] colombiano leído[b] y admirado en todo el mundo

Gabriel García Márquez, o «Gabo», como lo llamaban, es sin duda[c] el escritor colombiano más famoso del mundo. Su obra[d] literaria fue una de las más influyentes del siglo XX. Empezó trabajando como periodista[e] y escribió cuentos,[f] novelas y ensayos;[g] luego, en 1982, recibió el Premio Nobel de Literatura. Su obra más famosa es *Cien años de soledad*, ejemplo de un estilo literario que se llama realismo mágico. La novela narra la historia de una familia a través de[h] varias generaciones.

¿Puede nombrar usted a algunos escritores muy importantes de su país? ¿Cuál es su escritor favorito?

[a]*writer* [b]*read* [c]sin... *without a doubt* [d]*body of work* [e]*journalist* [f]*short stories* [g]*essays* [h]a... *throughout*

D. El programa de radio. *Te escucho* es un programa de radio que da consejos sobre todo tipo de problemas. Hoy son problemas relacionados con el uso y abuso de la tecnología. En parejas, imaginen que ustedes son los presentadores del programa. Lean lo que dicen los siguientes radioyentes (*listeners*) y preparen las respuestas que ustedes creen que los moderadores del programa deben darles.

1. **Habla Hortensia:** «Soy una chica de 20 años. Acabo de mudarme a esta ciudad y tengo pocos amigos aquí. Pero no me siento sola porque siempre estoy conectada a internet. Mi madre dice que no es normal que yo pase tantas horas en la computadora y que no salga con los amigos. ¿Qué piensan ustedes? ¿Qué me recomiendan?»
2. **Habla la Sra. Silva:** «Mi esposo es un hombre bueno y responsable. Pero la mayor parte del tiempo que pasa en casa, está en el estudio, en internet. Yo no comprendo por qué pasa tanto tiempo en eso. Estoy preocupada y también aburrida. ¿Qué me recomiendan que haga? ¿Qué le debo decir a mi esposo?»
3. **Habla Guillermo, un joven de 17 años:** «Mi hermano de 13 años está en Facebook, lo que es normal. Pero ayer descubrí que pone fotos de él y de toda la familia en internet. Yo no quiero que ponga fotos de nosotros, pero él dice que las fotos son suyas (*his*). Hay una foto horrible de mi madre. No quiero decírselo a mis padres porque tengo miedo de que le quiten la computadora a mi hermano. Pero no sé qué otra cosa puedo hacer. ¿Cuáles son mis opciones? ¿Es mejor que no haga nada?»

Estrategia

Empiecen sus consejos con cláusulas como las siguientes.

Te/Le recomendamos/ sugerimos que...
Es importante/urgente/ necesario que...
Dudamos que...

Paso 2. Ahora piensen en un problema con la tecnología que sea similar a los del **Paso 1.** Descríbanlo por escrito (*in writing*). El resto de la clase les va a hacer sugerencias sobre cómo resolverlo.

E. Intercambios

Paso 1. Complete las siguientes oraciones lógicamente... ¡y con sinceridad!

1. Mis padres (hijos, abuelos,...) insisten en que (yo) ______.
2. Mi mejor amigo/a (esposo/a, novio/a,...) desea que (yo) ______.
3. Prefiero que mis amigos ______.
4. No quiero que mis amigos ______.
5. Es urgente que (yo) ______.
6. Es necesario que mi mejor amigo/a (esposo/a, novio/a,...) ______.

Paso 2. En parejas, entrevístense para saber cómo completaron las oraciones del **Paso 1.** Luego díganle a la clase algo que ustedes tienen en común.

MODELO: ¿En qué insisten tus padres?

Vocabulario útil

desconectar	**quitar** to take away
limitar	**supervisar**

F. Prevención de los peligros (*dangers*) de la tecnología

Paso 1. Todo el mundo sabe que las tecnologías de la información y la comunicación (TIC) presentan problemas para muchas personas, especialmente para los niños y adolescentes. Haga una lista de cinco recomendaciones básicas para los padres.

Piense en las siguientes ideas:

- el uso de los aparatos en general
- el tiempo y los lugares de acceso
- el uso de los datos personales y las contraseñas
- el acceso a las redes sociales
- el uso de la cámara

Use el siguiente modelo para sus recomendaciones: mandatos de **usted** para los padres o una expresión de influencia + **que sus hijos** + subjuntivo para los hijos.

MODELOS: Prohíban que sus hijos usen...
Es necesario que su hijo / sus hijos limite(n)...

Paso 2. Ahora, en parejas, compartan (*share*) sus consejos. Luego díganle a la clase los cinco mejores consejos de ustedes.

Todo junto

A. Lengua y cultura: La ciudad de Cartagena, Colombia

Paso 1. Completar. Complete the following passage with the correct forms of the words in parentheses, as suggested by context. When two possibilities are given, select the correct word. **¡OJO!** As you conjugate the verbs in this activity, put the infinitives preceded by I: in the imperfect. Other verbs will be present indicative, present subjunctive, or infinitive as determined by the context.

Mayra y Joaquín son dos colombianos que viven en mi ciudad. Los dos ______ (ser / estar[1]) de Cartagena, una ______ (grande[2]) ciudad colombiana que ______ (ser / estar[3]) en el mar Caribe. De niña, Mayra ______ (I: vivir[4]) en la parte más antigua ______ (en la / de la[5]) ciudad, el Centro Amurallado[a] colonial. La familia de Joaquín______ (tener[6]) un apartamento en Bocagrande, la zona ______ (más / mejor[7]) moderna de Cartagena. Sin embargo, los dos les hacen las ______ (mismo[8]) recomendaciones a las personas ______ (que / quienes[9]) desean visitar la ciudad.

Mayra y Joaquín ______ (ser / estar[10]) de acuerdo en que el Centro Amurallado tiene ______ (mucho[11]) cosas que ver. Por eso, los dos recomiendan ______ (que / lo que[12]) los turistas en Cartagena ______ (dar[13]) un paseo por ese centro histórico de la ciudad. También es necesario ______ (que / —[14]) vean y admiren las fortalezas y las murallas.[b] ¿______ (Saber / Conocer[15]) ustedes que algunas miden veinte metros de ancho[c]? ¡______ (Ser / Estar[16]) impresionantes! Además[d] ______ (ser / haber[17]) playas muy chéveres, como la playa de La Boquilla* y el Parque Natural Corales del Rosario, en la isla Barú.† Por la noche Mayra y Joaquín ______ (sugerir[18]) que los turistas visiten un restaurante en la Boquilla y que ______ (pedir[19]) mariscos. Luego deben ______ (ir[20]) a un club a bailar cumbia.

©Dave G. Houser/Getty Images

Unos edificios de apartamentos muy modernos en Bocagrande

[a]Centro... *Walled Center* [b]fortalezas... *forts and walls* [c]miden... *are 20 meters thick* [d]*In addition*

Paso 2. Comprensión

1. ¿De qué ciudad son Mayra y Joaquín?
2. ¿Qué es lo que distingue la geografía de esta ciudad?
3. ¿En qué partes de la ciudad vivían los dos de niños?
4. ¿Qué recomiendan Mayra y Joaquín que hagan los turistas que visitan Cartagena?

Paso 3. En acción

Ahora, en parejas, hagan una serie de recomendaciones para las personas que visitan su ciudad y su universidad.

Vocabulario útil

Verbos/frases para recomendar	Ideas	Lugares	
proponer	**comer en**	**la colina**	hill
recomendar (ie)	**dar un paseo por**	**la fuente**	fountain
sugerir (ie) (i)	**subir/bajar por/a**	**el puente**	bridge
es buena idea/interesante	**ir a/ver/visitar**	**la torre**	tower

MODELO: Les recomendamos que suban a la colina Foss porque desde allí hay una vista muy bonita de la universidad.

*La Boquilla *is a fishing village outside of* Cartagena; *it has a long, secluded beach with restaurants and bars.*

†La isla Barú *is about ten minutes by motorboat from* Cartagena. *It has white sand beaches, crystal clear water, and big coral reefs.*

B. Proyecto: Cómo mejorar la contaminación acústica

No hay duda (*doubt*) de que vivimos en un mundo con mucho ruido. Por eso, en parejas, van a crear unas reglas (*rules*) para mejorar (*improve*) la situación en algún lugar concreto.

Vocabulario útil

la ambulancia	
el claxon	(car) horn
el despertador	alarm clock
el megáfono	loudspeaker
el ronquido	snoring
la sirena	
el sonido	sound
el taladro (eléctrico)	(electric) drill
el timbre	ring (*on a phone, door, etc.*)
el volumen	volume

Paso 1. Preparación. Hagan dos listas: una de cosas que causan ruido y la otra de espacios o situaciones que son especialmente ruidosos (*noisy*). La ilustración les puede dar algunas ideas.

Paso 2. Desarrollo. (*Development.*) Ahora elijan uno de los espacios o situaciones que ustedes creen que pueden mejorar, pensando especialmente en la gente joven. Hagan una lista de recomendaciones o reglas sobre lo que se debe o no se debe hacer para reducir el nivel de ruido. Usen mandatos de **tú**.

Paso 3. Presentación. Finalmente, elijan un buen título para su lista y, si es posible, añadan una imagen. Luego impriman su lista y preséntenla a la clase.

¡Ahora, yo!

A. Entrevista. Use de modelo las preguntas y respuestas de la página 357 de este capítulo para hablar de la zona donde usted vive y de los aparatos que usted usa diariamente para mantener sus relaciones sociales.

B. Proyecto audiovisual. Filme dos entrevistas con estudiantes o personal (*personnel*) de habla española en su universidad. Sus entrevistados deben hablar de los usos que hacen de la tecnología. Use como modelo las entrevistas de estudiantes ecuatorianos en el Programa 12 de *Salu2*.

«¡No sin mi celular!» Segmento 2

Antes de mirar

¿En qué sitios web y buscadores entra usted con frecuencia? ¿En qué proveedores de correo electrónico tiene usted una cuenta (*account*)?

Este segmento

Laura trae un reportaje sobre el uso de la tecnología entre los estudiantes universitarios de Quito. Para terminar, Ana y Víctor hablan de mensajes de texto.

«Yo creo que falta desarrollar (*it's necessary to develop*) un poco lo que es el wifi aquí en Quito. Pero ha incrementado (*has increased*) bastantísimo (*a lot*) el uso del wifi en todo lo que son lugares públicos... »

Vocabulario del segmento

han decidido	have decided	**inalámbrico/a**	wireless
te des cuenta	you realize	**resumir**	to summarize
el uso	**el hábito**	**crear**	to create
la investigación	research	**la prueba**	test
los deberes	**la tarea**	**pertenecer**	to belong
agradar	**gustar**	**ni pudo**	couldn't even (do it)
la costumbre	**el hábito**	**anticuado/a**	antiquated, old-fashioned
¡claro!	of course!		

Fragmento del guion

El mundo ha sufrido[a] un gran cambio tecnológico desde que... o sea,[b] desde los últimos veinte años. Ahora nos podemos comunicar con cualquier[c] persona en el mundo en cuestión de segundos.[d] Podemos hacer videollamadas con cualquier persona al otro lado del Atlántico, podemos hablar con gente en Europa, con gente en África... Y hace diez, quince años[e] eso era casi imposible, o costaba mucho hacer una llamada internacional. Ahora es gratuito.[f]

[a]ha... *experienced* [b]o... *I mean* [c]*any* [d]en... *in a matter of seconds* [e]hace... *ten, fifteen years ago* [f]*free*

Después de mirar

A. ¿Está claro? ¿Cierto o falso? Corrija las oraciones falsas.

	CIERTO	FALSO
1. Sarita, la hija de Víctor, ya tiene un iPhone y una página de Facebook.	☐	☐
2. Facebook es la red social más popular entre los jóvenes ecuatorianos.	☐	☐
3. Estos jóvenes universitarios no pueden conectarse en la universidad.	☐	☐
4. Víctor lee los texteos con facilidad (*easily*).	☐	☐

B. Un poco más. Complete las siguientes oraciones con información del video.

1. Los sitios de internet que más visitan los estudiantes son ______.
2. En el Ecuador, hay acceso wifi en ______.

C. Y ahora, ustedes. En parejas, estudien los dos mensajes de texto que aparecen en el programa y luego preparen un mensaje similar suyo (*of your own*) para el resto de la clase. ¡Inventen nuevas convenciones!

- Ola, q tal? q acs ste finde? Yamam pq es el qmple d mi hno ste finde y kiero acr 1 fiesta. Bsossssss.
- Hsta ntoncs salu2 muy cordials d td el ekipo d ste programa.

MUNDO HISPANO

Enfoque cultural: Colombia

Antes de leer

¿Conoce usted a sus vecinos? ¿Qué relación mantiene con ellos? ¿Hablan con frecuencia o solo se saludan?

Los barrios colombianos

Es común que los vecinos de un barrio colombiano desarrollen[a] una relación estrecha[b] con los otros vecinos y que hasta[c] organicen juntos fiestas y celebraciones en el barrio para fechas especiales. Es normal saber los nombres de muchos de los vecinos del barrio, no solo los[d] del edificio o de la calle donde uno vive. Con frecuencia, la gente habla de los amigos del barrio como un grupo distinto,[e] parecido[f] a los amigos del colegio,[g] de la universidad o del trabajo. En el barrio, es normal ver grupos de personas que charlan[h] juntas, en la plaza o en una esquina[i] o simplemente en la puerta de un edificio o tienda. Por eso el barrio es un lugar de intensa vida social, especialmente para las personas que no trabajan fuera de casa o para las personas mayores. Y, por supuesto,[j] para los niños.

[a]*develop* [b]*close* [c]*even* [d]*those* [e]*distinct, separate* [f]*similar* [g]*grade/high school* [h]*are chatting* [i]*corner* [j]por... *of course*

En otros países hispanos

- **En todo el mundo hispanohablante** Lo común es que haya una plaza central, rodeada de[a] algunos de los edificios más importantes de la ciudad, como el ayuntamiento[b] o la catedral. Estas plazas centrales frecuentemente reciben el nombre de plaza Mayor o plaza de Armas. Había plazas de este tipo en España antes de la conquista de América. Los españoles llevaron el diseño[c] a sus nuevas ciudades americanas.
- **En México y la Argentina** Varias ciudades hispanas tienen metro, pero los[d] de México y la Argentina son notables. El[e] de Buenos Aires es el más antiguo del hemisferio sur. Su construcción comenzó en 1913. Pero el más impresionante es sin duda el metro de la Ciudad de México. Es el segundo metro en longitud[f] de Norteamérica y el mayor de Latinoamérica. Por el número de pasajeros, es el quinto[g] del mundo. Su sistema para nombrar las estaciones es muy colorido y eficiente. Usa palabras y dibujos, para que las personas analfabetas[h] también puedan interpretarlo.

[a]rodeada... *surrounded by* [b]*town hall* [c]*design* [d]*those* [e]*That (i.e.* el metro*)* [f]*length*

[g]*fifth* [h]para... *so that people who can't read*

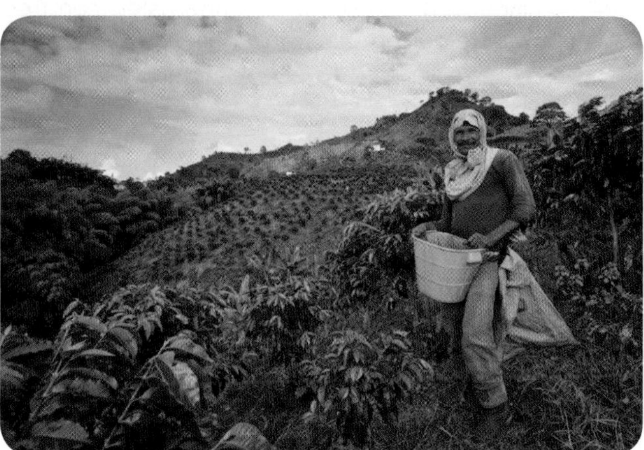

©Jane Sweeney/The Image Bank/Getty Images

Un cafetal (*coffee plantation*) colombiano

Un símbolo colombiano: El café

El café colombiano es famoso en todo el mundo y tiene su propia denominación de origen: Café de Colombia. El país tiene varias zonas cafeteras, que están por toda su geografía. Colombia es el tercer[a] país productor de café del mundo, y los Estados Unidos es el principal consumidor del café colombiano. Sin duda, parte de la fama del café colombiano se debe a la exitosa campaña publicitaria[b] con la figura de Juan Valdez, un personaje[c] ficticio que representa a los campesinos[d] y cafeteros[e] colombianos desde[f] 1959.

[a]*third* [b]exitosa... *successful ad campaign* [c]*character* [d]*farm workers* [e]*coffee producers* [f]*since*

Comprensión

1. ¿Por qué es importante el barrio en la vida de una ciudad hispana?
2. ¿Por qué hay una plaza central en las ciudades latinoamericanas?
3. ¿Cuál es el metro más antiguo de Latinoamérica? ¿Y el más impresionante?
4. ¿Qué contribuye a que sea famoso el café colombiano?
5. ¿Qué país es el principal consumidor del café colombiano?

En acción

Describa la plaza más importante o famosa de su ciudad. ¿Cómo se llama? ¿Por qué o de quién recibió ese nombre? ¿Qué edificios están allí?

Lectura

Antes de leer

Conteste las siguientes preguntas.

1. ¿En qué tipo de lugar vive usted ahora? ¿En una ciudad grande o en una ciudad pequeña? ¿En una zona residencial, rural o agrícola? ¿Y el lugar donde vivía de niño/a?
2. ¿De qué maneras influye en usted el lugar donde vive ahora (o vivía de niño/a) en cuanto a (*as far as*) las siguientes ideas?
   - sus preferencias en cuanto a la comida
   - la manera en que se viste
   - cómo pasa su tiempo libre
   - cómo se relaciona con otras personas
   - sus necesidades materiales
   - sus ideas políticas y sociales

«Cuadrados° y ángulos», de Alfonsina Storni

°*Squares*

Casas enfiladas,[a] casas enfiladas,
casas enfiladas.
Cuadrados, cuadrados, cuadrados.
Casas enfiladas.
Las gentes ya tienen el alma[b] cuadrada,
ideas en fila[c]
y ángulos en la espalda.[d]
Yo misma he vertido[e] ayer una lágrima,[f]
Dios mío, cuadrada.

[a]*in a straight row* [b]*soul* [c]en... *in single file* [d]la... *their backs* [e]Yo... *I myself shed* [f]*tear*

Comprensión

A. Elementos del poema. Identifique los siguientes aspectos del poema.

1. las palabras y frases que se repiten
2. los versos (*lines*) que describen las casas
3. el tipo de lugar que describe el poema
4. los versos que describen a las personas
5. los versos que se refieren a la poeta misma (*herself*)

B. Comentario. Conteste las siguientes preguntas para expresar su opinión como lector(a) (*reader*).

1. ¿Qué efecto tiene la repetición en este poema?
2. ¿Qué relación existe entre las personas y las casas?
3. ¿Qué tipo de persona es la poeta? ¿Qué efecto tiene en ella el ambiente que describe?
4. ¿Cree usted que la poeta se refiere solo a un lugar determinado? ¿O cree que se refiere a un problema más grande?
5. ¿Cree usted que la poeta podría (*could*) ser más feliz en un ambiente diferente? ¿En cuál?

Vocabulario útil

la arquitectura	**el sentido** sense
la monotonía	**sensible** sensitive

Proyecto: Un poema sobre un lugar

Paso 1. Piense en un lugar que no le gusta nada (o si prefiere, uno que le gusta mucho). Visualice ese lugar y haga una lista de algunos de los elementos de ese lugar. También describa la reacción emocional que puedan tener las personas cuando están en ese lugar y el efecto que ese lugar tiene en usted cuando está allí.

Paso 2. De las frases e ideas que anotó para el **Paso 1**, elija las más interesantes y escriba un poema como el (*that*) de Alfonsina Storni. Use la repetición de frases para ayudar a sus lectores a visualizar el lugar y a comprender cómo se sienten las personas cuando están allí.

Paso 3. En grupos, compartan sus poemas. ¿Son suficientemente descriptivos para que (*so that*) todos los miembros del grupo puedan visualizar los lugares y comprender los sentimientos que provocan en el autor / la autora del poema?

Textos orales

Vocabulario para escuchar

emitimos	we air
se trata del	we're talking about
la bienvenida	welcome
los radioyentes	radio listeners
los detalles	details
cómo no	of course
una pandemia	pandemic
la máquina	machine
conocida	known
monitorizar	to monitor
mejorar	to improve

Un doctor habla de un proyecto tecnológico

Antes de escuchar

Empareje cada término médico con su definición.

1. _______ un componente necesario para el funcionamiento del cuerpo que es regulado (*regulated*) por la insulina
2. _______ un órgano del cuerpo humano
3. _______ una hormona que produce el páncreas

a. la glucosa
b. la insulina
c. el páncreas

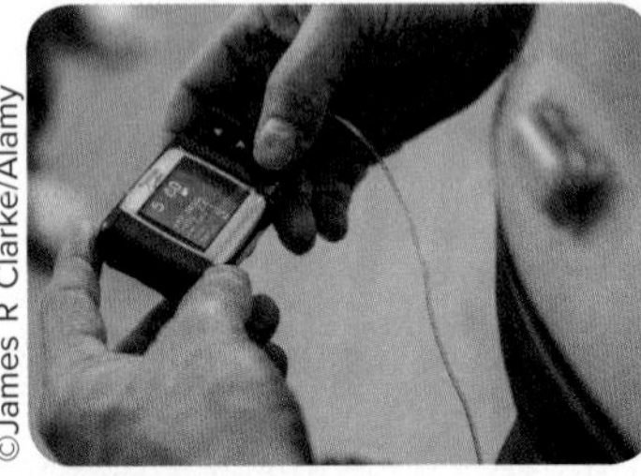

©James R Clarke/Alamy

Dos herramientas (*tools*) útiles en la lucha contra (*struggle against*) la diabetes: un monitor continuo de glucosa y una bomba (*pump*) de insulina

Comprensión

A. La diabetes. Empareje la información de las dos columnas.

1. _______ la característica de diabetes tipo 1
2. _______ el porcentaje de la población adulta mundial que va a sufrir de diabetes en el futuro
3. _______ el nombre común de la diabetes tipo 1
4. _______ el porcentaje de pacientes diabéticos que sufren de diabetes tipo 1
5. _______ el porcentaje de la población adulta mundial que sufre de diabetes en la actualidad

a. casi el 7%
b. casi el 8%
c. el 10%
d. la diabetes juvenil
e. la ausencia total de insulina

B. Más detalles. Conteste las siguientes preguntas.

1. ¿Dónde ocurre esta conversación? ¿Cómo se llama el programa?
2. ¿Qué es el páncreas artificial? ¿Qué tipo de personas lo necesitan?
3. ¿Existe ya esa máquina?
4. ¿Por qué es un gran proyecto?

En acción

Nombre y describa un aparato médico que, en su opinión, es muy útil. Explique también cuál es su función principal.

Proyecto en su comunidad

Entreviste a una persona hispana de su universidad o ciudad sobre su ciudad de origen y el barrio donde vivía en su país.

Preguntas posibles

- ¿Qué tipo de ciudad es? ¿Es grande o pequeña? ¿antigua o moderna?
- ¿Hay buenas vistas desde algún punto de la ciudad? ¿Hay un buen sistema de transporte público, como autobuses o metro?
- ¿Dónde vivía su familia? ¿En el centro o en las afueras? ¿en un barrio histórico o moderno? ¿en una casa individual o en un apartamento?
- ¿Cómo es (o era) la vida del barrio? (Pida detalles.)

Escritura

Proyecto: La educación universitaria: ¿presencial o a distancia?

©MBI/Alamy

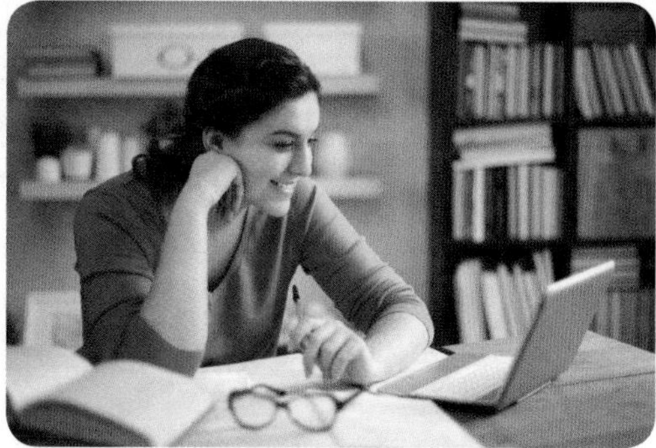

©elenaleonova/Getty Images

¿Prefiere usted las clases presenciales o a distancia?

Antes de escribir

Piensen en las opciones que existen hoy para obtener un título universitario: presencial (es decir, asistiendo a una universidad, según la manera tradicional) o a distancia, gracias a internet. ¿Cuál es el método más usado? ¿Qué ventajas y desventajas tiene cada opción? ¿Cuál fue la opción que ustedes eligieron (*chose*)? ¿Están contentos/as con su decisión? En parejas**,** hagan una lista de argumentos a favor y en contra de cada una de las dos opciones para obtener un título universitario: de forma presencial o a distancia. Deben incluir ejemplos específicos para apoyar (*support*) sus argumentos.

A escribir

Ahora use las ideas de **Antes de escribir** para comparar las dos opciones educativas. O, si lo prefiere, puede defender una de ellas. Hay más ayuda en Connect.

Más ideas para su portafolio

- Publique algo en español en su muro (*wall*) de Facebook. Luego saque una foto de su post e inclúyala en su portafolio, con una explicación de lo que escribió.
- Incluya un anuncio de celulares en español, de internet o de una revista o periódico. Explique lo que le gusta del anuncio y del producto o servicio mismo (*itself*) y también si el producto o servicio es comparable con lo que hay en este país.
- Si ha estado jugando (*you have been playing*) Practice Spanish: Study Abroad, en Quest 9 usted tuvo que decidir dónde quedarse cuando estaba de vacaciones en Colombia. Ahora haga un breve video dándoles consejos a los turistas que quieran visitar la ciudad donde usted vive. ¿Dónde deben quedarse? ¿en un hotel? ¿en una tienda de campaña? ¿en una pensión (*hostel*)? ¿con usted? Explique por qué. ¿Qué servicios (*amenities*) ofrece este lugar?

©McGraw-Hill Education

Sugerencia: You are now ready to play Quest 9 in **Practice Spanish: Study Abroad.**

EN RESUMEN En este capítulo

AFTER STUDYING THIS CHAPTER I CAN. . .

- ☐ talk about my neighborhood and living arrangements (358)
- ☐ talk about technology and technological equipment (360–361)
- ☐ give informal commands and directions (364–366)
- ☐ form the present subjunctive and understand its main uses (369–372)
- ☐ use the present subjunctive to express influence (375–376)
- ☐ recognize/describe at least 2–3 aspects of Colombian cultures

Gramática en breve

33. *Tú* Commands

Negative **tú** commands = "opposite" vowel

-ar → **-es**

-er/-ir → **-as**

Affirmative **tú** commands = **usted** form of the present indicative

-ar → **-a**

-er/-ir → **-e**

34. Present Subjunctive: An Introduction

Endings: "opposite" vowel

-ar: -e, -es, -e, -emos, -éis, -en

-er/-ir: -a, -as, -a, -amos, -áis, -an

Structure:

①		②
first subject = **indicative**	**que**	second subject = **subjunctive**

35. Uses of the Subjunctive: Influence

①		②
INFLUENCE first subject = **indicative**	**que**	second subject = **subjunctive**

Vocabulario

Los verbos

alegrarse (de)	to be glad, happy (about)
dudar	to doubt
esperar	to hope
haber (*inf. of* **hay**)	(there is, there are)
insistir (en)	to insist (on)
mandar	to order
permitir	to permit, allow
prohibir (prohíbo)	to prohibit, forbid

Repaso: desear, pedir (pido) (i), preferir (prefiero) (i), querer (quiero), recomendar (recomiendo), sugerir (sugiero) (i)

La tecnología

el archivo	(computer) file
la arroba	@
los auriculares	earphones/headphones
el buscador	search engine
el buzón de voz	voice mailbox
el canal	channel
la carpeta	(computer) folder
la contraseña	password
el correo electrónico	e-mail
el disco duro	hard drive
el equipo (electrónico)	(electronic) equipment
el espacio (de almacenamiento)	(storage) space
la impresora	printer
la página web	web page
la pantalla (grande/plana)	(big/flat) screen (monitor)
el ratón	mouse
la red social	social network
el sitio web	website
el teléfono fijo	landline

Cognados: el android, la app, el blog, la cámara, el CD, el CD-ROM, el chateo, el control remoto, el documento, el DVD, el e-mail, el escáner, Facebook (*m.*), **el fax, la fotocopia, la fotocopiadora, el internet, el iPhone, la memoria, la memoria USB, el módem, el radio, el teléfono celular, la televisión (plasma), el tuit, Twitter** (*m.*), **el video, el wifi**

Repaso: la computadora (portátil), la ropa, el teléfono, la televisión

almacenar	to store; to save
apagar (gu)	to turn off *(a machine)*
bajar	to download
buscar (qu) en internet	to look up on the internet

cambiar (de)	to change
descargar (gu)	to download
encender (ie)	to turn on (*a machine*)
entrar/estar en Facebook /en internet	to go on Facebook / online
fallar	to "crash" (*computer*)
funcionar	to work, function; to run (*machines*)
grabar	to record; to tape
guardar	to keep; to save (*documents*)
imprimir	to print
manejar	to operate *(a machine)*
navegar (gu) la red	to surf the internet
obtener (*like* tener)	to get, obtain
publicar (qu)	to post (*as on Facebook*); to publish

Cognados: conectarse, copiar, hacer clic, instalar, tuitear

Repaso: buscar (qu), conseguir (*like* seguir), entrar, estar, mandar un mensaje, poner (to turn on [an appliance])

En el centro de una ciudad

las afueras	outskirts; suburbs
el alquiler	rent
el ascensor	elevator
la avenida	avenue
el barrio	neighborhood
la calefacción	heat
la calle	street
el/la dueño/a	landlord, landlady
el edificio de apartamentos	apartment building
la farmacia	pharmacy
el gas	gas (*residential; not for cars*)
el gasto	expense
el gimnasio	gym
el/la inquilino/a	tenant; renter
la parada del autobús	bus stop
la parada del metro	subway stop
el piso	floor (*of a building*)
el primer piso	first floor (*second story*)
el segundo piso	second floor (*third story*)
la planta baja	ground floor
el/la portero/a	building manager; doorman
la residencia de ancianos	nursing home
el/la vecino/a	neighbor
la vista (a, de)	view (of)
la vivienda	housing
la zona	zone; area

Cognados: la electricidad, el supermercado

Repaso: el apartamento, la casa, el centro, la ciudad, la dirección, el/la dueño/a (*owner*)**, la escuela, la plaza**

alquilar	to rent
mudarse	to move (*residences*)

Otros sustantivos

los/las demás	others
la mentira	lie
el/la usuario/a	user

Repaso: la montaña

Los adjetivos

actual	current
plano/a	flat

Repaso: electrónico/a, grande

Palabras adicionales

es urgente que + subjunctive	it's urgent that
es importante que + subjunctive	it's important that

Repaso: es mejor/ necesario *(a machine)* to surf the internet

Vocabulario personal

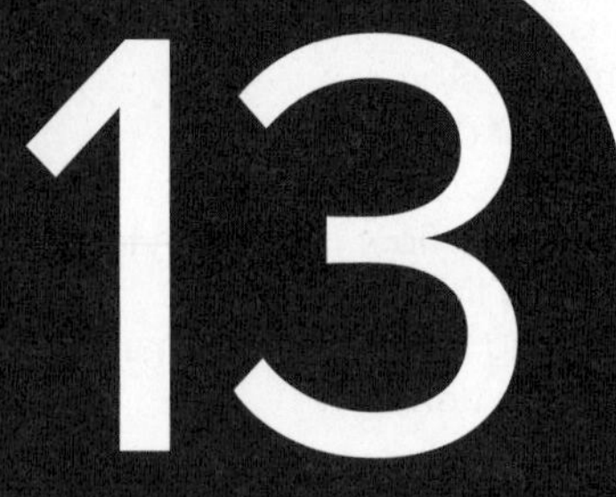

13 El arte y la cultura

En este capítulo

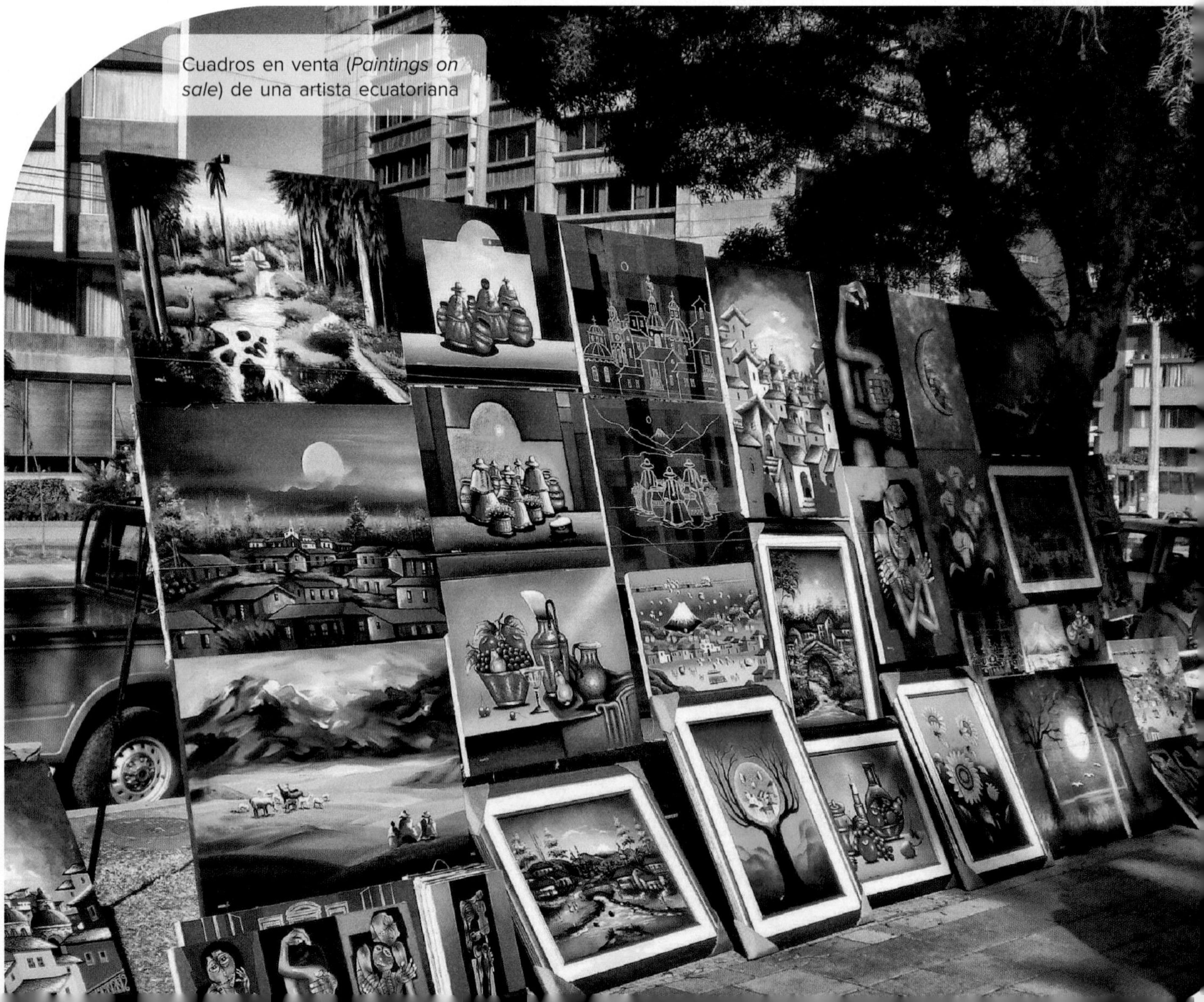

Cuadros en venta (*Paintings on sale*) de una artista ecuatoriana

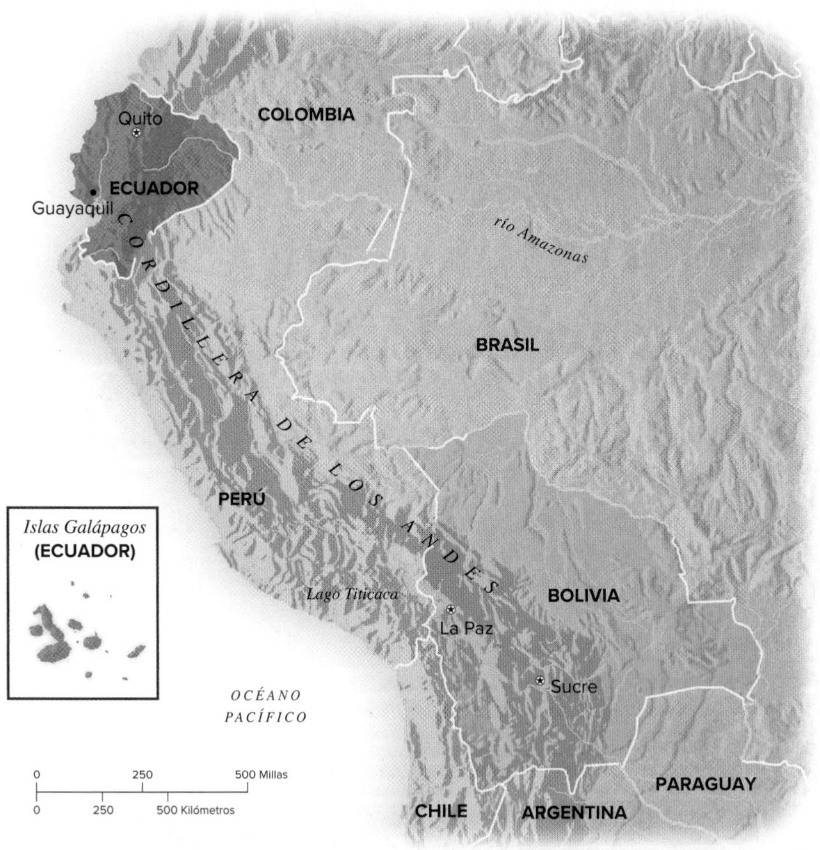

EL ECUADOR

16,9 (coma nueve) millones de habitantes

- Las Islas Galápagos, donde Darwin empezó a idear su teoría de la evolución, son territorio ecuatoriano.
- El Ecuador y Bolivia tienen una geografía impresionante, caracterizada por la cordillera de los Andes y la Amazonia.
- Los dos países tienen un alto porcentaje de población indígena y mestiza.

BOLIVIA

11,2 (coma dos) millones de habitantes

- Bolivia (como el Paraguay) no tiene litoral (costa) marítimo.

ENTREVISTA

- ¿Le interesa el arte en general? ¿Qué tipo de expresión artística le interesa más? ¿Le fascina la pintura, la escultura, la arquitectura, la danza, el cine, el teatro o el diseño de moda[a]? ¿O prefiere alguna otra?
- ¿Hay museos en su ciudad? ¿De qué tipo?
- ¿Hay artesanía típica de su región, como la cerámica o textiles o de otro tipo?

[a]diseño... *fashion design*

Ismael Pérez Mendizábal contesta las preguntas.

- Bueno, la verdad es que depende. Me encanta el cine y también me interesa la literatura porque me gusta mucho leer. Y... pues, claro,[a] me gusta la música pop y para bailar. Pero las otras artes no me interesan tanto.
- Sí, claro. Hay museos muy buenos y de diferentes enfoques.[b] Por ejemplo, hay el Museo Nacional sobre la historia de Colombia. Y también está el Museo de Arte Moderno de Bogotá. Y el Museo del Oro, que tiene la mejor colección en todo el mundo de piezas metalúrgicas de la época precolombina. Y el Maloka, un museo interactivo de ciencias. ¡Es bien chévere[c]!
- En Colombia hay mucha tradición de artesanías, ya desde[d] la época precolombina. Hay mucho trabajo textil por todo el país.

[a]*of course* [b]*emphases* [c]bien... *really cool* [d]ya... *dating from*

VOCABULARIO: PREPARACIÓN

You can hear the pronunciation of theme vocabulary words and phrases in the Connect eBook.

Las artes*

La expresión artística	Los artistas	Los verbos		Las obras artísticas
la arquitectura	**el arquitecto / la arquitecta**	**diseñar**	to design	**el edificio**
el baile / la danza	**el bailarín / la bailarina**	**bailar**		**el baile, el ballet, la danza**
el cine / el teatro / la ópera	**el actor / la actriz** **el director / la directora** **el dramaturgo / la dramaturga** playwright	**actuar (actúo)** **dirigir (dirijo)**	 to direct	**la película, la obra de teatro, la ópera**
el dibujo	**el/la dibujante**	**dibujar**	to draw	**el dibujo**
la escultura	**el escultor / la escultora**	**esculpir**	to sculpt	**la escultura**
la literatura	**el autor / la autora** **el escritor / la escritora** **el/la novelista** **el/la poeta**	**escribir**		**la obra de teatro, la novela, el poema**
la pintura	**el pintor / la pintora**	**pintar**		**el cuadro, la pintura**

The word* **arte *is both masculine and feminine. The masculine articles and adjectives are normally used with* **arte** *in the singular while the feminine ones are used in the plural. Note that* **las artes** *often refers to "the arts" in general:* **Guillermo es estudiante *de arte moderno*. Me gustan mucho *las artes gráficas*.**

Más sobre las obras artísticas

las entradas	tickets (*to a performance, movie…*)
el espectáculo	show
la fotografía	photography
el/la guía	guide
el guion	script
la imagen	image
el museo	museum
la obra (de arte)	work (of art)
la obra de teatro	play
la obra maestra	masterpiece
el papel	role
el siglo	century

Cognados: la comedia, el concierto, el drama, la escena, el mural

Otros verbos

crear	to create
tejer	to weave

La tradición cultural

la artesanía	arts and crafts
la cerámica	pottery; ceramics
las ruinas	ruins
los tejidos	woven goods
folclórico/a	traditional

Así se dice

Various words are used to describe comedians: **el/la comediante, el/la humorista,** or **el cómico / la cómica.**

An alternative spelling of **folclórico/a** is **folklórico/a.**

Comunicación

A. Obras de arte

Paso 1. ¿Qué clase de arte representan las siguientes obras y qué son?

1. la catedral de una gran ciudad
2. las obras de Diego Rivera y Frida Kahlo
3. la Estatua de la Libertad
4. *El cascanueces* (*The Nutcracker*)
5. las obras de los directores Alfonso Cuarón y Guillermo del Toro
6. *La bohème* y *La traviata*
7. las pirámides aztecas y mayas
8. *Don Quijote* y *Hamlet*
9. *Las meninas*, de Diego Velázquez
10. «*El cuervo* (*The Raven*)», de Edgar Allan Poe
11. las imágenes de los actores en las revistas o en internet
12. las obras de Selena Gómez o de Lady Gaga

Paso 2. Ahora dé otros ejemplos de obras en cada una de las categorías artísticas que usted mencionó en el **Paso 1.**

Nota comunicativa

Más sobre los gustos y preferencias

You already know a number of verbs for talking about what you like and don't like: **gustar, encantar, interesar, molestar.** As you know, these verbs are used with indirect object pronouns, and the verb always agrees with the thing or things liked or disliked, not with the person whose preferences are being described.

Here are some additional verbs that are used like **gustar.**

- **aburrir** — **Me aburre** el baile moderno.
  Modern dance is boring to me (*bores me*).
- **atraer** — A Juan **le atraen** las ruinas incas.
  Juan is drawn to (*attracted by*) *Incan ruins.*
- **fascinar** — **Nos fascinan** las artesanías indígenas.
  We're fascinated by (We love) indigenous handicrafts.

You can use some of these verbs in **Comunicación B.**

B. Encuesta (*Poll*): ¿Te gustan los eventos culturales?

Paso 1. Haga por lo menos cinco preguntas usando las siguientes ideas como base. Use verbos de la **Nota comunicativa** de la página 391.

MODELO: la ópera → ¿Te aburre la ópera?

1. el ballet clásico
2. los museos de arte moderno
3. las obras de teatro
4. los grandes museos como *The Smithsonian* o *The Natural History Museum*
5. los conciertos de música clásica
6. los recitales de poesía en algún café
7. las películas extranjeras
8. la ópera
9. ¿ ?

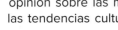

Paso 2. Ahora use las preguntas del **Paso 1** para entrevistar a cinco compañeros de clase para saber su opinión sobre las manifestaciones artísticas mencionadas en sus preguntas. ¿Qué puede usted decir sobre las tendencias culturales de la clase?

Nota cultural

La arquitectura en el mundo hispano

La arquitectura de los países hispanohablantes refleja la variedad de herencias[a] estéticas a través de[b] los siglos: las[c] que ya estaban en el continente antes de la llegada de los españoles y las que estos[d] trajeron.

- **Los pueblos indígenas** Estos pueblos crearon obras arquitectónicas impresionantes en la época prehispánica. Los grandes imperios azteca, maya e inca, entre otros, construyeron edificios y ciudades que les fascinaron a los españoles. Algunos ejemplos: Machu Picchu, la ciudad sagrada[e] de los incas en el Perú, y los centros urbanos de Tikal en Guatemala (maya) y Teotihuacán en México (azteca).
- **Los españoles** Los españoles trajeron a América los estilos artísticos europeos del momento y los aplicaron a las ciudades que inmediatamente empezaron a construir: edificios civiles y religiosos que compiten en belleza[f] con los edificios europeos. Ejemplos: la catedral de Quito (1567, el Ecuador) y la de la Ciudad de México (1571).

  Parte de la tradición estética de los españoles incluía el estilo que dejaron los musulmanes[g] durante los 800 años que ocuparon España (del siglo VIII al siglo XV). Un ejemplo de esa herencia es el uso de los azulejos,[h] muy común ahora en todo el mundo hispanohablante, para decorar las paredes y otras partes de los edificios.
- **Las ciudades modernas:** En la actualidad,[i] la arquitectura sigue transformando ciudades a ambos[j] lados del Atlántico. La Ciudad de México, la Ciudad de Panamá, Santiago de Chile, Buenos Aires y Madrid son algunos ejemplos más sobresalientes[k] de las grandes ciudades modernas, en donde los rascacielos[l] conviven[m] con edificios representativos de la larga historia de cada país. Los viejos edificios se renuevan[n] y se modifican para darles nuevos usos, de tal manera que[ñ] siguen siendo parte activa en la vida de cada ciudad.

©mediacolor's/Alamy

La iglesia (*Church*) de San Francisco, en Quito, Ecuador, del siglo XVII.

¿Cuáles son los edificios o complejos arquitectónicos sobresalientes en su estado o ciudad?

[a]*heritages* [b]*a... across* [c]*those* [d]*they (the Spanish)* [e]*sacred* [f]*beauty* [g]*Muslims* [h]*tiles* [i]*En... Currently* [j]*both* [k]*outstanding* [l]*skyscrapers* [m]*coexist* [n]*se... are being renovated* [ñ]*de... so that*

C. ¿Qué hacen?

Paso 1. Haga oraciones completas, usando una palabra o frase de cada columna. **¡OJO!** Hay más de una posibilidad en algunos casos.

MODELO: La compositora compone música para una película.

el/la compositor(a)	+	bailar	+	música, canciones, musicales
el/la artesano/a		componer		novelas, poesía
el actor / la actriz		dirigir		en el ballet
el/la director(a)		diseñar		cerámica
el/la músico/a		escribir		edificios y casas
el bailarín / la bailarina		esculpir		papeles en la televisión
el/la dramaturgo/a		hacer		guiones
el/la pintor(a)		interpretar		tejidos
el/la escritor(a)		mirar		con actores
el/la arquitecto/a		pintar		obras de teatro
el/la poeta		tocar		cuadros
		trabajar		instrumentos

Paso 2. Ahora, con dos o tres compañeros, dé nombres de artistas en cada categoría. ¿Cuántos artistas hispanos pueden nombrar?

D. Entrevista

Paso 1. Complete las siguientes oraciones de manera que sean ciertas para usted.

1. Me gusta mucho _______ (una actividad relacionada con el arte).
2. El arte que más me interesa como espectador(a) es _______.
3. (No) Tengo talento artístico para _______.
4. (No) Me gusta ir a mercados y ferias de artesanía. Allí (no) compro _______.
5. En la universidad, los espectáculos que más me interesan son _______.
6. En cuanto a (*As for*) música, prefiero _______. Mi canción/artista/cantante favorito/a es _______.

Vocabulario útil

el *country*
el *hip hop*
el jazz
la música de los años 50 (60,...)
el pop
el *rap*
el rock (clásico)

Paso 2. Ahora, en parejas, hablen de sus preferencias artísticas, usando como base las oraciones del **Paso 1** y después díganle a la clase las preferencias que ustedes tienen en común.

E. *Ternura.* Después de leer **Algo sobre... Oswaldo Guayasamín** y contemplar su obra, complete las siguientes ideas.

1. El cuadro *Ternura* muestra (*shows*)...
2. *Ternura* refleja (*reflects*)...
3. (No) Me gusta el cuadro *Ternura* porque...
4. Es importante que los artistas...
5. Creo que Guayasamín quiere que...

Algo sobre...

Oswaldo Guayasamín

El pintor y escultor Oswaldo Guayasamín (1919–1999) es un artista ecuatoriano mundialmente reconocido[a] y admirado. Era hijo de padre quechua y madre mestiza. Por eso su obra, que se considera expresionista, tiene toques[b] indigenistas. Sus pinturas y esculturas hablan del sufrimiento[c] y las injusticias que soportan[d] los seres[e] humanos.

Piense en una de sus pinturas o esculturas favoritas. ¿Qué sentimientos refleja? ¿Por qué le gusta a usted esa obra?

[a]mundialmente... *recognized throughout the world* [b]*touches, elements* [c]*suffering* [d]*withstand, bear* [e]*beings*

©age fotostock/Alamy

Ternura (Tenderness), un cuadro de la serie «Mientras viva siempre te recuerdo», que Guayasamín dedicó a su madre y a todas las madres del mundo

Los ordinales

primer(o/a)	first	**sexto/a**	sixth
segundo/a	second	**séptimo/a**	seventh
tercer(o/a)	third	**octavo/a**	eighth
cuarto/a	fourth	**noveno/a**	ninth
quinto/a	fifth	**décimo/a**	tenth

- The masculine singular form of ordinals is often used to organize instructions or items in a list.

  Primero, den un paseo por el centro de Quito. **Segundo**, les recomiendo que visiten la casa de Guayasamín. **Tercero**, tomen el teleférico para ver una vista magnífica de la ciudad.
- When they accompany a noun, ordinals are adjectives and they must agree in number and gender. Ordinals usually precede the nouns: **el <u>cuarto</u> concierto, la <u>quinta</u> película.**
- When they precede masculine singular nouns, **primero** and **tercero** shorten to **primer** and **tercer**: **el <u>primer</u> día**, **el <u>tercer</u> mes**.
- As in English, ordinal numbers are sometimes abbreviated. The endings of the abbreviations show gender and number agreement: **el 1er grado, la 3ª persona, el 5º guion**. When agreement is not needed, as in instructions, ordinals are abbreviated as **1º**, **2º**, **3º**, and so on.

Comunicación

A. ¿Cultura, yo?

Paso 1. Veamos (*Let's see*) si usted tiene interés en la cultura o no. Ordene las siguientes actividades según sus preferencias y hábitos, empezando por **1º.**

_______ ir al cine a ver las últimas películas en inglés
_______ ver películas extranjeras dobladas (*dubbed*) o subtituladas
_______ visitar museos, preferentemente en visitas guiadas
_______ comprar o sacar de la biblioteca libros de ficción
_______ ver obras de teatro
_______ bailar en clubes y fiestas
_______ ver programas de la tele
_______ ir a conciertos de música clásica/*jazz*
_______ ir a conciertos de música pop/rock/*country*
_______ leer o escribir poesía

Paso 2. Ahora, en parejas, entrevístense sobre sus cinco actividades favoritas. Usen números ordinales.

MODELO: Mi actividad favorita es ir a ver películas extranjeras subtituladas. Mi **segunda** actividad favorita es…

B. Autorretrato (*Self-portrait*) de un(a) estudiante. Complete las oraciones.

1. Soy estudiante de _______ año.
2. Estoy en mi _______ semestre/trimestre de español.
3. Los lunes, mi primera clase es la (*that*) de _______, a la(s) _______ (hora). Mi segunda clase es la de _______, a la(s) _______.
4. Con frecuencia, soy la _______ persona en llegar a la clase de español.
5. Soy la _______ persona de mi familia que asiste a una universidad. Y soy la _______ persona de mi familia que asiste a *esta* universidad.

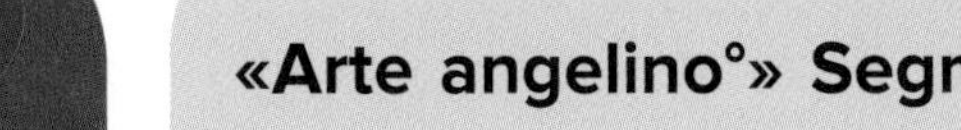

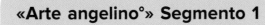

«Arte angelino°» Segmento 1

de Los Ángeles

Antes de mirar

¿Le interesa a usted la arquitectura? ¿Conoce la obra de algún arquitecto importante? ¿Dónde es frecuente encontrar arquitectura interesante?

- ☐ en casas y edificios de apartamentos
- ☐ en edificios del gobierno (*government*)
- ☐ en edificios de uso civil (como museos, por ejemplo)
- ☐ en iglesias (*churches*) y templos
- ☐ otros tipos de edificios y lugares

El templo de la Sagrada (*Sacred*) Familia, la obra inacabada (*unfinished*) del arquitecto Antoni Gaudí

Este segmento

En este segmento hay un reportaje sobre la obra del famoso arquitecto español Antoni Gaudí.

Vocabulario del segmento

fines del siglo XX	the end of the 20th century
principios de	the beginning of
reconocido/a	well-known
catalán/catalana	from **Cataluña** (Catalonia, Spain)
pertenecer (pertenezco)	to belong
la naturaleza	nature
el diseño	design
fijarse en	to notice; to pay attention to
la serpiente	snake
todavía no ha terminado	is still not complete

Después de mirar

A. ¿Está claro? Las siguientes oraciones sobre el arquitecto Antoni Gaudí son falsas. Corríjalas.

1. Gaudí fue un arquitecto ecuatoriano.
2. Solo construyó edificios en Barcelona.
3. Solo construyó iglesias y templos.
4. Los edificios de Gaudí incluyen muchos elementos de tipo industrial.

B. Un poco más. Conteste las siguientes preguntas.

1. ¿Qué elementos caracterizan las obras de Gaudí?
2. ¿Qué estilos combina el templo de la Sagrada Familia?
3. ¿Cuándo se comenzó a construir el templo? ¿Para qué año se espera que esté terminado?

C. Y ahora, ustedes. En parejas, descríbanse mutuamente algún edificio de su interés, ya sea (*whether it be*) en su ciudad de origen o en otra. ¿Por qué les gustan esos edificios? ¿Qué parte o aspecto de cada edificio es su favorito? ¿Son históricamente importantes los edificios? ¿Cuándo los visitaron por última vez?

GRAMÁTICA

¿Recuerda usted?

Review what you know about the present subjunctive by answering the following questions.

1. Is the subjunctive used in one- or two-clause sentences?
2. Is it used in the main (independent) or subordinate (dependent) clause?
3. Is it used before or after the word **que**?
4. When the subjunctive is used, is the subject the same in both clauses?
5. What verb form follows an impersonal expression when there is no change of subject?
6. Influence is one "cause" of the subjunctive. What are two more subjunctive "triggers"?

You will learn about those two subjunctive "triggers" in **Gramáticas 36** and **37.**

36 Expressing Feelings

Use of the Subjunctive (Part 3): Emotion

Gramática en acción: Diego y Lupe oyen tocar a los mariachis

DIEGO: Ay, ¡cómo me encanta esta música!

LUPE: **Me alegro de que** te guste.

DIEGO: Y **yo me alegro de que** estemos aquí. ¿Sabes el origen de la palabra **mariachi**?

LUPE: No... ¿Lo sabes tú?

DIEGO: Bueno, una de las teorías es que viene del siglo XIX, cuando los franceses ocuparon México. Ellos contrataban a grupos de músicos para tocar en las bodas. Y como los mexicanos no podían pronunciar bien la palabra francesa *mariage,* pues acabaron por decir **mariachi.** Y de allí viene el nombre de los grupos.

Ciudad de México

©DreamPictures/Blend Images/Getty Images

LUPE: ¡Qué fascinante! **Me sorprende que** sepas tanto de nuestra historia.

DIEGO: Pues, todo buen antropólogo debe saber un poco de historia también, ¿no?

¿Y a usted?

1. **¿Le sorprende que** la palabra mariachi venga del francés?
2. **¿Le sorprende que** tantas personas estudien español en su universidad?
3. **¿Se alegra de que** haya mucha información cultural en esta clase?

Diego and Lupe hear mariachis play *DIEGO: Oh, how I love this music! LUPE: I'm glad you like it. DIEGO: And I'm glad we're here. Do you know the origin of the word* ***mariachi****? LUPE: No . . . Do you? DIEGO: Well, one of the theories is that it comes from the nineteenth century, when the French occupied Mexico. They used to hire groups of musicians to play at weddings. And since Mexicans couldn't correctly pronounce the French word mariage, they ended up saying* ***mariachi.*** *And that's where the name of the groups comes from. LUPE: How fascinating! I'm surprised (that) you know so much about our history. DIEGO: Well, all good anthropologists should also know a bit of history, shouldn't they?*

① EMOTION		②
first subject = **indicative**	**que**	second subject = **subjunctive**

1. The Concept of Emotion

Another "trigger" for the use of the subjunctive in the subordinate clause is the concept of *emotion* (**la emoción**). The subject of the main clause *is glad, fears, hopes*, and so on, that the subject of the subordinate clause does something, expressed by a verb in the subjunctive. The verb in the main clause is always in the indicative.

Esperamos que usted **pueda** asistir.
We hope (that) you'll be able to come.

Tengo miedo de que mi abuelo **esté** muy enfermo.
I'm afraid (that) my grandfather is very ill.

Es una lástima que no **den** conciertos.
It's a shame (that) they're not putting on any concerts.

2. Verbs of Emotion

Here are some verbs of emotion. The ones marked with * are new.

alegrarse de	to be happy about
esperar	to hope; to expect
***lamentar**	to regret; to feel sorry
***sentir (siento) (i)**	to regret; to feel sorry
***temer**	to fear, be afraid
tener miedo (de)	to be afraid (of)

Temo que María **se caiga** mientras baila.
I'm afraid (that) María will fall while she's dancing.

3. Verbs of Emotion Like *gustar*

Gustar and similar verbs are frequently used to express emotion. If there is a change of subject in the subordinate clause, the subjunctive will be used. Only the verb marked with * is new. Notice that a subordinate clause is viewed as a singular subject, so **gusta** (not **gustan**) is used in the sentences.

¡OJO!

Remember that these verbs are used with indirect object pronouns in Spanish.

encantar	**molestar**
fascinar	***sorprender** to surprise
gustar	

Me (Te/Le...) encanta/fascina/gusta/molesta/ sorprende que...
I'm (You're/He's...) very glad/fascinated/pleased/ annoyed/surprised that...

Me molesta que las entradas del museo **sean** tan caras.
It bothers me that museum entrance fees are so expensive.

Nos sorprende que este cantante **tenga** tanto éxito.
I'm surprised that this singer is so successful.

4. Impersonal Expressions of Emotion

When a new subject is introduced after a generalization of emotion, it is followed by the subjunctive in the subordinate clause. Here are some general expressions of emotion.

¡OJO!

As you know, when there is no second subject, the infinitive follows verbs of emotion and impersonal expressions of emotion:

Me alegro de / Siento / Tengo miedo de estar aquí. **Es absurdo/bueno/extraño estar** aquí.

es absurdo que...	it's absurd that . . .
es extraño que...	it's strange that . . .
¡qué extraño que... !	how strange that . . . !
es increíble que...	it's incredible that . . .
es mejor/bueno/ malo que...	it's better/good/ bad that . . .
es normal que...	it's normal that . . .
es terrible que...	it's terrible that . . .
es una lástima que...	it's a shame that . . .
¡qué lástima que... !	what a shame that . . . !

Es terrible que la cantante **esté** enferma.
It's awful (that) the singer is ill.

¡Qué extraño que **haya** pocos turistas en las ruinas hoy!
How strange (that) there are so few tourists at the ruins today!

Summary of Emotion

emotion + **que** + change of subject → **subjunctive**

Práctica y comunicación

A. Opiniones sobre el cine

Paso 1. Autoprueba. Diga si en español se debe usar el subjuntivo o el infinitivo en la cláusula subordinada de las siguientes oraciones.

MODELO: I'm surprised you're here. → **subjuntivo**

1. I'm sorry you're angry.
2. I'm sorry to anger you.
3. We're happy to get this present.
4. We're afraid the guide will change the trip.
5. It's great they want to buy the sculpture.
6. I'm not interested in working with that director.
7. I'm thrilled they're visiting us.

Paso 2. Complete las siguientes oraciones incompletas con las cláusulas principales más apropiadas para expresar su opinión.

ORACIONES INCOMPLETAS

1. _______ que muchas películas sean violentas.
2. _______ que algunos actores ganen (*earn*) tanto dinero.
3. _______ que haya más representación de actores de otras razas.
4. _______ que no haya muchos papeles interesantes para mujeres de más de 50 años.
5. _______ que gasten millones de dólares en hacer películas mientras que hay gente que se muere de hambre.
6. _______ que _______ (nombre de un actor / una actriz) sea tan famoso/a.

CLÁUSULAS PRINCIPALES

a. Me molesta
b. Es increíble/extraordinario
c. Es ridículo
d. Espero
e. Me sorprende
f. Es absurdo/ilógico

Paso 3. Ahora, en parejas, túrnense para entrevistarse sobre las ideas del **Paso 2.** Luego díganle al resto de la clase una opinión que tienen en común.

MODELO: **E1:** ¿Te molesta que muchas películas sean violentas?
E2: Sí, me molesta mucho. ¿Y a ti?
E1: A mí también. →
A los dos nos molesta que muchas películas sean violentas.

©Ana Nance/Redux

Sin título, del pintor aymara Roberto Mamani Mamani (Bolivia, 1962 -)

B. Comentarios sobre el arte

Paso 1. Complete las siguientes opiniones sobre esta pintura de Roberto Mamani Mamani. Use la forma apropiada de los verbos entre paréntesis.

1. Este pintor es famoso. Me sorprende que su pintura le _______ (gustar) a la gente. Temo que sus obras _______ (ser) demasiado extrañas para mí. Es una lástima que _______ (haber) tantas obras de arte que yo no comprendo.

Prác. A, Paso 1: Answers: *1. subjuntivo 2. infinitivo 3. infinitivo 4. subjuntivo 5. subjuntivo 6. infinitivo 7. subjuntivo*

2. ¡Me encanta esta pintura! ¡Qué lástima que _______ (haber) gente que no aprecia el arte. Me alegro de que esta pintura _______ (estar) en este libro, porque no yo conocía la obra de Mamani Mamani. Me sorprende que (él) no _______ (tener) más fama fuera de (*outside of*) Bolivia.

Paso 2. Ahora, en parejas, entrevístense sobre sus opiniones de esta pintura. Deben explicar lo que les gusta más y lo que les gusta menos.

Nota comunicativa

Cómo expresar los deseos con *ojalá*

Ojalá is one way to express *I hope* in Spanish. It comes from the Arabic meaning *if Allah wishes*, and it is similar to English *God willing* and Spanish **quiera Dios (si Dios quiere)**.

As an expression of emotion, **ojalá** is followed by the present subjunctive. **Ojalá** is invariable in form and the use of **que** with it is optional.

Ojalá can also be used alone as an interjection in response to a question.

You will use **ojalá (que)** in **Práctica C.**

¡Ojalá (que) yo **gane** la lotería algún día!
I hope (that) I win the lottery some day!

¡Ojalá (que) haya paz en el mundo algún día!
I hope (that) there will be peace in the world some day!

Ojalá (que) no **pierdan** tu equipaje.
I hope (that) they don't lose your luggage.

—¿Te va a ayudar Julio a estudiar para el examen?
—**¡Ojalá!**

C. Una noche en la ópera. Dos amigos van a la ópera. Usando **ojalá**, diga lo que temen y lo que esperan.

MODELO: las entradas / no costar mucho →
Ojalá (que) las entradas no **cuesten** mucho.

1. los escenarios: ser fantásticos
2. haber subtítulos en inglés
3. el director (*conductor*): estar preparado
4. los músicos: tocar bien
5. nuestros asientos: no estar lejos del escenario
6. (nosotros) llegar a tiempo

D. Situaciones

Paso 1. Las siguientes personas están pensando en otra persona o en algo que van a hacer. ¿Qué emociones sienten? ¿Qué temen? Conteste las preguntas según los dibujos.

1.

1. Jorge piensa en su amiga Estela. ¿Por qué piensa en ella? ¿Dónde está? ¿Qué siente Jorge? ¿Qué espera? ¿Qué espera Estela? ¿Espera que la visiten los amigos? ¿que le manden algo?

2. ¿Dónde quiere pasar las vacaciones Mariana? ¿Espera que alguien la acompañe? ¿Dónde espera que estén juntos? ¿Qué teme Mariana? ¿Qué espera?

2.

Paso 2. Ahora, en parejas, comparen sus respuestas del **Paso 1.** ¿Tuvieron los/las dos la misma impresión de los dibujos?

Expresiones

es bueno/ malo que **es extraño/ increíble que** **es normal que** **es una lástima que** **lamento que** **me sorprende que**	+ **subjuntivo**
creo que **es obvio que** **es verdad que** **la realidad es que** **(yo) sé que**	+ **indicativo**

E. ¿Cómo es nuestra sociedad? Diga lo que usted opina de las siguientes declaraciones. Empiece sus opiniones con las **Expresiones** indicadas o con cualquier (*any*) otra.

MODELO: Los futbolistas profesionales ganan sueldos (*salaries*) fenomenales →
Es increíble que los futbolistas **ganen** sueldos fenomenales.

1. Muchas personas viven para trabajar. No saben descansar.
2. La nuestra (*Ours*) es una sociedad de consumidores.
3. Juzgamos (*We judge*) a los otros por las cosas materiales que tienen.
4. Las personas ricas tienen mucho prestigio en esta sociedad.
5. Las mujeres generalmente no ganan tanto dinero como los hombres por hacer igual trabajo.
6. Algunas obras de arte cuestan millones de dólares.
7. Para mucha gente joven, ver videos en YouTube es más atractivo que leer libros.
8. Hay discriminación contra la gente mayor en ciertas profesiones.

F. Esta universidad. Diga lo que usted opina de las siguientes declaraciones respecto a lo que ocurre en esta universidad. Use frases como: **Me gusta que…, Me molesta que…, Es terrible que…, Sé que…**

MODELO: Gastan mucho / poco dinero en construir nuevos edificios. →
Me molesta que gasten mucho dinero en construir nuevos edificios.

1. Se les da mucha / poca importancia a los deportes.
2. El precio de la matrícula es exagerado / muy bajo.
3. Se ofrecen muchos / pocos cursos en mi especialización.
4. Es necesario estudiar ciencias / lenguas para graduarse.
5. Hay muchos / pocos requisitos (*requirements*) para graduarse.
6. En general, hay mucha / poca gente en las clases.

Algo sobre…

la Amazonia y los Andes

Es sorprendente que el Ecuador y Bolivia, sin tener territorios adyacentes,[a] compartan[b] tantas características geográficas. Para empezar, los dos países tienen territorio en la Amazonia, una inmensa zona que se extiende por[c] un total de nueve naciones sudamericanas. Además[d] la cordillera de los Andes cruza Bolivia y el Ecuador y hace que sus capitales sean las capitales más altas del mundo. La Paz está a 12.000 pies (3.650 metros) sobre el nivel del mar. Sucre y Quito están a más de 9.000 pies (2.800 metros).

 **¿Cuáles son los factores geográficos más importantes de su país? ¿Y de su estado?**

[a]*adjacent* [b]*share* [c]*through* [d]*In addition*

La cordillera de los Andes y la Amazonia, que dominan el mapa de Sudamérica

37 Expressing Uncertainty

Use of the Subjunctive (Part 4): Doubt and Denial

Gramática en acción: El traje tradicional de las bolivianas

Unas mujeres bolivianas con su ropa tradicional, en La Paz

¿Cuánto sabe usted de la ropa que llevan las indígenas bolivianas? ¿Cree que son ciertas o falsas las siguientes declaraciones? Las respuestas están al pie de la página.

1. **Es verdad que** los sombreros hongo son una parte del traje tradicional de las indígenas del altiplano boliviano.
2. **Es probable que** sea muy frecuente ver a bolivianas que llevan sombrero hongo.
3. **Dudo que** los pantalones sean parte del traje tradicional de las bolivianas del altiplano.
4. **No creo que** el uso de los sombreros hongo sea una tradición inca.
5. En Bolivia, **es obvio que** llevar sombrero es una buena protección contra el sol.

¿Y usted?

1. ¿Le gusta el traje tradicional de las mujeres bolivianas? ¿Cree que es hermoso (*beautiful*)? ¿práctico?
2. ¿Le sorprende que las bolivianas indígenas lleven sombrero?

① DOUBT/DENIAL		②
first subject = **indicative**	**que**	second subject = **subjunctive**

1. **The Concepts of Doubt and Denial**
   The concepts of *doubt* (**la duda**) and *denial* (**la negación**) are also "triggers" for the use of the subjunctive in the subordinate clause. The subject of the main clause *doubts, does not believe, denies,* and so on, that the subject of the subordinate clause does something, expressed by a verb in the subjunctive. The verb in the main clause is always in the indicative.

No creo que **sean** cuadros de Goya.
I don't believe (that) they're paintings by Goya.

Es imposible que la actriz **salga** al escenario ahora.
It's impossible for the actress to go on (stage) now.

The traditional costume of Bolivian women *How much do you know about the clothing that indigenous Bolivian women wear? Do you think that the following statements are true or false? The answers are at the bottom of the page.* **1.** *It's true that bowler hats are a part of the traditional costume of indigenous women of the Bolivian high plateau.* **2.** *It's likely that one frequently sees Bolivian women who are wearing bowler hats.* **3.** *I doubt that pants are part of the traditional costume of women from the high plateau.* **4.** *I don't think that the use of bowler hats is an Inca tradition.* **5.** *In Bolivia, it's obvious that wearing a hat is good protection from the sun.*

Respuestas: **1.** *cierto: Muchas indígenas bolivianas lo llevan.* **2.** *cierto: Bolivia tiene el porcentaje más alto de población indígena en toda América. Por eso es muy normal ver a mujeres que llevan ropa tradicional.* **3.** *cierto: La pollera, un tipo de falda con mucho vuelo (flare) y colores, es la ropa típica de las indígenas bolivianas.* **4.** *cierto: Es una tradición colonial.* **5.** *cierto: La región del altiplano boliviano está tan alta que la exposición a los rayos solares es un problema serio. Por eso, el sombrero es una protección ideal para la cara, y también protege a los habitantes del frío.*

2. **Verbs and Expressions of Doubt (versus Certainty)**

Here are some verbs and expressions that imply doubt. They are followed by subjunctive in the subordinate clause if there is a change of subject. New verbs and expressions are marked with *.

verb or expression of doubt → **subjunctive** in subordinate clause with different subject

***no creer**	to disbelieve
dudar	to doubt
***no estar seguro/a de**	to be uncertain of
no pensar (pienso)	to not think
***no es seguro que...**	it's not certain / a sure thing that . . .
***(no) es posible que...**	it's (not) possible that . . .
***(no) es probable/ improbable que...**	it's (not) probable/ improbable that . . .

Mis padres **dudan** que yo **pueda** conseguir una entrada ahora.
My parents doubt that I can get a ticket now.

No es seguro que Emma **toque** en el concierto.
It's not certain that Emma will play in the concert.

No creo que nadie **sepa** la verdad.
I don't think (that) anyone knows the truth.

In contrast, verbs and expressions of *certainty* (**la certeza**) and *belief* (**la creencia**) are followed by the indicative in the subordinate clause when there is another subject, because they express what the speaker knows to be the reality or to be true. They express affirmation.

verb or expression of certainty → **indicative** in subordinate clause with different subject

creer	to believe
***estar seguro/a de**	to be certain of
no dudar	to believe (not doubt)
pensar (pienso)	to think
***es cierto que**	it's certain that
***es seguro que**	it's certain / a sure thing that
***es verdad que**	it's true that

Mis padres **creen / están seguros de** que puedo conseguir una entrada ahora.
My parents believe / are sure that I can get a ticket today.

Es verdad que Emma toca en el concierto.
It's certain that Emma plays in the concert.

Pienso que todo el mundo sabe la verdad.
I think everyone knows the truth.

¡OJO!

When used in questions, these verbs may be followed by either the indicative or the subjunctive in the dependent clause, depending on the level of certainty implied.

¿**Crees** que es auténtica la pieza?
Do you think (that) the piece is authentic? (I think it's possible that it is.)

¿**Crees** que **sea** auténtica la pieza?
Do you think (that) the piece is authentic? (I'm doubtful that it is.)

3. **Verbs and Expressions of Denial**

These are always followed by the subjunctive in the dependent clause because they negate the reality or truth of what follows them. They express negation. Only **negar** is new.

verb or expression of denial → **subjunctive** in subordinate clause with different subject

***negar (niego) (gu)**	to deny
es imposible que...	it's impossible that ...
no es verdad que...	it's not true that ...

Niego / Es imposible / No es verdad que todo el mundo **sepa** la verdad.
I deny / It's impossible / It isn't true that everyone knows the truth.

4. Infinitive with no Change of Subject

All of these verbs and expressions are generally followed by the infinitive when there is no change of subject.

Creo / No creo saber la verdad.
Niego / Es imposible saber la verdad.

> **¡OJO!**
>
> An exception: it is very common for **creer, dudar,** and **pensar** to be followed by a conjugated verb, indicative or subjunctive, when there is no change of subject.

No creo / Dudo / No pienso que (yo) **sepa** la verdad.
Creo / Pienso / No dudo que (yo) **sé** la verdad.

Práctica y comunicación

Summary of Doubt and Denial

doubt/denial + **que** + change of subject → **subjunctive**

A. Preferencias artísticas

Paso 1. Autoprueba. Indique las frases que expresan duda o negación.

_____ **1.** Dudamos que...
_____ **2.** Estoy segura de que...
_____ **3.** Niega que...
_____ **4.** Es cierto que...
_____ **5.** No es posible que...
_____ **6.** No creen que...
_____ **7.** No es cierto que...
_____ **8.** Pensamos que...

Paso 2. Exprese su opinión sobre las siguientes declaraciones. Empiece su opinión con una de las cláusulas principales de la lista y cambie el verbo de la cláusula subordinada al subjuntivo si es necesario.

Cláusulas principales

(No) Creo/Dudo que...
(No) Es cierto que...
(No) Estoy seguro/a de que...
(No) Es posible/probable que...

MODELO: **1.** A la mayoría de la gente le gusta ir a los museos de arte. →
No creo que a la mayoría de la gente le **guste** ir a los museos de arte.

1. A la mayoría de la gente le gusta ir a los museos de arte.
2. Todos mis amigos prefieren el teatro al cine.
3. La arquitectura le fascina a muchísimas personas.
4. Me encanta regalar artesanía.
5. Voy a conciertos de música clásica con frecuencia.
6. *El cascanueces* (*The Nutcracker*) es el ballet más famoso del mundo.
7. La música es la expresión artística más popular entre la gente joven.
8. Un videoblog se puede considerar una forma de arte.

Paso 3. Ahora, en parejas, túrnense para hacerse preguntas sobre sus opiniones del **Paso 2.** Luego díganle a la clase una opinión que tienen en común.

MODELO: **E1:** No creo que a mucha la gente le guste ir a los museos de arte. ¿Y tú?
E2: Yo tampoco. →
No creemos / Ninguno de nosotros dos cree que a mucha gente le guste ir a los museos de arte.

B. Una vasija (*vessel*) en el museo. Haga oraciones completas para expresar las especulaciones de dos antropólogos sobre una nueva pieza que está en el museo.

Estrategia

primer verbo = indicativo
segundo verbo = ¿indicativo o subjuntivo?

Habla el profesor Martín:

1. «creer / que / ser una vasija de la civilización inca»
2. «ser obvio / que / estar hecha de barro (*made of clay*)»
3. «ser posible / que / el diseño (*design*): representar algo en especial»
4. «¿creer / que / ser una pieza auténtica?»

(Continúa.)

Una vasija incaica

Source: Yale University Art Gallery

Prác. A, Paso 1: **Answers:** *Duda o negación:* **1, 3, 5, 6, 7**

Habla la profesora Figueroa:

5. «no creer / que / ser una vasija inca»
6. «ser probable / que / ser una pieza auténtica de la civilización tihuanaco»
7. «dudar / que / el diseño: simbolizar algo en especial»

Una turista en el mercado de Otavalo, Ecuador

C. En un mercado de artesanía. ¿Cómo puede reaccionar un turista en un mercado como el mercado de Otavalo, Ecuador? Complete las oraciones, pensando en los precios y en los regalos que a los turistas les gusta comprar para llevar de recuerdos (*as souvenirs*).

1. ¡Es fantástico (que)... !
2. No creo que los precios del mercado...
3. Dudo mucho que estos vendedores...
4. Estoy seguro/a de que...
5. No es muy probable que...
6. Creo que los otavaleños...

Vocabulario útil

la figurita de cerámica ceramic figurine
la muñeca doll
el poncho

Algo sobre...

el Lago Titicaca

El Lago Titicaca

El Perú y Bolivia comparten[a] el lago Titicaca, que se encuentra en los Andes centrales. Este lago es muy importante para Bolivia, ya que[b] el país no tiene salida al mar.[c] Está a 12.500 pies (3.800 metros) sobre el nivel del mar, lo que lo hace el lago navegable más alto del mundo. El lago Titicaca es el segundo lago más grande de Sudamérica, después del lago de Maracaibo.

¿Hay lagos navegables en este país? ¿Y lagos compartidos[d] con otro país?

[a]*share* [b]ya... *since* [c]no... *is landlocked* [d]*shared*

Nota comunicativa

Verbos que requieren preposiciones

You learned in earlier chapters that when two verbs occur in a series (one right after the other), the second verb is usually the infinitive.

Prefiero/Pienso ***cenar*** a las siete. — *I prefer/intend to eat at seven.*

Some Spanish verbs, however, require that a preposition or other word be placed before the second verb (still the infinitive). You have already used many of the Spanish verbs that have this feature. New vocabulary is indicated with *.

- The following verbs require the preposition **a** before an infinitive.

aprender a	**empezar (empiezo) (c) a**	**invitar a**	**venir a**
ayudar a	**enseñar a**	**ir a**	**volver (vuelvo) a**

Mis padres me **enseñaron a bailar.** — *My parents taught me to dance.*

- These verbs or verb phrases require **de** before an infinitive.

acabar de — **dejar de** — **tener ganas de**
***acordarse (me acuerdo) de** (*to remember*) — ***tratar de** (*to try to*)

Siempre **tratamos de llegar** puntualmente. — *We always try to arrive on time.*

- **Insistir** requires **en** before an infinitive.

Insisten en venir esta noche. — *They insist on coming over tonight.*

- Two verbs require **que** before an infinitive: ***hay que, tener que.**

Both of them express obligation, but only **tener que** can be conjugated in all persons. **Hay que** is invariable (like **hay**), but of course it can be used in other tenses and moods (**había**, **haya**).

Hay que ver el nuevo museo. — *You (One) must/should see the new museum.*

You will use these verbs in **Práctica D.**

D. En los próximos cinco años... En parejas, hagan oraciones para expresar lo que ustedes creen que les puede ocurrir en el futuro próximo (*near*). Hay que usar una palabra o frase de cada columna o terminar la oración con una idea propia (*of your own*). ¿Cuántas respuestas similares tienen ustedes?

¿INDICATIVO, SUBJUNTIVO O INFINITIVO?

(no) creo que... (no) dudo que... es (im)posible que... (no) estoy seguro/a de que... (no) es cierto que... tengo que...	+	(yo) { acordarse de aprender a dejar de empezar a ir a tratar de volver a	+	ser famoso/a estar casado/a (*married*) ganar la lotería jugar a la lotería pintar cuadros fumar tener hijos terminar mis estudios esculpir ¿ ?

38 Expressing Influence, Emotion, Doubt, and Denial

The Subjunctive (Part 5): A Summary

Gramática en acción: Las islas Galápagos

Lea **Algo sobre... las islas Galápagos**. Luego complete las oraciones, eligiendo (*choosing*) con lógica un verbo principal.

©FAN Travelstock/Alamy

La iguana terrestre de las islas Galápagos

Quiero (que)...
Espero (que)...
Es fascinante (que)... } + <u>**subjuntivo**</u> / **infinitivo**

Dicen que...
Sé que...
Es obvio que... } + **indicativo**

1. ...<u>haya</u> tantas especies endémicas.
2. ...las islas Galápagos están en el Pacífico.
3. ...es un lugar especial para los biólogos.
4. ...<u>estén</u> muy protegidas.
5. ...el Ecuador las <u>siga</u> protegiendo.

¿Y usted? ¿Quiere ir a las Galápagos algún día? ¿Quiere visitar el Ecuador?

Algo sobre...

las islas Galápagos

©Cleveland Metroparks Zoo/McGraw-Hill Education

Una tortuga galápago, la especie de tortuga más grande del mundo

El archipiélago de las islas Galápagos está formado por unas 19 islas y más de 40 islotes.[a] Son territorio del Ecuador, país que las protege rigurosamente. Están a casi 600 millas (1.000 km.) de la costa ecuatoriana, en el océano Pacífico. La isla más grande es Isabela. El nombre del archipiélago le viene de las tortugas gigantes que son endémicas de estas islas. Además de[b] las tortugas galápagos, hay pingüinos, cormoranes, iguanas, leones marinos y otros animales. La variedad de especies endémicas de las Galápagos sirvió de base a la teoría de la evolución de Darwin.

¿? ¿Cuál es el archipiélago más grande de este país? ¿Por qué es conocido[c] o visitado?

[a]*islets* [b]Además... *Besides* [c]*well-known*

①	②
INFLUENCE / EMOTION / DOUBT OR DENIAL	que + **subjunctive** / **infinitive**

①	②
INFORMATION / BELIEF / CERTAINTY	que + **indicative** / **infinitive**

This section will help you review what you have already learned about using the subjunctive and when to use the indicative or the infinitive instead.

1. **The Subjunctive in Two-clause Sentences**

Remember that, in Spanish, the subjunctive occurs primarily in the second clause of two-clause sentences, with a different subject in each clause. If there is no change of subject, an infinitive follows the first verb.

Quiero / **Es necesario** } que **los estudiantes** **saquen** una buena nota.
I want / *It's necessary for* } ***the students*** *to get a good grade.*
Quiero / **Es necesario** } **sacar** una nota buena.
I want / *It's necessary* } *to get a good grade.*

---

2. **Subjunctive "Triggers": Influence, Emotion, Doubt or Denial**

The main clause must also contain an expression of *influence, emotion,* or *doubt* or *denial* for the subjunctive to occur in the subordinate clause. If there is no such expression, the indicative is used.

The verb **decir** is a subjunctive "trigger" (first sentence to the right) when it conveys an order. When **decir** conveys information rather than influence (second sentence), it triggers the indicative.

Similarly, **creer** conveys certainty or belief (third sentence) but **no creer** conveys denial (fourth sentence). When **creer** affirms rather than denies information, it is followed by the indicative.

Dicen que **cante** Carlota.
They say that Carlota should sing.

Dicen que Julio **canta** muy mal; por eso **quieren** que **cante** Carlota.
They say that Julio sings very badly; that's why they want Carlota to sing.

Yo creo que Julio **canta** muy bien.
I think that Julio sings very well.

No creo que Carlota **cante** mejor que él.
I don't think that Carlota sings better than he (does).

¡OJO!

Remember to look for the "triggers," not just for specific verbs. If you see the verbs **decir** or **creer** in the main clause, you must think about how they are used.

---

3. **Influence +** ***indirect object pronoun***

Some expressions of influence are frequently used with indirect object pronouns. The indirect object pronoun in the main clause indicates the subject of the subordinate clause, as in the sample sentences: **Nos → (nosotros) vayamos.**

Nos dicen / **Nos** piden / **Nos** recomiendan } que **vayamos** al concierto.
They tell us to / *They ask us to* / *They recommend that we* } *go to the concert.*

---

4. **Same Subject → Infinitive**

Remember that verbs and expressions of influence, emotion, and doubt/denial are usually followed by an infinitive when there is no change of subject.

Es importante **practicar** todos los días.
It's important to practice every day.

Esta noche pienso **estudiar** para el examen.
Tonight I plan (intend) to study for the test.

5. Noun Clauses

The uses of the subjunctive that you have learned so far fall into the general category of the use of the subjunctive in *noun clauses* (**las cláusulas nominales**). The noun clause is the second (subordinate) clause in the sentence, the one that contains the subjunctive. It is called a noun clause because it functions like a noun in the sentence, usually as the direct object of the verb in the main clause but sometimes (with **gustar**) as the subject.

In the first two pairs of sentences to the right, the subordinate clause is the direct object of the main verb, answering the question *what?*

He wants *what?* → that they stop playing
They hope *what?* → that there will be many spectators

In the third pair of sentences, the subordinate clause is the subject of the verb **gustar.**

What isn't pleasing? → that ticket prices are high

A subordinate clause is viewed as a singular subject in Spanish, so **gusta** (not **gustan**) is used in the sentence.

cláusula subordinada nominal = complemento directo

—¿Qué quiere el director de la orquesta?
—Quiere **que los músicos dejen de tocar.**
"What does the orchestra director want?"
"He wants the musicians to stop playing."

—¿Qué esperan los músicos?
—Esperan **que haya muchos espectadores en el concierto.**
"What do the musicians want?"
"They hope (that) there will be many spectators at the concert."

cláusula subordinada nominal = sujeto

—¿Qué no les gusta a los espectadores?
—No les gusta **que las entradas sean muy caras.**
"What don't the spectators like?"
"They don't like tickets to be (that ticket prices are) so expensive."

Práctica y comunicación

Summary of Subjunctive

influence, emotion, doubt/denial + **que** + change of subject → **subjunctive**

A. Lo que deseo

Paso 1. Autoprueba. ¿Qué necesitan las siguientes cláusulas principales en la cláusula subordinada: subjuntivo, indicativo o depende?

1. El director de cine quiere que los espectadores...
2. Los artistas esperan que la gente...
3. Ojalá que...
4. Mis profesores piensan que lo más importante...
5. Yo no creo que lo más importante...
6. Mi madre dice que...

Paso 2. Termine las frases de la Columna A con una idea de la Columna B. A veces hay que conjugar el verbo y a veces no.

COLUMNA A	COLUMNA B
1. Quiero que...	**a.** graduarme en esta universidad en cuatro años
2. Espero...	**b.** tener un buen trabajo después de graduarme
3. Ojalá (que)...	**c.** sacar una buena nota en esta clase
4. Pienso...	**d.** ganar dinero como artista algún día
5. No creo que...	**e.** mi profesor(a) de español: dar mucha tarea
6. Digo que...	**f.** hablar español con soltura (*fluently*) en el futuro
	g. mis compañeros de clase: practicar el español durante el almuerzo.

Paso 3. Ahora, en parejas, túrnense para hacerse preguntas sobre las ideas del **Paso 2.** Luego díganle a la clase una idea que tienen en común.

MODELO: **E1:** ¿Quieres que tus compañeros de clase practiquen el español durante el almuerzo?
E2: Sí, quiero que lo practiquen durante el almuerzo. → Queremos que nuestros compañeros de clase practiquen el español durante el almuerzo.

Prác. A, Paso 1: Answers: *1. subjuntivo 2. subjuntivo 3. subjuntivo 4. indicativo 5. subjuntivo 6. depende*

©DEA/G Dagli Orti/Getty Images

Las meninas, de Diego Velázquez (España, 1599–1660)

B. En el Museo del Prado. Explique con oraciones completas por qué es buena idea tener la ayuda de un(a) guía en un museo.

1. Quiero que el guía…
   a. enseñarme los cuadros más famosos de Velázquez
   b. explicarme algunos detalles de los cuadros
   c. saber mucho sobre la vida del pintor
2. Me sorprende que muchos cuadros de Velázquez…
   a. tener como tema la vida cotidiana (*everyday*)
   b. estar en otros museos fuera de (*outside of*) España
   c. ser de la familia real (*royal*) de Felipe IV
3. Es posible que el guía…
   a. recomendarme algunos libros sobre la vida y el arte del pintor
   b. preguntarle a un colega si sabe algo más sobre Velázquez
   c. no tener más tiempo para hablar conmigo

C. ¡Qué maravilla de robot! Imagine que usted tiene un robot último modelo que va a hacer todo lo que usted le diga, especialmente las cosas que usted odia o que son difíciles. ¿Qué le va a mandar al robot que haga? Haga oraciones completas.

Le voy a decir que… Le voy a mandar que…	+	escribirme el informe (*report*) para la clase de historia hacerme el proyecto de arquitectura poner la mesa asistir por mí a todas las clases pagar mis cuentas ir por mí al trabajo ¿ ?

D. El lugar ideal para vivir

Paso 1. Piense en el lugar ideal para vivir. ¿Es una casa o un apartamento? ¿Está en una ciudad grande o pequeña? ¿Qué actividades culturales ofrece la ciudad? Lea la siguiente lista de factores e indique los que son indispensables para usted, más otros dos que no estén en la lista.

- ☐ casa con jardín grande
- ☐ apartamento grande
- ☐ apartamento con vista
- ☐ buenos museos
- ☐ cerca de una universidad importante
- ☐ buena orquesta y teatros
- ☐ muchos cines
- ☐ cerca de un gran centro comercial
- ☐ parques
- ☐ zonas naturales cerca de usted
- ☐ ¿ ?
- ☐ ¿ ?

Paso 2. Ahora, en parejas, describan el lugar ideal para vivir para cada uno de ustedes. Usen las siguientes frases como modelo. ¿En cuántos detalles coincidieron los dos?

MODELOS: Deseo que mi casa/apartamento…
No quiero vivir en…
(No) Me importa (mucho) (que)…
Es importante que la casa / el apartamento…
(No) Es absolutamente necesario que…
Espero (que)…

Todo junto

A. Lengua y cultura: En un museo, contemplando una obra de Fernando Botero

Paso 1. Completar. A guide and some visitors discuss a work by Fernando Botero. Complete the following dialogue with the correct form of the words in parentheses, as suggested by context. When two possibilities are given in parentheses, select the correct word or phrase. Conjugate the verbs in the present indicative, the **ustedes** command form, the present subjunctive, or the preterite, or leave them in the infinitive, if appropriate.

©Iberfoto/Superstock

Pareja bailando, de Fernando Botero (Colombia, 1932 -). Botero pintó varios cuadros sobre el mismo tema y con el mismo título.

GUÍA: Y ahora, vamos a ver una obra de Fernando Botero. _______ (Pasar[1]) ustedes por aquí, por favor. También les pido que _______ (dejar[2]) suficiente espacio para todos. Y bien, aquí estamos _______ (delante / detrás[3]) de _______ (este / esto[4]) cuadro _______ (de el / del[5]) pintor y escultor colombiano Fernando Botero. Mucha gente cree que Botero _______ (estar / ser[6]) el artista _______ (latinoamericano / latinoamericana[7]) más reconocido[a] del mundo. Un detalle curioso sobre Botero, que mucha gente no _______ (conocer / saber[8]): _______ (*él*: empezar[9]) su vida profesional como torero.[b] Pero pronto su familia _______ (descubrir[10]) que su vocación era la pintura. _______ (Estar / Ser[11]) obvio que sus figuras no son una copia exacta de la realidad, ¿verdad?

VISITANTE 1: ¿ _______ (Por qué / Porque[12]) son tan gordas sus figuras?

GUÍA: Es el estilo muy personal de Botero de representar la realidad. También _______ (le / se[13]) gusta hacer crítica social y política con humor. Pero a veces solo representa una escena cotidiana,[c] algo trágico o íntimo. Su estilo _______ (le / se[14]) llama el boterismo. ¿ _______ (Le / Les[15]) gusta a ustedes?

VISITANTE 1: No _______ (*yo*: conocer / saber[16])... Me _______ (gusta / gustan[17]) los colores y la escena, pero no me gusta que las figuras _______ (ser[18]) tan obesas. Me sorprende que Botero _______ (ser[19]) tan famoso internacionalmente.

VISITANTE 2: Pues _______ (a mí / yo[20]) no me sorprende. Para mí, hay sensualidad y movimiento en esas figuras.

---

[a]*well-known* [b]*bullfighter* [c]*everyday*

Paso 2. Comprensión. ¿Quién pudo decir lo siguiente: el guía, la visitante 1 o el visitante 2?

	EL GUÍA	VISITANTE 1	VISITANTE 2
1. «Prefiero las figuras más realistas.»	☐	☐	☐
2. «Me encanta que estas figuras sean voluminosas y redondas (*round*).»	☐	☐	☐
3. «Es posible que Botero quiera mostrarnos la sensualidad del baile.»	☐	☐	☐
4. «Quiero que todos me sigan ahora, por favor.»	☐	☐	☐

Paso 3. En acción

Dé sus propias opiniones sobre el cuadro. Después compárelas a las opiniones de una persona de la clase. ¿Coinciden en algo?

Expresiones útiles

Me gusta/sorprende/ molesta que...
Es interesante que...
Es obvio que...

B. Proyecto: Presentación oral sobre una obra de arte

©garrykosoff/123RF ©Merlot Levert/Shutterstock ©AntonovVitalii/Shutterstock ©hanohiki/Shutterstock

En este proyecto, va a comentar una obra de arte visual que le gusta o que le interesa por alguna razón. Recuerde que hay muchas formas de expresión artística: la pintura, la escultura, la arquitectura...

Paso 1. Preparación. Elija a un(a) artista del mundo hispanohablante y una obra suya (*of his/hers*) en concreto. En este capítulo hay información sobre varios pintores hispanohablantes (Botero, Guayasamín, Mamani Mamani y Velázquez), pero es posible que usted conozca a otros. Aquí tiene algunos nombres adicionales.

José Clemente Orozco	Wilfredo Lam	Remedios Varo
Francisco de Goya	Antonio Gaudí	Alfredo Matta
Antonio Berni	Doris Salcedo	Frida Kahlo

Paso 2. Investigación. (*Research.*) Haga una investigación sobre el/la artista y la obra que usted escogió en el **Paso 1**. Asegúrese de (*Be sure to*) obtener la siguiente información básica: época; tipo de arte y estilo principal del/de la artista; título de la obra en español; año en que fue creada (pintada, esculpida, construida...). También debe buscar información sobre el significado (*meaning*) de la obra: ¿Qué representa? ¿Cree que contiene un mensaje (*message*)? También piense en por qué le gusta la obra.

Paso 3. Presentación. Combine la información de los **Pasos 1** y **2** para crear una presentación de aproximadamente dos minutos. Su objetivo es explicarles una obra a personas que probablemente no la conocen y no saben mucho de arte. Debe comunicar su interés en la obra y su visión personal de ella. Finalmente, haga su presentación en clase.

Estrategia

Before you present, consider what makes a presentation attractive and interesting:

- Good organization
- Interesting information and explanation, just the right amount of complexity and depth for your audience
- Comprehensibility, a function of appropriate vocabulary, correct grammar, and clear pronunciation

¡Ahora, yo!

A. Entrevista. Use de modelo las preguntas y respuestas de la página 389 de este capítulo para hablar sobre las artes y las artesanías que a usted le interesan y el lugar donde se pueden ver en su ciudad.

B. Proyecto audiovisual. Haga un fotomontaje con voz en off (*voice-over*) sobre la obra de un artista hispano / una artista hispana cuya (*whose*) obra le interesa mucho a usted.

©Daniel Ernst/Getty Images

SALU

«Arte angelino» Segmento 2

Antes de mirar

¿Qué sabe usted de los murales como expresión artística? En su opinión, ¿son ejemplos del arte abstracto o son una expresión de mensajes políticos o sociales? ¿Hay arte mural en su campus o en su ciudad? ¿Dónde se puede ver? ¿Cómo es?

Este segmento

Laura presenta un reportaje sobre el movimiento muralista de la ciudad de Los Ángeles.

La Ofrenda (*Offering*), de Yreina Cervantes (1988), un tributo a la fuerza y la lucha (*struggle*) de los campesinos (*farmers*) del movimiento de la United Farm Workers, especialmente a una de sus líderes, Dolores Huerta

Vocabulario del segmento

establecer (establezco)	to establish
a través de	through
tener que ver	to have to do
sea	be it
el muro	wall
mide media milla	it's half a mile long
tardar... en	to take (*time*) to (*do something*)
la campaña de concientización	consciousness-raising campaign
llamar la atención	to get (*someone's*) attention
el motivo de orgullo	source of pride
se nos acabó el tiempo	our time is up

Fragmento del guion

Es muy feo cuando empiezan a marcar y rayar[a] los murales. Y eso pasa, puede ser, cada otra noche, de... No se sabe. Hay tantos[b] jóvenes que no saben la historia del muralismo y no saben que estas obras de arte les pertenecen[c] a ellos y les pertenecen a sus comunidades. Es historia de ellos. Y realmente quisiéramos[d] que ellos entiendan eso.

[a]*scratch* [b]*so many* [c]*belong* [d]*we'd like*

Después de mirar

A. ¿Está claro? ¿Cierto o falso? Corrija las oraciones falsas.

	CIERTO	FALSO
1. SPARC, el Centro Social y Público de Recursos Artísticos, está en Los Ángeles.	☐	☐
2. Pilar Castillo es una muralista angelina.	☐	☐
3. El movimiento muralista es exclusivo de la comunidad chicana/mexicana de Los Ángeles.	☐	☐
4. Baca trabajó sola en la creación de su mural *El Gran Muro*.	☐	☐

B. Un poco más. Conteste las siguientes preguntas.

1. ¿De dónde viene la influencia original del movimiento muralista angelino? ¿Cómo se adapta esta influencia a la realidad de Los Ángeles?
2. ¿Qué serio problema enfrentan (*face*) los murales? ¿Qué es necesario hacer para resolver esta situación?

C. Y ahora, ustedes. En parejas, preparen un reportaje sobre un edificio de la universidad o de su ciudad que sea particularmente interesante. Mencionen cuándo se construyó, el estilo y otros detalles del edificio, como, por ejemplo, quién lo diseñó, qué departamento o grupo lo ocupa ahora y si se construyó con otro fin (*purpose*) en otra época. No olviden decir si el edificio es un motivo de orgullo (*pride*) para la universidad o la ciudad y por qué.

MUNDO HISPANO

Enfoque cultural: El Ecuador y Bolivia

Antes de leer

¿Cuáles son los museos más importantes de su ciudad, su estado o su país? ¿Los conoce? ¿Cuál es su favorito?

Las artes en el Ecuador y Bolivia

Tanto el Ecuador como Bolivia son países multiculturales, donde diferentes grupos étnicos contribuyen a las artes en general.

En el Ecuador, la institución encargada de apoyar y promover[a] la cultura es La Casa de la Cultura Ecuatoriana Benjamín Carrión (CCE), una red nacional de bibliotecas, cines, museos, teatros y publicaciones, con sede[b] en Quito. Su misión es de «[p]reservar, promover,[c] fomentar,[d] investigar y difundir[e] el arte, ciencia y patrimonio cultural ecuatoriano» para fortalecer[f] la identidad nacional del país.

En Bolivia, la editorial[g] Yerba Mala[h] Cartonera es una iniciativa a destacar.[i] Publican las obras de todo tipo de escritores locales, en libros impresos[j] en papel ordinario y con tapas[k] recicladas de las cajas de cartón que se botan[l] en los supermercados. Los autores mismos[m] venden sus libros en lugares públicos, al precio de un boliviano ($0,14, aproximadamente). Y si alguien no tiene plata,[n] se lo regalan, para difundir la cultura.

[a]encargada... *in charge of supporting and promoting* [b]*headquarters* [c]*to promote* [d]*to encourage* [e]*to spread* [f]*strengthen* [g]*publishing house* [h]Yerba... *Weeds* [i]*highlight* [j]*printed* [k]*covers* [l]cajas... *cardboard boxes that are thrown away* [m]*themselves* [n]dinero

En otros países hispanos

- **En España y México** Uno de los museos de arte más importantes del mundo es el Museo del Prado, en Madrid. Allí se puede admirar las obras de Velázquez y Goya, entre otros muchos artistas españoles y europeos anteriores al siglo XX. El Museo Nacional de Antropología, en la Ciudad de México, es uno de los mejores del mundo en su género.[a] En este museo se puede admirar y apreciar la excelencia de la artesanía y arquitectura de los pueblos indígenas mesoamericanos.
- **En los Estados Unidos** En Nueva York está el Museo del Barrio, dedicado a la obra de artistas latinos, con énfasis en el arte puertorriqueño.

[a]*category, genre*

Juan Evo Morales, de ascendencia aymara, Presidente de Bolivia desde 2006

Un símbolo ecuatoriano y boliviano: La diversidad étnica y lingüística

El Ecuador y Bolivia son países que han logrado[a] preservar un gran porcentaje de su población indígena. Esto es sin duda una gran parte de la riqueza cultural y orgullo[b] nacional de ambos[c] países. Además,[d] el encuentro entre los españoles y los indígenas dio como resultado una mezcla[e] racial que hoy es el sustrato[f] más grande de la población de estos dos países (y de Latinoamérica en general).

[a]han... *have succeeded in* [b]*pride* [c]*both* [d]*Besides* [e]*mixture* [f]*ethnic background*

Comprensión

1. ¿Qué institución está encargada de fomentar la cultura ecuatoriana?
2. ¿Quiénes son los autores de los libros de la editorial Yerba Mala Cartonera?
3. ¿Cuáles son algunos de los museos famosos del mundo hispanohablante? ¿Cuál es la especialidad de cada una?
4. ¿Qué caracteriza a la mayoría de la población de Bolivia y el Ecuador?

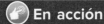

 En acción

Haga una breve descripción de su museo favorito o del museo más importante de su ciudad o estado: cómo se llama, dónde está, en qué se especializa y por qué recomienda usted que se visite.

Lectura

Antes de leer

1. ¿Qué hacen los poetas? ¿Dónde y cuándo escriben?
2. En su opinión, ¿es fácil o difícil ser poeta?
3. ¿Cree usted que, en general, los poetas tienen otro trabajo además del de (*besides that of*) escribir poemas?

«Sale caro ser poeta», de Gloria Fuertes

Sale caro, señores, ser poeta.
La gente va y se acuesta tan tranquila
—que después del trabajo da buen sueño—.[a]
Trabajo como esclavo llego a casa,
me siento ante[b] la mesa sin cocina,
me pongo a meditar lo que sucede.[c]
La duda me acribilla[d] todo espanta[e];
comienzo a ser comida por las sombras[f]
las horas se me pasan sin bostezo
el dormir se me asusta[g] se me huye[h]
—escribiendo me da la madrugada—.[i]
Y luego los amigos me organizan recitales.[j]
a los que acudo[k] y leo como tonta,
y la gente no sabe de esto nada.
Que me dejo la linfa[l] en lo que escribo
me caigo de la rama[m] de la rima
asalto las trincheras[n] de la angustia
me nombran su héroe los fantasmas,[ñ]
me cuesta[o] respirar cuando termino.
Sale caro señores ser poeta.

[a]que... *after work one gets good and sleepy* [b]*at* [c]me... *I start to meditate about what's happening* [d]*harasses* [e]*frightens* (*me*) [f]*shadows* [g]se... *is frightened away* [h]se... (el dormir) *flees from me* [i]me... *gets me to morning* [j]*readings* (*of my poetry*) [k]a... *which I attend* [l]me... *I leave my lymph glands* (*i.e., my heart and soul*) [m]*branch* [n]asalto... *I assail the trenches* [ñ]me... *ghosts call me their hero* [o]me... *it's hard for me*

Vocabulario para leer

el bostezo yawn
el esclavo slave
salir caro to be expensive

Comprensión

A. ¿Dónde lo dice? Dé el número de los versos (*lines*) del poema donde aparece la siguiente información.

1. ¿Tiene más de un trabajo la poeta?
2. ¿Cuándo escribe su poesía?
3. ¿Pasa rápido el tiempo mientras escribe?
4. ¿Se siente tranquila cuando escribe?
5. ¿Tiene audiencia esta poeta?
6. ¿Entiende el público cuánto trabaja la poeta?
7. ¿Es fácil el trabajo de poeta, según dice la poeta misma (*herself*)?

B. Preguntas

1. ¿Qué cree Ud que significa «esto» en «la gente no sabe de esto nada» (verso 14)?
2. ¿Por qué cree usted que después de escribir sus poemas le cuesta respirar (verso 19)?
3. Si la autora cree que «sale caro ser poeta», ¿por qué se dedica a (*does she work on*) escribir poesías? ¿Le parece a usted lógico?

Proyecto: Sale caro el trabajo artístico

Mucha gente tiene una noción idealizada de cómo es la vida y del trabajo de los artistas. Pero el trabajo artístico puede ser duro.

Paso 1. Elija una forma de expresión artística que le interesa (la arquitectura, el baile, el cine, etcétera). Considere y describa el proceso de creación y exposición (*exhibition*) de esa forma de arte.

Paso 2. Del proceso que describió en el **Paso 1**, ¿cuáles son—en su opinión—los pasos más difíciles? ¿Qué pasos cree usted que los artistas disfrutan *(enjoy)* más?

Paso 3: Busque en internet y lea una biografía breve de un(a) artista que trabaja con el tipo de arte que usted eligió. ¿Cómo corresponde esta biografía a las ideas que usted expresó en el **Paso 2**?

Textos orales

Una reseña° de la película *La vida de Susana Jiménez*

°*review*

Antes de escuchar

¿Le gusta el cine? ¿Tiene un género (*genre*) preferido de películas: las de acción, de artes marciales, de aventura, de ciencia ficción, de horror, de suspenso, de guerra (*war*), las comedias, los dramas, las musicales? En su opinión, ¿qué características necesita tener una película para que (*so that*) sea interesante y/o buena? ¿Lee usted en el periódico o en internet reseñas de las películas antes de verlas? ¿Las lee después de verlas? ¿O no las lee nunca?

Vocabulario para escuchar

el punto de vista	point of view
trata de	deals with
inesperado/a	unexpected
el argumento	plot
la actuación	performance
cursi	in poor taste; trite
al elegir	when she chose
recrea	it recreates

Comprensión

A. ¿Cierto o falso? ¿Qué dicen los críticos de la película? Corrija las oraciones falsas.

	CIERTO	FALSO
1. El hombre piensa que es una película que se debe ver.	☐	☐
2. La mujer piensa que es una película recomendable.	☐	☐
3. Los dos críticos piensan que la actriz principal es buena.	☐	☐
4. Los críticos están de acuerdo: el guion es bueno.	☐	☐

B. Más detalles. Conteste las siguientes preguntas.

1. Según la mujer, ¿cuál es el problema principal de la película?
2. ¿Cuáles son unos aspectos positivos de la película, según los críticos?

En acción

Haga una sinopsis de su película favorita, incluyendo una recomendación sobre el tipo de público que debe verla. Incluya el título en español, el año que salió (*it came out*) y los nombres del director / de la directora y de los actores principales.

Proyecto en su comunidad

Entreviste a una persona hispana de su universidad o ciudad sobre el arte y la artesanía de su país de origen.

Preguntas posibles

- ¿Cuáles son los artistas más conocidos (*best known*) de su país? ¿A qué tipo de arte se dedican?
- ¿Qué tipo de artesanía se hace en su país? ¿y en su ciudad o región? ¿Tiene muestras (*examples*) de esta artesanía en su casa?
- ¿Hay muchas oportunidades de asistir a eventos culturales (por ejemplo, exposiciones en museos, conciertos, espectáculos de danza, teatro o cine) en su país? Por lo general, ¿son baratas o caras las entradas para los eventos culturales?
- ¿Cuáles son los eventos culturales que usted prefiere? ¿Asiste a ellos con frecuencia?

Escritura

Proyecto: Un ensayo sobre la expresión artística en las escuelas

Antes de escribir

Paso 1. En parejas, piensen en los siguientes aspectos de la importancia del arte.

1. ¿Qué significa la palabra **arte**? ¿Cómo puede afectar el arte la vida de una persona?
2. ¿Cómo/Dónde se debe aprender las diversas formas de arte? ¿En la escuela o en el tiempo libre?
3. En general, ¿qué formas de arte se promueven (*are promoted*) y se enseñan en las escuelas públicas? ¿Creen que se enseñan de manera suficiente?

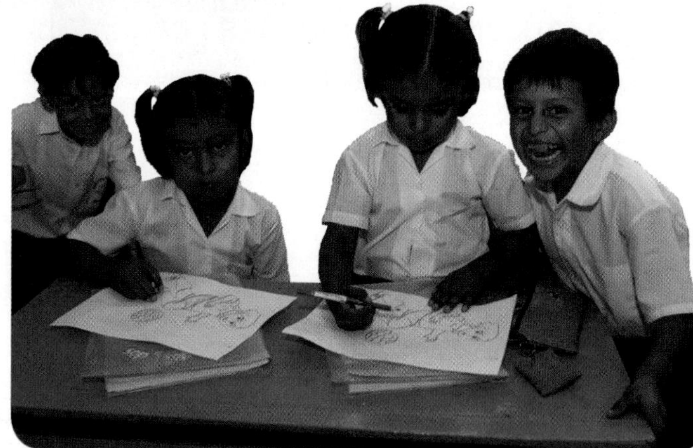

Unos niños en una clase de arte, en el Ecuador

Paso 2. Luego, hagan una lista de argumentos a favor de la idea de apoyar (*supporting*) y enseñar las artes en las escuelas públicas y otra de argumentos en contra.

A escribir

Ahora use las ideas de **Antes de escribir** para escribir un ensayo a favor o en contra de la enseñanza de las artes en las escuelas públicas. Hay más ayuda en Connect.

Más ideas para su portafolio

- Incluya una imagen de una de sus obras de arte favoritas (de arquitectura, escultura, pintura, cine, música o lo que sea). Explique por qué le gusta y cómo la descubrió.
- Incluya la imagen de alguna obra artística que usted ya ha hecho (*have made*) recientemente o antes de llegar a la universidad. Explique si se siente orgulloso/a (*proud*) de ella y por qué. Dé detalles sobre la obra: cuándo y por qué la hizo, dónde está o quién la tiene ahora, etcétera. Si no tiene ninguna obra suya (*of your own*) que comentar, hable de una obra hecha (*made*) por un pariente u otra persona.
- Si ha estado jugando (*you have been playing*) Practice Spanish: Study Abroad, en Quest 10 usted aprendió sobre algunos remedios caseros (*home remedies*) tradicionales de Colombia. En parejas, escriban un diálogo en el cual (*which*) una persona trata de ayudar a su amigo enfermo recomendándole unos remedios caseros populares en su país. El amigo / La amiga debe reaccionar a las sugerencias, expresando su opinión. Ensayen (*Rehearse*) bien y luego presenten su diálogo a la clase.

Sugerencia: You are now ready to play Quest 10 in **Practice Spanish: Study Abroad.**

EN RESUMEN En este capítulo

AFTER STUDYING THIS CHAPTER I CAN. . .

- ☐ talk about creative endeavors of all kinds (390–391)
- ☐ express the order of things (394)
- ☐ use the present subjunctive to express emotion (396–397)
- ☐ use the present subjunctive to express doubt and denial (401–403)
- ☐ use the indicative or the subjunctive in noun clauses (405–407)
- ☐ recognize/describe at least 2–3 aspects of Ecuadorian and Bolivian cultures

Gramática en breve

36. Uses of the Subjunctive: Emotion

① EMOTION		②
first subject = **indicative**	**que**	second subject = **subjunctive**

37. Uses of the Subjunctive: Doubt and Denial

① DOUBT AND DENIAL		②
first subject = **indicative**	**que**	second subject = **subjunctive**

38. The Subjunctive: A Summary

①		②
influence / emotion / doubt or denial	**que**	**subjunctive**
information / certainty or belief	**que**	**indicative**

Vocabulario

Los verbos

aburrir (*like* gustar)	to bore
acordarse (me acuerdo) (de)	to remember
atraer (*like* traer) (*like* gustar)	to draw, attract
fascinar (*like* gustar)	to fascinate
ganar	to earn (*income*)
lamentar	to regret; to feel sorry
negar (niego) (gu)	to deny
no creer	to disbelieve
sentir (siento) (i)	to regret; to feel sorry
sorprender (*like* gustar)	to surprise
temer	to fear, be afraid
tratar de + *inf.*	to try to (*do something*)

Repaso: alegrarse de, creer, dudar, encantar, esperar, gustar, molestar, pensar, tener miedo de

La expresión artística

el baile	dance
el cuadro	painting (*specific piece*)
la danza	dance
el dibujo	drawing
las entradas	tickets (*to a performance, movie...*)
el escenario	stage; scenery
la escultura	sculpture
el espectáculo	show
la fotografía	photography
el guion	script
la imagen	image
la obra de arte	work (of art)
la obra de teatro	play
la obra maestra	masterpiece
el papel	role
la pintura	painting *(in general; specific piece)*

Cognados: la arquitectura, las artes (*pl.*), el ballet, la comedia, el drama, la escena, el mural, la música, el musical, la novela, la ópera, el poema

Repaso: el arte, la canción, el cine, el concierto, el edificio, la foto(grafía), la literatura, el museo, la película, el siglo, el teatro

actuar (actúo)	to act
componer (compongo) (*like* poner)	to compose
crear	to create
dibujar	to draw
dirigir (dirijo)	to direct
diseñar	to design
esculpir	to sculpt
tejer	to weave

Cognado: pintar

Repaso: bailar, cantar, escribir

Las personas

el actor, la actriz (*pl.* actrices)	actor
el bailarín, la bailarina	dancer
el/la cantante	singer
el/la compositor(a)	composer
el/la dibujante	drawer
el/la director(a)	director; conductor
el/la dramaturgo/a	playwright
el/la escritor(a)	writer
el/la escultor(a)	sculptor
el/la espectador(a)	spectator; *pl.* audience
el/la guía	guide
el/la músico/a	musician
la orquesta	orchestra
el/la pintor(a)	painter

Cognados: el/la arquitecto/a, el/la artista, el/la autor(a), el/la novelista, el/la poeta, el público

La tradición cultural

la artesanía	arts and crafts
la cerámica	pottery; ceramics
los tejidos	woven goods

Cognado: la ruina

Los adjetivos

folclórico/a	traditional

Cognados: artístico/a, clásico/a, moderno/a

Los números ordinales

primer(o/a)	**sexto/a**
segundo/a	**séptimo/a**
tercer(o/a)	**octavo/a**
cuarto/a	**noveno/a**
quinto/a	**décimo/a**

Palabras adicionales

es... + indicative	it's . . .
cierto que	certain that
seguro que	certain/a sure thing that
verdad que	true that
es... + subjunctive	it's . . .
absurdo que	absurd that
extraño que	strange that
¡qué extraño que...!	how strange that . . . !
(im)posible que	(im)possible that
(im)probable que	(un)likely, (im)probable that
increíble que	incredible that
normal que	normal that
terrible que	terrible that
es una lástima que + subjunctive	it's a shame that
¡qué lástima que... !	what a shame that . . .!
hay que + *inf.*	it is necessary to (*do something*)
no es... + subjunctive	it's not . . .
(im)probable que	(im)probable that
posible que	possible that
seguro que...	certain / a sure thing that
(no) estar seguro de	to be (un)certain of
ojalá (que)	I hope (that)

Repaso: es mejor/bueno/malo que, primero (*adv.*)

Vocabulario personal

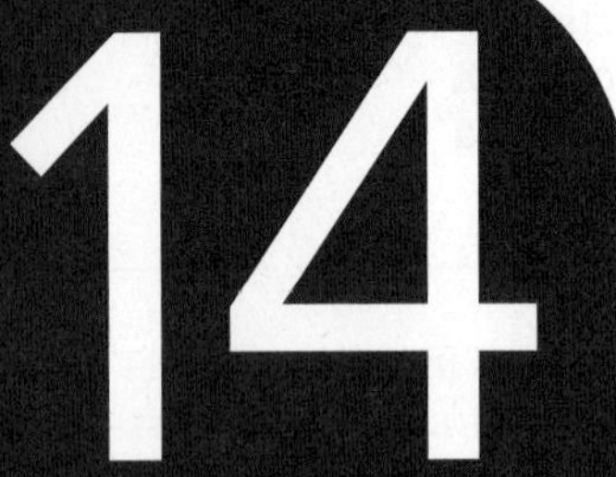

14 Las presiones° de la vida

Las... *Pressures*

En este capítulo

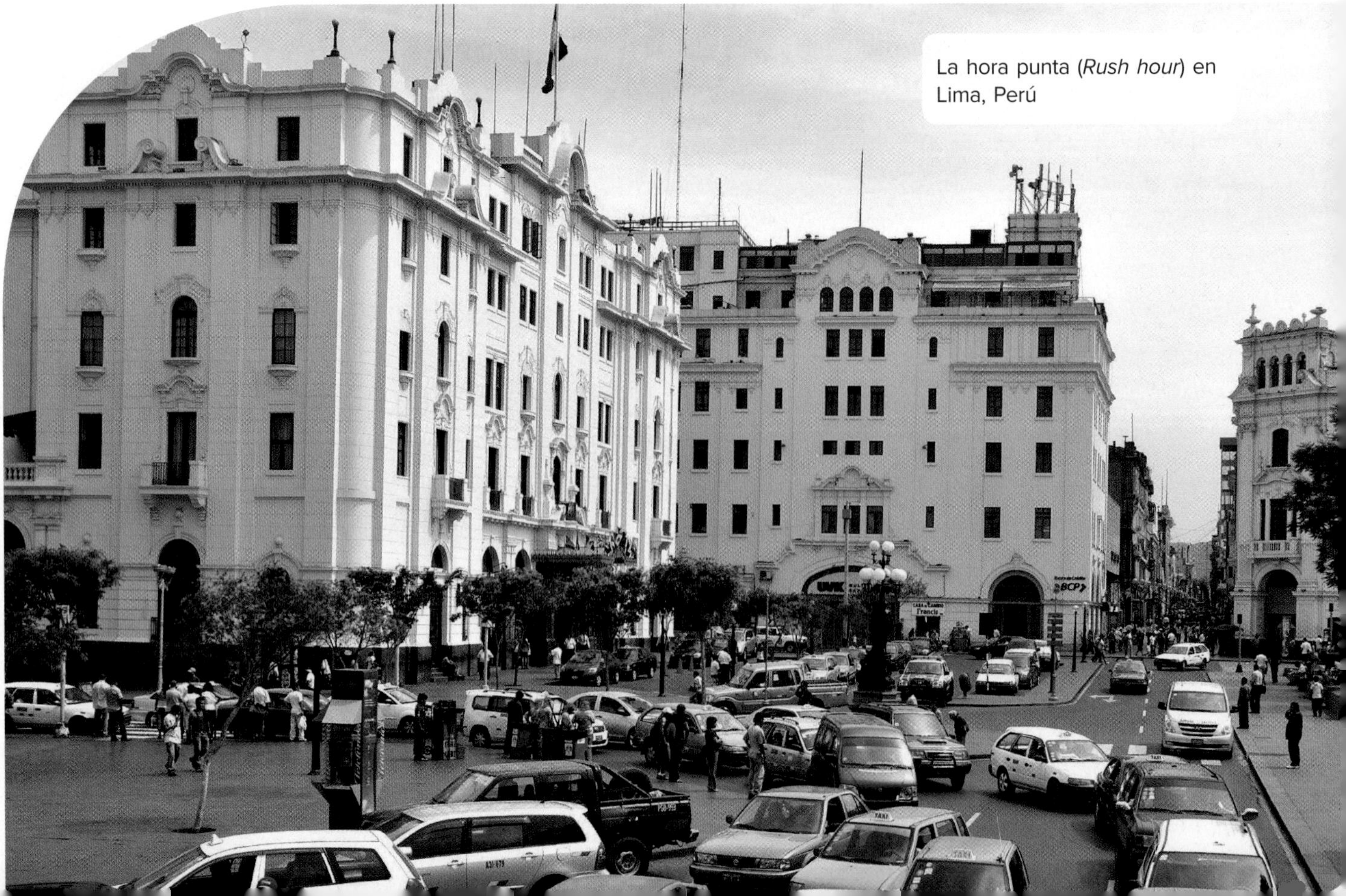

La hora punta (*Rush hour*) en Lima, Perú

EL PERÚ

32,6 (coma seis) millones de habitantes

- El Perú es otro de los países andinos que tiene costa en el océano Pacífico y territorio amazónico. También tiene una zona desértica al sur.
- Lima, la capital del Perú, es una inmensa ciudad de más de 9 millones de habitantes. Es la quinta entre las ciudades más grandes de Latinoamérica y una de las treinta ciudades más grandes del mundo.
- El Perú es un país multiétnico: más del 25% de su población es amerindia, principalmente quechua, seguida por[a] un gran porcentaje de mestizos, después blancos y, finalmente, negros, asiáticos (de origen chino y japonés) y árabes.

[a]seguida... *followed by*

ENTREVISTA

- ¿Cree usted que la vida moderna de hoy día es motivo de muchas presiones? ¿Y la vida estudiantil?
- En su opinión, ¿tenemos hoy más presiones en la vida diaria que hace 50 años[a]? Explique su respuesta.
- ¿Qué hace usted para calmarse cuando se siente muy estresado/a?

[a]que... *than 50 years ago*

Ismael Pérez Mendizábal contesta las preguntas.

- No hay duda de que el ritmo[a] de la vida de hoy día es la causa de que suframos muchas presiones y mucho estrés, tanto si[b] estás trabajando o estudiando. A muchos jóvenes nos preocupa salir bien en la universidad porque es difícil conseguir un buen trabajo cuando terminas.
- Yo diría[c] que tenemos más presiones hoy. En realidad no creo que la vida ahora sea más difícil que hace 50 años,[d] pero sí creo que vivimos con más tensión día a día. Y también nos causan estrés las expectativas[e] que tenemos para nuestro futuro.
- Pues, hago lo normal, creo. Salgo con mis amigos para distraerme,[f] duermo una siesta si puedo. También trato de hacer deporte, como correr o levantar pesas, porque eso me hace sentirme mejor físicamente.

[a]*rhythm* [b]tanto... *regardless of whether* [c]*would say* [d]hace... *50 years ago* [e]*expectations* [f]*take my mind off things*

VOCABULARIO: PREPARACIÓN

You can hear the pronunciation of theme vocabulary words and phrases in the Connect eBook.

Las presiones de la vida académica

la agenda	personal calendar
la ansiedad	anxiety
el calendario	calendar (*of the year*)
el estrés	stress
el horario	schedule
el informe (oral/escrito)	(oral/written) report
el plazo	deadline
el programa (del curso)	(course) syllabus
la prueba	quiz; test
la tarea	homework
el trabajo	job, work; report, (piece of) work
el trabajo de tiempo completo/parcial	full-time/part-time job
estresante	stressful
acordarse (me acuerdo) (de)	to remember
corregir (corrijo) (i)*	to grade; to correct
devolver (like **volver**) **(algo a alguien)**	to return (something to someone)
entregar (gu)	to turn/hand in
estacionar	to park
estar (muy) estresado/a	to be (very) stressed, be under (a lot of) stress
llegar (gu) a tiempo / tarde	to arrive on time/late
olvidar	to forget
pedir (pido) (i) disculpas	to apologize
recoger (recojo)*	to collect; to pick up
sacar (qu) buenas/malas notas	to get good/bad grades
ser (in)flexible	to be (in)flexible
sufrir (de)	to suffer (from)
tener / estar bajo muchas presiones	to have/be under a lot of pressure
tomar apuntes	to take notes (*academic*)

Para pedir y aceptar disculpas

la disculpa	apology
Disculpa. / Discúlpame.	Pardon me. I'm sorry. (*fam.*)
Disculpe. / Discúlpeme.	Pardon me. I'm sorry. (*form.*)
pedir (pido) (i) disculpas	to apologize
Fue sin querer.	I didn't mean (to do) it.
Lo siento (mucho).	I'm (very) sorry.
Perdón.	Pardon me. I'm sorry.
Está bien.	It's fine. It's O.K.
No hay problema.	No problem.

Note the present indicative conjugation of* **corregir: corrijo, corriges, corrige, corregimos, corregís, corrigen and **recoger: recojo, recoges, recoge, recogemos, recogéis, recogen.**

Así se dice

la nota = la calificación
el plazo = la fecha límite
estacionar = aparcar (*Sp.*), parquear (*Mex.*)

la tarjeta de identificación nacional = la cédula de ciudadanía (*Col.*), el documento nacional de identidad (DNI) (*Arg., Per., Sp.*)

Comunicación

A. Asociaciones

Paso 1. ¿Qué palabras asocia usted con los siguientes verbos? Pueden ser sustantivos o verbos, antónimos o sinónimos.

1. estacionar
2. recoger
3. acordarse
4. entregar
5. sacar
6. sufrir
7. pedir
8. llegar

Paso 2. ¿Qué palabras o situaciones asocia usted con los siguientes sustantivos?

1. el calendario
2. el despertador
3. las notas
4. las pruebas
5. el plazo
6. el horario
7. los informes
8. las llaves
9. la tarjeta de identificación
10. las disculpas
11. las presiones
12. la inflexibilidad
13. los apuntes
14. el trabajo

B. Situaciones

Paso 1. En parejas, emparejen las preguntas o comentarios con las respuestas apropiadas.

PREGUNTAS/COMENTARIOS

1. _____ —Anoche no me acordé de poner el despertador.
2. _____ —No puedes estacionar el coche aquí sin permiso.
3. _____ —¿Sacaste buena nota en la prueba?
4. _____ —Ramiro no está bien. Es obvio que está estresado.
5. _____ —Discúlpeme, profesor, pero aquí tiene mi trabajo sobre la Unión Europea.
6. _____ —Disculpa, pero no puedo hablar contigo ahora. Tengo que terminar el programa de curso para el semestre que viene y corregir todos estos trabajos finales.

RESPUESTAS

a. —Siento que tengas tanto trabajo. ¿Qué crees que es más urgente que hagas en este momento?
b. —Ya lo sé, pero no me importa. Estoy cansado de buscar estacionamiento por todo el campus.
c. —¡No te puedo creer! ¿Otra vez? ¿A qué hora llegaste al trabajo entonces?
d. —¿Pero no se acordó de que el plazo era ayer? Es la última vez que le acepto un informe tarde.
e. —Muy buena, pero es una sorpresa. No tuve tiempo para estudiar.
f. —¡Pero, hombre! Si el pobre tiene un trabajo de tiempo completo, y además (*besides*) toma tres cursos este semestre…

Paso 2. Ahora inventen un contexto para cada diálogo. ¿Dónde están las personas que hablan? ¿En una oficina? ¿en clase? ¿Quiénes son?

MODELO: **1.** → Las personas que hablan están en el trabajo (en una oficina). Probablemente están almorzando. Son compañeros de trabajo; se conocen, pero no son amigos…

C. Listas personales. Cree sus propias listas personales para este semestre/ trimestre: una con las cinco cosas que más ansiedad le provocan (*cause you*) y otra con las cinco cosas que más le gustan. Recuerde usar los ordinales (**primero, segundo...**).

D. La educación universitaria

Paso 1. Con frecuencia se oye a las personas mayores hablar de los años universitarios con nostalgia: años de libertad, sin responsabilidades, sin las presiones de la vida que vienen después. ¿Ve usted así la época universitaria? En parejas, comenten (*discuss*) este tema. Usen las siguientes preguntas como guía.

1. ¿Tienen muchas presiones los estudiantes universitarios?
2. ¿Qué les causa estrés a ustedes? Ordenen las causas de su estrés. (La primera causa de nuestro estrés es...)
3. ¿Son más divertidos los años universitarios que los años de la escuela secundaria? ¿Por qué?
4. ¿Les preocupa a ustedes el costo de la matrícula? ¿Es difícil para ustedes o para su familia pagarla?
5. ¿Creen ustedes que la vida va a ser mejor después de graduarse en la universidad? Expliquen su respuesta.

Paso 2. Ahora lean las siguientes citas (*quotes*) sobre la vida, la educación y el éxito (*success*) y contesten las preguntas.

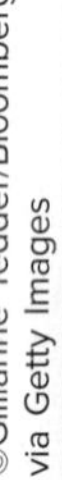

«El éxito se mide[a] en si usaste tu cabeza tanto como tu corazón, si fuiste generoso, si amaste[b] a los niños y a la naturaleza, si te preocupaste por los ancianos. Es acerca de tu bondad,[c] tu deseo de servir, tu capacidad de escuchar y tu valor sobre la conducta.[d]»

Carlos Slim Helú, hombre de negocios (*business*) mexicano

«El destino es una mezcla[e] de la preparación y la suerte.[f]»

Luis Miguel, cantante mexicano

«Les digo con todo mi corazón, con toda mi vida. Yo no tengo talento natural. No soy un genio. Pero mis padres a pesar de[g] ser tan humildes[h] me dieron educación.»

©Michael Tran/FilmMagic/
Getty Images

Edward James Olmos, actor mexicoamericano

[a]se... *is measured* [b]*you loved* [c]acerca... *about your kindness* [d]valor... *courage in the way you act*
[e]*mix* [f]*luck* [g]a... *in spite of* [h]*poor*

1. ¿Qué creen ustedes que es más importante para triunfar en la vida, tener talento natural o preparación?
2. ¿Creen que va a ayudarles a encontrar un buen trabajo la educación que están recibiendo?
3. ¿Son importantes las buenas notas para conseguir un buen trabajo? ¿O creen que es suficiente obtener un título universitario, no importa con qué notas?
4. ¿Cómo creen ustedes que se debe medir (*measure*) el éxito individual en la vida?

¡Qué mala suerte!°

¡Qué... *What bad luck!*

Los accidentes

doler (duele) (*like* **gustar**)	to hurt, ache
equivocarse (qu) (de)	to make a mistake (about/with)
hacerse daño en	to hurt one's (*body part*)
levantarse con el pie izquierdo	to get up on the wrong side of the bed
ocurrir, pasar	to happen
pegar (gu)	to hit, strike
pegar(se) (gu) con/contra	to run/bump into/against
tener buena/mala suerte	to have good/bad luck; to be (un)lucky

¡Qué + *adjective***!**	How . . . !
distraído/a	absent-minded, distracted
¡Qué distraído!	How absent-minded!
torpe	clumsy
¡Qué torpe!	How clumsy!
¡Qué + *noun***!**	What (a) . . . !
¡Qué desastre!	What a mess! What a disaster!
¡Qué dolor!	It hurts! (*lit.*, What pain!)

Reacciones emocionales (opcional)

- Para expresar dolor, sorpresa o compasión

¡Ay! Ouch! Oops!
¡Uy! Oops! Oh!
¡No puede ser! No way!
¡No me diga(s)! No! No way!
¿Qué le vamos a hacer? What can you do (about it)?
¡Cuánto lo siento!
¡Qué bonito/feo/bien!
¡Qué horror!
¡Qué maravilla! (*How wonderful!*)
¡Qué pena/lástima (*shame*)**!**
¡Qué terrible/triste!

- Con referencia a la suerte

¡Buena suerte! Good luck!
¡Qué mala suerte! Such bad luck!
¡Que te/le vaya bien! Hope it goes well!

Así se dice

chocar con/contra = darse con/contra
distraído/a = despistado/a
hacerse daño en = lastimarse en
romperse = quebrarse

Note that the first person singular of **caer** (to fall) *is irregular:* **caigo.** *The present participle is* **cayendo.**

†**Romper** *means* to break. *It is generally used with* **se: Se rompió la ventana.**

Comunicación

A. Accidentes y tropiezos (*mishaps*)

Paso 1. ¿Le pasaron a usted alguna de las siguentes cosas en los últimos meses? Modifique las oraciones, usando palabras afirmativas y negativas, para que sean (*so that they are*) verdaderas para usted.

MODELOS: Me caí por las escaleras (*stairs*) de ______. **Nunca** me caí por las escaleras de **mi casa.**

1. Me caí por las escaleras de ______.
2. No me acordé de hacer la tarea para la clase de ______.
3. Me equivoqué al contestar (*when I answered*) una pregunta en la clase de ______.
4. El despertador sonó, pero no me desperté.
5. Soy un poco torpe. Rompí sin querer ______ (algo) de ______ (alguien).
6. Choqué con un/una ______ y me hice daño en el/la ______ (parte del cuerpo).
7. Olvidé el plazo para entregar un informe de ______ (materia).
8. Olvidé devolverle el/la ______ (algo) a ______ (alguien).
9. Iba un poco distraído/a y me equivoqué de puerta en el edificio ______.

Paso 2. Ahora, usando las oraciones del **Paso 1** como guía, entrevístense sobre los accidentes que les han ocurrido (*have happened*) en la vida. También deben preguntarle a su compañero/a si le pasaron otros desastres.

MODELO: ¿Te caíste por las escaleras? ¿Te hiciste daño?
¿Qué (más) te pasó/ocurrió?

SegurVita
La vida te da sorpresas...
SEGURO DE ACCIDENTES Y VIAJE
Protégete y protege a las personas que dependen de ti.

B. Un anuncio para un seguro. La palabra **seguro** no solo significa *sure.* También quiere decir *insurance.* Lea este anuncio de un seguro de accidentes y conteste las preguntas.

1. ¿Qué significa en inglés el nombre de la compañía?
2. ¿Qué tipos de accidentes se ven en los dibujos?
3. ¿Tiene usted un seguro de accidentes?

Nota cultural

Megalópolis estresantes... y pueblitos relajantes

Muchas capitales de los países hispanohablantes son hoy día inmensas megalópolis con muchos millones de habitantes. En algunas de estas ciudades llega a concentrarse[a] más del 25% de la población total del país, como es el caso de Buenos Aires (Argentina), Lima (Perú) y Santiago (Chile).

Obviamente, el estrés causado por la congestión del tráfico en estas ciudades es altísimo. Pero el exceso de tráfico conlleva[b] el problema de encontrar estacionamiento (más estrés). Algunas de estas ciudades tienen un centro histórico muy antiguo[c] en el que[d] la circulación[e] y el estacionamiento son prácticamente imposibles. Y, por supuesto[f] hay que recordar el problema de la contaminación.

Para compensar el estrés de la vida urbana, mucha gente que emigró a la ciudad en busca de[g] mejores oportunidades laborales mantiene su conexión con su pueblo, su pequeña ciudad de origen. Allí vuelven con frecuencia a ver a sus parientes, a la celebración de fiestas o simplemente a relajarse.[h]

©tose/iStock/Getty Images

Un pueblo tranquilo en los Andes peruanos

Las ciudades hispanohablantes más grandes

Área metropolitana	población (millones)
Ciudad de México	23
Buenos Aires	16
Lima	10
Bogotá	10
Santiago	7
Madrid	6

¿Cuáles son las megalópolis de los Estados Unidos? ¿Cree usted que es estresante vivir en una? ¿Por qué?

[a]llega... *becomes concentrated* [b]*brings with it* [c]*old* [d]el... *which* [e]*driving* [f]por... *of course* [g]en... *in search of* [h]*relax*

C. ¿Qué le vamos a hacer? (*What can one do?*) Indique lo que puede pasar o algo que una persona puede hacer en cada una de las siguientes situaciones. También indique expresiones que se pueden decir en cada caso.

MODELO: Una estudiante choca contra el escritorio de un compañero de clase. →
Lo que puede pasar: La estudiante se hace daño en la pierna o el pie y se cae. Las cosas del escritorio de su compañero también se caen.
Se puede decir: ¡Ay¡ ¡Qué torpe soy! ¡Perdón! ¡Fue sin querer!

1. A alguien le duele mucho la cabeza.
2. Una persona que va distraída choca con otra en la cafetería.
3. Una persona torpe se cae mientras lleva la computadora en la mano.
4. Un compañero de clase se equivocó en muchas preguntas en el último examen.
5. Una amiga se hizo daño mientras jubaga a su deporte favorito.
6. Un amigo se levantó con el pie izquierdo.

Nota comunicativa

Más sobre los adverbios: adjetivo + *-mente*

You already know the most common Spanish adverbs: words like **bien/mal, mucho/poco, siempre/nunca...**

Adverbs that end in *-ly* in English usually end in **-mente** in Spanish. The suffix **-mente** is added to the feminine singular form of adjectives. Note that the accent mark on the stem word (if there is one) is retained.

ADJETIVO	ADVERBIO	INGLÉS
rápida	**rápidamente**	*rapidly*
fácil	**fácilmente**	*easily*
paciente	**pacientemente**	*patiently*

You will use adverbs in **Práctica D.**

¡OJO!

solamente	only
últimamente	lately

D. ¿Cómo lo hacen?

Paso 1. Explique cómo hace usted las siguientes acciones, usando un adverbio basado en los adjetivos de la lista de **Vocabulario útil.**

MODELO: estudiar para las clases →
Para mis clases, estudio **constantemente.**

1. vestirse para una fiesta formal
2. esperar a los amigos que llegan tarde
3. estudiar para las clases
4. estar confundido/a en la clase de ______
5. hacer la tarea de español
6. llegar a la clase de español
7. escuchar música
8. bailar reguetón

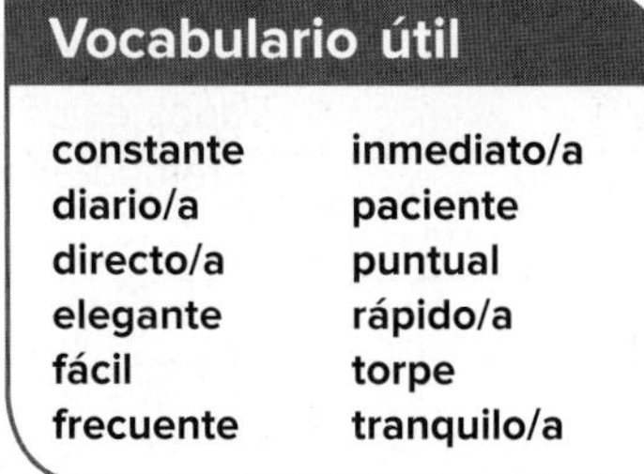

Vocabulario útil

constante	**inmediato/a**
diario/a	**paciente**
directo/a	**puntual**
elegante	**rápido/a**
fácil	**torpe**
frecuente	**tranquilo/a**

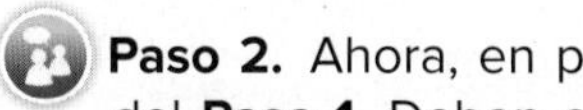

Paso 2. Ahora, en parejas, túrnense para entrevistarse sobre las acciones del **Paso 1.** Deben obtener información interesante y personal de su compañero/a.

MODELOS: estudiar para las clases → ¿Cómo estudias para tus clases en general? ¿Y para la clase de español?

Paso 3. Díganle a la clase por lo menos un detalle interesante de su compañero/a.

«¡Ay, qué estrés!» Segmento 1

Este profesor opina que siempre hay algo que perturbe (*bothers*) la mente de los estudiantes, ya sea (*be it*) lo cotidiano (*everyday things*), ya sea el nivel (*level*) económico de la familia, ya sea el tránsito (tráfico), ya sea la presión que ejercen (*exert*) los profesores en sus materias.

Antes de mirar

¿Cree usted que, en general, hay muchos estudiantes estresados en su universidad? ¿Cuáles son las cosas más estresantes para usted? ¿Qué aspectos de la vida universitaria le estresan más? ¿Qué época del año académico le provoca (*causes*) más estrés?

Este segmento

Este segmento incluye el principio del programa y un reportaje de Laura de entrevistas con estudiantes mexicanos sobre el estrés y sus causas.

Vocabulario del segmento

de nuevo	**otra vez**	**el apoyo**	support
restar a	to take away from	**mismo/a**	same; very
¿cómo anda... ?	how is ... ?	**el/la chico/a**	young person
la seguridad	security, safety	**podría**	could
presentar	to take (*a test*)	**igual salgo**	I may even leave
el parcial	midterm (exam)	**la carga**	load
el extraordinario	make-up (exam)	**la calificación**	**la nota**
la temporada	season		

Después de mirar

A. ¿Está claro? ¿Cierto o falso? Corrija las oraciones falsas.

	CIERTO	FALSO
1. La única presión que sufre Víctor tiene que ver (*has to do*) con el tráfico.	☐	☐
2. Ningún estudiante cree que el tráfico sea una causa de estrés.	☐	☐
3. Un profesor opina que conseguir dinero para poder pagarse los estudios genera estrés.	☐	☐
4. Varios estudiantes mencionan que sienten estrés durante la temporada de fútbol.	☐	☐

B. Un poco más. Conteste las siguientes preguntas.

1. ¿En qué es comparable la Ciudad de México con Los Ángeles?
2. ¿En qué época del año académico tuvieron lugar (*took place*) las entrevistas? ¿Cómo lo sabe usted?
3. ¿Qué presiones mencionan los estudiantes y los profesores?

C. Y ahora, ustedes. En parejas, comparen las respuestas de los jóvenes mexicanos con la realidad de los estudiantes en su universidad. ¿En qué son semejantes y en qué son diferentes? ¿Sufren los estudiantes de su universidad algún tipo de presiones que no se menciona en el programa?

GRAMÁTICA

39 Telling How Long or How Long Ago Something Happened

Hace... que: Another Use of **hacer**

Gramática en acción: Cusco, una ciudad histórica

©Yadid Levy/Robert Harding World Imagery/ Getty Images

La Plaza de Armas de la bella (*beautiful*) ciudad de Cusco, con vista de la Catedral y la Iglesia de la Compañía de Jesús

Cusco fue la capital del imperio de los incas. Luego, durante la dominación española, fue una importante ciudad colonial.

1. La ciudad de Cusco continúa habitada desde hace más de 3.000 años. Esto la hace la ciudad más antigua de Sudamérica.
2. Hace aproximadamente 500 años que los conquistadores españoles llegaron a Cusco por primera vez. La convirtieron en una ciudad importante de su imperio.

¿Y los Estados Unidos?

¿Cuánto tiempo hace que... ?

1. son un país independiente
2. tienen cincuenta estados
3. se independizaron de Inglaterra
4. hubo elecciones presidenciales

con el presente: (*it*) *has been happening for* [*time*]

hace + *present*, **desde hace** + *present*

Hace un año que **estudio** español.

Estudio español **desde hace** un año.

I've been studying Spanish for one year.

con el pretérito: (*it*) *happened* [*time*] *ago*

hace + *preterite*, *preterite* + **hace**

Hace un año que **empecé** a estudiar español.

Empecé a estudiar español **hace** un año.

I started studying Spanish a (*one*) *year ago.*

1. **Hace** + *time*

   In Spanish, a phrase with **hace** + *time* is used to express two perspectives on time.

   - With the *present* tense, the **hace** phrase tells how long something *has been happening*. (English uses the present perfect progressive tense for this: *has/have been* verb + *-ing for ...*)

Hace dos años **que estudio** en esta universidad.
Estudio en esta universidad **desde hace** dos años.
I've been studying at this university for two years.

¡OJO!

Use **que** when the **hace** phrase comes before the verb, **desde hace** when it comes after.

(Continúa.)

Cusco, a historic city *Cusco was the capital of the Inca Empire. Then, during the Spanish occupation, it was an important colonial city.*
1. *The city of Cusco has been continually inhabited for more than 3,000 years. That makes it the oldest city in South America.*
2. *The Spanish conquistadors arrived in Cusco for the first time about 500 years ago. They made it into an important city in their empire.*

- With the *preterite*, the **hace** phrase tells how long *ago* something *happened.*

  When the **hace** phrase comes before the verb, **que** is used with it.

> **¡OJO!**
>
> In this context, the word **hace** is invariable with a present tense or a preterite tense verb.

Hace dos años **que me gradué** en la escuela secundaria.
Me gradué en la escuela secundaria **hace** dos años.
I graduated from high school two years ago.

Hace dos años que **vivo** en el Perú.
Hace dos años que **fui** al Perú.

---

2. **Questions with *hace***

   The question **¿Cuánto tiempo hace que... ?** is used with both structures, with the present and the preterite. You can answer a question of this kind just by saying the time.

   - + *present tense* = to ask how long something *has been happening*
   - + *preterite tense* = to ask how long *ago* something *happened*

—**¿Cuánto tiempo hace que vives** aquí?
—Dos meses.
"*How long have you been living here?*"
"(*For*) *Two months.*"

—**¿Cuánto tiempo hace que te mudaste** aquí?
—Dos meses.
"*How long ago did you move here?*"
"*Two months ago.*"

Summary of Uses of *hace*

hace + *time* + **que** + *present* *present* + **desde hace** + *time*	= *has/have been doing*
hace + *time* + **que** + *preterite* *preterite* + **hace** + *time*	= *ago*

Práctica y comunicación

A. Información personal

Paso 1. Autoprueba. Empareje las oraciones con el equivalente apropiado.

a. *for x years* **b.** *x years ago*

1. _______ Hace dos años que te conozco.
2. _______ Te conocí hace dos años.
3. _______ Hace tres años que tomé cálculo.
4. _______ Hace tres años que estudio español.

Paso 2. Complete las siguientes oraciones con información personal.

1. Hace _______ que mi familia vive en el estado / la ciudad de _______.
2. Hace _______ que yo vivo en este estado.
3. Hace _______ que empecé a estudiar en esta universidad.
4. Me duché / Me bañé hace _______.
5. Vi a mi mejor amigo/a hace _______.
6. Hace _______ que practico/hago _______ (deporte o pasatiempo).

Paso 3. Ahora, en parejas, túrnense para entrevistarse sobre las ideas del **Paso 2.** Luego díganle al resto de la clase algo que tienen en común.

MODELO: **E1:** ¿Dónde vive tu familia? ¿Cuánto tiempo hace que vive en ese estado?
E2: Mi familia vive en Nevada desde hace 10 años. ¿Y tu familia?
E1: Mi familia vive en Oklahoma. Vive allí desde hace 10 años también.

B. Situaciones: ¿De qué tiene ganas?

Paso 1. Lea las siguientes situaciones. Luego indique cuánto tiempo hace que existe la situación. Finalmente, explique qué tiene(n) ganas de hacer la persona / las personas en cada circunstancia. Siga el modelo.

MODELO: Marina se levantó a las 8 de la mañana y es la una de la tarde. No tuvo tiempo de comer nada entre clase y clase. → **Hace** cinco horas **que** no come. **Tiene ganas de** comer.

Prác. A, Paso 1: Answers: 1. a 2. b 3. b 4. a

1. Manuela empezó a escribir un informe a las 5 de la tarde. Ahora son las 8 de la noche y todavía sigue escribiendo.
2. Usted y sus amigos llegaron a una fiesta a las 9 de la noche. Son las 4 de la mañana y todavía están en la fiesta.
3. Usted todavía tiene el mismo coche que tenía en el tercer año de la escuela secundaria ¡en 2011!
4. Empezó a llover el miércoles. Hoy es domingo y sigue lloviendo.

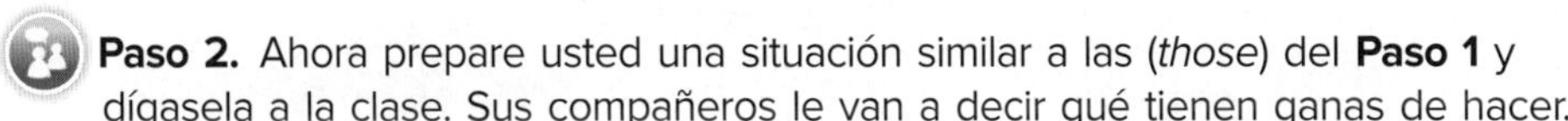

Paso 2. Ahora prepare usted una situación similar a las (*those*) del **Paso 1** y dígasela a la clase. Sus compañeros le van a decir qué tienen ganas de hacer.

C. Eventos históricos. ¿Cuánto tiempo hace que pasaron los siguientes eventos? Haga oraciones completas con las palabras indicadas. Si es necesario, mire los años en que pasaron estos eventos.*

MODELO: el primer hombre / llegar a la luna →
Hace más de cincuenta años que el primer hombre **llegó** a la luna.

1. Cristóbal Colón / llegar a América
2. la Segunda Guerra (*War*) Mundial / terminar
3. Michael Jackson / morir
4. el presidente actual / ser elegido (*to be elected*)
5. el profesor / la profesora de español / empezar a enseñar en esta universidad

D. Intercambios

Paso 1. Haga preguntas basadas en las siguientes ideas. **¡OJO!** Algunas requieren un verbo en el presente y otras un verbo en el pretérito.

MODELOS: vivir en esta ciudad →
¿Cuánto tiempo hace que **vives** en esta ciudad?
visitar a sus abuelos la última vez →
¿Cuánto tiempo hace que **visitaste** a tus abuelos la última vez?

1. vivir en esta ciudad
2. asistir a esta universidad
3. vivir en su apartamento/casa/residencia
4. estudiar español
5. escribir el último trabajo para una de sus clases
6. conocer a su mejor amigo/a
7. visitar a sus abuelos (a ¿ ?) la última vez
8. sacar una mala nota

Paso 2. Ahora use las preguntas del **Paso 1** para entrevistar a un compañero o una compañera de clase. Luego díganle a la clase un detalle interesante.

¿Recuerda usted?

You have learned a number of uses for the word **se.** Match each function of **se** with the appropriate sentence.

1. _____ Los niños tienen que bañar**se** ahora.
2. _____ Los amigos **se** quieren mucho.
3. _____ ¿El regalo? **Se** lo di a Ana ayer.
4. _____ Aquí **se** habla español.

a. to express *one* or *you*
b. to replace the indirect object pronoun **le** or **les** before **lo/la/los/las**
c. to express a reflexive action
d. to express a reciprocal action

In **Gramática 40** you will learn another use for the word **se.**

***Prác. C:* Los años:** MODELO: 1969 **1.** 1492 **2.** 1945 **3.** 2009 **4.** ¿ ? **5.** ¿ ?

Algo sobre...

la marinera

©Ernesto Benavides/AFP/Getty Images

¡En esta marinera el hombre baila en un caballo!

Como casi todos los países hispanohablantes, el Perú también tiene su danza particular,[a] que es un símbolo nacional: la marinera. Es un baile originario de la costa (de ahí[b] su nombre), y se baila en pareja. Es un baile de cortejo,[c] en el que[d] típicamente el hombre trata de seducir a la mujer.

Hay varios tipos de marinera, según la región. Por ejemplo, la marinera limeña, es decir, de la ciudad de Lima, se baila con un pañuelo[e] en la mano. En la hermosa ciudad colonial de Trujillo, hay un famoso concurso[f] anual de marineras.

¿Hay algún tipo de música o folclore en su país en que participen caballos u otros animales?

[a]*unique* [b]de... *that's where... comes from* [c]*courtship* [d]el... *which* [e]*handkerchief* [f]*contest*

40 Expressing Unplanned or Unexpected Events

Another Use of **se**

Gramática en acción: Un día terrible

1. A Diego se le cayó la taza de café.

2. A Antonio se le olvidaron los libros.

3. A Antonio y a Diego se les olvidó apagar las luces del coche.

¿Y usted?

¿También pasó un día terrible ayer? Para describir su día, indique si las siguientes oraciones son ciertas o falsas.

	CIERTO	FALSO
1. Se me perdió algo.	☐	☐
2. Se me olvidó hacer algo importante.	☐	☐
3. Se me cayeron algunas cosas.	☐	☐
4. Se me rompió algo de valor (*value*).	☐	☐

El *se* accidental

A + Noun (A + Pronoun)	**se**	**Indirect Object Pronoun**	**Verb**	**Subject**
A Antonio	se	le	olvid**an**	las llaves muchas veces.
A Carmen y a mí	se	nos	olvid**ó**	cerrar el coche con llave.
A los estudiantes	se	les	olvid**ó**	el examen.
(A mí)	Se	me	olvid**a**	entregar la tarea a veces.
(A ti)	Se	te	olvid**aba**	la tarea con frecuencia cuando eras pequeño.
(A nosotros)	Se	nos	olvid**aron**	los informes ayer.
(A ustedes/ellos/ellas)	Se	les	olvid**a**	estudiar los fines de semana.

1. Using *se* to Express Accidental Events

Unplanned or unexpected events (*I dropped ... , We lost ... , You forgot ...*) are frequently expressed in Spanish with **se** and a third person form of the verb. The event is viewed as happening *to* someone—the unwitting "victim" of the action. This structure is called the *accidental* ***se*** (**el *se* accidental**).

Se **me** **cayó** el papel.
I dropped the paper. (The paper slipped out of my hands. [I didn't drop it on purpose.])

Se **te** **olvidó** llamar a tu hija.
You forgot to call your daughter. (Calling your daughter slipped your mind.)

A mi hermano **se** **le** **olvidaron** las llaves.
My brother forgot the keys. (It slipped his mind to bring them.)

A terrible day 1. *Diego dropped a cup of coffee.* ***2.*** *Antonio forgot his books.* ***3.*** *Antonio and Diego forgot to turn off the car headlights.*

2. **Agreement with the Subject**

In these kinds of sentences, as with **gustar** and similar verbs, the subject of the sentence is the thing that is dropped, forgotten, and so on. The subject usually follows the verb.

- When the subject is singular, the verb will be singular, even if the "victim" is plural.
- When the subject is plural, the verb will be plural, even if the "victim" is singular.

> **¡OJO!**
>
> Remember that an infinitive is a singular subject:
> **A los niños se les olvidó llamar a su madre.**

Se me **cayó la computadora**.
My computer fell.

Se me **cayeron los libros**.
My books fell.

Al niño **se le olvidó el cumpleaños** de su madre.
The child forgot his mother's birthday.

A los niños **se les olvidó el cumpleaños** de su madre.
The children forgot their mother's birthday.

A Antonio **se le perdieron los apuntes.**
Antonio forgot his notes.

A Antonio y Diego **se les perdieron los apuntes.**
Antonio and Diego forgot their notes.

3. **Parts of the Sentence**

- An accidental **se** sentence must have:

(No) **Se** *IO pronoun* *verb* *subject*

Notice that **no** comes before **se.**

- When the "victim" is specifically named (with a noun or a person's name), the sentence will also have an **a** + *name/noun* phrase**: a Tomás / a los Sres. Pérez / al gato / a los niños.**

A + *name/noun* **(no)** **se** *IO pronoun* *verb* *subject*

Se le rompió el brazo.
He/She broke his/her arm.

No se le rompió el brazo.
He/She didn't break his/her arm.

A Ana / **A la niña** se **le** rompió el brazo.
Ana / The child broke her arm.

- The indirect object pronoun can be clarified or emphasized with an **a** + *pronoun* phrase: **a mí, a ti, a usted/él/ella, a nosotros, a vosotros, a ustedes/ellos/ellas.**

A + *pronoun* **(no)** **se** *IO pronoun* *verb* *subject*

- The phrase **a** + *name/noun/pronoun* can appear at the beginning or the end of the **se** sentence.

¡Y luego **a ti** se **te** cae el café! ¡Y luego se **te** cae el café **a ti**!
*And then **you** drop the coffee!*

A ella se **le** rompió el brazo.
She broke her arm.

A ella/Ana se **le** olvidó el informe.
Se **le** olvidó el informe **a ella/a Ana**.

¡**A mí** todo se **me** olvida!
¡Se **me** olvida todo **a mí**!

4. **Verbs Frequently Used with *se***

Here are some verbs frequently used in this construction. The verbs marked with * are new.

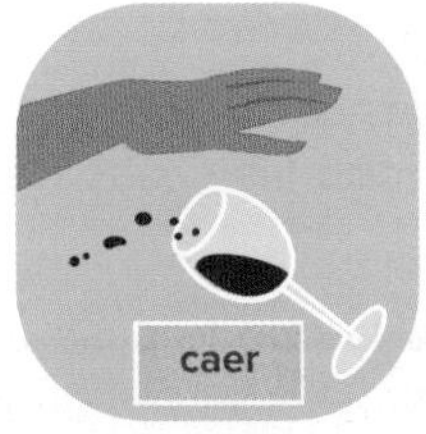

***acabar**	to finish; to run out of
caer	to fall; to drop
olvidar	to forget
perder (pierdo)	to lose
***quedar**	to remain, be left
romper	to break

5. **Accident Versus Intent**

This structure is used to emphasize the accidental nature of an event. When the speaker wishes to emphasize *who* committed the act, or that the act was intentional, that person becomes the subject of the verb and the **se** structure is not used.

Se me rompió el plato.
The plate broke on me. (accidentally)

(Yo) Rompí el plato.
I broke the plate. (emphasizes either who broke the plate or the intentionality of the act)

Summary of *el se accidental*

a + *noun* + **se** + *indirect object pronoun* + *verb* + *subject*
(**a** + *pronoun*) **se** + *indirect object pronoun* + *verb* + *subject*

Práctica y comunicación

A. ¿Algo deliberado o accidental?

Paso 1. Autoprueba. Empareje las oraciones de las dos columnas.

1. _______ No encuentro las llaves.	**a.** Se te rompió.
2. _______ Tu calculadora no funciona.	**b.** Se me acabó.
3. _______ Paco no entregó la tarea.	**c.** Se me perdieron.
4. _______ Necesito comprar leche.	**d.** Se le olvidó.

Paso 2. Indique si a usted le ocurrieron los siguientes accidentes o hizo las siguientes acciones.

1. ☐ Se me rompió algo de otra persona sin querer.
2. ☐ Rompí algo de alguien, con intención de hacerlo.
3. ☐ Se me cayó un plato de comida sin querer.
4. ☐ Tiré (*I threw*) comida a la basura porque no me gustaba.
5. ☐ Se me perdió algo de un ex novio / una ex novia.
6. ☐ Quemé (*I burned*) o rompí algo de un ex novio / una ex novia.

Paso 3. Ahora, en parejas, túrnense para entrevistarse sobre las acciones del **Paso 2.** Luego díganle al resto de la clase algo que tienen en común.

MODELO: **E1:** ¿Se te rompió algo de otra persona sin querer?
E2: Sí. ¿Y a ti se te rompió algo de otra persona sin querer?
E1: También. → A nosotros se nos rompieron cosas de otras personas sin querer.

B. ¡Qué distraída!

Paso 1. Hortensia es muy distraída y siempre se le olvida hacer muchas cosas importantes antes de salir de viaje. Empareje los olvidos (*lapses*) de Hortensia con las consecuencias.

OLVIDOS	CONSECUENCIAS
1. ______ Se le olvida cerrar la puerta de su casa.	**a.** Va a perder el trabajo.
2. ______ Se le olvida pagar las cuentas.	**b.** No va a poder leer los documentos de inmigración.
3. ______ Se le olvida cancelar el correo (*mail*).	**c.** Le van a suspender el servicio de la electricidad y del gas… ¡y cancelar sus tarjetas de crédito!
4. ______ Se le olvida pedirle permiso a su jefa (*boss*).	**d.** Alguien le va a robar las cosas de valor (*value*).
5. ______ Se le olvidan las gafas de leer.	**e.** No va a tener dónde pasar la noche.
6. ______ Se le olvida hacer reserva en un hotel.	**f.** Todos van a saber que no está en casa.

Paso 2. Ahora ponga las oraciones de las dos columnas en el pretérito, para narrar lo que le pasó a Hortensia cuando fue al Perú.

MODELO: 1. Se le olvida cerrar la puerta. Alguien le va a robar las cosas de valor.
→ Se le **olvidó** cerrar la puerta. Por eso alguien le **robó** las cosas de valor.

C. Una mañana terrible. Complete la siguiente descripción de lo que le pasó a Pablo ayer. **¡OJO!** Use el **se** accidental.

Pablo tuvo una mañana terrible. Primero _______ (olvidar[1]) poner el despertador. Se levantó tarde y se vistió rápidamente. No cerró bien su maletín;[a] por eso _______ (caer[2]) unos papeles importantes. Recogió los papeles y subió al coche, pero después de cinco minutos, _______ (acabar[3])

[a]*briefcase*

***Prác. A, Paso 1:** Answers: 1. c 2. a 3. d 4. b*

la gasolina y se le paró[b] el coche. Dejó el coche en la calle y decidió ir a pie. Llevaba el maletín en una mano y las llaves y un documento urgente en la otra. Desgraciadamente, en el camino[c] _______ (perder[4]) el documento. Cuando llegó a la oficina, buscó a su jefe[d] para entregarle el documento pero no podía encontrarlo entre sus papeles. Cansado y enojado, cerró el maletín sin cuidado y _______ (romper[5]) los lentes.

[b]se... (*the car*) *stopped on him* [c]en... *on the way* [d]*boss*

D. Unos dichos (*colloquial expressions*) hispanos. El **se** accidental se usa en muchos dichos en español. En parejas, traten de dar su equivalente en inglés. Luego emparejen los dichos con la situación apropiada.

DICHOS

a. Se le hace la boca agua.
b. Se le hacía tarde.
c. Se le cayó el alma (*soul*) a los pies.
d. Se le fue la lengua.
e. Se le acabó la paciencia.
f. Se le cae la baba (*drool*) por (algo o alguien).

SITUACIONES

1. La clase empezaba a las dos. Eran las dos menos veinte y Raúl todavía estaba en la ducha. A Raúl _____
2. Ramón le contó a María un secreto, pero María se lo dijo a Luisa. A María _____
3. La hija de Carmen es preciosa. A Carmen _____
4. Julio tiene muchísimas ganas de comer la comida de su madre. ¡Qué rica! Solo de pensarlo, a Julio _____
5. «¡Ya no más! (*Enough already!*)», gritó (*screamed*) la madre. «Vete a tu cuarto ahora mismo.» A la madre _____
6. Una joven tuvo un grave accidente. A su padre _____

E. ¡Desastres por todas partes (*everywhere*)!

Paso 1. ¿Es usted una persona distraída o torpe? Indique las oraciones que describen lo que le pasa a usted. Cambie algunos de los detalles de las oraciones si es necesario. **¡OJO!** Se usa el presente para hablar de acciones típicas.

1. ☐ Con frecuencia se me caen los libros (los platos,...).
2. ☐ Se me pierden constantemente las llaves (los calcetines,...).
3. ☐ Siempre se me rompen los lentes (las lámparas,...).
4. ☐ A veces se me quedan los libros (los cuadernos,...) en el salón de clase.
5. ☐ Se me olvida fácilmente mi horario (el nombre de alguien,...).

Paso 2. ¿Es usted igual ahora que cuando era más joven? Complete cada oración del **Paso 1** para describir cómo era de niño/a. **¡OJO!** Use el imperfecto.

MODELO: De niño/a, (no) se me **caían** los libros con frecuencia.

Paso 3. Ahora compare sus respuestas con las (*those*) de un compañero o una compañera. ¿Quién es más distraído/a o torpe ahora? ¿Quién era así de niño/a?

F. Encuesta (*Poll*): Accidentes de la semana

Paso 1. Haga una lista de cinco accidentes o cosas que ocurren con frecuencia en la vida diaria y que a nosotros nos parecen desastres. Debe usar por lo menos tres verbos diferentes.

MODELO: perder las llaves de la casa o apartamento

Paso 2. Ahora hágales cinco preguntas a cinco personas de la clase sobre los accidentes o desastres del **Paso 1.** Luego dígale a la clase cuál fue el accidente o desastre más común.

MODELO: perder las llaves de la casa o apartamento →
La semana pasada, ¿se te perdieron las llaves de la casa o apartamento?

Algo sobre...

el cajón

©Xinhua/Alamy

Un grupo que toca el cajón peruano

El cajón es un instrumento de percusión similar a una caja.[a] Originalmente fue creado[b] por los descendientes de esclavos africanos en la zona costera[c] peruana. Hoy es un instrumento muy popular que se usa en la música afroperuana y también en la música de otros países, incluyendo el flamenco en España.

¿Qué instrumento musical considera usted más emblemático de su país? ¿En qué tipo de música se utiliza?

[a]*box* [b]*created* [c]*coastal*

¿Recuerda usted?

Review what you know about **por** and **para** by completing these sentences.

1. ¡Gracias para/por el regalo!
2. Esta comida es para/por ti.
3. ¿Trabajas para/por la noche?
4. Tomo cinco clases. Para/Por eso tengo mucha tarea.
5. Para/Por aprender, hay que estudiar.
6. Dame el plato, para/por favor.
7. ¡Para/Por fin conocí al novio de mi compañera!
8. El informe es para/por mañana.

You will learn more about using these prepositions in **Gramática 41.**

41 *¿Por o para?*

A Summary of Their Uses

Gramática en acción: Ideas sobre la educación

¡Que no haya niñ@s sin una buena educación!

Escuelas públicas

financiadas por tod@s

con acceso para tod@s

A

Unidos[a] por la educación para asegurar[b] el futuro de nuestros hijos

Asociación de Madres y Padres de Alumnos de Escuelas Primarias

B [a]*United* [b]*secure*

Lea los anuncios sobre la educación. ¿Cuál de los dos anuncios expresa las siguientes ideas sobre la educación?

1. La educación nos conecta.
2. La educación no debe ser solo para algunas personas.
3. Un buen sistema educativo es muy importante para el progreso de un país.
4. Los ciudadanos (*citizens*) de un país son parte del sistema educativo.
5. Un buen sistema educativo es una tarea nacional.

¿Y usted?

Para usted, ¿qué otras cosas son «de tod@s y para tod@s»?

You have been using **por** and **para** since you started to study Spanish. Each preposition has some English equivalents that are unique to it, making it easy to decide between them in those cases. However, both **por** and **para** can mean *for*, depending on the context. You already know much of the information in this section.

Por

1. Unique Meanings of *por*

The preposition **por** has a number of English equivalents that are not expressed with *for* in English. **Para** can never express these meanings.

• *by / by means of*	El libro fue escrito **por Mario Vargas Llosa.** *The book was written by Mario Vargas Llosa.* Nos hablamos **por teléfono** mañana. *We'll talk by (on the) phone tomorrow.*
• *through/along*	Me gusta pasear **por el parque** y **por la playa.** *I like to stroll through the park and along the beach.*
• *during/in* (time of day)	Trabajo **por la mañana.** *I work in the morning.*
• *because of / due to*	Estoy nervioso **por la entrevista.** *I'm nervous because of the interview.*

2. For = *Por*

When it expresses *for,* **por** looks back at the *reason* or *cause* for something. To remember this, think of the interrogative **¿por qué?** = *why?* and the expressions **por eso...** (*that's why...*) and **gracias por...** (*thanks for...*).

• *for = for the sake of, on behalf of*	Lo hago **por ti.** *I'm doing it for you (for your sake).*
• *for = in place of*	No puedo tomar el examen **por ti.** *I can't take the exam for you (in your place).*
• *for = in exchange for*	Piden 1.000 dólares **por el coche.** *They're asking $1,000 for the car.* **Gracias por todo.** *Thanks for everything.*
• *for = period of time* (often omitted)	Vivieron allí (**por**) **un año.** *They lived there for a year.*

3. Fixed Expressions with *por*

Por is used in the expressions to the right, some of which (like **por eso** and **por si acaso**) express the *reason* or *cause* of something. The expressions marked with * are new.

***por Dios**	for heaven's sake
***por ejemplo**	for example
por eso	that's why
por favor	please
por fin	finally
por lo general	generally, in general
por lo menos	at least
***por primera/última vez**	for the first/last time
***por si acaso**	just in case
***¡por supuesto!**	of course!
***por todas partes**	everywhere

Para

1. Unique Meaning of *para*

The preposition **para** has one English equivalent that is not expressed with *for* in English. **Por** can never express this meaning.

- *in order to + infinitive*

Regresaron pronto **para estudiar.**
They returned soon (in order) to study.

Estudian **para conseguir** un buen trabajo.
They're studying (in order) to get a good job.

---

2. For = *Para*

When it expresses *for,* **para** looks ahead, toward the *goal, purpose,* or *destination* of something. To remember this, think of the interrogative **¿para qué?** = *for what purpose?*

- *for = destined for / to be given to*

Todo esto es **para ti.**
All this is for you.

Le di un libro **para su hijo.**
I gave her a book for her son.

- *for = by* (deadline, specified future time)

Para mañana, estudien ***por*** y ***para.***
For tomorrow, study **por** *and* **para.**

La composición es **para el lunes.**
The composition is for Monday.

- *for = toward / in the direction of*

Salió **para el Perú** ayer.
She left for Peru yesterday.

- *for = to be used for, purpose*

El dinero es **para la matrícula.**
The money is for tuition.

Es un vaso **para agua.**
It's a water glass.

> **¡OJO!**
>
> Compare the second example to **un vaso de agua** = *a glass (full) of water.*

- *for = as compared with / in relation to others*

Para mí, el español es fácil.
For me, Spanish is easy.

Para (ser) **extranjera**, habla muy bien el inglés.
For (being) a foreigner, she speaks English very well.

- *for = in the employ of, in preparation for*

Trabajan **para el gobierno.**
They work for the government.

Estudio **para (la carrera de) dentista.**
I'm studying to be (for a career as) a dentist.

Summary of *por* and *para*

por: reason or cause
for; by / by means of, through / along, during / in, because of / due to

para: goal, purpose, or destination
for; in order to

Práctica y comunicación

A. *¿Por o para?*

Paso 1. Autoprueba. ¿Con qué preposición asocia usted las siguientes frases?

1. _____ gracias
2. _____ una fecha en el futuro
3. _____ durante
4. _____ la persona que creó algo
5. _____ con el propósito (*purpose, goal*) de
6. _____ en lugar de otra persona
7. _____ a causa de
8. _____ a lo largo de (*along*)
9. _____ trabajar en una compañía
10. _____ pagar dinero
11. _____ en comparación con otros
12. _____ una carrera

***Prác. A, Paso 1:* Answers:** *1.* por *2.* para *3.* por *4.* por *5.* para *6.* por *7.* por *8.* por *9.* para *10.* por *11.* para *12.* para

Paso 2. Complete las siguientes oraciones con **por** o **para.**

1. ¿_____ qué organización o compañía trabaja tu padre/madre?
2. ¿Estudias mejor _____ la mañana o _____ la tarde?
3. ¿_____ qué calles pasas para llegar a esta clase?
4. ¿Cuánto pagaste _____ tu celular?
5. ¿_____ qué sirve hablar español en los Estados Unidos?
6. ¿_____ cuándo es la próxima tarea de español?
7. ¿_____ qué profesión estudias?
8. ¿Estás nervioso/a _____ el examen final en esta clase?

Paso 3. Ahora, en parejas, túrnense para hacer y contestar las preguntas del **Paso 2.** Luego díganle a la clase algo que tienen en común.

B. Situaciones

Paso 1. Complete las siguientes oraciones con **por** o **para.** Luego empareje las preguntas/situaciones con las respuestas apropiadas.

PREGUNTAS/SITUACIONES

1. _____ —¡Uf! Vengo de jugar un partido de basquetbol. ¡Jugamos _____ dos horas!
2. _____ —¿No vas a comer nada? _____ lo menos un sándwich.
3. _____ —¡Cuánto lo siento, don Javier! Sé que llegué tarde a la cita. Discúlpeme.
4. _____ —Es imposible que tome el examen hoy, _____ muchas razones.
5. _____ —¿No lo oíste? Juana acaba de tener un accidente horrible.
6. _____ —¡Pero, papá, quiero ir!
7. _____ —Ay, Mariana, ¿sabes que hubo un tornado? Murieron dos personas.

RESPUESTAS

a. —¡ _____ Dios! ¡Qué desgracia!
b. —Te digo que no, _____ última vez.
c. —No se preocupe. Lo importante es que _____ fin está aquí.
d. —¡ _____ Dios! ¿Qué pasó? ¿Está bien?
e. —No, gracias. No tengo mucha hambre y además (*besides*) tengo que irme en seguida.
f. —¿ _____ ejemplo? Dígame...
g. —Ah, _____ eso tienes tanto calor.

Paso 2. Ahora, en parejas, lean las preguntas/situaciones y respuestas. Luego inventen un breve contexto para cada diálogo. ¿Dónde están las personas que hablan? ¿Quiénes son? ¿Por qué dicen lo que dicen?

C. Una organización por la equidad

Paso 1. Lea la siguiente descripción de una ONG (organización no gubernamental) que promueve (*promotes*) la equidad en la educación. Luego explique por qué se usa **por** y **para** en cada contexto.

Paso 2. Ahora, en parejas, usen las siguientes ideas y el vocabulario del texto en el **Paso 1** para hablar de su participación en organizaciones o asociaciones. Hagan otras preguntas pertinentes para obtener información relevante.

Hablen de...

1. si son miembros de alguna asociación u ONG y qué causa defiende o promueve
2. por qué les interesa esa causa
3. qué tipo de personas la integran (*are members of it*)
4. cómo colaboran ustedes
5. dónde se puede encontrar más información sobre esa organización o asociación

ASOCIACIÓN POR LA EQUIDAD EDUCATIVA
por una educación justa e inclusiva

Para algunas personas el acceso a la educación es muy difícil. Por eso surgió[a] la Asociación por la Equidad Educativa, una ONG que está integrada[b] por estudiantes, educadores, personas expertas en educación, madres y padres que aspiran a que haya mayor igualdad de oportunidades educativas para todo el mundo, sin distinciones. Esta asociación trabaja para crear opciones educativas y promover[c] la coordinación de iniciativas diversas. AEE está presente en muchas escuelas y universidades por todo el país.

Para obtener más información, entra en www.equidadeducativa.com.

[a]*emerged* [b]una... *an NGO made up, consisting of* [c]*promote*

Algo sobre...

Mario Vargas Llosa

Mario Vargas Llosa (Arequipa, Perú, 1936–) es uno de los escritores e intelectuales de la lengua castellana[a] más famosos e influyentes de las últimas generaciones. Su reconocimiento[b] es mundial. Novelista y ensayista, Vargas Llosa ha recibido[c] numerosos premios,[d] entre ellos el Premio Nobel de Literatura. El tono de sus obras va de lo trágico a lo más cómico, pero sus obras más importantes se enfocan en el abuso del poder[e] en los gobiernos,[f] especialmente las dictaduras.

¿Puede usted nombrar a algunos escritores de su país que se consideran influyentes en todo el mundo?

[a]española [b]*recognition* [c]ha... *has received* [d]*awards, prizes* [e]*power* [f]*governments*

©Jonathan Nackstrand/AFP/Getty Images

Mario Vargas Llosa, quien recibió el Premio Nobel de Literatura en 2010

D. Más sobre Mario Vargas Llosa. Complete las siguientes oraciones con la preposición apropiada para saber más sobre este importante escritor peruano.

1. Mario Vargas Llosa recibió el Premio Nobel _______ (por / para) sus novelas.
2. Es obvio que _______ (para / por) el año 2010 Vargas Llosa ya era famoso.
3. _______ (Para / Por) este escritor, la estabilidad democrática de Latinoamérica es muy importante.
4. _______ (Para / Por) ser escritor, Vargas Llosa es muy famoso _______ (para / por) mucha gente.
5. _______ (Para / Por) sus ensayos, podemos saber de sus preocupaciones políticas y sociales.
6. _______ (Para / Por) muchos críticos y expertos, Vargas Llosa es uno de los mejores escritores de la lengua castellana de los últimos cincuenta años.

E. Entreviste a su profesor(a). Hágale preguntas a su profesor(a) para saber la siguiente información.

1. la tarea para mañana y para la semana que viene
2. lo que hay que estudiar para el próximo examen
3. si para él/ella son interesantes o aburridas las ciencias
4. lo que piensa de la pronunciación de ustedes, para ser principiantes (*beginners*)
5. qué deben hacer ustedes para mejorar su pronunciación del español
6. cuánto tiempo deben ustedes dedicar todos los días a practicar el español

F. Preguntas con *por* y *para*

Paso 1. Complete las siguientes frases con **por** o **para.**

1. prepararse _____ una profesión
2. estar nervioso/a _____ algo
3. trabajar _____ una compañía
4. hablar _____ teléfono con frecuencia
5. tener algo que hacer _____ mañana
6. pasear _____ el campus
7. tener algo que comprar _____ su casa/apartamento/cuarto
8. la idea de pagar mil dólares _____ un abrigo
9. tener algo que hacer _____ alguien
10. la idea de vivir en un sitio _____ toda la vida

Paso 2. Ahora, en parejas, hagan y contesten preguntas, usando las frases del **Paso 1.**

MODELO: prepararse _______ una profesión →
¿Sabes para qué profesión estás preparándote?

Todo junto

A. Lengua y cultura: De turismo por el Perú

Paso 1. Completar. Complete the following passage with the correct form of the words in parentheses, as suggested by context. When two possibilities are given in parentheses, select the correct word. **¡OJO!** As you conjugate the verbs in this activity, use the **usted** command when you see *comm:* in front of the infinitive. For other verbs, you will decide whether to use the present indicative or subjunctive, the preterite or imperfect, or simply the infinitive. Context will indicate which forms to use.

Machu Picchu, la ciudad imperial de los incas durante el siglo XV (1400–1500)

¿Le interesa la historia? ¿Le ______ (gusta / gustan[1]) los lugares espirituales? Entonces, ______ (*comm:* ir[2]) a Machu Picchu. ______ (Son / Están[3]) las ruinas de una antigua ciudad inca que ______ (es / está[4]) en ______ (el / la[5]) corazón de los Andes, cerca de Cusco. No es fácil ______ (llegue / llegar[6]) a ese lugar. ______ (Por / Para[7]) eso ______ (se / la[8]) llaman «la ciudad perdida[a] de los incas.» En el pasado, ______ (ser[9]) a la vez[b] lugar de refugio y de vacaciones de los reyes[c] y nobles incas. Después de la llegada de los españoles, esta ciudad fue ignorada y ______ (estar[10]) oculta[d] hasta que Hiram Bingham, un profesor y explorador estadounidense, la ______ (encontrar[11]) en 1911. ______ (Hacer[12]) un siglo[e] que Machu Picchu es un sitio famoso y un atractivo destino turístico ______ (por / para[13]) muchas personas de todas partes del mundo.

Pero Machu Picchu no ______ (es / está[14]) el único lugar interesante que se puede visitar en el Perú. Si visita ______ (el / la[15]) país con tiempo suficiente, le recomendamos que ______ (hacer[16]) una excursión ______ (por / para[17]) la selva.[f] También ______ (*comm:* viajar[18]) al desierto de Atacama, el lugar más árido ______ (en el / del[19]) mundo que está en Chile. Además,[g] ______ (*comm:* pasar[20]) unos días en las playas de Mancora y Cabo Blanco. ______ (*Comm:* Hacer[21]) un viaje fabuloso que ______ (nunca / siempre[22]) va a olvidar. Esperamos que ______ (*usted:* poder[23]) ir con alguien muy especial para ______ (usted / ustedes[24]). ______ (Sabemos / Conocemos[25]) que el Perú ______ (les / los[26]) va a fascinar.

[a]*lost* [b]*a... at the same time* [c]*kings* [d]*hidden* [e]*century* [f]*jungle* [g]*In addition*

Paso 2. Comprensión. Las siguientes oraciones son falsas. Corríjalas con información de la lectura.

1. El actual rey del Perú vive en Machu Picchu.
2. Es fácil llegar a Machu Picchu.
3. Hiram Bingham fue un explorador español.
4. Machu Picchu es el único sitio de interés turístico en el Perú.
5. Para los turistas, no es nada atractivo viajar al Perú.

Paso 3. En acción

Ahora, en parejas, piensen en algún lugar considerado sagrado o espiritual en su campus, ciudad, estado o país. ¿Quiénes lo consideran así (*that way*)? ¿Por qué? ¿Lo visita mucha gente? ¿De dónde son esos visitantes?

ENCUESTA

B. Proyecto: Encuesta sobre la vida universitaria

¿Cómo es la vida de los estudiantes en su campus? ¿Lo pasan bien en general o sufren de mucho estrés por las presiones académicas o sociales?

Paso 1. Preparación. En parejas, elijan uno de los siguientes temas relacionados con la vida universitaria para encuestar a sus compañeros de clase:

- una semana típica
- un semestre o trimestre típico
- «accidentes» frecuentes
- las presiones que sufren los estudiantes

Piensen bien en el objetivo (u objetivos) de su encuesta. Por ejemplo, si el tema es la semana típica, la encuesta puede enfocarse en la cantidad y el tipo de trabajo que hacen los estudiantes durante una semana.

Preparen una serie de 3 a 5 preguntas específicas, que pueden tener una variedad de formatos. Para ser más útiles, las preguntas deben incluir una escala o pedir información personal.

MODELOS: —¿Te sientes estresado/a esta semana? Contesta con un número del 1 al 5. 1 significa nada o casi nada y 5 significa muchísimo.
—Ordena las siguientes cosas de mayor a menor según la ansiedad que te causan: los exámenes, la vida social…

Paso 2. Encuesta. Háganles sus preguntas a varios compañeros de clase. Antes de empezar a preguntar, deben tener un plan para apuntar (*write down*) las respuestas.

Paso 3. Análisis de datos. Con la información de la encuesta, preparen una breve presentación y análisis de los datos. Incluyan una valoración (*assessment*) del grupo sobre los datos.

Vocabulario útil

la importancia
la necesidad

demostrar (demuestro)	to show
sugerir (sugiero) (i) + indicativo	to suggest; to show

según
x veces al día / a la semana / al mes

¡Ahora, yo!

A. Use de modelo las preguntas y respuestas de la página 419 de este capítulo para hablar de las presiones que usted sufre y lo que hace para reducir su nivel de estrés.

B. Filme dos entrevistas con personas de su universidad (estudiantes, profesores o personal universitario) que hablan del estrés que sufren y sus causas.

«¡Ay, qué estrés!» Segmento 2

Antes de mirar

Indique todas las cosas que usted asocia con las supersticiones o creencias (*beliefs*). ¿Cree usted en alguna?

_______ los amuletos
_______ pasar por debajo de una escalera (*ladder*)
_______ un gato negro
_______ cruzar los dedos
_______ un trébol (*clover*) de cuatro hojas
_______ rezar (*to pray*) a Dios
_______ otro

Ana le tiene cariño a (*is fond of*) este objeto que le regaló su abuela: « ...sin darme cuenta (*without realizing it*) lo toco cuando estoy nerviosa. Y como creo que tienes envidia de mí, le pedí a mi mamá que me mandara (*to send*) uno para ti».

Este segmento

Laura entrevista a varios jóvenes mexicanos sobre sus supersticiones y creencias. Luego Ana le da un objeto especial a Víctor.

Vocabulario del segmento

podría hacerse rico/a	could become rich	**prevenir (like venir)**	to prevent
las horas punta	rush hours	**encomendarse a Dios (me encomiendo)**	to entrust (oneself) to God
dispuesto/a	ready and willing	**fuerte**	hard
invertir (invierto) (i)	to invest	**San Miguel Arcángel**	St. Michael the Archangel
evitar	to avoid	**proteger (protejo)**	to protect
mejorar	to improve	**contra todo mal**	against all evil
la fe	**la religión**		

Fragmento del guion

Bueno, yo creo que aquí sí se van a reír porque sí tengo muchas cosas que, entre comillas,[a] me ayudan a pasar mis exámenes y dentro de ellas están los amuletos y mis creencias religiosas personales, no que... Bueno, aquí se van a percatar[b] que son bastantes[c] cosas que significan muchas cosas en chino, este, hindú, este, en hebreo, este tibetano, cristiano, este... O sea,[d] viene un poquito de todo, que es como que... una protección general hacia[e] lo que... en general, no tanto para la escuela como para la vida diaria.

[a]entre... *in quotation marks* [b]*notice* [c]*quite a lot of* [d]O... *That is* [e]*toward*

Después de mirar

A. ¿Está claro? Las siguientes oraciones son falsas. Corríjalas.

1. La mayoría de los estudiantes entrevistados es superticiosa.
2. Ninguno de los estudiantes del reportaje es religioso.
3. Es obvio que Víctor es supersticioso.
4. Ana dice que tiene un amuleto que le pertenecía (*used to belong*) a su abuela.

B. Un poco más. Haga una lista de todos los objetos, amuletos y acciones que mencionan los estudiantes supersticiosos del reportaje.

C. Y ahora, ustedes. En parejas, hablen de si ustedes son superticiosos o no. Si lo son, ¿qué amuletos tienen o qué hacen ustedes para tener buena suerte y evitar la mala suerte? Si no son supersticiosos, expliquen por qué.

MUNDO HISPANO

Enfoque cultural: El Perú

Antes de leer

¿Qué cuestiones (*topics*) sociales son motivo de ansiedad entre la gente de su ciudad, estado o país?

Las preocupaciones de los peruanos

Como ocurre en todos los países, hay múltiples cuestiones que les causan ansiedad a los peruanos. El tema de la educación es una de estas cuestiones. La educación pública requiere una mayor inversión[a] de dinero para que[b] el sistema sea más efectivo y sirva a todos. Además,[c] se necesita que los maestros[d] tengan mejores salarios.

El tema de los salarios es otra de las serias preocupaciones de muchos peruanos. En el Perú existe la Remuneración Mínima Vital, que es el salario mínimo establecido[e] por la ley.[f] Es el salario que recibe gran parte de los trabajadores[g] peruanos, pero que para muchos de ellos no resulta suficiente para cubrir[h] sus gastos cotidianos.[i]

[a]*investment* [b]para... *so that* [c]*In addition* [d]*teachers* [e]*established* [f]*law* [g]*workers* [h]*cover* [i]*daily*

En otros países hispanos

- **La emigración** Casi todos los países hispanohablantes han sufrido[a] condiciones políticas y económicas que provocaron la emigración de su gente. Con frecuencia los hispanohablantes emigran a otro país donde se habla español. Este es el caso de España. Durante la Guerra[b] Civil española (1936–1939), muchos españoles se exiliaron a México y la Argentina. En cambio,[c] en la última década del siglo XX y la primera del XXI, España, por su bonanza económica, se convirtió en un país receptor de inmigrantes latinoamericanos. Sin embargo, con la crisis reciente de la economía española, muchos jóvenes españoles volvieron a mirar a Latinoamérica como una opción.
- **En todo el mundo hispanohablante** Según las creencias populares, los siguientes acontecimientos[d] traen mala suerte.

[a]han... *have experienced* [b]*War* [c]En... *On the other hand* [d]*events*

- romper un espejo[e] (¡Esto significa siete años de mala suerte!)
- pasar por debajo de una escalera[f]
- derramar[g] sal (Hay un «antídoto»: tirar[h] un poco de la sal derramada por encima del hombro[i] izquierdo.)
- cruzarse con un gato negro en el camino[j]
- los días martes 13

[e]*mirror* [f]*ladder* [g]*to spill* [h]*to throw* [i]por... *over the shoulder* [j]*path*

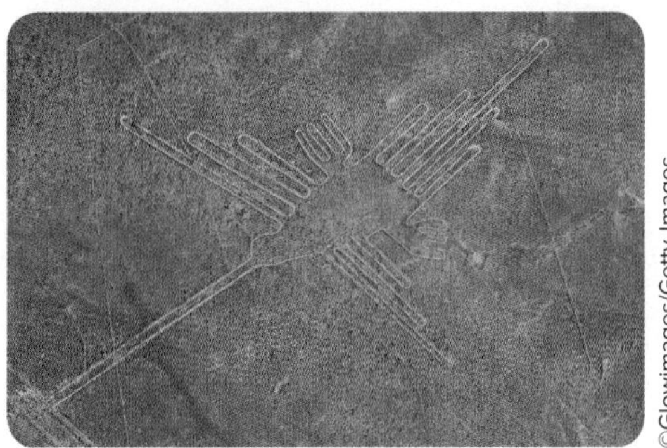

©Glowimages/Getty Images

Una vista aérea de las increíbles líneas de Nazca, Perú

Un símbolo peruano: La herencia indígena

El imperio inca duró aproximadamente un siglo (XV). Fue el mayor dominio territorial en toda América, anterior a[a] la llegada de los españoles. Pero los incas no fueron ni[b] el primer pueblo ni el único[c] en dejar su huella[d] en lo que es hoy el Perú, como lo demuestran las impresionantes líneas de la cultura nazca (entre los siglos I y VII). Su propósito[e] es todavía un misterio. En la actualidad, los pueblos indígenas tienen una importante presencia en el país. Se calcula que un 25% de la población peruana es amerindia. Algunas comunidades indígenas, como los quechuas y los aymaras, están extendidas por varios países andinos.

[a]anterior... *before* [b]ni... *ni neither ... nor* [c]el... *the only one* [d]*mark, footprint* [e]*purpose*

Comprensión

1. ¿Qué cuestiones les causan ansiedad a los peruanos?
2. ¿Qué es la Remuneración Mínima Vital?
3. ¿Cuáles son tres de las supersticiones que en el mundo hispano se asocian con la mala suerte?
4. ¿A qué países emigran los hispanohablantes en tiempos de necesidad?
5. Dé el nombre de dos pueblos amerindios en el Perú en la actualidad.
6. Dé el nombre de dos culturas prehispánicos que existían en lo que hoy es el Perú.

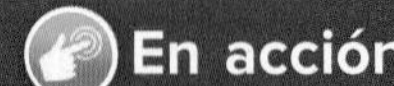

En acción

Haga una investigación (*research*) sobre un movimiento migratorio de hispanohablantes y luego haga una breve presentación al resto de la clase.

Lectura

Antes de leer

¿Qué opina su profesor(a) de su trabajo en la universidad? Lea las siguientes preguntas y contéstelas como usted cree que su profesor(a) las contestaría (*would answer*). Luego entrevístelo/la para saber lo que piensa.

1. De todas las actividades de su trabajo, ¿cuáles le gustan más?
2. ¿Qué es lo más aburrido de su trabajo? ¿Lo más estresante?
3. ¿Se siente frustrado/a con su trabajo a veces? ¿Qué hace entonces?

«OH», de Mario Benedetti

Jefe[a]
usté está aburrido
aburrido de veras[b]
hace veintiocho años
que sabe sus asientos[c]
que comprueba los saldos[d]
y revuelve[e] el café.

Está aburrido
jefe
se le nota[f] en los ojos
en la voz[g]
en las órdenes
en el paso[h]
en las mangas[i]
en los setenta rubros[j]
de letra redondilla.[k]

Jefe
usté está aburrido
nadie lo sabe
nadie.

Pero ahora que está solo
ahora que no ven Ellos
desahóguese[l]
grite[m]
discuta[n]
diga mierda[ñ]
dé golpes[o] en la mesa
vuélvase insoportable[p]
por favor
diga no
diga no muchas veces
hasta quedarse ronco.[q]

No cuesta nada[r]
jefe
haga la prueba.[s]

[a]*Boss* [b]de... *truly* [c]*ledger entries* [d]comprueba... *you check the balance sheets* [e]*stir* [f]se... *it's obvious* [g]*voice* [h]el... *your way of walking* [i]*little errors* [j]*headings (in a spreadsheet)* [k]*rounded* [l]*let it out* [m]*scream* [n]*argue* [ñ]*shit* [o]dé... *slam your fist* [p]vuélvase... *become unbearable* [q]quedarse... *you get hoarse* [r]No... *You can do it (lit., It doesn't cost anything)* [s]haga... *give it a try*

Comprensión

A. Para comprender el poema. Seleccione la opción correcta y explique su respuesta.

1. Este poema fue escrito _______ (por / para) un jefe.
2. Al jefe _______ (le gusta / no le gusta) su trabajo.
3. En la segunda estrofa (*stanza*) del poema, el poeta dice que la actitud del jefe es _______ (visible / invisible).
4. En la tercera estrofa, el poeta dice que la actitud del jefe es _______ (visible / invisible).
5. El poeta le recomienda al jefe que _______ (exprese / no exprese) sus sentimientos.

B. Para interpretar el poema. Conteste las siguientes preguntas según su opinión.

1. ¿Son contradictorias las estrofas 2 y 3?
2. ¿Cree usted que todas las personas que hacen el mismo trabajo por veintiocho años vayan a sentirse tan aburridas como este jefe? ¿Por qué?
3. ¿Muestra el poeta una actitud de intolerancia o muestra compasión hacia el jefe?
4. ¿Por qué cree usted que el poeta le habla al jefe usando la forma **usté** en vez de **usted**?

Proyecto: ¿Qué hacer cuando uno se siente aburrido?

El poema de este capítulo describe a un jefe aburrido en su trabajo. Sentirse así (*like that*) en los estudios o en el trabajo nos pasa a todos a veces. ¿Qué debemos hacer cuando nos sentimos así?

Paso 1. Describa una situación que suele *(tends)* ocurrir en sus clases o en su trabajo en la que (*which*) usted se siente muy aburrido/a. Explique por qué se siente así y cómo se comporta (*you behave*) en estas situaciones.

Paso 2. En parejas, intercambien sus descripciones e inventen consejos para su compañero/a.

Paso 3. Ahora comparen sus consejos y elijan los dos consejos más útiles, originales o divertidos para decírselos al resto de la clase.

Textos orales

La depresión entre los adolescentes

Antes de escuchar

Piense en una persona que usted conoce bien o en una persona famosa que sufre o ha sufrido (*has suffered*) de depresión. ¿Cómo se siente o sentía? ¿Qué hizo para mejorarse?

Vocabulario para escuchar

la tristeza	sadness	**deprimido/a**	depressed
el estado de ánimo	mood	**la desesperanza**	hopelessness
el comportamiento	behavior	**emocionar**	to get (*someone*) excited about (*something*)
enfrentarse a	to face		
hacer frente a	to face up to	**el peso**	weight
el aprendizaje	learning	**evitar**	to avoid
el acoso	harassment; bullying	**tratable**	treatable

Comprensión

A. Hablando de la depresión. ¿Qué dice el Dr. Carvajal sobre la depresión? Las siguientes oraciones son falsas. Corríjalas.

1. Todo el mundo (*Everyone*) sufre de depresión.
2. La depresión tiene solo una causa.
3. Uno de los síntomas de la depresión es querer estar siempre con los amigos y la familia.
4. La depresión es una de las enfermedades menos tratables.

B. Más detalles. Conteste las siguientes preguntas.

1. ¿Cuáles son tres de las causas de la depresión?
2. ¿Cuáles son tres de los síntomas de la depresión?
3. Según el Dr. Carvajal, ¿qué es lo primero que se debe hacer cuando un joven está deprimido?

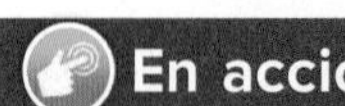

En acción

Usando la información de **Textos orales** y otra información que usted sepa o encuentre, prepare un breve mensaje sobre la depresión orientado a los estudiantes de la escuela secundaria o de la universidad. Incluya los síntomas más típicos de la depresión y lo que se debe hacer para combatirla.

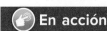

Proyecto en su comunidad

Entreviste a una persona hispana de su universidad o ciudad sobre lo que más les causa estrés a él/ella y a otras personas de su comunidad.

Preguntas posibles

- ¿Cuáles son los problemas que más les preocupan a usted y a su familia o a sus amigos? ¿Hay alguno que les cause más estrés que las otras?
- Si vive en una ciudad grande, ¿son el tráfico y el estacionamiento problemas para usted?
- ¿Qué presiones tiene la gente joven de su familia o comunidad? ¿Les preocupa su acceso a la universidad? ¿Por qué?
- ¿Qué actividades hace usted para relajarse (*relax*)?
- ¿Es usted una persona torpe o distraída? ¿Se le olvida hacer unas cosas o pierde cosas con bastante frecuencia? ¿Tiene accidentes relacionados con el estrés?

Escritura

Proyecto: Un ensayo sobre las presiones de la vida estudiantil

A lo largo de este capítulo ha habido (*there have been*) muchas oportunidades para hablar de las causas del estrés que sufren las personas. Ahora usted va a concentrarse en las presiones de los estudiantes de su universidad, para escribir un artículo para el periódico universitario.

©JGI/Jamie Grill/Getty Images

¿Triste, estresada o deprimida?

Antes de escribir

Llene (*Fill in*) la siguiente tabla con las presiones que usted cree que lo/la afectan más. Luego entreviste a dos compañeros para saber las opiniones de ellos.

Las presiones...	académicas	sociales	financieras	familiares
usted				
compañero/a 1				
compañero/a 2				

A escribir

Ahora, analice la información de **Antes de escribir**, saque algunas conclusiones y dé algunos consejos. ¿Cómo es que las presiones pueden afectar los estudios y la vida de un estudiante? ¿Qué pueden o deben hacer los estudiantes para prepararse o para aliviar estas presiones? Hay más ayuda en Connect.

Más ideas para su portafolio

- Incluya la imagen de un lugar al que (*to which*) usted puede volar con su mente para escaparse temporalmente (*temporarily*) de la realidad. Diga dónde está y descríbalo. ¿Lo conoce en personal o solo es un lugar que desea visitar?
- Haga una lista de las cosas que usted asocia con la buena suerte en su vida. Si usted no es nada supersticioso/a, puede hablar de las palabras que usted asocia con tres momentos agradables de su vida. Piense en eventos importantes o familiares, en canciones o lugares especiales, etcétera.
- Si ha estado jugando (*you have been playing*) Practice Spanish: Study Abroad, en Quest 10 usted ayudó a su amigo cuando se cayó y se hizo daño en el brazo. Ahora imagine una situación parecida (*similar*) y escriba un guion entre un médico / una médica y un(a) paciente que tuvo otro tipo de accidente. ¿Qué pasó? ¿Cuáles son las heridas (*injuries*) del/de la paciente? ¿Qué consejos recibe? Interprete la situación en clase con un compañero o una compañera.

©McGraw-Hill Education

Sugerencia: You are now ready to play Quest 10 in **Practice Spanish: Study Abroad.**

EN RESUMEN En este capítulo

AFTER STUDYING THIS CHAPTER I CAN . . .

- ☐ talk about the typical things that cause stress in life (420–421)
- ☐ talk about accidents (423)
- ☐ use **hace** + time to express how something has been happening or how long ago something happened (427–428)
- ☐ express some actions as unexpected or unintended events (430–431)
- ☐ use **por** and **para** accurately in more contexts (434–436)
- ☐ recognize/describe at least 2–3 aspects of Peruvian cultures

Gramática en breve

33. Hace + *time*

hace = has/have been doing

hace + *time* + **que** + *present*

present + **desde hace** + *time*

hace = ago

hace + *time* + **que** + *preterite*

preterite + **hace** + *time*

34. Accidental *se*

a + *noun* + **se** + *indirect object pronoun* + *verb* + *subject*

(**a** + *pronoun*) **se** + *indirect object pronoun* + *verb* + *subject*

35. *¿Por o para?*

por = reason, cause

by / by means of — *through/along*

because of / due to — *during/in* (time of day)

for = in exchange for, for the sake of / on behalf of, in place of, for (*period of time*)

para = goal, purpose, destination

in order to + *inf.*

for = destined for / to be given to, by (*future time*), toward / in the direction of, to be used for, as compared with / in relation to others, in the employ of, in preparation for

Vocabulario

Los verbos

acabar — to finish; to run out of
aceptar — to accept
quedar — to remain, be left

Repaso: olvidar, perder (pierdo), pedir (pido) (i)

Las presiones de la vida académica

la agenda — personal calendar
la ansiedad — anxiety
los apuntes — notes (*academic*)
el despertador — alarm clock
el estrés — stress
el horario — schedule
el informe (oral/escrito) — (oral/written) report
el plazo — deadline
el programa (del curso) — (course) syllabus
la prueba — quiz; test
la tarjeta de identificación — identification card, ID
el trabajo — report, (piece of) work
el trabajo de tiempo completo/parcial — full-time/part-time job

la presión — pressure

Cognado: el calendario

Repaso: el examen, la llave, la nota, la tarea, el trabajo (*job; work*)**, la vida**

corregir (corrijo) (i) — to grade; to correct
devolver (like volver) (algo a alguien) — to return (something to someone)
estacionar — to park
estar bajo muchas presiones — to be under a lot of pressure
estar (muy) estresado/a — to be (very) stressed, under (a lot of) stress
recoger (recojo) — to collect; to pick up
sacar (qu) — to get (*grades*)
sufrir (de) — to suffer (from)
tener muchas presiones — to have a lot of pressure

Repaso: acordarse (me acuerdo) (de), entregar (gu), llegar (gu) a tiempo / tarde, olvidar, tomar

Los accidentes

caer (caigo) — to fall; to drop
caerse — to fall down
chocar (qu) con/contra — to run into, bump against
equivocarse (qu) (de) — to make a mistake (about/with)

estar/ir distraído/a	to be distracted
hacerse daño	to hurt oneself
hacerse daño en	to hurt one's (*body part*)
lastimarse	to hurt (*a body part*)
levantarse con el pie izquierdo	to get up on the wrong side of the bed
ocurrir	to happen
pedir (pido) (i) disculpas	to apologize
pegar (gu)	to hit, strike
pegarse (gu) con/contra	to run, bump into/against
romper(se)	to break
tener buena/mala suerte	to have good/bad luck; to be (un)lucky

Repaso: doler (duele), pasar

la disculpa	apology
Disculpa. Discúlpame.	Pardon me. I'm sorry. (*fam.*)
Disculpe. Discúlpeme.	Pardon me. I'm sorry. (*form.*)
Fue sin querer.	I didn't mean (to do) it.
Lo siento (mucho).	I'm (very) sorry.
No hay problema.	No problem.

Repaso: está bien perdón

Los adjetivos

distraído/a	absentminded, distracted
escrito/a	written
estresado/a	stressed out, under stress
estresante	stressful
torpe	clumsy
universitario/a	(of the) university

Cognados: académico/a, (in)flexible, oral, parcial

Repaso: primero/a, último/a

Otros sustantivos

el desastre	disaster
el dolor	pain
las escaleras	stairs
la luz (*pl.* **luces**)	light
la taza	cup

Repaso: el dolor

Palabras adicionales

bajo (*prep.*)	under
hace + *time* + **que** + *preterite*; *preterite* + **hace** + *time*	ago
hace + *time* + **que** + *present*; *present* + **desde hace** + *time*	to have been (*doing something*) for (*time*)
por	by
por Dios	for heaven's sake
por ejemplo	for example
por primera/última vez	for the first/last time
por si acaso	just in case
¡por supuesto!	of course!
por todas partes	everywhere
¡qué + *adj.***!**	how + *adj.*!
¡qué + *noun***!**	what (a) + *noun*!
solamente	only
últimamente	lately
-mente	-ly (*adverbial suffix*)

Repaso: gracias por, para, por (because of; through; in; for)**, por eso, por favor, por fin, por la mañana/tarde/noche, por lo general, por lo menos, por teléfono**

Vocabulario personal

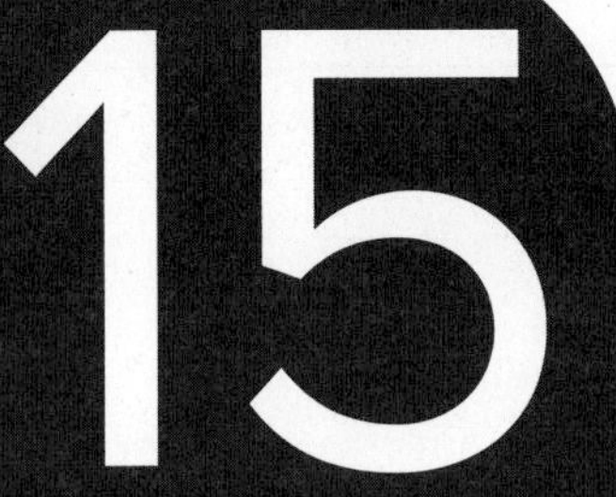

15 La naturaleza y el medio ambiente°

La... *Nature and the environment*

En este capítulo

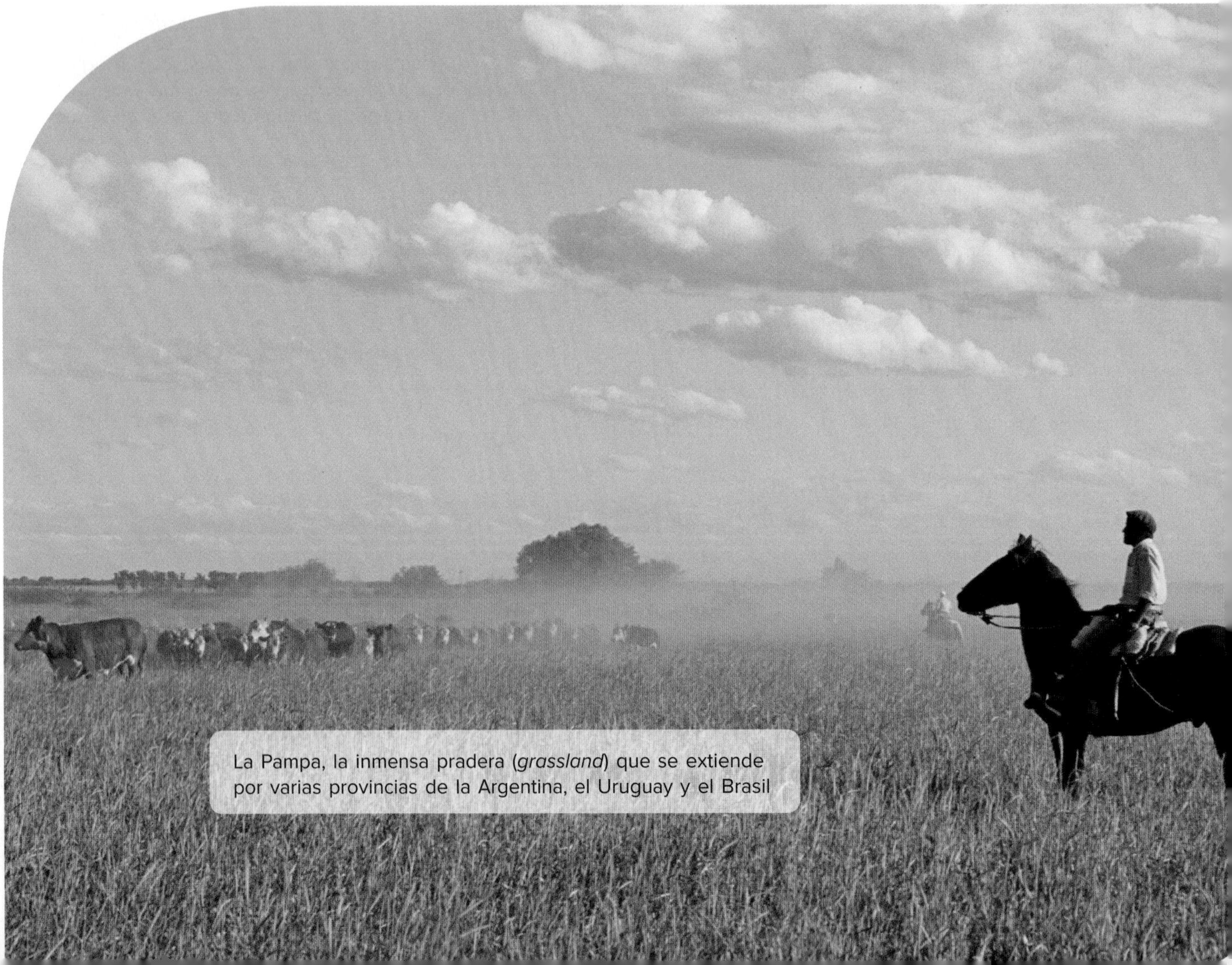

La Pampa, la inmensa pradera (*grassland*) que se extiende por varias provincias de la Argentina, el Uruguay y el Brasil

LA ARGENTINA

44,8 (coma ocho) millones de habitantes

EL URUGUAY

3,5 (tres y medio) millones de habitantes

- La Argentina y el Uruguay son dos países del Cono Sur, el triángulo de territorio sudamericano que está al sur del Trópico de Capricornio.
- El Uruguay y la Argentina están unidos por la historia y la cultura. Las capitales de estos países están en el inmenso estuario del Río de la Plata.

ENTREVISTA

- ¿Cómo llega usted al campus? ¿Necesita usted un coche para llegar a la universidad o al trabajo?
- ¿Le gusta a usted estar en contacto con la naturaleza? ¿Qué actividades hace cuando está al aire libre?
- ¿Hay mucha contaminación en el área donde usted vive? ¿Es la contaminación un problema que le preocupa?

 **Gabriela Romano Acosta contesta las preguntas.**

- Voy en colectivo[a] al trabajo. Trabajo en la Facultad de Farmacia y Bioquímica de la Universidad de Buenos Aires, que está en la Ciudad Universitaria. Es más práctico llegar en transporte público porque el estacionamiento[b] es un problema.
- ¡Me encanta estar en contacto con la naturaleza! Mis abuelos tienen una finca[c] cerca de la ciudad de Córdoba. Cuando los visito, paso mucho tiempo al aire libre, haciendo tareas agrícolas[d] o simplemente caminando y disfrutando del[e] aire limpio.
- ¡Claro! En Buenos Aires hay problemas de contaminación porque es una ciudad inmensa. Y sí, la contaminación me preocupa, especialmente la calidad del aire que respiramos todos los días.

[a]autobús [b]*parking* [c]*farm* [d]*agricultural* [e]disfrutando... *enjoying the*

©Daniel Ernst/iStock/Getty Images

VOCABULARIO: PREPARACIÓN

You can hear the pronunciation of theme vocabulary words and phrases in the Connect eBook.

La ciudad y el campo°

° countryside

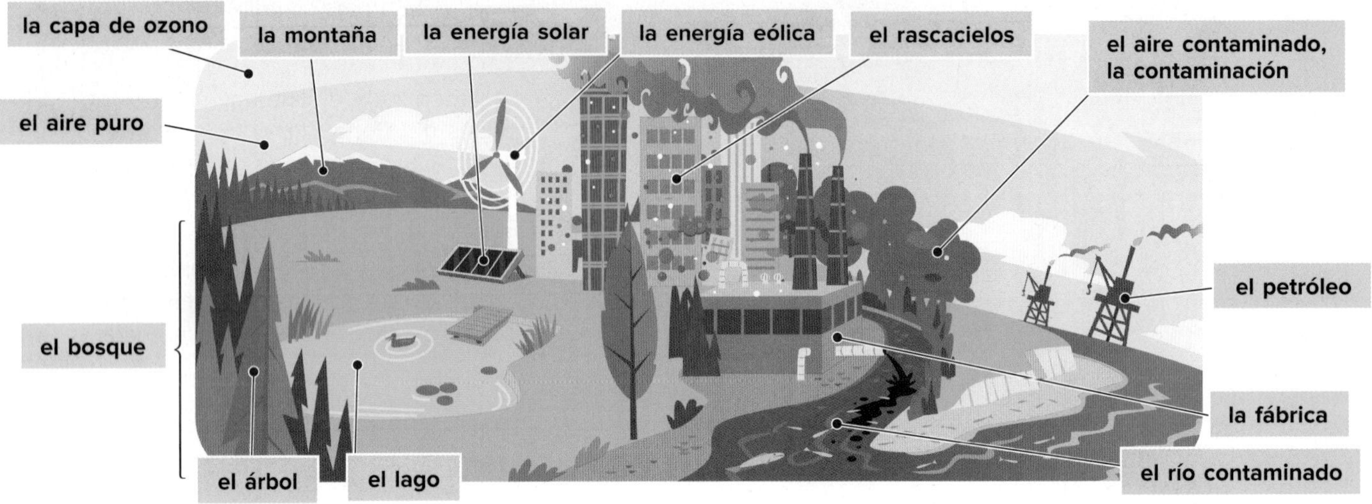

Los recursos naturales°	Los... *Natural resources*
la energía	energy
eólica	wind
renovable	renewable
el medio ambiente	environment
la naturaleza	nature
el reciclaje	recycling
la Tierra	Earth

Cognados: la energía eléctrica/nuclear/solar, el planeta

bello/a	beautiful
contaminado/a	contaminated, polluted
puro/a	pure

Los animales	
la ballena	whale
el caballo	horse
la especie (en peligro de extinción)	(endangered) species
el gato	cat
el pájaro	bird
el perro	dog
el pez (*pl.* peces)	fish
el toro	bull
la vaca	cow

Cognados: el elefante, el gorila

doméstico/a	domesticated, tame
salvaje	wild

El desarrollo°	El... *Development*
el agricultor / la agricultora	farmer
la agricultura	farming, agriculture
el campesino / la campesina	farmer; field laborer
el delito	crime
la densidad	density
la falta	lack; absence
la finca	farm
el gobierno	government
la población	population
el ritmo lento / acelerado de la vida	slow / fast pace of life
el servicio	service
el transporte	transportation
acelerado/a	fast, accelerated
público/a	public
acabar	to finish, run out (of); to use up completely
conservar	to save, conserve
construir*	to build
contaminar	to pollute
desarrollar	to develop
destruir (*like* construir)	to destroy
fabricar (qu)	to manufacture
proteger (protejo)	to protect
reciclar	to recycle

Note the present indicative conjugation of **construir: construyo, construyes, construye, construimos, construís, construyen.**

Comunicación

A. ¿En la ciudad o en el campo?

Paso 1. ¿Con qué relaciona usted las siguientes ideas, con la ciudad o con el campo?

	LA CIUDAD	EL CAMPO
1. El aire es más puro; hay menos contaminación.	☐	☐
2. La naturaleza es más bella.	☐	☐
3. El ritmo de la vida es más acelerado.	☐	☐
4. Hay más delitos.	☐	☐
5. Los servicios profesionales (financieros, legales...) son más accesibles	☐	☐
6. Hay pocos medios de transporte públicos.	☐	☐
7. Hay menos densidad de población.	☐	☐
8. Hay falta de viviendas.	☐	☐

Paso 2. Ahora, en parejas, den dos ideas más que ustedes asocian con la ciudad y con el campo.

B. Definiciones. Defina las siguientes palabras en español.

MODELO: el agricultor → Es el dueño de una finca.

1. la fábrica
2. el campesino
3. la falta
4. la finca
5. la naturaleza
6. la población
7. el río
8. el rascacielos
9. el agricultor

Así se dice

la fábrica = la factoría
la finca = la granja, el rancho, la estancia

El árbol is also called **el palo** in Mexico, Central America, and the Caribbean. The names of at least two California cities contain the word **palo:** Palo Alto and Palos Verdes.

Nota cultural

Programas medioambientales

En muchos países del mundo es necesario equilibrar[a] la protección del medio ambiente con los objetivos del desarrollo económico. En muchos casos, la explotación de recursos naturales es la mayor fuente de ingresos[b] para la economía de un país. Los gobiernos latinoamericanos están conscientes de la necesidad de proteger el medio ambiente y de conservar los recursos naturales. Los siguientes son algunos de los muchos programas medioambientales que existen en los países hispanohablantes.

- En las grandes ciudades de varios países (Bolivia, Chile, Colombia, el Ecuador, Honduras y México, entre otros) se han establecido[c] programas de restricción vehicular, que tratan de regular la cantidad de tráfico en determinadas horas o días. Se basan en un sistema que limita el uso de un vehículo según su placa.[d] Además de[e] reducir el tráfico diario en la ciudad, estos programas pueden mejorar[f] la calidad del aire.
- En muchos países hispanohablantes (la Argentina, el Uruguay, España y México, entre otros) existen programas de reciclaje, basados en sistemas de separación de basura. Es decir que, según su clase, los materiales se depositan en contenedores[g] de colores diferentes: el papel y el cartón[h] en un contenedor; el vidrio,[i] el metal y el plástico en otro; y en algunos casos los desperdicios de materia orgánica,[j] en otro.

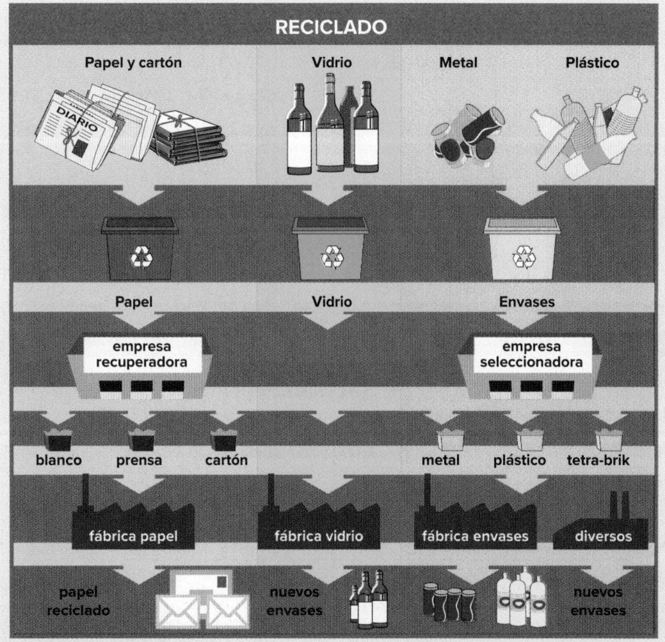

¿Qué programas medioambientales hay en su ciudad o estado?

[a]*to balance* [b]fuente... *source of income* [c]se... *have been established* [d]*license plate* [e]Además... *Besides* [f]*improve* [g]*containers, receptacles* [h]*cardboard* [i]*glass* [j]los... *organic waste matter*

 **C. ¿Cuánto saben ustedes de los animales?**

En parejas, clasifiquen los siguientes animales según las categorías de la tabla. **¡OJO!** Algunos pueden estar en más de un grupo. Luego traten de añadir otros animales en cada categoría.

LOS ANIMALES: **el águila, el camello, el cocodrilo, el cóndor, la cucaracha, el delfín, el hipopótamo, el jaguar, la jirafa, el león, el mosquito, el orangután, la ostra, la rata, el rinoceronte, el tigre**

Animales...			
domésticos	**salvajes**	**en peligro de extinción**	**insectos**

 **D. Problemas medioambientales**

Paso 1. En parejas, indiquen cuáles de los siguientes problemas y temas afectan a su ciudad, estado o país. Añadan por lo menos un tema que ustedes consideren importante.

AFECTA A...	MI CIUDAD	MI ESTADO	MI PAÍS
1. la contaminación del aire	☐	☐	☐
2. la destrucción de la capa de ozono	☐	☐	☐
3. la deforestación de los bosques	☐	☐	☐
4. el desarrollo de energías renovables	☐	☐	☐
5. la falta de transporte público adecuado	☐	☐	☐
6. el ritmo acelerado de la vida	☐	☐	☐
7. la falta de protección de los espacios naturales	☐	☐	☐
8. ¿ ?	☐	☐	☐

Paso 2. Ahora escojan dos de estos temas y explíquenle a la clase una de las causas del problema y una de las cosas que es necesario hacer para resolverlo.

 **E. Opiniones.** Con toda la clase, comenten las siguientes opiniones. Pueden usar las siguientes expresiones para aclarar (*clarify*) su posición con respecto a cada tema. **¡OJO!** Todas las expresiones requieren el uso del subjuntivo.

Vocabulario útil

Es / Me/Nos parece { **necesario/esencial que...** / **importantísimo que...** / **absurdo que...** }

Me opongo / Nos oponemos a que... I am / We are against . . .
No creo/creemos que...

1. Para conservar energía debemos reciclar todo lo posible.
2. Es mejor calentar (*to heat*) las casas con estufas de leña (*wood stoves*) que con gas o electricidad.
3. Se debe crear más parques urbanos, estatales y nacionales.
4. La protección del medio ambiente no debe impedir la explotación de los recursos naturales.
5. Para evitar la contaminación urbana, debemos limitar el uso de los coches a ciertos días de la semana.
6. El gobierno debe ponerles multas (*fines*) muy graves a las compañías e individuos que causan la contaminación.

F. **Anuncios medioambientales**

Paso 1. Lea los siguientes anuncios y conteste las preguntas.

Aprenda a ahorrar
Los recursos son cosa de todos
MAYOR AHORRO = MEJOR PLANETA
Si hay luz natural
¿por qué gastar electricidad?

Ahorrá dinero y usá energía limpia
Instalá un calentador[a] solar
SOLESLUZ

©iStockphoto/Getty Images

[a]*heater*

1. ¿Qué cosa sugieren los anuncios que ahorremos?
2. ¿Puede usted explicar el uso de la imagen de la bombilla (*light bulb*) en el anuncio de la izquierda?
3. ¿Qué significa en inglés «MAYOR AHORRO = MEJOR PLANETA»? ¿Con qué palabras juega el anuncio?
4. ¿Qué imagen predomina en el anuncio de Solesluz? ¿Por qué es apropiada esta imagen?

Vocabulario útil

ahorrar	to save
el panel solar	

Paso 2. En grupos, hablen de lo que ustedes hacen personalmente para conservar los recursos naturales. Deben considerar las siguientes ideas y añadir otras. Luego díganle a la clase algunas de las ideas interesantes de su grupo.

1. el reciclaje
2. apagar/encender las luces
3. caminar en vez de manejar (*instead of driving*)
4. pasear en bicicleta
5. consumir lo que se produce localmente
6. usar menos papel

Algo sobre...

la Pampa

La Pampa es una inmensa región sudamericana de praderas[a] que abarca[b] desde el sur del Brasil, casi todo el Uruguay y parte considerable del territorio argentino. La palabra «pampa», que viene de la lengua quechua, significa llanura.[c]

La Pampa se divide en subregiones según el clima y la ubicación.[d] Pero en general es una zona dedicada a la explotación[e] del ganado[f] y de la agricultura, especialmente de granos como la soja, el trigo[g] y el maíz.

¿Qué zona de este país se dedica especialmente a la explotación del ganado y al cultivo de granos?

[a]*grasslands* [b]*includes* [c]*plain* [d]*location* [e]*development* [f]*cattle* [g]*wheat*

La Pampa: un territorio multinacional

Los vehículos

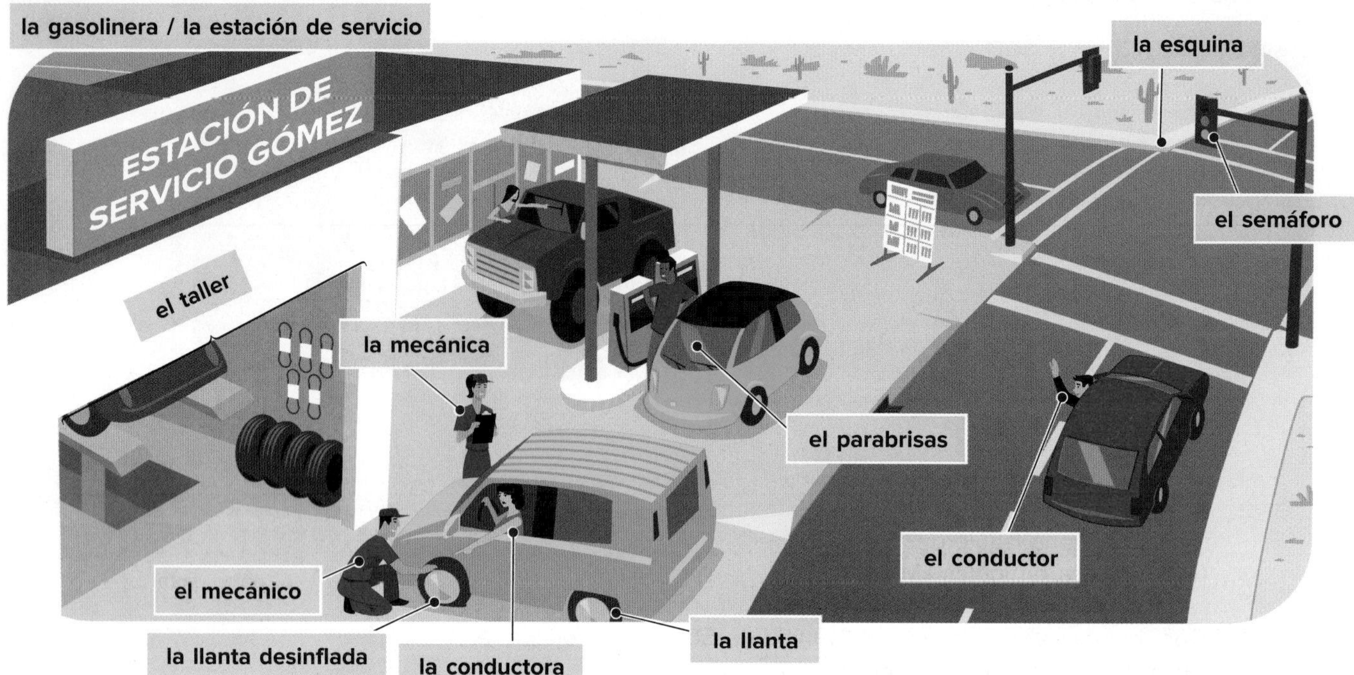

la acera	sidewalk
la autopista	freeway, interstate
la avenida	avenue
la calle	street
la camioneta	(mini)van
la carretera	highway
la circulación, el tránsito	traffic
el coche/carro (descapotable, híbrido, todoterreno)	(convertible, hybrid, all-terrain) car
el estacionamiento	parking place/lot
los frenos	brakes
la licencia de manejar/conducir	driver's license
la moto(cicleta)	motorcycle
el tanque	tank

Cognados: el auto(móvil), la batería, la bicicleta, la gasolina, el SUV, el tráfico

arrancar (qu)	to start up (*a car*)
arreglar	to fix, repair
chocar (qu) con	to run into, collide (with)
estacionar	to park
gastar (mucha/ poca gasolina)	to use (a lot of / little gas)
llenar	to fill (up)
manejar, conducir (conduzco)*	to drive
obedecer (obedezco)*	to obey
parar	to stop
revisar el aceite	to check the oil
tocar (qu) la bocina	to honk the horn

Cognado: reparar

Así se dice

el estacionamiento = el aparcamiento, el parking
la licencia de manejar/conducir = el carnet de conducir, el permiso de manejar
la llanta = la rueda
arrancar = encender el motor
estacionar = aparcar (*Sp.*), parquear (*Col., Mex.*)

There are many ways to express *car* in Spanish. You already know **el coche. El carro** is frequently used. **El automóvil,** or simply **el auto,** is perhaps the most generic word, understood in all parts of the Spanish-speaking world.

Like the verb* **conocer, conducir *and* **obedecer** *have a spelling change in the* **yo** *form of the present indicative:* **conozco, conduzco, obedezco.** *This spelling change is also used in all forms of the present subjunctive.*

Comunicación

A. Definiciones

Paso 1. Empareje las definiciones con las palabras y frases.

DEFINICIONES

1. _____ Se pone en el tanque.
2. _____ Se llenan de aire.
3. _____ Lubrica el motor.
4. _____ Es necesaria para arrancar el motor.
5. _____ Es necesario cambiarla cuando no tiene aire suficiente.
6. _____ Se usan para parar el coche.
7. _____ El policía nos la pide cuando nos para el coche.

PALABRAS Y FRASES

a. los frenos
b. la batería
c. una llanta desinflada
d. la gasolina
e. las llantas
f. el aceite
g. la licencia

Paso 2. Ahora, siguiendo el modelo de las definiciones del **Paso 1**, dé una definición de las siguientes palabras.

1. el semáforo
2. la circulación
3. estacionar
4. el conductor
5. la gasolinera
6. la autopista
7. la carretera
8. el taller

B. Entrevista: Un conductor responsable

Paso 1. Entreviste a un compañero o una compañera para saber con qué frecuencia hace las siguientes cosas.

1. dejar la licencia en casa cuando va a manejar
2. acelerar (*to speed up*) cuando ve a un policía
3. tomar bebidas alcohólicas y después manejar
4. respetar el límite de velocidad o excederlo
5. estacionar el coche donde dice «Prohibido estacionar»
6. revisar el aceite y la batería
7. seguir todo derecho (*straight*) a toda velocidad cuando no sabe llegar a su destino
8. adelantar (*to pass*) tres carros a la vez (*at the same time*)
9. mandar mensajes electrónicos mientras maneja
10. no parar cuando el semáforo está en rojo

Paso 2. Ahora, con el mismo compañero o compañera, haga una lista de diez de las cosas que debe hacer —o no debe hacer— un conductor responsable. Pueden usar frases del Paso 1, si quieren.

MODELOS: Es importante que el conductor **respete** el límite de velocidad.
No exceda el límite de velocidad.
Respetar / **No exceder** el límite de velocidad.

Paso 3. Ahora analice usted sus propias costumbres y cualidades como conductor(a). ¡Diga la verdad! ¿Es usted un conductor o una conductora responsable?

C. Intercambios. En parejas, hagan y contesten preguntas sobre su coche o el (*that*) de su familia o de un amigo.

1. la marca (*make*) y el modelo de su coche y la placa (*license plate*) que tiene
2. dónde lo estaciona
3. cuánto tiempo hace que lo tiene y cuánto tiempo más piensa tenerlo
4. si el coche expresa su personalidad o si es solo un medio de transporte para usted
5. si el coche tiene nombre

Nota comunicativa

Frases para indicar cómo llegar a un lugar

Since you know how to form informal (**tú**) and formal (**usted/ustedes**) commands, you should be able to give simple directions in Spanish.

doblar	to turn	**por (la calle/avenida...)**	on, through (. . . street/avenue)
seguir (sigo) (i)	to keep on going		
a la derecha/izquierda	to the right/left	**(todo) derecho/recto**	straight ahead
		¿Cómo se llega a... ?	How do you get to . . . ?

You will practice giving directions in **Comunicación C** and **D.**

D. En el centro de Montevideo

Paso 1. Complete las siguientes instrucciones sobre cómo llegar a varios sitios en Montevideo.

Centro de Montevideo

[a]*Port* [b]*Dock* [c]*Pier*

1. **Del Museo Histórico Nacional al Mercado del Puerto:** Salga del Museo y vaya ________ (a la derecha / a la izquierda). ________ (Siga todo recto por / Doble en) la Avenida Uruguay hasta la calle Pérez Castellano. Allí doble ________ (a la derecha / a la izquierda) y ________ (siga / doble) hasta la calle Cerro Largo. El Mercado está enfrente.
2. **Del Mercado del Puerto hasta la Plaza Zabala:** Saliendo del Mercado, tome la calle Pérez Castellano y ________ (doble / siga todo recto) hasta llegar a la calle Mercedes. Allí, doble ________ (a la derecha / a la izquierda) y siga hasta llegar a la Plaza.

Paso 2. Ahora dé usted las instrucciones sobre cómo llegar de la Plaza Zabala a la Plaza de la Constitución y de esa plaza a la Plaza España.

 **E. ¿Cómo se llega a... ?**

Paso 1. En parejas, escriban o den verbalmente direcciones para ir desde su campus a los siguientes lugares. Usen mandatos con **tú.**

1. a un cine que está cerca del campus
2. al centro de la ciudad
3. a un centro comercial popular
4. a un restaurante bien conocido (*well-known*)

Paso 2. Ahora lean las direcciones del **Paso 1** a la clase pero sin dar el nombre del destino. La clase lo va a tratar de adivinar (*guess*).

SALU2 «EcoSalu2» Segmento 1

Antes de mirar

Mucha gente toma medidas (*measures*) para reducir el consumo de energía en su casa. Indique cuáles de las siguientes medidas toma usted o su familia.

- ☐ usar bombillas (*light bulbs*) de bajo consumo
- ☐ mantener baja la temperatura de la calefacción en la casa
- ☐ mantener apagadas (*turned off*) las luces que no son necesarias
- ☐ no calentar (*to heat*) el agua de la piscina (alberca)
- ☐ instalar páneles solares en la casa

Laura enseña esta casa que fue remodelada para producir menos impacto medioambiental.

Este segmento

En este segmento Víctor y Ana introducen el tema del medio ambiente y Laura presenta un reportaje sobre una casa que fue remodelada para hacerla más ecológica.

Vocabulario del segmento

el nivel	level	**no ha pagado ni un centavo**	has not paid one penny
mejorar	to improve	**contar (cuento) con**	to rely on
en cuanto a	as far as . . . is concerned	**asegurar**	to ensure
lograr	to achieve	**el ahorro**	saving
el techo	roof	**el hogar**	home, household
quedan cubiertas	are covered		

Después de mirar

A. ¿Está claro? Las siguientes oraciones son falsas. Corríjalas.

1. La casa está al norte de Colorado.
2. Es una casa nueva.
3. Las casas viejas nunca son estructuralmente sólidas.
4. Los páneles solares no son suficientes para cubrir (*covering*) las necesidades de esta familia
5. Esta familia paga poco dinero a la compañía eléctrica.

B. Un poco más. Conteste las siguientes preguntas.

1. ¿Qué le pasa a Ana hoy?
2. Según Víctor, ¿dónde no debe vivir Ana?
3. ¿Qué medidas de ahorro energético ha tomado (*has taken*) la familia de la casa remodelada?

C. Y ahora, ustedes. En parejas, hablen sobre las medidas de ahorro energético que ha tomado (*has taken*) su universidad. ¿Son suficientes? ¿Qué otras medidas son recomendables para su campus?

GRAMÁTICA

¿Recuerda usted?

As you know, the Spanish present participle, like its English equivalent, does not change according to the subject of a sentence.

Cecilia } está cantand<u>o</u>, bebiend<u>o</u>, durmiend<u>o</u>.
Juan

Give the English equivalent of the following:

cantar: cantando **beber: bebiendo** **dormir: durmiendo**

In both English and Spanish, there is another kind of participle: the past participle. Like the present participle, it does not change its form when used as a verb. But it can also be used as an adjective. A number of adjectives you learned to use with **estar** are actually past participles.

Here are some past participle adjectives. Can you explain how they are formed?

1. **-ar** verbs: **cansado/a, cerrado/a, encantado/a, pasado/a, resfriado/a**
2. **-er/-ir** verbs: **aburrido/a, divertido/a, querido/a**
3. irregular verbs: **abierto/a, escrito/a**

You will learn more about past participles and how they are used in **Gramática 42** and **43.**

42 *Más descripciones*

Past Participle Used as an Adjective

Gramática en acción: Algunos refranes y dichos en español

a. En boca <u>cerrada</u> no entran moscas.

b. Estar tan <u>aburrido</u> como una ostra.

c. Cuando está <u>abierto</u> el cajón, el más <u>honrado</u> es ladrón.

Comprensión

Empareje estas oraciones con el refrán o dicho que explican.

1. _____ Es posible que una persona buena sienta la tentación de hacer algo malo si la oportunidad se le presenta.
2. _____ Hay que ser prudente. A veces es mejor no decir nada para evitar (*avoid*) problemas.
3. _____ Ejemplifican el aburrimiento (*boredom*) porque llevan una vida tranquila... siempre igual.

A few Spanish proverbs and sayings a. *Into a closed mouth no flies enter.* ***b.*** *To be as bored as an oyster.* ***c.*** *When the drawer is open, the most honest person is (can become) a thief.*

The Past Participle / **El participio pasado**		
verbos en *-ar*	**verbos en *-er/-ir***	
hablar → hablado spoken	**comer → comido** eaten	**vivir → vivido** lived

the past participle / **el participio pasado** = the form of a verb used with *to have* in English to form the perfect tenses (*I have written, I had written. . .*)

Forming the Past Participle / **Cómo se forma el participio pasado**

1. Regular Forms

The past participle of most English verbs ends in *-ed: to walk → walked, to close → closed.* Many, however, are irregular: *to sing* → sung, *to write* → *written.*

In Spanish, the *past participle* (**el participio pasado**) is formed by adding **-ado** to the stem of regular **-ar** verbs, and **-ido** to the stem of regular **-er** and **-ir** verbs.

An accent mark is used on the past participle of **-er/-ir** verbs with stems ending in **-a, -e,** or **-o**.

El participio pasado
-ar → -ado
-er/-ir: → -ido

Pronunciation hint: **-d-** = [ð], like English *th*

caer	**→ caído**	**oír**	**→ oído**
creer	**→ creído**	**(son)reír**	**→ (son)reído**
leer	**→ leído**	**traer**	**→ traído**

2. Irregular Forms

Some Spanish verbs have irregular past participles. Only the verbs with * are new.

> **¡OJO!**
>
> The past participle of most compound verbs (such as **descubrir**) that have an irregular root verb (in this case, **cubrir**) have the same irregularity in the past participle: **(des)cubierto.**

abrir:	**abierto**	**morir:**	**muerto**
***cubrir:** (to cover)	**cubierto**	**poner:**	**puesto**
decir:	**dicho**	***resolver:** (to solve, resolve)	**resuelto**
***descubrir:** (to discover)	**descubierto**	**romper:**	**roto**
escribir:	**escrito**	**ver:**	**visto**
hacer:	**hecho**	**volver:**	**vuelto**

The Past Participle as an Adjective / **El participio pasado como adjetivo**

1. Used as an Adjective

In both English and Spanish, the past participle can be used as an adjective to modify a noun. Like other Spanish adjectives, the past participle must agree in number and gender with the noun modified.

Viven en **una casa construida** en 1920.
They live in a house built in 1920.

El español es solo una de **las lenguas habladas** en los Estados Unidos.
Spanish is only one of the languages spoken in the United States.

2. With *estar*

The past participle is frequently used with **estar** to describe conditions that are the result of a previous action.

El lago **está contaminado.**
The lake is polluted.

Todos los peces **estaban cubiertos** de crudo.
All the fish were covered with crude oil.

> **¡OJO!**
>
> English past participles often have the same form as the past tense.
>
> *I **closed** the book.*
> *The thief stood behind the **closed** door.*
>
> The Spanish past participle is never identical in form or use to a past tense.

Cerré la puerta. Ahora la puerta está **cerrada.**
*I **closed** the door. Now the door is **closed.***

Resolvieron el problema. Ahora el problema está **resuelto.**
*They **solved** the problem. Now the problem is **solved.***

Summary of Past Participle

-ar:	-ado/a
-er/-ir:	-ido/a

Vocabulario útil

estar parado/a	to be standing up
estar sentado/a	to be sitting

Algo sobre...

el mate

©Viviane Ponti/Lonely Planet Images/Getty Images/Getty Images

El mate, una tradición en la Argentina y el Uruguay

El mate es también conocido como la yerba[a] mate. Es un tipo de infusión[b] inmensamente popular en la Argentina y el Uruguay. Se toma tradicionalmente en un recipiente[c] también llamado «mate», hecho de una calabaza,[d] y con una bombilla, que es una pajilla[e] de metal para sorber[f] la infusión. El mate con frecuencia se comparte entre familiares y amigos.

En su opinion, ¿cuál es la bebida más popular de este país? ¿Cuál es la bebida que usted prefiere?

[a]*small plant, grass* [b]*herbal tea* [c]*container* [d]*gourd* [e]*straw* [f]*suck*

Práctica y comunicación

A. En este momento

Paso 1. Autoprueba. Dé el infinitivo de los siguientes participios pasados.

1. estudiadas
2. leído
3. vistos
4. dicha
5. abiertas
6. bebido

Paso 2. Use uno de los participios entre paréntesis en la forma apropiada para describir las siguientes cosas y personas del salón de clase.

1. la puerta y las ventanas del salón de clase (cerrado / abierto)
2. los libros de texto de los estudiantes (cerrado / abierto)
3. las luces (apagado / encendido)
4. el proyector (apagado / encendido)
5. los estudiantes (sentado / parado)
6. el profesor / la profesora (sentado / parado)

Paso 3. Ahora, en parejas, den ejemplos de las siguientes ideas.

MODELOS: 1. algo que puede estar cerrado o abierto →
Una puerta puede estar cerrad**a** o abiert**a**.
Algo que puede estar cerrad**o** o abiert**o** es una puerta.

1. algo que puede estar cerrado o abierto y que no está en el salón de clase
2. un edificio del campus bien diseñado
3. algo contaminado
4. el transporte público más usado en su ciudad
5. algo deseado por muchos estudiantes
6. el mejor libro escrito en inglés
7. una cosa rota en su casa/cuarto

B. ¿Cuánto sabe de la Argentina y del Uruguay? Para saber más, complete las siguientes oraciones con el participio pasado de uno de los siguientes infinitivos.

VERBOS: **acelerar, celebrar, conquistar (*to conquer*), desarrollar, escribir, establecer (*to establish*), preferir, reconocer (*to recognize*), separar, traer**

1. La Argentina y el Uruguay son dos países muy ______.
2. Los dos países están ______ por el estuario del Río de la Plata.
3. El gaucho es una figura ______ como símbolo nacional.
4. En la Pampa, hay grandes fincas ______ en la época colonial.
5. El mate es la bebida ______ de los argentinos y uruguayos.
6. Los guaraníes son un pueblo indígena ______ por los españoles.
7. Muchos guaraníes murieron a causa de enfermedades ______ por los europeos.
8. «El Aleph» es un cuento ______ por el famoso escritor argentino Jorge Luis Borges.
9. El carnaval de Montevideo, ______ por cuarenta días, es una de las celebraciones más largas del mundo.
10. En Buenos Aires y Montevideo, el ritmo de la vida es muy ______.

Prác. A, Paso 1: Answers: *1. estudiar 2. leer 3. ver 4. decir 5. abrir 6. beber*

C. Comentarios sobre nuestro mundo. Complete cada párrafo con el participio pasado de los verbos de cada lista.

VERBOS: **desperdiciar (*to waste*), destruir, hacer, reciclar**

Todos los días, se bota[a] a la basura aproximadamente media libra[b] de papel por persona. Todo ese papel _______[1] constituye un gran número de árboles _______.[2] Esto es un buen motivo para convencer a sus compañeros de estudio y de trabajo de no imprimir papel innecesariamente. También debe recordarles que solo se puede completar el ciclo del reciclaje si se compran productos _______[3] con materiales _______.[4]

[a]se... *people throw* [b]media... *half a pound*

VERBOS: **agotar (*to exhaust*), comprometer con (*to commit to*), convencer, limitar, preparar**

El petróleo como fuente[a] de energía no está _______[5] todavía,[b] pero su duración[c] es _______[6]. Desafortunadamente, todavía no estamos _______[7] para sustituirlo[d] completamente con otras energías renovables. El problema es que muy pocos países están verdaderamente[e] _______[8] con la reducción de emisiones de carbono y no están _______[9] de que es necesario que cambiemos la manera en que consumimos energía.

[a]*source* [b]*yet* [c]su... *the amount of time it will last* [d]*replace it* [e]*really*

D. ¡Ojo alerta! Las cocinas de los dibujos A y B se diferencian (*differ*) en por lo menos siete detalles. En parejas, encuéntrenlos todos. Si pueden, usen adjetivos que son participios pasados para describir los detalles.

A.

B.

Vocabulario útil

el grifo	faucet
agitar	
cortar	
(des)ordenar	to (dis)organize

E. ¿Hecho o por hacer todavía (*yet to be done*)?

Paso 1. Haga oraciones completas que sean verdaderas para usted. Use un participio pasado como adjetivo, según el modelo. Si usted no tiene ninguna de estas cosas, diga **«No tengo... »**, según el modelo.

MODELOS: una tarea para la clase de _______ →
Mi tarea para la clase de inglés **ya** está escrita.
Mi tarea para la clase de inglés **no** está escrita **todavía**.
No tengo que hacer ninguna tarea escrita para ninguna clase.

1. un informe (oral/escrito) para la clase de _______
2. una presentación oral para la clase de _______
3. los problemas para la clase de matemáticas _______
4. ¿ ?

Vocabulario útil

escribir
investigar (gu) to research
organizar (c)
preparar
resolver (resuelvo)

Paso 2. Ahora, en parejas, comparen sus respuestas. Díganle a la clase algo que tienen en común.

43 *¿Qué has hecho?*

Perfect Forms: Present Perfect Indicative and Present Perfect Subjunctive

Gramática en acción: Una llanta desinflada

¿Qué ha pasado? ¡Ay, no! ¡Una llanta desinflada! ¡Nunca he cambiado una llanta desinflada!

¿Y usted?

Diga si ha hecho lo siguiente alguna vez (*ever*).

1. ¿Le ha cambiado una llanta desinflada a un carro? (Le **he...** / **Nunca** le **he...**)
2. ¿Le ha revisado el aceite al coche?
3. ¿Le ha reparado otras cosas al coche?
4. ¿Ha tenido un accidente automovilístico?
5. ¿Ha excedido el límite de velocidad en la autopista?

Present Perfect Indicative / **El presente perfecto de indicativo**

haber + past participle (-ar → -**ado**, -er/-ir → -**ido**)			
he	I have		
has	you have		
ha	you have / he/she has	conserv**ado**	conserved
hemos	we have	proteg**ido**	protected
habéis	you have	constru**ido**	built
han	you/they have		

¡OJO!

Remember that some verbs have irregular past participles: **abierto, cubierto, dicho...**

1. Present Perfect Indicative

In English, to say *I have* (*written, spoken . . .*), you use a present tense form of *to have* plus the past participle. This compound tense is called the *present perfect*. The Spanish equivalent, **el presente perfecto**, is formed with present tense forms of **haber** plus the past participle.

In general, the Spanish present perfect tense is used just like the English present perfect.

¿**Has ido** al zoo de San Diego?
Have you been to the San Diego zoo?

El accidente en la autopista nos **ha retrasado**.
The accident on the highway has delayed us.

¿Ya **has escrito** el ensayo?
Have you written the essay yet?

¡OJO!

Haber is the only verb that can be used with the past participle to form the Spanish present perfect, which is never formed with **tener**. However, **tener** *can* be conjugated in the present perfect, using **haber,** of course.

He tenido muchos problemas con el carro desde que tuve el accidente.
I have had many problems with the car since I had the accident.

A flat tire *What has happened? Oh, no! A flat tire! I've never changed a flat tire!*

2. Form and Placement

Here is how **el presente perfecto** is formed.

- The masculine singular form of the past participle is *always* used.
- **Haber** and the past participle are never separated and their order never changes.
- **No** and object pronouns always come before the form of **haber, no** first, then the pronouns.

> **¡OJO!**
>
> Remember that **acabar** + **de** + *infinitive*—not the present perfect tense—is used to state that something *has just happened.*

Ella **ha cambiado** llantas varias veces.
She's changed tires several times.

¿**Han cambiado** ustedes una llanta alguna vez?
¿Ustedes **han cambiado** una llanta alguna vez?
Have you ever changed a tire?

Todavía **no he** escrito el ensayo.
I haven't written the essay yet.

—¿**Le han** dado el coche a su hija ya?
—No, **no se lo han** dado todavía.
"Have they given the car to their daughter already?" "No, they haven't given it to her yet."

Acabo de mandar el ensayo.
I've just sent the essay.

3. Present Perfect of *hay*

The present perfect form of **hay** is **ha habido.** It is invariable, and it expresses both *there has been* and *there have been.*

Ha habido mucha discusión sobre este tema.
There has been a lot of discussion about this topic.

Ha habido muchos accidentes en esta esquina.
There have been many accidents at this corner.

Present Perfect Subjunctive / **El presente perfecto de subjuntivo**

To express *I have written* (*spoken* ...) in a context that requires the subjunctive, use the present subjunctive forms of **haber** to form the *present perfect subjunctive* (**el presente perfecto de subjuntivo**).

The English equivalent of the Spanish present perfect subjunctive will vary according to the context, as shown in the examples. It can be either the simple past (*built, came, did*) or the present perfect (*have built, have come, have done*).

haya hablado	**hayamos vivido**
hayas comido	**hayáis abierto**
haya dicho	**hayan tenido**

Es bueno que **haya cambiado** usted el aceite.
It's good (*that*) *you changed* (*have changed*) *the oil.*

Me alegro de que **hayas venido.**
I'm glad (*that*) *you've come* (*you came*).

Es posible que **haya habido** un grave problema ecológico.
It's possible (*that*) *there was* (*has been*) *a serious ecological problem.*

Práctica y comunicación

A. ¿Una vida interesante?

Paso 1. Autoprueba. Dé la forma indicada de **haber.**

INDICATIVO:
1. yo ________
2. tú ________
3. nosotros ________

SUBJUNTIVO:
4. yo ________
5. ella ________
6. ellos ________

Ahora dé el participio pasado de los siguientes verbos.

7. arrancar ________
8. conducir ________
9. conservar ________
10. construir ________
11. obedecer ________
12. proteger ________
13. morir ________
14. romper ________
15. ver ________

> **Summary of Present Perfect**
>
> Indicative: **he, has, ha, hemos, habéis, han** + *past participle*
> Subjunctive: **haya, hayas, haya, hayamos, hayáis, han** + *past participle*

(*Continúa.*)

Prác. A, Paso 1: Answers: *1. he 2. has 3. hemos 4. haya 5. haya 6. hayan 7. arrancado 8. conducido 9. conservado 10. construido 11. obedecido 12. protegido 13. muerto 14. roto 15. visto*

Paso 2. Diga si usted ha hecho alguna vez las siguientes cosas o no. Siga el modelo.

MODELO: hacer un viaje al extranjero →
(No) He hecho un viaje al extranjero.

1. hacer un viaje al extranjero
2. montar en camello
3. comprar un auto nuevo
4. ocupar un cargo (*position*) político
5. tener una mascota
6. ver una película en español
7. escribir un poema
8. romperse el brazo o la pierna

Paso 3. Ahora, en parejas, hagan y contesten preguntas sobre las acciones del **Paso 2.** Luego díganle al resto de la clase una o dos acciones que tienen en común.

MODELO: hacer un viaje al extranjero →
E1: ¿**Has hecho** un viaje al extranjero?
E2: Sí, **he viajado** a México. ¿Y tú?
E1: Yo también **he viajado** a México. →
Los/Las dos **hemos viajado** a México.

B. El auto de Carmina. Carmina acaba de comprarse un auto usado. Describa lo que le ha pasado a Carmina, según el modelo.

MODELO: ir a la agencia de compra-venta →
Ha ido a la agencia de compra-venta.

1. pedirle ayuda a un amigo
2. ver diferentes coches y compararlos
3. mirar uno baratísimo
4. revisarle las llantas
5. conducirlo para probarlo
6. pensarlo y regresar a la agencia
7. decidir comprarlo
8. comprarlo
9. volver a casa
10. llevar a sus amigas al cine en su coche

C. ¡No lo creo!

Paso 1. Complete las siguientes oraciones con la forma apropiada del presente perfecto (indicativo o subjuntivo). Luego indique cuál de las oraciones de cada par expresa su opinión sobre sus compañeros de clase. Luego su profesor(a) va a hacerles preguntas a todos para saber cuál es la verdad en cada caso.

1. Creo que alguien en esta clase _______ las pirámides de Egipto. (ver) ☐
   Es dudoso que alguien _______ las pirámides de Egipto. (ver) ☐
2. Estoy seguro/a de que por lo menos uno de mis compañeros _______ una montaña alta. (escalar) ☐
   No creo que nadie _______ una montaña alta. (escalar) ☐
3. Creo que alguien _______ autostop en un viaje. (hacer) ☐
   Dudo que alguien _______ autostop en un viaje. (hacer) ☐
4. Creo que alguien _______ en paracaídas. (saltar) ☐
   Es improbable que alguien _______ en paracaídas. (saltar) ☐
5. Estoy seguro/a de que alguien _______ el metro en Nueva York. (tomar) ☐
   No creo que nadie _______ el metro neoyorquino. (tomar) ☐

Vocabulario útil

el paracaídas	parachute
escalar	to climb
hacer autostop	to hitchhike
saltar	to jump

Paso 2. Ahora complete las siguientes ideas sobre las actividades de sus compañeros esta semana. **¡OJO!** Hay que usar el indicativo o el subjuntivo.

1. (No) Creo que todos _______ un examen. (tener)
2. (No) Estoy seguro/a de que todos mis compañeros _______ varios mensajes. (escribir)
3. (No) Dudo que muchos compañeros _______ más de 100 videos en YouTube. (ver)
4. Es probable que nadie _______ un hueso (*bone*). (romperse)
5. Es obvio que nadie _______. (morir)

 **D. Opiniones sobre el medio ambiente**

Paso 1. ¿Qué se ha hecho en los últimos años para proteger el medio ambiente? En parejas, hagan oraciones completas en el presente perfecto de indicativo. Sus oraciones pueden ser afirmativas o negativas, según su opinión.

MODELO: este país: **desarrollar** nuevas formas de energía renovable →
Este país (no) **ha desarrollado** nuevas formas de energía renovable.

1. este país: **desarrollar** la energía eólica/solar
2. la población de esta ciudad: **reciclar** el papel, el plástico y el vidrio (*glass*) con regularidad
3. los seres humanos (*humans*): **proteger** muchas especies de animales
4. varios países: **destruir** zonas naturales para construir más viviendas
5. el aire de esta ciudad: **contaminarse** más
6. este estado: **construir** muchas carreteras nuevas

Paso 2. Ahora añadan un comentario personal a sus oraciones del **Paso 1.** Puede ser una explicación (con el indicativo) o una reacción personal (con el subjuntivo).

MODELOS: Este país no ha desarrollado suficientemente sus fuentes de energía renovable **porque tenemos mucho petróleo.**
Es terrible que este país no **haya desarrollado** suficientemente sus fuentes de energía renovable todavía.

E. Entrevista: ¿Lo has hecho o no?

Paso 1. Indique si usted ha hecho o no las siguientes cosas, según el modelo. Añada una cosa interesante que usted ha hecho ya y otra que no ha hecho todavía, pero que quiere hacer.

MODELOS: **visitar** la Argentina o el Uruguay →
He visitado la Argentina una vez.
Nunca **he visitado** la Argentina, pero sí **he visitado** el Uruguay.

1. **bailar** el tango
2. **manejar** un Alfa Romeo
3. **escribir** un poema
4. **actuar** en una obra teatral
5. **conocer** a una persona famosa
6. **caerse** de la bicicleta/moto(cicleta)
7. ¿ ?
8. ¿ ?

Paso 2. Ahora, usando como base las actividades del **Paso 1,** complete las siguientes oraciones con referencia a sus compañeros de clase o a su profesor(a). **¡OJO!** Tiene que decidir si va a usar el indicativo o el subjuntivo en estas oraciones.

MODELO: Creo que... → Creo que **la profesora ha manejado** un Alfa Romeo.

1. Creo que...
2. Dudo que...
3. Es probable que...
4. Estoy seguro/a de que...
5. Ojalá que...

 **Paso 3.** Lea sus oraciones del **Paso 2** a la clase entera. La persona nombrada en la oración va a decir si la oración es cierta o falsa.

Algo sobre...

el tango

©Daniel Garcia/AFP/Getty Images

Una pareja que baila un tango en Buenos Aires

El tango es sin duda uno de los bailes hispanos más conocidos en todo el mundo. Es netamente[a] argentino y uruguayo, ya que[b] nació[c] en la zona del Río de la Plata. Es un baile muy sensual que se baila en pareja. Con frecuencia la letra de los tangos es sentimental: habla de conflictos amorosos o de tristes recuerdos de los años pasados. El instrumento básico del tango, y el más tradicional, es el bandoneón, un tipo de acordeón.

 **¿Le gusta a usted bailar en pareja? ¿Qué baila? ¿algún baile latino?**

[a]*distinctly* [b]ya... *since*
[c]*it originated*

Nota comunicativa

El pluscuamperfecto: *había* + *participio pasado*

Use the past participle with the imperfect forms of **haber (había, habías, había, habíamos, habíais, habían)** to talk about what you had—or had not—done before a given time in the past. This form, called the *past perfect* (**el pluscuamperfecto**), is used like its English equivalent.

Antes de graduarme en la escuela secundaria, no **había estudiado** español.	*Before graduating from high school, I hadn't studied Spanish.*
Antes de 2002, mi hermana menor no **había nacido**.	*Before 2002, my youngest sister hadn't been born yet.*
Para agosto de 2020 ya **habíamos obtenido** la licencia de manejar.	*By August 2020, we had already gotten our driver's license.*

You will use the past perfect in **Práctica F** and **G**.

Vocabulario útil

empezar (empiezo) la universidad	
nacer (nazco)	to be born
recibir una multa	to get a fine
terminar la escuela secundaria	

F. Fechas importantes en su vida

Paso 1. ¿Qué había hecho o no había hecho usted para las siguientes fechas?

1. para julio de 2001
2. antes de enero de 2010
3. antes del verano de 2015
4. para la primavera de 2018
5. antes del verano pasado
6. para septiembre de este año

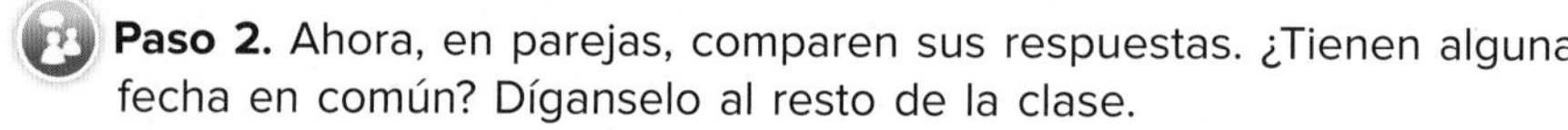

Paso 2. Ahora, en parejas, comparen sus respuestas. ¿Tienen alguna fecha en común? Díganselo al resto de la clase.

G. Intercambios

Paso 1. En parejas, hagan y contesten preguntas basadas en las siguientes frases. Inventen por lo menos una pregunta original.

MODELO: ¿qué cosa? / no **haber** aprendido a hacer antes del año pasado →
E1: ¿Qué cosa no **habías aprendido** a hacer antes del año pasado?
E2: Pues... no **había aprendido** a nadar. Aprendí a nadar este año en la clase de natación.

1. ¿qué cosa? / no **haber** aprendido a hacer antes de este semestre/trimestre
2. ¿qué materia? / no **haber** estudiado antes de venir a esta universidad
3. ¿qué deporte? / (no) **haber** practicado mucho antes de cumplir 16 años
4. ¿qué libro clásico o importante? / no **haber** leído antes de venir a esta universidad
5. ¿qué decisión? / no **haber** tomado antes de cumplir 18 años
6. ¿a quién de las personas importantes en su vida? / no **haber** conocido antes de venir a la universidad
7. ¿ ?

Paso 2. Ahora díganle a la clase algo de su historia personal que ustedes tienen en común. Si no tienen nada en común, cada uno debe contarle a la clase algo interesante de la vida de su compañero/a.

Todo junto

A. Lengua y cultura: El Parque Nacional Los Glaciares

Paso 1. Completar. Complete the following paragraphs with the correct form of the words in parentheses, as suggested by context. When two possibilities are given, select the correct word. Form adverbs with **-mente,** as needed. **¡OJO!** *PP:* = present perfect (indicative or subjunctive) *P/I:* = preterite or imperfect. Other infinitives are either present subjunctive or must remain in the infinitive form.

Algunos aspectos de la cultura y de la geografía de la Argentina son bien conocidos por todos. Seguro que ustedes _______ (*PP:* ver[1]) bailar el tango, porque es un baile que se _______ (*PP:* hacer[2]) muy popular _______ (reciente[3]) entre los bailes de salón.[a] Y casi todos _______ (saben / conocen[4]) qué es la Pampa y quiénes _______ (son / estar[5]) los gauchos.

Pero es fácil _______ (olvidar[6]) que la Argentina es un país larguísimo que se extiende desde la selva[b] tropical en la frontera[c] con el Brasil hasta la Antártida. _______ (Por / Para[7]) eso el país tiene una increíble variedad climática y geográfica.

El monte (*Mt.*) Fitz Roy, en la Patagonia

Si usted es aficionado/a al ecoturismo, _______ (se / le[8]) aconsejamos que _______ (visitar[9]) el Parque Nacional Los Glaciares, en _______ (el / la[10]) región de la Patagonia, al sur del país. El gobierno argentino _______ (*P/I:* crear[11]) el parque en 1937, y en 1982 la UNESCO _______ (lo / la[12]) _______ (*P/I:* declarar[13]) Patrimonio Natural de la Humanidad. Allí, en las 600.000 hectáreas[d] del parque, los visitantes pueden explorar impresionantes glaciares. Es posible _______ (escalar[14]) montañas de hielo[e] con grandes precipicios, que es un desafío[f] aun[g] para los _______ (mejor[15]) escaladores.[h]

[a]bailes... *ballroom dances* [b]*jungle* [c]*border* [d]*hectares (1 hectare = 2.47 acres)* [e]*ice* [f]*challenge* [g]*even* [h]*climbers*

Paso 2. Comprensión. Conteste las siguientes preguntas.

1. ¿Qué aspectos de la cultura argentina son bien conocidos?
2. ¿Por qué hay gran variedad climática y geográfica en la Argentina?
3. ¿En qué región está el Parque Nacional Los Glaciares?
4. ¿Por qué es tan (*so*) bueno el Parque para el alpinismo *(mountain climbing)*?

Paso 3. En acción

En parejas, comparen la Argentina con los Estados Unidos (o con su país de origen) en cuanto a (*with regard to*) la diversidad geográfica y climática. ¿Son comparables? ¿Cómo y por qué? Den ejemplos específicos.

B. Proyecto: Viñetas°

°*Cartoons*

¿Tienen ustedes talento para crear viñetas? ¡Vamos a ver!

[a]*Welcome* [b]me... *they sent me*

[c]aunque... *although adults* [d]historias... *scary stories*

Paso 1. Preparación. En parejas, estudien las dos viñetas en esta página. ¿En qué se enfocan? ¿Son cómicas? ¿críticas? ¿Conocen ustedes algunas viñetas similares? ¿Dónde las encuentran?

Paso 2. Investigación. Busquen dos viñetas en inglés sobre el medio ambiente o el tráfico y los conductores. Escriban el texto en español para cada una. O mejor aun (*even better*), creen sus propias viñetas. No se preocupen por el dibujo: si no son buenos dibujantes, simplemente describan la escena con palabras.

Paso 3. Presentación. Presenten sus viñetas a la clase.

¡Ahora, yo!

A. Entrevista. Use de modelo las preguntas y respuestas de la página 449 de este capítulo para hablar de sus preocupaciones por el medioambiente (si las tiene) y de su necesidad del coche o de su uso en su vida diaria.

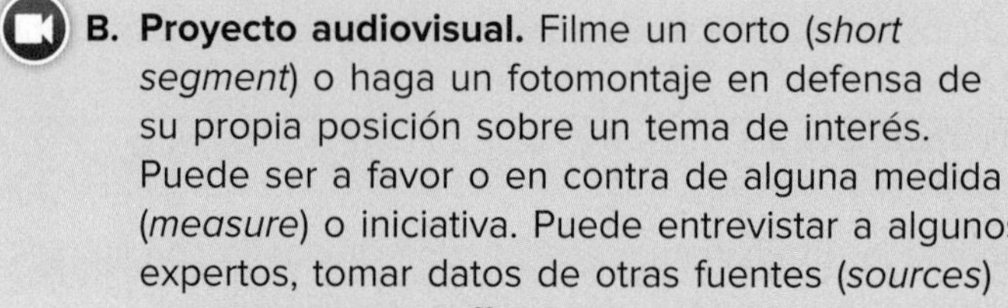

B. Proyecto audiovisual. Filme un corto (*short segment*) o haga un fotomontaje en defensa de su propia posición sobre un tema de interés. Puede ser a favor o en contra de alguna medida (*measure*) o iniciativa. Puede entrevistar a algunos expertos, tomar datos de otras fuentes (*sources*) y usar su voz en off.

«EcoSalu2» Segmento 2

Antes de mirar

Indique las oraciones que, en su opinión, son ciertas en relación con su ciudad.

1. ________ Hay buenos carriles (*lanes*) para las bicicletas.
2. ________ Hay suficiente estacionamiento para las bicicletas.
3. ________ Hay demasiado tráfico.
4. ________ Hay suficiente estacionamiento para los coches.
5. ________ Hay un buen sistema de transporte público.

La Avenida de la Reforma en la Ciudad de México, ocupada por cientos de ciclistas un domingo

Este segmento

Laura presenta un reportaje sobre la iniciativa de muchas ciudades para promover (*promote*) el uso de las bicicletas y reducir el uso de los coches. Al final, Ana y Víctor cierran el programa.

Vocabulario del segmento

qué hacer	what to do	**quedarse atrás**	to lag behind
a corto plazo	(in the) short term	**experimentar**	to experience
no solo... sino que	not only . . . but	**mejorar**	to improve
reportar	to create, produce	**la calidad**	quality
la red vial	road system	**ilimitado/a**	unlimited
la bici	**la bicicleta**	**por muy buen camino**	in the right direction
de manera que	so that		

Fragmento del guion

En el Distrito Federal, el programa se llama Ecobici. Por solo 300 pesos[a] anuales, menos de 30 dólares, puedes alquilar bicicletas de manera ilimitada por períodos de menos de 45 minutos. La ciudad cuenta con[b] 90 cicloestaciones, es decir, lugares donde estacionar la bici de forma práctica y segura.

[a]*Mexican currency* [b]cuenta... tiene

Después de mirar

A. ¿Está claro? Complete las siguientes oraciones según el programa.

1. Bicing es una iniciativa en ________ (Barcelona / Buenos Aires).
2. Hay iniciativas similares en otras ciudades ________ (españolas / españolas y europeas).
3. Ecobici es un programa para ________ (alquilar / comprar) bicicletas.
4. En el D.F. (La Ciudad de México) hay ________ (muchos / pocos) carriles para las bicicletas.
5. Los domingos la avenida de la Reforma ________ (se abre a las bicicletas y a los coches / se cierra a los coches).

B. Un poco más. Conteste las siguientes preguntas.

1. ¿Qué se ha construido en Barcelona para facilitar el uso de las bicicletas?
2. ¿Qué opciones incluye la iniciativa Bicing? ¿y la iniciativa Ecobici?
3. ¿Por qué son muy positivas estas iniciativas sobre el uso de la bicicleta?

C. Y ahora, ustedes. En grupos, hablen de las iniciativas que presenta Laura para la reducción de tráfico. ¿Hay alguna iniciativa similar en este país? ¿Y en su ciudad? Si no la tiene, ¿creen ustedes que la necesita? Justifiquen sus respuestas.

MUNDO HISPANO

Enfoque cultural: la Argentina y el Uruguay

Antes de leer

¿Qué ejemplos de belleza (*beauty*) natural hay en la zona donde usted vive?

Dos países con gran belleza natural

Tanto el Uruguay como la Argentina son países orgullosos[a] de la diversidad de su naturaleza. De norte a sur y de este a oeste, la Argentina tiene formidables atracciones naturales. Al norte, en la frontera con el Brasil y el Paraguay, están las cataratas[b] del Iguazú, una de las maravillas del mundo natural. Al sur se encuentra el impresionante glaciar Perito Moreno. Al oeste, en la frontera con Chile, la cordillera[c] de los Andes ostenta[d] el pico[e] más alto de todo el continente americano: el monte Aconcagua, de 6.962 metros (22.841 pies) de altura. En el centro, en un territorio compartido[f] con el Uruguay, se encuentra la Pampa, una interminable planicie[g] de tierras para el ganado[h] y el cultivo de granos. Al sur profundo, la Argentina continúa más allá del Estrecho de Magallanes[i] hasta la misma Antártida.

Por su parte, el Uruguay contiene los Humedales de Santa Lucía y del Este. Son tierras cubiertas de agua que mantienen ecosistemas de gran valor[j] medioambiental y el mayor parque de ombúes[k] del mundo.

[a]*proud* [b]*waterfalls* [c]*mountain range* [d]*is proud to show off* [e]*summit* [f]*shared* [g]*plain* [h]*cattle* [i]Estrecho... *Straight of Magellan* [j]*value* [k]*large shade trees*

En otros países hispanos

- **En Costa Rica, Colombia, el Ecuador, México, el Perú y Venezuela** Estas naciones están entre los diecisiete países megadiversos identificados por el Centro de Monitoreo de Conservación Ambiental, un organismo[a] del Programa de las Naciones Unidas para el Medio Ambiente (el PNUMA). Los países megadiversos, en su mayoría tropicales, son países que tienen el mayor porcentaje de biodiversidad en el planeta.

[a]*agency*

- **En España** En la actualidad, este país europeo está invirtiendo[b] en el desarrollo de las energías eólica y solar, ya que[c] el país disfruta de[d] innumerables horas de sol y buenas zonas de viento.

[b]*investing* [c]ya... *since* [d]disfruta... *enjoys*

©Cristian Lazzari/iStock/Getty Images

Vista aérea de Buenos Aires y el Río de la Plata

Un símbolo argentino y uruguayo: El Río de la Plata

El Río de la Plata es un río formado por la confluencia de dos ríos: el río Paraná y el río Uruguay. Este río se convierte en un gran estuario al entrar en el Atlántico. Es la frontera natural entre el Uruguay y la Argentina, y las capitales de estos países están junto a[a] estas aguas. El adjetivo derivado del Río de la Plata, «rioplatense», se usa para referirse a las personas y cosas de esta región de las dos naciones, que es una zona cultural y lingüística.

[a]junto... *next to*

Comprensión

1. ¿Qué destino turístico se destaca (*stands out*) en la Argentina?
2. ¿Qué región es parte tanto de la Argentina como del Uruguay?
3. ¿Qué países hispanos se clasifican como megadiversos? ¿Por qué lo son?
4. ¿Qué tipos de energías renovables son importantes en España ahora?
5. ¿Cuál es la frontera natural entre la Argentina y el Uruguay?

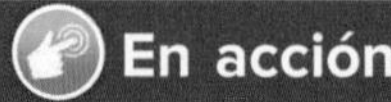

En acción

Describan uno o dos accidentes (*features*) geográficos que su país comparte (*shares*) con un país vecino. Luego mencionen las especies de animales o plantas que son autóctonas (*native*) de esas zonas geográficas.

Lectura

Antes de leer

La novela ***Asalto al paraíso*** describe la conquista de Costa Rica por los españoles y su impacto en las culturas indígenas de allí. El fragmento que usted va a leer consiste en los dos primeros párrafos del libro. Pa-brú Presbere, el protagonista indígena, se está preparando para una ceremonia espiritual guiado por (*led by*) el Kapá, un jefe (*chief*) religioso indígena. El Kapá describe algunas de las diferencias entre las creencias (*beliefs*) espirituales de la cultura indígena y la religión católica.

En preparación para la lectura, conteste las siguientes preguntas sobre el catolicismo.

1. ¿Es una religión monoteísta o politeísta?
2. Para los católicos, ¿dónde vive Dios (*God*): en la tierra, en el infierno o en el cielo (*heaven*)? ¿Y las personas?
3. ¿Cuántos «mundos» diferentes hay según la creencia católica? ¿Cuáles son?

Vocabulario para leer

arriba	above
abajo	below
satisfecho/a	satisfied

Extracto de la novela *Asalto al paraíso*, de Tatiana Lobo

Pa-brú Presbere sueña a[a] Surá, Señor del Mundo Más Abajo. Antes de comenzar el ayuno[b] comió el último pedazo[c] de plátano permitido, y alimentó el fuego[d] con la última ramita seca de cedro dulce.[e] La cueva[f] se iluminó. Quizá[g] cerca, quizá lejos, caminó la danta sagrada.[h] Puso atención a las últimas palabras del Kapá:

«Así es[i] —dijo éste—. El orden de las cosas está dispuesto[j] de esta manera; hay tres mundos hacia arriba, con rocas, nubes, vientos y estrellas.[k] Sibú vive por allí. Y hay tres mundos para abajo, donde vive el señor Surá... Las cosas verdaderas están en los mundos inferiores: de allá abajo nace[l] la vida, allá abajo el hombre tiene su raíz[m]; y también su cabeza, porque abajo regresamos al morir. Este es el misterio que los hombres de musgo en las quijadas[n] no pueden comprender. Ellos ordenan el universo al revés,[ñ] tienen un único dios en el cielo, y no ven que Sibú es imposible sin Surá. Engañados[o] por su dios solitario, caminan con sus largos vestidos, de aquí para allá, de allá para acá: nunca se asientan,[p] nunca están satisfechos... ».

[a]sueña... *dreams of* [b]*fast* [c]*piece* [d]alimentó... *he fed the fire* [e]ramita... *dry branch of sweet cedar* [f]*cave* [g]*Perhaps* [h]danta... *sacred tapir* [i]Así... *It's like this* [j]*arranged* [k]*stars* [l]*is born* [m]*root, origin* [n]de... *with moss on their jaws* [ñ]al... *backwards* [o]*Deceived* [p]nunca... *they never settle down*

Comprensión

A. Resumen del texto. Empareje cada elemento con la cultura que representa.

CULTURAS

1. ________ los indígenas de Costa Rica
2. ________ los españoles

SUS PERSONAS Y CREENCIAS RELIGIOSAS

a. Hay seis mundos, tres arriba y tres abajo.
b. Hay un solo Dios que vive en el cielo.
c. Hay dos Señores, Sibú y Surá, cada uno responsable por tres mundos.
d. Las personas no están tranquilas, quizá porque buscan a su dios.
e. Hay un Kapá.
f. Las personas viven abajo, donde la vida es real.
g. Los hombres tienen barba.

B. Interpretación. Conteste las siguientes preguntas.

1. Este texto implica que la persona que escucha al Kapá se preparó para una ceremonia espiritual. ¿Qué hizo para prepararse para esta experiencia?
2. Este texto incluye una fuerte (*strong*) crítica de la fe (*faith*) católica y posiblemente de todas las religiones monoteístas. ¿Dónde se ve la crítica en el texto?
3. A pesar de (*Despite*) las diferencias entre las dos religiones que se contrastan en el breve fragmento, también hay algunos paralelismos. ¿Cuáles son?

 Proyecto: Los pueblos° indígenas de Latinoamérica

°peoples

La conquista de Latinoamérica por los españoles tuvo como uno de sus objetivos dominar e incluso exterminar las culturas indígenas del continente americano. Sin embargo, muchos pueblos indígenas han sobrevivido (*survived*) el «asalto» y siguen conservando sus culturas. Para este proyecto, usted va a investigar la situación de un grupo indígena en el mundo de hoy y luego hacer una presentación a la clase.

Paso 1: Seleccione un pueblo indígena que habita en una región latinoamericana (incluyendo el Caribe).

Paso 2: Busque la siguiente información sobre el pueblo: su(s) nombre(s), lengua(s) que hablan, territorio donde viven y datos demográficos básicos, modo de vida, algunas tradiciones culturales y creencias espirituales y religiosas, la relación que tienen con el pueblo mayoritario y/o con el gobierno de su país y los problemas que enfrentan (*they face*). Incluya algunas imágenes y mapas.

Paso 3: Organice la información y prepare una presentación para la clase.

 Textos orales

Una campaña° para Greenpeace en la radio

°campaign

Vocabulario para escuchar

hacer campaña	to have a campaign
el partido político	political party
las pilas	batteries

Antes de escuchar

¿Qué problemas medioambientales le preocupan a usted? ¿Le preocupan más los problemas locales o los internacionales? ¿Es usted miembro/a de alguna organización dedicada a la protección del medio ambiente?

¡OJO!

En la Argentina y el Uruguay, así como en muchos países centroamericanos, se usa el pronombre personal **vos** en vez del (*instead of the*) pronombre **tú**. Los mandatos informales con **vos** tienen formas diferentes de los mandatos con **tú**. En el programa de radio, usted va a escuchar algunos de estos mandatos.

escuchá = escucha
pensá = piensa
unite = únete
hacete = hazte
ayudá = ayuda
andá = anda (*go*)
defendé = defiende

Comprensión

A. ¿Cierto o falso? Indique si las siguientes oraciones son ciertas o falsas. Corrija las falsas.

	CIERTO	FALSO
1. Greenpeace tiene una organización en la Argentina.	☐	☐
2. Greenpeace recibe dinero de varios gobiernos.	☐	☐
3. Greenpeace solo se preocupa por los problemas de la contaminación del aire y el agua.	☐	☐
4. Greenpeace solo busca miembros que contribuyan con dinero a la organización.	☐	☐

B. Más detalles. Conteste las siguientes preguntas.

1. ¿Cómo se llama el programa? ¿En qué tipo de estación de radio se presenta?
2. ¿Para qué tipo de oyentes (*listeners*) es este programa? ¿Por qué dice usted eso?
3. ¿Cómo trata de convencer el locutor (*host*) del programa a sus oyentes (*listeners*) de que es importante hacerse miembro de Greenpeace?
4. ¿Cuáles son dos de los temas que preocupan a Greenpeace?

En acción

Busque la página web de Greenpeace Argentina. Lea algunas de las noticias que reporta la organización allí y haga un resumen de tres de ellas para decírselo a la clase.

Proyecto en su comunidad

Entreviste a una persona hispana de su universidad o ciudad sobre cuestiones medioambientales relacionados con su país de origen.

Preguntas posibles

- ¿Hay problemas de contaminación en su ciudad o país de origen? ¿Qué los causa?
- ¿Qué está haciendo el país para preservar los recursos naturales? ¿Y para disminuir la contaminación?
- ¿Ve un cambio en la actitud de las personas de su país o ciudad con relación a la conservación de los recursos naturales?
- ¿Hay programas de reciclaje? ¿Cree que son efectivos?

Escritura

Proyecto: Un ensayo sobre los efectos del cambio° climático

°*change*

Como usted sabe, hay un debate internacional sobre el cambio climático y lo que las naciones deben hacer para cambiar esta situación. En este capítulo, va a escribir un ensayo en el que (which) defiende su postura (position) personal sobre el tema.

Antes de escribir

En parejas, piensen en el tema del cambio climático. ¿Hay más de una postura con respecto al tema? Según algunos científicos, ¿cuáles son las causas del cambio climático? ¿Cuáles son sus efectos? ¿Qué opinan las personas que no están de acuerdo con la idea del cambio climático?

Hagan una lista de los cuatro o cinco efectos del cambio climático que, en su opinión, son más problemáticos. También hagan una lista de los argumentos de los defensores del cambio climático, y otra, de los que (*those who*) se oponen a este concepto.

©unmillonedeelefantes/Shutterstock

¿Van a sobrevivir (*survive*) el cambio clímático los pingüinos?

A escribir

Ahora defina su postura personal y defiéndala en un su ensayo. Hay más ayuda en Connect.

Más ideas para su portafolio

- Incluya una lista de las cosas que usted ha hecho en su vida de las que se siente más orgulloso/a (*proud*) y otra lista de las cosas que no ha hecho todavía pero que desea hacer.
- Lo más... Incluya una lista de las cosas más raras o extraordinarias ¡o peores! que usted ha visto (hecho, comido...) en su vida.
- Si ha estado jugando Practice Spanish: Study Abroad, en Quest 9 usted aprendió de tres medios de transporte público en Colombia: el minibús, el autobús y el superbús. ¿Cuál es la diferencia entre ellos? ¿Ha tomado usted el autobús en un país hispanohablante o en el país donde usted vive? Escriba un párrafo sobre su experiencia. Si ha tomado el autobús en ambos (*both*) lugares, haga una comparación entre las dos experiencias.

©McGraw-Hill Education

Sugerencia: You are now ready to play Quest 9 in **Practice Spanish: Study Abroad.**

EN RESUMEN En este capítulo

AFTER STUDYING THIS CHAPTER I CAN . . .

- ☐ talk about natural and urban environments (450–451)
- ☐ talk about cars and driving (454)
- ☐ describe with adjectives that are also past participles (458–459)
- ☐ use the present and past perfect to express what *has* and *had happened* (462–463, 466)
- ☐ recognize/describe at least 2–3 aspects of Argentine and Uruguayan cultures

Gramática en breve

42. Past Participle Used As Adjective

Regular Past Participles

-ar → -ado/a
-er/-ir → -ido/a

Irregular Past Participles

abierto/a, cubierto/a, descubierto/a, dicho/a, escrito/a, hecho/a, muerto/a, puesto/a, resuelto/a, roto/a, visto/a, vuelto/a

43. Present Perfect Indicative and Subjunctive

Present Perfect Indicative		***Present Perfect Subjunctive***	
present indicative of **haber** + *past participle*		present subjunctive of **haber** + *past participle*	
he	**hemos**	**haya**	**hayamos**
has	**habéis**	**hayas**	**hayáis**
ha	**han**	**haya**	**hayan**

Past Perfect Indicative

imperfect of **haber** + *past participle*

había	**habíamos**
habías	**habíais**
había	**habían**

Vocabulario

Los verbos

cubrir	to cover
descubrir (*like* **cubrir**)	to discover
evitar	to avoid
resolver (like volver)	to solve, resolve

Los recursos naturales

el bosque	forest
la energía (eólica, renovable)	(wind, renewable) energy
el lago	lake
el medio ambiente	environment
la naturaleza	nature
el reciclaje	recycling
el río	river
la Tierra	Earth
el recurso natural	natural resource

Cognados: el aire, la energía eléctrica/nuclear/solar, el petróleo, el planeta

Repaso: el árbol, la montaña

conservar	to save, conserve
construir	to build
contaminar	to pollute
desarrollar	to develop
destruir (*like* **construir**)	to destroy
fabricar (qu)	to manufacture
proteger (protejo)	to protect
reciclar	to recycle

Repaso: acabar

El desarrollo

el/la agricultor(a)	farmer
la agricultura	farming, agriculture
el/la campesino/a	farmer; field laborer
el campo	field; countryside
la capa de ozono	ozone layer
el delito	crime
la densidad	density
el desarrollo	development
la fábrica	factory
la falta	lack; absence
la finca	farm
el gobierno	government
la población	population
el rascacielos	skyscraper
el ritmo lento / acelerado de la vida	slow / fast pace of life
el servicio	service

Repaso: la ciudad, la contaminación, el transporte, la vida

Los animales

la ballena	whale
la especie (en peligro de extinción)	(endangered) species
el pez (*pl.* **peces**)	fish
el toro	bull

la vaca	cow

Cognados: el elefante, el gorila

Repaso: el caballo, el gato, el pájaro, el perro

Los vehículos

la estación de servicio	gas station
los frenos	brakes
la gasolinera	gas station
la llanta (desinflada)	(flat) tire
el/la mecánico/a	mechanic
el parabrisas	windshield
el taller	(repair) shop
el tanque	tank

Cognados: el auto(móvil), la batería, el carro, la gasolina, la moto(cicleta), el SUV

Repaso: el aceite, la bicicleta, la camioneta, el coche, el vehículo

arrancar (qu)	to start up (*a car*)
arreglar	to fix, repair
gastar	to use (*gas*)
llenar	to fill (up)
revisar	to check

Cognado: reparar

En la carretera

la acera	sidewalk
la autopista	freeway, interstate
la bocina	horn (*car*)
la circulación	traffic
el/la conductor(a)	driver
la esquina	(street) corner
el estacionamiento	parking place/lot
la licencia de manejar/conducir	driver's license
el límite de velocidad	speed limit
el/la policía	police officer
el semáforo	traffic signal
el tránsito	traffic
la carretera	highway

Cognado: el tráfico

Repaso: la avenida, la calle

conducir	to drive
doblar	to turn
manejar	to drive
obedecer (obedezco)	to obey
parar	to stop
seguir (sigo) (i)	to keep on going
tocar (qu)	to honk

Repaso: chocar (qu) (con), estacionar

¿Cómo se llega a... ?	How do you get to . . . ?
(todo) derecho/recto	straight ahead

Repaso: a la derecha, a la izquierda, por (through)

Los adjetivos

acelerado/a	fast, accelerated
bello/a	beautiful
contaminado/a	contaminated, polluted
descapotable	convertible
doméstico/a	domesticated, tame
lento	slow
renovable	renewable
salvaje	wild
todoterreno (*inv.*)	all-terrain

Cognados: híbrido/a, natural, público/a, puro/a

Palabras adicionales

alguna vez	ever

Vocabulario personal

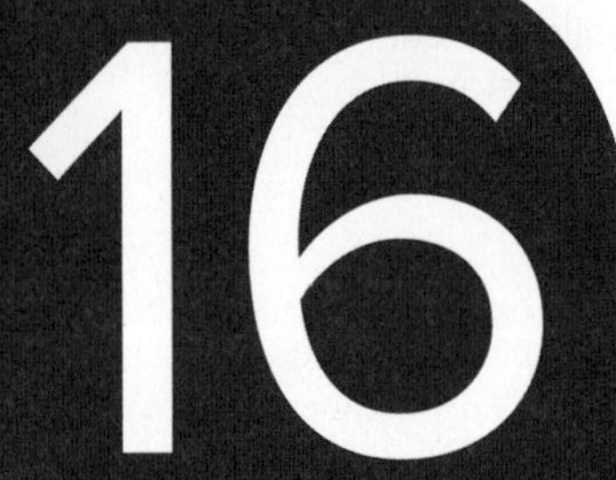

16 La vida social y afectiva

En este capítulo

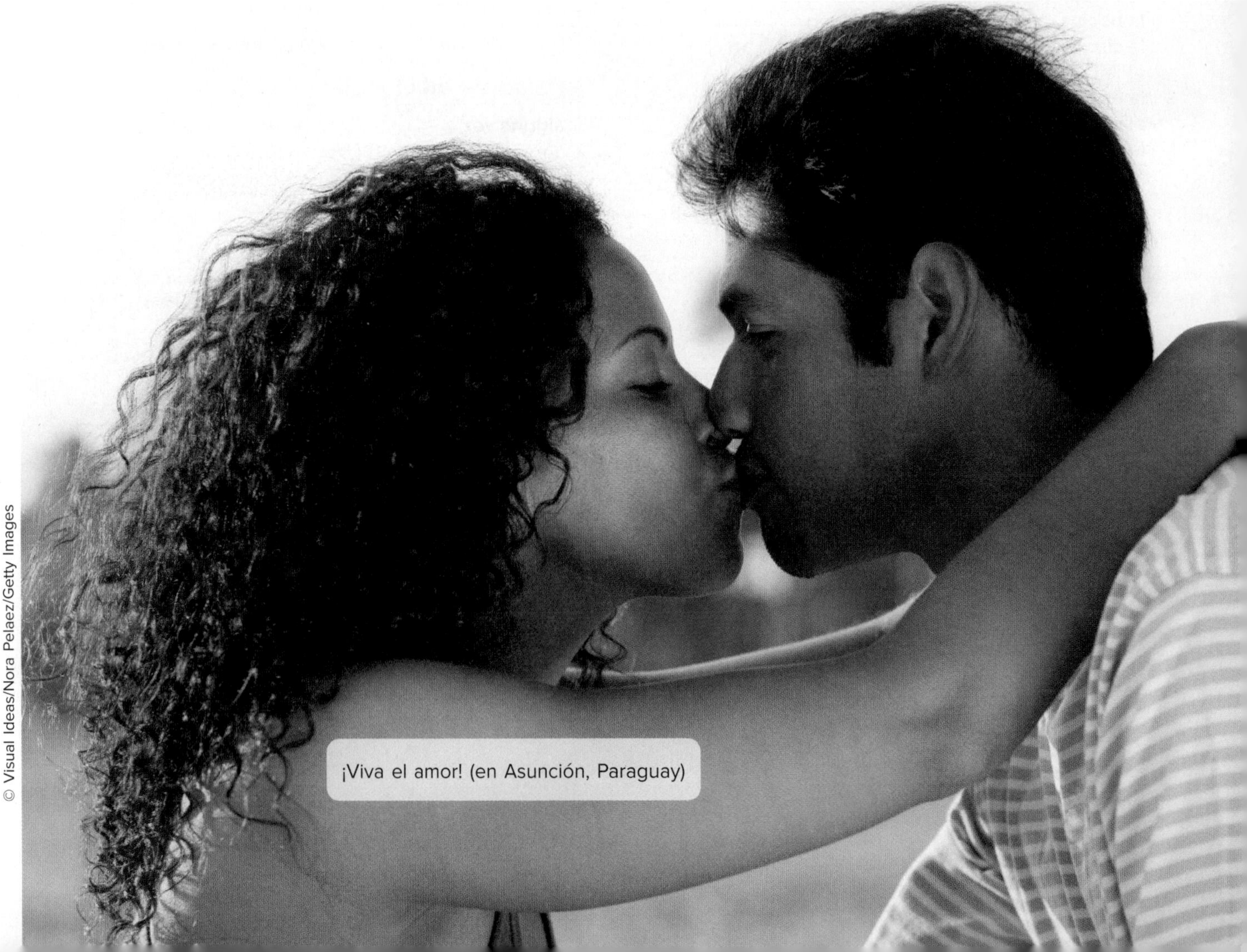

¡Viva el amor! (en Asunción, Paraguay)

EL PARAGUAY

6,9 (coma nueve) millones de habitantes

- El Paraguay es uno de los dos países sudamericanos que no tiene salida[a] al mar. (El otro es Bolivia.)
- Los guaraníes son el pueblo indígena que habitaba en el territorio que hoy es el Paraguay, así como[b] en partes del noreste de la Argentina, el sureste de Bolivia y el suroeste del Brasil.
- El nombre «Paraguay» viene de la lengua guaraní. También es el nombre de uno de los grandes ríos que atraviesan[c] el país. El otro es el río Paraná.

[a]*access* [b]así... *as well as* [c]*cross*

ENTREVISTA

- ¿Tiene usted pareja? ¿novio o novia? ¿esposo o esposa? ¿O sale con alguien?
- En este momento, ¿cuál es la relación social más importante de su vida? ¿Es una relación romántica o una de amistad? ¿O es su relación con su familia?
- ¿Cree usted en el amor a primera vista? ¿Y en el amor para toda la vida? En su opinión, ¿qué es necesario para que[a] haya una relación feliz y duradera[b] entre una pareja?

[a]para... *so that* [b]*lasting*

Gabriela Romano Acosta contesta las preguntas.

- Sí, tengo pareja. Bueno, es algo reciente. Empecé a salir con un chico de la universidad hace un mes más o menos. No es nada serio... por ahora. Pero está bien. Es lindo.[a]
- En este momento, mi familia y mis amigos de siempre son lo más importante. En el futuro, espero tener un compañero e hijos y que ellos sean lo más importante de mi vida. Pero, por ahora, es pronto para eso.
- ¡Ay, no sé! Creo que uno puede enamorarse[b] a primera vista, pero no creo que eso sea suficiente para que el amor dure[c] para siempre. Es difícil que el amor dure toda la vida, ¿no? Pero es bonito pensar que puede ser. Y para eso es necesario que las dos personas de la pareja se comprendan y se apoyen[d] mutuamente.

[a]Es... *It's nice* [b]*fall in love* [c]*lasts* [d]se... *support each other*

VOCABULARIO: PREPARACIÓN

You can hear the pronunciation of theme vocabulary words and phrases in the Connect eBook.

Las relaciones sentimentales

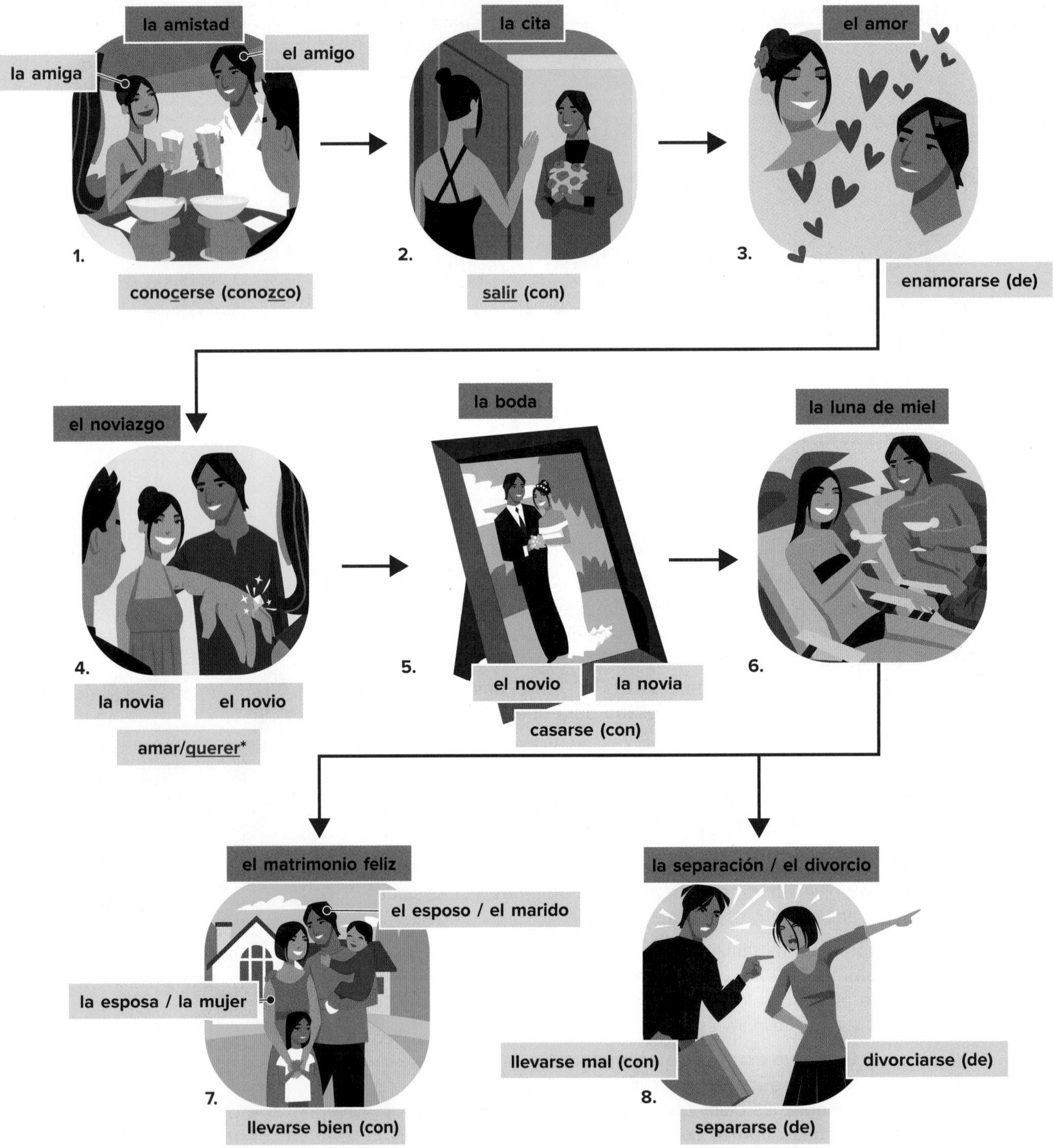

*__Amar__ *and* __querer__ *both mean to love, but* __amar__ *can imply more romantic passion in some dialects of Spanish.*

Las etapas° de la vida

Las... *Stages*

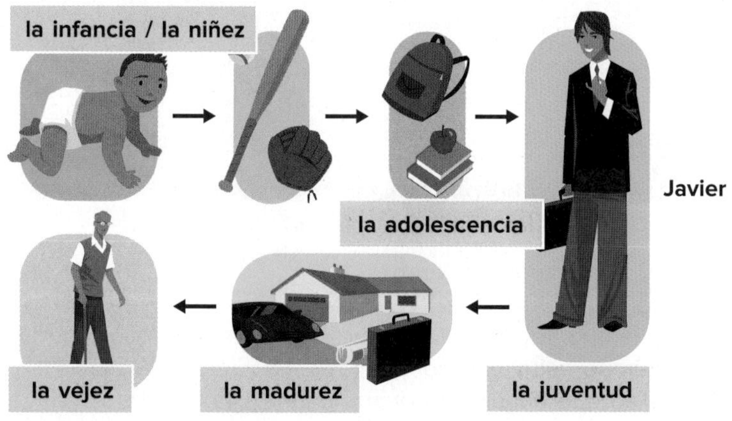

la muerte	death
nacer (nazco)	to be born
crecer (crezco)	to grow
morir (muero) (u)	to die

Comunicación

A. Etapas de la vida

Paso 1. Relacione las siguientes palabras y frases con las distintas etapas de la vida de una persona. **¡OJO!** Hay más de una relación posible en algunos casos.

1. el amor
2. los nietos
3. los juguetes (*toys*)
4. no poder comer sin ayuda
5. los hijos en la universidad
6. los granos (*pimples*)
7. la universidad
8. la boda

Paso 2. Ahora dé una definición o descripción de las siguientes etapas de la vida. Pueden ser descripciones serias o divertidas.

MODELOS: La infancia es cuando una persona tiene menos de dos años.
La infancia es la etapa de la vida en que solo te importa comer, dormir y jugar.

1. la niñez **2.** la adolescencia **3.** la madurez **4.** la vejez

B. Etapas de su vida

Paso 1. Describa lo que usted hacía, hace o piensa hacer, y sus sentimientos, en cada etapa de su vida.

MODELO: mi niñez → **Vivía** en Oklahoma. **Tuve** una niñez feliz. Siempre...

1. mi niñez
2. mi adolescencia
3. mi juventud
4. mi madurez
5. mi vejez

Paso 2. Ahora, en parejas o en grupos, comparen sus descripciones. Luego díganle a la clase lo que ustedes tienen en común.

Estrategia

Para hablar de cada etapa de la vida, es apropiado usar diferentes tiempos verbales. Ejemplos:

- **el pasado:** el pretérito, el imperfecto, el presente perfecto
- **la época actual:** el presente, el presente progresivo
- **el futuro: ir + a** + *infinitive*

Algo sobre...

el Gran Chaco

El Gran Chaco es una inmensa altiplanicie[a] aluvial[b] formada por los ríos Paraguay y Pilcomayo. Ocupa gran parte del Paraguay, además de[c] parte de Bolivia, la Argentina y el Brasil. Su nombre, que viene del quechua, significa tierra de caza.[d] Es una región poco poblada, pero curiosamente hay varias ciudades fundadas por colonias menonitas, alemanas y rusas que llegaron en la década de 1920.

¿Hay en este país alguna región transnacional, es decir, que va más allá de las fronteras nacionales?

[a]*high plateau* [b]*alluvial, formed by river deposits* [c]además... *in addition to* [d]*hunting*

SALU'

«Cosas del amor» Segmento 1

« ...él siempre me apoya (*supports*) en todo lo que yo quiera hacer. Y sin él, la verdad,... ya no soy completa».

Antes de mirar

¿Qué sabe usted de la historia romántica de sus padres o madres (o abuelos)? Conteste las siguientes preguntas.

1. ¿Dónde y cómo se conocieron?
2. ¿Fue amor a primera vista?
3. ¿Cuánto tiempo llevan juntos (*have they been together*)? ¿O cuánto tiempo estuvieron juntos?
4. ¿Cree usted que hacen una buena pareja? ¿Por qué?

Este segmento

Este segmento incluye unas entrevistas que Laura les hace a varias parejas para saber cómo se conocieron. El segmento termina con la historia de Víctor y su esposa.

Vocabulario del segmento

¡Qué asco!	How disgusting!
maravilloso/a	wonderful
acudir a	to attend, go to
casualmente	by chance
coincidir	to be (*somewhere*) at the same time by chance
cerquita de	very near to
inesperado/a	unexpected
nos dimos la mirada	**nos miramos**

Después de mirar

A. ¿Está claro? Empareje cada pareja con la descripción de cómo se conocieron.

LAS PAREJAS	¿CÓMO SE CONOCIERON?
1. _____ primera pareja	**a.** Trabajaron juntos en un proyecto en la comunidad.
2. _____ segunda pareja	**b.** Se conocieron en una fiesta.
3. _____ tercera pareja	**c.** Se conocieron en un baile en Ciudad Delicias, donde él tocaba.
4. _____ Víctor y su esposa	**d.** Se vieron cuando ella estaba haciendo fotocopias.

B. Un poco más. Conteste las siguientes preguntas.

1. ¿Dónde viven todas las parejas que se ven en el segmento?
2. La mayoría de las parejas, ¿creen o no en el amor a primera vista?
3. ¿Está casada Ana? ¿Por qué cree usted eso?

C. Y ahora, ustedes En parejas, hablen de la idea del amor a primera vista. ¿Creen en ello (*that concept*)? ¿Han tenido esa experiencia alguna vez? Expliquen sus respuestas y, si pueden, den ejemplos específicos.

GRAMÁTICA

¿Recuerda usted?

Before studying **Gramática 44,** review the indefinite and negative words that you learned in **Gramática 19 (Cap. 7).** Remember that **alguien** and **nadie** take the personal **a** when they are used as direct objects.

Busco **a alguien** de la familia.	*I'm looking for someone from the family.*
No veo **a nadie** en el salón de baile.	*I don't see anyone in the dance hall.*

Give the opposite of the following words.
1. nada **2.** algunos **3.** alguien

44 *¿Hay alguien que... ? ¿Hay un lugar donde... ?*

The Subjunctive (Part 6): The Subjunctive After Nonexistent and Indefinite Antecedents

Gramática en acción: Los buenos padres

©Maskot/Image Source

- Un buen padre, así como una buena madre, es **alguien que quiere** a sus hijos de manera incondicional, **se preocupa** por su formación y les **enseña** a ser personas útiles en la vida.
- Todos los niños **necesitan madres y padres que** los quieran incondicionalmente, los eduquen y los cuiden.

¿Y usted?

Complete las siguientes oraciones.

1. No hay nadie que me quiera más que mi(s) _______.
2. Mi madre/padre es la persona que me enseñó a _______.
3. La persona que se preocupa más por mí en la actualidad es mi _______.

①		②
definite/existing antecedent	**que**	**indicative**
indefinite/nonexisting antecedent	**que**	**subjunctive**

the antecedent / **el antecedente** = a word or phrase modified by an adjective clause

Good parents ■ *A good father, just like a good mother, is someone who loves his/her children unconditionally, worries about their education, and teaches them to live useful lives (i.e., be useful in life).* ■ *All children need mothers and fathers who love them unconditionally, educate them, and take care of them.*

1. Adjective Clauses and Antecedents

As you know, noun clauses function like nouns in a sentence. Adjective clauses function like adjectives: they modify/describe a noun or a pronoun. In the sentences to the right, the nouns *car* and *house* (*for sale*) are modified by dependent adjective clauses. The noun that is modified is called the *antecedent* (**el antecedente**) of the dependent clause.

I have a **car that gets good gas mileage.**
Is there a **house for sale that is closer to the city**?

2. Indicative with Existing Antecedents

The indicative is used in the adjective clause when it refers to or modifies something that the speaker knows exists.

DEFINITE/EXISTING ANTECEDENT: INDICATIVE

Vi un coche que me **gusta** y que no **es** caro.
I saw a car (that) I like and that's not expensive.

Hay algo aquí que **quiero** ver.
There's something here that I want to see.

Estoy buscando un libro que **estaba** aquí.
I'm looking for a book that was here.

3. Subjunctive with Nonexistent and Indefinite Antecedents

Sometimes the antecedent of an adjective clause is something that does not exist from the point of view of the speaker, or something whose existence is indefinite, uncertain, or just not yet identified. In these cases, the subjunctive must be used in the adjective (dependent) clause in Spanish.

INDEFINITE/NONEXISTENT ANTECEDENT: SUBJUNCTIVE

No hay nadie aquí que **hable** guaraní.
There is no one here who speaks Guaraní.

Busco a alguien que **hable** guaraní.
I'm looking for someone who speaks Guaraní. (That person may exist, but I don't know for sure.)

No conozco a nadie que **hable** guaraní.
I don't know anyone who speaks Guaraní.

Necesito un coche que no **gaste** mucha gasolina.
I need a car that doesn't use much gas. (The car may exist, but I haven't identified it yet.)

4. Adjective Clauses That Describe a Place

When the adjective clause describes a place, the word **donde** (rather than **que**) introduces the adjective clause.

INDEFINITE ANTECEDENT: SUBJUNCTIVE

Buscamos un restaurante donde sirvan comida chilena auténtica.
We're looking for a restaurant where they serve authentic Chilean food.

5. Questions Versus Answers with Adjective Clauses

The *subjunctive* is used in the dependent clause in a question about something that the speaker does not know exists for certain. However, the indicative or the subjunctive may be used in the answer, depending on whether the person who answers the question is sure of the existence of the antecedent or not.

QUESTION: SUBJUNCTIVE

—¿**Hay algo** aquí que te **guste**?
"Is there anything here that you like?"

DEFINITE ANTECEDENT: INDICATIVE

—Sí, **hay varios bolsos** que me **gustan.**
"Yes, there are several purses that I like."

NEGATIVE ANTECEDENT: SUBJUNCTIVE

—No, **no hay nada** aquí que me guste**.**
"No, there's nothing here that I like."

6. **Use of the Personal *a***

Remember that the personal **a** is used only before specific persons or animals. It is not used before unknown or nonspecific persons.

UNKNOWN PERSON: SUBJUNCTIVE

Busco **un estudiante** que **sepa** francés.
I'm looking for a student who knows French. (I don't know of any.)

KNOWN PERSON: INDICATIVE

Busco **al** estudiante que **sabe** francés.
I'm looking for the student who knows French. (I know there's one in our office.)

DIRECT OBJECT

¿Conoces **a alguien** que sepa francés?
Do you know someone who speaks French?

NOT DIRECT OBJECT

No hay **nadie** aquí que sepa francés.
There's no one here who speaks French.

> **¡OJO!**
>
> The personal **a** is always used before **alguien** and **nadie** when they are direct objects.

Práctica y comunicación

Summary of Nonexistent and Indefinite Antecedents

existing, definite → indicative
nonexistent, indefinite → subjunctive

A. Hablando de la gente que conocemos

Paso 1. Autoprueba. Indique cuáles de las siguientes oraciones expresan antecedentes indefinidos o inexistentes.

1. A friend is looking for a counselor who speaks Spanish.
2. I have a friend who is a marriage counselor.
3. I don't know of a good counselor who has an office downtown.
4. I'm looking for the counselor who helped us the last time.

Paso 2. Indique las oraciones que sean verdaderas para usted y cambie las otras para que (*so that*) sean verdaderas.

MODELO: Conozco a alguien que va a casarse este año. →
No conozco a **nadie** que **vaya** a casarse este año.

	CIERTO	FALSO
1. Conozco a alguien que va a casarse este año.	☐	☐
2. Tengo un amigo íntimo / una amiga íntima que está casado/a.	☐	☐
3. Conozco a alguien que está recién casado.	☐	☐
4. Tengo un pariente cercano (*close*) que se está divorciando.	☐	☐
5. Tengo un buen amigo que es viudo.	☐	☐
6. Conozco a una estudiante de mi año que está en su viaje de luna de miel.	☐	☐
7. No conozco a nadie que haya roto con su novio/a este año.	☐	☐
8. Sé de alguien que sale con una persona famosa.	☐	☐

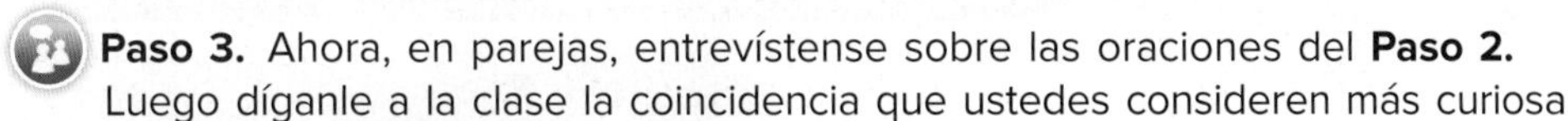

Paso 3. Ahora, en parejas, entrevístense sobre las oraciones del **Paso 2.** Luego díganle a la clase la coincidencia que ustedes consideren más curiosa.

B. Hablando de bodas

Paso 1. Complete las siguientes oraciones según lo que se ve en el dibujo.

1. Hay un hombre que _______ (está / esté) sacando una foto.
2. Hay una persona que _______ (está / esté) llorando.
3. Hay un hombre que _______ (está / esté) sonriendo.
4. Hay dos niñas que se _______ (están / estén) peleando.
5. No hay nadie que _______ (está / esté) cantando.
6. ¿Hay alguien que _______ (está / esté) tirando (*throwing*) arroz?

(*Continúa*)

***Prác. A, Paso 1:* Answers:** *1, 3*

Paso 2. Ahora complete las siguientes oraciones según su experiencia. Use el indicativo o el subjuntivo, según el caso.

En las bodas que yo he visto,...

1. hay / no hay mucha gente de otros estados que... (asistir)
2. hay personas / no hay nadie que... (dar buenos regalos)
3. hay / no hay una ceremonia que... (ser en la iglesia)
4. hay gente / no hay nadie que... (tirar arroz)
5. siempre hay alguien / nunca hay nadie que... (llorar)
6. ¿ ?

C. Una encuesta (*poll*). ¿Qué sabe usted de los compañeros de su clase de español? Pregúnteles si saben hacer lo siguiente o a quién le ocurre lo siguiente. Deben levantar la mano solo los que puedan contestar afirmativamente. Luego la persona que hizo la pregunta debe hacer un comentario apropiado. Siga el modelo.

MODELO: hablar chino →
En esta clase, ¿hay alguien que **hable** chino?
(*Nadie levanta la mano.*) No hay nadie que **hable** chino.
(*Alguien levanta la mano.*) Hay una (dos) persona(s) que **habla(n)** chino.

1. hablar ruso / japonés
2. saber tocar la viola / el violín
3. conocer a un actor / una actriz
4. saber preparar comida vietnamita/tailandesa
5. celebrar su cumpleaños hoy / nunca celebrar su cumpleaños
6. cantar en la ducha / la ópera
7. bailar tango/salsa
8. ¿ ?

D. Intercambios

Paso 1. Complete las siguientes declaraciones de acuerdo con su vida real y sus deseos.

1. Tengo un amigo / una amiga que...
2. No conozco a nadie que...
3. Este verano quiero tener un trabajo que...
4. En las próximas vacaciones no quiero hacer nada que...
5. Busco un compañero / una compañera en la vida que...
6. En este mundo, no hay nada que sea más importante que...
7. Este semestre/trimestre tengo cursos que...
8. El próximo semestre/trimestre quiero tomar cursos que...

Paso 2. Ahora, en parejas, hagan y contesten preguntas basadas en las declaraciones del **Paso 1.** Luego díganle a la clase las coincidencias o diferencias más interesantes que ustedes tienen.

Algo sobre...

la represa[a] de Itaipú

La represa de Itaipú es una obra de ingeniería impresionante. Es la central[b] hidroeléctrica que genera más electricidad en el mundo. Es el resultado de un proyecto binacional entre el Paraguay y el Brasil que explota el río Paraná, la frontera[c] natural entre los dos países. La represa, que se abrió en 1984, provee[d] casi toda la energía que necesita el Paraguay y un cuarto de la energía que consume el Brasil.

¿Cuáles son algunas de las obras de ingeniería más importantes de los Estados Unidos? ¿Hay alguna que esté en su estado?

[a]*dam* [b]*power station* [c]*border* [d]*provides*

©Mike Goldwater/Alamy

La represa de Itaipú, entre el Paraguay y el Brasil

45 *Lo hago para que tú...*

The Subjunctive (Part 7): The Subjunctive After Conjunctions of Purpose and Contingency

Gramática en acción: Relaciones familiares y sociales

A.

B.

C.

¿A qué dibujo corresponde cada una de las siguientes oraciones? ¿Quién las dice?

1. _______ «Aquí tienes la tarjeta de crédito, pero úsala solo **en caso de que** haya una emergencia, ¿eh?» (¿el abuelo o la nieta?)
2. _______ «Deja ya de jugar. No te permito que juegues **antes de que** termines la tarea. ¿Me entiendes?» (¿la madre o el hijo?)
3. _______ «Quiero casarme contigo **para que** estemos siempre juntos y no salgas más con Raúl.» (¿Marco o Ariadna?)

¿Y usted?

¿Alguien...

1. le ha dado dinero para que usted pague la matrícula de la universidad?
2. le ha ofrecido un trabajo fabuloso antes de que usted se gradúe?
3. le ha dicho que quiere casarse con usted con tal de que (*provided that*) usted lo/la ame?

①		②
indicative	conjunction of contingency or purpose	**subjunctive**

a conjunction / **una conjunción** = a word or phrase that connects other words, phrases, or clauses

1. Conjunctions of Purpose and Contingency

The conjunctions at the right express *purpose* (**el propósito**) or *contingency* (**la contingencia**), that is, when one action depends on another = *I'll do X unless Y occurs.* The dependent clauses introduced by them function as adverbs in the sentence.

When there is a change of subject, the Spanish subjunctive is *always* used in the dependent clause introduced by these conjunctions.

Las conjunciones de propósito y contingencia	
a menos que	unless
antes (de) que	before
con tal (de) que	provided (that), as long as
en caso de que	in case
para que	so that, in order that
sin que	without; unless

(Continúa.)

Family and social relationships *To which drawing does each of the following sentences correspond? Who is saying them?* **1.** *"Here's the credit card, but use it only in case there's an emergency, OK?"* **2.** *"Stop playing right now. I don't allow you to play before you finish your homework. Do you understand me?"* **3.** *"I want to marry you so that we can always be together and (so that) you don't go out with Raúl again."*

Note in the examples:

- Each conjunction contains the word **que,** which is obligatory in Spanish but optional in some cases in English.
- There is a change of subject in the dependent clause (the one introduced by the conjunction).

Yo voy **con tal (de) que** ellos **vengan** conmigo.
I'm going, provided (that) they go with me.

En caso de que llegue Juan, dile que ya salí.
In case Juan arrives, tell him (that) I already left.

No voy a la fiesta **sin que** tú **vengas** conmigo.
I won't go to the party unless you go with me.

---

2. **Order of the Clauses**

An adverbial clause that expresses purpose and contingency may precede or follow the main clause, separated by a comma, just as in English. Here are the sentences from Point 1 with the adverbial clause in a different position.

Con tal (de) que ellos **vengan** conmigo, yo voy.
Dile a Juan que ya salí, **en caso de que llegue**.
Sin que tú **vengas** conmigo a la fiesta, yo no voy.

. **Same Subject = *preposition* + *infinitive***

When there is no change of subject, a *preposition* + *infinitive* phrase is often used to express purpose or contingency, rather than a *conjunction* + *subjunctive*. Only **a menos que** does not have a prepositional equivalent.

PREPOSITIONS: **antes de, con tal de, en caso de, para, sin** + infinitive
CONJUNCTIONS: **antes (de) que, con tal (de) que, en caso de que, para que, sin que** + subjunctive

Estoy aquí **para aprender.** (subject = **yo**)
Estoy aquí **para que** ustedes **aprendan.** (subjects = **yo, ustedes**)

Coma usted algo **antes de salir.** (subject = **usted**)
Coma usted algo **antes de que salgamos.** (subjects = **usted, nosotros**)

Podemos salir **con tal de tener** tiempo. (subject = **nosotros**)
Podemos salir **con tal de que tengas** tiempo. (subjects = **nosotros, tú**)

Es difícil salir con los amigos **sin gastar** dinero. (subject = **impersonal**)
Es difícil salir con los amigos **sin que gastemos** dinero. (subjects = **impersonal, nosotros**)

Summary of Conjunctions of Purpose and Contingency

a menos que, antes (de) que, con tal (de) que, en caso de que, para que, sin que + change of subject → subjunctive

Práctica y comunicación

A. ¿Buenos amigos y buenas parejas?

Paso 1. Autoprueba. Empareje las conjunciones con su significado en inglés.

1. _______ para que
2. _______ antes (de) que
3. _______ con tal (de) que
4. _______ a menos que
5. _______ en caso de que
6. _______ sin que

a. *without; unless*
b. *unless*
c. *before*
d. *provided (that), as long as*
e. *in case*
f. *so that, in order that*

Paso 2. Complete las siguientes oraciones con la conjunción o preposición apropiada en cada caso. **¡OJO!** Algunas oraciones necesitan **que** y otras no.

1. Les hago favores a mis amigos _______ que sea posible.
2. Trato de escuchar y comprender a mis amigos _______ juzgarlos (*judging them*).
3. Llevo a mis amigos a casa cuando beben demasiado _______ no conduzcan.
4. Nunca les miento a mis amigos, _______ que sea necesario para su beneficio.
5. _______ tener problemas personales, busco el apoyo de mis mejores amigos.
6. Nunca les doy consejos a mis amigos _______ me los pidan.

Prác. A, Paso 1: Answers: 1. f ***2.*** c ***3.*** d ***4.*** b ***5.*** e ***6.*** a

Paso 3. Ahora, en parejas, túrnense para entrevistarse sobre las ideas del **Paso 2.** Luego díganle a la clase algo que tienen en común o en que son radicalmente diferentes.

MODELO: **E1:** ¿Les haces favores a tus amigos con tal de que sea posible?
E2: Sí. ¿Y tú?
E1: Yo también. → Les hacemos favores a nuestros amigos con tal de que sea posible.

B. Un fin de semana romántico

Paso 1. Un matrimonio está planeando hacer una escapada (*getaway*) de fin de semana para esquiar. Combine las siguientes ideas para explicar sus planes.

MODELO: Quieren pasar tres días esquiando _______ (con tal de / con tal de que) su hija no se enferme. →
Quieren pasar tres días esquiando **con tal de que** su hija no se enferm**e**.

1. Desean ir sin su hija _______ (para / para que) poder celebrar su aniversario de boda de una manera especial.
2. Van a pasar el fin de semana esquiando _______ (con tal de / con tal de que) los abuelos puedan quedarse con la niña.
3. No pueden ir _______ (sin / sin que) los abuelos se queden con la niña.
4. El plan es salir temprano el sábado _______ (menos / a menos que) estén muy cansados el viernes por la noche.
5. Es importante que lleguen a la estación de esquí _______ (antes de / antes de que) empiece a nevar.
6. Llevan cadena (*chains*) para las llantas _______ (en caso de / en caso de que) haya mucha nieve en las montañas.
7. Piensan regresar el lunes _______ (antes de / antes de que) sea de noche.

Paso 2. Diga si las siguientes oraciones son ciertas o falsas o si no se menciona la infomación, según el **Paso 1**.

	CIERTO	FALSO	NO SE MENCIONA
1. Los esposos acaban de casarse.	☐	☐	☐
2. Casi siempre salen de vacaciones con su hija.	☐	☐	☐
3. Los dos se preocupan mucho por su hija.	☐	☐	☐
4. Piensan que va a ser muy fácil llegar a la estación de esquí y regresar a casa.	☐	☐	☐

C. Relaciones sociales. Hay relaciones sociales de muchos tipos en donde unos dependen de otros. Complete las siguientes oraciones con el presente de subjuntivo para describir algunas de ellas.

1. A algunos abuelos les gusta mimar (*to spoil*) a sus nietos con tal de que los padres... _______ (permitirlo)
2. Los padres esperan que los padrinos (*godparents*) cuiden a sus hijos en caso de que ellos... _______ (morirse)
3. Los buenos amigos siempre saben lo que necesitamos antes de que... _______ (decírselo)
4. Los amigos paraguayos se reúnen afuera para tomar el tereré con tal de que... _______ (hacer buen tiempo)
5. Los estudiantes no estudian sin que los profesores... _______ (darles tarea)
6. Las parejas se llevan bien a menos que... _______ (haber entre ellos una gran diferencia de opiniones)
7. Los padres trabajan para que sus hijos... _______ (tener lo que necesitan)

Estrategia

cambio de sujeto → **subjuntivo**
sin cambio de sujeto → infinitivo

Algo sobre...

el té paraguayo

©EPA European Pressphoto Agency b.v./Alamy

El tereré, la bebida nacional del Paraguay

El té paraguayo o tereré es una bebida que tiene como base la yerba mate. Como en la Argentina y el Uruguay, se bebe en un tipo de taza[a] que tradicionalmente se hace de una calabaza,[b] aunque[c] hoy día se hace de muchos otros materiales. En el Paraguay esta taza se llama una «guampa». A diferencia del mate argentino y uruguayo, el tereré paraguayo se prepara con agua fría o jugo de fruta.

¿Hay bebidas que usted relacione con ciertos países? ¿Qué bebida asocia con los Estados Unidos?

[a]*cup* [b]*gourd* [c]*although*

Nota comunicativa

¿Para qué? / para (que)... and *¿por qué? / porque...*

These words are all close in meaning, but they are used for different purposes. Their use is similar to the use of their English equivalents.

¿Para qué?	What for? For what purpose?	**¿Por qué?**	Why? For what reason?
para que (*conj.*)	so that	**porque...**	because . . .
para (*prep.*)	(in order) to		

Compare the use of these words in the following sentences.

—¿**Para qué** necesitas ahora la lista de invitados a la boda?

— **Para** confirmar el número de invitados que van a asistir. Y **para que** el dueño del restaurante sepa exactamente cuántos invitados van a venir.

—¿**Por qué** estás tan nervioso?

—¡**Porque** me caso en una semana!

You will use these words and phrases in **Práctica D.**

D. **Razones para hacer las cosas que hacemos.** Empareje las frases de las dos columnas para hacer oraciones completas.

1. _____ Las universidades tienen cursos que son requisitos para...
2. _____ Los profesores corrigen tareas para...
3. _____ Estudiamos español para...
4. _____ Trabajamos en parejas en clase para...
5. _____ Los profesores organizan actividades en grupo en clase para que...

a. los estudiantes tengan más oportunidad de hablar español.
b. poder comunicarnos con mucha más gente.
c. que los estudiantes tengan un conocimiento amplio (*broad knowledge*) del mundo.
d. darles a los estudiantes más ayuda.
e. hablar más en clase.

¡OJO!

¿Por qué... ? / Porque... → *indicative*
para... + *infinitive*
para que... → *subjunctive*

Paso 2. Ahora, en parejas, den explicaciones sobre la razón de las siguientes situaciones.

1. Estudiamos en la universidad para (que) / porque...
2. La universidad cuesta mucho dinero para (que) / porque...
3. Los profesores les dan tarea a los estudiantes para (que) / porque...
4. Los estudiantes quieren sacar buenas notas para (que) / porque...

E. Intercambios

Paso 1. Complete las siguientes oraciones usando una conjunción de contingencia y propósito o una preposición: **a menos que, antes de (que), con tal de (que), en caso de (que), para (que), sin (que).**

MODELO: Voy a graduarme en esta universidad... → Voy a graduarme en esta universidad en dos años **a menos que saque malas notas en varias clases.**

1. Voy a graduarme en esta universidad...
2. (No) Voy a casarme con mi novio/a actual... (Mi hijo/a [no] va a casarse con su novio/a actual...)
3. Espero tener un buen trabajo en dos o tres años...
4. Deseo tener hijos/nietos...
5. Voy a quedarme en este estado...

Paso 2. Ahora, en parejas o grupos, comparen sus oraciones. Luego díganle a la clase cuáles de sus ideas son muy similares o muy diferentes.

SALU «Cosas del amor» Segmento 2

Antes de mirar

¿Conoce usted a alguien que haya encontrado pareja a través de (*through*) un servicio de internet? ¿Ha usado usted este tipo de servicio alguna vez? ¿Qué pasó? Si no ha usado tal (*such a*) servicio, ¿usaría (*would you use*) uno de estos en el futuro?

«...estoy convencida de que en la vida es necesario un equilibrio entre lo profesional y lo personal».

Este segmento

En este segmento, se muestran los videos de una mujer y dos hombres que buscan pareja. Ana y Víctor les piden a los telespectadores que escojan a uno de los dos hombres para que salga con la mujer.

Vocabulario del segmento

la carrera	career	**a pesar de mi físico**	despite my physical appearance
conversador(a)	conversationalist	**cansarse de**	to get tired of
sería el sueño de toda mi vida	would be my life's dream	**¿A qué esperas?**	What are you waiting for?
ponerse en contacto	to get in contact	**el aspecto**	appearance
aburrirse como una ostra	to be bored to death	**el sentido del humor**	sense of humor
no me falta trabajo	I don't lack for work	**formar un hogar**	to settle down
reconocer (reconozco)	to recognize	**disponible**	available
la ropa interior	underwear	**el/la concursante**	contestant
		diremos	we'll tell

Fragmento del guion

Nuestros tres participantes colocaron[a] sus perfiles[b] en un sitio de internet para buscar pareja y los tres nos dieron permiso para mostrar sus videos y participar en este programa. Aquí están.

[a]*placed* [b]*profiles*

Después de mirar

A. ¿Está claro? Complete las siguientes oraciones según el programa.

1. *El juego del amor* es la versión en español de ______.
2. Los participantes en *El juego del amor* se llaman ______.
3. ______ va(n) a decidir cuál es la mejor pareja para Yolanda.

B. Un poco más. Conteste las siguientes preguntas.

1. ¿Cuál es la profesión de los tres participantes que buscan pareja?
2. ¿Qué observación sobre Víctor les hace Ana a las telespectadoras, a manera de chiste (*as a joke*)?

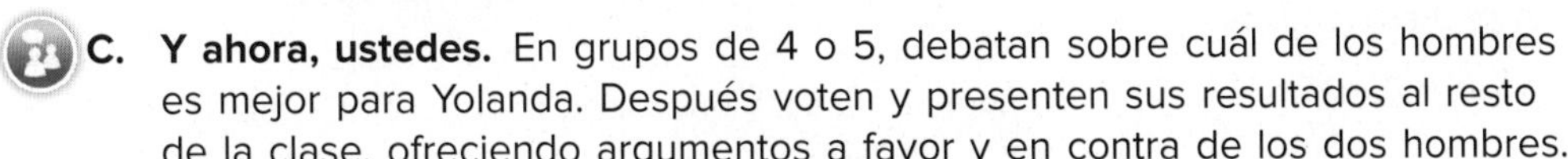

C. Y ahora, ustedes. En grupos de 4 o 5, debatan sobre cuál de los hombres es mejor para Yolanda. Después voten y presenten sus resultados al resto de la clase, ofreciendo argumentos a favor y en contra de los dos hombres.

MUNDO HISPANO

Enfoque cultural: El Paraguay

Antes de leer

Hay relaciones sentimentales de muchos tipos. ¿Qué expresiones usa usted en inglés para referirse a los diferentes tipos de relaciones entre parejas?

El concepto de noviazgo

En el Paraguay, como en casi todo el mundo hispanohablante, el concepto de noviazgo es un poco diferente del de[a] este país. «Tener novio/a» o «estar de novio/a» indica que una relación es seria y formal, con miras al[b] futuro. Novio y novia, además,[c] son los términos que se aplican a las personas que se casan durante la ceremonia de la boda. Como el noviazgo ya señala un compromiso,[d] no es tan frecuente usar la palabra prometido/a[e] para referirse a los novios que van a casarse.

Cuando las relaciones entre dos personas son informales, se dice que andan[f] o salen juntos, o simplemente que la persona tiene un amigo o amiga. Con frecuencia se usa la palabra pareja para referirse a una persona que convive[g] con otra sin casarse. Por ejemplo, se dice: «Te presento a mi pareja.»

[a]*del... from that of* [b]*con... (one that is) looking ahead to the* [c]*in addition* [d]*señala... indicates a commitment* [e]*fiancé/fiancée* [f]*lit., are walking* [g]*cohabits*

En otros países hispanos

- **En todo el mundo hispanohablante** Es muy común ver demostraciones de afecto entre una pareja en parques, plazas y calles, lo cual[a] a veces resulta chocante[b] a algunas personas de otras culturas. Pero es necesario recordar que la mayoría de los jóvenes vive con su familia y no tiene muchas oportunidades de intimidad.[c]
- **En España y otros países** El concepto de «la cita» no es común entre los jóvenes. Para muchos jóvenes españoles, la idea de una cita les suena[d] demasiado formal. Desde que[e] los chicos empiezan a salir sin sus padres, lo típico es salir en grupos, en los cuales[f] se forman parejas. Pero todavía prefieren salir en grupo a tomar algo en un bar por la noche o a tomar un café por la tarde.

[a]*lo... which* [b]*shocking* [c]*privacy* [d]*les... sounds to them* [e]*Desde... From the time that* [f]*en... in which*

©Studio Works/Alamy

La moneda (*currency*) oficial del Paraguay es el guaraní. Su símbolo es el ₲.

Un símbolo paraguayo: La cultura guaraní

Los guaraníes, un pueblo originario de la región amazónica, se asentaron[a] en lo que hoy es el Paraguay (y zonas adyacentes[b] de Bolivia, el Brasil y la Argentina) varios siglos antes de la llegada de los españoles. La cultura guaraní continúa muy presente en la actualidad. El Paraguay es uno de los países racialmente más homogéneos de Latinoamérica, debido a que[c] la inmensa mayoría de la población es mestiza, de ascendencia guaraní y española. Además,[d] más del 80% de la población del país es bilingüe: habla español y guaraní. Se puede decir que el Paraguay es un país ejemplar[e] en cuanto a[f] la conservación e integración de su herencia ancestral con la más reciente cultura española.

[a]*se... settled* [b]*adjacent, nearby* [c]*debido... due to the fact that* [d]*In addition* [e]*exemplary* [f]*en... in terms of*

Comprensión

1. ¿En qué es diferente el concepto de novio/a del (*from that*) de *boyfriend/girlfriend*?
2. ¿Qué palabra se refiere a las personas que conviven en una relación amorosa sin estar casados?
3. ¿Por qué es normal que los jóvenes demuestren su cariño en público?
4. ¿Qué costumbre de este país no es común entre los jóvenes de varios países hispanohablantes?
5. ¿Por qué es homogénea la población paraguaya?

En acción

En parejas, hagan una lista de los cinco lugares de la ciudad donde está su universidad para que unos turistas extranjeros tengan una cita romántica mientras visitan el estado.

Lectura

Antes de leer

¿Cuáles son algunas de las ventajas de conocer a la gente por internet? ¿Tiene esto sus desventajas también? ¿Cuáles son?

Vocabulario para leer

la belleza	beauty	**el espíritu**	spirit
cibernauta	**por internet**	**la mirada**	view, opinion
encendido/a	passionate	**proponer (like poner)**	to propose
enriquecer (enriquezco)	to enrich	**la réplica**	response
enviar (envío)	**mandar**	**el sufrimiento**	suffering

«Amor cibernauta», de Diego Muñoz Valenzuela

Se conocieron por la red. Él era tartamudo[a] y tenía un rostro[b] de neandertal: cabeza enorme, frente abultada,[c] ojos separados, redondos[d] y rojos, dientes de conejo[e] que sobresalían[f] de una boca enorme y abierta, cuerpo endeble[g] y barriga[h] prominente. Ella estaba inválida del cuello hacia abajo[i] y dictaba los mensajes al computador con una voz hermosa, pausada[j] y clara que no parecía tener nada que ver[k] con ella; tenía el cuerpo de una muñeca maltratada.[l] Fue un amor a primer intercambio de mensajes: hablaron de la armonía del universo y de los sufrimientos terrestres, de la necesidad del imperio[m] de la belleza y de los abyectos afanes[n] de los mercaderes de la guerra,[ñ] de la abrumadora[o] generosidad del espíritu humano que contradice la miseria[p] de unos pocos. Leían incrédulos[q] las réplicas donde encontraban una mirada equivalente del mundo, no igual, similar aunque[r] enriquecida por historias y percepciones diferentes. Durante meses evitaron hablar de sí mismos,[s] menos aún de[t] la posibilidad de encontrarse en un sitio real y no virtual. Un día él le envió la foto digitalizada de un galán.[u] Ella le retribuyó con la imagen de una bailarina. Él le escribió encendidos versos de amor que ella leyó embelesada.[v] Ella le envió canciones con su propia voz,[w] él lloró de emoción al escuchar esa música maravillosa. Él le narraba con gracia[x] su agitada vida social, burlándose agudamente[y] de los mediocres. Ella le enviaba descripciones pormenorizadas[z] de sus giras[aa] por el mundo con compañías famosas. Ninguno de los dos jamás propuso encontrarse en el mundo real. Fue un amor verdadero, no virtual, como los que suelen acontecernos[bb] en ese lugar que llamamos realidad.

[a]Él... *He was a stutterer* [b]*face* [c]frente... *a bulging forehead* [d]*round* [e]*rabbit* [f]*protruded* [g]*rickety* [h]*belly* [i]inválida... *paralyzed from the neck down* [j]*slow* [k]no... *didn't seem to have anything in common* [l]una... *a beat-up doll* [m]*reign* [n]*ambitions* [ñ]los... *the merchants of war* [o]*overwhelming* [p]*stinginess* [q]sin creer [r]*although* [s]evitaron... *they avoided talking about themselves* [t]menos... *even less about* [u]un... un hombre muy atractivo [v]*entranced* [w]*voice* [x]con... *gracefully* [y]burlándose... *pointedly making fun* [z]*detailed* [aa]*tours* [bb]los... *those that tend to happen to us*

Comprensión

A. Un resumen del cuento. Seleccione la opción apropiada, según el cuento.

1. El hombre del cuento es (muy feo / muy guapo).
2. La mujer (tiene / no tiene) una discapacidad (*disability*) física.
3. Primero, los dos mandan mensajes sobre (temas románticos / la vida y el mundo).
4. Por su intercambio de mensajes, sienten (mucha / poca) armonía entre sí (*between them*).
5. Cuando por fin se comunican detalles sobre su apariencia y su vida, envían información (falsa / verdadera).
6. Los dos (eventualmente / nunca) se conocen en persona.

B. ¿Qué piensa usted? Conteste las siguientes preguntas.

1. ¿Por qué cree usted que se dijeron mentiras sobre sí mismos? ¿Era eso necesario?
2. Los cibernautas del cuento se mintieron muchas veces. Sin embargo, a pesar de (*in spite of*) las mentiras, ¿cree usted que había algo verdadero en sus mensajes?
3. ¿Por qué el hombre y la mujer del cuento no tienen nombres?

Proyecto: Cartas de cibernautas en un sitio de citas (*dating website*)

Para este proyecto, va a crear un perfil (*profile*) ficticio para un sitio de citas por internet y va a contestar al perfil de una persona de su interés.

Paso 1. Invente un personaje (como un avatar) y escriba su perfil. Debe incluir lo siguiente por lo menos: nombre, género (*gender*), profesión, intereses, cualidades personales, aficiones y cualquier (*any*) otro detalle importante.

Paso 2. Lea los perfiles de las demás personas de la clase y elija un perfil. Asumiendo la personalidad del personaje que usted ha inventado, escríbale un mensaje. En el mensaje, descríbase a sí mismo/a, explique por qué le interesa esa persona y hágale unas preguntas. Mándele su mensaje.

Paso 3. Lea el mensaje que recibe y contéstelo.

Textos orales

Un anuncio para Naranjas, un sitio web para encontrar pareja

Antes de escuchar

¿Cómo se puede encontrar a la pareja ideal? Según su experiencia, ¿es difícil conocer a personas que podrían (*could*) ser su pareja? ¿Qué es necesario o fundamental para que haya una buena relación entre una pareja?

©Foodcollection

Vocabulario para escuchar

la media naranja	better half	**lograr**	to achieve
el éxito	success	**duradero/a**	long-lasting
el cuestionario	questionnaire	**los valores**	values
los pilares	pillars, bases	**la afinidad**	compatibility
cualquier	any	**elegir (elijo)**	to select
los terapeutas	therapists	**inscríbete gratis**	register for free
los investigadores	researchers	**el perfil**	profile
los compatibles	**las personas compatibles**	**la soledad**	loneliness
comprobado/a	demonstrated		

Comprensión

A. La información correcta. Las siguientes oraciones son falsas. Corríjalas.

1. El cuestionario de Naranjas se hace con papel y lápiz.
2. El éxito de este sitio está basado en las reuniones con los terapeutas.
3. La afinidad de valores e intereses no es importante para una buena relación entre dos personas.
4. Es necesario pagar para inscribirse.

B. Más detalles. Conteste las siguientes preguntas.

1. ¿Qué ventajas ofrece Naranjas sobre otros sitios?
2. ¿Por qué es importante el cuestionario de Naranjas?
3. ¿Qué ofrece gratis Naranjas?
4. ¿Cuál es la oferta para los nuevos miembros?
5. ¿Por qué cree usted que este sitio se llama Naranjas?

En acción

Escriba un perfil de usted misma/o para un sitio web que empareja (*matches*) personas. No tiene que ser para una relación romántica. También puede ser para encontrar compañeros de casa o de cuarto. Aquí hay unas sugerencias.

- Busco ______ (compañero/a, pareja, ...) para ______ (compartir [*to share*] casa / cuarto / la vida...)
- Soy ______ (un hombre / una mujer / una persona) de ______ años que... (varias características)
- Me gustan las personas que...
- No me gusta la gente que...
- En general, me llevo bien con todo el mundo, a menos que/con tal de que...

Proyecto en su comunidad

Entreviste a una persona hispana de su universidad o ciudad sobre las relaciones afectivas en su país.

Preguntas posibles

- ¿Qué palabras cariñosas se usan con más frecuencia entre padres e hijos en su país de origen? ¿Y entre esposos o novios? ¿Y entre amigos?
- ¿Cómo se celebra una boda típica en su país?
- ¿Cuál es el porcentaje de divorcios? ¿Es más alto que el (*that*) de este país o más bajo? Comparado con lo que era hace veinte o treinta años, ¿ha cambiado recientemente?

Escritura

Consejos sentimentales

En este capítulo usted va a escribir una columna de consejos sobre las relaciones personales. Para empezar, decida si quiere escribir sobre relaciones románticas o amistosas.

Una relación de más de cuarenta años

Antes de escribir

En parejas, hablen de las cualidades más importantes para mantener una buena amistad o una relación amorosa. Hablen también de los problemas más comunes con que se enfrentan (*are faced*) los amigos o las parejas.

A escribir

Ahora use las ideas de **Antes de escribir** para desarrollar su ensayo. Hay más ayuda en Connect.

Más ideas para su portafolio

- Incluya la foto de alguien con quien tiene una relación especial. Explique lo que esta persona representa para usted y dé otros detalles: las cualidades que usted admira de esta persona, cómo se conocieron, qué les gusta hacer juntos, etcétera.
- Escriba un párrafo sobre una pareja especial en su vida (sus padres, sus abuelos, unos amigos...). Describa la relación entre ellos: su historia, cómo han influido en la vida de usted, por qué son muy importantes para usted. Si es posible, incluya una foto de la pareja.
- Si ha estado jugando Practice Spanish: Study Abroad, en Quest 11 usted supo que fue la poesía de Pablo Neruda que inspiró a doña Jiménez a escribir. Busque y lea el poema «Oh Tierra, espérame» de Neruda y después haga un breve análisis literario. ¿De qué se trata (*is about*) el poema? ¿Cómo describe el poema la relación entre el ser humano y la naturaleza? Escriba su propio poema que contenga sus ideas y sus sentimientos sobre el medio ambiente.

Sugerencia: You are now ready to play Quest 11 in **Practice Spanish: Study Abroad.**

EN RESUMEN En este capítulo

AFTER STUDYING THIS CHAPTER I CAN. . .

- ☐ talk about relationships (478–479)
- ☐ talk about the stages of one's life (481)
- ☐ use the indicative or subjunctive after antecedents to describe things and people in complex sentences (483–485)
- ☐ express contingency and purpose in complex sentences using the subjunctive (487–488)
- ☐ recognize/describe at least 2–3 aspects of Paraguayan cultures

Gramática en breve

44. The Subjunctive After Nonexistent and Indefinite Antecedents

①		②
definite/existing antecedent	**que**	**indicative**

Hay alguien/algo que...

①		②
indefinite/ nonexistent antecedent	**que**	**subjunctive**

No hay nadie/nada que...
¿Hay alguien/algo que... ?

45. The Subjunctive After Conjunctions of Purpose and Contingency

①		②
indicative	conjunction of purpose or contingency	**subjunctive**

Conjunctions: **a menos que, antes (de) que, con tal (de) que, en caso de que, para que, sin que**

Vocabulario

Las relaciones sentimentales

amar	to love
casarse (con)	to marry
conocerse (conozco)	to meet
enamorarse (de)	to fall in love (with)
llevarse bien/mal (con)	to get along well/poorly (with)
querer	to love
romper (con)	to break up (with)

Cognados: divorciarse (de), separarse (de)

Repaso: pelear (con), salir (con)

la amistad	friendship
el amor	love
la boda	wedding (ceremony)
el cariño	affection
la iglesia	church
la luna de miel	honeymoon
el matrimonio	marriage; married couple
la mezquita	mosque
la novia	fiancée; bride
el noviazgo	engagement period
el novio	fiancé; groom
el/la viudo/a	widower/widow

Cognados: el divorcio, la separación, el templo

Repaso: el/la amigo/a, la cita, el/la esposo/a, el marido, la mujer (*wife*), **el/la novio/a** (*boy/girlfriend*), **la pareja**

amistoso/a	friendly
enamorado/a (de)	in love (with)
recién casado/a	newlywed
estar casado/a (con)	to be married (to)
ser casado/a	to be a married person
ser soltero/a	to be a single person

Cognados: divorciado/a (de), separado/a (de)

Repaso: cariñoso/a, feliz (*pl.* **felices**)

Las etapas de la vida

la infancia	infancy; childhood
la juventud	youth
la madurez	middle age
la muerte	death
la niñez (*pl.* **niñeces**)	infancy; childhood
la vejez	old age
la etapa	stage, phase

Cognado: la adolescencia

Repaso: la vida

crecer (crezco)	to grow
nacer (nazco)	to be born

Repaso: morir (muero) (u)

Las conjunciones

a menos que	unless
antes (de) que	before
con tal (de) que	provided (that), as long as
en caso de que	in case
para que	so that, in order that
sin que	without; unless

Las preposiciones

con tal de	provided
en caso de	in case

Repaso: antes de, para, sin

Palabras adicionales

bastante	rather, sufficiently; enough
¿para qué... ?	for what purpose?, what for?

Repaso: para, ¿por qué?, porque

Vocabulario personal

17 ¿Trabajar para vivir o vivir para trabajar?

En este capítulo

Durante la cosecha (*harvest*) de uvas Chardonnay, en Chile

CHILE

18,5 (coma cinco) millones de habitantes

- Chile es un país muy largo y angosto[a] que tiene casi todos los tipos de climas, con excepción del tropical. Se extiende desde el desierto de Atacama, el lugar más seco[b] del mundo, hasta la Antártida.
- La minería, especialmente del cobre,[c] representa una gran parte del producto nacional bruto[d] de Chile.
- Los vinos chilenos, producidos en la zona central del país, están entre los mejores del mundo. De hecho,[e] Chile ocupa el cuarto lugar entre los mayores exportadores de vino a los Estados Unidos

[a]*narrow* [b]más... *driest* [c]*copper* [d]producto... *gross national income* [e]De... *In fact*

ENTREVISTA

- En este momento de su vida, ¿trabaja usted y estudia o solo estudia?
- Si ha trabajado, ¿cómo ha sido su experiencia laboral? ¿Qué trabajos ha tenido?
- ¿Qué condiciones y beneficios laborales considera usted importantes? ¿Un seguro[a] de salud? ¿un horario flexible? ¿muchos días de vacaciones al año? ¿la posibilidad de viajar o trabajar desde la casa?

[a]*insurance*

Gabriela Acosta Romano contesta las preguntas.

- Estoy trabajando como asistente de laboratorio desde que[a] terminé la carrera de química el año pasado. Pero el curso[b] próximo voy a empezar una maestría.[c]
- Aparte de[d] trabajar en el laboratorio, he sido tutora de niños y, antes, en el verano trabajaba en la finca de mis abuelos haciendo labores agrícolas[e] o empacando[f] las verduras para la venta.[g]
- Supongo[h] que las normales: un buen horario, un mes de vacaciones pagadas, seguro de salud... El trabajo de laboratorio no se puede hacer en casa. Pero sí es posible tener flexibilidad de horario.

[a]desde... *since* [b]año académico [c]*master's (degree)* [d]Aparte... *Besides* [e]labores... *agricultural work, chores* [f]*packing* [g]*sale* [h]*I suppose*

VOCABULARIO: PREPARACIÓN

You can hear the pronunciation of theme vocabulary words and phrases in the Connect eBook.

Las profesiones y los oficios°

°*trades*

el maestro (la maestra) (de escuela)

la médica (el médico)

el plomero (la plomera)

la cocinera (el cocinero)

el peluquero (la peluquera)

la soldado (el soldado)

Las profesiones

el abogado / la abogada	lawyer
el/la asistente de vuelo	flight attendant
el bibliotecario / la bibliotecaria	librarian
el consejero / la consejera	counselor
el contador / la contadora	accountant
el enfermero / la enfermera	nurse
el hombre / la mujer de negocios	businessperson
el ingeniero / la ingeniera	engineer
el/la periodista	journalist
el sicólogo / la sicóloga	psychologist
el/la siquiatra	psychiatrist
el trabajador social / la trabajadora social	social worker
el traductor / la traductora	translator

Cognados: el/la analista de sistemas, el/la artista, el/la astronauta, el/la dentista, el diseñador gráfico / la diseñadora gráfica, el fotógrafo / la fotógrafa, el/la militar, el profesor / la profesora, el programador / la programadora, el secretario / la secretaria, el veterinario / la veterinaria

Los oficios

el amo/ama de casa	housekeeper
el cajero / la cajera	(check-out) cashier; (bank) teller
el camarero / la camarera	waiter/waitress
el dependiente / la dependienta	clerk
el obrero / la obrera	worker, laborer
el técnico / la técnica	technician
el vendedor / la vendedora	salesperson

Cognados: el/la electricista, el mecánico / la mecánica

¡OJO!

If the vocabulary needed to describe your (intended) career is not listed here, look it up in a dictionary or ask your instructor.

Comunicación

A. ¿A quién necesita usted?

Paso 1. ¿A quién se debe llamar o con quién se debe consultar en estas situaciones? **¡OJO!** Hay más de una respuesta posible en algunos casos.

1. La tubería del agua (*plumbing*) de la cocina no funciona bien.
2. Usted acaba de tener un accidente automovilístico; el conductor del otro coche dice que usted tuvo la culpa (*blame*).
3. Por las muchas presiones de su vida profesional y personal, usted tiene serios problemas afectivos.
4. Usted es el dueño o la dueña de un restaurante y necesita a alguien que prepare la comida.
5. Usted quiere que alguien le construya un muro (*wall*) en el jardín.
6. Usted conoce los detalles de un escándalo local y quiere divulgarlos.

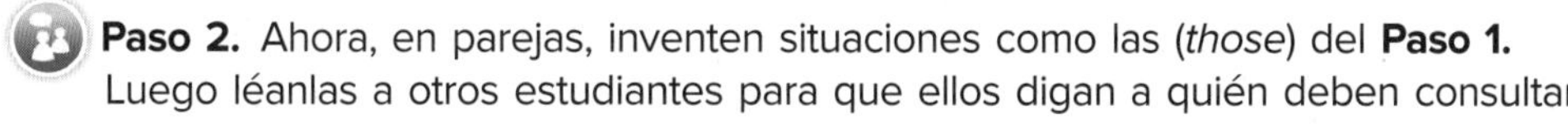

Paso 2. Ahora, en parejas, inventen situaciones como las (*those*) del **Paso 1.** Luego léanlas a otros estudiantes para que ellos digan a quién deben consultar.

B. Asociaciones. ¿Qué profesiones u oficios asocian ustedes con estas frases? Consulten la lista de profesiones y oficios y usen el **Vocabulario útil**. Digan también si conocen personalmente a alguien que haga cada tipo de trabajo.

1. creativo/rutinario
2. muchos/pocos años de preparación o experiencia
3. buen sueldo / sueldo regular
4. mucha/poca responsabilidad
5. mucho/poco prestigio
6. flexibilidad / «de nueve a cinco»
7. mucho/poco tiempo libre
8. peligroso (*dangerous*) / seguro
9. en el pasado, solo para hombres/mujeres
10. todavía solo para hombres/mujeres

Así se dice

el/la contador(a) = el/la contable (*Sp.*)
el/la periodista = el/la reportero/a
el/la plomero/a = el/la fontanero/a (*Sp.*)

Vocabulario útil

actor/actriz
arquitecto/a
camarero/a
cantinero/a (*bartender*)
carpintero/a
chófer
detective
niñero/a
pintor(a)
poeta
policía
político/a
presidente/a
sacerdote (*priest*), **pastor(a), rabino/a**
senador(a)

Nota cultural

Nuevas tendencias del español para evitar el sexismo lingüístico

Con el incremento de posiciones y cargos[a] ocupados por mujeres en todos los ámbitos[b] profesionales y de poder,[c] el debate por eliminar el sexismo en la lengua española se ha intensificado.

- Se evita usar exclusivamente la forma masculina para designar a grupos de personas de los dos sexos.
- Se usan palabras que incluyen a personas de los dos sexos, como las siguientes:

  el estudiantado[d] = estudiantes (hombres y mujeres)
  el profesorado[e] = profesores y profesoras
  la infancia = niños y niñas
  la tercera edad, las personas mayores = ancianos y ancianas

- En muchos ambientes laborales, se evita dar el tratamiento de «señorita» a todas las mujeres y se prefiere el[f] de «señora», para no hacer distinción entre las mujeres solteras y las casadas, al igual que[g] esta distinción no se hace entre los hombres.
- La aplicación de la forma femenina a algunos cargos importantes, títulos y profesiones se ha estabilizado a medida que[h] las mujeres han conquistado estos puestos: jefa,[i] médica, ministra, presidenta.

[a]*posts* [b]*arenas* [c]*power* [d]*student body, the students* [e]*faculty, the professors* [f]*that* [g]al... *just as* [h]a... *as* [i]*boss*

©Marcelo Hernandez/LatinContent/Getty Images

Michelle Bachelet, presidenta de Chile dos veces (2006–2010 y 2014–2018) y anteriormente Ministra de Salud y Ministra de Defensa

- Para integrar en una sola[j] palabra las formas masculina y femenina, se han empezado a usar terminaciones inclusivas, como e, x, o @ (el símbolo de la arroba). Por ejemplo: lxs / les / l@s jóvenes = los jóvenes y las jóvenes. La limitación de esta forma es que es solo un recurso gráfico.[k]

Aunque queda mucho por hacer[l] para eliminar el sexismo en la lengua española, se han dado grandes pasos en todos los países y a todos los niveles.

¿Conoce usted algún ejemplo de sexismo en su lengua materna?

[j]*single* [k]un... *a graphic solution* [l]Aunque... *Although much remains to be done*

Vocabulario útil

las comunicaciones
la contabilidad accounting
el derecho law
la gerontología
la ingeniería
el *marketing*/mercadeo
la organización administrativa
la pedagogía/enseñanza
la retórica speech
la sociología

C. ¿Qué preparación se necesita para ser... ? En parejas, piensen en las carreras (*majors*) y materias específicas que se deben o se pueden estudiar para prepararse para cada profesión de la siguiente lista.

MODELO: profesor(a) de una lengua extranjera → Debe estudiar por lo menos dos lenguas extranjeras o lingüística. Es necesario que hable una de las lenguas perfectamente. También debe estudiar literatura, historia y geografía.

1. traductor(a) en la ONU (Organización de las Naciones Unidas)
2. reportero deportivo / reportera deportiva en la televisión
3. contador(a) para un grupo de abogados
4. periodista para una revista de ecología
5. trabajador(a) social, especializado/a en los problemas de los ancianos
6. maestro/a de primaria, especializado/a en la educación bilingüe

El mundo laboral

el/la aspirante	job candidate; applicant
el empleo/trabajo	job; position
bien/mal pagado	well-/poorly paying
de tiempo completo/parcial	full-/part-time
la empresa	corporation; business
el gerente / la gerente	manager
el jefe / la jefa	boss
el puesto	job; position
el salario	pay, wages (*often per hour*)
la solicitud	job application (*form*)
el sueldo	salary
conseguir (*like* seguir) un empleo	to get a job
despedir (*like* pedir)	to let (*someone*) go; to fire (*someone*) (*from a job*)
graduarse (me gradúo) (en)	to graduate (from)
jubilarse	to retire (*from a job*)
llenar (un formulario)	to fill out (a form)
renunciar (a)	to resign (from)
solicitar	to apply for (*a job*)

Así se dice

el trabajo de tiempo parcial = la jornada de tiempo parcial
el empleo = el puesto, el trabajo

Comunicación

A. Definiciones. Defina las siguientes palabras y frases en español.

MODELO: la empresa → una compañía grande, como IBM™ o Ford™

1. el currículum
2. renunciar
3. la aspirante
4. el gerente
5. el sueldo
6. llenar una solicitud

B. Pasos para conseguir un empleo

Paso 1. En parejas, hagan una lista de las acciones que típicamente se hacen durante el proceso de buscar empleo.

MODELO: antes de la entrevista de trabajo →
Se miran los avisos clasificados para encontrar puestos interesantes.

1. antes de la entrevista de trabajo
2. al principio (*at the beginning*) de la entrevista
3. durante la entrevista
4. después de la entrevista

Paso 2. Ahora, en parejas, narren lo que hicieron para conseguir su empleo actual o el último empleo que han tenido. Si alguno/a de ustedes no tiene trabajo, esa persona debe narrar lo que va a hacer para conseguirlo.

MODELO: Necesitaba un trabajo de tiempo parcial en la universidad. Por eso fui al centro de orientación profesional de la universidad...

Vocabulario útil

los avisos clasificados classified ads
los beneficios
la carta de recomendación
el centro de orientación profesional career center
el/la recepcionista

C. Preguntas para una entrevista

Paso 1. En parejas, escriban una lista de cinco de las preguntas que pueden hacer los entrevistadores en el proceso de seleccionar candidatos para una variedad de trabajos. **¡OJO!** Usen **tú** o **usted** en sus preguntas de manera consistente. No hagan preguntas sobre la identidad racial, preferencias sexuales, edad, religión y afiliación política de los candidatos.

Paso 2. Ahora, en parejas, hagan una lista de las cosas que los candidatos deben saber bien antes de aceptar una oferta (*offer*) de trabajo.

Estrategia

una secuencia de acciones = el pretérito
los detalles de fondo (*background*) = el imperfecto.

Una cuestión de dinero

el interés	interest
el préstamo	loan
el presupuesto	budget
el recibo	receipt
ahorrar	to save (*money*)
cobrar	to cash (*a check*); to charge (*someone for an item or service*)
depositar	to deposit
ganar	to earn
gastar	to spend (*money*)
pagar (gu) a plazos / con cheque / en efectivo	to pay in installments / by check / in cash
prestar	to lend
sacar (qu)	to withdraw, take out

el cajero automático
BANCO POPULAR
la factura / la cuenta
TELÉFONO
el banco
la moneda
el billete
el cheque
BANCO POPULAR
el efectivo
la tarjeta bancaria / la tarjeta de crédito/débito

Así se dice

depositar dinero = ingresar dinero, poner dinero en una cuenta
pagar en efectivo = pagar al contado

Comunicación

A. El mes pasado. Piense en sus finanzas personales del mes pasado. ¿Fue un mes típico? ¿Tuvo dificultades al final del mes o todo le salió bien?

©Ronald Patrick/Bloomberg via Getty Images

Un cajero automático del Banco Santander, Chile. ¿Hay uno donde usted vive?

Paso 1. Indique las respuestas apropiadas, según su experiencia.

	SÍ	NO
1. Hice un presupuesto al principio del mes.	☐	☐
2. Deposité más dinero en el banco del que (*than what*) saqué.	☐	☐
3. Saqué dinero del cajero automático más de tres veces.	☐	☐
4. Pagué todas mis cuentas a tiempo.	☐	☐
5. Les pedí un préstamo a mis padres.	☐	☐
6. Almorcé en casa para ahorrar un poco.	☐	☐
7. Gasté mucho dinero en divertirme.	☐	☐
8. Le presté dinero a un amigo.	☐	☐
9. Usé la tarjeta de crédito solo un par de veces.	☐	☐
10. No gasté dinero en el café de Starbucks™.	☐	☐

Paso 2. Pensando todavía en sus respuestas, diga tres cosas que usted debe hacer para mejorar su situación económica.

MODELO: Debo hacer un presupuesto mensual (*monthly*).

B. Diálogos

Paso 1. Empareje las preguntas de la izquierda con las respuestas de la derecha.

1. _____ ¿Cómo prefiere usted pagar?
2. _____ ¿Hay algún problema con la cuenta?
3. _____ Me da una identificación, por favor. Necesito verla para que usted pueda cobrar su cheque.
4. _____ ¿Va a depositar este cheque o prefiere cobrarlo?
5. _____ ¿Le pongo el recibo en la bolsa (*bag*)?

a. Deposítelo, por favor.
b. No, mejor me lo da a mí.
c. Voy a pagar en efectivo.
d. Sí, señora. Usted me cobró demasiado por el postre.
e. Aquí la tiene.

Paso 2. Ahora, en parejas, inventen un contexto posible para cada diálogo. ¿Dónde están las personas que hablan? ¿En un banco? ¿en una tienda? ¿Qué hacen? ¿Quiénes son? ¿Clientes? ¿cajeros? ¿dependientes?

C. Situaciones. En parejas, describan lo que pasa en los siguientes dibujos. Usen estas preguntas como guía.

- ¿Quiénes son estas personas?
- ¿Dónde están?
- ¿Cómo van a pagar?
- ¿Qué van a hacer después de pagar?

1.

2.

Nota comunicativa

Más pronombres posesivos

In Spanish, *stressed possessives* (**las formas tónicas de los posesivos**) come after the noun, which is always preceded by a definite or indefinite article.

Es **un** amigo **mío.**	*He's a friend of mine.*

Stressed possessives are often used in Spanish to contrast one thing with another.

Esta es **la** cuenta **mía** y esa es **la suya.**	*This is my bill and that's (that one is) yours (his, hers, yours).*

As you can see in the preceding example (**la suya**) and in the following one, stressed possessives can also be used without the noun. Sometimes the article is omitted.*

—¿De quién es este libro?	*"Whose book is this?"*
—Es **mío.**	*"It's mine."*

Here are the forms of the stressed possessives.

mío/a(s)	my, (of) mine	**nuestro/a(s)**	our, (of) yours
tuyo/a(s)	your, (of) yours	**vuestro/a(s)**	your, (of) yours
suyo/a(s)	your, (of) yours, his, of (his), her, (of) hers	**suyo/a(s)**	your, (of) yours their, (of) theirs

You will use stressed possessives in **Comunicación D** and **E.**

¡OJO!

The **nosotros/as** and **vosotros/as** forms are identical to the possessives you already know.

D. Comparaciones. Compare los siguientes aspectos de su vida con lo que pasa en general.

1. Las clases de esta universidad son ________ (fáciles / regulares / difíciles). Creo que las mías...
2. Las clases aquí son ________ (grandes / pequeñas). Pienso que la nuestra...
3. En esta ciudad, los alquileres son ________ (altos / regulares). Creo que...
4. La familia es ________ (un apoyo [*support*] / una molestia) cuando uno tiene problemas. En general...
5. Muchas ciudades modernas ________ (tienen / no tienen) serios problemas con la contaminación. ...
6. Las finanzas son ________ (fáciles / difíciles) de manejar. ...

 **E. Información personal**

Paso 1. En parejas, túrnense para hacer y contestar preguntas, usando posesivos en sus respuestas según el modelo.

MODELO: Mi banco es... → Mi banco es University Bank. **¿Y el tuyo**?

1. Mi banco es...
2. Mis facturas mensuales (*monthly*) para los gastos de vivienda (no) son muy altas.
3. Hoy (no) tengo mucho dinero en mi cuenta corriente (*checking account*).
4. Mi celular es un...
5. Mi consejero académico / consejera académica es...
6. Un amigo mío / Una amiga mía juega en un equipo de...

Paso 2. Ahora díganle a la clase una cosa interesante sobre su compañero/a.

**See Appendix 3 (More About Stressed Possessives) for more information about using the stressed possessive forms.*

«Los hispanos que admiramos» Segmento 1

Proporcionar (*To provide*) cuidado médico a todas las personas que lo necesiten es un compromiso (*commitment*) personal y un orgullo (*pride*) tanto para (*as much for*) esta doctora como para (*as for*) el resto del personal de su clínica.

Antes de mirar

Las personas que usted más admira, ¿son famosas? ¿A qué se dedican? (*What do they do?*) Puede indicar más de una categoría, pero no las indique todas. Limítese a cuatro.

1. ☐ médico/a, dentista o enfermero/a
2. ☐ maestro/a o profesor(a)
3. ☐ hombre/mujer de negocios
4. ☐ ama/o de casa
5. ☐ deportista
6. ☐ actor/actriz, cantante o artista de otro tipo
7. ☐ trabajador(a) social
8. ☐ político/a
9. ☐ otro: ________

Este segmento

El programa está dedicado a las personas hispanas que son admiradas por otros hispanos. Este segmento incluye una entrevista con una doctora que trabaja en una clínica de Los Ángeles.

Vocabulario del segmento

en respuesta a nuestra petición	responding to our request	**diría**	I would say
efectivamente	actually	**si no estuviéramos**	if we weren't
los seres queridos	loved ones	**acudirían**	they would come
acudir	venir	**dar gusto**	to give pleasure
proporcionar	dar	**disfrutar**	to enjoy
la gente necesitada	needy people	**el seguro**	insurance
la amabilidad	kindness	**la meta**	goal
ya que	since	**tener confianza**	creer
		lograr	to achieve

Después de mirar

A. ¿Está claro? Complete las siguientes oraciones con información del programa.

1. Los telespectadores nombraron a las personas que admiran por medio de (*via*) ________.
2. El programa recibió ________ de nombres de personas admiradas.
3. La Dra. Zaragoza-Kaneki es una angelina de origen ________.
4. En su clínica, más del _____ por ciento de los pacientes es de origen hispano, y el _____ por ciento de todos los pacientes no habla inglés.
5. Su deseo para la clínica es obtener recursos federales para ________.

B. Un poco más. Conteste las siguientes preguntas.

1. ¿Entre qué horas está abierta la clínica?
2. ¿Por qué escogió la Dra. Zaragoza-Kaneki su profesión?
3. ¿Cuál es una de las metas importantes para la doctora?

C. Y ahora, ustedes. En parejas, imaginen que tienen la oportunidad de entrevistar a la Dra. Zaragoza-Kaneki. Hagan una lista de cinco preguntas que les gustaría hacerle.

GRAMÁTICA

¿Recuerda usted?

Before studying the future tense in **Gramática 46,** review **Gramática 3 (Cap. 2)** and **Gramática 11 (Cap. 4),** where you learned ways of expressing future actions. Then indicate which of the following sentences can be used to express a future action.

1. ☐ Trabajé hasta las dos.
2. ☐ Trabajo a las dos.
3. ☐ Voy a trabajar a las dos.
4. ☐ Trabajaba a las dos.
5. ☐ Estoy trabajando.
6. ☐ He trabajado a las dos.

46 Talking About the Future

Future Verb Forms

Gramática en acción: ¿Cómo será su futuro?

Alicia, 20 años

Alicia, 10 años

- Seré rica y famosa porque escribiré un blog que tendrá millones de seguidores.
- Todo el mundo en Middletown me conocerá.
- Viajaré mucho con mi mejor amiga y con mi familia.
- Viviré en Nueva York, Londres y París.

¿Y usted?

1. ¿Será usted rico/a y famoso/a algún día? ([No] Seré...)
2. ¿Dónde vivirá en 10 años?
3. ¿Viajará mucho?

So far, you have been expressing future actions in Spanish mostly with the present tense or with **ir** + **a** + *infinitive*. But Spanish also has a future tense, like English (*I will . . . , you will . . .*). In Spanish the *future* (**el futuro**) is used to express strong intentions and dreams.

Future of Regular Verbs / **El futuro de los verbos regulares**					
hablar		**comer**		**vivir**	
hablaré	**hablaremos**	**comeré**	**comeremos**	**viviré**	**viviremos**
hablarás	**hablaréis**	**comerás**	**comeréis**	**vivirás**	**viviréis**
hablará	**hablarán**	**comerá**	**comerán**	**vivirá**	**vivirán**

What will your future be like? • *I'll be rich and famous because I'll write a blog that will have millions of followers.* • *Everyone in Middletown will know me.* • *I'll travel a lot with my best friend and with my family.* • *I'll live in New York, London, and Paris.*

1. Future Tense Endings

In English the *future* (**el futuro**) is a compound tense, formed with the auxiliary (helping) verbs *will* or *shall*: *I will speak, you* ***shall*** *do what I say*, and so on. The Spanish future is a simple verb form (only one word). It is formed by adding the identical set of future endings to **-ar, -er,** and **-ir** infinitives. No auxiliary verbs are needed.

Las terminaciones del futuro

infinitivo +	**-é**	**-emos**
	-ás	**-éis**
	-á	**-án**

---

2. Irregular Future Forms

Here are the most common Spanish verbs that are irregular in the future. The future endings are attached to their irregular stems.

decir: diré, dirás, dirá, diremos, diréis, dirán

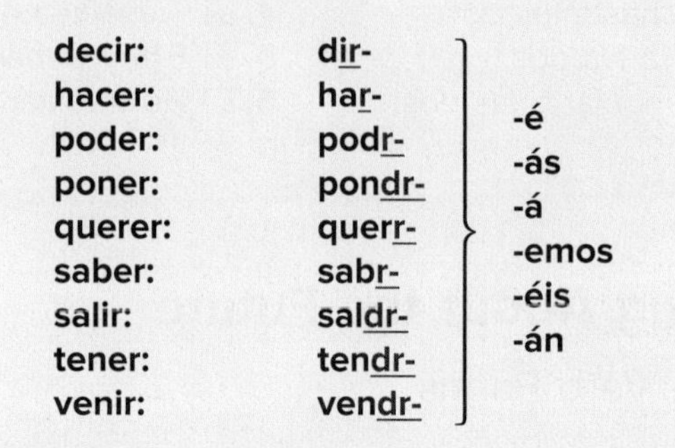

decir:	**dir-**	**-é**
hacer:	**har-**	**-ás**
poder:	**podr-**	**-á**
poner:	**pondr-**	**-emos**
querer:	**querr-**	**-éis**
saber:	**sabr-**	**-án**
salir:	**saldr-**	
tener:	**tendr-**	
venir:	**vendr-**	

---

3. The future of *hay* → *habrá (haber)*

As in the present and past (indicative and subjunctive), one word, **habrá,** meaning *there will be,* is used for singular and plural.

Spanish also has a *future perfect tense* (**el futuro perfecto**) that is used to express what *will have occurred* by a certain time in the future. The future perfect is formed with all persons of **haber**, like all other perfect tenses. The future forms of **haber** are **habré / habrás / habrá / habremos / habréis / habrán**. You will not practice this tense in ***Puntos de partida***, but you can find a more detailed presentation of it in Appendix 4 (Additional Perfect Tenses).

Habrá quince nuevos **empleados** el próximo mes.
There will be 15 new employees next month.

Habrá una gran **demanda** para profesionales en el campo de la salud.
There will be a great demand for professionals in the medical field.

---

4. Using the Future Tense

The Spanish future tense is mostly used to express serious goals and projects farther into the future, as when expressing dreams and aspirations, as seen in **Gramática en acción.**

Remember that you have already been using other tenses to express actions that refer to the near future.

- the simple present indicative
- **ir** + **a** + infinitive
- the simple present subjunctive

Trabajaré mucho y **me haré** rico.
I'll work very hard, and I'll get rich.

La empresa **contratará** cien nuevos empleados.
The company will hire a hundred new employees.

Nos vemos mañana a las ocho.
We'll see each other tomorrow at 8:00.

Voy a llevar una chaqueta para la entrevista.
I will wear (am going to wear) a jacket to the interview.

No creo que ella **consiga** ese puesto.
I don't think (that) she'll get that job.

5. **Expressing Willingness**

When the English *will* refers not to future time, but to the *willingness* of someone to do something, Spanish does not use the future but rather the verbs **querer** or **poder,** or simply the present tense of any verb. In this context, **querer** has almost the force of a command.

¿**Quieres/Puedes** cerrar la puerta, por favor?
Will/Could you please close the door?

¿**Cierras** la puerta, por favor?
Can you close the door, please?

Práctica y comunicación

A. Un sábado típico

Paso 1. Autoprueba. Dé la forma apropiada del futuro de los siguientes verbos.

1. yo vivir______
2. ella dir______
3. ellos saldr______
4. ustedes vendr______
5. nosotros comer______
6. tú querr______

Paso 2. Haga oraciones sobre cómo será su vida en los próximos 10–15 años, usando el tiempo futuro y las siguientes frases. Añada detalles y use la palabra **no** cuando sea necesaria.

MODELO: ser _______ (profesión) →
(No) **Seré** profesor universitario / profesora universitaria.

1. ser _______ (profesión)
2. conseguir una maestría (*masters*) o un doctorado (*Ph.D.*)
3. vivir en un país hispanohablante
4. conducir un coche deportivo
5. tener _______ (número) hijos.
6. participar activamente en la política (local, estatal o nacional)
7. casarse a los _______ años.

Paso 3. Ahora, en parejas, entrevístense sobre las ideas del **Paso 2.** Luego díganle a la clase algo que tienen en común o en lo que son muy diferentes.

MODELO: ser ________ (profesión) →
E1: ¿**Serás** profesora universitaria?
E2: No, **seré** analista de sistemas.
E2: Pues yo sí **seré** profesor universitario.

B. ¿Qué harán? Explique lo que harán las siguientes personas en su trabajo futuro. Luego, para cada grupo, diga qué profesión se describe.

MODELO: yo / darles consejos a los estudiantes →
Les **daré** consejos a los estudiantes.

1. yo
   - hablar bien el español
   - pasar mucho tiempo en la biblioteca
   - escribir artículos sobre la literatura latinoamericana
   - enseñar clases en español
2. tú
   - trabajar en una oficina y en la corte
   - ganar mucho dinero
   - tener muchos clientes
   - cobrar por muchas horas de trabajo
3. Felipe
   - ver a muchos pacientes
   - resolver muchos problemas mentales
   - leer a Freud y a Jung
   - hacerle un sicoanálisis a un paciente
4. Susana y Juanjo
   - pasar mucho tiempo sentados
   - usar el teclado (*keyboard*) constantemente
   - inventar nuevos programas
   - mandarles mensajes electrónicos a todos los amigos

Summary of the future

Infinitive + **-é, -ás, -á, -emos, -éis, -án**

Algo sobre...

«Gracias a la vida»

©GDA/AP Photo

Violeta Parra, en concierto

La canción «Gracias a la vida» es famosa en todo el mundo hispanohablante. Fue compuesta por la cantautora y folclorista chilena Violeta Parra (1917–1967). Es un himno[a] a la vida que habla de las cosas importantes y cotidianas[b] que muchas veces olvidamos. Muchos cantantes de todo el mundo han cantado esta canción, incluyendo la folclorista estadounidense Joan Baez y, más recientemente, Michael Bublé.

Aparte del[c] himno nacional, ¿hay alguna canción que usted considere un símbolo de su país? ¿Cuál es?

[a] *hymn, anthem* [b] *daily*
[c] Aparte... *Besides the*

Prác. A, Paso 1: Answers: 1. viviré 2. dirá 3. saldrán 4. vendrán 5. comeremos 6. querrás

C. Este mes

Paso 1. Describa lo que usted hará o no hará este mes en cuanto a (*as far as*) sus finanzas.

MODELO: (no) gastar más/menos este mes → (No) **Gastaré** menos este mes.

1. (no) gastar más/menos este mes
2. (no) pagar a tiempo todas mis cuentas
3. (no) hacer un presupuesto y / pero (no) seguirlo
4. (no) depositar mucho / poco dinero en mi cuenta
5. (no) cobrar un cheque de mi empleo / un pariente
6. (no) seguir usando mis tarjetas de crédito
7. (no) pedirles dinero a mis amigos / padres / hijos
8. (no) buscar un trabajo de tiempo completo / parcial

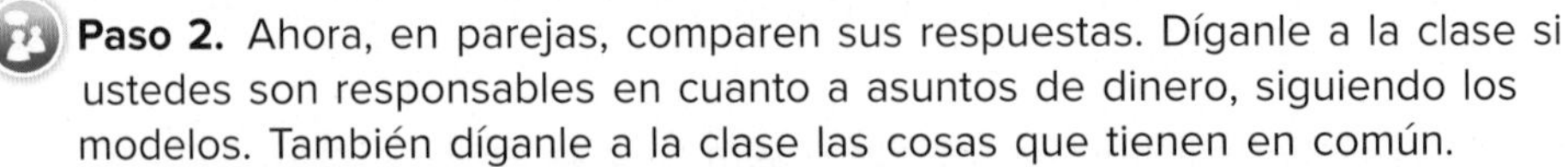

Paso 2. Ahora, en parejas, comparen sus respuestas. Díganle a la clase si ustedes son responsables en cuanto a asuntos de dinero, siguiendo los modelos. También díganle a la clase las cosas que tienen en común.

MODELOS: Dylan y yo somos muy responsables con nuestro dinero porque...
Dylan es muy responsable con su dinero, pero yo tengo que aprender a ser más responsable con el mío porque...

D. El horóscopo

Paso 1. ¿Creen ustedes en la astrología? Es posible que no, pero eso no importa para esta actividad. En parejas, hagan una lista de los temas y verbos que con frecuencia aparecen en los horóscopos.

Paso 2. Ahora escojan dos signos del Zodiaco y escriban predicciones para los próximos siete días basadas en cada uno de esos dos signos. ¡Sean creativos y demuestren su sentido del humor!

MODELO: Miércoles: Conocerás a una persona muy interesante en una clase o en una fiesta.

Paso 3. Finalmente, lean a la clase las predicciones para los signos que escogieron. ¿Cuáles son las reacciones de sus compañeros de clase ante (*to*) sus predicciones?

E. El mundo del año 2200

Paso 1. ¿Cómo será el mundo del futuro? En parejas, hagan una lista de cosas que ustedes creen que van a ser diferentes para el año 2200 (por ejemplo: el transporte, la comida, la vivienda). Piensen también en temas globales (por ejemplo: la política, los problemas que presenta la capa de ozono). Consulten la lista de **Vocabulario útil** en la próxima página y usen un diccionario si es necesario.

Vocabulario útil

la colonización
el espacio
la estación espacial
los OVNIs (Objetos Voladores No Identificados)
la pobreza poverty
el robot
el satélite
el transbordador espacial space shuttle
la vida artificial

diseñar
eliminar

intergaláctico/a
interplanetario/a
sintético/a

Paso 2. A base de su lista, hagan una serie de predicciones para el futuro.

MODELO: La gente **comerá** (**Comeremos**) comidas sintéticas.

Nota comunicativa

Cómo expresar probabilidad con el futuro

Estela, en el aeropuerto

Cecilia, en la carretera

—¿Dónde **estará** Cecilia? ¿Qué le **pasará**?	*"I wonder where Cecilia is."* (*"Where can Cecilia be?"*) *"I wonder what's up with her."* (*"What can be wrong?"*)
—**Estará** en un lío de tráfico.	*"She's probably* (*must be*) *in a traffic jam."* (*"I bet she's in a traffic jam."*)

In Spanish, the future can also be used to express probability or conjecture about what is happening now. This use of the future is called the *future of probability* (**el futuro de probabilidad**). Note in the preceding examples that the English cues for expressing probability (*probably, I bet, must be, I wonder, Where can . . . ?,* and so on) are not directly expressed in Spanish. Their sense is conveyed in Spanish simply by the use of the future form of the verb.

You will use the future of probability in **Práctica F.**

Algo sobre...

la Isla de Pascua

La Isla de Pascua, llamada Rapa Nui en la lengua indígena, es una isla chilena que es parte de la Polinesia. De hecho,[a] es la isla más aislada de las islas polinésicas y esto ha permitido que la cultura del pueblo rapanui haya mantenido características únicas. La Isla de Pascua tiene una población de aproximadamente 5.000 habitantes y es hoy día un centro turístico importante. Su mayor atracción sin duda son los misteriosos moáis, inmensas estatuas de piedra cuyo[b] significado no se comprende todavía.

©Mago World Image/age fotostock

Los moáis, la imagen más famosa de la Isla de Pascua

En su opinión, ¿cuál es el lugar más misterioso o espiritual de su país? ¿Lo ha visitado usted?

[a]De... *In fact* [b]*whose*

F. Predicciones. ¿Quiénes serán las personas en las siguientes fotos? ¿Qué estarán haciendo? ¿Dónde estarán? En parejas, usen lo que saben de Chile e inventen todos los detalles que puedan.

Vocabulario útil

la bodega	wine cellar
la cata de vino	wine tasting
la Isla de Pascua	Easter Island
el moái	*monolithic statue on Easter Island*
probar (pruebo)	to taste
el pueblo rapanui	people of Easter Island
la viña	vineyard

©Michael Snell/Robert Harding Picture Library/SuperStock

1.

©Lee Foster/Alamy

2.

¿Recuerda usted?

In **Gramática 45 (Cap. 16),** you learned about a series of adverbial conjunctions that always require the use of the subjunctive in the dependent clause. There are six such conjunctions. Complete the following phrases to name them all.

1. a ______ que = *unless*
2. ______ (de) que = *before*
3. con ______ (______) que = *provided that, as long as*
4. en ______ de que = *in case*
5. ______ que = *so that*
6. ______ que = *without; unless*

You will learn more about using one of these conjunctions and about others like it in **Gramática 47.**

47 Expressing Future or Pending Actions

The Subjunctive (Part 8): The Subjunctive and Indicative After Conjunctions of Time

Gramática en acción: Planes para el futuro

1. Después de graduarme, tendré que buscar trabajo. **Tan pronto como** tenga trabajo, ganaré mucho dinero y pagaré los préstamos de la universidad.
2. **En cuanto** me jubile, jugaré al golf por lo menos tres veces por semana. ¡Pero desgraciadamente quedan quince años **hasta que** me jubile!
3. Cuando trabajaba, siempre estaba cansado. Ahora me siento mejor que nunca. ¡Y voy a jugar al golf **hasta que** tenga 100 años!

¿Y usted?

1. ¿Buscará trabajo **antes de** graduarse o **después de** graduarse?
2. ¿Tendrá que pagar préstamos **cuando** se gradúe?
3. **Cuando** tenga un trabajo, ¿estará más cansado/a que ahora?

①		②
FUTURE/PENDING ACTION: **indicative** (present, future, command)	adverbial conjunction of time +	**subjunctive**

①		②
HABITUAL/COMPLETED ACTION: **indicative** (present, past)	adverbial conjunction of time +	**indicative**

1. **Adverbial Conjunctions of Time**

Future events are often expressed in Spanish in two-clause sentences in which the dependent clause is introduced by a conjunction of time. The most common ones are listed at the right.

Las conjunciones de tiempo			
antes (de) que	before	**en cuanto**	as soon as
cuando	when	**hasta que**	until
después (de) que	after	**tan pronto como**	as soon as

Plans for the future 1. *After I graduate, I'll have to look for a job. As soon as I have a job, I'll earn lots of money, and I'll pay off my university loans.* ***2.*** *As soon as I retire, I'll play golf at least three times a week. But unfortunately it'll be fifteen more years until I retire!* ***3.*** *When I was still working, I was always tired. Now I feel better than ever. And I'm going to play golf until I'm 100 (years old)!*

2. Use of the Indicative After Time Conjunctions

The indicative is used when the dependent clause introduced by a time conjunction describes a habitual action (present or past) or a completed event in the past.

> **¡OJO!**
>
> Clauses that start with a time conjunction can appear before or after the main clause. If they appear before, they are usually followed by a comma.

HABITUAL ACTIONS: INDICATIVE

Siempre pago las cuentas **en cuanto recibo** mi cheque.
I always pay bills as soon as I get my check.

Tan pronto como recibía mi cheque, lo depositaba en el banco.
As soon as I got my check, I would (used to) deposit it in the bank.

COMPLETED PAST ACTION: INDICATIVE

El mes pasado pagué las cuentas **en cuanto recibí** mi cheque.
Last month I paid my bills as soon as I got my check.

Cuando recibí el cheque, lo deposité.
When I got the check, I deposited it.

---

3. Use of the Subjunctive After Time Conjunctions

The subjunctive is used when the dependent clause introduced by a time conjunction describes an event that has not happened yet. This happens even when there is no change of subject in the dependent clause, as in the examples.

> **¡OJO!**
>
> When the present subjunctive is used in this way to express pending future actions, the *main-clause* verb is in the present indicative or future, or is a command.

MAIN CLAUSE: PRESENT INDICATIVE OR FUTURE

Debo depositar el dinero **tan pronto como** lo **reciba.**
I should deposit the money as soon as I get it.

Pagaré las cuentas **en cuanto reciba** mi cheque.
I'll pay the bills as soon as I get my check.

Pague usted las cuentas **en cuanto** las **reciba.**
Pay bills as soon as you get them.

This use of the subjunctive is very frequent in Spanish in clauses that begin with **Cuando...**

Cuando sea grande/mayor... *When I'm older . . .*

Cuando tenga tiempo... *When I have the time . . .*

---

4. *Antes (de) que + subjunctive*

As you know, the subjunctive is always used after the time conjunction **antes (de) que**. You can review this usage in **Gramática 45 (Cap. 16).**

No puedo comprar nada **antes de que** me **paguen**.
I can't buy anything until they pay me.

Antes de que lleguen los candidatos, los entrevistadores deben leer las solicitudes y currículums de cada uno.
Before candidates arrive, interviewers should read the applications and resumés of each one.

---

5. Preposition + *infinitive*

When there is no change of subject, the prepositions **antes de, después de,** and **hasta** are often used instead of the conjunctions **antes (de) que, después (de) que,** and **hasta que.**

¡Claro que no puedo depositar el dinero **antes de recibir** el cheque!
Of course I can't deposit the money before receiving the check!

Después de tener la entrevista, me sentí muy tranquila.
After having the interview, I felt very calm.

Summary of Time Conjunctions

	FUTURE/PENDING
antes de que	subjunctive
all other conjunctions of time	subjunctive
	HABITUAL/PAST
antes de que	subjunctive
all other conjunctions of time	indicative

Práctica y comunicación

A. ¿Futuro o presente?

Paso 1. Autoprueba. Indique cuáles de las siguientes oraciones indican una acción futura, que debe ser expresada con el subjuntivo en español.

	ACCIÓN FUTURA
1. I'll call as soon as I get home.	☐
2. We always interview applicants after we check their references.	☐
3. Some people apply for graduate school as soon as they enter their senior year.	☐
4. They won't deposit the check until you sign it.	☐

Prác. A, Paso 1: Answers 1, 4

Paso 2. Indique si las siguientes oraciones expresan una acción habitual (**H**) o futura (**F**). Luego complételas con la forma apropiada del indicativo o del subjuntivo e indique las (*those*) que son verdaderas (**V**) para usted.

	H	F	V
1. Estudio muchos días hasta que ________ (ser) las dos de la mañana.	☐	☐	☐
2. Mañana voy a estudiar hasta que ________ (ser) las dos de la mañana.	☐	☐	☐
3. Necesito actualizar (*to update*) mi currículum tan pronto como ________ (tener) tiempo.	☐	☐	☐
4. Generalmente actualizo el currículum cuando ________ (terminar) el año académico.	☐	☐	☐
5. No voy a buscar empleo hasta que ________ (graduarse).	☐	☐	☐
6. Voy a buscar empleo antes de ________ (graduarse).	☐	☐	☐
7. En cuanto ________ (*yo*: tener) un rato libre esta semana, voy a ir al centro de orientación profesional.	☐	☐	☐

Paso 3. Ahora, en parejas, entrevístense sobre las oraciones del **Paso 2.**

MODELO: **E1:** ¿Estudias muchos días hasta que son las dos de la mañana?
E2: Sí, y algunos días hasta que son las tres.
E1: Yo también.

B. Decisiones económicas

Paso 1. Lea las siguientes oraciones sobre Rigoberto e indique si se trata de (*each is about*) una acción habitual (**H**) o de una acción futura (**F**). Luego escoja la frase que complete mejor cada oración.

H	F	
☐	☐	**1.** ___ Rigoberto se va a comprar un auto en cuanto... **a.** ahorre suficiente dinero. **b.** ahorra suficiente dinero.
☐	☐	**2.** ___ Siempre usa su tarjeta de crédito cuando... **a.** no tenga dinero en efectivo. **b.** no tiene dinero en efectivo.
☐	☐	**3.** ___ Pagará su préstamo estudiantil tan pronto como... **a.** consiga un trabajo. **b.** consigue un trabajo.
☐	☐	**4.** ___ No puede pagar sus cuentas este mes hasta que... **a.** su hermano le devuelva el dinero que le prestó. **b.** su hermano le devuelve el dinero que le prestó.

Paso 2. Ahora diga cómo maneja usted sus propios asuntos económicos. Indique si la oración describe una acción habitual (**H**) o una acción futura (**F**).

H	F	
☐	☐	**1.** En cuanto tenga más dinero, voy a comprarme _____.
☐	☐	**2.** Cuando no tengo dinero en efectivo, siempre uso _____.
☐	☐	**3.** Tan pronto como consiga un trabajo, voy a _____.
☐	☐	**4.** Este mes, voy a _____ antes de que se me olvide.
☐	☐	**5.** En cuanto _____, empezaré a buscar trabajo.

Estrategia

Use un sustantivo en las oraciones 1 y 2. Use un infinitivo en las oraciones 3 y 4. En la oración 5, debe usar el subjuntivo.

C. Cosas de la vida. Las siguientes oraciones describen algunos aspectos de la vida de Mariana. Complételas con la forma apropiada de los infinitivos.

1. Hace cuatro años, cuando Mariana ________ (graduarse) en la escuela secundaria, sus padres ________ (darle) una computadora. El año que viene, cuando ________ (graduarse) en la universidad, ________ (darle) un carro.
2. Cuando ________ (ser) niña, Mariana ________ (querer) ser actriz. Cuando ________ (tener) 18 años, ________ (decidir) ser enfermera. Cuando ________ (terminar) su carrera este año, ________ (poder) encontrar un buen empleo.
3. Antes Mariana siempre ________ (pagar) sus cuentas con cheque. Ahora las ________ (pagar) por internet en cuanto le ________ (*ellos:* depositar) el sueldo en su cuenta.
4. Mariana ________ (tener) que comprar un regalo para la boda de unos amigos. No puede comprarlo hasta que su hermana le ________ (devolver) el dinero que Mariana le ________ (prestar).

Algo sobre...

los mapuches

Un grupo de mapuches, con la bandera[a] que los representa

Los mapuches son un pueblo originario de lo que hoy es Chile y parte de la Argentina. Forman el grupo indígena numéricamente más importante de Chile (hay aproximadamente un millón y medio de ellos). Se calcula que han estado en el territorio chileno desde el año 500 a. e. c.[b] o antes. Como casi todos los pueblos indígenas de las Américas, los mapuches reivindican[c] territorios y más reconocimiento[d] por parte del[e] gobierno, a fin de mejorar[f] la situación socioeconómica de muchos de ellos y proteger su cultura.

¿Cree usted que las reivindicaciones de los mapuches son diferentes o similares a las[g] de algunos pueblos indígenas de los Estados Unidos?

[a]*flag* [b]*before common era* [c]*claim* [d]*recognition* [e]por... *from the* [f]a... *in order to improve* [g]*those*

D. Los planes de David

Paso 1. David va a graduarse en sociología en la Universidad de Chile, en Santiago. Describa sus planes, haciendo oraciones completas con las siguientes frases y usando las conjunciones de tiempo en **negrilla**.

MODELO: querer tener un buen empleo / **tan pronto como** / graduarse →
David **querrá** tener un buen empleo tan pronto como **se gradúe.**

1. estar buscando un empleo / **antes de** / graduarse
2. independizarse de sus padres / **en cuanto** / ser posible
3. **cuando** / ahorrar dinero, / poder viajar a la Patagonia con su novia
4. **después de** / trabajar por un tiempo, / estudiar para obtener un doctorado
5. estudiar el mapudungún, la lengua de los mapuches, / **hasta que** / poder hablarlo bien
6. pero /**antes de que** / todo esto ser realidad, / necesitar estudiar mucho

Paso 2. Ahora use las ideas apropiadas del **Paso 1** para hablar de sus propios planes para el futuro. Haga los cambios necesarios.

MODELO: querer tener un buen empleo / **tan pronto como** / graduarse →
Querré tener un buen empleo tan pronto como **me gradúe.**

E. Descripciones. En parejas, completen la oración que acompaña cada escena. Luego completen las oraciones con información personal.

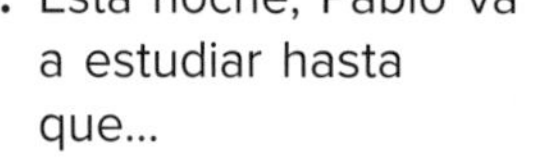

1. Esta noche, Pablo va a estudiar hasta que...

¿Y ustedes?

- Esta noche, voy a estudiar hasta que...
- Siempre estudio hasta que...
- Anoche estudié hasta que...

2. Los Sres. Castro van a cenar tan pronto como...

¿Y ustedes?

- Esta noche, voy a cenar tan pronto como...
- Generalmente ceno cuando / antes de (que)...
- Anoche cené tan pronto como / después de (que)...

F. Intercambios

Paso 1. Invente preguntas que a usted le gustaría hacerles a sus compañeros de clase sobre el futuro en general y sobre el futuro de ellos en particular.

MODELO: ¿Cuántos años tendrás... ? / cuando / jubilarse →
¿Cuántos años tendrás cuando **te jubiles**?

¿Cómo será tu vida... ? ¿Dónde vivirás... ? ¿Qué harás... ? ¿Cuántos años tendrás... ?	+	cuando	+	la humanidad: colonizar otros planetas los científicos: descubrir una cura para casi todos los casos de cáncer las mujeres: tener igualdad de oportunidades, de verdad haber paz en todas partes del mundo ¿ ? graduarse tener suficiente dinero para casarse / tener hijos / ¿ ? jubilarse ¿ ?

Paso 2. En parejas, entrevístense usando las preguntas que crearon en el **Paso 1.** Luego díganle a la clase algo interesante de su conversación.

MODELO: **E1:** ¿Cuántos años tendrás cuando te jubiles?
E2: Probablemente tendré más de 65 años cuando me jubile. Voy a ser maestro y creo que no voy a ganar mucho dinero. Por eso no voy a poder jubilarme antes.

Todo junto

A. Lengua y cultura: Trabajos para estudiantes universitarios

Paso 1. Completar. Complete the following paragraphs with the correct form of the words in parentheses, as suggested by context. When two possibilities are given in parentheses, select the correct word. *P / I*: will show you when to use the preterite or the imperfect. Conjugate all other infinitives in the future, present indicative, or subjunctive, or leave them in the infinitive form.

La necesidad de dinero es un problema para muchos estudiantes en todas partes del mundo. En la mayoría de los países hispanohablantes, _________ (el / la[1]) sistema universitario es gratuito. Además,[a] es natural que los estudiantes _________ (vivir[2]) con sus familias, _________ (por qué / porque[3]) la mayoría no _________ (irse[4]) a _________ (estudiar[5]) a otras ciudades. _________ (*Ellos:* Estudiar[6]) en _________ (el / la[7]) universidad más cercana.[b]

Sin embargo, muchos estudiantes no buscan trabajo de tiempo completo hasta que _________ (*ellos:* terminar[8]) sus estudios universitarios. Y, así como en este país, hay estudiantes que _________ (conseguir[9]) trabajo de tiempo parcial antes de _________ (terminar / terminen[10]) la escuela secundaria. A continuación se puede leer las experiencias laborales de algunos estudiantes durante la época universitaria.

Una joven paraguaya: «Desde los 16 años, _________ (*yo:* trabajar[11]) en una oficina. Así puedo _________ (cobrar / pagar[12]) la matrícula en la universidad y mi ropa y gastos personales y también _________ (*yo:* poder[13]) colaborar un poquito con la economía familiar.»

Un joven chileno: «Cuando _________ (*P / I: yo*: ser / estar[14]) estudiante universitario, _________ (*P / I:* trabajar[15]) como fotógrafo. _________ (*P / I: Yo*: Sacar[16]) fotos en bodas, bautizos y primeras comuniones. Era un _________ (bueno[17]) trabajo _________ (por / para[18]) un estudiante, porque _________ (*P / I: yo:* tener[19]) _________ (de / que[20]) trabajar los fines de semana pero casi nunca los días de clase.»

Una estudiante uruguaya de la escuela secundaria: «Tan pronto como las clases _________ (terminar[21]) este verano, _________ (*yo:* empezar[22]) a trabajar en la tienda de mi tía y _________ (ganar[23]) un poco de dinero. No quiero que mis padres _________ (tener[24]) que pagarlo todo cuando yo _________ (ser / estar[25]) en la universidad.»

©Jon Arnold Images Ltd/Alamy

Universidad de Chile, en Santiago

[a]*Besides* [b]más... *nearest*

(Continúa.)

Paso 2. Comprensión. Conteste las siguientes preguntas.

1. ¿Qué necesidad comparten los estudiantes de todo el mundo?
2. ¿Es caro o barato el sistema universitario de los países hispanos?
3. ¿Dónde vive la mayoría de los estudiantes hispanos?
4. ¿Qué trabajos se describen en estos párrafos?

Paso 3. En acción

Ahora, en parejas, hablen de los trabajos que tienen los estudiantes universitarios en este país mientras que estudian. ¿Cuáles son los más comunes? Hablen también de sus propios trabajos si es que trabajan.

B. Proyecto: Mucho más que un título

Todos los trabajos implican mucho más que un solo tipo de actividad o aptitud. En este proyecto, van a usar su conocimiento y creatividad para crear un perfil (*profile*), serio o cómico, sobre algunas profesiones y ocupaciones.

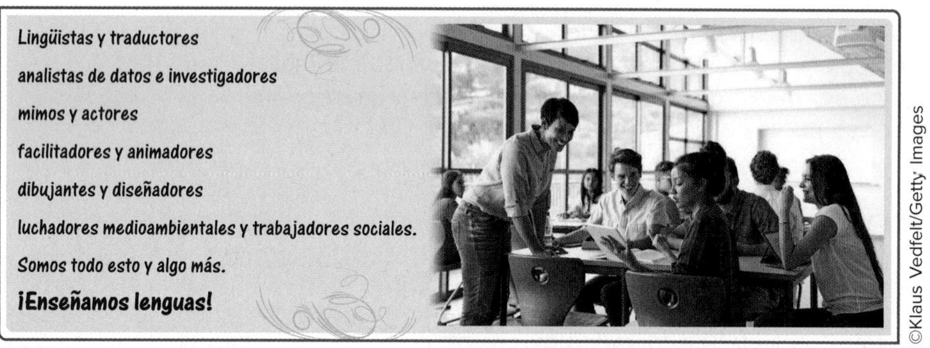

Lingüistas y traductores
analistas de datos e investigadores
mimos y actores
facilitadores y animadores
dibujantes y diseñadores
luchadores medioambientales y trabajadores sociales.
Somos todo esto y algo más.
¡Enseñamos lenguas!

©Klaus Vedfelt/Getty Images

Paso 1. Preparación. En parejas, elijan una o dos ocupaciones profesionales. Consideren no solo los trabajos tradicionales (médicos, enfermeros, abogados...), sino (*but*) también los que han surgido (*those that have emerged*) en los últimos veinte años. Después de decidir en cuál de las profesiones se van a enfocar, hagan una lista de todo lo que saben de ellas: ¿Qué actividades realizan (*achieve*) esos profesionales? ¿Qué aptitudes deben tener? ¿Qué deben saber? ¿Tienen que tener algún estilo de vida determinado?

Paso 2. Creación. Ahora hagan un perfil creativo de esas profesiones. Antes de empezar, elijan el objetivo para crearlo. Algunas posibilidades:

- la facultad de una universidad que promueve (*is promoting*) una carrera para atraer estudiantes
- un organismo del gobierno que considera necesario que en el país haya más especialistas en ese campo
- un artículo para una revista sobre profesiones antiguas y nuevas
- una viñeta (*cartoon*) cómica

Luego adapten la información de su lista a un formato adecuado para su proyecto.

MODELOS: los maestros y profesores de lenguas →

Son personas que estudian una o varias lenguas. Saben interpretarlas, traducirlas y analizar la cultura de los lugares en donde se hablan. También sabes enseñárselas a otras personas.

Hazte profesor de español si quieres ayudar a otras personas para que puedan comunicarse con más de 500 millones de personas en 21 países.

Recuerden ser consistentes con el formato y elegir un estilo en particular (serio, cómico o irónico).

Paso 3. Competición. Compartan su perfil con toda la clase. De todos los perfiles de la clase, ¿cuáles les parece que son los mejores? ¿Por qué?

¡Ahora, yo!

A. Entrevista. Use de modelo las preguntas y respuestas de la página 501 de este capítulo para hablar de su experiencia laboral y de las condiciones de trabajo que usted tiene ahora o desea tener en el futuro.

B. Proyecto audiovisual. Filme 2–3 entrevistas en las que (*which*) los entrevistados hablen de las personas que más admiran y expliquen por qué.

©Daniel Ernst/iStock/Getty Images

«Los hispanos que admiramos» Segmento 2

Antes de mirar

¿Cuánto sabe usted de la música de los países hispanohablantes? Relacione los siguientes tipos de música con el país que más se asocia con ellos y con los instrumentos con que se toca.

MÚSICA	LUGAR	INSTRUMENTOS
la música andina (de los Andes) el flamenco la salsa	Puerto Rico el Perú España	el piano, el cajón (*box-shaped percussion instrument*), la flauta, el *shaker*, las castañuelas (*castanets*), el charango (*stringed instrument*), la guitarra

Este segmento

Ana y Víctor entrevistan al compositor de la música de *Salu2*, Nico Barry, quien habla del proceso creativo y de la música autóctona (*indigenous*) de varios países.

Nico Barry en su estudio, con su charango: «Los instrumentos, los toco todos yo... »

Vocabulario del segmento

de mayor	as a grown-up
ponerle una cara a	to put a face with
Es todo un honor.	It's a great honor.
investigar (gu)	to research
el ritmo	rhythm
o sea	that is
suceder	to take place
el montuno	*Cuban rhythm*
vas llevando	[with it] you carry
relleno/a de	filled with
así	like this
grabar	to record
los termino reemplazando	I end up replacing them

Fragmento del guion

Obviamente, el flamenco es la música, parte de la música autóctona de España. Usaría[a] muchas guitarras españolas; como percusión usaría el cajón o las castañuelas. O en países como... totalmente diferentes, como Perú, usaría mucho el charango, que es más andino. Los ritmos, usaría muchísimos de los ritmos andinos; usaría más flautas, o bombos legüeros,[b] que son unos bombos muy grandes hechos con piel de vaca.[c]

[a] *I would use* [b] bombos... *wooden bass drums* [c] piel... *cowhide*

Después de mirar

A. ¿Está claro? Complete las siguientes oraciones con información del programa.

1. De pequeña, Ana quería ser ________.
2. De pequeño, Víctor quería ser ________.
3. Nico compone música para ________.
4. El *shaker* de Nico está relleno de ________.

B. Un poco más. Conteste las siguientes preguntas.

1. ¿Por qué admiran Ana y Víctor a Nico Barry?
2. ¿Qué hace Nico para componer la música de *Salu2*?

C. Y ahora, ustedes. En parejas, piensen en otros trabajos relacionados con un programa informativo de televisión. ¿Les gustaría tener algunos de estos trabajos en el futuro? ¿Cuáles? ¿Por qué les parecen atractivos?

MUNDO HISPANO

Enfoque cultural: Chile

Antes de leer

¿Cree usted que hay muchas personas preocupadas por la seguridad de su empleo hoy día? ¿Por qué existe esta preocupación?

El mundo del trabajo en Chile

Chile es uno de los países del mundo en donde la gente más trabaja. Como ocurre en otras partes del mundo, parte del problema es que algunos necesitan más de un trabajo para sobrevivir.[a] Pero existe también una minoría que tiene salarios altos. La realidad es que hay una brecha[b] salarial en el país. Según un reciente Informe de Salarios de la Organización Internacional del Trabajo, un trabajador chileno que cobra un sueldo alto gana casi 8 veces más que un trabajador que cobra uno bajo. Los abogados, médicos, ingenieros, empresarios, ejecutivos de bancos y congresistas[c] tienen las profesiones mejor pagadas. Y los obreros, maestros, trabajadores agrícolas y empleados públicos están entre las ocupaciones que no tienen buena remuneración.

[a]*survive* [b]*gap* [c]*congressional representatives*

En otros países hispanos

- **En algunos países hispanohablantes** La Real Academia Española de la Lengua define la palabra «trabajólico/a» como «Que trabaja afanosa[a] y compulsivamente». Curiosamente, la Real Academia identifica este adjetivo como una expresión chilena. En general, el hecho[b] de trabajar mucho o en exceso, de ser una persona trabajólica o creer que trabajar mucho es una buena cualidad son contrarios a la manera de pensar de los hispanos. Para la mayoría de estos, hay que trabajar para vivir, pero nunca al revés.[c]
- **En España** En este país, como en muchos otros países europeos, los trabajadores disfrutan de[d] buenos beneficios laborales que están establecidos por la ley.[e] Por ejemplo, un mes de vacaciones al año es el mínimo legal.

[a]*eagerly* [b]*act* [c]al... *the other way around* [d]disfrutan... tienen [e]*law*

Otro ejemplo es la licencia[f] por maternidad o paternidad, que la ley garantiza[g] con cuatro meses, además de[h] otros beneficios asociados. Además, España tiene un sistema nacional de salud que cubre prácticamente a toda la población.

[f]*leave* [g]*guarantees* [h]además... *in addition to*

Los majestuosos Andes, que cruzan todo Chile de norte a sur

Un símbolo chileno: Los Andes

Esta gran cordillera[a] es una imagen constante en la diversa geografía chilena y representa su frontera[b] natural con Bolivia y la Argentina. Los Andes son muy visibles porque el territorio de Chile es tan angosto[c] que en su punto más ancho[d] de este a oeste solo mide 180 kilómetros.[e]

[a]*mountain range* [b]*border* [c]*narrow* [d]más... *widest* [e]180... *112 miles*

Comprensión

1. ¿Cómo es la brecha salarial en Chile?
2. ¿Qué significa la palabra trabajólico/a?
3. ¿De qué beneficios disfrutan los trabajadores españoles por ley?
4. ¿En qué dirección la cordillera de los Andes atraviesa Chile?
5. ¿Cómo es Chile, un país ancho o estrecho (*narrow*)?

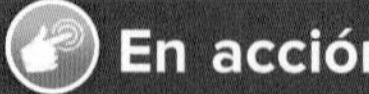 En acción

Haga una lista de todos los beneficios laborales que usted pueda imaginar. Luego, indique los (*those*) que considera más importantes. ¿Cree usted que hay algún beneficio laboral que deba ser protegido por la ley (*law*)? ¿Cuál es? Explique por qué debe protegerse.

Lectura

Antes de leer

Conteste las siguientes preguntas.

1. Mire el cuadro del pintor chileno Roberto Matta en esta página y también busque otros cuadros suyos en internet. ¿Le gustan? Explique por qué.
2. Piense en la creación de un cuadro. ¿Qué cree usted que el/la artista hace primero?

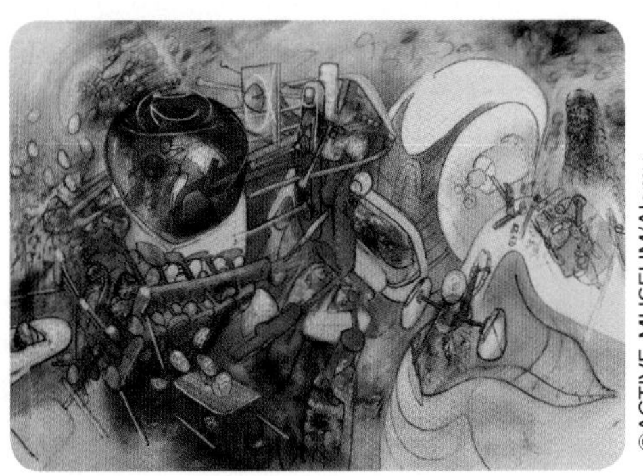

Detalle de *Los poderes (*powers*) del desorden*, de Roberto Matta

«La oportunidad de Salomón Bobadilla», de Tito Matamala

El amigo Salomón Bobadilla me lo había prometido[a] desde hacía muchos años.[b] Siempre esperó su oportunidad, y un día la oportunidad llegó, cuando la universidad pudo vanagloriarse[c] de traer a su Casa del Arte una exposición retrospectiva de Roberto Matta. Y a Roberto Matta en persona para la inauguración.

—Es mi oportunidad, repitió Salomón Bobadilla, ansioso.

No me pregunten cómo se consiguió una chaqueta y una corbata, y menos podré[d] explicar cómo Salomón Bobadilla pudo infiltrarse entre los exclusivos asistentes al cóctel con que se abría la muestra artística.

Allí, en medio de[e] autoridades[f] civiles y militares, Salomón Bobadilla se acercó furtivamente[g] al maestro. Y cuando al fin estuvo a un metro de distancia, como si fuese[h] un invitado de largo abolengo,[i] le preguntó:

—Don Roberto, ¿cuándo va a pasar sus pinturas en limpio[j]?

Eso tenía[k] Salomón Bobadilla: siempre cumplía sus promesas.

[a]había... *had promised* [b]desde... *many years ago* [c]*boast* [d]menos... *even less will I be able*
[e]en... *in the midst of* [f]*authorities* [g]se... *stealthily approached* [h]como... *as if he were*
[i]un... *a guest used to such events* [j]pasar... *create the final version of your paintings*
[k]Eso... *That's one thing you can really say about*

Vocabulario para leer

ansioso/a	anxious
el/la asistente	attendee
la exposición	exhibition
la inauguración	opening
el maestro	master
la muestra	show
cumplir una promesa	to keep a promise

Roberto Matta = un famoso pintor abstracto chileno

Comprensión

A. La exposición. ¿Qué podemos inferir (*infer*) de este microcuento?

	CIERTO	FALSO
1. Roberto Matta es un artista muy famoso.	☐	☐
2. La exposición de Matta en la Casa del Arte fue un evento importante para la universidad.	☐	☐
3. Muchas personas importantes de la sociedad asistieron a la inauguración.	☐	☐
4. Salomón Bobadilla asiste a inauguraciones de arte exclusivas con frecuencia.	☐	☐
5. Bobadilla no se vistió apropiadamente para la inauguración.	☐	☐
6. Matta no pudo asistir a la inauguración de su exposición.	☐	☐
7. Bobadilla decidió no hablar con Matta.	☐	☐

B. Su opinión

1. ¿Cree usted que a Bobadilla le gusta el arte de Matta?
2. ¿Piensa que la pregunta de Bobadilla era apropiada? ¿seria?
3. ¿Cómo cree usted que el pintor reaccionó a la pregunta de Bobadilla?

Vocabulario útil

abajo	down, down below
arriba	up, up top
en el fondo	in the background

Proyecto: La recreación de una obra de arte

Paso 1. Elija un cuadro de Roberto Matta o uno de otro pintor hispano que le gusta mucho. Llévelo a la clase—impreso (*printed*) en una hoja de papel o como versión digital en su computadora—pero no se lo enseñe a nadie.

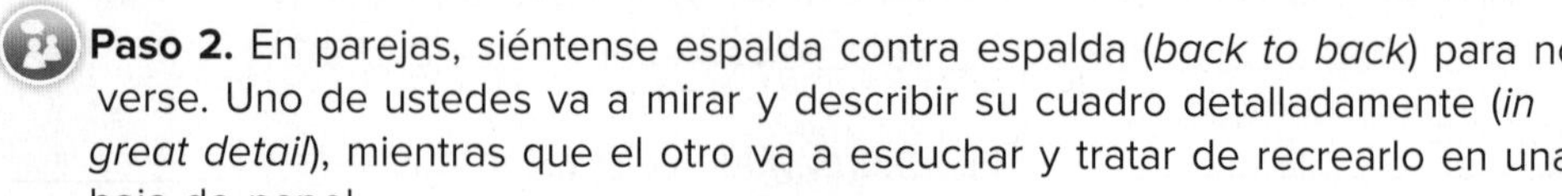

Paso 2. En parejas, siéntense espalda contra espalda (*back to back*) para no verse. Uno de ustedes va a mirar y describir su cuadro detalladamente (*in great detail*), mientras que el otro va a escuchar y tratar de recrearlo en una hoja de papel.

Paso 3. Finalmente, comparen el cuadro original con la reproducción. ¿Son similares? ¿Qué diferencias hay? Repitan el proceso, cambiando de papeles (*roles*).

Textos orales

Mundo laboral

Antes de escuchar

¿Qué debe o puede hacer una persona para prepararse para una entrevista de trabajo? ¿Es normal que alguien se ponga nervioso cuando sabe que tiene una entrevista?

Vocabulario para escuchar

la petición	request	**averigüe**	find out
cualquier	any	**asegúrese**	be sure
la formación	education, training	**la cartera**	portfolio; folder
la carrera	career	**hacer falta**	to need
acerca de	about	**el agradecimiento**	thanks

Comprensión

A. Sugerencias específicas. Haga por lo menos una sugerencia para cada momento del proceso de una entrevista laboral.

1. varios días antes de la entrevista
2. el día antes de la entrevista
3. el mismo día, antes de la entrevista
4. durante la entrevista
5. después de la entrevista

B. El programa de radio. Conteste las siguientes preguntas.

1. ¿Por qué se repite la programación de la semana anterior?
2. Según el programa, ¿cuál es la mejor manera de reducir el estrés de una entrevista?
3. ¿Dónde se puede encontrar el texto del programa?

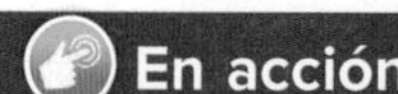

En acción

Haga una lista de las cosas que usted hizo antes de su última entrevista de trabajo. ¿Sentía que estaba bien preparado/a para la entrevista? ¿Cómo se sintió al final de la entrevista?

Proyecto en su comunidad

Entreviste a una persona hispana de su universidad o ciudad sobre algunos temas laborales.

Preguntas posibles

- ¿A qué se dedica? (¿Cuál es su trabajo?) ¿Cuánto tiempo hace que se dedica a eso? ¿Le gusta su trabajo? ¿Por qué?
- ¿Vino a este país por razones de trabajo?
- ¿Cómo es la situación laboral en su país de origen?
- ¿Qué piensa de la situación laboral en este país hoy día? ¿Cree que es mejor que cuando llegó a este país o peor?

Escritura

Proyecto: Un trabajo ideal

En este capítulo usted va a describir un trabajo que, en su opinion, es ideal.

Antes de escribir

En parejas, piensen en las características que debe tener un trabajo ideal. Incluyan muchos aspectos diferentes: el tipo de trabajo/profesión, el sueldo, el horario, el lugar de trabajo, etcétera. Describan el impacto que este empleo puede tener en la comunidad y en la sociedad. Hablen también de la persona ideal para ocupar ese puesto. Es posible que no estén de acuerdo en varias cosas, pero esta conversación los ayudará a planear su ensayo.

Haciendo un proyecto en una oficina

A escribir

Ahora use las ideas de **Antes de escribir** para escribir su ensayo. Hay más ayuda en Connect.

Más ideas para su portafolio

- Incluya un aviso clasificado de un trabajo que le interese aunque (*even if*) esté en inglés. Puede traducirlo si quiere. Debe explicar por qué le interesa ese trabajo.
- Escriba un párrafo sobre una persona que tiene una profesión que usted admira. Describa el trabajo que hace y explique por qué usted admira a esa persona.
- Si ha estado jugando Practice Spanish: Study Abroad, en Quest 11 usted supo que la cattleya es la flor nacional colombiana. Busque en internet la planta o el animal nacional de otro país hispanohablante y haga un afiche (*poster*) con una foto y su propia descripción. ¿Por qué cree usted que escogieron esta planta o animal como representante del país?

Sugerencia: You are now ready to play Quest 11 in **Practice Spanish: Study Abroad.**

EN RESUMEN En este capítulo

AFTER STUDYING THIS CHAPTER I CAN. . .

- ☐ name many professions (502)
- ☐ talk about finding and having a job (504)
- ☐ talk about money and finances (505)
- ☐ express future plans using the future (509–511)
- ☐ express probability using the future (513)
- ☐ use time conjunctions to talk about actions in the past, present, and future (515–516)
- ☐ recognize/describe at least 2–3 aspects of Chilean cultures

Gramática en breve

46. The Future

Infinitive + **-é, -ás, -á, -emos, -éis, -án**

Irregular forms: **dir-, habr-, har-, podr-, pondr-, querr-, sabr-, saldr-, tendr-, vendr-** + *future endings*

47. The Subjunctive After Conjunctions of Time

	Future/ Pending	**Habitual/ Past**
most conjunctions of time	subjunctive	indicative
antes (de) que	subjunctive	subjunctive

Conjunctions: **antes (de) que, cuando, después (de) que, en cuanto, hasta que, tan pronto como**

Vocabulario

Las profesiones y los oficios

el/la abogado/a lawyer
el amo/ama de casa housekeeper
el/la cajero/a (check-out) cashier; (bank) teller
el/la cocinero/a cook; chef
el/la contador(a) accountant
el hombre / la mujer de negocios businessperson
el/la ingeniero/a engineer
el/la maestro/a (de escuela) schoolteacher
el/la obrero/a worker, laborer
el/la peluquero/a hairstylist
el/la periodista journalist
el/la plomero/a plumber
el/la sicólogo/a psychologist
el/la siquiatra psychiatrist
el/la soldado soldier
el/la técnico/a technician
el/la trabajador(a) social social worker
el/la traductor(a) translator
el/la vendedor(a) salesperson

el oficio trade (*type of job*)

Cognados: el/la analista de sistemas, el/la astronauta, el/la diseñador(a) gráfico/a, el/la electricista, el/la fotógrafo/a, el/la militar, el/la programador(a), el/la veterinario/a

Repaso: el/la artista, el/la asistente de vuelo, el/la bibliotecario/a, el/la camarero/a, el/la consejero/a, el/la dentista, el/la dependiente/a, el/la enfermero/a, el/la mecánico/a, el/la médico/a, el/la profesor(a), el/la secretario/a

El mundo laboral

el/la aspirante job candidate; applicant
el currículum resumé
el empleo job; position
bien/mal pagado well-/poorly paid
la empresa corporation; business
la entrevista interview
el/la entrevistado/a interviewee
el/la entrevistador(a) interviewer
el formulario form (*to fill out*)
el/la gerente manager
el/la jefe/a boss
el puesto job; position
el salario pay, wages (*often per hour*)
la solicitud job application (*form*)
el sueldo salary

Repaso: de tiempo completo/parcial, el mundo, el trabajo

despedir (*like* **pedir**) to let (*someone*) go; to fire (*someone*) (*from a job*)
graduarse (me gradúo) (en) to graduate (from)
hacer una entrevista to conduct an interview
jubilarse to retire (*from a job*)
llenar to fill out (*a form*)
renunciar (a) to resign (from)
solicitar to apply for (*a job*)
tener una entrevista to have an interview

Repaso: conseguir (*like* **seguir**)

Una cuestión de dinero

ahorrar	to save (*money*)
cobrar	to cash (*a check*); to charge (*someone for an item or service*)
sacar (qu)	to withdraw, take out

Cognados: depositar

Repaso: devolver (*like* **volver**)**, ganar, gastar, pagar (gu), prestar**

el banco	bank
el billete	bill (*money*)
el cajero automático	automatic teller machine (ATM)
el cheque	check
la cuenta	account
el efectivo	cash
la factura	bill
el interés	interest
la moneda	coin
el préstamo	loan
el presupuesto	budget
el recibo	receipt
la tarjeta bancaria / la tarjeta de débito	credit/debit card

Repaso: la cuenta, el dinero, la tarjeta de crédito

a plazos	in installments
con cheque	by check
en efectivo	in cash

Los adjetivos

laboral	work, work-related

Las formas posesivas

mío/a(s)	mine, of mine
tuyo/a(s)	yours, of yours (*fam. sing.*)
suyo/a(s)	your, of yours (*form., sing./pl.*); his, of his; hers, of hers; their, of theirs
nuestro/a(s)	ours, of ours
vuestro/a(s)	yours, of yours (*fam. pl.*)

Las conjunciones de tiempo

después (de) que	after
en cuanto	as soon as
hasta que	until
tan pronto como	as soon as

Repaso: antes (de) que, cuando

Palabras adicionales

al principio de	at the beginning of

Vocabulario personal

18 La actualidad

En este capítulo

Manifestación (*Demonstration*) en la Puerta del Sol, Madrid

ESPAÑA

47 millones de habitantes

- España es un país donde muchas culturas se han encontrado a través de su milenaria[a] historia. Los fenicios, griegos, romanos y árabes son solo algunos de los más influyentes.
- El nombre del país viene de *Hispania,* el nombre en latín que los romanos le dieron al territorio español cuando era una provincia de su imperio.
- España es un país diverso en geografía, clima y culturas. De hecho,[b] existen otras lenguas oficiales junto al[c] español, como el catalán, el gallego y el vasco.

[a]a... *throughout its thousand-year* [b]De... *In fact* [c]junto... *besides*

ENTREVISTA

- ¿Es importante para usted estar al día[a] en cuanto a[b] lo que pasa en el mundo?
- ¿Qué medios de comunicación usa principalmente para mantenerse informado/a? ¿La radio y la televisión? ¿la prensa[c]? ¿internet?
- ¿Votó en las últimas elecciones? ¿Cree que es importante votar?

[a]al... *up to date* [b]en... *as far as* [c]*press*

Javier Aguirre Pereira contesta las preguntas.

- Sí, para mí es importante estar al día sobre lo que pasa en mi país y en el mundo. Y también en mi ciudad, claro.
- Me mantengo informado sobre la actualidad de diferentes maneras. Normalmente, escucho las noticias en el coche camino a[a] la oficina o de vuelta[b] a casa. Pero también leo el periódico impreso[c] o por internet. Y en casa vemos el telediario a la hora de cenar.
- ¡Por supuesto que sí![d] He votado en todas las elecciones desde que soy mayor de edad.[e] No siempre me gustan los candidatos, la verdad. Pero creo que votar es una responsabilidad en una democracia, no solo un derecho.[f]

[a]camino... *on the way to* [b]de... *on the way back* [c]*printed*
[d]¡Por... *Of course!* [e]mayor... *old enough to vote* [f]*right*

VOCABULARIO: PREPARACIÓN

You can hear the pronunciation of theme vocabulary words and phrases in the Connect eBook.

Las noticias

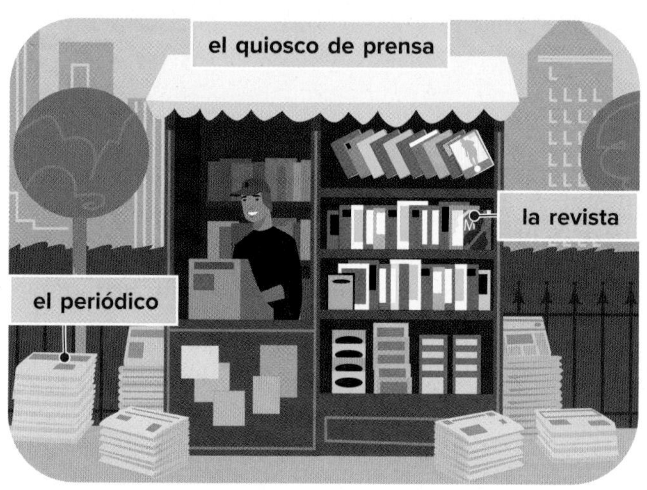

Los acontecimientos°	Los... *Events, Happenings*
el asesinato	assassination
asesinar	to assassinate
matar	to kill
el desastre (natural)	(natural) disaster
la esperanza	hope, wish
mantener (*like* tener)	to maintain; to keep
la guerra	war
la huelga	strike (*labor*)
la lucha	fight; struggle
luchar	to fight
el medio de comunicación	medium of communication (*pl.* mass media)
la muerte	death
la paz (pl. **paces)**	peace
la prensa	(print) press; news media

Cognados: el ataque (terrorista), el blog, la bomba, la erupción, la radio, la televisión, el terrorismo, el/la terrorista

El noticiero°	El... *Newscast*
comunicar(se) (qu) (con)	to communicate (with)
enterarse (de)	to find out; to learn (about)
estar al día	to be up to date
ofrecer (ofrezco)	to offer

Cognado: informar

Comunicación

A. En tertulia. La tertulia es la tradición hispana de reunirse regularmente con un grupo de amigos/colegas para hablar de las noticias del día y otros temas interesantes de la actualidad y comentarlos.

Paso 1. ¿De qué tipo de noticias le interesaría más a usted (*would most interest you*) hablar en una tertulia?

1. ☐ las noticias sobre la política internacional
2. ☐ las noticias sobre la política nacional
3. ☐ las noticias locales de su ciudad o estado
4. ☐ las noticias sobre desastres o tragedias
5. ☐ las noticias de interés humano
6. ☐ las noticias de deportes
7. ☐ las noticias financieras o de negocios
8. ☐ las noticias sobre el arte y la cultura
9. ☐ ¿ ?

Paso 2. Ahora, en grupos de cinco o seis, comparen sus respuestas. ¿Hay temas que les interesen a casi todos los estudiantes de su grupo? ¿Hay temas que no le interesen a nadie?

Paso 3. Con toda la clase, hagan una lista de los medios de comunicación que se usan hoy en día. Luego, pónganlos en orden de popularidad en el mundo de hoy, empezando por el más popular.

B. ¿Quién sabe más? En grupos de tres o cuatro, den un ejemplo actual o histórico de las siguientes cosas o personas.

MODELO: un reportero → Jorge Ramos Ávalo

1. un reportero / una reportera
2. un asesinato
3. una huelga o una lucha
4. una guerra
5. un desastre natural
6. otro tipo de desastre (por ejemplo, un accidente)
7. un ataque terrorista
8. un canal de televisión o estación de radio

C. Definiciones

Paso 1. Dé las palabras definidas.

1. un programa que nos informa diariamente de lo que pasa en el mundo
2. una muerte violenta causada intencionadamente
3. un medio de comunicación que presenta la información por escrito
4. la persona que investiga y presenta una noticia
5. una persona que emplea la violencia para causar pánico
6. cuando los obreros dejan de trabajar para protestar por su situación laboral o por su salario
7. una persona que está presente cuando ocurre algo y lo ve todo

Paso 2. Ahora, en parejas, definan las siguientes palabras en español.

1. la guerra	**4.** ofrecer
2. la muerte	**5.** luchar
3. el terrorismo	**6.** estar al día

Paso 3. Lean a la clase las definiciones que crearon en el **Paso 2** para que sus compañeros adivinen (*guess*) la palabra definida.

Así se dice

el acontecimiento = el evento, el hecho, el suceso
estar al día = estar al tanto, estar al corriente
la huelga = el paro

D. Ustedes y los medios de comunicación. En parejas, expresen y justifiquen su opinión sobre las siguientes ideas.

1. El interés por los *reality shows* demuestra que el público no se interesa realmente en los problemas actuales del mundo.
2. La prensa de los países democráticos es con frecuencia irresponsable y parcial.
3. Ver la televisión o YouTube es una pérdida (*waste*) de tiempo.
4. Hay demasiado sexo y violencia en las películas y los programas de televisión.
5. El internet es una fuente (*source*) de información tan buena como los otros medios de comunicación.

Vocabulario útil

creer que + *indicative*
no creer que + *subjunctive*
dudar que + *subjunctive*
no dudar que + *indicative*
esperar que + *subjunctive*

estar de acuerdo con/en que + *indicative*
no estar de acuerdo con/en que + *subjunctive*
es una lástima / probable / increíble que + *subjunctive*

El gobierno y la responsabilidad cívica

Las personas

el ciudadano / la ciudadana	citizen
los/las demás	(the) others
el dictador / la dictadora	dictator
el rey / la reina	king/queen

Cognados: el/la representante al congreso, el senador / la senadora

Los conceptos

el deber	responsibility; obligation
el derecho	right
la (des)igualdad	(in)equality
la dictadura	dictatorship
la discriminación	discrimination
la ley	law
el partido (político)	(political) party
la política	politics; policy
el servicio militar	military service

Las acciones

durar	to last
ganar	to win
obedecer (obedezco)	to obey
perder (pierdo)	to lose
postularse (para un cargo / como candidato/a)	to run (for a position / as a candidate)
votar	to vote

Así se dice

postularse (para un cargo político como candidato/a) = presentarse (como candidato/a a un cargo político)

Comunicación

A. ¿Quién sabe más de la política?

Paso 1. ¿Cuánto sabe usted de la política? Dé un ejemplo de las siguientes categorías.

1. un país con un rey o una reina
2. un país que tenga o haya tenido una dictadura
3. un dictador o una dictadora
4. un cargo político que dure dos / cuatro / seis años
5. el mes típico para votar en este país
6. un político o una política muy conocido/a hoy en día
7. un partido político de este país
8. un derecho esencial de todos los ciudadanos de este país
9. una causa de la desigualdad social o política

Paso 2. En parejas, comparen sus respuestas del **Paso 1.** Luego díganle a la clase cuál de ustedes pudo dar ejemplos en más categorías y qué respuestas tienen en común.

Nota cultural

El panorama social y político en el mundo hispano

Aquí hay algunos datos de interés sobre los países de habla española.

- **La mayoría de edad:** En el mundo hispano en general se llega a la mayoría de edad[a] a los 18 años, que es la edad en que la ley permite consumir bebidas alcohólicas y obtener el permiso de manejar.
- **El servicio militar:** Hoy día el servicio militar es voluntario en España y la Argentina y obligatorio en la mayoría de los otros países. Sin embargo «obligatorio» no significa que todo el mundo lo haga o que todo el mundo lo haga de manera igual.
- **Las mujeres en el ejército:** Las mujeres pueden ser militares en la Argentina, Colombia, Chile, México y España.
- **Las mujeres en la política:** A pesar de[b] la fama del machismo que existe en la cultura hispana y aunque[c] no hay igualdad en la representación de cargos del gobierno, las mujeres han llegado a ser presidentas en varios países (Chile, la Argentina, Costa Rica, Nicaragua y Panamá) y también vicepresidentas y primeras ministras, incluso ministras de Defensa aun[d] siendo civiles (en Chile y en España). Además[e] hay numerosas juezas[f] y mujeres que ocupan otros cargos políticos de importancia.

¿En cuáles de estos datos hay grandes similaridades entre su país y los países hispanohablantes?

©People and Politics/Alamy

Sonia Sotomayor, primera jueza hispana de la Corte Suprema de los Estados Unidos

[a]mayoría... *legal age* [b]A... *In spite of* [c]*although* [d]*even* [e]*Besides* [f]*judges*

©Emilk Kask/AFP/Getty Images

Los reyes de España, Felipe VI y Letizia, saludando en un acto público

B. El gobierno de España. Complete el siguiente párrafo sobre España con las palabras de la lista.

ciudadano	los demás	rey
ejército	monarquía	servicio militar
gobierno	políticos	vota
igualdad	reina	

España es un país democrático, con principios de ________[1] muy similares a los principios que existen en países con democracias bien establecidas, como los Estados Unidos y el Canadá. Sin embargo, una diferencia es el tipo de ________[2]. En España existe una ________[3] parlamentaria, lo que significa que hay un ________[4] y una ________[5]. Los reyes son figuras representativas, sin poder ejecutivo. Nadie ________[6] por el rey, pero sí se vota para elegir al presidente y todos ________[7] cargos ________[8]. España tiene un ________[9] voluntario; es decir, que no hay ________[10] obligatorio para ningún ________[11].

C. ¿Qué opina usted? En parejas, den su opinión sobre las siguientes ideas. Las palabras y expresiones del **Vocabulario útil** los ayudarán a expresar bien sus opiniones.

1. En este país, se permite que consumamos demasiado petróleo (energía, carne, azúcar).
2. Votar es un deber, no un privilegio.
3. En este país, la igualdad de todos no es una realidad todavía.
4. Es posible que una dictadura sea una buena alternativa a la democracia en algunos casos.
5. El personal a cargo (*in charge*) de los servicios básicos de un país (por ejemplo, del agua) no debe tener derecho a declararse en huelga.

Vocabulario útil

Aunque... Although ...
De hecho,... In fact ...
En mi opinión...
Por un lado... On the one hand ...
Por otro lado... On the other hand ...
Sin embargo... However ...

Algo sobre...

la diversidad lingüística de España

España, por su larga y complicada historia, tiene regiones con marcadas diferencias unas de otras, incluyendo diferencias lingüísticas. No solo hay dialectos sino[a] también lenguas diferentes. El español, también llamado el castellano tanto en España como en algunos países latinoamericanos, es la lengua mayoritaria; se habla por todo el país. Pero hay otras lenguas que se hablan y son cooficiales en sus regiones. El catalán se habla en Cataluña (donde también hay otra lengua oficial, el aranés) y tiene variantes oficiales en Valencia y las islas Baleares. El gallego se habla en Galicia, la región al noroeste de la penísula que hace frontera con Portugal. Y también tiene numerosos hablantes el vasco o euskera, que se habla en el País Vasco (con regiones en España y Francia). Es interesante notar que el español, el catalán y el gallego son lenguas romances, es decir, derivadas del latín. En contraste, el vasco no lo es y es muy diferente de los otros idiomas de la península ibérica. En la tabla, se comparan tres palabras comunes en las cuatro lenguas.

español o castellano	catalán	gallego	vasco
hola	hola	ola	kaixo
adiós	adéu	adeus	agur
gracias	gràcies	grazas	eskerrik asko

¿Cree usted que hay diferencias lingüísticas muy marcadas en los Estados Unidos? Si las hay, ¿puede explicar a qué se deben?

[a]*but*

Mapa lingüístico de España que muestra dónde se hablan las cuatro lenguas oficiales del país

SALU

«¡Noticias!» Segmento 1

Antes de mirar

¿Qué medios de comunicación usa usted para estar al corriente (*up-to-date*) de lo que pasa en el mundo?

☐ internet
☐ los noticieros de la radio
☐ los noticieros de la televisión
☐ los periódicos
☐ otros medios impresos (*print*)
☐ otros

Como estudia comunicación, esta joven mexicana desea verse inmersa en información sobre la política y la sociedad, para saber a qué atenerse (*to deal with*).

Este segmento

En este segmento se habla de cómo la gente se entera de las noticias en una serie de entrevistas con profesores y estudiantes universitarios mexicanos.

Vocabulario del segmento

disfrutar	to enjoy	**el afán**	interest
apenas	hardly ever	**el temblor**	earthquake
la fuente	source	**podría**	it could
mediante	though, via	**el ámbito**	area
estar suscrito/a	to be a subscriber	**englobar**	to encompass the whole world
la cadena	(TV) station		
prender	to turn on (*an appliance*)	**la belleza**	beauty
aparte	besides	**regir (rijo) (i)**	to rule; to matter
el adelanto	advancement		

Después de mirar

A. ¿Está claro? Las siguientes oraciones son falsas. Corríjalas.

1. A Ana le encanta leer el periódico los domingos.
2. Ana se entera de las noticias por la radio.
3. El primer profesor está suscrito a un periódico.
4. El segundo profesor cree que los estudiantes están bien informados de las noticias políticas y económicas.

B. Un poco más. Conteste las siguientes preguntas.

1. ¿Qué medio de comunicación usan más los jóvenes del programa?
2. Según el segundo profesor, ¿sobre qué temas están informados los jóvenes?

C. Y ahora, ustedes. En grupos, hablen de cómo ustedes se enteran de las noticias. ¿Creen que están al día? ¿Qué tipos de noticias les interesan más? ¿Cómo se comparan ustedes con los jóvenes mexicanos entrevistados en el segmento?

GRAMÁTICA

¿Recuerda usted?

The forms of the past subjunctive, which you will learn in **Gramática 48,** are based on the third person plural of the preterite. Here is a brief review of that preterite form.

- regular **-ar** verbs: **-ar** → **-aron**
- regular **-er/-ir** verbs: **-er/-ir** → **-ieron**
- **-ir** stem-changing verbs: **e** → **i, o** → **u** in the stem: **pidieron, durmieron**
- verbs whose stem ends in a vowel (**leer, construir,** and so on): **-ieron** → **-yeron**: **leyeron, construyeron**
- irregular preterite stems: **quisieron, hicieron, dijeron,** and so on
- four totally irregular verbs: **ser/ir** → **fueron, dar** → **dieron, ver** → **vieron**

Give the third person plural of the preterite for these infinitives.

1. hablar	**5.** perder	**9.** estar	**13.** traer	**17.** decir
2. comer	**6.** dormir	**10.** tener	**14.** dar	**18.** creer
3. vivir	**7.** reír	**11.** destruir	**15.** saber	**19.** ir
4. jugar	**8.** leer	**12.** mantener	**16.** vestirse	**20.** poder

48 *Queríamos que todo el mundo votara*

The Subjunctive (Part 9): The Past Subjunctive

Gramática en acción: Las últimas elecciones

Indique las condiciones que eran verdaderas para usted sobre las últimas elecciones en su país o estado.

En las últimas elecciones…

1. ☐ yo no tenía edad para votar.
2. ☐ yo tenía edad para votar, pero no voté.
3. ☐ para mí era importante que votara mucha gente.
4. ☐ yo dudaba que ganara uno de los candidatos que yo apoyaba, ¡pero sí ganó!
5. ☐ no se postuló ningún candidato que me convenciera o me entusiasmara de verdad.
6. ☐ en mi estado no hubo clases para los niños, para que las escuelas primarias sirvieran de centros electorales.

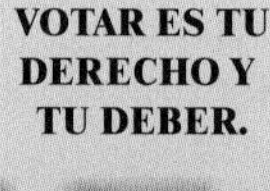
VOTAR ES TU
DERECHO Y
TU DEBER.

¡No faltes[a]!

©Lisa S./Shutterstock

[a]¡No… *Show up!*

Although Spanish has two simple indicative past tenses (preterite and imperfect), it has only one simple subjunctive past tense, the *past subjunctive* (**el imperfecto de subjuntivo**). Generally speaking, this tense is used in the same situations as the present subjunctive but to talk about past events. The exact English equivalent depends on the context in which it is used.

Past Subjunctive of Regular Verbs / El imperfecto de subjuntivo de los verbos regulares

hablar: hablar~~on~~		comer: comier~~on~~		vivir: vivier~~on~~	
hablara	habláramos	comiera	comiéramos	viviera	viviéramos
hablaras	hablarais	comieras	comierais	vivieras	vivierais
hablara	hablaran	comiera	comieran	viviera	vivieran

The last elections *Indicate the conditions that were true for you about the last elections in your country or state. In the last elections…* **1.** *I wasn't old enough to vote.* **2.** *I was old enough to vote, but I didn't vote.* **3.** *it was important to me that many people voted.* **4.** *I doubted that one of the candidates that I supported would win, but he did win!* **5.** *no candidate ran who won me over or about whom I got really enthusiastic.* **6.** *in my state there were no classes for children, so that elementary schools could serve as polling places.*

Forms of the Past Subjunctive / **Las formas del imperfecto de subjuntivo**

1. **Past Subjunctive Endings**

   As you can see in the chart on the previous page, the past subjunctive endings are identical for **-ar, -er,** and **-ir** verbs. Those endings are added to the past subjunctive stem: the third person plural of the preterite minus -**on.** For this reason, the forms of the past subjunctive reflect all of the irregularities of the third person preterite (points 2–4, below).

   An alternate form of the past subjunctive ends in **-se**: **hablase, hablases, hablase, hablásemos, hablaseis, hablasen.** This form will not be practiced in ***Puntos de partida.***

Las terminaciones del imperfecto de subjuntivo			
verbos en -ar		**verbos en -er / -ir**	
-ara	**-áramos**	**-iera**	**-iéramos**
-aras	**-arais**	**-ieras**	**-ierais**
-ara	**-aran**	**-iera**	**-ieran**

2. **The Past Subjunctive of Stem-changing Verbs**

   - **-ar** and **-er** verbs: no change

     empezar: empezar~~on~~ → **empezara, empezaras,...**
     volver: volvier~~on~~ → **volviera, volvieras,...**

   - **-ir** verbs: All persons of the past subjunctive have the vowel change of the third person plural of the preterite.

   Remember that the stem change for the third person preterite of **-ir** verbs is shown in parentheses in vocabulary lists. It is this change that occurs in *all* persons of the past subjunctive.

   pedir (pido) (i): pidier~~on~~ →

pidiera	**pidiéramos**
pidieras	**pidierais**
pidiera	**pidieran**

   dormir (duermo) (u): durmier~~on~~ →

durmiera	**durmiéramos**
durmieras	**durmierais**
durmiera	**durmieran**

3. **The Past Subjunctive of Verbs with Spelling Changes**

   All persons of the past subjunctive reflect the change from **i** to **y** between two vowels.

   i → y (caer, construir, creer, destruir, leer, oír)

   Other preterite spelling changes (**c → qu, g → gu, z → c**) do not occur in the past subjunctive because those changes do not appear in the third person plural of the preterite: **buscaron, pagaron, empezaron**.

   creer: creyer~~on~~ →

creyera	**creyéramos**
creyeras	**creyerais**
creyera	**creyeran**

4. **The Past Subjunctive of Verbs with Irregular Preterites**

   The same formula (endings are added to the third person plural of the preterite) applies to all irregular verbs.

   dar: dier~~on~~ →

diera	**diéramos**
dieras	**dierais**
diera	**dieran**

dar:	dier~~on~~ → **diera,...**	**querer:**	quisier~~on~~ → **quisiera,...**
decir:	dijer~~on~~ → **dijera,...**	**saber:**	supier~~on~~ → **supiera,...**
estar:	estuvier~~on~~ → **estuviera,...**	**ser:**	fuer~~on~~ → **fuera,...**
hacer:	hicier~~on~~ → **hiciera,...**	**tener:**	tuvier~~on~~ → **tuviera,...**
ir:	fuer~~on~~ → **fuera,...**	**traer:**	trajer~~on~~ → **trajera...**
poder:	pudier~~on~~ → **pudiera,...**	**venir:**	vinier~~on~~ → **viniera,...**
poner:	pusier~~on~~ → **pusiera,...**		

5. **The Imperfect Subjunctive of *hay* → *hubiera (haber)***
As in the present/past (indicative and subjunctive) and future, one word, **hubiera,** meaning *there was / were* or *there would be*, is used for singular and plural.

Spanish also has a *past perfect subjunctive* (**el pluscuamperfecto de subjuntivo**). The past perfect subjunctive is formed with all persons of **haber**, like all other perfect tenses. The past perfect subjunctive forms of **haber** are **hubiera / hubieras / hubiera / hubiéramos / hubierais / hubieran**. You will not practice this tense in ***Puntos de partida***, but you can find a more detailed presentation of it in Appendix 4 (Additional Perfect Tenses).

Nadie esperaba que **hubiera un huracán** en abril.
No one expected (that) there would be a hurricane in April.

Dudo que **hubiera** más de **cien personas** en la protesta.
I doubt (that) there were more than 100 people in the protest.

Uses of the Past Subjunctive / **Los usos del imperfecto de subjuntivo**

1. **Expressing Past Events**
The past subjunctive usually has the same uses as the present subjunctive, but for talking about the past. Compare the pairs of sentences at the right. The first sentence in each pair is in the present tense, the second in the past.

El presidente **quiere** que los ciudadanos **se enteren** de la tragedia inmediatamente.
The president wants the citizens to find out about the tragedy immediately.
El presidente **quería** que los ciudadanos **se enteraran** de la tragedia inmediatamente.
The president wanted the citizens to find out about the tragedy immediately.

Siento que mis padres no **puedan** estar allí esta noche.
I'm sorry (that) my parents can't be there tonight.
Sentí que mis padres no **pudieran** estar allí anoche.
I was sorry (that) my parents couldn't be there last night.

Dudamos que esos países **mantengan** la paz.
We doubt (that) those countries will keep the peace.
Dudábamos que esos países **mantuvieran** la paz.
We doubted (that) those countries would keep the peace.

---

2. **Subjunctive "Triggers"**
Remember that the subjunctive is used after:
(1) expressions of influence, emotion, and doubt/denial
(2) nonexistent and indefinite antecedents
(3) conjunctions of contingency and purpose, as well as those of time

(1) **¿Era necesario** que **regatearas**?
Was it necessary for you to bargain?

(1) **Temí** que no **pudieran** ir a Granada.
I was afraid (that) they couldn't go to Granada.

(1) **No creía** que **hubiera** tiempo para hacerlo.
I didn't think (that) there was time to do it.

(2) **No había nadie** que **pudiera** resolverlo.
There wasn't anyone who could (might have been able to) solve it.

(3) Los padres **trabajaron** mucho **para que** sus hijos **asistieran** a la universidad.
The parents worked hard so that their children could (might) go to the university.

(3) Anoche, **íbamos** a salir **en cuanto llegara** Felipe.
Last night, we were going to leave as soon as Felipe arrived.

---

3. **Past Subjunctive of *querer* to Express Requests**
The past subjunctive of the verb **querer** is often used to make a request sound more polite.

Quisiéramos hablar con usted en seguida.
We would like to speak with you immediately.

Quisiera un café, por favor.
I would like a cup of coffee, please.

Práctica y comunicación

Summary of the Imperfect Subjunctive

Third person plural of the preterite minus **-on** + **-a, -as, -a, -amos, -ais, -an**

A. Cuando era adolescente

Paso 1. Autoprueba. Dé la forma del pasado de subjuntivo de los siguientes verbos.

1. quise
2. tuve
3. salí
4. supe
5. estuve
6. traje
7. pedí
8. leí

Paso 2. Complete las oraciones con el pasado de subjuntivo para que sean verdaderas para usted cuando usted tenía más o menos 13 años.

(No) Era obligatorio que yo...

1. ________ (ir) a un servicio religioso ________ (en la iglesia / la mezquita / el templo...)
2. ________ (sacar) buenas notas para poder recibir el estipendio (*allowance*) semanal
3. ________ (poner) la mesa con frecuencia
4. ________ (leer) casi todos los días
5. ________ (mantener) mi cuarto ordenado

Mis padres no querían que... / A mis padres no les importaba que...

6. ________ (*yo:* tener) novio o novia
7. ________ (*yo:* estar) solo/a en casa
8. ________ (*yo:* mirar) la tele o cualquier (*any*) pantalla por más de dos horas al día
9. ________ (*yo:* comer) demasiada (*too much*) comida rápida
10. mis amigos ________ (venir) a casa cuando ellos no estaban

Paso 3. Ahora, en parejas, entrevístense sobre las ideas del **Paso 2.** Luego díganle a la clase algo que tenían en común o que era muy diferente para cada uno de ustedes.

MODELO: **E1:** Cuando tenías 13 años, ¿era necesario que fueras a un servicio religioso?
E2: No, para mí no era necesario. ¿Y para ti?
E1: Para mí tampoco. / Para mí sí.

B. Noticias

Paso 1. Empareje cada idea de la **Columna A** con una de la **Columna B.** Luego conjugue el verbo de la **Columna B** en el presente de subjuntivo para formar una oración completa y lógica.

COLUMNA A

1. ______ El Presidente pide que la Guardia Nacional...
2. ______ El Congreso ha votado una nueva ley para que...
3. ______ La policía va de puerta en puerta buscando a alguien que...
4. ______ La Ministra de Defensa dice que espera que...
5. ______ La Corte Suprema proclama que no es legal que...
6. ______ Los bomberos (*firefighters*) van a rescatar (*rescue*) a la víctima antes de que...

COLUMNA B

a. ________ (saber) algo del crimen
b. ________ (caerse) el edificio
c. ________ (haber) más ayuda económica para los estudiantes
d. ________ (ir) al lugar del desastre natural
e. los sospechosos ________ (estar) detenidos sin pruebas (*proof*)
f. la intervención militar ________ (ser) corta

Paso 2. Ahora ponga las oraciones del **Paso 1** en el pasado, usando el pretérito del verbo principal y haciendo otros cambios necesarios.

MODELO: Para no ir a la huelga, los obreros exigen que la compañía les dé un aumento de sueldo. → Para no ir a la huelga, los obreros **exigieron** que la compañía les **diera** un aumento de sueldo.

©Evrim Aydin/Anadolu Agency/Getty Images

Una sesión en el Congreso español

***Prác. A, Paso 1: Answers: 1.** quisiera **2.** tuviera **3.** saliera **4.** supiera **5.** estuviera **6.** trajera **7.** pidiera **8.** leyera*

C. Acontecimientos históricos

Vocabulario útil

grupos de Asia / de África / del Medio Oriente
los españoles y los portugueses
los irlandeses
los colonos ingleses en los Estados Unidos / Australia
los cuáqueros Quakers

Paso 1. Complete las siguientes oraciones con la forma correcta del imperfecto de subjuntivo de uno de los verbos de la lista. Si puede, nombre un grupo al que puede referirse cada oración.

haber **poder** **practicar** **seguir** **tener**

1. Las leyes de su país de origen no permitían que este grupo _______ libremente su religión.
2. Estas personas esperaban que _______ oro y plata en América.
3. El rey no quería que estos criminales _______ viviendo en su país.
4. Estos inmigrantes buscaban un país donde _______ tener paz y prosperidad.
5. Este grupo buscaba un país donde sus miembros no _______ que pasar hambre.

Paso 2. Ahora exprese algunos acontecimientos de la historia de los Estados Unidos, haciendo oraciones completas con los siguientes elementos. **¡OJO!** El verbo en la primera cláusula debe estar en el pasado.

1. Inglaterra: _______ (desear) / que / los colonos: _______ (conseguir) más tierras en Norteamérica
2. los indígenas americanos: _______ (temer) / que / los colonos: _______ (quitarles) sus tierras
3. el rey de Inglaterra: _______ (querer) / que / los colonos: _______ (pagar) impuestos (*taxes*)
4. los estadounidenses: _______ (ir) a la guerra / para que / México: _______ (darles) parte de su territorio
5. los estados del sur: no _______ (gustarles) / que / los estados del norte: _______ (controlar) las leyes
6. los abolicionistas: _______ (desear) / que / todas las personas del país: _______ (tener) los mismos derechos

Paso 3. Ahora, en parejas, contesten la siguiente pregunta: ¿Qué buscaban los primeros inmigrantes que llegaron a lo que es hoy los Estados Unidos?

Buscaban un lugar donde...

Vocabulario útil

poder practicar su religión
haber abundantes recursos naturales
haber menos restricciones / más libertad política y personal
tener que pagar menos impuestos (*taxes*)

D. Hace más de cien años.

Combine ideas de las dos columnas para describir cómo era la vida a finales del siglo XIX y principios del siglo XX.

COLUMNA A

Las leyes prohibían que...
Los padres esperaban que sus hijas...
Las mujeres tenían que aceptar esposos que...
Los hombres buscaban esposas que...
No había muchas personas que...

COLUMNA B

casarse jóvenes
tener muchos hijos
personas de razas diferentes: casarse
personas de origen africano: ser candidatos políticos
las mujeres: votar
tomar todas las decisiones
aceptar sus decisiones
poder imaginar ¿ ? (un derecho o una situación actual)

Algo sobre...

el flamenco

El flamenco no es la música típica de todas las regiones españolas, pero es sin duda la música que más se asocia con España a nivel internacional. Tiene su origen en Andalucía, la región más al sur, y lleva la marca indeleble del pueblo gitano.[a]

El flamenco es un género musical de gran diversidad que va desde canciones muy lentas y tristes a muy animadas y alegres. Los cantantes de flamenco se llaman cantaores y el instrumento tradicional es la guitarra acompañada de las palmas.[b] Los bailaores, que son los bailarines de flamenco, también hacen música con el taconeo[c] de sus zapatos.

Un espectáculo de flamenco, con una bailaora, un cantaor y otros músicos

¿Hay algún género musical en este país que incluya instrumentos musicales, canciones y bailes al mismo tiempo?

[a]*Romani* [b]acompañada... *accompanied by clapping* [c]*stamping*

E. Una encuesta (*poll*)

Paso 1. Haga cinco oraciones completas con elementos de cada columna. Trate de no repetir muchos elementos.

MODELO: Cuando yo era niña, mi hermana mayor no permitía que yo jugara con sus videojuegos.

cuando yo era niño/a cuando yo era adolescente (13 o 14 años) cuando yo estaba en el último año de la escuela secundaria	+	(yo) mi madre/padre mis padres mi mejor amigo/a mi hermano/a mis hermanos (no) era necesario/imposible ¿ ?	+	tener miedo de (que)... (no) querer (que)... necesitar un trabajo para (que)... prohibir que... (no) permitir que... (no) gustar (que)... ¿ ?

Paso 2. Ahora convierta sus oraciones del **Paso 1** en preguntas generales sobre los temas que usted escogió. Use las preguntas para encuestar (*poll*) a cinco compañeros de clase para ver si tuvieron experiencias similares.

MODELO: Cuando eras niño, ¿te permitían tus hermanos que jugaras con sus videojuegos?

Paso 3. Dígale a la clase por lo menos dos detalles interesantes de su encuesta.

F. Con mucha cortesía

Paso 1. Lea el dibujo y conteste las preguntas.

1. ¿Dónde está el niño?
2. ¿Qué hora será?
3. ¿Qué problema tiene el niño?
4. ¿Cómo demuestra (*shows*) el niño que es muy cortés y considerado?
5. ¿Por qué usa el niño tanta cortesía?

No te preocupes, mamá; no me pasa nada. Solo quisiera saber si podría volver otra vez[a] más tarde, en caso de que tuviera sed o me pasara algo.

[a]otra... *again*

(Continúa.)

Paso 2. Ahora, en parejas, inventen cómo pedirían (*you would ask for*) lo que necesitan en las siguientes situaciones.

1. Usted quiere el número de teléfono de una persona que acaba de conocer. Habla con un amigo de él/ella.
2. Ustedes quieren saber cuándo es el examen final en esta clase y qué va a incluir.
3. Usted necesita una extensión del plazo para la tarea de este capítulo.
4. Usted necesita una carta de recomendación del profesor / de la profesora.
5. Usted ha llamado a un amigo a las diez de la noche para invitarlo a salir, pero él ya estaba dormido y usted lo ha despertado.
6. Usted llega a casa muy enfermo/a, con tos y fiebre. Debe guardar cama. Pero la persona con quien vive le ha preparado una fiesta sorpresa de cumpleaños. Todos sus amigos lo/la saludan cuando entra.

Nota comunicativa

Cómo expresar deseos imposibles

In **Capítulo 13,** you learned to use **ojalá (que)** + *present subjunctive* to express hopes that can become a reality.

ojalá (que) + *present subjunctive* = *I hope*

Ojalá (que) saque una buena nota en este curso.

Ojalá (que) encuentre trabajo tan pronto como me gradúe.

Ojalá (que) can also be used with the *past subjunctive* to express wishes about things that are not likely to occur or that are impossible.

ojalá (que) + *past subjunctive* = *I wish*

Ojalá (que) pudiera ir a la playa este fin de semana. (*You can't because the semester/quarter isn't over yet. And, unless you live on the East or West Coast, the beach may be far away.*)

Ojalá (que) todos los estudiantes **pudieran** pasar el verano en un país hispanohablante. (*It's obvious that that's not possible for everyone.*)

Remember that the expression **ojalá** comes from the Arabic meaning *if Allah wishes*. It is similar to English *God willing* and Spanish **quiera Dios (si Dios quiere)**.

You will use **ojalá (que)** with the past subjunctive in **Práctica G.**

G. ¡Ojalá!

Paso 1. Complete las siguientes oraciones lógicamente.

1. Ojalá que (yo) tuviera...
2. Ojalá que (yo) pudiera...
3. Ojalá inventaran una máquina que...
4. Ojalá solucionaran el problema de...
5. Ojalá que en esta universidad fuera posible...

Paso 2. ¿Qué dirían (*would say*) estas personas en las siguientes situaciones?

1. el presidente / la presidenta de un país en guerra
2. un político / una política, durante una campaña electoral muy disputada
3. una persona que está muy enferma
4. un niño que quiere un juguete (*toy*) de último modelo muy caro (¡piense en lo que usted deseaba de niño/a!)
5. un(a) estudiante que tiene que pedir un préstamo para pagar la matrícula

¿Recuerda usted?

In **Gramática 49** you will learn the forms and uses of the conditional. You have already learned one conditional form: **me gustaría (Capítulo 8)**. Review what you know by giving the English equivalent of the following sentence.

Hoy **me gustaría** ir al museo.

Knowing the future, which you studied in **Gramática 46 (Capítulo 17)**, will help you learn the conditional. Can you provide the correct future forms of the following verbs?

1. (yo) viajar
2. (ellos) beber
3. (tú) ir
4. (usted) venir
5. (nosotros) hacer
6. (ella) poner

49 Expressing What You Would Do

Conditional Verb Forms

Gramática en acción: Un mundo utópico

En un mundo ideal...

- habría paz en todos los países.
- el medio ambiente no estaría contaminado.
- todas las personas tendrían los mismos derechos y libertades.
- nadie cometería ningún acto criminal.
- ningún niño sufriría de hambre ni de enfermedades.

¿Y usted?

¿Cómo sería un mundo ideal si usted pudiera cambiarlo? ¿Qué más características añadiría usted?

En mi mundo ideal,

1. (no) habría ________.
2. todo el mundo podría ________.
3. nadie tendría ________.
4. yo sería ________ (profesión/adjetivo)

The phrase **me gustaría** expresses what you *would like* to (do, say, and so on). The verb **gustaría** is a conditional form. You will learn to form the *conditional* (**el condicional**) of all verbs in this section.

Conditional of Regular Verbs / **El condicional de los verbos regulares**					
hablar		**comer**		**vivir**	
hablaría	**hablaríamos**	**comería**	**comeríamos**	**viviría**	**viviríamos**
hablarías	**hablaríais**	**comerías**	**comeríais**	**vivirías**	**viviríais**
hablaría	**hablarían**	**comería**	**comerían**	**viviría**	**vivirían**

A perfect world *In an ideal world ... • there would be peace in all countries. • the environment would not be polluted. • everyone would have the same rights and freedoms. • no one would engage in any criminal acts. • no child would be hungry or sick.*

1. **Conditional Endings**

In English the conditional, like the future, is a compound tense, formed with the auxiliary (helping) verb *would: I* ***would*** *speak, you* ***would*** *do,* and so on.

The Spanish *conditional* (**el condicional**), like the future, is a simple verb form (only one word). It is formed by adding the identical set of conditional endings to **-ar, -er,** and **-ir** infinitives. No auxiliary verb is needed.

Las terminaciones del condicional		
infinitivo +	-ía	-íamos
	-ías	-íais
	-ía	-ían

2. **Irregular Conditional Forms**

Verbs that form the future on an irregular stem use the same stem to form the conditional.

decir: diría, dirías, diría, diríamos, diríais, dirían

decir:	**dir-**	
hacer:	**har-**	
poder:	**podr-**	**-ía**
poner:	**pondr-**	**-ías**
querer:	**querr-**	**-ía**
saber:	**sabr-**	**-íamos**
salir:	**saldr-**	**-íais**
tener:	**tendr-**	**-ían**
venir:	**vendr-**	

3. **The Conditional of *hay* → *habría (haber)***

As in the present/past (indicative and subjunctive) and future, one word, **habría,** meaning *there would be*, is used for singular and plural.

Spanish also has a *past perfect conditional* (**el condicional perfecto).** The past perfect conditional is formed with all persons of **haber,** like all other perfect tenses. The conditional perfect forms of **haber** are **habría / habrías / habría / habríamos / habríais / habrían**. You will not practice this tense in ***Puntos de partida***, but you can find a more detailed presentation of it in Appendix 4 (Additional Perfect Tenses).

No **habría más de 10 personas** en la sala.
There wouldn't be more than 10 people in the room.

Los trabajadores anunciaron que **habría una huelga.**
The workers announced that there would be a strike.

4. **Uses of the Conditional**

Most uses of the Spanish conditional are the same as those of the conditional in English.

- to express what you *would* do in a particular situation or given a particular set of circumstances

—Manuel, ¿**hablarías** español en Portugal?
—No, **hablaría** portugués.
"Manuel, would you speak Spanish in Portugal?"
"No, I would speak Portuguese."
—¿**Irías** a la playa en las islas Canarias?
—Sí, claro. Me **gustaría** nadar allí.
"Would you go to the beach in the Canary Islands?"
"Yes, of course. I would like to swim there."

- to report what someone said that he/she/they *was/were going to do*, that is, to express the future from the point of view of the past

MANUEL: —Iré a Madrid en enero. → Manuel dijo que **iría** a Madrid en enero.
MANUEL: "I'll go to Madrid in January." → Manuel said that he would go to Madrid in January.
ANITA Y CARLOS: —Iremos a la manifestación esta noche. → Anita y Carlos dijeron que **irían** a la manifestación esta noche.
ANITA AND CARLOS: "We'll go to the demonstration tonight." → Anita and Carlos said that they would go to the demonstration tonight.

5. Another Way to Express *would*

Remember that *would* = *used to* (a habitual action) is expressed with the imperfect tense in Spanish.

Manuel **iba** a España todos los veranos.
Manuel would (used to) go to Spain every summer.

Práctica y comunicación

Summary of the Conditional

Infinitive + **-ía, -ías, -ía, -íamos, -íais, -ían**

A. ¿Qué haría usted en España?

Paso 1. Autoprueba. Complete las siguientes formas del condicional.

1. salir: sal_____ía **3.** querer: que_____ías **5.** tener: ten_____ía
2. hacer: ha_____íamos **4.** decir: d_____ían **6.** poder: po_____ía

Paso 2. Para describir un posible viaje a España, complete las siguientes oraciones con la forma apropiada del condicional y la información indicada.

1. _______ (ir) a España con _______
2. _______ (viajar) en _______ (mes o estación) porque _______
3. _______ (hablar) español todo el tiempo para _______
4. _______ (comer) _______ (plato[s], comidas)
5. _______ (ver) un espectáculo de _______
6. _______ (querer) _______ (infinitivo) durante el viaje
7. _______ (gustar) conocer a _______ durante mi visita
8. no _______ (poder) volver a casa sin _______ (infinitivo)

Paso 3. Ahora, en parejas, entrevístense sobre las oraciones del **Paso 1.** Luego añadan a la lista dos cosas más que harían en su viaje y díganselas a la clase.

MODELO: **E1:** ¿Con quién irías a España?
E2: Iría con mi hermana mayor, porque habla español y juntas nos divertimos mucho. ¿Y tú?

Algo sobre...

las tapas

Las tapas son pequeños platos de comida que se toman como aperitivos o en lugar del almuerzo o la cena. Es una distintiva manera española no solo de comer sino[a] de socializar en los muchos bares que existen en cualquier[b] ciudad del país. Las tapas son siempre comida salada[c] (nunca postres). Pueden ser platos fríos o calientes, simples o complicados. El concepto de las tapas ha alcanzado[d] ahora cierta popularidad en los Estados Unidos y en otros países.

¿? En su opinión, ¿cuál es una de las comidas o tipo de comida más distintivamente estadounidense?

[a]*but also* [b]*any* [c]con sal [d]*achieved*

©Image Source

Algunas de las tapas típicas españolas: calamares (*squid*) fritos, camarones, sardinas, aceitunas (*olives*) y mejillones (*mussels*)

B. ¿Es posible escapar?

Paso 1. Cuente la siguiente fantasía de una pareja, dando la forma condicional de los verbos.

Necesitamos salir de todo esto... Pensamos que _______ (deber[1]) ir al Caribe... No _______ (trabajar[2])... _______ (Poder[3]) nadar todos los días... _______ (Tomar[4]) el sol en la playa... _______ (Beber[5]) el agua de un coco... _______ (Ver[6]) bellos lugares naturales... El viaje _______ (ser[7]) ideal...

Pero... , tarde o temprano, _______ (tener[8]) que volver a lo de siempre... a los rascacielos de la ciudad... al tráfico... al medio ambiente contaminado... al trabajo... _______ (Poder[9]) usar tarjetas de crédito, como dice el anuncio —pero ¡_______ (tener[10]) que pagar después!

(Continúa.)

Prác. A, Paso 1: **Answers: 1.** *saldría* **2.** *haríamos* **3.** *querrías* **4.** *dirían* **5.** *tendría* **6.** *podría*

Paso 2. Comprensión. ¿Cierto, falso o no lo dice? Corrija las oraciones falsas.

	CIERTO	FALSO	NO LO DICE.
1. Esta pareja trabaja en una ciudad grande.	☐	☐	☐
2. No les interesan los deportes acuáticos.	☐	☐	☐
3. Pueden pagar este viaje de sueños al contado (*in cash*).	☐	☐	☐
4. Quiseran hacer el viaje con sus padres.	☐	☐	☐

C. ¿Qué dijo?

Paso 1. Repita lo que dijeron las siguientes personas.

MODELO: María: —Llegaré el lunes por la noche. →
María **dijo que llegaría** el lunes por la noche.

1. Tomás: —Estaré en el café a las 2.
2. Marta y Clara: —Vamos a hacer una fiesta este sábado.
3. La profesora de español: —Salgo para Madrid el 9 de junio.
4. Los padres: —Nos vemos en casa de los abuelos.
5. Usted: —No podré ir al cine con ustedes.
6. Yo: —No tener tiempo para ir de compras.

Paso 2. Ahora, en parejas, digan lo que dijeron algunas personas o noticieros recientemente, usando un elemento de cada columna.

MODELO: el pronóstico del tiempo →
El pronóstico del tiempo **dijo que** este fin de semana **haría** buen tiempo.

COLUMNA A	COLUMNA B
el pronóstico del tiempo	haber un examen el día _____
el profesor / la profesora de español	hacer buen/mal tiempo ______ (día / el fin de semana)
otro profesor / otra profesora	(no) haber un examen final
su padre/madre	(no) venir a visitarme pronto
su mejor amigo/a	ser necesario escribir un ensayo sobre ______
	querer estudiar juntos para un examen
	¿ ?

Nota comunicativa

Cláusulas con *si*

To express hypothetical situations, Spanish uses sentences with **si** (*if*) clauses, just like English.*

***if* CLAUSE**	**RESULT**
si + *past subjunctive*	*conditional*
Si yo **pudiera,**	**iría** a España de vacaciones.
If I could,	*I would go to Spain on vacation.*
Si yo **fuera** tú,	no **haría** eso.
If I were you,	*I wouldn't do that.*

You are already familiar with **si** clauses with the present indicative. They present actions that are habitual in the present or likely to happen.

¡OJO!

The present subjunctive is never used after **si.**

Si ahorro suficiente dinero, **iré** de vacaciones a España.
If I save enough money, I'll go to Spain on vacation.

You will create **si**-clause sentences in **D** through **H.**

These contrary-to-fact situations express speculations about the present and the future. The perfect forms of the conditional and the past subjunctive are used to speculate about the past; that is, what* would have *happened if a particular event had occurred:* Si **hubiera tenido el dinero, **habría hecho** el viaje. (*If **I had had** the money, **I would have made** the trip.) You will find a more detailed presentation of this structure in Appendix 4 (Additional Perfect Tenses).*

D. ¿Qué haría usted?

Paso 1. Complete las siguientes declaraciones lógicamente.

1. Si yo quisiera comprar comida, iría a ______.
2. Si necesitara comprar un libro, iría a ______.
3. Si necesitara consultar un libro, iría a ______.
4. Si tuviera sed en este momento, tomaría ______.
5. Si tuviera que emigrar, iría a ______.
6. Si fuera a ______, tendría que viajar en ______.
7. Si tuviera suficiente dinero, compraría ______.
8. Si pudiera, me gustaría ______.

Paso 2. Ahora, en parejas, túrnense para comparar sus oraciones del **Paso 1**. Luego díganle a la clase lo que ustedes tienen en común.

E. Situaciones

Paso 1. Empareje los siguientes dibujos con las descripciones. Luego complete las descripciones, conjugando los verbos y añadiendo los detalles necesarios.

a.

b.

c.

d.

_____ 1. Miriam ______ (ir) en coche al trabajo como siempre si su coche no ______ (tener) un serio problema con los frenos. Si su padre ______ (vivir) cerca, ______ (poder) arreglarlo él, pero (él)...

_____ 2. Si el avión no ______ (ser) tan pequeño, la Sra. Blanco no ______ (tener) tanto miedo. ______ (Preferir) ir en coche, pero es un caso de emergencia: su hijo...

_____ 3. Si Mariana ______ (tener) suficiente dinero, ahora mismo ______ (comprar) ese traje pantalón. ______ (Ser) ideal para... (un evento o una situación)

_____ 4. Si la compañera de casa de Julia ______ (poder) llevarla al trabajo, Julia ______ (seguir) durmiendo hasta las ocho por lo menos. Y Julia no ______ (estar) tan cansada si...

Paso 2. Ahora imagine una solución para cada situación. Use el futuro para expresar lo que pasará. ¡Sea imaginativo/a!

MODELO: Mariana le pedirá dinero a... Esta persona no se lo dará / se lo dará como regalo de cumpleaños.

 F. **¿En qué circunstancias lógicas... ?** En parejas, hagan y contesten preguntas sobre los siguientes temas.

MODELO: comprar un coche nuevo →
E1: ¿En qué circunstancias **comprarías** un coche nuevo?
E2: **Compraría** un coche nuevo **si tuviera** más dinero.

1. dejar de estudiar en esta universidad
2. emigrar a otro país
3. estudiar otro idioma
4. no obedecer a tus padres / a tu jefe/a
5. votar por _______ para presidente/a
6. ser candidato/a para presidente/a
7. casarse / divorciarse
8. no decirle la verdad a un amigo / una amiga

 G. **¿Qué haría si... ?**

Paso 1. En parejas, inventen soluciones para los siguientes dilemas.

1. Si su mejor amigo/a le pidiera 500 dólares para algo muy urgente.
2. Si uno de sus profesores o profesoras le dijera que no ha cancelado el examen final de su curso.
3. Si su novio/a le propusiera que se casaran inmediatamente. (O si su esposo/a le propusiera que se divorciaran en seguida.)
4. Si de pronto tuviera un millón de dólares hoy.

Paso 2. Ahora inventen una situación bien difícil de resolver que la clase tiene que solucionar. ¡Sean imaginativos!

 H. **Si el mundo fuera diferente...** ¿Qué ocurriría si el mundo fuera diferente? En parejas, hablen de las siguientes circunstancias.

MODELO: Si yo fuera la única *(only)* persona en el mundo... →
- **tendría** que aprender a hacer muchas cosas.
- **sería** la persona más importante —y más ignorante— del mundo.

1. Si yo pudiera tener solamente un amigo o amiga, _______.
2. Si yo tuviera que pasar un año en una isla desierta, _______.
3. Si yo fuera _______ (otra persona), _______.
4. Si el presidente / la presidenta fuera _______, _______.
5. Si yo viviera en (nombre de país), _______.

©Ricardo Rubio/Europa Press News/Getty Images

La vicepresidenta del gobierno español, Carmen Calvo

Todo junto

A. Lengua y cultura: Maneras de practicar el español fuera de clase

Paso 1. Completar. Complete the following paragraphs with the correct form of the words in parentheses, as suggested by context. When two possibilities are given, select the correct word. **¡OJO!** As you conjugate verbs, decide whether to use the subjunctive (present, present perfect, or past) or the indicative (present, present perfect, future, preterite, or imperfect). For items flagged with *comm.*, use a command. Start out in the present.

Claro está que usted habla español en clase. También es probable que lo _______ (hablar[1]) con su profesor(a) cada vez que lo/la _______ (ver[2]) en el campus de la universidad. Pero _______ (por / para[3]) hablar español con soltura,[a] usted tiene que practicar más.

«¡Ojalá que _______ (*yo:* poder[4]) practicar español fuera de clase!» ¿_______ (*pres. perf.:* Decir[5]) usted eso alguna vez? Pues hay muchas maneras de hacerlo. Por ejemplo, los compañeros de una misma clase de español siempre pueden hablar español cuando _______ (verse[6]) para no _______ (perder[7]) _______ (ninguno[8]) oportunidad de practicar. Otra idea es _______ (mirar[9]) una telenovela[b] o _______ (un / una[10]) programa de noticias en español. También puede escuchar la radio cuando _______ (manejar[11]). Lo importante es dedicar un rato[c] a escuchar español auténtico con frecuencia.

Muchas personas _______ (sentirse[12]) muy frustradas con esta actividad _______ (por qué/porque[13]) no pueden comprenderlo todo. Pero _______ (haber[14]) que recordar que no es necesario entender cada una de las palabras que se oyen. Para los estudiantes principiantes,[d] es suficiente identificar _______ (el / la[15]) tema y _______ (alguno[16]) palabras y expresiones. Si usted _______ (escuchar[17]) español habitualmente en los medios de comunicación, _______ (aprender[18]) mucho... y rápidamente.

Otra actividad útil es leer el periódico o una revista de actualidad en español. _______ (*comm., Usted:* Buscar[19]) un sitio en internet. _______ (Por / Para[20]) ejemplo, muchos gobiernos tienen páginas relacionadas con el turismo.

Finalmente, _______ (*comm., usted:* recordar[21]) su propia comunidad. Es muy posible que usted _______ (vivir[22]) en una ciudad o estado que tiene una comunidad hispana. Le sugerimos que _______ (*usted:* visitar[23]) tiendas o supermercados hispanos para que _______ (*usted:* ver[24]) las cosas que se venden allí. ¡Leer la lista de los ingredientes de cualquier producto es un ejercicio de lectura!

[a]con... *fluently* [b]*soap opera* [c]un... *a bit of time* [d]*beginning*

Paso 2. Comprensión. Conteste las siguientes preguntas.

1. Además de (*Besides*) hablar español en clase, ¿qué cosas puede usted hacer para practicar el idioma fuera de (*outside of*) la clase?
2. ¿Es buena o mala la idea de mirar la televisión en español? ¿Qué tipos de programas se recomienda ver?
3. ¿Es necesario que un estudiante entienda cada una de las palabras de lo que oye en los medios de comunicación?
4. ¿Qué tipos de lecturas puede usted conseguir en español para practicar más?

©Hermes Mereghetti Studio/Alamy

Una página de la edición electrónica de *El País*, un periódico de España

(Continúa.)

Paso 3. En acción

Ahora, en parejas, hablen sobre su futuro con respecto al español. Las siguientes preguntas les darán algunas ideas para su conversación.

1. ¿Van a tomar otra clase de español el próximo semestre/trimestre? ¿Por qué sí o por qué no?
2. ¿Piensan estudiar en un país hispanohablante? ¿En dónde? ¿Cuándo?
3. ¿Creen que en el futuro usarán el español en su trabajo? ¿Por qué?

B. Proyecto: Una encuesta sobre decisiones personales

¿Creen ustedes que conocen bien a sus compañeros de clase? ¡Es posible que les sorprendan algunas respuestas!

¿Qué preguntas les quiere usted hacer a sus compañeros de clase?

Paso 1. Preparación. En parejas, preparen cuatro preguntas que presenten dilemas personales. Piensen en temas importantes en la vida, como la familia, los estudios, el trabajo, el medio ambiente y las relaciones sociales. Usen el condicional para indicar la cualidad hipotética de sus preguntas. También pueden usar oraciones hipotéticas con **si**.

MODELOS: ¿**Podrías** pasar más de una semana sin mirar el celular?
Si **tuvieras** la opción de irte a otra universidad, ¿**te irías**?

Vocabulario útil

vivir permanentemente en este estado / esta ciudad
tener más de dos hijos / adoptar hijos
presentarse como candidato político / candidata política a nivel estatal
prestar (*to do*) servicio militar
poder vivir sin la televisión / la computadora / el celular

Paso 2. Encuesta. Ahora entrevisten a todas las personas que puedan de la clase. Recuerden apuntar (*to take down notes*) de las respuestas.

Paso 3. Información. Finalmente, preparen una breve presentación con los resultados de su encuesta. Añadan un comentario personal a cada una de las respuestas que van a presentar.

MODELO: (No) Nos sorprendió que la mayoría de la clase pensara que no podría pasar más de una semana sin mirar el celular.

¡Ahora, yo!

A. Entrevista. Use de modelo las preguntas y respuestas de la página 529 de este capítulo para decir si es importante para usted estar al día de lo que pasa en el mundo y qué hace para enterarse de las noticias.

B. Producción audiovisual. Filme una entrevista que le hace a una persona que trabaja de voluntario/a en alguna organización local o de la universidad.

«¡Noticias!» Segmento 2

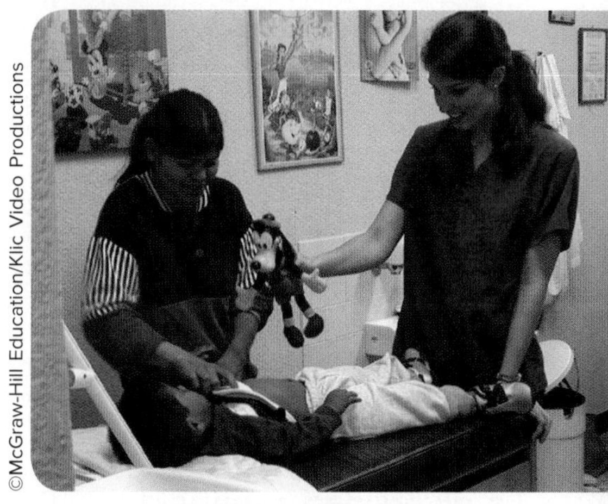

«Y al final, ¿ellos qué es lo que se llevan (*they [the volunteers] take away*)? Se llevan la sensación de haber ayudado (*having helped*), pero la mayoría se va con la idea de que ellos aprendieron más de lo que dieron.»

Antes de mirar

¿Hace o ha hecho usted trabajo de voluntario? ¿En qué tipo de organización?

☐ una organización religiosa
☐ una escuela primaria, media o secundaria
☐ una residencia de ancianos
☐ un refugio para perros y gatos
☐ una organización sin fines de lucro (*non-profit*)

Este segmento

Laura presenta un reportaje sobre un programa para voluntarios extranjeros en Guatemala.

Vocabulario del segmento

sumo/a	great
el analfabetismo	illiteracy
mejorar	to improve
atender	to take care of
el alivio	relief
colocar (qu)	to place
llenarse	to get filled up
bien satisfecho/a	very satisfied
Chinautla, Antigua	**ciudades guatemaltecas**
antiguo/a	former
valorar	to value
la pobreza	poverty
maravilloso/a	wonderful

Fragmento del guion

HERMANO[a] LUVÍN: Diario[b] atendemos noventa a cien ancianos, en los cuales les damos alimentación que consta[c] de un almuerzo, que para ellos es desayuno, almuerzo y cena, porque no tienen dónde más comer.[d] Fuera de eso,[e] les prestamos el servicio de baño.[f] Ellos vienen de la calle, sucios, vueltos nada.[g] Y les damos ropa, les damos el baño para que cambien y para que se bañen y queden distintos. También le[s] damos la parte espiritual, como motivación para que su autoestima[h] se eleve un poco y piensen que son importantes para la sociedad, aunque vivan en las circunstancias que viven.

[a]*BROTHER (in a religious order)* [b]*On a daily basis* [c]alimentación... *nourishment that consists* [d]no... *they have nowhere else to eat* [e]Fuera... *In addition* [f]les... *we provide them with bathing facilities* [g]vueltos... *reduced to nothing* [h]*self-esteem*

Después de mirar

A. ¿Está claro? Las siguientes oraciones son falsas. Corríjalas.

1. CCS es una compañía de negocios internacionales.
2. Los voluntarios atienden solo a ancianos.
3. CCS coloca a todos los voluntarios en la misma organización.
4. Los voluntarios de CCS no viajan.

B. Un poco más. Conteste las siguientes preguntas.

1. ¿Qué problemas endémicos tiene Guatemala?
2. Según una codirectora de CCS, ¿qué aprenden los voluntarios?
3. Además de (*Besides*) ayudar a las personas necesitadas (*in need*), ¿qué otras actividades hacen los voluntarios?

C. Y ahora, ustedes. Obviamente, no hay que ir a otro país para ayudar a las personas necesitadas. En parejas, hablen de los tipos de ayuda que uno puede dar como voluntario en este país y dónde lo puede hacer. ¿Hay áreas especialmente necesitadas en su estado? ¿Qué tipo de ayuda necesitan?

MUNDO HISPANO

Enfoque cultural: España

Antes de leer

¿Cuáles son las ventajas y desventajas cuando hay gran diversidad en un solo (*single*) país?

La diversidad española

España es un país de una gran diversidad geográfica y cultural. En el país conviven[a] regiones con identidades bien definidas a lo largo de[b] una historia milenaria.[c] Estas diferencias incluyen hasta lenguas diferentes.

Con la Constitución de 1978, España reconoce[d] esta diversidad, constituyéndose[e] como un Estado de las autonomías: diecisiete regiones que funcionan de manera descentralizada, no muy diferente del sistema federativo estadounidense.

La diversidad de España es una fuente[f] de innumerables tensiones lingüísticas, políticas, presupuestarias,[g] etcétera. Pero también es motivo de orgullo[h] general, porque con un territorio un poco más pequeño que el tamaño[i] de Texas, España es un país de intensos contrastes.

[a]*coexist* [b]a... *throughout* [c]*thousand-year* [d]*recognizes* [e]*organizing itself* [f]*source* [g]*budgetary* [h]*pride* [i]*size*

En todo el mundo hispano

- **En muchos países americanos hispanohablantes** En 2010, muchos países celebraron el bicentenario del proceso de su independencia de España. Esa lucha, que empezó en la mayoría de los casos a principios del siglo XIX, duró alrededor de[a] quince años y culminó con la creación de los nuevos estados americanos.
- **En la Argentina, el Paraguay y el Uruguay** Junto con el Brasil, estos países firmaron un tratado[b] para formar el Mercado Común del Sur, o MERCOSUR. Es un acuerdo[c] que fomenta[d] la libre circulación de productos y servicios. En la actualidad MERCOSUR tiene más países asociados: Bolivia, Chile, Colombia, el Ecuador y el Perú.

[a]alrededor... *about* [b]firmaron... *signed a treaty* [c]*agreement* [d]*encourages*

©Pixtal/age fotostock

Hay estatuas de don Quijote de la Mancha y Sancho Panza por todo el país. Estas están en la Plaza de España, en Madrid.

Un símbolo español: Don Quijote de la Mancha y Sancho Panza

El ingenioso hidalgo[a] *Don Quijote de la Mancha*,[b] de Miguel de Cervantes, es una de las obras cumbres[c] de la literatura mundial. Se considera la primera novela moderna y es el libro más editado y traducido del mundo, después de la Biblia.

La novela cuenta la historia de don Quijote, un señor mayor que se vuelve loco[d] y decide hacerse[e] caballero andante[f] como los de las novelas[g] que le encanta leer. Por eso toma un escudero,[h] Sancho Panza, que en realidad es solo un campesino local. Sancho intenta disuadir a su señor de meterse en líos.[i] Juntos pasarán por una larga serie de aventuras que revelan la naturaleza humana. Don Quijote es un símbolo del espíritu humano que siempre lucha por algo noble, aunque[j] sean causas perdidas, mientras que Sancho Panza es símbolo de lealtad.[k]

[a]*gentleman* [b]*region in the center of Spain* [c]obras... *masterpieces* [d]se... *goes mad* [e]*to become* [f]caballero... *a knight errant* [g]como... *like the ones in the novels* [h]*squire* [i]de... *from getting himself into trouble* [j]*although* [k]*loyalty*

Comprensión

1. ¿Cómo está dividida España administrativamente?
2. ¿De qué año es la Constitución española actual?
3. ¿Cuántos siglos hace que son independientes muchas naciones latinoamericanas?
4. ¿Qué es MERCOSUR?
5. ¿Por qué es importante la novela *Don Quijote de la Mancha*?
6. ¿Qué simbolizan don Quijote y Sancho?

En acción

En parejas, decidan cuáles son los grandes íconos humanos de su país. Pueden ser personajes (*characters*) de ficción, como don Quijote y Sancho, o personajes reales e históricos.

Lectura cultural

Antes de leer

Usted va a leer unos artículos de la Constitución española que vienen de la sección de «Derechos y libertades». Empiece leyendo solamente los títulos de los artículos 14, 15 y 16 y trate de predecir (*predict*) algunos de los derechos y libertades permitidos por esta Constitución. En su opinión, ¿hay alguno de los tres artículos en particular que sea más importante, o cree usted que los tres tienen la misma importancia? Explique su respuesta.

Vocabulario para leer

la confesión	faith	**la pena**	punishment
la creencia	belief	**la pena de muerte**	death penalty
el culto	worship	**penal**	criminal (*adj.*)
el individuo	individual	**el trato**	treatment

Constitución española, Capítulo segundo. Derechos y libertades

Artículo 14. Igualdad ante la ley

Los españoles son iguales ante la ley, sin que pueda prevalecer discriminación alguna por razón[a] de nacimiento,[b] raza, sexo, religión, opinión o cualquier[c] otra condición o circunstancia personal o social.

SECCIÓN 1ª. De los derechos fundamentales y de las libertades públicas

Artículo 15. Derecho a la vida

Todos tienen derecho a la vida y a la integridad física y moral, sin que, en ningún caso, puedan ser sometidos a[d] tortura ni a penas o tratos inhumanos o degradantes. Queda abolida[e] la pena de muerte, salvo lo que puedan disponer[f] las leyes penales militares para tiempos de guerra.

Artículo 16. Libertad ideológica y religiosa

1. Se garantiza la libertad ideológica, religiosa y de culto de los individuos y las comunidades sin más limitación, en sus manifestaciones, que la necesaria para el mantenimiento[g] del orden público protegido por la ley.
2. Nadie podrá ser obligado a declarar[h] sobre su ideología, religión o creencias.
3. Ninguna confesión tendrá carácter estatal. Los poderes públicos tendrán en cuenta[i] las creencias religiosas de la sociedad española y mantendrán las consiguientes relaciones de cooperación con la Iglesia Católica y las demás confesiones.

[a]sin... *without the possibility of any discrimination on the grounds* [b]*birth* [c]*any* [d]sometidos... *subjected to* [e]Queda... *Is abolished* [f]salvo... *except as stipulated by* [g]el... *maintaining* [h]*testify* [i]tendrán... *will take into account*

Comprensión

A. Los derechos y libertades en España. Según los Artículos 14, 15 y 16 de la Constitución española, ¿son ciertas o falsas las siguientes afirmaciones? Indique el artículo al que corresponda (*matches*) cada afirmación y corrija las afirmaciones falsas.

	CIERTO	FALSO
1. En España, las mujeres tienen más libertad que los hombres.	☐	☐
2. Excepto en situaciones de guerra, el gobierno no puede torturar a ningún individuo.	☐	☐
3. El gobierno puede obligar a sus ciudadanos a expresar sus ideas políticas o religiosas.	☐	☐
4. En España, las cárceles (*jails*) no tienen el derecho de tratar a los prisioneros de forma inhumana.	☐	☐
5. En España existe la pena de muerte.	☐	☐
6. España se establece como un país católico.	☐	☐

(Continúa.)

B. Pensando como abogado/a constitucional. Imagine que usted es abogado/a y que tiene clientes en las siguientes situaciones. ¿Qué artículos de la Constitución española puede usted citar para ayudarlos? **¡OJO!** Recuerde que a veces es necesario que los abogados y jueces (*judges*) interpreten artículos de la Constitución, ya que (*since*) ninguna constitución contempla todas las posibles situaciones.

1. Su cliente cree que ha sido discriminado por pertenecer (*belonging*) a una religión minoritaria.
2. Su cliente está en la cárcel (*jail*) y dice que los otros presos (*prisoners*) abusan de él.
3. Su cliente es transgénero y es víctima de discriminación en el trabajo.

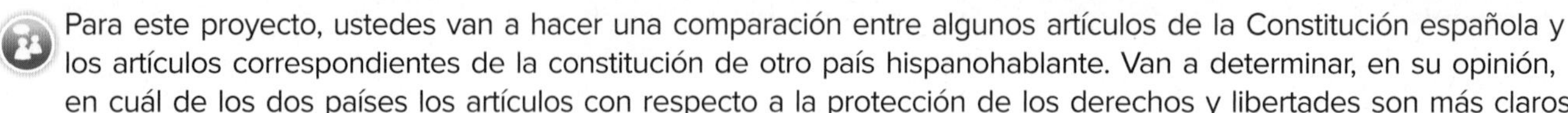

Proyecto: Una comparación entre los derechos y libertades de dos constituciones

Para este proyecto, ustedes van a hacer una comparación entre algunos artículos de la Constitución española y los artículos correspondientes de la constitución de otro país hispanohablante. Van a determinar, en su opinión, en cuál de los dos países los artículos con respecto a la protección de los derechos y libertades son más claros.

Paso 1. En parejas, elijan la constitución de otro país hispanohablante y busquen las secciones que correspondan a los artículos 14, 15 y 16 de la Constitución española. ¿Qué semejanzas y diferencias hay entre ellas?

Paso 2. Busquen en internet la Constitución española entera y lean en ella otro artículo sobre los derechos y libertades. Luego busquen la sección correspondiente en la constitución del otro país. De nuevo (*Once again*), identifiquen las semejanzas y diferencias.

Paso 3. Preparen una breve presentación sobre las semejanzas y diferencias entre las dos constituciones. Después de escuchar todas las presentaciones, determinen entre todos si hay algunos países que le garanticen más derechos y libertades al individuo.

Textos orales

Una breve historia de España

Antes de escuchar

¿Qué sabe usted de la historia de España? Seguro que sabe que tuvo un gran imperio, pero ¿sabía que en ese país hubo una guerra civil, como en los Estados Unidos? ¿Cómo cree que es el país en la actualidad, pobre o rico? ¿moderno o tradicional?

El acueducto de Segovia, construido por los romanos

Vocabulario para escuchar

autóctono/a	indígena	**tras**	after
la huella	trace; mark	**listo/a**	ready
la caída	fall	**pasar de ser**	to go from being
el imperio	empire	**creciente**	growing
a lo largo de	throughout	**milenario/a**	thousand-year
el reino	kingdom	**acoger**	to welcome

Comprensión

A. Una breve historia. Lea primero la **Estrategia** en la siguiente página. Escriba el siglo al que corresponden los eventos.

1. Los griegos, fenicios y otros pueblos se establecieron en la península ibérica antes del siglo ________ d.C.
2. Los romanos dominaron la península ibérica desde el siglo ________ hasta el siglo ________
3. La invasión de los árabes ocurrió en el siglo ________.
4. Los árabes fueron expulsados de la península ibérica en el siglo ________.
5. El país que hoy se conoce como España comenzó en el siglo ________.
6. El final del gran imperio español ocurrió en el siglo ________.
7. España tuvo una guerra civil en el siglo ________.

B. La España de hoy. ¿Cómo es España hoy? Use palabras de la conferencia y sus propias palabras para describir la España de hoy.

1. el gobierno **2.** la economía **3.** la población

 En acción

Compare lo que estaba pasando en España con lo que estaba pasando en su país al mismo tiempo (*at the same time*) en cuatro momentos del pasado.

Por ejemplo: En el siglo VIII ocurrió la invasión árabe de la península ibérica, pero no hubo ninguna invasión importante en Norteamérica.

Estrategia

- Para indicar los siglos en español, se usan los números romanos. Por ejemplo, el siglo XV = el siglo quince (*1400s*).
- a. e. c. = antes de la era común (antes de Cristo)/ e. c. = era común (después de Cristo)

 Proyecto en su comunidad

Entreviste a una persona hispana de su universidad o ciudad sobre el gobierno de su país de origen y sobre sus preferencias políticas.

Preguntas posibles

- ¿Qué tipo de gobierno hay en su país? ¿Ha habido algún cambio grande en la estructura del gobierno en los últimos años? ¿Y en las últimas décadas?
- ¿Quién es el presidente o la presidenta del país? ¿Hay un congreso y un senado?
- ¿Cuáles son los partidos políticos más importantes? Si hay más de dos partidos, ¿se forman coaliciones de partidos para gobernar?
- ¿Estaba afiliado/a a algún partido en su país? ¿Votó alguna vez? ¿En qué elecciones?

 Escritura

 Proyecto: Un ensayo sobre la mayoría de edad°

mayoría... *legal age*

¿Cuál es su opinión sobre la mayoría de edad? ¿Está de acuerdo con la idea de que haya una edad mínima para tener derecho a ciertas actividades? ¿Coincide su opinión con la (*that*) de muchos de sus compañeros?

Antes de escribir

 En parejas, hagan una lista de los puntos que uno debe considerar para escribir un ensayo sobre el tema de la mayoría de edad. Luego preparen una serie de preguntas basadas en esas consideraciones y úsenlas para encuestar a cinco de sus compañeros.

©VectorPic/Shutterstock

A escribir

Después de hacer su encuesta, use las respuestas para escribir el ensayo. Hay más ayuda en Connect.

Más ideas para su portafolio

- Haga una lista de las cosas que usted haría durante un viaje ideal a un país hispanohablante en las próximas vacaciones.
- Si usted pudiera, ¿qué cosas cambiaría en el mundo? Haga una lista de cinco o seis cosas que usted haría. Puede ser una lista seria o cómica.
- Si ha estado jugando Practice Spanish: Study Abroad, en Quest 12 usted participó en una actividad que usó varios dichos y refranes de países hispanohablantes. Investigue otros refranes en español y trate de interpretarlos. Después, compárelos con refranes de su cultura de origen. ¿Hay semejanzas y correspondencias entre los refranes de diferentes culturas, o nota usted diferencias? ¿Qué importancia cultural tienen los refranes en general? Presente algunos refranes en clase y pídales a sus compañeros que den sus interpretaciones.

Sugerencia: You are now ready to play Quest 12 in **Practice Spanish: Study Abroad.**

EN RESUMEN En este capítulo

AFTER STUDYING THIS CHAPTER I CAN. . .

- ☐ talk about current events (530)
- ☐ talk about government and civic responsibilities (532)
- ☐ express situations in the past that require the subjunctive (536–538)
- ☐ talk about hypothetical events using the conditional (543–545)
- ☐ recognize/describe at least 2–3 aspects of Spanish culture

Gramática en breve

48. The Past Subjunctive

Third person plural preterite minus **-on** + **-a, -as, -a, -amos, -ais, -an**

49. The Conditional

Infinitive + **-ía, -ías, -ía, -íamos, -íais, -ían**

Irregular forms: **dir-, habr-, har-, podr-, pondr-, querr-, sabr-, saldr-, tendr-, vendr-** + *conditional endings*

Vocabulario

Las noticias

el acontecimiento	event, happening
el asesinato	assassination
el choque	collision, crash
la esperanza	hope, wish
la estación de radio	radio station
la guerra	war
la huelga	strike (*labor*)
la lucha	fight; struggle
la manifestación	demonstration; march
el medio de comunicación	medium of communication (*pl.* mass media)
el noticiero	newscast
la paz (*pl.* **paces**)	peace
la prensa	(print) press; news media
el quiosco de prensa	newsstand
el/la testigo	witness

Cognados: el ataque (terrorista), la bomba, la erupción, el/la reportero/a, el terrorismo, el/la terrorista, la víctima

Repaso: el blog, el canal (de televisión), el desastre, la muerte, las noticias, el periódico, la radio, la revista, la televisión

asesinar	to assassinate
comunicarse (qu) (con)	to communicate (with)
enterarse (de)	to find out; to learn (about)
estar al día	to be up to date
luchar	to fight
mantener (*like* **tener**)	to maintain; to keep
matar	to kill

Cognado: informar

Repaso: ofrecer (ofrezco)

El gobierno y la responsabilidad cívica

el cargo	(political) office
el centro	center (*political*)
el/la ciudadano/a	citizen
el deber	responsibility; obligation
el derecho	right
la (des)igualdad	(in)equality
el/la dictador(a)	dictator
la dictadura	dictatorship
el ejército	army
la ley	law
el partido	political party
la política	politics; policy
el/la político/a	politician
el rey / la reina	king/queen
el servicio militar	military service

Cognado: el/la candidato/a, el concepto, la discriminación, el/la representante al congreso, el/la senador(a)

Repaso: los/las demás, la derecha, el gobierno, la izquierda, el soldado / la soldado

durar	to last
postularse (para un cargo / como candidato/a)	to run (for a position / as a candidate)

Cognado: votar

Repaso: ganar, obedecer (obedezco), perder (pierdo)

Los adjetivos

Cognados: cívico/a, político/a

Repaso: natural

Vocabulario personal

LECTURA CULTURAL FINAL

El español en el resto del mundo

A lo largo de[a] dieciocho capítulos, se ha presentado en *Puntos de partida* el inmenso y variado mundo hispanohablante, desde[b] los Estados Unidos hasta el Cono Sur en las Américas y, dentro de Europa, en España.

Pero el español es una lengua importante en otros países también. En África, sobrevive[c] bien arraigado[d] en la Guinea Ecuatorial, así como[e] en las ciudades norteafricanas de Ceuta y Melilla, que son territorio español. En Oceanía,* en las islas Filipinas, la lengua española es parte de su herencia[f] colonial, aunque[g] ya no es una lengua oficial en ese país. Y también hay que mencionar el Canadá, país donde hay una creciente[h] inmigración hispanohablante.

[a]A... *Throughout* [b]*from* [c]*it survives* [d]*established* [e]así... *as well as* [f]*heritage* [g]*although* [h]*growing*

The term* **Oceanía *refers to the islands of the tropical Pacific Ocean, including Polynesia, Australia, and New Zealand, as well as the Philippines and other island groups.*

LA GUINEA ECUATORIAL

La Guinea Ecuatorial es uno de los países más pequeños de África, pero también es uno de los más prósperos, debido a los yacimientos[a] de petróleo que se encuentran en su territorio. Fue colonia española desde[b] 1778 hasta 1968, y desde 1844 el español es una de sus lenguas oficiales, además del[c] francés y el portugués.

Aunque[d] tradicionalmente el país no se considera un país hispano, la realidad es que la mayoría de la población habla español, especialmente en la capital, Malabo. El español es también la lengua de varios escritores ecuatoguineanos, que se están abriendo camino[e] en el mundo literario hispanohablante.

La influencia de España en la Guinea Ecuatorial, así como[f] pasó en los países americanos de habla española, fue mucho más allá[g] de lo lingüístico. Es evidente en la religión (ya que[h] en el país existe una inmensa mayoría católica), en el sistema de apellidos que se usa (dos apellidos: primero el[i] del padre y luego el de la madre) y hasta[j] en la comida (entre otros platos, las empanadas).

[a]debido... *due to the deposits* [b]*from* [c]además... *in addition to* [d]*Although* [e]que... *who are making a name for themselves* [f]así... *as* [g]más... *beyond* [h]ya... *since* [i]*that* [j]*even*

Malabo, la capital de la Guinea Ecuatorial

LAS ISLAS FILIPINAS

Las islas Filipinas son un archipiélago formado por más de 7.000 islas en el océano Pacífico. Fueron territorio español por más de 300 años. El fin de la colonización española ocurrió en 1898, cuando España cedió[a] el control de las Filipinas a los Estados Unidos, como consecuencia de la guerra hispanoamericana. Aunque[b] el español era la primera lengua oficial del país, el uso del español disminuyó[c] con la ocupación estadounidense y se perdió en la gran mayoría de la población. Sin embargo, los nombres y apellidos de muchos filipinos, así como[d] los nombres de muchos lugares y cosas de uso cotidiano,[e] son españoles, testimonio de la gran influencia de la lengua española en el país.

La Universidad de Santo Tomás, fundada por los frailes dominicanos (*Dominican friars*) en 1611

La herencia de España ha quedado reflejada[f] también en la cocina filipina, en la que se combinan las influencias española, china y del sudeste asiático. En las islas Filipinas se preparan muchos platos que mantienen el nombre en español y que son adaptaciones de recetas españolas tradicionales, como la paella, el cocido,[g] el lechón asado[h] y la torta, similar a la españolísima tortilla de patatas, por solo nombrar algunos.

[a]*gave up* [b]*Although* [c]*declined* [d]así… *just like* [e]*everyday* [f]ha… *can still be seen reflected* [g]*stew* [h]lechón… *roasted suckling pig*

Cartel (*Poster*) para la *Hispanic Fiesta* de 2010

EL CANADÁ

Se estima que en el Canadá vive hoy entre medio millón y un millón de hispanohablantes, cuya mayoría[a] se concentra en la zona de las ciudades de Toronto y Hamilton. También hay comunidades hispanas importantes en el oeste del país, porque a finales[b] del siglo XIX hubo una ola[c] inmigratoria de argentinos y chilenos a la provincia de Alberta.

Los hispanocanadienses disfrutan de[d] acceso a numerosos medios de comunicación en español. Además,[e] hay en el Canadá varios festivales y eventos que conmemoran la presencia hispana en el país. Uno de los más importantes es la Hispanic Fiesta, que se celebra anualmente en el mes de agosto en Toronto. Allí se encuentra comida de todas partes del mundo hispanohablante, se puede escuchar música andina y mexicana, entre otras formas musicales, y ver demostraciones de tango, flamenco y otros bailes.

[a]cuya… *the majority of whom* [b]a… *at the end* [c]*wave* [d]disfrutan… *enjoy* [e]*Besides*

Comprensión

1. ¿En qué continentes y regiones del mundo se habla español como lengua oficial?
2. ¿En qué países tiene el español una presencia actual o histórica muy importante, aunque (*although*) no es la lengua oficial?
3. ¿Qué colonia española se independizó de España en el siglo XX?
4. En general, ¿en qué se nota la influencia española en la Guinea Ecuatorial, las Filipinas y el Canadá?

APPENDIX 1 Glossary of Grammatical Terms

ADJECTIVE A word that describes a noun or pronoun.	una casa **grande** *a* ***big*** *house* Ana es **inteligente.** *Ana is* ***smart.***
Demonstrative adjective An adjective that points out a particular noun.	**este** chico, **esos** libros, **aquellas** personas ***this*** *boy,* ***those*** *books,* ***those*** *people* (*over there*)
Interrogative adjective An adjective used to form questions.	¿**Qué** cuaderno? ***Which*** *notebook?* ¿**Cuáles** son los carteles que buscas? Which ones are the posters (that) you're looking for?
Possessive adjective (unstressed) An adjective that indicates possession or a special relationship.	**sus** coches ***their*** *cars* **mi** hermana ***my*** *sister*
Possessive adjective (stressed) An adjective that more emphatically describes possession.*	Es **una** amiga **mía.** *She's* ***my*** *friend. / She's a friend* ***of mine.*** Es **un** coche **suyo.** *It's* ***her*** *car. / It's a car* ***of hers.***
ADVERB A word that describes an adjective, a verb, or another adverb.	Roberto es **muy** alto. *Roberto is* ***very*** *tall.* María escribe **bien.** *María writes* ***well.*** Van **demasiado** rápidamente. *They are going* ***too*** *quickly.*
ARTICLE A determiner that sets off a noun. **Definite article** An article that indicates a specific noun.	**el** país ***the*** *country* **la** silla ***the*** *chair* **las** mujeres ***the*** *women*
Indefinite article An article that indicates an unspecified noun.	**un** chico ***a*** *boy* **una** ciudad ***a*** *city* **unas** zanahorias (***some***) *carrots*

*See Appendix 3 on page A-7 for a more detailed explanation.

CLAUSE A construction that contains a subject and a verb.	
Main (Independent) clause A clause that can stand on its own because it expresses a complete thought.	**Busco una muchacha.** ***I'm looking for a girl.*** Si yo fuera rica, **me compraría una casa.** *If I were rich,* ***I would buy a house.***
Subordinate (Dependent) clause A clause that cannot stand on its own because it does not express a complete thought.	Busco a la muchacha **que juega al tenis.** *I'm looking for the girl* ***who plays tennis.*** **Si yo fuera rica,** me compraría una casa. ***If I were rich,*** *I would buy a house.*
COMPARATIVE The form of adjectives and adverbs used to compare two nouns or actions.	Luis es **menos hablador que** Julián. *Luis is* ***less talkative than*** *Julián.* Luis corre **más rápido que** Julián. *Luis runs* ***faster than*** *Julián.*
CONJUGATION The different forms of a verb for a particular tense or mood. A present indicative conjugation:	(yo) **hablo** · (nosotros/as) **hablamos** (tú) **hablas** · (vosotros/as) **habláis** (usted) **habla** · (ustedes) **hablan** (él/ella) **habla** · (ellos/as) **hablan** *I speak* · *we speak* *you (fam. sing.) speak* · *you (fam. pl.) speak* *you (form. sing.) speak* · *you (pl.) speak* *he/she speaks* · *they speak*
CONJUNCTION An expression that connects words, phrases, or clauses.	Cristóbal **y** Diana *Cristóbal* ***and*** *Diana* Hace frío, **pero** hace buen tiempo. *It's cold,* ***but*** *it's nice out.*
DIRECT OBJECT The noun or pronoun that receives the action of a verb.	Veo **la caja.** *I see* ***the box.*** **La** veo. *I see* ***it.***
GENDER A grammatical category of words. In Spanish, there are two genders: masculine and feminine.	(see table below)
IMPERATIVE *See* Mood.	
IMPERFECT (*IMPERFECTO*) In Spanish, a verb tense that expresses a past action with no specific beginning or ending.	**Nadábamos** con frecuencia. *We* ***used to swim*** *often.*

	MASCULINE	FEMININE
ARTICLES AND NOUNS:	**el** disco compacto	**la** cinta
PRONOUNS:	**él**	**ella**
ADJECTIVES:	bonito, listo	bonita, lista
PAST PARTICIPLES:	El informe está **escrito.**	La composición está **escrita.**

IMPERSONAL CONSTRUCTION One that contains a third person singular verb but no specific subject in Spanish. The subject of English impersonal constructions is generally *it.*	**Es importante** que... ***It is important** that . . .* **Es necesario** que... ***It is necessary** that . . .*
INDICATIVE *See* Mood.	
INDIRECT OBJECT The noun or pronoun that indicates *for who(m)* or *to who(m)* an action is performed. In Spanish, the indirect object pronoun is usually included, even when the indirect object is explicitly stated as a noun.	Marcos **le** da el suéter **a Raquel**. / Marcos **le** da el suéter. *Marcos gives the sweater **to Raquel.** / Marcos gives **her** the sweater.*
INFINITIVE The form of a verb introduced in English by *to: to play, to sell, to come.* In Spanish dictionaries, the infinitive form of the verb appears as the main entry.	Luisa va a **comprar** un periódico. *Luisa is going **to buy** a newspaper.*
MOOD A set of categories for verbs indicating the attitude of the speaker toward what he or she is saying.	
Imperative mood A verb form expressing a command.	¡**Ten** cuidado! ***Be** careful!*
Indicative mood A verb form denoting actions or states considered facts.	**Voy** a la biblioteca. ***I'm going** to the library.*
Subjunctive mood A verb form, uncommon in English, used in Spanish primarily in subordinate clauses after expressions of desire, doubt, or emotion. Spanish constructions with the subjunctive have many possible English equivalents.	Quiero que **vayas** inmediatamente. *I want you **to go** immediately.*
NOUN A word that denotes a person, place, thing, or idea. Proper nouns are capitalized names.	**abogado, ciudad, periódico, libertad, Luisa** ***lawyer, city, newspaper, freedom, Luisa***
NUMBER	
Cardinal number A number that expresses an amount.	**una** silla, **tres** estudiantes ***one** chair, **three** students*
Ordinal number A number that indicates position in a series.	la **primera** silla, el **tercer** estudiante *the **first** chair, the **third** student*
PAST PARTICIPLE The form of a verb used in compound tenses (*see* Perfect Tenses). Used with forms of *to have* or *to be* in English and with **ser, estar,** or **haber** in Spanish.	**comido, terminado, perdido** ***eaten, finished, lost***

PERFECT TENSES Compound tenses that combine the auxiliary verb **haber** with a past participle.	
Present perfect indicative This form uses a present indicative form of **haber.** The use of the Spanish present perfect generally parallels that of the English present perfect.	No **he viajado** nunca a México. ***I've*** *never* ***traveled*** *to Mexico.*
Past perfect indicative This form uses **haber** in the imperfect tense to talk about something that had or had not been done before a given time in the past.	Antes de 2008, **no había estudiado** español. *Before 2008,* ***I hadn't studied*** *Spanish.*
Present perfect subjunctive This form uses the present subjunctive of **haber** to express a present perfect action when the subjunctive is required.	¡Ojalá que Marisa **haya llegado** a su destino! *I hope* (*that*) *Marisa* ***has arrived*** *at her destination!*

PERSON The form of a pronoun or verb that indicates the person involved in an action.

	SINGULAR	PLURAL
FIRST PERSON:	***I*** **/ yo**	***we*** **/ nosotros/as**
SECOND PERSON:	***you*** **/ tú, usted**	***you*** **/ vosotros/as, ustedes**
THIRD PERSON:	***he, she*** **/ él, ella**	***they*** **/ ellos, ellas**

PREPOSITION A word or phrase that specifies the relationship of one word (usually a noun or pronoun) to another. The relationship is usually spatial or temporal.	**a** la escuela ***to*** *school* **cerca de** la biblioteca ***near*** *the library* **con** él ***with*** *him* **antes de** la medianoche ***before*** *midnight*
PRESENT PARTICIPLE The verb form that ends in *-ing* in English. Used with forms of *to be* in English and with **estar** in Spanish to form the progressive.	**hablando, comiendo, pidiendo** ***speaking, eating, asking***
PRETERITE (*PRETÉRITO*) In Spanish, a verb tense that expresses a past action with a specific beginning and ending.	**Salí** para Roma el jueves. ***I left*** *for Rome on Thursday.*
PROGRESSIVE The verb that expresses continuing or developing action.	Julio **está durmiendo** ahora. *Julio* ***is sleeping*** *now.* Anita **estaba comiendo** cuando sonó el teléfono. *Anita* ***was eating*** *when the phone rang.*
PRONOUN A word that refers to a person (I, you) or that is used in place of one or more nouns.	¿Ana? **Ella** no está aquí. Ana? ***She*** isn´t here.
Demonstrative pronoun A pronoun that singles out a particular person, place, thing, or idea.	Aquí están dos libros. **Este** es interesante, pero **ese** es aburrido. *Here are two books.* ***This one*** *is interesting, but* ***that one*** *is boring.*
Interrogative pronoun A pronoun used to ask a question.	¿**Quién** es él? ¿**Qué** prefieres? ***Who*** *is he?* ***What*** *do you prefer?*

Object pronoun A pronoun that replaces a direct object noun or an indirect object noun. Both direct and indirect object pronouns can be used together in the same sentence.	Si **me** llamas más tarde, **te** doy el número de teléfono de David. *If you call **me** later, I'll give **you** David's phone number.* Veo a **Alejandro.** Lo veo. *I see **Alejandro.** I see **him.***
However, when the pronouns **le** or **les** appear before **lo, la, los,** or **las, le** or **les** changes to **se.**	Le doy **el libro a Juana.** *I give the book **to Juana.*** Se **lo** doy (a ella). *I give **it** to **her.***
Reflexive pronoun A pronoun that represents the same person as the subject of the verb.	**Me** miro en el espejo. *I look at **myself** in the mirror.*
Relative pronoun A pronoun that introduces a dependent clause and denotes a noun already mentioned.	El hombre con **quien** hablaba era mi vecino. *The man with **whom** I was talking was my neighbor.* Aquí está el bolígrafo **que** buscas. *Here is the pen (**that**) you're looking for.*
Subject pronoun A pronoun representing the person, place, thing, or idea performing the action of a verb.	**Lucas y Julia** juegan al tenis. ***Lucas and Julia** are playing tennis.* **Ellos** juegan al tenis. ***They** are playing tennis.*
SUBJECT The word(s) denoting the person, place, thing, or idea performing an action or existing in a state.	**Sara** trabaja aquí. ***Sara** works here.* ¡**Buenos Aires** es una ciudad magnífica! ***Buenos Aires** is a great city!* Mis **libros** y mi **computadora** están allí. *My **books** and my **computer** are over there.*
SUBJUNCTIVE *See* Mood.	
SUPERLATIVE The form of an adjective or adverb that expresses an extreme. In English, the superlative is marked by *most, least,* or *-est.*	Escogí **el vestido más caro.** *I chose **the most expensive** dress.* Ana es **la persona menos habladora** que conozco. *Ana is **the least talkative person** I know.*
TENSE The form of a verb indicating time: present, past, or future.	Raúl **era, es** y siempre **será** mi mejor amigo. *Raúl **was, is,** and always **will be** my best friend.*
VERB A word that reports an action or state.	Maribel **llegó.** *Maribel **arrived.*** La niña **estaba** cansada. *The child **was** tired.*
Auxiliary verb A verb in conjuction with a participle to convey distinctions of tense and mood. In Spanish, one auxiliary verb is **haber.**	**Han** viajado por todas partes del mundo. *They **have** traveled everywhere in the world.*
Reflexive verb A verb whose subject and object are the same.	Juan **se corta** la cara cuando **se afeita.** *Juan **cuts himself** when he **shaves (himself).***

APPENDIX 2 Using Adjectives as Nouns

Nominalization means using an adjective as a noun. In Spanish, adjectives can be nominalized in a number of ways, all of which involve dropping the noun that accompanies the adjective, then using the adjective in combination with an article or other word. One kind of adjective, the demonstrative, can simply be used alone. In most cases, these usages parallel those of English, although the English equivalent may be phrased differently from the Spanish.

Article + Adjective

Simply omit the noun from an *article* + *noun* + *adjective* phrase.

el **libro** azul ⟶ **el azul** (*the blue one*)
la **hermana** casada ⟶ **la casada** (*the married one*)
el **señor** mexicano ⟶ **el mexicano** (*the Mexican* [*one*])
los **pantalones** baratos ⟶ **los baratos** (*the inexpensive ones*)

You can also drop the first noun in an *article* + *noun* + **de** + *noun* phrase.

la **casa** de Julio ⟶ **la de Julio** (*Julio's*)
los **coches** del Sr. Martínez ⟶ **los del Sr. Martínez** (*Mr. Martínez's*)

In both cases, the construction is used to refer to a noun that has already been mentioned. The English equivalent uses *one* or *ones,* or a possessive without the noun.

— ¿Necesitas el **libro** grande?
— No. Necesito **el pequeño.**
"Do you need the big book?"
"No. I need the small one."

— ¿Usamos el **coche** de Ernesto?
— No. Usemos **el de Ana.**
"Shall we use Ernesto's car?"
"No. Let's use Ana's."

Note that in the preceding examples the noun is mentioned in the first part of the exchange (**libro, coche**) but not in the response or rejoinder.

Note also that a demonstrative can be used to nominalize an adjective: **este rojo** (*this red one*), **esos azules** (*those blue ones*).

Lo + Adjective

As seen in **Capítulo 11, lo** combines with the masculine singular form of an adjective to describe general qualities or characteristics. The English equivalent is expressed with words like *part* or *thing.*

lo mejor — *the best thing* (*part*), *what's best*
lo mismo — *the same thing*
lo cómico — *the funny thing* (*part*), *what's funny*

Article + Stressed Possessive Adjective

The stressed possessive adjectives—but not the unstressed possessives—can be used as possessive pronouns: **la maleta suya** ⟶ **la suya.** The article and the possessive form agree in gender and number with the noun to which they refer.

Este es mi **banco.** ¿Dónde está **el suyo**?
This is my bank. Where is yours?

Sus **bebidas** están preparadas; **las nuestras,** no.
Their drinks are ready; ours aren't.

No es la **maleta** de Juan; es **la mía.**
It isn't Juan's suitcase; it's mine.

Note that the definite article is frequently omitted after forms of **ser: ¿Esa maleta? Es suya.**

Demonstrative Pronouns

The demonstrative adjective can be used alone, without a noun. An accent mark can be added to the demonstrative pronoun (**éste, ése, aquél**) to distinguish it from the demonstrative adjectives if context does not make meaning clear.

Necesito este diccionario y **ese** (**ése**).
I need this dictionary and that one.

Estas señoras y **aquellas** (**aquéllas**) son las hermanas de Sara, ¿no?
These women and those (*over there*) *are Sara's sisters, aren't they?*

It is acceptable in modern Spanish, according to the **Real Academia Española,** to omit the accent on demonstrative pronouns when context makes the meaning clear and no ambiguity is possible.

APPENDIX 3 More About Stressed Possessives

When in English you would emphasize the possessive with your voice or with *of mine* (*of yours, of his*, and so on), you will use the *stressed possessives* (**las formas tónicas de los posesivos**) in Spanish. As the term implies, they are more emphatic than the *unstressed forms* (**las formas átonas de los posesivos**).

The stressed forms follow the noun, and the noun *must* be preceded by a definite or indefinite article or by a demonstrative adjective. The stressed forms agree with the noun modified in number and gender. In the following examples, boldface italic type in the English translations indicates voice stress.

Es **su** perro.	*It's her dog.*

But:

Es **un** perro **suyo.**	*It's **her** dog (i.e., not ours). It's a dog of hers.*
El perro **suyo** se llama King.	***Her** dog is named King.*
Ese perro **suyo** es bravo.	*That dog of **hers** is fierce.*

Es **su** maleta.	*It's **his** suitcase.*

But:

Es **una** maleta **suya.**	*It's **his** suitcase.*
La maleta **suya** está perdida.	***His** suitcase (i.e., not ours) is lost.*
Esa maleta **suya** está perdida.	*That suitcase of his is lost.*

The stressed possessives are often used as nouns. See **Appendix 2: Using Adjectives as Nouns.**

APPENDIX 4 Additional Perfect Forms (Indicative and Subjunctive)

As you know, some indicative verb tenses have corresponding perfect forms in the indicative and subjunctive moods. Here is the present tense system.

el presente:	yo hablo, como, pongo
el presente perfecto:	yo he hablado, comido, puesto
el presente perfecto de subjuntivo:	(que) yo haya hablado, comido, puesto

Other indicative forms that you have learned also have corresponding perfect indicative and subjunctive forms. Here are the most important ones, along with examples of their use. In each case, the tense or mood is formed with the appropriate form of **haber.**

El pluscuamperfecto de subjuntivo

yo:	hubiera hablado, comido, vivido, *and so on*
tú:	hubieras hablado, comido, vivido, *and so on*
usted/él/ella:	hubiera hablado, comido, vivido, *and so on*
nosotros:	hubiéramos hablado, comido, vivido, *and so on*
vosotros:	hubierais hablado, comido, vivido, *and so on*
ustedes/ellos/ellas:	hubieran hablado, comido, vivido, *and so on*

These forms correspond to **el pluscuamperfecto de indicativo** (*past perfect indicative*) (**Capítulo 15**). The **pluscuamperfecto de subjuntivo** is most frequently used in **si** clause sentences, along with the conditional perfect. See examples in the second column.

El futuro perfecto

yo:	habré hablado, comido, vivido, *and so on*
tú:	habrás hablado, comido, vivido, *and so on*
usted/él/ella:	habrá hablado, comido, vivido, *and so on*
nosotros:	habremos hablado, comido, vivido, *and so on*
vosotros:	habréis hablado, comido, vivido, *and so on*
ustedes/ellos/ellas:	habrán hablado, comido, vivido, *and so on*

These forms correspond to **el futuro** (**Capítulo 17**) and are most frequently used to tell what *will have already happened* at some point in the future. (In contrast, the future is used to tell what *will happen.*)

Mañana **hablaré** con Miguel.
I'll speak with Miguel tomorrow.

Para las tres, ya **habré hablado** con Miguel.
By 3:00, I'll already have spoken with Miguel.

El año que viene **visitaremos** a los nietos.
We'll visit our grandchildren next year.

Para las Navidades, ya **habremos visitado** a los nietos.
We'll already have visited our grandchildren by Christmas.

El condicional perfecto

yo:	habría hablado, comido, vivido, *and so on*
tú:	habrías hablado, comido, vivido, *and so on*
usted/él/ella:	habría hablado, comido, vivido, *and so on*
nosotros:	habríamos hablado, comido, vivido, *and so on*
vosotros:	habríais hablado, comido, vivido, *and so on*
ustedes/ellos/ellas:	habrían hablado, comido, vivido, *and so on*

These forms correspond to **el condicional** (**Capítulo 18**). They are frequently used to tell what *would have happened* at some point in the past. (In contrast, the conditional tells what one *would do.*)

Yo **hablaría** con Miguel.
I would speak with Miguel (if I were you, at some point in the future).

Yo **habría hablado** con Miguel.
I would have spoken with Miguel (if I had been you, at some point in the past).

***Si* Clause: Sentences About the Past**

You have learned (**Capítulo 18**) to use the past subjunctive and conditional to speculate about the present in **si** clause sentences: what *would happen* if a particular event *were* (or *were not*) to occur.

Si **tuviera** el tiempo, **aprendería** francés.
If I had the time, I would learn French.

The perfect forms of the past subjunctive and the conditional are used to speculate about the past: what *would have happened* if a particular event *had* (or *had not*) occurred.

En la escuela superior, si **hubiera tenido** el tiempo, **habría aprendido** francés.
In high school, if I had had the time, I would have learned French.

A. Regular Verbs: Simple Tenses

Infinitive Present Participle Past Participle	INDICATIVE					SUBJUNCTIVE		IMPERATIVE
	Present	Imperfect	Preterite	Future	Conditional	Present	Imperfect	
hablar hablando hablado	hablo hablas habla hablamos habláis hablan	hablaba hablabas hablaba hablábamos hablabais hablaban	hablé hablaste habló hablamos hablasteis hablaron	hablaré hablarás hablará hablaremos hablaréis hablarán	hablaría hablarías hablaría hablaríamos hablaríais hablarían	hable hables hable hablemos habléis hablen	hablara hablaras hablara habláramos hablarais hablaran	habla tú, no hables hable usted hablemos hablad, no habléis hablen
comer comiendo comido	como comes come comemos coméis comen	comía comías comía comíamos comíais comían	comí comiste comió comimos comisteis comieron	comeré comerás comerá comeremos comeréis comerán	comería comerías comería comeríamos comeríais comerían	coma comas coma comamos comáis coman	comiera comieras comiera comiéramos comierais comieran	come tú, no comas coma usted comamos comed, no comáis coman
vivir viviendo vivido	vivo vives vive vivimos vivís viven	vivía vivías vivía vivíamos vivíais vivían	viví viviste vivió vivimos vivisteis vivieron	viviré vivirás vivirá viviremos viviréis vivirán	viviría vivirías viviría viviríamos viviríais vivirían	viva vivas viva vivamos viváis vivan	viviera vivieras viviera viviéramos vivierais vivieran	vive tú, no vivas viva usted vivamos vivid, no viváis vivan

B. Regular Verbs: Perfect Tenses

INDICATIVE										SUBJUNCTIVE			
Present Perfect		Past Perfect		Preterite Perfect		Future Perfect		Conditional Perfect		Present Perfect		Past Perfect	
he has ha hemos habéis han	hablado comido vivido	había habías había habíamos habíais habían	hablado comido vivido	hube hubiste hubo hubimos hubisteis hubieron	hablado comido vivido	habré habrás habrá habremos habréis habrán	hablado comido vivido	habría habrías habría habríamos habríais habrían	hablado comido vivido	haya hayas haya hayamos hayáis hayan	hablado comido vivido	hubiera hubieras hubiera hubiéramos hubierais hubieran	hablado comido vivido

C. Irregular Verbs

Infinitive Present Participle Past Participle	INDICATIVE					SUBJUNCTIVE		IMPERATIVE
	Present	Imperfect	Preterite	Future	Conditional	Present	Imperfect	
andar andando andado	ando andas anda andamos andáis andan	andaba andabas andaba andábamos andabais andaban	anduve anduviste anduvo anduvimos anduvisteis anduvieron	andaré andarás andará andaremos andaréis andarán	andaría andarías andaría andaríamos andaríais andarían	ande andes ande andemos andéis anden	anduviera anduvieras anduviera anduviéramos anduvierais anduvieran	anda tú, no andes ande usted andemos andad, no andéis anden
caber cabiendo cabido	quepo cabes cabe cabemos cabéis caben	cabía cabías cabía cabíamos cabíais cabían	cupe cupiste cupo cupimos cupisteis cupieron	cabré cabrás cabrá cabremos cabréis cabrán	cabría cabrías cabría cabríamos cabríais cabrían	quepa quepas quepa quepamos quepáis quepan	cupiera cupieras cupiera cupiéramos cupierais cupieran	cabe tú, no quepas quepa usted quepamos cabed, no quepáis quepan

C. Irregular Verbs (*continued*)

Infinitive Present Participle Past Participle	INDICATIVE					SUBJUNCTIVE		IMPERATIVE
	Present	Imperfect	Preterite	Future	Conditional	Present	Imperfect	
caer cayendo caído	caigo caes cae caemos caéis caen	caía caías caía caíamos caíais caían	caí caíste cayó caímos caísteis cayeron	caeré caerás caerá caeremos caeréis caerán	caería caerías caería caeríamos caeríais caerían	caiga caigas caiga caigamos caigáis caigan	cayera cayeras cayera cayéramos cayerais cayeran	cae tú, no caigas caiga usted caigamos caed, no caigáis caigan
creer creyendo creído	creo crees cree creemos creéis creen	creía creías creía creíamos creías creían	creí creíste creyó creímos creísteis creyeron	creeré creerás creerá creeremos creeréis creerán	creería creerías creería creeíamos creeríais creerían	crea creas crea creamos creáis crean	creyera creyeras creyera creyéramos creyerais creyeran	cree tú, no creas crea usted creamos creed, no creáis crean
dar dando dado	doy das da damos dais dan	daba dabas daba dábamos dabais daban	di diste dio dimos disteis dieron	daré darás dará daremos daréis darán	daría darías daría daríamos daríais darían	dé des dé demos deis den	diera dieras diera diéramos dierais dieran	da tú, no des dé usted demos dad, no deis den
decir diciendo dicho	digo dices dice decimos decís dicen	decía decías decía decíamos decíais decían	dije dijiste dijo dijimos dijisteis dijeron	diré dirás dirá diremos diréis dirán	diría dirías diría diríamos diríais dirían	diga digas diga digamos digáis digan	dijera dijeras dijera dijéramos dijerais dijeran	di tú, no digas diga usted digamos decid, no digáis digan

C. Irregular Verbs (*continued*)

Infinitive Present Participle Past Participle	INDICATIVE					SUBJUNCTIVE		IMPERATIVE
	Present	Imperfect	Preterite	Future	Conditional	Present	Imperfect	
estar estando estado	estoy estás está estamos estáis están	estaba estabas estaba estábamos estabais estaban	estuve estuviste estuvo estuvimos estuvisteis estuvieron	estaré estarás estará estaremos estaréis estarán	estaría estarías estaría estaríamos estaríais estarían	esté estés esté estemos estéis estén	estuviera estuvieras estuviera estuviéramos estuvierais estuviera	está tú, no estés esté usted estemos estad, no estéis estén
haber habiendo habido	he has ha hemos habéis han	había habías había habíamos habíais habían	hube hubiste hubo hubimos hubisteis hubieron	habré habrás habrá habremos habréis habrán	habría habrías habría habríamos habríais habrían	haya hayas haya hayamos hayáis hayan	hubiera hubieras hubiera hubiéramos hubierais hubieran	
hacer haciendo hecho	hago haces hace hacemos hacéis hacen	hacía hacías hacía hacíamos hacíais hacían	hice hiciste hizo hicimos hicisteis hicieron	haré harás hará haremos haréis harán	haría harías haría haríamos haríais harían	haga hagas haga hagamos hagáis hagan	hiciera hicieras hiciera hiciéramos hicierais hicieran	haz tú, no hagas haga usted hagamos haced, no hagáis hagan
ir yendo ido	voy vas va vamos vais van	iba ibas iba íbamos ibais iban	fui fuiste fue fuimos fuisteis fueron	iré irás irá iremos iréis irán	iría irías iría iríamos iríais irían	vaya vayas vaya vayamos vayáis vayan	fuera fueras fuera fuéramos fuerais fueran	ve tú, no vayas vaya usted vayamos id, no vayáis vayan

C. Irregular Verbs (*continued*)

Infinitive Present Participle Past Participle	INDICATIVE					SUBJUNCTIVE		IMPERATIVE
	Present	Imperfect	Preterite	Future	Conditional	Present	Imperfect	
oír oyendo oído	oigo oyes oye oímos oís oyen	oía oías oía oíamos oíais oían	oí oíste oyó oímos oísteis oyeron	oiré oirás oirá oiremos oiréis oirán	oiría oirías oiría oiríamos oiríais oirían	oiga oigas oiga oigamos oigáis oigan	oyera oyeras oyera oyéramos oyerais oyeran	oye tú, no oigas oiga usted oigamos oíd, no oigáis oigan
poder pudiendo podido	puedo puedes puede podemos podéis pueden	podía podías podía podíamos podíais podían	pude pudiste pudo pudimos pudisteis pudieron	podré podrás podrá podremos podréis podrán	podría podrías podría podríamos podríais podrían	pueda puedas pueda podamos podáis puedan	pudiera pudieras pudiera pudiéramos pudierais pudieran	
poner poniendo puesto	pongo pones pone ponemos ponéis ponen	ponía ponías ponía poníamos poníais ponían	puse pusiste puso pusimos pusisteis pusieron	pondré pondrás pondrá pondremos pondréis pondrán	pondría pondrías pondría pondríamos pondríais pondrían	ponga pongas ponga pongamos pongáis pongan	pusiera pusieras pusiera pusiéramos pusierais pusieran	pon tú, no pongas ponga usted pongamos poned, no pongáis pongan
querer queriendo querido	quiero quieres quiere queremos queréis quieren	quería querías quería queríamos queríais querían	quise quisiste quiso quisimos quisisteis quisieron	querré querrás querrá querremos querréis querrán	querría querrías querría querríamos querríais querrían	quiera quieras quiera queramos queráis quieran	quisiera quisieras quisiera quisiéramos quisierais quisieran	quiere tú, no quieras quiera usted queramos quered, no queráis quieran

C. Irregular Verbs (*continued*)

Infinitive Present Participle Past Participle	INDICATIVE					SUBJUNCTIVE		IMPERATIVE
	Present	Imperfect	Preterite	Future	Conditional	Present	Imperfect	
saber sabiendo sabido	sé sabes sabe sabemos sabéis saben	sabía sabías sabía sabíamos sabíais sabían	supe supiste supo supimos supisteis supieron	sabré sabrás sabrá sabremos sabréis sabrán	sabría sabrías sabría sabríamos sabríais sabrían	sepa sepas sepa sepamos sepáis sepan	supiera supieras supiera supiéramos supierais supieran	sabe tú, no sepas sepa usted sepamos sabed, no sepáis sepan
salir saliendo salido	salgo sales sale salimos salís salen	salía salías salía salíamos salíais salían	salí saliste salió salimos salisteis salieron	saldré saldrás saldrá saldremos saldréis saldrán	saldría saldrías saldría saldríamos saldríais saldrían	salga salgas salga salgamos salgáis salgan	saliera salieras saliera saliéramos salierais salieran	sal tú, no salgas salga usted salgamos salid, no salgáis salgan
ser siendo sido	soy eres es somos sois son	era eras era éramos erais eran	fui fuiste fue fuimos fuisteis fueron	seré serás será seremos seréis serán	sería serías sería seríamos seríais serían	sea seas sea seamos seáis sean	fuera fueras fuera fuéramos fuerais fueran	sé tú, no seas sea usted seamos sed, no seáis sean
tener teniendo tenido	tengo tienes tiene tenemos tenéis tienen	tenía tenías tenía teníamos teníais tenían	tuve tuviste tuvo tuvimos tuvisteis tuvieron	tendré tendrás tendrá tendremos tendréis tendrán	tendría tendrías tendría tendríamos tendríais tendrían	tenga tengas tenga tengamos tengáis tengan	tuviera tuvieras tuviera tuviéramos tuvierais tuvieran	ten tú, no tengas tenga usted tengamos tened, no tengáis tengan

C. Irregular Verbs (*continued*)

Infinitive Present Participle Past Participle	INDICATIVE					SUBJUNCTIVE		IMPERATIVE
	Present	Imperfect	Preterite	Future	Conditional	Present	Imperfect	
traer trayendo traído	traigo traes trae traemos traéis traen	traía traías traía traíamos traíais traían	traje trajiste trajo trajimos trajisteis trajeron	traeré traerás traerá traeremos traeréis traerán	traería traerías traería traeríamos traeríais traerían	traiga traigas traiga traigamos traigáis traigan	trajera trajeras trajera trajéramos trajerais trajeran	trae tú, no traigas traiga usted traigamos traed, no traigáis traigan
venir viniendo venido	vengo vienes viene venimos venís vienen	venía venías venía veníamos veníais venían	vine viniste vino vinimos vinisteis vinieron	vendré vendrás vendrá vendremos vendréis vendrán	vendría vendrías vendría vendríamos vendríais vendrían	venga vengas venga vengamos vengáis vengan	viniera vinieras viniera viniéramos vinierais vinieran	ven tú, no vengas venga usted vengamos venid, no vengáis vengan
ver viendo visto	veo ves ve vemos veis ven	veía veías veía veíamos veíais veían	vi viste vio vimos visteis vieron	veré verás verá veremos veréis verán	vería verías vería veríamos veríais verían	vea veas vea veamos veáis vean	viera vieras viera viéramos vierais vieran	ve tú, no veas vea usted veamos ved, no veáis vean

D. Stem-Changing and Spelling Change Verbs

Infinitive Present Participle Past Participle	INDICATIVE					SUBJUNCTIVE		IMPERATIVE
	Present	Imperfect	Preterite	Future	Conditional	Present	Imperfect	
pensar (pienso) pensando pensado	pienso piensas piensa pensamos pensáis piensan	pensaba pensabas pensaba pensábamos pensabais pensaban	pensé pensaste pensó pensamos pensasteis pensaron	pensaré pensarás pensará pensaremos pensaréis pensarán	pensaría pensarías pensaría pensaríamos pensaríais pensarían	piense pienses piense pensemos penséis piensen	pensara pensaras pensara pensáramos pensarais pensaran	piensa tú, no pienses piense usted pensemos pensad, no penséis piensen
volver (vuelvo) volviendo vuelto	vuelvo vuelves vuelve volvemos volvéis vuelven	volvía volvías volvía volvíamos volvíais volvían	volví volviste volvió volvimos volvisteis volvieron	volveré volverás volverá volveremos volveréis volverán	volvería volverías volvería volveríamos volveríais volverían	vuelva vuelvas vuelva volvamos volváis vuelvan	volviera volvieras volviera volviéramos volvierais volvieran	vuelve tú, no vuelvas vuelva usted volvamos volved, no volváis vuelvan
dormir (duermo) (u) durmiendo dormido	duermo duermes duerme dormimos dormís duermen	dormía dormías dormía dormíamos dormíais dormían	dormí dormiste durmió dormimos dormisteis durmieron	dormiré dormirás dormirá dormiremos dormiréis dormirán	dormiría dormirías dormiría dormiríamos dormiríais dormirían	duerma duermas duerma durmamos durmáis duerman	durmiera durmieras durmiera durmiéramos durmierais durmieran	duerme tú, no duermas duerma usted durmamos dormid, no durmáis duerman
sentir (siento) (i) sintiendo sentido	siento sientes siente sentimos sentís sienten	sentía sentías sentía sentíamos sentíais sentían	sentí sentiste sintió sentimos sentisteis sintieron	sentiré sentirás sentirá sentiremos sentiréis sentirán	sentiría sentirías sentiría sentiríamos sentiríais sentirían	sienta sientas sienta sintamos sintáis sientan	sintiera sintieras sintiera sintiéramos sintierais sintieran	siente tú, no sientas sienta usted sintamos sentid, no sintáis sientan
pedir (pido) (i) pidiendo pedido	pido pides pide pedimos pedís piden	pedía pedías pedía pedíamos pedíais pedían	pedí pediste pidió pedimos pedisteis pidieron	pediré pedirás pedirá pediremos pediréis pedirán	pediría pedirías pediría pediríamos pediríais pedirían	pida pidas pida pidamos pidáis pidan	pidiera pidieras pidiera pidiéramos pidierais pidieran	pide tú, no pidas pida usted pidamos pedid, no pidáis pidan

D. Stem-Changing and Spelling Change Verbs (*continued*)

Infinitive Present Participle Past Participle	INDICATIVE					SUBJUNCTIVE		IMPERATIVE
	Present	Imperfect	Preterite	Future	Conditional	Present	Imperfect	
reír (río) (i) riendo reído	río ríes ríe reímos reís ríen	reía reías reía reíamos reíais reían	reí reíste rio reímos reísteis rieron	reiré reirás reirá reiremos reiréis reirán	reiría reirías reiría reiríamos reiríais reirían	ría rías ría riamos riáis rían	riera rieras riera riéramos rierais rieran	ríe tú, no rías ría usted riamos reíd, no riáis rían
seguir (sigo) (i) siguiendo seguido	sigo sigues sigue seguimos seguís siguen	seguía seguías seguía seguíamos seguíais seguían	seguí seguiste siguió seguimos seguisteis siguieron	seguiré seguirás seguirá seguiremos seguiréis seguirán	seguiría seguirías seguiría seguiríamos seguiríais seguirían	siga sigas siga sigamos sigáis sigan	siguiera siguieras siguiera siguiéramos siguierais siguieran	sigue tú, no sigas siga usted sigamos seguid, no sigáis sigan
construir (construyo) construyendo construido	construyo construyes construye construimos construís construyen	construía construías construía construíamos construíais construían	construí construiste construyó construimos construisteis construyeron	construiré construirás construirá construiremos construiréis construirán	construiría construirías construiría construiríamos construiríais construirían	construya construyas construya construyamos construyáis construyan	construyera construyeras construyera construyéramos construyerais construyeran	construye tú, no construyas construya usted construyamos construid, no construyáis construyan
conducir (conduzco) conduciendo conducido	conduzco conduces conduce conducimos conducís conducen	conducía conducías conducía conducíamos conducíais conducían	conduje condujiste condujo condujimos condujisteis condujeron	conduciré conducirás conducirá conduciremos conduciréis conducirán	conduciría conducirías conduciría conduciríamos conduciríais conducirían	conduzca conduzcas conduzca conduzcamos conduzcáis conduzcan	condujera condujeras condujera condujéramos condujerais condujeran	conduce tú, no conduzcas conduzca usted conduzcamos conducid, no conduzcáis conduzcan

VOCABULARIES

This **Spanish-English Vocabulary** contains all the words that appear in the text, with the following exceptions: (1) most close or identical cognates that do not appear in the chapter vocabulary lists; (2) most conjugated verb forms; (3) diminutives ending in **-ito/a;** (4) absolute superlatives in **-ísimo/a;** (5) most adverbs ending in **-mente,** and (6) words listed or glossed in the **Vocabulario del segmento** and **Fragmento del guion** features of the **Salu2** sections. Active vocabulary is indicated by the number of the chapter in which a word or given meaning is first listed (**1** = **Capítulo 1**); vocabulary that is glossed in the text is not considered to be active vocabulary and is not numbered. Only meanings that are used in the text are given. The **English-Spanish Vocabulary** is based on the chapter lists of active vocabulary.

The gender of nouns is indicated, except for masculine nouns ending in **-o** and feminine nouns ending in **-a.** Because **ch** and **ll** are no longer considered separate letters, words beginning with **ch** and **ll** are found as they would be found in English. The letter **ñ** follows the letter **n: añadir** follows **anuncio,** for example.

Irregular verbs found in the verb charts of Appendix 5 are set in red and underlined: **andar**. No changes are indicated for them in these vocabularies. Verbs with stem changes or spelling changes in the *present tense* show the **yo** form of the present tense in parentheses with the stem-vowel or spelling changes indicated in text in red and underlined: **sentarse (me siento); conocer (conozco); escoger (escojo); actuar (actúo).** Verbs with stem changes in the third person *preterite* and the *present participle* show the stem vowel in red and underlined (**i** or **u**) in parentheses after the present tense **yo** form: **preferir (prefiero) (i); morirse (me muero) (u).** Verbs with any other spelling changes in the first person *preterite* or *present subjunctive* show the change in parentheses: **buscar (qu); pagar (gu); empezar (empiezo) (c); averiguar (ü).**

The following abbreviations are used:

adj.	adjective	*interj.*	interjection
adv.	adverb	*inv.*	invariable form
Arg.	Argentina	*L.A.*	Latin America
C.A.	Central America	*m.*	masculine
Carib.	Caribbean	*Mex.*	Mexico
Col.	Colombia	*n.*	noun
conj.	conjunction	*obj.* (*of prep.*)	object (of a preposition)
def. art.	definite article	*pl.*	plural
d.o.	direct object	*poss.*	possessive
f.	feminine	*p.p.*	past participle
fam.	familiar	*prep.*	preposition
form.	formal	*pron.*	pronoun
gram.	grammatical term	*refl. pron.*	reflexive pronoun
Guat.	Guatemala	*s.*	singular
ind. art.	indefinite article	*sl.*	slang
inf.	infinitive	*Sp.*	Spain
i.o.	indirect object	*sub. pron.*	subject pronoun

Spanish-English Vocabulary

A

a to; at (*with time*) (1); **a base de** based on; **a causa de** because of; **a continuación** following; **a este respecto** in this regard; **a la derecha de** to the right of (6); **a la izquierda de** to the left of (6); **a la moda** in fashion, in a stylish way; **a la(s)...** at . . . (*time of day*) (1); **a menos que** unless (16); **a partir de** beyond (4); **a pesar de** in spite of; **a plazos** in installments (17); **¿a qué hora... ?** at what time . . . ? (1); **a solas** alone; **a tiempo** on time (8); **a través de** across, through; throughout; **¿a usted le gusta... ?** do you (*form. s.*) like . . . ? (1); **a veces** sometimes, at times (3); **a ver** let's see

abacería grocery store

abajo below; underneath

abandonar to abandon

abarcar (qu) to cover (*a topic*)

abarrotes *m. pl.* groceries

abecedario alphabet

abierto/a (*p.p. of* **abrir**) open (6)

abogado/a lawyer (17)

abogar (gu) to advocate

abolengo lineage

abolicionista *m., f.* abolitionist

aborto abortion

abrazar(se) (c) to embrace (11)

abrazo hug, embrace

abreviatura abbreviation

abrigo coat (4)

abril *m.* April (6)

abrir (*pp.* **abierto**) to open (3)

abrumador(a) overwhelming

absoluto/a absolute

abstenerse (*like* **tener**) to refrain

absurdo/a absurd; **es absurdo que** + *subjunctive* it's absurd that (13)

abuelo/a grandfather/grandmother (3); *m. pl.* grandparents (3)

abundante abundant

aburrido/a bored (6); **ser aburrido/a** to be boring (10)

aburrimiento boredom

aburrir (*like* **gustar**) to bore (13); **aburrirse** to get bored (10)

abuso abuse

abyecto/a wretched

acá here

acabar to finish (14); to run out of (14); **acabar de** + *inf.* to have just (*done something*) (7)

academia academy

académico/a *adj.* academic (14); **año académico** school year; **vida académica** academic life (14)

acampar to camp; **tienda de acampar** tent

acaso: por si acaso just in case (14)

acatar to obey

acceso access

accesorio accessory

accidente *m.* accident (14)

acción *f.* action; **Día** (*m.*) **de (Acción de) Gracias** Thanksgiving

aceite (*m.*) **(de oliva)** (olive) oil (7)

acelerado/a fast, accelerated (15); **ritmo acelerado de la vida** fast pace of life (15)

acelerar to accelerate; to speed up

acento accent; **acento diacrítico** diacritical mark; **acento ortográfico** accent mark

acentuación *f.* accent mark

acentuado/a accentuated

aceptable acceptable

aceptar to accept (14)

acera sidewalk (15)

acerca de *prep.* about, concerning, regarding

acercarse (qu) (a) to come near to

acertar (acierto) to guess correctly

ácido acid

acompañar to accompany

acondicionado/a: aire (*m.*) **acondicionado** air conditioning

aconsejable advisable

aconsejar to advise

acontecer to occur

acontecimiento event, happening (18)

acordarse (me acuerdo) (de) to remember (13)

acordeón *m.* accordion

acoso harassment, bullying

acostarse (me acuesto) to go to bed (5)

acostumbrarse (a) to become accustomed (to); to get used (to)

acribillar to bombard

acrílico/a acrylic

actitud *f.* attitude

actividad *f.* activity

activo/a active

acto act

actor *m.* actor (13)

actriz *f.* (*pl.* **actrices**) actor (13)

actuación *f.* performance

actual *adj.* current, present-day (12)

actualidad: en la actualidad currently, right now (10)

actualizar (c) to update

actuar (actúo) to act (13)

acuario aquarium

Acuario Aquarius

acuático/a aquatic

acudir (a) to go (to)

acueducto aqueduct

acuerdo agreement; **(no) estar de acuerdo** to (dis)agree (3)

acumular to accumulate

adaptación *f.* adaptation

adaptarse (a) to adapt (to)

adecuado/a appropriate

adelante forward

adelgazar (c) to lose weight

además *adv.* moreover; **además de** *prep.* besides

adentro inside

adicción *f.* addiction

adicional additional (1)

adiós good-bye (1)

adivinar to guess (9)

adjetivo *gram.* adjective (3); **adjetivo de nacionalidad** adjective of nationality (3); **adjetivo posesivo** possessive adjective (3)

administración *f.* administration; **administración de empresas** business administration (2)

administrar to administer; to manage; to run

admiración *f.* admiration

admirar to admire

admitir to admit

adolescencia adolescence (16)

adolescente *m., f.* adolescent, teenager; **de adolescente** as an adolescent (10)

¿adónde? where (to)? (4)

adoptar to adopt

adoquinado/a cobblestoned

adorar to adore

adquirir to acquire

adquisitivo/a: poder (*m.*) **adquisitivo** purchasing power

aduana customs (*at a border*) (8); **pasar por la aduana** to go/pass through customs (8)

adulto/a adult

adverbio *gram.* adverb

adverso/a adverse

advertencia warning

adyacente adjacent

aéreo/a aerial

aeróbico/a: hacer ejercicios aeróbicos to do aerobics (11)

aerolínea airline

aeropuerto airport (8)

afán *m.* effort

afanoso/a laborious, hard

afectación *f.* affectation

afectar to affect

afectivo/a: estado afectivo emotional state (9)

afecto affection

afeitarse to shave (5)

afición *f.* hobby (10)

aficionado/a fan (10); **ser aficionado/a (a)** to be a fan (of) (10)
afiliación *f.* affiliation
afiliado/a (a) affiliated (with)
afín related
afinidad *f.* compatibility
afirmación *f.* statement
afirmar to affirm
afirmativo/a affirmative
afluente affluent
afortunado/a fortunate, lucky
africano/a *n., adj.* African
afroamerindo/a *n., adj.* Afro-Amerindian
afroantillano/a Afro-Antillian
afroperuano/a Afro-Peruvian
afuera *adv.* outdoors (6)
afueras *f. pl.* outskirts (12); suburbs (12)
agencia agency; **agencia de compra-venta (de coches)** used car dealership; **agencia de viajes** travel agency
agenda personal calendar
agente *m., f.* agent (8); **agente de viajes** travel agent
ágil agile
agitar to agitate
agnóstico/a agnostic
agobiado/a overwhelmed
agosto August (6)
agotar to empty; to drain
agradable agreeable, pleasant
agradar (*like* **gustar**) to please
agradecimiento *n.* thanks
agregar (gu) to add
agresivo/a aggressive
agrícola *adj. m., f.* agricultural
agricultor(a) farmer (15)
agricultura farming, agriculture (15)
agrio/a bitter
agroturismo agritourism
agroturista *m., f.* agritourist
agroturístico/a *adj.* of rural tourism
agrupar to group
agua *f.* (*but* **el agua**) **(mineral)** (mineral) water (7)
aguacate *m.* avocado (7)
aguar (ü) to dilute; water down
agudo/a sharp
águila *f.* (*but* **el águila**) eagle
agujero hole
ahí there
ahijado/a godson/goddaughter
ahora now (2); **ahora mismo** right now (6)
ahorrar to save (*money*) (17)
ahorro savings
ahorros: cuenta de ahorros savings account
aimara *n.* Aymara
airado/a angry; annoyed
aire *m.* air (15); **aire acondicionado** air conditioning; **al aire libre** outdoors (10)
ajedrez *m.* chess; **jugar (juego) (gu) al ajedrez** to play chess (10)
ajo garlic
al (*contraction of* **a** + **el**) to the (4); **al** + *inf.* while (*doing something*); **al aire** (*m.*) **libre** outdoors (10); **al alcance** within reach; **al instante** right away; **al lado de** alongside of (6); **al menos** at least; **al principio de** at the beginning of (17)
alameda tree-lined avenue
alberca swimming pool (*Mex.*)
álbum *m.* album
alcance: al alcance within reach
alcanzar (c) to reach; to achieve
alce *m.* elk; moose
alcoba bedroom (5)
alcohol *m.* alcohol
alcohólico/a alcoholic; **bebida alcohólica** alcoholic beverage
alegrarse (de) to be glad, happy (about) (12)
alegre happy (6)
alemán *m.* German (*language*) (2)
alemán, alemana *n., adj.* German (3)
Alemania Germany
alergia allergy
alérgico/a allergic
alerta: ojo alerta eagle eye
alfabeto alphabet
alfombra rug (5)
algo something, anything (7)
algodón *m.* cotton (4); **de algodón** *adj.* (made of) cotton (4)
alguien someone, anyone (7)
algún (alguna/os/as) some, any (7); **alguna vez** once; ever (15)
alimentación *f.* diet
alimenticio/a of eating
alimento food
aliviar to alleviate
allá (way) over there (4)
allí there (4)
alma *m.* soul
almacén *m.* department store (4)
almacenamiento: **espacio de almacenamiento** storage space (12)
almacenar to store (12); to save (12)
almohada pillow
almorzar (almuerzo) (c) to have lunch (5)
almuerzo lunch (7)
¿aló? hello? (*telephone greeting*)
alojarse to lodge
alpinismo mountain climbing; **practicar (qu) el alpinismo** to mountain climb
alquilar *v.* to rent (12)
alquiler *n. m.* rent (12)
alrededor (de) around
alternar to take turns
alternativa *n.* alternative
alternativo/a *adj.* alternative
altiplanicie *f.* high plateau
altiplano high plateau
altitud *f.* height; altitude
alto/a tall (3); **de alta costura** high fashion; **de alto riesgo** high risk
altura altitude
alucinante incredible
alumno/a student
aluvial alluvial
amabilidad *f.* kindness
amable kind (3); nice (3)
amanecer *m.* dawn
amar to love (16)
amarillo/a yellow (4)
amasijo dough; mixture
Amazonas *m. s.* Amazon (River)
amazónico/a *adj.* Amazonian; **Selva Amazónica** Amazon Jungle
ambiental environmental
ambiente *m.* atmosphere; environment; **medio ambiente** environment (15)
ambigüedad *f.* ambiguity
ámbito area
ambos/as both
ambulante *adj.* traveling
América: América Latina Latin America; **Estados** (*m. pl.*) **Unidos de América** United States of America
americano/a American; **fútbol** (*m.*) **americano** football
amerindo/a *n., adj.* Amerindian
amigo/a friend (2)
amistad *f.* friendship (16)
amistoso/a friendly (16)
amo/a (*but* **el ama**) **de casa** housekeeper (17)
amoníaco ammonia
amor *m.* love (16)
amoroso/a loving
ampliar (amplío) to widen
amplio/a wide; large; spacious
amueblado/a furnished
amueblar to furnish
amuleto charm; amulet
amurallado/a walled
analfabetismo *n.* illiteracy
analfabeto/a illiterate
análisis *m. inv.* analysis
analista *m., f.* analyst; **analista de sistemas** systems analyst (17)
analizar (c) to analyze
ananá *m.* pineapple
anaranjado/a orange (4)
ancho/a wide
anciano/a *n.* old person; *adj.* old; ancient; **residencia de ancianos** nursing home (12)

Andalucía Andalusia
andaluz(a) *n., adj.* Andalusian
andante: caballero andante knight-errant
andar to walk; **andar en bicicleta** to ride a bicycle; **cinta de andar** treadmill
andino/a Andean
android *m.* android (12)
anécdota anecdote
anémico/a anemic
anfibio amphibian
anfitrión, anfitriona host (*of an event*) (9)
ángel *m.* angel
angelino/a *adj.* from Los Angeles; *n.* person from Los Angeles
angloparlante *adj.* English-speaking
anglosajón, anglosajona Anglo Saxon
angosto/a narrow
ángulo angle
angustia anguish
anillo ring
ánima *f.* (*but* **el ánima**) soul
animado/a lively; animated; **dibujos** (*m. pl.*) **animados** cartoons
animal *m.* animal (15); **animal de peluche** stuffed animal; **animal doméstico** pet
animar(se) to cheer up; **animarse a** to get up the courage to (*do something*)
ánimo: estado de ánimo state of mind
aniversario anniversary
anoche *adv.* last night (11)
anónimo/a anonymous
ansiedad *f.* anxiety (14)
ansioso/a anxious
antártico/a *adj.* Antarctic
Antártida Antarctica
ante *prep.* before; in front of
anteayer *adv.* the day before yesterday (5)
antecedente *m. gram.* antecedent
anteojos *m. pl.* glasses (11)
antepenúltimo/a third from the end
anterior previous, preceding
antes *adv.* before; **antes de** *prep.* before (5); **antes de Cristo (a.C.)** before Christ (B.C.); **antes (de) que** *conj.* before (16)
antibiótico antibiotic (11)
anticipar to anticipate
anticipo advance
anticuado/a antiquated
antídoto antidote
antiguo/a old; ancient; former
antillano/a *adj.* of/from the Antilles
Antillas (*f. pl.*) **Mayores** Greater Antilles
antipático/a unpleasant, unlikeable (*people*) (3)
antojo appetizer
antónimo antonym
antropología anthropology
antropólogo/a anthropologist
anual annual
anualmente annually
anunciar to announce (8)
anuncio announcement; advertisement
añadir to add
año year (6); **año académico** school year; **año bisiesto** leap year; **el año entrante** next year; **Año Nuevo** New Year; **año pasado** last year; **el año que viene** next year; **cumplir años** to have a birthday (9); **fin** (*m.*) **de año** end of the year (9); **tener... años** to be . . . years old (3)
apagar (gu) to turn off (*a machine*) (12)
apagón *m.* blackout
aparato appliance (10); **aparato doméstico** home appliance (10)
aparcamiento parking place; parking lot
aparcar (qu) to park
aparecer (aparezco) to appear
apariencia appearance
apartamento apartment (2); **edificio de apartamentos** apartment building (12)
aparte also
apellido surname
apenas barely
aperitivo appetizer
apetecer (apetezco) (*like* **gustar**) to appeal to
apetito appetite
apio celery
aplicación *f.* application
aplicar (qu) to apply
aportar to contribute
apóstol *m., f.* apostle
apoyar to support
apoyo support; help
app *f.* app(lication) (12)
apreciar to appreciate
aprender to learn (3); **aprender a** + *inf.* to learn how to (*do something*) (3)
aprendizaje *m.* learning
apropiado/a appropriate
aproximadamente approximately
aproximado/a approximate
aptitud *f.* aptitude
apuntar to write down; **apuntarse** to enroll; to add one's name to the list
apuntes *m. pl.* notes (*academic*) (14)
aquel, aquella *adj.* that ([way] over there) (4); *pron.* that one ([way] over there)
aquello (*neuter pron.*) that ([way] over there) (4)
aquellos/as *adj.* those ([way] over there) (4) *pron.* those ones ([way] over there)
aquí here (2)
árabe *m.* Arabic (*language*); *n., adj. m., f.* Arab
Arabia Saudita Saudi Arabia
arábico/a *adj.* Arabic
arado *n.* plow
araña spider
árbol *m.* tree (9); **árbol genealógico** family tree
arcángel *m.* archangel
archipiélago archipelago
archivo (computer) file (12)
arco arch
ardilla squirrel
área *f.* (*but* **el área**) area, region
arena sand
arepa *patty made of cornmeal and flour and stuffed with different foods*
aretes *m. pl.* earrings (4)
argentino/a *n., adj.* Argentine
argumento argument; plot
árido/a arid, dry
aristocrático/a aristocratic
arma *f.* (*but* **el arma**) weapon
armado/a: fuerzas armadas (*f. pl.*) armed forces
armar un bochinche to throw a (loud) party
armario armoire, free-standing closet (5)
armonía harmony
arpa *f.* (*but* **el arpa**) harp
arqueológico/a archaeological
arquitecto/a architect (13)
arquitectónico/a architectural
arquitectura architecture (13)
arraigado/a deeply rooted
arrancar (qu) to start up (*a car*) (15)
arreglar to fix, repair (15)
arrepentido/a sorry; repentant
arriba (de) *prep.* above
arroba @ (12)
arrodillarse to kneel
arrogancia arrogance
arrogante arrogant
arroz *m.* (*pl.* **arroces**) rice (7)
arruinar to ruin
arte *m.* art (2); **artes** *f. pl.* the arts (13); **bellas artes** fine arts; **obra de arte** work of art (13)
arteria artery
arterial: presión (*f.*) **arterial** blood pressure
artesanía arts and crafts (13)
artesano/a artisan
Ártico *adj.* Arctic
artículo article; **artículo (in)definido** *gram.* (in)definite article
artista *m., f.* artist (13)
artístico/a artistic (13); **expresión** (*f.*) **artística** artistic expression (13)
arvejas *f. pl.* green peas (7)

asado/a roast(ed) (7); grilled (7); **lechón** (*m.*) **asado** roast suckling pig; **pollo asado** roast chicken (7)

asaltar to rob

asamblea assembly

ascendencia ancestry, descent

ascensor *m.* elevator (12)

asco: ¡qué asco! yuck!

asegurar to assure; **asegurarse (de que)** to make certain (that)

asentamiento settlement

asentarse (me asiento) to settle

asesinar to assassinate (18)

asesinato assassination (18); murder

asesino *m., f.* murderer

así thus; so; **así como** as well as; **así que** therefore, consequently, so

asiático/a *adj.* Asian

asiento seat (8)

asignar to assign

asimismo additionally

asistencia sanitaria health care

asistente (*m., f.*) **de vuelo** flight attendant (8)

asistir (a) to attend, go to (*a class, function*) (3)

asma *m.* asthma

asociación *f.* association

asociado/a associated; **estado libre asociado** commonwealth

asociar to associate

aspecto aspect

aspiradora vacuum cleaner (10); **pasar la aspiradora** to vacuum (10)

aspirante *m., f.* job candidate; applicant (17)

aspirar to vacuum

aspirina aspirin

astronauta *m., f.* astronaut (17)

asumir to assume

asunto matter

asustar to scare

atacar (qu) to attack

ataque (*m.*) **(terrorista)** (terrorist) attack (18)

atar to tie

Atenas Athens

atención *f.* attention; **poner atención** to pay attention

atender (atiendo) to look after

atenerse (*like* **tener**) to deal with

ateo/a atheist

ático attic

Atlántico Atlantic

atleta *m., f.* athlete

atmosférico/a atmospheric

átomo atom

atracción *f.* attraction

atractivo/a attractive

atraer (*like* **traer**) (*like* **gustar**) to draw, to attract (13)

atrás *adv.* back, backward; behind; **de atrás** backwards

atrasado/a (*with* **estar**) late (8)

atravesar (atravieso) to go through

atributo attribute

atún *m.* tuna (7)

audaz (*pl.* **audaces**) bold, daring

audiencia audience

auditivo/a aural

aula *f.* (*but* **el aula**) classroom

aumentar to increase

aumento raise

aun *adv.* even

aún *adv.* still, yet

aunque although

auriculares *m. pl.* headphones

auscultar to listen (*with a stethoscope*)

ausencia absence

ausente absent

austeridad *f.* austerity

australiano/a *n., adj.* Australian

auténtico/a authentic

autobiográfico/a autobiographical

autobús *m.* bus (8); **estación** (*f.*) **de autobuses** bus station (8); **ir en autobús** to go/travel by bus (8); **parada del autobús** bus stop (12)

autóctono/a indigenous

autoestima self-esteem

automático/a automatic; **cajero automático** automatic teller machine (ATM) (17)

auto(móvil) *m.* auto(mobile)

automovilístico/a *adj.* automobile (15)

automutilación *f.* self-mutilation

autonomía autonomy; region

autónomo/a autonomous

autopista freeway, interstate (15)

autoprueba self-test

autor(a) author (13)

autoridad *f.* authority

autorizado/a authorized

autorretrato self-portrait

autostop: hacer autostop to hitchhike

autosuficiencia self-sufficiency

autosuficiente self-sufficient

auxiliar to help; to assist

avance *m.* preview

avanzado/a advanced

ave *f.* (*but* **el ave**) bird

avenida avenue (12)

aventura adventure

aventurero/a adventurous

aventurismo adventure tourism

aventurista *m., f.* adventure tourist

avergonzado/a embarrassed (9)

averiguar (ü) to find out

avión *m.* airplane (8); **ir en avión** to go/travel by plane (8); **volar (vuelo) en avión** to fly (8); to go by plane (8)

avisar to warn

aviso warning

¡ay! *interj.* ah!; ouch!

ayer yesterday (5); **ayer fue (miércoles...)** yesterday was (Wednesday . . .) (5)

ayuda help (7)

ayudante *m., f.* assistant

ayudar to help (7); **ayudar a** + *inf.* to help to (*do something*) (7)

ayuntamiento local government

azteca *n., adj. m., f.* Aztec

azúcar *m.* sugar (7)

azul blue (4)

azulejo tile

B

baba saliva; **se le cae la baba por** he/she is drooling over

bacán: ¡qué bacán! fantastic!

bahía bay

bailable danceable

bailaor(a) flamenco dancer

bailar to dance (2)

bailarín, bailarina dancer (13)

baile *m.* dance (13)

bajada ebb; dip

bajar to lower; to download (12); **bajarse (de)** to get down (from) (8); to get off (of) (*a vehicle*) (8)

bajareque *n.* mud wall

bajo *prep.* under (14); **estar bajo muchas presiones** to be under a lot of pressure (14)

bajo/a short (*in height*) (3); low

balcón *m.* balcony

ballena whale (15)

ballet *m.* ballet (13)

baloncesto basketball

banana banana (7)

banano banana tree

bancario/a: tarjeta bancaria debit card (17)

banco bank (17)

banda band

bandeja tray

bandera flag

bandoneón *m.* large concertina

bañarse to take a bath, bathe (5)

bañera bathtub (5)

baño bathroom (5); **traje** (*m.*) **de baño** swimsuit (4)

bar *m.* bar; **ir a un bar** to go to a bar (10)

barato/a inexpensive (4)

barba beard

barbacoa barbecue (7)

barcelonés, barcelonesa of Barcelona (*Sp.*)

barco boat, ship (8); **ir en barco** to go/travel by boat, ship (8)

barra bar

barrer (el piso) to sweep (the floor) (10)

barriga belly

barrio neighborhood (12)

barro mud
basarse en to base one's ideas/ opinions on
base *f.* base; **a base de** based on; **base de datos** data base; **con base en** based on
básico/a basic
basquetbol *m.* basketball (10)
bastante rather, sufficiently; enough (16)
bastar to be enough
basura trash (10); **sacar (qu) la basura** to take out the trash (10)
bata robe
batalla battle
batería battery (15)
bautizo baptism
bebé *m., f.* baby
beber to drink (3)
bebida drink (5); **bebida alcohólica** alcoholic beverage
beca scholarship
béisbol *m.* baseball (10)
beisbolista *m., f.* baseball player
Bélgica Belgium
belleza beauty
bello/a beautiful (15); **bellas artes** (*f. pl.*) fine arts
bendecir (*like* **decir**) to bless; **que Dios te bendiga** God bless you
bendito/a blessed
beneficio benefit
besar to kiss; **besarse** to kiss each other (11)
beso kiss
bestia beast
Biblia Bible
biblioteca library (2)
bibliotecario/a librarian (2)
bicentenario bicentennial
bicho insect
bici *f.* bike
bicicleta bicycle; **andar en bicicleta** to ride a bicycle; **pasear en bicicleta** to ride a bicycle (10)
bien *adv.* well (1); **caerle bien a alguien** to make a good impression on someone; **empleo bien pagado** well-paid job/position (17); **está bien** it's fine, OK (6); **estar bien** to be well; to be comfortable (*temperature*) (6); **llevarse bien (con)** to get along well (with) (16); **muy bien** fine, very well (1); **pasarlo bien** to have a good time (9); **portarse bien** to behave (9); **salir bien** to come/turn out well (5); to do well (5)
bienes raíces *m. pl.* real estate
bienestar *m.* well-being (11)
bienvenida *n.* welcome
bienvenido/a *adj.* welcome
bife *m.* beef
bilingüe bilingual
billete *m.* bill (*money*) (17); ticket (*Sp.*) (8); **billete de ida** one-way ticket (8); **billete de ida y vuelta** round- trip ticket (8); **billete electrónico** e-ticket (8)
binacional binational
biodiversidad *f.* biodiversity
biografía biography
biología biology
bioluminiscencia bioluminescence
bioquímica biochemistry
bisabuelo/a great-grandfather/ great-grandmother
bisiesto/a: año bisiesto leap year
bisonte *m.* bison
bistec *m.* steak (7)
blanco/a white (4); **pizarrón** (*m.*) **blanco** whiteboard (2); **vino blanco** white wine (7)
blando/a soft
blog *m.* blog (12)
bloqueador (*m.*) **solar** sunscreen (8)
bloqueo de llamadas call blocker
bluejeans *m. pl.* jeans
blusa blouse (4)
boca mouth (11)
bocadillo sandwich (*Sp.*)
bochinche: armar un bochinche to throw a (loud) party
bocina horn (*car*) (15)
boda wedding (*ceremony*) (16)
bodega grocery store (*Carib.*)
bogotano/a *adj.* from Bogotá, Colombia
bola ball
bolero love song
boleto ticket (*L.A.*) (8); **boleto de ida** one-way ticket (8); **boleto de ida y vuelta** round-trip ticket; **boleto electrónico** e-ticket (8)
bolígrafo pen (2)
bolívar *m. Venezuelan currency unit*
boliviano/a *n., adj.* Bolivian
bolso purse (4)
bomba bomb (18)
bombardeo bombing
bombero/a firefighter
bombilla light bulb
bombo legüero *Argentine drum*
bonanza boom (*economic*)
bongó bongo
bonito/a (*people and things*) pretty (3)
boricua *n., adj.* Puerto Rican
Borinquen *indigenous name of Puerto Rico*
borinqueño/a *adj.* Puerto Rican
borrador *m.* draft (of a document)
borrasca storm
bosque *m.* forest (15); **bosque tropical lluvioso** tropical rain forest
bostezo yawn
botanas *f. pl.* (*Mex.*) appetizers (9)
botanía botany
botánico/a botanical
botar to throw out
botas *f. pl.* boots (4)
botella bottle
botón *m.* button
boxeador(a) boxer
brasileño/a *n., adj.* Brazilian
brazo arm (11)
brecha gap; **brecha digital** digital gap; **brecha salarial** wage gap
Bretaña: Gran Bretaña Great Britain
breve brief
británico/a British
bronce *m.* bronze
broncear to tan
bruja witch
brujo wizard; warlock
bruto/a: producto nacional bruto gross national product
bucear to scuba dive; to snorkel
budismo Buddhism
budista *n., adj. m., f.* Buddhist
buen, bueno/a good (3); **¡buen provecho!** bon appetit! (7); enjoy your meal! **buenas noches** good night (1); **buenas tardes** good afternoon (1); **buenos días** good morning (1); **lo bueno** the good news/thing (11); **hace (muy) buen tiempo** it's (very) good weather (6); it's (very) nice out (6); **muy buenas** good afternoon/ evening (1); **tener buena suerte** to have good luck (14); to be lucky (14)
buey *sl.* dude (*Mex.*)
bufanda scarf
burlarse de to make fun of
buscador *m.* search engine (12)
buscar (qu) to look for (2); **buscar en internet** to look up on the internet (12)
búsqueda search
buzón (*m.*) **de voz** voice mailbox (12)

C

caballero knight; **caballero andante** knight-errant
caballo horse (10); **montar a caballo** to ride a horse (10)
caber to fit (*into an area*)
cabeza head (11); **dolor** (*m.*) **de cabeza** headache
cabina cabin (*on a ship*) (8)
cacerola casserole dish
cacique, cacica chief
cada *inv.* each, every (5); **cada vez más** increasingly; **cada vez mayor** greater and greater
cadena chain
caer (caigo) to fall (14); to drop (14); **caer en** to fall on (*day of the week*); **caerle bien/mal a alguien** to make a

good/bad impression on someone; **caerse** to fall down (14); **se le cae la baba por** he/she is drooling over
café *m.* coffee (2); *adj.* **(de) color café** brown (4)
cafeína caffeine
cafetal *m.* coffee plantation
cafetera coffeemaker (10)
cafetería cafeteria (2)
cafetero/a coffee plantation worker
caída fall (*from a height*)
caimán *m.* alligator
caja box
cajero/a (check-out) cashier; (bank) teller (17); **cajero automático** automatic teller machine (ATM) (17)
cajón *m.* drawer
calabaza pumpkin; squash
calabozo prison cell
calamar *m.* squid
calcetines *m. pl.* socks (4)
calculadora calculator (2)
calcular to calculate
cálculo calculus
calefacción *f.* heat (12)
calendario calendar (14)
calentador(a) *adj.* warming
calentar (caliento) to warm
calidad *f.* quality (*excellence*)
cálido/a hot
caliente hot (*in temperature, not taste*) (7)
calificación *f.* grade
caligrafía calligraphy; handwriting
callar to silence
calle *f.* street (12)
callejero/a *adj.* (of the) street
calma calm
calmarse to calm down
calor *m.* heat; **hace (mucho) calor** to be very hot (6); **tener (mucho) calor** to be (very) warm, hot (6)
caloría calorie
caluroso/a hot
cama bed (5); **guardar cama** to stay in bed (11); **hacer la cama** to make the bed (10); **tender (tiendo) la cama** to make the bed
cámara camera (12)
camarero/a waiter/waitress (7)
camarones *m. pl.* shrimp (7)
cambiar (de) to change (12)
cambio change; **cambio climático** climate change
camélidos *m. pl.* (*zool.*) Camelidae
camello camel
caminadora treadmill (11)
caminar to walk (10)
caminata: dar una caminata to hike (10); to go for a hike (10)
caminero/a: furia caminera road rage
camino road; path
camión *m.* truck
camioneta (mini) van (8)
camisa shirt (4)
camiseta T-shirt (4)
campamento campsite
campaña campaign; **tienda de campaña** tent (8)
campeón, campeona champion
campeonato championship
campesino/a farmer; field laborer (15)
camping *m.* campground (8); **hacer *camping*** to go camping (8)
campo field (15); countryside (15)
Canadá Canada; **Día** (*m.*) **del Canadá** Canada Day
canadiense *n., adj. m., f.* Canadian
canal *m.* channel (12)
canario canary
cancelar to cancel
cáncer *m.* cancer
cancha field; court (*tennis*)
canción *f.* song (7)
candidato/a candidate (18); **postularse como candidato/a** to run as a candidate (18)
cansado/a tired (6)
cansancio fatigue
cantante *m., f.* singer (13)
cantaor(a) flamenco singer
cantar to sing (2)
cantautor(a) singer, songwriter
cantidad *f.* quantity
cantinero/a bartender
caña sugar cane
cañonazo cannon shot
capa layer (15); **capa de ozono** ozone layer (15)
capacidad *f.* capacity
capaz (*pl.* **capaces)** able
Caperucita Roja Little Red Ridinghood
capilla chapel
capital *f.* capital city (6)
capitán, capitana captain
capítulo chapter
Capricornio Capricorn
cara face
caracola large shell
característica *n.* characteristic
característico/a *adj.* characteristic
caracterizar (c) to characterize
caramañola *torpedo-shaped meat pie of Colombia and Panama*
cárcel *f.* jail
cardinal: punto cardinal cardinal point (6)
cardiólogo/a cardiologist
carga load; **carga de trabajo** workload
cargo (political) office (18); **postularse para un cargo** to run for a position (18)
Caribe *m.* Caribbean; **mar** (*m.*) **Caribe** Caribbean Sea
caribeño/a Caribbean
caricatura caricature
cariño affection (16)
cariñoso/a affectionate (6)
carnaval *m.* carnival
carne *f.* meat (7)
carnet (*m.*) **de identificación / de identidad** identification card
carnicería butcher's shop
caro/a expensive (4)
carpa tent
carpeta (computer) folder (12)
carpintero/a carpenter
carrera career
carreta cart, wagon
carretera highway (15)
carretilla wheelbarrow
carril *m.* lane
carro (descapotable) (convertible) car (15)
carta letter (3); card; **jugar (juego) (gu) a las cartas** to play cards (10)
cartera wallet (4); handbag (4)
cartón *m.* cardboard
casa house, home (3); **amo/a** (*but* **el ama) de casa** housekeeper (17); **casa natal** house where someone was born; **en casa** at home (2); **limpiar la casa** to clean (the) house (10); **regresar a casa** to go home (2)
casabe *m.* *tortilla-type bread made of cassava*
casado/a married; **estar casado/a (con)** to be married (to) (16); **recién casado/a (con)** newlywed (to) (16); **ser casado/a** to be a married person (16)
casarse (con) to marry (16)
cascanueces *m. inv.* nutcracker
caserío hamlet; farmhouse
casero/a home-made
casi *adv.* almost (3); **casi nunca** almost never (3)
caso case; **en caso de** *prep.* in case (16); **en caso de que** *conj.* in case (16)
castaño/a brown (chestnut-colored)
castañuelas *f. pl.* castinets
castellano Spanish (language)
castigar (gu) to punish
cata (de vino) (wine) tasting
catalán *m.* Catalan (*language*); **catalán, catalana** *adj.* Catalan
catálogo catalogue
Cataluña Catalonia
catarata waterfall
catarro cold (*health condition*)
catedral *f.* cathedral
categoría category
catolicismo Catholicism
católico/a *n., adj.* Catholic
catorce fourteen (1)

caucásico/a Caucasian
causa cause; **a causa de** because of
causar to cause
cava cellar
cazador(a) hunter
cazar (c) to hunt
CD *m.* CD (compact disc) (12)
CD-ROM *m.* CD-ROM (12)
cebolla onion (7)
cédula identity card
celda cell (*prison*)
celebración *f.* celebration
celebrar to celebrate (6)
celíaco/a gluten intolerant
celos *m. pl.* jealousy
celta *n., adj. m., f.* Celtic
celular: (teléfono) celular *m.* cell phone (2)
cementerio cemetery
cena dinner, supper (7)
cenar to have (eat) dinner, supper (7)
Cenicienta Cinderella
centavo cent
centígrado Celsius
céntrico/a central
centro center (*political*) (18); downtown (4); **centro comercial** shopping mall (4)
Centroamérica Central America
centroamericano/a Central American
cepillarse los dientes to brush one's teeth (5)
cerámica pottery (13); ceramics (13)
cerca *adv.* near, nearby, close; **cerca de** *prep.* close to (6)
cercano/a *adj.* close, near
cerdo pork (7); **chuleta de cerdo** pork chop (7)
cereal *m.* cereal (7)
cerebro brain (11)
ceremonia ceremony
cero zero (1)
cerrado/a closed (6)
cerrar (cierro) to close (5); **cerrarse** to close; to finish
cerro hill
certeza certainty
cerveza beer (7)
césped *m.* lawn; grass
cesto basket
ceviche *m. raw fish dish*
champán *m.* champagne (9)
champiñones *m. pl.* mushrooms (7)
chanclas *f. pl.* flip-flops (4)
chaqueta jacket (4)
charango *stringed instrument*
charco puddle
charlar to chat
chatear to chat
chateo *n.* chat (12)
chauchas *f. pl.* green beans (*Arg.*)
cheque *m.* check (17); **con cheque** by check (17)
chequeo check-up (11)
chévere *sl.* cool
chibcha *n., adj. m., f. indigenous people of the Colombian Andes*
chicha *natural fruit soft drink*
chicle *m.* gum
chico/a guy/girl (4)
chileno/a *n., adj.* Chilean
chino Chinese (*language*)
chino/a *n., adj.* Chinese
chisme *m.* gossip
chiste *m.* joke (8)
chocante shocking
chocar (qu) con/contra to run into, bump against (14)
chocolate *m.* chocolate
chofer *m., f.* driver
choque *m.* collision, crash (18)
chuleta (de cerdo) (pork) chop (7)
churro *strip of fried dough*
cibernauta *adj.* of the internet; *n. / m., f.* internet user
ciclismo bicycling (10)
ciclo cycle
ciclón *m.* cyclone
ciego/a blind
cien one hundred (3)
ciencia science (2); **ciencia ficción** science fiction; **ciencias** *(f. pl.)* **naturales** natural sciences (2); **ciencias** *(f. pl.)* **políticas** political science (2); **ciencias** *(f. pl.)* **sociales** social sciences (2)
científico/a scientist
ciento one hundred (4); **ciento dos** one hundred two (4); **ciento noventa y nueve** one hundred ninety-nine (4); **ciento uno/a** one hundred one (4)
cierto/a true (13); **es cierto que** + *indicative* it's certain that (13)
ciervo deer; stag
cifra figure, number
cigarrillo cigarette
cinco five (1)
cincuenta fifty (3)
cine *m. s.* movies (5); movie theater (5)
cineasta *m., f.* filmmaker
cinematográfico/a *adj.* movie, film
cinta: cinta de andar/correr treadmill; **cinta rodante** treadmill
cinturón *m.* belt (4)
circulación *f.* traffic (15)
circular to circulate
círculo circle
circunstancia circumstance
cirugía surgery
cisne *m.* swan
cita appointment (11); date (11)
citar to cite, quote
ciudad *f.* city (3)
ciudadano/a citizen (18)
cívico/a civic (18); **responsabilidad** (*f.*) **cívica** civic duty (18)
civil civil; **guerra civil** civil war
civilización *f.* civilization
clarificar (qu) to clarify
claro/a clear
clase *f.* class (*of students*) (2); class, course (*academic*) (2); **compañero/a (de clase)** classmate (2); **dar clases** to teach class; **salón** (*m.*) **de clase** classroom (2)
clásico/a classic(al) (13)
clasificar (qu) to classify
cláusula *gram.* clause
clave *f. n., adj.* key
clic: hacer clic to click (12)
clicar (qu) to click
cliente/a client (2)
clima *m.* climate (6)
climático/a *adj.* climate; **cambio climático** climate change
clínica clinic
cliquear to click
clóset *m.* closet
coalición *f.* coalition
cobrar to cash (*a check*) (17); to charge (*someone for an item or service*) (17)
cobre *m.* copper
coche *m.* car (3); **agencia de compra-venta (de coches)** used car dealership; **coche descapotable** convertible (car) (15)
cochera garage; carport
cochinilla cochineal
cocido/a *adj.* cooked
cocina kitchen (5); cuisine (7)
cocinar to cook (7)
cocinero/a cook (17); chef (17)
coco coconut
cocodrilo crocodile
cóctel *m.* cocktail party
codiciado/a coveted
código code
codirector(a) codirector
codo elbow
coexistir to coexist
coger (cojo) to take (*things*) (*Sp.*)
cognado *gram.* cognate
coherente coherent
cohesión *f.* cohesion
coincidencia coincidence
coincidir to coincide
cola line (*of people*) (8); **hacer cola** to stand in line (8)
colaborar to collaborate
colección *f.* collection
coleccionar to collect
colectivo bus
colega *m., f.* colleague
colegio school
colérico/a furious
colesterol *m.* cholesterol

coletilla tag (*as in* tag question)

colgar (cuelgo) (gu) to post (*on the internet*)

colina hill

collar *m.* necklace

colmado small grocery store (*Carib.*)

colocar (qu) to place

colombiano/a Colombian

colonia colony

colonización *f.* colonization

colonizador(a) colonist

colonizar (c) to colonize

colono/a settler

coloquial colloquial

color *m.* color (4); *adj.* **(de) color café** brown (4)

colorado/a red-colored

colorido/a colorful

columna column

comadre *f.* godmother

combatir to combat

combinación *f.* combination

combinar to combine

comedia comedy (13)

comediante *m., f.* comedian

comedor *m.* dining room (5)

comentar to talk about

comentario comment

comentarista *m., f.* commentator

comenzar (comienzo) (c) to begin; **comenzar a** + *inf.* to begin to (*do something*)

comer to eat (3); **comerse** to eat up

comercial: centro comercial shopping mall (4)

comercio business, commerce; **libre comercio** free trade

comestibles *m. pl.* groceries, foodstuff (7)

cometa *m.* comet

cometer to commit

cómico/a funny; **tira cómica** comic strip

comida food (7); meal (7); **comida rápida** fast food

comienzo beginning

comillas *f. pl.* quotation marks

como like; as; **así como** as well as; **tan... como** as . . . as (6); **tanto como** as much as (6); **tanto/a(os/as)... como** as much/many . . . as (6)

¿cómo? how?; what? (1); **¿cómo es usted?** what are you (*form. s.*) like? (1); **¿cómo está?** how are you (*form. s.*)? (1); **¿cómo estás?** how are you (*fam. s.*)? (1); **¿cómo se llama usted?** what is your (*form. s.*) name? (1); **¿cómo se llega a... ?** how do you get to . . . ? (15); **¿cómo te llamas?** what is your (*fam. s.*) name? (1)

cómoda bureau (5); dresser (5)

comodidad *f.* convenience

cómodo/a comfortable (4)

compacto/a: disco compacto (**CD** *m.*) compact disc (CD) (12)

compadre *m.* godfather

compañero/a companion; friend; **compañero/a (de clase)** classmate (2); **compañero/a de cuarto** roommate (2)

compañía company

comparación *f.* comparison (6)

comparar to compare

comparativo/a comparative

compartir to share

compasión *f.* compassion

compensar to make up for

competencia competition

competente competent

competición *f.* competition

competitivo/a competitive

complejo/a complex

complemento (in)directo *gram.* (in)direct object

completar to complete

completo/a complete; **trabajo de tiempo completo** full-time job (14)

complicación *f.* complication

componer (*like* **poner**) to compose (13)

comportamiento behavior

composición *f.* composition

compositor(a) composer (13)

compostero composter

compra-venta: agencia de compra-venta (de coches) used car dealership

comprador(a) buyer

comprar to buy (2); **comprar por internet** to buy online (4)

compras: de compras shopping (4); **ir de compras** to go shopping (4)

comprender to understand (3)

comprensible understandable

comprensión *f.* understanding; comprehension

comprensivo/a *adj.* understanding

comprobar (compruebo) to prove

comprometido/a committed

compuesto/a composed; compound (*gram.*)

compulsivo/a compulsive

computación *f.* computer science (2)

computadora (portátil) (laptop) computer (2)

común common

comunicación *f.* communication; *pl.* communication (*subject*) (2); **medio de comunicación** medium of communication (18)

comunicarse (qu) (con) to communicate (with) (18)

comunicativo/a communicative

comunidad *f.* community

comunión *f.* communion

comunitario/a *adj.* community

con with (2); **chocar (qu) con** to run into, bump against (14); **comunicarse (qu) (con)** to communicate (with) (18); **con base en** based on; **con cheque** by check (17); **con cuidado** carefully; **con frecuencia** frequently (2); **con permiso** excuse me (1); **¿con qué frecuencia... ?** how often . . . ? (3); **con respecto a** regarding; **con tal de** *prep.* provided (16); **con tal (de) que** *conj.* provided (that), as long as (16); **darse con** to run into; **pegarse (gu) con** to run/bump into (14)

conceder to concede

concentración *f.* concentration

concentrar to concentrate

concepto concept (18)

conciencia conscience

concienciación *f. n.* conscious-raising

concierto concert (10); **ir a un concierto** to go to a concert (10)

conciso/a concise

conclusión *f.* conclusion

concordancia *gram.* agreement

concreto: en concreto in particular

concursante *m., f.* contestant

concurso contest

condenado/a condemned

condición *f.* condition

condicional *gram.* conditional

cóndor *m.* condor

conducción *f.* driving

conducir (conduzco) to drive (15); **licencia de conducir** driver's license (15)

conductor(a) driver (15)

conectar to connect; **conectarse** to connect (12)

conector *m.* connector

conejo/a rabbit

conexión *f.* connection

conferencia lecture

confesional confessional

confianza confidence

confiar (confío) to trust

configurar to configure

confirmar to confirm

conflicto conflict

confluencia *n.* coming-together

confundido/a confused

congelado/a frozen (6); very cold (6)

congelador *m.* freezer (10)

congestión *f.* congestion

congresista *m., f.* member of congress

congreso congress; **representante** (*m., f.*) **al congreso** congressional representative (18)

conjugación *f. gram.* conjugation

conjugar (gu) *gram.* to conjugate

conjunción *f. gram.* conjunction (16);

conjunción de tiempo conjunction of time (17)
conjunto group
conllevar to involve
conmemorar to commemorate
conmigo with me (6)
Cono Sur Southern Cone
conocer (conozco) to know (*a person*) (7); be acquainted, familiar with (*a place*) (7); to meet (*a person*) (7); **conocerse** to meet (16)
conocimiento knowledge
conquista conquest
conquistador(a) conqueror
consciente conscious, aware
consecuencia consequence
consecutivo/a consecutive
conseguir (*like* **seguir**) to get (9); to obtain (9); **conseguir** + *inf.* to succeed in (*doing something*) (9)
consejero/a advisor (2)
consejo (piece of) advice (7)
conservación *f.* conservation
conservacionista conservationist
conservador(a) conservative
conservar to save; to conserve (15)
consideración *f.* consideration
considerar to consider
consigo with himself, herself, themselves
consiguiente: por consiguiente as a result
consistencia consistency
consistir (en) to consist (of)
constante constant
constar (de) to consist of
constatar to confirm
constipado/a: estar constipado/a to have a cold
constitución *f.* constitution
constituir (*like* **construir**) to constitute
construcción *f.* construction
construir (construyo) to build (15)
consuelo consolation
consulta consultation
consultar to consult
consultorio (medical) office (11); consultation
consumidor(a) consumer
consumir to consume
consumo consumption
contabilidad *f.* accounting
contable *m., f.* accountant (*Sp.*)
contacto contact; **lentes** (*m. pl.*) **de contacto** contact lenses (11); **mantenerse** (*like* **tener**) **en contacto** to stay in touch
contador(a) accountant (17)
contaminación *f.* pollution (6); **hay (mucha) contaminación** there's (lots of) pollution (6)
contaminado/a contaminated, polluted (15)
contaminar to pollute (15)
contar (cuento) to tell (8); to narrate (8)
contemplación *f.* contemplation
contemplar to contemplate
contemporáneo/a contemporary
contenedor *m.* container
contener (*like* **tener**) to contain
contenido contents
contento/a content, happy (6)
contestar to answer (7)
contexto context
contigo with you (*fam.*) (6)
continente *m.* continent
contingencia contingency
continuación: a continuación following
continuar (continúo) to continue (6)
contra against; **chocar (qu)/pegarse (gu) contra** to run into; to bump against (14); **darse contra** to run into
contrabajo double bass (*musical instrument*)
contradecir (*like* **decir**) to contradict
contraer (*like* **traer**) to contract
contrario contrary
contrarrestar to resist
contraseña password (12)
contrastar to contrast
contraste *m.* contrast
contrastivo/a contrasting
contribución *f.* contribution
contribuir (*like* **construir**) to contribute
control *m.* control (8); **control de seguridad** security (check) (8); **control remoto** remote control (12); **pasar por el control de seguridad** to go/pass through security (check) (8)
controlador(a) controller
controlar to control
convencer (convenzo) to convince
convención *f.* convention; system
conversación *f.* conversation
conversar to converse
convertir (convierto) (i) to convert
convivencia cohabitation; living together
convivir to live together
coordinar to coordinate
copa (wine) glass
Copa del Mundo World Cup (*soccer*); **Copa Mundial** World Cup (*soccer*)
copia copy; **hacer copia** to copy
copiar to copy (12)
copioso/a copious
coquí *m. small frog of Puerto Rico*
corazón *m.* heart (11)
corbata tie (4)
cordillera mountain range
coreano/a *n., adj.* Korean
cormorán cormorant (*aquatic bird*)
coro chorus
corona crown
corporación *f.* corporation
correcto/a correct
corregir (corrijo) (i) to correct (14); to grade (14)
correo mail; **correo electrónico** e-mail (12)
correr to run (10); **cinta de correr** treadmill
correspondencia correspondence
corresponder (a) to correspond (to)
correspondiente *m., f.* correspondent; *adj.* corresponding
corrido *Mexican folk song*
corriente: cuenta corriente checking account; **estar al corriente** to be up to date
cortar to cut
cortejo courting
cortés *m., f.* polite
cortesía courtesy; **expresión** (*f.*) **de cortesía** courteous expression (1)
cortijo country house
cortina curtain
corto *n.* short segment (*film*)
corto/a short (*in length*) (3); **pantalones** (*m. pl.*) **cortos** shorts (4)
cosa thing (5)
cosecha harvest; crop
cosechar to harvest
cosmético/a cosmetic
cosmopolita *m., f.* cosmopolitan
cosmovisión *f.* world view
costa coast
costar (cuesto) to cost; **¿cuánto cuesta(n)?** how much does it (do they) cost? (4)
costarricense *n., adj. m., f.* Costa Rican
costero/a coastal
costo cost
costoso/a expensive
costumbre *f.* custom
costura: de alta costura high fashion
cotidiano/a daily
country *m.* country music
creación *f.* creation
crear to create (13)
creatividad *f.* creativity
creativo/a creative
crecer (crezco) to grow (16)
crecimiento *n.* rise, growth
credencial *f.* identity card
crédito credit; **tarjeta de crédito** credit card (7)
creencia belief
creer (en) to think (3); to believe (in) (3); **no creer** to not think/believe (13)
creíble believable
crema cream
cremoso/a creamy
creyente *m., f.* believer

criado/a servant
criatura child
crimen *m.* (*pl.* **crímenes**) crime
criollo/a *n., adj.* creole
cristal *m.* glass
cristianismo Christianity
cristiano/a *n., adj.* Christian
Cristo Christ; **antes de Cristo (a.C.)** before Christ (B.C.); **después de Cristo (a.D.)** Anno Domini (A.D.)
crítica criticism
criticar (qu) to criticize
crítico/a critic
crónica chronicle
crónico/a chronic
cronológico/a chronological
croqueta croquette
crucero cruise (ship) (8)
crudo/a raw
cruz *f.* (*pl.* **cruces**) cross; **Día** (*m.*) **de la Cruz** Day of the Cross
cruzar (c) to cross; **cruzarse con** to cross paths with
cuaderno notebook (2)
cuadrado *n.* square
cuadrado/a *adj.* square
cuadro painting (*specific piece*) (13); **de cuadros** plaid (4)
cuajar to fit in
cual: el/la cual, lo cual, los/las cuales which
¿cuál(es)? what? (2); which? (2); **¿cuál es la fecha de hoy?** what's today's date? (6); **¿cuál es tu onda?** what's your style?
cualidad *f.* quality (*characteristic*)
cualquier *adj. inv.* any
cuando when
¿cuándo? when? (2)
cuanto: en cuanto as soon as (17); **en cuanto a** regarding
¿cuánto? how much? (2); **¿cuánto cuesta(n)?** how much does it (do they) cost? (4); **¿cuánto tiempo hace que... ?** how long ago (*did something happen*)? / for how long (*has something been happening*)?
¿cuántos/as? how many? (2)
cuáquero/a *n.* Quaker
cuarenta forty (3)
Cuaresma Lent
cuartel *m.* barracks
cuarto room (2); one-fourth; quarter (*of an hour*); **compañero/a de cuarto** roommate (2); **menos cuarto** a quarter to (*hour*) (1); **y cuarto** a quarter (fifteen minutes) after (*the hour*) (1)
cuarto/a *adj.* fourth (13)
cuate *sl. m., f.* buddy, pal
cuatro four (1)
cuatrocientos/as four hundred (4)
cubano/a *n., adj.* Cuban
cubanoamericano/a *n., adj.* Cuban American
cubierto/a (*p.p. of* **cubrir**) covered
cubiertos *m. pl.* cutlery
cubrir (*p.p.* **cubierto**) to cover (15)
cucaracha cockroach
cuchara spoon
cucharada spoonful
cuchillo knife
cuello neck
cuenta check, bill (7); **cargar (gu) a una cuenta** to charge to an account (17); **cuenta corriente** checking account
cuento story
cuerda string
cuero leather (4); **de cuero** leather (4)
cuerpo (humano) (human) body (11)
cuervo crow
cuestión *f.* question (*issue*); matter (17)
cuestionable questionable
cuestionario questionnaire
cuidado care; *interj.* careful!; **con cuidado** carefully; **tener cuidado** to be careful
cuidar a to care for; **cuidar de** to take care of (11); **cuidarse** to take care of oneself (11)
culebra snake
culinario/a culinary
culminar to culminate
culpa fault; **tener la culpa** to be at fault
cultivar to cultivate
cultivo cultivation
culto cult; **rendir (rindo) (i) culto** to worship
cultrún *m. ceremonial Mapuche drum*
cultura culture
cultural cultural; **tradición** (*f.*) **cultural** cultural tradition (13)
cumbia *Colombian folk dance now popular throughout Latin America*
cumbre *f.* summit
cumpleaños *m. inv.* birthday (6); **pastel** (*m.*) **de cumpleaños** birthday cake (9)
cumplir to fulfill; **cumplir años** to have a birthday (9)
cuñado/a brother-in-law, sister-in-law
cupo quota; capacity (*space*)
cupón *m.* coupon
cura cure
curación *f.* cure
curar to cure
curativo/a curing, curative
curioso/a curious
currículum *m.* résumé (17)
cursi in poor taste; trite
curso course; **programa** (*m.*) **del curso** course syllabus (14)
cuyo/a whose

D

dama lady
danza dance (13)
daño: hacerse daño to hurt oneself (14); **hacerse daño en** to hurt one's (*body part*) (14)
dar to give (8); **dar clases** to teach class; **dar un paseo** to take a walk (10); **dar una caminata** to hike; to go for a hike (10); **darle una fiesta (a alguien)** to give (someone) a party (9); to have a party (for someone) (9); **darse con/contra** to run into; **darse la mano** to shake hands (11)
darwinista *m., f.* Darwinian
datar de to date back to
datos *m. pl.* data; **base** (*f.*) **de datos** data base
de of (1); from (1); **de adolescente** *adj.* adolescent (10) **de algodón** *m.* (made of) cotton (4); **de alta costura** high fashion; **de alto riesgo** high risk; **de atrás** backwards; **de compras** shopping (4); **de cuadros** plaid (4); **de cuero** leather (4); **¿de dónde eres (tú)?** where are you (*fam. s.*) from? (1); **¿de dónde es (usted)?** where are you (*form. s.*) from? (1); **de estatura mediana** of medium height; **de exposición** expository; **de forma presencial** in person; **de la mañana** in the morning, A.M. (1); **de la noche** in the evening, P.M. (1); **de la tarde** in the afternon, P.M. (1); **de lana** wool (4); **de lunares** polka-dot (4); **de manera que** so that, in such a way that; **de modo que** in such a way that; **de nada** you're welcome (1); **de niño/a** as a child (10); **de oro** gold (4); **de plata** silver (4); **¿de quién?** whose? (3); **de rayas** striped (4); **de remate** hopeless(ly); **de repente** suddenly (11); **de seda** silk (4); **de todo** everything (4); **de todo tipo** of all kinds; **de vacaciones** on vacation (8); **¿de veras?** really?; **de viaje** on a trip, traveling (8); **es de...** it is made of . . . (4); **estar de vacaciones** to be on vacation (8)
debajo de below (6)
debate *m.* debate
debatir to debate
deber *n. m.* responsibility (18); obligation (18)
deber *v.* + *inf.* should, must, ought to (*do something*) (3)
debido/a a due to; because of

débito debit; **tarjeta de débito** debit card (17)
década decade
decadencia decadence
decente decent
decidir to decide
décimo/a tenth (13)
decimotercer(o/a) thirteenth
decir to say (8); to tell (8); **eso quiere decir...** that means . . . (11)
decisión *f.* decision
declaración *f.* statement
declarar to state
decoración *f.* decoration
decorar to decorate
decorativo/a decorative
dedicarse (qu) (a) to dedicate oneself (to)
dedo (de la mano) finger (11); **dedo del pie** toe (11)
deducir (*like* **conducir**) to deduce
defender (defiendo) to defend
defensa defense
defensor(a) defender
deficiencia deficiency
deficiente deficient
definición *f.* definition
definido: artículo definido *gram.* definite article
definir to define
degustar to taste
dejar to leave; to let, allow; to quit (17); **dejar de** + *inf.* to stop (*doing something*) (11)
del (*contraction of* **de** + **el**) of the; from the (3)
delante de in front of (6)
delegación *f.* delegation
delfín *m.* dolphin
delgado/a thin, slender (3)
deliberado/a deliberate
delicia delicacy
delicioso/a delicious
delito crime (15)
demanda demand
demás: los/las demás the rest, others (12)
demasiado *adv.* too (9)
demasiado/a *adj.* too much (9); too many (9)
democracia democracy
demócrata *m., f.* democrat
democrático/a democratic
demonio demon, devil
demora delay (8)
demostración *f.* demonstration
demostrar (demuestro) to demonstrate
demostrativo/a *gram.* demonstrative (4)
denominación *f.* denomination
densidad *f.* density (15)
dentista *m., f.* dentist (11)
dentro *adv.* inside; **dentro de** *prep.* inside; within; in (*time*)
departamento department
dependencia dependence
depender (de) to depend (on)
dependiente/a clerk (2)
deporte *m.* sport (10); **practicar (qu) un deporte** to play a sport
deportista *m., f.* athlete
deportivo/a *adj.* sporting, sports (10); sports-loving (10)
depositar to deposit (17)
depósito deposit
depresión *f.* depression
deprimido/a depressed
derecha *n.* right side; **a la derecha de** to the right of (6)
derecho right (18); **(todo) derecho** straight ahead (15)
derivación *f.* branch, offshoot
derivarse (de) to derive (from)
derramar to spill
desacuerdo disagreement
desafío challenge
desagradable disagreeable
desahogarse (gu) to let off steam; to vent
desamor *m.* lack of affection
desaparecer (desaparezco) to disappear
desarrollar to develop (15)
desarrollo development (15)
desastre *m.* disaster (14)
desastroso/a disastrous
desayunar to have (eat) breakfast (7)
desayuno breakfast (7)
descansar to rest (5)
descanso rest
descapotable: coche/carro descapotable convertible (car) (15)
descargar (gu) to download (12)
descendiente *m., f.* descendent
descentralizado/a decentralized
descifrar to decipher; to figure out
desconectar to unplug; to disconnect
desconocido/a unknown
descontento/a unhappy
descortés *m., f.* rude, impolite
describir (*p.p.* **descrito**) to describe
descripción *f.* description
descriptivo/a descriptive
descrito/a (*p.p. of* **describir**) described
descubierto/a (*p.p. of* **descubrir**) discovered
descubrimiento discovery
descubrir (*p.p.* **descubierto**) to discover (15)
desde *prep.* from; since
desear to want (2)
desempleo unemployment
deseo wish
desequilibrio imbalance
desértico/a *adj.* desert
desesperanza desperation
desfile *m.* parade
desgracia misfortune; disgrace
desgraciadamente unfortunately (11)
deshumanización *f.* dehumanization
desierto desert
designación *f.* designation
designar to appoint; to designate
desigualdad *f.* inequality (18)
desilusión *f.* disillusion
desinflado/a: llanta desinflada flat tire (15)
desocupado/a empty; available
desordenado/a messy (6)
desorganizado/a unorganized
despacio *adv.* slowly
despedida farewell
despedir (*like* **pedir**) to let (*someone*) go (17); to fire (*someone*) (*from a job*) (17); **despedirse (de)** to say good-bye (to) (9)
despejado/a clear (*sky*)
desperdiciar to waste
desperdicio waste
despertador *m.* alarm clock (14)
despertarse (me despierto) to wake up (5)
despierto/a (*p.p. of* **despertar**) awake
despistado/a absent-minded; forgetful
después *adv.* then, later next (5); **después de** *prep.* after (5); **después de Cristo (a.D.)** Anno Domini (A.D.); **después (de) que** *conj.* after (17)
destacar (qu) to emphasize; **destacarse** to stand out
destino destination (8); destiny
destrucción *f.* destruction
destruir (*like* **construir**) to destroy (15)
desventaja disadvantage
detalle *m.* detail (9)
detective *m., f.* detective
detenerse (*like* **tener**) to stop
determinación *f.* determination
determinado/a specific
determinante decisive
determinar to determine
detestar to detest
detrás de behind (6)
deuda debt
devolver (*like* **volver**) to return (*something to someone*) (14)
devoto/a devout
día *m.* day (2); **buenos días** good morning (1); **Día de (Acción de) Gracias** Thanksgiving; **Día de la Cruz** Day of the Cross; **Día de la Madre** Mother's Day; **Día de los Difuntos** Day of the Dead; **Día de Muertos** Day of the Dead; **Día de San Patricio** St. Patrick's Day; **Día de San Valentín** St. Valentine's Day; **Día del Padre**

Father's Day; **día festivo** holiday (9); **Día Internacional de la No Violencia Contra la Mujer** International Day for the Elimination of Violence against Women; **días de la semana** days of the week (5); **estar al día** to be up to date (18); **¿qué día es hoy?** what day is today? (5); **todos los días** every day (2)
diabetes (*f. inv.*) **(juvenil)** (childhood) diabetes
diabético/a diabetic
diablo devil
diacrítico/a: acento diacrítico diacritical mark
diagnosticar (qu) to diagnose
diágrafo group of letters that represent a single sound
dialecto dialect
diálogo dialogue
diamante *m.* diamond
diariamente daily
diario/a daily (5)
dibujante *m., f.* drawer (*person*) (13)
dibujar to draw (13)
dibujo drawing (13); **dibujos** (*m. pl.*) **animados** cartoons
diccionario dictionary (2)
dicho saying
diciembre *m.* December (6)
dictador(a) dictator (18)
dictadura dictatorship (18)
dictar to dictate
diecinueve nineteen (1)
dieciocho eighteen (1)
dieciséis sixteen (1)
diecisiete seventeen (1)
diente *m.* tooth (5); **cepillarse los dientes** to brush one's teeth (5)
dieta dieta (7); **estar a dieta** to be on a diet (7)
dietético/a *adj.* diet
diez ten (1)
diferencia difference; **a diferencia de** unlike
diferenciado/a differentiated
diferente different
difícil hard, difficult (6)
dificultad *f.* difficulty
difundir to disseminate
difunto/a dead; **Día** (*m.*) **de los Difuntos** Day of the Dead
digestión *f.* digestion
digital digital; **brecha digital** digital gap
dígito digit
dignidad *f.* dignity
dilema *m.* dilemma
diligente diligent
dimensión *f.* dimension
diminutivo *gram. n.* diminutive
Dinamarca Denmark
dinero money (2)
dinoflagelado *type of marine plankton*
dios *m. s.* god; **Dios** God; **por Dios** for heaven's sake (14)
diosa goddess
diptongo *gram.* diphthong
dirección *f.* address (7)
directo/a direct; **complemento directo** *gram.* direct object
director(a) director (13); conductor (13)
directorio directory
dirigir (dirijo) to direct (13)
discapacidad *f.* disability
discapacitado/a disabled
disco disc; **disco duro** hard drive (12)
discoteca discotheque; **ir a una discoteca** to go to a disco (10)
discriminación *f.* discrimination (18)
disculpa apology (14); excuse; **pedir (pido) (i) disculpas** to apologize (14)
disculpar to excuse, pardon; **disculpa, discúlpame** pardon me (*fam. s.*) (14); I'm sorry (*fam. s.*) (14); **disculpe, discúlpeme** pardon me (*form. s.*) (14); I'm sorry (*form. s.*) (14)
discurso speech
discusión *f.* argument; discussion
discutir con (alguien) por/sobre (algo) to argue with (someone) about (something) (9)
diseñador(a) (gráfico/a) (graphic) designer (17)
diseñar to design (13)
diseño design
disfraz *m.* (*pl.* **disfraces**) costume, disguise
disfrutar (de) to enjoy
disminuir (*like* **construir**) to diminish
disparar to shoot
dispensario clinic
disponible available
disposición *f.* disposition
dispositivo device
dispuesto/a ready; prepared (*to do something*)
disputarse to compete for
distancia distance
distante distant
distinción *f.* distinction
distintivo/a distinctive
distinto/a different
distracción *f.* distraction
distraer (*like* **traer**) to distract
distraído/a absentminded (14); distracted (14); **estar/ir distraído/a** to be distracted (14)
distribuido/a distributed
distrito district
disuadir to dissuade
diversidad *f.* diversity
diversión *f.* fun activity (10)
diverso/a diverse
divertido/a fun (10); **ser divertido/a** to be fun (10)
divertirse (me divierto) (i) to have a good time; to enjoy oneself (5)
dividirse to be divided
divorciado/a (de) divorced (from) (16)
divorciarse (de) to get divorced (from) (16)
divorcio divorce (16)
divulgar (gu) to divulge
doblar to turn (15)
doble *m.* double
doce twelve (1)
dócil docile
doctor(a) doctor
doctorado doctorate
documento document
dólar *m.* dollar (4)
doler (duele) (*like* **gustar**) to hurt (11); to ache (11)
dolor (*m.*) **(de)** pain, ache (in) (11); **dolor de cabeza** headache; **tener dolor de** to have a pain/ache in (11)
doméstico/a domestic, related to the home (10); domesticated, tame (15); **animal** (*m.*) **doméstico** pet; **aparato doméstico** home appliance (10); **quehacer** (*m.*) **doméstico** household chore (10); **tarea doméstica** household chore
domicilio home
dominación *f.* domination
dominar to control; to dominate
domingo Sunday (5)
dominicano/a *n., adj.* Dominican
dominio control
don *m. title of respect used with a man's first name*
donar to donate
donde where
¿dónde? where? (1); **¿de dónde eres (tú)?** where are you (*fam. s.*) from? (1); **¿de dónde es usted?** where are you (*form. s.*) from? (1)
doña *title of respect used with a woman's first name*
dormir (duermo) (u) to sleep (5); **dormir la siesta** to take a nap (5); **dormirse** to fall asleep (5)
dormitorio bedroom
dos two (1); **dos veces** twice (11)
doscientos/as two hundred (4)
drama *m.* drama (13)
dramático/a dramatic
dramatizar(c) to dramatize
dramaturgo/a playwright (13)
droga drug
dromedario dromedary
ducha *n.* shower
ducharse to take a shower (5)
duda *n.* doubt

dudar to doubt (12)
dudoso/a doubtful
duelo duel
dueño/a landlord, landlady (12); owner (7)
dulce *adj.* sweet
dulces *m. pl.* sweets (7); candy (7)
duración *f.* duration
duradero/a lasting
durante during (5)
durar to last (18)
duro/a hard; **disco duro** hard drive (12)
DVD *m.* DVD (12)

E

e and (*before words beginning with the sound* **i-**) (3)
echar to throw out
ecocasa ecological house
ecología ecology
ecológico/a ecological
ecologista *m., f.* ecologist
economía economy; *s.* economics (2)
económico/a economical
economista *m., f.* economist
ecoturismo ecotourism
ecoturista *m., f.* ecotourist
ecoturístico/a *adj.* ecotourist
ecuador *m.* equator
ecuatoguineano/a of or from Equatorial Guinea
ecuatoriano/a Ecuadoran
edad *f.* age
edificio building (2); **edificio de apartamentos** apartment building (12)
editar to edit
editorial *f.* publishing house
educación *f.* education
educador(a) educator
educarse (qu) to be educated
educativo/a educational
efectivo cash (17); **en efectivo** in cash (17)
efectivo/a effective
efecto effect
efectuar (efectúo) to carry out, execute
eficiencia efficiency
eficiente efficient
Egipto Egypt
egoísmo selfishness
egoísta *m., f.* selfish
ejecutivo/a *n., adj.* executive
ejemplar exemplary
ejemplificar (qu) to exemplify
ejemplo example (14); **por ejemplo** for example (14)
ejercer (ejerzo) to apply, exercise
ejercicio exercise (5); **hacer ejercicio** to exercise (5); **hacer ejercicios aeróbicos** to do aerobics (11)
ejército army (18)
el *def. art. m. s.* the; **el cual** which; **el lunes (martes...)** on Monday (Tuesday . . .) (5); **el primero de** the first of (*month*) (6); **el próximo (martes...)** next (Tuesday . . .) (5)
él *sub. pron.* he (2)
elaboración *f.* elaboration
elección *f.* choice; *pl.* election
electricidad *f.* electricity (12)
electricista *m., f.* electrician (17)
eléctrico/a electrical; **energía eléctrica** electrical energy (15)
electrónica electronic equipment
electrónico/a electronic; **billete** (*m.*) (*Sp.*) / **boleto** (*L.A.*) **electrónico** e-ticket (8); **equipo electrónico** electronic equipment (12)
elefante *m.* elephant (15)
elegante elegant
elegir (elijo) (i) to select; to elect
elemento element
elevado/a high
elevador *m.* elevator
elevarse to rise
eliminar to eliminate
ella *sub. pron.* she (2)
ello: por ello therefore
ellos/as *sub. pron.* they (2); *obj.* (*of prep.*) them (2)
e-mail *m.* e-mail (12)
embarazada pregnant
embargo: sin embargo nevertheless (6)
embarque: puerta de embarque boarding gate (8); **tarjeta de embarque** boarding pass (8)
emberá Embera person
emblema *m.* emblem
emblemático/a emblematic
embotellamiento traffic jam
embutido sausage
emergencia emergency
emigración *f.* emigration
emigrante *m., f.* emigrant
emigrar to emigrate
emisario/a emissary
emitir to emit
emoción *f.* emotion (9)
emocionado/a excited
emocional emotional
emocionante exciting
emocionarse to get excited
emoticono emoticon
empacar (qu) to pack
empanada *turnover pie or pastry*
emparedado sandwich
emparejar to match
empezar (empiezo) (c) to begin, start (5); **empezar a** + *inf.* to begin to (*do something*) (5)
empleado/a employee
empleador(a) employer
emplear to use; to employ
empleo job, position (17); **empleo bien/mal pagado** well-/poorly paid job/position (17); **empleo de tiempo completo/parcial** full-/part-time job/position (17)
empresa corporation (17); business (17); **administración** (*f.*) **de empresas** business administration (2)
empresario/a businessman/woman
en in (1); on (1); at (*a place*) (1); **en casa** at home (2); **en caso de** *prep.* in case (16); **en caso de que** *conj.* in case (16); **en cuanto** as soon as (17); **en efectivo** in cash (17); **en la actualidad** currently, right now (10); **en negrilla** boldface; **en onda** in style; **en punto** on the dot (*time*) (1); **en rebaja** on sale; **en resumen** in summary; **en seguida** immediately (5); **en vez de** instead of
enamorado/a (de) in love (with) (16)
enamorarse (de) to fall in love (with) (16)
enano/a dwarf
encantado/a pleased to meet you (1); enchanted
encantar (*like* **gustar**) to like very much (8); to love (8)
encanto charm
encapuchado/a hooded
encarcelado/a incarcerated
encargado/a in charge
encender (enciendo) to turn on (*a machine*) (12); to light
encerado blackboard
encima de on top of (6)
encomendarse (me encomiendo) a to commend yourself to
encontrar (encuentro) to find (9); **encontrarse (con)** to meet (*someone somewhere*) (11)
encuentro encounter
encuesta survey
encuestar to survey
endeble unstable
endémico/a endemic
enemigo enemy
energía energy (15); **energía eléctrica** electrical energy (15); **energía eólica** wind energy (15); **energía nuclear** nuclear energy (15); **energía renovable** renewable energy (15); **energía solar** solar energy (15)
enérgico/a energetic
enero January (6)
enfado anger
énfasis *m. inv.* emphasis
enfático/a emphatic
enfatizar (c) to emphasize
enfermarse to get sick (11)
enfermedad *f.* illness, sickness (11)

enfermero/a nurse (11)
enfermo/a sick (6)
enfilado/a in a line
enfocar (qu) to focus
enfoque *m.* focus
enfrentar(se) (a) to face
enfrente de *prep.* in front of; across from; facing
englobar to encompass
engordar to gain weight; to fatten
enhorabuena congratulations
enojado/a angry (9); upset (9)
enojarse con (alguien) por (algo) to get angry with (someone) about (something) (9)
enorme enormous
enriquecer (enriquezco) to enrich
ensalada salad (7)
ensayar to test
ensayista *m., f.* essayist
ensayo essay
enseñanza teaching
enseñar to teach (2); **enseñar a** + *inf.* to teach to (*do something*)
ensuciarse to get dirty
entender (entiendo) to understand (5)
enterarse (de) to find out (18); to learn (about) (18)
entero/a entire
enterrado/a buried
entidad *f.* entity
entonces then, in that case
entrada entrance; ticket (*to a performance, movie . . .*) (12)
entrante: el año entrante next year
entrañable moving, touching
entrar to enter; **entrar en internet** to go on the internet (12); **entrar en Facebook** to go onto Facebook (12)
entre *prep.* between (6); among (6)
entregar (gu) to hand in (8)
entrenador(a) trainer, coach
entrenamiento training
entrenar to practice (10); to train (10)
entresemana during the week
entrevista interview (17)
entrevistado/a interviewee (17)
entrevistador(a) interviewer (17)
entrevistar to interview
entusiasmar to enthuse
envase *m.* container
envenenar to poison
enviar (envío) to send
envidia envy
envuelto/a covered
eólico/a: energía eólica wind energy (15)
episodio chapter
epitafio epitaph
época era, time (*period*)
equilibrar to balance
equilibrio balance
equipaje *m.* baggage, luggage (8); **facturar el equipaje** to check baggage (8)
equipar to equip
equipo team (10); equipment (12); **equipo electrónico** electronic equipment (12)
equivalente *m.* equivalent
equivaler (*like* **salir**) to equal
equivocarse (qu) (de) to make a mistake (about/with) (14)
eructar to burp, belch
erupción *f.* eruption (18)
escala stop (8); **hacer escala** to make a stop (8)
escalador(a) climber
escalar to climb
escalera staircase; *pl.* stairs (14); ladder
escándalo scandal
escanear to scan
escáner *m.* scanner (12)
escapar(se) (de) to escape (from)
escaparate *m.* store (display) window
escaso/a scarce
escena scene (13)
escenario stage (13); scenery (13)
esclavitud *f.* slavery
esclavo/a slave
esclusa lock (*of a canal*)
escoba broom
escoger (escojo) to choose; to select
escolar *adj.* school
Escorpión *m.* Scorpio
escribir (*p.p.* **escrito**) to write (3)
escrito/a (*p.p. of* **escribir**) written (14); **informe** (*m.*) **escrito** written report (14)
escritor(a) writer (13)
escritorio desk (2)
escuálido/a scrawny
escuchar to listen (to) (2)
escuela school (10); **escuela primaria** elementary school; **escuela secundaria** high school; **maestro/a de escuela** schoolteacher (17)
esculpir to sculpt
escultor(a) sculptor (13)
escultura sculpture (13)
ese/a *adj.* that (4)
esencia essence
esencial essential
esfuerzo effort
eso (*neuter pron.*) that (4); **eso quiere decir...** that means . . . (11); **por eso** for that reason (3)
esos/as *adj.* those (4)
espacial *adj.* space; **nave** (*f.*) **espacial** spaceship; **transbordador** (*m.*) **espacial** space shuttle
espacio space (10); **espacio de almacenamiento** storage space (12)
espacioso/a spacious
espalda back
espantapájaros *m. inv.* scarecrow
espantar to scare
español *m.* Spanish (*language*) (2)
español(a) *n.* Spaniard; *adj.* Spanish (3)
espárragos *m. pl.* asparagus (7)
especial special
especialidad *f.* specialty
especialización *f.* major (*academic*); specialization
especializarse (c) (en) to major (in)
especie *f.* species (15); **especie en peligro de extinción** endangered species (15)
especificar (qu) to specify
específico/a specific
espectacular spectacular
espectáculo show (13)
espectador(a) spectator (13); *pl.* audience (13)
especulación *f.* speculation
espejo mirror
espera wait; **llamada de espera** call-waiting; **sala de espera** waiting room (8)
esperanza hope, wish (18)
esperar to wait (for) (7); to expect (7); to hope (12)
espeso/a thick
espinaca spinach
espíritu *m.* spirit
espiritual spiritual
esplendor *m.* splendor
esposado/a handcuffed
esposo/a husband/wife (3)
esqueleto skeleton
esquema *m.* outline
esquí *m.* skiing (10)
esquiador(a) skier
esquiar (esquío) to ski (10)
esquina (street) corner (15)
esta noche tonight (6)
estabilidad *f.* stability
estable stable
establecer (establezco) to establish
estación *f.* station (8); season (6); **estación de autobuses** bus station (8); **estación de radio** radio station (18); **estación de servicio** gas station (15); **estación de trenes** train station (8)
estacionamiento parking place/lot (15)
estacionar to park (14)
estadio stadium
estadística *s.* statistics
estadístico/a statistical
estado state (3); **estado afectivo** emotional state (9); **estado de ánimo** state of mind; **estado libre asociado** commonwealth; **Estados** (*m. pl.*) **Unidos de América** United States of America

estadounidense *n., adj.* U.S. (3)
estancia stay (*in a hotel*)
estante *m.* bookshelf (5)
estar to be (2); **¿cómo está?** how are you (*form. s.*)? (1); **¿cómo estás?** how are you (*fam. s.*)? (1); **está bien** it's fine, OK (6); **está de moda** it's trendy (hot) (4); **está (muy) nublado** it's (very) cloudy, overcast (6); **estar a dieta** to be on a diet (7); **estar al corriente** to be up to date; **estar al día** to be up to date (18); **estar bajo muchas presiones** to be under a lot of pressure (14); **estar bien** to be comfortable (*temperature*) (6); **estar casado/a (con)** to be married (to) (16); **estar** distraido/a to be distracted (14); **estar de vacaciones** to be on vacation (8); **estar (muy) estresado/a** to be (very) stressed, under (a lot of) stress (14); **(no) estar de acuerdo** to (dis)agree (3); **(no) estar seguro/a de** to be (un)certain of (13)
estatal *adj.* state, of the government
estatua statue
estatura height; **de estatura mediana** of medium height
este *m.* east (6)
este/a *adj.* this (3)
estéreo stereo
estereotípico/a stereotypical
estereotipo stereotype
estético/a aesthetic
estilizado/a slender
estilo style
estimar to estimate
estipendio stipend
estipular to stipulate
estirar to stretch
esto (*neuter pron.*) this (3)
estómago stomach (11)
estornudo sneeze
estos/as *adj.* these (3)
estrategia strategy
estrecho *n.* straight; **Estrecho de Magallanes** Strait of Magellan
estrella star
estrépito crashing
estrés *m. inv.* stress (14)
estresado/a stressed out, under stress (14); **estar (muy) estresado/a** to be (very) stressed, under (a lot of) stress (14)
estresante stressful (14)
estresar to cause stress
estricto/a strict
estrofa verse (*poem*)
estructura structure
estructurar to structure
estuario estuary
estudiantado student body
estudiante *m., f.* student (2)
estudiantil *adj.* (of) student(s)
estudiar to study (2)
estudio office (*in a home*) (5); studio (*television*); *pl.* studies (*education*)
estudioso/a studious
estufa stove (5)
estupendo/a stupendous
etapa stage, phase (16); **etapa de la vida** life stage (16)
etcétera etcetera
eterno/a eternal
ético/a ethical
etnia ethnicity
étnico/a ethnic
etnolingüístico/a ethnolinguistic
Europa Europe
europeo/a *n., adj.* European
euskera *m.* Basque (*language*)
evaluación *f.* evaluation
evangélico/a *n., adj.* evangelical
evangelismo evangelism
evento event
evidencia evidence
evidente evident
evitar to avoid (15)
evolución *f.* evolution
exacto/a exact
exagerado/a exaggerated
examen *m.* exam, test (4)
examinar to examine
exceder to exceed
excelencia excellence
excelente excellent
excepción *f.* exception
excepcional exceptional
excepto except
excesivo/a excessive
exceso excess
exclamar to exclaim
excluir (*like* **construir**) to exclude
exclusivo/a exclusive
excursión *f.* excursion
excusa excuse
exigente demanding
exigir (exijo) to demand
exiliarse to go into exile
existencia existence
existir to exist
éxito success; **tener éxito** to be successful
exitoso/a successful
exótico/a exotic
expandir to expand
expectativa expectation
expedición *f.* expedition
experiencia experience
experto/a expert
explicación *f.* explanation
explicar (qu) to explain (8)
exploración *f.* exploration
explorador(a) explorer
explotación *f.* exploitation
explotar to exploit
exponer (*like* **poner**) (*p.p.* **expuesto**) to display; to propose
exportador(a) exporter
exportar to export
exposición *f.* exposition; **de exposición** expository
expresar to express
expresión *f.* expression (1); **expresión artística** artistic expression (13); **expresión de cortesía** courteous expression (1)
expresionista expressionist
expresivo/a expressive
expulsar to expel
expulsión *f.* expulsion
exquisito/a exquisite
extender (extiendo) to extend
extensión *f.* extension
externo/a external
extinción *f.* extinction (15); **especie** (*f.*) **en peligro de extinción** endangered species (15)
extinguirse (me extingo) to become extinct
extracto extract
extranjero/a *n.* foreigner (2); *adj.* foreign; **ir al extranjero** to go abroad (8); **lengua extranjera** foreign language (2)
extrañar to miss
extraño/a strange; **es extraño que** + *subjunctive* it's strange that (13); **¡qué extraño que...** + *subjunctive*! how strange that . . . ! (13)
extraordinario/a extraordinary
extravagante extravagant
extremo/a extreme
extrovertido/a extrovert(ed)

F

fábrica factory (15)
fabricar (qu) to manufacture (15)
fábula fable
fabuloso/a fabulous
Facebook *m.* Facebook (12); **entrar en Facebook** to go into Facebook (12)
fácil easy (6)
facilidad *f.* ease
facilitar to facilitate
factor *m.* factor
factura bill (17)
facturar el equipaje to check baggage (8)
facultad *f.* department (*university*)
falda skirt (4)
fallar to crash (*computer*) (12)
falso/a false
falta lack (15); absence (15)

faltar (a) to be absent (from) (9); to not attend (9)
fama fame
familia family (3)
familiar *adj.* (of the) family
famoso/a famous
fantasía fantasy
fantasma *m.* ghost
fantástico/a fantastic
farmacéutico/a pharmacist (11)
farmacia pharmacy (12)
faro lighthouse
fascinante fascinating
fascinar (*like* **gustar**) to fascinate (13)
fastidioso/a tedious
fatal *sl.* bad, awful
fatalista *m., f.* fatalist
fauna animal species
fauno faun
favor *m.* favor; **a favor de** in favor of; **por favor** please (1)
favorito/a favorite
fax *m.* FAX (12)
fe *f.* faith
febrero February (6)
fecha date (*calendar*) (6); **¿cuál es la fecha de hoy?** what's today's date? (6); **fecha límite** deadline; **¿qué fecha es hoy?** what's today's date? (6)
federación *f.* federation
federativo/a federative
felicidades *f. pl.* congratulations
felicitaciones *f. pl.* congratulations
felicitar to congratulate
feliz (*pl.* **felices**) happy (9)
femenino/a feminine
fenicio/a Phoenician
fénix *m.* phoenix
fenomenal phenomenal
fenómeno phenomenon
feo/a ugly (3)
feria fair
feriado/a: día (*m.*) **feriado** holiday
fertilidad *f.* fertility
festejar to celebrate
festividad *f.* festival
festivo/a festive, celebratory (9); **día** (*m.*) **festivo** holiday (9)
ficción *f.* fiction; **ciencia ficción** science fiction
ficticio/a fictitious
fiebre *f.* fever (11); **tener fiebre** to have a fever
fiel faithful (3)
fiesta party (2); **darle / hacerle una fiesta (a alguien)** to give (someone) a party (9); to have a party (for someone) (9); **fiesta patronal** party dedicated to a patron saint
fiestero/a happy; fond of parties
figura figure
fijarse (en) to notice
fijo/a set, fixed (4); **precio fijo** fixed, set price (4); **teléfono fijo** landline (12)
fila line
Filadelfia Philadelphia
filantrópico/a philanthropic
Filipinas *f. pl.* Philippines
filipino/a *n., adj.* Philippine
filmar to film; to record
filosofía philosophy (2)
filosófico/a philosophical
fin *m.* end (9); **a fines de** at the end of; **fin de año** end of the year (9); **fin de semana** weekend (2); **por fin** finally (5); **sin fines de lucro** non-profit
final *m.* end
finalmente finally (5)
financiar to finance
financiero/a financial
finanzas *f. pl.* finances
finca farm (15)
Finlandia Finland
fino/a fine
firmar to sign
física physics (2)
físico/a physical
flaco/a skinny
flamenco *music and dance form of southern Spain*
flan *m.* (baked) custard (7)
flauta flute
flexibilidad *f.* flexibility
flexible flexible (14)
flor *f.* flower (8)
flora plant species
flota fleet
folclore folklore
folclórico/a traditional (13)
folclorista *m., f.* folklorist
folklórico/a traditional
fomentar to encourage; to promote
fondo background; fund; bottom
fontanero/a plumber (*Sp.*)
forma form (4); shape (4); way; **de forma presencial** in person
formación *f.* formation; education, training
formar to form
formato format
formidable tremendous
fórmula formula
formulario form (*to fill out*) (17)
fortalecer (fortalezco) to strengthen
fortaleza fort
fosforescente phosphorescent
foto(grafía) *f.* photo(graph) (8); **sacar (qu) fotos** to take photos (8)
fotocopia photocopy (12)
fotocopiadora copy machine (12)
fotocopiar to photocopy
fotografía photography (13); **foto(grafía)** *f.* photo(graph) (13)
fotógrafo/a photographer (17)
fotomontaje *m.* photo montage
fragmentado/a fragmented
fragmento fragment; excerpt
francés *m.* French (*language*) (2)
francés, francesa *n.* French person; *adj.* French
Francia France
franja stripe, band; border, fringe
frase *f.* phrase; sentence
fraternidad *f.* fraternity
frecuencia frequency (2); **con frecuencia** frequently (2); **¿con qué frecuencia... ?** how often . . . ? (3)
frecuente frequent
frecuentemente frequently (11)
frenos *m. pl.* brakes (15)
frente a facing; **hacer frente a** to face up to
fresa strawberry
fresco/a fresh (7); *n.*
fresco: hace fresco it's cool (weather) (6)
frigorífico refrigerator
frijoles *m. pl.* beans (7)
frío: hace (mucho) frío it's (very) cold (*weather*) (6); **tener (mucho) frío** to be (very) cold (6)
frío/a *adj.* cold (6)
frito/a fried (7); **papa frita** French fried potato (7)
frituras *f. pl.* fried food
frontera border
frotar to rub
frustración *f.* frustration
frustrado/a frustrated
fruta fruit (7); **jugo de fruta** fruit juice (7)
frutería fruit store, stand
frutilla strawberry
fruto fruit
fuego fire
fuente *f.* source; fountain; serving dish
fuera *adv.* outside
fuerza force; **fuerzas** (*f. pl.*) **armadas** armed forces
fumador(a) smoker (8); **sala de fumadores** smoking area (8)
fumar to smoke (8); **sala de fumar** smoking area (8)
funcionamiento *n.* functioning, working
funcionar to work (12); to function (12); to run (*machines*) (12)
fundación *f.* foundation
fundador(a) founder
fundar to found
furia rage; **furia al volante** road rage; **furia caminera** road rage
furioso/a furious, angry (6)
fútbol *m.* soccer (10); **fútbol americano** football (10)
futbolista *m., f.* soccer player
futuro *n.* future
futuro/a *adj.* future

G

gabinete *m.* cabinet
gafas *f. pl.* glasses (4); **gafas de sol** sunglasses (4)
gaita *Colombian indigenous flute*
galán *m.* handsome man
gallego Galician (*language*)
galleta cookie (7)
gallo/a rooster, hen; **Misa del Gallo** Midnight Mass
galope *m. traditional dance of Paraguay*
galopera *traditional dance of Paraguay*
gambas *f. pl.* shrimp (*Sp.*)
ganador(a) winner
ganancia earning
ganar to win (10); to earn (*income*) (13)
ganas: tener ganas de + *inf.* to feel like (*doing something*) (4)
gandules *m. pl.* pigeon peas
ganga bargain (4)
garaje *m.* garage (5)
garantizar (c) to guarantee
garbanzos *m. pl.* chickpeas (7)
garganta throat (11)
garifunas *m. pl.* Black Caribs (*descendents of Carib indigenous people and African slaves in Honduras*)
gas *m.* gas (*residential, not for cars*) (12)
gaseosa soft drink
gasolina gasoline (15)
gasolinera gas station (15)
gastar to spend (*money*) (9); to use (*gas*) (15)
gasto expense (12)
gastronómico/a gastronomic
gato cat (3)
gaucho *Argentine cowboy*
gazpacho *cold tomato soup of southern Spain*
gemelo/a twin
genealógico/a: árbol (*m.*) **genealógico** family tree
generación *f.* generation
general general; **en general** in general; **por lo general** generally (5)
generar to generate; to create
genérico/a generic
género genre; gender
generosidad *f.* generosity
generoso/a generous
gente *f. s.* people (8)
genuinamente genuinely
geografía geography
geográfico/a geographic
geología geology
geométrico/a geometric
gerente *m., f.* manager (17)
gerundio *gram.* gerund
gigante *adj.* giant
gimnasio gym(nasium) (12)
ginecólogo/a gynecologist
gira tour
gitano/a *n., adj.* Romani
globalización *f.* globalization
gobernador(a) governor
gobierno government (15)
gol *m.* goal (*soccer*)
golf *m.* golf (10)
golfo gulf
golpe *m.* blow; **golpe de estado** coup d'état
gordo/a fat (3)
gorila *m.* gorilla (15)
gorra baseball cap (4)
gótico/a Gothic
grabadora (tape) recorder/player
grabar to record (12); to tape (12)
gracia grace
gracias thank you (1); **Día** (*m.*) **de (Acción de) Gracias** Thanksgiving; **gracias por** + *noun/inf.* thanks for (9); **muchas gracias** thank you very much (1)
grado grade, year (*in school*); degree (*temperature*)
graduarse (me gradúo) (en) to graduate (from) (17)
gráfico/a graphic (17); **diseñador(a) gráfico/a** graphic (17)
grafiti *m.* graffiti
gramática grammar
gramo gram
gran, grande large, big; great (3); **Gran Bretaña** Great Britain; **pantalla grande** big screen (monitor) (12)
granero barn
granizo hail
granja farm
grano grain
grasa fat
gratis *inv.* free (of charge)
gratuito/a free (of charge)
grave serious
Grecia Greece
griego/a *n., adj.* Greek
grifo faucet
gripa flu (*Mex.*)
gripe *f.* flu (11)
gris gray (4)
gritar to shout
grito shout; cry
grueso/a thick
grupo group; band
guagua bus (*Carib.*)
guaguanco *subgenre of rumba*
guampa *cup made from a hollowed bull's horn used to drink* mate; *cup used to drink* **tereré**
guanábana soursop (*tropical fruit*)
guancasco *traditional dance of the Lenca of Honduras*
guante *m.* glove
guapo/a handsome, good-looking (*people*) (3)
guaraní *m. indigenous language of South America*
guardacostas *m. inv.* Coast Guard
guardar to keep (12); to save (*documents*) (12); **guardar cama** to stay in bed (11); **guardar un puesto** to save a place (*in line*) (8)
guatemalteco/a *n., adj.* Guatemalan
gubernamental governmental
guerra war (18); **guerra civil** civil war
guerrero/a warrior
guía *m., f.* guide (13)
guiado/a guided
guion *m.* script (13)
güiro *Latin American musical instrument*
guitarra guitar
guitarrista *m., f.* guitarist
gustar to be pleasing (8); **¿a usted le gusta... ?** do you (*form. s.*) like . . . ? (1); **me gustaría (mucho)...** I would (really) like . . . (8); **(no,) no me gusta...** (no,) I don't like . . . (1); **(sí,) me gusta...** (yes), I like . . . (1); **¿te gusta... ?** do you (*fam. s.*) like . . . ? (1)
gusto like, preference; *pl.* likes (1); **mucho gusto** nice to meet you (1)

H

haber (*inf. of* **hay**) (there is, there are) (12); **hay (mucha) contaminación** there's (lots of) pollution (6)
habichuelas *f. pl.* beans
habilidad *f.* ability
habitación *f.* bedroom
habitante *m., f.* inhabitant
habitar to inhabit
hábito habit
hablante *m., f.* speaker
hablar to speak; to talk (2); **hablar con soltura** to speak fluently; **hablar por teléfono** to talk on the phone (2)
hacer to do; to make (5); **hace** + *time* + **que** + *present* to have been (*doing something*) for (*time*) (14); **hace** + *time* + **que** + *preterite* ago (14); *present* + **desde hace** + *time* to have been (*doing something*) for (*time*) (14); *preterite* + **hace** + *time* ago (14); **hace (muy) buen/mal tiempo** it's very good/bad weather (6); **hace (mucho) calor** it's (very) hot (weather) (6.); **hace (mucho) fresco** it's cool (very) (weather) (6.); **hace (mucho) frío** it's (very) cold (*weather*) **hace (mucho) sol** it's (very) sunny (6); **hace (mucho) viento** it's (very) windy (6); **hacer autostop** to hitchhike; **hacer *camping*** to go camping (8);

hacer clic to click (12) **hacer cola** to stand in line (8); **hacer ejercicio** to exercise (5); **hacer ejercicios aeróbicos** to do aerobics (11); **hacer (el método) Pilates** to do Pilates (11); **hacer (el) yoga** to do yoga (10); **hacer escala** to make a stop (8); **hacer frente a** to face up to; **hacer la cama** to make the bed (10); **hacer la(s) maleta(s)** to pack one's suitcase(s) (8); **hacer parada** to make a stop (8); **hacer planes (*m.*) para** + *inf.* to make plans to (*do something*) (10); **hacer reserva** to make a reservation; **hacer un pícnic** to have a picnic (10); **hacer un viaje** to take a trip (5); **hacer una juerga** to throw a party; **hacer una pregunta** to ask a question (5); **hacerle una fiesta (a alguien)** to give (someone) a party (9); to have a party (for someone) (9); **hacerse daño** to hurt oneself (14); **hacerse daño en** to hurt one's (*body part*) (14); **¿qué tiempo hace?** what's the weather like? (6)
hacia *prep.* towards
hada *f.* **(***but* **el hada)** fairy
hallaca *Venezuelan meat pastry*
hamaca hammock
hambre *f.* hunger (7); **pasar hambre** to go hungry; **tener (mucha) hambre** to be (very) hungry (7)
hamburguesa hamburger (7)
harina flour
hasta *adv.* until; even; *prep.* until; **hasta luego** see you later (1); **hasta mañana** see you tomorrow (1); **hasta pronto** see you soon; **hasta que** *conj.* until (17)
hay there is/are (1); **¿hay?** is there / are there? (1); **hay que** + *inf.* it is necessary to (*do something*) (13); **no hay** there is/are not (1); **no hay de qué** you're welcome (1); **no hay problema** no problem (14)
hebreo Hebrew (*language*)
hecho *n.* fact (9); event (9)
hecho/a (*p.p. of* **hacer**) made
hectárea *land measure equal to 2.5 acres*
helado ice cream (7)
heliconia *flowering tropical plant*
hemisferio hemisphere
herbolario/a herbalist
heredar to inherit
herencia inheritance
hermanastro/a stepbrother, stepsister
hermano/a brother/sister (3); *m. pl.* siblings (3)
hermoso/a beautiful
héroe *m.* hero
heroína heroine
hervir (hiervo) (i) to boil
híbrido/a hybrid (15)
hidalgo nobleman
hidroeléctrico/a hydroelectric
hielo ice
hierba grass
hígado liver
hijastro/a stepson, stepdaughter
hijo/a son/daughter (3); *m. pl.* children (3)
himno hymn; **himno nacional** national anthem
hipopótamo hippopotamus
hispánico/a Hispanic
hispano/a Hispanic (3)
Hispanoamérica Hispanic America
hispanoamericano/a *adj.* Hispanic American
hispanohablante *adj. m., f.* Spanish-speaking
historia history (2); story (8)
historiador(a) historian
histórico/a historical
hockey *m.* hockey (10)
hogar *m.* home
hoja leaf
hola hi (1); hello (1)
Holanda Holland
hombre *m.* man (2); **hombre de negocios** businessman (17)
homeópata *m., f.* homeopath
homeopático/a homeopathic
homogeneidad *f.* homogeneity
homogéneo/a homogenous
hondureño/a *n., adj.* Honduran
honesto/a honest
hongo mushroom; toadstool; fungus; **sombrero hongo** bowler hat, derby
honor *m.* honor
honrado/a honest; honorable
hora hour; time (1); **¿a qué hora... ?** at what time . . . ? (1); **es hora de...** it's time to . . . ; **hora punta** peak hour **¿qué hora es?** what time is it? (1)
horario schedule (14)
horchata *Mexican drink made from rice*
hormona hormone
horno oven; **horno de microondas** microwave oven (10)
horóscopo horoscope
horror *m.* horror
hospital *m.* hospital
hospitalario/a hospitable
hospitalidad *f.* hospitality
hospitalización *f.* hospitalization
hotel *m.* hotel
hoy today (1); **¿cuál es la fecha de hoy?** what's today's date? (6); **¿qué día es hoy?** what day is today? (5); **¿qué fecha es hoy?** what's today's date? (6)
huelga strike (*labor*) (18)
huella mark; (finger)print
huerto orchard
hueso bone
huésped *m., f.* guest
huevo egg (7)
huipil *m. traditional Mayan blouse*
huir (*like* **construir**) to flee
humanidad *f.* humanity; *pl.* humanities (2)
humanista *n., adj.* humanist
humanitario/a humanitarian
humanizar (c) to make more human
humano/a human (11); **cuerpo humano** human body (11); **ser (*m.*) humano** human being
humedad *f.* humidity
húmedo/a humid
humilde humble
humorístico/a humorous
huracán *m.* hurricane

I

ibérico/a *adj.* Iberian
íbero/a *n.* Iberian
icónico/a iconic
ícono icon
ida: billete (*m.*) (*Sp.*) / **boleto** (*L.A.*) **de ida** one-way ticket (8); **billete** (*m.*) (*Sp.*) / **boleto** (*L.A.*) **de ida y vuelta** round-trip ticket (8)
idealista *m., f.* idealistic
idear to think up; to conceive (*idea*)
idéntico/a identical
identidad *f.* identity; **carnet** (*m.*) **de identidad** identification card
identificación *f.* identification (14); **carnet** (*m.*) **de identificación** identification card; **tarjeta de identificación** identification card, ID (14)
identificar(se) (qu) to identify (oneself)
idioma *m.* language
idiomático/a idiomatic
ídolo idol
iglesia church (16)
ignorante ignorant
ignorar to ignore
igual same; equal
igualdad *f.* equality (18)
igualitario/a egalitarian
igualmente likewise (1); same here (1)
ilimitado/a unlimited
ilógico/a illogical
iluminar to light up
ilusorio/a false
ilustrar to illustrate
ilustrativo/a illustrative
imagen *f.* image (13)
imaginación *f.* imagination
imaginar(se) to imagine
imaginativo/a imaginative
imitar to imitate

impaciente impatient
impacto impact
impedimento impediment
impedir (*like* **pedir**) to impede
imperfecto *gram.* imperfect
imperio empire
impermeable *m.* raincoat (4); *adj.* impermeable
impertinente impertinent
implementar to implement
implicar (qu) to imply
imponer (*like* **poner**) to impose
importancia importance
importante important (12); **es importante que** + *subjunctive* it's important that (12)
importar (*like* **gustar**) to matter; to be important
imposible impossible (13); **es imposible que** + *subjunctive* it's impossible that (13); **no es imposible que** + *subjunctive* it's not impossible (13)
impresión *f.* impression
impresionante impressive
impresionar to impress
impreso/a printed
impresora printer (12)
imprimir to print (12)
improbable unlikely (13); **es improbable que** + *subjunctive* it's unlikely, improbable that (13); **no es improbable que** + *subjunctive* it's not improbable that (13)
improvisar to improvise
impuesto tax
impulsivo/a impulsive
inalámbrico/a wireless
inauguración *f.* inauguration
inca *n. m., f.* Inca; *adj. m., f.* Incan
incaico/a *adj.* Inca
incapacidad *f.* inability
incendio fire
incidente *m.* incident
incienso incense
inclinación *f.* inclination
inclinarse to lean
incluir (*like* **construir**) to include
incómodo/a uncomfortable
incompleto/a incomplete
inconcebible inconceivable
inconveniencia inconvenience
inconveniente *n. m; adj.* inconvenient
incorporar to incorporate; to include
incorrecto/a incorrect
incrédulo/a incredulous
increíble incredible (13); **es increíble que** + *subjunctive* it's incredible that (13)
incrementar to increase
incremento increment
indefinido/a indefinite; **artículo indefinido** *gram.* indefinite article; **palabra indefinida y negativa** *gram.* indefinite and negative word (7)
indeleble indelible
independencia independence
independiente Independent
independizarse (c) to become independent
indescriptible indescribable
indicación *f.* instruction; direction
indicar (qu) to indicate
indicativo *gram.* indicative
índice *m.* index
Índico Indian (Ocean)
indiferente indifferent
indígena *n. m., f.* indigenous person; *adj. m., f.* indigenous
indigenista *m., f. pertaining to indigenous topics and themes*
indio/a *n., adj.* Indian
indirecto/a indirect; **complemento indirecto** *gram.* indirect object
indiscreto/a indiscreet
indispensable indispensible, essential
indistinto/a indistinct
individualidad *f.* individuality
individuo *n.* individual
individuo/a *adj.* individual
industria industry
inesperado/a unexpected
inexistente nonexistent
infancia infancy (16); childhood (16)
infantil *adj.* child, children's
infatigable tireless
infección *f.* infection
inferir (infiero) (i) to infer
infiltrarse to infiltrate
infinitivo *gram.* infinitive
inflexible inflexible (14)
inflexibilidad *f.* inflexibility
influencia influence
influir (*like* **construir**) to influence
influyente influential
infografía computer graphic
información *f.* information
informar to inform (18)
informática computer science
informativo/a informative
informe (*m.*) **(oral/escrito)** (oral/written) report (14)
infraestructura infrastructure
infrecuente infrequent
infusión *f.* infusion
ingeniería engineering
ingeniero/a engineer (17)
ingenioso/a ingenious
Inglaterra England
inglés *m.* English (*language*) (2)
inglés, inglesa *n., adj.* English (3)
ingrediente *m.* ingredient
ingresar to deposit (*in an account*)
ingreso income
inicial *f.* initial (*letter*)
iniciar to start
iniciativa initiative
inicio beginning
injusticia injustice
injusto/a unfair
inmediato/a immediate
inmenso/a immense
inmerso/a immersed
inmigración *f.* immigration
inmigrante *n., m., f.* immigrant
inmobiliario/a *adj.* real estate; property
inmóvil unmoving
innecesario/a unnecessary
innumerable countless
inocente innocent
inolvidable unforgettable
inquilino/a tenant (12); renter (12)
inscribir(se) (*p.p.* **inscrito**) **(en)** to sign up; to register (for)
inscripción *f.* inscription
inscrito/a (*p.p. of* **inscribir**) registered
insecto insect
insistir (en) to insist (on) (12)
insoportable unbearable
inspiración *f.* inspiration
instalación *f.* facility
instalar to install (12)
instantáneo/a instantaneous
instante: al instante right away
institución *f.* institution
instituto institute
instrucciones *f. pl.* instructions
instructor(a) instructor
instrumento instrument
insulina insulin
insulto insult
integración *f.* integration
integrarse to integrate oneself
intelectual intellectual
inteligencia intelligence
inteligente intelligent (3)
intención *f.* intention
intencionadamente intentionally
intensidad *f.* intensity
intensificar (qu) to intensify
intenso/a intense
intentar to attempt (to)
interacción *f.* interaction
interactivo/a interactive
intercambiar to exchange
intercambio exchange
interés *m.* interest (17)
interesante interesting
interesar (*like* **gustar**) to interest (*someone*) (8)
intergaláctico/a intergalactic
interior interior; inner (4); **ropa interior** underwear (4)
intermedio/a intermediate
interminable endless
internacional international; **Día** (*m.*) **Internacional de la No Violencia**

Contra la Mujer International Day for the Elimination of Violence against Women
internauta *m., f.* internet user
internet *m.* internet (12); **buscar (qu) en internet** to look up on the internet (12); **entrar en internet** to go on the internet (12)
interno/a internal
interplanetario/a interplanetary
interpretación *f.* interpretation
interpretar to interpret
interrogación: signo de interrogación question mark
interrogativo/a *gram.* interrogative (1)
interrumpir to interrupt
interrupción *f.* interruption
intervención *f.* intervention
intimidad *f.* intimacy
íntimo/a intimate; close
intolerancia intolerance
intranquilidad *f.* restlessness
introducción *f.* introduction
introducir (*like* **conducir**) to introduce
inundación *f.* flood
inútil useless
invadido/a invaded
inválido/a disabled
invasión *f.* invasion
invasor(a) *adj.* invading
inventar to invent
inversión *f.* investment
invertir (invierto) (i) to invest
investigación *f.* investigation; research
investigador(a) researcher
investigar (gu) to investigate; to research
invierno winter (6)
invitación *f.* invitation
invitado/a guest (9)
invitar to invite (7)
invocar (qu) to invoke
inyección *f.* injection (11); **ponerle una inyección** to give (*someone*) a shot (11)
iPhone *m.* iPhone (12)
ir to go (4); **ir a** + *inf.* to be going to (*do something*) (4); **ir a un bar** to go to a bar (10); **ir a un concierto** to go to a concert (10); **ir a un museo** to go to a museum (10); **ir a una discoteca** to go to a disco (10); **ir al extranjero** to go abroad (8); **ir al teatro** to go to the theater (10) **ir de compras** to go shopping (4); **ir de safari** to go on a safari; **ir de vacaciones a...** to go on vacation to/in . . . (8); **ir distraído/a** to be distracted (14); **ir en...** to go/travel by . . . (8); **ir en autobús** to go/travel by bus (8); **ir en avión** to go/travel by plane (8); **ir en barco** to go/travel by boat, ship (8); **ir en tren** to go/travel by train (8); **irse** to leave; **vamos** let's go (4)
ira al manejar road rage
iraní (*pl.* **iraníes**) *n., adj.* Iranian
iraquí (*pl.* **iraquíes**) *n., adj.* Iraqi
iridiscencia iridescence
Irlanda Ireland
irlandés, irlandesa *n., adj.* Irish
ironía irony
irónico/a ironic
irresponsable irresponsible
-ísimo/a adj., adv. very very (9)
isla island (6)
Islandia Iceland
islote *m.* islet
israelí (*pl.* **israelíes**) *n., adj.* Israeli
Italia Italy
italiano Italian (*language*) (2)
italiano/a *n., adj.* Italian
itinerario itinerary
-ito/a *diminuitive suffix* (10)
izquierda *n.* left-hand side; **a la izquierda de** to the left of (6)
izquierdo/a *adj.* left (14); **levantarse con el pie izquierdo** to get up on the wrong side of the bed (14)

J

jaguar *m.* jaguar
jamaica hibiscus
jamás never (7)
jamón *m.* ham (7)
Japón *m.* Japan
japonés *m.* Japanese (*language*)
japonés, japonesa *n., adj.* Japanese
jarabe *m.* (cough) syrup (11)
jardín *m.* garden (5)
jarra jar
jazz *m.* jazz
jeans *m. pl.* blue jeans (4)
jefe/a boss (17)
jerarquía hierarchy
jersey *m.* sweater; pullover
jirafa giraffe
jornada de tiempo parcial part-time job
joropo *folkloric music of Venezuela*
joven *n. m., f.* (*pl.* **jóvenes**) youth; *adj.* young (3); **de joven** as a youth (10)
joyería jewelry
jubilarse to retire (17)
judaísmo Judaism
juego game; **Juegos Olímpicos** Olympic Games
juerga party; **hacer una juerga** to have/throw a party
jueves *m. inv.* Thursday (5)
jugador(a) player (10)
jugar (juego) (gu) (a, al) to play (*a game, sport*) (5); **jugar a las cartas / a los videojuegos / al ajedrez** to play cards/videogames/chess (10)
jugo (de fruta) (fruit) juice (7)
juguete *m.* toy
julio July (6)
junio June (6)
junto a *prep.* near
juntos/as together (8)
jurar to swear (*oath*)
justicia justice
justificación *f.* justification
justificar (qu) to justify
justo/a fair
juvenil *adj.* youth; youthful; **diabetes** (*f.*) **juvenil** childhood diabetes
juventud *f.* youth (16)
juzgar (gu) to judge

K

kaki: color (*m.*) **kaki** khaki
kilo(gramo) kilo(gram)
kilómetro kilometer

L

la *def. art. f. s.* the; *d.o. f. s.* you (*form.*); her, it; **a la(s)...** at . . . (*time of day*) (1); **la cual** which
labor *f.* work, job
laboral *adj.* work, work-related (17)
laboratorio laboratory
lácteo/a *adj.* dairy
lado side; **al lado de** alongside of (6); **por otro lado** on the other hand; **por un lado** on one hand
ladrar to bark
ladrón, ladrona thief
lagarto lizard
lago lake (15)
lágrima tear
lamentar to regret (13); to feel sorry (13)
laminado/a laminated
lámpara lamp (5)
lana wool (4); **de lana** wool (4)
langosta lobster (7)
lapicero pen
lápiz *m.* (*pl.* **lápices**) pencil (2)
largo/a long (3)
las *def. art. s. pl.* the; *d.o. f. pl.* you (*form. pl.*); **a la(s)...** at . . . (*time of day*) (1); **las cuales** which
lasaña lasagne
lástima shame; **es una lástima que** + *subjunctive* it's a shame that (13); **¡qué lástima que...** + *subjunctive*! what a shame that . . . ! (13)
lastimarse to hurt (*a body part*) (14)
lata can
latín *m.* Latin (*language*)
latino/a *adj.* Latin; **América Latina** Latin America

Latinoamérica Latin America
latinoamericano/a *n., adj.* Latin American
lavabo (bathroom) sink (5)
lavadora washing machine (10)
lavandería laundry
lavaplatos *m. inv.* dishwasher (10)
lavar to wash (10); **lavarse** to wash (oneself)
le *indir. obj. pron.* to/for him/her; to/for you (*s. form.*); to/for it; **¿(a usted) le gusta... ?** do you (*form. s.*) like . . . ? (1)
lealtad *f.* loyalty
lección *f.* lesson
leche *f.* milk (7)
lechón *m.* suckling pig; **lechón asado** roast suckling pig
lechuga lettuce (7)
lector(a) reader
lectura reading
leer (*like* **creer**) to read (3)
legislación *f.* legislation
legumbre *f.* legume
lejos *adv.* far; **lejos de** *prep.* far from (6)
lema *m.* motto
lempira *currency of Honduras*
lengua language (2); tongue (11); **lenguas extranjeras** (*f. pl.*) foreign languages (2); **sacar (qu) la lengua** to stick out one's tongue (11)
lentes *m. pl.* glasses (11); **lentes de contacto** contact lenses (11)
lentillas *f. pl.* contact lenses (*Sp.*)
lento/a slow (15); **ritmo lento de la vida** slow pace of life (15)
león *m.* lion; **león marino** sea lion
leopardo leopard
letra letter (*of the alphabet*); lyrics (*of a song*) (7)
levantar to raise; to lift (11); **levantar pesas** to lift weights (11); **levantarse** to get up (out of bed) (5); to stand up (5); **levantarse con el pie izquierdo** to get up on the wrong side of the bed (14)
leve *adj.* light
ley *f.* law (18)
leyenda legend
libanés, libanesa lebanese
liberar(se) to free (oneself)
libertad *f.* freedom, liberty
libertador(a) liberator
libra pound (*measurement*)
libre free, unoccupied (10); **al aire** (*m.*) **libre** outdoors (10); **estado libre asociado** commonwealth; **libre comercio** free trade; **ratos** (*m. pl.*) **libres** spare (free) time (10); **tiempo libre** free time (10)
librería bookstore (2)
libro (de texto) (text) book (2)
licencia license (15); **licencia de manejar/conducir** driver's license (15)
licor *m.* liqueur
licuar (licúo) to liquefy
líder *m., f.* leader
liga league
ligero/a light, not heavy (7)
lima lime
limeño/a *adj.* from Lima, Peru
limitación *f.* limitation
limitar to limit
límite *m.* limit; **fecha límite** deadline; **límite de velocidad** speed limit (15)
limón *m.* lemon
limonada lemonade
limonero lemon tree
limosina limousine
limpiar (la casa) to clean (the) house (10)
limpieza cleanliness
limpio/a clean (6)
lindo/a pretty
línea line
lingüístico/a linguistic
linterna flashlight
lío problem; trouble; **meterse en líos** to get into trouble
liquidación *f.* liquidation
líquido liquid
Lisboa Lisbon
lista list
listo/a smart (3); clever (3); **estar listo/a** to be ready
literario/a literary
literatura literature (2)
litoral *m.* coast
llamada call; **bloqueo de llamadas** call blocker
llamar to call (7); **¿cómo se llama usted?** what is your (*form. s.*) name? (1); **¿cómo te llamas?** what is your (*fam. s.*) name? (1); **llamarse** to be called (5); **me llamo...** my name is . . . (1)
llanero *Venezuelan cowboy*
llanero/a of or pertaining to the plains
llano *n.* plain
llanta (desinflada) (flat) tire (15)
llanura *n.* plain
llave *f.* key (5)
llegada arrival (8)
llegar (gu) to arrive (3); **¿cómo se llega a... ?** how do you get to . . . ? (15); **llegar a ser** to become
llenar to fill (*a car*) (15); to fill out (*a form*) (17)
lleno/a full
llevar to wear (4); to carry (4); to take (4); **llevar una vida sana/tranquila** to lead a healthy/calm life (11); **llevarse bien/mal (con)** to get along well/poorly (with) (16)
llorar to cry (9)
llover (llueve) to rain (6); **llueve** (it's raining) (6)
lluvia rain
lluvioso/a *adj.* rainy; of rain; **bosque** (*m.*) **tropical lluvioso** tropical rain forest
lo *d.o. m. s.* you (*form.*); him; it; **lo bueno** the good news/thing (11); **lo cual** which; **lo malo** the bad news/thing (11); **lo que** what, that which (5); **lo siento (mucho)** I'm (very) sorry (14); **lo suficiente** enough (11); **por lo general** generally (5); **por lo menos** at least (9); **por lo regular** in general
lobo/a wolf
localidad *f.* ticket to a movie
localización *f.* location
loco/a crazy (6)
locutor(a) commentator
lógico/a logical
logotipo logo
lograr to achieve
logro achievement
Londres London
longitud *f.* longitude
los *def. art. m. pl.* the; *d.o. m. pl.* you (*form. pl.*) them; **los cuales** which; **los lunes (los martes...)** on Mondays (Tuesdays . . .) (5)
lotería lottery
lubricar (qu) to lubricate
lucha fight (18); struggle (18)
luchar to fight (18)
lucro: sin fines de lucro non-profit
luego then, later next (5); **hasta luego** see you later (1)
lugar *m.* place (2)
lujo luxury
lujoso/a luxurious
luminiscente luminescent
luminoso/a lit up
luna moon (16); **luna de miel** honeymoon (16)
lunares: de lunares polka-dot (4)
lunes *m. inv.* Monday (5); **el lunes** on Monday (5); **los lunes** on Mondays (5); **el lunes que viene** next Monday (5)
Luxemburgo Luxembourg
luz *f.* (*pl.* **luces**) light (14)

M

madera wood
madrastra stepmother
madre *f.* mother (3); **Día** (*m.*) **de la Madre** Mother's Day
madrileño/a of or pertaining to Madrid
madrina godmother
madrugada dawn
madurez *f.* middle age (16)

maduro/a mature
maestría master's degree
maestro/a (de escuela) schoolteacher (17); *adj.* master; **obra maestra** masterpiece (13)
Magallanes: Estrecho de Magallanes Strait of Magellan
mágico/a *adj.* magic
magnífico/a magnificent
mago wizard
mahones *m. pl.* jeans
maíz *m.* (*pl.* **maíces**) corn
mal *adv.* poorly (2); **caerle mal a alguien** to make a bad impression on someone; **empleo mal pagado** poorly paid job/position (17); **llevarse mal (con)** to get along poorly (with) (16); **pasarlo mal** to have a bad time (9); **portarse mal** to misbehave (9); **salir mal** to come/turn out poorly (5); to do poorly (5)
mal, malo/a *adj.* bad (3); **hace (muy) mal tiempo** it's (very) bad weather (6); **lo malo** the bad news/thing (11); **tener mala suerte** to have bad luck (14); to be unlucky (14)
maleducado/a spoiled
malestar *m.* discomfort
maleta suitcase (8); **hacer la(s) maleta(s)** to pack one's suitcase(s) (8)
maletero porter (8)
malvado/a evil
mamá mother, mom (3)
mami mom, mommy
mamífero mammal
mancha stain
mandar to send (2); to order (12); **mandar un mensaje (de texto)** to (send a) text (2)
mandarín *m.* Mandarin (*language*)
mandato command (7)
manejar to drive; to operate (a *machine*) (12); **ira al manejar** road rage; **licencia de manejar** driver's license (15)
manera way, manner; **de manera que** so that, in such a way that
manga sleeve
manifestación *f.* demonstration (18); march (18)
maniquí *m.* mannequin
mano *f.* hand (11); **darse la mano** to shake hands (11)
mansión *f.* mansion
mantener (*like* **tener**) to maintain (18); to keep (18); **mantenerse en contacto** to stay in touch
mantequilla butter (7)
manzana apple (7); (city) block
mañana tomorrow (1); **de la mañana** in the morning, A.M. (1); **hasta mañana** see you tomorrow (1); **pasado mañana** the day after tomorrow (5); **por la mañana** in the morning (2)
mapa *m.* map
mapudungun *m. language of the Mapuche people*
máquina machine
mar *m.* sea (8); **mar Caribe** Caribbean Sea
maracuyá *m.* passion fruit
maratón *m.* marathon
maravilla wonder, marvel
maravillar to delight
maravilloso/a marvelous
marca brand; label
marcar (qu) to mark
marcial martial
mareado/a dizzy (11); nauseated (11)
marido husband (3)
marihuana marijuana
marinera *folkloric dance of coastal Peru*
marino/a marine; **león** (*m.*) **marino** sea lion
mariscos *m. pl.* shellfish (7)
marítimo/a maritime; sea, marine
marketing *m.* marketing
marrón *adj. m., f.* brown
martes *m. inv.* Tuesday (5); **los martes** on Tuesdays (5)
Marruecos Morocco
marzo March (6)
más more (2); **cada vez más** increasingly; **más de** + *number* more than + *number* (6); **más... que** more (-er) . . . than (6)
masa mass; dough
máscara mask
mascota pet (3)
masculino/a masculine
masivo/a massive
masticar (qu) to chew
matar to kill (18)
mate *m. traditional drink of Argentina*
matemáticas *f. pl.* math (2)
materia subject area (2); material (4)
materialidad *f.* material aspect; outward appearance
materialista *m., f.* materialistic
maternidad *f.* maternity
materno/a maternal
matinal *adj.* morning
matriarcado matriarchy
matriarcal matriarchal
matrícula tuition (2)
matricularse to enroll; to register
matrimonio marriage (16); married couple (16)
máximo/a maximum
maya *n., adj. m., f.* Mayan
mayo May (6)
mayor older (6); oldest; greater; greatest; **mayor(es) que** older than (6); **Antillas** (*f. pl.*) **Mayores** Greater Antilles; **cada vez mayor** greater and greater
mayoría majority
mayoritariamente primarily
mayoritario/a *adj.* majority
mayúscula capital (letter), uppercase
me *d.o.* me; *i.o.* to/for me; *refl. pron.* myself; **me gustaría (mucho)...** I would (really) like . . . (8); **me llamo...** my name is . . . (1); **(no,) no me gusta...** (no,) I don't like . . . (1); **(sí,) me gusta...** (yes), I like . . . (1)
mecánico/a mechanic (15)
mecanización *f.* mechanization
mecanografía typing
medalla medal
mediano/a: de estatura mediana of medium height
medianoche *f.* midnight (6)
mediante *prep.* by, with
medias *f. pl.* stockings (4)
medicamento medicine
medicina medicine (11)
médico/a (medical) doctor (3)
medio *n.* medium; means; *pl.* mass media (18); **medio ambiente** environment (15); **medio de comunicación** medium of communication (18); **medio de transporte** means of transportation (8)
medio/a *adj.* half; middle; average; **media naranja** better half; **y media** half past (*the hour*) (1)
medioambiental environmental
medioambiente *m.* environment
mediodía *m.* noon (6)
medir (mido) (i) to measure
meditar to meditate
megadiverso/a megadiverse
megalópolis *f.* super-city
mejor better (6); best (6); **es mejor** it's better (12); **mejor(es) que** better than (6)
mejora improvement
mejorar(se) to improve; to get better
mellizo/a fraternal twin
melódico/a melodious
memoria memory (12); **memoria USB** pen drive (12)
mencionar to mention
menonito/a *adj.* Mennonite
menor younger (6); youngest; less; least; **menor(es) que** younger than (6)
menorá menorah
menos less; least; minus; **a menos que** *conj.* unless (16); **al menos** at least; **menos cuarto** a quarter to (*hour*) (1); **menos de** + *number* fewer than + *number* (6); **menos quince** fifteen

minutes till (*hour*) (1); **por lo menos** at least (9)
mensaje *m.* message; **mandar un mensaje (de texto)** to (send a) text (2)
mensual monthly
mente *f.* mind
-mente -ly (*averbial suffix*) (14)
mentir (miento) (i) to lie
mentira lie (12)
menú *m.* menu (7)
menudo: a menudo *adv.* often
mercadeo marketing
mercader *m., f.* merchant
mercado market(place) (4)
mercadotecnia marketing
merecer (merezco) to deserve
merendar (meriendo) to snack (7)
merengue *m. dance from the Dominican Republic*
merienda snack (7)
mes *m.* month (6)
mesa table (2); **poner la mesa** to set the table (10); **quitar la mesa** to clear the table (10)
meseta plateau
mesita end table (5)
mesoamericano/a *n., adj.* Meso-American
mestizaje *m.* mixing of races
meta goal
metáfora metaphor
metal *m.* metal
metálico/a metallic
metalúrgico/a metallurgical
meteorológico/a meteorological
meter to put (into); to place; **meterse en líos** to get into trouble
método method; **hacer (el método) Pilates** to do Pilates (11)
metro subway; **parada del metro** subway stop (12)
metrópoli *f.* metropolis
metropolitano/a urban
mexicano/a Mexican (3)
mexicoamericano/a Mexican American
mezcla mix
mezclar to mix
mezclilla denim
mezquita mosque (16)
mí *obj. of prep.* me (6)
mi(s) *poss. adj.* my (3)
microbio microbe
microcuento very short story
microondas: horno de microondas microwave oven (10)
microorganismo microorganism
miedo fear (4); **tener miedo (de)** to be afraid (of) (4)
miel *f.* honey (16); **luna de miel** honeymoon (16)
miembro/a member
mientras while (10)
miércoles *m. inv.* Wednesday (5); **ayer fue miércoles...** yesterday was Wednesday . . . (5)
mierda shit
mil (one) thousand (4)
milagro miracle
milenario/a thousand-year
mililitro milliliter
militar *n. m., f.* soldier; (17) *adj.* military; **servicio militar** military service (18)
milla mile
millón one million (4)
millonario/a millionaire
mimar to spoil; to pamper
mineral: agua *f.* (*but* **el agua**) **(mineral)** (mineral) water (7)
minidiálogo minidialogue
mínimo minimum
ministerio ministry
ministro/a minister
minoría minority
minuto minute
mío/a(s) *poss. adj.* my; *poss. pron.* mine, (of) mine (17)
mirada look
mirar to look at (3); to watch (3); **mirar la tele(visión)** to watch television (3)
misa mass; **Misa del Gallo** midnight mass
miseria misery
misil *n.* missile
misión *f.* mission
mismo/a same (6); **ahora mismo** right now (6)
misterio mystery
misterioso/a mysterious
mitad *f.* half
mixto/a mixed
moái *m. statue on Easter Island, Chile*
mochila backpack (2)
moda fashion; style; **a la moda** in fashion, in a stylish way; **es de última moda** it's trendy (hot) (4); **está de moda** it's trendy (hot) (4)
modales *m. pl.* manners
modelar to model
modelo model, example
módem *m.* modem (12)
moderación *f.* moderation
modernidad *f.* modernity
modernismo modernism
modernista *m., f.* modernist
moderno/a modern (13)
modificar (qu) to modify
modismo idiom
modista dressmaker
modo way, matter; mode; *gram.* mood; **de modo que** in such a way that
mole *m. Mexican sauce*
molestar (*like* **gustar**) to bother (11)
molestia *n.* bother
molesto/a annoyed (6)
molino: rueda de molino treadmill
momento moment
momia mummy
monarquía monarchy
monasterio monastery
moneda coin (17); currency
monedero coin purse
monitor *m.* monitor
monitorizar (c) to monitor
mono monkey
monolingüe *adj.* monolingual
monoparental *adj.* single-parent
monopatín *m.* skateboard
monotonía monotony
monótono/a monotonous
monovolumen *m.* minivan
monstruo monster
montaje *m.* montage
montaña mountain (8)
montañoso/a mountainous
montar to ride; **montar a caballo** to ride a horse (10); **montar en bicicleta** to ride a bicycle (10)
montón: un montón a lot
montuno *traditional hat of Panama*
monumento monument
morado/a purple (4)
morales *f. pl.* morals
morderse (me muerdo) to bite
moreno/a brunet(te) (3)
morir(se) ([me] muero) (u) (*p.p.* **muerto**) to die (9)
moro/a *n.* Moor; *adj.* Moorish
mosaico mosaic
mosca fly
mostrador *m.* counter (8)
mostrar (muestro) to show (8)
motivación *f.* motivation
motivo motive
moto(cicleta) *f.* motorcycle (15)
motor *m.* motor
mover (muevo) to move
móvil mobile
movimiento movement
muchacho/a young boy/girl
muchísimo an awful lot (8)
mucho *adv.* much (2); a lot (2); **lo siento mucho** I'm very sorry (14); **me gustaría mucho...** I would really like . . . (8)
mucho/a a lot (of) (3); *pl.* many (3); **estar bajo muchas presiones** to be under a lot of pressure (14); **hace (mucho) calor** it's (very) hot (6); **hace (mucho) fresco** it's (very) cool (6); **hace (mucho) frío** it's (very) cold (6); **hace (mucho) sol** it's (very) sunny (6); **hace (mucho) viento** it's (very) windy (6); **hay (mucha) contaminación** there's (lots of)

pollution (6) **muchas gracias** thank you very much (1); **(mucho) gusto** nice to meet you (1); **tener (mucha) hambre** to be (very) hungry (7); **tener (mucha) sed** to be (very) thirsty (7); **tener muchas presiones** to have a lot of pressure (14); **tener (mucho) calor** to be very warm, hot (6); **tener (mucho) frío** to be very cold (6)
mudanza *n.* move
mudarse to move (*residence*) (12)
mueble *m.* piece of furniture (5)
muela molar, back tooth (11)
muerte *f.* death (16)
muerto/a (*p.p. of* **morir [muero] [u]**) dead; **Día** (*m.*) **de Muertos** Day of the Dead
mujer *f.* woman (2); wife (3); **Día** (*m.*) **Internacional de la No Violencia Contra la Mujer** International Day for the Elimination of Violence against Women; **mujer de negocios** businesswoman (17); **mujer soldado** female soldier (17)
mula mule
mulato/a mulatto
multa fine
multilingüe multilingual
multinacional multinational
múltiple multiple
multiplicarse (qu) to multiply; to grow in number
multirracial multiracial
mundial *adj.* world; **Copa Mundial** World Cup
mundo world (3); **Copa del Mundo** World Cup (soccer)
municipio municipality
muñeca doll
mural *m.* mural (13)
muralismo muralism
muralista *m., f.* muralist
muralla city wall
murciélago bat
muro wall
músculo muscle
museo museum (10); **ir a un museo** to go to a museum (10)
música music (13)
musical musical (13)
músico *m., f.* musician (13)
musulmán, musulmana Muslim
mutuo/a mutual
muy very (1); **muy bien** fine, very well (1); **muy buenas** good afternoon/ evening (1)

N

nacer (nazco) to be born (16)
nacimiento birth
nación *f.* nation; **Organización** (*f.*) **de Naciones Unidas (ONU)** United Nations (U.N.)
nacional national; **himno nacional** national anthem; **producto nacional bruto** gross national product
nacionalidad *f.* nationality; **adjetivo de nacionalidad** adjective of nationality (3)
nada nothing, not anything (7); **de nada** you're welcome (1); **para nada** at all (8)
nadar to swim (8)
nadie no one, nobody, not anybody (7)
náhuatl *m.* Nahuatl (*language of the Aztecs*)
nana *fam.* grandma
naranja orange (7); **media naranja** better half
nariz *f.* (*pl.* **narices**) nose (11)
narración *f.* narration
narrador(a) narrator
narrar to narrate
natación *f.* swimming (10)
natal: casa natal house where someone was born
nativo/a native
natural natural; **ciencias** (*f. pl.*) **naturales** natural sciences (2); **recurso natural** natural resource (15)
naturaleza nature (15)
naturópata *m., f.* naturopath
náufrago shipwreck
nave (*f.*) **espacial** spaceship
navegable navigable
navegación *f.* navigation
navegar (gu) to navigate (12); **navegar la red** to surf the internet
Navidad *f.* Christmas (9)
navideño/a *adj.* Christmas
neblina mist; fog
necesario/a necessary (3)
necesidad *f.* need, necessity
necesitar to need (2)
negación *f.* negation
negar (niego) (gu) to deny (13)
negativo/a negative; **palabra indefinida y negativa** *gram.* indefinite and negative word (7)
negociar to negotiate
negocio business; **hombre** (*m.*) **de negocios** businessman (17); **mujer** (*f.*) **de negocios** businesswoman (17)
negrilla: en negrilla boldface
negro/a black (4)
neoyorquino/a *adj.* pertaining to New York
nerviosismo nervousness
nervioso/a nervous (6)
neumático tire (*automobile*)
neutralizar (c) to neutralize
neutro/a neutral
nevar (nieva) to snow (6); **nieva** it's snowing (6)
nevera refrigerator
ni neither; nor; **ni... ni** neither . . . nor
nicaragüense *n., adj. m., f.* Nicaraguan
niebla fog
nieto/a grandson/granddaughter (3)
ningún (ninguna) no, not any (7)
niñero/a baby-sitter (10)
niñez *f.* (*pl.* **niñeces**) infancy (16); childhood (16)
niño/a small child (3); boy/girl (3); **de niño/a** as a child (10)
nivel *m.* level
no no (1); **no creer** + *subjunctive* to not think/believe (13); **no es seguro/(im) posible, (im)probable** it's not certain / a sure thing/(im)possible, (im)probable (13); **no estar de acuerdo** to disagree (3); **no estar seguro/a de** to not be sure of (13); **no hay** there is/are not (1); **no hay de qué** you're welcome (1); **no hay problema** no problem (14); **no obstante** however; **no tener razón** to be wrong (4); **ya no** no longer
¿no? right, don't they (you...)? (4)
noche *f.* night; **buenas noches** goodnight (1); **de la noche** in the evening, P.M. (1); **esta noche** tonight (6); **por la noche** at night, in the evening (2)
Nochebuena Christmas Eve (9)
Nochevieja New Year's Eve (9)
nombrar to name
nombre *m.* name (7)
nopal *m. cactus*
noreste *m.* northeast
norma rule; norm
normal normal; **es normal que** + *subjunctive* it's normal that (13)
normalidad *f.* normality
noroeste *m.* northwest
norte *m.* north (6)
Norteamérica North America
norteamericano/a North American
nos *d. o. pron.* us; *i. o. pron.* to/for us; *refl. pron.* ourselves; **nos vemos** see you around (1)
nosotros/as *subj. pron.* we (2); *obj.* (*of prep.*) us (2)
nota grade (*academic*) (5); note
notar to note; to notice
noticias *f. pl.* news (5)
noticiero newscast (18)
notificación *f.* notification
novecientos/as nine hundred (4)
novela novel (13)
novelista *m., f.* novelist (13)
noveno/a ninth (13)

noventa ninety (3)
noviazgo engagement period (16)
noviembre *m.* November (6)
novio/a boyfriend/girlfriend (6); fiancé(e) (16); groom/bride (16)
nube *f.* cloud
nublado/a cloudy; **está (muy) nublado** it's (very) cloudy, overcast (6)
nuclear: energía nuclear nuclear energy (15)
nuestro/a(s) *poss. adj.* our (3); *poss. pron.* ours, of ours (17)
nueve nine (1)
nuevo/a new (3); **Año Nuevo** New Year; **Nueva York** New York
numérico/a numerical
número number (1); **número ordinal** ordinal number (13)
numeroso/a numerous
nunca never (3); **casi nunca** almost never (3)
nupcial nuptial; **votos** (*m. pl.*) **nupciales** wedding vows
nutritivo/a nutritious

O

o or (1)
obedecer (obedezco) to obey (15)
obispo bishop
objetivo *n.* objective
objeto object (2)
obligación *f.* obligation
obligado/a customary
obligatorio/a obligatory
obra work; **obra de arte** work of art (13); **obra de teatro** play (13); **obra maestra** masterpiece (13); **obra teatral** play
obrero/a worker, laborer (17)
observación *f.* observation
observar to observe
obstáculo obstacle
obstante: no obstante however
obtener (*like* **tener**) to get, obtain (12)
obvio/a obvious
ocasión *f.* occasion
ocasionar to cause
océano ocean (8); **océano Pacífico** Pacific Ocean
ochenta eighty (3)
ocho eight (1)
ochocientos/as eight hundred (4)
octavo/a eighth (13)
octubre *m.* October (6)
oculista *m., f.* ophthalmologist
oculto/a hidden
ocupación *f.* occupation
ocupado/a busy (6)
ocupar to hold; to occupy
ocurrir to occur (14)
odiar to hate (8)
oeste *m.* west (6)
ofensivo/a offensive
off: voz en off voice-over
oficial official
oficina office (2)
oficio trade (*type of job*) (17)
ofrecer (ofrezco) to offer (8)
ofrenda *n.* offering
oído inner ear (11)
oír to hear (5); to listen to (*music, the radio*) (5)
ojalá (que) I hope (that) (13)
ojo eye (11); **¡ojo!** *interj.* watch out!; **ojo alerta** eagle eye
olímpico/a: Juegos (*m. pl.*) **Olímpicos** Olympic Games
oliva: aceite (*m.*) **de oliva** olive oil (7)
olor *m.* odor
olvidar to forget (9)
omnipresente omnipresent
once eleven (1)
onda wave; **¿cuál es tu onda?** what's your style?; **en onda** in style; **¿qué onda?** what's new/happening?
onomatopeya onomatopoeia
onomatopéyico/a onomatopoeic
ONU *f.* **(Organización** [*f.*] **de Naciones Unidas)** U.N. (United Nations)
opción *f.* option
opcional optional
ópera opera (13)
operación *f.* operation
opinar to think; to have/express an opinion
opinión *f.* opinion
oponerse (a) (*like* **poner**) to oppose
oportunidad *f.* opportunity
optar (por) to opt (for)
optimista *m., f.* optimist; *adj.* optimistic
opuesto/a opposite
oración *f.* *gram.* sentence (2)
oral oral (14); **informe** (*m.*) **oral** oral report (14)
órale *interj. sl.* wow
orangután *m.* orangutan
órbita orbit
orden *m.* order
ordenado/a neat (6)
ordenador *m.* computer (*Sp.*)
ordenar to put in order
ordinal: número ordinal ordinal number (13)
ordinario/a ordinary
oreja (outer) ear (11)
orgánico/a organic
organismo organism
organización *f.* organization
organizar (c) to organize
órgano organ
orgullo pride
orgulloso/a proud
orientación *f.* orientation
oriental eastern
origen *m.* origin
originario/a native
originarse de to come from
oriundo/a native
oro gold (4); **de oro** gold (4)
orquesta orchestra (13)
orquídea orchid
ortografía spelling
ortográfico/a: acento ortográfico accent mark
oscuridad *f.* darkness
oso/a bear
ostra oyster
otavaleno/a *resident of Otavalo (Ecuador)*
otoño fall, autumn (6)
otorgar (gu) to grant
otro/a other, another (3); **otra vez** again; **por otro lado** on the other hand
oveja sheep
ozono: capa de ozono ozone layer (15)

P

paciencia patience
paciente *n. m., f.* patient (11); *adj.* patient
pacífico/a pacific; **océano Pacífico** Pacific Ocean
padrastro stepfather
padre *m.* father (3); *m. pl.* parents (3); **Día** (*m.*) **del Padre** Father's Day
padrino godfather
paella *Spanish dish made with rice, shellfish, and often chicken, and flavored with saffron*
pagado/a: empleo bien/mal pagado well-/poorly paid job/position (17)
pagar (gu) to pay (for) (2)
página page; **página web** webpage (12)
país *m.* country (3)
pájaro bird (3)
Pakistán Pakistan
pakistaní *m., f.* (*pl.* **pakistaníes**) Pakistani
palabra word (1); **palabra indefinida y negativa** *gram.* indefinite and negative word (7)
palacio palace
palestino/a Palestinian
palma palm tree
palmera palm tree
palo stick
palomitas *f. pl.* popcorn
pampa plain (*geography, Arg.*)
pan *m.* bread (7); **pan tostado** toast (7)
panadería bakery
panameño/a *n., adj.* Panamanian
páncreas *m. inv.* pancreas
pandemia pandemic
pandilla gang

pánel (*m.*) **solar** solar panel
panhispano/a Pan-Hispanic
pánico panic
panorama *m.* panorama
pantalla (grande/plana) (big/flat) screen (monitor) (12)
pantalones *m. pl.* pants (4); **pantalones cortos** shorts (4)
pañuelo handkerchief
papa (frita) (French fried) potato (7)
papá *m.* father, dad (3)
papel *m.* paper (2); role (13)
papi *m.* dad, daddy
par *m.* pair
para (intended) for; in order to (3); **para** + *inf.* (*do something*) (3); **para nada...** at all (8); **para que** so that, in order that (16)
parabrisas *m. inv.* windshield (15)
paracaídas *m. inv.* parachute
paracaidismo skydiving
parada stop (8); **hacer parada** to make a stop (8); **parada del autobús** bus stop (12); **parada del metro** subway stop (12)
paraguayo/a *n., adj.* Paraguayan
parar to stop (15)
parcial partial (14); **empleo de tiempo parcial** part-time job/position (17); **trabajo de tiempo parcial** part-time job (14)
pardo/a brown
parecer (parezco) (*like* **gustar**) to seem; **parecerse (a)** to resemble
pared *f.* wall (5)
pareja partner (3); significant other (3); couple (3)
paréntesis *m. inv.* parentheses
pariente *m.* relative (3)
parlamentario/a parliamentary
parque *m.* park
parqueadero parking lot
parquear to park
párrafo paragraph
parranda *Christmas party* (*Cuba*)
parrilla grill
parte *f.* part (5); **por todas partes** everywhere (14)
participación *f.* participation
participante *m., f.* participant
participar to participate
particular particular; unique; **en particular** particularly
partida: punto de partida starting point
partido game, match (10); political party (18)
partir: a partir de beyond (4)
pasado/a past, last (11); **el año pasado** last year; **pasado mañana** the day after tomorrow (5)
pasaje *m.* fare, price (*of a transportation ticket*) (8)
pasajero/a passenger (8)
pasaporte *m.* passport (8)
pasar to spend (*time*) (6); to happen (6); **pasar hambre** to go hungry; **pasar la aspiradora** to vacuum (10); **pasar las vacaciones en...** to spend one's vacation in . . . (8); **pasar por el control de seguridad** to go/pass through security (check) (8); **pasar por la aduana** to go/pass through customs (8); **pasar tiempo** to spend time (6); **pasarlo bien/mal** to have a good/bad time (9)
pasatiempo pastime (10)
Pascua Easter (9)
pasear to take a walk, stroll; to go for a ride; **pasear en bicicleta** to ride a bicycle (10)
paseo walk, stroll; **dar un paseo** to take a walk (10)
pasillo aisle (8)
pasión *f.* passion
paso step
pastel *m.* cake (7); pie (7); **pastel de cumpleaños** birthday cake (9)
pastilla pill (11)
pastor(a) minister
pata leg (*of an animal*)
patata potato
paternidad *f.* paternity
paterno/a paternal
patinaje *m.* skating (10)
patinar to skate (10)
patio patio (5); yard (5)
patojo/a *sl.* young man/woman (*Guat.*)
patriarcal patriarchal
Patricio: Día (*m.*) **de San Patricio** St. Patrick's Day
patrimonio patrimony
patriota *m., f.* patriot
patriótico/a patriotic
patronal: fiesta patronal *party dedicated to patron saint*
pavo turkey (7)
paz *f.* (*pl.* **paces**) peace (18)
peca freckle
pecho chest
pedazo piece
pedir (pido) (i) to ask for (5); to order (5); **pedir disculpas** to apologize (14)
pegar (gu) to hit, strike (14); **pegarse con/contra** to run, bump into/against (14)
peinarse to comb/brush one's hair (5)
Pekín Peking
pelado/a *sl.* young man/woman (*Col.*)
pelear to fight (10)
pelícano pelican
película movie (5)
peligro danger (15); **especie** (*f.*) **en peligro de extinción** endangered species (15)
peligroso/a dangerous
pelo hair; **teñirse (me tiño) (i) el pelo** to dye one's hair; **tomarle el pelo** to pull someone's leg
pelota ball (10)
pelotero/a baseball player
peluche: animal (*m.*) **de peluche** stuffed animal
peluquero/a hairstylist (17)
pena pity
pendiente *m.* earring (*Sp.*)
península peninsula
pensar (pienso) (de/en) to think (about) (5); **pensar** + *inf.* to intend, plan to (*do something*) (5); **pensar que** to think that (5)
penúltimo/a next to last
peor worse (6); **peor(es) que** worse than (6)
pepino cucumber (7)
pequeño/a small (3)
percatarse to realize
percepción *f.* perception
percibir to perceive
percusión *f.* percussion
perder (pierdo) to lose; to miss (*an event*) (5)
perdón excuse me (1)
perdonar to forgive
perdurable lasting
peregrinación *f.* pilgrimage
perezoso/a lazy (3)
perfección *f.* perfection
perfecto/a perfect
pérfido/a treacherous
perfil *m.* profile
perforación *f.* drilling (*well*)
perfume *m.* perfume
periódico newspaper (3)
periodismo journalism
periodista *m., f.* journalist (17)
período period (*of time*)
permanecer (permanezco) to remain, stay
permanente permanent
permiso permission; permit; **(con) permiso** excuse me (1); **permiso de manejar** driving permit
permitir to permit, allow (12)
pero but (1)
perro dog (3)
persecución *f.* persecution
perseguir (*like* **seguir**) to chase; to pursue
persona person (2)
personaje *m.* character (*book, movie*)
personal (*m.*) **médico** medical personnel (11)
personal *adj.* personal; **pronombre** (*m.*) **personal** *gram.* personal pronoun (2)
personalidad *f.* personality
perspectiva perspective

persuasivo/a persuasive
pertenecer (pertenezco) a to belong to
perturbar to perturb, bother
peruano/a *n., adj.* Peruvian
pesado/a boring (10); heavy
pesar to weigh; **a pesar de** in spite of
pesas: levantar pesas to lift weights (11)
pescadería fish market
pescado fish (*cooked*) (7)
pescar (qu) to fish
pesimista *m., f.* pessimistic
peso weight
pestaña eyelash
petición *f.* request
petróleo petroleum, oil (15)
petrolero/a *adj.* oil; petroleum
pez *m.* (*pl.* **peces**) fish (*live*) (15)
picante hot, spicy (7)
picar (qu) to bite; to sting
pícnic: hacer un pícnic to have a picnic (10)
pico peak
pie *m.* foot (11); **dedo del pie** toe (11); **levantarse con el pie izquierdo** to get up on the wrong side of the bed (14)
piedra stone
piel *f.* skin
pierna leg (11)
pieza piece
pila battery; **ponerse las pilas** to get one's act together; to energize oneself
pilar *m.* pillar
Pilates: hacer (el método) Pilates to do Pilates (11)
píldora pill
piloto *m., f.* pilot (8)
pimienta pepper (*condiment*) (7)
pingüino penguin
pino pine (tree)
pinola *m. typical Nicaragua drink*
pintar to paint (13)
pintor(a) painter (13)
pintura painting (*in general*; *specific piece*) (12)
piña pineapple
pirámide *f.* pyramid
piraña piranha
Pirineos *m. pl.* Pyrenees
piscina swimming pool (5)
Piscis *m.* Pisces
pisco *alcoholic beverage of Peru and Chile*
piso floor (*of a building*) (12); floor (*of a room*); **barrer el piso** to sweep the floor (10); **primer piso** first floor (second story) (12); **segundo piso** second floor (third story) (12)
pizarra chalkboard
pizarrón *m.* **(blanco)** (white)board (2)
placa license plate
placer *m.* pleasure
plan *m.* plan (10); **hacer planes para** + *inf.* to make plans to (*do something*) (10)
planchar to iron (10)
planeación *f.* planning
planear to plan
planeta *m.* planet (15)
planetario/a planetary
plano map (*of a city*); blueprint
plano/a flat (12); **pantalla plana** flat screen (monitor) (12)
planta plant
planta baja ground floor (12)
plantación *f.* plantation
plasma: televisión plasma plasma television (*f.*) (12)
plástico plastic
plata *n.* silver (4); **de plata** *adj.* silver (4)
plátano plantain
platino platinum
plato dish (*food prepared in a particular way*) 7; course (7); plate (5); **plato principal** main course (7)
playa beach (6)
plaza plaza, square (4)
plazo deadline (14); **a plazos** in installments (17)
pleno/a complete; full
plomero/a plumber (17)
pluma pen
plurinacional multinational
población *f.* population (15)
pobre poor (3)
pobreza poverty
poco (a) little (2); few (4); **un poco (de)** a little bit (of) (2)
poder *v.* to be able, can (4)
poder *n. m.* power; **poder adquisitivo** purchasing power
poderoso/a powerful
poema *m.* poem (13)
poesía poetry
poeta *m., f.* poeta (13)
poético/a poetic
polaco/a Polish
policía *m., f.* police officer (15); *f.* police (*force*); **mujer** (*f.*) **policía** policewoman
polinésico/a Polynesian
política politics (18); policy (18)
político/a *n.* politician (18); *adj.* political; **ciencias** (*f. pl.*) **políticas** political science (2)
pollera *indigenous skirt of the Andes*
pollo chicken (7); **pollo asado** roast chicken (7); **pollo frito** fried chicken
polvo dust
poner to put (5); to place (5); to turn on (*an appliance*) (5); **poner atención** to pay attention; **poner la mesa** to set the table (10); **ponerle una inyección** to give (*someone*) a shot (11); **ponerse** to put on (*an article of clothing*) (5); **ponerse** + *adj./adv.* to become, get + *adj./adv.* (9); **ponerse las pilas** to get one's act together; to energize oneself; **ponerse rojo/a** to blush (9)
popularidad *f.* popularity
por about (6); because of (6); through (8); for (8); by (14); **gracias por** + *noun/inf.* thanks for (9); **por consiguiente** as a result; **por Dios** for heaven's sake (14); **por ejemplo** for example (14); **por otro lado** on the other hand; **por ello** therefore; **por eso** for that reason (3); **por favor** please (1); **por fin** finally (5); **por la mañana** in the morning (2); **por la noche** at night, in the evening (2); **por la tarde** in the afternoon (2); **por lo general** generally (5); **por lo menos** at least (9); **por lo regular** in general; **por primera/última vez** for the first/last time (14); **por si acaso** just in case (14); **¡por supuesto!** of course! (14); **por todas partes** everywhere (14); **por un lado** on one hand
porcentaje *m.* percentage
porción *f.* portion, part
pormenorizado/a detailed
poro pore
porotos *m. pl.* beans
¿por qué? why? (3)
porque because (3)
portafolio portfolio
portarse bien/mal to (mis)behave (9)
portátil portable (2); **computadora portátil** laptop (computer) (2); **ordenador** (*m.*) **portátil** (*Sp.*) laptop computer
portero/a building manager (12); doorman (12)
portón *m.* front door; gate
portugués *m.* Portuguese (*language*)
portugués, portuguesa *n., adj.* Portuguese
posar to pose
posesión *f.* possession
posesivo/a possessive (17); **adjetivo posesivo** *gram.* possessive adjective (3)
posibilidad *f.* possibility
posible possible (3); **es posible que** + *subjunctive* it's possible that (13); **no es posible que** + *subjunctive* it's not possible that (13)
posición *f.* position
positivo/a positive
posponer (*like* **poner**) to postpone
postal: tarjeta postal postcard (8)
posterior later, subsequent
postre *m.* dessert (7)

postularse to run (18); **postularse como candidato/a** to run as a candidate (18); **postularse para un cargo** to run for a position (18)
postura posture
potencia power
potencial *m.* potential; *adj.* potential
práctica practice
practicar (qu) to practice (2); **practicar el alpinismo** to mountain climb; **practicar un deporte** to play a sport
práctico/a practical
pradera meadow
preadolescencia preadolescence
precedente *m.* precedent
preceder to precede
precio (fijo) (fixed, set) price (4)
precioso/a precious
precipicio precipice
precipitado/a hasty
precisamente precisely
precolombino/a pre-Columbian
predicción *f.* prediction
predominante predominant
predominar to predominate
preescolar *adj.* preschool
preferencia preference (1)
preferir (prefiero) (i) to prefer (4)
pregunta question (5); **hacer una pregunta** to ask a question (5)
preguntar to ask (*a question*) (8)
prehispánico/a pre-Hispanic (*before the arrival of the Spanish*)
prehistórico/a prehistoric
premio prize
prenda article of clothing
prender to fasten
prensa (print) press (18); news media (18); **quiosco de prensa** newsstand (18)
prensado/a pressed
preocupación *f.* worry
preocupado/a worried (6)
preocupar(se) to worry
preparación *f.* preparation
preparar to prepare (7); **prepararse** to prepare oneself; to get ready
preparatoria **(prepa)** pre-university study
preposición *f. gram.* preposition (5)
prescribir to prescribe
preseleccionado/a pre-selected
presencia presence
presencial: de forma presencial in person
presentación *f.* presentation
presentador(a) presenter; (television) anchor
presentar to introduce; to present
presente *m.* present (*time*); *gram.* present tense; *adj.* present
preservar to preserve
presidencia presidency
presidencial presidential
presidente/a president
presión *f.* pressure (14); **estar bajo muchas presiones** to be under a lot of pressure (14); **tener muchas presiones** to have a lot of pressure (14)
preso/a prisoner
préstamo loan (17)
prestar to lend (8)
prestigioso/a prestigious
presupuestario/a budgetary
presupuesto budget (17)
pretérito *gram.* preterite
preuniversitario/a pre-university
prevenir (*like* **venir**) to warn
primario/a primary; first; elementary; **escuela primaria** elementary school
primavera spring (6)
primero *adv.* first (5)
primer(o/a) first (5); **por primera vez** for the first time (14); **el primero de** the first of (*month*) (6); **primer piso** first floor (second story) (12)
primo/a cousin (3); *m. pl.* cousins (3)
princesa princess
principal main; **plato principal** main course (7)
príncipe *m.* prince
principiante *m., f.* beginner; novice
principio beginning; **al principio de** at the beginning of (17)
priorizar (c) to prioritize
prisa: tener prisa to be in a hurry (4)
privacidad *f.* privacy
privado/a private
privilegio privilege
probabilidad *f.* probability
probable probable (13); **es probable que** + *subjunctive* it's likely, probable that (13); **no es probable que** + *subjunctive* it's not probable that (13)
probar (pruebo) to try, taste
problema *m.* problem; **no hay problema** no problem (14)
problemático/a problematic
procedimiento procedure
procesión *f.* procession
proceso process
proclamar to proclaim
procurar to procure
producción *f.* production
producir (*like* **conducir**) to produce
productivo/a productive
producto product; **producto nacional bruto** gross national product
productor(a) producer
profesión *f.* profession (17)
profesional *n. m., f.* professional, person with a profession; *adj.* professional
profesionista *n. m., f.* professional, person with a profession
profesor(a) professor (1)
profesorado faculty
profundidad *f.* depth
profundo/a deep
programa *m.* program; **programa (del curso)** (course) syllabus (14)
programación *f.* programming
programador(a) programmer (17)
progresivo/a progressive
progreso progress
prohibir (prohíbo) to prohibit, forbid (12)
proliferación *f.* proliferation
promedio average
promesa promise
prometer to promise (8)
prominente prominent
promover (promuevo) to promote
pronombre *m. gram.* pronoun (2); **pronombre personal** *gram.* personal pronoun (2); **pronombre relativo** *gram.* relative pronoun
pronosticar (qu) to forecast
pronóstico forecast
pronto *adv.* soon; **hasta pronto** see you soon; **tan pronto como** *conj.* as soon as (17)
pronunciación *f.* pronunciation
pronunciar to pronounce
propiedad *f.* property; characteristic
propio/a own, one's own (4)
proponer (*like* **poner**) to propose
proporción *f.* proportion
proporcionar to provide
propósito purpose
prórroga extension
protagonista *m., f.* protagonist
protección *f.* protection
protector(a) protective
proteger (protejo) to protect (15)
proteína protein
protestante *n., adj. m., f.* Protestant
protestantismo Protestantism
protestar to protest
provecho: ¡buen provecho! bon appetit! (7); enjoy your meal! (7)
proveedor(a) provider
proveer (*like* **creer**) to provide
proverbio proverb
providencia providence
provincia province
provocar **(qu)** to cause
próximo/a next; **el próximo (martes...)** next (Tuesday . . .) (5); **la próxima semana** next week (5)
proyección *f.* projection
proyecto project
prudente prudent
prueba quiz (14); test (14); proof
publicación *f.* publication

publicar (qu) to post (*as on Facebook*) (12); to publish (12)
publicidad *f.* publicity
publicitario/a *adj.* advertising
público *n.* audience (13)
público/a *adj.* public (15); **transporte** (*m.*) **público** public transportation
pueblo town
puente *m.* bridge
puerco pig
puerta door (2); **puerta de embarque** boarding gate (8)
puerto port (8)
puertorriqueño/a *n., adj.* Puerto Rican
pues *conj.* well
puesto job; position; place (*in line*) (8)
pulgada inch
pulido/a polished
pulmones *m. pl.* lungs (11)
pulpería grocery store (*C.A.*)
pulpo octopus
punto point; **a punto de** + *inf.* about to + *inf.;* **en punto** on the dot (*time*) (1); **hora punta** peak hour; **punto cardinal** cardinal point (6); **punto de partida** starting point; **punto de vista** point of view
puntuación *f.* punctuation
pupusa *thick stuffed corn tortilla*
puro cigar
puro/a pure (15)
púrpura *n.* purple
purpúreo/a *adj.* purple

Q

que that, which (3); who (3); **así que** therefore, consequently, so; **hasta que** *conj.* until; **que Dios te bendiga** God bless you; **ya que** since
¿qué? what? which? (1); **¿a qué hora... ?** at what time . . . ? (1); **¿con qué frecuencia... ?** how often . . . ? (3); **¿por qué?** why? (3)
¡qué... ! what . . . !; **¡qué** + *adj.***!** how + *adj.*! (14); **¡qué** + *noun***!** what (a) + *noun* (14); **¡qué bacán!** fantastic!
quebrarse (me quiebro) to break
quedar to remain, be left (14); **quedarse** to stay, remain (*in a place*) (6)
quehacer (*m.*) **doméstico** household chore (10)
quejarse (de) to complain (about) (8)
quemada *n.* burn
quemar to burn
querer to want (4); to love (16); **eso quiere decir...** that means . . . (11); **fue sin querer** I didn't mean (to do) it (14); **quererse** to love each other (11); to be fond of each other (11)
querido/a dear (6)
queso cheese (7)
quetzal *currency of Guatemala*
quien who; whom
¿quién(es)? who? whom? (1); **¿de quién?** whose? (3)
química chemistry (2)
quince fifteen (1); **menos quince** fifteen minutes until (*hour*) (1); **y quince** fifteen minutes after (*the hour*) (1)
quinceañera young woman's fifteenth birthday party (9); young woman who is turning fifteen
quinientos/as five hundred (4)
quinto/a fifth (13)
quiosco de prensa newsstand (18)
quiropráctico/a chiropractor
quitar to remove; **quitar la mesa** to clear the table (10); **quitarse** to take off (*an article of clothing*) (5)
quizás *adv.* perhaps

R

rabia rutera road rage
ración *f.* portion
radiante bright, shining, radiant
radical *m. gram.* root
radio *m.* radio (*apparatus*) (12); *f.* radio (*medium*) (18); **estación** (*f.*) **de radio** radio station (18)
radioyente *m., f.* radio listener; *m. pl.* radio audience
raíz *f.* (*pl.* **raíces**) root
rama branch
rana frog
ranchera *traditional music of Mexico*
rancho ranch
rap *m.* rap music
rapanui *n. m., f. indigenous person of Easter Island*
rápido *adv.* quickly
rápido/a fast; **comida rápida** fast food
rápidos *m. pl.* rapids
raqueta racket
raro/a rare; strange
rascacielos *m. inv.* skyscraper (15)
rata rat
rato while, short time; **ratos libres** (*m. pl.*) spare (free) time (10)
ratón *m.* mouse (12)
raya: de rayas striped (4)
rayar to scratch
raza race (*ethnic*)
razón *f.* reason; **no tener razón** to be wrong (4); **tener razón** to be right (4)
reacción *f.* reaction
reaccionar to react
real royal; real
realidad *f.* reality
realismo realism
realista *m., f.* realistic
realizar (c) to achieve; to attain
rebaja sale, reduction (4); *pl.* sales, reductions (4); **en rebaja** on sale
rebanada slice
rebasar to pass (*a vehicle*)
rebelde *n. m., f.* rebel; *adj.* rebellious
rebelión *f.* rebellion
recado message
recámara bedroom
recepción *f.* reception
recepcionista *m., f.* receptionist
receptor *m.* receiver; recipient
receta recipe (7); prescription (11)
recetar to prescribe
recibir to receive (3)
recibo receipt (17)
reciclaje *m.* recycling (15)
reciclar to recycle (15)
recién recently (16); **recién casado/a** newlywed (16)
reciente recent
recipiente *m.* container
recíproco/a reciprocal
recitar to recite
recoger (recojo) to collect (14); to pick up (14)
recomendable recommendable
recomendación *f.* recommendation
recomendar (recomiendo) to recommend (8)
reconocer (*like* **conocer**) to recognize
reconocimiento recognition
reconquista reconquest
reconstituido/a remarried; hybrid (*of a family*)
reconstituir (*like* **construir**) to reconstitute; to reconstruct
recordar (recuerdo) to remember (9)
recrear to recreate
recreo recess
recto/a straight; **(todo) recto** straight ahead (15)
rector(a) university president
recuerdo memory
recuperación *f.* recuperation
recuperador(a) recuperative
recuperar to recuperate
recurso resource (15); **recurso natural** natural resource (15)
red *f.* network; internet; **navegar (gu) la red** to surf the internet; **red social** social network (12)
redacción *f.* editing
redactar to write; to edit
reducción *f.* reduction
reducir (*like* **conducir**) to reduce
reemplazar (c) to replace
referencia reference
referirse (me refiero) (i) (a) to refer (to)
refinado/a refined
reflejar to reflect

reflexivo/a reflexive; **verbo reflexivo** *gram.* reflexive verb (5)
reforma change
refrán *m.* saying, proverb
refresco soft drink (7)
refrigerador *m.* refrigerator (10)
refrigeradora refrigerator
refugio refuge
regalar to give (*as a gift*) (8)
regalo present, gift (3)
regatear to haggle (4); to bargain (4)
regateo bartering
reggae *m.* reggae
régimen *m.* regime
región *f.* region
regir (rijo) (i) to govern
registración *f.* registration
registrar to register
registro register; record
regla rule
regresar to return (*to a place*) (2); **regresar a casa** to go home (2)
regulador(a) regulator
regular *adj.* so-so (1); **por lo regular** in general; *v.* to regulate
regularidad *f.* regularity
reina queen (18)
reinar to reign
reino kingdom
reírse (río) (i) (de) to laugh (about) (9)
reiterar to reiterate
reivindicación *f.* vindication
reivindicar (qu) to reclaim
reja bar (*of prison*)
relación *f.* relation; relationship; **relación sentimental** emotional relationship (16)
relacionar to relate
relajado/a relaxed
relajante relaxing
relajarse to relax
relámpago lightning
relativo/a: pronombre (*m.*) **relativo** *gram.* relative pronoun
relevante relevant
religión *f.* religion
religioso/a religious
relleno/a filled
reloj *m.* watch (4)
remarcar (qu) to remark
remate: de remate hopeless(ly)
remedio remedy
remodelado/a remodeled
remoto/a: control (*m.*) **remoto** remote control (12)
remuneración *f.* remuneration
renovable renewable (15); **energía renovable** renewable energy (15)
renovar (renuevo) to renew
rentar to rent (*Mex.*)
renunciar (a) to resign (from) (17)
reparar to repair (15)
repasar to review
repaso review
repeler to repel
repente: de repente suddenly (11)
repetición *f.* repetition
repetir (repito) (i) to repeat
repetitivo/a repetitive
reportaje *m.* report (*on a news show*)
reportar to report
reportero/a reporter (18)
represa dam
representación *f.* representation
representante *n. m., f.* representative; **representante al congreso** congressional representative (18)
representar to represent
representativo/a *adj.* representative
república republic
republicano/a republican
requerir (requiero) (i) to require
requisito requirement
rescatar to rescue
reseña review (*book, movie*)
reserva reserve; reservation (*Sp.*); **hacer reserva** to make a reservation
resfriado *n.* cold (*illness*) (11)
resfriado/a *adj.* congested, stuffed up (11)
resfriarse (me resfrío) to catch/get a cold (11)
residencia dormitory (2); **residencia de ancianos** nursing home (12)
residente *m., f.* resident
residuos *m. pl.* waste
resistente resistant; strong
resistir to resist
resolver (resuelvo) (*p.p.* **resuelto**) to solve (15); to resolve (15)
respectivo/a respective
respecto: a este respecto in this regard; **(con) respecto a** regarding
respetar to respect
respeto respect
respiración *f.* breathing
respirar to breathe (11)
responder to respond
responsabilidad *f.* responsibility (18); **responsabilidad cívica** civic duty (18)
responsable responsible
respuesta answer (6)
restablecimiento re-establishment; restoration
restaurante *m.* restaurant (7)
resto rest, remainder
restricción *f.* restriction
resuelto/a (*p.p. of* **resolver**) resolved
resultado result
resumen *m.* summary; **en resumen** in summary
resumir to summarize
resurrección *f.* resurrection
retribuir (*like* **contribuir**) to reward
retrospectivo/a retrospective
retumbar to resound
reunión *f.* meeting
reunirse (me reúno) (con) to get together (with) (9)
revelar to reveal
revés: al revés backwards
revisar to check (15)
revista magazine (3)
revolucionario/a revolutionary
revolver (*like* **volver**) to stir
rey *m.* king (18)
rezar (c) to pray
Ricitos de Oro Goldilocks
rico/a rich (3); tasty, savory; rich (*in calories*) (7)
ridículo/a ridiculous
riesgo risk; **de alto riesgo** high risk
rígido/a rigid
rima rhyme
rimar to rhyme
rincón *m.* corner
rinoceronte *m.* rhinoceros
riñón *m.* kidney
río river (15)
rioplatense *adj., m., f.* from the **Río de la Plata** area
riqueza richness
risa laughter
ritmo rhythm; **ritmo lento / acelerado de la vida** slow / fast pace of life (15)
rito rite; ritual
robar to rob; to steal
robo theft; robbery
rodante: cinta rodante treadmill
rodeado/a (de) surrounded (by)
rodear to go around
rojo/a red (4); **ponerse rojo/a** to blush (9)
Roma Rome
romano/a Roman
romántico/a romantic
romper(se) (*p.p.* **roto**) to break (14); **romper (con)** to break up (with) (16)
ron *m.* rum
ropa clothing (4); **ropa interior** underwear (4)
ropero wardrobe
rosa rose; **rosa té** tea rose
rosado/a pink (4)
rosario rosary
rostro face
roto/a (*p.p. of* **romper**) broken
rotulador *m.* felt-tipped pen
rubio/a blond(e) (3)
rueda wheel, tire; **rueda de molino** treadmill
ruido noise (5)
ruidoso/a noisy
ruina ruin (13)

ruso Russian (*language*)
ruso/a *n., adj.* Russian
ruta route
rutero/a: rabia rutera road rage
rutina routine (5)
rutinario/a *adj.* routine (11)

S

sábado Saturday (5)
saber (sé) to know (*facts, information*) (7); **saber** + *inf.* to know how to (*do something*) (7)
sabiduría wisdom
sabio/a wise
sabor *m.* flavor
sabroso/a tasty
sacar (qu) to get (*grades*) (14); to withdraw, take out (17); **sacar dinero** to withdraw money; **sacar fotos / fotografías** to take photos (8); **sacar la basura** to take out the trash (10); **sacar la lengua** to stick out one's tongue (11)
sacerdote *m.* priest
safari: ir de safari to go on a safari
Sagitario Sagittarius
sagrado/a sacred
sal *f.* salt (7)
sala living room (5); **sala de espera** waiting room (8); **sala de fumadores/ de fumar** smoking area (8); **sala de urgencias** emergency room
salarial: brecha salarial wage gap
salario pay, wages (*often per hour*) (17)
salchicha sausage (7); hot dog (7)
salida departure (8)
salir (de) to leave (*a place*) (5); **salir bien/mal** to come/turn out well/ poorly (5); to do well/poorly (5); **salir (con)** to go out (with) (5); **salir de vacaciones** to leave on vacation (8); **salir (para)** to leave (for) (*a place*) (5)
salmón *m.* salmon (7)
salón (*m.*) **de clase** classroom (2)
salsa sauce (7); salsa (*music*)
salsero/a *adj.* salsa (*music*)
saltar to jump
salud *f.* health (11)
saludable healthy
saludarse to greet each other (11)
saludo greeting (1)
salvadoreño/a *n., adj.* Salvadoran
salvaje wild (15)
salvar to save
san, santo/a *n.* saint; **Día** (*m.*) **de San Patricio** St. Patrick's Day; **Día** (*m.*) **de San Valentín** St. Valentine's Day
sanador(a) healer
sancocho *stew made with meat, cassava, and plantains*
sandalias *f. pl.* sandals (4)
sandía watermelon
sándwich *m.* sandwich (7)
sangre *f.* blood (11)
sangriento/a bloody
sanitario/a health; **asistencia sanitaria** health care
sano/a healthy (11); **llevar una vida sana** to lead a healthy life (11)
santo saint
santo/a holy
santuario sanctuary
sarcástico/a sarcastic
sartén *f.* skillet
satélite *m.* satellite
satírico/a satirical
satisfacción *f.* satisfaction
satisfactorio/a satisfactory
satisfecho/a satisfied
Saudito/a: Arabia Saudita Saudi Arabia
sazonar to season
secadora clothes dryer (10)
secar(se) (qu) to dry (oneself)
sección *f.* section
seco/a dry
secretario/a secretary (2)
secreto *n.* secret
secreto/a *adj.* secret
secuencia sequence
secundario/a secondary; **escuela secundaria** high school
sed *f.* thirst (7); **tener (mucha) sed** to be (very) thirsty (7)
seda silk (4); **de seda** *adj.* silk (4)
sedentario/a sedentary
seducir (*like* **conducir**) to seduce
segmento segment
seguida: en seguida immediately (5)
seguidor(a) follower
seguimiento following
seguir (sigo) (i) to continue (6); to keep on going (15)
según according to (3)
segundo/a second (13); **segundo piso** second floor (third story) (12)
seguridad *f.* security; safety; **control** (*m.*) **de seguridad** security (check) (8); **pasar por el control de seguridad** to go/pass through security (check) (8)
seguro *n.* insurance
seguro/a *adj.* sure, certain (6); **es seguro que** + *indicative* it's certain/a sure thing that (13) **no es seguro que** + *subjunctive* it's not sure that (13); **no estar seguro/a de** to not be sure of (13)
seis six (1)
seiscientos/as six hundred (4)
selección *f.* selection; choice
seleccionador(a) *adj.* selection
seleccionar to select; to choose
selva jungle; **Selva Amazónica** Amazon Jungle
selvático/a *adj.* jungle
semáforo traffic signal (15)
semana week; **días** (*m. pl.*) **de la semana** days of the week (5); **fin** (*m.*) **de semana** weekend (2); **la próxima semana** next week (5); **la semana que viene** next week (5); **una vez a la semana** once a week (3)
semanal *m., f.* weekly
sembrar (siembro) to sow, plant
semejante similar
semejanza similarity
semestre *m.* semester
semi-cerrado/a semiclosed
semilla seed
senado senate
senador(a) senator (18)
sencillo/a simple
senda path
senderismo *n.* hiking
sendero path
sensación *f.* sensation
sensibilidad *f.* sensitivity
sensible sensitive
sentarse (me siento) to sit down (5)
sentido sense
sentimental: relación (*f.*) **sentimental** emotional relationship (16)
sentimiento feeling, emotion
sentir (siento) (i) to regret (13); to feel sorry (13); **lo siento (mucho)** I'm (very) sorry (14); **sentirse** + *adj./adv.* to feel + *adj./adv.* (9)
señalar to note; to point out
señor (Sr.) *m.* man; Mr.; sir (1)
señora (Sra.) woman; Mrs.; ma'am (1)
señorita (Srta.) young woman; Miss; Ms. (1)
separación *f.* separation (16)
separado/a (de) separated (from) (16)
separarse (de) to separate (from) (16)
septiembre *m.* September (6)
séptimo/a seventh (13)
ser to be (1); **ayer fue (miércoles...)** yesterday was (Wednesday . . .) (5); **¿cómo es usted?** what are you (*form. s.*) like? (1); **¿de dónde eres (tú)?** where are you (*fam. s.*) from? (1); **¿de dónde es (usted)?** where are you (*form. s.*) from? (1); **de última moda** it's trendy (hot) (4); **eres** you are (1); **es** he/ she is, you (*form. s.*) are (1); **es absurdo que** + *subjunctive* it's absurd that (13); **es cierto que** + *indicative* it's certain that (13); **es de...** it is made of . . . (4); **es extraño que** + *subjunctive* it's strange that (13); **es importante que** + *subjunctive* it's important that (12); **es (im)posible que** + *subjunctive* it's (im)possible that (13); **es (im)probable que** + *subjunctive*

it's (un)likely, (im)probable that (13); **es increíble que** + *subjunctive* it's incredible that (13); **es la una** it's one o'clock (1); **es mejor** it's better (12); **es necesario** it's necessary (12); **es normal que** + *subjunctive* it's normal that (13); **es seguro que** + *indicative* it's certain / a sure thing that (13); **es terrible que** + *subjunctive* it's terrible that (13); **es una lástima que** + *subjunctive* it's a shame that (13); **es urgente *que*** + *subj.* it's urgent that (12); **es verdad que** + *indicative* it's true that (13); **fue sin querer** I didn't mean (to do) it (14); **llegar (gu) a ser** to become; **no es (im)probable que** + *subjunctive* it's not (im)probable that (13); **no es posible que** + *subjunctive* it's not posible that (13); **no es seguro que** + *subj.* it is not certain / a sure thing that (13); **pasar de ser** to go from being; **¿qué hora es?** what time is it? (1); **ser aburrido/a** to be boring (10); **ser aficionado/a (a)** to be a fan (of) (10); **ser casado/a** to be a married person (16); **ser divertido/a** to be fun (10); **ser en** + *place* to take place in/at (*a place*) (9); **son las...** it's . . . o'clock (1); **(yo) soy de...** I am from . . . (1)

ser (*m.*) **humano** human being

serie *f.* series

serio/a serious

serpiente *f.* snake

servicio service (15); **estación** (*f.*) **de servicio** gas station (15); **servicio militar** military service (18)

servilleta napkin

servir (sirvo) (i) to serve (5); **servir para** to be used for (5)

sesenta sixty (3)

sesión *f.* session

setecientos/as seven hundred (4)

setenta seventy (3)

sevillano/a of or pertaining to Seville

sexismo sexism

sexo sex

sexto/a sixth (13)

si if (4); **por si acaso** just in case (14)

sí yes (1); **sí, me gusta...** yes, I like . . . (1)

sicología psychology (2)

sicólogo/a psychologist (17)

siempre always (3)

sierra mountain

siesta nap; **dormir (duermo) (u) la siesta** to take a nap (5)

siete seven (1)

siglo century (10)

significado meaning

significar (qu) to mean

significativo/a significant

signo sign

siguiente following (5)

sílaba syllable

silencio silence

silla chair (2)

sillón *m.* armchair (5)

simbólico/a symbolic

simbolizar (c) to symbolize

símbolo symbol

similaridad *f.* similarity

similitud *f.* similarity

simpático/a nice, likeable (*people*) (3)

sin without (5); **fue sin querer** I didn't mean (to do) it (14); **sin duda** without a doubt; **sin embargo** nevertheless (6); **sin que** *conj.* without; unless (16)

sinagoga synagogue

sinceridad *f.* sincerity

sincero/a sincere

sino but (rather); **sino que** *conj.* but (rather)

sinónimo synonym

sintético/a synthetic

síntoma *m.* symptom (11)

siquiatra *m., f.* psychiatrist (17)

sísmico/a seismic

sismorresistente earthquake resistant

sistema *m.* system (17); **analista** (*m., f.*) **de sistemas** systems analyst (17)

sistemático/a systematic

sitio place, location (12); **sitio web** website (12)

situación *f.* situation

situado/a situated

situarse (me sitúo) to situate oneself; to be placed (*in time*)

snowboard *m.* snowboarding

soberano/a sovereign

sobre *prep.* about (4); on; on top of; over

sobremesa after-dinner conversation

sobrenatural *adj.* supernatural

sobresaliente outstanding

sobresalir (*like* **salir**) to stand out

sobreviviente *adj., m., f.* surviving

sobrevivir to survive

sobrino/a nephew/niece (3)

social social; **ciencias** (*f. pl.*) **sociales** social sciences (2); **red** (*f.*) **social** social network (12); **trabajador(a) social** social worker (17)

socialismo socialism

socialista *n., adj. m., f.* socialist

socializar (c) to socialize

sociedad *f.* society

socioeconómico/a socioeconomic

sociología sociology (2)

sodio sodium

sofá *m.* couch (5)

soja soybean

sol *m.* sun (6); **gafas** (*f. pl.*) **de sol** sunglasses (4); **hace (mucho) sol** it's (very) sunny (6); **tomar el sol** to sunbathe (8)

solamente only (14)

solar solar (8); **bloqueador** (*m.*) **solar** sunscreen (8); **energía solar** solar energy (15); **pánel** (*m.*) **solar** solar panel

solas: a solas alone

soldado *m., f.* soldier

soleado/a sunny

soledad *f.* solitud

soler (suelo) to tend to

solicitante *m., f.* applicant

solicitar to apply for (*a job*) (17)

solicitud *f.* job application (*form*) (17)

sólido/a solid

solitario/a solitary, lonely

solo *adv.* only (2)

solo/a *adj.* alone (5)

soltero/a single, not married (16)

soltura: hablar con soltura to speak fluently

solución *f.* solution

sombra shadow; shade

sombrero hat (4); **sombrero hongo** bowler hat, derby

sonar (sueno) to ring (10); to sound (10)

sonido sound

sonreír (*like* **reír**) to smile (9)

sopa soup (7)

soportar to bear

sor *f.* sister (*religious*)

sorber to absorb

sorprendente surprising

sorprender (*like* **gustar**) to surprise (13)

sorpresa surprise

sospechoso/a suspicious

sostenible sustainable

sostenido/a held

su(s) *poss. adj.* his, her, its, your (*form. s.*); their, your (*form. pl.*) (3)

suave mild, smooth, soft

subir (a) to go up; to get on (*a vehicle*) (8)

subjuntivo *gram.* subjunctive

subordinado/a: cláusula subordinada *gram.* subordinate clause

subregión *f.* subregion

substituir (*like* **construir**) to substitute

subtítulo subtitle

suburbio suburb

suceder to occur; to happen

suceso happening

sucesor(a) successor

sucio/a dirty (6)

sudadera sweatshirt (4)

Sudamérica South America

sudamericano/a South American

Suecia Sweden

sueco/a Swedish

suegro/a father-in-law, mother-in-law
sueldo salary (17)
suelo floor (*of a room*)
sueño dream; **tener sueño** to be sleepy (4)
suerte *f.* luck (14); **tener buena/mala suerte** to have good/bad luck (14); to be (un)lucky (14)
suéter *m.* sweater (4)
suficiente enough (11); **lo suficiente** enough (11)
sufijo *gram.* suffix
sufrimiento suffering
sufrir (de) to suffer (from) (14)
sugerencia suggestion
sugerir (sugiero) (i) to suggest (9)
suicidio suicide
suizo/a Swiss
sujeto *gram.* subject
sumo/a supreme
superar to overtake
superhombre *m.* superman
superlativo *gram.* superlative
supermercado supermarket (12)
superstición *f.* superstition
supersticioso/a superstitious
supervisor(a) supervisor
suplemento supplement
suponer (*like* **poner**) to suppose
supremo/a supreme
supuesto: ¡por supuesto! of course! (14)
sur *m.* south (6)
sureste *m.* southeast
surfear to surf (10)
suroeste *m.* southwest
surrealismo surrealism
surrealista *adj. m., f.* surrealist
suscripción *f.* subscription
suspender to suspend
suspenso suspense
sustantivo *gram.* noun (2)
sustrato essence
sutil subtle
SUV *m.* SUV (15)
suyo/a(s) *poss. adj.* your (*form. s., pl.*) (17); his, her, its, their (17); *poss. pron.* (of) your, yours (*form. s., pl.*) (17); (of) his, her, its, their (17); (of) theirs (17)

T

tabaco tobacco
tabla table; chart
tableta tablet
tabú *f.* taboo
tacón *m.* heel
taconeo heel tap
tailandés, tailandesa Thai
Tailandia Thailand
taíno/a *pre-Hispanic culture of the Caribbean*
tal such, such a; **con tal de** *prep.* provided (16); **con tal (de) que** *conj.* provided (that), as long as (16); **¿qué tal?** how are you? (1); **tal como** just as; **tal vez** perhaps
taladro drill
talento talent
talla size
taller *m.* (repair) shop (15)
tamal *m.* tamale
tamalada *get-together to make and eat tamales*
tamaño size
también also (1)
tambor *m.* drum
tambora African drum
tampoco neither, not either (7)
tan *adv.* so; as; **tan... como** as . . . as (6); **tan pronto como** as soon as (17)
tanque *m.* tank (15)
tanto/a *adj.* as much, so much; such (a); *pl.* so many; as many; **tanto como** as much as (6); **tanto/a(os/as)... como** as much/many . . . as (6)
tapa lid
tapar to cover
tapas *f. pl.* appetizers (9)
tapir *m.* tapir
taquigrafía shorthand
tardar to be long / take (a long) time
tarde *adv.* late (2)
tarde *f.* afternoon (1); **buenas tardes** good afternoon (1); **de la tarde** in the afternoon, P.M. (1); **por la tarde** in the afternoon (2)
tarea homework (5); **tarea doméstica** household chore
tarjeta card (8); **tarjeta bancaria / de débito** debit card (17); **tarjeta de crédito** credit card (7); **tarjeta de embarque** boarding pass (8); **tarjeta de identidad** identification card; **tarjeta de identificación** identification card, ID (14); **tarjeta postal** postcard (8)
tarta cake
tartamudo/a stutterer
tata *fam.* grandpa
tatuaje *m.* tattoo
taza cup (14)
te *dir. obj. pron.* you (*s. fam.*); *indir. obj. pron.* to/for you (*s. fam.*); *refl. pron.* yourself (*s. fam.*); **¿te gusta...?** do you (*fam. s.*) like . . . ? (1)
té *m.* tea (7); **rosa té** tea rose
teatral theatrical; **obra teatral** play
teatro theater; **ir al teatro** to go to the theater (10); **obra de teatro** play (13)
techo roof
teclado keyboard
técnico/a technician (17)
tecnología technology (12)
tecnológico/a technological
teja tile
tejedor(a) weaver
tejer to weave (13)
tejido weaving; *pl.* woven goods (13); textiles
tela cloth
tele *f.* T.V.
telediario news program
telefonear to phone
telefonía telephone systems
telefónico/a *adj.* telephone
teléfono (celular) (cell) phone (2); **hablar por teléfono** to talk on the phone (2); **teléfono fijo** landline (12)
telegrama *m.* telegram
telenovela soap opera
telespectador(a) television viewer
televidente *m., f.* television viewer
televisión (*f.*) (**plasma**) (plasma) television (12); **mirar la tele(visión)** to watch television (3)
televisor *m.* television set
tema *m.* theme, topic
temblar (tiemblo) to tremble
temblor *m.* trembling
temer to fear, be afraid (13)
temperatura temperature (11); **tomarle la temperatura** to take someone's temperature (11)
templo temple (16)
temporada season (*hunting, fashion, etc.*)
temporal temporary
temprano *adv.* early (2)
tendencia tendency
tender (tiendo): tender la cama to make the bed
tenedor *m.* fork
tener to have (4); **no tener razón** to be wrong (4); **tener... años** to be . . . years old (3); **tener buena/mala suerte** to have good/bad luck (14); to be (un)lucky (14); **tener cuidado** to be careful; **tener dolor de** to have a pain/ache in (11); **tener éxito** to be successful; **tener fiebre** to have a fever; **tener ganas de** + *inf.* to feel like (*doing something*) (4); **tener la culpa** to be at fault; **tener miedo (de)** to be afraid (of) (4); **tener (mucha) hambre** to be (very) hungry (7); **tener (mucha) sed** to be (very) thirsty (7); **tener muchas presiones** to have a lot of pressure (14); **tener (mucho) calor** to be (very) warm, hot (6); **tener (mucho) frío** to be (very) cold (6); **tener prisa** to be in a hurry (4); **tener que** + *inf.* to have to (*do something*) (4); **tener razón** to be right (4); **tener sueño** to be sleepy (4)
tenis *m. inv.* tennis (10); *pl.* tennis shoes (4)

tensión *f.* tension; **tensión arterial** blood pressure

tentación *f.* temptation

tentempié *m.* snack

teñirse (me tiño) (i) el pelo to dye one's hair

teoría theory

terapeuta *m., f.* therapist

terapia therapy

tercer(o/a) third (13)

tereré *m. traditional Paraguayan drink*

terminación *f. gram.* ending

terminal *m.* station, terminal

terminar to finish

término term

termómetro thermometer

ternura tenderness

terraza terrace

terremoto earthquake

terreno piece of land

terrestre *adj.* earth

terrible terrible (13); **es terrible que** + *subjunctive* it's terrible that (13)

territorio territory

terrorismo terrorism (18)

terrorista *m., f.* terrorist (18); **ataque** (*m.*) **terrorista** (terrorist) attack (18)

tertulia get-together

tesis *f. inv.* thesis

testigo *m., f.* witness (18)

testimonio testimony

texteo text (message)

textil *adj.* textile

texto text; **libro de texto** textbook (2); **mandar un mensaje (de texto)** to send a text (2)

ti (*obj. of prep.*) you (*fam.*) (6)

tibetano/a Tibetan

tiempo weather (6); time (6); *gram.* tense; **a tiempo** on time (8); **conjunción** (*f.*) **de tiempo** conjunction of time (17); **empleo de tiempo completo/parcial** full-/part-time job/position (17); **hace (muy) buen/mal tiempo** it's (very) good/bad weather (6); **jornada de tiempo parcial** part-time job; **¿qué tiempo hace?** what's the weather like? (6); **tiempo libre** free time (10); **trabajo de tiempo completo/parcial** full/part-time job (14)

tienda shop, store (4); **tienda de acampar** tent; **tienda (de campaña)** tent (8)

tierra land

Tierra Earth (15)

tigre *m.* tiger

tihuanaco/a Tiwanakan (*of or pertaining to the pre-Columbian Tiwanaku civilization of Bolivia*)

tilma poncho; shawl

timbre *m.* doorbell

tímido/a shy

tina bathtub

tinieblas *f. pl.* darkness

tinto/a: vino tinto red wine (7)

tío/a uncle/aunt (3); *m. pl.* aunts and uncles (3)

típico/a typical

tipo type, kind; **de todo tipo** of all kinds

tira cómica comic strip

tirar to throw

tiritar to shiver

títere *m.* puppet

título title

toalla towel (5)

toallero towel rack

tocar (qu) to touch; to play (*a musical instrument*) (2); to honk (15); **tocarle a uno** to be someone's turn (10)

todavía still (6); yet

todo *n.* everything; **de todo** everything (4); **de todo tipo** of all kinds

todo/a *adj.* all (3); every (3); **por todas partes** everywhere (14); **todo derecho/recto** straight ahead (15); **todos los días** every day (2)

todoterreno *inv.* all-terrain (15)

tolerante tolerant

tomar to take (2); to drink (2); **tomar el sol** to sunbathe (8); **tomar unas vacaciones** to take a vacation (8); **tomarle el pelo** to pull (someone's) leg; **tomarle la temperatura** to take someone's temperature (11)

tomate *m.* tomato (7)

tono tone

tonto/a silly, foolish (3)

toque *f.* touch

torno: en torno a around

toro bull (15)

torpe clumsy (14)

torre *f.* tower

torta sandwich (*Mex.*)

tortilla potato omelet (*Sp.*); *thin unleavened cornmeal or flour pancake* (*Mex.*)

tortuga turtle

tos *f.* cough (11)

tosco/a rustic; crude

toser to cough (11)

tostado/a toasted (7); **pan** (*m.*) **tostado** toast (7)

tostadora toaster (10)

tostones *m. pl. crispy fried plantain slices*

totalidad *f.* totality

trabajador(a) *adj.* hardworking (3)

trabajador(a) *n.* worker (17); **trabajador(a) social** social worker (17)

trabajar to work (2)

trabajo work (10); job (10); report, (piece of) work (14); **carga de trabajo** workload; **trabajo de tiempo completo/parcial** full-/part-time job (14)

trabajólico/a workaholic

trabalenguas *m. inv.* tongue twister

tractor *m.* tractor

tradición *f.* tradition (13); **tradición cultural** cultural tradition (13)

tradicional traditional

traducción *f.* translation

traducir (*like* **conducir**) to translate

traductor(a) translator (17)

traer to bring (5)

tráfico traffic (15)

tragedia tragedy

trágico/a tragic

traje *m.* suit (4); **traje de baño** swimsuit (4)

trámite *m.* step; procedure

tranquilo/a calm (9); **llevar una vida tranquila** to lead a calm life (11)

transatlántico *n.* ocean liner

transbordador (*m.*) **espacial** space shuttle

transformar to transform

transición *f.* transition

tránsito traffic (15)

transmitir to pass on; to transmit

transnacional international

transporte *m.* transportation (8); **medio de transporte** means of transportation (8); **transporte público** public transportation

tras *prep.* after

trasero/a back, rear

trasladarse to move

trastienda back room (*of a store*)

tratable treatable

tratado treaty

tratamiento treatment (11)

tratar de + *inf.* to try to (*do something*) (13); **tratar de** + *noun* to deal with + *noun*

través: a través de across; through; throughout

travieso/a mischievous

trayectoria trajectory; path

trébol *m.* clover

trece thirteen (1)

treinta thirty (1); **y treinta** thirty minutes past (*the hour*) (1)

tren *m.* train (8); **estación** (*f.*) **de trenes** train station (8); **ir en tren** to go/travel by train (8)

tres three (1)

trescientos/as three hundred (4)

triángulo triangle

tribu *f.* tribe

tributo tribute

trigo wheat

trilogía trilogy
trimestre *m.* trimester
triste sad (6)
tristeza sadness
triunfar to triumph
trofeo trophy
trompeta trumpet
tropical tropical; **bosque** (*m.*) **tropical lluvioso** tropical rain forest
trópico *n.* tropics
tropiezo mistake
trotadora treadmill
trozo piece
trucha trout
trueno thunder
tú *subj. pron.* you (*fam. s.*) (2); **¿de dónde eres (tú)?** where are you (*fam. s.*) from? (1); **¿y tú?** and you (*fam. s.*)? (1)
tu(s) your (*fam. s.*) (3)
tuit *m.* tweet (12)
tuitear to tweet
tumba tomb
tuna cactus fruit
turismo tourism
turista *n. m., f.* tourist
turístico/a *adj.* tourist
turnarse to take turns
turno shift (*on a job*)
turrón *m. type of candy traditionally eaten at Christmas*
tutor(a) tutor
tuyo/a(s) *poss. adj.* your (*fam. s.*); *poss. pron.* yours, of yours (*fam. s.*) (17)
Twitter *m.* Twitter (12)

U

u or (*before words beginning with the sound* **o-**) (3)
ubicar (qu) to locate
ucraniano/a Ukranian
¡uf! *interj.* oof!; whew!
últimamente lately (14)
último/a last, final (14); latest (4); **es de última moda** it's trendy (hot) (4); **por última vez** for the last time (14)
ultramoderno/a ultramodern
un, uno/a one (1); *ind. art.* a, an; **un millón (de)** one million (4); **un poco (de)** a little bit (of) (2); **una vez a la semana** once a week (3)
unánime unanimous
único/a *adj.* only; unique
unidad *f.* unity
unido/a united; **Estados** (*m. pl.*) **Unidos de América** United States of America; **Naciones** (*f. pl.*) **Unidas** United Nations; **Organización** (*f.*) **de Naciones Unidas (ONU)** United Nations (U.N.)
unificar (qu) to unify
unión *f.* union
unir to join (together); to unite; **unirse a** to join (*a cause, organization*)
universidad *f.* university (2)
universitario/a *adj.* (of the) university (14)
universo universe
urbanistico/a *adj.* of urban development
urbano/a urban
urgencias: sala de urgencias emergency room
urgente urgent (12); **es urgente que** + *subjunctive* it's urgent that (12)
uruguayo/a *n., adj.* Uruguayan
usar to wear (4); to use (4)
USB: memoria USB pen drive (12)
uso use
usted (Ud., Vd.) *sub. pron.* you (*form. s.*) (2); *obj.* (*of prep.*) you (*form. s.*) (2); **¿a usted le gusta... ?** do you (*form. s.*) like . . . ? (1); **¿cómo es usted?** what are you (*form. s.*) like? (1); **¿cómo se llama usted?** what is your (*form. s.*) name? (1); **¿de dónde es usted?** where are you (*form. s.*) from? (1); **¿y usted?** and you (*form. s.*)? (1)
ustedes (Uds., Vds.) *sub. pron.* you (*form. pl.*); *obj.* (*of prep.*) you (*form pl.*) (2)
usuario/a user (12)
útil useful
utilidad *f.* utility
utilizar (c) to use; to utilize
uva grape
¡uy! *interj.* oh!; ah!

V

vaca cow (15)
vacaciones *f. pl.* vacation (8); **de vacaciones** on vacation (8); **estar de vacaciones** to be on vacation (8); **ir de vacaciones a...** to go on vacation to/in. . . (8); **pasar las vacaciones en...** to spend one's vacation in . . . (8); **salir de vacaciones** to leave on vacation (8); **tomar unas vacaciones** to take a vacation (8)
vacuna vaccine (11); **ponerle una vacuna** to give someone a vaccination (11)
vacunación *f.* vaccination
vacunarse to get a shot
vainilla vanilla
valenciano/a Valencian
Valentín: Día (*m.*) **de San Valentín** St. Valentine's Day
valiente courageous
valioso/a valuable
valle *m.* valley
vallenato *Colombian folk music*
valor *m.* value
valorar to value
valorización *f.* appreciation
vals *m. inv.* waltz
vampiro vampire
vanagloriarse to brag
vandalismo vandalism
vapor *m.* mist
vaquero/a cowboy/cowgirl
variación *f.* variation
variante variant
variar (varío) to vary
variedad *f.* variety
varios/as several
vasco/a *n., adj.* Basque
vasija earthenware pot; vessel
vaso (drinking) glass
vasto/a vast
vecindario neighborhood
vecino/a neighbor (12)
vegano/a *n., adj.* vegan
vegetariano/a *n., adj.* vegetarian
vehículo vehicle (15)
veinte twenty (1)
veinticinco twenty-five (1)
veinticuatro twenty-four (1)
veintidós twenty-two (1)
veintinueve twenty-nine (1)
veintiocho twenty-eight (1)
veintiséis twenty-six (1)
veintisiete twenty-seven (1)
veintitrés twenty-three (1)
veintiún, veintiuno/a twenty-one (1)
vejez *f.* (*pl.* **vejeces**) old age (16)
vela candle (9)
velocidad *f.* speed (15); **límite** (*m.*) **de velocidad** speed limit (15)
vena vein
vendedor(a) salesperson (17)
vender to sell (3)
Venecia Venice
venerar to revere; to venerate
venezolano/a *n., adj.* Venezuelan
venir to come (4); **el año que viene** next year; **el lunes** (*m.*) **que viene** next Monday (5); **la semana que viene** next week (5)
venta sale
ventaja advantage
ventana window (2)
ventanilla small window (*on a plane*) (8)
ver (*p.p.* **visto**) to see (5); **a ver** let's see; **nos vemos** see you around (1)
verano summer (6)
veras: ¿de veras? really
verbo *gram.* verb (2); **verbo reflexivo** *gram.* reflexive verb (5)
verdad *f.* truth; **es verdad que** it's true that (13)
¿verdad? right, don't they (you...)? (4)
verdadero/a true; real
verde green (4)
verduras *f. pl.* vegetables (7)
vergonzoso/a shameful

vergüenza embarrassment
verificar (qu) to verify
versión *f.* version
verso verse; line of a poem
verter (vierto) (i) to spill; to shed (*a tear*)
vestido dress (4)
vestir (visto) (i) to dress; **vestirse** to get dressed (5)
veterano/a *n.* veteran
veterinario/a veterinarian (17)
vez *f.* (*pl.* **veces**) time; **a veces** sometimes, at times (3); **alguna vez** once; ever (15); **cada vez más** increasingly; **cada vez mayor** greater and greater; **dos veces** twice (11); **en vez de** instead of; **otra vez** again; **por primera/última vez** for the first/last time (14); **tal vez** perhaps; **una vez** once; **una vez a la semana** once a week (3)
viajar to travel (8)
viaje *m.* trip (5); **agencia de viajes** travel agency; **agente de viajes** travel agent; **de viaje** on a trip, traveling (8); **hacer un viaje** to take a trip (5)
viajero/a traveler
vial *adj.* road
vicepresidente/a vice president
víctima victim (18)
victoria victory
vicuña vicuna (llama)
vida life (11); **vida académica** academic life (14); **llevar una vida sana/ tranquila** to lead a healthy/calm life (11); **ritmo lento / acelerado de la vida** slow / fast pace of life (15)
video video (12)
videocasetera video cassette recorder
videojuego videogame; **jugar (juego) (gu) a los videojuegos** to play videogames (10)
videollamada video call
videoturismo videotourism
vidrio glass
viejo/a old (3)
viento wind (6); **hace (mucho) viento** it's (very) windy (6)
viernes *m. inv.* Friday (5)
vietnamita *n., adj. m., f.* Vietnamese
vikingo/a Viking
vinagre *m.* vinegar
vino (blanco, tinto) (white, red) wine (7)
violación *f.* violation
violencia violence; **Día** (*m.*) **Internacional de la No Violencia Contra la Mujer** International Day for the Elimination of Violence against Women
violento/a violent
violín *m.* violin
Virgen *f.* Virgin (Mary)
virreinato viceroyalty
virus *m. inv.* virus
visión *f.* vision
visita visit (11)
visitante *m., f.* visitor
visitar to visit (10)
víspera eve
vista view (12); **punto de vista** point of view
viudo/a widower/widow (16)
vivienda housing (12)
vivir to live (3)
vivo/a lively; bright (*of colors*)
vocabulario vocabulary
vocal *f.* vowel
voga: en voga in vogue
volante *m.* steering wheel; **furia al volante** road rage
volar (vuelo) to fly; **volar en avión** to fly (8); to go by plane (8)
volcán *m.* volcano
volcánico/a volcanic
voleibol *m.* volleyball (10)
voltear to turn (over)
volumen *m.* volume
voluntario/a volunteer
volver (vuelvo) (*p.p.* **vuelto**) to return (*to a place*) (5); **volver a** + *inf.* to (*do something*) again (5)
vos *subj. pron.* you (*fam. s. C.A., S.A.*)
vosotros/as *sub. pron.* you (*fam. pl. Sp.*); *obj.* (*of prep.*) you (*fam. pl. Sp.*) (2)
votación *f.* vote; voting
votante *m., f.* voter
votar to vote (18)
votos (*m. pl.*) **nupciales** wedding vows
voz *f.* (*pl.* **voces**) voice (12); **buzón** *m.* **de voz** voice mailbox (12); **voz en off** voice over
vudú *m.* voodoo
vuelo flight (8); **asistente** (*m., f.*) **de vuelo** flight attendant (8)
vuelta: billete *m.* (*Sp.*) / **boleto** (*L.A.*) **de ida y vuelta** round-trip ticket (8)
vuelto/a (*p.p. of* **volver**) returned
vuestro/a(s) your (*fam. pl. Sp.*) (3); *poss. pron.* your, of yours (*fam. pl. Sp.*) (17)

W

web: página web webpage (12); **sitio web** website (12)
wifi *m.* wifi (12)

Y

y and (1); **y cuarto** a quarter (fifteen minutes) after (*the hour*) (1); **y media** half past (*the hour*) (1); **y quince** fifteen minutes after (*the hour*) (1); **y treinta** thirty minutes past (*the hour*) (1) **¿y tú?** and you (*fam. s.*)? (1); **¿y usted?** and you (*form. s.*)? (1)
ya already (9); **ya no** no longer; **ya que** since
yacimiento deposit (*mineral*)
yerba herb
yerno son-in-law
yo *sub. pron.* I (2); **yo soy de...** I am from . . . (1)
yoga *m.* yoga; **hacer (el) yoga** to do yoga (10)
yogur *m.* yogurt (7)
yuca cassava, manioc; **¡qué yuca!** how difficult!

Z

zalamería flattery
zampoña *South American panpipe*
zanahoria carrot (7)
zancudo mosquito
zapatería shoe store
zapato shoe (4); *pl.* shoes (4)
zarzuela *traditional Spanish operetta*
zócalo central plaza (*Mex.*)
Zodíaco Zodiac
zona zone (12); area (12)
zoología zoology
zumo juice (*Sp.*)

VOCABULARIES

English-Spanish Vocabulary

A

@ **arroba** (12)
A.M. **de la mañana** (1)
able: to be able **poder** (4)
about **por** (6); **sobre** (4)
abroad: to go abroad **ir al extranjero** (8)
absence **falta** (15)
absent: to be absent (from) **faltar (a)** (9)
absentminded **distraído/a** (14)
absurd: it's absurd that **es absurdo que** + *subjunctive* (13)
academic **académico/a** (14); academic life **vida académica** (14)
accelerated **acelerado/a** (15); **ritmo acelerado de la vida** fast pace of life (15)
accept **aceptar** (14)
accident **accidente** *m.* (14)
according to **según** (3)
account **cuenta** (17)
accountant **contador(a)** (17)
ache *n.* (in) **dolor (de)** (11); *v.* **doler (duele)** (*like* **gustar**) (11); to have an ache in **tener dolor de** (11)
acquainted: to be acquainted with **conocer (conozco)** (7)
act *v.* **actuar (actúo)** (13)
activity: fun activity **diversión** *f.* (10)
actor **actor** *m.* (13); **actriz** *f.* (*pl.* **actrices**)
additional **adicional** (1)
address **dirección** *f.* (7)
adjective *gram.* **adjetivo** (3); adjective of nationality **adjetivo de nacionalidad** (3); possessive adjective **adjetivo posesivo** (3)
administration: business administration **administración** (*f.*) **de empresas** (2)
adolescence **adolescencia** (16)
adolescent: as an adolescent **de adolescente** (10)
advice (piece of) **consejo** (7)
advisor **consejero/a** (2)
aerobics: to do aerobics **hacer ejercicios aeróbicos** (11)
affection **cariño** (16)
affectionate **cariñoso/a** (6)
afraid: to be afraid (of) **tener miedo (de)** (4), **temer** (13)
after *prep.* **después de** (5); *conj.* **después (de) que** (17)
afternoon: good afternoon **buenas tardes** (1); **muy buenas** (1); in the afternoon **de la tarde** (1), **por la tarde** (2)
afterward **luego** (5); afterwards **después** (5)
agent **agente** *m., f.* (8)
ago **hace** + *time* + **que** + *preterite* (14); *preterite* + **hace** + *time* (14)
agree **estar de acuerdo** (3)
agriculture **agricultura** (15)
ahead: straight ahead **(todo) derecho** (15), **todo recto** (15)
air **aire** *m.* (15)
airplane **avión** *m.* (8)
airport **aeropuerto** (8)
aisle **pasillo** (8)
alarm clock **despertador** *m.* (14)
all **todo/a** (3)
all-terrain **todoterreno** *inv.* (15)
allow **permitir** (12)
almost **casi** *inv.* (3); almost never **casi nunca** (3)
alone **solo/a** (5)
alongside of **al lado de** (6)
already **ya** (9)
also **también** (1)
always **siempre** (3)
am: I am **soy** (1); I am from **soy de** (1)
America: of the United States of America *n., adj.* **estadounidense** (3)
among *prep.* **entre** (6)
analyst: systems analyst **analista** (*m., f.*) **de sistemas** (17)
and **y** (1); **e** (*before words beginning with the sound* **i-**) (3); and you? **¿y tú?** *fam. s.* (1), **¿y usted?** *form. s.* (1)
android **android** *m.* (12)
angry **enojado/a** (9); **furioso/a** (6); to get angry with (someone) about (something) **enojarse con (alguien) por (algo)** (9)
animal **animal** *m.* (15)
announce **anunciar** (8)
annoyed **molesto/a** (6)
another **otro/a** (3)
answer *n.* **respuesta** (6); *v.* to answer **contestar** (7)
antibiotic **antibiótico** (11)
anxiety **ansiedad** *f.* (14)
any **algún (alguna/os/as)** (7); not any **ningún (ninguna)** (7)
anybody: not anybody **nadie** (7)
anyone **alguien** (7)
anything **algo** (7); not anything **nada** (7)
apartment **apartamento** (2); apartment building **edificio de apartamentos** (12)
apologize **pedir (pido) (i) disculpas** (14)
apology **disculpa** (14)
app(lication) **app** *f.* (12)
appetizers **botanas** *f. pl.* (*Mex.*) (9); **tapas** *f. pl.* (9)
apple **manzana** (7)
appliance: home appliance **aparato doméstico** (10)
applicant **aspirante** *m., f.* (17)
application (*form*) **solicitud** *f.* (17)
apply for (*a job*) **solicitar** (17)
appointment **cita** (11)
April **abril** *m.* (6)
architect **arquitecto/a** (13)
architecture **arquitectura** (13)
are: you (*fam. s.*) are **eres** (1); you (*form. s.*) are **es** (1)
area **zona** (12); smoking area **sala de fumadores/de fumar** (8)
argue with (someone) about (something) **discutir con (alguien) por/sobre (algo)** (9)
arm **brazo** (11)
armchair **sillón** *m.* (5)
armoire **armario** (5)
army **ejército** (18)
arrival **llegada** (8)
arrive **llegar (gu)** (3)
art **arte** *m.* (2); arts and crafts **artesanía** (13); the arts **artes** *f. pl.* (13); work of art **obra de arte** (13)
artist **artista** *m., f.* (13)
artistic **artístico/a** (13); artistic expression **expresión** (*f.*) **artística** (13)
as: as . . . as **tan... como** (6); as a child **de niño/a** (10); as a youth **de adolescente** (10); as long as *conj.* **con tal (de) que** (16); as much as **tanto como** (6); as much/many . . . as **tanto/a(os/as)... como** (6); as soon as **en cuanto** (17), **tan pronto como** (17)
ask (a question) **hacer una pregunta** (5), **preguntar** (8); to ask for **pedir (pido) (i)** (5)
asleep: to fall asleep **dormir(se) ([me] duermo) (u)** (5)
asparagus **espárragos** *m. pl.* (7)

assassinate **asesinar** (18)
assassination **asesinato** (18)
astronaut **astronauta** *m., f.* (17)
at **en** (1); at . . . (*time of day*) **a la(s)...** (1); at all **(para) nada** (8); at home **en casa** (2); at least **por lo menos** (9); at the beginning of **al principio de** (17); at times **a veces** (3); at what time . . . ? **¿a qué hora... ?** (1)
attack **ataque** *m.* (18); terrorist attack **ataque** (*m.*) **terrorista** (18)
attend (*class, function*) **asistir (a)** (3); to not attend **faltar (a)** (9)
attendant: flight attendant **asistente** (*m., f.*) **de vuelo** (8)
attract **atraer** (*like* **traer**) (*like* **gustar**) (13)
audience **espectadores** *m. pl.* (13); **público** (13)
August **agosto** (6)
aunt **tía** (3); aunts and uncles **tíos** *m. pl.* (3)
author **autor(a)** (13)
automatic teller machine (ATM) **cajero automático** (17)
auto(mobile) **auto(móvil)** *m.* (15)
autumn **otoño** (6)
avenue **avenida** (12)
avocado **aguacate** *m.* (7)
avoid **evitar** (15)
awful: an awful lot **muchísimo** (8)

B

babysitter **niñero/a** (10)
back tooth **muela** (11)
backpack **mochila** (2)
bad **mal, malo/a** (3); (very) bad (weather) out **(muy) mal tiempo** (6); the bad news/thing **lo malo** (11); to have a bad time **pasarlo mal** (9); to have bad luck **tener mala suerte** (14)
badly: to come/turn out badly **salir mal** (5)
baggage **equipaje** *m.* (8); to check baggage **facturar el equipaje** (8)
baked custard **flan** *m.* (7)
ball **pelota** (10)
ballet **ballet** *m.* (13)
banana **banana** (7)
bank **banco** (17)
bar: to go to a bar **ir a un bar** (10)
barbecue **barbacoa** (7)
bargain *n.* **ganga** (4); *v.* **regatear** (4)
baseball **béisbol** *m.* (10); baseball cap **gorra** (4)
basketball **basquetbol** *m.* (10)
bath: to take a bath **bañarse** (5)
bathe **bañarse** (5)
bathroom **baño** (5); bathroom sink **lavabo** (5)
bathtub **bañera** (5)
battery **batería** (15)
be **estar** (2); **ser** (1), (3); to be . . . years old **tener... años** (3); to be a fan (of) **ser aficionado/a (a)** (10); to be a married person **ser casado/a** (16); to be able **poder** (4); to be absent (from) **faltar (a)** (9); to be afraid **temer** (13); to be afraid (of) **tener miedo (de)** (4); to be boring **ser aburrido/a** (10); to be born **nacer (nazco)** (16); to be certain of **estar seguro/a de** (13); to be (very) cold **tener (mucho) frío** (6); to be comfortable (*temperature*) **estar bien** (6); to be distracted **ir distraído/a** (14); to be fond of each other **quererse** (11); to be fun **ser divertido/a** (10); to be happy (about) **alegrarse (de)** (12); to be (very) hungry **tener (mucha) hambre** (7); to be in a hurry **tener prisa** (4); to be left **quedar** (14); to be lucky **tener buena suerte** (14); to be married (to) **estar casado/a (con)** (16); to be on a diet **estar a dieta** (7); to be on vacation **estar de vacaciones** (8); to be right **tener razón** (4); to be sleepy **tener sueño** (4); to be (very) stressed, under (a lot of) stress **estar (muy) estresado/a** (14); to be (very) thirsty **tener (mucha) sed** (7); to be under a lot of pressure **estar bajo muchas presiones** (14); to be uncertain of **no estar seguro/a de**; to be unlucky **tener mala suerte** (14); to be up to date **estar al día** (18); to be used for **servir (sirvo) (i) para** (5); to be (very) warm, hot **tener (mucho) calor** (6); to be wrong **no tener razón** (4)
beach **playa** (6)
beans **frijoles** *m. pl.* (7)
beautiful **bello/a** (15)
because **porque** (3); because of **por** (6)
become + *adj./adv.* **ponerse** + *adj./adv.* (9)
bed **cama** (5); to get out of bed **levantarse** (5); to get up on the wrong side of the bed **levantarse con el pie izquierdo** (14); to go to bed **acostarse (me acuesto)** (5); to make the bed **hacer la cama** (10); to stay in bed **guardar cama** (11)
bedroom **alcoba** (5)
beer **cerveza** (7)
before *prep.* **antes** (5); **antes de** (16); *conj.* **antes (de) que** (16)
begin **empezar (empiezo) (c)** (5); to begin to (*do something*) **empezar a** + *inf.* (5)
beginning: at the beginning of **al principio de** (17)
behave **portarse bien** (9)
behind *prep.* **detrás de** (6)
believe (in) **creer (en)** (3); to not believe **no creer** (13)
below *prep.* **debajo de** (6)
belt **cinturón** *m.* (4)
best **mejor** (6); better than **mejor(es) que** (6)
better **mejor** (6)
between *prep.* **entre** (6)
beyond **a partir de** (4)
bicycle **bicicleta** (10); to ride a bicycle **montar en bicicleta** (10); **pasear en bicicleta** (10)
bicycling **ciclismo** (10)
big **gran, grande** (3); big screen (monitor) **pantalla grande** (12)
bill (*restaurant*) **cuenta** (7); **factura** (17); (*money*) **billete** *m.* (17)
bird **pájaro** (3)
birthday **cumpleaños** *m. inv.* (6); birthday cake **pastel** (*m.*) **de cumpleaños** (9); to have a birthday **cumplir años** (9)
black **negro/a** (4)
blog **blog** *m.* (12)
blond(e) **rubio/a** (3)
blood **sangre** *f.* (11)
blouse **blusa** (4)
blue **azul** (4)
blue jeans ***jeans*** *m. pl.* (4)
blush *v.* **ponerse rojo/a** (9)
board **pizarrón** *m.* (2)
boarding: boarding gate **puerta de embarque** (8); boarding pass **tarjeta de embarque** (8)
boat **barco** (8); to go/travel by boat **ir en barco** (8)
body: human body **cuerpo humano** (11)
bomb **bomba** (18)
bon appetit! **¡buen provecho!** (7)
book **libro** (2)
bookshelf **estante** *m.* (5)
bookstore **librería** (2)
boots **botas** *f. pl.* (4)
bore **aburrir** (*like* **gustar**) (13)
bored **aburrido/a** (6); to get bored **aburrirse** (10)
boring **pesado/a** (10); to be boring **ser aburrido/a** (10)
born: to be born **nacer (nazco)** (16)
bother **molestar** (*like* **gustar**) (11)
boy **niño** (3); **chico** (4)
boyfriend **novio** (6)
brain **cerebro** (11)
brakes **frenos** *m. pl.* (15)
bread **pan** *m.* (7)
break **romper(se)** (14); to break up (with) **romper (con)** (16)
breakfast **desayuno** (7); to have (eat) breakfast **desayunar** (7)

breathe **respirar** (11)
bride **novia** (16)
bring traer (5)
brother **hermano** (3)
brown **(de) color café** (4)
brunet(te) **moreno/a** (3)
brush one's hair **peinarse** (5); to brush one's teeth **cepillarse los dientes** (5)
budget **presupuesto** (17)
build **construir** (15)
building **edificio** (2); apartment building **edificio de apartamentos** (12); building manager **portero/a** (12)
bull **toro** (15)
bump against **chocar (qu) con/contra** (14); **pegarse (gu) con/contra** (14)
bureau **cómoda** (5)
bus **autobús** *m.* (8); bus station **estación** (*f.*) **de autobuses** (8); bus stop **parada del autobús** (12); to go/travel by bus **ir en autobús** (8)
business **empresa** (17); business administration **administración** (*f.*) **de empresas** (2)
businessman **hombre** (*m.*) **de negocios** (17)
businesswoman **mujer** (*f.*) **de negocios** (17)
busy **ocupado/a** (6)
but **pero** (1)
butter **mantequilla** (7)
buy **comprar** (2); **comprar por internet** to buy online (4)
by **por** (14); by check **con cheque** (17)

C

cabin (*on a ship*) **cabina** (8)
cafeteria **cafetería** (2)
cake **pastel** *m.* (7); birthday cake **pastel de cumpleaños** (9)
calculator **calculadora** (2)
calendar **calendario** (14); personal calendar **agenda** (14)
call **llamar** (7); to be called **llamarse** (5)
calm **tranquilo/a** (9); to lead a calm life **llevar una vida tranquila** (11)
camera **cámara** (12)
campground ***camping*** *m.* (8)
camping: to go camping **hacer *camping*** (8)
can (*be able*) **poder** (4)
candidate (*for a job*) **aspirante** *m., f.* (17); (*political*) **candidato/a** (18); to run as a candidate **postularse como candidato/a** (18)
candle **vela** (9)
candy **dulces** *m. pl.* (7)
cap (baseball) **gorra** (4)
capital city **capital** *f.* (6)
car **coche** *m.* (3); **carro** (15); convertible car **coche/carro descapotable** (15)
card: (post)card **tarjeta (postal)** (8); credit card **tarjeta de crédito** (7); debit card **tarjeta bancaria** (17), **tarjeta de débito** (17); identification card **tarjeta de identificación** (14); to play cards **jugar (juego) (gu) a las cartas** (10)
cardinal point **punto cardinal** (6)
care: to take care of **cuidar de** (11); to take care of oneself **cuidarse** (11)
carrot **zanahoria** (7)
carry **llevar** (4)
case: in case *prep.* **en caso de** (16); in that case *adv.* **entonces** (8); *conj.* **en caso de que** (16); just in case **por si acaso** (14)
cash (*a check*) **cobrar** (17); *n.* **efectivo** (17); in cash **en efectivo** (17)
cashier (check-out) **cajero/a** (17)
cat **gato** (3)
catch a cold **resfriarse (me resfrío)** (11)
CD **CD** *m.* (12)
CD-ROM **CD-ROM** *m.* (12)
celebrate **celebrar** (6)
celebratory **festivo/a** (9)
cell phone **teléfono celular** (2)
center (*political*) **centro** (18)
century **siglo** (10)
ceramics **cerámica** *s.* (13)
cereal **cereal** *m.* (7)
certain **seguro/a** (6); it's certain that **es cierto que** + *indicative* (13); **estar seguro/a de** to be certain of (13)
chair **silla** (2)
champagne **champán** *m.* (9)
change **cambiar (de)** (12)
channel **canal** *m.* (12)
charge (*someone for an item or service*) **cobrar** (17)
chat *n.* **chateo** (12)
check (*bank*) **cheque** *m.* (17); (*restaurant*) **cuenta** (7); by check **con cheque** (17); *v.* **revisar** (15); to check baggage **facturar el equipaje** (8)
check-up **chequeo** (11)
cheese **queso** (7)
chef **cocinero/a** (17)
chemistry **química** (2)
chess: to play chess **jugar (juego) (gu) al ajedrez** (10)
chicken **pollo** (7); roast chicken **pollo asado** (7)
chickpeas **garbanzos** *m. pl.* (7)
child: as a child **de niño/a** (10); small child **niño/a** (3)
childhood **infancia** (16); **niñez** *f.* (16)
children **hijos** *m. pl.* (3)
chop: (pork) chop **chuleta (de cerdo)** (7)
chore: household chore **quehacer** (*m.*) **doméstico** (10)
Christmas **Navidad** *f.* (9)
Christmas Eve **Nochebuena** *f.* (9)
church **iglesia** (16)
citizen **ciudadano/a** (18)
city **ciudad** *f.* (3)
civic duty **responsabilidad** (*f.*) **cívica** (18)
class (*of students*) **clase** *f.* (2); (*academic*) **clase** *f.* (2)
classic(al) **clásico/a** (13)
classmate **compañero/a (de clase)** (2)
classroom **salón** (*m.*) **de clase** (2)
clean *adj.* **limpio/a** (6); to clean (house) **limpiar (la casa)** (10)
clear the table **quitar la mesa** (10)
clerk **dependiente/a** (2)
clever **listo/a** (3)
click *v.* **hacer clic** (*m.*) (12)
client **cliente/a** (2)
climate **clima** *m.* (6)
clock: alarm clock **despertador** *m.* (14)
close **cerrar (cierro)** (5)
close to *prep.* **cerca de** (6)
closed **cerrado/a** (6)
closet (*free-standing*) **armario** (5)
clothes dryer **secadora** (10)
clothing **ropa** (4)
cloudy: it's (very) cloudy **está (muy) nublado** (6)
clumsy **torpe** (14)
coat **abrigo** (4)
coffee **café** *m.* (2)
coffeemaker **cafetera** (10)
cognate **cognado** (2)
coin **moneda** (17)
cold (*illness*) **resfriado** *n.* (11); it's (very) cold (*weather*) **hace (mucho) frio** (6); to be (very) cold **tener (mucho) frío** (6); to catch/get a cold **resfriarse (me resfrío)** (11); very cold **congelado/a** (6)
collect **recoger (recojo)** (14)
collision **choque** *m.* (18)
color **color** *m.* (4)
comb one's hair **peinarse** (5)
come **venir** (4); to come out badly **salir mal** (5); to come out well **salir bien** (5)
comedy **comedia** (13)
comfortable **cómodo/a** (4); to be comfortable (*temperature*) **estar bien** (6)
coming (*time*) **que viene** (5)
command **mandato** (7)
communicate (with) **comunicarse (qu) (con)** (18)
communication (*subject*) **comunicaciones** *f. pl.* (2); medium of communication **medio de comunicación** (18)
comparison **comparación** *f.* (6)
complain (about) **quejarse (de)** (8)
compose **componer** (*like* **poner**) (13)
composer **compositor(a)** (13)

computer **computadora** (2); computer file **archivo** (12); computer folder **carpeta** (12); computer science **computación** *f.* (2); laptop (computer) **computadora portátil** (2)
concept **concepto** (18)
concert **concierto** (10); to go to a concert **ir a un concierto** (10)
conductor **director(a)** (13)
congested (*with a cold*) *adj.* **resfriado/a** (11)
congratulations! **¡felicitaciones!** (9)
congressional representative **representante** (*m., f.*) **al congreso** (18)
conjunction *gram.* **conjunción** *f.* (17); conjunction of time **conjunción** (*f.*) **de tiempo** (17)
connect **conectarse** (12)
conserve **conservar** (15)
contact lenses **lentes** (*m. pl.*) **de contacto** (11)
contaminated **contaminado/a** (15)
content *adj.* **contento/a** (6)
continue **continuar (continúo)** (6); **seguir (sigo) (i)** (6)
control: remote control **control** (*m.*) **remoto** (12)
convertible car **coche/carro descapotable** (12)
cook *v.* **cocinar** (7); *n.* **cocinero/a** (17)
cookie **galleta** (7)
cool: it's (very) cool (weather) **hace (mucho) fresco** (6)
copy *n.*: copy machine **fotocopiadora** (12); *v.* **copiar** (12); **hacer (foto)copia** (12)
corner (*street*) **esquina** (15)
corporation **empresa** (17)
correct *v.* **corregir (corrijo) (i)** (14)
cost: how much does it (do they) cost? **¿cuánto cuesta(n)?** (4)
cotton *n.* **algodón** *m.* (4); **de algodón** *adj.* (4)
couch **sofá** *m.* (5)
cough *n.* **tos** *f.* (11); cough syrup **jarabe** *m.* (11); *v.* **toser** (11)
counter **mostrador** *m.* (8)
country **país** *m.* (3)
countryside **campo** (15)
couple **pareja**; (3); married couple **matrimonio** (16)
course (*academic*) **clase** *f.* (2); (*of a meal*) **plato** (7); course syllabus **programa** (*m.*) **del curso** (14); main course **plato principal** (7); of course! **¡por supuesto!** (14)
courteous expression **expresión** (f.) **de cortesía** (1)
courtesy **cortesía** (1)
cousin **primo/a** (3); *m. pl.* **primos** (3)
cover **cubrir** (*p.p.* **cubierto**) (15)
cow **vaca** (15)
craft: arts and crafts **artesanía** (13)
crash *n.* **choque** *m.* (18); *v.* (*computer*) **fallar** (12)
crazy **loco/a** (6)
create **crear** (13)
credit card **tarjeta de crédito** (7)
crime **delito** (15)
cruise (ship) **crucero** (8)
cry **llorar** (9)
cucumber **pepino** (7)
cuisine **cocina** (7)
cultural **cultural** (13); cultural tradition **tradición** (*f.*) **cultural** (13)
cup **taza** (14)
current *adj.* **actual** (12)
currently **en la actualidad** (10)
custard: baked custard **flan** *m.* (7)
customs (*at a border*) **aduana** (8); to go/pass through customs **pasar por la aduana** (8)

D

dad **papá** *m.* (3)
daily **diario/a** (5)
dance *n.* **baile** *m.* (13); **danza** (13); *v.* **bailar** (2)
dancer **bailarín, bailarina** (13)
date **cita** (11); (*calendar*) **fecha** (6); to be up to date **estar al día** (18); what's today's date? **¿cuál es la fecha de hoy?** (6), **¿qué fecha es hoy?** (6)
daughter **hija** (3)
day **día** *m.* (2); day after tomorrow **pasado mañana** (5); days of the week **días** (*m. pl.*) **de la semana** (5); every day **todos los días** (2); the day before yesterday **anteayer** (5); what day is today? **¿qué día es hoy?** (5)
deadline **plazo** (14)
dear **querido/a** (6)
death **muerte** *f.* (16)
debit card **tarjeta bancaria**, **tarjeta de débito** (17)
December **diciembre** *m.* (6)
delay **demora** (8)
demonstration **manifestación** *f.* (18)
demonstrative *gram.* **demostrativo/a** (4)
density **densidad** *f.* (15)
dentist **dentista** *m., f.* (11)
deny **negar (niego) (gu)** (13)
department store **almacén** *m.* (4)
departure **salida** (8)
deposit **depositar** (17)
design **diseñar** (13)
designer: graphic designer **diseñador(a) gráfico/a** (17)
desk **escritorio** (2)
dessert **postre** *m.* (7)
destination **destino** (8)
destroy **destruir** (*like* **construir**) (15)
detail **detalle** *m.* (9)
develop **desarrollar** (15)
development **desarrollo** (15)
dictator **dictador(a)** (18)
dictatorship **dictadura** (18)
dictionary **diccionario** (2)
die **morir(se) ([me] muero) (u)** (9)
diet: to be on a diet **estar a dieta** (7)
difficult **difícil** (6)
dining room **comedor** *m.* (5)
dinner **cena** (7); to have (eat) dinner **cenar** (7)
direct **dirigir (dirijo)** (13)
director **director(a)** (13)
dirty **sucio/a** (6)
disagree **no estar de acuerdo** (3)
disaster **desastre** *m.* (14)
disc: compact disc (CD) **disco compacto** (**CD** *m.*) (12)
disco: to go to a disco **ir a una discoteca** (10)
discover **descubrir** (*p.p.* **descubierto**) (15)
discrimination **discriminación** *f.* (18)
dish (*food prepared in a particular way*) **plato** (7)
dishwasher **lavaplatos** *m. inv.* (10)
distracted **distraído/a** (14); to be distracted **ir distraído/a** (14)
divorce *n.* **divorcio** (16); *v.* **divorciarse (de)** (16)
divorced (from) **divorciado/a (de)** (16)
dizzy **mareado/a** (11)
do **hacer** (5); do you like . . . ? **¿a usted le gusta... ?** *form. s.* (1); to do aerobics **hacer ejercicios** (*m. pl.*) **aeróbicos** (11); to (*do something*) again **volver a** + *inf.* (5); to do Pilates **hacer (el método) Pilates** (11); to do poorly **salir mal** (5); to do well **salir bien** (5); to do yoga **hacer (el) yoga** (10)
doctor (*medical*) **médico/a** (3)
document **documento** (12)
dog **perro** (3)
dollar **dólar** *m.* (4)
domestic, related to the home **doméstico/a** (10)
domesticated **doméstico/a** (15)
don't they (you...)? **¿no?** (4), **¿verdad?** (4)
door **puerta** (2)
doorman **portero/a** (12)
dormitory **residencia** (2)
dot: on the dot (*time*) **en punto** (1)
doubt **dudar** (12)
download **bajar** (12); **descargar (gu)** (12)
downtown **centro** (4)
drama **drama** *m.* (13)
draw **dibujar** (13); (*attract*) **atraer** (*like* **traer**) (*like* **gustar**) (13)
drawer (*person*) **dibujante** *m., f.* (13)
drawing **dibujo** (13)
dress **vestido** (4)

dressed: to get dressed **vestirse (me visto) (i)** (5)

dresser **cómoda** (5)

drink *n.* **bebida** (5); soft drink **refresco** (7); *v.* **beber** (3); **tomar** (2)

drive *n.:* hard drive **disco duro** (12); *v.* **manejar** (12); **conducir (conduzco)** (15)

driver **conductor(a)** (15); driver's license **licencia de manejar/conducir** (15)

drop **caer** (14)

dryer: clothes dryer **secadora** (10)

during **durante** (5)

duty: civic duty **responsabilidad** (*f.*) **cívica** (18)

DVD **DVD** *m.* (12)

E

e-mail **e-mail** *m.* (12); **correo electrónico** (12)

e-ticket **billete** (*m.*) (*Sp.*) / **boleto** (*L.A.*) **electrónico** (8)

each **cada** *inv.* (5)

ear **oreja** (11); inner ear **oído** (11)

early *adv.* **temprano** (2)

earn (*income*) **ganar** (13)

earphones **auriculares** *m., pl.* (12)

earrings **aretes** *m. pl.* (4)

Earth **Tierra** (15)

east **este** *m.* (6)

Easter **Pascua** (9)

easy **fácil** (6)

eat **comer** (3); to eat breakfast **desayunar** (7); to eat dinner, supper **cenar** (7); to eat lunch **almorzar (ue) (c)** (5)

economics **economía** (2)

economy **economía** (2)

egg **huevo** (7)

eight **ocho** (1)

eight hundred **ochocientos/as** (4)

eighteen **dieciocho** (1)

eighth **octavo/a** (13)

eighty **ochenta** (3)

either: not either **tampoco** (7)

electrical **eléctrico/a** (15); electrical energy **energía eléctrica** (15)

electrician **electricista** *m., f.* (17)

electricity **electricidad** *f.* (12)

electronic equipment **equipo electrónico** (12)

elephant **elefante** *m.* (15)

elevator **ascensor** *m.* (12)

eleven **once** (1)

embarrassed **avergonzado/a** (9)

embrace **abrazarse (c)** (11)

emotion **emoción** *f.* (9)

emotional **afectivo/a** (9); emotional relationship **relación** (*f.*) **sentimental** (16); emotional state **estado afectivo** (9)

end of the year **fin** (*m.*) **de año** (9)

end table **mesita** (5)

endangered species **especie** (*f.*) **en peligro de extinción** (15)

energy **energía** (15); electrical energy **energía eléctrica** (15); nuclear energy **energía nuclear** (15); renewable energy **energía renovable** (15); solar energy **energía solar** (15); wind energy **energía eólica** (15)

engagement period **noviazgo** (16)

engineer **ingeniero/a** (17)

English (*language*) **inglés** *n. m.* (2); *n., adj.* **inglés, inglesa** (3)

enjoy oneself **divertirse (me divierto) (i)** (5)

enough **bastante** (16), **suficiente** (11); **lo suficiente** (11)

environment **medio ambiente** (15)

equality **igualdad** *f.* (18)

equipment **equipo** (12); electronic equipment **equipo electrónico** (12)

eruption **erupción** *f.* (18)

evening: good evening **buenas noches** (1); **muy buenas** (1); in the evening **de la noche** (1); **por la noche** (2)

event **acontecimiento** (18); **hecho** (9)

ever **alguna vez** (15)

every **cada** *inv.* (5); **todo/a** (3); every day **todos los días** (2)

everything **de todo** (4)

everywhere **por todas partes** (14)

exam **examen** *m.* (4)

example: for example **por ejemplo** (14)

excuse me **(con) permiso** (1), **perdón** (1)

exercise *n.* **ejercicio** (5); *v.* **hacer ejercicio** (5)

expect **esperar** (7)

expense **gasto** (12)

expensive **caro/a** (4)

explain **explicar (qu)** (8)

expression (phrase) **expresión** *f.* (1); artistic expression **expresión artística** (13)

extinction **extinción** *f.* (15)

eye **ojo** (11)

F

Facebook **Facebook** *m.* (12); to go into Facebook **entrar en Facebook** (12)

fact **hecho** (9)

factory **fábrica** (15)

faithful **fiel** (3)

fall (*season*) *n.* **otoño** (6); *v.* **caer** (14); to fall asleep **dormir(se) ([me] duermo) (u)** (5); to fall down **caerse** (14); to fall in love (with) **enamorarse (de)** (16)

familiar: to be familiar with **conocer (conozco)** (7)

family **familia** (3)

fan: to be a fan (of) **ser aficionado/a (a)** (10)

far from **lejos de** (6)

fare **pasaje** *m.* (8)

farm **finca** (15)

farmer **agricultor(a)** (15), **campesino/a** (15)

farming **agricultura** (15)

fascinate **fascinar** (like **gustar**) (13)

fast **acelerado/a** (15)

fat **gordo/a** (3)

father **padre** *m.* (3), **papá** *m.* (3)

FAX **fax** *m.* (12)

fear *n.* **miedo** (4); *v.* **temer** (13)

February **febrero** (6)

feel **sentir (siento) (i)** (13); feel + *adj./adv.* **sentirse (me siento) (i)** + *adj./adv.* (9); to feel like (*doing something*) **tener ganas de** + *inf.* (4); to feel sorry **lamentar** (13)

female housekeeper **ama** (*f.*) (*but* **el ama**) **de casa** (17)

female soldier **mujer** (*f.*) **soldado** (17)

festive **festivo/a** (9)

fever **fiebre** *f.* (11)

few **poco/a** (4)

fiancé **novio** (16)

fiancée **novia** (16)

field **campo** (15); field laborer **campesino** (15)

fifteen **quince** (1); fifteen minutes until (*hour*) **menos cuarto/quince** (1); young woman's fifteenth birthday party **quinceañera** (9)

fifth **quinto/a** (13)

fifty **cincuenta** (3)

fight *n.* **lucha** (18); *v.* **luchar** (18), **pelear** (10)

file (*computer*) **archivo** (12)

fill (*a car*) **llenar** (15); to fill out (*a form*) **llenar** (17)

final **último/a** (4)

finally **por fin** (5), **finalmente** (5)

find **encontrar (encuentro)** (9); to find out (about) **enterarse (de)** (18)

fine **muy bien** (1); it's fine **está bien** (6)

finger **dedo (de la mano)** (11)

finish **acabar** (14)

fire (*someone*) (*from a job*) **despedir** (*like* **pedir**) (17)

first *adv.* **primero** (5); first *adj.* **primero/a** (5); first floor (second story) **primer piso** (12); for the first time **por primera vez** (14); the first of (*month*) **el primero de** (6)

fish (*cooked*) **pescado** (7); (*live*) **pez** *m.* (*pl.* **peces**) (15)

five **cinco** (1)

five hundred **quinientos/as** (4)

fix **arreglar** (15)

fixed price **precio fijo** (4)

flat: **plano/a** (12) flat screen (*monitor*) **pantalla plana** (12); flat tire **llanta desinflada** (15)
flexible **flexible** (14)
flight **vuelo** (8); flight attendant **asistente** (*m., f.*) **de vuelo** (8)
flip-flops **chanclas** *f. pl.* (4)
floor (*of a building*) **piso** (12); first/second floor (second/third story) **primer/segundo piso** (12); ground floor **planta baja** (12); to sweep the floor **barrer el piso** (10)
flower **flor** *f.* (8)
flu **gripe** *f.* (11)
fly *v.* **volar (vuelo) en avión** (8)
folder (*computer*) **carpeta** (12)
following *adj.* **siguiente** (5)
fond: to be fond of each other **quererse** (11)
food **comida** (7)
foodstuff **comestibles** *m. pl.* (7)
foolish **tonto/a** (3)
foot **pie** *m.* (11)
football **fútbol** (*m.*) **americano** (10)
for **para** (3); **por** (8); for example **por ejemplo** (14); for heaven's sake **por Dios** (14); for that reason **por eso** (3); for what purpose? **¿para qué... ?** (16); what for? **¿para qué... ?** (16)
forbid **prohibir (prohíbo)** (12)
foreign **extranjero/a** (2); foreign language **lengua extranjera** (2)
foreigner **extranjero/a** (2)
forest **bosque** *m.* (15)
forget **olvidar** (9)
form **forma** (4); (*to fill out*) **formulario** (17)
forty **cuarenta** (3)
four **cuatro** (1)
four hundred **cuatrocientos/as** (4)
fourteen **catorce** (1)
fourth *adj.* **cuarto/a** (13)
free (*unoccupied*) **libre** (10); free time **ratos** (*m. pl.*) **libres** (10), **tiempo libre** (10)
freeway **autopista** (15)
freezer **congelador** *m.* (10)
French (*language*) **francés** *m.* (2); French fried potato **papa frita** (7)
frequently **con frecuencia** (2); **frecuentemente** (11)
fresh **fresco/a** (7)
Friday **viernes** *m. inv.* (5)
fried **frito/a** (7); French fried potato **papa frita** (7)
friend **amigo/a** (2)
friendly **amistoso/a** (16)
friendship **amistad** *f.* (16)
from **de** (1); from the **del** (3); I am from . . . **(yo) soy de...** (1); where are you from? **¿de dónde eres (tú)?** *fam. s.* (1); **¿de dónde es usted?** *form. s.* (1)
front: in front of **delante de** (6)
frozen **congelado/a** (6)
fruit **fruta** (7); fruit juice **jugo de fruta** (7)
full-time job **empleo de tiempo completo** (17); **trabajo de tiempo completo** (14)
fun: fun activity **diversión** *f.* (10); to be fun **ser divertido/a** (10)
function **funcionar** (12)
furious **furioso/a** (6)
furniture (*piece*) **mueble** *m.* (5)

G

game **partido** (10)
garage **garaje** *m.* (5)
garden **jardín** *m.* (5)
gas (*residential, not for cars*) **gas** *m.* (12)
gas station **estación** (*f.*) **de servicio** (15), **gasolinera** (15)
gasoline **gasolina** (15)
gate: boarding gate **puerta de embarque** (8)
generally **por lo general** (5)
German (*language*) **alemán** *m.* (2); *n., adj.* **alemán, alemana** (3)
get **obtener** (*like* **tener**) (12); get + *adj./adv.* **ponerse** + *adj./adv.* (9); how do you get to . . . ? **¿cómo se llega a... ?** (15); to get **conseguir** (*like* **seguir**) (9); to get (*grades*) **sacar (qu)** (14); to get a cold **resfriarse (me resfrío)** (11); to get along poorly (with) **llevarse mal (con)** (16); to get along well (with) **llevarse bien (con)** (16); to get angry (with) **enojarse (con)** (9); to get bored **aburrirse** (10); to get down (from) **bajarse (de)** (8); to get dressed **vestirse (me visto) (i)** (5); to get off (of) (*a vehicle*) **bajarse (de)** (8); to get on (*a vehicle*) **subir (a)** (8); to get sick **enfermarse** (11); to get together (with) **reunirse (me reúno) (con)** (9); to get up (out of bed) **levantarse** (5); to get up on the wrong side of the bed **levantarse con el pie izquierdo** (14)
gift **regalo** (3)
girl **chica** (4); **niña** (3)
girlfriend **novia** (6)
give **dar** (8); to give (*as a gift*) **regalar** (8); to give (someone) a party **darle/hacerle una fiesta (a alguien)** (9); to give (*someone*) a shot / a vaccination **ponerle una inyección//una vacuna** (11)
glad: to be glad about **alegrarse de** (12)
glasses **anteojos** *m. pl.* (11), **lentes** *m. pl.* (11)
go **ir** (4); let's go **vamos** (4); to be going to (*do something*) **ir a** + *inf.* (4); to go abroad **ir al extranjero** (8); to go by boat/ship **ir en barco** (8); to go by bus **ir en autobús** (8); to go by plane **ir/volar (vuelo) en avión** (8); to go by train **ir en tren** (8); to go camping **hacer *camping*** (8); to go for a hike **dar una caminata** (10); to go home **regresar a casa** (2); to go on the internet **entrar en internet** (12); to go on vacation to/in . . . **ir de vacaciones a...** (8); to go onto Facebook **entrar en Facebook** (12); to go out (with) **salir (con)** (5); to go shopping **ir de compras** (4); to go through customs **pasar por la aduana** (8); to go through security (check) **pasar por el control de seguridad** (8); to go to (*a class, function*) **asistir (a)** (3); to go to a bar **ir a un bar** (10); to go to a concert **ir a un concierto** (10); to go to a disco **ir a una discoteca** (10); to go to a museum **ir a un museo** (10); to go to bed **acostarse (me acuesto)** (5); to go to the theater **ir al teatro** (10); to go up **subir (a)** (8); to go/travel by train **ir en tren** (8)
gold *n.* **oro** (4); *adj.* **de oro** (4)
golf **golf** *m.* (10)
good **buen, bueno/a** (3); good afternoon **buenas tardes** (1); good afternoon/evening **muy buenas** (1); good morning **buenos días** (1); good night **buenas noches** (1); the good news/thing **lo bueno** (11); it's (very) good weather **hace (muy) buen tiempo** (6); to have a good time **pasarlo bien** (9), **divertirse (me divierto) (i)** (5); to have good luck **tener buena suerte** (14)
good-bye **adiós** (1); to say good-bye (to) **despedir(se)** (*like* **pedir**) **(de)** (9)
good-looking (*people*) **guapo/a** (3)
goods: woven goods **tejidos** *m. pl.* (13)
gorilla **gorila** *m.* (15)
government **gobierno** (15)
grade (*academic*) **nota** (5); *v.* **corregir (corrijo) (i)** (14)
graduate (from) **graduarse (me gradúo) (*en*)**
granddaughter **nieta** (3)
grandfather **abuelo** (3)
grandmother **abuela** (3)
grandparents **abuelos** *m. pl.* (3)
grandson **nieto** (3)
graphic designer **diseñador(a) gráfico/a** (17)
gray **gris** (4)
great **gran, grande** (3)
green **verde** (4)
green peas **arvejas** *f. pl.* (7)
greet each other **saludarse** (11)
greeting **saludo** (1)
grilled **asado/a** (7)

groceries **comestibles** *m. pl.* (7)
groom **novio** (16)
ground floor **planta baja** (12)
grow **crecer (crezco)** (16)
guess **adivinar** (9)
guest **invitado/a** (9)
guy **chico** (4)
gym **gimnasio** (12)
guide **guía** *m., f.* (13)

H

haggle **regatear** (4)
hair: to brush one's hair **peinarse** (5)
hairstylist **peluquero/a** (17)
half past (*the hour*) **y media** (1)
ham **jamón** *m.* (7)
hamburger **hamburguesa** (7)
hand **mano** *f.* (11); to shake hands **darse la mano** (11)
hand in **entregar (gu)** (8)
handbag **cartera** (4)
handsome (*people*) **guapo/a** (3)
happen **pasar** (6); **ocurrir** (14)
happening **acontecimiento** (18)
happy **alegre** (6), **contento/a** (6); **feliz** (*pl.* **felices**) (9); to be happy (about) **alegrarse (de)** (12)
hard **difícil** (6)
hard drive **disco duro** (12)
hardworking **trabajador(a)** (3)
hat **sombrero** (4)
hate **odiar** (8)
have **tener** (4); (*auxiliary verb*) **haber** (12); to have a bad time **pasarlo mal** (9); to have a birthday **cumplir años** (9); to have a good time **divertirse (me divierto) (i)** (5), **pasarlo bien** (9); to have (a lot of) pressure **tener muchas presiones** (14); to have a pain/ache in **tener dolor de** (11); to have a party (for someone) **darle / hacerle una fiesta (a alguien)** (9); to have a picnic **hacer un pícnic** (10); to have a snack **merendar (meriendo)** (7); to have bad luck **tener mala suerte** (14); to have been (*doing something*) for (*time*) **hace** + *time* + **que** + *present* (14); *present* + **desde hace** + *time* (14); to have breakfast **desayunar** (7); to have dinner, supper **cenar** (7); to have good luck **tener buena suerte** (14); to have just (*done something*) **acabar de** + *inf.* (7); to have lunch **almorzar (almuerzo) (c)** (5); to have to (*do something*) **tener que** + *inf.* (4)
he *sub. pron.* **él** (2); he is **es** (1)
head **cabeza** (11)
headphones **auriculares** *m., pl.* (12)
health **salud** *f.* (11)
healthy **sano/a** (11); to lead a healthy life **llevar una vida sana** (11)
hear **oír** (5)
heart **corazón** *m.* (11)
heat **calefacción** *f.* (12)
heaven: for heaven's sake **por Dios** (14)
heavy: not heavy **ligero/a** (7)
hello **hola** (1)
help *n.* **ayuda** (7); *v.* **ayudar** (7); to help to (*do something*) **ayudar a** + *inf.* (7)
her *poss. adj.* **su(s)** (3); her, (of) hers *poss. adj., poss. pron.* **suyo/a(s)** (17)
here **aquí** (2)
hi **hola** (1)
highway **carretera** (15)
hike: to hike, go for a hike **dar una caminata** (10)
his *poss. adj.* **su(s)** (3); his, of his *poss. adj., poss. pron.* **suyo/a(s)** (17)
Hispanic **hispano/a** (3)
history **historia** (2)
hit **pegar (gu)** (14)
hobby **afición** *f.* (10)
hockey **hockey** *m.* (10)
holiday **día** (*m.*) **festivo** (9)
home *n.* **casa** (3); at home **en casa** (2); nursing home **residencia de ancianos** (12); to go home **regresar a casa** (2); *adj.* (*related to the home*) **doméstico/a** (10)
home appliance **aparato doméstico** (10)
homework **tarea** (5)
honeymoon **luna de miel** (16)
honk **tocar (qu)** (15)
hope **esperanza** (18); I hope (that) **ojalá (que)** (13); to hope **esperar** (12)
horn (*car*) **bocina** (15)
horse: to ride a horse **montar a caballo** (10)
host (*of an event*) **anfitrión, anfitriona** (9)
hot (*spicy*) **picante** (7); (*in temperature, not taste*) **caliente** (7); it's (very) hot (weather) **hace (mucho) calor** (6); it's hot (trendy) **está de moda** (4); **es de última moda** (4); to be (very) hot **tener (mucho) calor** (6)
hot dog **salchicha** (7)
house **casa** (3)
household chore **quehacer** (*m.*) **doméstico** (10)
housekeeper: female housekeeper **ama** (*f.*) (*but* **el ama**) **de casa** (17); male housekeeper **amo de casa** (17)
housing **vivienda** (12)
how + *adj.*! **¡qué** + *adj.***!** (14); how strange that . . . ! **¡qué extraño que... !** (13)
how? **¿cómo?** (1); how are you ? **¿cómo está(s)?** (1); **¿qué tal?** (1); how do you get to . . . ? **¿cómo se llega a... ?** (15); how many? **¿cuántos/as?** (2); how much? **¿cuánto?** (2); how much does it (do they) cost? **¿cuánto cuesta(n)?** (4); how often . . . ? **¿con qué frecuencia... ?** (3)
human **humano/a** (11); human body **cuerpo humano** (11)
humanities **humanidades** *f. pl.* (2)
hungry: to be (very) hungry **tener (mucha) hambre** (7)
hurry: to be in a hurry **tener prisa** (4)
hurt **doler (duele)** (*like* **gustar**) (11); to hurt oneself **hacerse daño** (14); to hurt (*a body part*) lastimarse (14); to hurt one's (*body part*) **hacerse daño en** (14)
husband **esposo** (3), **marido** (3)
hybrid **híbrido/a** (15)

I

I *sub. pron.* **yo** (2); I am **soy** (1); I am from . . . **(yo) soy de...** (1); I didn't mean (to do it) **fue sin querer** (14); I hope (that) **ojalá (que)** (13); I would (really) like . . . **me gustaría (mucho)...** (8); **(no,) no me gusta...** (no,) I don't like . . . (1); **(sí,) me gusta...** (yes,) I like . . . (1); I'm sorry/ pardon me **disculpa, discúlpame** *fam. s.* (14); **disculpe, discúlpeme** *form. s.* (14); I'm (very) sorry **lo siento (mucho)** (14)
ice cream **helado** (7)
ID **tarjeta de identificación** (14)
identification card **tarjeta de identificación** (14)
if **si** (4)
illness **enfermedad** *f.* (11)
image **imagen** *f.* (13)
immediately **en seguida** (5)
important: it's important that **es importante que** + *subjunctive* (12)
impossible **imposible** (13); it's impossible that **es imposible que** + *subjunctive* (13); it's not impossible **no es imposible que** + *subjunctive* (13)
improbable **improbable** (13); it's improbable that **es improbable que** + *subjunctive* (13); it's not improbable **no es improbable que** + *subjunctive* (13)
in **en** (1); in case **en caso de (que)** (16); in that case *adv.* **entonces** (8); in cash **en efectivo** (17); in front of **delante de** (6); in love (with) **enamorado/a (de)** (16); in order that **para que** (16); in order to (*do something*) **para** + *inf.* (3); in the afternoon **de la tarde** (1); in the evening **de la noche** (1); in the morning **de la mañana** (1); in the morning/afternoon/evening **por la mañana/tarde/noche** (2)

incredible **increíble** (13); it's incredible that **es increíble que** + *subjunctive* (13)

indefinite and negative word *gram.* **palabra indefinida y negativa** (7)

inequality **desigualdad** *f.* (18)

inexpensive **barato/a** (4)

infancy **infancia** (16), **niñez** *f.* (16)

inflexible **inflexible** (14)

inform **informar** (18)

injection **inyección** *f.* (11)

inner ear **oído** (11)

insist (on) **insistir (en)** (12)

install **instalar** (12)

installments: in installments **a plazos** (17)

intelligent **inteligente** (3)

intend to (*do something*) **pensar (pienso)** + *inf.* (5)

intended for **para** (3)

interest *n.* **interés** *m.* (17); *v.* to interest (*someone*) **interesar** (*like* **gustar**) (8)

internet **internet** *m.* (12); **red** (*f.*) (12); to go on the internet **entrar en internet** (12); to look up on the internet **buscar (qu) en internet** (12); to surf the internet; **navegar (gu) la red** (12)

interrogative *gram.* **interrogativo/a** (2); interrogative word **palabra interrogativa** (2)

interstate **autopista** (15)

interview **entrevista** (17)

interviewee **entrevistado/a** (17)

interviewer **entrevistador(a)** (17)

invite **invitar** (7)

iPhone **iPhone** *m.* (12)

iron *v.* **planchar** (10)

island **isla** (6)

issue **cuestión** *f.* (17)

it is... (*time*) **es la...** (1), **son las...** (1)

it's: it's absurd that **es absurdo que** + *subjunctive* (13); it's certain that **es cierto que** + *indicative* (13); it's certain / a sure thing that **es seguro que** + *indicative* (13); it's (im)possible that **es (im)posible que** + *subjunctive* (13); it's (im)probable that **es (im)probable que** + *subjunctive* (13); it's normal that **es normal que** + *subjunctive* (13); it's not certain / a sure thing that **no es seguro que** + *subjunctive* (13); it's not (im)probable that **no es (im)probable que** + *subjunctive* (13); it's not possible that **no es posible que** + *subjunctive* (13); it's strange that **es extraño que** + *subjunctive* (13); it's terrible that **es terrible que** + *subjunctive* (13); it's true that **es verdad que** + *indicative* (13); **no es (im)probable que** + *subjunctive* it's not (im) probable that (13); **no es posible que** + *subjunctive* it's not posible that (13); **¡qué extraño que... !** how strange that . . . ! (13); **¡qué lástima que... !** what a shame that . . . ! (13)

Italian (*language*) **italiano** (2)

its *poss. adj.* **su(s)** (3); (of) its *poss. adj., poss. pron.* **suyo/a(s)** (17)

J

jacket **chaqueta** (4)

January **enero** (6)

jeans ***jeans*** *m. pl.* (4)

job **empleo** (17), **trabajo** (10); full-time job **empleo de tiempo completo** (17), **trabajo de tiempo completo** (14); job application (*form*) **solicitud** *f.* (17); part-time job **empleo de tiempo parcial** (17), **trabajo de tiempo parcial** (14); poorly paid job **empleo mal pagado** (17); well-paid job **empleo bien pagado** (17)

joke **chiste** *m.* (8)

journalist **periodista** *m., f.* (17)

juice **jugo** (7); fruit juice **jugo de fruta** (7)

July **julio** (6)

June **junio** (6)

just in case **por si acaso** (14)

K

keep **guardar** (12); **mantener** (*like* **tener**) (18); to keep on going **seguir (sigo) (i)** (15)

key **llave** *f.* (5)

kill **matar** (18)

kind **amable** (3)

king **rey** *m.* (18)

kiss: to kiss each other **besarse** (11)

kitchen **cocina** (5)

know (*a person*) **conocer (conozco)** (7); (*facts*) **saber** (7); to know how to (*do something*) **saber** + *inf.* (7)

L

laborer **obrero/a** (17); field laborer **campesino/a** (15)

lack **falta** (15)

lake **lago** (15)

lamp **lámpara** (5)

landlady **dueña** (12)

landline **teléfono fijo** (12)

landlord **dueño** (12)

language **lengua** (2); foreign language **lengua extranjera** (2)

laptop (computer) **computadora portátil** (2)

large **gran, grande** (3)

last **pasado/a** (11); **último/a** (4); for the last time **por última vez** (14); last night *adv.* **anoche** (11); to last **durar** (18)

late *adj.* **atrasado/a** (8); *adv.* **tarde** (2)

lately **últimamente** (14)

later **después** (5); **luego** (5); see you later **hasta luego** (1)

latest (new) **ultimo/a** (4)

laugh **reírse (de)** (9)

law **ley** *f.* (18)

lawyer **abogado/a** (17)

layer: ozone layer **capa de ozono** (15)

lazy **perezoso/a** (3)

lead a calm/healthy life **llevar una vida tranquila/sana** (11)

learn **aprender** (3); to learn (about) **enterarse (de)** (18); to learn how to (*do something*) **aprender a** + *inf.* (3)

least: at least **por lo menos** (9)

leather *n.* **cuero** (4); *adj.* **de cuero** (4)

leave (*a place*) **salir (de)** (5); to leave for (*a place*) **salir para** (5); to leave on vacation **salir de vacaciones** (8)

left: to the left of **a la izquierda de** (6); to be left **quedar** (like **gustar**) (14)

leg **pierna** (11)

lend **prestar** (8)

lenses: contact lenses **lentes** (*m. pl.*) **de contacto** (11)

less than **menos que** (6); less. . . than **menos... que** (6); less than + *number* **menos de** + *number* (6)

let (*someone*) go **despedir** (*like* **pedir**) (17)

let's go **vamos** (4)

letter **carta** (3)

lettuce **lechuga** (7)

librarian **bibliotecario/a** (2)

library **biblioteca** (2)

license: driver's license **licencia de manejar/conducir** (15)

lie **mentira** (12)

life **vida** (11); academic life **vida académica** (14); slow / fast pace of life **ritmo lento / acelerado de la vida** (15)

lift weights **levantar pesas** (11)

light *n.* **luz** *f.* (*pl.* **luces**) (14); *adj.* light (*not heavy*) **ligero/a** (7)

like *n.* **gusto** (1); do you like . . . ? **¿te gusta... ?** *fam. s.* (1); **¿a usted le gusta... ?** *form. s.* (1); I would (really) like . . . **me gustaría (mucho)...** (8); (no,) I don't like . . . **(no,) no me gusta** (1); to like **gustar** (8); to like very much **encantar** (*like* **gustar**) (8); what are you like? **¿cómo es usted?** *form. s.* (1); yes, I like . . . **sí, me gusta...** (1)

likeable (*people*) **simpático/a** (3)

likely: it's likely that **es probable que** + *subjunctive* (13)

likewise **igualmente** (1)

limit: speed limit **límite** (*m.*) **de velocidad** (15)

line (*of people*) **cola** (8); to stand in line **hacer cola** (8)

listen to (*music, the radio*) **oír** (5); to listen (to) **escuchar** (2)

literature **literatura** (2)
little *adv.* (a) little **poco** (2); (adjective suffix) **-ito/a** (10); a little bit (of) **un poco (de)** (2); *adj.* **poco/a** (4)
live **vivir** (3)
living room **sala** (5)
loan **préstamo** (17)
lobster **langosta** (7)
long **largo/a** (3)
look at **mirar** (3); to look for **buscar (qu)** (2); to look up on the internet **buscar (qu) en internet** (12)
lose **perder (pierdo)** (5)
lot: a lot *adv.* **mucho** (2); a lot *adj.* (of) **mucho/a** (3); an awful lot **muchísimo** (8); there's lots **hay mucho/a** (6); to be under (a lot of) stress **estar (muy) estresado/a** (14); to have a lot of pressure **tener muchas presiones** (14)
love *n.* **amor** *m.* (16); *adj.* in love (with) **enamorado/a (de)** (16); *v.* **amar** (16); **querer** (16); **encantar** (*like* **gustar**) (8); to fall in love (with) **enamorarse (de)** (16); to love each other **quererse** (11)
luck: to have bad/good luck **tener mala/buena suerte** (14)
lucky: to be lucky **tener buena suerte** (14)
luggage **equipaje** *m.* (8)
lunch *n.* **almuerzo** (7); to have lunch **almorzar (almuerzo) (c)** (5)
lungs **pulmones** *m. pl.* (11)
-ly (*adverbial suffix*) **-mente** (14)
lyrics (*of a song*) **letra** (7)

M

ma'am **señora (Sra.)** (1)
machine: automatic teller machine (ATM) **cajero automático** (17)
made: it is made of . . . **es de...** (4)
magazine **revista** (3)
mailbox: voice mailbox **buzón** (*m.*) **de voz** (12)
main course **plato principal** (7)
maintain **mantener** (*like* **tener**) (18)
make **hacer** (5); to make a mistake (about) **equivocarse (qu) (de)** (14); to make plans to (*do something*) **hacer planes** (*m.*) **para** + *inf.* (10); to make a stop **hacer escala/parada** (8); to make the bed **hacer la cama** (10)
male housekeeper **amo de casa** (17)
mall: shopping mall **centro comercial** (4)
man **hombre** *m.* (2); *business man* **hombre de negocios** (17)
manager **gerente** *m., f.* (17); building manager **portero/a** (12)
manufacture **fabricar (qu)** (15)
many **muchos/as** (3); as many . . . as **tanto/a(os/as) ... como** (6); how many? **¿cuántos/as?** (2)
march **manifestación** *f.* (18)
March **marzo** (6)
market(place) **mercado** (4)
marriage **matrimonio** (16)
married: to be a married person **ser casado/a** (16); to be married (to) **estar casado/a (con)** (16)
marry **casarse (con)** (16)
mass media **medios** *m. pl.* (18)
masterpiece **obra maestra** (13)
match (*game*) **partido** (10)
material **materia** (4)
math **matemáticas** *f. pl.* (2)
matter **cuestión** *f.* (17)
May **mayo** (6)
me *obj. of prep.* **mí** (6); with me **conmigo** (6)
meal **comida** (7)
mean: I didn't mean (to do) it **fue sin querer** (14); that means . . . **eso quiere decir...** (11)
means of transportation **medio de transporte** (8)
meat **carne** *f.* (7)
mechanic **mecánico/a** (15)
medical **médico/a** (11); medical office **consultorio** (11); medical personnel **personal** (*m.*) **médico** (11)
medicine **medicina** (11)
medium of communication **medio de comunicación** (18)
meet (*a person*) **conocer (conozco)** (7); **conocerse (conozco)** (16); nice to meet you **mucho gusto** (1); to meet (*someone somewhere*) **encontrarse (me encuentro) (con)** (11)
memory **memoria** (12)
menu **menú** *m.* (7)
messy **desordenado/a** (6)
Mexican **mexicano/a** (3)
microwave oven **horno de microondas** (10)
middle age **madurez** *f.* (16)
midnight **medianoche** *f.* (6)
military *adj.* **militar** (18); military service **servicio militar** (18)
milk **leche** *f.* (7)
million: one million **un millón (de)** (4)
mine, (of) mine *poss. adj., poss. pron.* **mío/a(s)** (17)
mineral water **agua** (*f.*, but **el agua**) **mineral** (7)
minivan **camioneta** (8)
minute: fifteen minutes until (*hour*) **menos quince** (1); thirty minutes past (*the hour*) **y treinta** (1)
misbehave **portarse mal** (9)
miss (*an event*) **perder (pierdo)** (5)
Miss **señorita (Srta.)** (1)
mistake: to make a mistake (about) **equivocarse (qu) (de)** (14)
modem **módem** *m.* (12)
modern **moderno/a** (13)
molar **muela** (11)
mom **mamá** (3)
Monday **lunes** *m. inv.* (5); next Monday **el lunes que viene** (5); on Monday **el lunes** (5); on Mondays **los lunes** (5)
money **dinero** (2)
monitor **pantalla** (12); big screen monitor **pantalla grande** (12); flat screen monitor **pantalla plana** (12)
month **mes** *m.* (6)
moped **moto(cicleta)** *f.* (15)
more **más** (2); more than **más que** (6); more . . . than **más... que** (6); more than + *number* **más de** + *number* (6)
morning: good morning **buenos días** (1); in the morning **por la mañana** (2); **de la mañana** (1)
mosque **mezquita** (16)
mother **madre** *f.* (3); **mamá** (3)
motorcycle **moto(cicleta)** *f.* (15)
mountain **montaña** (8)
mouse **ratón** *m.* (12)
mouth **boca** (11)
move (*residence*) **mudarse** (12)
movie **película** (5); movie theater **cine** *m.* (5); movies **cine** *m. s.* (5)
Mr. **señor (Sr.)** *m.* (1)
Mrs. **señora (Sra.)** (1)
Ms. **señorita (Srta.)** (1)
much **mucho** (2); as much . . . as **tanto/a(os/as)... como** (6); as much as **tanto como** (6); how much? **¿cuánto?** (2); how much does it (do they) cost? **¿cuánto cuesta(n)?** (4)
mural **mural** *m.* (13)
museum **museo** (13); to go to a museum **ir a un museo** (10)
mushrooms **champiñones** *m. pl.* (7)
music **música** (13)
musical *n. m.* **musical** (13)
musician **músico/a** (13)
must (*do something*) **deber** + *inf.* (3)
my *poss. adj.* **mi(s)** (3); *poss. adj., poss. pron.* **mío/a(s)** (17)

N

name **nombre** *m.* (7); my name is . . . **me llamo...** (1); what is your name? **¿cómo se llama usted?** *form. s.* (1); **¿cómo te llamas?** *fam. s.* (1)
nap: to take a nap **dormir (duermo) (u) la siesta** (5)
narrate **contar (cuento)** (8)
nationality **nacionalidad** *f.* (3); adjective of nationality **adjetivo de nacionalidad** (3)

natural **natural** (15); natural resource **recurso natural** (15); natural sciences **ciencias** (*f. pl.*) **naturales** (2)
nature **naturaleza** (15)
nauseated **mareado/a** (11)
navigate **navegar (gu)** (12)
neat **ordenado/a** (6)
necessary **necesario/a** (3); it is necessary to (*do something*) **hay que** + *inf.* (13)
need **necesitar** (2)
negative: indefinite and negative word *gram.* **palabra indefinida y negativa** (7)
neighbor **vecino/a** (12)
neighborhood **barrio** (12)
neither **tampoco** (7)
nephew **sobrino** (3)
nervous **nervioso/a** (6)
network: social network **red** (*f.*) **social** (12)
never **jamás** (7), **nunca** (3); almost never **casi nunca** (3)
nevertheless **sin embargo** (6)
new **nuevo/a** (3)
New Year's Eve **Nochevieja** (9)
newlywed **recién casado/a** (16)
news **noticias** *f. pl.* (5); news media **prensa** (18); the bad news **lo malo** (11); the good news **lo bueno** (11)
newscast **noticiero** (18)
newspaper **periódico** (3)
newsstand **quiosco de prensa** (18)
next *adv.* **luego** (5); **después** (5); *adj.* **próximo/a** (5); next (Tuesday . . .) **el próximo (martes...)** (5); next Monday **el lunes** (*m.*) **que viene** (5); next week **la próxima semana** (5), **la semana que viene** (5)
nice (*people*) **amable** (3), **simpático/a** (3); nice to meet you **mucho gusto** (1); it's (very) nice out **hace (muy) buen tiempo** (6)
niece **sobrina** (3)
night: at night **de la noche** (1), **por la noche** (2); last night *adv.* **anoche** (11)
nine **nueve** (1)
nine hundred **novecientos/as** (4)
nineteen **diecinueve** (1)
ninety **noventa** (3)
ninth **noveno/a** (13)
no **no** (1); **ningún (ninguna)** (7); no, I don't like . . . **(no,) no me gusta** (1); no problem **no hay problema** (14)
no one **nadie** (7)
nobody **nadie** (7)
noise **ruido** (5)
noon **mediodía** *m.* (6)
normal **normal** (13); it's normal that **es normal que** + *subjunctive* (13)
north **norte** *m.* (6)
nose **nariz** *f.* (*pl.* **narices**) (11)
not any **ningún (ninguna)** (7)
not married **soltero/a** (16)
notebook **cuaderno** (2)
notes (*academic*) **apuntes** *m. pl.* (14)
nothing **nada** (7)
noun *gram.* **sustantivo** (2)
novel **novela** (13)
novelist **novelista** *m., f.* (13)
November **noviembre** *m.* (6)
now **ahora** (2); right now **ahora mismo** (6)
nuclear energy **energía nuclear** (15)
number **número** (1); ordinal number *gram.* **número ordinal** (13)
nurse **enfermero/a** (11)
nursing home **residencia de ancianos** (12)

O

o'clock: it's . . . o'clock **es la... , son las...** (1)
obey **obedecer (obedezco)** (15)
object **objeto** (2)
obligation **deber** *m.* (18)
obtain **obtener** (*like* **tener**) (12); **conseguir** (*like* **seguir**) (9)
ocean **océano** (8)
October **octubre** *m.* (6)
of **de** (1); of course! **¡por supuesto!** (14); of the **del** (3)
off: to turn off **apagar (gu)** (12)
offer **ofrecer (ofrezco)** (8)
office **oficina** (2); (*in a home*) **estudio** (5); (*medical*) **consultorio** (11); (*political*) **cargo** (18)
often: how often . . . ? **¿con qué frecuencia... ?** (3)
oil (*cooking*) **aceite** *m.* (7); (*fuel*) **petróleo** (15)
OK: it's OK **está bien** (6)
old **viejo/a** (3); old age **vejez** *f.* (16)
older (than) **mayor(es) (que)** (6)
olive oil **aceite** (*m.*) **de oliva** (7)
on **en** (1); on a trip **de viaje** (8); on Monday **el lunes** (5); on the dot (*time*) **en punto** (1); on time **a tiempo** (8); on top of **encima de** (6); on Tuesdays **los martes** (5); on vacation **de vacaciones** (8)
once a week **una vez a la semana** (3)
one **uno** (1); it's one o'clock **es la una** (1)
one hundred **cien** (3); (*used with* 101–199); **ciento** (4)
one hundred ninety-nine **ciento noventa y nueve** (4)
one hundred one **ciento uno/a** (4)
one hundred two **ciento dos** (4)
one million **un millón (de** + *noun*) (4)
one thousand **mil** (4)
one-way ticket **billete** *m.* (*Sp.*) / **boleto** (*L.A.*) **de ida** (8)
onion **cebolla** (7)
online: to buy online **comprar en internet** (4)
only *adv.* **solo** (2); **solamente** (14)
open *v.* **abrir** (*p.p.* **abierto**) (3); *adj.* **abierto/a** (6)
opera **ópera** (13)
operate (*a machine*) **manejar** (12)
opinion: to have an opinion about/that **pensar (pienso) de/that** (5)
or **o** (1); **u** (*before words beginning with the sound* **o-**) (3)
oral **oral** (14); oral report **informe** (*m.*) **oral** (14)
orange *n.* **naranja** (7); *adj.* **anaranjado/a** (4)
orchestra **orquesta** (13)
order **mandar** (12); (*in a restaurant*) **pedir (pido) (i)** (5); in order to (*do something*) **para** + *inf.* (3); in order that **para que** (16)
ordinal number *gram.* **número ordinal** (13)
other **otro/a** (3); others **los/las demás** (12); significant other **pareja** (3)
ought to (*do something*) **deber** + *inf.* (3)
our *poss. adj.* **nuestro/a(s)** (3); our, of ours *poss. adj., poss. pron.* **nuestro/a(s)** (17)
outdoors *adv.* **afuera** (6); **al aire libre** (10)
outer ear **oreja** (11)
outskirts **afueras** *f. pl.* (12)
oven: microwave oven **el horno de microondas** (10)
overcast: it's (very) overcast **está (muy) nublado** (6)
own, one's own **propio/a** (4)
owner **dueño/a** (7)
ozone layer **capa de ozono** (15)

P

p.m. **de la noche** (1); **de la tarde** (1)
pace: slow / fast of life **lento / acelerado ritmo de la vida** (15)
pack one's suitcase(s) **hacer la(s) maleta(s)** (8)
page: webpage **página web** (12)
paid: well/poorly paid job/position **empleo bien/mal pagado** (17)
pain (in) **dolor** *m.* **(de)** (11); to have a pain in **tener dolor de** (11)
paint **pintar** (13)
painter **pintor(a)** (13)
painting (*in general; specific piece*) **pintura** (13); (*specific piece*) **cuadro** (13)
pants **pantalones** *m. pl.* (4)
paper **papel** *m.* (2)

pardon me **con permiso** (1); **disculpa, discúlpame** *fam. s.* (14); **disculpe, discúlpeme** *form. s.* (14)

parents **padres** *m. pl.* (3)

park **estacionar** (14)

parking lot/place **estacionamiento** (15)

part **parte** *f.* (5)

part-time job/position **empleo de tiempo parcial** (17), **trabajo de tiempo parcial** (14)

partner **pareja** (3)

party **fiesta** (2); political party **partido** (18); to give (someone) a party **darle/hacerle una fiesta (a alguien)** (9); to have a party (for someone) **darle/hacerle una fiesta (a alguien)** (9)

pass *n.*: boarding pass **tarjeta de embarque** (8)

pass *v.*: pass through customs **pasar por la aduana** (8); to pass through security (check) **pasar por el control de seguridad** (8)

passenger **pasajero/a** (8)

passport **pasaporte** *m.* (8)

password **contraseña** (12)

past **pasado/a** (11)

pastime **pasatiempo** (10)

patient **paciente** *n. m., f.* (11)

patio **patio** (5)

pay *n.* (*often per hour*) **salario** (17); *v.* to pay (for) **pagar (gu)** (2)

pea: green peas **arvejas** *f. pl.* (7)

peace **paz** *f.* (*pl.* **paces**) (18)

pen **bolígrafo** (2); pen drive **memoria USB** pen drive (12)

pencil **lápiz** *m.* (*pl.* **lápices**) (2)

people **gente** *f. s.* (8)

pepper (*condiment*) **pimienta** (7)

permit **permitir** (12)

person **persona** (2)

personal: personal calendar **agenda** (14); personal pronoun *gram.* **pronombre** (*m.*) **personal** (2)

personnel: medical personnel **personal** (*m.*) **médico** (11)

pet **mascota** (3)

petroleum **petróleo** (15)

pharmacist **farmacéutico/a** (11)

pharmacy **farmacia** (12)

phase **etapa** (16)

philosophy **filosofía** (2)

phone **teléfono** (2); cell phone **teléfono celular** (2); to talk on the phone **hablar por teléfono** (2)

photo(graph) **foto(grafía)** (8); to take photos **sacar (qu) fotos/fotografías** (8)

photocopier **fotocopiadora** (12)

photocopy **fotocopia** (12)

photographer **fotógrafo/a** (17)

photo(graph) **foto(grafía)** *f.* (13)

photography **fotografía** (13)

physics **física** (2)

pick up **recoger (recojo)** (14)

picnic: to have a picnic **hacer un pícnic** (10)

pie **pastel** *m.* (7)

piece: piece of advice **consejo** (7); piece of furniture **mueble** *m.* (5)

Pilates: to do Pilates **hacer (el método) Pilates** (11)

pill **pastilla** (11)

pilot **piloto** *m., f.* (8)

pink **rosado/a** (4)

place *n.* **lugar** *m.* (2); (*in line*) **puesto** (8); parking place **estacionamiento** (15); *v.* **poner** (5); to take place in/at (*a place*) **ser en** + *place* (9)

plaid **de cuadros** (4)

plan **plan** *m.* (10); to plan to (*do something*) **pensar (pienso)** + *inf.* (5); to make plans to (*do something*) **hacer planes para** + *inf.* (10)

plane **avión** *m.* (8); to fly; to go/travel by plane **volar (vuelo) en avión** (8); **ir en avión** (8)

planet **planeta** *m.* (15)

plasma television **televisión** (*f.*) **plasma** (12)

plate **plato** (5)

play (*dramatic*) *n.* **drama** *m.* (13), **obra de teatro** (13); (*a game, sport*) *v.* **jugar (juego) (gu) (a, al)** (5); (*a musical instrument*) **tocar (qu)** (2); to play cards **jugar (juego) (gu) a las cartas** (10); to play chess **jugar (juego) (gu) al ajedrez** (10); to play videogames **jugar (juego) (gu) a los videojuegos** (10)

player **jugador(a)** (10)

playwright **dramaturgo/a** (13)

plaza **plaza** (4)

pleasantry **expresión** (*f.*) **de cortesía** (1)

please **por favor** (1)

pleased to meet you **encantado/a** (1), **mucho gusto** (1)

pleasing: to be pleasing **gustar** (8)

plumber **plomero/a** (17)

poem **poema** *m.* (13)

poet **poeta** *m., f.* (13)

point: cardinal point **punto cardinal** (6)

police officer **policía** *m., f.* (15)

policy **política** (18)

political: political office **cargo** (18); political party **partido** (18); political science **ciencias** (*f. pl.*) **políticas** (2)

politician **político/a** (18)

politics **política** *s.* (18)

polka-dot **de lunares** (4)

pollute **contaminar** (15)

polluted **contaminado/a** (15)

pollution: there's (lots of) pollution **hay (mucha) contaminación** *f.* (6)

pool **piscina** (5)

poor **pobre** (3); poorly paid job/position **empleo mal pagado** (17); to do poorly (5); to do/turn out poorly **salir mal** (5)

poorly *adv.* **mal** (2); to get along poorly (with) **llevarse mal (con)** (16)

population **población** *f.* (15)

pork chop **chuleta de cerdo** (7)

port **puerto** (8)

porter **maletero** (8)

position **empleo** (17); full-time / part-time position **empleo de tiempo completo / parcial** (17), **trabajo de tiempo parcial** (14); poorly paid position **empleo mal pagado** (17); to run for a position **postularse para un cargo** (18); well-paid position **empleo bien pagado** (17)

possessive **posesivo/a** (17); possessive adjective *gram.* **adjetivo posesivo** (3)

possible **posible** (3); it's not possible **no es posible que** + *subjunctive* (13); it's possible that **es posible que** + *subjunctive* (13)

post (*as on Facebook*) **publicar (qu)** (12)

postcard **tarjeta postal** (8)

potato **papa** (7); French fried potato **papa frita** (7)

pottery **cerámica** (13)

practice (*play*) **practicar (qu)** (2); (*train*) **entrenar** (10)

prefer **preferir (prefiero) (i)** (4)

preference **preferencia** (1)

prepare **preparar** (7)

preposition *gram.* **preposición** *f.* (5)

prescription **receta** (11)

present **regalo** (3)

press (*print*) **prensa** (18)

pressure **presión** *f.* (14); to be under a lot of pressure **estar bajo muchas presiones** (14); to have a lot of pressure **tener muchas presiones** (14)

pretty (*people and things*) **bonito/a** (3)

price (*of a transportation ticket*) **pasaje** *m.* (8); (fixed, set) price **precio (fijo)** (4)

print **imprimir** (12)

printer **impresora** (12)

probable **probable** (13); it's not probable **no es probable que** + *subjunctive* (13); it's probable that **es probable que** + *subjunctive* (13)

problem: no problem **no hay problema** (14)

profession **profesión** *f.* (17)

professor **profesor(a)** (1)

programmer **programador(a)** (17)

prohibit **prohibir (prohíbo)** (12)
promise **prometer** (8)
pronoun: personal pronoun *gram.* **pronombre** (*m.*) **personal** (2)
protect **proteger (protejo)** (15)
provided *prep.* **con tal de** (16); provided (that) *conj.* **con tal (de) que** (16)
psychiatrist **siquiatra** *m., f.* (17)
psychologist **sicólogo/a** (17)
psychology **sicología** (2)
public *n.* **público** (13); *adj.* **público/a** (15)
publish **publicar (qu)** (12)
pure **puro/a** (15)
purple **morado/a** (4)
purpose: for what purpose? **¿para qué?** (16)
purse **bolso** (4)
put **poner** (5); to put on (*an article of clothing*) **ponerse** (5)

Q

quarter: a quarter (fifteen minutes) after (*the hour*) **y cuarto/quince** (1); a quarter to (*hour*) **menos cuarto/quince** (1)
queen **reina** (18)
question **pregunta** (5); to ask a question **hacer una pregunta** (5), **preguntar** (8)
quit **dejar** (17)
quiz **prueba** (14)

R

radio (apparatus) **radio** *m.* (12); radio station **estación** (*f.*) **de radio** (18)
rain **llover (llueve)** (6); it rains, it's raining **llueve** (6)
raincoat **impermeable** *m.* (4)
rather **bastante** (16)
read **leer** (*like* **creer**) (3)
really: I would really like . . . **me gustaría mucho...** (8)
reason: for that reason **por eso** (3)
receipt **recibo** (17)
receive **recibir** (3)
recipe **receta** (7)
recommend **recomendar (recomiendo)** (8)
record **grabar** (12)
recycle **reciclar** (15)
recycling **reciclaje** *m.* (15)
red **rojo/a** (4); red wine **vino tinto** (7)
reduction **rebajas** *f. pl.* (4)
reflexive verb *gram.* **verbo reflexivo** (5)
refrigerator **refrigerador** *m.* (10)
regret **lamentar** (13), **sentir (siento) (i)** (13)
relationship: emotional relationship **relación** (*f.*) **sentimental** (16)
relative **pariente** *m.* (3)
remain (*in a place*) **quedarse** (6); to remain; to be left **quedar** (14)
remember **acordarse (me acuerdo) (de)** (13); **recordar (recuerdo)** (9)
remote control **control** (*m.*) **remoto** (12)
renewable **renovable** (15); renewable energy **energía renovable** (15)
rent *n.* **alquiler** *m.* (12); *v.* to rent **alquilar** (12)
renter **inquilino/a** (12)
repair **arreglar** (15), **reparar** (15); repair shop **taller** *m.* (15)
report **informe** *m.* (14), **trabajo** (14); oral report **informe oral** (14); written report **informe escrito** (14)
reporter **reportero/a** (18)
representative: congressional representative **representante** (*m., f.*) **al congreso** (18)
resign (from) **renunciar (a)** (17)
resolve **resolver (resuelvo)** (15)
resource: natural resource **recurso natural** (15)
responsibility **deber** *m.* (18), **responsabilidad** *f.* (18)
rest **descansar** (5)
restaurant **restaurante** *m.* (7)
résumé **currículum** *m.* (17)
retire (*from a job*) **jubilarse** (17)
return (*something to someone*) **devolver** (*like* **volver**) (14); (*to a place*) **regresar** (2), **volver (vuelvo)** (5); to return home **regresar a casa** (2)
review **repaso** (2)
rice **arroz** *m.* (*pl.* **arroces**) (7)
rich (*wealthy*) **rico/a** (3); (*in calories*) **rico/a** (7)
ride: to ride a bicycle **montar en bicicleta** (10); **pasear en bicicleta** (10); to ride a horse **montar a caballo** (10)
right (*legal*) **derecho** (18); **¿no?** (4), **¿verdad?** (4); right now **ahora mismo** (6); right now (*currently*) **en la actualidad** (10); to be right **tener razón** (4); to the right of **a la derecha de** (6)
ring **sonar (suena)** (10)
river **río** (15)
roast(ed) **asado/a** (7); roast chicken **pollo asado** (7)
role (*in a play, an event*) **papel** *m.* (13)
room **cuarto** (2); waiting room **sala de espera** (8)
roommate **compañero/a de cuarto** (2)
round-trip ticket **billete** *m.* (*Sp.*) / **boleto** (*L.A.*) **de ida y vuelta** (8)
routine **rutina** (5); *adj.* **rutinario/a** (11)
rug **alfombra** (5)
ruin **ruina** (13)
run **correr** (10); (*machines*) **funcionar** (12); to run out of **acabar** (14); to run as a candidate **postularse como candidato/a** (18); to run for a position **postularse para un cargo** (18); to run into **chocar (qu) contra/con** (14); **pegarse (gu) con/contra** (14)

S

sad **triste** (6)
sake: for heaven's sake **por Dios** (14)
salad **ensalada** (7)
salary **sueldo** (17)
sales **rebajas** *f. pl.* (4)
salesperson **vendedor(a)** (17)
salmon **salmón** *m.* (7)
salt **sal** *f.* (7)
same **mismo/a** (6); same here (likewise) **igualmente** (1)
sandals **sandalias** *f. pl.* (4)
sandwich **sándwich** *m.* (7)
Saturday **sábado** (5)
sauce **salsa** (7)
sausage **salchicha** (7)
save **conservar** (15); to save a place in line **guardar un puesto** (8); (*documents*) **almacenar** (12), **guardar** (12); (*money*) **ahorrar** (17)
savory **rico/a** (7)
say **decir** (8); to say good-bye (to) **despedirse** (*like* **pedir**) **(de)** (9)
scanner **escáner** *m.* (12)
scene **escena** (13)
scenery **escenario** (13)
schedule **horario** (14)
school **escuela** (10)
schoolteacher **maestro/a de escuela** (17)
science **ciencia** (2); computer science **computación** *f.* (2); natural sciences **ciencias** (*f. pl.*) **naturales** (2); political science **ciencias** (*f. pl.*) **políticas** (2); social sciences **ciencias** (*f. pl.*) **sociales** (2)
screen **pantalla** (12); big screen (monitor) **pantalla grande** (12); flat screen (monitor) **pantalla plana** (12)
script **guion** *m.* (13)
sculpt **esculpir** (13)
sculptor **escultor(a)** (13)
sculpture **escultura** (13)
sea **mar** *m.* (8)
search engine **buscador** *m.* (12)
season (*of the year*) **estación** *f.* (6)
seat **asiento** (8)
second **segundo/a** (13); second floor (third story) **segundo piso** (12)
secretary **secretario/a** (2)

security (check) **control** (*m.*) **de seguridad** (8); to go/pass through security (check) **pasar por el control de seguridad** (8)
see **ver** (5); see you around **nos vemos** (1); see you later **hasta luego** (1); see you tomorrow **hasta mañana** (1)
sell **vender** (3)
senator **senador(a)** (18)
send a text **mandar un mensaje (de texto)** (2)
sentence *gram.* **oración** *f.* (2)
separate (from) **separarse (de)** (16)
separated from **separado/a (de)** (16)
separation **separación** *f.* (16)
September **septiembre** *m.* (6)
serve **servir (sirvo) (i)** (5)
service **servicio** (15); military service **servicio militar** (18)
set price **precio fijo** (4)
set the table **poner la mesa** (10)
seven **siete** (1)
seven hundred **setecientos/as** (4)
seventeen **diecisiete** (1)
seventh **séptimo/a** (13)
seventy **setenta** (3)
shake hands **darse la mano** (11)
shame **lástima** (13); it's a shame that **es una lástima que** + *subjunctive* (13); what a shame that . . . ! **¡qué lástima que...** + *subjunctive***!** (13)
shape **forma** (4)
shave **afeitarse** (5)
she *sub. pron.* **ella** (2); she is **es** (1)
shellfish **mariscos** *m. pl.* (7)
ship **barco** (8); cruise ship **crucero** (8); to go/travel by ship **ir en barco** (8)
shirt **camisa** (4)
shoes **zapatos** *m. pl.* (4)
shop **tienda** (4); repair shop **taller** *m.* (15)
shopping **de compras** (4); shopping mall **centro comercial** (4); to go shopping **ir de compras** (4)
short (*in height*) **bajo/a** (3); (*in length*) **corto/a** (3)
shorts **pantalones** (*m. pl.*) **cortos** (4)
shot: to give (*someone*) a shot **ponerle una inyección** (11)
should (*do something*) **deber** + *inf.* (3)
show *n.* **espectáculo** (13); *v.* **mostrar (muestro)** (8)
shower: to take a shower **ducharse** (5)
shrimp **camarones** *m., pl.* (7)
siblings **hermanos** *m. pl.* (3)
sick **enfermo/a** (6); to get/become sick **enfermarse** (11)
sickness **enfermedad** *f.* (11)
sidewalk **acera** (15)
signal: traffic signal **semáforo** (15)
significant other **pareja** (3)
silk *n.* **seda** (4); *adj.* **de seda** (4)
silly **tonto/a** (3)
silver *n.* **plata** (4); *adj.* **de plata** (4)
sing **cantar** (2)
singer **cantante** *m., f.* (13)
single, not married **soltero/a** (16)
sink: bathroom sink **lavabo** (5)
sir **señor (Sr.)** *m.* (1)
sister **hermana** (3)
sit down **sentarse (me siento)** (5)
six **seis** (1)
six hundred **seiscientos/as** (4)
sixteen **dieciséis** (1)
sixth **sexto/a** (13)
sixty **sesenta** (3)
skate *v.* **patinar** (10)
skating **patinaje** *m.* (10)
ski **esquiar (esquío)** (10)
skiing **esquí** *m.* (10)
skirt **falda** (4)
skyscraper **rascacielos** *m. inv.* (15)
sleep **dormir (duermo) (u)** (5)
sleepy: to be sleepy **tener sueño** (4)
slender **delgado/a** (3)
slow **lento/a** (15); slow pace of life **ritmo lento de la vida** (15)
small **pequeño/a** (3); (*adjective suffix*) **-ito/a** (10); small child **niño/a** (3)
smart **listo/a** (3)
smile **sonreír** (*like* **reír**) (9)
smoke **fumar** (8)
smoking area **sala de fumadores / de fumar** (8)
snack **merienda** (7); to have a snack **merendar (meriendo)** (7)
snow **nevar (nieva)** (6); it snows, it's snowing **nieva** (6)
so that **para que** (16)
so-so **regular** (1)
soccer **fútbol** *m.* (10)
social: social network **red** (*f.*) **social** (12); social sciences **ciencias** (*f. pl.*) **sociales** (2); social worker **trabajador(a) social** (17)
sociology **sociología** (2)
socks **calcetines** *m. pl.* (4)
soft drink **refresco** (7)
solar energy **energía solar** (15)
soldier **militar** *m., f.* (17); **soldado** *m., f.* (17)
solve **resolver (resuelvo)** (15)
some **algún (alguna/os/as)** (7)
someone **alguien** (7)
something **algo** (7)
sometimes **a veces** (3)
son **hijo** (3)
song **canción** *f.* (7)
soon: as soon as **en cuanto** (17), **tan pronto como** (17)
sorry: to feel sorry **lamentar** (13), **sentir (siento) (i)** (13); I'm (very) sorry **lo siento (mucho)** (14)
sound **sonar (suena)** (10)
soup **sopa** (7)
south **sur** *m.* (6)
space: storage space **espacio de almacenamiento** (12)
Spanish (*language*) **español** *m.* (2); *n., adj.* **español, española** (3)
spare (free) time **ratos** (*m. pl.*) **libres** (10)
speak **hablar** (2)
species **especie** *f.* (15); endangered species **especie en peligro de extinción** (15)
spectator **espectador(a)** (13)
speed **velocidad** *f.* (15); speed limit **límite** (*m.*) **de velocidad** (15)
spend (*money*) **gastar** (9); (*time*) **pasar** (6); to spend one's vacation in . . . **pasar las vacaciones en...** (8); to spend time **pasar tiempo** (6)
spicy **picante** (7)
sport **deporte** *m.* (10)
sporting *adj.* **deportivo/a** (10)
sports *adj.*, sports-loving *adj.* **deportivo/a** (10)
spring (*season*) **primavera** (6)
square **plaza** (4)
stage **escenario** (13); (*phase*) **etapa** (16); life stage **etapa de la vida** (16)
stairs **escaleras** *f. pl.* (14)
stand: stand up **levantarse** (5); to stand in line **hacer cola** (8)
start **empezar (empiezo) (c)** (5); to start up (*a car*) **arrancar (qu)** (15)
state **estado** (3); emotional state **estado afectivo** (9)
station **estación** *f.* (8); bus station **estación de autobuses** (8); gas station **estación de servicio** (15); radio station **estación de radio** (18); train station **estación de trenes** (8)
stay **quedarse** (6); to stay in bed **guardar cama** (11)
steak **bistec** *m.* (7)
stick out one's tongue **sacar (qu) la lengua** (11)
still **todavía** (6)
stockings **medias** *f. pl.* (4)
stomach **estómago** (11)
stop *n.* **escala** (*in a trip*) (8); bus stop **parada del autobús** (12); subway stop **parada del metro** (12); to make a stop **hacer escala/parada** (8); to stop **parar** (15); to stop (*doing something*) **dejar de** + *inf.* (11)
storage (space) **(espacio de) almacenamiento** (12)
store *n.* **tienda** (4) department store **almacén** *m.* (4); *v.* (*computer*) **almacenar** (12)
story **historia** (8)
stove **estufa** (5)
straight ahead **(todo) derecho** (15), **todo recto** (15)

strange: how strange that . . . ! **¡qué extraño que...** + *subjunctive***!** (13); it's strange that **es extraño que** + *subjunctive* (13)
street **calle** *f.* (12)
street corner **esquina** (15)
stress **estrés** *m.* (14); to be under (a lot of) stress **estar (muy) estresado/a** (14); under stress, stressed out **estresado/a** (14)
stressed: to be (very) stressed **estar (muy) estresado/a** (14)
stressful **estresante** (14)
strike (*labor*) **huelga** (18); *v.* **pegar (gu)** (14)
striped **de rayas** (4)
struggle **lucha** (18)
student **estudiante** *m., f.* (2)
study **estudiar** (2)
stuffed up (*with a cold*) **resfriado/a** *adj.* (11)
subject area **materia** (2)
suburbs **afueras** *f. pl.* (12)
subway stop **parada del metro** (12)
succeed in (*doing something*) **conseguir** (*like* **seguir**) + *inf.* (9)
suddenly **de repente** (11)
suffer **sufrir (de)** (14)
sufficiently **bastante** (16)
sugar **azúcar** *m.* (7)
suggest **sugerir (sugiero) (i)** (9)
suit **traje** *m.* (4)
suitcase **maleta** (8); to pack one's suitcase(s) **hacer la(s) maleta(s)** (8)
summer **verano** (6)
sunbathe **tomar el sol** (8)
Sunday **domingo** (5)
sunglasses **gafas** (*f. pl.*) **de sol** (4)
sunny: it's (very) sunny **hace (mucho) sol** (6)
sunscreen **bloqueador** (*m.*) **solar** (8)
supermarket **supermercado** (12)
supper **cena** (7); to have (eat) supper **cenar** (7)
sure **seguro/a** (6); it's a sure thing that **es seguro que** + *indicative* (13); it's not sure **no es seguro que** + *subjunctive* (13)
surf **surfear** (10)
surprise **sorprender** (*like* **gustar**) (13)
SUV **SUV** *m.* (15)
sweater **suéter** *m.* (4)
sweatshirt **sudadera** (4)
sweep (the floor) **barrer (el piso)** (10)
sweets **dulces** *m. pl.* (7)
swim **nadar** (8)
swimming **natación** *f.* (10); swimming pool **piscina** (5)
swimsuit **traje** (*m.*) **de baño** (4)
syllabus **programa** (*m.*) **del curso** (14)
symptom **síntoma** *m.* (11)
syrup: cough syrup **jarabe** *m.* (11)
systems analyst **analista** (*m., f.*) **de sistemas** (17)

T

T-shirt **camiseta** (4)
table **mesa** (2); to clear the table **quitar la mesa** (10); to set the table **poner la mesa** (10)
take **tomar** (2); **llevar** (4); to take a bath **bañarse** (5); to take a nap **dormir (duermo) (u) la siesta** (5); to take a shower **ducharse** (5); to take a trip **hacer un viaje** (5); to take a vacation **tomar unas vacaciones** (8); to take a walk **dar un paseo** (10); to take care of **cuidar de** (11); to take care of oneself **cuidarse** (11); to take off (*an article of clothing*) **quitarse** (5); to take out **sacar (qu)** (17); to take out the trash **sacar (qu) la basura** (10); to take photos **sacar (qu) fotos/fotografías** (8); to take place at/in (*a place*) **ser en** + *place* (9); to take someone's temperature **tomarle la temperatura** (11)
talk **hablar** (2); to talk on the phone **hablar por teléfono** (2)
tall **alto/a** (3)
tame **domesticado/a** (15)
tank **tanque** *m.* (15)
tape **grabar** (12)
tasty **rico/a** (7)
tea **té** *m.* (7)
teach **enseñar** (2)
teacher: school teacher **maestro/a de escuela** (17)
team **equipo** (10)
technician **técnico/a** (17)
technology **la tecnología** (12)
teeth: to brush one's teeth **cepillarse los dientes** (5)
television: (plasma) television **televisión** (*f.*) **(plasma)** (12); to watch television **mirar la tele(visión)** (3)
tell **contar (cuento)** (8); **decir** (8)
teller (bank) **cajero/a** (17); automatic teller machine (ATM) **cajero automático** (17)
temperature **temperatura** (11); to take someone's temperature **tomarle la temperatura** (11)
temple **templo** (16)
ten **diez** (1)
tenant **inquilino/a** (12)
tennis **tenis** *m.* (10)
tennis shoes **tenis** *m. pl.* (4)
tent **tienda (de campaña)** (8)
tenth **décimo/a** (13)
terrible **terrible** (13); it's terrible that **es terrible que** + *subjunctive* (13)
terrorism **terrorismo** (18)
terrorist **terrorista** *m., f.* (18); terrorist attack **ataque** (*m.*) **terrorista** (18)
test **examen** *m.* (4); **prueba** (14)
text (*electronic*) **mensaje** *m.* (2); to (send a) text **mandar un mensaje (de texto)** (2)
textbook **libro de texto** (2)
than: better than **mejor(es) que** (6); less . . . than **menos... que** (6); less than + *number* **menos de** + *number* (6); more . . . than **más... que** (6); more than + *number* **más de** + *number* (6); older than **mayor(es) que** (6); worse than **peor(es) que** (6); younger than **menor(es) que** (6)
thank you (very much) **(muchas) gracias** (1); thanks for **gracias por** + *inf./ noun* (9)
that *conj.* **que** (3); that *adj., pron.* **ese/a** (4); *neuter pron.* **eso** (4); that ([way] over there) *adj., pron.* **aquel, aquella** (4); that ([way] over there) *neuter pron.* **aquello** (4); that means . . . **eso quiere decir...** (11); that which **lo que** (5)
theater **teatro** (10); to go to the theater **ir al teatro** (10)
their *poss. adj.* **su(s)** (3); (of) theirs *poss. adj., poss pron.* **suyo/a(s)** (17)
them *obj.* (*of prep.*) **ellos/as** (2)
then **luego** (5); **después** (5); **entonces** (8)
there **allí** (4)
there: (way) over there **allá** (4)
there is/are **hay** (1); is there / are there? **¿hay?** (1); there is/are not **no hay** (1); there's (lots of) **hay (mucho/a[s])** (6); infinitive form of **hay haber** (12)
these *adj., pron.* **estos/as** (3)
they *sub. pron.* **ellos/as** (2)
thin **delgado/a** (3)
thing **cosa** (5); the bad thing **lo malo** (11); the good thing **lo bueno** (11)
think **creer** (3); to not think **no creer** (13); to think (about) **pensar (pienso) (de/en)** (5); to think that **pensar (pienso) que** (5)
third **tercer(o/a)** (13)
thirsty: to be (very) thirsty **tener (mucha) sed** (7)
thirteen **trece** (1)
thirty **treinta** (1); thirty minutes past (*the hour*) **y treinta** (1)
this *adj., pron.* **este/a** (3); *neuter pron.* **esto** (3)
those *adj., pron.* **esos/as** (4); those ([way] over there) *adj., pron.* **aquellos/as** (4)
three **tres** (1)
three hundred **trescientos/as** (4)
throat **garganta** (11)
through **por** (8)
Thursday **jueves** *m. inv.* (5)

ticket **billete** *m.* (*Sp.*) **/ boleto** (*L.A.*) (8); one-way ticket **billete/bolleto de ida** (8); round-trip ticket **billete/boleto de ida y vuelta** (8); (*to a performance, movie . . .*) **entrada** (12)

tie **corbata** (4)

time **tiempo** (6); at what time . . . ? **¿a qué hora... ?** (1); at times **a veces** (3); conjunction of time **conjunción** (*f.*) **de tiempo** (17); for the first/last time **por primera/última vez** (14); free time **ratos** (*m. pl.*) **libres** (10); **tiempo libre** (10); on time **a tiempo** (8); to have a bad time **pasarlo mal** (9); to have a good time **divertirse (me divierto) (i)** (5); **pasarlo bien** (9); to spend time **pasar tiempo** 6); what time is it? **¿qué hora es?** (1)

tire **llanta** (15); flat tire **llanta desinflada** (15)

tired **cansado/a** (6)

to **a** (1); to the **al** (4); to the left of **a la izquiera de** (6); to the right of **a la derecha de** (6)

toast **pan tostado** (7)

toasted **tostado/a** (7)

toaster **tostadora** (10)

today **hoy** (1); what day is today? **¿qué día es hoy?** (5); what's today's date? **¿cuál es la fecha de hoy?** (6), **¿qué fecha es hoy?** (6)

toe **dedo del pie** (11)

together **juntos/as** (8); to get together (with) **reunirse (me reúno) (con)** (9)

tomato **tomate** *m.* (7)

tomorrow **mañana** (1); see you tomorrow **hasta mañana** (1); the day after tomorrow **pasado mañana** (5)

tongue **lengua** (11); to stick out one's tongue **sacar (qu) la lengua** (11)

tonight **esta noche** (6)

too (much) **demasiado** *adv.* (9)

tooth **diente** *m.* (5); back tooth **muela** (11); to brush one's teeth **cepillarse los dientes** (5)

top: on top of **encima de** (6)

towel **toalla** (5)

trade (*type of job*) **oficio** (17)

tradition: cultural tradition **tradición** (*f.*) **cultural** (13)

traditional **folclórico/a** (13)

traffic **circulación** *f.* (15), **tráfico** (15), **tránsito** (15); traffic signal **semáforo** (15)

train **tren** *m.* (8); to go/travel by train **ir en tren** (8); to train **entrenar** (10); train station **estación** (*f.*) **de trenes** (8)

translator **traductor(a)** (17)

transportation: means of transportation **medio de transporte** (8)

trash **basura** (10); to take out the trash **sacar (qu) la basura** (10)

travel **viajar** (8); to travel by boat/ship **ir en barco** (8); to travel by bus **ir en autobús** (8); to travel by plane **ir en avión** (8)

traveling **de viaje** (8)

treadmill **caminadora** (11)

treatment **tratamiento** (11)

tree **árbol** *m.* (9)

trendy: it's trendy **está de moda** (4), **es de última moda** (4)

trip **viaje** *m.* (5); on a trip **de viaje** (8); to take a trip **hacer un viaje** (5)

true: it's true that **es verdad que** + *indicative* (13)

try to (*do something*) **tratar de** + *inf.* (13)

Tuesday **martes** *m. inv.* (5); on Tuesdays **los martes** (5)

tuition **matrícula** (2)

tuna **atún** *m.* (7)

turkey **pavo** (7)

turn **doblar** (15); to be someone's turn **tocarle (qu) a uno** (10); to turn on (*a machine*) **encender (enciendo)** (12); to turn off (*machine*) **apagar (gu)** (12); to turn on (*appliance*) **poner** (10); to turn out badly **salir mal** (5); to turn out well **salir bien** (5)

tweet *n.* **tuit** *m.* (12); *v.* **twitear** (12)

twelve **doce** (1)

twenty **veinte** (1)

twenty-eight **veintiocho** (1)

twenty-five **veinticinco** (1)

twenty-four **veinticuatro** (1)

twenty-nine **veintinueve** (1)

twenty-one **veintiuno** (1)

twenty-seven **veintisiete** (1)

twenty-six **veintiséis** (1)

twenty-three **veintitrés** (1)

twenty-two **veintidós** (1)

twice **dos veces** (11)

Twitter **Twitter** *m.* (12)

two **dos** (1)

two hundred **doscientos/as** (4)

U

ugly **feo/a** (3)

uncertain: to be uncertain of **no estar seguro/a de**; to be certain of (13)

uncle **tío** (3); aunts and uncles **tíos** *m. pl.* (3)

under stress **estresado/a** (14); to be under a lot of stress **estar (muy) estresado/a** (14); to be under a lot of pressure **estar bajo muchas presiones** (14)

understand **comprender** (3); **entender (entiendo)** (5)

underwear **ropa interior** (4)

unfortunately **desgraciadamente** (11)

United States: of the United States of America *n., adj.* **estadounidense** (3)

university *n.* **universidad** *f.* (2); *adj.* **universitario/a** (14)

unless *conj.* **a menos que** (16); **sin que** (16)

unlikeable (*people*) **antipático/a** (3)

unlikely: it's unlikely that **es improbable que** + *subjunctive* (13)

unlucky: to be unlucky **tener mala suerte** (14)

unoccupied **libre** (10)

unpleasant (*people*) **antipático/a** (3)

until *prep.* **hasta** (1); *conj.* **hasta que** (17)

up: to be up to date **estar al día** (18)

upset **enojado/a** (9)

urgent **urgente** (12); it's urgent (that) **es urgente que** (12)

us *obj.* (*of prep.*) **nosotros/as** (2)

use **usar** (4); (*gas*) **gastar** (15); to be used for **servir (sirvo) (i) para** (5)

user **usuario/a** (12)

V

vacation: on vacation **de vacaciones** (8); to be on vacation **estar de vacaciones** (8); to go on vacation to/in . . . **ir de vacaciones a...** (8); to leave on vacation **salir de vacaciones** (8); to spend one's vacation in . . . **pasar las vacaciones en...** (8); to take a vacation **tomar unas vacaciones** (8)

vaccination **vacuna** (11)

vacuum cleaner **aspiradora** (10); to vacuum **pasar la aspiradora** (10)

van **camioneta** (8)

vegetables **verduras** *f. pl.* (7)

vehicle **vehículo** (15)

verb *gram.* **verbo** (2); reflexive verb *gram.* **verbo reflexivo** (5)

very *adv.* **muy** (1); very much **muchísimo**; very very **-ísimo** (9); very well **muy bien** (1); to be (very) stressed **estar (muy) estresado/a** (14)

veterinarian **veterinario/a** (17)

victim **víctima** (18)

video **video** (12); videogame **videojuego** (10); to play videogames **jugar (juego) (gu) a los videojuegos** (10)

view **vista** (12)

visit **visita** (11)

voice mailbox **buzón** (*m.*) **de voz** (12)

volleyball **voleibol** *m.* (10)

vote **votar** (18)

W

wages (*often per hour*) **salario** (17)
wait (for) **esperar** (7)
waiter/waitress **camarero/a** (7)
waiting room **sala de espera** (8)
wake up **despertarse (me despierto)** (5)
walk **caminar** (10); to take a walk **dar un paseo** (10)
wall **pared** *f.* (5)
wallet **cartera** (4)
want **desear** (2); **querer** (4)
war **guerra** (18)
was **fue** (5)
wash **lavar** (10)
washing machine **lavadora** (10)
watch *n.* **reloj** *m.* (4); *v.* **mirar** (3); to watch (a program, movie) **ver** (5); to watch television **mirar la tele(visión)** (3)
water **agua** *f.* (*but* **el agua**) (7); mineral water **agua mineral** (7)
way over there **allá** (4)
we *sub. pron.* **nosotros/as** (2)
wear **llevar** (4); **usar** (4)
weather **tiempo** (6); what's the weather like? **¿qué tiempo hace?** (6); it's (very) good/bad weather **hace (muy) buen/mal tiempo** (6)
weave **tejer** (13)
webpage **página web** (12)
website **sitio web** (12)
wed: newly wed **recién casado/a** (16)
wedding (*ceremony*) **boda** (16)
Wednesday **miércoles** *m. inv.* (5)
week **semana** (5); days of the week **días** (*m. pl.*) **de la semana** (5); next week **la próxima semana** (5), **la semana que viene** (5); once a week **una vez a la semana** (3)
weekend **fin** (*m.*) **de semana** (2)
weight: to lift weights **levantar pesas** (11)
welcome: you're welcome **de nada** (1), **no hay de qué** (1)
well **bien** (1); to get along well (with) **llevarse bien (con)** (16) very well **muy bien** (1); to come/turn out well **salir bien** (5); to do well **salir bien** (5)
well-being **bienestar** *m.* (11)
well-paid job/position **empleo bien pagado** (17)
west **oeste** *m.* (6)
whale **ballena** (15)
what (that which) **lo que** (5)
what? **¿cómo?** (1); **¿cuál?** (2); **¿qué?** (1); at what time? **¿a qué hora... ?** (1); for what purpose? **¿para qué... ?** (16); what (a) + *noun*! **¡qué** + *noun*! (14); what a shame that . . . ! **¡qué lástima que...** + *subjunctive*! (13); what are you like? **¿cómo es usted?** *form. s.* (1); what day is today? **¿qué día es hoy?** (5); what for? **¿para qué... ?** (16); what is your name? **¿cómo se llama usted?** *form. s.* (1); **¿cómo te llamas?** *fam. s.* (1); what time is it? **¿qué hora es?** (1); what's the weather like? **¿qué tiempo hace?** (6); what's today's date? **¿cuál es la fecha de hoy?** (6), **¿qué fecha es hoy?** (6)
when? **¿cuándo?** (2)
where? **¿dónde?** (1); where (to)? **¿adónde?** (4); where are you from? **¿de dónde eres (tú)?** *fam. s.* (1); **¿de dónde es usted?** *form. s.* (1)
which *conj.* **que** (3)
which? **¿cuál?** (2)
while **mientras** (10)
white **blanco/a** (4); white wine **vino blanco** (7)
whiteboard **pizarrón** (*m.*) **blanco** (2)
who *rel. pron.* **que** (3)
who? **¿quién?** (1)
whose? **¿de quién?** (3)
why? **¿por qué?** (3)
widow **viuda** (16)
widower **viudo** (16)
wife **esposa** (3), **mujer** *f.* (3)
wifi **wifi** *m.* (12)
wild **salvaje** (15)
win **ganar** (10)
wind **viento** (6); wind energy **energía eólica** (15)
window **ventana** (2); small window (*on a plane*) **ventanilla** (8)
windshield **parabrisas** *m. inv.* (15)
windy: it's (very) windy **hace (mucho) viento** (6)
wine (white, red) **vino (blanco, tinto)** (7)
winter **invierno** (6)
wish **esperanza** (18)
with **con** (2); with me **conmigo** (6); with you *fam. s.* **contigo** (6)
withdraw (*from an account*) **sacar (qu)** (17)
without *prep.* **sin** (5); *conj.* **sin que** (16)
witness **testigo** *m., f.* (18)
woman **mujer** *f.* (2); business woman **mujer de negocios** (17)
wool *n.* **lana** (4); *adj.* **de lana** (4)
word **palabra** (1); indefinite and negative word *gram.* **palabra indefinida y negativa** (7); interrogative word **palabra interrogativa** (2)
work (*labor*) **trabajo** (10); (piece of) **trabajo** (14); to work (function) **funcionar** (12); to work (*at a job*) **trabajar** (2); work of art **obra de arte** (13); *adj.* **laboral** (17)
worker **obrero/a** (17); social worker **trabajador(a) social** (17)
world **mundo** (3)
worried **preocupado/a** (6)
worse **peor** (6); worse than **peor(es) que** (6)
woven goods **tejidos** *m. pl.* (13)
write **escribir** (*p.p.* **escrito**) (3)
writer **escritor(a)** (13)
written **escrito/a** (*p.p. of* **escribir**) (14); written report **informe** (*m.*) **escrito** (14)
wrong: to be wrong **no tener razón** (4); to get up on the wrong side of the bed **levantarse con el pie izquierdo** (14)

Y

yard **patio** (5)
year **año** (6); (*in school*) **grado** (10); end of the year **fin** (*m.*) **de año** (9); to be . . . years old **tener... años** (3)
yellow **amarillo/a** (4)
yes **sí** (1)
yesterday **ayer** (5); yesterday was . . . **ayer fue...** (5); the day before yesterday *adv.* **anteayer** (5)
yet **todavía** (15)
yoga: to do yoga **hacer (el) yoga** (10)
yogurt **yogur** *m.* (7)
you *sub. pron.* **tú** *fam. s.* (2); **usted (Ud.)** *form. s.* (2); **vosotros/as** *fam. pl.* (*Sp.*) (2); **ustedes (Uds.)** *form. pl.* (2); *obj. of prep.* **ti** *fam. s.* (6); **usted** *form. s.; ustedes* (*Uds.*) *form. pl.* (6); and you? **¿y tú?** *fam. s.* (1); **¿y usted?** *form. s.* (1); how are you? **¿cómo está(s)?** (1), **¿qué tal?** (1); with you *fam. s.* **contigo** (6); you are *fam. s.* **eres** (1), *form. s.* **es** (1)
young **joven** (3); young woman **señorita (Srta.)** (1)
younger (than) **menor (que)** (6)
your *poss. adj.* **tu(s)** *fam. s.* (3); **su(s)** *form. s., pl.* (3); **vuestro/a(s)** *fam. pl.* (*Sp.*) (3); your, (of) yours *poss. adj., poss. pron.* **tuyo/a(s)** *fam. s.* (17); **suyo/a(s)** *form. s., pl.* (17); **vuestro/a(s)** *fam. pl.* (*Sp.*) (17)
you're welcome **de nada** (1), **no hay de qué** (1)
youth **juventud** *f.* (16)

Z

zero **cero** (1)
zone **zona** (12)

INDEX

In this index, cultural notes, authors of the literature presentations (**Lectura**), and vocabulary topic groups are listed by individual topic as well as under those headings.

D

E

F

G

H

I

Q

R

S

MANDATOS° Y FRASES COMUNES EN EL SALÓN DE CLASE

°*Commands*

Los estudiantes

Practice saying these sentences aloud. Then try to give the Spanish as you look at the English equivalents.

Tengo una pregunta (que hacer).	*I have a question (to ask).*
¿Cómo se dice *page* en español?	*How do you say "page" in Spanish?*
Otra vez, por favor. No entiendo.	*(Say that) Again, please. I don't understand.*
¿Cómo?	*What (did you say)?*
¡(Espere,) Un momento, por favor! No sé (la respuesta).	*(Wait,) Just a minute, please! I don't know (the answer).*
(Sí,) Cómo no.	*(Yes,) Of course.*

Los profesores

After you read these Spanish sentences, cover the English equivalents and say what each expression means.

¿Hay preguntas?	*Are there any questions?*
¿Qué opina/cree usted?	*What do you think?*
Escuchen.	*Listen.*
Repitan.	*Repeat.*
Lean (en voz alta).	*Read (aloud).*
Escriban/Completen (la siguiente oración).	*Write/Complete (the next sentence).*
Contesten en español.	*Answer in Spanish.*
Preparen (el ejercicio) para mañana.	*Prepare (the exercise) for tomorrow.*
Abran el libro en la página ________.	*Open your book to page ________.*
Cierren el cuaderno.	*Close your notebook.*
Saquen (un papel).	*Take out (a sheet of paper).*
Levanten la mano si...	*Raise your hand if . . .*
Vayan a la pizarra.	*Go to the board.*
Pregúntele a otro estudiante ________.	*Ask another student ________.*
Dele ________ a ________.	*Give ________ to ________.*
Busque un compañero/una compañera./Busque una persona para trabajar en pareja.	*Look for a partner.*
Haga la actividad con dos compañeros.	*Do the activity with two classmates.*
Formen grupos de cinco estudiantes.	*Get into groups of five students.*
En parejas...	*In pairs . . .*

SELECTED VERB FORMS

Regular Verbs | Simple Tenses and Present Perfect (Indicative)

	PRESENT	PRETERITE	IMPERFECT	PRESENT PERFECT
hablar	hablo	hablé	hablaba	he hablado
comer	como	comí	comía	he comido
vivir	vivo	viví	vivía	he vivido

Common Irregular Verbs | Present and Preterite (Indicative)

caer	caigo	caí	**poner**	pongo	puse
dar	doy	di	**querer**	quiero	quise
decir	digo	dije	**saber**	sé	supe
estar	estoy	estuve	**ser**	soy	fui
hacer	hago	hice	**tener**	tengo	tuve
ir	voy	fui	**traer**	traigo	traje
oír	oigo	oí	**venir**	vengo	vine
poder	puedo	pude	**ver**	veo	vi

Irregular Verbs | Imperfect (Indicative)

ir	iba	**ser**	era	**ver**	veía

Regular Verbs | Simple Tenses and Present Perfect (Subjunctive)

	PRESENT	IMPERFECT	PRESENT PERFECT
hablar	hable	hablara	haya hablado
comer	coma	comiera	haya comido
vivir	viva	viviera	haya vivido

Regular and Irregular Verbs | Future and Conditional

hablar	hablaré	hablaría
comer	comeré	comería
vivir	viviré	viviría

decir	diré	diría	**querer**	querré	querría
hacer	haré	haría	**saber**	sabré	sabría
poder	podré	podría	**tener**	tendré	tendría
poner	pondré	pondría	**venir**	vendré	vendría

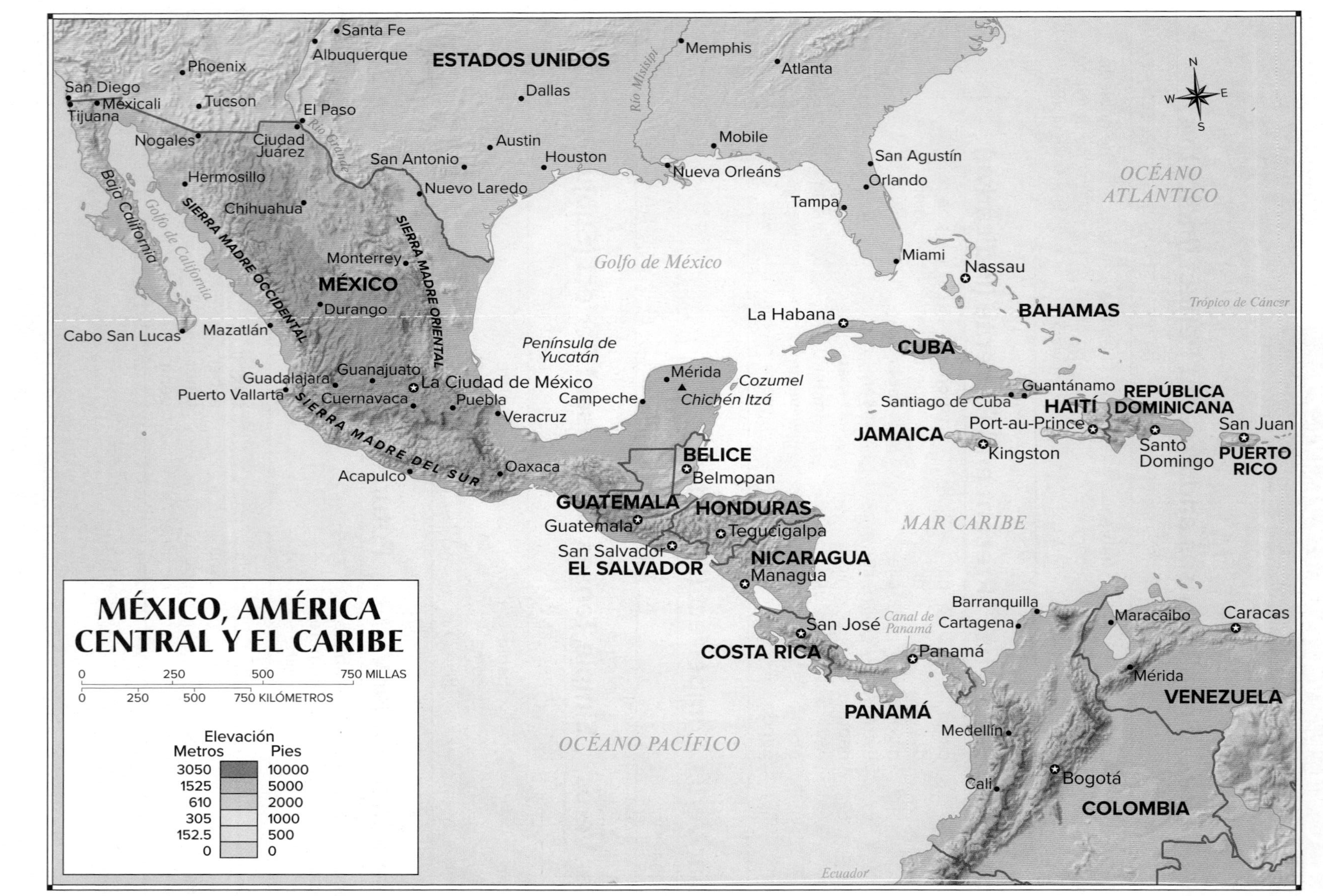
MÉXICO, AMÉRICA CENTRAL Y EL CARIBE
0 250 500 750 MILLAS
0 250 500 750 KILÓMETROS
Elevación
Metros Pies
3050 10000
1525 5000
610 2000
305 1000
152.5 500
0 0
ESTADOS UNIDOS
MÉXICO
GUATEMALA
BELICE
HONDURAS
EL SALVADOR
NICARAGUA
COSTA RICA
PANAMÁ
COLOMBIA
VENEZUELA
CUBA
BAHAMAS
JAMAICA
HAITÍ
REPÚBLICA DOMINICANA
PUERTO RICO
OCÉANO ATLÁNTICO
OCÉANO PACÍFICO
Golfo de México
MAR CARIBE
Golfo de California
Baja California
Trópico de Cáncer
Ecuador
Río Misisipí
Río Grande
SIERRA MADRE OCCIDENTAL
SIERRA MADRE ORIENTAL
SIERRA MADRE DEL SUR
Península de Yucatán
Canal de Panamá
Santa Fe
Albuquerque
Phoenix
San Diego
Tijuana
Mexicali
Tucson
El Paso
Ciudad Juárez
Nogales
Dallas
Austin
San Antonio
Houston
Memphis
Atlanta
Mobile
Nueva Orleáns
San Agustín
Orlando
Tampa
Miami
Nassau
Nuevo Laredo
Hermosillo
Chihuahua
Monterrey
Durango
Mazatlán
Cabo San Lucas
Guanajuato
Guadalajara
Puerto Vallarta
Cuernavaca
La Ciudad de México
Puebla
Veracruz
Oaxaca
Acapulco
Campeche
Mérida
Chichén Itzá
Cozumel
Belmopan
Guatemala
San Salvador
Tegucigalpa
Managua
San José
Panamá
La Habana
Santiago de Cuba
Guantánamo
Port-au-Prince
Kingston
Santo Domingo
San Juan
Barranquilla
Cartagena
Maracaibo
Caracas
Mérida
Medellín
Cali
Bogotá
N
E
S
W

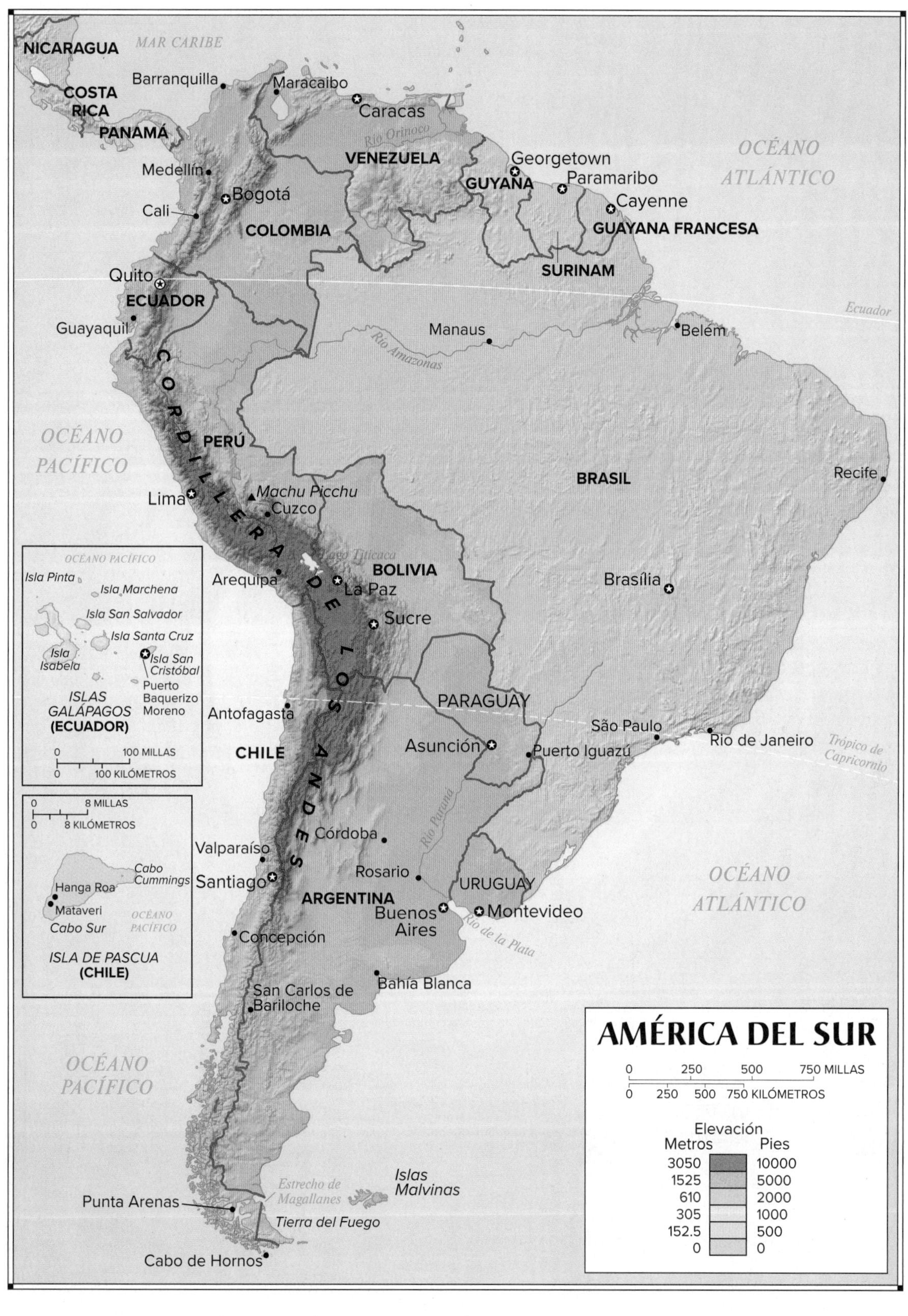
AMÉRICA DEL SUR
NICARAGUA
MAR CARIBE
COSTA RICA
PANAMÁ
Barranquilla
Maracaibo
Caracas
Río Orinoco
VENEZUELA
Medellín
Bogotá
Cali
COLOMBIA
Georgetown
GUYANA
Paramaribo
Cayenne
GUAYANA FRANCESA
SURINAM
OCÉANO ATLÁNTICO
Quito
ECUADOR
Guayaquil
Ecuador
Manaus
Río Amazonas
Belém
CORDILLERA DE LOS ANDES
OCÉANO PACÍFICO
PERÚ
Lima
Machu Picchu
Cuzco
BRASIL
Recife
Lago Titicaca
BOLIVIA
Arequipa
La Paz
Sucre
Brasília
PARAGUAY
Antofagasta
Asunción
São Paulo
Rio de Janeiro
Trópico de Capricornio
Puerto Iguazú
CHILE
Córdoba
Río Paraná
Valparaíso
Rosario
URUGUAY
Santiago
ARGENTINA
Buenos Aires
Montevideo
Río de la Plata
OCÉANO ATLÁNTICO
Concepción
Bahía Blanca
San Carlos de Bariloche
OCÉANO PACÍFICO
Estrecho de Magallanes
Islas Malvinas
Punta Arenas
Tierra del Fuego
Cabo de Hornos
OCÉANO PACÍFICO
Isla Pinta
Isla Marchena
Isla San Salvador
Isla Santa Cruz
Isla Isabela
Isla San Cristóbal
Puerto Baquerizo Moreno
ISLAS GALÁPAGOS (ECUADOR)
0 100 MILLAS
0 100 KILÓMETROS
0 8 MILLAS
0 8 KILÓMETROS
Cabo Cummings
Hanga Roa
Mataveri
Cabo Sur
OCÉANO PACÍFICO
ISLA DE PASCUA (CHILE)
0 250 500 750 MILLAS
0 250 500 750 KILÓMETROS
Elevación
Metros Pies
3050 10000
1525 5000
610 2000
305 1000
152.5 500
0 0

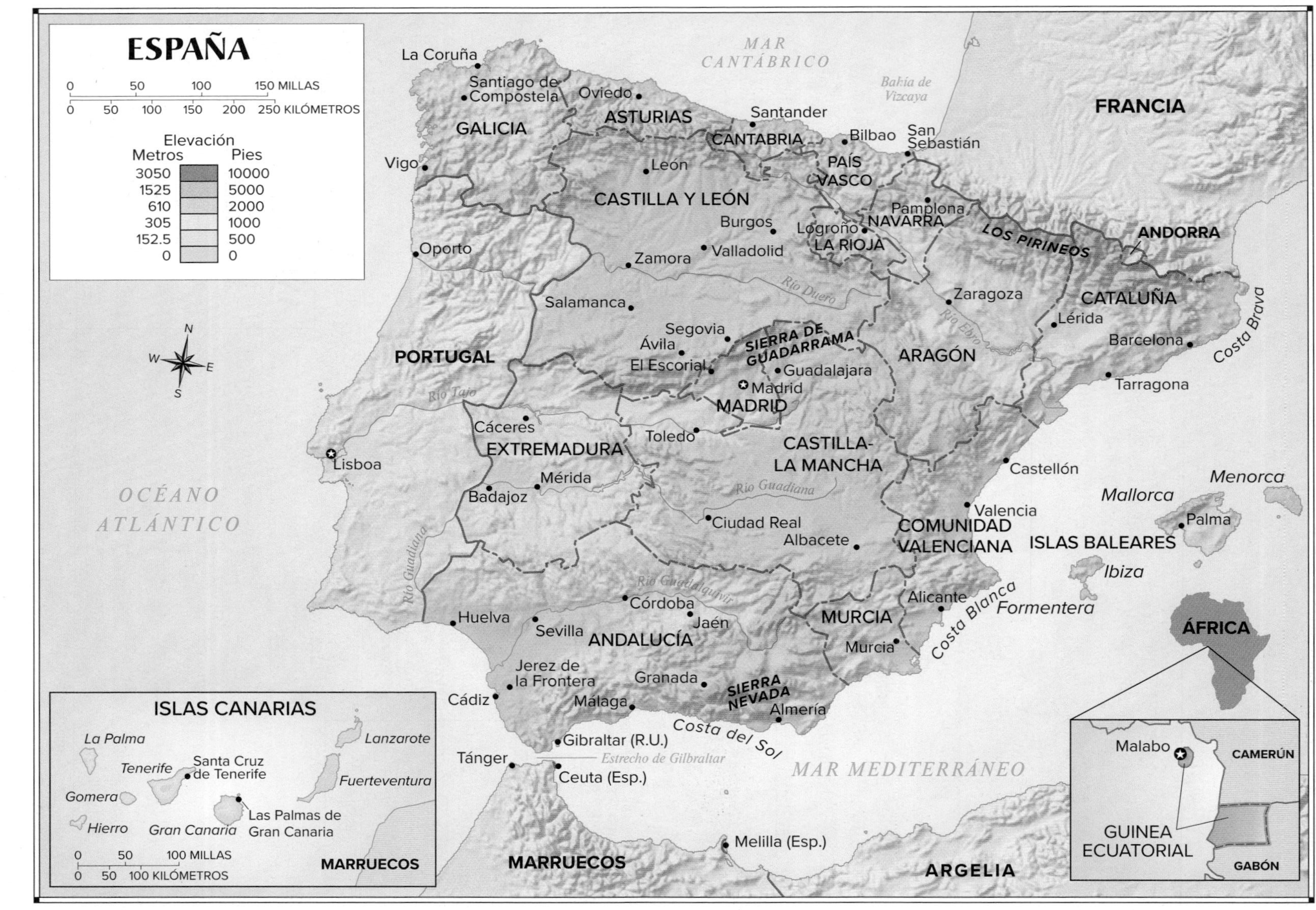
ESPAÑA
0 50 100 150 MILLAS
0 50 100 150 200 250 KILÓMETROS
Elevación
Metros Pies
3050 10000
1525 5000
610 2000
305 1000
152.5 500
0 0
N
W
E
S
MAR CANTÁBRICO
Bahía de Vizcaya
OCÉANO ATLÁNTICO
MAR MEDITERRÁNEO
FRANCIA
PORTUGAL
ANDORRA
MARRUECOS
ARGELIA
GALICIA
ASTURIAS
CANTABRIA
PAÍS VASCO
NAVARRA
LA RIOJA
CASTILLA Y LEÓN
ARAGÓN
CATALUÑA
MADRID
CASTILLA-LA MANCHA
EXTREMADURA
COMUNIDAD VALENCIANA
MURCIA
ANDALUCÍA
ISLAS BALEARES
LOS PIRINEOS
SIERRA DE GUADARRAMA
SIERRA NEVADA
La Coruña
Santiago de Compostela
Vigo
Oporto
Oviedo
León
Santander
Bilbao
San Sebastián
Pamplona
Logroño
Burgos
Valladolid
Zamora
Salamanca
Segovia
Ávila
El Escorial
Guadalajara
Madrid
Toledo
Zaragoza
Lérida
Barcelona
Tarragona
Castellón
Valencia
Albacete
Ciudad Real
Cáceres
Mérida
Badajoz
Lisboa
Huelva
Sevilla
Córdoba
Jaén
Granada
Jerez de la Frontera
Cádiz
Málaga
Almería
Murcia
Alicante
Gibraltar (R.U.)
Estrecho de Gilbraltar
Tánger
Ceuta (Esp.)
Melilla (Esp.)
Río Duero
Río Ebro
Río Tajo
Río Guadiana
Río Guadalquivir
Costa Brava
Costa Blanca
Costa del Sol
Mallorca
Menorca
Palma
Ibiza
Formentera
ISLAS CANARIAS
La Palma
Tenerife
Santa Cruz de Tenerife
Gomera
Hierro
Gran Canaria
Las Palmas de Gran Canaria
Lanzarote
Fuerteventura
0 50 100 MILLAS
0 50 100 KILÓMETROS
MARRUECOS
ÁFRICA
Malabo
CAMERÚN
GUINEA ECUATORIAL
GABÓN